Tolerable Upper Intake Levels(UL[a])

Vitamins

Life-Stage Group	Vitamin A (μg/d)[b]	Vitamin C (mg/d)	Vitamin D (μg/d)	Vitamin E (mg/d)[c,d]	Niacin (mg/d)[d]	Vitamin B₆ (mg/d)	Folate (μg/d)[d]	Choline (g/d)
Infants								
0–6 mo	600	ND[e]	25	ND	ND	ND	ND	ND
7–12 mo	600	ND	25	ND	ND	ND	ND	ND
Children								
1–3 y	600	400	50	200	10	30	300	1.0
4–8 y	900	650	50	300	15	40	400	1.0
Males, Females								
9–13 y	1,700	1,200	50	600	20	60	600	2.0
14–18 y	2,800	1,800	50	800	30	80	800	3.0
19–70 y	3,000	2,000	50	1,000	35	100	1,000	3.5
>70 y	3,000	2,000	50	1,000	35	100	1,000	3.5
Pregnancy								
≤18 y	2,800	1,800	50	800	30	80	800	3.0
19–50 y	3,000	2,000	50	1,000	35	100	1,000	3.5
Lactation								
≤18 y	2,800	1,800	50	800	30	80	800	3.0
19–50 y	3,000	2,000	50	1,000	35	100	1,000	3.5

Elements

Life-Stage Group	Boron (mg/d)	Calcium (g/d)	Copper (μg/d)	Fluoride (mg/d)	Iodine (μg/d)	Iron (mg/d)	Magnesium (mg/d)[f]	Manganese (mg/d)	Molybdenum (μg/d)	Nickel (mg/d)	Phosphorus (g/d)	Selenium (μg/d)	Vanadium (μg/d)[g]	Zinc (mg/d)
Infants														
0–6 mo	ND	ND	ND	0.7	ND	40	ND	ND	ND	ND	ND	45	ND	4
7–12 mo	ND	ND	ND	0.9	ND	40	ND	ND	ND	ND	ND	60	ND	5
Children														
1–3 y	3	2.5	1,000	1.3	200	40	65	2	300	0.2	3	90	ND	7
4–8 y	6	2.5	3,000	2.2	300	40	110	3	600	0.3	3	150	ND	12
Males, Females														
9–13 y	11	2.5	5,000	10	600	40	350	6	1,100	0.6	4	280	ND	23
14–18 y	17	2.5	8,000	10	900	45	350	9	1,700	1.0	4	400	ND	34
19–70 y	20	2.5	10,000	10	1,100	45	350	11	2,000	1.0	4	400	1.8	40
>70 y	20	2.5	10,000	10	1,100	45	350	11	2,000	1.0	3	400	1.8	40
Pregnancy														
≤18 y	17	2.5	8,000	10	900	45	350	9	1,700	1.0	3.5	400	ND	34
19–50 y	20	2.5	10,000	10	1,100	45	350	11	2,000	1.0	3.5	400	ND	40
Lactation														
≤18 y	17	2.5	8,000	10	900	45	350	9	1,700	1.0	4	400	ND	34
19–50 y	20	2.5	10,000	10	1,100	45	350	11	2,000	1.0	4	400	ND	40

Data from: Adapted from the Dietary Reference Intakes series, National Academies Press. Copyright 1997, 1998, 2000, 2001, by the National Academy of Sciences. These reports may be accessed via www.nap.edu. Courtesy of the National Academies Press, Washington, D.C.

[a] UL = The maximum level of daily nutrient intake that is likely to pose no risk of adverse effects. Unless otherwise specified, the UL represents total intake from food, water, and supplements. Due to lack of suitable data, ULs could not be established for vitamin K, thiamin, riboflavin, vitamin B₁₂, pantothenic acid, biotin, or carotenoids. In the absence of ULs, extra caution may be warranted in consuming levels above recommended intakes.

[b] As preformed vitamin A only.

[c] As α-tocopherol; applies to any form of supplemental α-tocopherol.

[d] The ULs for vitamin E, niacin, and folate apply to synthetic forms obtained from supplements, fortified foods, or a combination of the two.

[e] ND = Not determinable due to lack of data of adverse effects in this age group and concern with regard to lack of ability to handle excess amounts. Source of intake should be from food only to prevent high levels of intake.

[f] The ULs for magnesium represent intake from a pharmacological agent only and do not include intake from food and water.

[g] Although vanadium in food has not been shown to cause adverse effects in humans, there is no justification for adding vanadium to food, and vanadium supplements should be used with caution. The UL is based on adverse effects in laboratory animals, and this data could be used to set a UL for adults but not children and adolescents.

Improve Your Grade!

Access included with any new book.

www.pearsonhighered.com/thompsonmanore

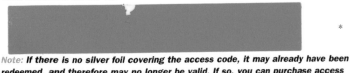

Help your students get IT!

Excellent! An excellent addition [the In Depth section] to the book—this has been missing in the past. I really like the way the vitamins and minerals are presented by function, but it was difficult to teach without an overview—this new mini-chapter covers that overview—it is well done.

—Janet Peterson, Professor at *Linfield College*

I moved to Thompson/Manore/Vaughan's functional approach because my students were having a difficult time with the vitamins and minerals chapters. Since adopting the text, test scores have improved significantly.

—Andrea Villarreal, Professor at *Mesa Community College*

Making nutrition real

The Science of Nutrition, **Second Edition** is uniquely organized using an applied approach, which organizes vitamins and minerals based on their functions and effects on the body. This applied approach is most evident in the functional organization of the micronutrient (vitamin and mineral) chapters.

Rather than requiring students to simply memorize all the vitamins and minerals and their characteristics, the authors present them organized around their functions (such as fluid and electrolyte balance, antioxidant function, bone health, energy metabolism, and blood and immunity health) so that students can understand their effects on the body.

JANICE L. THOMPSON

MELINDA M. MANORE

LINDA A. VAUGHAN

THE SCIENCE OF
NUTRITION

SECOND EDITION

Table of Contents

NEW! In Depth mini chapters cover the four key areas of Alcohol, Vitamins & Minerals, Phytochemicals and Functional Foods, and Disordered Eating, offering instructors flexibility in incorporating them into their course.

Functional Approach

In Chapters 8–12, vitamins and minerals are presented by their functions, allowing instructors to go into greater depth on processes and to demonstrate how micronutrients work.

Nutri-Cases

These short case studies feature five recurring characters that help students relate to and apply the material they learned in the chapter. Two Nutri-Cases appear in each chapter.

NEW! Nutri-Case Character, Judy

Judy is a new Nutri-Case character. She is Hannah's mother and struggles with poor eating habits, overweight, and borderline diabetes. We also use Judy and Hannah to illustrate the effects of family environment and eating patterns.

Hannah has been updated to an 18-year-old college freshman, living at home and struggling with her weight.

Gustavo
59 years old

Theo
21 years old

Liz
20 years old

See for Yourself

Take a piece of lined paper and divide it into four equal columns, labeled as follows:

☐ Food Item
☐ Serving Size
☐ Time of Day
☐ Location

The document you create will resemble a standard form used for a 24-hour dietary recall. Fill it out as carefully and thoroughly as you can, listing each food you ate yesterday, beginning and ending at midnight.

Now answer the following questions:

1. How confident are you that you documented every single item that you ate all day yesterday?
2. How confident are you that you recalled accurately the serving size of each food you ate?
3. Given your experience filling out a 24-hour dietary recall, what would you identify as the main limitations of this assessment tool?

NEW! See For Yourself

This self-assessment feature appears at the end of each chapter and offers brief, targeted activities that emphasize active learning and applied skills, and provides opportunities for students to learn about their own nutrition and health habits.

An applied approach leads to learning

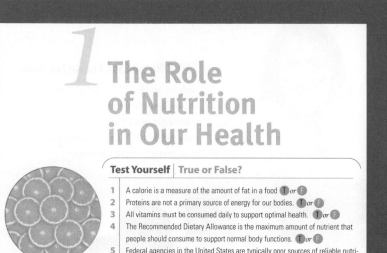

1 The Role of Nutrition in Our Health

Test Yourself | **True or False?**

1. A calorie is a measure of the amount of fat in a food. **T** or **F**
2. Proteins are not a primary source of energy for our bodies. **T** or **F**
3. All vitamins must be consumed daily to support optimal health. **T** or **F**
4. The Recommended Dietary Allowance is the maximum amount of nutrient that people should consume to support normal body functions. **T** or **F**
5. Federal agencies in the United States are typically poor sources of reliable nutrition information. **T** or **F**

Test Yourself answers are located after the chapter Summary.

The applied approach allows instructors to go into greater depth on processes such as energy and metabolism, while targeted features encourage students to apply what they learn.

Nutrition Myth or Fact?

These feature boxes dispel common misconceptions and help students to critically evaluate information they get from advertising, mass media, and their peers.

Test Yourself

These brief quizzes at the beginning of each chapter pique students' interest in the topics to be covered by raising and dispelling common misperceptions about nutrition. The answers to these questions can be found at the end of each chapter.

Nutrition Myth or Fact?

Can Vitamin C Prevent the Common Cold?

What do you do when you feel a cold coming on? If you are like many people, you drink a lot of orange juice or take vitamin C supplements to ward it off. Do these tactics really help prevent a cold?

It is well known that vitamin C is important for a healthy immune system. A deficiency of vitamin C can seriously weaken the immune cells' ability to detect and destroy invading microbes, increasing susceptibility to many diseases and illnesses—including the common cold. Many people have taken vitamin C supplements to prevent the common cold, basing their behavior on its actions of enhancing our immune function. Interestingly, scientific studies do not support this action. A recent review of many of the studies of vitamin C and the common cold found that people taking vitamin C regularly in an attempt to ward off the common cold experienced as many colds as people who took a placebo. However, the *duration* of their colds was significantly reduced—by 8% in adults and 13.6% in children.[1] Timing appears to be impor-

tant, though: Taking vitamin C after the onset of cold symptoms did not reduce either the duration or severity of the cold. Interestingly, taking vitamin C supplements regularly did reduce the number of colds experienced in marathon runners, skiers, and soldiers participating in exercises done under extreme environmental conditions.

The amount of vitamin C taken in these studies was at least 200 mg per day, with many using doses as high as 4,000 mg per day (more than 40 times the RDA), with no harmful effects noted in those studies that reported adverse events.

In summary, it appears that, for most people, taking vitamin C supplements regularly will not prevent colds, but may reduce their duration. Consuming a healthful diet that includes excellent sources of vitamin C will also help you maintain a strong immune system. Taking vitamin C after the onset of cold symptoms does not appear to help, so next time you feel a cold coming on, you may want to think twice before taking extra vitamin C.

NUTRITION DEBATE

71

Will Revising the USDA Food Guide Pyramid Help You Find the Perfect Diet?

As you learned in this chapter, the previous USDA Food Guide Pyramid (FGP) was revised in 2005. MyPyramid was developed to address many of the limitations of the previous FGP. For instance, one major criticism was that the older FGP was overly simple and did not help consumers make appropriate choices within each food group. MyPyramid has addressed this concern by instructing consumers to choose foods that are lower in fat and added sugar and higher in fiber, as well as by providing many specific examples of healthful foods in each food group. Another criticism was that the previous FGP did not emphasize the need for regular physical activity. In contrast, the left side of MyPyramid includes a graphic of a person climbing stairs to highlight the importance of daily physical activity.

Despite these improvements upon the previous FGP, MyPyramid's reception has been lukewarm. Indeed, many of the same criticisms once leveled at the FGP persist, as does a fundamental doubt that such a tool can really help Americans design and maintain a healthful diet. Let's explore some of the specific concerns nutrition and public health experts have raised since the release of MyPyramid.

One major criticism is that the serving sizes suggested in MyPyramid are unrealistic or do not coincide with typical serving sizes of foods listed on food labels. For instance, one serving of a muffin as defined in MyPyramid is 1 oz-equivalent, but most muffins available to consumers range from 2 oz to 8 oz!

The way that foods are packaged is also confusing to consumers. Unless people read food labels carefully, it is easy to consume an entire package of a food that contains multiple servings and assume that the entire package is equal to one serving. For example, it is common to find soft drinks sold in 20-fl.-oz bottles. Although the serving size listed on the label is 8 fl. oz, and total servings per bottle is listed as 2.5, most people just drink the entire bottle in one sitting and assume they had one soft drink.

Although the serving size of a muffin in MyPyramid is 1 oz-equivalent, many muffins sold today range in size from 2 oz to 8 oz.

A second criticism of MyPyramid is that it has not gone far enough to encourage people to consume more healthful foods. For instance, low-fat and low-calorie food choices are not clearly defined in each food category: The 1-oz-equivalent servings of meat, poultry, fish, dry beans, eggs, and nuts suggested in MyPyramid are not differentiated by their fat content or by the type of fat they contain. Fish is low in fat and contains a more healthful type of fat than that found in red meats. In addition, although nuts are relatively high in fat, the type of fat in nuts is more healthful than that found in meats. MyPyramid fails to point out these differences, treating all foods in the meat, poultry, fish, dry beans, eggs, and nuts group as equivalent choices. In addition, MyPyramid recommends that at least half the grains eaten each day should be from whole-grain sources, allowing for eating half of your grain sources from refined foods. In reality, it is more healthful to eat virtually all your grains from whole-grain foods.

A third criticism is that a person must have access to the Internet and the ability to maneuver through Web-based programming in order to effectively use MyPyramid. Although it may be hard for many people to imagine, a considerable number of Americans still do not have access to the Internet, and many of those who do are not comfortable using interactive programming. As a stand-alone graphic, MyPyramid is quite limited in its usefulness as a stand-alone graphic. Without the capacity to access and manipulate the interactive components on the Internet at www.MyPyramid.gov, individuals cannot personalize MyPyramid.

A fourth criticism is that MyPyramid does not graphically illustrate the principles it claims to represent. For example, by simply looking at the MyPyramid graphic, a consumer cannot know that the varying widths of bands represent how much of that food group to consume. In addition, varying the widths of each band from wider at the bottom to narrower at the top of MyPyramid is supposed to communicate the message that we should eat more of certain foods and less of others in each of the food categories, but it's doubtful that consumers pick up on that message. Similarly, it's questionable whether consumers will notice the yellow band and link it with the oil drop below the graphic in the text. In short, a number of nutrition experts feel that the MyPyramid graphic on its own is not particularly useful, as it is difficult to understand how to use it unless the graphic is linked with the text and supplemented with information provided on the Web site.

Think about it; prior to taking this class, did you use the previous FGP or the new MyPyramid to help you design a healthful diet? It may be that you had not even seen

Problems with accessing or navigating the Internet can prevent people from using MyPyramid.

Because of these limitations and criticisms, many nutrition experts doubt that MyPyramid can halt the current obesity epidemic or significantly contribute to improving the health of Americans. Although MyPyramid is grounded in science, new research emphasizes the importance of eating specific nutrients and whole foods that promote health and prevent disease—concepts that MyPyramid does not adequately address. The Healthy Eating Pyramid is an alternative pyramid developed by researchers at the Harvard School of Public Health that has been identified as one example of a better tool for designing a healthful diet (see Web Links at the end of this chapter for the URL). Following the design of the previous Food Guide Pyramid, the Healthy Eating Pyramid highlights healthful food choices and emphasizes daily exercise and weight control. A recent study shows that people eating a diet based on the Healthy Eating Pyramid reduced their risk for heart disease two times more than people eating a diet based on the previous FGP.* Because of the recent release of MyPyramid, no studies are yet available comparing the effectiveness of the Healthy Eating Pyramid to MyPyramid in reducing chronic disease risk.

As you can imagine, a great deal of time, effort, and money was invested in the new message, content, and design of MyPyramid. In making this investment, nutrition experts at the USDA intended that MyPyramid would help reduce the alarmingly high obesity rates in the United States. The primary assumption made by these experts was that people would actually use MyPyramid to design their diets. In fact, however, the extent to which people use MyPyramid in their daily lives is debatable.

these pyramids, or if you did, you had no idea how to use them. This is the case for many Americans. Our work with community members throughout the United States has shown us that some people have no idea what MyPyramid or the previous FGP are, and many of those who have tried to use them find them confusing because of the limitations just discussed. In addition, the pyramid shape does not make sense to many consumers. Furthermore, many people find any type of graphic image too vague—they need specific menus and recipes to follow and prefer to buy diet books that provide this information. Still others do not use the pyramids because they view them as another confusing mandate from experts who are out of touch with how "real" people eat and how they live their lives.

It is obvious that we need to address the obesity epidemic effectively. In doing so, one of the major challenges we face is to design nutrition recommendations and tools that millions of Americans can, and will, use. Until easier-to-use and more accessible guidelines are available and their impact on the rates of obesity and chronic disease is assessed, this debate will continue.

Critical Thinking Questions

▶ What do you think?

▶ Do you feel that the revised MyPyramid has adequately addressed the flaws of the previous USDA Food Guide Pyramid?

▶ Do you think that MyPyramid can help people design a healthful diet?

▶ Do you think it can help people to lose weight, and reduce our population's rate of obesity and chronic disease?

Will MyPyramid help you select the most healthful option when you eat?

Nutrition Debates

This end-of-chapter feature contains in-depth, multi-sided coverage of current events and hot topics, pulled from the frontlines of the ever-changing nutritional field. The debates encourage students to be more informed and discriminating consumers of nutrition and health information, and to think deeply about complex issues. The **Second Edition** features new Critical Thinking Questions after each debate.

70

Art helps students visualize and analyze

The rich art and photo program includes high-quality, accurate images and illustrations that help students visualize and focus on the core information they need to learn.

Salivary glands

Esophagus

1 Mouth
- Chewing stimulates secretion of saliva from salivary glands
- Salivary amylase breaks down starch into shorter polysaccharides and maltose

5 Liver
- Monosaccharides travel to liver in bloodstream via the portal vein, are converted to glucose, and then transported to cells to provide energy
- Excess glucose is stored as glycogen in liver

2 Stomach
- Salivary amylase is destroyed by acids
- No carbohydrate digestion takes place in the stomach

3 Pancreas
- Pancreatic amylase is secreted into small intestine

6 Large intestine
- Some carbohydrates pass into large intestine undigested
- Bacteria ferment some undigested carbohydrate
- Remaining fiber is excreted in feces

4 Small intestine
- Pancreatic amylase breaks down remaining starch into maltose
- Specific enzymes (maltase, sucrase, lactase) in small intestine break down disaccharides into monosaccharides
- All monosaccharides are absorbed by small intestine and enter bloodstream

Enhanced Figurative Art

Improved art helps students better visualize important processes in the body and provides a vivid colorful interior design.

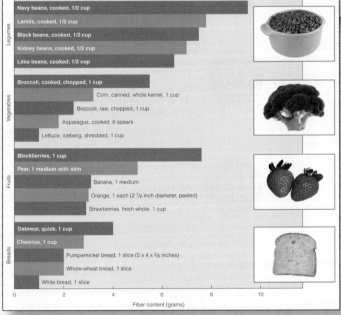

Updated Food Source Diagrams

Revised diagrams provide clearer and enlarged pictures of the food sources of key nutrients.

Updated Meal Planning Art

Many new photos of specific meals have been added to help students grasp important pedagogical concepts.

Meals with Foods High in Nutrient Density

Breakfast
1 cup cooked oatmeal with
½ cup skim milk
1 slice whole-wheat toast with
1 tsp. butter
6 fl. oz grapefruit juice

Snack
1 peeled orange
1 cup nonfat yogurt

Lunch
Turkey sandwich
3 oz turkey breast
2 slices whole-grain bread
2 tsp. Dijon mustard
3 slices fresh tomato
2 leaves red leaf lettuce
1 cup baby carrots with broccoli crowns
20 fl. oz (2.5 cups) water

Snack
½ whole-wheat bagel
1 tbsp. peanut butter
1 medium apple

Dinner
Spinach salad
1 cup fresh spinach leaves
¼ cup diced tomatoes
¼ cup diced green pepper
½ cup kidney beans
1 tbsp. fat-free Italian salad dressing
3 oz broiled chicken breast
½ cup cooked brown rice
½ cup steamed broccoli
8 fl. oz (1 cup) skim milk

Meals with Foods Low in Nutrient Density

Breakfast
1 cup puffed rice cereal with
½ cup whole milk
1 slice white toast with
1 tsp. butter
6 fl. oz grape drink

Snack
1 12-oz can orange soft drink
1.5 oz cheddar cheese

Lunch
Hamburger
3 oz regular ground beef
1 white hamburger bun
2 tsp. Dijon mustard
1 tbsp. tomato ketchup
2 leaves iceberg lettuce
1 snack-sized bag potato chips
20 fl. oz cola soft drink

Snack
3 chocolate sandwich cookies
1 12-oz can diet soft drink
10 Gummi Bears candy

Dinner
Green salad
1 cup iceberg lettuce
¼ cup diced tomatoes
1tsp. green onions
¼ cup bacon bits
1 tbsp. regular Ranch salad dressing
3 oz beef round steak, breaded and fried
½ cup cooked white rice
½ cup sweet corn
8 fl. oz (1 cup) iced tea

Figure 2.4 A comparison of one day's meals that contain foods high in nutrient density to meals that contain foods low in nutrient density.

All the tools you need in one convenient place

www.mynutritionlab.com

MyNutritionLab is the online course management system that makes it easy for you to organize your class, personalize your students' educational experience, and push their learning to the next level. MyDietAnalysis 4.0 will be available as a single sign-on to MyNutritionLab. MyNutritionLab makes learning easy for students with its simple navigation on a chapter-by-chapter basis.

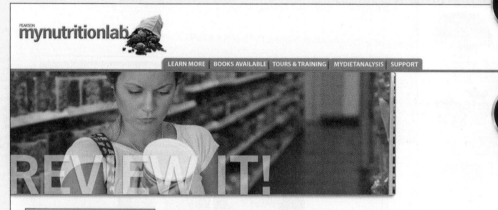

Study It

This section contains access to extra math and chemistry assistance specific to nutrition with *Get Ready for Nutrition.*

See It

Students can access more than 15 videos to extend their learning on important nutrition topics.

Do It

Hands-on activities related to the text include Careers in Nutrition Interviews, questions for Two Points of View, and Clinical Cases for each chapter.

Read It

This section includes chapter objectives to guide student learning, plus the new Pearson eText. Pearson eText is easy for students to read. Users can create notes, highlight text in different colors, create book marks, zoom, click hyperlinked words and phrases to view definitions, and view in single-page or two-page view. Pearson eText also links students to associated media files, enabling them to view an animation as they read the text.

Review It

Contains quizzes for each chapter, along with access to flashcards that are available as downloads to a mobile phone.

Motivate students to assess their own diets

www.mydietanalysis.com

MyDietAnalysis was developed by the nutrition database experts at ESHA Research, Inc. and is tailored for use in college nutrition courses. It offers an accurate, reliable, and easy-to-use program for your students' diet analysis needs. MyDietAnalysis features a database of nearly 20,000 foods and multiple reports. Available on CD-ROM or online, the program allows students to track their diet and activity, and generate and submit reports electronically. MyDietAnalysis is also available as a single sign-on to MyNutritionLab.

Reports

NEW! Features of MyDietAnalysis 4.0

MyDietAnalysis 4.0 is coming for your spring semester classes! You will be able to track when your students have completed their diet analysis project, and your students' errors will be reduced. Ask your Pearson rep for more information!

- Set up a roster of students and see when they have completed their projects, all within MyDietAnalysis's easy-to-use interface.

- View a class-wide nutritional average. MyDietAnalysis will allow you to see a nutritional profile of your entire class, enabling you to base your lecture on your students' needs.

- Video assistance covers the topics students struggle with most. Students take a quiz after each video to ensure they understand how to set up and use the program.

Diet Tracker

The Companion Website has been reorganized into five sections: **See It, Read It, Study It, Review It,** and **Do It.** The website also features Chapter Summaries, Critical Thinking questions, Chapter Quizzes, Cumulative Quizzes, Careers in Nutrition interviews, questions related to Two Points of View, eLearn links, Web Links, Flashcards, a glossary, and Clinical Cases.

Additional teaching and learning resources

Instructor Resource DVD (IR-DVD)

This valuable teaching resource offers everything you need to create lecture presentations and course materials, including JPEG and PowerPoint® files of all the art, tables, and selected photos from the text, and "stepped-out" art for selected figures from the text, as well as animations for the majors nutrition course.

The IR-DVD allows for "click and play" in the classroom— no downloading required, and also includes:

· PowerPoint lecture outlines with embedded links to animations and *ABC News* Lecture Launcher Videos

· Jeopardy-type quiz show

· Instructor Manual

· Test Bank Microsoft® Word files and TestGen® Computerized Test Bank

· Questions for Classroom Response Systems (CRS) in PowerPoint format, allowing you to import the questions into your own CRS

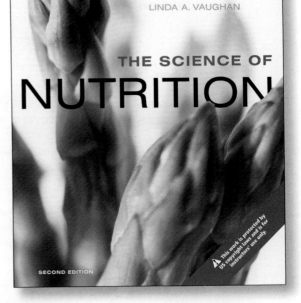

INSTRUCTOR RESOURCE DVD

JANICE L. THOMPSON
MELINDA M. MANORE
LINDA A. VAUGHAN

THE SCIENCE OF
NUTRITION

SECOND EDITION

Janice Thompson, co-author of *The Science of Nutrition,* **Second Edition,** *Nutrition: An Applied Approach,* **Second Edition,** and *Nutrition for Life,* **Second Edition,** eases instructors into teaching with the Functional Approach.

ABC News Video Clips

These 15 video clips, created in partnership with *ABC News,* range from 5–10 minutes in length and can be used to stimulate classroom discussion. Digital versions of the videos are integrated into the PowerPoint lecture outline, and are available in a separate, full-screen version.

For Instructors

Instructor Manual
978-0-321-66757-1 • 0-321-66757-3

Printed Test Bank
978-0-321-66758-8 • 0-321-66758-1

Instructor Resource DVD
978-0-321-66759-5 • 0-321-66759-X

Great Ideas! Active Ways to Teach Nutrition
978-0-321-59646-8 • 0-321-59646-3

MyDietAnalysis 4.0 Premium Website
www.mydietanalysis.com

TestGen® Computerized Test Bank
978-0-321-66764-9 • 0-321-66764-6

Course Management Options :

MyNutritionLab
MyNutritionLab with MyDietAnalysis
www.mynutritionlab.com

WebCT
www.pearsonhighered.com/elearning

Blackboard
www.pearsonhighered.com/elearning

For Students

Companion Website
www.pearsonhighered.com/thompsonmanore

MyDietAnalysis 4.0 Student Access Kit
978-0-321-66814-1 • 0-321-66814-6

MyDietAnalysis 3.0 Stand-alone CD-ROM
978-0-321-66769-4 • 0-321-66769-7

Food Composition Table
978-0-321-66793-9 • 0-321-66793-X

Eat Right!
Healthy Eating in College and Beyond

Eat Right! Healthy Eating in College and Beyond by Janet Anderson, et al.

ISBN-13: 978-0-8053-8288-4
ISBN-10: 0-8053-8288-7

This handy, full-color 80-page booklet provides practical guidelines, tips, shopper's guides, and recipes students can use to put healthy eating guidelines into action. Topics include how to choose healthy foods in a cafeteria, dorm room, and fast food restaurant; eating on a budget; weight management tips; vegetarian alternatives; and guidelines on alcohol and health.

The Science of Nutrition
Second Edition

Janice L. Thompson, Ph.D., FACSM
University of Bristol
University of New Mexico

Melinda M. Manore, Ph.D., RD, CSSD, FACSM
Oregon State University

Linda A. Vaughan, Ph.D., RD
Arizona State University

Benjamin Cummings

Boston Columbus Indianapolis New York San Francisco Upper Saddle River
Amsterdam Cape Town Dubai London Madrid Milan Munich Paris Montréal Toronto
Delhi Mexico City São Paulo Sydney Hong Kong Seoul Singapore Taipei Tokyo

Acquisitions Editor: Sandra Lindelof
Project Editor: Susan Scharf
Development Manager: Barbara Yien
Development Editor: Laura Bonazzoli
Art Development Editor: Laura Southworth
Media Producer: Sarah Young-Dualan
Editorial Assistant: Brianna Paulson
Managing Editor: Deborah Cogan
Production Supervisor: Beth Masse
Production Management and Composition: S4Carlisle
    Publishing Services

Copyeditor: Kirsten Balayti
Senior Photo Editor: Donna Kalal
Interior Designer: Derek Bacchus
Cover Designer: Riezebos Holzbaur Design Group
Illustrators: Precision Graphics
Photo Researcher: Kristin Piljay
Image Rights and Permissions Manager: Zina Arabia
Manufacturing Buyer: Jeff Sargent
Senior Marketing Manager: Neena Bali
Cover Photo Credit: Boden/Ledingham

Credits can be found on page CR-1.

Library of Congress Cataloging-in-Publication Data

Thompson, Janice, 1962-
  The science of nutrition / Janice L. Thompson, Melinda M. Manore, Linda A. Vaughan. — 2nd ed.
      p. cm.
  Includes bibliographical references and index.
  ISBN 978-0-321-64316-2
1. Nutrition—Textbooks. I. Manore, Melinda, 1951- II. Vaughan, Linda A. (Linda Ann) III. Title.

TX354.T47 2011
613.2—dc22   2009041909

ISBN-10: 0-321-64316-X (Student edition)
ISBN-13: 978-0-321-64316-2 (Student edition)
ISBN-10: 0-321-66698-4 (Professional copy)
ISBN-13: 978-0-321-66698-7 (Professional copy)

 2 3 4 5 6 7 8 9 10—WBC—13 12 11 10
Manufactured in the United States of America.

Benjamin Cummings
    is an imprint of

www.pearsonhighered.com

Dedication

This book is dedicated to my amazing family, friends, and colleagues—you provide constant support, encouragement, and unconditional love. It is also dedicated to my students—you continue to inspire me, challenge me, and teach me. —**JLT**

This book is dedicated to my wonderful colleagues, friends, and family—your guidance, support, and understanding have allowed this book to happen. —**MMM**

This book is dedicated to my strong circle of family, friends, and colleagues. Year after year, your support and encouragement sustain me. —**LAV**

About the Authors

Janice L. Thompson, Ph.D., FACSM

University of Bristol
University of New Mexico

Janice Thompson earned a doctorate in exercise physiology and nutrition at Arizona State University. She is currently Professor of Public Health Nutrition at the University of Bristol in the Department of Exercise and Health Sciences and is also an adjunct faculty member at the University of New Mexico Health Sciences Center. Her research focuses on designing and assessing the impact of nutrition and physical activity interventions to reduce the risks for obesity, cardiovascular disease, and type 2 diabetes in high-risk populations. She also teaches nutrition and research methods courses and mentors graduate research students.

Janice is a Fellow of the American College of Sports Medicine (ACSM) and a member of the American Society for Nutrition (ASN), the British Association of Sport and Exercise Science (BASES), and The Nutrition Society. Janice won an undergraduate teaching award while at the University of North Carolina, Charlotte. In addition to *The Science of Nutrition*, Janice coauthored the Benjamin Cummings textbooks *Nutrition: An Applied Approach* and *Nutrition for Life* with Melinda Manore.

Janice loves hiking, yoga, traveling, and cooking and eating delicious food. She likes almost every vegetable except fennel and believes chocolate should be listed as a food group.

Melinda M. Manore, Ph.D., RD, CSSD, FACSM
Oregon State University

Melinda Manore earned a doctorate in human nutrition with a minor in exercise physiology at Oregon State University (OSU). She is the past chair of the Department of Nutrition and Food Management at OSU and is currently a professor in the Department of Nutrition and Exercise Sciences. Prior to her tenure at OSU, she taught at Arizona State University for 17 years. Melinda's area of expertise is nutrition and exercise, especially the role of diet and exercise in health and prevention of chronic disease, exercise performance, weight control, and micronutrient needs. She has a special focus on the energy and nutritional needs of active women and girls across the life cycle.

Melinda is an active member of the American Dietetic Association (ADA) and the American College of Sports Medicine (ACSM). She is the past chair of the ADA Research Committee and the Research Dietetic Practice Group and served on the ADA Obesity Steering Committee. She is a Fellow and current Vice-President of the ACSM.

Melinda is also a member of the American Society of Nutrition (ASN) and the North American Association for the Study of Obesity (NAASO) and serves as chair of the USDA Nutrition and Health Committee for Program Guidance and Planning. Melinda writes the nutrition column and is an associate editor for the ACSM's *Health and Fitness Journal,* serves on editorial boards of numerous research journals, and has won awards for excellence in research and teaching. She has also coauthored the Benjamin Cummings textbooks *Nutrition: An Applied Approach* and *Nutrition for Life* with Janice Thompson.

Melinda is an avid walker, hiker, and former runner who loves to garden, cook, and eat great food. She is also an amateur birder.

Linda A. Vaughan, Ph.D., RD
Arizona State University

Linda Vaughan is a professor and past chair of the Department of Nutrition at Arizona State University. Linda earned a doctorate in agricultural biochemistry and nutrition at the University of Arizona. She currently teaches, advises graduate students, and conducts research about independent-living older adults and the nutrient content of donated and distributed food from community food banks. Her area of specialization is older adults and life-cycle nutrition.

Linda is an active member of the American Dietetic Association (ADA), the American Society of Nutrition (ASN), and the Arizona Dietetic Association. She has served as chair of the Research and Dietetic Educators of Practitioners practice groups of the American Dietetic Association. Linda has received numerous awards, including the Arizona Dietetic Association Outstanding Educator Award (1997) and the Arizona State University Supervisor of the Year award (2004).

Linda enjoys swimming, cycling, and baking bread in her free time.

Welcome to *The Science of Nutrition, Second Edition!*

As nutrition researchers and educators, we know that the science of nutrition is constantly evolving. Our goal as authors is to provide students and instructors with the most recent and scientifically accurate nutrition information available.

Learning to Avoid Nutrition Confusion

What should I eat? In this information age, answers to that question are available 24 hours a day: on the Internet, television, and radio, in books, newspapers, and magazines, and on billboards and posters and the sides of vending machines. Even food packages offer nutrition advice. From research studies with contradictory findings to marketing claims for competing products, potential sources of confusion abound.

You're probably not fooled by the ads for diets and supplements in your e-mail inbox, but what kinds of nutrition messages *can* you trust? Which claims are backed up by scientific evidence, and of those, which are relevant to you? How can you evaluate the various sources of nutrition information and find out whether the advice they provide is accurate and reliable? How can you navigate the Internet to find nutrition facts and avoid nutrition myths? How can you develop a way of eating that's right for you—one that supports your physical activity, allows you to maintain a healthful weight, and helps you avoid chronic disease? And if you're pursuing a career in nutrition or another healthcare field, how can you continue to obtain the most current and valid information about food and physical activity as you work with individual clients?

Why We Wrote This Book

The Science of Nutrition, second edition, began with the conviction that both students and instructors would benefit from an accurate, clear, and engaging textbook that links nutrients with their functional benefits. As instructors, we recognized that students have a natural interest in their bodies, their health, their weight, and their success in sports and other activities. We developed this text to demonstrate how nutrition relates to these interests. *The Science of Nutrition,* second edition, empowers you to reach your personal health and fitness goals while also teaching you about the scientific evidence linking nutrition with disease. This information will be vital to your success as you build a career in nutrition or another health-related discipline. You'll also learn how to debunk nutrition myths and how to distinguish nutrition fact from fiction. Throughout the chapters, material is presented in lively narrative that is scientifically sound and that continually links the evidence with these goals. Information on current events and recent and ongoing research keeps the inquisitive spark alive, illustrating that nutrition is not a "dead" science but rather a source of spirited ongoing debate.

The content of *The Science of Nutrition,* second edition, is designed for nutrition and other science and healthcare majors, but it is also applicable and accessible to students in the liberal arts. We present the "science of nutrition" in a conversational style with engaging features that encourage you to apply the material to your own life and to the lives of future clients. To support visual learning, the writing is supplemented by illustrations and photos that are attractive, effective, and always level-appropriate. As teachers, we are familiar with the myriad challenges of presenting nutrition information in the classroom. We have therefore developed an exceptional ancillary package with a variety of tools to assist instructors in successfully meeting these challenges. We hope to contribute to the excitement of teaching and learning about nutrition: a subject that affects every one of us; a subject so important and relevant that correct and timely information can make the difference between health and disease.

A multitude of features throughout this new edition challenge you to think about how the recommendations of different nutritional experts (and others who may be less-than-expert, such as the media) apply to your unique health issues, activity level, energy requirements, food preferences, and lifestyle. For example, the Nutrition Myth or Fact? boxes explore the science supporting or challenging common beliefs about foods, and the Highlight boxes explore research across a range of important, specific nutritional issues. The end-of-chapter Nutrition Debates cover multi-sided aspects of hot topics and nutritional controversies, and the Nutrition Label Activities help students understand how to interpret food label information so they can make better nutritonal choices. In providing these features, in addition to new features listed below, we hope that by the time you finish this book, you'll feel more confident and engaged in making decisions about your diet and physical activity.

Nutri-Case: You Play the Expert!

In addition to the features mentioned above, our updated Nutri-Case feature provides readers with a chance to evaluate the nutrition-related beliefs and behaviors of five people representing a range of backgrounds and nutritional challenges. As you encounter them, keep in mind that these case scenarios are for instructional purposes, and not intended to suggest that students using this text are qualified to offer nutritional advice to others. In the real world, only properly trained and licensed health professionals are qualified to provide nutritional counseling. Take a moment to get acquainted with our Nutri-Case characters here.

Hannah

Hi, I'm Hannah. I'm 18 years old and in my first year at Valley Community College. I haven't made up my mind yet about my major. All I know for sure is that I don't want to work in a hospital like my mom! I got good grades in high school, but I'm a little freaked out by college so far. There's so much homework, plus one of my courses has a lab, plus I have to work part-time because my mom doesn't have the money to put me through school . . . Sometimes I feel like I just can't handle it all. And when I get stressed out, I eat. I've already gained 10 pounds and I haven't even finished my first semester!

Theo

Hi, I'm Theo. Let's see, I'm 21, and my parents moved to the Midwest from Nigeria 11 years ago. The first time I ever played basketball, in middle school, I was hooked. I won lots of awards in high school and then got a full scholarship to the state university, where I'm a junior studying political science. I decided to take a nutrition course because, last year, I had a hard time making it through the playing season, plus keeping up with my classes and homework. I want to have more energy, so I thought maybe I'm not eating right. Anyway, I want to figure out this food thing before basketball season starts again.

Liz

I'm Liz, I'm 20, and I'm a dance major at the School for Performing Arts. Last year, two other dancers from my class and I won a state championship and got to dance in the New Year's Eve celebration at the governor's mansion. This spring, I'm going to audition for the City Ballet, so I have to be in top condition. I wish I had time to take a nutrition course, but I'm too busy with dance classes and rehearsals and teaching a dance class for kids. But it's okay, because I get lots of tips from other dancers and from the Internet. Like last week, I found a Web site especially for dancers that explained how to get rid of bloating before an audition. I'm going to try it for my audition with the City Ballet!

Judy

I'm Judy, Hannah's mother, and I'm a nurse's aide at Valley Hospital. Back when Hannah was a baby, I dreamed of going to college so I could be a registered nurse. But then my ex and I split up, and Hannah and me, we've been in survival mode ever since. I'm proud to have raised my daughter without any handouts, and I do good work, but the pay never goes far enough and it's exhausting. I guess that's partly because I'm out of shape, and my blood sugar's high, too. Most nights, I'm so tired at the end of my shift that I just pick up some fast food for supper. I know I should be making home-cooked meals, but like I said, I'm in survival mode.

Gustavo

Hello. My name is Gustavo. Around 46 years ago, when I was 13, I came to the United States from Mexico with my parents and three sisters to pick crops in California, and now I manage a large vineyard. They ask me when I'm going to retire, but I can still work as hard as a man half my age. Health problems? None. Well, maybe my doctor tells me my blood pressure is high, but that's normal for my age! I guess what keeps me going is thinking about how my father died 6 months after he retired. He had colon cancer, but he never knew it until it was too late. Anyway, I watch the nightly news and read the papers, so I keep up on what's good for me, "Eat less salt" and all that stuff. I'm doing great!

Throughout this text, you'll read about these five characters as they grapple with myriad nutrition-related challenges in their lives. As you do, you might find that they remind you of people you know, and you may also discover you have something in common with one or more of them. Our hope is that by applying the information you learn in this course to their situations, you will deepen your understanding of the importance of nutrition in your own life.

New in the Second Edition

Four new **In Depth** "mini chapters" cover the key areas of Alcohol, Vitamins and Minerals, Phytochemicals and Functional Foods, and Disordered Eating, and offer instructors flexibility in using them in their course. The Vitamins and Minerals In Depth specifically serves as an overview of micronutrient basics prior to the first functional chapter, while the other In Depths provide a focused presentation of other key content for students.

The **Nutri-Case** character of Hannah (whom you met above, and who in the first edition was a young child) has now been re-imagined as an 18-year-old first-year college student, living at home and struggling with her weight. A new Nutri-Case character, Judy, has been added, replacing Nadia from the first edition. Judy is Hannah's mother, and suffers from poor eating habits, overweight, and borderline diabetes. Together, Hannah and Judy highlight many common nutritional issues that run in and through families, such as the home environment and shared eating patterns.

See for Yourself is a new self-assessment feature at the end of each chapter offering brief, targeted activities that emphasize active learning and applied skills, and provide students the opportunityto learn about their own nutrition and health habits.

Revised **Nutrition Debates** encourage students to become better-informed and discriminating consumers of nutrition information. In this new edition they are more clinically based and include an added **Critical Thinking** component at the end of each debate.

Chapter material on **Digestion, Metabolism,** and **Bone Health** feature updated content reflecting current research and recommendations, enhancing the text's relevance and clarity.

Enhanced **figurative art** throughout the book helps students better visualize important processes in the body.

Updated **Food Source Diagrams** provide pictures of the best food sources for each nutrient so that they are more easily identifiable.

A newly redesigned open-access **Companion Website** offers students an even easier-to-navigate site organized by learning areas, including: **See It, Read It, Study It, Review It,** and **Do It.** The **Study It** section, via a pass code, provides additional targeted help with access to an **Online Study Guide**, additional math and chemistry help with the **Get Ready for Nutrition** ebook and pre/post quizzing, and Janice Thompson's new and stimulating short videos on the ten toughest concepts in nutrition.

A newly redesigned **MyNutritionLab** takes advantage of the reorganization of online materials by learning area, as with the Companion Website just described. In addition, MyNutritionLab also includes the myEBook, *ABC News* videos, and forty nutrition animations.

Instructors have more help than ever with a syllabus converter, an .rtf version of the Test Bank that can easily be imported into Respondus and other testing programs, and peer teaching ideas with the print supplement *Great Ideas in Nutrition* along with the new Teaching Nutrition Community.

The Visual Walkthrough at the front of the book provides additional information on the new features in the second edition. For specific changes to each chapter, see below.

Chapter 1

- Moved the vitamins/minerals overview to the new In Depth on Vitamins and Minerals.
- Added two new Nutri-Cases, Theo and Liz.
- Deleted a redundant narrative section on career options in nutrition.
- Substantially expanded information previously in the Nutrition Debate on nutrition research and the scientific method, and placed it in the body of the chapter.
- Added a new Nutrition Debate on nutrigenomics.
- Added a new See for Yourself self-assessment developed around a 24-hour dietary recall.

Chapter 2

- Revised and updated chapter-opening Test Yourself questions.
- Added new chapter opener content focusing on the health effects of a poor quality diet.
- Edited the discussion of the concept of moderation in a healthy diet.
- Deleted Table 2.1 (not essential for student learning).
- Expanded the discussion on label claims and added a discussion of structure/function claims.
- Deleted Table 2.3 (the information is now thoroughly covered in the text).
- Deleted Table 2.4 (not applicable to the target audience).
- Emphasized information on USDA Food Guide, and clarified that MyPyramid is the graphic representation of the USDA Food Guide.
- Deleted the discussion of the food groups in MyPyramid (the information can be easily found on the MyPyramid website).
- Deleted the narrative on limitations of MyPyramid within the chapter (the information is covered in the Nutrition Debate on this topic).
- Replaced Tables 2.6 and 2.7 with figures that more engagingly illustrate sample diets across various energy intakes, and comparison of meals either high or low in energy density.
- Deleted the Latin American Diet Pyramid and retained the Asian and Vegetarian Pyramids as examples; retained Mediterranean Diet Pyramid and inserted content into the Highlight box on the health benefits of the Mediterranean Diet.
- Updated information on portion sizes and added the related You Do The Math feature.
- Added new Figure 2.8 on increasing portion sizes.
- Deleted the discussion of various diet plans and inserted the content into other chapters.
- Moved the content on the Meal Exchange System to the appendix.
- Added the See for Yourself feature on label reading related to nutrient, health, and structure/function claims.
- Added/revised two new Nutri-Cases.
- Added/updated the Nutrition Debate on revising the USDA Food Guide Pyramid.

Chapter 3

- Enhanced and updated the art in Figures 3.2, 3.3, 3.4, 3.5, 3.6, 3.8, 3.10. 3.11, and 3.18.
- Improved the pedagogy in the discussion on factors influencing eating behaviors and the accompanying figure in the opening narrative section.
- Added a new Nutri-Case, Judy.
- Updated the research on the sense of taste.
- Redrew the figure comparing peristalsis and segmentation.
- Revised and updated the research on food allergies, celiac disease, and irritable bowel syndrome.
- Deleted the Highlight box on medications used in heartburn and GERD.
- Moved the previous See for Yourself to the print supplements and added a new one wherein students keep a log to determine whether they eat in response to external or internal cues.
- Added a new Nutrition Debate: Should All School-Age Children Be Screened for Celiac Disease?

- Moved the narrative within the former Nutrition Debate on probiotics to the new In Depth on phytochemicals and functional foods.
- Added/revised two new Nutri-Cases.

Chapter 4

- Enhanced and updated the art in Figures 4.6 and 4.11.
- Revised the chapter title to be more appropriate for and specific to carbohydrates.
- Updated and developed new Test Yourself questions.
- Provided new chapter opener content on type 2 diabetes.
- Updated and revised the discussion of fiber to reduce repetition within the chapter.
- Revised and updated Figure 4.10 for more engaging illustration of the concept.
- Added new Figure 4.12 on how fiber may reduce blood cholesterol.
- Replaced Table 4.4 on fiber content of common foods with new Figure 4.15.
- Replaced Table 4.5 on comparison of two high-carbohydrate diets with new Figure 4.16.
- Deleted the Highlight box on Risk Factors for Type 2 Diabetes, and revised it into the See For Yourself assessment of readers' diabetes risks.
- Added/revised two new Nutri-Cases.
- Added a new Nutrition Debate on high-fructose corn syrup and the obesity epidemic.

In Depth: Alcohol

- This new "mini-chapter" has been added in this edition to focus on the effects of alcohol from a nutritional perspective.

Chapter 5

- Enhanced and updated the art in Figure 5.8.
- Added/revised two new Nutri-Cases.
- Added/updated end of chapter Nutrition Debate on the role nutrition professionals play in shaping debates about foods.

Chapter 6

- Enhanced and updated the art in Figures 6.8 and 6.11.
- Revised Test Yourself question 3.
- Updated chapter opener content on current athletes who are vegetarians.
- Revised and clarified information on protein quality scores.
- Added new Figure 6.6 on protein turnover.
- Replaced former Table 6.2 on complementary food combinations with new Figure 6.9.
- Replaced Figure 6.10 (single photo of edema) with revised Figure 6.12 illustrating the role of proteins in energy balance and comparing a non-edemic and edemic foot.
- Added new Figure 6.14 on nitrogen balance.
- Converted Table 6.4 on protein intakes of athletes into textual narrative.
- Reduced the size of Table 6.3 (protein content of common foods).
- Revised and clarified information on why people may eat vegetarian diets.
- Replaced the previous vegetarian pyramid with new Figure 6.15.
- Condensed chapter summary material.
- Added a new See for Yourself feature: Tips for Adding Legumes to Your Daily Diet.

- Added a new Nutrition Debate on the environmental benefits of eating less meat.
- Added/revised two new Nutri-Cases.

Chapter 7

- Added/revised two new Nutri-Cases.
- Added a new end of chapter Nutrition Debate on carnitine supplements.

In Depth: Vitamins and Minerals: Micronutrients with Macro Powers

- This new "mini-chapter" has been added in this edition to serve as a traditional overview of micronutrient basics prior to the innovative "applied approach" to the content in Chapters 8, 9, 10, 11, and 12.

Chapter 8

- Added/revised two new Nutri-Cases.
- Added a new end of chapter Nutrition Debate on treating premenstrual syndrome with vitamin B_6.

Chapter 9

- Enhanced and updated the art in Figures 9.4 and 9.7.
- Added new Figure 9.9, an enhanced graph showing food sources of potassium.
- Added new Figure 9.10, an enhanced graph showing food sources of phosphorous.
- Added/revised two new Nutri-Cases.
- Added a new end of chapter Nutrition Debate on the hype and reality behind sports beverages.

Chapter 10

- Moved information on phytochemicals to the expanded In Depth on phytochemicals.
- Updated Test Yourself questions.
- Added new chapter opener content to make it more applicable to college/university lifestyles.
- Condensed the background information on antioxidants.
- Deleted Table 10.1 for redundancy.
- Deleted Table 10.2 and replaced it with nutrient summary content in the margin.
- Deleted Table 10.3 and replaced it with the Highlight box: Nutritional Factors That Increase Our Risk for Cancer.
- Deleted Table 10.4 (information is now presented in In Depth on phytochemicals).
- Updated and enhanced food source Figures 10.4, 10.7, 10.9, 10.13, and 10.15.
- Condensed the discussion of selenium.
- Revised and updated the discussion of cancer.
- Added new Figure 10.18 of normal lungs and smoker's lungs.
- Updated the Highlight box: Disorders Linked to Tobacco Use, and added figures illustrating mouth cancer and premature wrinkling.
- Added new Figure 10.20, and the related discussion of human papillomavirus in relation to cancer.
- Added new Figure 10.21 on melanoma in the discussion on skin cancer.
- Deleted the Highlight box on Cancer Prevention Recommendations and replaced it with the new See for Yourself assessment feature with an American Cancer Society quiz.

- Edited and updated information on macular degeneration and cataracts.
- Revised Figure 10.22 to illustrate visual changes with eye disorders.
- Updated the Nutrition Debate on vitamin and mineral supplementation.
- Added/revised two new Nutri-Cases.

In Depth: Phytochemicals and Functional Foods

- This new "mini-chapter" has been added in this edition to develop and highlight this important nutritional area for students.

Chapter 11

- Added new Test Yourself questions 4 and 5.
- Updated chapter opener content.
- Deleted Table 11.2 and replaced with nutrient summary in the margin.
- Updated and enhanced food source Figures 1.6, 11.10, 11.13, and 11.14.
- Added new Figure 11.7 on serving sizes and energy content of various foods containing same amount of calcium as an 8 fl oz glass of milk.
- Revised and condensed the Highlight box on calcium supplements.
- Added new Figure 11.9, a map of the United States showing geographical location of 40° latitude.
- Updated chapter information on vitamin D recommendations.
- Added a new Nutrition Debate on the controversy surrounding whether to increase current vitamin D recommendations.
- Revised and condensed the discussion on treatments for osteoporosis.
- Added a new See for Yourself feature on assessing calcium supplements in regards to the cost and amount of calcium as compared to eating calcium-rich foods.
- Added/revised two new Nutri-Cases.

Chapter 12

- Added/revised two new Nutri-Cases.
- Added/revised/updated end-of-chapter Nutrition Debate on the pros and cons of using zinc lozenges in treating cold symptoms.

Chapter 13

- Enhanced and updated the art in Figure 13.13.
- Added/revised two new Nutri-Cases.
- Added/revised/updated end-of-chapter Nutrition Debate on the details and physical effects of high protein diets.

In Depth: Disordered Eating

- This new "mini-chapter" has been added in this edition to specifically cover critical content on disordered eating and its consequences in a fuller and more comprehensive way than previously done.

Chapter 14

- Condensed information on components of a sound fitness program, the FIT principle, and warm-up and cool-down.
- Deleted the Highlight box: Life or Death Consequences Related to Sports Nutrition.

- Revised chapter-opening Test Yourself questions.
- Converted former Table 14.2 into new Figure 14.3 with photos.
- Converted former Table 14.8 into new Figure 14.13 on Symptoms of Dehydration During Heavy Exercise.
- Redesigned Figure 14.8 (formerly Figure 14.7) to include illustrations of activities.
- Redesigned Figure 14.12 (formerly Figure 14.11) to more clearly illustrate the concept of the effects of low-carbohydrate diet on muscle glycogen stores.
- Updated a Nutri-Case to include new character, Judy.
- Merged Recaps throughout the chapter for greater clarity and ease of integration.
- Deleted former Table 14.3: Physical Activity Guidelines for Achieving Health versus Physical Fitness.
- Updated the Nutrition Debate: How Much Physical Activity Is Enough?
- Added/revised two new Nutri-Cases.

Chapter 15

- Enhanced and updated the art in Figure 15.5.
- Updated chapter content regarding current information on food contaminations and on related government interventions.
- Added chapter content on marine toxins.
- Added new figure on bioaccumulation.
- Added content on new methods of packaging, and added new figure.
- Added the discussion on the use of antibiotics in animals raised for food and related issues.
- Added a new Highlight box: Food Safety at a Barbecue.
- Added/revised two new Nutri-Cases.
- Added/revised/updated Nutrition Debate on genetically modified organisms.

Chapter 16

- Added/revised two new Nutri-Cases.
- Added/revised/updated Nutrition Debate on issues and controversies surrounding breastfeeding.

Chapter 17

- Enhanced and updated the art in Figures 17.6 and 17.10.
- Added/revised two new Nutri-Cases.
- Added/revised/updated Nutrition Debate on issues and controversies surrounding vitamin D supplementation.

Chapter 18

- Added/revised two new Nutri-Cases.
- Added/revised/updated Nutrition Debate on longevity diets.

Chapter 19

- Added/revised two new Nutri-Cases.
- Added/revised/updated Nutrition Debate on the effects of tariffs and subsidies on food growers around the world.

Appendices and Back Matter

- Updated and developed former Appendix A, Nutrient Values of Foods, into a stand-alone, full supplement: *The Food Composition Table*.
- Added new Figure A.11, Metabolism Overview.
- Enhanced and updated the art in Figures C.2, C.6, C.10, D.11, D.13, and D.17.
- Dropped Appendix E, Nutrition and Physical Activity Recommendations for Canadians (the material is represented in our Canada edition).
- Dropped Appendix G, Traditional Organization of Nutrients (the material is now covered within the text).
- The Answers to Review Questions now include complete answers to all the end-of-chapter Review Questions, in print form at the end of the text.

Supplemental Resources for Instructors and Students

For the Instructor

Instructor's Manual

978-0-321-66757-1 / 0-321-66757-3

This resource lets instructors create engaging lectures and additional activities with chapter summaries; objectives; lecture outlines; key terms; and activity ideas, including a diet analysis activity and a Nutrition Debate activity for each chapter, in addition to The Real Deal activities that engage students with improving their daily nutrition in the real world.

Printed and Computerized Test Banks

978-0-321-66758-8 / 0-321-66758-1

The Test Bank, available in both print and computerized formats, provides short-answer, multiple-choice, true/false, matching, and essay questions for material from each text chapter. The computerized test bank is provided within the IR-DVD.

Instructor Resource DVD

978-0-321-66759-5 / 0-321-66759-X

The Instructor Resource DVD (IR-DVD) offers everything instructors need to create lecture presentations and other course materials, including JPEG and PowerPoint® files of all the art, tables, and selected photos from the text, with the ability to edit labels and view "stepped-out" art for selected figures from the text. The IR-DVD also includes in each chapter PowerPoint® lecture outlines with embedded links to ABC News Lecture Launcher Videos, a Jeopardy-type quiz show, Instructor's Manual, Test Bank, and questions for Classroom Response Systems (CRS) in PowerPoint® format, allowing professors to import these questions into their own CRS. It also includes a new video series with Janice Thompson, the lead author, geared especially for students that reviews the toughest topics covered in the text and provides strategies for dealing with them.

Great Ideas: Active Ways to Teach Nutrition

978-0-321-59646-8 / 0-321-59646-3

This updated, revised booklet compiles the best ideas from nutrition instructors across the country on innovative ways to teach nutrition topics with an emphasis on active learning.

Broken into useful pedagogic areas including targeted and general classroom activities and an overview of active learning principles, this booklet provides creative ideas for teaching nutrition concepts, along with tips and suggestions for classroom activities that can be used to teach almost any topic.

MyDietAnalysis 4.0 Online

978-0-321-66813-4 / 0-321-66813-8

MyDietAnalysis offers an accurate, reliable, and easy-to-use program for your students' diet analysis needs. Developed by the nutrition database experts at ESHA Research, Inc. and tailored for use in college nutrition courses, MyDietAnalysis features a database of nearly 20,000 foods and multiple reports. MyDietAnalysis is available at a significant discount when packaged with the text. The new 4.0 online version additionally features videos with assessment quizzes to reduce student error, professor/student relationship to help with tracking paperless reports, the ability to see class statistics, and even more ethnic foods.

MyDietAnalysis 3.0 CD-ROM

MyDietAnalysis offers an accurate, reliable, and easy-to-use program for your students' diet analysis needs. Developed by the nutrition database experts at ESHA Research, Inc. and tailored for use in college nutrition courses, MyDietAnalysis features a database of nearly 20,000 foods and multiple reports. MyDietAnalysis is available at a significant discount when packaged with the text. The 3.0 CD-ROM builds on its easy-use interface and unique assessment activity and includes the following features: serving size help, more ethnic foods, and a unique annotation feature on reports so students can respond to the assignment right on the report.

Rich Text File version of the Test Bank

A Rich text file version of the Test Bank is provided for easy import into Respondus along with other computerized testing programs.

MyNutritionLab Instructor Access Kit

978-0-321-66790-8 / 0-321-66790-5

Powered by CourseCompass™, MyNutritionLab includes everything needed to teach introductory nutrition in one convenient place, with content that can be customized for each course. Students and instructors can easily access case studies, animations, RSS feeds, study tools, an e-book, quizzes, a gradebook, ABC News videos, and much more. Content is easily navigated by learning areas, including: **See It, Read It, Study It, Review It, Do It.** The **Study It** sections provide students with extra help in three ways: access to the Online Study Guide, extra math and chemistry preparation with the Get Ready for Nutrition diagnostics, and Janice Thompson's concise videos on the toughest topics in nutrition.

MyNutritionLab with MyDietAnalysis Instructor Access Kit

978-0-321-66737-3 / 0-321-66737-9

Powered by CourseCompass™, MyNutritionLab includes everything needed to teach introductory nutrition in one convenient place with content that can be customized for each course. Students and instructors can easily access case studies, animations, RSS feeds, study tools, an e-book, quizzes, a gradebook, and much more. Content is easily navigated by learning areas, including: **See It, Read It, Study It, Review It, Do It.** The **Study It** sections give students extra help in three ways: access to the Online Study Guide, extra math and chemistry preparation with the Get Ready for Nutrition diagnostics, and Janice Thompson's concise videos on the toughest topics in nutrition.

WebCT Premium

978-0-321-66763-2 / 0-321-66763-8

www.pearsonhighered.com/webct
WebCT includes the entire Companion website, plus instructor resources and a Tutor Center link.

BlackBoard Premium

978-0-321-66762-5 / 0-321-66762-X

www.pearsonhighered.com/blackboard
BlackBoard includes the entire Companion Website, plus instructor resources and a Tutor Center link.

Teaching Nutrition Community

www.pearsonhighered.com/nutritioncommunity
This site offers a one-stop resource for connecting with fellow educators, sharing ideas, and keeping up-to-date on the latest happenings in the world of nutrition education.

For the Student

MyDietAnalysis 4.0

Via online access code card

MyDietAnalysis 3.0 CD-ROM

978-0-321-66769-4 / 0-321-66769-7

MyDietAnalysis offers an accurate, reliable, and easy-to-use program for students' diet analysis needs. Developed by the nutrition database experts at ESHA Research, Inc. and tailored for use in college nutrition courses, MyDietAnalysis features a database of nearly 20,000 foods and multiple reports. MyDietAnalysis is available at a significant discount when packaged with the text. The 3.0 CD-ROM features multiple profiles, a unique activity assessment, and a user-friendly interface. The new 3.0 online version additionally features serving size help, more ethnic foods, and a unique annotation feature on reports so students can respond to the assignment right on the report.

MyNutritionLab Student Access Kit

978-0-321-66789-2 / 0-321-66789-1

MyNutritionLab with MyDietAnalysis Student Access Kit

978-0-321-66792-2 / 0-321-66792-1

Companion Website

978-0-321-66760-1 / 0-321-66760-3

www.pearsonhighered.com/thompson
The *Science of Nutrition*, second edition, Companion Website offers students chapter and cumulative quizzes with immediate feedback, Web links, flashcards, a glossary, new RSS feeds, answers to review questions, suggested answers to the Nutri-Cases, further discussion and exercises related to the Nutrition Debates, and examples of clinical case studies for each chapter. It also includes a new video series with Janice Thompson, the lead author, geared especially for students that reviews the toughest topics covered in the text and provides

strategies for dealing with them. The site is additionally enhanced with its easy-to-navigate organization by learning area: **See It, Read It, Study It, Review It, Do It**. The **Study It** sections contain access to the Student Study Guide. The Study Guide will help students get the best grade possible with terminology questions, text outlines, study questions, completion exercises, practice tests, and critical thinking sections for each chapter.

Eat Right! Healthy Eating in College and Beyond
978-0-8053-8288-4 / 0-8053-8288-7

This handy, full-color, eighty-page booklet provides students with practical guidelines, tips, shopper's guides, and recipes so they can start putting healthy eating guidelines into action. Written specifically for students, topics include: healthy eating in the cafeteria, dorm room, and fast food restaurants; eating on a budget; weight-management tips; vegetarian alternatives; and guidelines on alcohol and health.

Acknowledgments

It is eye-opening to write a textbook and to realize that the work of so many people contributes to the final product. There are numerous people to thank, and we'd like to begin by extending our thanks to the fabulous staff at Pearson Benjamin Cummings for their incredible support and dedication to this book. Publisher Frank Ruggirello committed extensive resources to ensure the quality of this text, and his support and enthusiasm helped us maintain the momentum we needed to complete this project. Our acquisitions editor, Sandy Lindelof, provided unwavering vision, support, and guidance throughout the process of writing and publishing this book. We could never have completed this text without the exceptional writing and organizational skills of Laura Bonazzoli, our developmental editor and co-writer. Laura's energy, enthusiasm, and creativity significantly enhanced the quality of this textbook. We want to express our sincere gratitude to our project editor, Susan Scharf. We know that managing all the aspects of a textbook is a bit like herding cats. Susan worked tirelessly to improve the text and steer us on our course, and kept us sane with her patience, sense of humor, and excellent editorial instincts. We are also indebted to art development editor Laura Southworth, who developed a spectacular art program for the text and then enhanced it even more in this edition with thoughtful improvements and the careful attention to detail that we have come to expect. Our thanks also to Marie Beaugureau and Deirdre Espinoza, for their guidance and support in this and previous editions. Brianna Paulson, editorial assistant extraordinaire, provided superior editorial and administrative support that we would have been lost without.

Multiple talented players helped build this book in the production and design process as well. Beth Masse, our talented production supervisor, and the resourceful Norine Strang and her colleagues at S4Carlisle Publishing Services, kept manuscripts moving throughout the process, and expertly tracked the many important details in this complex project. We'd also like to thank Debbie Cogan, senior managing editor, for her guidance and assistance; Derek Bacchus, design manager, who developed the elegant interior for this edition; and Donna Kalal, senior art and photo coordinator, who supervised the photo program. Yvo Riezebos surpassed himself by creating yet another stunning cover. Kristin Piljay performed research for many of the excellent photos that appear in this edition.

We can't go without thanking the marketing and sales teams who have been working so hard to get this book out to those who will benefit most from it, especially senior marketing manager Neena Bali and the excellent Pearson Marketing Communications team for their enthusiastic support and innovative ideas. Thanks also to Brooke Suchomel, market development manager, who coordinated class testing, nutrition forums, and conducted extensive market research to ensure our writing efforts met the needs of students and instructors.

We would also like to again express our gratitude to Carole Conn from the University of New Mexico, for her contribution to the immunity content in the previous edition. And our goal of meeting instructor and student needs could not have been realized without the team of educators and editorial staff who worked on the substantial supplements package for *The Science of Nutrition*. Sarah Young-Dualan, media producer, expertly supervised all aspects of the media program and the Companion Website, with assistance from the ever-resourceful Brianna Paulson, who also managed development of the print supplements. Media authors and contributors were Jeanne S. Boone (Palm Beach Community College, South); Kathy D. Munoz (Humboldt State University); Deborah Bella (Oregon State University); LuAnn Soliah (Baylor University); and Carol Friesen (Ball State University). Thanks also to Nicole George-O'Brien and Matthew Monte, for their contributions to and assistance with the media products. Print supplements authors and contributors include Janet Peterson (Linfield College), who wrote the Test Bank; Katie Wiedman (University of St. Francis), for the Instructor Manual; Colleen Loveland (Dallas County Community College) developed the Study Guide; Elizabeth Quintana (West Virginia University) developed the PowerPoint Lecture Slides, and also reviewed the Test Bank accuracy; and Patricia Munn (Metropolitan Community Colleges, Longview) reviewed the Test Bank accuracy. Thanks also to Diane Moyer (Metropolitan State College of Denver) for her expert review of the Food Composition Table. Our gratitude to all for their valuable contributions to this edition.

We would also like to thank the many colleagues, friends, and family members who helped us along the way. Janice would specifically like to thank her supportive and hard-working colleagues at the University of Bristol. She says, "Their encouragement and enthusiasm keep me going through seemingly endless deadlines. My family and friends have been so incredibly wonderful throughout my career. Mom, Dianne, Pam, Steve, Aunt Judy, and cousin Julie are always there for me to offer a sympathetic ear, a shoulder to cry on, and endless encouragement. Although my Dad is no longer with us, his unwavering love and faith in my abilities inspired me to become who I am. I am always amazed that my friends and family actually read my books to learn more about nutrition—thanks for your never-ending support! You are incredible people who keep me sane and healthy and help me to remember the most important things in life." Melinda would specifically like to thank her husband, Steve Carroll, for the patience and understanding he has shown through this process—once again. He has learned that there is always another chapter due! Melinda would also like to thank her family, friends, and professional colleagues for their support and listening ear through this whole process. You have all helped make life a little easier during this incredibly busy time. Linda would like to acknowledge the unwavering support of her family and friends, a solid network of love and understanding that keeps her afloat. She would also like to thank Janice and Melinda for providing the opportunity to learn and grow through the process of writing this book.

Janice L. Thompson

Melinda M. Manore

Linda A. Vaughan

Reviewers

Kim Aaronson
Truman College

Amy Allen-Chabot
Anne Arundel Community College

Kim Archer
Stephen F. Austin State University

Julianne Arient
Triton College

Deborah Bella
Oregon State University

Jenna A. Bell-Wilson
Ohio State University

Jeanne Boone
Palm Beach Community College

John Capeheart
University of Houston, Downtown

Erin Caudill
Southeast Community College

Dorothy Chen-Maynard
California State University, San Bernadino

Susan Chou
American River College

Susan Cooper
Montana State University, Great Falls College of Technology

Jennifer Coppola
Sacramento City College

Ava Craig-Waite
Sacramento City College

Robert Cullen
Illinois State University

Norma Daly
Community College of Denver

Evelyn Elshaw
South Puget Sound Community College

Karon Felten
University of Nevada, Reno

Pam Fletcher
TVI Community College

Susan Gaumont
Chandler-Gilbert Community College

Jill Golden
Orange Coast College

Susan Gollnick
California Polytechnic State University, San Luis Obispo

Jana Gonsalves
California Polytechnic State University, San Luis Obispo

Gloria Gonzalez
Pensacola Junior College

Mel Govindan
Fitchburg State College

Charlene Hamilton
University of Delaware

Donna Handley
University of Rhode Island

Leslie Hayden-Malloy
San Francisco State University

Susan Helm
Pepperdine University

Kimberly Henige
University of Southern California

James Hollis
Purdue University

Julie Hood
Central Oregon Community College

Rafida Idris
Alcorn State University

Karen Israel
Anne Arundel Community College

Allen Knehans
University of Oklahoma

Jennifer Koslo
Glendale Community College

Robert Lee
Central Michigan University

Janet Levins
Pensacola Junior College

Rosanna Licht
Palm Beach Community College

Colleen Loveland
Dallas County Community College

Kim Lower
Collin County Community College

Rose Martin
Pennsylvania State University

Jean McCurry
Cascadia Community College

Kim McMahon
Utah State University

Glen F. McNeil
Fort Hays State University

Monica Meadows
University of Texas, Austin

Gina Marie Morris
Frank Phillips College

Judith Myhand
Louisiana State University

Anna Page
Johnson County Community College

Erwina Peterson
Yakima Valley Community College

Janet Peterson
Linfield College

Judi Phillips
Del Mar College

Elizabeth Quintana
West Virginia University

Scott Reaves
California Polytechnic State University, San Luis Obispo

Ruth Reed
Juniata College

Christina Reiter
Metropolitan State College of Denver

Andrew Rorschach
University of Houston

Zara Rowlands
Youngstown State University

Denise Russo
Cabrillo College

Janet Sass
Northern Virginia Community College, Annandale

Mollie Smith
California State University, Fresno

LuAnn Soliah
Baylor University

Carol Stinson
University of Louisville

Fred Surgent
Frostburg State University

Jo Taylor
Southeast Community College

Carol Turner
New Mexico State University

Elizabeth Vargo
Community College of Allegheny County

Andrea Villarreal
Phoenix College

Eric Vlahov
University of Tampa

Daryle Wane
Pasco-Hernando Community College

Dana Wassmer
Cosumnes River College

Suzy Weems
Stephen F. Austin State University

Katie Wiedman
University of Saint Francis

Jessie Yearwood
Dallas County Community College District

Gloria Young
Virginia State University

Jane Ziegler
Cedar Crest College

Nutrition Forum and Focus Group Participants

Janet Anderson
Utah State University

Mary Beck
Owens Community College

Michael Bizeau
Colorado State University

Jeanne Boone
Palm Beach Community College

Lorrie Brilla
Western Washington University

Tricia Davidson
Sussex County Community College

Alice Fly
Indiana University

Rachel Freiberg
Canada College

Trish Froehlich
Palm Beach Community College

Sherrie Frye
University of North Carolina

Teresa Fung
Simmons College

Kimberly Henige
University of Southern California

Peter Henkel
Johnson & Wales University

Karen Israel
Anne Arundel Community College

Carol Johnston
Arizona State University, East Campus

Jay Kandiah
Ball State University

Rose Martin
Pennsylvania State University

Monica Meadows
University of Texas

Huanbiao Mo
Texas Women's University

Owen Murphy
University of Colorado Boulder

Janet Peterson
Linfield College

Janet Sass
Northern Virginia Community College

Carrie Schroeder McConnell
Metropolitan State College of Denver

Victoria Smith
North Hennepin Community College

Bernice Spurlock
Hinds Community College

Jennifer Weddig
Metropolitan State College of Denver

Brief Contents

Contents

Contents

Contents

Contents

Contents

Contents

Contents

Contents

Chapter 15: Food Safety and Technology: Impact on Consumers 581

Contents

Chapter 16: Nutrition Through the Life Cycle: Pregnancy and the First Year of Life 619

Chapter 17: Nutrition Through the Life Cycle: Childhood and Adolescence 665

Contents

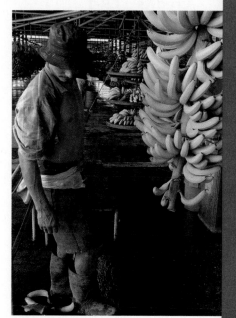

Contents

Appendices

The Science of Nutrition | Second Edition

1 The Role of Nutrition in Our Health

Test Yourself | True or False?

1 A calorie is a measure of the amount of fat in a food. **T** *or* **F**

2 Proteins are not a primary source of energy for our bodies. **T** *or* **F**

3 All vitamins must be consumed daily to support optimal health. **T** *or* **F**

4 The Recommended Dietary Allowance is the maximum amount of nutrient that people should consume to support normal body functions. **T** *or* **F**

5 Federal agencies in the United States are typically poor sources of reliable nutrition information. **T** *or* **F**

Test Yourself answers are located in the Chapter Review.

Chapter Objectives *After reading this chapter, you will be able to:*

1. Define the term *nutrition*, p. 4.

2. Discuss why nutrition is important to health, pp. 6–9.

3. Identify the six classes of nutrients essential for health, pp. 9–14.

4. Identify the Dietary Reference Intakes for nutrients, pp. 15–17.

5. Describe the process for assessing an individual's nutritional status, pp. 18–21.

6. Discuss the four steps of the scientific method, pp. 22–24.

7. List at least four sources of reliable and accurate nutrition information, pp. 28–30.

Marilyn is 58 years old and works as a clerk at a small gift shop. During the last year, she has noticed that she is becoming increasingly tired at work and feels short of breath when performing tasks that she used to do easily, such as stocking shelves. This morning, she had her blood pressure checked for free at a local market and was told by the woman conducting the test that the reading was well above average. Assuming the woman's white lab coat meant that she was a healthcare professional, Marilyn asked her whether or not high blood pressure could explain her fatigue. The woman replied that fatigue was certainly a symptom and advised Marilyn to see her physician. When Marilyn explained that she had no health insurance and little expendable income, the woman said, "Well, I'm not a physician, but I *am* a nutritionist, and I can certainly tell you that the best thing you can do to reduce your high blood pressure is to lose weight. We're running a special all month on our most popular weight-loss supplement. You take it 30 minutes before a meal and, since it's high in fiber, it makes you feel satisfied with less food. I can personally recommend it, because it helped me to lose 30 pounds."

Marilyn wasn't convinced that she needed to lose weight. Sure, she was stocky, but she'd been that way all her life, and her fatigue had only started in the past year. But then she remembered that lately she'd been having trouble getting her rings on and off and that her shoes were feeling tight. So maybe the nutritionist was right. Noticing Marilyn wavering, the nutritionist added, "A few weeks after I started taking this product, my blood pressure went from sky-high to perfectly normal." She certainly looked slender and healthy, and her personal testimonial convinced Marilyn to spend $12 of her weekly grocery budget on the smallest-size bottle of the supplements.

What do you think of the advice Marilyn received? Was the nutritionist's assessment of her nutritional status adequate? Was the treatment plan sound? Just what is a "nutritionist" anyway? In this chapter, we'll begin to answer these questions as we explore the role of nutrition in human health, identify the six classes of nutrients, and describe what constitutes a professional assessment of a person's nutritional status. You'll also learn how to evaluate nutrition-related research studies, and how to distinguish science from scams. But first, let's take a quick look at the evolution of nutrition as a distinct scientific discipline.

What Is the Science of Nutrition and How Did It Evolve?

Although many people think that *food* and *nutrition* mean the same thing, they don't. **Food** refers to the plants and animals we consume. These foods contain the energy and nutrients our bodies need to maintain life and support growth and health. **Nutrition,** in contrast, is a science. Specifically, it is the science that studies food and how food nourishes our bodies and influences our health. It identifies the processes by which we consume, digest, metabolize, and store the nutrients in foods, and how these nutrients affect our bodies. Nutrition also involves studying the factors that influence our eating patterns, making recommendations about the amount we should eat of each type of food, maintaining food safety, and addressing issues related to the global food supply.

When compared with other scientific disciplines such as chemistry, biology, and physics, nutrition is a relative newcomer. The cultivation, preservation, and preparation of food has played a critical role in the lives of humans for millennia, but in the West, the recognition of nutrition as an important contributor to health has developed slowly only during the past 400 years.

It started when researchers began to make the link between diet and illness. For instance, in the mid-1700s, long before vitamin C itself had been identified, researchers discovered that the vitamin C–deficiency disease *scurvy* could be prevented by consuming citrus fruits. By the mid-1800s, the three energy-providing nutrients—carbohydrates, lipids, and proteins—had been identified, as well as a number of essential minerals. Nutrition was coming into its own as a developing scientific discipline.

Still, vitamins were entirely unrecognized, and some fatal diseases that we now know to be due to vitamin deficiency were then thought to be due to infection. For instance, when

The study of nutrition encompasses everything about food.

food   The plants and animals we consume.

nutrition   The scientific study of food and how it nourishes the body and influences health.

Highlight
Solving the Mystery of Pellagra

In the first few years of the 20th century, Dr. Joseph Goldberger successfully controlled outbreaks of several fatal infectious diseases, from yellow fever in Louisiana to typhus in Mexico. So it wasn't surprising that, in 1914, the Surgeon General of the United States chose him to tackle another disease thought to be infectious that was raging throughout the South. Called *pellagra,* the disease was characterized by a skin rash, diarrhea, and mental impairment. At the time, it afflicted more than 50,000 people each year, and in about 10% of cases it resulted in death.

Pellagra is often characterized by a scaly skin rash.

Goldberger began studying the disease by carefully observing its occurrence in groups of people. He asked, if it is infectious, then why would it strike children in orphanages and prison inmates yet leave their nurses and guards unaffected? Why did it overwhelmingly affect impoverished mill workers and share croppers while leaving their affluent (and well-fed) neighbors healthy? Could a dietary deficiency cause pellagra? To confirm his hunch, he conducted a series of trials in which he fed afflicted orphans and prisoners, who had been consuming a limited, corn-based diet, a variety of nutrient-rich foods, including meats. They recovered. Moreover, orphans and inmates who did not have pellagra and ate the new diet did not develop the disease. Finally, Goldberger recruited eleven healthy prison inmates, who in return for a pardon of their sentence, agreed to consume a corn-based diet. After five months, six of the eleven developed pellagra.

Still, many skeptics were unable to give up the idea that pellagra was an infectious disease. So to prove that pellagra was not spread by germs, Goldberger and his colleagues deliberately injected and ingested patients' scabs, nasal secretions, and other bodily fluids. He and his team remained healthy.

Although Goldberger could not identify the precise component in the new diet that cured pellagra, he eventually found an inexpensive and widely available substance, brewer's yeast, that when added to the diet prevented or reversed the disease. Shortly after Goldberger's death in 1937, scientists identified the precise nutrient that was deficient in the diet of pellagra patients: niacin, one of the B-vitamins, which is plentiful in brewer's yeast.

Data from: Kraut, A. Dr. Joseph Goldberger and the war on pellagra. National Institutes of Health, Office of NIH History. Retrieved February 2009, from http://history.nih.gov/exhibits/goldberger; and H. Markel. 2003. The New Yorker who changed the diet of the South. *New York Times,* August 12, p. D5.

Dutch scientist Christian Eijkman began studying the fatal nerve disease *beriberi* in the 1880s, he conducted experiments designed to ferret out the causative bacterium. Finally, Eijkman discovered that replacing the polished white rice in a patient's diet with whole-grain brown rice cured the disease. Still, he surmised that something in the brown rice conferred resistance to the beriberi "germ." It was not until the 20th century that the substance missing in polished rice—the B-vitamin *thiamin*—was identified and beriberi was definitively classified as a deficiency disease.[1] Another B-vitamin, niacin, was discovered through the work of Dr. Joseph Goldberger in the early 1900s. The accompanying Highlight box describes Dr. Goldberger's daring work.

Nutrition research continued to focus on identifying and preventing deficiency diseases through the first half of the 20th century. Then, as the higher standard of living after World War II led to an improvement in the American diet, nutrition research began pursuing a new objective: supporting wellness and preventing and treating **chronic diseases**—that is, diseases that come on slowly and can persist for years, often despite treatment. Chronic diseases of particular interest to nutrition researchers include heart disease, obesity, type 2 diabetes, and various cancers. This new research has raised as many questions as it has answered, and we still have a great deal to learn about the relationship between nutrition and chronic disease.

chronic disease A disease characterized by a gradual onset and long duration, with signs and symptoms that are difficult to interpret, and which respond poorly to medical treatment.

In the closing decades of the 20th century, an exciting new area of nutrition research began to emerge. Reflecting our growing understanding of genetics, *nutrigenomics* seeks to uncover links between our genes, our environment, and our diet. The Nutrition Debate on pages 35–38 describes this new field of research in detail.

How Does Nutrition Contribute to Health?

Proper nutrition can help us improve our health, prevent certain diseases, achieve and maintain a desirable weight, and maintain our energy and vitality. When you consider that most people eat on average three meals per day, this results in almost 11,000 opportunities during a 10-year period to affect our health through nutrition. The following section provides more detail on how nutrition supports health and wellness.

Nutrition Is One of Several Factors Supporting Wellness

Traditionally, **wellness** was defined simply as the absence of disease. However, as we have learned more about our health and what it means to live a healthful lifestyle, our definition has expanded. Wellness is now considered to be a multidimensional process, one that includes physical, emotional, and spiritual health (**Figure 1.1**). Wellness is not an end point in our lives, but rather is an active process we work with every day.

In this book, we focus on two critical aspects of wellness: nutrition and physical activity. The two are so closely related that you can think of them as two sides of the same coin: our overall state of nutrition is influenced by how much energy we expend doing daily activities, and our level of physical activity has a major impact on how we use the nutrients in our food. We can perform more strenuous activities for longer periods of time when we eat a nutritious diet, whereas an inadequate or excessive food intake can make us lethargic. A poor diet, inadequate or excessive physical activity, or a combination of these also can lead to serious health problems. Finally, several studies have suggested that healthful nutrition and regular physical activity can increase feelings of well-being and reduce feelings of anxiety and depression. In other words, wholesome food and physical activity just plain feel good!

A Healthful Diet Can Prevent Some Diseases and Reduce Your Risk for Others

Nutrition appears to play a role—from a direct cause to a mild influence—in the development of many diseases (**Figure 1.2**). As we noted earlier, poor nutrition is a direct cause of

wellness A multidimensional, lifelong process that includes physical, emotional, and spiritual health.

Figure 1.1 Many factors contribute to an individual's wellness. Primary among these are a nutritious diet and regular physical activity.

Diseases in which nutrition plays some role	Osteoporosis Osteoarthritis Some forms of cancer

Diseases with a strong nutritional component	Type 2 diabetes Heart disease High blood pressure Obesity

Diseases caused by nutritional deficiencies or toxicities	Pellagra Scurvy Iron-deficiency anemia Other vitamin and mineral deficiencies Nutrient toxicities

Figure 1.2 The relationship between nutrition and human disease. Notice that whereas nutritional factors are only marginally implicated in the diseases of the top row, they are strongly linked to the development of the diseases in the middle row and truly causative of those in the bottom row.

deficiency diseases such as scurvy and pellagra. Thus, early nutrition research focused on identifying the causes of nutrient-deficiency diseases and means to prevent them. These discoveries led nutrition experts to develop guidelines for nutrient intakes that are high enough to prevent deficiency diseases, and to lobby for fortification of foods with nutrients of concern. These measures, along with a more abundant and reliable food supply, have ensured that the majority of nutrient-deficiency diseases are no longer of concern in developed countries. However, they are still major problems in many developing nations (see Chapter 19, Global Nutrition).

In addition to directly causing disease, poor nutrition can have a more subtle influence on our health. For instance, it can contribute to the development of brittle bones, a disease called *osteoporosis,* as well as to the progression of some forms of cancer. These associations are considered mild; however, poor nutrition is also strongly associated with three chronic diseases that are among the top ten causes of death in the United States (**Figure 1.3**). These

Disease

Diseases of the heart	632
Cancer	559
Stroke	137
Chronic respiratory disease	124
Unintentional injuries	122
Diabetes mellitus	72
Alzheimer's disease	72
Influenza and pneumonia	56
Inflammatory kidney disease	45
Blood poisoning	34

0   100   200   300   400   500   600   700
Number of deaths (in thousands)

Figure 1.3 Of the ten leading causes of death in the United States in 2006, three—heart disease, stroke, and diabetes—are strongly associated with poor nutrition. In addition, nutrition plays a limited role in the development of some forms of cancer.

Figure 1.4   These diagrams illustrate the increase in obesity rates across the United States from 1994 to 2007 as documented in the Behavioral Risk Factor Surveillance System. Obesity is defined as a body mass index greater than or equal to 30, or approximately 30 lb overweight for a 5′4″ woman. (Graphics from: Centers for Disease Control and Prevention, U.S. Obesity Trends 1985 to 2007, available at www.cdc.gov/nccdphp/dnpa/obesity/trends/maps.)

are heart disease, stroke, and diabetes. In one study, poor diet and physical inactivity were found to be directly responsible for about 16% of all deaths in the year 2000.[2]

It probably won't surprise you to learn that the primary link between poor nutrition and mortality is obesity. That is, obesity is fundamentally a consequence of eating more calories than are expended. At the same time, obesity is a well-established risk factor for heart disease, stroke, type 2 diabetes, and some forms of cancer. Unfortunately, the prevalence of obesity has dramatically increased throughout the United States during the past 20 years (**Figure 1.4**). Throughout this text, we will discuss in detail how nutrition and physical activity affect the development of obesity and other chronic diseases.

Healthy People 2020 Identifies Nutrition-Related Goals for the United States

Because of its importance to the wellness of all Americans, nutrition has been included in the national health promotion and disease prevention plan of the United States. Revised every decade, *Healthy People* is an agenda that promotes optimal health and disease prevention across the United States. *Healthy People 2020*, launched in January 2010, identifies a set of goals and objectives that we hope to reach as a nation by the year 2020.[3] This agenda was developed by a team of experts from a variety of federal agencies under the direction of the Department of Health and Human Services. Input was gathered from a large number of individuals and organizations, including hundreds of national and state health organizations, and the general public was asked to share its ideas.

The two overarching goals of *Healthy People* are (1) to increase quality and years of healthy life and (2) to eliminate health disparities. These goals are supported by hundreds of more specific goals and objectives. The importance of nutrition is underscored by the number of nutrition-related objectives in the agenda. Other objectives address physical activity and the problem with overweight and obesity, both of which are of course influenced by nutrition.

Table 1.1 identifies some of the specific goals and objectives related to nutrition and physical activity from *Healthy People 2010*. A version of this table derived from *Healthy People 2020* is available on our Web site at www.pearsonhighered.com/thompsonmanore.

Table 1.1 Nutrition and Fitness Goals and Objectives from *Healthy People 2010*

Focus Area	Goal	Objective Number and Description
Nutrition and overweight	Promote health and reduce chronic disease associated with diet and weight.	19–1. Increase the proportion of adults who are at a healthy weight from 42% to 60%.
		19–2. Reduce the proportion of adults who are obese from 23% to 15%.
		19–5. Increase the proportion of persons aged 2 years and older who consume at least two daily servings of fruit from 28% to 75%.
		19–6. Increase the proportion of persons aged 2 years and older who consume at least three daily servings of vegetables, with at least one-third being dark-green or orange vegetables, from 3% to 50%.
		19–9. Increase the proportion of persons aged 2 years and older who consume no more than 30% of calories from total fat from 33% to 75%.
Physical activity and fitness	Improve health, fitness, and quality of life through daily physical activity.	22–1. Reduce the proportion of adults who engage in no leisure-time physical activity from 40% to 20%.
		22–2. Increase the proportion of adults who engage regularly, preferably daily, in moderate physical activity for at least 30 minutes per day from 15% to 30%.
		22–4. Increase the proportion of adults who perform physical activities that enhance and maintain muscular strength and endurance from 18% to 30%.
		22–5. Increase the proportion of adults who perform physical activities that enhance and maintain flexibility from 30% to 43%.

Data from: U.S. Department of Health and Human Services. 2000. *Healthy People 2010: Understanding and Improving Health.* 2d ed. Washington, DC: U.S. Governmental Printing Office. Available at www.health.gov/healthypeople.

RECaP

Food refers to the plants and animals we consume, whereas nutrition is the scientific study of food and how food affects our bodies and our health. Nutrition is an important component of wellness and is strongly associated with physical activity. In the past, nutrition research focused on the prevention of nutrient-deficiency diseases such as scurvy and pellagra; currently, a great deal of nutrition research is dedicated to identifying dietary patterns that can lower the risk for chronic diseases such as type 2 diabetes and heart disease. *Healthy People 2020* is a health promotion and disease prevention plan for the United States.

What Are Nutrients?

We enjoy eating food because of its taste, smell, and the pleasure and comfort it gives us. However, we rarely stop to think about what our food actually contains. Foods are composed of many chemical substances, some of which are not useful to the body, and others of which are critical to human growth and function. These latter chemicals are referred to as **nutrients.** The six groups of nutrients found in foods are (**Figure 1.5**):

- carbohydrates
- lipids (including fats and oils)
- proteins
- vitamins
- minerals
- water

As you may know, the term *organic* is commonly used to describe foods that are grown with little or no use of chemicals. But when scientists describe individual nutrients as **organic,** they mean that these nutrients contain an element called *carbon* that is an essential component of all living organisms. Carbohydrates, lipids, proteins, and vitamins are organic, because they contain carbon. Minerals and water are **inorganic** because they do not contain carbon. Both organic and inorganic nutrients are equally important for sustaining

nutrients Chemicals found in foods that are critical to human growth and function.

organic A substance or nutrient that contains the element carbon.

inorganic A substance or nutrient that does not contain carbon.

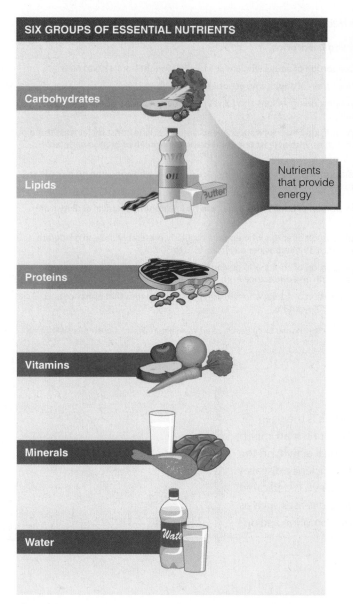

SIX GROUPS OF ESSENTIAL NUTRIENTS

Carbohydrates

Lipids

Proteins

Vitamins

Minerals

Water

Nutrients that provide energy

Figure 1.5   The six groups of nutrients found in the foods we consume.

life but differ in their structures, functions, and basic chemistry. You will learn more about the details of these nutrients in subsequent chapters; a brief review is provided here.

Carbohydrates, Lipids, and Proteins Provide Energy

Carbohydrates, lipids, and proteins are the only nutrients in foods that provide energy. By this we mean that these nutrients break down and reassemble into a fuel that the body uses to support physical activity and basic physiologic functioning. Although taking a multivitamin and a glass of water might be beneficial in some ways, it will not provide you with the energy you need to do your 20 minutes on the stair-climber! The energy nutrients are also referred to as **macronutrients.** *Macro* means "large," and thus macronutrients are those nutrients needed in relatively large amounts to support normal function and health.

Alcohol is found in certain beverages and foods, and it provides energy—but it is not considered a nutrient. This is because it does not support the regulation of body functions or the building or repairing of tissues. In fact, alcohol is considered to be both a drug and a toxin. Details about alcohol are provided in the *In Depth* look on pages 154–165.

We express energy in units of *kilocalories* (kcal). Refer to the Highlight box "What Is a Kilocalorie?" for a definition of this term. Both carbohydrates and proteins provide 4 kcal per gram, alcohol provides 7 kcal per gram, and lipids provide 9 kcal per gram. Thus, for every gram of lipids we consume, we obtain more than twice the energy as compared with a gram of carbohydrate or protein. Refer to the You Do the Math box on page 12 to learn how to calculate the energy contribution of carbohydrates, lipids, and proteins in one day's diet.

Carbohydrates Are a Primary Fuel Source

Carbohydrates are the primary source of fuel for the human body, particularly for neurologic functioning and physical exercise (**Figure 1.6**). A close look at the word *carbohydrate* reveals the chemical structure of this nutrient. *Carbo-* refers to carbon, and *-hydrate* refers to water. You may remember that water is made up of hydrogen and oxygen. Thus, carbohydrates are composed of chains of carbon, hydrogen, and oxygen.

macronutrients   Nutrients that the body requires in relatively large amounts to support normal function and health. Carbohydrates, lipids, and proteins are macronutrients.

carbohydrates   The primary fuel source for the body, particularly for the brain and for physical exercise.

Carbohydrates

• Primary source of energy for the body
• Composed of carbon, hydrogen, and oxygen

Figure 1.6   Carbohydrates are a primary source of energy for our bodies and are found in a wide variety of foods.

Highlight

What Is a Kilocalorie?

Have you ever wondered what the difference is between the terms *energy, kilocalories,* and *calories?* Should these terms be used interchangeably, and what do they really mean? The brief review provided in this highlight should broaden your understanding. First, some precise definitions:

■ *Energy* is defined as the capacity to do work. We derive energy from the energy-containing nutrients in the foods we eat—namely, carbohydrates, lipids, and proteins.

■ A *kilocalorie* (kcal) is the amount of heat required to raise the temperature of 1 kilogram (kg) of water by 1 degree Celsius (°C). It is a unit of measurement that nutrition researchers use to quantify the amount of energy in food that can be supplied to the body. For instance, the energy found in 1 gram (g) of carbohydrate is equal to 4 kcal. *Kilo-* is a prefix used in the metric system to indicate

1,000 (think of *kilometer* or *kilobytes*). Thus, technically speaking, 1 kilocalorie is equal to 1,000 calories.

■ But what, then, is a *calorie* (cal)? In science, the term *Calorie*, with a capital "C," is used to indicate a kilocalorie. However, for the sake of simplicity, nutrition labels and publications intended for consumers use the term *calorie* with a lowercase "c" to represent the unit of kilocalories. So if the wrapper on an ice cream bar states that it contains 150 calories, it actually contains 150 kilocalories.

It is most appropriate to use the term *energy* when you are referring to the general concept of energy intake or energy expenditure. If you are discussing the specific *units* related to energy, it is most correct to use either *kilocalories* or *Calories*. In this textbook, we use the term *kilocalorie* (or *kcal*) as a unit of energy; we use the term *calorie* only when providing information related to food labels.

Carbohydrates are found in a wide variety of foods: rice, wheat, and other grains, as well as vegetables and fruits. Carbohydrates are also found in *legumes* (foods that include lentils, beans, and peas), seeds, nuts, and milk and other dairy products. Fiber is also classified as a type of carbohydrate. Carbohydrates and their role in health are the focus of Chapter 4.

Lipids Provide Energy and Other Essential Nutrients

Lipids are another important source of energy for the body (**Figure 1.7**). Lipids are a diverse group of organic substances that are largely insoluble in water. Lipids include triglycerides, phospholipids, and sterols. Like carbohydrates, lipids are composed mainly of carbon, hydrogen, and oxygen (and in phospholipids, phosphorus and sometimes nitrogen); however, they contain proportionately much less oxygen and water than do carbohydrates. This quality partly explains why they yield more energy per gram than either carbohydrates or proteins.

Triglycerides (more commonly known as fats) are by far the most common lipid in foods. They are composed of an alcohol molecule called *glycerol* attached to three acid

Carbohydrates are the primary source of fuel for the body, particularly for the brain.

Lipids

- Major form of stored energy
- Important source of energy at rest and during low-intensity exercise
- Composed of carbon, hydrogen, and oxygen
- Foods containing lipids also provide fat-soluble vitamins and essential fatty acids

Figure 1.7 Lipids are an important energy source during rest and low-intensity exercise. Foods containing lipids also provide other important nutrients.

lipids A diverse group of organic substances that are insoluble in water; includes triglycerides, phospholipids, and sterols.

You Do the Math

Calculating Energy Contribution of Carbohydrates, Lipids, and Proteins

One of the most useful skills to learn as you study nutrition is how to determine the percentage of the total energy someone eats that comes from carbohydrates, lipids, or proteins. This data is an important first step in evaluating the quality of an individual's diet. Fortunately, a simple equation is available to help you calculate these values.

To begin, you need to know how much total energy someone consumes each day, as well as how many grams of carbohydrates, lipids, and proteins. You also need to know the kilocalorie (kcal) value of each of these nutrients: the energy value for carbohydrates and proteins is 4 kcal per gram, the energy value for alcohol is 7 kcal per gram, and the energy value for lipids is 9 kcal per gram. Working along with the following example will help you perform the calculations:

1. Let's say you have completed a personal diet analysis for your mother, and she consumes 2,500 kcal per day. From your diet analysis you also find that she consumes 300 g of carbohydrates, 90 g of lipids, and 123 g of proteins.

2. To calculate her percentage of total energy that comes from carbohydrates, you must do two things:

   a. Take her total grams of carbohydrate and multiply by the energy value for carbohydrate to determine how many kilocalories of carbohydrate she has consumed.

   300 g of carbohydrate $\times$ 4 kcal/g = 1,200 kcal of carbohydrate

   b. Take the kilocalories of carbohydrate she has consumed, divide this number by the total number of kilo-

calories she has consumed, and multiply by 100. This will give you the percentage of total energy that comes from carbohydrate.

   (1,200 kcal/2,500 kcal) $\times$ 100 = 48% of total energy from carbohydrate

3. To calculate her percentage of total energy that comes from lipids, you follow the same steps but incorporate the energy value for lipids:

   a. Take her total grams of lipids and multiply by the energy value for lipids to find the kilocalories of lipids consumed.

   90 g of fats $\times$ 9 kcal/g = 810 kcal of lipids

   b. Take the kilocalories of lipids she has consumed, divide this number by the total number of kilocalories she consumed, and multiply by 100 to get the percentage of total energy from lipids.

   (810 kcal/2,500 kcal) $\times$ 100 = 32.4% of total energy from lipids

4. Now try these steps to calculate the percentage of the total energy she has consumed that comes from proteins.

   These calculations will be useful throughout this course as you learn more about how to design a healthful diet. Later in this book, you will learn how to estimate someone's energy needs and determine the appropriate amount of energy to consume from carbohydrates, fats, and proteins.

Lipids are an important energy source for our bodies at rest and can be broken down for energy during periods of fasting, for example, while we are asleep.

molecules called *fatty acids*. As we'll discuss throughout this book, triglycerides in foods exert different health effects according to the type of fatty acids they contain. Some fatty acids are associated with an increased risk of chronic disease, whereas others—including essential fatty acids—are protective of our health. Triglycerides are an important energy source when we are at rest and during low- to moderate-intensity exercise. The human body is capable of storing large amounts of triglycerides as adipose tissue, or body fat. These fat stores can be broken down for energy during periods of fasting, such as while we are asleep. Foods that contain lipids are also important in providing fat-soluble vitamins.

Phospholipids are a type of lipid that contains phosphate. The body synthesizes phospholipids, and they are found in a few foods. Cholesterol is a form of lipid that is synthesized in the liver and other body tissues. It is also available in foods of animal origin such as meat and eggs. Chapter 5 provides a thorough review of lipids.

Proteins Support Tissue Growth, Repair, and Maintenance

Proteins also contain carbon, hydrogen, and oxygen, but they differ from carbohydrates and lipids in that they contain the element *nitrogen* (**Figure 1.8**). Within proteins, these four elements assemble into small building blocks known as *amino acids*. We break down dietary

Proteins

- Support tissue growth, repair, and maintenance

- Composed of carbon, hydrogen, oxygen, and nitrogen

Figure 1.8 Proteins contain nitrogen in addition to carbon, hydrogen, and oxygen. Proteins support the growth, repair, and maintenance of body tissues.

proteins into amino acids and reassemble them to build our own body proteins—for instance, the proteins in muscles and blood.

Although proteins can provide energy, they are not usually a primary energy source. Proteins play a major role in building new cells and tissues, maintaining the structure and strength of bone, repairing damaged structures, and assisting in regulating metabolism and fluid balance.

Proteins are found in many foods. Meats and dairy products are primary sources, as are seeds, nuts, and legumes. We also obtain small amounts of protein from vegetables and whole grains. Proteins are explored in detail in Chapter 6.

Vitamins Assist in the Regulation of Physiologic Processes

Vitamins are organic compounds that assist in the regulation of the body's physiologic processes. Contrary to popular belief, vitamins do not contain energy (or kilocalories); however, they do play an important role in the release and utilization of the energy found in carbohydrates, lipids, and proteins. They are also critical in building and maintaining healthy bone, blood, and muscle; supporting our immune system so we can fight illness and disease; and ensuring healthy vision. Because we need relatively small amounts of these nutrients to support normal health and body functions, the vitamins (in addition to minerals) are referred to as **micronutrients.** Some vitamins can be destroyed by heat, light, excessive cooking, exposure to air, and an alkaline (or basic) environment.

Vitamins are classified according to their solubility in water as either **fat-soluble** or **water-soluble** vitamins (Table 1.2). This classification is based upon their solubility in water, which affects how vitamins are absorbed, transported, and stored in body tissues. As our bodies cannot synthesize most vitamins, we must consume them in our diets. Both fat-soluble and water-soluble vitamins are essential for our health and are found in a variety of foods. Learn more about vitamins in the *In Depth* look on pages 281–284. Chapters 8 through 12 discuss individual vitamins in detail.

Fat-soluble vitamins are found in a variety of fat-containing foods, including dairy products.

proteins The only macronutrient that contains nitrogen; the basic building blocks of proteins are amino acids.

vitamins Organic compounds that assist in regulating physiologic processes.

micronutrients Nutrients needed in relatively small amounts to support normal health and body functions. Vitamins and minerals are micronutrients.

fat-soluble vitamins Vitamins that are not soluble in water but soluble in fat. These include vitamins A, D, E, and K.

water-soluble vitamins Vitamins that are soluble in water. These include vitamin C and the B-vitamins.

Table 1.2 Overview of Vitamins

Type	Names	Distinguishing Features
Fat soluble	A, D, E, and K	Soluble in fat
		Stored in the human body
		Toxicity can occur from consuming excess amounts, which accumulate in the body
Water soluble	C, B-vitamins (thiamin, riboflavin, niacin, vitamin B_6, vitamin B_{12}, pantothenic acid, biotin, and folate)	Soluble in water
		Not stored to any extent in the human body
		Excess excreted in urine
		Toxicity generally only occurs as a result of vitamin supplementation

Table 1.3 Overview of Minerals

Type	Names	Distinguishing Features
Major minerals	Calcium, phosphorus, sodium, potassium, chloride, magnesium, sulfur	Needed in amounts greater than 100 mg/day in our diets Amount present in the human body is greater than 5 g (or 5,000 mg)
Trace minerals	Iron, zinc, copper, manganese, fluoride, chromium, molybdenum, selenium, iodine	Needed in amounts less than 100 mg/day in our diets Amount present in the human body is less than 5 g (or 5,000 mg)

Peanuts are a good source of magnesium and phosphorus, which play an important role in formation and maintenance of the skeleton.

Minerals Assist in the Regulation of Many Body Functions

Minerals are inorganic substances, meaning that they do not contain carbon. Some important dietary minerals include sodium, potassium, calcium, magnesium, zinc, and iron. Minerals differ from the macronutrients and vitamins in that they are not broken down during digestion or when the body uses them to promote normal function; and unlike certain vitamins, they are not destroyed by heat or light. Thus, all minerals maintain their structure no matter what environment they are in. This means that the calcium in our bones is the same as the calcium in the milk we drink, and the sodium in our cells is the same as the sodium in our table salt.

Minerals have many important physiologic functions. They assist in fluid regulation and energy production, are essential to the health of our bones and blood, and help rid the body of harmful by-products of metabolism. Minerals are classified according to the amounts we need in our diet and according to how much of the mineral is found in the body. The two categories of minerals in our diets and bodies are the **major minerals** and the **trace minerals** (Table 1.3). Learn more about minerals in the *In Depth* look on pages 284–287. Chapters 8 through 12 discuss individual minerals in detail.

Water Supports All Body Functions

Water is an inorganic nutrient that is vital for our survival. We consume water in its pure form, in juices, soups, and other liquids, and in solid foods such as fruits and vegetables. Adequate water intake ensures the proper balance of fluid both inside and outside of our cells and also assists in the regulation of nerve impulses and body temperature, muscle contractions, nutrient transport, and excretion of waste products. Because of the key role that water plays in our health, Chapter 9 focuses on water and its function in the body.

RECAP

The six essential nutrient groups found in foods are carbohydrates, lipids, proteins, vitamins, minerals, and water. Carbohydrates, lipids, and proteins are energy nutrients. Carbohydrates are the primary energy source; lipids provide fat-soluble vitamins and essential fatty acids and act as energy-storage molecules; and proteins support tissue growth, repair, and maintenance. Vitamins are organic compounds that assist with regulating a multitude of body processes. Minerals are inorganic elements that have critical roles in virtually all aspects of human health and function. Water is essential for survival and is important for regulating nerve impulses and body temperature, muscle contractions, nutrient transport, and excretion of waste products.

minerals   Inorganic substances that are not broken down during digestion and absorption and are not destroyed by heat or light. Minerals assist in the regulation of many body processes and are classified as major minerals or trace minerals.

major minerals   Minerals we need to consume in amounts of at least 100 mg per day and of which the total amount in our bodies is at least 5 g.

trace minerals   Minerals we need to consume in amounts less than 100 mg per day and of which the total amount in our bodies is less than 5 g.

What Are the Current Dietary Recommendations and How Are They Used?

Now that you know what the six classes of nutrients are, you are probably wondering how much of each a person needs each day. But before you can learn more about specific nutrients and how to plan a healthful diet, you need to become familiar with current dietary standards and how these standards shape nutrition recommendations.

The Dietary Reference Intakes Identify a Healthy Person's Nutrient Needs

In the past, the dietary standards in the United States were referred to as the *Recommended Dietary Allowances* (RDAs), and the standards in Canada were termed the *Recommended Nutrient Intakes* (RNIs). These standards defined recommended intake values for various nutrients and were used to plan diets for both individuals and groups. As noted earlier, they were adopted with the goal of preventing nutrient-deficiency diseases; however, in developed countries like the United States and Canada, these diseases are now extremely rare. Thus, nutrition scientists have developed a new set of reference values aimed at preventing and reducing the risk of chronic disease and promoting optimal health. These new reference values in both the United States and Canada are known as the **Dietary Reference Intakes (DRIs)** (**Figure 1.9**). These standards include and expand upon the former RDA values, and set new recommendation standards for nutrients that do not have RDA values.

The DRIs are dietary standards for healthy people only; they do not apply to people with diseases or those who are suffering from nutrient deficiencies. Like the RDAs and RNIs, they identify the amount of a nutrient needed to prevent deficiency diseases in healthy individuals, but they also consider how much of this nutrient may reduce the risk for chronic diseases in healthy people. The DRIs establish an upper level of safety for some nutrients and represent one set of values for both the United States and Canada.

The DRIs for most nutrients consist of four values:

- Estimated Average Requirement (EAR)
- Recommended Dietary Allowance (RDA)
- Adequate Intake (AI)
- Tolerable Upper Intake Level (UL)

In the case of energy and the macronutrients, different standards are used. The standards for energy and the macronutrients include the Estimated Energy Requirement (EER) and the Acceptable Macronutrient Distribution Ranges (AMDR). The definitions for each of these DRI values are presented in the following section.

The Estimated Average Requirement Guides the Recommended Dietary Allowance

The first step in determining our nutrient requirements is to calculate the EAR. The **Estimated Average Requirement (EAR)** represents the average daily nutrient intake level estimated to meet the requirement of half of the healthy individuals in a particular life stage or gender group.[4] **Figure 1.10** provides a graph representing this value. As an example, the EAR for iron for women between the ages of 19 and 30 years represents the average daily intake of iron that meets the requirement of half of the women in this age group. The EAR

Dietary Reference Intakes (DRIs) A set of nutritional reference values for the United States and Canada that applies to healthy people.

Estimated Average Requirement (EAR) The average daily nutrient intake level estimated to meet the requirement of half of the healthy individuals in a particular life stage or gender group.

Figure 1.9 The Dietary Reference Intakes (DRIs) for all nutrients. Note that the Estimated Energy Requirement (EER) only applies to energy, and the Acceptable Macronutrient Distribution Ranges (AMDR) apply to the macronutrients.

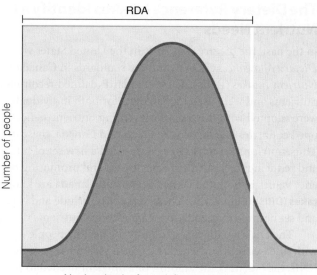

Figure 1.10   The Estimated Average Requirement (EAR) represents the average daily nutrient intake level that meets the requirements of half of the healthy individuals in a given group.

Figure 1.11   The Recommended Dietary Allowance (RDA). The RDA represents the average daily nutrient intake level that meets the requirements of almost all (97% to 98%) healthy individuals in a given life stage or gender group.

is used by scientists to define the Recommended Dietary Allowance (RDA) for a given nutrient. Obviously, if the EAR meets the needs of only half the people in a group, then the recommended intake will be higher.

The Recommended Dietary Allowance Meets the Needs of Nearly All Healthy People

Recommended Dietary Allowance (RDA) was the term previously used to refer to *all* nutrient recommendations in the United States. The RDA is now considered one of many reference standards within the larger umbrella of the DRIs. The RDA represents the average daily nutrient intake level that meets the nutrient requirements of 97% to 98% of healthy individuals in a particular life stage and gender group (**Figure 1.11**).[4] For example, the RDA for iron is 18 mg per day for women between the ages of 19 and 30 years. This amount of iron will meet the nutrient requirements of almost all women in this age category.

Again, scientists use the EAR to establish the RDA. In fact, if an EAR cannot be determined for a nutrient, then this nutrient cannot have an RDA. When this occurs, an Adequate Intake value is determined for a nutrient.

The Adequate Intake Is Based on Estimates of Nutrient Intakes

The **Adequate Intake (AI)** value is a recommended average daily nutrient intake level based on observed or experimentally determined estimates of nutrient intake by a group of healthy people.[4] These estimates are assumed to be adequate and are used when the evidence necessary to determine an RDA is not available. There are numerous nutrients that have an AI value, including calcium, vitamin D, vitamin K, and fluoride. More research needs to be done on human requirements for the nutrients assigned an AI value so that an EAR, and subsequently an RDA, can be established.

In addition to establishing RDA and AI values for nutrients, an upper level of safety for nutrients, or Tolerable Upper Intake Level, has also been defined.

The Tolerable Upper Intake Level Is the Highest Level That Poses No Health Risk

The **Tolerable Upper Intake Level (UL)** is the highest average daily nutrient intake level likely to pose no risk of adverse health effects to almost all individuals in a particular life stage

Recommended Dietary Allowance (RDA)   The average daily nutrient intake level that meets the nutrient requirements of 97% to 98% of healthy individuals in a particular life stage and gender group.

Adequate Intake (AI)   A recommended average daily nutrient intake level based on observed or experimentally determined estimates of nutrient intake by a group of healthy people.

Tolerable Upper Intake Level (UL)   The highest average daily nutrient intake level likely to pose no risk of adverse health effects to almost all individuals in a particular life stage and gender group.

Table 1.4 Acceptable Macronutrient Distribution Ranges (AMDR) for Healthful Diets

Nutrient	AMDR*
Carbohydrate	45–65%
Fat	20–35%
Protein	10–35%

*AMDR values expressed as percent of total energy or as percent of total calories.

Data from: Institute of Medicine, Food and Nutrition Board. 2005. *Dietary Reference Intakes for Energy, Carbohydrates, Fiber, Fat, Fatty Acids, Cholesterol, Protein, and Amino Acids (Macronutrients).* Washington, DC: National Academies Press. Reprinted by permission.

and gender group.[4] This does not mean that we should consume this intake level or that we will receive more benefits from a nutrient by meeting or exceeding the UL. In fact, as our intake of a nutrient increases in amounts above the UL, the potential for toxic effects and health risks increases. The UL value is a helpful guide to assist you in determining the highest average intake level that is deemed safe for a given nutrient. Note that there is not enough research to define the UL for all nutrients.

The Estimated Energy Requirement Is the Intake Predicted to Maintain a Healthy Weight

The **Estimated Energy Requirement (EER)** is defined as the average dietary energy intake that is predicted to maintain energy balance in a healthy adult. This dietary intake is defined by a person's age, gender, weight, height, and level of physical activity that is consistent with good health.[5] Thus, the EER for an active person is higher than the EER for an inactive person even if all other factors (age, gender, and so forth) are the same.

The Acceptable Macronutrient Distribution Ranges Are Associated with Reduced Risk for Chronic Diseases

The **Acceptable Macronutrient Distribution Ranges (AMDR)** are ranges of intakes for a particular energy source that is associated with reduced risk of chronic disease while providing adequate intakes of essential nutrients.[5] The AMDR is expressed as a percentage of total energy or as a percentage of total kcal. The AMDR also has a lower and upper boundary; if we consume nutrients above or below this range, there is a potential for increasing our risk for poor health. The AMDRs for carbohydrate, fat, and protein are listed in Table 1.4.

Diets Based on the DRIs Promote Wellness

The primary goal of dietary planning is to develop an eating plan that is nutritionally adequate, meaning that the chances of consuming too little or too much of any nutrient are very low. By eating a diet that provides nutrient intakes that meet the RDA or AI values, a person is more likely to maintain a healthy weight, support his or her daily physical activity, and prevent nutrient deficiencies and toxicities.

The DRI values are listed in a table on the inside cover of this book; they are also reviewed with each nutrient as it is introduced throughout this text. Find your own life-stage group and gender in the left-hand column, then simply look across to see each nutrient's value that applies. Using the DRI values in conjunction with diet planning tools such as the Dietary Guidelines for Americans or the USDA Food Guide will ensure a healthful and adequate diet. Chapter 2 provides details on how you can use these tools to develop a healthful diet.

RECAP

The Dietary Reference Intakes (DRIs) are dietary standards for nutrients established for healthy people in a particular life stage or gender group. The Estimated Average Requirement (EAR) represents the nutrient intake level that meets the

Knowing your daily Estimated Energy Requirement (EER) is a helpful step toward maintaining a healthful body weight. Your EER is defined by your age, gender, weight, height, and physical activity level.

Estimated Energy Requirement (EER) The average dietary energy intake that is predicted to maintain energy balance in a healthy adult.

Acceptable Macronutrient Distribution Ranges (AMDR) A range of intakes for a particular energy source that is associated with reduced risk of chronic disease while providing adequate intakes of essential nutrients.

requirement of half of the healthy individuals in a group. The Recommended Dietary Allowance (RDA) represents the level that meets the requirements of 97% to 98% of healthy individuals in a group. The Adequate Intake (AI) is based on estimates of nutrient intake by a group of healthy people when there is not enough information to set an RDA. The Tolerable Upper Intake Level (UL) is the highest daily nutrient intake level that likely poses no health risk. The Estimated Energy Requirement (EER) is the average daily energy intake that is predicted to maintain energy balance in a healthy adult. The Acceptable Macronutrient Distribution Ranges (AMDR) are intakes associated with reduced risk of chronic disease and adequate intakes of essential nutrients.

How Do Nutrition Professionals Assess the Nutritional Status of Clients?

Before nutrition professionals can make valid recommendations about a client's diet, they need to have a thorough understanding of a client's current nutritional status, including weight, ratio of lean body tissue to body fat, and intake of energy and nutrients. The results of this assessment are extremely important, because they will become the foundation of any dietary or lifestyle changes that are recommended and will provide a baseline against which the success of any recommended changes are evaluated. For instance, if assessments reveal that an adolescent client is 20 lb underweight and consumes less than half the recommended amount of calcium each day, these baseline data are used to support a recommendation of increased energy and calcium intake and to evaluate the success of these recommendations in the future.

A client's nutritional status may fall anywhere along a continuum from healthy to imbalanced. Nutrition professionals use three terms to describe serious nutritional problems: **Malnutrition** refers to a situation in which a person's nutritional status is out of balance; the individual is either getting too much or too little of a particular nutrient or energy over a significant period of time. **Undernutrition** refers to a situation in which someone consumes too little energy or too few nutrients over time, causing significant weight loss or a nutrient-deficiency disease. **Overnutrition** occurs when a person consumes too much energy or too much of a given nutrient over time, causing conditions such as obesity, heart disease, or nutrient toxicity.

Nutrition professionals use a number of tools to determine the nutritional status of a client. As you read about these in the following section, keep in mind that no one method is sufficient to indicate malnutrition. Instead, a combination of tools is used to confirm the presence or absence of nutrient imbalances.

A Physical Examination Is Conducted by a Healthcare Provider

Physical examinations should be conducted by a trained healthcare provider such as a physician, nurse, nurse practitioner, or physician assistant. The tests conducted during the examination depend on the client's medical history, disease symptoms, and risk factors. Typical tests may include vital signs (pulse, blood pressure, body temperature, and respiration rate), auscultation of heart and lung sounds, and laboratory analysis of blood and/or urine samples. Nutritional imbalances may be detected by examining the client's hair, skin, tongue, eyes, and fingernails.

A person's age and health status determine how often he or she needs a physical examination. It is typically recommended that a healthy person younger than 30 years of age have a thorough exam every 2 to 3 years. Adults aged 30 to 50 years should have an examination every 1 to 2 years, and individuals older than 50 years of age should have an exam on a yearly basis. However, individuals with established diseases or symptoms of malnutrition may require more frequent examinations.

malnutrition A nutritional status that is out of balance; an individual is either getting too much or not enough of a particular nutrient or energy over a significant period of time.

undernutrition A situation in which too little energy or too few nutrients are consumed over time, causing significant weight loss or a nutrient-deficiency disease.

overnutrition A situation in which too much energy or too much of a given nutrient is consumed over time, causing conditions such as obesity, heart disease, or nutrient-toxicity symptoms.

Questionnaires Elicit Subjective Information

Health-history questionnaires are tools that assist in cataloging a person's history of health, illness, drug use, exercise, and diet. These questionnaires are typically completed just prior to the physical examination by a nurse or other healthcare professional, or the patient may be asked to complete one independently. The questions included in health-history questionnaires usually relate to the following:

- Demographic information, including name, age, contact information, and self-reported height and body weight
- Current medication status, potential drug allergies, and history of drug use
- Family history of disease
- Personal history of illnesses, injuries, and surgeries
- History of menstrual function (for females)
- Exercise history
- Socioeconomic factors such as education level, access to shopping and cooking facilities, marital status, and racial/ethnic background

In addition, specific questionnaires can be used to assess a person's nutrient and energy intakes. Examples include a diet history, 24-hour dietary recalls, food-frequency questionnaires, and diet records. As you read about each of these tools, bear in mind that they are all subjective; that is, they rely on a person's ability to self-report. The accuracy of the data cannot be empirically verified, as it can, for example, by repeating a measurement of a person's weight. Of these tools, the one or two selected by nutrition professionals will depend on what questions they wish to answer, the population they are working with, and the available resources. Following is a brief description of each.

Diet History

A diet history is typically conducted by a trained nutrition professional. Diet history information is gathered using either an interview process or a questionnaire. Information that is generally included in the diet history includes current weight, usual weight, and body weight goals; factors affecting appetite and food intake; typical eating patterns (including time, place, dietary restrictions, frequency of eating out, and so forth); disordered eating behaviors (if any); economic status; educational level; living, cooking, and food-purchasing arrangements; medication and/or dietary supplement use; and physical activity patterns. A diet history can help identify any nutrition or eating problems and highlight a person's unique needs.

Twenty-Four-Hour Dietary Recalls

The 24-hour dietary recall is used to assess recent food intake. A trained nutrition professional interviews the person and records all of the person's responses. The person recalls all of the foods and beverages consumed in the previous 24-hour period. Information that the person needs to know to provide an accurate recall includes serving sizes, food-preparation methods, and brand names of convenience foods or fast foods that were eaten. The 24-hour recall has serious limitations, including the fact that it does not give an indication of a person's typical intake; other limitations include reliance on a person's memory and his or her ability to estimate portion sizes.

Food-Frequency Questionnaires

Food-frequency questionnaires can assist in determining a person's typical dietary pattern over a predefined period of time, such as 1 month, 6 months, or 1 year. These questionnaires include lists of foods with questions regarding the number of times these foods are eaten during the specified time period. Some questionnaires only assess qualitative information, meaning they include only a list of typical foods that are eaten but do not include amounts of foods eaten. Semiquantitative questionnaires are also available; these assess specific foods eaten and the quantity consumed.

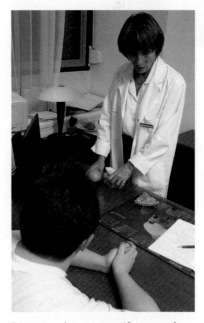

Diet records are a specific type of questionnaire, usually involving some training from a nutrition professional to ensure accuracy.

Diet Records

A diet record is a list of all foods and beverages consumed over a specified time period, usually 3 to 7 days. The days selected for recording the person's diet should be representative of typical dietary and activity patterns.

The client is responsible for filling out the record accurately, and both training and take-home instructions are essential. The record is more accurate if all foods consumed are weighed or measured, labels of all convenience foods are saved, and labels of supplements are provided. Providing a food scale and measuring utensils can also assist people in improving the information obtained from diet records.

Although diet records can provide a reasonably good estimate of a person's energy and nutrient intakes, they are challenging to complete accurately and in sufficient detail. Because of this burden, people may change their intake to simplify completing the diet record. They may also change their intake simply because they know it will be analyzed; for example, a client who typically eats ice cream after dinner might forego this indulgence for the duration of the diet record. In addition, analyses are time-consuming and costly.

Anthropometric Assessments Provide Objective Data

Anthropometric assessments are, quite simply, measurements of human beings (*anthropos* is a Greek word meaning "human"). The most common anthropometric measurements used include height and body weight. Other measurements that may be taken include head circumference in infants and circumference of limbs. It is critical that the person taking anthropometric measurements is properly trained and uses the correct tools. Measurements are then compared with standards specific for a given age and gender. This allows health practitioners to determine if a person's body size or growth is normal for his or her age and gender. Repeated measurements can also be taken on the same person over time to assess trends in nutritional status and growth.

Although not technically considered an anthropometric assessment tool, body composition may also be measured. That is, the health practitioner will use one of several available methods to determine the ratio of fat tissue to nonfat tissue (or lean body mass) of which the client's body is composed. Specific details about body composition assessment are discussed in Chapter 13.

Think back to the advice that the nutritionist gave to Marilyn in our chapter-opening scenario. Now that you have learned about both subjective and objective methods for assessing a person's nutritional status, you probably recognize that the nutritionist failed to perform even a rudimentary nutritional assessment; instead, she based her weight-loss recommendation solely on a measurement of Marilyn's blood pressure! Later in this chapter, we'll explore what the term *nutritionist* really means and discuss what it means to work within one's scope of practice. But for now, let's look at an example of how healthcare professionals use subjective and objective assessments to determine malnutrition.

A Finding of Malnutrition Requires Further Classification

If the results of nutrition assessment lead to a finding of malnutrition, the nutrition professional classifies the finding further as overnutrition or undernutrition. Overnutrition is further classified as overweight or obesity (see Chapter 13). Nutrient deficiencies are further classified as *primary* or *secondary*. **Primary deficiency** occurs when a person does not consume enough of a nutrient in the diet; thus, the deficiency occurs as a direct consequence of an inadequate intake. **Secondary deficiency** occurs when a person cannot absorb enough of a nutrient in his or her body, when too much of a nutrient is excreted from the body, or when a nutrient is not utilized efficiently by the body. Thus, a secondary deficiency is secondary to, or a consequence of, some other disorder.

Symptoms of a nutrient deficiency are not always obvious. A deficiency in its early stages, when few or no symptoms are observed, is referred to as a **subclinical deficiency.** The symptoms of a subclinical deficiency are typically **covert,** meaning they are hidden and require laboratory tests or other invasive procedures to detect. Once the symptoms of a nutri-

Measuring height is a common anthropometric assessment, and when repeated over time can help determine a person's nutritional status.

primary deficiency A deficiency that occurs when not enough of a nutrient is consumed in the diet.

secondary deficiency A deficiency that occurs when a person cannot absorb enough of a nutrient, excretes too much of a nutrient from the body, or cannot utilize a nutrient efficiently.

subclinical deficiency A deficiency in its early stages, when few or no symptoms are observed.

covert symptom A symptom that is hidden from a client and requires laboratory tests or other invasive procedures to detect.

ent deficiency become obvious, they are referred to as **overt.** In the following example, notice that several nutrition assessment tools are used together to determine the presence of a nutrient deficiency.

Bob is a 70-year-old man who has come to his healthcare provider to discuss a number of troubling symptoms. He has been experiencing numbness and tingling in his legs and feet, loses his balance frequently, has memory loss and occasionally feels disoriented, and has intermittent periods of blurred vision. A health history is taken and reveals that Bob has mild hypertension, but he has been regularly physically active and was in good health until the past 6 months. A physical examination shows him to be underweight for his height, with pale skin, and experiencing tremors in his hands. His memory is also poor upon examination. Bob's physician orders some laboratory tests and refers him to the clinic's dietitian, who takes a diet history. During the history, Bob reveals that, a year ago, he began wearing dentures that have made it difficult for him to chew properly. He reports that over time he "gave up on eating anything tough, especially meat." When asked if he eats fish, he says that he has never eaten it as he does not like the taste. Also, he avoids consuming dairy products because they cause stomach upset, intestinal gas, and diarrhea. When asked if he takes any supplements, Bob explains that he is on a limited income and cannot afford them.

Laboratory test results reveal that Bob is suffering from a deficiency of vitamin B_{12}. This deficiency is primary in nature, as Bob is not consuming meats, fish, or dairy products, which are the primary sources of vitamin B_{12} in our diets. He also does not take a supplement containing vitamin B_{12}. By the time Bob visited his healthcare provider, he was suffering from a clinical deficiency and was showing overt symptoms.

RECAP

Malnutrition refers to a person's nutritional status being out of balance; undernutrition is a situation in which someone consumes too little energy or too few nutrients over time, and overnutrition occurs when a person consumes too much energy or too much of a nutrient. Assessment tools that can be used to determine if malnutrition exists include a physical examination, a health-history questionnaire, a diet history, a 24-hour dietary recall, a food-frequency questionnaire, a diet record, and anthropometric measures.

Theo
Nutri-Case

"When I was trying out for the basketball team, I had to have a physical with the team's physician. I was weighed and they took my pulse and my blood pressure, and I had to have some blood tests—the usual stuff. But on top of all that, they made me fill out this weird form telling them how often I eat certain things. They asked me about all sorts of things like pizza and soft drinks—but good things, too, like fruits and oatmeal. And they wanted me to try to remember for the last 6 months! Six months? I can barely remember what I ate for dinner last night! And why did they want to know all that anyway?"

Based on his description, what kind of nutritional assessment tool do you think Theo was asked to complete? What drawbacks of this tool do Theo's comments reveal? Why do you think he was asked to complete this assessment?

Research Study Results: Who Can We Believe?

"Eat more carbohydrates! Fats cause obesity!"

"Eat more protein and fat! Carbohydrates cause obesity!"

Do you ever feel overwhelmed by the abundant and often conflicting advice in media reports related to nutrition? If so, you are not alone. In addition to the "high-carb,

overt symptom A symptom that is obvious to a client, such as pain, fatigue, or a bruise.

low-carb" controversy, we've been told that calcium supplements are essential to prevent bone loss and that calcium supplements have no effect on bone loss; that high fluid intake prevents constipation and that high fluid intake has no effect on constipation; that coffee and tea could be bad for our health and that both can be beneficial! How can you navigate this sea of changing information? What constitutes valid, reliable evidence, and how can you determine whether or not research findings apply to you?

To become a more informed critic of product claims and nutrition news items, you need to understand the research process and how to interpret the results of different types of studies. Let's now learn more about research.

Research Involves Applying the Scientific Method

When confronted with a claim about any aspect of our world, from "The Earth is flat" to "Carbohydrates cause obesity," scientists, including nutritionists, must first consider whether or not the claim can be tested. In other words, can evidence be presented to substantiate the claim, and if so, what data would qualify as evidence? Scientists worldwide use a standardized method of looking at evidence called the *scientific method*. This method ensures that certain standards and processes are used in evaluating claims. The scientific method usually includes the following steps, which are described in more detail below and summarized in **Figure 1.12**:

- The researcher makes an *observation* and description of a phenomenon.
- The researcher proposes a *hypothesis* or educated guess to explain why the phenomenon occurs.
- The researcher develops an *experimental design* that will test the hypothesis.
- The researcher *collects and analyzes data* that will either support or reject the hypothesis.
- If the data do not support the original hypothesis, then an *alternative hypothesis* is proposed and tested.
- If the data support the original hypothesis, then a *conclusion* is drawn.
- The experiment must be *repeatable*, so other researchers can obtain similar results.
- Finally, a *theory* is proposed offering a conclusion drawn from repeated experiments that have supported the hypothesis time and time again.

Figure 1.12   The scientific method, which forms the framework for scientific research. **Step 1:** Observations are made regarding some phenomenon, which lead researchers to ask a question. **Step 2:** A hypothesis is generated to explain the observations. **Step 3:** An experiment is conducted to test the hypothesis. Observations are made during the experiment, and data are generated and documented. **Step 4:** The data may either support or refute the hypothesis. If the data support the hypothesis, more experiments are conducted to test and confirm support for the hypothesis. A hypothesis that is supported after repeated testing may be called a theory. If the data do not support the hypothesis, the hypothesis is either rejected or modified and then retested.

Observation of a Phenomenon Initiates the Research Process

The first step in the scientific method is the observation and description of a phenomenon. As an example, let's say you are working in a healthcare office that caters to mostly older adult clients. You have observed that many of these clients have high blood pressure, but some have normal blood pressure. After talking with a large number of clients, you notice a pattern developing in that the clients who report being more physically active are also those having lower blood pressure readings. This observation leads you to question the relationship that might exist between physical activity and blood pressure. Your next step is to develop a *hypothesis*, or possible explanation for your observation.

A Hypothesis Is a Possible Explanation for an Observation

A **hypothesis** is also sometimes referred to as a research question. In this example, your hypothesis might be, "Adults over age 65 with high blood pressure who begin and maintain a program of 45 minutes of aerobic exercise daily will experience a decrease in blood pressure." Your hypothesis must be written in such a way that it can be either supported or rejected. In other words, it must be testable.

An Experiment Is Designed to Test the Hypothesis

An *experiment* is a scientific study that is conducted to test a hypothesis. A well-designed experiment should include several key elements:

- The *sample size* or the number of people being studied should be adequate enough to ensure that the results obtained are not due to chance alone. For example, would you be more likely to believe a study that tested 5 people or 500?
- Having a *control group* is essential for comparison between treated and untreated individuals. A control group is a group of people who are as much like the treated group as possible except with respect to the *variable* being tested. For instance, in your study, 45 minutes daily of aerobic exercise would be the variable; the experimental group would consist of people over age 65 with high blood pressure who perform the exercise, and the control group would consist of people of the same age with high blood pressure who do not exercise. Using a control group helps a researcher to judge if a particular treatment has worked or not.
- A good experimental design also attempts to control for other variables that may coincidentally influence the results. For example, what if someone in your study was on a diet, smoked, or took blood-pressure-lowering medication? Because any of these factors could affect the results, researchers try to design experiments that have as many *constants* as possible. In doing so, they increase the chance that their results will be valid. To use an old saying, you can think of validity as "Comparing apples to apples."

Data Are Collected and Analyzed to Determine Whether They Support or Reject the Hypothesis

As part of the design of the experiment, the researcher must determine the type of data to collect and how it will be collected. For example, in your study the data being collected are blood pressure readings. These values could be collected by a person or a machine, but because the data will be closely scrutinized by other scientists, they should be as accurate as technology allows. In this case, an automatic blood pressure gauge would provide more reliable and consistent data than blood pressure measurements taken by research assistants.

Once the data have been collected, they must be interpreted or analyzed. Often, the data will begin to make sense only after being organized and put into different forms, such as tables or graphs, that reveal patterns that at first were not obvious. In your study, you can create a graph comparing blood pressure readings from both your experimental group and your control group to see if there is a significant difference between the blood pressure readings of those who exercised and those who did not.

hypothesis   An educated guess as to why a phenomenon occurs.

Most Hypotheses Need to Be Refined

Remember that a hypothesis is basically a guess as to what causes a particular phenomenon. Rarely do scientists get it right the first time. The original hypothesis is often refined after the initial results are obtained, usually because the answer to the question is not clear and leads to more questions. When this happens, an alternative hypothesis is proposed, a new experiment is designed, and the new hypothesis is tested.

An Experiment Must Be Repeatable

One research study does not prove or disprove a hypothesis. Ideally, multiple experiments are conducted over many years to thoroughly test a hypothesis. Indeed, repeatability is a cornerstone of scientific investigation. Supporters and skeptics alike must be able to replicate an experiment and arrive at similar conclusions or the hypothesis becomes invalid. Have you ever wondered why the measurements used in scientific textbooks are always in the metric system? The answer is repeatability. Scientists use the metric system because it is a universal system and thus allows repeatability in any research facility worldwide.

Unfortunately, media reports on the findings of a research study that has just been published rarely include a thorough review of the other studies conducted on that topic. Thus, you should never accept one report in a newspaper or magazine as absolute fact on any topic.

A Theory May Be Developed Following Extensive Research

If the results of multiple experiments consistently support a hypothesis, then scientists may advance a **theory.** A theory represents a scientific consensus (agreement) as to why a particular phenomenon occurs. Although theories are based on data drawn from repeated experiments, they can still be challenged and changed as the knowledge within a scientific discipline evolves. For example, at the beginning of this chapter, we said that the prevailing theory held that beriberi was an infectious disease. Experiments were conducted over several decades before their consistent results finally confirmed that the disease was due to thiamin deficiency. We continue to apply the scientific method to test hypotheses and challenge theories today.

RECAP

The steps in the scientific method are (1) observing a phenomenon, (2) creating a hypothesis, (3) designing and conducting an experiment, and (4) collecting and analyzing data that support or refute the hypothesis. If the data are rejected, then an alternative hypothesis is proposed and tested. If the data support the original hypothesis, then a conclusion is drawn. A hypothesis that is supported after repeated experiments may be called a theory.

Different Types of Research Studies Tell Us Different Stories

Establishing nutrition guidelines and understanding the role of nutrition in health involve constant experimentation. Depending upon how the research study is designed, we can gather information that tells us different stories. Let's take a look at the different types of research.

Epidemiological Studies

Epidemiological studies are also referred to as observational studies. They involve assessing nutritional habits, disease trends, or other health phenomena of large populations and determining the factors that may influence these phenomena. However, these studies can only indicate relationships between factors, not specifically a cause-and-effect relationship. For example, let's say that an epidemiological study finds that the blood pressure values of physically active older adults are lower than those of inactive older adults. These results do not

theory   A scientific consensus, based on data drawn from repeated experiments, as to why a phenomenon occurs.

indicate that regular physical activity reduces blood pressure or that inactivity causes high blood pressure. All these results can tell us is that there is a relationship between higher physical activity and lower blood pressure in older adults.

Model Systems

Humans are not very good experimental models because it is difficult to control for all of the variables that affect their lives. Humans also have long life spans, so it would take a long time to determine the effects of certain nutritional studies. For these reasons, laboratory studies generally involve experiments with animals. In many cases, animal studies provide preliminary information that can assist us in designing and implementing human studies. Animal studies also are used to conduct research that cannot be done with humans. For instance, it is possible to study nutritional deficiencies in animals by causing a deficiency and studying its adverse health effects over the life span of the animal; this type of experiment is not acceptable to perform with humans.

Animals with relatively short reproduction times can be studied when researchers need to look at the effects of specific drugs or treatments over many generations. Such animals can also be bred so they display specific traits such as certain diseases or metabolic conditions. One drawback of animal studies is that the results may not apply directly to humans. Another drawback is the ethical implications of studies involving animals, especially when the research reduces the animal's quality of life.

Human Studies

The two primary types of studies conducted with humans include case control studies and clinical trials. *Case control studies* are epidemiological studies done on a smaller scale. Case control studies involve comparing a group of individuals with a particular condition (for instance, older adults with high blood pressure) to a similar group without this condition (for instance, older adults with low blood pressure). This comparison allows the researcher to identify factors other than the defined condition that differ between the two groups. By identifying these factors, researchers can gain a better understanding of things that may cause and help prevent disease. In the case of your experiment, you may find that older adults with low blood pressure are not only more physically active, but also eat more fruits and vegetables and less sodium. These findings would indicate that other factors in addition to physical activity may play a role in affecting the blood pressure levels of older adults.

Clinical trials are tightly controlled experiments in which an intervention is given to determine its effect on a certain disease or health condition. Interventions may include medications, nutritional supplements, controlled diets, or exercise programs. Clinical trials include the experimental group, whose members are given the intervention, and the control group, whose members are not given the intervention. The responses of the intervention group are compared to those of the control group. In the case of your experiment, you could assign one group of older adults with high blood pressure to an exercise program and assign a second group to a program in which no exercise is done. After the intervention phase was completed, you could compare the blood pressure of the people who exercised to those who did not. If the blood pressure of the intervention group decreased significantly and the blood pressure of the control group did not, then you could propose that the exercise program caused a decrease in blood pressure.

Among clinical trials, the type considered most likely to produce valid, reliable data is the *double-blind, placebo-controlled study*. In a double-blind study, neither researchers nor participants know which group is really getting the treatment. Blinding helps prevent the researchers from seeing only the results they want to see. A *placebo* is an imitation treatment that has no scientifically recognized therapeutic value, for instance, a sugar pill that looks, feels, smells, and tastes identical to the medication being tested. In a double-blind, placebo-controlled study, neither the researchers providing the treatment nor the study participants receiving it know whether the treatment being administered is the one being tested or a placebo.

Epidemiological studies indicate relationships between factors, such as between exercise and blood pressure in older adults, but cannot prove cause and effect.

Another important variable that cannot be overlooked in clinical trials is the effect of participation in the study on the subject's state of mind. This is known as the *psychosomatic effect* or *placebo effect*. Sometimes, just knowing they're in a study will cause individuals to experience physiological changes that they may interpret as therapeutic. For example, because the older adults in your study know they are part of a study concerning high blood pressure, they may subconsciously be more relaxed and content because they feel validated and important. They may therefore show a decrease in blood pressure. Similarly, people who take an "herbal supplement" believing that it will help relieve their insomnia may fall asleep more easily because of that belief, even if the pill that they swallow is actually a placebo.

Use Your Knowledge of Research to Help You Evaluate Media Reports

How can all of this research information assist you in becoming a better consumer and critic of media reports? By having a better understanding of the research process and types of research conducted, you are more capable of discerning the truth or fallacy within media reports. Keep the following points in mind when examining any media report:

- Who is reporting the information? Is it an article in a newspaper, magazine, or on the Internet? If the report is made by a person or group who may financially benefit from you buying their products, you should be skeptical of the reported results. Also, many people who write for popular magazines and newspapers are not trained in science and are capable of misinterpreting research results.
- Who conducted the research, and who paid for it? Was the study funded by a company that stands to profit from certain results? Are the researchers receiving goods, personal travel funds, speaking fees, or other perks from the research sponsor, or do they have investments in companies or products related to their study? If the answer to any of these questions is yes, there exists a conflict of interest between the researchers and the funding agency. If a conflict of interest does exist, it may seriously compromise the researchers' ability to conduct unbiased research and report the results in an accurate and responsible manner.

To become a more informed critic of nutrition reports in the media, and a smarter consumer, you need to understand the research process and how to interpret the results of different types of studies.

- Is the report based on reputable research studies? Did the research follow the scientific method, and were the results reported in a reputable scientific journal? Ideally, the journal is peer-reviewed; that is, the articles are critiqued by other specialists working in the same scientific field. A reputable report should include the reference, or source of the information, and should identify researchers by name. This allows the reader to investigate the original study and determine its merit. Some reputable nutrition journals are identified later in this chapter.

- Is the report based on testimonials about personal experiences? Are sweeping conclusions made from only one study? Be aware of personal testimonials, as they are fraught with bias. In addition, one study cannot answer all of our questions or prove any hypothesis, and the findings from individual studies should be placed in their proper perspective.

- Are the claims in the report too good to be true? Are claims made about curing disease or treating a multitude of conditions? If something sounds too good to be true, it probably is. Claims about curing diseases or treating many conditions with one product should be a signal to question the validity of the report.

As you may know, *quackery* is the misrepresentation of a product, program, or service for financial gain. Marilyn, the woman with high blood pressure from our opening story, was a victim of quackery. She probably would not have purchased that weight-loss supplement if she had understood that it was no more effective in promoting weight loss than a generic fiber supplement costing less than half the price. Throughout this text we provide you with information to assist you in becoming a more educated consumer regarding nutrition. You will learn about labeling guidelines, the proper use of supplements, and whether various nutrition topics are myths or facts. Armed with the information in this book, plus plenty of opportunities to test your knowledge, you will become more confident when trying to evaluate nutrition claims.

RECAP

Epidemiological studies involve large populations, model studies involve animals, and human studies include case control studies and clinical trials. Each type of study can be used to gather a different kind of data. When evaluating media reports, consider who is reporting the information, who conducted and paid for the research, whether or not the research was published in a reputable journal, and whether it involves testimonials or makes claims that sound too good to be true. Quackery is the misrepresentation of a product, program, or service for financial gain.

Nutrition Advice: Whom Can You Trust?

After reading this chapter, you can see that nutrition is a relatively new science that plays a critical role in preserving health and preventing and treating disease. As recognition of this vital role has increased over the past few decades, the public has become more and more interested in understanding how nutrition affects their health. One result of this booming interest has been the publication of an almost overwhelming quantity of nutritional information and claims on television infomercials; on Web sites; in newspapers, magazines, newsletters, and journals; on product packages; and via many other forums. "The noise level is extraordinary," says Marion Nestle, a professor of nutrition at New York University. "I expect health claims from every food in the supermarket."[6] Most individuals do not have the knowledge or training to interpret and evaluate the reliability of this information and thus are vulnerable to misinformation and potentially harmful quackery.

Nutrition professionals are in a perfect position to work in a multitude of settings to counsel and educate their clients and the general public about sound nutrition practices. The following discussion identifies some key characteristics of reliable sources of nutrition information.

Trustworthy Experts Are Educated and Credentialed

It is not possible to list here all of the types of health professionals who provide reliable and accurate nutrition information. The following is a list of the most common groups:

- *Registered dietitian (or RD):* To become a **registered dietitian (RD)** requires a minimum of a bachelor's degree, completion of a supervised clinical experience, a passing grade on a national examination, and maintenance of registration with the American Dietetic Association (in Canada, the Dietitians of Canada). Individuals who complete the education, experience, exam, and registration are qualified to provide nutrition counseling in a variety of settings. For a list of individuals who are registered dietitians in your community, you can look in the yellow pages of your phone book or contact the American Dietetic Association at www.eatright.org.

- *Licensed dietitian:* A licensed dietitian is a dietitian meeting the credentialing requirement of a given state in the United States to engage in the practice of dietetics.[7] Each state in the United States has its own laws regulating dietitians. These laws specify which types of licensure or registration a nutrition professional must obtain in order to provide nutrition services or advice to individuals. Individuals who practice nutrition and dietetics without the required license or registration can be prosecuted for breaking the law.

- *Nutritionist:* This term generally has no definition or laws regulating it. In some cases, it refers to a professional with academic credentials in nutrition who may also be an RD.[7] In other cases, the term may refer to anyone who thinks he or she is knowledgeable about nutrition. There is no guarantee that a person calling himself or herself a nutritionist is necessarily educated, trained, and experienced in the field of nutrition. It is important to research the credentials and experience of any individual calling himself or herself a nutritionist. In the chapter-opening scenario, how might Marilyn have determined whether or not the "nutritionist" was qualified to give her advice?

- *Professional with an advanced degree* (a master's degree [MA or MS] or doctoral degree [PhD]) *in nutrition:* Many individuals hold an advanced degree in nutrition and have years of experience in a nutrition-related career. For instance, they may teach at community colleges or universities or work in fitness or healthcare settings. Unless these individuals are licensed or registered dietitians, they are not certified to provide clinical dietary counseling or treatment for individuals with disease. However, they are reliable sources of information about nutrition and health.

- *Physician:* The term *physician* encompasses a variety of healthcare professionals. A medical doctor (MD) is educated, trained, and licensed to practice medicine in the United States. However, MDs typically have very limited experience and training in the area of nutrition. Medical students in the United States are not required to take any nutrition courses throughout their academic training, although some may take courses out of personal interest. On the other hand, a number of individuals who started their careers in nutrition go on to become medical doctors and thus have a solid background in nutrition. Nevertheless, if you require a dietary plan to treat an illness or disease, most medical doctors will refer you to an RD or licensed nutritionist. In contrast, an osteopathic physician, referred to as a doctor of osteopathy (DO), may have studied nutrition extensively, as may a naturopathic physician, a homeopathic physician, or a chiropractor. Thus, it is prudent to determine a physician's level of expertise rather than assuming that he or she has extensive knowledge of nutrition.

Government Sources of Information Are Usually Trustworthy

Many government health agencies have come together in the past 20 years to address the growing problem of nutrition-related disease in the United States. These organizations are funded with taxpayer dollars, and many of these agencies provide financial support for re-

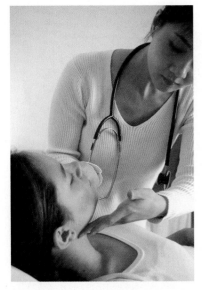

Medical doctors may have limited experience and training in the area of nutrition, but they can refer clients to a registered dietitian (RD) or licensed dietitian to assist them in meeting their dietary needs.

registered dietitian (RD)   A professional designation that requires a minimum of a bachelor's degree in nutrition, completion of a supervised clinical experience, a passing grade on a national examination, and maintenance of registration with the American Dietetic Association (in Canada, the Dietitians of Canada). RDs are qualified to work in a variety of settings.

search in the areas of nutrition and health. Thus, these agencies have the resources to organize and disseminate the most recent and reliable information related to nutrition and other areas of health and wellness. A few of the most recognized and respected of these government agencies are discussed here.

The Centers for Disease Control and Prevention

The **Centers for Disease Control and Prevention (CDC)** is considered the leading federal agency in the United States that protects human health and safety. Located in Atlanta, Georgia, the CDC works in the areas of health promotion, disease prevention and control, and environmental health. The CDC's mission is to promote health and quality of life by preventing and controlling disease, injury, and disability. Among its many activities, the CDC supports two large national surveys that provide us with important nutrition and health information.

The **National Health and Nutrition Examination Survey (NHANES)** is conducted by the National Center for Health Statistics and the CDC. The NHANES tracks the nutrient consumption of Americans and includes carbohydrates, lipids, proteins, vitamins, minerals, fiber, and other food components. Nutrition and other health information is gathered from interviews and examinations using 24-hour dietary recalls, food-frequency questionnaires, and dietary interviews. The database for the NHANES survey is extremely large, and an abundance of research papers have been generated from it. To learn more about the NHANES, see the Web Links at the end of this chapter.

The **Behavioral Risk Factor Surveillance System (BRFSS)** was established by the CDC to track lifestyle behaviors that increase our risk for chronic disease. The world's largest telephone survey, the BRFSS gathers data at the state level at regular intervals. Although the BRFSS includes questions related to injuries and infectious diseases, it places a particularly strong focus on the health behaviors that increase our risk for the nation's leading killers: heart disease, stroke, cancer, and diabetes. These health behaviors include:[8]

- Lack of adequate physical activity
- Consuming a diet that is low in fiber and high in fat
- Using tobacco and alcohol
- Not getting medical care that is known to save lives, such as regular Pap smears, mammograms, flu shots, and screening for cancer of the colon and rectum

These behaviors are of particular interest because it is estimated that four out of ten deaths (or 40%) in the United States can be attributed to smoking, alcohol misuse, lack of physical activity, and eating an unhealthful diet.[8]

The National Institutes of Health

The **National Institutes of Health (NIH)** is the world's leading medical research center, and it is the focal point for medical research in the United States. The NIH is one of the agencies of the Public Health Service, which is part of the U.S. Department of Health and Human Services. The mission of the NIH is to uncover new knowledge that leads to better health for everyone. This mission is accomplished by supporting medical research throughout the world and by fostering communication of this information. The NIH has many institutes and centers that focus on a broad array of nutrition-related health issues. Some of these institutes include:

- National Cancer Institute (NCI)
- National Heart, Lung, and Blood Institute (NHLBI)
- National Institute of Diabetes and Digestive and Kidney Diseases (NIDDK)
- National Center for Complementary and Alternative Medicine (NCCAM)

The headquarters of the NIH is located in Bethesda, Maryland. To find out more about the NIH, see the Web Links at the end of this chapter.

Lifestyle behaviors, such as eating an unhealthful diet, can increase your risk for chronic disease.

Centers for Disease Control and Prevention (CDC) The leading federal agency in the United States that protects the health and safety of people. Its mission is to promote health and quality of life by preventing and controlling disease, injury, and disability.

National Health and Nutrition Examination Survey (NHANES) A survey conducted by the National Center for Health Statistics and the CDC; this survey tracks the nutrient and food consumption of Americans.

Behavioral Risk Factor Surveillance System (BRFSS) The world's largest telephone survey that tracks lifestyle behaviors that increase our risk for chronic disease.

National Institutes of Health (NIH) The world's leading medical research center and the focal point for medical research in the United States.

Professional Organizations Provide Reliable Nutrition Information

A number of professional organizations represent nutrition professionals, scientists, and educators. These organizations publish cutting-edge nutrition research studies and educational information in journals that are accessible at most university and medical libraries. Some of these organizations include:

- *The American Dietetic Association (ADA):* This is the largest organization of food and nutrition professionals in the United States and the world. The mission of this organization is to promote nutrition, health, and well-being. The Canadian equivalent is Dietitians of Canada. The ADA publishes a professional journal called the *Journal of the American Dietetic Association.*
- *The American Society for Nutrition (ASN):* The ASN is the premier research society dedicated to improving quality of life through the science of nutrition. The ASN fulfills its mission by fostering, enhancing, and disseminating nutrition-related research and professional education activities. The ASN publishes a professional journal called the *American Journal of Clinical Nutrition.*
- *The Society for Nutrition Education (SNE):* The SNE is dedicated to promoting healthy, sustainable food choices in communities through nutrition research and education. The primary goals of the SNE are to educate individuals, communities, and professionals about nutrition education and to influence policy makers about nutrition, food, and health. The professional journal of the SNE is the *Journal of Nutrition Education and Behavior.*
- *The American College of Sports Medicine (ACSM):* The ACSM is the leading sports medicine and exercise science organization in the world. The mission of the ACSM is to advance and integrate scientific research to provide educational and practical applications of exercise science and sports medicine. Many members are nutrition professionals who combine their nutrition and exercise expertise to promote health and athletic performance. *Medicine and Science in Sports and Exercise* is the professional journal of the ACSM.
- *The North American Association for the Study of Obesity (NAASO):* NAASO is the leading scientific society dedicated to the study of obesity. It is committed to encouraging research on the causes and treatments of obesity and to keeping the medical community and public informed of new advances. The official NAASO journal is *Obesity Research,* which is intended to increase knowledge, stimulate research, and promote better treatment of people with obesity.

For more information on any of these organizations, see the Web Links at the end of this chapter.

RECaP

The Centers for Disease Control and Prevention is the leading federal agency in the United States that protects human health and safety. The CDC supports two large national surveys that provide important nutrition and health information: the National Health and Nutrition Examination Survey (NHANES) and the Behavioral Risk Factor Surveillance System (BRFSS). The National Institutes of Health is the leading medical research agency in the world. The American Dietetic Association, the American Society for Nutritional Sciences, the Society for Nutrition Education, the American College of Sports Medicine, and the North American Association for the Study of Obesity are examples of professional organizations that provide reliable nutrition information.

Liz
Nutri-Case

"Am I ever sorry I caught the news last night right before going to bed! They had a report about this study that had just come out saying that ballet dancers are at some super-abnormally high risk for fractures! I couldn't sleep thinking about it, and then today in dance class, every move I made, I was freaking out about breaking my ankle. I can't go on being afraid like this!"

What information should Liz find out about the fracture study to evaluate its merits? Identify *at least* two factors she should evaluate. Let's say that her investigation of these factors leads her to conclude that the study is trustworthy: what else should she bear in mind about the research process that would help her take a more healthy perspective when thinking about this single study?

See for Yourself

Take a piece of lined paper and divide it into four equal columns, labeled as follows:

☐ Food Item
☐ Serving Size
☐ Time of Day
☐ Location

The document you create will resemble a standard form used for a 24-hour dietary recall. Fill it out as carefully and thoroughly as you can, listing each food you ate yesterday, beginning and ending at midnight.

Now answer the following questions:

1. How confident are you that you documented every single item that you ate all day yesterday?
2. How confident are you that you recalled accurately the serving size of each food you ate?
3. Given your experience filling out a 24-hour dietary recall, what would you identify as the main limitations of this assessment tool?

Chapter Review

Test Yourself | Answers

1. **F** A calorie is a measure of the energy in a food. More precisely, a kilocalorie is the amount of heat required to raise the temperature of 1 kilogram of water by 1 degree Celsius.

2. **T** Carbohydrates and lipids are the primary energy sources for the body.

3. **F** Most water-soluble vitamins need to be consumed daily. However, we can consume foods that contain fat-soluble vitamins less frequently because our bodies can store these vitamins.

4. **F** The Recommended Dietary Allowance is the average daily nutrient intake level that meets the nutrient requirements of 97% to 98% of healthy individuals in a particular life stage and gender group.

5. **F** Other good sources are professional organizations in the field of nutrition research and education and individuals who are licensed or registered as nutrition professionals.

Summary

- Nutrition is the scientific study of food and how food nourishes the body and influences health.

- Early nutrition research focused on identifying, preventing, and treating nutrient-deficiency diseases. As the Western diet improved, obesity and its associated chronic diseases became an important subject for nutrition research. In the late 20th century, nutrigenomics emerged as a new field of nutrition research.

- Nutrition is an important component of wellness. Healthful nutrition plays a critical role in eliminating deficiency disease and can help reduce our risks for various chronic diseases.

- *Healthy People 2020* is a national health agenda that focuses on health promotion and disease prevention; its two primary goals are to increase quality and years of life and to eliminate health disparities in the U.S. population.

- Nutrients are chemicals found in food that are critical to human growth and function.

- The six essential nutrients found in the foods we eat are: carbohydrates, lipids, and proteins, which provide energy and are known as the macronutrients; vitamins and minerals, which are micronutrients; and water.

- Carbohydrates are composed of carbon, hydrogen, and oxygen. Carbohydrates are the primary energy source for the human body, particularly for the brain.

- Lipids provide us with fat-soluble vitamins and essential fatty acids in addition to storing large quantities of energy.

- Proteins can provide energy if needed, but they are not a primary fuel source. Proteins support tissue growth, repair, and maintenance.

- Vitamins assist with the regulation of body processes.

- Minerals are inorganic substances that are not changed by digestion or other metabolic processes.

- Water is critical to support numerous body functions, including fluid balance, conduction of nervous impulses, and muscle contraction.

- The Dietary Reference Intakes (DRIs) are reference standards for nutrient intakes for healthy people in the United States and Canada.

- The DRIs include the Estimated Average Requirement, the Recommended Dietary Allowance, the Adequate Intake, the Tolerable Upper Intake Level, the Estimated Energy Requirement, and the Acceptable Macronutrient Distribution Range.

- Malnutrition occurs when a person's nutritional status is out of balance. Undernutrition occurs when someone consumes too little energy or nutrients, and overnutrition occurs when too much energy or too much of a given nutrient is consumed over time.

- Nutrition assessment methods include a physical examination, health-history questionnaire, dietary intake tools, and anthropometric assessments. Specific dietary intake tools include a diet history, 24-hour recalls, food-frequency questionnaires, and diet records.

- A primary nutrient deficiency occurs when a person does not consume enough of a given nutrient in the diet. A secondary nutrient deficiency occurs when a person cannot absorb enough of a nutrient, when too much of a nutrient is excreted, or when a nutrient is not efficiently utilized.

- The steps in the scientific method are (1) observing a phenomenon, (2) creating a hypothesis, (3) designing and conducting an experiment, and (4) collecting and analyzing data that support or refute the hypothesis.

- A hypothesis that is supported after repeated experiments may be called a theory.

- Epidemiological studies involve large populations, model studies involve animals, and human studies include case control studies and clinical trials. A double-blind, placebo-controlled study is considered the most trustworthy form of clinical trial.

- When evaluating media reports, consider who is reporting the information, who conducted and paid for the research, whether or not the research was published in a reputable journal, and whether it involves testimonials or makes claims that sound too good to be true. Quackery is the misrepresentation of a product, program, or service for financial gain.

- Potentially good sources of reliable nutrition information include individuals who are registered dietitians, licensed nutritionists, or who hold an advanced degree in nutrition. Medical professionals such as physicians, osteopaths, and registered nurses have variable levels of training in nutrition.

- The Centers for Disease Control and Prevention (CDC) is the leading federal agency that protects the health and safety of Americans.

- The National Health and Nutrition Examination Survey (NHANES) is a survey conducted by the CDC and the National Center for Health Statistics that tracks the nutritional status of people in the United States.

- The Behavioral Risk Factor Surveillance System (BRFSS) was established by the CDC and is the world's largest telephone survey; the BRFSS gathers data at the state level on the health behaviors and risks of Americans.

- The National Institutes of Health (NIH) is the leading medical research agency in the world. The mission of NIH is to uncover new knowledge that leads to better health for everyone.

Review Questions

1. Vitamins A and C, thiamin, calcium, and magnesium are considered
   a. water-soluble vitamins.
   b. fat-soluble vitamins.
   c. energy nutrients.
   d. micronutrients.

2. Malnutrition plays a role in which of the following?
   a. obesity
   b. iron-deficiency anemia
   c. scurvy
   d. all of the above

3. Ten grams of fat
   a. contain 40 kcal of energy.
   b. contain 90 kcal of energy.
   c. constitute the Dietary Reference Intake for an average adult male.
   d. constitute the Tolerable Upper Intake Level for an average adult male.

4. Which of the following assessment methods provides objective data?
   a. 24-hour dietary recall
   b. history of illnesses, injuries, and surgeries
   c. measurement of height
   d. diet record

5. Which of the following statements about hypotheses is true?
   a. Hypotheses can be proven by clinical trials.
   b. If the results of multiple experiments consistently support a hypothesis, it is confirmed as fact.
   c. "A high-protein diet increases the risk for porous bones" is an example of a valid hypothesis.
   d. "Many inactive people have high blood pressure" is an example of a valid hypothesis.

6. **True or false?** Fat-soluble vitamins provide energy.

7. **True or false?** Carbohydrates, lipids, and proteins all contain carbon, hydrogen, and oxygen.

8. **True or false?** The Recommended Dietary Allowance represents the average daily intake level that meets the requirements of almost all healthy individuals in a given life stage or gender group.

9. **True or false?** An epidemiological study is a clinical trial in which a large population participates as members of the experimental and control groups.

10. **True or false?** Nutrition-related reports in the *Journal of the American Dietetic Association* are likely to be trustworthy.

11. Explain the role of the control group in a clinical trial.

12. Compare the Estimated Average Requirement with the Recommended Dietary Allowance.

13. Imagine that you are in a gift shop and meet Marilyn, from the chapter-opening scenario. Learning that you are studying nutrition, she tells you of her experience and states that the supplements "didn't seem to do much of anything." She asks you, "How can I find reliable nutrition information?" How would you answer?

14. Your mother, who is a self-described "chocolate addict," phones you. She has read in the newspaper a summary of a research study suggesting that the consumption of a moderate amount of bittersweet chocolate reduces the risk of heart disease in older women. You ask her who funded the research. She says she doesn't know and asks you why it would matter. Explain why such information is important.

15. Intrigued by the idea of a research study on chocolate, you obtain a copy of the full report. In it, you learn that:
    - twelve women participated in the study;
    - the women's ages ranged from 65 to 78;
    - the women had all been diagnosed with high blood pressure;
    - they all described themselves as sedentary; and
    - six of the twelve smoked at least half a pack of cigarettes a day, but the others did not smoke.

    Your mother is 51 years old, walks daily, and takes a weekly swim class. Her blood pressure is on the upper end of the normal range. She does not smoke. Identify at least three aspects of the study that would cause you to doubt its relevance to your mother.

Web Links

www.healthypeople.gov
Healthy People 2020
Search this site for a list of objectives that identify the most significant preventable threats to health in the United States and establish national goals to reduce these threats.

www.eatright.org
American Dietetic Association (ADA)
Obtain a list of registered dietitians in your community from the largest organization of food and nutrition professionals in the United States. Information about careers in dietetics is also available at this site.

www.cdc.gov
Centers for Disease Control and Prevention (CDC)
Visit this site for additional information about the leading federal agency in the United States that protects the health and safety of people.

www.cdc.gov/nchs/express.htm
National Center for Health Statistics
From the CDC site, click the "National Data" link on the left to learn more about the National Health and Nutrition Examination Survey (also referred to as NHANES) and other national health surveys.

www.nih.gov
National Institutes of Health (NIH)
Find out more about the National Institutes of Health, an agency under the U.S. Department of Health and Human Services.

www.nutrition.org
The American Society for Nutrition (ASN)
Learn more about the American Society for Nutrition and its goal to improve quality of life through the science of nutrition.

www.sne.org
Society for Nutrition Education (SNE)
Go to this site for further information about the Society for Nutrition Education and its goals to educate individuals, communities, and professionals about nutrition education and influence policy makers about nutrition, food, and health.

www.acsm.org
American College of Sports Medicine (ACSM)
Obtain information about the leading sports medicine and exercise science organization in the world.

www.naaso.org
The North American Association for the Study of Obesity
Learn about this interdisciplinary society and its work to develop, extend, and disseminate knowledge in the field of obesity.

References

1. Carpenter, K. J. 2000. *Beriberi, White Rice, and Vitamin B: A Disease, a Cause, and a Cure.* Berkeley, CA: University of California Press.

2. Mokdad, A. H., J. S. Marks, D. F. Stroup, and J. L. Gerberding. 2004. Actual causes of death in the United States, 2000. *JAMA* 291:1238–1245.

3. U.S. Department of Health and Human Services. 2008. *Healthy People 2020: The Road Ahead.* Available at www.healthypeople.gov/hp2020/.

4. Institute of Medicine, Food and Nutrition Board. 2003. *Dietary Reference Intakes: Applications in Dietary Planning.* Washington, DC: National Academies Press.

5. Institute of Medicine, Food and Nutrition Board. 2002. *Dietary Reference Intakes for Energy, Carbohydrates, Fiber, Fat, Protein and Amino Acids (Macronutrients).* Washington, DC: National Academies Press.

6. Elliott, S. 2005. Got bread? A campaign offers an alternative to the low-carb craze. *New York Times,* February 1, p. C9.

7. Winterfeldt E. A., M. L. Bogle, and L. L. Ebro. 2005. *Dietetics. Practice and Future Trends.* 2nd ed. Sudbury, MA: Jones and Bartlett Publishers.

8. U.S. Department of Health and Human Services, Centers for Disease Control and Prevention. 2005. CDC at a glance. Health Risks in America: Behavioral Risk Factor Surveillance System 2004. Available at http://apps.nccd.cdc.gov/brfss/.

9. Watters, E. 2006. DNA is not destiny. *Discover* 27(11):32–75.

10. The NCMHD Center of Excellence for Nutritional Genomics. Retrieved April 2007 from http://nutrigenomics.ucdavis.edu.

11. Johnson, N., and J. Kaput. 2003. Nutrigenomics: An emerging scientific discipline. *Food Technology* 57(4):60–67.

12. Grierson, B. 2003. What your genes want you to eat. *New York Times,* May 4.

13. Underwood, A., and J. Adler. 2005. Diet and genes. *Newsweek,* January 17, p. 40.

14. Wallace, K. 2007. Diet, exercise may lower colon cancer risk [television broadcast]. CBS News, March 15.

15. Kaput, J., and R. Rodriguez. 2004. Nutritional genomics: The next frontier in the post-genomic era. *Physiological Genomics* 16:166–177.

16. Human Genome Project Information. 2008. How many genes are in the human genome? Retrieved February 2009 from www.ornl.gov/sci/techresources/Human_Genome/faq/genenumber.shtml.

17. Sterling, R. 2008. The on-line promotion and sale of nutrigenomic services. *Genet Med.,* November, 10(11):784–796.

Nutrigenomics: Personalized Nutrition or Pie in the Sky?

Agouti mice are specifically bred for scientific studies. These mice are normally yellow in color, obese, and prone to cancer and diabetes, and they typically have a short life span. When agouti mice breed, these traits are passed on to their offspring. Look at the picture of the agouti mice on this page; do you see a difference? The mouse on the right is obviously brown and of normal weight, but what you can't see is that it did not inherit its parents' susceptibility to disease and therefore will live a longer, healthier life. What caused this dramatic difference between parent and offspring? The answer is diet![9]

In 2000, researchers at Duke University found that when they changed the mother's diet just before conception, they could "turn off" the agouti gene, and any offspring born to that mother would appear normal.[9] As you might know, a *gene* is a segment of DNA, the substance responsible for inheritance, or the passing on of traits from parents to offspring, in both animals and humans. An organism's *genome* is its complete set of DNA, which is found packed into the nucleus of its body cells. Genes are precise regions of DNA that encode instructions for making specific proteins. In other words, genes are *expressed* in proteins; for instance, one way that the agouti gene is expressed is in the pigment proteins that produce yellow fur. We'll discuss genes and proteins in more detail in Chapter 6.

The Duke University researchers interfered with normal gene expression in their agouti mice by manipulating the mice's diet. Specifically, they fed the mother a diet that was high in methyl donors, compounds that can transfer a methyl group (CH_3) to another molecule. Methylation is thought to play a role in genetic expression. Sure enough, the methyl donors attached to the agouti gene and, in essence, turned it off. When the mother conceived, her offspring still carried the agouti gene on their DNA, but their cells no longer used the gene to make proteins. In short, the gene was no longer expressed; thus, the traits such as obesity that were linked to the agouti gene did not appear in the offspring.[9] These Duke University studies were some of the first to directly link a dietary intervention to a genetic modification and contributed significantly

Prompted only by a change in her diet before she conceived, an inbred agouti mouse (left) gave birth to a young mouse (right) that differed not only in appearance but also in its susceptibility to disease.

to the emerging science of *nutrigenomics* (or *nutritional genomics*).

What Is Nutrigenomics?

Nutrigenomics is a scientific discipline studying the interactions between genes, the environment, and nutrition.[10, 11] Scientists have known for some time that diet and environmental factors can contribute to disease, but what has not been understood before is *how*—namely, by altering how our genes are expressed. Until the late 20th century, scientists believed that the genes a person is born with determined his or her traits rigidly; in other words, that gene expression was not susceptible to outside influences. But the theory behind nutrigenomics is that genetic expression is indeed influenced—perhaps significantly—by foods we eat and substances in our environment to which our cells are exposed.

Nutrigenomics proposes that foods and environmental factors can act like a switch in body cells, turning on some genes while turning off others. When a gene is activated, it will instruct the cell to create a protein that will show up as a physical characteristic or functional ability, such as a protein that facilitates the storage of fat. When a gene is switched off, the cell will not create that protein, and the organism's form or function will differ. Some of the factors thought most likely to affect gene activation include tobacco, drugs, alcohol, environmental toxins, radiation, exercise, and the foods most common to an individual's diet.[10, 11]

In addition, nutrigenomics scientists are discovering that what we expose our genes to—such as food and smoke—can affect gene expression not only in the exposed organism but in his or her offspring.[9] In the Duke University study, switching off the agouti gene caused beneficial changes in the offspring mice. But sometimes flipping the switch can be harmful, as when paternal exposure to radiation causes changes in sperm cells that increase the likelihood of birth defects in the offspring.

In short, nutrigenomics proposes that foods and environmental factors can influence the expression of our genes and possibly influence the traits of our children. It's an intriguing theory—but beyond the agouti study, what evidence supports it?

Evidence for Nutrigenomics

Several observations over many decades certainly suggest that the theory has merit. For example, nutrition researchers have long noted that some people will lose weight on a specific diet and exercise program, whereas others following the same diet and exercise program will experience no weight loss or will even gain weight.[11, 12] The varying results are now thought to depend to a certain extent upon how the foods in that diet affect the study participants' genes.

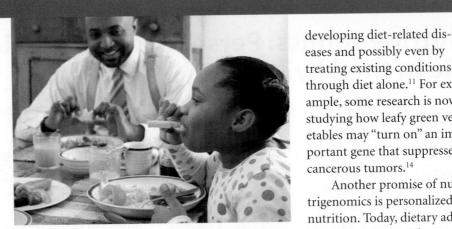

Nutrigenomics suggests that dietary and environmental factors can either activate or turn off some of the genes a person inherits from his or her parents.

Another example is smoking. Researchers have long understood that smoking is harmful to human health, but they now recognize that smokers with a particular set of genes have a much higher rate of mortality than smokers who do not have those genes.[13]

Scientists also point to evidence from population studies. For example, they observe that when different ethnic groups are exposed to a Western diet, the percentage of type 2 diabetes increases in some populations significantly more than in others. Also, the health disparities that exist between people in developed versus developing countries are known to be due in large part to their different access to appropriate nutrition.[10]

Evidence of nutrigenomics influencing future generations includes the breakthrough study of agouti mice, as well as recent historical data that suggest a link between the availability of food and type 2 diabetes. Researchers have found that when one generation experiences a food surplus during critical periods of reproductive development, their offspring are more likely to develop type 2 diabetes.[9]

Promises of Nutrigenomics

Currently, researchers involved in nutrigenomics are making predictions not unlike that of the famous inventor Thomas Edison: "The doctor of the future will give no medicine but will interest his patients in the care of the human frame, in diet, and in the cause and prevention of disease."

One promise of nutrigenomics is that it can assist people in optimizing their health by reducing their risk of developing diet-related diseases and possibly even by treating existing conditions through diet alone.[11] For example, some research is now studying how leafy green vegetables may "turn on" an important gene that suppresses cancerous tumors.[14]

Another promise of nutrigenomics is personalized nutrition. Today, dietary advice is based primarily on observations of large populations. Typically, these epidemiological studies do not consider variations within the group.[10, 11] But advice that is generally appropriate for a population might not be appropriate for every individual within that population. For example, most Americans are overweight or obese and need dietary advice that can help them lose weight. But some Americans are chronically underweight and need advice for increasing their energy intake. Advances in nutrigenomics could eliminate this concern by making it possible to provide each individual with a personalized diet. In this future world, you would provide a tissue sample to a healthcare provider who would send it to a lab for genetic analysis. The results would guide the provider in creating a diet tailored to your specific genetic makeup. By identifying both foods to eat and foods to avoid, this personalized diet would help you to turn on beneficial genes and turn off genes that could be harmful.

Another promise of nutrigenomics is increased understanding of the role of physical activity in human health. Recent research shows that exercise can influence genes involved in certain diseases, such as colon cancer. Dr. Anne McTiernan of the Fred Hutchinson Cancer Research Center in Seattle has found that exercise can reduce the risk of colon cancer by 50%. McTiernan has observed that study participants who exercised at least 4 hours a week turned abnormal-looking cells that had the potential to develop into polyps and even colon cancer into normal-functioning cells.[14] Thus, nutrigenomics is finding that the conventional advice to "eat a balanced diet and exercise" holds true for the majority of people.

A final promise of nutrigenomics is reduction in the global problem of health disparities. Information gained from comparing nutrient/gene interactions as well as environmental factors in different populations may help scientists address the problems of global malnutrition and disease in both developed and developing countries.[10]

Challenges of Nutrigenomics

If the promises of nutrigenomics strike you as pie in the sky, you're not alone. Many researchers caution, for example, that dietary "prescriptions" to prevent or treat chronic diseases would be extremely challenging because multiple genes may be involved, and environmental, emotional, and even social factors may also play a role.[15] In addition, genetics researchers currently believe that there are about 20,000 to 25,000 genes in human DNA, representing only about 2% of the human genome.[16] The remaining regions of DNA are considered non-coding but are thought to have other functions, many of which may influence nutrition and health. Moreover, the pathways for genetic expression are extremely complex, and turning on a gene may have a beneficial effect on one body function but a harmful effect on another. To complicate the matter further, other factors such as age, gender, and lifestyle will also affect how different foods interact with these different genetic pathways. In short, the number of variables that must be considered in order to develop a "personalized diet" is staggering.

Even by themselves, food interactions are extremely complicated because when one eats a meal, hundreds of nutrient compounds are consumed at one time. Think about all the ingredients found in just one food item, such as pancakes. Each one of these ingredients may interact with a variety of genes directly or indirectly in an uncontrollable and inestimable number of ways.[15] As an example, scientists have determined that at least 150 different genes are linked to type 2 diabetes, and 300 or more have been linked to obesity. Which of the ingredients consumed affect what gene and how? It will be years before researchers are capable of mapping out these complex interactions.[13]

This daunting complexity has not stopped companies from offering naïve consumers nutrigenomics products and services ranging from at-home testing kits to "personalized" diets. One study of online sales of nutrigenomics services called such practices premature and concluded that organizations did not provide adequate information about their offerings.[17] Considering these challenges, regulation of the nutrigenomics industry is a growing concern. But what agency should be responsible? Currently the Food and Drug Administration (FDA) monitors and regulates food production and food safety, as well as the safety of medications and many medical devices. In the absence of such oversight, the safety of nutrigenomics services is likely to become a real concern as increasing numbers of consumers fall prey to fraudulent or even dangerous dietary advice.

Another potential challenge facing the field of nutrigenomics, discrimination on the basis of an individual's DNA profile, may already have been surmounted. In 2007 the U.S. House of Representatives passed a bill that bans employers and insurance companies from discriminating against people based on their genetic makeup. Under this bill, genetic profiles cannot be used by insurance companies to deny insurance coverage or raise premiums, nor can employers terminate individuals from their jobs for having a genetic mutation.

When Will Nutrigenomics Become a Viable Healthcare Option?

Delivering on the promises of nutrigenomics will require a multidisciplinary approach involving researchers in genetics, nutrition, chemistry, molecular biology, physiology, pathology, sociology, ethics, and many more. The number and complexity of nutritional, environmental, and genetic interactions these scientists will have to contend with are so staggering that decades may pass before nutrigenomics is able to contribute significantly to human health.

Consumers will probably first encounter nutrigenomics in diagnostic testing. In this process, a blood or tissue sample of DNA will be genetically analyzed to determine how food and food supplements interact with that individual's genes and how a change in diet might affect those interactions. Genetic counseling will be required to help consumers understand the meaning and recommendations suggested by their genetic profile.[11]

Second, consumers will probably begin to see more specialized foods promoted for specific conditions. For example, consumers currently have an array of foods they can choose from if they want to lower their cholesterol or enhance their bone health. More such foods will likely be developed, and food packages of the future might even be coded for certain genetic profiles.

We may be decades away from a "personalized diet," but one thing is clear right now: Nutrigenomics is showing us the importance of nutrition and environmental factors in preserving our health. In doing so, nutrigenomics is changing not only the way we look at food but the science of nutrition itself.

Critical Thinking Questions

- Are personalized diets and food packages coded for certain genetic profiles part of our future?
- When you experience poor health, will you consult a nutrigenomics professional instead of a physician and get a prescription for foods instead of medicines?
- Will nutrigenomics advance preventive medicine and reduce our rate of obesity and other chronic diseases?
- If so, will it lower healthcare costs?
- In what other ways could nutrigenomics change the landscape of healthcare in America?

2 Designing a Healthful Diet

Test Yourself | True or False?

1. A healthful diet is made up predominantly of fruits and vegetables. **T** or **F**
2. All foods sold in the United States must display a food label. **T** or **F**
3. MyPyramid is the graphic representation of the U.S. Department of Agriculture (USDA) Food Guide and can be used by most Americans to design a healthful diet. **T** or **F**
4. The Dietary Guidelines for Americans recommend that all Americans should consume alcohol sensibly. **T** or **F**
5. It is impossible to eat a healthful diet when eating out. **T** or **F**

Test Yourself answers are located in the Chapter Review.

Chapter Objectives *After reading this chapter, you will be able to:*

1. Define the components of a healthful diet, *pp. 40–41.*

2. Read a food label and use the Nutrition Facts Panel to determine the nutritional adequacy of a given food, *pp. 42–45.*

3. Distinguish between label claims related to nutrient content, health, and body structure or function, *pp. 45–47.*

4. Describe the Dietary Guidelines for Americans and discuss how these guidelines can be used to design a healthful diet, *pp. 47–52.*

5. Identify the food groups, number of servings, and serving sizes included in the USDA Food Guide, *pp. 52–57.*

6. Define discretionary calories and discuss the role that discretionary calories play in designing a healthful diet, *pp. 54–55.*

7. Describe how the USDA Food Guide can be used to design a healthful diet, *pp. 52–57.*

8. Identify some challenges of using MyPyramid, *pp. 55–57.*

9. List at least four ways to practice moderation and apply healthful dietary guidelines when eating out, *p. 65.*

Each person needs to determine her or his own pattern of healthful eating.

Shivani and her parents moved to the United States from India when Shivani was 6 years old. Although delicate in comparison to her American peers, Shivani was healthy and energetic, excelling in school and riding her new bike in her suburban neighborhood. By the time Shivani entered high school, her weight had caught up to that of her American classmates. Now a college freshman, she has joined the more than 16% of U.S. teens who are overweight.[1] Shivani explains, "In India, the diet is mostly rice, lentils, and vegetables. Many people are vegetarians, and many others eat meat only once or twice a week, and very small portions. Desserts are only for special occasions. When we moved to America, I wanted to eat like all the other kids: hamburgers, French fries, sodas, and sweets. I gained a lot of weight on that diet, and now my doctor says my cholesterol, my blood pressure, and my blood sugar levels are all too high. I wish I could start eating like my relatives back in India again, but they don't serve rice and lentils at the dorm cafeteria."

What influence does diet have on health? What exactly qualifies as a "poor diet," and what makes a diet healthful? Is it more important to watch how much we eat, or what kinds of foods we choose? Is low-carb better, or low-fat? What do the national dietary guidelines advise, and do they apply to "real people" like you?

Many factors contribute to the confusion surrounding healthful eating. First, nutrition is a relatively young science. In contrast with physics, chemistry, and astronomy, which have been studied for thousands of years, the science of nutrition emerged around 1900, with the discovery of the first vitamin in 1897. The initial Recommended Dietary Allowance (RDA) values for the United States were published in 1941. Although we have made substantial discoveries in the area of nutrition during the past century, nutritional research is still considered to be in its infancy. Thus, a growing number of new findings on the benefits of foods and nutrients are discovered almost daily. These new findings contribute to regular changes in how a healthful diet is defined. Second, as stated in Chapter 1, the popular media typically report the results of only selected studies, usually the most recent. This practice does not give a complete picture of all the research conducted in any given area. Indeed, the results of a single study are often misleading. Third, there is no one right way to eat that is healthful and acceptable for everyone. We are individuals with unique needs, food preferences, and cultural influences. For example, a female athlete may need more iron than a sedentary male. One person might prefer to eat three cooked meals a day, whereas another might prefer to eat several smaller snacks, salads, and other quick foods. People following certain religious practices may limit or avoid foods like specific meats and dairy products. Thus, there are literally millions of different ways to design a healthful diet to fit individual needs.

Given all this potential confusion, it's a good thing there are nutritional tools to guide people in designing a healthful diet. In this chapter, we introduce these tools, including food labels, the Dietary Guidelines for Americans, the U.S. Department of Agriculture Food Guide (and its accompanying graphic MyPyramid), and others. Before exploring the question of how to design a healthful diet, however, it is important to understand what a healthful diet *is*.

What Is a Healthful Diet?

A **healthful diet** provides the proper combination of energy and nutrients. It has four characteristics: it is adequate, moderate, balanced, and varied. No matter if you are young or old, overweight or underweight, healthy or coping with illness, if you keep in mind these characteristics of a healthful diet, you will be able to consciously select foods that provide you with the appropriate combination of nutrients and energy each day.

A Healthful Diet Is Adequate

An **adequate diet** provides enough of the energy, nutrients, and fiber to maintain a person's health. A diet may be inadequate in only one area. For example, as just noted, many people in the United States do not eat enough vegetables and therefore are not consuming enough

healthful diet A diet that provides the proper combination of energy and nutrients and is adequate, moderate, balanced, and varied.

adequate diet A diet that provides enough of the energy, nutrients, and fiber to maintain a person's health.

of the fiber and micronutrients found in vegetables. However, their intake of protein, fat, and carbohydrate may be adequate. In fact, some people who eat too few vegetables are overweight or obese, which means that they are eating a diet that exceeds their energy needs.

On the other hand, a generalized state of undernutrition can occur if an individual's diet contains an inadequate level of several nutrients for a long period of time. To maintain a thin figure some individuals may skip one or more meals each day, avoid foods that contain any fat, and limit their meals to only a few foods such as a bagel, a banana, or a diet soda. This type of restrictive eating pattern practiced over a prolonged period can cause low energy levels, loss of bone and hair, impaired memory and cognitive function, and menstrual dysfunction in women.

A diet that is adequate for one person may not be adequate for another. For example, the energy needs of a small woman who is lightly active are approximately 1,700 to 2,000 kilocalories (kcal) each day, while a highly active male athlete may require more than 4,000 kcal each day to support his body's demands. These two individuals differ greatly in their activity level and in their quantity of body fat and muscle mass, which means they require very different levels of fat, carbohydrate, protein, and other nutrients to support their daily needs.

A Healthful Diet Is Moderate

Moderation is one of the keys to a healthful diet. **Moderation** refers to eating any foods in moderate amounts—not too much and not too little. If a person eats too much or too little of certain foods, health goals cannot be reached. For example, some people drink as much as 60 fluid ounces (or three 20-oz bottles) of soft drinks on some days. Drinking this much contributes an extra 765 kcal of energy to a person's diet. In order to allow for these extra kilocalories and avoid weight gain, a person would need to reduce his or her food intake. This could lead to a person cutting healthful food choices from his or her diet. In contrast, people who drink mostly water or other beverages that contain little or no energy can consume more nourishing foods that will support their wellness.

A Healthful Diet Is Balanced

A **balanced diet** is one that contains the combinations of foods that provide the proper proportions of nutrients. As you will learn in this course, the body needs many types of foods in varying amounts to maintain health. For example, fruits and vegetables are excellent sources of fiber, vitamin C, potassium, and magnesium. In contrast, meats are not good sources of fiber and these various nutrients. However, meats are excellent sources of protein, iron, zinc, and copper. By eating the proper balance of all healthful foods, including fruits, vegetables, and meats or meat substitutes, we can be confident that we are consuming the balanced nutrition we need to maintain health.

A Healthful Diet Is Varied

Variety refers to eating many different foods from the different food groups on a regular basis. With literally thousands of healthful foods to choose from, trying new foods on a regular basis is a fun and easy way to vary your diet. Eat a new vegetable each week or substitute one food for another, such as raw spinach on your turkey sandwich in place of iceberg lettuce. Selecting a wide variety of foods increases the likelihood of consuming the multitude of nutrients the body needs. As an added benefit, eating a varied diet prevents boredom and avoids the potential of getting into a "food rut." Later in this chapter, we provide suggestions for eating a varied diet.

A diet that is adequate for one person may not be adequate for another. A woman who is lightly active will require fewer kilocalories of energy per day than a highly active male.

RECAP

A healthful diet provides adequate nutrients and energy, and it includes sweets, fats, and salty foods in moderate amounts only. A healthful diet includes an appropriate balance of nutrients and a wide variety of foods.

moderation Eating any foods in moderate amounts—not too much and not too little.

balanced diet A diet that contains the combinations of foods that provide the proper proportions of nutrients.

variety Eating a lot of different foods each day.

Eating a new vegetable each week is a fun way to vary your diet. Kale is a member of the cabbage family and is an excellent source of calcium.

What Tools Can Help Me Design a Healthful Diet?

Many people feel it is impossible to eat a healthful diet. They may mistakenly believe that the foods they would need to eat are too expensive or not available to them or they may feel too busy to do the necessary planning, shopping, and cooking. Some people rely on dietary supplements to get enough nutrients instead of focusing on eating a variety of foods. But is it really that difficult to eat healthfully?

Although designing and maintaining a healthful diet is not as simple as eating whatever you want, most of us can improve our diets with a little practice and a little help. Let's look now at some tools for designing a healthful diet.

Reading Food Labels Can Be Easy and Helpful

To design and maintain a healthful diet, it's important to read and understand food labels. It may surprise you to learn that a few decades ago, there were no federal regulations for including nutrition information on food labels! The U.S. Food and Drug Administration (FDA) first established such regulations in 1973. These regulations were not as specific as they are today and were not required for many of the foods available to consumers. Throughout the 1970s and 1980s, consumer interest in food quality substantially grew, and many watchdog groups were formed to protect consumers from unclear labeling and false claims made by some manufacturers.

Public interest and concern about how food affects health became so strong that in 1990, the U.S. Congress passed the Nutrition Labeling and Education Act. This act specifies which foods require a food label, provides detailed descriptions of the information that must be included on the food label, and describes the companies and food products that are exempt from publishing complete nutrition information on food labels. For example, detailed food labels are not required for meat or poultry, as these products are regulated by the U.S. Department of Agriculture, not the FDA. In addition, foods such as coffee and most spices are not required to follow the FDA labeling guidelines, as they contain insignificant amounts of all the nutrients that must be listed in nutrition labeling.

Five Components Must Be Included on Food Labels

Five primary components of information must be included on food labels (**Figure 2.1**).

1. **A statement of identity:** The common name of the product or an appropriate identification of the food product must be prominently displayed on the label. This information tells us very clearly what the product is.
2. **The net contents of the package:** The quantity of the food product in the entire package must be accurately described. Information may be listed as weight (e.g., grams), volume (e.g., fluid ounces), or numerical count (e.g., 4 each).

In this text you will learn how to read labels, a skill that can help you to meet your nutritional goals.

3. **Ingredient list:** The ingredients must be listed by their common names, in descending order by weight. This means that the first product listed in the ingredient list is the predominant ingredient in that food. This information can be useful in many situations, such as when you are looking for foods that are lower in fat or sugar or when you are attempting to identify foods that contain whole-grain flour instead of processed wheat flour.
4. **The name and address of the food manufacturer, packer, or distributor:** This information can be used if you want to find out more detailed information about a food product and to contact the company if there is something wrong with the product or you suspect that it caused an illness.

Figure 2.1 The five primary components that are required for food labels. (© *ConAgra Brands, Inc.*)

5. **Nutrition information:** The Nutrition Facts Panel contains the nutrition information required by the FDA. This panel is the primary tool to assist you in choosing more healthful foods. An explanation of the components of the Nutrition Facts Panel follows.

How to Read and Use the Nutrition Facts Panel on Foods

Figure 2.2 shows an example of a **Nutrition Facts Panel.** You can use the information on this panel to learn more about an individual food, and you can also use the panel to compare one food with another. Let's start at the top of the panel and work our way down to better understand how to use this information.

1. **Serving size and servings per container:** describes the serving size in a common household measure (e.g., cup), a metric measure (e.g., grams), and how many servings are contained in the package. The FDA has defined serving sizes based on the amounts people typically eat for each food. However, keep in mind that the serving size listed on the package may not be the same as the amount *you* eat. You must factor in how much of the food you eat when determining the amount of nutrients that this food contributes to your actual diet.

2. **Calories and calories from fat per serving:** describes the total number of calories and the total amount of calories that come from fat per one serving of that food. By looking at this section of the label, you can determine if this food is relatively high in fat. For example, one serving of the food on this label (as prepared) contains 320 total calories, with 90 of those calories coming from fat. This means that this food contains 28% of its total calories as fat ([90 fat calories ÷ 320 total calories] × 100).

3. **List of nutrients:** describes various nutrients that are found in this food. Those nutrients listed toward the top, including total fat, saturated fat, *trans* fat, cholesterol, and

The serving size on a nutrition label may not be the same as the amount you eat.

Nutrition Facts Panel The label on a food package that contains the nutrition information required by the FDA.

Figure 2.2   The Nutrition Facts Panel contains a variety of information to help you select more healthful food choices.

sodium, are generally nutrients that we strive to limit in a healthful diet. Some of the nutrients listed toward the bottom are those we try to consume more of, including fiber, vitamins A and C, calcium, and iron.

4.   **Percent daily values (%DVs):** tells you how much a serving of food contributes to your overall intake of nutrients listed on the label. For example, 10 grams of fat constitutes 15% of an individual's total daily recommended fat intake. Because we are all individuals with unique nutritional needs, it is impractical to include nutrition information that applies to each person consuming a food. That would require thousands of labels! Thus, when defining the %DV, the FDA based its calculations on a 2,000-calorie diet. Even if you do not consume 2,000 calories each day, you can still use the %DV to figure out whether a food is high or low in a given nutrient. For example, foods that contain less than 5% DV of a nutrient are considered low in that nutrient, while foods that contain more than 20% DV are considered high in that nutrient. If you are trying to consume more calcium in your diet, select foods that contain more than 20% DV for calcium. In contrast, if you are trying to consume lower-fat foods, select foods that contain less than 5% or 10% fat. By comparing the %DV between foods for any nutrient, you can quickly decide which food is higher or lower in that nutrient without having to know anything about how many calories you need.

5.   **Footnote** (or lower part of panel): tells you that the %DVs are based on a 2,000-calorie diet and that your needs may be higher or lower based on your caloric needs.

percent daily values (%DVs)
Information on a Nutrition Facts Panel that identifies how much a serving of food contributes to your overall intake of nutrients listed on the label; based on an energy intake of 2,000 calories per day.

The remainder of the footnote includes a table with values that illustrate the differences in recommendations between a 2,000-calorie and 2,500-calorie diet; for instance, someone eating 2,000 calories should strive to eat less than 65 g of fat per day, whereas a person eating 2,500 calories should eat less than 80 g of fat per day. The table may not be present on the package if the size of the food label is too small. When present, the footnote and the table are always the same because the information refers to general dietary advice for all Americans rather than to a specific food.

Food Labels Can Display a Variety of Claims

Have you ever noticed a food label displaying a claim such as, "This food is low in sodium," or "This food is part of a heart-healthy diet"? The claim may have influenced you to buy the food even if you weren't sure what it meant. So let's take a look.

The FDA regulates two types of claims that food companies put on food labels: nutrient claims and health claims. Food companies are prohibited from using a nutrient or health claim that is not approved by the FDA.

The Daily Values on the food labels serve as a basis for nutrient claims. For instance, if the label states that a food is "low in sodium," this indicates that the particular food contains 140 mg or less of sodium per serving. Table 2.1 defines terms approved for use in nutrient claims.

Food labels are also allowed to display certain claims related to health and disease. The health claims that the FDA allows at the present time are listed in Table 2.2. To help consumers gain a better understanding of nutritional information related to health, the FDA has developed a Health Claims Report Card (**Figure 2.3**) that grades the level of confidence in a health claim based on current scientific evidence. For example, if current scientific evidence is not convincing, a particular health claim may have to include a disclaimer so that consumers are not misled. Complete the Nutrition Label Activity on page 48 to determine the strengths of certain health claims made on foods commonly consumed.

In addition to nutrient and health claims, labels may also contain structure-function claims. These are claims that can be made without approval from the FDA. While these claims can be generic statements about a food's impact on the body's structure and function, they cannot refer to a specific disease or symptom. Examples of structure-function claims include "Builds stronger bones," "Improves memory," "Slows signs of aging," and "Boosts your immune system." It is important to remember that these claims can be made with no proof, and thus there are no guarantees that any benefits identified in structure-function claims are true about that particular food.

This Cheerios label is an example of an approved health claim.

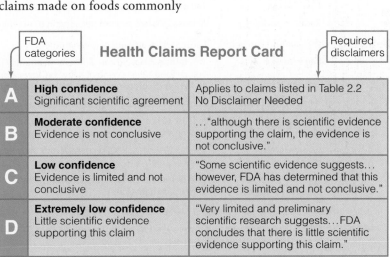

FDA categories	Health Claims Report Card	Required disclaimers
A	**High confidence** Significant scientific agreement	Applies to claims listed in Table 2.2 No Disclaimer Needed
B	**Moderate confidence** Evidence is not conclusive	…"although there is scientific evidence supporting the claim, the evidence is not conclusive."
C	**Low confidence** Evidence is limited and not conclusive	"Some scientific evidence suggests…however, FDA has determined that this evidence is limited and not conclusive."
D	**Extremely low confidence** Little scientific evidence supporting this claim	"Very limited and preliminary scientific research suggests…FDA concludes that there is little scientific evidence supporting this claim."

Figure 2.3   The U.S. Food and Drug Administration's Health Claims Report Card.

RecaP

The ability to read and interpret food labels is important for planning and maintaining a healthful diet. Food labels must list the identity of the food, the net contents of the package, the contact information for the food manufacturer or distributor, the ingredients in the food, and a Nutrition Facts Panel. The Nutrition Facts Panel provides specific information about calories, macronutrients, and selected vitamins and minerals. Food labels may also contain claims related to nutrients, health, and structure-function.

Table 2.1 United States Food and Drug Administration (FDA)–Approved Nutrient-Related Terms and Definitions

Nutrient	Claim	Meaning
Energy	Calorie free	Less than 5 kcal per serving
	Low calorie	40 kcal or less per serving
	Reduced calorie	At least 25% fewer kcal than reference (or regular) food
Fat and cholesterol	Fat free	Less than 0.5 g of fat per serving
	Low fat	3 g or less fat per serving
	Reduced fat	At least 25% less fat per serving than reference food
	Saturated fat free	Less than 0.5 g of saturated fat **AND** less than 0.5 g of *trans* fat per serving
	Low saturated fat	1 g or less saturated fat and less than 0.5 g *trans* fat per serving **AND** 15% or less of total kcal from saturated fat
	Reduced saturated fat	At least 25% less saturated fat **AND** reduced by more than 1 g saturated fat per serving as compared to reference food
	Cholesterol free	Less than 2 mg of cholesterol per serving **AND** 2 g or less saturated fat and *trans* fat combined per serving
	Low cholesterol	20 mg or less cholesterol **AND** 2 g or less saturated fat per serving
	Reduced cholesterol	At least 25% less cholesterol than reference food **AND** 2 g or less saturated fat per serving
Fiber and sugar	High fiber	5 g or more fiber per serving*
	Good source of fiber	2.5 g to 4.9 g fiber per serving
	More or added fiber	At least 2.5 g more fiber per serving than reference food
	Sugar free	Less than 0.5 g sugars per serving
	Low sugar	Not defined; no basis for recommended intake
	Reduced/less sugar	At least 25% less sugars per serving than reference food
	No added sugars or without added sugars	No sugar or sugar-containing ingredient added during processing
Sodium	Sodium free	Less than 5 mg sodium per serving
	Very low sodium	35 mg or less sodium per serving
	Low sodium	140 mg or less sodium per serving
	Reduced sodium	At least 25% less sodium per serving than reference food
Relative Claims	Free, without, no, zero	No or a trivial amount of given nutrient
	Light (or lite)	This term can have three different meanings: (1) a serving provides 1/3 fewer kcal than or half the fat of the reference food; (2) a serving of a low-fat, low-calorie food provides half the sodium normally present; or (3) lighter in color and texture, with the label making this clear (for example, light molasses)
	Reduced, less, fewer	Contains at least 25% less of a nutrient or kcal than reference food
	More, added, extra, or plus	At least 10% of the Daily Value of nutrient as compared to reference food (may occur naturally or be added); may only be used for vitamins, minerals, protein, dietary fiber, and potassium
	Good source of, contains, or provides	10% to 19% of Daily Value per serving (may not be used for carbohydrate)
	High in, rich in, or excellent source of	20% or more of Daily Value per serving for protein, vitamins, minerals, dietary fiber, or potassium (may not be used for carbohydrate)

*High-fiber claims must also meet the definition of low fat; if not, then the level of total fat must appear next to the high-fiber claim.

Data from: U.S. Food and Drug Administration. Center for Food Safety and Applied Nutrition. 2004. *A Food Labeling Guide.* Appendix A and Appendix B. Available at www.cfsan.fda.gov/~dms/flg-6a.html and www.cfsan.fda.gov/~dms/flg-6b.html.

Gustavo

Nutri-Case

"Until last night, I hadn't stepped inside of a grocery store for 10 years, maybe more. But then my wife fell and broke her hip and had to go to the hospital. On my way home from visiting her, I remembered that we didn't have much food in the house, so I thought I'd do a little shopping. Was I ever in for a shock. I don't know how my wife does it, choosing between all the different brands, reading those long labels. She never went to school past sixth grade, and she doesn't speak

Table 2.2 United States Food and Drug Administration–Approved Health Claims on Labels

Disease/Health Concern	Nutrient	Example of Approved Claim Statement
Osteoporosis	Calcium	Regular exercise and a healthy diet with enough calcium help teens and young adult white and Asian women maintain good bone health and may reduce their high risk of osteoporosis later in life.
Coronary heart disease	Saturated fat and cholesterol Fruits, vegetables, and grain products that contain fiber, particularly soluble fiber Soluble fiber from whole oats, psyllium seed husk, and beta glucan soluble fiber from oat bran, rolled oats (or oatmeal), and whole-oat flour Soy protein Plant sterol/stanol esters Whole-grain foods	Diets low in saturated fat and cholesterol and rich in fruits, vegetables, and grain products that contain some types of dietary fiber, particularly soluble fiber, may reduce the risk of heart disease, a disease associated with many factors.
Cancer	Dietary fat Fiber-containing grain products, fruits and vegetables Fruits and vegetables Whole-grain foods	Low-fat diets rich in fiber-containing grain products, fruits, and vegetables may reduce the risk of some types of cancer, a disease associated with many factors.
Hypertension and stroke	Sodium Potassium	Diets containing foods that are a good source of potassium and that are low in sodium may reduce the risk of high blood pressure and stroke.*
Neural tube defects	Folate	Healthful diets with adequate folate may reduce a woman's risk of having a child with a brain or spinal cord defect.
Dental caries	Sugar alcohols	Frequent between-meal consumption of foods high in sugars and starches promotes tooth decay. The sugar alcohols in [name of food] do not promote tooth decay.

*Required wording for this claim. Wordings for other claims are recommended model statements but are not required verbatim.

Data from: U.S. Food and Drug Administration. Center for Food Safety and Applied Nutrition. 2005. *A Food Labeling Guide.* Appendix C. Available at www.cfsan.fda.gov/~dms/flg-6c.html.

English very well either! I bought a frozen chicken pie for my dinner, but it didn't taste right. So I got the package out of the trash and read all the labels, and that's when I realized there wasn't any chicken in it at all! It was made out of tofu! This afternoon, my daughter is picking me up, and we're going to do our grocery shopping together!"

Given what you've learned about FDA food labels, what parts of a food package should Gustavo read before he makes a choice? What else can he do to make his grocery shopping easier? Imagine that, like Gustavo's wife, you have only limited skills in mathematics and reading. In that case, what other strategies might you use when shopping for nutritious foods?

Dietary Guidelines for Americans

The **Dietary Guidelines for Americans** are a set of principles developed by the U.S. Department of Agriculture and the U.S. Department of Health and Human Services to assist Americans in designing a healthful diet and lifestyle.[2] They are updated every 5 years, and the current guidelines were published in 2005. A complete description of the guidelines is provided on the inside front cover of this text. You can look to these general directives for assistance with eating a healthful diet and altering your physical activity habits to help reduce the risks for chronic diseases.

Following is a brief description of each of the chapters and key recommendations of the Dietary Guidelines for Americans. Refer to Table 2.3 for specific examples of how you might alter your current diet and physical activity habits to meet some of these guidelines.

Adequate Nutrients Within Calorie Needs

It is important to consume adequate nutrients to promote health while staying within energy needs. Key recommendations include consuming a variety of nutrient-dense foods and beverages within and among the basic food groups while choosing foods that are limited in

Dietary Guidelines for Americans A set of principles developed by the U.S. Department of Agriculture and the U.S. Department of Health and Human Services to assist Americans in designing a healthful diet and lifestyle. These guidelines are updated every 5 years.

Nutrition Label Activity

How Do Health Claims on Food Labels Measure Up?

The U.S. Food and Drug Administration has published a Health Claims Report Card to assist consumers in deciphering health claims on food labels (Figure 2.3). As you can see, a grade of "A" is given to claims that are based on high scientific agreement. These claims can be displayed on a label unaccompanied by any label disclaimer. In contrast, claims given grades "B" to "D" are based on inconclusive and/or limited scientific evidence and must be accompanied by a disclaimer. Notice that the claims reported in Table 2.2 are based on high scientific agreement.

Included below is a food label displaying health claims. Look at this label: based on the Health Claims Report Card criteria listed in Figure 2.3, what level of confidence do scientists currently have about these health claims? Taking this level of confidence into consideration, would you use this product if you were concerned about your risk for heart disease? Why or why not?

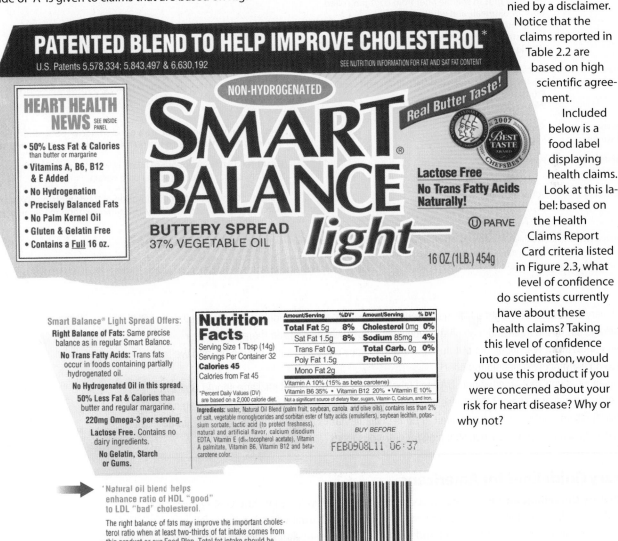

Table 2.3 Ways to Incorporate the Dietary Guidelines for Americans into Your Daily Life

If You Normally Do This:	Try Doing This Instead:
Watch television when you get home at night	Do 30 minutes of stretching or lifting of hand weights in front of the television
Drive to the store down the block	Walk to and from the store
Go out to lunch with friends	Take a 15- or 30-minute walk with your friends at lunchtime 3 days each week
Eat white bread with your sandwich	Eat whole-wheat bread or some other bread made from whole grains
Eat white rice or fried rice with your meal	Eat brown rice or try wild rice
Choose cookies or a candy bar for a snack	Choose a fresh nectarine, peach, apple, orange, or banana for a snack
Order French fries with your hamburger	Order a green salad with low-fat salad dressing on the side
Spread butter or margarine on your white toast each morning	Spread fresh fruit compote on whole-grain toast
Order a bacon double cheeseburger at your favorite restaurant	Order a turkey burger or grilled chicken sandwich without the cheese and bacon, and add lettuce and tomato
Drink non-diet soft drinks to quench your thirst	Drink iced tea, ice water with a slice of lemon, seltzer water, or diet soft drinks
Eat salted potato chips and pickles with your favorite sandwich	Eat carrot slices and crowns of fresh broccoli and cauliflower dipped in low-fat or nonfat ranch dressing

saturated and *trans* fats, cholesterol, added sugars, salt, and alcohol. **Nutrient-dense foods** are foods that give the highest amount of nutrients for the least amount of energy (or calories). **Figure 2.4** compares one day of meals that are high in nutrient density to meals that are low in nutrient density. This example can assist you in selecting the most nutrient-dense foods when planning your meals.

People can meet their recommended intakes within energy needs by adopting a balanced eating pattern, such as the USDA Food Guide discussed later in this chapter or the DASH Eating Plan discussed in Chapter 9.

Weight Management

Being overweight or obese increases the risk for many chronic diseases, including heart disease, type 2 diabetes, stroke, and some forms of cancer. Key recommendations include maintaining body weight in a healthful range by balancing calories from foods and beverages with calories expended. Also, to prevent gradual weight gain over time, Americans should make small decreases in food and beverage calories and increase physical activity.

Physical Activity

Key recommendations include engaging in regular physical activity and reducing sedentary activities to promote health, psychological well-being, and a healthful body weight. People are also encouraged to achieve physical fitness by including cardiovascular conditioning, stretching exercises for flexibility, and resistance exercises or calisthenics for muscle strength and endurance. By accumulating at least 30 minutes of moderate physical activity most, preferably all, days of the week, Americans can reduce their risk for chronic diseases. Moderate physical activity includes walking, riding a bike, mowing the lawn with a push mower, or performing heavy yard work or housework. Other activities that are beneficial include those that build strength, such as lifting weights, groceries, or other objects, carrying your golf clubs while you walk around the course, and participating in yoga or other flexibility activities.

The 30-minute guideline is a minimum; people who are already doing more activity than this should continue on their healthful path. For most people, greater health benefits

Being physically active for at least 30 minutes each day can reduce your risk for chronic diseases.

nutrient-dense foods Foods that give the highest amount of nutrients for the least amount of energy (or calories).

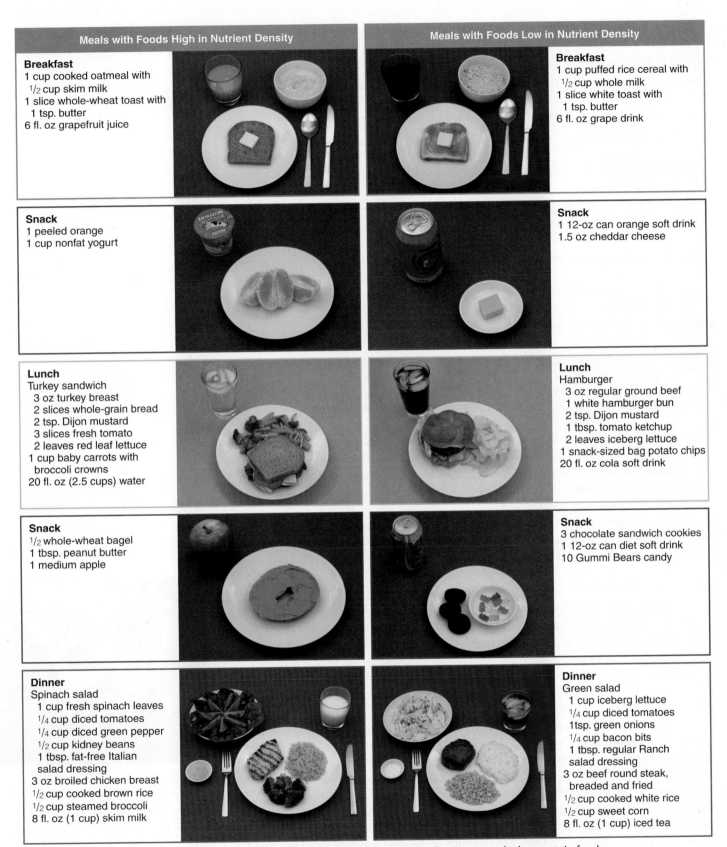

Meals with Foods High in Nutrient Density	Meals with Foods Low in Nutrient Density

Breakfast
1 cup cooked oatmeal with
  1/2 cup skim milk
1 slice whole-wheat toast with
  1 tsp. butter
6 fl. oz grapefruit juice
	Breakfast
	1 cup puffed rice cereal with
	  1/2 cup whole milk
	1 slice white toast with
	  1 tsp. butter
	6 fl. oz grape drink

Snack 1 peeled orange 1 cup nonfat yogurt	**Snack** 1 12-oz can orange soft drink 1.5 oz cheddar cheese

Lunch
Turkey sandwich
  3 oz turkey breast
  2 slices whole-grain bread
  2 tsp. Dijon mustard
  3 slices fresh tomato
  2 leaves red leaf lettuce
1 cup baby carrots with
  broccoli crowns
20 fl. oz (2.5 cups) water
	Lunch
	Hamburger
	  3 oz regular ground beef
	  1 white hamburger bun
	  2 tsp. Dijon mustard
	  1 tbsp. tomato ketchup
	  2 leaves iceberg lettuce
	1 snack-sized bag potato chips
	20 fl. oz cola soft drink

Snack 1/2 whole-wheat bagel 1 tbsp. peanut butter 1 medium apple	**Snack** 3 chocolate sandwich cookies 1 12-oz can diet soft drink 10 Gummi Bears candy

Dinner
Spinach salad
  1 cup fresh spinach leaves
  1/4 cup diced tomatoes
  1/4 cup diced green pepper
  1/2 cup kidney beans
  1 tbsp. fat-free Italian
  salad dressing
3 oz broiled chicken breast
1/2 cup cooked brown rice
1/2 cup steamed broccoli
8 fl. oz (1 cup) skim milk
	Dinner
	Green salad
	  1 cup iceberg lettuce
	  1/4 cup diced tomatoes
	  1tsp. green onions
	  1/4 cup bacon bits
	  1 tbsp. regular Ranch
	  salad dressing
	3 oz beef round steak,
	  breaded and fried
	1/2 cup cooked white rice
	1/2 cup sweet corn
	8 fl. oz (1 cup) iced tea

Figure 2.4 A comparison of one day's meals that contain foods high in nutrient density to meals that contain foods low in nutrient density.

can be obtained by engaging in physical activity that is of more vigorous intensity or longer duration. If someone is currently inactive, 30 minutes is a realistic and healthful goal. Being physically active 60 to 90 minutes per day on most days of the week is recommended to prevent weight gain and to promote weight loss in those who are overweight.

Food Groups to Encourage

Eating a variety of fruits and vegetables is important to ensure that we consume the various nutrients we need to enhance health. A few of the nutrients provided by fruits and vegetables include vitamin A, vitamin C, folate, and potassium. Key recommendations include consuming a sufficient amount of fruits and vegetables each day while staying within energy needs. In addition, people are encouraged to choose a variety of fruits and vegetables, selecting from all five vegetable subgroups: dark-green, orange, legumes, starchy vegetables, and other vegetables. Americans are also encouraged to eat 3 or more ounces of whole-grain foods each day, and to consume 3 cups per day of low-fat or fat-free milk or equivalent milk products.

Fats

Fat is an important part of a healthful diet because it provides energy, and fats in foods contain important nutrients such as essential fatty acids and fat-soluble vitamins. However, because fats are energy-dense, eating a diet high in total fat can lead to overweight and obesity. In addition, eating a diet high in saturated fats, *trans* fats, and cholesterol is linked to an increased risk for heart disease. Thus, it is important to minimize intake of these fats. Key recommendations include consuming less than 10% of calories from saturated fats and less than 300 mg/day of cholesterol. *Trans* fat intake should be as low as possible. Total fat intake should be 20% to 35% of total energy intake, with most fats coming from fish, nuts, and vegetable oils. People are also encouraged to select low-fat or fat-free meat and milk products. See Chapter 5 for more information about types of fats and dietary recommendations.

Carbohydrates

High-carbohydrate foods are an important source of energy and essential nutrients. Key recommendations include choosing fiber-rich fruits, vegetables, and whole grains often and choosing and preparing foods and beverages with little added sugars. It is important to moderate the intake of foods high in sugar and starch, because these foods promote tooth decay. To reduce the risk of dental caries (or cavities), it is recommended that people practice good oral hygiene and consume foods and beverages that contain sugar and starch less frequently.

Sodium and Potassium

Sodium and potassium are both major minerals that are essential for health in appropriate amounts. Whereas potassium consumption is linked to healthful blood pressure levels, excessive sodium consumption is linked to high blood pressure in some people. Eating a lot of sodium also can cause some people to lose calcium from the bones, which could increase the risk for bone loss and bone fractures. Table salt contains the mineral sodium, but much of the salt that is consumed in the diet comes from processed and prepared foods. Key recommendations include consuming less than 2,300 mg of sodium (the amount in approximately 1 tsp. of salt) per day, choosing and preparing foods with little salt, and consuming potassium-rich foods such as fruits and vegetables. Ways to decrease salt intake include eating fresh, plain frozen, or canned vegetables without salt added; limiting intake of processed meats such as cured ham, sausage, bacon, and most canned meats; and looking for foods with labels that say "low-sodium." In addition, adding little or no salt to foods at home and limiting the intake of salty condiments such as ketchup, mustard, pickles, soy sauce, and olives can help reduce salt intake.

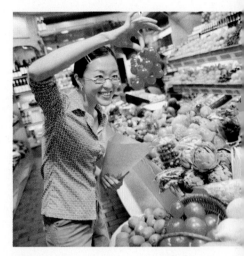

When grocery shopping, try to select foods that are moderate in total fat, sugar, and salt.

Eating a diet rich in whole-grain foods, such as whole-wheat bread and brown rice, can enhance your overall health.

Alcoholic Beverages

Alcohol provides energy, but it does not contain any nutrients. In the body, it depresses the nervous system and is toxic to liver and other body cells. Drinking alcoholic beverages in excess can lead to serious health and social problems. Key recommendations include drinking sensibly and in moderation for those who choose to drink. Moderation is defined as no more than one drink per day for women and no more than two drinks per day for men. People who should not drink alcohol include those who cannot restrict their intake, women of childbearing age who may become pregnant, pregnant and lactating women, children and adolescents, individuals taking medications that can interact with alcohol, people with certain medical conditions, and people who are engaging in activities that require attention, skill, or coordination. To learn more about whether or not alcohol can be part of a healthful diet, refer to the *In Depth* look on alcohol on pages 154–165.

Food Safety

A healthful diet is one that is safe from food-borne illnesses like those caused by microorganisms and their toxins. Food safety is discussed in more detail in Chapter 15. Important tips to remember include storing and cooking foods at the proper temperatures, avoiding unpasteurized juices and milk products and raw or undercooked meats and shellfish, and washing hands and cooking surfaces before cooking and after handling raw meats, shellfish, and eggs.

RECAP

The Dietary Guidelines for Americans emphasize healthful food choices and physical activity behaviors. The guidelines include achieving a healthful weight; being physically active each day; eating whole-grain foods, fruits, and vegetables daily; eating foods low in saturated and *trans* fat and cholesterol and moderate in total fat; moderating sugar intake; eating less salt; eating more potassium-rich foods; keeping foods safe to eat/and drinking alcohol in moderation, if at all.

The USDA Food Guide

The U.S. Department of Agriculture (USDA) pyramid-based food guidance system is another tool that can guide you in designing a healthful diet. It was created in 2005 to provide a conceptual framework for the types and amounts of foods that make up a healthful diet. It is important to remember that the USDA Food Guide is an evolving document, and it will continue to change as we learn more about the roles of specific nutrients and foods in promoting health and preventing certain diseases.

The graphic representation for the USDA Food Guide is called **MyPyramid** (**Figure 2.5**). This graphic is a revision of the previous USDA Food Guide Pyramid. MyPyramid is an interactive, personalized guide that people can access on the Internet to assess their current diet and physical activity levels and to plan appropriate changes. MyPyramid is intended to help Americans:

- eat in moderation,
- eat a variety of foods,
- consume the right proportion of each recommended food group,
- personalize their eating plan,
- increase their physical activity, and
- set goals for gradually improving their food choices and lifestyle.

Six Food Groups in the USDA Food Guide

The six food groups emphasized in the USDA Food Guide are grains, vegetables, fruits, oils, milk, and meat and beans. These are represented in the pyramid graphic with bands of six different colors (see Figure 2.5).

MyPyramid   The graphic representation of the USDA Food Guide.

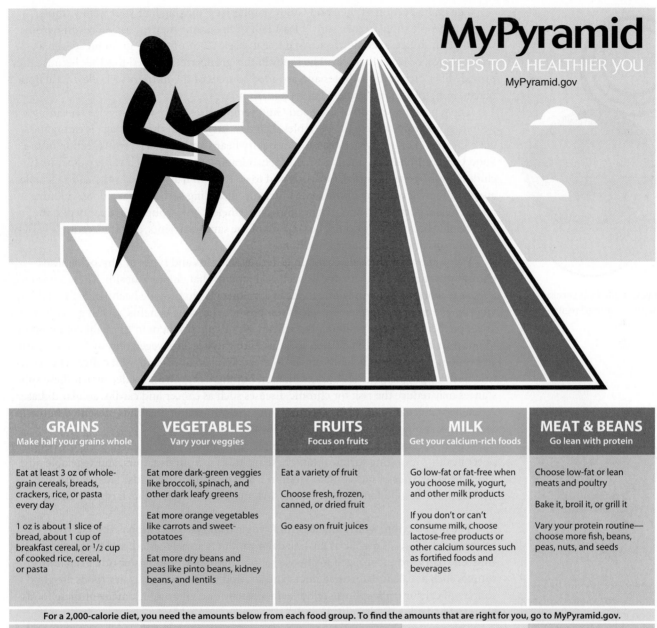

MyPyramid
STEPS TO A HEALTHIER YOU
MyPyramid.gov

GRAINS	VEGETABLES	FRUITS	MILK	MEAT & BEANS
Make half your grains whole	Vary your veggies	Focus on fruits	Get your calcium-rich foods	Go lean with protein
Eat at least 3 oz of whole-grain cereals, breads, crackers, rice, or pasta every day 1 oz is about 1 slice of bread, about 1 cup of breakfast cereal, or 1/2 cup of cooked rice, cereal, or pasta	Eat more dark-green veggies like broccoli, spinach, and other dark leafy greens Eat more orange vegetables like carrots and sweet-potatoes Eat more dry beans and peas like pinto beans, kidney beans, and lentils	Eat a variety of fruit Choose fresh, frozen, canned, or dried fruit Go easy on fruit juices	Go low-fat or fat-free when you choose milk, yogurt, and other milk products If you don't or can't consume milk, choose lactose-free products or other calcium sources such as fortified foods and beverages	Choose low-fat or lean meats and poultry Bake it, broil it, or grill it Vary your protein routine—choose more fish, beans, peas, nuts, and seeds

For a 2,000-calorie diet, you need the amounts below from each food group. To find the amounts that are right for you, go to MyPyramid.gov.

Eat 6 oz every day	Eat 2¹/₂ cups every day	Eat 2 cups every day	Get 3 cups every day; for kids aged 2 to 8, it's 2	Eat 5¹/₂ oz every day

Find your balance between food and physical activity
- Be sure to stay within your daily calorie needs.
- Be physically active for at least 30 minutes most days of the week.
- About 60 minutes a day of physical activity may be needed to prevent weight gain.
- For sustaining weight loss, at least 60 to 90 minutes a day of physical activity may be required.
- Children and teenagers should be physically active for 60 minutes every day, or most days.

Know the limits on fats, sugars, and salt (sodium)
- Make most of your fat sources from fish, nuts, and vegetable oils.
- Limit solid fats like butter, margarine, shortening, and lard, as well as foods that contain these.
- Check the Nutrition Facts label to keep saturated fats, *trans* fats, and sodium low.
- Choose food and beverages low in added sugars. Added sugars contribute calories with few, if any, nutrients.

MyPyramid.gov
STEPS TO A HEALTHIER YOU

U.S. Department of Agriculture
Center for Nutrition Policy and Promotion
April 2005
CNPP-15

USDA is an equal opportunity provider and employer.

Figure 2.5   MyPyramid, the Graphic of the 2005 USDA Food Guide.
People can visit the MyPyramid Web site to assess their current diet and physical activity levels and plan changes in their food intake and physical activity patterns. To create your own personalized MyPyramid, go to www.MyPyramid.gov.

Some of your daily fruit servings can come from canned fruits.

Seafood, meat, poultry, dry beans, eggs, and nuts are examples of foods that are high in protein.

phytochemicals   Chemicals found in plants (*phyto-* is from the Greek word for "plant"), such as pigments and other substances, that may reduce our risk for diseases such as cancer and heart disease.

discretionary calories   A term used in the USDA Food Guide that represents the extra amount of energy you can consume after you have met all of your essential needs by consuming the most nutrient-dense foods that are low fat or fat free and that have no added sugars.

The grains section of the Food Guide emphasizes "making half your grains whole," meaning people should make sure at least half of the grains they eat each day come from whole-grain sources. People are advised to eat at least 3 oz of whole-grain bread, cereal, crackers, rice, or pasta each day. The foods in this group are clustered together because they provide fiber-rich carbohydrates and are good sources of the nutrients riboflavin, thiamin, niacin, iron, folate, zinc, protein, and magnesium.

The vegetables section of the Food Guide emphasizes "vary your veggies," meaning people should eat a variety of vegetables each day. Included in this message is eating more dark-green and orange vegetables and more dry beans and peas. The fruits section of the Food Guide emphasizes "focus on fruits," encouraging people to eat a variety of fruits (including fresh, frozen, canned, or dried) and to go easy on fruit juices. Fruits and vegetables are good sources of many of the same nutrients, including carbohydrate, fiber, vitamins A and C, folate, potassium, and magnesium. Nevertheless, the groups are separated in the Food Guide because they do not contain all of the same nutrients, and thus eating a variety of *both* fruits and vegetables is important.

Fruits and vegetables also contain differing amounts and types of **phytochemicals**— naturally occurring plant chemicals such as pigments that enhance health. These substances appear to work together in whole foods in a unique way to provide health benefits. Taking vitamin and mineral supplements does not provide the same benefits as eating whole foods, as supplements may not contain phytochemicals or contain them in the right combinations to optimize their effect. In addition to fruits and whole grains, vegetables such as soy, garlic, and onions contain phytochemicals, as do green and black teas and even coffee. The scientific study of phytochemicals is in its infancy, but there is growing evidence that these substances may reduce the risk for chronic diseases such as cancer and cardiovascular disease. A detailed explanation of phytochemicals and their impact on health is presented in the *In Depth* look at phytochemicals on pages 398–407.

The oils section of the Food Guide emphasizes "know your fats," encouraging people to select health-promoting forms of fat. These include fat from fish, nuts, and vegetable oils. These healthy types of fats contain vitamin E and essential fatty acids. This section also stresses limiting solid fats such as butter, stick margarine, shortening, lard, and visible fat on meat.

The milk section, which includes milk, yogurt, and cheese, emphasizes "get your calcium-rich foods." Low-fat or fat-free dairy products are suggested, and those who cannot consume dairy are encouraged to choose lactose-free dairy products or other calcium sources such as calcium-fortified juices and soy and rice beverages. Dairy foods are good sources of calcium, phosphorus, riboflavin, protein, and vitamin B_{12}; many of these foods are also fortified with vitamins D and A.

The meat and beans section, which includes meat, poultry, fish, dry beans, eggs, and nuts, emphasizes "go lean on protein." Low-fat or lean meats and poultry are encouraged, as is use of cooking methods such as baking, broiling, or grilling. People are also encouraged to vary their meat group choices to include more fish, beans, nuts, and seeds. This group comprises foods that are good sources of protein, phosphorus, vitamin B_6, vitamin B_{12}, magnesium, iron, zinc, niacin, riboflavin, and thiamin. Notice that legumes, which include dried beans, peas, and lentils, are included both in the meat and beans section and in the vegetables section. This is because legumes are good sources of fiber, contain many of the vitamins found in vegetables, and are also good sources of protein and of some of the minerals found in meat and poultry.

Concept of Discretionary Calories

One new concept introduced in the 2005 USDA Food Guide is that of **discretionary calories.** Discretionary calories represent the extra amount of energy a person can consume after he or she has met all essential needs by consuming nutrient-dense foods. The number of discre-

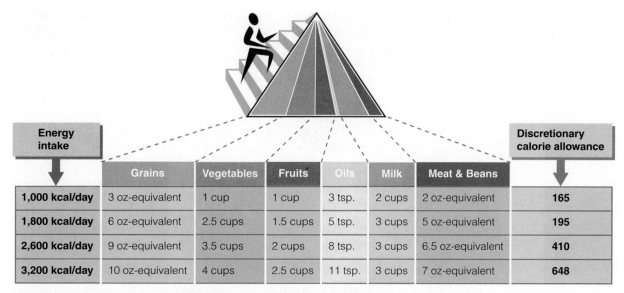

Energy intake	Grains	Vegetables	Fruits	Oils	Milk	Meat & Beans	Discretionary calorie allowance
1,000 kcal/day	3 oz-equivalent	1 cup	1 cup	3 tsp.	2 cups	2 oz-equivalent	**165**
1,800 kcal/day	6 oz-equivalent	2.5 cups	1.5 cups	5 tsp.	3 cups	5 oz-equivalent	**195**
2,600 kcal/day	9 oz-equivalent	3.5 cups	2 cups	8 tsp.	3 cups	6.5 oz-equivalent	**410**
3,200 kcal/day	10 oz-equivalent	4 cups	2.5 cups	11 tsp.	3 cups	7 oz-equivalent	**648**

Figure 2.6   Sample diets from MyPyramid at four different energy intakes.

tionary calories you can eat depends on your age, gender, and physical activity level. This number is small for most people, between about 100 to 300 kcal/day. Foods that use up discretionary calories include butter, margarine, lard, salad dressings, mayonnaise, sour cream, cream, and gravy. High-sugar foods such as candies, desserts, gelatin, soft drinks, fruit drinks, and alcoholic beverages are also included in the discretionary calorie allowance. People might also decide to use their discretionary calories to eat more healthful foods.

Number of Servings in the USDA Food Guide

The USDA Food Guide also helps someone decide *how much* of each food he or she should eat. The number of servings for each food section is determined based on the recommended calorie level. **Figure 2.6** shows the daily amount of food from each section at four different energy intake levels. As you can see in this figure, people who need more energy need to eat more foods from each food group of MyPyramid. A term used here that may be new to you is **ounce-equivalent** (or oz-equivalent). This term is used to define a serving size that is 1 oz, or equivalent to an ounce, for the grains and meats and beans section. Let's now discuss exactly what is meant by serving size when using the USDA Food Guide.

Serving Size in the USDA Food Guide

What is considered a serving size for the foods recommended in the USDA Food Guide? **Figure 2.7** shows examples of the number of cups or oz-equivalent servings recommended for a 2,000-kcal food intake pattern and the amounts that are equal to 1 cup or 1 oz-equivalent for foods in each group. An oz-equivalent serving from the grains group is defined as 1 slice of bread, 1 cup of ready-to-eat cereal, or 1/2 cup of cooked rice, pasta, or cereal. One cup of vegetables is equal to 2 cups of raw leafy vegetables such as spinach or equal to 1 cup of chopped raw or cooked vegetables such as broccoli. An oz-equivalent serving of meat is 1 oz-equivalent; thus, 3 oz of meat is equal to 3 oz-equivalents. One egg, 1 tablespoon peanut butter, and 1/4 cup cooked dry beans are also considered 1 oz-equivalents from the meat and beans group. Although it may seem unnatural and inconvenient to measure food servings, understanding the size of a serving is critical to planning a nutritious diet.

It is important to understand that no national standardized definition for a serving size for any food exists. A serving size as defined in the USDA Food Guide may not be equal to a

ounce-equivalent   (or oz-equivalent) A term used to define a serving size that is 1 oz, or equivalent to an ounce, for the grains section and the meats and beans section of the USDA Food Guide.

Food group	Number of cups or oz-equivalents for a 2,000-kcal food intake pattern	Examples of amounts equal to 1 cup or 1 oz-equivalent			
Milk group	3 cups	1 cup (8 fl. oz) milk	1 cup (8 fl. oz) yogurt	1.5 oz hard cheese	1 cup of ice cream
Meat and beans group	5.5 oz-equivalents	1 oz pork loin chop	1 oz chicken breast without skin	¹/₄ cup pinto beans	¹/₂ oz almonds
Vegetables group	2.5 cups	1 cup (8 fl. oz) tomato juice	2 cups raw spinach	1 cup cooked broccoli	1 cup mashed potatoes
Fruits group	2 cups	1 cup (8 fl. oz) orange juice	1 cup strawberries	1 cup of pears	¹/₂ pink grapefruit
Grains group	6 oz-equivalents	1 (1 oz) slice of whole wheat bread	¹/₂ cup (1 oz) cooked brown rice	¹/₂ regular hamburger bun	2 pancakes (4" diameter)

Figure 2.7   Examples of serving sizes for foods in each food group of the USDA Food Guide for a 2,000-kcal food intake pattern. Here are some examples of household items that can help you to estimate serving sizes: 1.5 oz of hard cheese is equal to 4 stacked dice, 1 standard ice cream scoop is 1/2 cup, 3 oz of meat is equal in size to a deck of cards, and one-half of a regular hamburger bun is the size of a yo-yo.

serving size identified on a food label. For instance, the serving size for crackers in the USDA Food Guide is 3 to 4 small crackers, whereas a serving size for crackers on a food label can range from 5 to 18 crackers, depending on the size and weight of the cracker. When comparing serving sizes from the USDA Food Guide with serving sizes on packaged foods you eat, remember to check the Nutrition Facts Panel. Try the Nutrition Label Activity to determine whether the serving sizes listed on assorted food labels match the serving sizes that you normally consume.

Nutrition Label Activity

How Realistic Are the Serving Sizes Listed on Food Labels?

Many people read food labels to determine the energy (i.e., caloric) value of foods, but it is less common to pay close attention to the actual serving size that corresponds to the listed caloric value. To test how closely your "naturally selected" serving size meets the actual serving size of certain foods, try these label activities:

■ Choose a breakfast cereal that you commonly eat. Pour the amount of cereal that you would normally eat into a bowl. Before adding milk to your cereal, use a measuring cup to measure the amount of cereal you poured. Now read the label of the cereal to determine the serving size (for example, 1/2 cup or 1 cup) and the caloric value listed on the label. How do your "naturally selected" serving size and the label-defined serving size compare?

■ At your local grocery store, locate various boxes of snack crackers. Look at the number of crackers and total calo-

ries per serving listed on the labels of crackers such as regular Triscuits, reduced-fat Triscuits, Vegetable Thins, and Ritz crackers. How do the number of crackers and total calories per serving differ for the serving size listed on each box? How do the serving sizes listed in the Nutrition Facts Panel compare to how many crackers you would usually eat?

These activities are just two examples of ways to understand how nutrition labels can assist the consumer with making balanced and healthful food choices. As many people do not know what constitutes a serving size, they are inclined to consume too much of some foods (such as snack foods and meat) and too little of other foods (such as fruits and vegetables).

For items consumed individually, such as muffins, frozen burgers, bottled juices, and so on, the serving sizes in the USDA Food Guide are typically much smaller than the items we buy. In addition, serving sizes in restaurants, cafes, and movie theatres have grown substantially over the past 30 years.[3] This "super-sizing" phenomenon, now seen even at home, indicates a major shift in accessibility to foods and in accepted eating behaviors, and emphasizes the importance of becoming educated about portion size control. In addition to being a potentially important contributor to the rise in obesity rates around the world, this increase in serving size leads to confusion among consumers. This confusion is illustrated by the results of a study conducted by Young and Nestle[4] in which introductory nutrition students were asked to bring to class one sample of a "medium" bagel, baked potato, muffin, apple, or cookie. The weights of these foods were measured, and most of the foods the students brought to class well exceeded the USDA's definition of a serving size. Young and Nestle[5] report that the discrepancy in portion size of many common foods sold outside of the home in comparison to USDA standards is quite staggering—chocolate chip cookies are seven times larger than USDA standards, while steaks are more than twice as large, and a serving of cooked pasta in a restaurant is almost five times larger. Thus, when using diet-planning tools like food labels and the USDA Food Guide, it is essential to learn the definition of serving size for the tool you are using, and *then* measure your food intake to determine whether you are meeting the guidelines. Refer to the You Do the Math activity on pages 58–59 to estimate how much physical activity you would need to do in order to expend the excess energy you consume because of increasing food portion sizes.

Ethnic Variations of MyPyramid

As MyPyramid has recently been released to the general public, there are not yet variations developed for diverse populations. However, you can easily fit foods that meet your specific ethnic, religious, or other lifestyle preferences into your own personal MyPyramid. In addition, adaptations of the previous version of the USDA Food Guide Pyramid can

You Do the Math

How Much Exercise Is Needed to Combat Increasing Food Portion Sizes?

Although the causes of obesity are complex and multifactorial, it is speculated that one reason obesity rates are rising around the world is a combination of increased energy intake due to expanding food portion sizes and a reduction in overall daily physical activity. This activity should help you to better understand how portion sizes have increased over the past 20 years and how much physical activity you would need to do to expend the excess energy resulting from these larger portion sizes.

The two photos in **Figure 2.8** give examples of foods whose portion sizes have increased substantially. A bagel 20 years ago had a diameter of approximately 3 inches and contained 140 kcal. A bagel in today's society is about 6 inches in diameter and contains 350 kcal. Similarly, a cup of coffee 20 years ago was 8 fl. oz and was typically served with a small amount of whole milk and sugar. It contained about 45 kcal. A standard coffee mocha commonly consumed today is 16 fl. oz and contains 350 kcal; this excess energy comes from the addition of sugar, milk, and flavored syrup.

On her morning break at work, Judy routinely consumes a bagel and a coffee drink like the ones described here. Judy has type 2 diabetes, and her doctor has advised her to lose weight. How much physical activity would Judy need to do to "burn" this excess energy? Let's do some simple math to answer this question.

1. Calculate the excess energy Judy consumes from both of these foods:

   a. Bagel: 350 kcal in larger bagel – 140 kcal in smaller bagel = 210 kcal extra

   b. Coffee: 350 kcal in large coffee mocha – 45 kcal in small regular coffee = 305 kcal extra
   Total excess energy for these two larger portions = 515 kcal

2. Judy has started walking each day in an effort to lose weight. Judy currently weighs 200 lb. Based on her relatively low fitness level, Judy walks at a slow pace (approximately 2 miles per hour); it is estimated that walking at this pace expends 1.2 kcal per pound of body weight per hour. How long does Judy need to walk each day to expend 515 kcal?

20 years ago   **Today**

3-inch diameter, 140 calories   6-inch diameter, 350 calories

(a) Bagel

8 fluid ounces, 45 calories   16 fluid ounces, 350 calories

(b) Coffee

Figure 2.8   Examples of increases in food portion sizes over the past 20 years. **(a)** A bagel has increased in diameter from 3 inches to 6 inches; **(b)** a cup of coffee has increased from 8 fl. oz to 16 fl. oz, and now commonly contains calorie-dense flavored syrup as well as steamed whole milk.

   a. First, calculate how much energy Judy expends if she walks for a full hour by multiplying her body weight by the energy cost of walking per hour = 1.2 kcal/lb body weight × 200 lb = 240 kcal

b. Next, you need to calculate how much energy she expends each minute she walks by dividing the energy cost of walking per hour by 60 minutes = 240 kcal/hour ÷ 60 minutes/hour = 4 kcal/minute

c. To determine how many minutes she would need to walk to expend 515 kcal, divide the total amount of energy she needs to expend by the energy cost of walking per minute = 515 kcal ÷ 4 kcal/minute = 103.75 minutes

Thus, Judy would need to walk for approximately 104 minutes, or about 1 hour and 45 minutes, to expend the excess energy she consumes by eating the larger bagel and coffee. If she wanted to burn off all of the energy in her morning snack, she would have to walk even longer, especially if she enjoyed her bagel with cream cheese!

Now use your own weight in these calculations to determine how much walking you would have to do if you consumed these same foods:

a. 1.2 kcal/lb × (your weight in pounds) = _____ kcal/hour

(If you walk at a brisk pace, use 2.4 kcal/lb.)

b. _____ kcal/hour ÷ 60 minutes/hour = _____ kcal/minute

c. 515 extra kcal in bagel and coffee ÷ _____ kcal/minute = _____ minutes

For more information about large portion sizes and the physical activities one needs to do to avoid weight gain, take the National Heart, Lung, and Blood Institute's Portion Distortion Quiz at http://hp2010.nhlbihin.net/portion/index.htm.

provide guidance in meeting diverse dietary needs. For instance, Houtkooper modified the previous Food Guide Pyramid to address the needs of athletes by including fluids as a new food category at the base of the pyramid, emphasizing the importance of daily fluid replacement for active people.[6] There are also pyramids for children and for adults over the age of 70 years.[7, 8]

There are also many ethnic and cultural variations of the Food Guide Pyramid. As you know, the population of the United States is culturally and ethnically diverse, and this diversity influences our food choices. Foods that we may typically consider a part of an Asian, Latin American, or Mediterranean diet can also fit into a healthful diet. Variations of the previous USDA Food Guide Pyramid that have been introduced include the Latin American Diet Pyramid and the Asian Diet Pyramid (**Figure 2.9**). There are also variations for Singapore, Malaysia, and Native Americans.[9] These variations illustrate that anyone can design a healthful diet to accommodate his or her individual food preferences.

Of these variations, the Mediterranean diet has enjoyed considerable popularity. Does it deserve its reputation as a healthful diet? Check out the Highlight box on page 61 to learn more about the Mediterranean diet.

RecaP

The USDA Food Guide can be used to plan a healthful, balanced diet that includes foods from the grains group, vegetables group, fruits group, milk group, oil group, and meat and beans group. The serving sizes of foods as defined in the USDA Food Guide typically are smaller than the amounts we normally eat or are served, so it is important to learn the definition of serving sizes when using the USDA Food Guide to design a healthful diet.

There are many ethnic and cultural variations of the USDA Food Guide. Its flexibility enables anyone to design a diet that meets the goals of adequacy, moderation, balance, variety, and nutrient density.

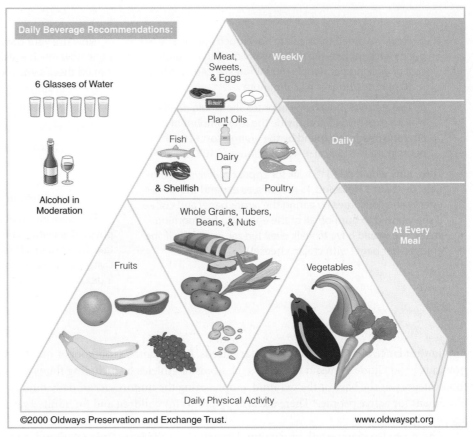

(a) Latin American diet pyramid

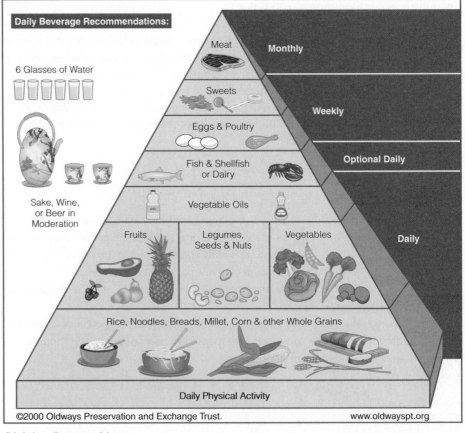

Figure 2.9 Ethnic and cultural variations of an earlier version of the USDA Food Guide Pyramid. **(a)** The Latin American Diet Pyramid and **(b)** the Asian Diet Pyramid. (© 2000 Oldways Preservation and Exchange Trust. The Food Issues Think Tank. Healthy Eating Pyramids & Other Tools. www.oldwayspt.org)

(b) Asian diet pyramid

Highlight

The Mediterranean Diet and Pyramid

A Mediterranean-style diet has received significant attention in recent years, as the rates of cardiovascular disease in many Mediterranean countries are substantially lower than rates in the United States. There is actually not a single Mediterranean diet, as this region of the world includes Portugal, Spain, Italy, France, Greece, Turkey, and Israel. Each of these countries has different dietary patterns; however, there are similarities that have led to speculation that this type of diet is more healthful than the typical U.S. diet:

■ Meat is eaten monthly, and eggs, poultry, fish, and sweets are eaten weekly, making the diet low in saturated fats and refined sugars.

■ The predominant fat used for cooking and flavor is olive oil, making the diet high in mono-unsaturated fats.

■ Foods eaten daily include: grains such as bread, pasta, couscous, and bulgur; fruits; beans and other legumes; nuts; vegetables; and cheese and yogurt. These choices make this diet high in fiber and rich in vitamins and minerals.

As you can see in **Figure 2.10,** the base of the Mediterranean Pyramid includes breads, cereals, and other grains, foods also emphasized in MyPyramid. Another similarity is the daily intake of fruits and vegetables. Finally, both pyramids highlight daily physical activity.

The two pyramids differ in several important aspects. The Mediterranean Pyramid recommends beans, other legumes, and nuts as daily sources of protein; fish, poultry, and eggs are eaten weekly; and red meat is eaten only about once each month. The Mediterranean Pyramid highlights cheese and yogurt as the primary dairy sources and recommends daily consumption of olive oil. Another feature of the Mediterranean diet is the inclusion of wine.

Interestingly, the Mediterranean diet is not lower in fat; in fact, about 40% of the total energy in this diet is derived from fat, which is much higher than the dietary fat recommendations made in the U.S. This fact has led some nutritionists to criticize the Mediterranean diet; however, supporters point out that the majority of fats in the Mediterranean diet are plant oils, which are more healthful than the animal fats found in the U.S. diet, and make the Mediter-

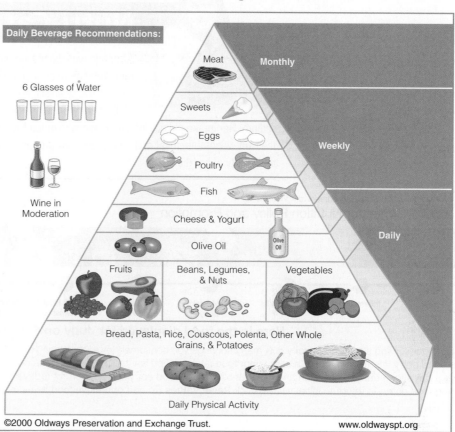

Figure 2.10 The Mediterranean Diet Pyramid. (© 2000 Oldways Preservation and Exchange Trust. The Food Issues Think Tank. Healthy Eating Pyramids & Other Tools. www.oldwayspt.org.)

ranean diet more protective against cardiovascular disease. The potential benefits of plant oils in reducing our cholesterol levels and our risk for heart disease are discussed in Chapter 5.

Can following a Mediterranean-style diet really improve your health? In June 1995, the *American Journal of Clinical Nutrition* reviewed the most recent findings on the Mediterranean diet. Renaud et al.[10] studied the effects of a Mediterranean diet on individuals living in Crete who were recovering from a heart attack. Researchers found that those who ate a Mediterranean diet had a much lower risk of recurrent heart attack and premature death than people who followed the heart-healthy diet prescribed by their doctors. In addition, Tavani and La Vecchia[11] reported that Italians who ate more fruits and vegetables as part of a Mediterranean diet had significantly lower risks of some types of cancers, particularly in the mouth, esophagus, stomach, lung, and intestines. A recent study found that people who consumed a Mediterranean diet were significantly less likely to be obese than people who did not.[12] These studies indicate that eating a Mediterranean-style diet that includes more fruits and vegetables, less meat, and few high-fat dairy products can reduce the risks for obesity, heart disease, and some cancers.

Judy
Nutri-Case

After she was diagnosed with type 2 diabetes, Judy used the MyPyramid Web site to analyze one day of her diet. **Figure 2.11** shows the results of this analysis. As you can see, Judy's diet as compared to the 2005 Dietary Guidelines was too high in total fat, saturated fat, and sodium. Her intake did not match the recommended MyPyramid because she ate too few foods from the fruit, vegetable, meat and beans, and milk groups. What specific foods could Judy eat to improve the quality of her diet?

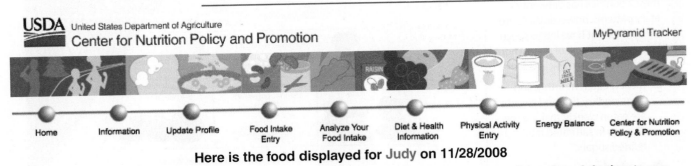

USDA United States Department of Agriculture
Center for Nutrition Policy and Promotion

MyPyramid Tracker

| Home | Information | Update Profile | Food Intake Entry | Analyze Your Food Intake | Diet & Health Information | Physical Activity Entry | Energy Balance | Center for Nutrition Policy & Promotion |

Here is the food displayed for Judy on 11/28/2008

Select your serving sizes and specify how many servings you consumed for each. When you are done, click on **Save & Analyze** to save your food entry information and to analyze your food intake. If you want to make more than one day's food entry, click on **Return to Login** to save a day's food entry information and make another day's food entry. For a record of today's food entry, click **Print Food Record** prior to saving food entry. To return to initial values, click **Reset Values**. To add or remove food items, click on **Enter Foods**.

Foods Consumed	Select Serving Size	Number of Servings (Enter a number (e.g. 1.5))
BAGEL, W/ RAISINS	1 large (3-1/2" to 3-3/4" dia) ▼	2
CREAM CHEESE	1 tablespoon ▼	2
WATER	1 fl oz ▼	16
APPLE (APPLES), FRESH	1 medium (2-3/4 dia) (approx 3 per lb) ▼	1
HAM, FRESH, LEAN ONLY	1 thin slice (approx 4-1/2 x 2-1/2 x 1/8) ▼	6
BREAD, MARBLE RYE & PUMPERNICKEL	1 regular slice ▼	2
MUSTARD	1 teaspoon ▼	2
MAYONNAISE, REGULAR	1 tablespoon ▼	1
RED LEAF LETTUCE	1 small leaf ▼	2
POTATO CHIPS, BAKED	10 chips ▼	3
LETTUCE SALAD, W/ CHEESE, TOMATO/CARROTS, NO DRESSING	1 cup ▼	2
SALAD DRESSING, LOW CALORIE	1 tablespoon ▼	2
HERSHEY BAR	1 Big Block bar (2.2 oz) ▼	1
COFFEE, MADE FROM GROUND, REGULAR, FLAVORED	1 fl oz ▼	20
CHEDDAR OR COLBY, LOWFAT CHEESE	1 slice (1 oz) ▼	1

| Save & Analyze | Enter Foods | Return to Login | Reset Values |

Print Food Record

(a) Judy's diet for one day

Figure 2.11 Analysis of one day of Judy's diet using MyPyramid Tracker. When Judy entered her diet into MyPyramid tracker, her diet for this day was too low in fruit, grains, milk, and meat and beans and was too high in total and saturated fat. As you can see, Judy's personal pyramid stats do not match the recommended MyPyramid guidelines, as she ate too few foods from the fruit, grains, milk, and meat and beans groups. *Data from:* USDA, Center for Nutrition Policy and Promotion, www.MyPyramidtracker.gov.

The 2005 Dietary Guidelines (DG) Recommendations
for Judy on 2/14/2009

Click directly on the 😊 😐 ☹ emoticon (face) for more detailed dietary information.

Dietary Guidelines Recommendations	Emoticon	Number of cup/ oz. Equ. Eaten	Number of cup/oz. Equ. Recommended
Grain	😊	7.5 oz equivalent	6 oz equivalent
Vegetable	😐	2 cup equivalent	2.5 cup equivalent
Fruit	☹	0.1 cup equivalent	1.5 cup equivalent
Milk	☹	1.2 cup equivalent	3 cup equivalent
Meat and Beans	😐	4.5 oz equivalent	5 oz equivalent

Dietary Guidelines Recommendations	Emoticon	Amount Eaten	Recommendation or Goal
Total Fat	☹	41.1% of total calories	20% to 35%
Saturated Fat	☹	14.4% of total calories	less than 10%
Cholesterol	😊	202 mg	less than 300 mg
Sodium	😐	2770 mg	less than 2300 mg
Oils	*	*	*
Discretionary calories (solid fats, added sugars, and alcohol)	*	*	*

* Calculations for oils and discretionary calories from foods are under revision.

More information about the Dietary Guidelines for Americans 2005
(To view this document you need Adobe Acrobat Reader)

(b) Judy's Tracker results

Comparison of Your Intake with
MyPyramid Recommendations for Judy

Your Pyramid Stats

Milk Intake — 1.2 cup equivalent
Milk Recommendation — 3 cup equivalent
Meat and Beans Intake — 4.5 oz equivalent
Meat and Beans Recommendation — 5 oz equivalent
Vegetables Intake — 2 cup equivalent
Vegetables Recommendation — 2.5 cup equivalent
Fruits Intake — 0.1 cup equivalent
Fruits Recommendation — 1.5 cup equivalent
Grains Intake — 7.5 oz equivalent
Grains Recommendation — 6 oz equivalent

Pyramid Categories	Percent Recommendation
Milk	40%
Meat and Beans	90%
Vegetables	80%
Fruits	7%
Grains	125%

(c) Judy's comparison of nutrient intake to MyPyramid recommendations

Can Eating Out Be Part of a Healthful Diet?

Foods served at fast-food chains are often high in calories, total fat, and sodium. McDonald's popular sausage, egg, and cheese McGriddles™ breakfast sandwiches, for example, contain 560 calories, 32 g of fat, and 1,290 mg of sodium.

How many times each week do you eat out? A report from the Pew Research Center states that about one-third of Americans eat out once per week, while another one-third eat out two or more times per week.[13] Almost half (47%) of men and 35% of women surveyed report eating a meal at a fast-food restaurant at least once per week. Restaurant sales for 2003 exceeded $426 billion. Over the past 20 years, there has been phenomenal growth in the restaurant industry, particularly in the fast-food market. During this same time period, rates of obesity have increased by more than 60%, and now an estimated 66% of U.S. adults are either overweight or obese.[14]

The Hidden Costs of Eating Out

Table 2.4 shows an example of foods served at McDonald's and Burger King restaurants. As you can see, a regular McDonald's hamburger has only 270 kcal, whereas the Big Xtra with cheese has 810 kcal. A meal of the Quarter Pounder with cheese, Super Size French fries, and a Super Size Coke provides 1,550 kcal. This meal has enough energy to support an entire day's needs for a small, lightly active woman! Similar meals at Burger King and other fast-food chains are also very high in calories, not to mention total fat and sodium.

Fast-food restaurants are not alone in serving large portions. Most sit-down restaurants also serve large meals that may include bread with butter, a salad with dressing, sides of vegetables and potatoes, and free refills of sugar-filled drinks. Combined with a high-fat appetizer like potato skins, fried onions, fried mozzarella sticks, or buffalo wings, it is easy to eat more than 2,000 kcal at one meal!

Does this mean that eating out cannot be a part of a healthful diet? Not necessarily. By becoming an educated consumer and making wise meal choices while dining out, you can enjoy both a healthful diet and the social benefits of eating out.

Table 2.4 Nutritional Value of Selected Fast Foods

Menu Item	Kcal	Fat (g)	Fat (% kcal)	Sodium (mg)
McDonald's				
Hamburger	270	9	29.6	600
Cheeseburger	320	13	37.5	830
Quarter Pounder	430	21	44.2	840
Quarter Pounder with cheese	530	30	50.9	1,310
Big Mac	570	32	49.1	1,100
Big Xtra	710	46	59.2	1,400
Big Xtra with cheese	810	55	60.5	1,870
French fries, small	210	10	42.8	135
French fries, medium	450	22	44.4	290
French fries, large	540	26	42.6	350
Burger King				
Hamburger	320	15	43.8	520
Cheeseburger	360	19	47.2	760
Whopper	660	40	54.5	900
Whopper with cheese	760	48	56.6	1,380
Double Whopper	920	59	57.6	980
Bacon Cheeseburger	400	22	50.0	940
Bacon Double Cheeseburger	620	38	54.8	1,230
French fries, small	250	13	48.0	550
French fries, medium	400	21	47.5	820
French fries, king size	590	30	45.8	1,180

The Healthful Way to Eat Out

Most restaurants, even fast-food restaurants, offer lower-fat menu items that you can choose. For instance, eating a regular McDonald's hamburger, a small order of French fries, and a diet beverage or water provides 480 kcal and 19 g of fat (or 35% of kcal from fat). To provide some vegetables for the day, you could add a side salad with low-fat or nonfat salad dressing. Other fast-food restaurants also offer smaller portions, sandwiches made with whole-grain bread, grilled chicken or other lean meats, and side salads. Many sit-down restaurants offer "lite" menu items such as grilled chicken and a variety of vegetables, which are usually a much better choice than eating from the regular menu.

Here are some other suggestions on how to eat out in moderation. Practice some of these suggestions every time you eat out:

- Avoid coffee drinks made with syrups, as well as those made with cream, whipping cream, or whole milk; select reduced-fat or skim milk in your favorite coffee drink.
- Avoid eating appetizers that are breaded, fried, or filled with cheese or meat; you may want to skip the appetizer completely. Alternatively, you may want to order a healthful appetizer as an entrée instead of a larger meal.
- Share an entrée with a friend! Many restaurants serve entrées large enough for two people.
- Order broth-based soups instead of cream-based soups.
- Order any meat dish grilled or broiled, and avoid fried or breaded meat dishes.
- If you order a meat dish, select lean cuts of meat, such as chicken or turkey breast, extra-lean ground beef, pork loin chop, or filet mignon.
- Order a meatless dish filled with vegetables and whole grains. Avoid dishes with cream sauces and a lot of cheese.
- Order a salad with low-fat or nonfat dressing served on the side. Many restaurants smother their salads in dressing, and you will eat less by controlling how much you put on the salad.
- Order steamed vegetables on the side instead of potatoes or rice. If you order potatoes, make sure you get a baked potato (with very little butter or sour cream on the side).
- Order beverages with few or no calories, such as water, tea, or diet drinks.
- Eat no more than half of what you are served, and take the rest home for another meal.
- Skip dessert or share one dessert with a lot of friends! Another healthful alternative is to order fresh fruit for dessert.

Table 2.5 lists examples of low-fat foods you can choose when you eat out.[15] Although provided as examples for people with diabetes, they are useful for anyone who is interested in making more healthful food choices while eating out. By choosing healthful foods and appropriate portion sizes, you can eat out regularly and still maintain a healthful body weight.

When ordering your favorite coffee drink, avoid those made with flavored syrups, cream, or whipping cream, and request reduced-fat or skim milk instead.

Eating out can be part of a healthful diet, if you are careful to choose wisely.

Table 2.5 Low-Fat Food Choices Available in Restaurants

Appetizers	Salads	Breads	Entrée	Fats	Desserts
Minestrone soup Chicken soup with vegetables Raw celery and carrots with low-fat or nonfat ranch dressing	Tossed with mixed greens, lettuce, tomato, cucumber Spinach salad with crab meat, raw vegetables, and nonfat salad dressing	Whole-grain rolls Corn tortillas Whole-wheat or pumpernickel bread	Baked halibut with thyme and fresh-squeezed lemon Grilled skinless chicken breast with tomato salsa	Diet margarine Low-fat/low-calorie salad dressing Low-fat sour cream or yogurt	Fresh fruit Fruit sorbet Fat-free or low-fat yogurt

Data adapted from: American Diabetes Association. 2007. *Your Guide to Eating Out.* Available at www.diabetes.org/nutrition-and-recipes/nutrition/eatingoutguide.jsp.

RECaP

Healthful ways to eat out include choosing menu items that are smaller in size, ordering meats that are grilled or broiled, avoiding fried foods, choosing items with steamed vegetables, avoiding energy-rich appetizers and desserts, and eating less than half of the food you are served.

Hannah
Nutri-Case

"At least once a week, I go to the sub shop near campus for lunch. I used to order a chicken breast sandwich and a garden salad. I figured the salad is good for me, and since it's veggies, it can't be more than 100 calories, right? Guess again! Last week when I was waiting in line to order, I started reading the nutrition information they've got posted on the wall. I almost freaked out! The sandwich was okay, but that measly little packet of ranch dressing I always put on my salad? It has 320 calories—that's more than the sandwich! From now on, I'm skipping the salad!"

Are you surprised by the number of calories in a packet of regular ranch salad dressing? What do you think of Hannah's plan to skip the salad from now on? Is there a different action she could take that would enable her to include a vegetable choice in her lunch for fewer calories?

See for Yourself

Go to your local grocery store and compile a list of ten examples of nutrient, health, or structure–function claims made on the labels of various foods. Record the name of the food, the actual claim, and any information related to supporting the claim given on the packaging. For each item, note whether or not you found the claim convincing enough to persuade you that the item would be part of a healthful diet.

Chapter Review

Test Yourself | Answers

1　Ⓕ　A healthful diet can come in many forms, and particular attention must be paid to adequacy, variety, moderation, and balance. While consuming at least 5 servings of fruits and vegetables each day is important to maintain optimal health, a healthful diet should also include whole grains and cereals, meat or meat substitutes, dairy or dairy substitutes, and small amounts of healthful fats.

2　Ⓕ　Detailed food labels are not required for meat or poultry, as these products are regulated by the U.S. Department of Agriculture, and coffee and most spices are not required to have food labels, as they contain insignificant amounts of all the nutrients that must be listed on food labels.

3 Ⓣ MyPyramid is the graphic representation of the USDA Food Guide and can be used by most Americans to design a healthful diet. This tool is flexible and allows for modifications as needed; there are also many ethnic variations available.

4 Ⓕ The Dietary Guidelines for Americans recommend that people who choose to drink should do so sensibly and in moderation. Moderation is defined as no more than one drink per day for women and no more than two drinks per day for men.

5 Ⓕ Eating out poses many challenges to healthful eating, but it is possible to eat a healthful diet when dining out. Ordering and/or consuming smaller portion sizes, selecting foods that are lower in fat and added sugars, and selecting eating establishments that serve more healthful foods can assist you in eating healthfully while dining out.

Summary

- A healthful diet is adequate, moderate, balanced, and varied.

- The U.S. Food and Drug Administration (FDA) regulates the content of food labels; food labels must contain a statement of identity, the net contents of the package, the contact information of the food manufacturer or distributor, an ingredient list, and nutrition information.

- The Nutrition Facts Panel on a food label contains important nutrition information about serving size; servings per package; total calories and calories of fat per serving; a list of various macronutrients, vitamins, and minerals; and the % Daily Values for the nutrients listed on the panel.

- The FDA regulates nutrient and health claims found on food labels; however, claims that a food contributes to body structure or function are not regulated.

- The Dietary Guidelines are general directives about healthful eating and physical activity and include aiming for a healthful weight; being physically active each day; consuming adequate nutrients within calorie needs; eating whole-grain foods, fruits, and vegetables each day; keeping food safe to eat; choosing foods lower in saturated fat, *trans* fat, and cholesterol and moderate in total fat; moderating your intake of sugar; eating less salt; eating more potassium-rich foods; and drinking alcoholic beverages in moderation, if at all.

- The USDA Food Guide was created in 2005 to provide a conceptual framework for the types and amounts of foods that make up a healthful diet. MyPyramid is an interactive Web-based tool that is the graphic representation of the USDA Food Guide. The groups in the USDA Food Guide and MyPyramid include grains, fruits, vegetables, oil, milk, and meat and beans.

- Specific serving sizes are defined for foods in each group of the USDA Food Guide. There is no standard definition for a serving size, and the serving sizes defined in the pyramid are generally smaller than those listed on food labels or the servings generally sold to consumers.

- There are many ethnic and cultural variations of the previous USDA Food Guide Pyramid, including the Mediterranean, Latin American, and Asian Diet Pyramids.

- Eating out is challenging because of the high fat content and large serving sizes of many fast-food and sit-down restaurant menu items.

- Behaviors that can improve the quality of your diet when eating out include choosing lower-fat meats that are grilled or broiled, eating vegetables and salads as side or main dishes, asking for low-fat salad dressing on the side, skipping high-fat desserts and appetizers, and drinking low-calorie or noncaloric beverages.

Review Questions

1. The Nutrition Facts Panel identifies which of the following?
   a. all of the nutrients and calories in the package of food
   b. the Recommended Dietary Allowance for each nutrient found in the package of food
   c. a footnote identifying the Tolerable Upper Intake Level for each nutrient found in the package of food
   d. the % Daily Values of selected nutrients in a serving of the packaged food

2. An adequate diet is defined as a diet that
   a. provides enough energy to meet minimum daily requirements.
   b. provides enough of the energy, nutrients, and fiber to maintain a person's health.
   c. provides a sufficient variety of nutrients to maintain a healthful weight and to optimize the body's metabolic processes.
   d. contains combinations of foods that provide healthful proportions of nutrients.

3. The USDA Food Guide recommends eating
   a. at least half your grains as whole grains each day.
   b. 6 to 11 servings of milk, cheese, and yogurt each day.
   c. 200 kcal to 500 kcal of discretionary calories each day.
   d. 2 to 3 servings of fruit juice each day.

4. The Dietary Guidelines for Americans recommends which of the following?
   a. choosing and preparing foods without salt
   b. consuming two alcoholic beverages per day
   c. being physically active each day
   d. following the Mediterranean diet

5. What does it mean to choose foods for their nutrient density?
   a. Dense foods such as peanut butter or chicken are more nutritious choices than transparent foods such as mineral water or gelatin.
   b. Foods with a lot of nutrients per calorie such as fish are more nutritious choices than foods with fewer nutrients per calorie such as candy.

   c. Calorie-dense foods such as cheesecake should be avoided.
   d. Fat makes foods dense, and thus foods high in fat should be avoided.

6. **True or false?** The USDA has written a standardized definition for a serving size for most foods.

7. **True or false?** Structure–function claims on food labels must be approved by the FDA.

8. **True or false?** Discretionary calories are the extra amount of energy a person can consume after meeting all essential needs through eating nutrient-dense foods.

9. **True or false?** The USDA Food Guide classifies beans, peas, and lentils in both the vegetables group and the meat and beans group.

10. **True or false?** About half of all Americans eat out at least once a week.

11. Defend the statement that no single diet can be appropriate for every human being.

12. You work for a food company that is introducing a new variety of soup. Design a label for this new soup, including all five label components required by the FDA.

13. Explain why the USDA Food Guide identifies a range in the number of suggested daily servings of each food group instead of telling us exactly how many servings of each food to eat each day.

14. If the label on a box of cereal claims that the cereal is "High in fiber," at least how much fiber does it provide per serving?

15. You are chatting with your nutrition classmate, Sylvia, about her attempts to lose weight. "I tried one of those low-carb diets," Sylvia confesses, "but I couldn't stick with it because bread and pasta are my favorite foods! Now I'm on the Mediterranean diet. I like it because it's a low-fat diet, so I'm sure to lose weight, plus I can eat all the bread and pasta that I want!" Do you think Sylvia's assessment of the Mediterranean diet is accurate? Why or why not?

Web Links

www.fda.gov
U.S. Food and Drug Administration (FDA)
Learn more about the government agency that regulates our food and first established regulations for nutrition information on food labels.

www.healthierus.gov/dietaryguidelines
Dietary Guidelines for Americans
Use these guidelines to make changes in your food choices and physical activity habits to help reduce your risk for chronic disease.

www.MyPyramid.gov
USDA MyPyramid Steps to a Healthier You
Use the MyPyramid Tracker on this Web site to assess the overall quality of your diet based on the USDA MyPyramid.

www.oldwayspt.org
Oldways Preservation and Exchange Trust
Find different variations of ethnic and cultural food pyramids.

http://hp2010.nhlbihin.net/portion
The National Institutes of Health (NIH) Portion Distortion Quiz
Take this short quiz to see if you know how today's food portions compare with those of 20 years ago.

www.diabetes.org
The American Diabetes Association
Find out more about the nutritional needs of people living with diabetes as well as meal-planning exchange lists.

www.eatright.org
The American Dietetic Association
Visit the food and nutrition information section of this Web site for additional resources to help you achieve a healthful lifestyle.

www.hsph.harvard.edu
The Harvard School of Public Health
Search this site to learn more about the Healthy Eating Pyramid, an alternative to the USDA Food Guide Pyramid.

References

1. Ogden C. L., M. D. Carroll, and K. M. Flegal. 2008. High body mass index for age among US children and adolescents, 2003–2006. *JAMA* 299(20):2401–2405.

2. U.S. Department of Health and Human Services (USDHHS) and U.S. Department of Agriculture (USDA). 2005. *Dietary Guidelines for Americans, 2005.* 6th ed. Washington, DC: U.S. Government Printing Office. Available at www.healthierus.gov/dietaryguidelines.

3. Nielsen, S. J., and B. M. Popkin. 2003. Patterns and trends in food portion sizes, 1977–1998. *JAMA* 289(4):450–453.

4. Young, L. R., and M. Nestle. 1998. Variation in perceptions of a "medium" food portion: Implications for dietary guidance. *J. Am. Diet. Assoc.* 98:458–459.

5. Young, L. R., and M. Nestle. 2002. The contribution of expanding portion sizes to the US obesity epidemic. *Am. J. Pub. Health* 92(2):246–249.

6. Houtkooper, L. 1994. *Winning Sports Nutrition Training Manual.* Tucson: University of Arizona Cooperative Extension.

7. U.S. Department of Agriculture (USDA). 1999. The Food Guide Pyramid for Young Children. Available at www.usda.gov/cnpp/KidsPyra/.

8. Tufts University. 2002. Tufts Food Guide Pyramid for Older Adults. Available at http://nutrition.tufts.edu/pdf/guidelines.pdf.

9. Food and Nutrition Information Center. 2006. Dietary guidance. Ethnic/Cultural Food Pyramid. Available at http://fnic.nal.usda.gov/nal_display/index.php?info_center=4&tax_level=3&tax_subject=256&topic_id=1348&level3_id=5732.

10. Renaud, S., M. de Lorgeril, J. Delaye, J. Guidollet, F. Jacquard, N. Mamelle, J.-L. Martin, I. Monjaud, P. Salen, and P. Toubol. 1995. Cretan Mediterranean diet for prevention of coronary heart disease. *Am. J. Clin. Nutr.* 61(suppl.):1360S–1367S.

11. Tavani, A., and C. La Vecchia. 1995. Fruit and vegetable consumption and cancer risk in a Mediterranean population. *Am. J. Clin. Nutr.* 61(suppl):1374S–1377S.

12. Panagiotakos, D. B., C. Chrysohoou, C. Pitsavos, and C. Stefanadis. 2006. Association between the prevalence of obesity and adherence to the Mediterranean diet: The ATTICA study. *Nutrition* 22(5):449–456.

13. Taylor, P., C. Funk, and P. Craighill. 2006. Eating more; enjoying less. Pew Research Center. A social trends report. Available at http://pewresearch.org/assets/social/pdf/Eating.pdf.

14. Ogden, C. L., M. D. Carroll, M. A. McDowell, and K. M. Flegal. 2007. *Obesity Among Adults in the United States—No Change Since 2003–2004.* NCHS data brief no 1. Hyattsville, MD: National Center for Health Statistics. Available at http://www.cdc.gov/nchs/data/databriefs/db01.pdf.

15. American Diabetes Association. 2007. Your guide to eating out. Available at www.diabetes.org/nutrition-and-recipes/nutrition/eatingoutguide.jsp.

16. McCullough, M. L., D. Feskanich, M. J. Stampfer, E. L. Giovannucci, E. B. Rimm, F. B. Hu, D. Spiegelman, D. J. Hunter, G. A. Colditz, and W. C. Willett. 2002. Diet quality and major chronic disease risk in men and women: moving toward improved dietary guidance. *Am. J. Clin. Nutr.* 76(6):1261–1271.

Will Revising the USDA Food Guide Pyramid Help You Find the Perfect Diet?

As you learned in this chapter, the previous USDA Food Guide Pyramid (FGP) was revised in 2005. MyPyramid was developed to address many of the limitations of the previous FGP. For instance, one major criticism was that the older FGP was overly simple and did not help consumers make appropriate choices within each food group. MyPyramid has addressed this concern by instructing consumers to choose foods that are lower in fat and added sugar and higher in fiber, as well as by providing many specific examples of healthful foods in each food group. Another criticism was that the previous FGP did not emphasize the need for regular physical activity. In contrast, the left side of MyPyramid includes a graphic of a person climbing stairs to highlight the importance of daily physical activity.

Despite these improvements upon the previous FGP, MyPyramid's reception has been lukewarm. Indeed, many of the same criticisms once leveled at the FGP persist, as does a fundamental doubt that such a tool can really help Americans design and maintain a healthful diet. Let's explore some of the specific concerns nutrition and public health experts have raised since the release of MyPyramid.

One major criticism is that the serving sizes suggested in MyPyramid are unrealistic or do not coincide with typical serving sizes of foods listed on food labels. For instance, one serving of a muffin as defined in MyPyramid is 1 oz-equivalent, but most muffins available to consumers range from 2 oz to 8 oz!

The way that foods are packaged is also confusing to consumers. Unless people read food labels carefully, it is easy to consume an entire package of a food that contains multiple servings and assume that the entire package is equal to one serving. For example, it is common to find soft drinks sold in 20-fl.-oz bottles. Although the serving size listed on the label is 8 fl. oz, and total servings per bottle is listed as 2.5, most people just drink the entire bottle in one sitting and assume they had one soft drink.

Although the serving size of a muffin in MyPyramid is 1 oz-equivalent, many muffins sold today range in size from 2 oz to 8 oz.

A second criticism of MyPyramid is that it has not gone far enough to encourage people to consume more healthful foods. For instance, low-fat and low-calorie food choices are not clearly defined in each food category. The 1-oz-equivalent servings of meat, poultry, fish, dry beans, eggs, and nuts suggested in MyPyramid are not differentiated by their fat content or by the type of fat they contain. Fish is low in fat and contains a more healthful type of fat than that found in red meats. In addition, although nuts are relatively high in fat, the type of fat in nuts is more healthful than that found in meats. MyPyramid fails to point out these differences, treating all foods in the meat, poultry, fish, dry beans, eggs, and nuts group as equivalent choices. In addition, MyPyramid recommends that at least half the grains eaten each day should be from whole-grain sources, allowing for eating half of your grain sources from refined foods. In reality, it is more healthful to eat virtually all your grains from whole-grain foods.

A third criticism is that a person must have access to the Internet and the ability to maneuver through Web-based programming in order to effectively use MyPyramid. Although it may be hard for many people to imagine, a considerable number of Americans still do not have access to the Internet, and many of those who do are not comfortable using interactive programming. MyPyramid is quite limited in its usefulness as a stand-alone graphic. Without the capacity to access and manipulate the interactive components on the Internet at www.MyPyramid.gov, individuals cannot personalize MyPyramid.

A fourth criticism is that MyPyramid does not graphically illustrate the principles it claims to represent. For example, by simply looking at the MyPyramid graphic, a consumer cannot know that the varying widths of bands represent how much of that food group to consume. In addition, varying the widths of each band from wider at the bottom to narrower at the top of MyPyramid is supposed to communicate the message that we should eat more of certain foods and less of others in each of the food categories, but it's doubtful that consumers pick up on that message. Similarly, it's questionable whether consumers will notice the yellow band and link it with the oil drop below the graphic in the text. In short, a number of nutrition experts feel that the MyPyramid graphic on its own is not particularly useful, as it is difficult to understand how to use it unless the graphic is linked with the text and supplemented with information provided on the Web site.

Because of these limitations and criticisms, many nutrition experts doubt that MyPyramid can halt the current obesity epidemic or significantly contribute to improving the health of Americans. Although MyPyramid is grounded in science, new research emphasizes the importance of eating specific nutrients and whole foods that promote health and prevent disease—concepts that MyPyramid does not adequately address. The Healthy Eating Pyramid is an alternative pyramid developed by researchers at the Harvard School of Public Health that has been identified as one example of a better tool for designing a healthful diet (see Web Links at the end of this chapter for the URL). Following the design of the previous Food Guide Pyramid, the Healthy Eating Pyramid highlights healthful food choices and emphasizes daily exercise and weight control. A recent study shows that people eating a diet based on the Healthy Eating Pyramid reduced their risk for heart disease two times more than people eating a diet based on the previous FGP.[16] Because of the recent release of MyPyramid, no studies are yet available comparing the effectiveness of the Healthy Eating Pyramid to MyPyramid in reducing chronic disease risk.

As you can imagine, a great deal of time, effort, and money was invested in the new message, content, and design of MyPyramid. In making this investment, nutrition experts at the USDA intended that MyPyramid would help reduce the alarmingly high obesity rates in the United States. The primary assumption made by these experts was that people would actually use MyPyramid to design their diets. In fact, however, the extent to which people use MyPyramid in their daily lives is debatable.

Think about it; prior to taking this class, did you use the previous FGP or the new MyPyramid to help you design a healthful diet? It may be that you had not even seen these pyramids, or if you did, you had no idea how to use them. This is the case for many Americans. Our work with community members throughout the United States has shown us that some people have no idea what MyPyramid or the previous FGP are, and many of those who have seen these tools do not know how to use them. Others who have tried to use them find them confusing because of the limitations just discussed. In addition, the pyramid shape does not make sense to many consumers. Furthermore, many people find any type of graphic image too vague—they need specific menus and recipes to follow and prefer to buy diet books that provide this information. Still others do not use the pyramids because they view them as another confusing mandate from experts who are out of touch with how "real" people eat and how they live their lives.

It is obvious that we need to address the obesity epidemic effectively. In doing so, one of the major challenges we face is to design nutrition recommendations and tools that millions of Americans can, and will, use. Until easier-to-use and more accessible guidelines are available and their impact on the rates of obesity and chronic disease is assessed, this debate will continue.

Problems with accessing or navigating the Internet can prevent people from using MyPyramid.

Will MyPyramid help you select the most healthful option when you eat?

Critical Thinking Questions

- Do you feel that the revised MyPyramid has adequately addressed the flaws of the previous USDA Food Guide Pyramid?

- Do you think that MyPyramid can help people design a healthful diet?

- Do you think it can help people to lose weight, and reduce our population's rate of obesity and chronic disease?

3 The Human Body: Are We Really What We Eat?

Test Yourself | True or False?

1 Sometimes you may have an appetite even though you are not hungry. **T** *or* **F**

2 Your stomach is the primary organ responsible for telling you when you are hungry. **T** *or* **F**

3 If you eat only small amounts of food, over time, your stomach will permanently shrink. **T** *or* **F**

4 The entire process of digestion and absorption of one meal takes about 24 hours. **T** *or* **F**

5 Most ulcers result from a type of infection. **T** *or* **F**

Test Yourself answers are located in the Chapter Review.

Chapter Objectives *After reading this chapter, you will be able to:*

1. Distinguish between appetite and hunger, describing the mechanisms that stimulate each, *p. 74.*

2. Draw a picture of the gastrointestinal tract, including all major and accessory organs, *p. 79.*

3. Describe the contribution of each organ of the gastrointestinal tract to the digestion, absorption, and elimination of food, *pp. 80–84.*

4. Identify the source and function of the key enzymes involved in digesting foods, *p. 87.*

5. Identify the four major hormones involved in the regulation of the gastrointestinal tract and describe their primary action, *pp. 87–88.*

6. Discuss the roles of the gallbladder, pancreas, and liver in digestion, absorption, and processing of nutrients, *pp. 88–89.*

7. List and describe the four types of absorption that occur in the small intestine, *pp. 90–91.*

8. Describe the causes, symptoms, and treatments of gastroesophageal reflux disease, ulcers, food allergies, celiac disease, diarrhea, constipation, and irritable bowel syndrome, *pp. 97, 99, and 100–103.*

Two months ago, Andrea's lifelong dream of becoming a lawyer came one step closer to reality: She moved out of her parents' home in the Midwest to attend law school in Boston. Unfortunately, the adjustment to a new city, new friends, and her intensive course work was more stressful than she'd imagined, and Andrea has been experiencing insomnia and exhaustion. What's more, her always "sensitive stomach" has been getting worse: After every meal, she gets cramps so bad that she can't stand up, and twice she has missed classes because of sudden attacks of pain and diarrhea. She suspects that the problem is related to stress, and wonders if she is going to experience it throughout her life. She is even thinking of dropping out of school if that would make her feel well again.

Almost everyone experiences brief episodes of abdominal pain, diarrhea, or other symptoms from time to time. Such episodes are usually caused by food poisoning or an infection such as influenza. But do you know anyone who experiences these symptoms periodically for days, weeks, or even years? If so, has it made you wonder why? What are the steps in normal digestion and absorption of food, and at what points can the process break down?

We begin this chapter with a look at some of the factors that make us feel as if we want to eat. We then discuss the physiologic processes by which the body digests and absorbs food and eliminates waste products. Finally, we look at some disorders that affect these processes.

Why Do We Want to Eat What We Want to Eat?

You've just finished eating at your favorite Thai restaurant. As you walk back to the block where you parked your car, you pass a bakery window displaying several cakes and pies, each of which looks more enticing than the last, and through the door wafts a complex aroma of coffee, cinnamon, and chocolate. You stop. You know you're not hungry ... but you go inside and buy a slice of chocolate torte and an espresso anyway. Later that night, when the caffeine from the chocolate and espresso keep you awake, you wonder why you succumbed.

Two mechanisms prompt us to seek food: **Hunger** is a physiologic drive for food that occurs when the body senses that we need to eat. The drive is *nonspecific*; when you're hungry, a variety of different foods could satisfy you. If you've recently finished a nourishing meal, then hunger probably won't compel you toward a slice of chocolate torte. Instead, the culprit is likely to be **appetite,** a psychological desire to consume *specific* foods. It is aroused when environmental cues—such as the sight of chocolate cake or the smell of coffee—stimulate our senses, prompting pleasant emotions and often memories.

People commonly experience appetite in the absence of hunger. That's why you can crave cake and coffee even after eating a full meal. On the other hand, it is possible to have a physiologic need for food yet have no appetite. This state, called **anorexia,** can accompany a variety of illnesses from infectious diseases to mood disorders. It can also occur as a side effect of certain medications, such as the chemotherapy used in treating cancer patients. Although in the following sections we describe hunger and appetite as separate entities, ideally the two states coexist: we seek specific, appealing foods to satisfy a physiologic need for nutrients.

Foods that are artfully prepared, arranged, or ornamented, like the cakes and pies in this bakery display case, appeal to our sense of sight.

Hunger is a physiologic stimulus that prompts us to find food and eat.

hunger   A physiologic sensation that prompts us to eat.

appetite   A psychological desire to consume specific foods.

anorexia   An absence of appetite.

The Hypothalamus Prompts Hunger in Response to Various Signals

Because hunger is a physiologic stimulus that drives us to find food and eat, it is often felt as a negative or unpleasant sensation. The primary organ producing that sensation is the brain. That's right—it's not our stomachs, but our brains that tell us when we're hungry.

Hypothalamus

Pituitary gland

Figure 3.1 The hypothalamus triggers hunger by integrating signals from nerve cells throughout the body, as well as from messages carried by hormones.

The region of brain tissue that is responsible for prompting us to seek food is called the **hypothalamus** (**Figure 3.1**). It's located just above the pituitary gland and brain stem in a region of the brain responsible for regulating many types of involuntary activity. The hypothalamus triggers feelings of hunger or satiation (fullness) by integrating signals from nerve cells in other body regions and from chemical messengers called hormones. Even the amount and type of food we eat influence the hypothalamus to cause us to feel hungry or full. Let's now review these three types of signals generated from nerve cells, hormones, and the food we eat.

The Role of Nerve Cells

One hunger-regulating signal comes from special cells lining the stomach and small intestine that detect changes in pressure according to whether the organ is empty or distended with food. The cells relay these data to the hypothalamus. For instance, if you have not eaten for many hours and your stomach and small intestine do not contain food, these data are sent to the hypothalamus, which in turn prompts you to experience the sensation of hunger.

The Role of Hormones

Hormones are chemical messengers that are secreted into the bloodstream by one of the many *endocrine glands* of the body. Their presence in the blood helps regulate one or more body functions. Insulin and glucagon are two hormones produced in the pancreas. They are responsible for maintaining blood glucose levels. Glucose is our bodies' most readily available fuel supply. It's not surprising, then, that its level in our blood is an important signal regulating hunger. When we have not eaten for a while, our blood glucose levels fall, prompting a change in the level of insulin and glucagon. This chemical message is relayed to the hypothalamus, which then prompts us to eat in order to supply our bodies with more glucose.

After we eat, the hypothalamus picks up the sensation of a distended stomach, other signals from the gut, and a rise in blood glucose levels. When it integrates these signals, you have the experience of feeling full, or *satiated*. However, as we have noted, even though the brain sends us clear signals about hunger, most of us become adept at ignoring them ... and eat when we are not truly hungry.

In addition to insulin and glucagon, a variety of other hormones and hormone-like substances signal the hypothalamus to cause us to feel hungry or satiated. Examples of

hypothalamus A region of the brain below (*hypo*-) the thalamus and cerebral hemispheres and above the pituitary gland and brain stem where visceral sensations such as hunger and thirst are regulated.

hormone A chemical messenger that is secreted into the bloodstream by one of the many endocrine glands of the body. Hormones act as a regulator of physiologic processes at a site remote from the gland that secreted them.

hormones and hormone-like substances that stimulate food intake include neuropeptide Y and galanin, while those that create feelings of satiety include leptin, cholecystokinin, and serotonin.[1] More detail about the various hormones involved in digestion are provided later in this chapter. For information about the role of hormones in weight management, see Chapter 13.

The Role of Amount and Type of Food

Foods containing protein have the highest satiety value.[1] This means that a ham-and-egg breakfast will cause us to feel satiated for a longer period of time than will pancakes with maple syrup, even if both meals have exactly the same number of calories. High-fat diets have a higher satiety value than high-carbohydrate diets.

Another factor affecting hunger is how bulky the meal is—that is, how much fiber and water are within the food. Bulky meals tend to stretch the stomach and small intestine, which sends signals back to the hypothalamus telling us that we are full, so we stop eating. Beverages tend to be less satisfying than semisolid foods, and semisolid foods have a lower satiety value than solid foods. For example, if you were to eat a bunch of grapes, you would feel a greater sense of fullness than if you drank a glass of grape juice.

RecaP

In contrast to appetite, hunger is a physiologic sensation triggered by the hypothalamus in response to cues about stomach and intestinal distention and the levels of certain hormones and hormone-like substances. Foods containing protein have the highest satiety value, and bulky meals fill us up quickly, causing the distention that signals us to stop eating.

Environmental Cues Trigger Appetite

Whereas hunger is prompted by internal signals, appetite is triggered by aspects of our environment. The most significant factors influencing our appetite are sensory data, social and cultural cues, and learning (**Figure 3.2**).

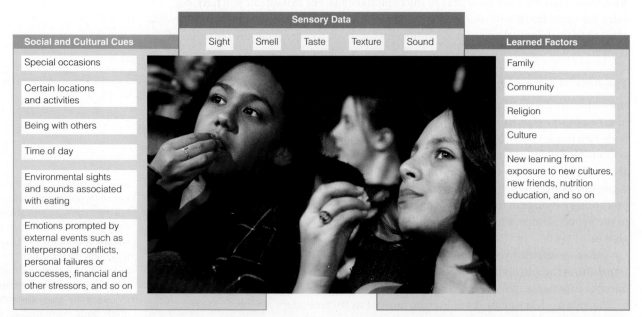

Figure 3.2 Appetite is a drive to consume specific foods, such as popcorn at the movies. It is aroused by social and cultural cues and sensory data, and influenced by learning.

The Role of Sensory Data

Foods stimulate our five senses. Foods that are artfully prepared, arranged, or ornamented, with several different shapes and colors, appeal to our sense of sight. Food producers know this and spend millions of dollars annually in the United States to promote and package their products in an appealing way.

The aromas of foods such as freshly brewed coffee and baked goods can also be powerful stimulants. Interestingly, the sense of smell is so acute that newborn babies can distinguish the scent of their own mother's breast milk from that of other mothers.[2] Much of our ability to taste foods actually comes from our sense of smell. This is why foods are not as appealing when we have a stuffy nose due to a cold. Certain tastes, such as sweetness, are almost universally appealing, whereas others, such as the astringent taste of foods like spinach and kale, are quite individual. Because many natural poisons and spoiled foods are bitter, our distaste for bitterness is thought to be protective.[3]

Texture, or "mouth feel," is also important in food choices, as it stimulates nerve endings sensitive to touch in our mouths and on our tongues. Do you prefer mashed potatoes, thick French fries, or rippled potato chips? Even your sense of hearing can be stimulated by foods, from the fizz of cola to the crunch of peanuts to the "snap, crackle, and pop" of Rice Krispies cereal.

The Role of Social and Cultural Cues

In addition to sensory cues, the brain's association with certain social events such as birthday parties or holiday gatherings can stimulate our appetite. At these times, our culture gives us permission to eat more than usual or to eat "forbidden" foods. Even when we feel full, these cues can motivate us to accept a second helping.

For some people, being in a certain location, such as at a baseball game or a movie theatre, can trigger appetite. Others may be triggered by certain activities such as watching television or studying, or at certain times of day associated with mealtimes. Many people feel an increase or decrease in appetite according to whom they are with; for example, they may eat more when at home with family members and less when out on a date. Even visual cues and sounds in the environment can trigger appetite. Do you start thinking about food every time you pass your refrigerator? When the bell sounds at the end of a class period, how many of your classmates head for the vending machines?

In some cases, appetite masks an emotional response to an external event. For example, after receiving a failing grade or arguing with a close friend, a person might experience a desire for food rather than a desire for emotional comfort. Many people crave food when they're frustrated, worried, or bored, or when they are at a party or other gathering where they feel anxious or awkward. Others subconsciously seek food as a "reward." For example, have you ever found yourself heading out for a burger and fries after handing in a term paper?

The Role of Learning

Pigs' feet, anyone? What about blood sausage, stewed octopus, or tripe? These are delicacies in various European cultures. Would you eat grasshoppers? If you'd grown up in certain parts of Africa or Central America you probably would. That's because your preference for particular foods is largely a learned response. The family, community, religion, and/or culture in which you are raised teach you what plant and animal products are appropriate to eat. If your parents fed you cubes of plain tofu throughout your toddlerhood, then you are probably still eating tofu now.

That said, early introduction to foods is not essential: we can learn to enjoy new foods at any point in our lives. Immigrants from developing nations settling in the United States or Canada often adopt a typical Western diet, especially when their traditional foods are not readily available. This happens temporarily when we travel: the last time you were away

Food preferences are influenced by the family and culture in which you are raised.

Digestion of a sandwich starts before you even take a bite.

from home, you probably enjoyed sampling a variety of dishes that are not normally part of your diet.

Food preferences also change when people learn what foods are most healthful in terms of nutrient density and prevention of chronic diseases. Since reading Chapters 1 and 2, has your diet changed at all? Chances are, as you learn more about the health benefits of specific types of carbohydrates, fats, and proteins, you'll quite naturally start incorporating more of these foods in your diet.

We can also "learn" to dislike foods we once enjoyed. For example, if we experience an episode of food poisoning after eating undercooked scrambled eggs, we might develop a strong distaste for all types of cooked eggs. Many adults who become vegetarians do so after learning about the treatment of animals in slaughterhouses: they might have eaten meat daily when young but no longer have any appetite for it.

ReCaP

In contrast to hunger, appetite is a psychological desire to consume specific foods. It is triggered when external stimuli arouse our senses, and often occurs in combination with social and cultural cues. Our preference for certain foods is largely learned from the culture in which we were raised, but our food choices can change with exposure to new foods or with new learning experiences.

Judy
Nutri-Case

My doctor says that if I lost some weight—at least 20 pounds—it would help get my blood sugar down. But when I diet, I end up feeling so hungry. Like yesterday at work, I ate a ham sandwich and a teensy bag of French fries from the cafeteria at lunch, and when I got home, I had just a can of chicken soup for dinner. But then I was watching TV and there was this commercial for a Mexican restaurant, and that made me realize how hungry I was for real food! So I fixed myself a bowl of chili and cheese, and that filled me up. And I don't feel guilty about it either! I mean, if you're hungry, then that means you need to eat!

What aspects of this scenario suggest that Judy's decision to fix herself a bowl of chili was prompted more by appetite than physical hunger? On the other hand, why do you think she didn't feel satiated after dinner, but the chili and cheese "filled her up"? Next time, what could Judy add to her chicken soup that might turn it into a meal that is both healthful and satisfying?

digestion   The process by which foods are broken down into their component molecules, either mechanically or chemically.

absorption   The physiologic process by which molecules of food are taken from the gastrointestinal tract into the circulation.

elimination   The process by which the undigested portions of food and waste products are removed from the body.

gastrointestinal (GI) tract   A long, muscular tube consisting of several organs: the mouth, esophagus, stomach, small intestine, and large intestine.

What Happens to the Food We Eat?

When we eat, the food we consume is digested, then the useful nutrients are absorbed, and, finally, the waste products are eliminated. But what does each of these processes really entail? In the simplest terms, **digestion** is the process by which foods are broken down into their component molecules, either mechanically or chemically. **Absorption** is the process of taking these products of digestion through the wall of the intestine. **Elimination** is the process by which the undigested portions of food and waste products are removed from the body.

The processes of digestion, absorption, and elimination occur in the **gastrointestinal (GI) tract,** the organs of which work together to process foods. The GI tract is a long tube: If held out straight, an adult GI tract would be close to 30 feet in length. Food within this tube is digested; in other words, food is broken down into molecules small enough to be absorbed by the cells lining the GI tract and thereby passed into the body.

The GI tract begins at the mouth and ends at the anus (**Figure 3.3**). It is composed of several distinct organs, including the mouth, esophagus, stomach, small intestine, and large intestine. The flow of food between these organs is controlled by muscular **sphincters,** which are tight rings of muscle that open when a nerve signal indicates that food is ready to pass into the next section. Surrounding the GI tract are several accessory organs, including the salivary glands, liver, pancreas, and gallbladder, each of which has a specific role in digestion and absorption of nutrients.

Now let's take a look at the role of each of these organs in processing the food we eat. Imagine that you ate a turkey sandwich for lunch today. It contained two slices of bread spread with mayonnaise, some turkey, two lettuce leaves, and a slice of tomato. Let's travel along with the sandwich and see what happens as it enters your GI tract and is digested and absorbed into your body.

Digestion Begins in the Mouth

Believe it or not, the first step in the digestive process is not your first bite of that sandwich. It is your first thought about what you wanted for lunch and your first whiff of turkey and freshly baked bread as you stood in line at the deli. In this **cephalic phase** of digestion, hunger and appetite work together to prepare the GI tract to digest food. The nervous system stimulates the release of digestive juices in preparation for food entering the GI tract, and sometimes we experience some involuntary movement commonly called "hunger pangs."

Figure 3.3 An overview of the gastrointestinal (GI) tract. The GI tract begins at the mouth and ends at the anus and is composed of numerous organs.

Now, let's stop smelling that sandwich and take a bite and chew! Chewing moistens the food and mechanically breaks it down into pieces small enough to swallow (**Figure 3.4**). The presence of food not only initiates mechanical digestion via chewing but also initiates chemical digestion through the secretion of hormones and other substances throughout the gastrointestinal tract. As the teeth cut and grind the different foods in the sandwich, more surface area of the foods is exposed to the digestive juices in the mouth. Foremost among these is **saliva,** which is secreted from the **salivary glands.**

Without saliva, we could not taste the foods we eat. That's because taste occurs when chemicals dissolved in saliva bind to chemoreceptors called *taste receptors* located in structures called *taste buds* on the surface of the tongue. Taste receptors are able to detect at least five distinct tastes: bitter, sweet, salty, sour, and *umami*, a savory taste due to the presence of glutamic acid, an amino acid that occurs naturally in meats and other protein-rich foods. Flavors, such as turkey or tomato, reflect complex combinations of these five basic tastes. As noted earlier, taste depends significantly on the sense of smell, called *olfaction*. To achieve olfaction, odorants dissolved in mucus bind to chemoreceptors in the nasal cavity called *olfactory receptor cells*. These cells then transmit their data to the olfactory bulb of the brain.

Saliva also initiates the chemical digestion of carbohydrates. It accomplishes this through the actions of salivary amylase, a digestive enzyme. **Enzymes** are complex chemicals, usually proteins, that induce chemical changes in other substances to speed up bodily processes. They can be reused because they essentially are unchanged by the chemical reactions they catalyze. Salivary amylase is only one of many enzymes that assist the body in digesting foods. We make hundreds of enzymes in our bodies, and not only digestion but many other biochemical processes could not happen without them. By the way, enzyme

sphincter A tight ring of muscle separating some of the organs of the GI tract and opening in response to nerve signals indicating that food is ready to pass into the next section.

cephalic phase The earliest phase of digestion in which the brain thinks about and prepares the digestive organs for the consumption of food.

saliva A mixture of water, mucus, enzymes, and other chemicals that moistens the mouth and food, binds food particles together, and begins the digestion of carbohydrates.

salivary glands A group of glands found under and behind the tongue and beneath the jaw that releases saliva continually as well as in response to the thought, sight, smell, or presence of food.

enzymes Small chemicals, usually proteins, that act on other chemicals to speed up body processes but are not changed during those processes.

Figure 3.4   Where your food is now: the mouth. Chewing moistens food and mechanically breaks it down into pieces small enough to swallow, while salivary amylase begins chemical digestion of carbohydrates.

names usually end in *-ase*, so they are easy to recognize as we go through the digestive process. Various amylases assist in the digestion of carbohydrates, lipases are involved with lipid digestion, and proteases help digest proteins.

Saliva contains many other components, including:

- bicarbonate, which helps neutralize acids
- mucus, which moistens the food and the oral cavity, ensuring that food easily travels down the esophagus
- antibodies, proteins that defend against bacteria entering the mouth
- lysozyme, an enzyme that inhibits bacterial growth in the mouth and may assist in preventing tooth decay

In reality, very little digestion occurs in the mouth. This is because we do not hold food in our mouths for very long and because all of the enzymes needed to break down foods are not present in saliva. Salivary amylase starts the digestion of carbohydrates in the mouth, and this digestion continues until food reaches the stomach. Once in the stomach, salivary amylase is no longer active because it is destroyed by the acidic environment of the stomach.

RECAP

The cephalic phase of digestion involves hunger and appetite working together before you take your first bite of food to prepare the GI tract for digestion and absorption. Chewing initiates mechanical digestion of food by breaking it into smaller components and mixing all nutrients together. Chewing also stimulates chemical digestion through the secretion of digestive juices such as saliva. Saliva allows for the sensation of taste, moistens food, and starts the process of carbohydrate digestion through the action of the enzyme salivary amylase. This action continues during the transport of food through the esophagus and stops when food reaches the acidic environment of the stomach.

The Esophagus Propels Food into the Stomach

The mass of food that has been chewed and moistened in the mouth is referred to as a **bolus.** This bolus is swallowed (**Figure 3.5**) and propelled to the stomach through the esophagus. Most of us take swallowing for granted. However, it is a very complex process

bolus   A mass of food that has been chewed and moistened in the mouth.

Soft palate

Bolus of food

Epiglottis
(open)

Esophagus
(closed)

Trachea

(a) Chewing

Epiglottis is open; esophagus is closed

Soft palate rises to close opening to nasal passages

Epiglottis
(closed)

Esophagus
(open)

Epiglottis bends to close off trachea and open esophagus

(b) Swallowing

Figure 3.5 Chewing and swallowing are complex processes. **(a)** During the process of chewing, the epiglottis is open and the esophagus is closed so that we can continue to breathe as we chew. **(b)** During swallowing, the epiglottis closes so that food does not enter the trachea and obstruct our breathing. The soft palate also rises to seal off the nasal passages to prevent aspiration of food or liquid into the sinuses.

involving voluntary and involuntary motion. A tiny flap of tissue called the *epiglottis* acts like a trapdoor covering the entrance to the trachea (or windpipe). The epiglottis is normally open, allowing us to breathe freely even while chewing (Figure 3.5a). As our bite of sandwich moves to the very back of the mouth, the brain is sent a signal to temporarily raise the soft palate and close the openings to the nasal passages, preventing aspiration of food or liquid into the sinuses (Figure 3.5b). The brain also signals the epiglottis to close during swallowing so food and liquid cannot enter the trachea. Sometimes this protective mechanism goes awry; for instance, when we try to eat and talk at the same time. When this happens, we experience the sensation of choking and typically cough involuntarily and repeatedly until the offending food or liquid is expelled from the trachea.

As the trachea closes, the sphincter muscle at the top of the esophagus, called the *upper esophageal sphincter*, opens to allow the passage of food. The **esophagus** then transports the food to the stomach (**Figure 3.6**). A muscular tube, the esophagus propels food along its

esophagus A muscular tube of the GI tract connecting the back of the mouth to the stomach.

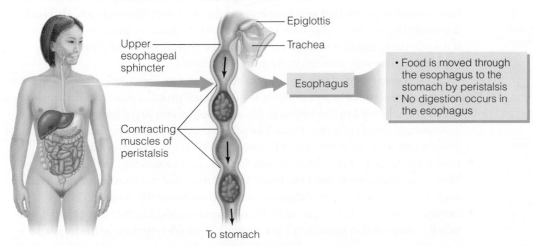

Upper esophageal sphincter

Epiglottis

Trachea

Esophagus

Contracting muscles of peristalsis

- Food is moved through the esophagus to the stomach by peristalsis
- No digestion occurs in the esophagus

To stomach

Figure 3.6 Where your food is now: the esophagus. Peristalsis, the rhythmic contraction and relaxation of both circular and longitudinal muscles in the esophagus, propels food toward the stomach. Peristalsis occurs throughout the GI tract.

length by contracting two sets of muscles: inner sheets of circular muscle squeeze the food, while outer sheets of longitudinal muscle push food along the length of the tube. Together, these rhythmic waves of squeezing and pushing are called **peristalsis.** We will see later in this chapter that peristalsis occurs throughout the GI tract.

Gravity also helps transport food down the esophagus, which is one reason why it is wise to sit or stand upright while eating. Together, peristalsis and gravity can transport a bite of food from the mouth to the opening of the stomach in 5 to 8 seconds. At the end of the esophagus is another sphincter muscle, the *gastroesophageal sphincter* (*gastro-* indicates the stomach), also referred to as the *lower esophageal sphincter,* which is normally tightly closed. When food reaches the end of the esophagus, this sphincter relaxes to allow the passage of food into the stomach. In some people, this sphincter is continually somewhat relaxed. Later in the chapter, we'll discuss this disorder and the unpleasant symptoms experienced when this sphincter does not function properly.

RECaP

Swallowing causes the nasal passages to close and the epiglottis to cover the trachea to prevent food from entering the sinuses and lungs. The upper esophageal sphincter opens as the trachea closes. The esophagus is a muscular tube that transports food from the mouth to the stomach via peristalsis. Gravity also helps move food toward the stomach. Once food reaches the stomach, the gastroesophageal sphincter opens to allow food into the stomach.

The Stomach Mixes, Digests, and Stores Food

The **stomach** is a J-shaped organ. Its size varies with different individuals; in general, its volume is about 6 fluid ounces (or 3/4 cup) when it is empty. The stomach wall contains four layers, the innermost of which is crinkled into large folds called *rugae* that flatten progressively to accommodate food. This allows the stomach to expand to hold about 4 cups of food and liquid.[4] As food is released into the small intestine, the rugae reform, and the stomach gradually returns to its baseline size.

Before any food reaches the stomach, the brain sends signals to the stomach to stimulate and prepare it to receive food. For example, the hormone *gastrin*, secreted by stomach-lining cells called *G cells*, stimulates gastric glands to secrete a digestive fluid referred to as **gastric juice.** Gastric glands are lined with two important types of cells—**parietal cells** and **chief cells**—that secrete the various components of gastric juice, as follows:

- *Hydrochloric acid (HCl)*, which is secreted by parietal cells, keeps the stomach interior very acidic—more so than citrus juices (**Figure 3.7**). This acidic environment kills any bacteria and/or germs that may have entered the body with the sandwich. HCl is also extremely important for digestion because it starts to denature proteins, which means it uncoils the bonds that maintain their structure. This is an essential preliminary step in breaking down the proteins in the turkey and bread.
- HCl also converts *pepsinogen*, an inactive enzyme secreted by chief cells, into the active enzyme *pepsin*, which begins to digest the denatured proteins into smaller components. Recall that salivary amylase begins to digest carbohydrates in the mouth. In contrast, proteins and lipids enter the stomach largely unchanged. Pepsin begins the digestion of protein and activates many other GI enzymes needed to digest your sandwich.
- *Gastric lipase,* secreted by the chief cells, is an enzyme responsible for lipid digestion. Thus, it begins to break apart the lipids in the turkey and mayonnaise in your sandwich. However, only minimal digestion of lipids occurs in the stomach.
- *Intrinsic factor,* secreted by parietal cells, is a protein critical to the absorption of vitamin B_{12} (discussed in more detail in Chapter 12), which is present in the turkey.

Because gastric juice is already present in the stomach, chemical digestion of proteins and lipids begins as soon as food enters (**Figure 3.8**). The stomach also plays a role in

peristalsis Waves of squeezing and pushing contractions that move food, chyme, and feces in one direction through the length of the GI tract.

stomach A J-shaped organ where food is partially digested, churned, and stored until released into the small intestine.

gastric juice Acidic liquid secreted within the stomach; it contains hydrochloric acid, pepsin, and other compounds.

parietal cells Cells lining the gastric glands that secrete hydrochloric acid and intrinsic factor.

chief cells Cells lining the gastric glands that secrete pepsinogen and gastric lipase.

Table 3.1 Digestive Enzymes Produced in the Gastrointestinal Tract and Their Actions

Organ Where Produced	Enzyme	Site of Action	Primary Action
Mouth	Salivary amylase	Mouth	Digests carbohydrates
Stomach	Pepsin	Stomach	Digests proteins
	Gastric lipase		Digests lipids
Pancreas	Proteases (trypsin, chymotrypsin, carboxypolypeptidase)	Small intestine	Digest proteins
	Elastase		Digests fibrous proteins
	Pancreatic lipase		Digests lipids
	Cholesterol esterase		Digests cholesterol
	Pancreatic amylase (amylase)		Digests carbohydrates
Small intestine	Carboxypeptidase, aminopeptidase, dipeptidase	Small intestine	Digest proteins
	Lipase		Digests lipids
	Sucrase		Digests sucrose
	Maltase		Digests maltose
	Lactase		Digests lactose

Hormones Assist in Regulating Digestion

As introduced earlier in this chapter, hormones are regulatory chemicals produced by endocrine glands. Hormones are released into the bloodstream and travel to target cells that contain the receptor protein specific to that given hormone. Generally, the receptor proteins for hormones are located on the cell membrane. When the hormone arrives at the target cell, it binds to the receptor protein and activates what is referred to as a *second messenger system* within the cell (**Figure 3.12**). This second messenger system achieves the targeted response, such as release of a particular digestive enzyme.

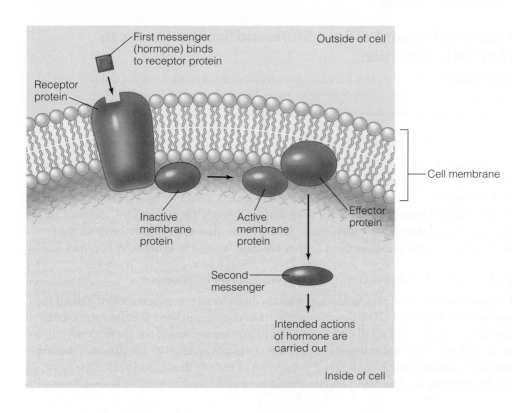

Figure 3.12 Hormones travel to target cells to initiate specific actions. When a hormone arrives at its target cell, it binds to the receptor protein on the cell membrane. This binding activates a protein on the interior cell membrane that initiates a second messenger system within the cell. The second messenger system then carries out the action directed by the hormone's "message."

Table 3.2 Hormones Involved in the Regulation of Digestion

Hormone	Production Site	Target Organ	Actions
Gastrin	Stomach	Stomach	Stimulates secretion of HCl and pepsinogen (inactive form of pepsin)
			Stimulates gastric motility
			Promotes proliferation of gastric mucosal cells
Secretin	Small intestine (duodenum)	Pancreas	Stimulates secretion of pancreatic bicarbonate (which neutralizes acidic chyme)
		Stomach	Decreases gastric motility
Cholecystokinin (CCK)	Small intestine (duodenum and jejunum)	Pancreas	Stimulates secretion of pancreatic digestive enzymes
		Gallbladder	Stimulates gallbladder contraction
		Stomach	Slows gastric emptying
Gastric inhibitory peptide (GIP)	Small intestine	Stomach	Inhibits gastric acid secretion
			Slows gastric emptying
		Pancreas	Stimulates insulin release

Regulation of the gastrointestinal tract involves the action of more than 80 hormones and hormone-like substances. Table 3.2 identifies four of the most important of these hormones and the actions they initiate. These are gastrin, secretin, cholecystokinin (CCK), and gastric inhibitory peptide (GIP). Two other hormones have recently received attention for their potential roles in digestion. Somatostatin acts to inhibit the release of various hormones and enzymes involved in digestion, and it is being used to treat pancreatic cancer and disorders of the gastrointestinal tract such as diarrhea.[7, 8] Ghrelin is a hormone secreted by cells in the gastrointestinal tract, and it has been identified as playing a role in eating behavior and weight regulation.[9] It may also have a beneficial effect on the cardiovascular system by improving blood flow and decreasing blood pressure. As the research studying the impact of ghrelin on obesity and cardiovascular health is in its infancy, there is still much to learn about this hormone.

Accessory Organs Produce, Store, and Secrete Chemicals That Aid in Digestion

The gallbladder, pancreas, and liver are considered accessory organs to the gastrointestinal tract. As you will learn in the following sections, these organs are critical to the production, storage, and secretion of enzymes and other substances that are involved in digestion.

The Gallbladder Stores Bile

As noted in Table 3.2, cholecystokinin (CCK) is released in the small intestine in response to the presence of proteins and lipids. This hormone signals the **gallbladder** to contract. The gallbladder is located beneath the liver (see Figure 3.3) and stores a greenish fluid, **bile,** produced by the liver. Contraction of the gallbladder sends bile through the *common bile duct* into the duodenum. Bile then *emulsifies* the lipids; that is, it reduces the lipids into smaller globules and disperses them so they are more accessible to digestive enzymes.

The Pancreas Produces Digestive Enzymes and Bicarbonate

The **pancreas** manufactures, holds, and secretes digestive enzymes. It is located behind the stomach (see Figure 3.3). The pancreas stores these enzymes in their inactive forms, and they are activated in the small intestine; this is important because if the enzymes were active in the pancreas, they would digest the pancreas. Enzymes secreted by the pancreas include *pancreatic amylase,* which continues the digestion of carbohydrates, and *pancreatic lipase,* which continues the digestion of lipids. *Proteases* secreted in pancreatic juice digest pro-

gallbladder A pear-shaped organ beneath the liver that stores bile and secretes it into the small intestine.

bile Fluid produced by the liver and stored in the gallbladder; it emulsifies lipids in the small intestine.

pancreas A gland located behind the stomach that secretes digestive enzymes.

teins. The pancreas is also responsible for manufacturing hormones that are important in metabolism. Insulin and glucagon, two hormones necessary to regulate the amount of glucose in the blood, are produced by the pancreas.

Another essential role of the pancreas is to secrete bicarbonate into the duodenum. Bicarbonate is a base and, like all bases, is capable of neutralizing acids. Recall that chyme leaving the stomach is very acidic. The pancreatic bicarbonate neutralizes this acidic chyme. This allows the pancreatic enzymes to work effectively and ensures that the lining of the duodenum is not eroded. When the acidic chyme first enters the duodenum, this portion of the small intestine is protected by mucus produced by special glands until the bicarbonate is released and has neutralized the chyme.

The Liver Produces Bile and Regulates Blood Nutrients

The **liver** is a triangular, wedge-shaped organ of about 3 lb of tissue that rests almost entirely within the protection of the rib cage on the right side of the body (see Figure 3.3). It is the largest digestive organ; it is also one of the most important organs in the body, performing more than 500 discrete functions. One important job of the liver is to synthesize many of the chemicals used by the body in carrying out metabolic processes. For example, the liver synthesizes bile, which, as we just discussed, is then stored in the gallbladder until needed for the emulsification of lipids.

Another important function of the liver is to receive the products of digestion via the **portal vein,** remove them from the bloodstream and process them for storage, and then release back into the bloodstream those nutrients needed throughout the body. For instance, after we eat a meal, the liver picks up excess glucose from the blood and stores it as glycogen, releasing it into the bloodstream when we need energy later in the day. It also stores certain vitamins and manufactures blood proteins. The liver can even make glucose when necessary to ensure that our blood levels stay constant. Thus, the liver plays a major role in regulating the level and type of fuel circulating in our blood.

Have you ever wondered why people who abuse alcohol are at risk for damaging the liver? That's because another of its functions is to filter the blood, removing wastes and toxins such as alcohol, medications, and other drugs. When you drink, your liver works hard to replace the cells poisoned with alcohol, but, over time, scar tissue forms. The scar tissue blocks the free flow of blood through the liver, so that any further toxins accumulate in the blood, causing confusion, coma, and, ultimately, death. Alcohol is discussed in the *In Depth* chapter on pages 154–165.

RecaP

Enzymes speed up the digestion of food through hydrolysis. Hormones act as chemical messengers to regulate digestion. The key hormones involved in digestion include gastrin, secretin, cholecystokinin, and gastric inhibitory peptide. The digestive accessory organs include the gallbladder, pancreas, and liver. The gallbladder stores bile, which is produced by the liver. Bile emulsifies lipids into pieces that are more easily digested. The pancreas synthesizes and secretes digestive enzymes that break down carbohydrates, lipids, and proteins. The liver processes all nutrients absorbed from the small intestine, regulates blood glucose levels, and stores glucose as glycogen.

How Does the Body Absorb and Transport Digested Nutrients?

Although some nutrient absorption occurs in the stomach and large intestine, the majority occurs in the small intestine. The small intestine is ideally equipped to handle this responsibility due to its extensive surface area and specialized absorptive cells. Let's now learn more about how we absorb the nutrients from our food.

liver The largest auxiliary organ of the GI tract and one of the most important organs of the body. Its functions include production of bile and processing of nutrient-rich blood from the small intestine.

portal vein A vessel that carries blood and various products of digestion from the digestive organs and spleen to the liver.

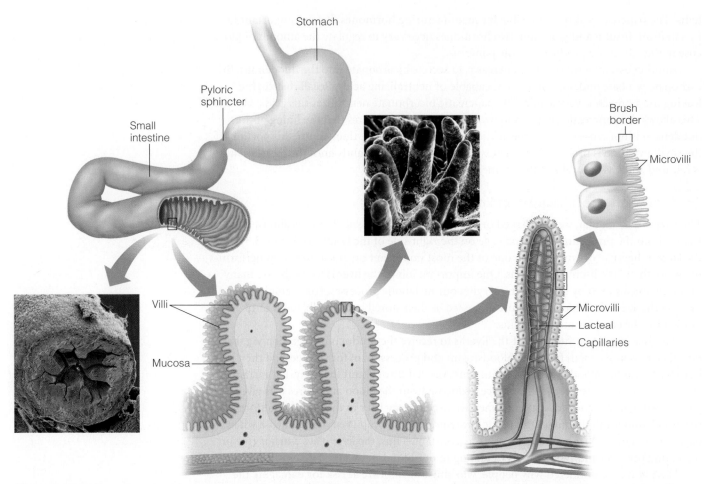

Figure 3.13 Absorption of nutrients occurs via the specialized lining of the small intestine. The lining of the small intestine is heavily folded and has thousands of finger-like projections called *villi*. The cells covering the villi end in hairlike projections called *microvilli* that together form the brush border. These features significantly increase the absorptive capacity of the small intestine.

A Specialized Lining Enables the Small Intestine to Absorb Food

The lining of the small intestine is especially well suited for absorption. If you looked at the inside of the lining, which is also referred to as the *mucosal membrane,* you would notice that it is heavily folded (**Figure 3.13**). This feature increases the surface area of the small intestine and allows it to absorb more nutrients than if it were smooth. Within these larger folds, you would notice even smaller finger-like projections called *villi,* whose constant movement helps them to encounter and trap nutrient molecules. The villi are composed of numerous specialized absorptive cells called **enterocytes.** Inside each villus are capillaries and a **lacteal,** which is a small lymph vessel. (The role of the lymphatic system is discussed shortly.) The capillaries and lacteals absorb some of the end products of digestion. Water-soluble nutrients are absorbed directly into the bloodstream, whereas fat-soluble nutrients are absorbed into lymph. Each enterocyte of each villus has hairlike projections called *microvilli.* The microvilli look like tiny brushes and are sometimes collectively referred to as the **brush border.** These intricate folds increase the surface area of the small intestine by more than 500 times, tremendously increasing its absorptive capacity as well.

Four Types of Absorption Occur in the Small Intestine

Nutrients are absorbed across the mucosal membrane and into the bloodstream or lymph via four mechanisms: passive diffusion, facilitated diffusion, active transport, and endocytosis. These are illustrated in **Figure 3.14**.

enterocytes Specialized absorptive cells in the villi of the small intestine.

lacteal A small lymph vessel located inside of the villi of the small intestine.

brush border A term that describes the microvilli of the small intestine's lining. These microvilli tremendously increase the small intestine's absorptive capacity.

Figure 3.14 The four types of absorption that occur in the small intestine. **(a)** In passive diffusion, nutrients pass through the enterocytes and into the bloodstream without the use of a carrier protein or the requirement of energy. **(b)** In facilitated diffusion, nutrients are shuttled across the enterocytes with the help of a carrier protein without the use of energy. **(c)** In active transport, energy is used along with a carrier protein to transport nutrients against their concentration gradient. **(d)** In endocytosis, a small amount of the intestinal contents is engulfed by the cell membrane of the enterocyte and released into the interior of the cell.

Passive diffusion is a simple process in which nutrients pass through the enterocytes and into the bloodstream without the use of a carrier protein or the requirement of energy (Figure 3.14a). Passive diffusion can occur when the wall of the intestine is permeable to the nutrient and the concentration of the nutrient in the GI tract is higher than its concentration in the enterocytes. Thus, the nutrient is moving from an area of higher concentration to an area of lower concentration. Lipids, water, vitamin C, and some minerals are absorbed via passive diffusion.

Facilitated diffusion occurs when nutrients are shuttled across the enterocytes with the help of a carrier protein (Figure 3.14b). This process is similar to passive diffusion in that it does not require energy and is driven by a concentration gradient. The monosaccharide fructose is transported via facilitated diffusion.

Active transport requires the use of energy to transport nutrients in combination with a carrier protein (Figure 3.14c). The energy derived from ATP and the assistance of the carrier protein allow for absorption of nutrients against their concentration gradient, meaning the nutrients can move from areas of low to high concentration. Glucose, galactose, sodium, potassium, magnesium, calcium, iron, and amino acids are some of the nutrients absorbed via active transport. In addition to being absorbed via passive diffusion, vitamin C can also be absorbed via active transport.

Endocytosis (also called pinocytosis) is a form of active transport by which a small amount of the intestinal contents is engulfed by the enterocyte's cell membrane and incorporated into the cell (Figure 3.14d). Some proteins and other large particles are absorbed in this way, as are the antibodies contained in breast milk.

Blood and Lymph Transport Nutrients and Wastes

Two circulating fluids transport nutrients and waste products throughout the body: Blood travels through the cardiovascular system, and lymph travels through the lymphatic system (**Figure 3.15**). The oxygen we inhale into our lungs is carried by our red blood cells. This oxygen-rich blood then travels to the heart, where it is pumped out to the body. Blood

passive diffusion The simple absorptive process in which nutrients pass through the enterocytes and into the bloodstream without the use of a carrier protein or the requirement of energy.

facilitated diffusion The absorptive process that occurs when nutrients are shuttled across the enterocytes with the help of a carrier protein.

active transport An absorptive process that requires the use of energy to transport nutrients and other substances in combination with a carrier protein.

endocytosis An absorptive process by which a small amount of the intestinal contents is engulfed by the cell membrane (also called pinocytosis).

Lymphatic capillaries

Lymph node

Capillaries in lungs
(pulmonary circuit)

Heart

Capillaries in body
(systemic circuit)

Lymph node

Figure 3.15 Blood travels through the cardiovascular system to transport nutrients and fluids and to pick up waste products. Lymph travels through the lymphatic system and transports most lipids and fat-soluble vitamins.

travels to all of our tissues to deliver nutrients and other materials and to pick up waste products. In the GI tract, blood in the capillaries picks up most nutrients, including water, that have been absorbed through the mucosal membrane of the small intestine. The lacteals have picked up most lipids and fat-soluble vitamins, as well as any fluids that have escaped from the capillaries, and these are now transported in the lymph. Lymph nodes are clusters of immune cells that filter microbes and other harmful agents from the lymph fluid (see Figure 3.15). The lymph eventually returns to the bloodstream in an area near the heart where the lymphatic and blood vessels join together.

As the blood leaves the GI system, it is transported to the liver, whose role in digestion was described earlier. The waste products picked up by the blood as it circulates around the body are filtered and excreted by the kidneys. In addition, much of the carbon dioxide remaining in the blood once it reaches the lungs is exhaled into the outside air, making room for oxygen to attach to the red blood cells and repeat this cycle of circulation again.

Recap

The mucosal membrane of the small intestine contains multiple villi and microvilli that significantly increase absorptive capacity. Nutrients are absorbed through one of four mechanisms: passive diffusion, facilitated diffusion, active transport, and endocytosis. Most nutrients and waste products are transported throughout the body via the blood, whereas lipids and fat-soluble vitamins are transported through lymph.

How Does the Body Coordinate and Regulate Digestion?

Now that you can identify the organs involved in digestion and absorption and the complex tasks they each perform, you might be wondering—who's the boss? In other words, what organ or system controls all of these interrelated processes? The answer is the neuromuscular system. Its two components, nerves and muscles, partner to coordinate and regulate the digestion and absorption of food and the elimination of waste.

The Muscles of the Gastrointestinal Tract Mix and Move Food

The purposes of the muscles of the GI tract are to mix food, ensure efficient digestion and optimal absorption of nutrients, and move the intestinal contents from the mouth toward the anus. Once we swallow a bolus of food, peristalsis begins in the esophagus and continues throughout the remainder of the gastrointestinal tract. Peristalsis is accomplished through the actions of circular muscles and longitudinal muscles that run along the entire GI tract (**Figure 3.16a**). The circular and longitudinal muscles continuously contract and relax, causing subsequent constriction and bulging of the tract. This action pushes the contents from one area to the next.

The stomach is surrounded by its own set of longitudinal, circular, and diagonal muscles that assist in digestion (see **Figure 3.17**, page 94). These muscles alternately contract and relax, churning the stomach contents and moving them toward the pyloric sphincter. The pyloric sphincter stays closed while gastric juices are secreted and the chyme is completely liquefied. Once the chyme is liquefied, the pyloric sphincter is stimulated to open, and small amounts of chyme are regularly pushed into the small intestine.

Water is readily absorbed along the entire length of the GI tract.

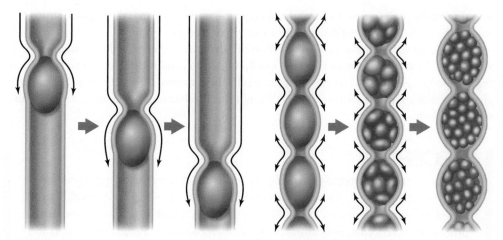

(a) Peristalsis   (b) Segmentation

Figure 3.16 Peristalsis and segmentation. **(a)** Peristalsis occurs through the actions of circular muscles and longitudinal muscles that run along the entire GI tract. These muscles continuously contract and relax, causing subsequent constriction and bulging of the tract, and push the intestinal contents from one area to the next. **(b)** Segmentation occurs through the rhythmic contraction of the circular muscles of the small intestine. This action squeezes the chyme, mixes it, and enhances its contact with digestive enzymes and enterocytes.

In the small intestine, a unique pattern of motility called **segmentation** occurs (Figure 3.16b). Segmentation, accomplished by the rhythmic contraction of circular muscles in the intestinal wall, squeezes the chyme, mixes it, and enhances its contact with digestive enzymes and enterocytes.

The colon also exhibits a unique pattern of motility, called **haustration,** in which the haustra contract sluggishly to move wastes toward the sigmoid colon. However, two or more times each day, a much stronger and more sustained **mass movement** of the colon occurs, pushing wastes forcibly toward the rectum.

The muscles of the GI tract contract at varying rates depending on their location and whether or not food is present. The stomach tends to contract more slowly, about three times per minute, whereas the small intestine may contract up to ten times per minute when chyme is present. The contractions of haustra are very slow, occurring at a rate of about two per hour. As with an assembly line, the entire GI tract functions together so that materials are moved in one direction, absorption of nutrients is maximized, and wastes are removed as needed.

In order to process the large amount of food we consume daily, we use both voluntary and involuntary muscles. Muscles in the mouth are primarily voluntary; that is, they are under our conscious control. Once we swallow, the involuntary muscles just described largely take over to propel food through the rest of the GI tract. This enables us to continue digesting and absorbing food while we're working, exercising, and even sleeping. Let's now identify the master controller behind these involuntary muscular actions.

Nerves Control the Contractions and Secretions of the Gastrointestinal Tract

The contractions and secretions of the gastrointestinal tract are controlled by nerves from three divisions of the nervous system:

- a specialized division localized in the wall of the gastrointestinal tract, called the **enteric nervous system (ENS)**
- the parasympathetic and sympathetic branches of the autonomic nervous system, which is part of the peripheral nervous system (PNS)
- the central nervous system (CNS), which includes the brain and spinal cord

Some digestive functions are carried out entirely within the ENS. For instance, control of peristalsis and segmentation is enteric, occurring without PNS or CNS involvement. In addition, enteric nerves regulate the secretions of the various digestive glands whose roles we have discussed in this chapter.

Enteric nerves also work in collaboration with the PNS and CNS. For example, we noted earlier in this chapter that in response to fasting, receptors in the stomach and

segmentation Rhythmic contraction of the circular muscles of the intestines that squeeze chyme, mix it, and enhance digestion and absorption of nutrients from the chyme.

haustration Involuntary, sluggish contraction of the haustra of the proximal colon that moves wastes toward the sigmoid colon.

mass movement Involuntary, sustained, forceful contraction of the colon that occurs two or more times a day to push wastes toward the rectum.

enteric nervous system The nerves of the GI tract.

intestinal walls (ENS receptors) stimulate peripheral nerves to signal the hypothalamus, part of the CNS. We then experience the sensation of hunger.

Finally, some functions, such as secretion of saliva, are achieved without enteric involvement. A variety of stimuli from the smell, sight, taste, and tactile sensations from food trigger special salivary cells in the CNS; these cells then increase PNS activity to the salivary glands. Activation of the salivary glands through this mechanism causes an increase of salivary secretions.

RECaP

The coordination and regulation of digestion are directed by the neuromuscular system. Voluntary muscles assist us with chewing and swallowing. Once food is swallowed, involuntary muscles of the GI tract function together so that materials are processed in a coordinated manner. Involuntary movements include the mixing and churning of chyme by muscles in the stomach wall, as well as peristalsis, segmentation, haustration, and mass movement. The enteric nerves of the GI tract work with the peripheral and central nervous systems to achieve digestion, absorption, and elimination of food.

What Disorders Are Related to Digestion, Absorption, and Elimination?

Considering the complexity of digestion, absorption, and elimination, it's no wonder that sometimes things go wrong. Disorders of the neuromuscular system, hormonal imbalances, infections, allergies, and a host of other disorders can disturb gastrointestinal functioning, as can merely consuming the wrong types or amounts of food for our unique needs. Whenever there is a problem with the GI tract, absorption of nutrients can be affected. If absorption of a nutrient is less than optimal for a long period of time, malnutrition can result. Let's look more closely at some GI tract disorders and what you might be able to do if they affect you.

Belching and Flatulence Are Common

Many people complain of problems with belching (or eructation) and/or flatulence (passage of intestinal gas). The primary cause of belching is swallowed air. Eating too fast, wearing improperly fitting dentures, chewing gum, sucking on hard candies or a drinking straw, and gulping food or fluid can increase the risk of swallowing air. To prevent or reduce belching, avoid these behaviors.

Although many people find *flatus* (intestinal gas) uncomfortable and embarrassing, its presence in the GI tract is completely normal, as is its expulsion. Flatus is a mixture of many gases, including nitrogen, hydrogen, oxygen, methane, and carbon dioxide. Interestingly, all of these are odorless. It is only when flatus contains sulfur that it causes the embarrassing odor associated with flatulence.

Foods most commonly reported to cause flatus include those rich in fibers, starches, and sugars, such as beans, dairy products, and some vegetables. The partially digested carbohydrates from these foods pass into the large intestine, where they are acted upon by bacteria, producing gas. Other food products that may cause flatus, intestinal cramps, and diarrhea include products made with the fat substitute olestra, sugar alcohols, and quorn (a meat substitute made from fungus).

Because many of the foods that can cause flatus are healthful, it is important not to avoid them. Eating smaller portions can help reduce the amount of flatus produced and passed. In addition, products such as Beano can offer some relief. Beano is an over-the-counter supplement that contains alpha-galactosidase, an enzyme that digests the complex sugars in gas-producing foods. Although flatus is generally normal, some people have mal-

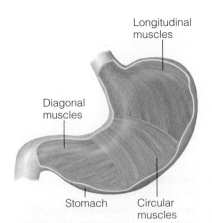

Figure 3.17 The stomach has longitudinal, circular, and diagonal muscles. These three sets of muscles aid digestion by alternately contracting and relaxing; these actions churn the stomach contents and move them toward the pyloric sphincter.

Longitudinal muscles

Diagonal muscles

Stomach

Circular muscles

absorption diseases that cause painful bloating and require medical treatment. Some of these disorders are described later in this section.

Heartburn and Gastroesophageal Reflux Disease (GERD) Are Caused by Reflux of Stomach Acid

When you eat food, your stomach secretes hydrochloric acid (HCl) to start the digestive process. In many people, the amount of HCl secreted is occasionally excessive or the gastroesophageal sphincter opens too soon. In either case, the result is that HCl seeps back up into the esophagus (**Figure 3.18**). Although the stomach lining is protected from HCl by a thick coat of mucus, the esophagus does not have this mucus coating. Thus, the HCl burns it. When this happens, a person experiences a painful sensation in the region of his or her chest above the sternum (breastbone). This condition is commonly called **heartburn.** People often take over-the-counter antacids to neutralize the HCl, thereby relieving the heartburn. A non-drug approach is to repeatedly swallow: This action causes any acid within the esophagus to be swept down into the stomach, eventually relieving the symptoms.

Gastroesophageal reflux disease (GERD) is a more painful type of heartburn that occurs more than twice per week. GERD affects about 19 million Americans and, like heartburn, occurs when HCl flows back into the esophagus. Although people who experience occasional heartburn usually have no structural abnormalities, many people with GERD have an overly relaxed or damaged esophageal sphincter or damage to the esophagus itself. Symptoms of GERD include persistent heartburn and acid regurgitation. Some people have GERD without heartburn and instead experience chest pain, trouble swallowing, burning in the mouth, the feeling that food is stuck in the throat, or hoarseness in the morning.[10]

The exact causes of GERD are unknown. However, a number of factors may contribute, including the following:[10]

- A *hiatal hernia,* which occurs when the upper part of the stomach lies above the diaphragm muscle. Normally, the diaphragm muscle separates the stomach from the chest and helps keep acid from coming into the esophagus. Stomach acid can more easily enter the esophagus in people with a hiatal hernia.

heartburn The painful sensation that occurs over the sternum when hydrochloric acid backs up into the lower esophagus.

gastroesophageal reflux disease (GERD) A painful type of heartburn that occurs more than twice per week.

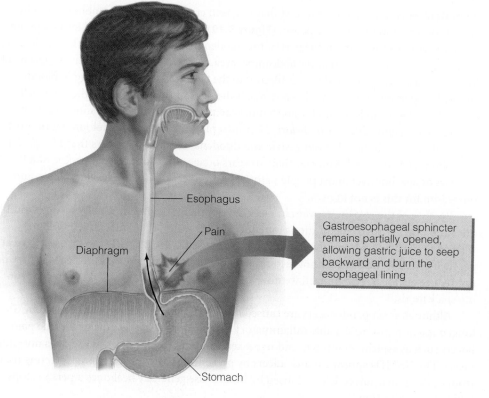

Figure 3.18 The mechanism of heartburn and gastroesophageal reflux disease is the same: Acidic gastric juices seep backward through an open or relaxed sphincter into the lower portion of the esophagus, burning its lining. The pain is felt above the sternum, over the heart.

Although the exact causes of gastroesophageal reflux disease (GERD) are unknown, smoking and being overweight may be contributing factors.

- Cigarette smoking.
- Alcohol use.
- Overweight.
- Pregnancy.
- Foods such as citrus fruits, chocolate, caffeinated drinks, fried foods, garlic and onions, spicy foods, and tomato-based foods such as chili, pizza, and spaghetti sauce.
- Large, high-fat meals. These meals stay in the stomach longer and increase stomach pressure, making it more likely that acid will be pushed up into the esophagus.
- Lying down within 1 to 2 hours after a meal. This is almost certain to bring on symptoms, because it positions the body so that it is easier for the stomach acid to back up into the esophagus.

There are ways to reduce the symptoms of GERD. One way is to identify the types of foods or situations that trigger episodes and then avoid them. Eating smaller meals also helps. After a meal, waiting at least 3 hours before lying down is recommended. Some people relieve their nighttime symptoms by elevating the head of the bed 4 to 6 inches, for instance by placing a wedge between the mattress and the box spring. This keeps the chest area elevated and minimizes the amount of acid that can back up into the esophagus. It is also suggested that if people smoke, they should stop, and if they are overweight, they should lose weight. Taking an antacid before a meal can help, and many prescription medications are available to treat GERD. The most effective medications currently available are called *proton pump inhibitors*; these drugs reduce the secretion of HCl from the stomach's parietal cells.

Left untreated, GERD can cause serious health problems, including bleeding and ulceration of the esophagus. Scar tissue can develop in the esophagus, making swallowing very difficult. Some people can also develop a condition called Barrett esophagus, which can lead to cancer. Asthma can also be aggravated or even caused by GERD.[10]

An Ulcer Is an Area of Erosion in the GI Tract

A **peptic ulcer** is an area of the GI tract that has been eroded away by a combination of hydrochloric acid and the enzyme pepsin (**Figure 3.19**). In almost all cases, it is located in the stomach area (*gastric ulcer*) or the part of the duodenum closest to the stomach (*duodenal ulcer*). It causes a burning pain in the abdominal area, typically 1 to 3 hours after eating a meal. In serious cases, eroded blood vessels bleed into the GI tract, causing vomiting of blood and/or blood in the stools, as well as anemia. If the ulcer entirely perforates the tract wall, stomach contents can leak into the abdominal cavity, causing a life-threatening infection.

The bacterium *Helicobacter pylori* (*H. pylori*) plays a key role in development of most peptic ulcers, which include both gastric and duodenal ulcers.[11] It appears that *H. pylori* infects about 20% of people younger than 40 years of age and about 50% of people older than 60 years of age; however, most people with *H. pylori* infection do not develop ulcers, and the reason for this is not known.[12]

Because of the role of *H. pylori* in ulcer development, treatment usually involves antibiotics and other types of medications to reduce gastric secretions. Antacids are used to weaken the gastric acid, and the same medications used to treat GERD can be used to treat peptic ulcers. Special diets are not recommended as often as they once were because they do not reduce acid secretion. In fact, we now know that ulcers are not caused by stress or eating spicy foods.

Although most peptic ulcers are caused by *H. pylori* infection, some are caused by prolonged use of nonsteroidal anti-inflammatory drugs (NSAIDs); these drugs include pain relievers such as aspirin, ibuprofen, and naproxen sodium. Acetaminophen use does not cause ulcers. The NSAIDs appear to cause ulcers by preventing the stomach from protecting itself from acidic gastric juices. Ulcers caused by NSAID use generally heal once a person stops taking the medication.[13]

Figure 3.19 A peptic ulcer.

peptic ulcer An area of the GI tract that has been eroded away by the acidic gastric juice of the stomach. The two main causes of peptic ulcers are *Helicobacter pylori* infection or use of nonsteroidal anti-inflammatory drugs.

Recap

Belching is commonly caused by behaviors that cause us to swallow air. Foods that may cause flatulence include those rich in fibers, starches, and sugars. Heartburn is caused by the seepage of gastric juices into the esophagus. Gastroesophageal reflux disease (GERD) is a painful type of heartburn that occurs more than twice per week. GERD can cause serious health consequences such as esophageal bleeding, ulcers, and cancer. Peptic ulcers are caused by erosion of the GI tract by hydrochloric acid and pepsin. The two major causes of peptic ulcers are *Helicobacter pylori* infection and the use of nonsteroidal anti-inflammatory drugs. Peptic ulcers are typically treated with antibiotics and other medications.

Some People Experience Disorders Related to Specific Foods

You check out the ingredients list on your energy bar, and you notice that it says, "Produced in a facility that processes peanuts." The carton of soy milk you're drinking from proclaims: "Gluten free!" What's all the fuss about? To some people, consuming certain food ingredients can be dangerous, even life-threatening. That's why the U.S. Food and Drug Administration requires food labels to identify any ingredients containing protein derived from the following eight foods: milk, eggs, fish, crustacean shellfish, tree nuts, peanuts, wheat, and soybeans.

Disorders related to specific foods can be clustered into three main groupings: food intolerances, food allergies, and a genetic disorder called celiac disease. We discuss these separately.

Food Intolerance

A **food intolerance** is a cluster of GI symptoms (often gas, pain, and diarrhea) that occur following consumption of a particular food. The immune system plays no role in intolerance, and although episodes are unpleasant, they are usually transient, resolving after the offending food has been eliminated from the body. An example is lactose intolerance. It occurs in people whose bodies do not produce sufficient quantities of the enzyme lactase, which is needed for the breakdown of the milk sugar lactose. (Lactose intolerance is discussed in more detail in Chapter 4.) People can also have an intolerance to wheat, soy, and other foods, but as with lactose intolerance, the symptoms pass once the offending food is out of the person's system.

Food Allergy

A **food allergy** is a hypersensitivity reaction of the immune system to a particular component (usually a protein) in a food. This reaction causes the immune cells to release chemicals that cause either limited or systemic (whole-body) inflammation. About 5% of infants and young children and 2% of adults experience food allergies.[14] Although this makes them much less common than food intolerances, food allergies can be far more serious. Approximately 30,000 consumers require emergency room treatment and 150 Americans die each year because of allergic reactions to foods.[14]

You may have heard stories of people being allergic to foods as common as peanuts. This is the case for Liz. She was out to dinner with her parents, celebrating her birthday, when the dessert cart came around. The caramel custard looked heavenly and was probably a safe choice, but she asked the waiter just to be sure that it contained no peanuts. He checked with the chef, then returned and assured her that, no, the custard was peanut-free—but within minutes of consuming it, Liz's skin became flushed, and she struggled to breathe. As her parents were dialing 911, she lost consciousness. Fortunately, the paramedics arrived within minutes and were able to resuscitate her. It was subsequently determined that, unknown to the chef, the spoon that his prep cook had used to scoop the baked custard into serving bowls had been resting on a cutting board where he had chopped

For some people, eating a meal of grilled shrimp with peanut sauce would cause a severe allergic reaction.

food intolerance Gastrointestinal discomfort caused by certain foods that is not a result of an immune system reaction.

food allergy An allergic reaction to food, caused by a reaction of the immune system.

peanuts for a different dessert. Just this small exposure to peanuts was enough to cause a severe allergic reaction in Liz.

How can a food that most people consume regularly, such as peanuts, shellfish, eggs, or milk, cause another person's immune system to react so violently? In Liz's case, a trace amount of peanut stimulated immune cells throughout her body to release their inflammatory chemicals. In many people, the inflammation is localized, so the damage is limited; for instance, a person's mouth and throat might itch whenever they eat cantaloupe. What made Liz's experience so terrifyingly different was that the inflammation was widespread. Thus, her airways became constricted and clogged with mucus, leading to respiratory collapse. At the same time, her blood vessels dilated and became so permeable that her blood pressure plummeted, leading to circulatory collapse. This state, called *anaphylactic shock*, is nearly always fatal if not treated immediately. For this reason, many people with known food allergies carry with them a kit containing an injection of a powerful stimulant called epinephrine. This drug can reduce symptoms long enough to buy the victim time to get emergency medical care.

Celiac Disease

Celiac disease, also known as *celiac sprue*, is a digestive disease that severely damages the lining of the small intestine and interferes with absorption of nutrients.[15] As in food allergy, the body's immune system causes the disorder. However, there is a strong genetic predisposition to celiac disease, with the risk now linked to specific gene markers.

In celiac disease, the offending food component is *gliadin*, a fraction of a protein called *gluten* that is found in wheat, rye, and barley. When people with celiac disease eat one of these grains, their immune system triggers an inflammatory response that erodes the villi of the small intestine. If the person is unaware of the disorder and continues to eat gluten, repeated immune reactions cause the villi to become greatly decreased so that there is less absorptive surface area. In addition, the enzymes located at the brush border of the small intestine become reduced. As a result, the person becomes unable to absorb certain nutrients properly—a condition known as *malabsorption*. Over time, malabsorption can lead to malnutrition (poor nutrient status). Deficiencies of fat-soluble vitamins A, D, E, and K, as well as iron, folic acid, and calcium, are common in those suffering from celiac disease, as are inadequate intakes of protein and total energy.[16]

Symptoms of celiac disease often mimic those of other intestinal disturbances such as irritable bowel syndrome (discussed shortly), and so the condition is often misdiagnosed. Some of the symptoms of celiac disease include fatty stools (due to poor fat absorption); frequent stools, either watery or hard, with an odd odor; cramping; anemia; pallor; weight loss; fatigue; and irritability. However, other puzzling symptoms do not appear to involve the GI tract. These include an intensely itchy rash called *dermatitis herpetiformis*, osteoporosis (poor bone density), infertility, epilepsy, anxiety, irritability, depression, and migraine headaches, among others.[16]

Diagnostic tests for celiac disease include a variety of blood tests that screen for the presence of immune proteins called antibodies, or for the genetic markers of the disease. However, the "gold standard" for diagnosis is a biopsy of the small intestine showing atrophy of the intestinal villi. Because long-term complications of undiagnosed celiac disease include an increased risk for intestinal cancer, early diagnosis can be life-saving. Unfortunately, celiac disease is currently thought to be widely underdiagnosed in the United States.[16] We'll explore some reasons for this in the Nutrition Debate on pages 108–109.

Currently there is no cure for celiac disease. Treatment is with a special diet that excludes all forms of wheat, rye, and barley. Oats are allowed, but they are often contaminated with wheat flour from processing, and even a microscopic amount of wheat can cause an immune response. The diet is especially challenging because many binding agents and other unfamiliar ingredients in processed foods are derived from gluten. Thus, nutritional counseling is essential. Fortunately, many gluten-free foods are now available.

For people with celiac disease, corn is a gluten-free source of carbohydrates.

celiac disease   A disorder characterized by an immune reaction that damages the lining of the small intestine when the individual is exposed to a component of a protein called gluten.

Crohn Disease and Colitis Are Inflammatory Disorders

Two inflammatory bowel diseases are Crohn disease and ulcerative colitis. The precise causes of these disorders are unknown, but both have been linked to an immune response to a virus or bacterium. Both also are associated with similar symptoms.

Crohn Disease

Crohn disease causes inflammation in the small intestine, usually the ileum, and affects the entire thickness of the wall. Some experts speculate that the inflammation is related to the reaction of the immune system to a virus or bacterium.

The symptoms of Crohn disease include diarrhea, abdominal pain, rectal bleeding, weight loss, and fever. People with this disease may also suffer from anemia due to the persistent bleeding that occurs, and children with Crohn disease can experience delayed physical and mental development. If allowed to progress, Crohn disease can cause blockage of the intestine and the development of ulcers that tunnel through the areas surrounding the inflammation, such as the bladder, vagina, skin, anus, or rectum. These tunnels are referred to as *fistulas,* and they become infected and commonly require surgical treatment. Crohn disease also results in deficiencies in protein, energy, and vitamins and is associated with arthritis, kidney stones, gallstones, and diseases of the liver.

Because it shares many of the same symptoms as other intestinal disorders, Crohn disease can be difficult to diagnose. Treatment may involve a combination of prescription drugs and nutritional supplements, as well as surgery to control inflammation, correct nutritional deficiencies, and relieve pain, diarrhea, and bleeding.[17]

Ulcerative Colitis

Ulcerative colitis is a chronic disease characterized by inflammation and ulceration of the mucosa, or innermost lining, of the colon. Ulcers form on the surface of the mucosa, where they bleed and produce pus and mucus. The causes of ulcerative colitis are unknown. Many of the scientists who study this disease believe it results from an interaction between an outside virus or bacterium and the immune system. This interaction might either trigger the disease or directly cause the damage to the intestinal wall.

The resulting symptoms are similar to Crohn disease and include diarrhea (which may be bloody), abdominal pain, weight loss, anemia, nausea, fever, and severe urgency to have a bowel movement. Complications of ulcerative colitis include profuse bleeding, rupture of the bowel, severe abdominal distention, dehydration, and nutritional deficiencies.

Treatment usually involves taking anti-inflammatory medications. Surgery may be needed for those people who do not successfully respond to pharmacologic treatment.[18] No particular foods cause ulcerative colitis, but it may be necessary for people with this disease to avoid foods that cause intestinal discomfort.

RECAP

Food intolerances are digestive problems caused by consumption of certain foods, but not due to an immune reaction. Food allergies are hypersensitivities to food ingredients caused by an immune reaction. Food allergies can cause mild symptoms, such as hives and swelling, or life-threatening inflammation and anaphylactic shock. People with celiac disease cannot eat gluten, a protein found in wheat, rye, and barley, as it causes an immune reaction that damages the lining of the small intestine and leads to malabsorption of nutrients and malnutrition. Crohn disease and ulcerative colitis are inflammatory bowel diseases. Crohn disease usually affects the entire thickness of the ileum of the small intestine, whereas colitis is an inflammation and ulceration of the innermost lining of the colon. The causes of Crohn disease and ulcerative colitis are unknown.

Crohn disease   A bowel disease that causes inflammation in the small intestine leading to diarrhea, abdominal pain, rectal bleeding, weight loss, and fever.

ulcerative colitis   A chronic disease of the large intestine, or colon, indicated by inflammation and ulceration of the mucosa, or innermost lining of the colon.

Liz
Nutri-Case

"I used to think my peanut allergy was no big deal, but ever since my experience at that restaurant last year, I've been pretty obsessive about it. For months afterward, I refused to eat anything that I hadn't prepared myself. I do eat out now, but I always insist that the chef prepare my food personally, with clean utensils, and I avoid most desserts. They're just too risky. Shopping is a lot harder too, because I have to check every label. The worst, though, is eating at my friends' houses. I have to ask them, do you keep peanuts or peanut butter in your house? Some of them are really sympathetic, but others look at me as if I'm a hypochondriac! I wish I could think of something to say to them to make them understand that this isn't something I have any control over."

What could Liz say in response to friends who don't understand the cause and seriousness of her food allergy? Do you think it would help Liz to share her fears with her doctor and discuss possible strategies? If so, why? In addition to shopping, dining out, and eating at friends' houses, what other situations might require Liz to be cautious about her food choices?

Diarrhea, Constipation, and Irritable Bowel Syndrome Are Functional Disorders

As their name implies, functional disorders affect the regular function of the gastrointestinal tract. Food may move through the small or large intestine too quickly or too slowly, prompting discomfort, bloating, or other symptoms.

Diarrhea

Diarrhea is the frequent (more than three times in one day) passage of loose, watery stools. Other symptoms may include cramping, abdominal pain, bloating, nausea, fever, and blood in the stools. Diarrhea is usually caused by an infection of the gastrointestinal tract, stress, food intolerances, reactions to medications, or an underlying bowel disorder or other chronic disease.[19]

Acute diarrhea lasts less than 3 weeks and is usually caused by an infection from bacteria, a virus, or a parasite. Chronic diarrhea, which lasts more than 3 weeks, affects about 3% to 5% of the U.S. population and is usually caused by allergies to cow's milk, irritable bowel syndrome (discussed shortly), lactose intolerance, celiac disease, or conditions such as Crohn disease or ulcerative colitis.

Whatever the cause, diarrhea can be harmful if it persists for a long period of time because the person can lose large quantities of water and electrolytes and become severely dehydrated. Table 3.3 reviews the signs and symptoms of dehydration, which is

Table 3.3 Signs and Symptoms of Dehydration in Adults and Children

Signs and Symptoms in Adults	Signs and Symptoms in Children
Thirst	Dry mouth and tongue
Light-headedness	No tears when crying
Less frequent urination	No wet diapers for 3 hours or more
Dark-colored urine	High fever
Fatigue	Sunken abdomen, eyes, or cheeks
Dry skin	Irritable or listless
	Skin that does not flatten when pinched and released

Data from: National Digestive Diseases Information Clearinghouse (NDDIC). 2001. Diarrhea. NIH publication no. 01–2749. Available online at http://digestive.niddk.nih.gov/ddiseases/pubs/diarrhea/index.htm

diarrhea A condition characterized by the frequent passage of loose, watery stools.

particularly dangerous in infants and young children. In fact, a child can die from dehydration in just a few days. Adults, particularly the elderly, can also become dangerously ill if severely dehydrated.

A condition referred to as *traveler's diarrhea* has become a common health concern due to the expansion in global travel.[20] Traveler's diarrhea is discussed in the accompanying Highlight box.

Constipation

At the opposite end of the spectrum is **constipation,** which is typically defined as a condition in which no stools are passed for two or more days; however, it is important to recognize that some people normally experience bowel movements only every second or third day. Thus, the definition of constipation varies from one person to another. In addition to being infrequent, the stools are usually hard, small, and difficult to pass.

Constipation is frequent in people who have disorders affecting the nervous system, which in turn affect the muscles of the large bowel, as they do not receive the appropriate neurologic signals needed for involuntary muscle movement to occur. For these individuals, drug therapy is often needed to keep the large bowel functioning.

Many people experience temporary constipation at some point in their lives in response to a variety of factors. Often people have trouble with it when they travel, when their schedule is disrupted, if they change their diet, or if they are on certain medications. Increasing fiber and fluid in the diet is one of the mainstays of preventing constipation. Five servings of fruits and vegetables each day and six or more servings of whole grains is helpful to most people. If you eat breakfast cereal, make sure you buy a cereal containing at least 2 to 3 g of fiber per serving. The dietary recommendation for fiber and the role it plays in maintaining healthy elimination is discussed in detail in Chapter 4. Staying well-hydrated by drinking lots of water is especially important when increasing fiber intake. Exercising also helps reduce the risk of constipation.

Irritable Bowel Syndrome

Irritable bowel syndrome (IBS) is a disorder that interferes with normal functions of the colon. Symptoms include abdominal cramps, bloating, and either constipation or diarrhea. It is one of the most common medical diagnoses, applied to approximately 20% of the U.S. population.[21] Three times more women than men are diagnosed with IBS, which typically first appears by early adulthood.[21]

IBS shows no sign of disease that can be observed or measured.[21] However, it appears that the colon is more sensitive to physiologic or emotional stress in people with IBS than in healthy people. Some researchers believe that the problem stems from conflicting messages between the central nervous system and the enteric nervous system. The immune system may also trigger symptoms of IBS. Whatever the cause, the normal movement of the colon appears to be disrupted. In some people with IBS, food moves too quickly through the colon and fluid cannot be absorbed fast enough, which causes diarrhea. In others, the movement of the colon is too slow and too much fluid is absorbed, leading to constipation. Some of the foods thought to cause physiologic stress linked to IBS include:

- Caffeinated drinks, such as tea, coffee, and colas
- Foods such as chocolate, alcohol, dairy products, and wheat
- Large meals

Some women with IBS find that their symptoms worsen during their menstrual period, indicating a possible link between reproductive hormones and IBS. Certain medications may also increase the risk.

The high prevalence of the diagnosis in the United States, along with the lack of any sign of physical disease, has led to charges that IBS is overdiagnosed or misdiagnosed. Some physicians do not even agree that IBS qualifies as a disease, pointing out that the stresses of everyday life have always led to digestive problems, and probably always will.[21] Other

Consuming caffeinated drinks is one of several factors that have been linked with irritable bowel syndrome (IBS), a disorder that interferes with normal functions of the colon.

constipation A condition characterized by the absence of bowel movements for a period of time that is significantly longer than normal for the individual.

irritable bowel syndrome A bowel disorder that interferes with normal functions of the colon. Symptoms are abdominal cramps, bloating, and constipation or diarrhea.

Highlight

Traveler's Diarrhea—What Is It and How Can I Prevent It?

Diarrhea is the rapid movement of fecal matter through the large intestine, often accompanied by large volumes of water. *Traveler's diarrhea* (also called *dysentery*) is experienced by people traveling to countries outside of their own and is usually caused by viral or bacterial infection. Diarrhea represents the body's way of ridding itself of the invasive agent. The large intestine and even some of the small intestine become irritated by the microbes and the resulting immune response. This irritation leads to increased secretion of fluid and increased peristalsis of the large intestine, causing watery stools and a higher-than-normal frequency of bowel movements.

People generally get traveler's diarrhea from consuming water or food that is contaminated with fecal matter. High-risk destinations include developing countries in Africa, Asia, Latin America, and the Middle East. However, hikers and others traveling in any remote region are at increased risk if they drink untreated water from lakes, rivers, and streams.

Traveler's diarrhea usually starts about 5 to 15 days after you arrive at your destination. Symptoms include fatigue, lack of appetite, abdominal cramps, and watery diarrhea. In some cases, you may also experience nausea, vomiting, and low-grade fever. Usually, this diarrhea passes within 4 to 6 days, and people recover completely. However, infants and toddlers, the elderly, and people with compromised immunity are at greater risk for serious illness resulting from traveler's diarrhea. This is also true for people with digestive disorders such as celiac disease and ulcers.[20]

What can you do to prevent traveler's diarrhea? Table 3.4 lists foods and beverages to avoid and those that are considered relatively safe when traveling. In general, it is smart to as-

When traveling in developing countries, it is wise to avoid food from street vendors.

sume that all local water is contaminated, including ice, so you should wipe all chilled bottles clean before drinking bottled beverages. Beverages made with boiling water are typically safe. Chemicals such as chorine bleach and iodine can be used to sterilize drinking water, but boiling is more effective.

If you do suffer from traveler's diarrhea, it is important to replace the fluid and nutrients lost as a result of the illness. Specially formulated oral rehydration solutions are usually available in most countries at local pharmacies or stores. Antibiotics may also be prescribed to kill the bacteria. Once treatment is initiated, the diarrhea should cease within 2 to 3 days. If the diarrhea persists for more than 10 days after the initiation of treatment, or if there is blood in your stools, you should return to a physician immediately to avoid serious medical consequences.

Table 3.4 Foods and Beverages Linked with Traveler's Diarrhea

Foods/Beverages That Can Cause Traveler's Diarrhea	Foods/Beverages Considered Safe to Consume
Tap water	Boiled tap water
Local bottled water	Brand-name bottled water
Iced tea	Hot coffee and hot tea
Unpasteurized dairy products or juices	Wine and beer
Ice (in alcoholic or nonalcoholic beverages)	Well-cooked foods
Undercooked or raw foods (includes meats, vegetables, and most fruits)	Fruit that can be peeled (for example, bananas and oranges)
Cooked foods that are no longer hot in temperature	
Shellfish	
Food from street vendors	

Data from: Stanley, S. L. 1999. Advice to travelers. In: Yamada, T. ed. *Textbook of Gastroenterology*, vol. 1, 3rd ed. Philadelphia: Lippincott Williams & Wilkins. Used with permission.

researchers argue that U.S. physicians too often apply the diagnosis of IBS before screening for more serious disorders. In more than one study, a significant percentage of patients who had been diagnosed with IBS were determined upon screening to have celiac disease; thus, some researchers are arguing that all diarrhea-predominant IBS patients should be screened for celiac disease.[22]

If you think you have IBS, it is important to have a complete physical examination to rule out any other health problems, including celiac disease. Treatment options include certain medications to treat diarrhea or constipation, stress management, regular physical activity, eating smaller meals, avoiding foods that exacerbate symptoms, eating a higher-fiber diet, and drinking at least six to eight glasses of water each day.[23] Although IBS is uncomfortable, it does not appear to endanger long-term health. However, severe IBS can be disabling and prevent people from leading normal lives; thus, accurate diagnosis and effective treatment are critical.

RecaP

Diarrhea is the frequent passage of loose or watery stools, whereas constipation is failure to have a bowel movement for two or more days or within a time period that is normal for the individual. Diarrhea should be treated quickly to avoid dehydration. Constipation often can be corrected by increasing your intake of fiber and water. Irritable bowel syndrome (IBS) causes abdominal cramps, pain, bloating, and constipation or diarrhea. Factors linked by some studies to exacerbation of IBS include stress, consumption of certain foods and fluids, large meals, and certain medications. IBS can be treated with medications and dietary and lifestyle changes.

See for Yourself

Do You Eat in Response to External or Internal Cues?

In this chapter, you learned the differences between appetite and hunger, as well as the influence of learning on food choices. So now you might be curious to investigate your own reasons for eating what and when you do. Whether you're trying to lose weight, gain weight, or maintain your current healthful weight, you'll probably find it intriguing to keep a log of the reasons behind your decisions about what, when, where, and why you eat. Are you eating in response to internal sensations telling you that your body *needs* food, or in response to your emotions, situation, or a prescribed diet? Keeping a "cues" log for 1 full week would give you the most accurate picture of your eating habits, but even logging 2 days of meals and snacks should increase your cue awareness.

Each day, every time you eat a meal, snack, or beverage other than water, make a quick note of:

- **When you eat.** Many people eat at certain times (for example, 6 PM) whether they are hungry or not.
- **What you eat, and how much.** A cup of yogurt and a handful of nuts? An apple? A 20-oz cola?

- **Where you eat.** At home at the dining room table, watching television, driving in the car, and so on.
- **With whom you eat.** Are you alone or with others? If with others, are they eating as well? Have they offered you food?
- **Your emotions.** Many people overeat when they are happy, especially when celebrating with others. Some people eat excessively when they are anxious, depressed, bored, or frustrated. Still others eat as a way of denying feelings because they don't want to identify and deal with them. For some, food becomes a substitute for emotional fulfillment.
- **Your sensations: what you see, hear, or smell.** Are you eating because you walked past the kitchen and spied that batch of homemade cookies, or smelled coffee roasting?
- **Any diet restrictions.** Are you choosing a particular food because it is allowed on your current diet plan? Or are you hungry, but drinking a diet soda to stay within a certain allowance of calories? Are you restricting yourself

continued

because you feel guilty about having eaten too much at another time?

- **Your physiologic hunger.** Rate your hunger on a scale from 1 to 5 as follows:

  1 = you feel full or even stuffed

  2 = you feel satisfied but not uncomfortably full

  3 = neutral; you feel no discernible satiation nor hunger

  4 = you feel hungry and want to eat

  5 = you feel strong physiologic sensations of hunger and need to eat

After keeping a log for 2 or more days, you might become aware of patterns you'd like to change. For example, maybe you notice that you often eat when you are not actually hungry but are worried about homework or personal relationships. Or maybe you notice that you can't walk past the snack bar without going in. This self-awareness may prompt you to take positive steps to change those patterns. For instance, instead of stifling your worries with food, sit down with a pen and paper and write down exactly what you are worried about, including steps you can take to address your concerns. And the next time you approach the snack bar, before going in, check with your gut: are you truly hungry? If so, then purchase a healthful snack, maybe a yogurt, a piece of fruit, or a bag of peanuts. If you're not really hungry, then take a moment to acknowledge the strength of this visual cue—and then walk on by.

Chapter Review

Test Yourself | Answers

1 **T** Sometimes you may have an appetite even though you are not hungry. These feelings are referred to as "cravings" and are associated with physical or emotional cues.

2 **F** Your brain, not your stomach, is the primary organ responsible for telling you when you are hungry.

3 **F** Even extreme food restriction, such as near-starvation, does not cause the stomach to permanently shrink. Likewise, the stomach doesn't permanently stretch. The folds in the wall of the stomach flatten as it expands to accommodate a large meal, but they reform over the next few hours as the food empties into the small intestine. Only after gastric surgery, when a very small stomach "pouch" remains, can stomach tissue stretch permanently.

4 **T** Although there are individual variations in how we respond to food, the entire process of digestion and absorption of one meal usually takes about 24 hours.

5 **T** Most ulcers result from an infection by the bacterium *Helicobacter pylori* (*H. pylori*). Contrary to popular belief, ulcers are not caused by stress or spicy food.

Summary

- Hunger is a physiologic drive that prompts us to eat.

- Appetite is a psychological desire to consume specific foods; this desire is influenced by sensory data, social and cultural cues, and learning.

- In response to signals from the gastrointestinal tract and from hormones, the hypothalamus causes us to feel hungry or satiated.

- Foods that contain fiber, water, and large amounts of protein have the highest satiety value.

- Digestion is the process of breaking down foods into molecules small enough to be transported into enterocytes, absorption is the process of taking molecules of food out of the gastrointestinal tract and into the circulation, and elimination is the process of removing undigested food and waste products from the body.

- In the mouth, chewing starts mechanical digestion of food. Saliva contains salivary amylase, an enzyme that initiates the chemical digestion of carbohydrates.

- Food moves down to the stomach through the esophagus via a process called peristalsis. Peristalsis involves rhythmic waves of squeezing and pushing food through the gastrointestinal tract.

- The stomach mixes and churns food together with gastric juices. Hydrochloric acid and the enzyme pepsin initiate protein digestion, and a minimal amount of fat digestion begins through the action of gastric lipase.

- The stomach periodically releases the partially digested food, referred to as chyme, into the small intestine.

- Most digestion and absorption of nutrients occur in the small intestine.

- The large intestine digests any remaining food particles, absorbs water and chemicals, and moves feces to the rectum for elimination.

- Enzymes guide the digestion of food via the process of hydrolysis. Most digestive enzymes are synthesized by the pancreas and small intestine.

- The four primary hormones that regulate digestion are gastrin, secretin, cholecystokinin, and gastric inhibitory peptide.

- The gallbladder stores bile and secretes it into the small intestine to assist with the digestion of lipids.

- The pancreas manufactures and secretes digestive enzymes into the small intestine. Pancreatic amylase digests carbohydrates, pancreatic lipase digests lipids, and proteases digest proteins. The pancreas also synthesizes two hormones that play a critical role in carbohydrate metabolism, insulin and glucagon.

- The liver processes all absorbed nutrients, alcohol, and drugs, and it stores various nutrients. The liver also synthesizes bile and regulates metabolism of monosaccharides, fatty acids, and amino acids.

- The lining of the small intestine has folds, villi, and microvilli that increase its surface area and absorptive capacity.

- The four types of absorption that occur in the small intestine are passive diffusion, facilitated diffusion, active transport, and endocytosis.

- The neuromuscular system involves coordination of the muscles as well as the enteric, peripheral, and central nervous systems to move food along the gastrointestinal tract and to control all aspects of digestion, absorption, and elimination.

- Belching results from swallowed air, and flatulence can be caused by consumption of foods rich in fibers, starches, and sugars, such as beans, dairy products, and some vegetables.

- Heartburn occurs when hydrochloric acid seeps into the esophagus and burns its lining. Gastroesophageal reflux disease (GERD) is a more painful type of heartburn that occurs more than twice per week.

- A peptic ulcer is an area in the stomach or duodenum that has been eroded away by hydrochloric acid and pepsin.

- Food allergies can cause either localized reactions such as a minor skin rash or systemic inflammation resulting in respiratory and circulatory collapse.

- People with celiac disease cannot eat gluten, a protein found in wheat, rye, and barley, as it causes an immune reaction that damages the lining of the small intestine and leads to malabsorption of nutrients and malnutrition.

- Crohn disease is an inflammatory bowel disease that usually affects the small intestine, whereas ulcerative colitis damages the mucosal lining of the colon. The causes of these diseases are unknown.

- Diarrhea is the frequent (more than three times per day) elimination of loose, watery stools. Constipation is a condition in which no stools are passed for two or more days or for a length of time considered abnormally long for the individual. Irritable bowel syndrome is a bowel disorder that interferes with normal functions of the colon, causing pain, diarrhea, and/or constipation.

Review Questions

1. Which of the following processes moves food along the entire GI tract?
   a. mass movement
   b. peristalsis
   c. haustration
   d. segmentation

2. Bile is a greenish fluid that
   a. is produced by the gallbladder.
   b. is stored by the pancreas.
   c. denatures proteins.
   d. emulsifies lipids.

3. The region of brain tissue that is responsible for prompting us to seek food is the
   a. pituitary gland.
   b. enteric nervous system.
   c. hypothalamus.
   d. thalamus.

4. Heartburn is caused by
   a. seepage of gastric acid into the esophagus.
   b. seepage of gastric acid into the cardiac muscle.
   c. seepage of bile into the stomach.
   d. seepage of salivary amylase into the stomach.

5. Which of the following foods is likely to keep a person satiated for the longest period of time?
   a. a bean and cheese burrito
   b. a serving of full-fat ice cream
   c. a bowl of rice cereal in whole milk
   d. a tossed salad with oil and vinegar dressing

6. **True or false?** Hunger is more physiologic, and appetite is more psychologic.

7. **True or false?** The nerves of the GI tract are collectively known as the enteric nervous system.

8. **True or false?** Vitamins and minerals are digested in the small intestine.

9. **True or false?** A person with celiac disease cannot tolerate milk or milk products.

10. **True or false?** Intestinal villi are composed of numerous specialized absorptive cells called enterocytes.

11. Explain why it can be said that you are what you eat.

12. Imagine that the lining of your small intestine were smooth, like the inside of a rubber tube. Would this design be efficient in performing the main function of this organ? Why or why not?

13. Why doesn't the acidic environment of the stomach cause it to digest itself?

14. Create a table comparing the area of inflammation, symptoms, and treatment options for celiac disease, Crohn disease, and ulcerative colitis.

15. After dinner, your roommate lies down to rest for a few minutes before studying. When he gets up, he complains of a sharp, burning pain in his chest. Offer a possible explanation for his pain.

Web Links

http://digestive.niddk.nih.gov
National Digestive Diseases Information Clearinghouse (NDDIC)
Explore this site to learn more about the disorders covered in this chapter.

www.healthfinder.gov
Health Finder
Search this site to learn more about disorders related to digestion, absorption, and elimination.

www.ific.org
International Food Information Council Foundation (IFIC)
Scroll down to "Food Safety Information" and click on the link for "Food Allergies and Asthma" for additional information on food allergies.

www.foodallergy.org
The Food Allergy & Anaphylaxis Network (FAN)
Visit this site to learn more about common food allergens.

www.csaceliacs.org
Celiac Sprue Association—National Celiac Disease Support Group
Get information on the Celiac Sprue Association, a national education organization that provides information and referral services for persons with celiac disease.

www.ccfa.org
Crohn's & Colitis Foundation of America
Search this site to learn more about the most recent research, news, and advocacy information for people with ulcerative colitis and Crohn disease.

References

1. Orr, J., and B. Davy. 2005. Dietary influences on peripheral hormones regulating energy intake: potential applications for weight management. *J. Am. Diet. Assoc.* 105:1115–1124.
2. Gardner, S. L., and E. Goldson. 2002. The neonate and the environment: impact on development. In: Merenstein, G. G., and S. L. Gardner, eds. *Handbook of Neonatal Intensive Care*, 5th ed., pp. 219–282. St. Louis: Mosby.
3. Marieb, E., and K. Hoehn. 2007. *Human Anatomy and Physiology*, 7th ed. San Francisco: Benjamin Cummings, p. 582.
4. Kim, D.-Y., M. Camilleri, J. A. Murray, D. A. Stephens, J. A. Levine, and D. D. Burton. 2001. Is there a role for gastric accommodation and satiety in asymptomatic obese people? *Obesity Res.* 9:655–661.
5. Germann, W. J., and C. L. Stanfield. 2005. *Principles of Human Physiology*, 2nd ed. San Francisco: Benjamin Cummings, p. 653.
6. Davidson, N. O. 2003. Intestinal lipid absorption. In: Yamada, T., D. H. Alpers, N. Kaplowitz, L. Laine, C. Owyang, and D. W. Powell, eds. *Textbook of Gastroenterology*, vol. 1. 4th ed. Philadelphia: Lippincott Williams & Wilkins.
7. Bajetta, E., C. Carnaghi, L. Ferrari, I. Spagnoli, V. Mazzaferro, and R. Buzzoni. 1996. The role of somatostatin analogues in the treatment of gastro-enteropancreatic endocrine tumors. *Digestion* 57(Suppl 1):72–76.
8. Farthing, M. J. The role of somatostatin analogues in the treatment of refractory diarrhea. *Digestion* 57(Suppl 1):107–113.
9. Eisenstein, J., and A. Greenberg. 2003. Ghrelin: Update 2003. *Nutr. Rev.* 61(3):101–104.
10. National Digestive Diseases Information Clearinghouse (NDDIC). 2003. Heartburn, hiatal hernia, and gastroesophageal reflux disease (GERD). NIH Publication No. 03–0882. Available online at http://digestive.niddk.nih.gov/ddiseases/pubs/gerd/index.htm.
11. Chan, F. K. L., and W. K. Leung. 2002. Peptic-ulcer disease. *Lancet* 360:933–941.
12. National Digestive Diseases Information Clearinghouse (NDDIC). 2002. H. pylori and peptic ulcer. NIH Publication No. 03–4225. Available online at http://digestive.niddk.nih.gov/ddiseases/pubs/hpylori/index.htm.
13. National Digestive Diseases Information Clearinghouse (NDDIC). 2002. NSAIDs and peptic ulcers. NIH Publication No. 02–4644. Available online at http://digestive.niddk.nih.gov/ddiseases/pubs/nsaids/index.htm.
14. U.S. Food and Drug Administration (FDA). December 20, 2005. FDA to require food manufacturers to list food allergens. *FDA News*. Available online at http://www.fda.gov/bbs/topics/NEWS/2005/NEW01281.html.
15. National Institutes of Health (NIH). June 26, 2008. Celiac disease awareness campaign. Available online at http://celiac.nih.gov/default.aspx.
16. National Institutes of Health (NIH). June 2004. *NIH consensus development conference on celiac disease.* Available online at http://consensus.nih.gov/2004/2004CeliacDisease118html.htm.
17. National Digestive Diseases Information Clearinghouse (NDDIC). 2003. Crohn's disease. NIH Publication No. 03–3410. Available online at http://digestive.niddk.nih.gov/ddiseases/pubs/crohns/index.htm.
18. Crohn's & Colitis Foundation of America (CCFA). 2005. Introduction to ulcerative colitis. Available online at http://www.ccfa.org/research/info/aboutuc.
19. National Digestive Diseases Information Clearinghouse (NDDIC). 2001. Diarrhea. NIH Publication No. 01–2749. Available online at http://digestive.niddk.nih.gov/ddiseases/pubs/diarrhea/index.htm.
20. DuPont, H. L. 2006. New insights and directions in traveler's diarrhea. *Gastroenterol. Clin. N. Am.* 35(2):337–353, viii–ix.
21. Lewis, C. July–August 2001. Irritable bowel syndrome: A poorly understood disorder. *FDA Consumer Magazine*. Available online at http://www.fda.gov/fdac/features/2001/401_ibs.html.
22. Mein, S. M., and U. Ladabaum. Serological testing for coeliac disease in patients with symptoms of irritable bowel syndrome: a cost-effective analysis. *Aliment Phamacol Ther* April 29, 2004 19(11):1199–1210; National Institutes of Health. March 12, 2002. Celiac disease meeting summary. DDICC meeting minutes. Available online at http://digestive.niddk.nih.gov/federal/ddicc/minutes_3-12-02.pdf.
23. National Digestive Diseases Information Clearinghouse (NDDIC). 2003. Irritable bowel syndrome. NIH Publication No. 03–693. Available online at http://digestive.niddk.nih.gov/ddiseases/pubs/ibs/index.htm.
24. Ladewig, P., M. London, and M. Davidson. 2006. *Contemporary Maternal–Newborn Nursing Care*, 6th edn. Upper Saddle River, NJ: Pearson Prentice Hall, p. 655.
25. National Digestive Diseases Information Clearinghouse (NDDIC). October 2005. Celiac disease. NIH Publication No. 06-4269. Available online at http://digestive.niddk.nih.gov.
26. Early, E. 2003. Celiac disease more prevalent in diabetic children. Medical College of Wisconsin. Available online at http://healthlink.mcw.edu/article/1009402816.html.
27. North American Society for Pediatric Gastroenterology, Hepatology, and Nutrition. 2005. Diagnosis and treatment of celiac disease in children: Clinical practice guideline summary. *Journal of Pediatric Gastroenterology and Nutrition* 40(1):1–19. Available online at http://www.naspghan.org.

Should All School-Age Children Be Screened for Celiac Disease?

A *screening test* is a diagnostic procedure that elicits data about the presence or absence of characteristic signs of a disorder. Every baby born in a U.S. hospital undergoes at least two screening tests within the first 48 hours of life.[24] These are for the metabolic disorder phenylketonuria, discussed in Chapter 4, and hypothyroidism, a disorder affecting the thyroid gland. Most school-age children in the United States are also screened for vision and hearing problems, learning disorders, excessive sleepiness, head lice, and other problems. With all this screening going on, should school-age children also be screened for celiac disease?

Researchers and healthcare professionals in favor of screening children for celiac disease point to several factors in support of their position. First, the prevalence in the United States is high enough to be of general concern: about 1% of the U.S. population, or 1 in every 300 Americans, is believed to have celiac disease.[15] This is in line with prevalence rates in Europe, where celiac disease is the most common genetic disease.[16]

In addition, celiac disease is thought to be greatly underdiagnosed. Three reasons for this are the following: many doctors and healthcare providers in the United States are not knowledgeable about celiac disease; only a small number of U.S. laboratories are experienced and skilled in testing for celiac disease; and celiac symptoms can be attributed to other problems.[25] Although in many people celiac disease presents as a "classic" syndrome of diarrhea, weight loss, abdominal bloating, and excessive intestinal gas, the symptoms are in reality highly variable, with some patients experiencing constipation, vomiting, or abdominal pain. In people with neurologic and other non-digestive symptoms, celiac disease may never even be considered without routine, population-wide screening.

Moreover, general screening both in Europe and in limited studies in the United States reveals a significant prevalence of "silent celiac disease"; that is, the individual is not aware of having symptoms, but has a positive antibody test and upon biopsy is shown to have atrophy of the intestinal villi. Although asymptomatic, the intestinal damage in these people puts them at risk for all of the complications of untreated celiac disease. In Italy, where the prevalence of celiac disease is about 1 in 250 people, all children are screened by age 6 so that even asymptomatic disease is caught early.[26] Guidelines for pediatricians from the North American Society for Pediatric Gastroenterology, Hepatology, and Nutrition (NASPGHAN) recommend that all children with type 1 diabetes be screened for celiac disease, as an association between the two diseases has been recognized for some time.[27] A recent U.S. study showed that at least 4.6% of children with type 1 diabetes also have celiac disease.[26] NASPGHAN also recommends that children with Down syndrome be screened.[27] In these children the prevalence is 5% to 12%.[16] In addition, NASPGHAN recommends testing for children with unexplained short stature, delayed puberty, and poor bone density.[27]

Further considerations in favor of routine screening are the potentially serious consequences of a missed diagnosis. In children, short stature results when childhood celiac disease prevents nutrient absorption during the years when nutrition is critical to a child's normal growth and development.[25] Children who are diagnosed and treated before their growth period ends may be able to catch up to the growth of their peers, but after that time, the short stature is irreversible. Other possible consequences of a missed diagnosis include an increased risk of depression, anxiety, learning disorders, epilepsy, autoimmune disorders, type 1 diabetes, thyroid disease, liver disease, poor bone density, and GI cancers.[25]

Finally, a simple blood test that is highly sensitive and specific to antibodies produced

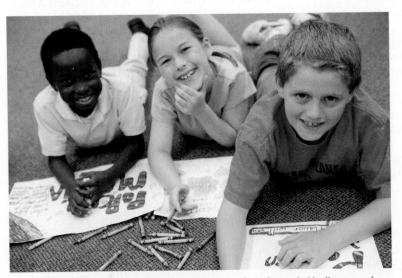

School-age children may have celiac disease and not know it. Undiagnosed celiac disease can lead to a variety of serious health problems as children grow.

A simple blood test can identify celiac disease.

in celiac disease is available. Routine screening would provide a financial incentive for laboratories to make the antibody test more widely available, benefiting all Americans.

Arguments against routine testing center on the invasiveness and questions of reliability of the available tests. Unlike the screening tests for vision, hearing, or head lice, the antibody test for celiac disease is invasive, requiring that the healthcare provider draw a small amount of blood. Some families object to invasive medical tests for religious or other reasons. Second, although the antibody test is considered generally reliable for diagnosing celiac disease, false negatives are not uncommon. Indeed, the reliability of the test for children younger than 5 is controversial.[25] The only definitive proof of celiac disease is via a biopsy of the small intestine that shows atrophy of the villi. Because few people would argue that all children should undergo a biopsy, should routine screening wait until a reliable but noninvasive test is developed?

Another area of controversy exists over the benefit of identifying people with "latent celiac disease," that is, people who test positive with the antibody screen but do not currently have symptoms or any damage to the intestinal villi. Do these people need to go on the highly restrictive gluten-free diet? Because current data do not indicate a clear benefit of a gluten-free diet in people with latent disease, this question is the subject of debate.[16]

Finally, the concept of routine screening itself is a matter of some controversy. While few would argue against simple, low-cost screening tests such as those for vision or hearing problems, some people hesitate when tests become more costly. The United States does not currently require screening of all children for type 1 or type 2 diabetes, obesity, or many other serious health problems, so why should the public be burdened with screening for celiac disease?

In 2004, the National Institutes of Health Consensus Development Conference on Celiac Disease concluded that, at this time, there are insufficient data to recommend routine screening for celiac disease. Instead, the Conference recommended further research into the benefits and cost-effectiveness of screening in the general population. Ongoing with this research, the Conference recommends heightened awareness of the disease; education of physicians, registered dietitians, and other healthcare providers is imperative.[16]

Critical Thinking Questions

■ Now that you've read the arguments for and against routine screening of American children for celiac disease, do you think that all children should have the test? Why or why not?

■ If you said yes, who should pay for it? Parents? School districts? The public health department?

■ Given the number of children who are home-schooled or in private schools, how could we ensure that all families were offered screening?

■ Would you be in favor of routine screening of children for type 2 diabetes, hypertension, obesity, and other disorders?

■ What factors seem most important to consider when deciding which diseases we screen for in American children?

4 Carbohydrates: Plant-Derived Energy Nutrients

Test Yourself | True or False?

1. Carbohydrates are the primary fuel source for the brain and body tissues. **T** *or* **F**

2. Carbohydrates are fattening. **T** *or* **F**

3. Type 2 diabetes is typically seen only in adults. **T** *or* **F**

4. Diets high in sugar cause hyperactivity in children. **T** *or* **F**

5. Alternative sweeteners, such as aspartame, are safe for us to consume. **T** *or* **F**

Test Yourself answers are located in the Chapter Review.

Chapter Objectives *After reading this chapter, you will be able to:*

1. Describe the difference between simple and complex carbohydrates, *pp. 113–116.*

2. Describe the difference between alpha and beta bonds, and discuss how these bonds are related to the digestion of fiber and lactose intolerance, *pp. 115–116.*

3. Compare and contrast soluble and insoluble fibers, *pp. 117–118.*

4. Discuss how carbohydrates are digested and absorbed by the body, *pp. 118–120.*

5. List four functions of carbohydrates in the body, *pp. 124–126*

6. Define the Acceptable Macronutrient Distribution Range for carbohydrates, the Adequate Intake for fiber, and the recommended intake of added sugars, *pp. 128–129.*

7. Identify the potential health risks associated with diets high in simple sugars, *pp. 130–131.*

8. List five foods that are good sources of carbohydrates, *pp. 133–134.*

9. Identify at least three alternative sweeteners, *pp. 136–140.*

10. Describe type 1 and type 2 diabetes, and discuss how diabetes differs from hypoglycemia, *pp. 140–144.*

It was a typical day at a large medical center in the Bronx, New York: two patients were having toes amputated, another had nerve damage, one was being treated for kidney failure, another for infection, and another was blind. Despite their variety, these problems were due to just one disease: diabetes. On an average day, nearly half of the inpatients at the medical center are there because of diabetes. And the problem isn't limited to the Bronx. Every day in the United States, 230 people with diabetes have surgery to remove toes, a foot, or an entire leg; 120 people with diabetes enter the final stage of kidney disease; and 55 go blind. A little over a decade ago, these complications, which typically develop about 10 to 15 years after the onset of the disease, were rarely seen in people younger than age 60. But now, as more and more children are being diagnosed with diabetes, experts are predicting that the typical patient will be more like Iris, one of the patients with diabetes at the Bronx medical center this day. Iris is 26 years old.[1]

What is diabetes, and why are we discussing it in a chapter on carbohydrates? Does the consumption of carbohydrates somehow lead to diabetes—or, for that matter, to obesity or any other disorder? Several popular diets—including the Zone Diet,[2] Sugar Busters,[3] and Dr. Atkins' New Diet Revolution[4]—claim that carbohydrates are bad for your health and advocate reducing **carbohydrate** consumption and increasing protein and fat intake. Are carbohydrates a health menace, and should we reduce our intake? If you noticed that a friend regularly consumed four or five soft drinks a day, plus chips, cookies, candy, and other high-carbohydrate snacks, would you say anything?

In this chapter, we explore the differences between simple and complex carbohydrates and learn why some carbohydrates are better than others. We also learn how the human body breaks down carbohydrates and uses them to maintain our health and to fuel our activity and exercise. Because carbohydrate metabolism sometimes does go wrong, we'll also discuss its relationship to some common health disorders.

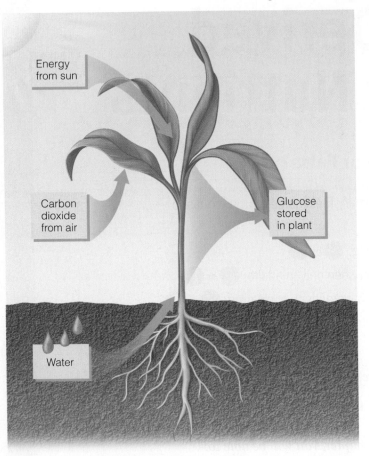

Figure 4.1   Plants make carbohydrates through the process of photosynthesis. Water, carbon dioxide, and energy from the sun are combined to produce glucose.

carbohydrate   One of the three macronutrients, a compound made up of carbon, hydrogen, and oxygen that is derived from plants and provides energy.

glucose   The most abundant sugar molecule, a monosaccharide generally found in combination with other sugars; the preferred source of energy for the brain and an important source of energy for all cells.

photosynthesis   A process by which plants use sunlight to fuel a chemical reaction that combines carbon and water into glucose, which is then stored in their cells.

What Are Carbohydrates?

As we mentioned in Chapter 1, carbohydrates are one of the three macronutrients. As such, they are an important energy source for the entire body and are the preferred energy source for nerve cells, including those of the brain. We will say more about their functions later in this chapter.

The term *carbohydrate* literally means "hydrated carbon." Water (H_2O) is made of hydrogen and oxygen, and when something is said to be *hydrated*, it contains water. Thus, the chemical abbreviation for carbohydrate (CHO) indicates the atoms it contains: carbon, hydrogen, and oxygen.

We obtain carbohydrates predominantly from plant foods such as fruits, vegetables, and grains. Plants make the most abundant form of carbohydrate, called **glucose,** through a process called **photosynthesis.** During photosynthesis, the green pigment of plants, called *chlorophyll,* absorbs sunlight, which provides the energy needed to fuel the manufacture of glucose. As shown in **Figure 4.1**, water absorbed from the earth by the roots of plants combines with carbon dioxide present in the leaves to produce the carbohydrate glucose. Plants continually store glucose and use it to support their own growth. Then, when we eat plant foods, our bodies digest, absorb, and use the stored glucose.

What's the Difference Between Simple and Complex Carbohydrates?

Carbohydrates can be classified as *simple* or *complex*. Simple carbohydrates contain either one or two molecules, whereas complex carbohydrates contain hundreds to thousands of molecules.

Simple Carbohydrates Include Monosaccharides and Disaccharides

Simple carbohydrates are commonly referred to as *sugars*. Four of these sugars are called **monosaccharides** because they consist of a single sugar molecule (*mono*, meaning "one," and *saccharide*, meaning "sugar"). The other three sugars are **disaccharides**, which consist of two molecules of sugar joined together (*di*, meaning "two").

Glucose, Fructose, Galactose, and Ribose Are Monosaccharides

Glucose, fructose, and *galactose* are the three most common monosaccharides in our diet. Each of these monosaccharides contains 6 carbon atoms, 12 hydrogen atoms, and 6 oxygen atoms (**Figure 4.2**). Very slight differences in the structure of these three monosaccharides cause major differences in their level of sweetness.

Given what you've just learned about how plants manufacture glucose, it probably won't surprise you to discover that glucose is the most abundant monosaccharide found in our diets and in our bodies. Glucose does not generally occur by itself in foods but attaches to other sugars to form disaccharides and complex carbohydrates. In our bodies, glucose is the preferred source of energy for the brain, and it is a very important source of energy for all cells.

Fructose, the sweetest natural sugar, occurs naturally in fruits and vegetables. Fructose is also called *levulose*, or *fruit sugar*. In many processed foods, it is a component of *high-fructose corn syrup*. This syrup is made from corn and is used to sweeten soft drinks, desserts, candies, and jellies.

Galactose does not occur alone in foods. It joins with glucose to create lactose, one of the three most common disaccharides.

Ribose is a five-carbon monosaccharide. Very little ribose is found in our diets; our bodies produce ribose from the foods we eat, and ribose is contained in the genetic material of our cells: deoxyribonucleic acid (DNA) and ribonucleic acid (RNA).

In our bodies, glucose is the preferred source of energy for the brain.

simple carbohydrate Commonly called *sugar*; a monosaccharide or disaccharide such as glucose.

monosaccharide The simplest of carbohydrates. Consists of one sugar molecule, the most common form of which is glucose.

disaccharide A carbohydrate compound consisting of two monosaccharide molecules joined together.

fructose The sweetest natural sugar; a monosaccharide that occurs in fruits and vegetables; also called *levulose*, or *fruit sugar*.

galactose A monosaccharide that joins with glucose to create lactose, one of the three most common disaccharides.

ribose A five-carbon monosaccharide that is located in the genetic material of cells.

Monosaccharides		
Glucose	**Fructose**	**Galactose**
Most abundant sugar molecule in our diet; good energy source	Sweetest natural sugar; found in fruit, high-fructose corn syrup	Does not occur alone in foods; binds with glucose to form lactose

Figure 4.2 The three most common monosaccharides. Notice that all three monosaccharides contain identical atoms: 6 carbon, 12 hydrogen, and 6 oxygen. It is only the arrangement of these atoms that differs.

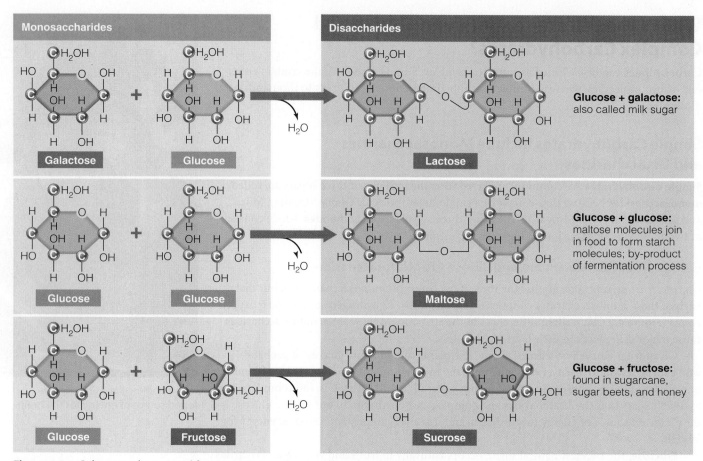

Figure 4.3   Galactose, glucose, and fructose join together in different combinations to make the disaccharides lactose, maltose, and sucrose.

Lactose, Maltose, and Sucrose Are Disaccharides

The three most common disaccharides found in foods are *lactose, maltose,* and *sucrose* (**Figure 4.3**). **Lactose** (also called *milk sugar*) consists of one glucose molecule and one galactose molecule. Interestingly, human breast milk has a higher amount of lactose than cow's milk, which makes human breast milk taste sweeter.

Maltose (also called *malt sugar*) consists of two molecules of glucose. It does not generally occur by itself in foods but rather is bound together with other molecules. As our bodies break these larger molecules down, maltose results as a by-product. Maltose is also the sugar that results from *fermentation* during the production of beer and liquor products. **Fermentation** is the anaerobic process in which an agent, such as yeast, causes an organic substance to break down into simpler substances and results in the production of adenosine triphosphate (ATP). Thus, maltose is formed during the anaerobic breakdown of sugar into alcohol. Contrary to popular belief, very little maltose remains in alcoholic beverages after the fermentation process; thus, alcoholic beverages are not good sources of carbohydrate.

Sucrose is composed of one glucose molecule and one fructose molecule. Because sucrose contains fructose, it is sweeter than lactose or maltose. Sucrose provides much of the sweet taste found in honey, maple syrup, fruits, and vegetables. Table sugar, brown sugar, powdered sugar, and many other products are made by refining the sucrose found in sugarcane and sugar beets. You will learn more about the different forms of sucrose commonly used in foods later in this chapter. Are honey and other naturally occurring forms of sucrose more healthful than manufactured forms? The Nutrition Myth or Fact? box investigates this question.

lactose   Also called *milk sugar,* a disaccharide consisting of one glucose molecule and one galactose molecule; found in milk, including human breast milk.

maltose   A disaccharide consisting of two molecules of glucose; does not generally occur independently in foods but results as a by-product of digestion; also called *malt sugar.*

fermentation   The anaerobic process in which an agent causes an organic substance to break down into simpler substances and results in the production of ATP.

sucrose   A disaccharide composed of one glucose molecule and one fructose molecule; sweeter than lactose or maltose.

Nutrition Myth or Fact?
Is Honey More Nutritious Than Table Sugar?

Liz's friend Tiffany is dedicated to eating healthful foods. She advises Liz to avoid sucrose and to eat foods that contain honey, molasses, or raw sugar. Like many people, Tiffany believes these sweeteners are more natural and nutritious than refined table sugar. How can Liz sort sugar fact from fiction?

Remember that sucrose consists of one glucose molecule and one fructose molecule joined together. From a chemical perspective, honey is almost identical to sucrose, because honey also contains glucose and fructose molecules in almost equal amounts. However, enzymes in bees'"honey stomachs" separate some of the glucose and fructose molecules, resulting in honey looking and tasting slightly different from sucrose. As you know, bees store honey in combs and fan it with their wings to reduce its moisture content. This also alters the appearance and texture of honey.

Honey does not contain any more nutrients than sucrose, so it is not a more healthful choice than sucrose. In fact, per tablespoon, honey has more calories (or energy) than table sugar. This is because the crystals in table sugar take up more space on a spoon than the liquid form of honey, so a tablespoon contains less sugar. However, some people argue that honey is sweeter, so you use less.

It is important to note that honey commonly contains bacteria that can cause fatal food poisoning in infants. The more mature digestive system of older children and adults is immune to the effects of these bacteria, but babies younger than 12 months should never be given honey.

Are raw sugar and molasses more healthful than table sugar? Actually, the "raw sugar" available in the United States is not really raw. Truly raw sugar is made up of the first crystals obtained when sugar is processed. Sugar in this form contains dirt, parts of insects, and other by-products that make it illegal to sell in the United States. The raw sugar products in American stores have actually gone through more than half of the same steps in the refining process used to make table sugar. Raw sugar has a more coarse tex-

ture than white sugar and is unbleached; in most markets it is also significantly more expensive.

Molasses is the syrup that remains when sucrose is made from sugarcane. It is reddish brown in color, with a distinctive taste that is less sweet than table sugar. It does contain some iron, but this iron does not occur naturally. It is a contaminant from the machines that process the sugarcane! Incidentally, blackstrap molasses is the residue of a third boiling of the syrup. It contains less sugar than light or dark molasses but more minerals.

Table 4.1 compares the nutrient content of white sugar, honey, blackstrap molasses, and raw sugar. As you can see, none of them contains many nutrients that are important for health. This is why highly sweetened products are referred to as "empty calories."

Table 4.1 Nutrient Comparison of Four Different Sugars

	Table Sugar	Raw Sugar	Honey	Molasses
Energy (kcal)	49	49	64	58
Carbohydrate (g)	12.6	12.6	17.3	14.95
Fat (g)	0	0	0	0
Protein (g)	0	0	0.06	0
Fiber (g)	0	0	0	0
Vitamin C (mg)	0	0	0.1	0
Vitamin A (IU)	0	0	0	0
Thiamin (mg)	0	0	0	0.008
Riboflavin (mg)	0.002	0.003	0.008	0
Folate (µg)	0	0	0	0
Calcium (mg)	0	0.042	1	41
Iron (mg)	0	0	0.09	0.94
Sodium (mg)	0	0	1	7
Potassium (mg)	0	0.25	11	293

Note: Nutrient values are identified for 1 tablespoon of each product.

Data from: U.S. Department of Agriculture, Agricultural Research Service. 2008. USDA national nutrient database for standard reference, release 21. Available online at http://www.nal.usda.gov/fnic/foodcomp.

The two monosaccharides that compose a disaccharide are attached by a bond between oxygen and one carbon on each of the monosaccharides (**Figure 4.4**). Two forms of this bond occur in nature: an **alpha bond** and a **beta bond.** As you can see in Figure 4.4a, sucrose is produced by an alpha bond joining a glucose molecule and a fructose molecule. The disaccharide maltose is also produced by an alpha bond. In contrast, lactose is

alpha bond A type of chemical bond that can be digested by enzymes found in the human intestine.

beta bond A type of chemical bond that cannot be easily digested by enzymes found in the human intestine.

(a)

(b)

Figure 4.4 The two monosaccharides that compose a disaccharide are attached by either an **(a)** alpha bond or **(b)** beta bond between oxygen and one carbon of each monosaccharide.

produced by a beta bond joining a glucose molecule and a galactose molecule (see Figure 4.4b). Alpha bonds are easily digestible by humans, whereas beta bonds are very difficult to digest and may even be non-digestible. As you will learn later in this chapter, many people do not possess enough of the enzyme lactase that is needed to break the beta bond present in lactose, which causes the condition referred to as *lactose intolerance*. Beta bonds are also present in high-fiber foods, leading to our inability to digest most forms of fiber.

RECAP

Carbohydrates contain carbon, hydrogen, and oxygen. Simple carbohydrates include monosaccharides and disaccharides. Glucose, fructose, galactose, and ribose are monosaccharides; lactose, maltose, and sucrose are disaccharides. In disaccharides, two monosaccharides are linked together with either an alpha bond or a beta bond. Alpha bonds are easily digestible by humans, whereas beta bonds are not easily digestible.

Complex Carbohydrates Include Oligosaccharides and Polysaccharides

Complex carbohydrates, the second major classification of carbohydrate, generally consist of long chains of glucose molecules. Technically, any carbohydrates with three or more monosaccharides are considered complex carbohydrates.

Oligosaccharides are carbohydrates that contain 3 to 10 monosaccharides (*oligo,* meaning "few"). Two of the most common oligosaccharides found in our diets are **raffinose** and **stachyose.** Raffinose is composed of galactose, glucose, and fructose. It is commonly found in beans, cabbage, brussels sprouts, broccoli, and whole grains. Stachyose is composed of two galactose molecules, a glucose molecule, and a fructose molecule. It is found in many beans and legumes.

Raffinose and stachyose are part of the raffinose family of oligosaccharides (RFOs).[5] Because humans do not possess the enzyme needed to break down these RFOs, they pass into the large intestine undigested. Once they reach the large intestine, they are fermented by bacteria that produce gases such as carbon dioxide, methane, and hydrogen. The product Beano® contains the enzyme alpha-galactosidase; this is the enzyme needed to break down the RFOs in the intestinal tract. Thus, this product can help to reduce the intestinal gas caused by eating beans and various vegetables.

Most **polysaccharides** consist of hundreds to thousands of glucose molecules (*poly,* meaning "many").[5] The polysaccharides include starch, glycogen, and most fibers (**Figure 4.5**).

Starch Is a Polysaccharide Stored in Plants

Plants store glucose not as single molecules but as polysaccharides in the form of **starch.** The two forms of starch are amylose and amylopectin (see Figure 4.5). Amylose is a straight chain of glucose molecules, whereas amylopectin is highly branched. Both forms of starch are found in starch-containing foods. The more open-branched structure of amylopectin increases its surface area and thus its exposure to digestive enzymes, resulting in it being more rapidly digested than amylose, which in turn results in amylopectin raising blood glucose more quickly than amylose.

Excellent food sources of starch include grains (wheat, rice, corn, oats, and barley), legumes (peas, beans, and lentils), and tubers (potatoes and yams). Our cells cannot use the complex starch molecules exactly as they occur in plants. Instead, the body must

complex carbohydrate A nutrient compound consisting of long chains of glucose molecules, such as starch, glycogen, and fiber.

oligosaccharides Complex carbohydrates that contain 3 to 10 monosaccharides.

raffinose An oligosaccharide composed of galactose, glucose, and fructose. Also called melitose, it is found in beans, cabbage, broccoli, and other vegetables.

stachyose An oligosaccharide composed of two galactose molecules, a glucose molecule, and a fructose molecule. Found in the Chinese artichoke and various beans and legumes.

polysaccharide A complex carbohydrate consisting of long chains of glucose.

starch A polysaccharide stored in plants; the storage form of glucose in plants.

break them down into the monosaccharide glucose, from which we can then fuel our energy needs.

Our bodies easily digest most starches, in which alpha bonds link the numerous glucose units; however, starches linked by beta bonds are largely indigestible and are called *resistant*. Technically, resistant starch is classified as a type of fiber. When our intestinal bacteria ferment resistant starch, a short-chain fatty acid called *butyrate* is produced. Consuming resistant starch may be beneficial: some research suggests that butyrate reduces the risk of cancer.[6] Legumes contain more resistant starch than do grains, fruits, or vegetables. This quality, plus their high protein and fiber content, makes legumes a healthful food.

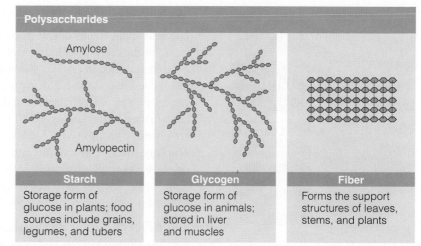

Figure 4.5 Polysaccharides, also referred to as complex carbohydrates, include starch, glycogen, and fiber.

Glycogen Is a Polysaccharide Stored by Animals

Glycogen is the storage form of glucose for animals, including humans. After an animal is slaughtered, most of the glycogen is broken down by enzymes found in animal tissues. Thus, very little glycogen exists in meat. As plants contain no glycogen, it is not a dietary source of carbohydrate. We can very quickly break down the glycogen stored in the body into glucose when we need it for energy. We store glycogen in our muscles and liver; the storage and use of glycogen are discussed in more detail on page 120.

Fiber Is a Polysaccharide That Gives Plants Their Structure

Like starch, fiber is composed of long polysaccharide chains; however, the body does not easily break down the bonds that connect fiber molecules. This means that most fibers pass through the digestive system without being digested and absorbed, so they contribute no energy to our diet. However, fiber offers many other health benefits (see page 126).

There are currently a number of definitions of fiber. Recently, the Food and Nutrition Board of the Institute of Medicine proposed three distinctions: *dietary fiber, functional fiber,* and *total fiber*.[5]

Tubers, such as these sweet potatoes, are excellent food sources of starch.

- **Dietary fiber** is the non-digestible parts of plants that form the support structures of leaves, stems, and seeds (see Figure 4.5). In a sense, you can think of dietary fiber as the plant's "skeleton."
- **Functional fiber** consists of non-digestible forms of carbohydrates that are extracted from plants or manufactured in a laboratory and have known health benefits. Functional fiber is added to foods and is the form found in fiber supplements. Examples of functional fiber sources you might see on nutrition labels include cellulose, guar gum, pectin, and psyllium.
- **Total fiber** is the sum of dietary fiber and functional fiber.

Fiber can also be classified according to its chemical and physical properties as soluble or insoluble.

Soluble Fibers   **Soluble fibers** dissolve in water. They are also **viscous,** forming a gel when wet, and they are fermentable; that is, they are easily digested by bacteria in the colon. Soluble fibers are typically found in citrus fruits, berries, oat products, and beans.

Research suggests that regular consumption of soluble fibers reduces the risks for cardiovascular disease and type 2 diabetes by lowering blood cholesterol and blood glucose levels. The possible mechanisms by which fiber reduces the risk for various diseases are discussed in more detail on pages 126–127.

glycogen A polysaccharide stored in animals; the storage form of glucose in animals.

dietary fiber The non-digestible carbohydrate parts of plants that form the support structures of leaves, stems, and seeds.

functional fiber The non-digestible forms of carbohydrate that are extracted from plants or manufactured in the laboratory and have known health benefits.

total fiber The sum of dietary fiber and functional fiber.

soluble fibers Fibers that dissolve in water.

viscous Term referring to a gel-like consistency; viscous fibers form a gel when dissolved in water.

Dissolvable laxatives are examples of soluble fiber.

Examples of soluble fibers include the following:

- *Pectins* contain chains of galacturonic acid and other monosaccharides. Pectins are found in the cell walls and intracellular tissues of many fruits and berries. They can be isolated and used to thicken foods such as jams and yogurts.
- *Gums* contain galactose, glucuronic acid, and other monosaccharides. Gums are a diverse group of polysaccharides that are viscous. They are typically isolated from seeds and are used as thickening, gelling, and stabilizing agents. Guar gum and gum arabic are common gums used as food additives.
- *Mucilages* are similar to gums and contain galactose, mannose, and other monosaccharides. Two examples include psyllium and carrageenan. Psyllium is the husk of psyllium seeds, which are also known as plantago or flea seeds. Carrageenan comes from seaweed. Mucilages are used as food stabilizers.

Insoluble Fibers   **Insoluble fibers** are those that do not typically dissolve in water. These fibers are usually nonviscous and cannot be fermented by bacteria in the colon. They are generally found in whole grains such as wheat, rye, and brown rice and are also found in many vegetables. These fibers are not associated with reducing cholesterol levels but are known for promoting regular bowel movements, alleviating constipation, and reducing the risk for a bowel disorder called diverticulosis (discussed later in this chapter). Examples of insoluble fibers include the following:

- *Lignins* are noncarbohydrate forms of fiber. Lignins are found in the woody parts of plant cell walls and are found in carrots and in the seeds of fruits and berries. Lignins are also found in brans (or the outer husk of grains such as wheat, oats, and rye) and other whole grains.
- *Cellulose* is the main structural component of plant cell walls. Cellulose is a chain of glucose units similar to amylose, but unlike amylose, cellulose contains beta bonds that are non-digestible by humans. Cellulose is found in whole grains, fruits, vegetables, and legumes. It can also be extracted from wood pulp or cotton, and it is added to foods as an agent for anti-caking, thickening, and texturizing of foods.
- *Hemicelluloses* contain glucose, mannose, galacturonic acid, and other monosaccharides. Hemicelluloses are found in plant cell walls and they surround cellulose. They are the primary component of cereal fibers and are found in whole grains and vegetables. Although many hemicelluloses are insoluble, some are also classified as soluble.

RᴇCᴀP

Complex carbohydrates include oligosaccharides and polysaccharides. The three types of polysaccharides are starch, glycogen, and fiber. Starch is the storage form of glucose in plants, while glycogen is the storage form of glucose in animals. Fiber forms the support structures of plants. Soluble fibers dissolve in water, are viscous, and can be digested by bacteria in the colon, whereas insoluble fibers do not dissolve in water, are not viscous, and cannot be digested.

How Do Our Bodies Break Down Carbohydrates?

Glucose is the form of sugar that our bodies use for energy, and the primary goal of carbohydrate digestion is to break down polysaccharides and disaccharides into monosaccharides that can then be converted to glucose. Chapter 3 provided an overview of digestion of the three types of macronutrients, as well as vitamins and minerals. Here, we focus specifically and in more detail on the digestion and absorption of carbohydrates. **Figure 4.6** provides a visual tour of carbohydrate digestion.

insoluble fibers   Fibers that do not dissolve in water.

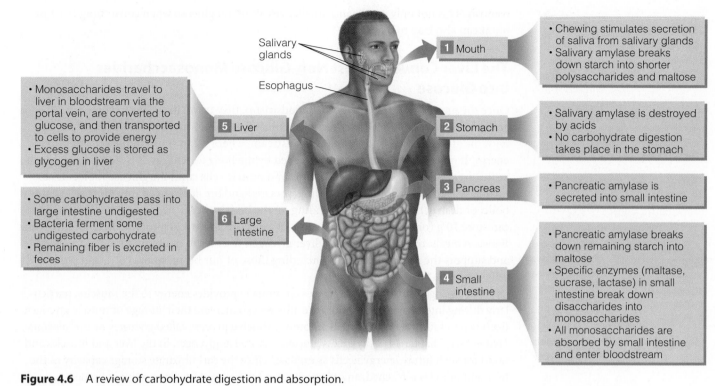

- Monosaccharides travel to liver in bloodstream via the portal vein, are converted to glucose, and then transported to cells to provide energy
- Excess glucose is stored as glycogen in liver

5 Liver

- Some carbohydrates pass into large intestine undigested
- Bacteria ferment some undigested carbohydrate
- Remaining fiber is excreted in feces

6 Large intestine

Salivary glands

Esophagus

1 Mouth
- Chewing stimulates secretion of saliva from salivary glands
- Salivary amylase breaks down starch into shorter polysaccharides and maltose

2 Stomach
- Salivary amylase is destroyed by acids
- No carbohydrate digestion takes place in the stomach

3 Pancreas
- Pancreatic amylase is secreted into small intestine

4 Small intestine
- Pancreatic amylase breaks down remaining starch into maltose
- Specific enzymes (maltase, sucrase, lactase) in small intestine break down disaccharides into monosaccharides
- All monosaccharides are absorbed by small intestine and enter bloodstream

Figure 4.6   A review of carbohydrate digestion and absorption.

Digestion Breaks Down Most Carbohydrates into Monosaccharides

Carbohydrate digestion begins in the mouth (Figure 4.6, step 1). As you saw in Chapter 3, the starch in the foods you eat mixes with your saliva during chewing. Saliva contains an enzyme called **salivary amylase,** which breaks down starch into smaller particles and eventually into the disaccharide maltose. The next time you eat a piece of bread, notice that you can actually taste it becoming sweeter; this indicates the breakdown of starch into maltose. Disaccharides are not digested in the mouth.

As the bolus of food leaves the mouth and enters the stomach, all digestion of carbohydrates ceases. This is because the acid in the stomach inactivates the salivary amylase enzyme (Figure 4.6, step 2).

The majority of carbohydrate digestion occurs in the small intestine. As the contents of the stomach enter the small intestine, an enzyme called *pancreatic amylase* is secreted by the pancreas into the small intestine (Figure 4.6, step 3). **Pancreatic amylase** continues to digest any remaining starch into maltose. Additional enzymes found in the microvilli of the mucosal cells that line the intestinal tract work to break down disaccharides into monosaccharides. Maltose is broken down into glucose by the enzyme **maltase.** Sucrose is broken down into glucose and fructose by the enzyme **sucrase.** The enzyme **lactase** breaks down lactose into glucose and galactose (Figure 4.6, step 4). Enzyme names are identifiable by the suffix *-ase.*

Once digestion of carbohydrates is complete, all monosaccharides are then absorbed into the mucosal cells lining the small intestine, where they pass through and enter into the bloodstream. Glucose and galactose are absorbed across the enterocytes via active transport using a carrier protein saturated with sodium. This process requires energy from the breakdown of ATP. Fructose is absorbed via facilitated diffusion and therefore requires no energy. (Refer back to Chapter 3 for a description of these transport processes.) The absorption of fructose takes longer than that of glucose or galactose. This slower absorption rate means that fructose stays in the small intestine longer and draws water into the intestines via

salivary amylase   An enzyme in saliva that breaks starch into smaller particles and eventually into the disaccharide maltose.

pancreatic amylase   An enzyme secreted by the pancreas into the small intestine that digests any remaining starch into maltose.

maltase   A digestive enzyme that breaks maltose into glucose.

sucrase   A digestive enzyme that breaks sucrose into glucose and fructose.

lactase   A digestive enzyme that breaks lactose into glucose and galactose.

osmosis. This not only results in a smaller rise in blood glucose when consuming fructose, but it can also lead to diarrhea.

The Liver Converts Most Non-Glucose Monosaccharides into Glucose

Once the monosaccharides enter the bloodstream, they travel to the liver, where fructose and galactose are converted to glucose (Figure 4.6, step 5). If needed immediately for energy, the glucose is released into the bloodstream, where it can travel to the cells to provide energy. If glucose is not immediately needed by the body for energy, it is stored as glycogen in the liver and muscles. Enzymes in liver and muscle cells combine glucose molecules to form glycogen (an anabolic, or building, process) and break glycogen into glucose (a catabolic, or destructive, process), depending on the body's energy needs. On average, the liver can store 70 g (or 280 kcal) and the muscles can store about 120 g (or 480 kcal) of glycogen. Between meals, our bodies draw on liver glycogen reserves to maintain blood glucose levels and support the needs of our cells, including those of our brain, spinal cord, and red blood cells (**Figure 4.7**).

The glycogen stored in our muscles continually provides energy to the muscles, particularly during intense exercise. Endurance athletes can increase their storage of muscle glycogen from two to four times the normal amount through a process called *glycogen*, or *carbohydrate*, *loading* (see Chapter 14). Any excess glucose is stored as glycogen in the liver and muscles and saved for such future energy needs as exercise. Once the carbohydrate storage capacity of the liver and muscles is reached, any excess glucose can be stored as fat in adipose tissue.

Fiber Is Excreted from the Large Intestine

As previously mentioned, humans do not possess enzymes in the small intestine that can break down fiber. Thus, fiber passes through the small intestine undigested and enters the large intestine, or colon. There, bacteria ferment some previously undigested carbohydrates, causing the production of gases such as hydrogen, methane, and sulfur and a few short-chain fatty acids such as acetic acid, butyric acid, and propionic acid. The cells of the large intestine use these short-chain fatty acids for energy. It is estimated that fermented fibers yield about 1.5 to 2.5 kcal/g.[5,6] This is less than the 4 kcal/g provided by carbohydrates that are digested

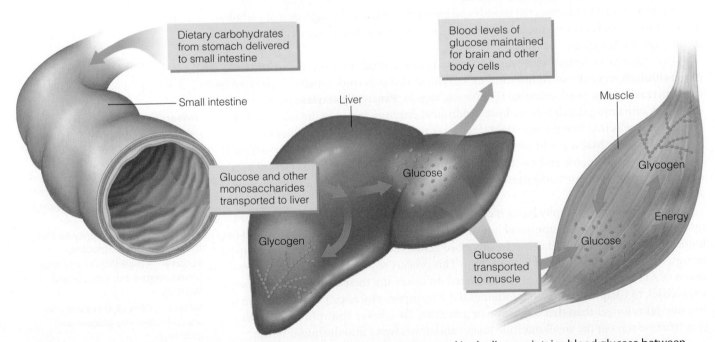

Figure 4.7 Glucose is stored as glycogen in both liver and muscle. The glycogen stored in the liver maintains blood glucose between meals; muscle glycogen provides immediate energy to the muscle during exercise.

and absorbed in the small intestine; the discrepancy is due to the fact that fermentation of the fibers in the colon is an anaerobic process, which yields less energy than the aerobic digestive process of other carbohydrates. Obviously, the fibers that remain totally undigested contribute no energy to our bodies. Fiber remaining in the colon adds bulk to our stools and is excreted in feces (Figure 4.6, step 6). In this way, fiber assists in maintaining bowel regularity. The health benefits of fiber are discussed later in this chapter (pages 126–128).

A Variety of Hormones Regulate Blood Glucose Levels

Our bodies regulate blood glucose levels within a fairly narrow range to provide adequate glucose to the brain and other cells. A number of hormones, including insulin, glucagon, epinephrine, norepinephrine, cortisol, and growth hormone, assist the body with maintaining blood glucose.

When we eat a meal, our blood glucose level rises. But glucose in our blood cannot help the nerves, muscles, and other tissues to function unless it can cross into their cells. Glucose molecules are too large to cross the cell membranes of our tissues independently. To get in, glucose needs assistance from the hormone **insulin,** which is secreted by the beta cells of the pancreas (**Figure 4.8a**). Insulin is transported in the blood to the cells of tissues throughout the body, where it stimulates special carrier proteins, called *glucose transporters,* located in cells. The arrival of insulin at the cell membrane stimulates glucose transporters to travel to the surface of the cell, where they assist in transporting glucose across the cell membrane and into the cell. Insulin can thus be thought of as a key that opens the gates of the cell membrane, enabling the transport of glucose into the cell interior, where it can be used for energy. Insulin also stimulates the liver and muscles to take up glucose and store it as glycogen.

When you have not eaten for some period of time, your blood glucose level declines. This decrease in blood glucose stimulates the alpha cells of the pancreas to secrete another hormone, **glucagon** (Figure 4.8b). Glucagon acts in an opposite way to insulin: it causes the liver to convert its stored glycogen into glucose, which is then secreted into the bloodstream and transported to the cells for energy. Glucagon also assists in the breakdown of body proteins to amino acids so the liver can stimulate **gluconeogenesis** (or "generating new glucose"), the production of glucose from amino acids.

Epinephrine, norepinephrine, cortisol, and growth hormone are additional hormones that work to increase blood glucose. Epinephrine and norepinephrine are secreted by the adrenal glands and nerve endings when blood glucose levels are low. They act to increase glycogen breakdown in the liver, resulting in a subsequent increase in the release of glucose into the bloodstream. They also increase gluconeogenesis. These two hormones are also responsible for our "fight or flight" reaction to danger; they are released when we need a burst of energy to respond quickly. Cortisol and growth hormone are secreted by the adrenal glands to act upon liver, muscle, and adipose tissue. Cortisol increases gluconeogenesis and decreases the use of glucose by muscles and other body organs. Growth hormone decreases glucose uptake by the muscles, increases our mobilization and use of fatty acids stored in our adipose tissue, and also increases the liver's output of glucose.

Normally, the effects of these hormones balance each other to maintain blood glucose within a healthy range. If this balance is altered, it can lead to health conditions such as diabetes (pages 140–144) or hypoglycemia (pages 144–145).

RECAP

Carbohydrate digestion starts in the mouth and continues in the small intestine. Glucose and other monosaccharides are absorbed into the bloodstream and travel to the liver, where non-glucose monosaccharides are converted to glucose. Glucose is either used by the cells for energy, converted to glycogen and stored in the liver and muscles for later use, or converted to fat and stored in adipose tissue. Various hormones are involved in regulating blood glucose. Insulin lowers blood glucose levels by facilitating the entry of glucose into cells. Glucagon, epinephrine, norepinephrine, cortisol, and growth hormone raise blood glucose levels by a variety of mechanisms.

insulin Hormone secreted by the beta cells of the pancreas in response to increased blood levels of glucose; facilitates uptake of glucose by body cells.

glucagon Hormone secreted by the alpha cells of the pancreas in response to decreased blood levels of glucose; causes breakdown of liver stores of glycogen into glucose.

gluconeogenesis The generation of glucose from the breakdown of proteins into amino acids.

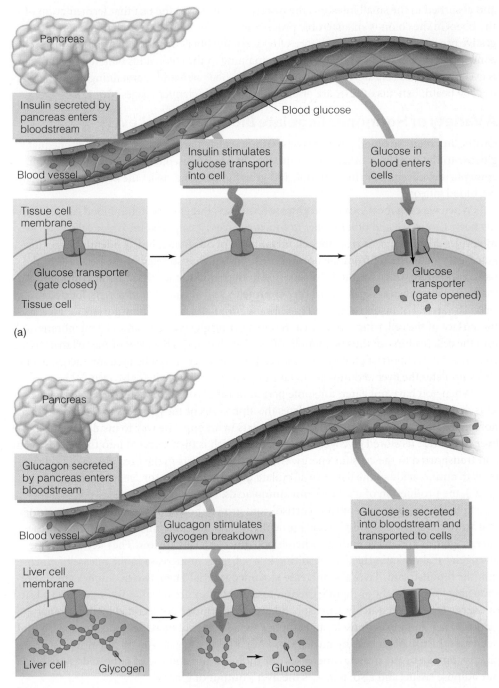

Figure 4.8 Regulation of blood glucose by the hormones insulin and glucagon. **(a)** When blood glucose levels increase after a meal, the pancreas secretes insulin. Insulin opens gates in the cell membranes of body tissues to allow the passage of glucose into the cell. **(b)** When blood glucose levels are low, the pancreas secretes glucagon. Glucagon enters the cell, where it stimulates the breakdown of stored glycogen into glucose. This glucose is then released into the bloodstream.

The Glycemic Index Shows How Foods Affect Our Blood Glucose Levels

glycemic index Rating of the potential of foods to raise blood glucose and insulin levels.

The **glycemic index** refers to the potential of foods to raise blood glucose levels. Foods with a high glycemic index cause a sudden surge in blood glucose. This in turn triggers a large increase in insulin, which may be followed by a dramatic drop in blood glucose. Foods with a low glycemic index cause low to moderate fluctuations in blood glucose. When foods are assigned a glycemic index value, they are often compared with the glycemic effect of pure glucose.

The glycemic index of a food is not always easy to predict. **Figure 4.9** ranks certain foods according to their glycemic index. Do any of these rankings surprise you? Most people assume that foods containing simple sugars have a higher glycemic index than starches, but this is not always the case. For instance, compare the glycemic index for apples and instant potatoes. Although instant potatoes are a starchy food, they have a glycemic index value of 83, while the value for an apple is only 36!

An apple has a much lower glycemic index (36) than a serving of white rice (56).

The type of carbohydrate, the way the food is prepared, and its fat and fiber content can all affect how quickly the body absorbs it. It is important to note that we eat most of our foods combined into a meal. In this case, the glycemic index of the total meal becomes more important than the ranking of each food.

For determining the effect of a food on a person's glucose response, some nutrition experts believe the **glycemic load** is more useful than the glycemic index. The glycemic load of a food is the total grams of carbohydrate it contains multiplied by the glycemic index of that particular carbohydrate. For instance, carrots are recognized as a vegetable having a relatively high glycemic index of about 68; however, the glycemic load of carrots is only 3.[7] This is because there is very little total carbohydrate in a serving of carrots. The low glycemic load of carrots means that carrot consumption is unlikely to cause a significant rise in glucose and insulin.

Why do we care about the glycemic index and glycemic load? Foods or meals with a lower glycemic load are a better choice for someone with diabetes because they will not

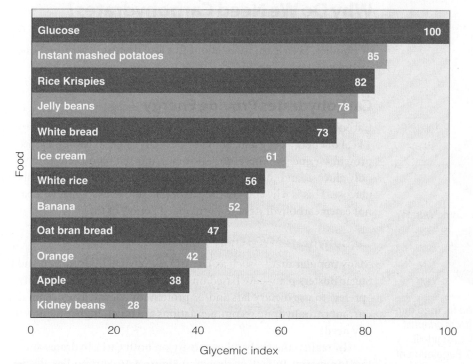

Figure 4.9 Glycemic index values for various foods as compared to pure glucose. (*Data adapted from:* Foster-Powell, K., S. H. A. Holt, and J. C. Brand-Miller. 2002. International table of glycemic index and glycemic load values. *Am. J. Clin. Nutr.* 76:5–56.)

glycemic load The amount of carbohydrate in a food multiplied by the glycemic index of the carbohydrate.

trigger dramatic fluctuations in blood glucose. They may also reduce the risk of heart disease and colon cancer because they generally contain more fiber, and it is known that fiber helps decrease fat levels in the blood. Recent studies have shown that people who eat lower-glycemic-index diets have higher levels of high-density lipoprotein, or HDL (a healthful blood lipid), and lower levels of low-density lipoprotein, or LDL (a blood lipid associated with increased risk for heart disease), and their blood glucose values are more likely to be normal.[8–10] Diets with a low glycemic index and load are also associated with a reduced risk for prostate cancer.[11] Despite some encouraging research findings, the glycemic index and glycemic load remain controversial. Many nutrition researchers feel that the evidence supporting their health benefits is weak. In addition, many believe the concepts of the glycemic index/load are too complex for people to apply to their daily lives. Other researchers insist that helping people to choose foods with a lower glycemic index/load is critical to the prevention and treatment of many chronic diseases. Until this controversy is resolved, people are encouraged to eat a variety of fiber-rich and less-processed carbohydrates such as beans and lentils, fresh vegetables, and whole-wheat bread, because we know these forms of carbohydrates are lower in glycemic load and they also contain a multitude of important nutrients.

Our red blood cells can use only glucose and other monosaccharides, and the brain and other nervous tissues primarily rely on glucose. This is why you get tired, irritable, and shaky when you have not eaten for a prolonged period of time.

RECAP

The glycemic index is a value that indicates the potential of foods to raise blood glucose and insulin levels. The glycemic load is the amount of carbohydrate in a food multiplied by the glycemic index of the carbohydrate in that food. Foods with a high glycemic index/load cause sudden surges in blood glucose and insulin, whereas foods with a low glycemic index/load cause low to moderate fluctuations in blood glucose. Diets with a low glycemic index/load are associated with a reduced risk for chronic diseases such as cardiovascular disease, type 2 diabetes, and prostate cancer.

Figure 4.10 Amounts of carbohydrate and fat used during light, moderate, and intense exercise. (*Data adapted from:* Romijn, J. A., E. F. Coyle, L. S. Sidossis, A. Gastaldelli, J. F. Horowitz, E. Endert, and R. R. Wolfe. 1993. Regulation of endogenous fat and carbohydrate metabolism in relation to exercise intensity and duration. *Am. J. Physiol.* 265 [Endocrinol. Metab. 28]:E380–E391.)

Why Do We Need Carbohydrates?

We have seen that carbohydrates are an important energy source for our bodies. Let's learn more about this and discuss other functions of carbohydrates.

Carbohydrates Provide Energy

Carbohydrates, an excellent source of energy for all of our cells, provide 4 kcal of energy per gram. Some of our cells can also use lipids and even protein for energy if necessary. However, our red blood cells can use only glucose, and the brain and other nervous tissues rely primarily on glucose. This is why you get tired, irritable, and shaky when you have not eaten carbohydrates for a prolonged period of time.

Carbohydrates Fuel Daily Activity

Many popular diets—such as Dr. Atkins' New Diet Revolution and the Sugar Busters plan—are based on the idea that our bodies actually "prefer" to use dietary fats and/or protein for energy. They claim that current carbohydrate recommendations are much higher than we really need.

In reality, the body relies mostly on both carbohydrates and fats for energy. In fact, as shown in **Figure 4.10**, our bodies always use some combination of carbohydrates and fats to fuel daily activities.

Fats are the predominant energy source used by our bodies at rest and during low-intensity activities such as sitting, standing, and walking. Even during rest, however, our brain cells and red blood cells still rely on glucose.

Carbohydrates Fuel Exercise

When we exercise, whether running, briskly walking, bicycling, or performing any other activity that causes us to breathe harder and sweat, we begin to use more glucose than lipids. Whereas lipid breakdown is a slow process and requires oxygen, we can break down glucose very quickly either with or without oxygen. Even during very intense exercise, when less oxygen is available, we can still break down glucose very quickly for energy. That's why when you are exercising at maximal effort, carbohydrates are providing the majority of the energy your body requires.

If you are physically active, it is important to eat enough carbohydrates to provide energy for your brain, red blood cells, and muscles. In Chapter 14, we discuss in more detail the carbohydrate recommendations for active people. In general, if you do not eat enough carbohydrate to support regular exercise, your body will have to rely on fat and protein as alternative energy sources (the consequences of which are discussed shortly). If you or someone you know is trying to lose weight, you may be wondering whether exercising at a lower intensity will result in more stored fat being burned for energy. This is a question that researchers are still trying to answer. Weight-loss studies show that, to lose weight and keep it off, it is important to exercise daily. A low-intensity activity such as walking is generally recommended because it is easy to do and can be done for longer periods of time than high-intensity exercise; thus, it can result in the expenditure of more energy. Also, we know that fat stores provide much of the energy we need for walking. However, a study of highly trained athletes found that they actually lost more body fat when they performed very-high-intensity exercise![12] Although the exact mechanism for this fat loss is unknown, the researchers speculated that very-high-intensity exercise activated enzymes that increased the metabolism of fat, leading to a reduction in body fat. Based on the evidence currently available, the recommended activities for weight loss combine aerobic-type exercises, such as walking, jogging, or bicycling, with strength-building exercises. (For more information on weight loss, see Chapter 13.)

Low Carbohydrate Intake Can Lead to Ketoacidosis

When we do not eat enough carbohydrates, the body seeks an alternative source of fuel for the brain and begins to break down stored fat. This process, called **ketosis,** produces an alternative fuel called **ketones.** The metabolic process of ketosis is discussed in more detail in Chapter 7.

Ketosis is an important mechanism for providing energy to the brain during situations of fasting, low carbohydrate intake, or vigorous exercise.[13] However, ketones also suppress appetite and cause dehydration and acetone breath (the breath smells like nail polish remover). If inadequate carbohydrate intake continues for an extended period of time, the body will produce excessive amounts of ketones. Because many ketones are acids, high ketone levels cause the blood to become very acidic, leading to a condition called **ketoacidosis.** The high acidity of the blood interferes with basic body functions, causes the loss of lean body mass, and damages many body tissues. People with untreated diabetes are at high risk for ketoacidosis, which can lead to coma and even death. (See pages 140–144 for further details about diabetes.)

Carbohydrates Spare Protein

If the diet does not provide enough carbohydrate, the body will make its own glucose from protein. As noted earlier, this process, called gluconeogenesis, involves breaking down the proteins in blood and tissues into amino acids, then converting them to glucose.

When our bodies use proteins for energy, the amino acids from these proteins cannot be used to make new cells, repair tissue damage, support the immune system, or perform

When we exercise at relatively high intensities, or perform any other activity that causes us to breathe harder and sweat, we begin to use more glucose than fat.

ketosis The process by which the breakdown of fat during fasting states results in the production of ketones.

ketones Substances produced during the breakdown of fat when carbohydrate intake is insufficient to meet energy needs. Provide an alternative energy source for the brain when glucose levels are low.

ketoacidosis A condition in which excessive ketones are present in the blood, causing the blood to become very acidic, which alters basic body functions and damages tissues. Untreated ketoacidosis can be fatal. This condition is found in individuals with untreated diabetes mellitus.

any of their other functions. During periods of starvation or when eating a diet that is very low in carbohydrate, our body will take amino acids from the blood first, and then from other tissues such as muscles and the heart, liver, and kidneys. Using amino acids in this manner over a prolonged period of time can cause serious, possibly irreversible, damage to these organs. (See Chapter 6 for more details on using protein for energy.)

Complex Carbohydrates Have Health Benefits

Complex carbohydrates contain fiber and other nutrients that can reduce the risk for obesity, heart disease, and diabetes. The relationship between carbohydrates and these chronic diseases is the subject of considerable controversy. Proponents of low-carbohydrate diets claim that eating carbohydrates makes you overweight and promotes changes in blood lipids and insulin that contribute to heart disease and diabetes. However, fat is more than twice as energy dense as carbohydrate, and anyone who consumes extra calories, whether in the form of sugar, starch, protein, or fat, may eventually become obese. As we'll discuss later in this chapter, studies indicate that people who are obese have a significantly increased risk of both heart disease and type 2 diabetes. On the other hand, eating carbohydrates that are high in fiber and other nutrients has been shown to reduce the risk for obesity, heart disease, and type 2 diabetes. Thus, all carbohydrates are not bad, and complex carbohydrates are significantly beneficial. Even a small amount of simple carbohydrate can be included in a healthful diet. People who are very active and need more calories can eat more simple carbohydrates, whereas those who are older, less active, or overweight should limit their consumption of simple carbohydrates and focus on complex carbohydrates.

Fiber Helps Us Stay Healthy

Although we cannot digest fiber, it is still an important substance in our diet. Research indicates that it helps us stay healthy and may play a role in preventing many digestive and chronic diseases. The potential benefits of fiber consumption include the following:

- May reduce the risk of colon cancer. While there is still some controversy surrounding this issue, many researchers believe that fiber binds cancer-causing substances and speeds their elimination from the colon. However, recent studies of colon cancer and fiber have shown that their relationship is not as strong as previously thought.
- Helps prevent hemorrhoids, constipation, and other intestinal problems by keeping our stools moist and soft. Fiber gives gut muscles "something to push on" and makes it easier to eliminate stools.
- Reduces the risk of *diverticulosis,* a condition that is caused in part by trying to eliminate small, hard stools. A great deal of pressure must be generated in the large intestine to pass hard stools. This increased pressure weakens intestinal walls, causing them to bulge outward and form pockets (**Figure 4.11**). Feces and fibrous materials can get trapped in these pockets, which become infected and inflamed. This painful condition is typically treated with antibiotics or surgery.
- May reduce the risk of heart disease by delaying or blocking the absorption of dietary cholesterol into the bloodstream (**Figure 4.12**). In addition, when soluble fibers are digested, bacteria in the colon produce short-chain fatty acids that may lower the production of low-density lipoprotein (or LDL) to healthful levels in our bodies.
- May enhance weight loss, as eating a high-fiber diet causes a person to feel more full. Fiber absorbs water, expands in our intestine, and slows the movement of food through the upper part of the digestive tract. People who eat a fiber-rich diet tend to eat fewer fatty and sugary foods.
- May lower the risk of type 2 diabetes. In slowing digestion and absorption, fiber also slows the release of glucose into the blood. It thereby improves the body's regulation of insulin production and blood glucose levels.

Brown rice is a good source of dietary fiber.

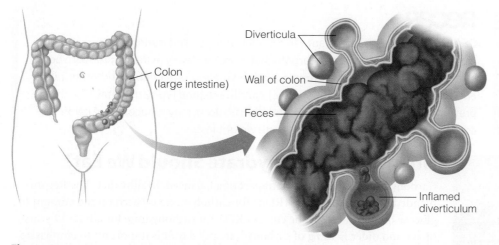

Figure 4.11 Diverticulosis occurs when bulging pockets form in the wall of the colon. These pockets become infected and inflamed, demanding proper treatment.

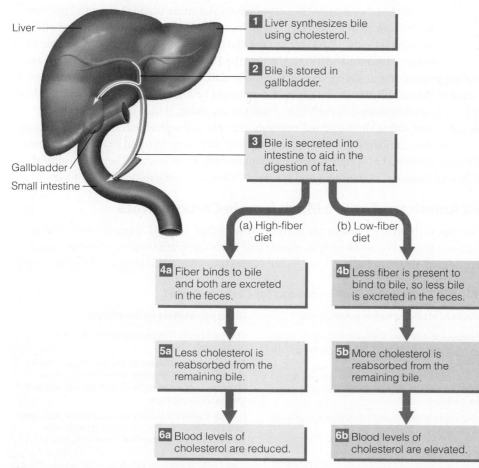

Figure 4.12 How fiber might help decrease blood cholesterol levels. **(a)** When eating a high-fiber diet, fiber binds to the bile that is produced from cholesterol, resulting in relatively more cholesterol being excreted in the feces. **(b)** When a lower-fiber diet is consumed, less fiber (and thus cholesterol) is bound to bile and excreted in the feces.

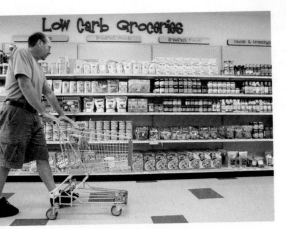

Many popular diets claim that current carbohydrate recommendations are much higher than we really need.

How Much Carbohydrate Should We Eat?

Carbohydrates are an important part of a balanced, healthy diet. The Recommended Dietary Allowance (RDA) for carbohydrate is based on the amount of glucose the brain uses.[5] The current RDA for carbohydrate for adults 19 years of age and older is 130 g of carbohydrate per day. It is important to emphasize that this RDA does not cover the amount of carbohydrate needed to support daily activities; it covers only the amount of carbohydrate needed to supply adequate glucose to the brain.

As introduced in Chapter 1, carbohydrates and the other macronutrients have been assigned an Acceptable Macronutrient Distribution Range (AMDR). This is the range of intake associated with a decreased risk of chronic diseases. The AMDR for carbohydrates is 45% to 65% of total energy intake.

Table 4.2 compares the carbohydrate recommendations from the Institute of Medicine with the Dietary Guidelines for Americans related to carbohydrate-containing foods.[5, 14] As you can see, the Institute of Medicine provides specific numeric recommendations, whereas the Dietary Guidelines for Americans are general suggestions about eating fiber-rich carbohydrate foods. Most health agencies agree that most of the carbohydrates you eat each day should be high in fiber, whole grain, and unprocessed. As recommended in the USDA Food Guide, eating at least half your grains as whole grains and eating the suggested amounts of fruits and vegetables each day will ensure that you get enough fiber-rich carbohydrates in your diet. Keep in mind that fruits are predominantly composed of simple sugars and contain little or no starch. They are healthful food choices, however, as they are good sources of vitamins, some minerals, and fiber.

Most Americans Eat Too Much Simple Carbohydrate

The average carbohydrate intake per person in the United States is approximately 50% of total energy intake. For some people, almost half of this amount consists of simple sugars. Where does all this sugar come from? Some sugar comes from healthful food sources, such

Table 4.2 Dietary Recommendations for Carbohydrates

Institute of Medicine Recommendations[†]	Dietary Guidelines for Americans[‡]
Recommended Dietary Allowance (RDA) for adults 19 years of age and older is 130 g of carbohydrate per day.	Choose fiber-rich fruits, vegetables, and whole grains often.
The Acceptable Macronutrient Distribution Range (AMDR) for carbohydrate is 45–65% of total daily energy intake.	Choose and prepare foods and beverages with little added sugars or caloric sweeteners, such as amounts suggested by the USDA Food Guide and the DASH Eating Plan.
Added sugar intake should be 25% or less of total energy intake each day.	Reduce the incidence of dental caries by practicing good oral hygiene and consuming sugar- and starch-containing foods and beverages less frequently.

[†]Institute of Medicine, Food and Nutrition Board. 2005. *Dietary Reference Intakes for Energy, Carbohydrates, Fiber, Fat, Fatty Acids, Cholesterol, Protein, and Amino Acids (Macronutrients).* Washington, DC: The National Academy of Sciences. Reprinted by permission.

[‡]U.S. Department of Health and Human Services and U.S. Department of Agriculture. 2005. *Dietary Guidelines for Americans, 2005,* 6th ed. Washington, DC: U.S. Government Printing Office.

Highlight

Forms of Sugars Commonly Used in Foods

Brown sugar   A highly refined sweetener made up of approximately 99% sucrose and produced by adding to white table sugar either molasses or burnt table sugar for coloring and flavor.

Concentrated fruit juice sweetener   A form of sweetener made with concentrated fruit juice, commonly pear juice.

Confectioner's sugar   A highly refined, finely ground white sugar; also referred to as powdered sugar.

Corn sweeteners   A general term for any sweetener made with corn starch.

Corn syrup   A syrup produced by the partial hydrolysis of corn starch.

Dextrose   An alternative term for glucose.

Fructose   A monosaccharide that occurs in fruits and vegetables. Also called levulose, or fruit sugar.

Galactose   A monosaccharide that joins with glucose to create lactose.

Glucose   The most abundant monosaccharide; it is the preferred source of energy for the brain and an important source of energy for all cells.

Granulated sugar   Another term for white sugar, or table sugar.

High-fructose corn syrup   A type of corn syrup in which part of the sucrose is converted to fructose, making it sweeter than sucrose or regular corn syrup; most high-fructose corn syrup contains 42% to 55% fructose.

Honey   A sweet, sticky liquid sweetener made by bees from the nectar of flowers; contains glucose and fructose.

Invert sugar   A sugar created by heating a sucrose syrup with a small amount of acid. Inverting sucrose results in its breakdown into glucose and fructose, which reduces the size of the sugar crystals. Due to its smooth texture, it is used in making candies such as fondant and some syrups.

Lactose   A disaccharide formed by one molecule of glucose and one molecule of galactose. Occurs naturally in milk and other dairy products.

Levulose   Another term for fructose, or fruit sugar.

Maltose   A disaccharide consisting of two molecules of glucose. Does not generally occur independently in foods but results as a by-product of digestion. Also called malt sugar.

Mannitol   A type of sugar alcohol.

Maple sugar   A sugar made by boiling maple syrup.

Molasses   A thick brown syrup that is separated from raw sugar during manufacturing. It is considered the least refined form of sucrose.

Natural sweeteners   A general term used for any naturally occurring sweeteners, such as sucrose, honey, and raw sugar.

Raw sugar   The sugar that results from the processing of sugar beets or sugarcane. It is approximately 96% to 98% sucrose. True raw sugar contains impurities and is not stable in storage; the raw sugar available to consumers has been purified to yield an edible sugar.

Sorbitol   A type of sugar alcohol.

Turbinado sugar   The form of raw sugar that is purified and safe for human consumption. Sold as "Sugar in the Raw" in the United States.

White sugar   Another name for sucrose, or table sugar.

Xylitol   A type of sugar alcohol.

---

as fruit and milk. However, much of our simple sugar intake comes from **added sugars**—that is, sugars and syrups that are added to foods during processing or preparation.[5]

The most common source of added sugars in the U.S. diet is sweetened soft drinks; we drink an average of 40 gallons per person each year. Consider that one 12-oz sugared cola contains 38.5 g of sugar, or almost 10 teaspoons. If you drink the average amount, you are consuming more than 16,420 g of sugar (about 267 cups) each year! Other common sources of added sugars include cookies, cakes, pies, fruit drinks, and candy. In addition, a surprising number of processed foods you may not think of as "sweet" actually contain a significant amount of added sugar, including many brands of peanut butter and flavored rice mixes.

Added sugars are not chemically different from naturally occurring sugars. However, foods and beverages with added sugars have lower levels of vitamins and minerals than foods that naturally contain simple sugars. Because of these nutrient limitations, it is recommended that we choose and prepare foods and beverages with little added sugars. People who are very physically active are able to consume relatively more added sugars, while smaller or less active people should consume relatively less. The Nutrition Facts Panel includes a listing of total sugars, but a distinction is not generally made between added sugars and naturally occurring sugars. Thus, you need to check the ingredients list. (Refer to the Highlight: Forms of Added Sugars Commonly Used in Foods for a list of terms indicating

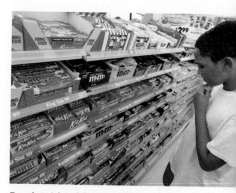

Foods with added sugars, such as candy, have lower levels of vitamins, minerals, and fiber than foods that naturally contain simple sugars.

added sugars   Sugars and syrups that are added to food during processing or preparation.

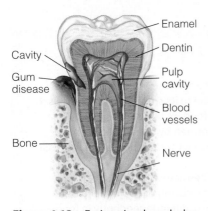

Figure 4.13 Eating simple carbohydrates can cause an increase in cavities and gum disease. This is because bacteria in the mouth consume simple carbohydrates present on the teeth and gums and produce acids, which eat away at these tissues.

added sugars.) To maintain a diet low in added sugars, limit foods in which a form of added sugar is listed as one of the first few ingredients on the label.[15]

Simple Carbohydrates Are Blamed for Many Health Problems

Why do simple carbohydrates have such a bad reputation? First, they are known to contribute to tooth decay. Second, they have been identified as a possible cause of hyperactivity in children. Third, many researchers believe that eating a lot of simple carbohydrates increases the levels of unhealthful lipids in our blood, increasing our risk for heart disease. High intakes of simple carbohydrates have also been blamed for causing diabetes and obesity. Let's now learn the truth about these accusations related to simple carbohydrates.

Sugar Causes Tooth Decay

Simple carbohydrates do play a role in dental problems because the bacteria that cause tooth decay thrive on them. These bacteria produce acids that eat away at tooth enamel and can eventually cause cavities and gum disease (**Figure 4.13**). Eating sticky foods that adhere to teeth—such as caramels, crackers, sugary cereals, and licorice—and sipping sweetened beverages over a period of time increase the risk of tooth decay. This means that people shouldn't slowly sip soda or juice and that babies should not be put to sleep with a bottle unless it contains water. As we have seen, even breast milk contains sugar, which can slowly drip onto the baby's gums. As a result, infants should not routinely be allowed to fall asleep at the breast.

To reduce your risk for tooth decay, brush your teeth after each meal and especially after drinking sugary drinks and eating candy. Drinking fluoridated water and using a fluoride toothpaste also will help protect your teeth.

There Is No Link Between Sugar and Hyperactivity in Children

Although many people believe that eating sugar causes hyperactivity and other behavioral problems in children, there is little scientific evidence to support this claim. Some children actually become less active shortly after a high-sugar meal! However, it is important to emphasize that most studies of sugar and children's behavior have only looked at the effects of sugar a few hours after ingestion. We know very little about the long-term effects of sugar intake on the behavior of children. Behavioral and learning problems are complex issues, most likely caused by a multitude of factors. Because of this complexity, the Institute of Medicine has stated that, overall, there currently does not appear to be enough evidence that eating too much sugar causes hyperactivity or other behavioral problems in children.[5] Thus, a Tolerable Upper Intake Level has not been set for sugar.

High Sugar Intake Can Lead to Unhealthful Levels of Blood Lipids

Research evidence suggests that consuming a diet high in simple sugars, particularly fructose, can lead to unhealthful changes in blood lipids. You will learn more about blood lipids (including cholesterol and lipoproteins) in Chapter 5. Briefly, higher intakes of simple sugars are associated with increases in our blood of both triglycerides and LDLs, which are commonly referred to as "bad cholesterol." At the same time, high simple sugar intake appears to *decrease* our HDLs, which are protective and are often referred to as "good cholesterol."[5, 16] These changes are of concern, as increased levels of triglycerides and LDLs and decreased levels of HDLs are known risk factors for heart disease. However, there is not enough scientific evidence at the present time to state with confidence that eating a diet high in simple sugars causes heart disease. Based on our current knowledge, it is prudent for a person at risk for heart disease to eat a diet low in simple sugars. Because high-fructose corn syrup is a component of many processed foods, careful label reading is advised.

High Sugar Intake Does Not Cause Diabetes but May Contribute to Obesity

There is no scientific evidence that eating a diet high in sugar causes diabetes. In fact, studies examining the relationship between sugar intake and type 2 diabetes are equivocal, reporting either no association between sugar intake and diabetes, an increased risk of diabetes associated with increased sugar intake and weight gain, or a decreased risk of diabetes with increased sugar intake.[17-19] However, people who have diabetes need to moderate their intake of sugar and closely monitor their blood glucose levels.

We have somewhat more evidence linking sugar intake with obesity. For example, a recent study found that overweight children consumed more sugared soft drinks than did children of normal weight.[20] Another study found that for every extra sugared soft drink consumed by a child per day, the risk of obesity increases by 60%.[21] We also know that if you consume more energy than you expend, you will gain weight. It makes intuitive sense that people who consume extra energy from high-sugar foods are at risk for obesity, just as people who consume extra energy from fat or protein gain weight. In addition to the increased potential for obesity, another major concern about high-sugar diets is that they tend to be low in nutrient density because the intake of high-sugar foods tends to replace that of more nutritious foods. The relationship between sugared soft drinks and obesity is highly controversial and discussed in more detail in the Nutrition Debate on pages 151–153.

RECaP

The RDA for carbohydrate is 130 g per day; this amount is sufficient only to supply adequate glucose to the brain. The AMDR for carbohydrate is 45% to 65% of total energy intake. Added sugars are sugars and syrups added to foods during processing or preparation. Our intake of simple sugars should be 25% or less of our total energy intake each day, with no more than 10% coming from added sugars. Sugar contributes to tooth decay but does not appear to cause hyperactivity in children. Higher intakes of simple sugars are associated with increases in triglycerides and low-density lipoproteins. Diets high in sugar are not confirmed to cause diabetes but may contribute to obesity.

Most Americans Eat Too Little Complex Carbohydrate

Do you eat enough complex carbohydrate each day? If you are like most people in the United States, you eat only about two servings of fruits or vegetables (including legumes) each day; this is far below the recommended amount.

Breads and cereals are another potential source of complex carbohydrates, and they're part of most Americans' diets. But are the breads and cereals you eat made with whole grains? If you're not sure, check out the ingredients lists on the labels of your favorite breads and breakfast cereals. Do they list *whole-wheat flour* or just *wheat flour*? And what's the difference? To help you answer this question, we've defined in Table 4.3 some terms commonly used on labels for breads and cereals. As you can see, whole-wheat flour is made from whole grains: only the husk of the wheat kernel has been removed. In contrast, the term *wheat flour* can be used to signify a flour that has been highly refined, with the bran and other fiber-rich portions removed.

In addition to stripping a grain of its fiber, the refining process reduces many of the grain's original nutrients. To make up for some of the lost nutrients, manufacturers sometimes enrich the product. **Enriched foods** are foods in which nutrients that were lost during processing have been added back so the food meets a specified standard. Notice that the terms *enriched* and *fortified* are not synonymous: **fortified foods** have nutrients added that did not originally exist in the food (or existed in insignificant amounts). For example, some breakfast cereals have been fortified with iron, a mineral that is not present in cereals naturally. **Figure 4.14** compares the nutrients and fiber in whole-grain bread versus enriched and unenriched white breads.

We Need at Least 25 Grams of Fiber Daily

How much fiber do we need? The Adequate Intake for fiber is 25 g per day for women and 38 g per day for men, or 14 g of fiber for every 1,000 kcal per day that a person eats. Most

Whole-grain foods provide more nutrients and fiber than foods made with enriched flour.

enriched foods Foods in which nutrients that were lost during processing have been added back so the food meets a specified standard.

fortified foods Foods in which nutrients are added that did not originally exist in the food or existed in insignificant amounts.

Table 4.3 Terms Used to Describe Grains and Cereals on Nutrition Labels

Term	Definition
Brown bread	Bread that may or may not be made using whole-grain flour. Many brown breads are made with white flour with brown (caramel) coloring added.
Enriched (or fortified) flour or grain	Enriching or fortifying grains involves adding nutrients to refined foods. In order to use this term in the United States, a minimum amount of iron, folate, niacin, thiamin, and riboflavin must be added. Other nutrients can also be added.
Refined flour or grain	Refining involves removing the coarse parts of food products; refined wheat flour is flour in which all but the internal part of the kernel has been removed.
Stone ground	Refers to a milling process in which limestone is used to grind any grain. Stone ground does not mean that bread is made with whole grain, as refined flour can be stone ground.
Unbleached flour	Flour that has been refined but not bleached; it is very similar to refined white flour in texture and nutritional value.
Wheat flour	Any flour made from wheat; includes white flour, unbleached flour, and whole-wheat flour.
White flour	Flour that has been bleached and refined. All-purpose flour, cake flour, and enriched baking flour are all types of white flour.
Whole-grain flour	A flour made from grain that is not refined; whole grains are milled in their complete form, with only the husk removed.
Whole-wheat flour	An unrefined, whole-grain flour made from whole wheat kernels.

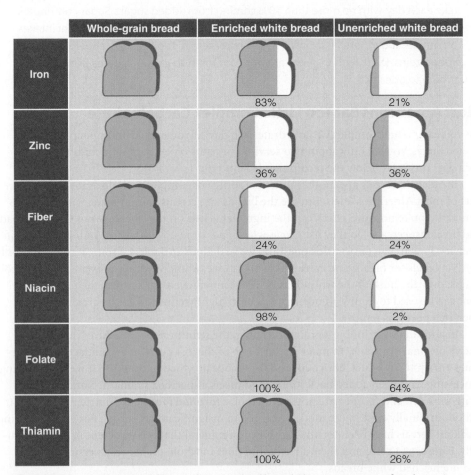

Figure 4.14 Nutrients and fiber in three kinds of bread. The percentages of each nutrient reported for enriched and unenriched white bread indicate the amount they contain as compared to the amount contained in whole-grain bread. For example, the white breads contain only 36% of the zinc found in whole-grain bread.

people in the United States eat only 12 to 18 g of fiber each day, getting only half of the fiber they need.[5] Although fiber supplements are available, it is best to get fiber from food because foods contain additional nutrients such as vitamins and minerals.

Eating the amounts of whole grains, vegetables, fruits, nuts, and legumes recommended in the USDA Food Guide will ensure that you eat adequate fiber. **Figure 4.15** lists some common foods and their fiber content. You can use this information to design a diet that includes adequate fiber.

It is important to drink plenty of fluid as you increase your fiber intake, as fiber binds with water to soften stools. Inadequate fluid intake with a high-fiber diet can actually result in hard, dry stools that are difficult to pass through the colon. At least eight 8-oz glasses of fluid each day are commonly recommended.

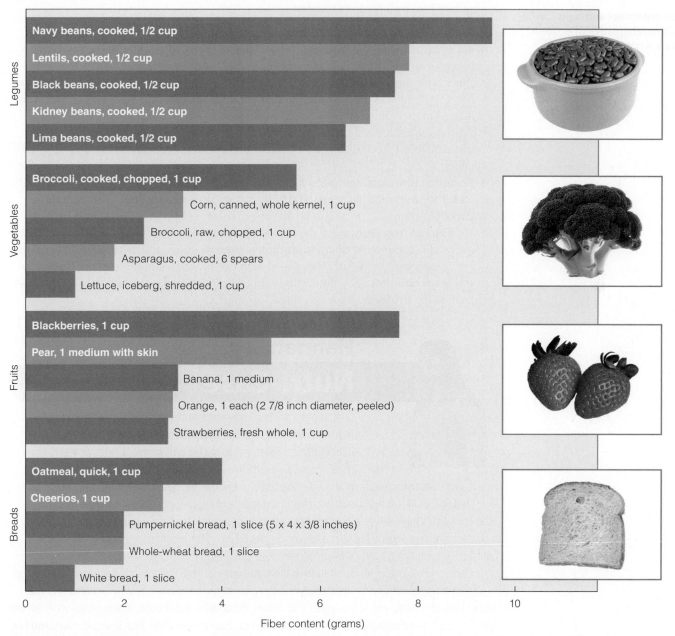

Figure 4.15 Fiber content of common foods. *Note:* The Adequate Intake for fiber is 25 g per day for women and 38 g per day for men. *Data from:* U.S. Department of Agriculture, Agricultural Research Service. 2008. USDA national nutrient database for standard reference, release 21. Nutrient Data Laboratory home page. Available online at http://www.ars.usda.gov/ba/bhnrc/ndl.

Frozen vegetables and fruits can be a healthful alternative when fresh produce is not available.

Can you eat too much fiber? Excessive fiber consumption can lead to problems such as intestinal gas, bloating, and constipation. Because fiber binds with water, it causes the body to eliminate more water in the feces, so a very-high-fiber diet could result in dehydration. Fiber also binds many vitamins and minerals, so a high-fiber diet can reduce our absorption of important nutrients such as iron, zinc, and calcium. In children, some elderly, the chronically ill, and other at-risk populations, extreme fiber intake can even lead to malnutrition—they feel full before they have eaten enough to provide adequate energy and nutrients. So whereas some societies are accustomed to a very-high-fiber diet, most people in the United States find it difficult to tolerate more than 50 g of fiber per day.

Hunting for Complex Carbohydrates

Figure 4.16 compares the food and fiber content of two diets, one high in complex, fiber-rich carbohydrates and the other high in simple carbohydrates. Here are some hints for selecting healthful carbohydrate sources:

- Select breads and cereals that are made with whole grains such as wheat, oats, barley, and rye (make sure the label says "whole" before the word *grain*). Choose foods that have at least 2 or 3 g of fiber per serving.
- Buy fresh fruits and vegetables whenever possible. When appropriate, eat foods such as potatoes, apples, and pears with the skin left on, as much of the fiber and nutrients are located in the skin.
- Frozen vegetables and fruits can be a healthful alternative when fresh produce is not available. Check frozen selections to make sure there is no extra sugar or salt added.
- Be careful when buying canned fruits and vegetables, as many are high in sodium and added sugar. Foods that are packed in their own juice are more healthful than those packed in syrup.
- Eat legumes frequently, every day if possible. Canned or fresh beans, peas, and lentils are excellent sources of fiber-rich carbohydrates, vitamins, and minerals. Add them to soups, casseroles, and other recipes—it is an easy way to eat more of them. If you are trying to consume less sodium, rinse canned beans to remove extra salt or choose low-sodium alternatives.

Hannah
Nutri-Case

"Last night, my mom called and said she'd be late getting home from work, so I made dinner. I was tired after my classes and I had a lot of homework to get to, so I kept it simple. I made us each a cheeseburger—no bun!—served with frozen French fries and some carrot sticks with guacamole on the side. We both had a cola, too. Later that night, though, when I was studying, I got a snack attack and raided a package of sugar-free cookies. I ate maybe three or four, but I didn't think it was a big deal because they're sugar-free. Then when I checked the package label this morning, I found out that each cookie has 90 calories! It bummed me out—until those cookies, I'd been doing pretty well on my new low-carb diet!"

Hannah takes public transportation to the community college she attends, and does not engage in regular physical activity. Without analyzing the precise grams of carbohydrate or number of calories in Hannah's meal, would you agree that before the cookies she'd been "doing pretty well" on her low-carb diet? In other words, would you describe her meal as low carb? Would you characterize her meal as low in energy? About how many grams of dietary fiber do you think were in the meal?

High Complex Carbohydrate Diet	High Simple Carbohydrate Diet
Breakfast: 1½ cups Cheerios / 1 cup skim milk / 2 slices whole-wheat toast with 1 tbsp. light margarine / 1 medium banana / 8 fl. oz fresh orange juice	**Breakfast:** 1½ cups Fruit Loops cereal / 1 cup skim milk / 2 slices white bread toasted, with 1 tbsp. light margarine / 8 fl. oz fresh orange juice
Lunch: 8 fl. oz low-fat blueberry yogurt / Tuna sandwich (2 slices whole-wheat bread; ¼ cup tuna packed in water, drained; 1 tsp. Dijon mustard; 2 tsp. low-calorie mayonnaise) / 2 carrots, raw, with peel / 1 cup raw cauliflower / 1 tbsp. peppercorn ranch salad dressing (for dipping vegetables)	**Lunch:** McDonald's Quarter Pounder— 1 sandwich / 1 large order French fries / 16 fl. oz cola beverage / 30 jelly beans
Snack: 3 cups non-fat popcorn	**Snack:** 1 cinnamon raisin bagel (3½ - inch diameter) / 2 tbsp. cream cheese / 8 fl. oz low-fat strawberry yogurt
Dinner: ½ chicken breast roasted / 1 cup brown rice, cooked / 1 cup cooked broccoli / Spinach salad (1 cup chopped spinach, 1 whole egg white, 2 slices turkey bacon, 3 cherry tomatoes, and 2 tbsp. creamy bacon salad dressing) / 2 baked apples (no added sugar)	**Dinner:** 1 whole chicken breast, roasted / 2 cups mixed green salad / 2 tbsp. ranch salad dressing / 1 serving macaroni and cheese / 12 fl. oz cola beverage / Cheesecake (⅑ of cake)
(No Snack)	**Late Night Snack:** 2 cups gelatin dessert (cherry flavored) / 3 raspberry oatmeal no-fat cookies

Nutrient Analysis:
2150 kcal
60% of energy from carbohydrates
22% of energy from fat
18% of energy from protein
38 grams of dietary fiber

Nutrient Analysis:
4012 kcal
60% of energy from carbohydrates
25% of energy from fat
15% of energy from protein
18.5 grams of dietary fiber

Figure 4.16 Comparison of two high-carbohydrate diets. (*Note*: Diets were analyzed using Food Processor Version 7.21 *Data from:* ESHA Research, Salem, OR.)

Nutrition Label Activity

Recognizing Carbohydrates on the Label

Figure 4.17 shows labels for two breakfast cereals. The cereal on the left (a) is processed and sweetened, whereas the one on the right (b) is a whole-grain product with no added sugar.

◼ Check the center of each label to locate the amount of total carbohydrate. For the sweetened cereal, the total carbohydrate is 26 g. For the whole-grain cereal, the total carbohydrate is almost the same, 27 g for a smaller serving size.

◼ Look at the information listed as subgroups under Total Carbohydrate. The label for the sweetened cereal lists all types of carbohydrates in the cereal: dietary fiber, sugars, and other carbohydrate (which refers to starches). Notice that this cereal contains 13 g of sugar—half of its total carbohydrates—but only 1 g of dietary fiber.

◼ The label for the whole-grain cereal lists dietary fiber. In contrast to the sweetened cereal, this product contains 4 g of fiber and only 1 g of sugar! Notice that on this label there is no amount listed for starches (or other carbohydrates). In this case, the amount of starch is the difference between the total carbohydrate and the sum of dietary fiber and sugars, or 27 g − 5 g = 22 g of starch.

◼ Now look at the percent values listed to the right of the Total Carbohydrate section. For both cereals (without milk), their percent contribution to daily carbohydrate is 9%. This does not mean that 9% of the calories in these cereals comes from carbohydrates. Instead, this percentage refers to the Daily Values listed at the bottom of each label. For a person who eats 2,000 calories, the recommended amount of carbohydrate each day is 300 g. One serving of each cereal contains 26–27 g, which is about 9% of 300 g.

◼ To calculate the percent of calories that comes from carbohydrate, do the following:

a. Calculate the *calories* in the cereal that come from carbohydrate. Multiply the total grams of carbohydrate per serving by the energy value of carbohydrate:

$$26 \text{ g of carbohydrate} \times 4 \text{ kcal/g} = 104 \text{ kcal}$$
$$\text{from carbohydrate}$$

b. Calculate the *percent of calories* in the cereal that come from carbohydrate. Divide the kcal from carbohydrate by the total calories for each serving:

$$(104 \text{ kcal/120 kcal}) \times 100 = 87\% \text{ calories}$$
$$\text{from carbohydrate}$$

Which cereal should you choose? Check the ingredients for the sweetened cereal. Remember that the ingredients are listed in the order from highest to lowest amount. The second and third ingredients listed are sugar and brown sugar, and the corn and oat flours are not whole-grain flours. Now look at the ingredients for the other cereal—it contains whole-grain oats. Although the sweetened product is enriched with more B vitamins, iron, and zinc, the whole-grain cereal packs 4 g of fiber per serving and contains no added sugars. Overall, it is a more healthful choice.

Try the Nutrition Label Activity above to learn how to recognize various carbohydrates on food labels. Armed with this knowledge, you are now ready to make more healthful food choices.

Recap

The Adequate Intake for fiber is 25 g per day for women and 38 g per day for men. Most Americans only eat half of the fiber they need each day. Foods high in fiber and complex carbohydrates include whole grains and cereals, fruits, and vegetables. The more processed the food, the fewer fiber-rich carbohydrates it contains.

What's the Story on Alternative Sweeteners?

Most of us love sweets but want to avoid the extra calories and tooth decay that go along with eating simple sugars. Remember that all carbohydrates, whether simple or complex, contain 4 kcal of energy per gram. Because sweeteners such as sucrose, fructose, honey, and brown sugar contribute energy, they are called **nutritive sweeteners.**

Other nutritive sweeteners include the *sugar alcohols* such as mannitol, sorbitol, isomalt, and xylitol. Popular in sugar-free gums, mints, and diabetic candies, sugar alcohols are less sweet than sucrose (**Figure 4.18**). Foods with sugar alcohols have health benefits that

nutritive sweeteners Sweeteners such as sucrose, fructose, honey, and brown sugar that contribute calories (or energy).

Nutrition Facts

Serving Size: 3/4 cup (30g)
Servings Per Package: About 14

Amount Per Serving	Cereal	Cereal With 1/2 Cup Skim Milk
Calories	120	160
Calories from Fat	15	15

	% Daily Value**	
Total Fat 1.5g*	2%	2%
Saturated Fat 0g	0%	0%
Trans Fat 0g		
Polyunsaturated Fat 0g		
Monounsaturated Fat 0.5g		
Cholesterol 0mg	0%	1%
Sodium 220mg	9%	12%
Potassium 40mg	1%	7%
Total Carbohydrate 26g	9%	11%
Dietary Fiber 1g	3%	3%
Sugars 13g		
Other Carbohydrate 12g		
Protein 1g		
Vitamin A	0%	4%
Vitamin C	0%	2%
Calcium	0%	15%
Iron	25%	25%
Thiamin	25%	25%
Riboflavin	25%	35%
Niacin	25%	25%
Vitamin B6	25%	25%
Folate	25%	25%
Zinc	25%	25%

* Amount in cereal. One-half cup skim milk contributes an additional 65mg sodium, 6g total carbohydrate (6g sugars), and 4g protein.
** Percent Daily Values are based on a 2,000 calorie diet. Your daily values may be higher or lower depending on your calorie needs:

	Calories	2,000	2,500
Total Fat	Less than	65g	80g
Sat. Fat	Less than	20g	25g
Cholesterol	Less than	300mg	300mg
Sodium	Less than	2,400mg	2,400mg
Potassium		3,500mg	3,500mg
Total Carbohydrate		300g	375g
Dietary fiber		25g	30g

Calories per gram:		2,500
Fat 9 • Carbohydrate 4 • Protein 4		

INGREDIENTS: Corn Flour, Sugar, Brown Sugar, Partially Hydrogenated Vegetable Oil (Soybean and Cottonseed), Oat Flour, Salt, Sodium Citrate (a flavoring agent), Flavor added [Natural & Artificial Flavor, Strawberry Juice Concentrate, Malic Acid (a flavoring agent)], Niacinamide (Niacin), Zinc Oxide, Reduced Iron, Red 40, Yellow 5, Red 3, Yellow 6, Pyridoxine Hydrochloride (Vitamin B6), Riboflavin (Vitamin B2), Thiamin Mononitrate (Vitamin B1), Folic Acid (Folate) and Blue 1.

(a)

Nutrition Facts

Serving Size: 1/2 cup dry (40g)
Servings Per Container: 13

Amount Per Serving	
Calories	150
Calories from Fat	25

	% Daily Value*
Total Fat 3g	5%
Saturated Fat 0.5g	2%
Trans Fat 0g	
Polyunsaturated Fat 1g	
Monounsaturated Fat 1g	
Cholesterol 0mg	0%
Sodium 0mg	0%
Total Carbohydrate 27g	9%
Dietary Fiber 4g	15%
Soluble Fiber 2g	
Insoluble Fiber 2g	
Sugars 1g	
Protein 5g	
Vitamin A	0%
Vitamin C	0%
Calcium	0%
Iron	10%

* Percent Daily Values are based on a 2,000 calorie diet. Your daily values may be higher or lower depending on your calorie needs:

	Calories	2,000	2,500
Total Fat	Less than	65g	80g
Sat. Fat	Less than	20g	25g
Cholesterol	Less than	300mg	300mg
Sodium	Less than	2,400mg	2,400mg
Total Carbohydrate		300g	375g
Dietary fiber		25g	30g

INGREDIENTS: 100% Natural Whole Grain Rolled Oats.

(b)

Figure 4.17 Labels for two breakfast cereals: **(a)** processed and sweetened cereal; **(b)** whole-grain cereal with no sugar added.

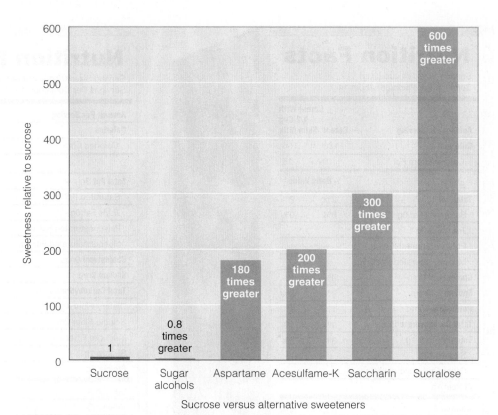

Figure 4.18   Relative sweetness of alternative sweeteners as compared to sucrose. (*Data adapted from:* Kroger M., K. Meister, and R. Kava. 2006. Low-calorie sweeteners and other sugar substitutes: A review of the safety issues. *Comp. Rev. Food Sci. Food Safety* 5:35–47.)

foods made with sugars do not have, such as a reduced glycemic response and decreased risk of dental caries. Also, because sugar alcohols are absorbed slowly and incompletely from the intestine, they provide less energy than sugar, usually 2 to 3 kcal of energy per gram. However, because they are not completely absorbed from the intestine, they can attract water into the large intestine and cause diarrhea.

Alternative Sweeteners Are Non-Nutritive

A number of other products have been developed to sweeten foods without promoting tooth decay and weight gain. As these products provide little or no energy, they are called **non-nutritive, or alternative, sweeteners.**

Limited Use of Alternative Sweeteners Is Not Harmful

Contrary to popular belief, alternative sweeteners have been determined as safe for adults, children, and individuals with diabetes. Women who are pregnant should discuss the use of alternative sweeteners with their healthcare provider. In general, it appears safe for pregnant women to consume alternative sweeteners in amounts within the Food and Drug Administration (FDA) guidelines.[22] The **Acceptable Daily Intake** (ADI) is an estimate made by the FDA of the amount of a sweetener that someone can consume each day over a lifetime without adverse effects. The estimates are based on studies conducted on laboratory animals, and they include a 100-fold safety factor. It is important to emphasize that actual intake by humans is typically well below the ADI.

Saccharin

Discovered in the late 1800s, *saccharin* is about 300 times sweeter than sucrose (see Figure 4.18). Evidence to suggest that saccharin may cause bladder tumors in rats surfaced

Contrary to recent media reports claiming severe health consequences related to consumption of alternative sweeteners, major health agencies have determined that these products are safe for us to consume.

non-nutritive sweeteners   Also called *alternative sweeteners;* manufactured sweeteners that provide little or no energy.

Acceptable Daily Intake (ADI)   An estimate made by the Food and Drug Administration of the amount of a non-nutritive sweetener that someone can consume each day over a lifetime without adverse effects.

in the 1970s; however, more than 20 years of scientific research has shown that saccharin is not related to bladder cancer in humans. Based on this evidence, in May 2000 the National Toxicology Program of the U.S. government removed saccharin from its list of products that may cause cancer. No ADI has been set for saccharin, and it is used in foods and beverages and sold as a tabletop sweetener. Saccharin is sold as Sweet n' Low (also known as "the pink packet") in the United States.

Acesulfame-K

Acesulfame-K (or acesulfame potassium) is marketed under the names Sunette and Sweet One. It is a calorie-free sweetener that is 175 times sweeter than sugar. It is used to sweeten gums, candies, beverages, instant tea, coffee, gelatins, and puddings. The taste of acesulfame-K does not change when it is heated, so it can be used in cooking. The body does not metabolize acesulfame-K, so it is excreted unchanged by the kidneys. The ADI for acesulfame-K is 15 mg per kg body weight per day. For example, the ADI in an adult weighing 150 pounds (or 68 kg) would be 1020 mg.

Aspartame

Aspartame, also called Equal ("the blue packet") and NutraSweet, is one of the most popular alternative sweeteners currently found in foods and beverages. Aspartame is composed of two amino acids: phenylalanine and aspartic acid. When these amino acids are separate, one is bitter and the other has no flavor—but joined together, they make a substance that is 200 times sweeter than sucrose. Although aspartame contains 4 kcal of energy per gram, it is so sweet that only small amounts are necessary, thus it ends up contributing little or no energy. Because aspartame is made from amino acids, its taste is destroyed with heat because the dipeptide bonds that bind the two amino acids are destroyed when heated (see Chapter 6); thus, it cannot be used in cooking.

A significant amount of research has been done to test the safety of aspartame. Although a number of false claims have been published, especially on the Internet, there is no scientific evidence to support the claim that aspartame causes brain tumors, Alzheimer's disease, or nerve disorders.

The ADI for aspartame is 50 mg per kg body weight per day. Table 4.4 shows how many servings of aspartame-sweetened foods have to be consumed to exceed the ADI. Although eating less than the ADI is considered safe, note that children who consume many powdered drinks, diet sodas, and other aspartame-flavored products could potentially exceed this amount. Drinks sweetened with aspartame are extremely popular among children and teenagers, but they are very low in nutritional value and should not replace more healthful beverages such as milk, water, and 100% fruit juice.

There are some people who should not consume aspartame at all: those with the disease *phenylketonuria (PKU)*. This is a genetic disorder that prevents the breakdown of the amino acid phenylalanine. Because the person with PKU cannot metabolize phenylalanine, it builds up to toxic levels in the tissues of the body and causes irreversible brain damage. In the United States, all newborn babies are tested for PKU; those who have it are placed on a

Table 4.4 The Amount of Food That a 50-Pound Child and a 150-Pound Adult Would Have to Consume Daily to Exceed the ADI for Aspartame

Food	50-lb Child	150-lb Adult
12 fl. oz carbonated soft drink	7	20
8 fl. oz powdered soft drink	11	34
4 fl. oz gelatin dessert	14	42
Packets of tabletop sweetener	32	97

Data from: International Food Information Council Foundation. 2003. Everything you need to know about aspartame. Available online at http://www.ific.org/publications/brochures/aspartamebroch.cfm.

phenylalanine-limited diet. Some foods that are common sources of protein and other nutrients for many growing children, such as meats and milk, contain phenylalanine. Thus, it is critical that children with PKU not waste what little phenylalanine they can consume on nutrient-poor products sweetened with aspartame.

Sucralose

The FDA has recently approved the use of *sucralose* as an alternative sweetener. It is marketed under the brand name Splenda and is known as "the yellow packet." It is made from sucrose, but chlorine atoms are substituted for the hydrogen and oxygen normally found in sucrose, and it passes through the digestive tract unchanged, without contributing any energy. It is 600 times sweeter than sucrose and is stable when heated, so it can be used in cooking. It has been approved for use in many foods, including chewing gum, salad dressings, beverages, gelatin and pudding products, canned fruits, frozen dairy desserts, and baked goods. Safety studies have not shown sucralose to cause cancer or to have other adverse health effects. The ADI for sucralose is 5 mg per kg body weight per day. For example, the ADI of sucralose in an adult weighing 150 pounds (or 68 kg) would be 340 mg.

Other Alternative Sweeteners

Truvia and PureVia are two zero-calorie sweeteners that have recently been designated by the FDA as safe for tabletop, food, and beverage use. These sweeteners are developed from a purified extract of the stevia plant, a plant native to South and Central America. The trade name for the purified stevia extract is cebiana. Truvia and PureVia are up to 300 times sweeter than sucrose.

> ## RECAP
>
> Alternative sweeteners can be used in place of sugar to sweeten foods. Most of these products do not promote tooth decay and contribute little or no energy. The alternative sweeteners approved for use in the United States are considered safe when eaten in amounts less than the acceptable daily intake.

What Disorders Are Related to Carbohydrate Metabolism?

Health conditions that affect the body's ability to absorb and/or use carbohydrates include diabetes, hypoglycemia, and lactose intolerance.

Diabetes: Impaired Regulation of Glucose

Hyperglycemia is the term referring to higher-than-normal levels of blood glucose. **Diabetes** is a chronic disease in which the body can no longer regulate glucose within normal limits, and blood glucose levels become dangerously high. It is imperative to detect and treat the disease as soon as possible because excessive fluctuations in glucose injure tissues throughout the body. As we noted at the beginning of this chapter, if not controlled, diabetes can lead to blindness, seizures, kidney failure, nerve disease, amputations, stroke, and heart disease. Uncontrolled diabetes can also lead to ketoacidosis, which may result in coma and death. Diabetes is the seventh leading cause of death in the United States.[23]

Approximately 24 million people in the United States—7.8% of the total population—are diagnosed with diabetes. It is speculated that another 5.7 million people have diabetes but do not know it. **Figure 4.19** shows the percentage of adults with diabetes from various ethnic groups in the United States.[24] As you can see, diabetes is more common in African Americans, Hispanic or Latino Americans, and American Indians and Alaska Natives.

hyperglycemia   A condition in which blood glucose levels are higher than normal.

diabetes   A chronic disease in which the body can no longer regulate glucose.

The two main forms of diabetes are type 1 and type 2. Some women develop a third form, *gestational diabetes,* during pregnancy; we will discuss this in more detail in Chapter 16.

In Type 1 Diabetes, the Body Does Not Produce Enough Insulin

Approximately 10% of people with diabetes have **type 1 diabetes,** in which the body cannot produce enough insulin. When people with type 1 diabetes eat a meal and their blood glucose rises, the pancreas is unable to secrete insulin in response. Glucose levels soar, and the body tries to expel the excess glucose by excreting it in the urine. In fact, the medical term for the disease is *diabetes mellitus* (from the Greek *diabainein,* "to pass through," and Latin *mellitus,* "sweetened with honey"), and frequent urination is one of its warning signs (see Table 4.5 for other symptoms). If blood glucose levels are not controlled, a person with type 1 diabetes will become confused and lethargic and have trouble breathing. This is because the brain is not getting enough glucose to properly function. As discussed earlier, uncontrolled diabetes can lead to ketoacidosis; left untreated, the ultimate result is coma and death.

The cause of type 1 diabetes is unknown, but it may be an *autoimmune disease.* This means that the body's immune system attacks and destroys its own tissues, in this case the beta cells of the pancreas.

Most cases of type 1 diabetes are diagnosed in adolescents around 10 to 14 years of age, although the disease can appear in infants, young children, and adults. It has a genetic link, so siblings and children of those with type 1 diabetes are at greater risk.[25]

The only treatment for type 1 diabetes is administration of insulin by injection or pump several times daily. Insulin is a hormone composed of protein, so it would be digested in the intestine if taken as a pill. Individuals with type 1 diabetes must also monitor their blood glucose levels closely to ensure that they remain within a healthful range (**Figure 4.20**). The Highlight box on page 142 describes how one young man with type 1 diabetes stays healthy.

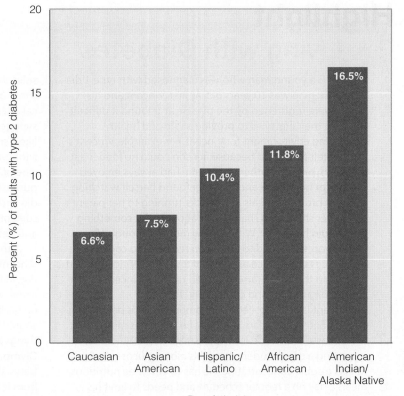

Figure 4.19 The percent of adults from various ethnic and racial groups with type 2 diabetes. (*Data adapted from:* the National Diabetes Information Clearinghouse [NDIC]. 2008. National diabetes statistics. National Institutes of Health [NIH] publication no. 08–3892. Available online at http://diabetes.niddk.nih.gov/dm/pubs/statistics/index.htm.)

Table 4.5 Signs and Symptoms of Type 1 and Type 2 Diabetes

Type 1 Diabetes	Type 2 Diabetes[†]
Frequent urination	Any of the type 1 signs and symptoms
Unusual thirst	Frequent infections
Extreme hunger	Blurred vision
Unusual weight loss	Cuts/bruises that are slow to heal
Extreme fatigue	Tingling/numbness in the hands or feet
Irritability	Recurring skin, gum, or bladder infections

Data adapted from: the American Diabetes Association. 2009. Diabetes symptoms. Available online at http://www.diabetes.org/diabetes-symptoms.jsp. Reprinted with permission.

[†]Some people with type 2 diabetes experience no symptoms.

Figure 4.20 Monitoring blood glucose requires pricking the fingers several times each day and measuring the blood glucose level using a glucometer.

type 1 diabetes A disorder in which the body cannot produce enough insulin.

Highlight
Living with Diabetes

Vincent is a young man who was diagnosed with type 1 diabetes when he was 10 years old. At first, Vincent and his family were frightened by the disease and found it difficult to adapt their lifestyles to provide a safe and health-promoting environment for Vincent. For example, Vincent's mother felt frustrated because her son could no longer eat the cakes, pies, and other sweets she had always enjoyed baking for her family, and his sister found herself watching over her brother's meals and snacks, running to her parents whenever she feared that he was about to eat something that would harm him. Within a few months, though, Vincent's mother learned to adapt her recipes and cooking techniques to produce a variety of foods that Vincent could enjoy, and the entire family learned to allow Vincent the responsibility for his food choices and his health.

Vincent is now a college sophomore and has been living with diabetes for 9 years, but what he still hates most about the disease is that food is always a major issue. Vincent is smart and a good student, but if his blood glucose declines, he has trouble concentrating. He has to eat three nutritious meals a day on a regular schedule and needs to limit his snacks unless his blood sugar is low. When his friends eat candy, chips, or other snacks, he can't join them. In general, he knows these dietary changes are very healthful, but sometimes he wishes he could eat like all of his friends. On the other hand, he cannot skip a meal, even if he isn't hungry. It is also important for Vincent to stay on a regular schedule for exercise and sleep.

Vincent must test his blood sugar many times each day. He has to prick his fingers to do this, and they get tender and develop calluses. During his first few years with diabetes, he had to give himself two to four shots of insulin each day. He learned to measure the insulin into a syringe, and he had to monitor where the shots were injected because each in-

Insulin pumps can help those with diabetes eat a wider range of foods.

sulin shot should be given in a different place on his body to avoid damaging the skin and underlying tissue. Technological advances now offer easier alternatives than a needle and syringe. Vincent uses an insulin infusion pump, which looks like a small pager and delivers insulin into the body through a long, thin tube in very small amounts throughout the day. One of Vincent's friends also has diabetes but can't use a pump; instead, he uses an insulin pen, which includes a needle and a cartridge of insulin. Now that Vincent uses the insulin pump, he can choose to eat more of the foods he loves and deliver his insulin accordingly.

Although diabetes is challenging, it does not prevent Vincent from playing soccer and basketball almost every day. In fact, he knows that people with diabetes should be active. As long as he takes his insulin regularly, keeps an eye on his blood sugar, drinks plenty of water, and eats when he should, he knows that he can play sports and do most of the things he wants to do. There are numerous professional and Olympic athletes and other famous people who have diabetes, showing that this disease should not prevent Vincent from leading a healthful life and realizing his dreams.

Currently, there is no cure for type 1 diabetes. However, there are many new treatments and potential cures being researched. The FDA has approved several devices that measure blood glucose without pricking the finger. Some of them can read glucose levels through the skin, and others insert a small needle into the body to monitor glucose continually. Tests are also being conducted on insulin nasal sprays and inhalers. Advances in genetic engineering may soon make it possible to transplant healthy beta cells into the pancreas of virtually anyone with type 1 diabetes, so that the normal cells will secrete insulin. Vincent looks forward to seeing major changes in the treatment of diabetes in the next few years.

In Type 2 Diabetes, Cells Become Less Responsive to Insulin

In **type 2 diabetes,** body cells become resistant (less responsive) to insulin. This type of diabetes develops progressively, meaning that the biological changes resulting in the disease occur over a long period of time.

Obesity is the most common trigger for a cascade of changes that eventually results in the disorder. It is estimated that 80% to 90% of the people with type 2 diabetes are overweight or obese. Specifically, the cells of many obese people are less responsive to insulin, exhibiting a condition called *insulin insensitivity* (or insulin resistance). The pancreas attempts to compensate for this insensitivity by secreting more insulin. At first, the

type 2 diabetes A progressive disorder in which body cells become less responsive to insulin.

increased secretion of insulin is sufficient to maintain normal blood glucose levels. However, over time, a person who is insulin insensitive will have to circulate very high levels of insulin to use glucose for energy, and this excessive production becomes insufficient for preventing a rise in fasting blood glucose. The resulting condition is referred to as **impaired fasting glucose**, meaning glucose levels are higher than normal but not high enough to lead to a diagnosis of type 2 diabetes. Some health professionals refer to this condition as *pre-diabetes*, as people with impaired fasting glucose are more likely to get type 2 diabetes than people with normal fasting glucose levels. Eventually the pancreas becomes incapable of secreting these excessive amounts of insulin, and the beta cells stop producing the hormone altogether. Thus, blood glucose levels may be elevated in a person with type 2 diabetes (1) because of insulin insensitivity, (2) because the pancreas can no longer secrete enough insulin, or (3) because the pancreas has entirely stopped insulin production.

Many factors can cause type 2 diabetes. Genetics plays a role, so relatives of people with type 2 diabetes are at increased risk. Obesity and physical inactivity also increase the risk. A cluster of risk factors referred to as the *metabolic syndrome* is also known to increase the risk for type 2 diabetes. The criteria for metabolic syndrome include having a waist circumference ≥88 cm (or 35 in.)[26] for women and ≥102 cm (or 40 in.) for men, elevated blood pressure, and unhealthful levels of certain blood lipids and blood glucose. Increased age is another risk factor: Most cases of type 2 diabetes develop after age 45, and almost 20% of Americans 65 years of age and older have diabetes.

Once commonly known as *adult-onset diabetes,* type 2 diabetes in children was virtually unheard of until recently. Unfortunately, the disease is increasing dramatically among children and adolescents, posing serious health consequences for them and their future children.[23]

Type 2 diabetes can be treated in a variety of ways. Weight loss, healthful eating patterns, and regular exercise can control symptoms in some people. More severe cases may require oral medications. These drugs work in either of two ways: they improve body cells' sensitivity to insulin or reduce the amount of glucose the liver produces. If a person with type 2 diabetes can no longer secrete enough insulin, the patient must take daily injections of insulin just like people with type 1 diabetes.

Jerry Garcia, a member of the band The Grateful Dead, had type 2 diabetes.

Lifestyle Choices Can Help Control or Prevent Diabetes

Type 2 diabetes is thought to have become an epidemic in the United States because of a combination of our poor eating habits, sedentary lifestyles, increased obesity, and an aging population. We can't control our age, but we can adopt a healthful diet, increase our physical activity, and maintain a healthful weight.

In general, people with diabetes should follow many of the same dietary guidelines recommended for those without diabetes. One difference is that people with diabetes may need to eat less carbohydrate and slightly more fat or protein to help regulate their blood glucose levels. Carbohydrates are still an important part of the diet, but their intake may need to be reduced. Precise nutritional recommendations vary according to each individual's responses to foods. In addition, people with diabetes should avoid alcoholic beverages, which can cause hypoglycemia. The symptoms of alcohol intoxication and hypoglycemia are very similar. The person with diabetes and his or her companions may confuse these conditions; this can result in a potentially life-threatening situation.

Moderate daily exercise may prevent the onset of type 2 diabetes more effectively than dietary changes alone.[27] See Chapter 14 for examples of moderate exercise programs. Exercise will also assist in weight loss, and studies show that losing only 10 to 30 pounds can reduce or eliminate the symptoms of type 2 diabetes.[28]

In summary, by eating a healthy diet, staying active, and maintaining a healthful body weight, you should be able to keep your risk for diabetes low.

impaired fasting glucose Fasting blood glucose levels that are higher than normal but not high enough to lead to a diagnosis of type 2 diabetes.

Judy
Nutri-Case

"Ever since my last doctor's visit, I've felt as if there's been a 'food cop' spying on me. Sometimes I feel like I have to look over my shoulder when I pull into the McDonald's parking lot. My doctor says I need to lose weight and get my blood sugar down, so I'm supposed to switch to healthy foods. When I ask what that means, he says, "Eat broiled fish! And salad instead of French fries! And have fruit with nonfat yogurt for dessert!" I didn't bother telling him I don't like that stuff and it doesn't fill me up and I don't have the money to buy it or the time to make it! That kind of diet is for movie stars. All the real people I know eat the same way I do."

In previous chapters, you've learned about the many factors influencing why we eat what we eat. Identify at least two factors that might be affecting Judy's food choices. Do you agree that the foods Judy's doctor recommended are not for "real people" like Judy? Why or why not?

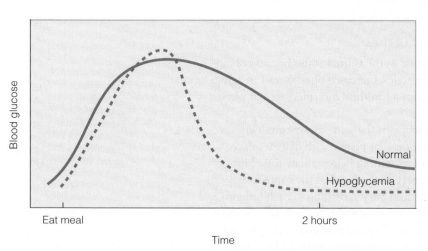

Figure 4.21   Changes in blood glucose after a meal for people with hypoglycemia (lower than normal) and without hypoglycemia (normal).

hypoglycemia   A condition marked by blood glucose levels that are below normal fasting levels.

Hypoglycemia: Low Blood Glucose

In **hypoglycemia,** fasting blood sugar falls to lower-than-normal levels (**Figure 4.21**). One cause of hypoglycemia is excessive production of insulin, which lowers blood glucose too far. People with diabetes can develop hypoglycemia if they inject too much insulin or if they exercise and fail to eat enough carbohydrates. Two types of hypoglycemia can develop in people who do not have diabetes: reactive and fasting.

Reactive hypoglycemia occurs when the pancreas secretes too much insulin after a high-carbohydrate meal. The symptoms of reactive hypoglycemia usually appear about 1 to 4 hours after the meal and include nervousness, shakiness, anxiety, sweating, irritability, headache, weakness, and rapid or irregular heartbeat. Although many people experience these symptoms from time to time, they are rarely caused by true hypoglycemia. A person diagnosed with reactive hypoglycemia must eat smaller meals more frequently to level out blood insulin and glucose levels.

Fasting hypoglycemia occurs when the body continues to produce too much insulin, even when someone has not eaten. This condition is usually secondary to another disorder such as cancer, liver infection, alcohol-induced liver disease, or a tumor in the pancreas. Its symptoms are similar to those of reactive hypoglycemia but occur more than 4 hours after a meal.

> ## Recap
>
> Hypoglycemia refers to lower-than-normal blood glucose levels. Reactive hypoglycemia occurs when the pancreas secretes too much insulin after a high-carbohydrate meal. Fasting hypoglycemia occurs when the body continues to produce too much insulin even when someone has not eaten.

Lactose Intolerance: Inability to Digest Lactose

Sometimes our bodies do not produce enough of the enzymes necessary to break down certain carbohydrates before they reach the colon. A common example is **lactose intolerance,** in which the body does not produce sufficient amounts of the enzyme lactase in the small intestine and therefore cannot digest foods containing lactose.

Lactose intolerance should not be confused with a milk allergy. People who are allergic to milk experience an immune reaction to the proteins found in cow's milk. Symptoms of milk allergy include skin reactions such as hives and rashes; intestinal distress such as nausea, vomiting, cramping, and diarrhea; and respiratory symptoms such as wheezing, runny nose, and itchy and watery eyes. In severe cases, anaphylactic shock can occur. In contrast, symptoms of lactose intolerance are limited to the GI tract and include intestinal gas, bloating, cramping, nausea, diarrhea, and discomfort. These symptoms resolve spontaneously within a few hours.

Although some infants are born with lactose intolerance, it is more common to see lactase enzyme activity decrease after 2 years of age. In fact, it is estimated that up to 70% of the world's adult population will lose some ability to digest lactose as they age. In the United States, lactose intolerance is more common in Native American, Asian, Hispanic, and African-American adults than in Caucasians.

Not everyone experiences lactose intolerance to the same extent. Some people can digest small amounts of dairy products, whereas others cannot tolerate any. Suarez and colleagues found that many people who reported being lactose intolerant were able to consume multiple small servings of dairy products without symptoms, which enabled them to meet their calcium requirements.[29] Thus, it is not necessary for everyone with lactose intolerance to avoid all dairy products; they may simply need to eat smaller amounts and experiment to find foods that do not cause intestinal distress.

People with lactose intolerance need to find foods that can supply enough calcium for normal growth, development, and maintenance of bones. Many can tolerate specially formulated milk products that are low in lactose, whereas others take pills or use drops that contain the lactase enzyme when they eat dairy products. Calcium-fortified soy milk and orange juice are excellent substitutes for cow's milk. Many lactose-intolerant people can also digest yogurt and aged cheese, as the bacteria or molds used to ferment these products break down the lactose during processing.

How can you tell if you are lactose intolerant? Many people discover that they have problems digesting dairy products by trial and error. But because intestinal gas, bloating, and diarrhea may indicate other health problems, you should consult a physician to determine the cause.

Tests for lactose intolerance include drinking a lactose-rich liquid and testing blood glucose levels over a 2-hour period. If you do not produce the normal amount of glucose, you are unable to digest the lactose present. Another test involves measuring hydrogen levels in the breath, as lactose-intolerant people breathe out more hydrogen when they drink a beverage that contains lactose.

Milk products, such as ice cream, are hard to digest for people who are lactose intolerant.

lactose intolerance A disorder in which the body does not produce sufficient lactase enzyme and therefore cannot digest foods that contain lactose, such as cow's milk.

See for Yourself

Calculate Your Risk for Type 2 Diabetes

To calculate your risk for developing type 2 diabetes, answer the following questions:

I am overweight.	Yes No
I am sedentary (I exercise fewer than three times a week).	Yes No
I have a close family member with type 2 diabetes.	Yes No
I am a member of one of the following groups:	Yes No

African American
Hispanic American (Latino)
Native American
Pacific Islander

I have had gestational diabetes, or I gave birth to at least one baby weighing more than 9 pounds.	Yes No
My blood pressure is 140/90 or higher, or I have been told that I have high blood pressure.	Yes No
My cholesterol levels are not normal. (See the discussion of cholesterol in Chapter 5.)	Yes No

The more "yes" responses you give, the higher your risk of developing type 2 diabetes. You cannot change your ethnicity or your family members' health, but you can take steps to maintain a healthful weight and increase your physical activity. For tips, see Chapters 13 and 14.

Data from: The National Diabetes Information Clearinghouse (NDIC). Available online at http://diabetes.niddk.nih.gov/dm/pubs/riskfortype2/.

Chapter Review

Test Yourself | Answers

1. **T** Our brains rely almost exclusively on glucose for energy, and our body tissues utilize glucose for energy both at rest and during exercise.

2. **F** At 4 kcal/g, carbohydrates have less than half the energy of a gram of fat. Eating a high-carbohydrate diet will not cause people to gain body fat unless their total diet contains more energy (or kcal) than they expend. In fact, eating a diet high in complex, fiber-rich carbohydrates is associated with a lower risk for obesity.

3. **F** Although specific estimates are not yet available, significantly higher rates of type 2 diabetes are now being reported in children and adolescents; these higher rates are attributed to increasing obesity rates in young people.

4. **F** There is no evidence that diets high in sugar cause hyperactivity in children.

5. **T** Contrary to recent reports claiming harmful consequences related to consumption of alternative sweeteners, major health agencies have determined that these products are safe for most of us to consume in limited quantities.

Summary

- Carbohydrates contain carbon, hydrogen, and oxygen. Plants make the carbohydrate glucose during photosynthesis.

- Simple sugars include mono- and disaccharides. The three primary monosaccharides are glucose, fructose, and galactose.

- Two monosaccharides joined together are called disaccharides. Glucose and fructose join to make sucrose; glucose and glucose join to make maltose; and glucose and galactose join to make lactose.

- The two monosaccharides that compose a disaccharide are attached by a bond between oxygen and one carbon on each of the monosaccharides. There are two forms of this bond: alpha bonds are easily digestible by humans, whereas beta bonds are very difficult to digest.

- Oligosaccharides are complex carbohydrates that contain 3 to 10 monosaccharides.

- Polysaccharides are complex carbohydrates that typically contain hundreds to thousands of monosaccharides. The three types of polysaccharides are starches, glycogen, and fiber.

- Starches are the storage form of glucose in plants.

- Glycogen is the storage form of glucose in humans. Glycogen is stored in the liver and in muscles.

- Dietary fiber is the non-digestible parts of plants, whereas functional fiber is a non-digestible form of carbohydrate extracted from plants or manufactured in the laboratory. Fiber may reduce the risk of many diseases and digestive illnesses.

- Carbohydrate digestion starts in the mouth, where chewing and an enzyme called salivary amylase start breaking down the carbohydrates in food.

- Digestion continues in the small intestine. Specific enzymes are secreted to break starches into smaller mono- and disaccharides. As disaccharides pass through the intestinal cells, they are digested into monosaccharides.

- Glucose and other monosaccharides are absorbed into the bloodstream and travel to the liver, where all non-glucose molecules are converted to glucose.

- Glucose is transported in the bloodstream to the cells, where it is either used for energy, stored in the liver or muscle as glycogen, or converted to fat and stored in adipose tissue.

- Insulin is secreted when blood glucose increases sufficiently, and it assists with the transport of glucose into cells.

- Glucagon, epinephrine, norepinephrine, cortisol, and growth hormone are secreted when blood glucose levels are low, and they assist with the conversion of glycogen to glucose, with gluconeogenesis, and with reducing the use of glucose by muscles and other organs.

- The glycemic index and the glycemic load are values that indicate how much a food increases glucose levels. High-glycemic foods can trigger detrimental increases in blood glucose for people with diabetes.

- All cells can use glucose for energy. The red blood cells, brain, and central nervous system prefer to use glucose exclusively.

- Using glucose for energy helps spare body proteins, and glucose is an important fuel for the body during exercise.

- Fiber helps us maintain the healthy elimination of waste products. Eating adequate fiber may reduce the risk of colon cancer, type 2 diabetes, obesity, heart disease, hemorrhoids, and diverticulosis.

- The Acceptable Macronutrient Distribution Range for carbohydrate is 45% to 65% of total energy intake. Our diets should contain less than 25% of total energy from simple sugars.

- High added-sugar intake can cause tooth decay, elevate triglyceride and low-density lipoprotein levels in the blood, and contribute to obesity. It does not appear to cause hyperactivity in children.

- The Adequate Intake for fiber is 25 g per day for women and 38 g per day for men, or 14 g of fiber for every 1,000 kcal of energy consumed.

- Foods high in fiber-rich carbohydrates include whole grains and cereals, fruits, and vegetables. Eating 6 to 11 servings of breads/grains and 5 to 9 servings of fruits and vegetables helps ensure that you meet your fiber-rich carbohydrate goals.

- Alternative sweeteners are added to some foods because they sweeten foods without promoting tooth decay and add little or no calories to foods.

- All alternative sweeteners approved for use in the United States are believed to be safe when eaten at levels at or below the Acceptable Daily Intake levels defined by the FDA.

- Diabetes is caused by insufficient insulin or by the cells becoming resistant or insensitive to insulin. It causes dangerously high blood glucose levels. The two primary types of diabetes are type 1 and type 2.

- A lower-than-normal blood glucose level is defined as hypoglycemia. There are two types: reactive and fasting. Reactive hypoglycemia occurs when too much insulin is secreted after a high-carbohydrate meal; fasting hypoglycemia occurs when blood glucose drops even though no food has been eaten.

- Lactose intolerance results from an insufficient amount of the lactase enzyme. Symptoms include intestinal gas, bloating, cramping, diarrhea, and discomfort.

Review Questions

1. The glycemic index rates
   a. the acceptable amount of alternative sweeteners to consume in 1 day.
   b. the potential of foods to raise blood glucose and insulin levels.
   c. the risk of a given food for causing diabetes.
   d. the ratio of soluble to insoluble fiber in a complex carbohydrate.

2. Carbohydrates contain
   a. carbon, nitrogen, and water.
   b. carbonic acid and a sugar alcohol.
   c. hydrated sugar.
   d. carbon, hydrogen, and oxygen.

3. The most common source of added sugar in the American diet is
   a. table sugar.
   b. white flour.
   c. alcohol.
   d. sweetened soft drinks.

4. Glucose, fructose, and galactose are
   a. monosaccharides.
   b. disaccharides.
   c. polysaccharides.
   d. complex carbohydrates.

5. Aspartame should not be consumed by people who have
   a. phenylketonuria.
   b. type 1 diabetes.
   c. lactose intolerance.
   d. diverticulosis.

6. **True or false?** Sugar alcohols are non-nutritive sweeteners.

7. **True or false?** Insulin and glucagon are both pancreatic hormones.

8. **True or false?** A person with lactose intolerance is allergic to milk.

9. **True or false?** Plants store glucose as fiber.

10. **True or false?** Salivary amylase breaks down starches into galactose.

11. Describe the role of insulin in regulating blood glucose levels.

12. Identify at least four ways in which fiber helps us maintain a healthy digestive system.

13. Your niece Lilly is 6 years old and is learning about MyPyramid in her first-grade class. She points out the "grains" group on the left side of the pyramid and proudly lists her favorite food choices from this group: "saltine crackers, pancakes, cinnamon toast, and spaghetti." Explain to Lilly, in words she could understand, the difference between fiber-rich carbohydrates and highly processed carbohydrates and why fiber-rich carbohydrates are more healthful food choices.

14. When Ben returns from his doctor's appointment with the news that he has been diagnosed with type 2 diabetes and must lose weight, his wife looks skeptical. "I thought that diabetes runs in families," she says. "No one in your family has diabetes, and your whole family is overweight! So how come your doctor thinks losing weight will solve your problems?" Defend the statement that obesity can trigger type 2 diabetes.

15. Create a table listing molecular composition and food sources of each of the following carbohydrates: glucose, fructose, lactose, and sucrose.

Web Links

www.eatright.org
American Dietetic Association
Visit this Web site to learn more about diabetes, low- and high-carbohydrate diets, and general healthful eating habits.

www.ific.org
International Food Information Council Foundation (IFIC)
Search this site to find out more about sugars and low-calorie sweeteners.

www.ada.org
American Dental Association
Go to this site to learn more about tooth decay as well as other oral health topics.

www.nidcr.nih.gov
National Institute of Dental and Craniofacial Research (NIDCR)

Find out more about recent oral and dental health discoveries, and obtain statistics and data on the status of dental health in the United States.

www.diabetes.org
American Diabetes Association
Find out more about the nutritional needs of people living with diabetes.

www.niddk.nih.gov
National Institute of Diabetes and Digestive and Kidney Diseases (NIDDK)
Learn more about diabetes, including treatment, complications, U.S. statistics, clinical trials, and recent research.

www.caloriecontrol.org/neotame.html
Calorie Control Council
This site provides information about reducing energy and fat in the diet, achieving and maintaining a healthy weight, and various low-calorie, reduced-fat foods and beverages.

References

1. Kleinfield, N. R. 2006. Diabetes and its awful toll quietly emerge as a crisis. *The New York Times.* January 9, 2006. http://www.nytimes.com/2006/01/09/nyregion/nyregionspecial5/09diabetes.html. (Accessed March 2007.)

2. Sears, B. 1995. *The Zone. A Dietary Road Map.* New York: Harper-Collins Publishers.

3. Steward, H. L., M. C. Bethea, S. S. Andrews, and L. A. Balart. 1995. *Sugar Busters! Cut Sugar to Trim Fat.* New York: Ballantine Books.

4. Atkins, R. C. 1992. *Dr. Atkins' New Diet Revolution.* New York: M. Evans & Company, Inc.

5. Institute of Medicine, Food and Nutrition Board. 2002. *Dietary Reference Intakes for Energy, Carbohydrates, Fiber, Fat, Protein and Amino Acids (Macronutrients).* Washington, DC: The National Academy of Sciences.

6. Topping, D. L., and P. M. Clifton. 2001. Short-chain fatty acids and human colonic function: Roles of resistant starch and non-starch polysaccharides. *Physiol. Rev.* 81:1031–1064.

7. Foster-Powell K., S. H. A. Holt, and J. C. Brand-Miller. 2002. International table of glycemic index and glycemic load values: 2002. *Am. J. Clin. Nutr.* 76:5–56.

8. Liu, S., J. E. Manson, M. J. Stampfer, M. D. Holmes, F. B. Hu, S. E. Hankinson, and W. C. Willett. 2001. Dietary glycemic load assessed by food-frequency questionnaire in relation to plasma high-density-lipoprotein cholesterol and fasting plasma triacylglycerols in postmenopausal women. *Am. J. Clin. Nutr.* 73:560–566.

9. Sloth B., I. Krog-Mikkelsen, A. Flint, I. Tetens, I. Björck, S. Vinoy, H. Elmståhl, A. Astrup, V. Lang, and A. Raben. 2004. No difference in body weight decrease between a low-glycemic-index and a high-glycemic-index diet but reduced LDL cholesterol after 10-wk ad libitum intake of the low-glycemic-index diet. *Am. J. Clin. Nutr.* 80:337–347.

10. Buyken, A. E., M. Toeller, G. Heitkamp, G. Karamanos, B. Rottiers, R. Muggeo, and M. Fuller. 2001. Glycemic index in the diet of European outpatients with type 1 diabetes: relations to glycated hemoglobin and serum lipids. *Am. J. Clin. Nutr.* 73:574–581.

11. Augustin L. S. A., C. Galeone, L. Dal Maso, C. Pelucchi, V. Ramazzotti, D. J. A. Jenkins, M. Montella, R. Talamini, E. Negri, S. Franceschi, and C. La Vecchia. 2004. Glycemic index, glycemic load and risk of prostate cancer. *Int. J. Cancer* 112: 446–450.

12. Tremblay, A., J. A. Simoneau, and C. Bouchard. 1994. Impact of exercise intensity on body fatness and skeletal muscle metabolism. *Metabolism* 43:814–818.

13. Pan, J. W., D. L. Rothman, K. L. Behar, D. T. Stein, and H. P. Hetherington. 2000. Human brain ß-hydroxybutyrate and lactate increase in fasting-induced ketosis. *J. Cereb. Blood Flow Metab.* 20:1502–1507.

14. U.S. Department of Health and Human Services and U.S. Department of Agriculture. 2005. *Dietary Guidelines for Americans, 2005,* 6th ed. Washington, DC: U.S. Government Printing Office.

15. U.S. Department of Health and Human Services (USDHHS) and U.S. Department of Agriculture (USDA). 2006. Eating healthier and feeling better using the Nutrition Facts Label. http://www.cfsan.fda.gov/~acrobat/nutfacts.pdf. (Accessed January 2009.)

16. Howard, B. V., and J. Wylie-Rosett. 2002. Sugar and cardiovascular disease. A statement for healthcare professionals from the Committee on Nutrition of the Council on Nutrition, Physical Activity, and Metabolism of the American Heart Association. *Circulation* 106:523–527.

17. Meyer, K. A., L. H. Kushi, D. R. Jacobs, J. Slavin, T. A. Sellers, and A. R. Folsom. 2000. Carbohydrates, dietary fiber, and incidence of type 2 diabetes in older women. *Am. J. Clin. Nutr.* 71:921–930.

18. Colditz, G. A., J. E. Manson, M. J. Stampfer, B. Rosner, W. C. Willett, and F. E. Speizer. 1992. Diet and risk of clinical diabetes in women. *Am. J. Clin. Nutr.* 55:1018–1023.

19. Schultz, M. B., J. E. Manson, D. S. Ludwig, G. A. Colditz, M. J. Stampfer, W. C. Willett, and F. B. Hu. 2004. Sugar-sweetened beverages, weight gain, and incidence of type 2 diabetes in young and middle-aged women. *JAMA.* 292:927–934.

20. Troiano, R. P., R. R. Briefel, M. D. Carroll, and K. Bialostosky. 2000. Energy and fat intakes of children and adolescents in the United States: Data from the National Health and Nutrition Examination Surveys. *Am. J. Clin. Nutr.* 72:1343S–1353S.

21. Ludwig, D. S., K. E. Peterson, and S. L. Gortmaker. 2001. Relation between consumption of sugar-sweetened drinks and childhood obesity: a prospective, observational analysis. *Lancet* 357:505–508.

22. Duffy, V. B., and G. H. Anderson. 1998. Use of nutritive and non-nutritive sweeteners—position of the ADA. *J. Am. Diet. Assoc.* 98:580–587.

23. Centers for Disease Control and Prevention (CDC). 2007. National diabetes fact sheet: 2007. Available online at http://www.cdc.gov/diabetes/pubs/pdf/ndfs_2007.pdf.

24. National Diabetes Information Clearinghouse (NDIC). 2008. National diabetes statistics. National Institutes of Health Publication No. 08–3892. Available online at http://diabetes.niddk.nih.gov/dm/pubs/statistics/index.htm.

25. American Diabetes Association. 2005. *The genetics of diabetes.* Available online at http://www.diabetes.org/genetics.jsp.

26. Grundy, S. M., J. I. Cleeman, S. R. Daniels, K. A. Donato, R. H. Eckel, B. A. Franklin, D. J. Gordon, R. M. Krauss, P. J. Savage, S. C. Smith, J. A. Spertus, and F. Costa. 2005. Diagnosis and management of the metabolic syndrome: An American Heart Association/National Heart, Lung, and Blood Institute scientific statement. *Circulation* 112(17):2735–2752.

27. Pan, X.-P., G.-W. Li, Y.-H. Hu, J. X. Wang, W. Y. Yang, Z. X. An, Z. X. Hu, J. Lin, J. Z. Xiao, H. B. Cao, P. A. Liu, X. G. Jiang, Y. Y. Jiang, J. P Wang, H. Zheng, H. Zhang, P. H. Bennett, and B. V. Howard. 1997. Effects of diet and exercise in preventing NIDDM in people with impaired glucose tolerance. *Diabetes Care* 20:537–544.

28. American College of Sports Medicine (ACSM). 2000. Position stand: Exercise and type 2 diabetes. *Med. Sci. Sports Exerc.* 32:1345–1360.

29. Suarez, F. L., J. Adshead, J. K. Furne, and M. D. Levitt. 1998. Lactose maldigestion is not an impediment to the intake of 1500 mg calcium daily as dairy products. *Am. J. Clin. Nutr.* 68:1118–1122.

30. Ogden, C. L., M. D. Carroll, and K. M. Flegal. 2008. High body mass index for age among US children and adolescents, 2003–2006. *JAMA* 299:2401–2405.

31. Elliott S. S., N. L. Keim, J. S. Stern, K. Teff, and P. J. Havel. 2002. Fructose, weight gain, and the insulin resistance syndrome. *Am. J. Clin. Nutr.* 76:911–922.

32. Bray G. A., S. J. Nielsen, and B. M. Popkin. 2004. Consumption of high-fructose corn syrup in beverages may play a role in the epidemic of obesity. *Am. J. Clin. Nutr.* 79:537–543.

33. Wilkinson Enns, C., S. J. Mickle, and J. D. Goldman. 2002. Trends in food and nutrient intakes by children in the United States. *Family Econ. Nutr. Rev.* 14:56–68.

34. Harnack, L., J. Stang, and M. Story. 1999. Soft drink consumption among U.S. children and adolescents: nutritional consequences. *J. Am. Diet. Assoc.* 99:436–441.

35. Ebbeling, C. B., H. A. Feldman, S. K. Osganian, V. R. Chomitz, S. H. Ellenbogen, and D. S. Ludwig. 2006. Effects of decreasing sugar-sweetened beverage consumption on body weight in adolescents: A randomized, controlled pilot study. *Pediatrics* 117:673–680.

36. Wolf, A., G. A. Bray, and B. M. Popkin. 2008. A short history of beverages and how our body treats them. *Obesity Rev.* 9:151–164.

37. Jacobson, M. F. 2004. Letter to the editor. High-fructose corn syrup and the obesity epidemic. *Am. J. Clin. Nutr.* 80:1081–1090.

38. Lê K.-A., D. Faeh, R. Stettler, M. Ith, R. Kreis, P. Vermathen, C. Boesch, E. Ravussin, and L. Tappy. 2006. A 4-wk high-fructose diet alters lipid metabolism without affecting insulin sensitivity or ectopic lipids in healthy humans. *Am. J. Clin. Nutr.* 84:1374–1379.

Is High-Fructose Corn Syrup the Cause of the Obesity Epidemic?

Almost every day in the news we see headlines about obesity: "More Americans Overweight!" "The Fattening of America," "Obesity Is a National Epidemic!" These headlines accurately reflect the state of weight in the United States. Over the past 30 years, obesity rates have increased dramatically for both adults and children. Obesity has become public health enemy number one, as many chronic diseases such as type 2 diabetes, heart disease, high blood pressure, and arthritis go hand in hand with obesity.

Of particular concern are the rising obesity rates in children. Recent evidence from the Centers for Disease Control and Prevention indicates that the prevalence of obesity is 12.4% in young children aged 2 to 5 years, 17% in children aged 6 to 11 years, and 17.6% in adolescents aged 12 to 19 years.[30]

It is estimated that the rate of overweight in children in the United States has increased 100% since the mid-1970s.

Why should we concern ourselves with fighting obesity in children? First, it is well established that the treatment of existing obesity is extremely challenging, and our greatest hope of combating this disease is through prevention. Most agree that prevention should start with children at a very early age. Second, approximately 30% of children who are obese will remain obese as adults, suffering all of the health problems that accompany this disease. Young children are now experiencing type 2 diabetes, high blood pressure, and high cholesterol at increasingly younger ages, only compounding the devastating effects of these illnesses as they get older. We have reached the point at which serious action must be taken immediately to curb this growing crisis.

How can we prevent obesity? This is a difficult question to answer. One way is to better understand the factors that contribute to obesity, and then take actions to alter these factors. We know of many factors that contribute to overweight and obesity. These include genetic influences, lack of adequate physical activity, and eating foods that are high in fat, added sugar, and energy. While it is easy to blame our genetics, they cannot be held entirely responsible for the rapid rise in obesity that has occurred over the past 30 years. Our genetic makeup takes thousands of years to change; thus, humans who lived 50 or 100 years ago have essentially the same genetic makeup as humans who live now. The fact that obesity rates have risen so dramatically in recent years illustrates that we need to look more closely at how our lifestyle changes over this same period have contributed to obesity.

One factor that has recently come to the forefront of nutrition research and policy making is the contribution of added sugars, particularly in the form of high-fructose corn syrup (HFCS), to overweight and obesity. As discussed earlier in this chapter, there is disagreement about whether added sugar does cause, and how much it might contribute to, obesity. Many nutrition researchers are beginning to draw attention to the potential role of HFCS in rising obesity rates. Before we discuss why these researchers are pointing to HFCS as a major cause of the obesity epidemic, it is important to understand what HFCS is and how it is metabolized in our bodies.

HFCS is made by first converting the starch in corn to glucose, and then converting some of the glucose to fructose through a process referred to as *enzymatic isomerization*. The result is an inexpensive corn-based syrup that has been used to replace sucrose and other simple sugars as a sweetener in foods and beverages. Fructose is sweeter than glucose. It is also metabolized differently from glucose, as it is absorbed farther down in the small intestine and, unlike glucose, it does not stimulate insulin release from the pancreas. It also enters the cell by a transport protein that does not require the presence of insulin.

Interestingly, brain cells do not have this transport protein; thus, unlike glucose, fructose cannot enter brain cells and stimulate satiety signals. In addition, consumption of fructose increases the production of triglycerides in the blood significantly more than glucose, and in animals can lead to excessive insulin production, resistance to insulin, and impaired glucose regulation—all factors that can lead to type 2 diabetes.[31]

How might the consumption of HFCS contribute to obesity? Bray et al.[32] speculate that HFCS could lead to increased obesity because of its effect on appetite regulation and its contribution to excessive energy intake. Both insulin and the hormone leptin inhibit food intake in humans, and as previously stated, fructose does not stimulate insulin release. As insulin increases the release of leptin, it is possible that consuming fructose results in lower circulating levels of both insulin and leptin, which results in an increase in appetite and food intake.

At the same time, HFCS could contribute to obesity because people consume significant amounts of excess energy in the form of HFCS-sweetened soft drinks and foods. Bray et al.[32] emphasize that HFCS is the sole caloric sweetener in sugared soft drinks and represents more than 40% of caloric sweeteners added to other foods and beverages in the United States. These researchers have linked the increased use and consumption of HFCS in beverages and foods with the rising rates of obesity since the 1970s, when HFCS was first developed and marketed (see the accompanying graph).

Consumption of sweetened soft drinks is thought to play a much greater role in obesity than consumption of sugary foods. Why? Evidence indicates that the body does not recognize the energy in sweetened beverages in the same way as it recognizes the energy in solid food. Studies suggest that when we snack on cookies, we unconsciously compensate for these calories by reducing our intake of other foods in the next several hours. But when we consume energy in the form of soft drinks and other sweetened beverages, we do not adjust our intake of foods accordingly.[33]

How significant a problem is soft drink consumption in children? Studies show that girls and boys ages 6 to 11 years drank about twice as many soft drinks in 1998 as compared to 1977, and consumption of milk over this same time period dropped by about 30%.[33] Equally alarming is the finding that one-fourth of a group of adolescents studied were heavy consumers of sugared soft drinks, drinking at least 26 oz of soft drinks each day. This

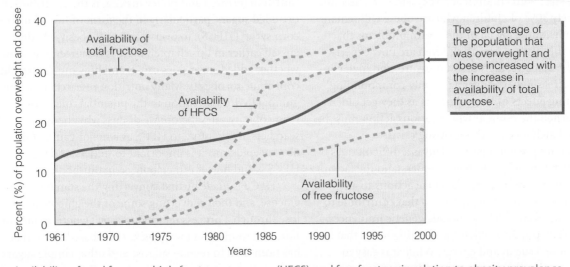

Availability of total fructose, high-fructose corn syrup (HFCS), and free fructose in relation to obesity prevalence in the United States. (*Data adapted from:* Bray, G. A., S. J. Nielsen, and B. M. Popkin. 2004. Consumption of high-fructose corn syrup in beverages may play a role in the epidemic of obesity. *Am. J. Clin. Nutr.* 79:537–543. Used with permission.)

intake is equivalent to almost 400 extra calories! As we might expect, consuming these liquid calories did not prompt the teens to reduce their energy intake in other ways; instead, they consumed more energy from all foods than other adolescents.[34] So it's not surprising that, according to another study, for each extra sugared soft drink that children consume each day, the risk of obesity increases by 60%.[21] A recent pilot intervention study found that replacing sweetened soft drinks with noncaloric beverages in the diets of 13- to 18-year-old adolescents resulted in a significant decrease in body mass index in the adolescents who were the most overweight when starting the study.[35]

In addition to providing significant quantities of nutritionally empty calories, soft drinks may also have a detrimental effect on bone density: soft drinks typically displace milk in the diet, and the phosphorus available in some sodas, whether sugared or diet, binds with calcium, causing it to be drawn out of the bones. This is especially harmful during childhood and adolescence, when bones are still growing.[36]

All of this alarming information has led to dramatic changes in soft drink availability in schools and at school-sponsored events. In 2006, the soft drink industry agreed to a voluntary ban on sales of all sweetened soft drinks in elementary and high schools, to take effect by the start of the 2009–2010 school year. Despite these positive changes in schools, foods and beverages containing HFCS are still widely available in the marketplace.

Although the evidence pinpointing HFCS as a major contributor to the obesity epidemic may appear strong, other nutrition professionals disagree with these speculations about HFCS. It has been proposed that soft drinks would have contributed to the obesity epidemic no matter whether the sweetener was sucrose or fructose and that their contribution to obesity is due to increased consumption resulting from massive increases in advertising, substantial increases in serving sizes of soft drinks, and virtually unlimited access to soft drinks throughout our everyday lives.[37] A recent study has also indicated that although 4 weeks of increased fructose consumption in humans does cause an increased production of triglycerides as previously stated, it does not cause weight gain or increased resistance to insulin.[38] Thus, it may be that animals respond differently than humans to diets high in fructose. It is entirely possible that the obesity epidemic has resulted from increased consumption of energy (pre-

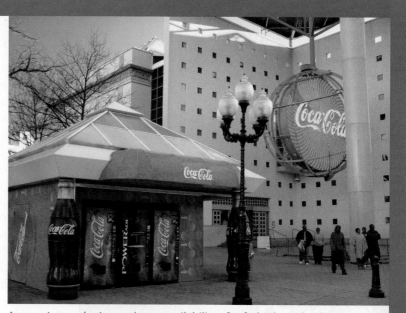

Aggressive marketing and easy availability of soft drinks make them a tempting choice for children and adults, adding HFCS and calories to their diets.

dominantly in the form of sweetened soft drinks and other high-energy foods) and a reduction in physical activity levels, and HFCS has nothing to do with this epidemic. Evidence to support this supposition stems from the fact that obesity rates are rising around the world, and many of the countries experiencing this epidemic do not use HFCS as a sweetener.

This issue is extremely complex, and it has been suggested that more research needs to be done in humans before we can fully understand how HFCS contributes to our diet and our health.[31]

Critical Thinking Questions

- After reading this, do you think HFCS is unhealthful and a major contributor to the obesity epidemic?

- Should HFCS be banned from our food supply? Why or why not?

- Should soft drink companies be encouraged to replace HFCS with sucrose or some other form of caloric sweetener?

- Should reducing soft drink consumption be up to individuals, or should it be mandatory for those at high risk for obesity?

- Should families, schools, and our government play a central role in controlling the types of foods and beverages offered to young people throughout their day?

As this controversy grows, it is more likely that average citizens will be asked to take a stand on this issue.

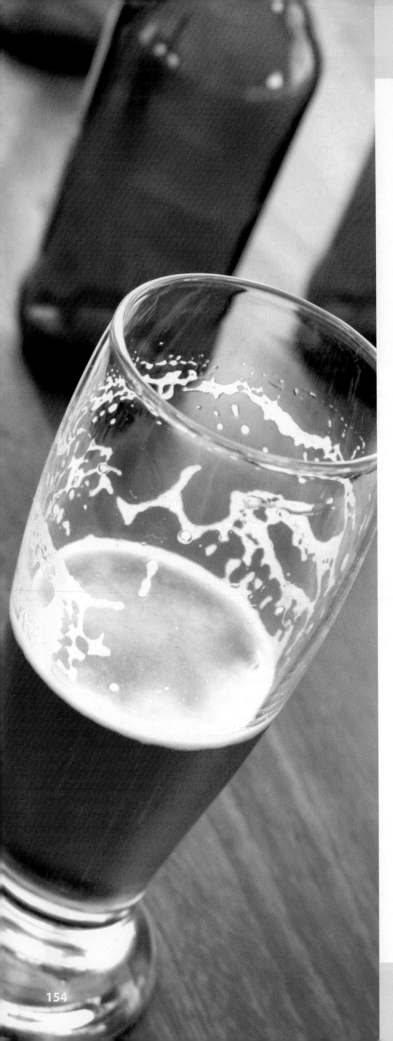

Read On.

No one should have to spend his 21st birthday in an emergency room, but that's what happened to Todd the night he turned 21. His friends took him off campus to celebrate, and, with their encouragement, he attempted to drink 21 shots before the bar closed at 2:00 A.M. Fortunately for Todd, when he passed out and couldn't be roused, his best friend noticed his cold, clammy skin and erratic breathing and drove him to the local emergency room. There, his stomach was pumped and he was treated for alcohol poisoning. He regained consciousness but felt sick and shaky for several more hours. Not everyone is so lucky. Some people with alcohol poisoning never wake up.

What makes excessive alcohol intake so dangerous, and why is moderate alcohol consumption often considered healthful? How can you tell if someone is struggling with alcohol addiction, and what can you do to help? What if that someone is you? We explore these questions *In Depth* here.

Alcohols are chemical compounds structurally similar to carbohydrates, with one or more hydroxyl (OH) groups. **Ethanol,** the specific type of alcohol found in beer, wine, and distilled spirits such as whiskey and vodka, has one hydroxyl group.

Throughout this discussion, the common term *alcohol* will be used to represent the specific compound *ethanol*.

The chemical structure of ethanol.

What Are the Health Benefits and Concerns of Moderate Alcohol Intake?

Alcohol intake is usually described as "drinks per day." A **drink** is defined as the amount of a beverage that provides 1/2 fluid ounce of pure alcohol. For example, 12 oz of beer, 10 oz of a wine cooler, 4–5 oz of wine, and 1½ oz of 80-**proof** whiskey, scotch, gin, or vodka are each equivalent to one drink (**Figure 1**).

---

alcohol Chemically, a compound characterized by the presence of a hydroxyl group; in common usage, a beverage made from fermented fruits, vegetables, or grains and containing ethanol.

ethanol A specific alcohol compound (C_2H_5OH) formed from the fermentation of dietary carbohydrates and used in a variety of alcoholic beverages.

drink The amount of an alcoholic beverage that provides approximately 0.5 fl. oz of pure ethanol.

proof A measure of the alcohol content of a liquid; 100-proof liquor is 50% alcohol by volume, 80-proof liquor is 40% alcohol by volume, and so on.

Alcohol

Want to find out . . .

- what "moderate drinking" really means?
- how many young Americans die in alcohol-related incidents each year?
- if you should be concerned about your alcohol intake?
- how to talk to someone who might have a drinking problem?

The 2005 Dietary Guidelines for Americans advise, "Those who choose to drink alcoholic beverages should do so sensibly and in moderation—defined as the consumption of up to one drink per day for women and up to two drinks per day for men." Notice that this definition of moderate drinking is based on a maximal daily intake; a person who does not drink any alcohol on weekdays but downs a six-pack of beer most Saturday nights would *not* be classified as a "moderate drinker"! The 2005 Dietary Guidelines for Americans also identify groups of individuals who should not consume alcohol at all, including women who are or may become pregnant and women who are breastfeeding. In addition, people with a history of alcoholism and those taking medications that interact with alcohol should not drink at all, nor should individuals driving, operating machinery, or engaged in other tasks that require attention and coordination.

As we discuss here, both health benefits and concerns are associated with moderate alcohol intake. When deciding if or how much alcohol to drink, you need to weigh the pros and cons of alcohol consumption against your own personal health history.

Benefits of Moderate Alcohol Intake

In most people, moderate alcohol intake offers some psychological benefits; it can reduce stress and anxiety while improving self-confidence. It can also have nutritional benefits: in the elderly, moderate use of alcohol can improve appetite and dietary intake.[1]

In addition, moderate alcohol consumption has been linked to lower rates of heart disease, especially in older adults and those already at risk for heart disease. Alcohol increases levels of the "good" type of cholesterol (HDL) while lowering the concentration of "bad" cholesterol (LDL); it also reduces the risk of abnormal clot formation in the blood vessels.[2] Recently, there has been a lot of interest in **resveratrol,** a phytochemical found in red wines and foods such as grapes and nuts. Some researchers, based on experiments with mice, are proposing that resveratrol may be able to lower our risk for certain chronic diseases such as diabetes, heart disease, and liver disease. However, if resveratrol is found to be effective in promoting human health, the amount needed would be so high that it would have to be given as a purified supplement, not in the form of red wine.

---

resveratrol A phytochemical known to play a role in limiting cell damage from the by-products of metabolic reactions. It is found in red wine and certain other plant-based foods.

Figure 1 What does one drink look like? A drink is equivalent to 1½ oz of distilled spirits, 4 to 5 oz of wine, 10 oz of wine cooler, or 12 oz of beer.

Concerns of Moderate Alcohol Intake

Not everyone responds to alcohol in the same manner. A person's age, genetic makeup, state of health, and use of medications can influence both immediate and long-term responses to alcohol intake, even at moderate levels. For example, some women appear to be at increased risk for breast cancer when consuming low to moderate amounts of alcohol. As few as two drinks per day can increase the risk of hypertension (high blood pressure) in some people, especially if the alcohol is consumed in the absence of food.[3] Moderate use of alcohol has also been linked to a higher rate of bleeding in the brain, resulting in what is termed *hemorrhagic stroke*.[4]

Another concern is the effect of alcohol on our waistlines! As we explained in Chapter 1, alcohol is not classified as a nutrient because it does not serve any unique metabolic role in humans. Although it provides virtually no nutritional value, it does provide energy: at 7 kcal/g, alcohol has a relatively high caloric content. Only fat (9 kcal/g) has more calories per gram. If you are watching your weight, it makes sense to strictly limit your consumption of alcohol to stay within your daily energy needs. Alcohol intake may also increase your *total* energy intake, increasing your risk of overweight or obesity. That's because alcoholic beverages, unlike solid foods, fail to trigger the satiety or "fullness" response, leading some people to overeat.[5]

The potential for drug–alcohol interactions is well known; many medications carry a warning label advising consumers to avoid alcohol while taking the drug. Alcohol magnifies the effect of certain painkillers, sleeping pills, antidepressants, and antianxiety medications and can lead to loss of consciousness. It also increases the risk of gastrointestinal bleeding in people taking aspirin or ibuprofen, as well as the risk of stomach bleeding and liver damage in people taking acetaminophen (Tylenol). In diabetics using insulin or oral medications to lower blood glucose, alcohol can exaggerate the drug's effect, leading to an inappropriately low level of blood glucose.

As you can see, there are both benefits and risks to moderate alcohol consumption. Experts agree that people who are currently consuming alcohol in moderation and who have low or no risk of alcohol addiction

Alcohol can interfere with and increase the risks of using various over-the-counter and prescription medications.

or medication interaction can safely continue their current level of use. Adults who abstain from alcohol, however, should not start drinking just for the possible health benefits. Individuals who have a personal or family history of alcoholism or fall into any other risk category should consider abstaining from alcohol use, even at a moderate level.

How Is Alcohol Metabolized?

Alcohol is absorbed directly from both the stomach and the small intestine; it does not require digestion prior to absorption. Consuming foods with some fat, protein, and fiber slows the absorption of alcohol and can reduce *blood alcohol concentration (BAC)* by as much as 50% compared to peak BAC when drinking on an empty stomach. Carbonated alcoholic beverages are absorbed very rapidly, which explains why champagne and sparkling wines are so quick to generate an alcoholic "buzz." As explained in the next paragraph, women often absorb 30% to 35% more of a given alcohol intake compared to men of the same size, which may explain why females often show a greater response to alcohol compared to males.

The process of alcohol metabolism will be discussed in detail in Chapter 7, but a brief overview will introduce you to the basics. While most alcohol is oxidized, or broken down, in the liver, a small amount is metabolized in the stomach before it has even been absorbed. The enzyme *alcohol dehydrognase* (ADH) triggers the first step in alcohol degradation, while *aldehyde dehydrogenase* (ALDH) takes the breakdown process one step farther (**Figure 2**). In women, ADH in the stomach is less active than in men; thus, women do not oxidize as much alcohol in their stomach, leaving up to 30% to 35% more intact alcohol to be absorbed.

Once absorbed, the alcohol moves through the bloodstream to the liver, where it is broken down at a fairly steady rate. On average, a healthy adult metabolizes the equivalent of one drink per hour. If someone drinks more than that, such as two or three alcoholic drinks in an hour, the excess alcohol is released back into the bloodstream, where it elevates BAC and triggers a variety of behavioral and metabolic reactions. Through the blood, alcohol is

IN DEPTH

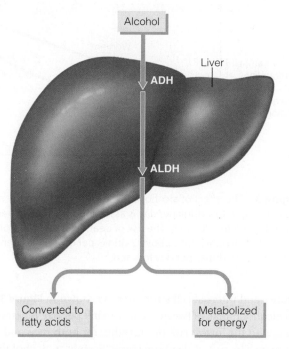

Figure 2 Metabolism of alcohol.

A person who steadily increases his or her alcohol consumption over time becomes more tolerant of a given intake of alcohol. Chronic drinkers experience *metabolic tolerance*, a condition in which the liver becomes more efficient in its breakdown of alcohol. This means that the person's BAC rises more slowly after consuming a certain number of drinks. In addition, chronic drinkers develop what is called *functional tolerance*, meaning they show few if any signs of impairment or intoxication even at high

Theo
Nutri-Case

"I was driving home from a post-game party last night when I was pulled over by the police. The officer said I seemed to be driving 'erratically' and asked me how many drinks I'd had. I told him I'd only had three beers, and explained that I was pretty tired from the game. Then, just to prove I was fine, I offered to count backward from a hundred, but I must have sounded sober, because he didn't make me do it. I can't believe he thought I was driving drunk! Still, maybe three beers after a game really is too much."

Do you think it is physiologically possible that Theo's driving might have been impaired even though he had consumed only three beers? To answer, you'll need to consider both Theo's body weight and the effect of playing a long basketball game. What other factors that influence the rate of alcohol absorption or breakdown could have affected Theo's BAC? How could all of these factors influence a decision about whether or not "three beers after a game really is too much"?

readily distributed throughout all body fluids and tissues, including the brain. Any time you consume more than one alcoholic beverage per hour, you are exposing every tissue in your body to the toxic effects of alcohol.

Despite what you may have heard, there is no effective intervention to speed up the breakdown of alcohol (Table 1). The key to keeping your BAC below the legal limit is to drink alcoholic beverages while eating a meal or large snack, to drink very slowly, no more than one drink per hour, and to limit your total consumption of alcohol on any one occasion.

Table 1 Myths About Alcohol Metabolism

The Claim	The Reality
Physical activity, such as walking around, will speed up the breakdown of alcohol.	Muscles don't metabolize alcohol; the liver does.
Drinking a lot of coffee will keep you from getting drunk.	Coffee does not cause alcohol to be excreted in the urine.
Using a sauna or steam room will force the alcohol out of your body.	Very little alcohol is lost in the sweat; the alcohol will remain in your bloodstream.
Herbal and nutritional products are available that speed up the breakdown of alcohol.	There is no scientific evidence that commercial supplements will increase the rate of alcohol metabolism; they will not lower blood alcohol levels.

BACs. As a result, these individuals may need to consume twice as much alcohol as when they first started drinking in order to reach the same state of euphoria.

What Is Alcohol Abuse?

Alcohol abuse is defined simply as the excessive consumption of alcohol, whether chronically or occasionally. Both chronic and occasional alcohol abuse can eventually lead to alcoholism.

Binge drinking, the consumption of five or more alcoholic drinks on one occasion (within a 3- to 5-hour span, for example), occurs in about 15% of U.S. adults and in youth as young as 12 years of age. Young males between the ages of 18 and 25 have the highest rate of binge drinking.[6, 7] Binge drinking by college students and other young adults (or even underage adolescents) increases the risk of potentially fatal falls, drownings, and automobile accidents. Acts of physical violence, including vandalism and physical and sexual assault, are also associated with binge drinking. The consequences also carry over beyond the actual binge: hangovers, which are discussed shortly, are practically inevitable given the amount of alcohol consumed.

Alcoholism is a disease characterized by chronic dependence on alcohol. It is characterized by:

- *Craving:* a strong need or urge to drink alcoholic beverages
- *Loss of control:* the inability to stop once drinking has begun
- *Physical dependence:* the presence of nausea, sweating, shakiness, and other signs of withdrawal after stopping alcohol intake
- *Tolerance:* the need to drink larger and larger amounts of alcohol to get the same "high" or pleasurable sensations associated with alcohol intake

What Are the Effects of Alcohol Abuse?

Alcohol is a drug. It exerts a narcotic effect on virtually every part of the brain, acting as a sedative and depressant. Alcohol also has the potential to act as a direct toxin; in high concentrations, it can damage or destroy cell mem-

alcohol abuse   The excessive consumption of alcohol, whether chronically or occasionally.

binge drinking   The consumption of five or more alcoholic drinks on one occasion.

alcoholism   A disease state characterized by chronic dependence on alcohol.

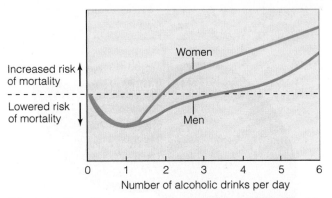

Figure 3   The effect of alcohol consumption on mortality risk. Consuming ½ to 1 drink per day is associated with the lowest mortality risk for all adults. The risk of death increases sharply at levels of alcohol intake above 2 drinks per day for women, and about 3½ drinks per day for men.

branes and internal cell structures. As shown in **Figure 3**, an alcohol intake between ½ and 1 drink per day is associated with the lowest risk of mortality for both men and women. The risk of death increases sharply as alcohol intake increases above 2 drinks per day for women, and 3½ drinks per day for men. These increased mortality risks are related to alcohol's damaging effects on the brain, the liver, and other organs, as well as its role in motor vehicle accidents and other traumatic injuries.

Alcohol Hangovers

Alcohol hangover is a frequent and extremely unpleasant consequence of drinking too much alcohol. It lasts up to 24 hours, and its symptoms include headache, fatigue, dizziness, muscle aches, nausea and vomiting, sensitivity to light and sound, and extreme thirst. Some people also experience depression, anxiety, irritability, and other mood disturbances. While some of the aftereffects of a binge may be due to nonalcoholic compounds known as congeners (found in red wines, brandy, and whiskey, for example), most of the consequences are directly related to the alcohol itself.

Some of the symptoms occur because of alcohol's effect as a *diuretic,* a compound that increases urine output. Alcohol inhibits the release of hormones that normally regulate urine production, elevating the loss of fluid and electrolytes and contributing to dizziness and lightheadedness. Alcohol irritates the lining of the stomach and increases gastric acid production, which may account for the

alcohol hangover   A consequence of drinking too much alcohol; symptoms include headache, fatigue, dizziness, muscle aches, nausea and vomiting, sensitivity to light and sound, extreme thirst, and mood disturbances.

abdominal pain, nausea, and vomiting seen in most hangovers. Alcohol also disrupts normal body metabolism, leading to low levels of blood glucose and elevated levels of lactic acid. These disturbances contribute to the characteristic fatigue, weakness, and mood changes seen after excessive alcohol intake. Finally, alcohol disrupts various biological rhythms, such as sleep patterns and cycles of hormone secretion, leading to an effect similar to that of jet lag.

Alcohol abuse can lead to a number of negative consequences.

While many folk remedies, including various herbal products, are claimed to prevent or reduce hangover effects, few have been proven effective. Drinking water or other nonalcoholic beverages will minimize the risk of dehydration, while consumption of toast or dry cereal will bring blood glucose levels back to normal. Getting adequate sleep can counteract the fatigue, and use of antacids may reduce nausea and abdominal pain. Whereas aspirin, acetaminophen, and ibuprofen might be useful for headaches, they may worsen stomach pain, increase risk of GI bleeding, and, over time, may increase risk of liver damage.

Reduced Brain Function

Alcohol is well known for its ability to alter behavior, mainly through its effects on the brain. Even at low intakes, alcohol impairs reasoning and judgment (Table 2). Alcohol also interferes with normal sleep patterns, alters sight and speech, and leads to loss of fine and gross motor skills such as handwriting, hand–eye

Table 2 Effects of Blood Alcohol Concentration (BAC) on Brain Activity

Blood Alcohol Concentration	Typical Response
0.02–0.05%	Feeling of relaxation, euphoria, relief
0.06–0.10%	Impaired judgment, fine motor control, and coordination; loss of normal emotional control; legally drunk in many states (at the upper end of the range)
0.11–0.15%	Impaired reflexes and gross motor control; staggered gait; legally drunk in all states; slurred speech
0.16–0.20%	Impaired vision; unpredictable behavior; further loss of muscle control
0.21–0.35%	Total loss of coordination; in a stupor
0.40% and above	Loss of consciousness; coma; suppression of respiratory response; death

coordination, and balance. Many people who drink experience unexpected mood swings, intense anger, or unreasonable irritation. Others react in the opposite direction, becoming sad, withdrawn, and lethargic. When teens or young adults chronically consume excessive amounts of alcohol, they may permanently damage brain structure and function.[8] Intellectual functioning and memory can be lost. In addition, early exposure to alcohol increases risk of future alcohol addiction and may contribute to lifelong deficits in memory, motor skills, and muscle coordination.[9,10]

Alcohol Poisoning

At very high intakes of alcohol, a person is at risk for **alcohol poisoning,** a metabolic state that occurs in response to binge drinking. At high BACs, the respiratory center of the brain is depressed. This reduces the level of oxygen reaching the brain and increases the individual's risk of death by respiratory or cardiac failure. Like Todd in our opening story, many binge drinkers lose consciousness before alcohol poisoning becomes fatal, but emergency care is often essential.

If someone passes out after a night of hard drinking, he or she should never be left alone to "sleep it off." Instead, the person should be placed on his or her side to prevent aspiration if vomiting occurs. The person should also be watched carefully for cold and clammy skin, a bluish tint to the skin, or slow, irregular breathing. If any of these signs become evident, or there is any reason to believe he or she has alcohol poisoning, seek emergency healthcare immediately.

Reduced Liver Function

The liver performs an astonishing number and variety of body functions, including nutrient metabolism, glycogen storage, the synthesis of many essential compounds, and the detoxification of medications and other potential poisons. As noted earlier, it is the main site of alcohol metabolism. When an individual's rate of alcohol intake exceeds the rate at which the liver can break the alcohol down, liver cells are damaged or destroyed. The longer the alcohol abuse continues, the greater the damage to the liver.

alcohol poisoning A potentially fatal condition in which an overdose of alcohol results in cardiac and/or respiratory failure.

(a)   (b)

Figure 4 Cirrhosis of the liver is often caused by chronic alcohol abuse. **(a)** A healthy liver. **(b)** A liver damaged by cirrhosis.

Fatty liver, a condition in which abnormal amounts of fat build up in the liver, is an early yet reversible sign of liver damage commonly linked to alcohol abuse. Once alcohol intake stops and a healthful diet is maintained, the liver is able to heal and resume normal function.

Alcoholic hepatitis is a more severe condition, resulting in loss of appetite, nausea and vomiting, abdominal pain, and jaundice (a yellowing of the skin and eyes, reflecting loss of liver function). Mental confusion and impaired immune response often occur with alcoholic hepatitis. While avoidance of alcohol and a healthful diet often result in full recovery, many people experience lifelong complications from alcoholic hepatitis.

Cirrhosis of the liver is often the result of long-term alcohol abuse; liver cells are scarred, blood flow through the liver is impaired, and liver function declines (**Figure 4**). This condition almost always results in irreversible damage to the liver and can be life-threatening. Blood pressure increases dramatically, large amounts of fluid are retained in the abdominal cavity, and metabolic wastes accumulate. In some cases, liver function fails completely, resulting in the need for a liver transplant or the likelihood of death.

Increased Risk of Chronic Disease

While moderate drinking may provide some health benefits, it is clear that chronically high intakes of alcohol dam-

---

fatty liver An early and reversible stage of liver disease often found in people who abuse alcohol and characterized by the abnormal accumulation of fat within liver cells; also called alcoholic steatosis.
alcoholic hepatitis Inflammation of the liver caused by alcohol; other forms of hepatitis can be caused by a virus or toxin.
cirrhosis of the liver End-stage liver disease characterized by significant abnormalities in liver structure and function; may lead to complete liver failure.

age a number of body organs and systems, increasing a person's risk of chronic disease and death:

- *Bone health.* Men and women who are alcoholics experience an increased loss of calcium in the urine, impaired vitamin D activation, and decreased production of certain hormones that enhance bone formation.[11]
- *Pancreatic injury and diabetes.* Alcohol damages the pancreas, which produces insulin, and decreases the body's ability to properly respond to insulin. The result is chronically elevated blood glucose levels and an increased risk of diabetes.
- *Cancer.* Research has most strongly linked alcohol intake to increased risk of cancer of the mouth and throat, esophagus, stomach, liver, colon, and female breast.[12] A recent study estimated that as many as 13% of cancers in a group of Japanese men were due to heavy drinking, complicated by smoking.[13]

Malnutrition

As alcohol intake increases to 30% or more of total energy intake, appetite is lost and intake of healthful foods declines. Over time, the diet becomes deficient in protein, fats, carbohydrates, vitamins A and C, and minerals such as iron, zinc, and calcium (**Figure 5**). End-stage alcoholics may consume as much as 90% of their daily energy intake from alcohol, displacing virtually all foods. Even if food intake is maintained, the toxic effects of alcohol lead to impaired food digestion, nutrient absorption, and nutrient metabolism.

Long-term exposure to alcohol damages not only the liver but also the stomach, small intestine, and pancreas. Alcohol increases gastric acid production, leading to stomach ulcers, gastric bleeding, and damage to the cells that produce gastric enzymes, mucus, and other proteins. The lining of the small intestine is also damaged by chronic alcohol abuse, reducing nutrient absorption, whereas damage to the pancreas reduces the production of pancreatic digestive enzymes. As a result, the digestion of foods and absorption of nutrients such as the fat-soluble vitamins (A, D, E, and K), vitamin B_6, folate, and zinc become inadequate, leading to malnutrition and inappropriate weight loss.

Not only are dietary intake, food digestion, and nutrient absorption negatively impacted by alcohol abuse, but so too is the ability of body cells to utilize nutrients. For example, even if an alcoholic were to take vitamin D sup-

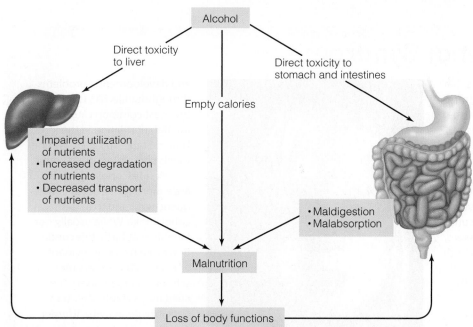

Figure 5 Alcohol-related malnutrition. Excess alcohol consumption contributes directly and indirectly to widespread nutrient deficiencies.

plements, his or her liver would be so damaged that its cells could not activate the vitamin D. Many chronic alcoholics are unable to synthesize the liver proteins that carry vitamins and minerals to target tissues. Other vitamins and minerals are negatively affected because the liver is too damaged to maintain normal nutrient storage capacity. Across the whole spectrum, from food intake to cell

Excessive alcohol intake greatly increases the risks for car accidents and other traumatic injuries.

nutrient metabolism, alcohol abuse increases risk of malnutrition.

Increased Risk of Traumatic Injury

Excessive alcohol intake is the leading cause of death for Americans under the age of 21. It is also the third leading cause of all U.S. deaths.[14] It has been estimated that as many as 6,000 young Americans die each year from alcohol-related motor vehicle accidents, suicides, and homicides. As previously noted, rates of physical and sexual assaults, vandalism, accidental falls, and drownings also increase when people are under the influence of alcohol.

Fetal and Infant Health Problems

No level of alcohol consumption is considered safe for pregnant women. Women who are or think they may be pregnant should abstain from all alcoholic beverages. As discussed in the Highlight box on page 162, fetal alcohol syndrome, which is caused by alcohol intake in a childbearing woman, is a critical problem in the United States.

Women who are breastfeeding should also abstain from alcohol because it easily passes into the breast milk at levels equal to blood alcohol concentrations. If consumed by the infant, the alcohol in breast milk can slow motor development, depress the central

Highlight

Fetal Alcohol Syndrome

The March of Dimes estimates that more than 40,000 babies are born each year with some type of alcohol-related defect.[15] Alcohol is a known **teratogen** (a substance that causes fetal harm) that readily crosses the placenta into the fetal bloodstream. Because the immature fetal liver can not effectively break down the alcohol, it accumulates in the fetal blood and tissues, increasing the risk for various birth defects. The effects of maternal alcohol intake are dose related: the more the mother drinks, the greater the potential harm to the fetus. In addition to the amount of alcohol consumed during pregnancy, the timing of the mother's alcohol intake influences the risk of fetal complications. Binge or frequent drinking during the first trimester of pregnancy is more likely to result in birth defects and other permanent abnormalities, whereas alcohol consumption in the third trimester typically results in low birth weight and growth retardation.

Fetal alcohol syndrome (FAS) is a condition characterized by malformations of the face, limbs, heart, and nervous system. The characteristic facial features persist throughout the child's life (Figure 6). Exposure to alcohol while in the womb impairs fetal growth; FAS babies are often underweight at birth and rarely normalize their growth after birth. Newborn and infant death rates are abnormally high, and those who do survive suffer from emotional, behavioral, social, learning,

Figure 6 A child with fetal alcohol syndrome (FAS). The facial features typical of children with FAS include a short nose with a low, wide bridge; drooping eyes with an extra skinfold; and a flat, thin upper lip. These external traits are typically accompanied by behavioral problems and learning disorders. The effects of FAS are irreversible.

and developmental problems throughout life. FAS is one of the most common causes of mental retardation in the United States and the only one that is completely preventable.

Fetal alcohol effects (FAE) are a more subtle set of consequences related to maternal alcohol intake. While usually not identified at birth, this condition often becomes evident when the child enters preschool or kindergarten. The child may exhibit, attention deficit/hyperactivity disorder, or impaired learning abilities. It is estimated that the incidence of FAE is ten times greater than that of FAS.

Can a pregnant woman safely consume any amount of alcohol? Although some pregnant women do have an occasional alcoholic drink with no apparent ill effects, there is no amount of alcohol known to be safe. In one recent study, researchers identified a number of subtle but long-term negative consequences of light to moderate alcohol consumption during pregnancy: children of women who had as little as one alcoholic drink a week during their pregnancy were more aggressive and more likely to engage in delinquent behaviors compared to children who had no fetal exposure to alcohol. The best advice regarding alcohol intake during pregnancy is to abstain if there is any chance of becoming pregnant, as well as throughout the pregnancy.

---

teratogen A compound known to cause fetal harm or danger.

fetal alcohol syndrome (FAS) A set of serious, irreversible alcohol-related birth defects characterized by certain physical and mental abnormalities.

fetal alcohol effects (FAE) A set of subtle consequences of maternal intake of alcohol, such as impaired learning and behavioral problems.

nervous system, and increase sleepiness in the child. Alcohol also reduces the mother's ability to produce milk, putting the infant at risk for malnutrition.

Taking Control of Your Alcohol Intake

Knowing that a moderate intake of alcohol may provide some health benefits and that excessive intake results in a wide range of problems, what can you do to control your drinking? The following are practical strategies that can help you avoid the negative consequences of excessive alcohol consumption:

- Think about WHY you are planning to drink. Is it to relax and socialize, or are you using alcohol to release stress? If the latter, try out some stress-reduction techniques that don't involve alcohol, such as exercise, yoga, meditation, or simply talking with a friend.
- Make sure you have a protein-containing meal or snack before your first alcoholic drink; having food in the stomach delays gastric emptying, which means more of the alcohol can be broken down in the stomach before it even gets the chance to be absorbed into the bloodstream.
- Rotate between alcoholic and nonalcoholic drinks. Start with a large glass of water, iced tea, or soda. Once your thirst has been satisfied, your rate of fluid intake will drop. Remember, a glass of pure orange juice doesn't look any different from one laced with vodka, so no one will even know what it is you are or are not drinking! Dilute hard liquor with large amounts of soda, water, juice, or iced tea. These diluted beverages are cheaper and lower in calories too!
- Whether or not your drink is diluted, sip slowly to allow your liver time to keep up with your alcohol intake.
- If your friends pressure you to drink, volunteer to be the designated driver. You'll have a "free pass" for the night in terms of saying no to alcoholic drinks.
- Decide in advance what your alcohol intake will be, and plan some strategies for sticking to your limit. If you are going to a bar, for example, bring only enough money to buy two beers and two sodas. If you are at a party, stay occupied dancing, sampling the food, or talking with friends, and stay as far away from the bar area as you can.

Should You Be Concerned About Your Alcohol Intake?

Even if you are not dependent on alcohol, you should be concerned about your alcohol intake if you engage in binge drinking or drink at inappropriate times (while pregnant, before or while driving a car, to deal with negative emotions, or while at work/school). If you answer "yes" to one or more of the following questions, provided by the National Institute on Alcohol Abuse and Alcoholism, you may have a problem with alcohol abuse:

- Have you ever felt you should cut down on your drinking?
- Have people annoyed you by criticizing your drinking?
- Have you ever felt bad or guilty about your drinking?
- Do you drink alone when you feel angry or sad?
- Has your drinking ever made you late for school or work?
- Have you ever had a drink first thing in the morning to steady your nerves or get rid of a hangover?
- Do you ever drink after promising yourself you won't?

If you think you have an alcohol problem, it is important for you to speak with a trusted friend, coach, teacher, counselor, or healthcare provider. In addition, many campuses have support groups that can help. Taking control of your alcohol intake will allow you to take control of your life.

Talking to Someone About Alcohol Addiction

You may suspect that a close friend or relative might be one of the nearly 14 million Americans who abuse alcohol or are dependent on alcohol.[16] If you notice that your friend or relative uses alcohol as the primary way to calm down, cheer up, or relax, that may be a sign of alcohol dependency or addiction. The appearance of tremors or other signs of withdrawal as well as the initiation of secretive behaviors when consuming alcohol are other indications that alcohol has become a serious problem.

Many people become defensive or hostile when asked about their use of alcohol; denial is very common. The single hardest step toward sobriety is often the first: accepting the fact that help is needed. Some people respond well when confronted by a single person, while others benefit more from a group intervention. There should be no blaming or shaming; alcohol addiction and dependency are medical conditions with a strong genetic component. The National Institute on Alcoholism and Alcohol Abuse suggests the following approaches when trying to get a friend or relative into treatment:

Stop covering up and making excuses.   Many times, family and friends will make excuses to others to protect the person from the results of his or her drinking. It is important, however, to stop covering for that person so he or she can experience the full consequences of inappropriate alcohol consumption.

Intervene at a vulnerable time.   The best time to talk to someone about problem drinking is shortly after an alcohol-related incident such as a DUI arrest, an alcohol-related traffic accident, or a public scene. Wait until the person is sober and everyone is relatively calm.

Be specific.   Tell the person exactly why you are concerned; use examples of specific problems associated with his or her drinking habits (e.g., poor school or work performance; legal problems; inappropriate behaviors). Explain what will happen if the person chooses not to get help—for example, no longer going out with the person if alcohol will be available, no longer riding with him or her in motor vehicles, moving out of a shared home, and so on.

Get help.   Professional help is available from community agencies, healthcare providers, online sites, school or worksite wellness centers, and some religious organizations. Several contacts and Web sites are listed at the end of this *In Depth*. If the person indicates a willingness to get help, call immediately for an appointment and/or immediately bring him or her to a treatment center. The longer the delay, the more likely it is that the person will experience a change of heart.

Enlist the support of others.   Whether or not the person agrees to get help, calling upon other friends and relatives can often be effective, especially if one has had alcohol-related problems of his or her own. Formal support groups such as Al-Anon and Alateen can provide additional information and guidance.

Treatment for alcohol-related problems works for many, but not all, individuals. "Success" is measured in small steps, and relapses are common. Most scientists agree that people who abuse alcohol cannot just "cut down." Complete avoidance of all alcoholic beverages is the only way for most people who abuse alcohol to achieve full and ongoing recovery.

Web Links

www.aa.org
Alcoholics Anonymous, Inc.
This site provides links to local AA groups and provides information on the AA program.

www.al-anon.alateen.org
Al-Anon Family Group Headquarters, Inc.
This site provides links to local Al-Anon and Alateen groups, which provide support for spouses, children, and other loved ones of people addicted to alcohol.

www.ncadd.org
National Council on Alcoholism and Drug Dependence, Inc.
Educational materials and information on alcoholism can be obtained from this site.

www.niaaa.nih.gov
National Institute on Alcohol Abuse and Alcoholism
Visit this Web site for information on the prevalence, consequences, and treatments of alcohol-related disorders. Information for healthcare providers, people struggling with alcohol abuse, and family members is available free of charge.

www.collegedrinkingprevention.gov
College Drinking: Changing the Culture
The NIAAA developed this Web site specifically for college students seeking information and advice on the subject of college drinking. Services include self-assessment questionnaires, answers to frequently asked questions, news articles, research, and links to support groups.

www.madd.org
Mothers Against Drunk Driving
Links to local chapters, statistics related to drunk driving, and prevention strategies are easily accessed from this site.

www.marchofdimes.com
March of Dimes
Information on fetal alcohol syndrome and fetal alcohol effects is available at this site.

References

1. Dufour, M. C., L. Archer, and E. Gordis. 1992. Alcohol and the elderly. *Clin. Geriatr. Med.* 8:127–141.

2. Gunzerath, L., V. Faden, S. Zakhari, and K. Warren. 2004. National Institute on Alcohol Abuse and Alcoholism Report on moderate drinking. *Alcohol. Clin. Exp. Res.* 28L:829–847.

3. Stranges, S., T. Wu, J. M. Born., et al. 2004. Relationship of alcohol drinking pattern to risk of hypertension. *Hypertension* 44:813–819.

4. Meister, K. A., E. M. Whelan, and R. Kava. 2000. The health effects of moderate alcohol intake in humans: An epidemiologic review. *Crit. Rev. Clin. Lab. Sci.* 37:261–296.

5. Caton, S. J., M. Ball, A. Ahern, et al. 2004. Dose-dependent effects of alcohol on appetite and food intake. *Physiol. Behav.* 81:51–58.

6. Nelson, D. E., T. S. Naimi, R. D. Brewer, J. Bolen, and H. E. Wells. 2004. Metropolitan-area estimates of binge drinking in the United States. *Am. J. Pub. Health* 94:663–671.

7. Naimi, T. S., R. D. Brewer, A. Mokdad, C. Denny, and M. K. Serdula. 2003. Binge drinking among US adults. *JAMA* 289:70–79.

8. Oscar-Berman, M., and K. Marinkovic. 2003. Alcoholism and the brain: An overview. *Alc. Res. Health* 27:161–173.

9. Brown, S. A., S. F. Tapert, E. Granholm, and D. C. Delis. 2000. Neurocognitive functioning of adolescents: Effects of protracted alcohol use. *Alc. Clin. Exp. Res.* 24:164–171.

10. National Institute on Alcohol Abuse and Alcoholism (NIAAA). 2006. Young adult drinking. *Alcohol Alert*, No. 68, April.

11. National Institute of Arthritis and Musculoskeletal and Skin Diseases (NIAMS). 2005. What people recovering from alcoholism need to know about osteoporosis. Available at http://www.niams.nih.gov/bone/hi/osteoporosis_alcohol.htm. (Accessed August 2009.)

12. Bagnardi, V., M. Blangiardo, C. La Vecchia, and G. Corrao. 2001. Alcohol consumption and the risk of cancer: A meta-analysis. *Alc. Res. Health* 25:263–270.

13. Inoue, M., and S. Tsugane for the JPHC Study Group. 2004. Impact of alcohol drinking on total cancer risk: Data from a large-scale population-based cohort study in Japan. *Brit. J. Cancer* 92:182–187.

14. National Institute on Alcohol Abuse and Alcoholism (NIAAA). 2005. A snapshot of high-risk college drinking consequences. Available at http://www.collegedrinkingprevention.gov/facts/snapshot.aspx. (Accessed August 2009.)

15. Sokol, R. J., et al. 2003. Fetal alcohol spectrum disorder. *JAMA* 290:2996–2999.

16. National Institute on Alcohol Abuse and Alcoholism (NIAAA). 2005. Alcohol: How to cut down on your drinking. Available at http://www.collegedrinkingprevention.gov/facts/cutdrinking.aspx. (Accessed August 2009.)

5 Lipids: Essential Energy-Supplying Nutrients

Test Yourself | True or False?

1 Fat is unhealthful, and we should consume as little as possible. **T** *or* **F**

2 Fat is an important fuel source during rest and exercise. **T** *or* **F**

3 Fried foods are relatively nutritious as long as vegetable shortening is used to fry the foods. **T** *or* **F**

4 Certain fats protect against heart disease. **T** *or* **F**

5 High-fat diets cause cancer. **T** *or* **F**

Test Yourself answers are located in the Chapter Review.

Chapter Objectives *After reading this chapter, you will be able to:*

1. List and describe the three types of lipids found in foods, *pp. 168–176.*

2. Discuss how the level of saturation of a fatty acid affects its shape and the form it takes, *pp. 170–171.*

3. Identify the primary difference between a *cis* fatty acid and a *trans* fatty acid, *pp. 171–172.*

4. Compare and contrast the two essential fatty acids, *pp. 172–174.*

5. Describe the steps involved in fat digestion, absorption, and transport, *pp. 176–180.*

6. List three functions of fat in the body, *p. 181.*

7. Define the recommended dietary intakes for total fat, saturated fat, and the two essential fatty acids, *pp. 184–185.*

8. Identify at least three food sources of omega-3 fatty acids, *pp. 188–189.*

9. Describe the role of dietary fat in the development of cardiovascular disease, *pp. 189–198.*

10. Identify lifestyle recommendations for the prevention or treatment of cardiovascular disease, *pp. 198–199.*

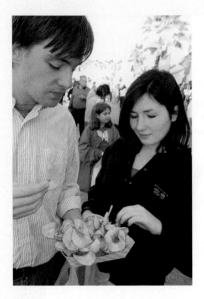

How would you feel if you purchased a bag of potato chips and were charged an extra 5% "fat tax"? What if you ordered fish and chips in your favorite restaurant only to be told that, in an effort to avoid lawsuits, fried foods were no longer being served? Sound surreal? Believe it or not, these and dozens of similar scenarios are being proposed, threatened, and defended in the current "obesity wars" raging around the globe. From Maine to California, from Iceland to New Zealand, local and national governments and healthcare policy advisors are scrambling to find effective methods for combating their rising rates of obesity. For reasons we explore in this chapter, many of their proposals focus on limiting consumption of foods high in saturated fats—for instance: requiring food vendors and manufacturers to reduce the portion size of high-fat foods; taxing or increasing the purchase price of these foods; levying fines on manufacturers who produce them; removing these foods from vending machines; banning advertisements of these foods to children; and using food labels and public service announcements to warn consumers away from these foods. At the same time, "food litigation" lawsuits have been increasing, including allegations against restaurant chains and food companies for failing to warn consumers of the health dangers of eating their energy-dense, high-saturated-fat foods.

Is saturated fat really such a menace? Does a diet high in saturated fat cause obesity, heart disease, or diabetes? What exactly *is* saturated fat anyway? And are other types of fat just as bad?

Although some people think that all dietary fat should be avoided, a certain amount of fat is absolutely essential for life and health. In this chapter, we'll discuss the function of fat in the human body, explain how dietary fat is digested, absorbed, transported, and stored, and help you distinguish between beneficial and harmful types of dietary fat. You'll also assess how much fat you need in your diet and learn about the role of dietary fat in the development of heart disease and other disorders.

What Are Lipids?

Lipids are a large and diverse group of substances that are distinguished by the fact that they are insoluble in water. Think of a salad dressing made with vinegar (which is mostly water) and olive oil—a lipid. Shaking the bottle *disperses* the oil but doesn't *dissolve* it; that's why it separates back out again so quickly. Lipids are found in all sorts of living things, from bacteria to plants to human beings. In fact, their presence on your skin explains why you can't clean your face with water alone—you need some type of soap to break down the insoluble lipids before you can wash them away. In this chapter, we focus on lipids that are found in foods and some of the lipids synthesized within the body.

Many different forms of lipids occur in the body and in foods. In the body, lipids are stored in adipose tissues that protect and insulate organs, are combined with phosphorus in cell membranes, and occur as steroids in bile salts, sex hormones, and other substances.[1] In foods, lipids occur as both fats and oils. These two forms are distinguished by the fact that fats, such as butter and lard, are solid at room temperature, whereas oils such as olive oil are liquid at room temperature. Dietary guidelines, food labels, and other nutrition information intended for the general public use the term *fats* when referring to the lipid content of diets and foods. We adopt this practice throughout this textbook, reserving the term *lipids* for discussions of chemistry and metabolism.

Three types of lipids are commonly found in foods and in the cells and tissues of the human body. These are triglycerides, phospholipids, and sterols. Let's take a look at each.

Triglycerides Are the Most Common Food-Based Lipid

Most of the fat we eat (95%) is in the form of triglycerides (also called triacylglycerols), which is the same form in which most body fat is stored. As reflected in the prefix *tri*, a **triglyceride** is a molecule consisting of *three* fatty acids attached to a *three*-carbon glycerol backbone (**Figure 5.1a**). **Fatty acids** are long chains of carbon atoms bound to each other as well as to hydrogen atoms. They are acids because they contain an acid group (carboxyl group) at one end of their chain. **Glycerol,** the backbone of a triglyceride molecule, is an al-

Some lipids, such as olive oil, are liquid at room temperature.

lipids A diverse group of organic substances that are insoluble in water; lipids include triglycerides, phospholipids, and sterols.

triglyceride A molecule consisting of three fatty acids attached to a three-carbon glycerol backbone.

fatty acids Long chains of carbon atoms bound to each other as well as to hydrogen atoms.

glycerol An alcohol composed of three carbon atoms; it is the backbone of a triglyceride molecule.

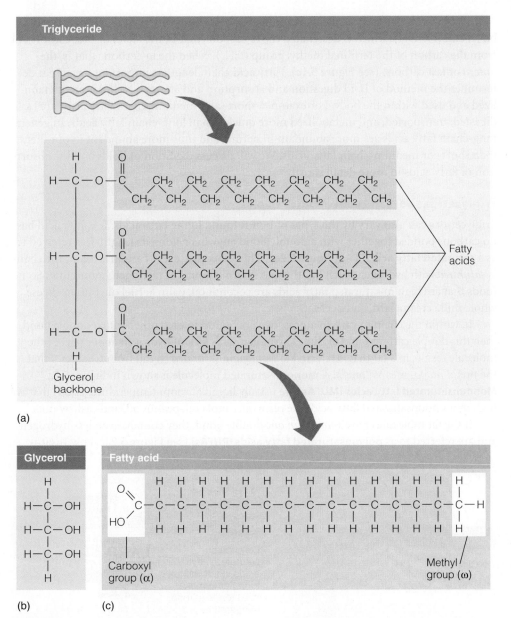

Figure 5.1 **(a)** A triglyceride consists of three fatty acids attached to a three-carbon glycerol backbone. **(b)** Structure of glycerol. **(c)** Structure of a fatty acid showing the carboxyl carbon (α) and the methyl carbon (ω) ends.

cohol composed of three carbon atoms (Figure 5.1b). One fatty acid attaches to each of these three carbons to make the triglyceride.

Triglycerides can be classified by their chain length (number of carbons in each fatty acid), by their level of saturation (how much hydrogen is attached to each carbon atom in the fatty acid chain), and by their shape, which is determined in some cases by how they are commercially processed. All of these factors influence how the triglyceride is used within the body and how it affects our health.

Triglycerides Vary in Chain Length

The fatty acids attached to the glycerol backbone can vary in the number of carbons they contain, a quality referred to as their *chain length.*

- **Short-chain fatty acids** are usually fewer than six carbon atoms in length.
- **Medium-chain fatty acids** are six to twelve carbons in length.
- **Long-chain fatty acids** are fourteen or more carbons in length.

short-chain fatty acids Fatty acids fewer than six carbon atoms in length.

medium-chain fatty acids Fatty acids that are six to twelve carbon atoms in length.

long-chain fatty acids Fatty acids that are fourteen or more carbon atoms in length.

The carbons of a fatty acid can be numbered beginning with the carbon of the carboxyl end (COOH), which is designated the α-carbon (that is, the *alpha* or first carbon), or from the carbon of the terminal methyl group (CH$_3$), called the ω-carbon (that is, the *omega* or last carbon) (see Figure 5.1c). Fatty acid chain length is important because it determines the method of lipid digestion and absorption and affects how lipids are metabolized and used within the body. For example, short- and medium-chain fatty acids are digested, transported, and metabolized more quickly than long-chain fatty acids. In general, long-chain fatty acids are more abundant in nature, and thus more abundant in our diet, than short- or medium-chain fatty acids. We will discuss digestion of lipids and the absorption of fatty acids in more detail shortly.

Triglycerides Vary in Level of Saturation

Triglycerides can also vary by the types of bonds found in the fatty acids. If a fatty acid has no carbons bonded together with a double bond anywhere along its length, it is referred to as a **saturated fatty acid (SFA)** (**Figure 5.2a**). This is because every carbon atom in the chain is *saturated* with hydrogen: Each has the maximum amount of hydrogen bound to it. Some foods that are high in saturated fatty acids are coconut oil, palm kernel oil, butter, cheese, whole milk, cream, lard, and beef fat.

If, within the chain of carbon atoms, two are bound to each other with a double bond, then this double carbon bond excludes hydrogen. This lack of hydrogen at *one* part of the molecule results in a fat that is referred to as *monounsaturated* (recall from Chapter 4 that the prefix *mono-* means "one"). A monounsaturated molecule is shown in Figure 5.2a. **Monounsaturated fatty acids (MUFAs)** are usually liquid at room temperature. Foods that are high in monounsaturated fatty acids are olive oil, canola oil, peanut oil, and cashew nuts.

If the fat molecules have *more than one* double bond, they contain even less hydrogen and are referred to as **polyunsaturated fatty acids (PUFAs)** (see Figure 5.2a). Polyunsatu-

saturated fatty acids (SFAs) Fatty acids that have no carbons joined together with a double bond; these types of fatty acids are generally solid at room temperature.

monounsaturated fatty acids (MUFAs) Fatty acids that have two carbons in the chain bound to each other with one double bond; these types of fatty acids are generally liquid at room temperature.

polyunsaturated fatty acids (PUFAs) Fatty acids that have more than one double bond in the chain; these types of fatty acids are generally liquid at room temperature.

(a)

Long-chain saturated fatty acids stack well together to make solid forms at room temperature.

(b)

Monounsaturated and polyunsaturated fatty acids do not stack well together because they are bent. These fatty acids are liquid at room temperature.

(c)

Figure 5.2 Examples of levels of saturation among fatty acids and how these levels of saturation affect the shape of fatty acids. **(a)** Saturated fatty acids are saturated with hydrogen, meaning they have no carbons bonded together with a double bond. Monounsaturated fatty acids contain two carbons bound by one double bond. Polyunsaturated fatty acids have more than one double bond linking carbon atoms. **(b)** Saturated fats have straight fatty acids packed tightly together and are solid at room temperature. **(c)** Unsaturated fats have "kinked" fatty acids at the area of the double bond, preventing them from packing tightly together; they are liquid at room temperature.

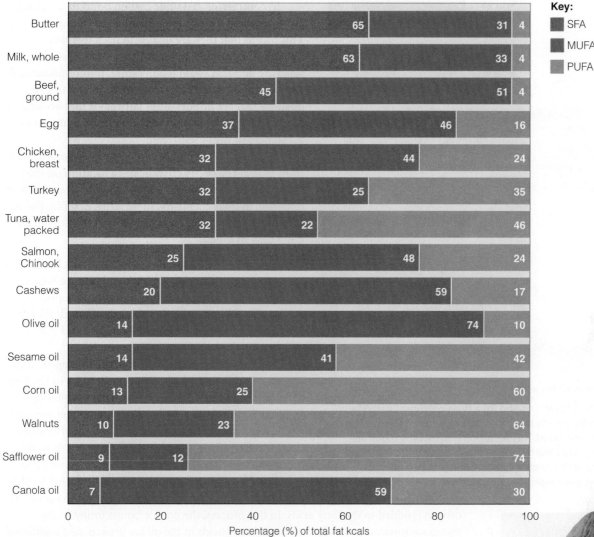

Key:
- ■ SFA
- ■ MUFA
- ■ PUFA

Food	SFA	MUFA	PUFA
Butter	65	31	4
Milk, whole	63	33	4
Beef, ground	45	51	4
Egg	37	46	16
Chicken, breast	32	44	24
Turkey	32	25	35
Tuna, water packed	32	22	46
Salmon, Chinook	25	48	24
Cashews	20	59	17
Olive oil	14	74	10
Sesame oil	14	41	42
Corn oil	13	25	60
Walnuts	10	23	64
Safflower oil	9	12	74
Canola oil	7	59	30

Percentage (%) of total fat kcals

Figure 5.3 Major sources of dietary fat.

rated fatty acids are also liquid at room temperature and include cottonseed, canola, corn, and safflower oils.

Foods vary in the types of fatty acids they contain. For example, animal fats provide approximately 40% to 60% of their energy from saturated fats, whereas plant fats provide 80% to 90% of their energy from monounsaturated and polyunsaturated fats (**Figure 5.3**). Notice that most oils are a good source of both MUFAs and PUFAs. Diets higher in plant foods will usually be lower in saturated fats than diets high in animal products. The impact that various types of fatty acids have on health will be discussed later in this chapter (beginning on page 185).

Carbon Bonding Affects Shape

Have you ever noticed how many toothpicks are packed into a small box? Two hundred or more! But if you were to break a bunch of toothpicks into V shapes anywhere along their length, how many could you then fit into the same box? It would be very few because the bent toothpicks would jumble together, taking up much more space. Molecules of saturated fat are like straight toothpicks: They have no double carbon bonds and always form straight, rigid chains. As they have no kinks, these chains can pack together tightly (Figure 5.2b). That is why saturated fats, such as the fat in meats, are solid at room temperature.

Walnuts and cashews are high in monounsaturated fatty acids.

(a) *cis* polyunsaturated fatty acid

(b) *trans* polyunsaturated fatty acid

Figure 5.4   Structure of **(a)** a *cis* and **(b)** a *trans* polyunsaturated fatty acid. Notice that *cis* fatty acids have both hydrogen atoms located on the same side of the double bond. This positioning makes the molecule kinked. In *trans* fatty acids, the hydrogen atoms are attached on diagonally opposite sides of the double carbon bond. This positioning makes them straighter and more rigid.

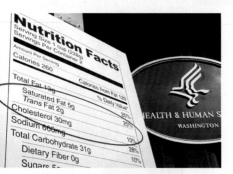

The U.S. Food and Drug Administration (FDA) requires that both saturated and *trans* fats be listed as separate line items on Nutrition Facts Panels for conventional foods and some dietary supplements. Research studies show that diets high in these fatty acids can increase the risk of cardiovascular disease.

hydrogenation   The process of adding hydrogen to unsaturated fatty acids, making them more saturated and thereby more solid at room temperature.

In contrast, each double carbon bond of unsaturated fats gives them a kink along their length (Figure 5.2c). This means that they are unable to pack together tightly—for example, to form a stick of butter—and instead are liquid at room temperature. Monounsaturated and polyunsaturated fatty acids are fluid and flexible, qualities that are important in fatty acids that become part of cell membranes, as well as in those that transport substances in the bloodstream.

Unsaturated fatty acids can occur in either a *cis* or a *trans* shape. The prefix *cis* indicates a location on the same side, whereas *trans* is a prefix that denotes across or opposite. In lipid chemistry, these terms describe the positioning of the hydrogen atoms around the double carbon bond, as follows:

- A *cis fatty acid* has both hydrogen atoms located on the same side of the double bond (**Figure 5.4a**). This positioning gives the *cis* molecule a pronounced kink at the double carbon bond. We typically find the *cis* fatty acids in nature and thus in foods like olive oil.
- In contrast, in a *trans fatty acid*, the hydrogen atoms are attached on diagonally opposite sides of the double carbon bond (Figure 5.4b). This positioning makes *trans* fatty acid fats straighter and more rigid, just like saturated fats. Although a limited amount of *trans* fatty acids is found in full-fat cow's milk, the majority of *trans* fatty acids are commercially produced by manipulating the fatty acid during food

processing. For example, in the **hydrogenation** of oils, such as corn or safflower oil, hydrogen is added to the fatty acids. In this process, the double bonds found in the monounsaturated and polyunsaturated fatty acids in the oil are broken, and additional hydrogen is inserted at diagonally opposite sides of the double bonds. This process straightens out the molecules, making the oil more solid at room temperature—and also more saturated. Thus, corn oil margarine is a partially hydrogenated fat made from corn oil. Margarines that are hydrogenated have more *trans* fatty acids than butter. The hydrogenation of fats helps foods containing these fats, such as cakes, cookies, and crackers, to resist rancidity, because the additional hydrogen reduces the tendency of the carbon atoms in the fatty acid chains to undergo oxidation.

Does the straight, rigid shape of the saturated and *trans* fats we eat have any effect on our health? Absolutely! Research during the past two decades has shown that both saturated and *trans* fatty acids raise blood cholesterol levels and appear to change cell membrane function and the way cholesterol is removed from the blood. For these reasons, diets high in saturated or *trans* fatty acids are associated with an increased risk of cardiovascular disease. Because of the concerns related to these fatty acids, food manufacturers are required to list the amount of saturated and *trans* fatty acids per serving on the Nutrition Facts Panel of food labels.

Some Triglycerides Contain Essential Fatty Acids

The length of the fatty acid chain (number of carbons) and the placement of the double bonds will determine the function of the fatty acid within the body. As noted earlier, the carbons of a fatty acid can be numbered beginning with the carbon of the terminal methyl group, called the ω-carbon (ω [omega] is the last letter in the Greek alphabet), or from the

Figure 5.5 The two essential fatty acids. **(a)** In linoleic acid (omega-6 fatty acid), counting from the terminal methyl group (the ω-carbon), the first double bond occurs at the sixth carbon. **(b)** In alpha-linolenic acid (omega-3 fatty acid), counting from the terminal methyl group (the ω-carbon), the first double bond occurs at the third carbon.

α-carbon of the beginning carboxyl group (α [alpha] is the first letter in the Greek alphabet). In **Figure 5.5**, we have illustrated this numbering system and have numbered the carbons from the ω-carbon. When synthesizing fatty acids, the body cannot insert double bonds before the ninth carbon from the ω-carbon.[2] For this reason, fatty acids with double bonds closer to the methyl end (at ω-3 and at ω-6) are considered **essential fatty acids (EFAs)**—because the body cannot synthesize them, they must be obtained from food.

essential fatty acids (EFAs) Fatty acids that must be consumed in the diet because they cannot be made by the body. The two essential fatty acids are linoleic acid and alpha-linolenic acid.

EFAs are precursors to important biological compounds called *eicosanoids* and are therefore essential to growth and health. Eicosanoids get their name from the Greek word *eicosa*, which means "twenty," as they are synthesized from fatty acids with twenty carbon atoms. They include prostaglandins, thromboxanes, and leukotrienes. Among the most potent regulators of cellular function in nature, eicosanoids are produced in nearly every cell within the body.[3] They help to regulate gastrointestinal tract motility, secretory activity, blood clotting, vasodilatation and vasoconstriction, vascular permeability, and inflammation. There must be a balance between the various eicosanoids to assure that the appropriate amount of blood clotting or dilation/constriction of the blood vessels occurs.

The body's synthesis of various eicosanoids depends on the abundance of the EFAs available as precursors and the enzymes within each pathway. The two essential fatty acids in our diet are linoleic acid and alpha-linolenic acid.

Linoleic Acid   **Linoleic acid,** also known as *omega-6 fatty acid,* is found in vegetable and nut oils such as sunflower, safflower, corn, soy, and peanut oil. If you eat lots of vegetables or use vegetable-oil-based margarines or vegetable oils, you are probably getting adequate amounts of this essential fatty acid in your diet. Linoleic acid is metabolized in the body to arachidonic acid, which is a precursor to a number of eicosanoids.

Alpha-Linolenic Acid   **Alpha-linolenic acid,** also known as *omega-3 fatty acid,* was only recognized to be essential in the mid-1980s. It is found primarily in dark green, leafy vegetables, flaxseeds and flaxseed oil, soybeans and soybean oil, walnuts and walnut oil, and canola oil. You may also have read news reports of the health benefits of the omega-3 fatty acids found in many fish. The two omega-3 fatty acids found in fish, shellfish, and fish oils are **eicosapentaenoic acid (EPA)** and **docosahexaenoic acid (DHA).** Fish that naturally contain more oil, such as salmon and tuna, are higher in EPA and DHA than lean fish such as cod or flounder. Research indicates that diets high in EPA and DHA stimulate the production of prostaglandins and thromboxanes that reduce inflammatory responses in the body, reduce blood clotting and plasma triglycerides, and thereby reduce an individual's risk of heart disease.

Shrimp are high in omega-3 fatty acid content.

RECAP

Fat is essential for health. Triglycerides are the most common fat found in food. A triglyceride is made up of glycerol and three fatty acids. These fatty acids can be classified based on chain length, level of saturation, and shape. The essential fatty acids, linoleic acid and alpha-linolenic acid, cannot be synthesized by the body and must be consumed in the diet.

linoleic acid   An essential fatty acid found in vegetable and nut oils; also known as omega-6 fatty acid.

alpha-linolenic acid   An essential fatty acid found in leafy green vegetables, flaxseed oil, soy oil, fish oil, and fish products; an omega-3 fatty acid.

eicosapentaenoic acid (EPA)   A metabolic derivative of alpha-linolenic acid.

docosahexaenoic acid (DHA)   A metabolic derivative of alpha-linolenic acid; together with EPA, it appears to reduce the risk of heart disease.

phospholipids   A type of lipid in which a fatty acid is combined with another compound that contains phosphate; unlike other lipids, phospholipids are soluble in water.

Phospholipids Combine Lipids with Phosphate

Along with the triglycerides just discussed, we also find **phospholipids** in the foods we eat. They are abundant, for example, in egg yolks, peanuts, and soybeans and are present in processed foods containing emulsifiers, additives that help foods stay blended.

Phospholipids consist of a glycerol backbone with fatty acids attached at the first and second carbons and another compound that contains phosphate attached at the third carbon (**Figure 5.6a**). Because phosphates are soluble in water, phospholipids are soluble in water, a property that enables them to assist in transporting fats in the bloodstream. We discuss this concept in more detail later in this chapter (page 178).

The phospholipids are unique in that they have a hydrophobic (water-avoiding) end, which is their lipid "tail," and a hydrophilic (water-attracting) end, which is their phosphate "head." In the cell membrane, this quality helps them to regulate the transport of substances into and out of the cell (see Figure 5.6b). Phospholipids also help with digestion of dietary fats. In the liver, phospholipids called *lecithins* combine with bile salts and electrolytes to make bile. As you recall from Chapter 3, bile emulsifies lipids. Note that the body manufactures phospholipids, so they are not essential to include in the diet.

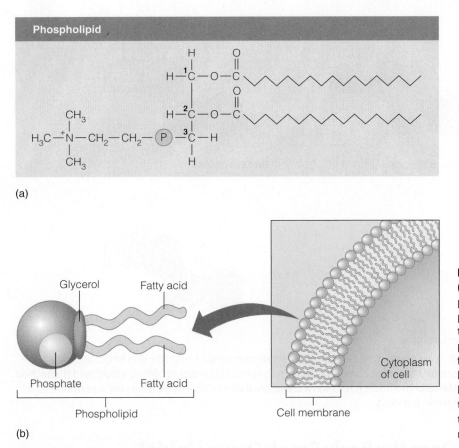

Phospholipid

(a)

(b)

Glycerol Fatty acid

Phosphate Fatty acid

Phospholipid

Cytoplasm of cell

Cell membrane

Figure 5.6 The structure of a phospholipid. **(a)** Detailed biochemical drawing of the phospholipid phosphatidylcholine, in which the phosphate is bound to choline and attached to the glycerol backbone at the third carbon. This phospholipid is commonly called lecithin and is found in foods such as egg yolks as well as in the body. **(b)** Phospholipids consist of a glycerol backbone with two fatty acids and a compound that contains phosphate. This diagram illustrates the placement of the phospholipids in the cell membrane structure.

Sterols Have a Ring Structure

Sterols are a type of lipid found in both plant and animal foods and produced in the body, but their multiple-ring structure is quite different from that of triglycerides or phospholipids (**Figure 5.7a**). Plants contain some sterols, but they are not very well absorbed. Plant sterols appear to block the absorption of dietary cholesterol, the most commonly occurring sterol in the diet (Figure 5.7b). In food, cholesterol is found primarily as cholesterol esters, in which a fatty acid is attached to the cholesterol ring structure (Figure 5.7c). Endogenous (dietary) cholesterol is found in the fatty part of animal products such as butter, egg yolks, whole milk, meats, and poultry. Lean meats and low- or reduced-fat milk, yogurt, and cheeses have little cholesterol.

It is not necessary to consume cholesterol because the body continually synthesizes it, mostly in the liver, adrenal cortex, reproductive tissues, and intestines. This continuous production is vital because cholesterol is part of every cell membrane, where it works in conjunction with fatty acids and phospholipids to help maintain cell membrane integrity and modulate fluidity. It is particularly plentiful in the neural cells that make up the brain, spinal cord, and nerves.

The body uses cholesterol, whether exogenous or endogenous, to make several important sterol compounds, including sex hormones (estrogen, androgens such as testosterone, and progesterone), adrenal hormones, and vitamin D. In addition, cholesterol is the precursor for the bile salts that are a primary component of bile, which helps emulsify the lipids in the gut prior to digestion. Thus, despite cholesterol's bad reputation, it is absolutely essential to human health.

RECAP

Phospholipids combine two fatty acids and a glycerol backbone with a phosphate-containing compound, making them soluble in water. Sterols have a multiple-ring structure; cholesterol is the most commonly occurring sterol in our diets.

sterols A type of lipid found in foods and the body that has a ring structure; cholesterol is the most common sterol that occurs in our diets.

(a) Sterol ring structure   **(b)** Cholesterol

(c) Cholesterol ester

Figure 5.7   Sterol structure. **(a)** Sterols are lipids that contain multiple ring structures. **(b)** Cholesterol is the most commonly occurring sterol in the diet. **(c)** When a fatty acid is attached to the cholesterol molecule, it is called a cholesterol ester. Cholesterol esters are a common form of cholesterol in our diets.

How Does the Body Break Down Lipids?

Because lipids are not soluble in water, they cannot enter the bloodstream easily from the digestive tract. Thus, their digestion, absorption, and transport within the body differ from those of carbohydrates and proteins, which are water-soluble substances.

The digestion and absorption of lipids were discussed in detail in Chapter 3, but we briefly review the process here (**Figure 5.8**). Dietary fats are usually mixed with other foods. Lingual lipase, a salivary enzyme released during chewing, plays a minor role in the breakdown of lipids in food, so most lipids reach the stomach intact (see Figure 5.8, step 1). The primary role of the stomach in lipid digestion is to mix and break up the lipid into smaller droplets. Because lipids are not soluble in water, these droplets typically float on top of the watery digestive juices in the stomach until they are passed into the small intestine (see Figure 5.8, step 2).

The Gallbladder, Liver, and Pancreas Assist in Fat Digestion

Because lipids are not soluble in water, their digestion requires the help of bile from the gallbladder and digestive enzymes from the pancreas. Recall from Chapter 3 that the gallbladder is a sac attached to the underside of the liver and the pancreas is an oblong-shaped organ sitting below the stomach. Both have a duct connecting them to the small intestine. As lipids enter the small intestine from the stomach, the gallbladder contracts and releases bile (see Figure 5.8, step 3). The contraction of the gallbladder is primarily caused by the release of cholecystokinin (CCK) (also called pancreozymin) from the duodenal mucosal cells into the circulation. Secretin, another hormone released from the duodenal mucosa, also plays a role in gallbladder contraction. These same gut hormones also cause the release of the pancreatic aqueous phase (bicarbonate and water) and the pancreatic digestive enzymes into the gut.

Although bile is stored in the gallbladder, it is actually produced in the liver. It is composed primarily of bile salts made from cholesterol, lecithins and other phospholipids, and

Fats and oils do not dissolve readily in water.

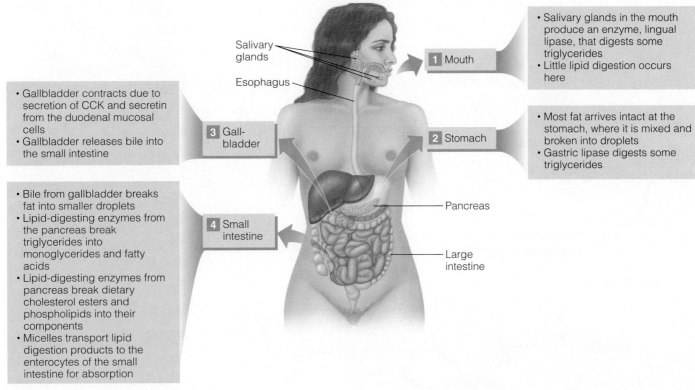

- Salivary glands in the mouth produce an enzyme, lingual lipase, that digests some triglycerides
- Little lipid digestion occurs here

Salivary glands

Esophagus

1 Mouth

- Gallbladder contracts due to secretion of CCK and secretin from the duodenal mucosal cells
- Gallbladder releases bile into the small intestine

3 Gall-bladder

2 Stomach

- Most fat arrives intact at the stomach, where it is mixed and broken into droplets
- Gastric lipase digests some triglycerides

- Bile from gallbladder breaks fat into smaller droplets
- Lipid-digesting enzymes from the pancreas break triglycerides into monoglycerides and fatty acids
- Lipid-digesting enzymes from pancreas break dietary cholesterol esters and phospholipids into their components
- Micelles transport lipid digestion products to the enterocytes of the small intestine for absorption

4 Small intestine

Pancreas

Large intestine

Figure 5.8 The process of lipid digestion.

electrolytes (for example, sodium, potassium, chloride, and calcium). *Lecithins* (also called phosphatidylcholine; see Figure 5.6a) are phospholipids in which a phosphate-containing compound and choline are combined and attached at the third carbon on the glycerol backbone. They are the primary emulsifiers in bile: The hydrophobic tails of lecithin molecules attract lipid droplets, clustering them together in tiny spheres, while the hydrophilic heads form a water-attracting shell. Lecithins enable bile to act much like soap, breaking up lipids into smaller and smaller droplets with a greater surface area. The more droplets there are, the greater the chance that digestive enzymes will be able to reach their target. Interestingly, lecithins are abundant in egg yolk, which is frequently used as an emulsifier in cooking—for instance, when oil and vinegar are combined to make mayonnaise.

At the same time the bile is mixing with the lipids to emulsify them, lipid-digesting enzymes produced in the pancreas travel through the pancreatic duct into the small intestine. Each lipid product requires a specific digestive enzyme or enzymes. For example, triglycerides require both pancreatic lipase and co-lipase for digestion. The co-lipase anchors the pancreatic lipase to the lipid droplet so that it can break the fatty acids away from their glycerol backbones. Each triglyceride molecule is broken down into two free fatty acids, which are removed from the first and third carbons on the glycerol backbone, and one *monoacylglyceride*, a glycerol molecule with one fatty acid still attached at the second carbon on the glycerol backbone (**Figure 5.9a**).

Specific enzymes also assist the digestion of cholesterol esters and phospholipids. As noted in Figure 5.7c, when a fatty acid is attached to cholesterol it is called a cholesterol ester. Some of the cholesterol in our diet is in this form; thus, we need cholesterol esterase, an enzyme released from the pancreas, to break the ester bond between cholesterol and its attached fatty acid and release a free cholesterol molecule and a free fatty acid. Phospholipase enzymes are responsible for breaking phospholipids into smaller parts. Thus, the end products of digestion are much smaller molecules that can be more easily captured and transported to the enterocytes for absorption.

Lecithins are abundant in egg yolk, which is used as an emulsifier in products such as mayonnaise.

(a) Triglyceride digestion

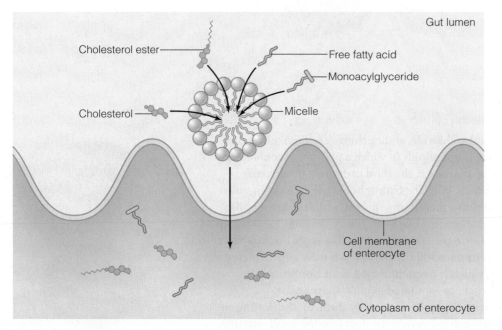

(b) Micelle transport into enterocyte

Figure 5.9 Lipid digestion and absorption. **(a)** In the presence of enzymes, triglycerides are broken down into fatty acids and monoacyl-glycerides. **(b)** These products, along with cholesterol and cholesterol esters, are trapped in the micelle, a spherical compound made up of bile salts and biliary phospholipids. The micelle then transports these lipid digestion products to the intestinal mucosal cell, and these products are then absorbed into the cell.

Absorption of Lipids Occurs Primarily in the Small Intestine

The majority of lipid absorption occurs in the mucosal lining of the small intestine with the help of micelles (see Figure 5.8, step 4). A **micelle** is a spherical compound made up of bile salts and biliary phospholipids that can capture the lipid digestion products, such as free fatty acids, free cholesterol, and the monoglycerides, and transport them to the enterocytes for absorption (Figure 5.9b). The micelle has a hydrophobic core and a hydrophilic surface, which is excellent for transporting lipids in the watery environment of the gut.

How do the absorbed lipids—which do not mix with water—get into the bloodstream? Within the enterocytes, the fatty acids and monoglycerides are reformulated back into triglycerides and then packaged into lipoproteins before they're released into the blood-

micelle A spherical compound made up of bile salts and biliary phospho-lipids that transports lipid digestion products to the intestinal mucosal cell.

stream. A **lipoprotein** is a spherical compound with triglycerides clustered in the center along with cholesterol esters, free cholesterol, and other hydrophobic lipids, and phospholipids and proteins forming the outside of the sphere (**Figure 5.10**). The specific lipoprotein produced in the enterocytes to transport lipids from a meal is called a **chylomicron.**

The process of forming a chylomicron begins with the re-creation of the triglycerides and the cholesterol esters in the enterocytes (**Figure 5.11**). These products are then loosely enclosed within an outer shell made of phospholipids and proteins. The chylomicron is now soluble in water because phospholipids and proteins are water soluble. Once chylomicrons are formed, they are transported out of the enterocytes to the lymphatic system, which empties into the bloodstream through the thoracic duct at the left subclavian vein in the neck. In this way, the dietary fat consumed in a meal is transported into the blood. Soon after a meal containing fat, there is an increase of chylomicrons in the blood as the fat is being transported into the body. For most individuals, chylomicrons are cleared rapidly from the blood, usually within 6 to 8 hours after a moderate-fat meal, which is why patients are instructed to fast overnight before having blood drawn for a laboratory analysis of blood lipid levels.

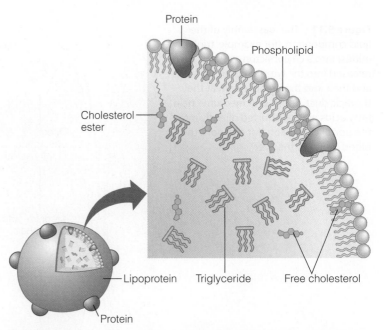

Figure 5.10 Structure of a lipoprotein. Notice that the fat clusters in the center of the molecule and the phospholipids and proteins, which are water-soluble, form the outside of the sphere. This enables lipoproteins to transport fats in the bloodstream.

As mentioned earlier, short- and medium-chain fatty acids (those less than fourteen carbons in length) can be transported in the body more readily than long-chain fatty acids. This is because short- and medium-chain fatty acids transported to the muscosal cells do not have to be re-formed into triglycerides and incorporated into chylomicrons (see Figure 5.11). Instead, they can travel in the portal bloodstream bound to either the transport protein albumin or a phospholipid. In general, our diets are low in short- and medium-chain fatty acids; however, they can be extracted from certain oils for clinical use in feeding patients who cannot digest long-chain fatty acids.

Fat Is Stored in Adipose Tissues for Later Use

After a meal, the chylomicrons, which are filled with dietary triglycerides, begin to circulate through the blood, looking for a place to deliver their load. There are three primary fates of these dietary triglycerides:

1. They can immediately be taken up and used as a source of energy for the cells, especially by the muscle cells.
2. They can be used to make lipid-containing compounds in the body.
3. They can be stored in the muscle or adipose tissue for later use. (See **Figure 5.12** for an illustration of an adipose cell.)

How do the triglycerides get out of the chylomicrons and into the cells of the body, such as the adipose or muscle cells? This process occurs with the help of an enzyme called **lipoprotein lipase,** or LPL, which is found on the outside of our cells. For example, when chylomicrons touch the surface of an adipose cell, they come into contact with LPL. As a result of this contact, LPL breaks apart the triglycerides in the core of the chylomicrons. This process frees individual fatty acids to move into the adipose cell. If the adipose cell needs the fat for energy, these fatty acids will be quickly used as fuel. If the cell doesn't need the fatty acids for immediate energy, they will have to be stored. However, cells cannot store individual fatty acids; instead, cells convert these fatty acids back into a triglyceride for storage. Because adipose cells are the only body cells that

Adipose tissue. During times of weight gain, excess fat consumed in the diet is stored in the adipose tissue.

lipoprotein A spherical compound in which fat clusters in the center and phospholipids and proteins form the outside of the sphere.

chylomicron A lipoprotein produced in the mucosal cell of the intestine; transports dietary fat out of the intestinal tract.

lipoprotein lipase An enzyme that sits on the outside of cells and breaks apart triglycerides so that their fatty acids can be removed and taken up by the cell.

Figure 5.11 The reassembly of the lipid components (for example, triglycerides) into a chylomicron, which is then released into the lymphatic circulation and then into the bloodstream at the thoracic duct. Short- and medium-chain fatty acids are transported directly into the portal circulation (for example, the blood going to the liver).

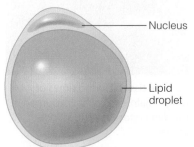

Figure 5.12 Diagram of an adipose cell.

have significant storage capacity for triglycerides, most fat not needed for energy is stored in adipose tissues for later use.

Although the primary storage site for triglycerides is the body's adipose tissues, if you are physically active, your body will preferentially store this extra fat in your muscle tissues. This ensures that, the next time you go out for a run, the fat will be readily available for energy. Thus, people who engage in physical activity are more likely to have extra triglyceride stored in the muscle tissue and to have less body fat—something many of us would prefer. Of course, fat stored in your adipose tissues can also be used for energy during exercise, but it must be broken down first and then transported to your muscle cells.

ReCaP

Fat digestion begins when fats are emulsified by bile. Lipid-digesting enzymes from the pancreas subsequently digest the triglycerides into two free fatty acids and one monoglyceride. These are transported into the intestinal mucosal cells with the help of micelles. Once inside the mucosal cells, triglycerides are re-formed and packaged into lipoproteins called chylomicrons. Dietary fat, in the form of triglycerides, is transported by the chylomicrons to cells within the body that need energy. Triglycerides stored in the muscle tissue are used as a source of energy during physical activity. Excess triglycerides are stored in the adipose tissue and can be used whenever the body needs energy.

Why Do We Need Lipids?

Lipids, in the form of dietary fat, provide energy and help our bodies perform essential physiologic functions.

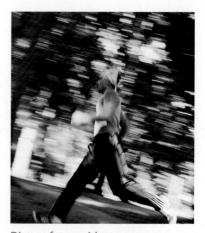

Dietary fat provides energy.

Lipids Provide Energy

Dietary fat is a primary source of energy because fat has more than twice the energy per gram as carbohydrate or protein. Fat provides 9 kilocalories (kcals) per gram, whereas carbohydrate and protein provide only 4 kcals per gram. This means that fat is much more energy dense. For example, 1 tablespoon of butter or oil contains approximately 100 kcals, whereas it takes 2.5 cups of steamed broccoli or 1 slice of whole-wheat bread to provide 100 kcals.

Lipids Are a Major Fuel Source When We Are at Rest

At rest, we are able to deliver plenty of oxygen to our cells so that metabolic functions can occur. Just as a candle needs oxygen for the flame to continue burning, our cells need oxygen to use fat for energy. Thus, approximately 30% to 70% of the energy used at rest by the muscles and organs comes from lipids.[4] The exact amount of energy coming from lipids at rest will depend on how much fat you are eating in your diet, how physically active you are, and whether you are gaining or losing weight. If you are dieting, more lipid will be used for energy than if you are gaining weight. During times of weight gain, more of the fat consumed in the diet is stored in the adipose tissue, and the body uses more dietary protein and carbohydrate as fuel sources at rest.

Lipids Fuel Physical Activity

Lipids are the major energy source during physical activity, and one of the best ways to lose body fat is to exercise and reduce energy intake. During aerobic exercise, such as running or cycling, lipids can be mobilized from any of the following sources of body fat: muscle tissue, adipose tissue, and blood lipoproteins. A number of hormonal changes signal the body to break down stored energy to fuel the working muscles. The hormonal responses, and the amount and source of the lipids used, depend on your level of fitness; the type, intensity, and duration of the exercise; and how well fed you are before you exercise.

For example, adrenaline (that is, epinephrine) strongly stimulates the breakdown of stored fat. Within minutes of beginning exercise, blood levels of epinephrine rise dramatically. Through a cascade of events, this surge of epinephrine activates an enzyme within adipose cells called *hormone-sensitive lipase.* This enzyme works to remove single fatty acids from the stored triglycerides. When all three free fatty acids on the glycerol backbone have been removed, the free fatty acids and the glycerol are released into the blood.

Epinephrine also signals the pancreas to *decrease* insulin production. This is important, because insulin inhibits fat breakdown. Thus, when the need for fat as an energy source is high, blood insulin levels are typically low. As you might guess, blood insulin levels are high when we are eating, because during this time our need for energy from stored fat is low and the need for fat storage is high.

The longer you exercise, the more fat you use for energy. Cyclists in a long-distance race make greater use of fat stores as the race progresses.

Once fatty acids are released from the adipose cells, they travel in the blood attached to the transport protein albumin, to the muscle cells. There, they enter the mitochondria, the cell's energy-generating structures, and use oxygen to produce ATP, which is the cell's energy source. Becoming more physically fit means you can deliver more oxygen to the muscle cells to use the fatty acids delivered there. In addition, you can exercise longer when you are fit.

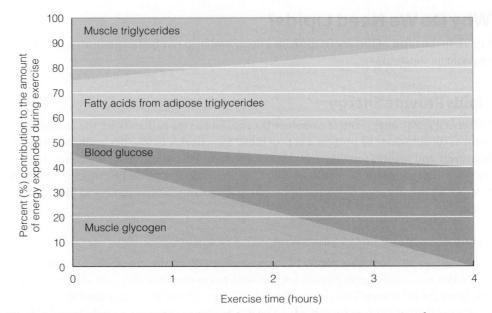

Figure 5.13 Various sources of energy used during exercise. As a person exercises for a prolonged period of time, fatty acids from adipose cells contribute relatively more energy than do carbohydrates stored in the muscle or circulating in the blood. (*Data from:* Coyle, E. F. 1995. Substrate utilization during exercise in active people. *Am. J. Clin. Nutr.* 61[Suppl.]:968S–979S. Used with permission.)

Because the body has only a limited supply of stored carbohydrate as glycogen in muscle tissue, the longer you exercise, the more fatty acids you use for energy. This point is illustrated in **Figure 5.13**. In this example, an individual is running for 4 hours at a moderate intensity. As the muscle glycogen levels become depleted, the body relies on fatty acids from the adipose tissue as a fuel source.

Fatty acids cannot be used to produce glucose; however, recall that the breakdown of triglycerides also frees molecules of glycerol into the bloodstream. Some of this free glycerol travels to the liver, where it can be used for the production of modest amounts of glucose (in the process of gluconeogenesis).

Body Fat Stores Energy for Later Use

The body stores extra energy in the form of body fat, which then can be used for energy at rest, during exercise, or during periods of low energy intake. Having a readily available energy source in the form of fat allows the body to always have access to energy even when we choose not to eat (or are unable to eat), when we are exercising, and while we are sleeping. The body has small amounts of stored carbohydrate in the form of glycogen—only enough to last about 1 to 2 days—and there is no place that the body can store extra protein. We cannot consider our muscles and organs as a place where "extra" protein is stored! For these reasons, the fat stored in adipose and muscle tissues is necessary to fuel the body between meals. Although too much stored adipose tissue can harm our health, some fat storage is essential to protect our health.

Essential Fatty Acids Are Components of Important Biological Compounds

As discussed earlier, EFAs are needed to make a number of important biological compounds. They also are important constituents of cell membranes, help prevent DNA damage, help fight infection, and are essential for fetal growth and development. In the growing fetus, EFAs are necessary for normal growth, especially for the development of the brain and visual centers.

Dietary Fat Enables the Transport of Fat-Soluble Vitamins

Dietary fat enables the absorption and transport of the fat-soluble vitamins (A, D, E, and K) needed by the body for many essential metabolic functions. The fat-soluble vitamins are transported in the gut to the intestinal cells for absorption as part of micelles, and they are transported in the blood to the body cells as part of chylomicrons.[5] The fat-soluble vitamins include vitamin A, which is important for normal vision and night vision. Vitamin D helps regulate blood calcium and phosphorus concentrations within normal ranges, which indirectly helps maintain bone health. Vitamin E keeps cell membranes healthy throughout the body, and vitamin K is important for proteins involved in blood clotting and bone health. We discuss these vitamins in detail in later chapters.

Lipids Help Maintain Cell Function and Provide Protection to the Body

Lipids, especially PUFAs and phospholipids, are a critical part of every cell membrane, where they help to maintain membrane integrity, determine what substances are transported in and out of the cell, and regulate what substances can bind to the cell. Thus, lipids strongly influence the function of cells.

In addition, lipids help maintain cell fluidity. For example, wild salmon live in very cold water and have high levels of omega-3 fatty acids in their cell membranes. These fatty acids stay fluid and flexible even at very low temperatures, thereby enabling the fish to swim in extremely cold water. In the same way, lipids help our membranes stay fluid and flexible. For example, red blood cells require flexibility to bend and move through the smallest capillaries in the body, delivering oxygen to all body cells.

PUFAs are also primary components of the tissues of the brain and spinal cord, where they facilitate the transmission of information from one cell to another. The body also uses lipids for the development, growth, and maintenance of these tissues.

Stored body fat also plays an important role in the body. Besides being the primary site of stored energy, adipose tissue pads the body and protects the organs, such as the kidneys and liver, when we fall or are bruised. Fat under the skin also acts as insulation to help retain body heat. Although we often think of body fat as "bad," it plays an important role in keeping the body healthy and functioning properly.

Adipose tissue pads the body and protects the organs when we fall or are bruised.

Fats Contribute to the Flavor and Texture of Foods

Dietary fat adds texture and flavor to foods. Fat makes salad dressings smooth and ice cream "creamy," and it gives cakes and cookies their moist, tender texture. Frying foods in melted fat or oil, as with doughnuts or French fries, gives them a crisp, flavorful coating; however, eating such foods regularly can be unhealthful because they are high in saturated and/or *trans* fatty acids.

Fats Help Us Feel Satiated Because They Are Energy Dense

We often hear that fats contribute to satiation and satiety. First, what does this mean? A food or nutrient is said to contribute to *satiation* if that food makes you feel full and causes you to stop eating. A food or nutrient is said to contribute to *satiety* if it contributes to a feeling of fullness that subsequently reduces the amount of food you eat at the next meal or lengthens the time between meals.

Fat adds texture and flavor to foods.

A number of research studies have compared the effects of fat and carbohydrate on both satiation and satiety. In general, this research has found little difference between these two macronutrients when energy intake has been controlled.[6, 7] However, research also indicates that the energy density of a food contributes significantly to both satiety and satiation. Because fats are more energy dense (kcal/g) than carbohydrate and protein, foods that contain a high proportion of fat are typically higher in energy density. For example, a cup of whole milk provides 8 g of fat and 146 kcal, whereas a cup of low-fat (1% fat) milk provides 2.4 g of fat and 102 kcal. For every gram of fat you consume, you get 2.25 times the amount of energy that you get with a gram of protein or carbohydrate.

In addition, high-fat foods are often very palatable, so it is easy to overeat them and end up consuming more calories than we would if foods with lower energy densities were selected. Satiety is also affected by the level of gastric distention produced by the food consumed and by how quickly food empties from the stomach, both of which factors can be affected by the energy density of the food.[6] The rate at which foods reach the satiety receptors in the gut and release satiety hormones can also be influenced by the energy density of the food.

RECAP

Dietary fats play a number of important roles within the body. (1) Dietary fats provide the majority of energy required at rest and are a major fuel source during exercise, especially endurance exercise. (2) Dietary fats provide essential fatty acids (linoleic and alpha-linolenic acid). (3) Dietary fats help transport the fat-soluble vitamins into the body. (4) Dietary fats help regulate cell function and maintain membrane integrity. (5) Stored body fat in the adipose tissue helps protect vital organs and pads the body. (6) Fats contribute to the flavor and texture of foods, and because fats are energy dense, they are one factor that contributes to the satiety we feel after a meal.

How Much Dietary Fat Should We Eat?

The latest research comparing low-carbohydrate to low-fat diets has made Americans wonder what, exactly, is a healthful level of dietary fat and what foods contain the most beneficial fats. We'll explore these issues here.

Dietary Reference Intake for Total Fat

The Acceptable Macronutrient Distribution Range (AMDR) for fat is 20% to 35% of total energy.[8] This recommendation is based on evidence indicating that higher intakes of fat increase the risk of obesity and its complications, especially heart disease and diabetes, but that diets too low in fat and too high in carbohydrate can also increase the risk of heart disease if they cause blood triglycerides to increase and high-density lipoprotein-cholesterol to decrease.[8] Within this range of fat intake, it is also recommended that we minimize our intake of saturated and *trans* fatty acids; these changes will lower our risk of heart disease.

Because carbohydrate is essential in replenishing glycogen, athletes and other physically active people are advised to consume less fat and more carbohydrate than sedentary people. Specifically, it is recommended that athletes consume 20% to 25% of their total energy from fat, 55% to 60% of energy from carbohydrate, and 12% to 15% of energy from protein.[9] This level of fat intake represents approximately 45 to 55 g per day of fat for an athlete consuming 2,000 kcals per day, and 78 to 97 g per day of fat for an athlete consuming 3,500 kcals per day.

Although many people trying to lose weight consume less than 20% of their energy from fat, this practice may do more harm than good, especially if they are also limiting energy intake (eating fewer than 1,500 kcals per day). Research suggests that very-low-fat diets, or those with less than 15% of energy from fat, do not provide additional health or performance benefits over moderate-fat diets and are usually very difficult to follow.[10] In fact, most people find they feel better, are more successful in weight maintenance, and are less preoccupied with food if they keep their fat intakes at 20% to 25% of energy intake. Additionally, people attempting to reduce their dietary fat frequently eliminate protein-rich foods, such as meat, dairy, eggs, and nuts. These foods are also potential sources of many essential vitamins and minerals important for good health and for maintaining an active lifestyle. Diets extremely low in fat may also be deficient in essential fatty acids.

Liz
Nutri-Case

"Lately I'm hungry all the time. I read on a Web site last night that if I limit my total fat intake to no more than 10% of my total calories, I can eat all the carbohydrate and protein that I want, and I won't gain weight. So I went right out to the yogurt shop down the street and ordered a large sundae with nonfat vanilla yogurt and fat-free chocolate syrup. I have to admit, though, that an hour or so after I ate it, I was hungry again. Maybe it's stress. . . ."

What do you think of Liz's approach to her persistent hunger? What have you learned in this chapter about the role of fats that might be important for Liz to consider?

Dietary Reference Intakes for Essential Fatty Acids

Dietary Reference Intakes (DRIs) for the two essential fatty acids were set in 2002:[8]

- *Linoleic acid.* The Adequate Intake (AI) for linoleic acid is 14 to 17 g per day for men and 11 to 12 g per day for women 19 years and older. Using the typical energy intakes for adult men and women, this translates into an AMDR of 5% to 10% of energy.
- *Alpha-linolenic acid.* The AI for alpha-linolenic acid is 1.6 g per day for adult men and 1.1 g per day for adult women. This translates into an AMDR of 0.6% to 1.2% of energy.

For example, an individual consuming 2,000 kcal per day should consume about 11 to 22 g per day of linoleic acid and about 1.3 to 2.6 g per day of alpha-linolenic acid. This level of intake would keep one within the 5:1 to 10:1 ratio of linoleic:alpha-linolenic acid recommended by the World Health Organization and supported by the Institute of Medicine.[8] Because these fatty acids compete for the same enzymes to produce various eicosanoids that regulate body functions, this ratio helps keep the eicosanoids produced in balance; that is, one isn't overproduced at the expense of another.

Most Americans Eat Within the Recommended Percentage of Fat but Eat the Wrong Types

Many nutrition experts have been recommending the reduction of dietary fat for more than 20 years. According to recent data, relative fat intake has decreased from 45% of total energy intake in 1965 to 33% of energy intake in 2000 for both men and women.[11] However, this reduction in the percentage of fat consumed is misleading because Americans are consuming 14% to 15% more energy overall. This additional energy comes mostly in the form of carbohydrates, and less in fats, but the end result is that daily fat consumption in absolute levels has not decreased; instead, it has *increased* slightly from 70.9 to 74.8 g/d.[12]

Of the dietary fat we eat, saturated and *trans* fats are most highly correlated with an increased risk of heart disease because they increase blood cholesterol levels by altering the way cholesterol is removed from the blood. Thus, the recommended intake of saturated fat is less than 10% of our total energy; unfortunately, our average intake of saturated fats is between 11% and 12% of energy.[13] The Institute of Medicine also recommends that we keep our intake of *trans* fatty acids to an absolute minimum.[8] Determining the actual amount of *trans* fatty acids consumed in America has been hindered by the lack of an accurate and comprehensive database of foods containing *trans* fatty acids. At the present time, a best guess as to the amount of *trans* fatty acid consumed in the United States comes from a recent national survey, which estimated our intake at 2.6% of our total fat intake.[14]

Don't Let the Fats Fool You

The last time you picked up a frozen dinner in the grocery store, did you stop and read the Nutrition Facts Panel on the box? If you had, you might have been shocked to learn how much saturated fat was in the meal. As we discuss here, many processed foods are hidden sources of fat, especially saturated and *trans* fats. In contrast, many whole foods, such as oils and nuts, are rich sources of the healthful fats our bodies need.

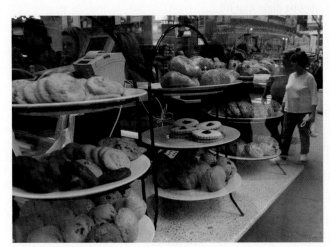

Baked goods are often high in invisible fats.

Watch Out for Invisible Fats

Americans not only eat lots of high-fat foods but also commonly add fat to foods to improve their taste. Added fats, such as oils, butter, cream, shortening, margarine, mayonnaise, and salad dressings are called **visible fats** because we can easily see that we are adding them to our food.

When we add cream to coffee or butter to pancakes, we know how much fat we are adding and what kind. In contrast, when fat is added in the preparation of a frozen entrée or a fast-food burger and fries, we are less aware of how much or what type of fat is actually there. In fact, we might not be aware that a food contains any fat at all. We call fats in prepared and processed foods **invisible fats** because they are hidden within the food. In fact, their invisibility often tricks us into choosing them over more healthful foods. For example, a slice of yellow cake is much higher in fat (40% of total energy) than a slice of angel food cake (1% of total energy). Yet many consumers assume that the fat content of these foods is the same, because they are both cake.

The majority of the fat in the average American diet is invisible. Foods that can be high in invisible fats are baked goods, regular-fat dairy products, processed meats or meats that are highly marbled or not trimmed, and most convenience and fast foods, such as hamburgers, hot dogs, chips, ice cream, French fries, and other fried foods.

Because high-fat diets have been associated with obesity, many Americans have tried to reduce their total fat intake. Food manufacturers have been more than happy to provide consumers with low-fat alternatives to their favorite foods. However, these lower-fat foods may not always have fewer calories. See the upcoming Highlight box "Low-Fat, Reduced-Fat, Nonfat . . . What's the Difference?" and Table 5.1.

Select Beneficial Fats

In general, it is prudent to switch to more healthful sources of fats without increasing your total fat intake. For example, use olive oil and canola oil in place of butter and margarine, and select fish more frequently instead of high-fat meat sources (hot dogs, hamburgers, sausage). Dairy products, including cheeses, can be high in saturated fats, so select low- and reduced-fat versions when possible. Read the Nutrition Label Activity, pages 190–191, "How Much Fat Is in This Food?" to learn how to calculate the calories from fat in the foods you buy.

Americans appear to get adequate amounts of omega-6 fatty acids, probably because of the high amount of salad dressings, vegetable oils, margarine, and mayonnaise we eat; however, our consumption of omega-3 fatty acids is more variable and can be low in the diets of people who do not eat dark green, leafy vegetables; fish or walnuts; soy products; canola oil; or flaxseeds or their oil. Table 5.2 on page 189 identifies the omega-3 fatty acid content of various foods.

visible fats Fat we can see in our foods or see added to foods, such as butter, margarine, cream, shortening, salad dressings, chicken skin, and untrimmed fat on meat.

invisible fats Fats that are hidden in foods, such as the fats found in baked goods, regular-fat dairy products, marbling in meat, and fried foods.

Highlight

Low-Fat, Reduced-Fat, Nonfat . . . What's the Difference?

Although most people love high-fat foods, we also know that eating too much fat isn't good for our health or our waistlines. Because of this concern, food manufacturers have produced a host of modified-fat foods—so you can have your cake and eat it too! In fact, it is now estimated that there are more than 7,000 different fat-modified foods on the market.[15] This means that similar foods may come in a wide range of fat contents. For example, you can purchase full-fat, low-fat, or fat-free milk; ice cream; sour cream; cheese; and yogurt.

In Table 5.1, we list a number of full-fat foods with their lower-fat alternatives. These products, if incorporated in the diet on a regular basis, can significantly reduce the amount of fat consumed but may or may not reduce the amount of energy consumed. For example, drinking nonfat milk (86 kcals and 0.5 g of fat per serving) instead of whole milk (150 kcals and 8.2 g of fat per serving) will dramatically reduce both fat and energy intake. However, eating fat-free Fig Newton cookies (3 cookies have 204 kcals and 0 g of fat) instead of regular Fig Newton cookies (3 cookies have 210 kcals and 4.5 g of fat) does not significantly reduce your energy intake, even though it reduces your fat intake by 4.5 g per serving.

Thus, those who think that they can eat all the low-fat foods they want without gaining weight are mistaken. The reduced fat is often replaced with added carbohydrate, resulting in a very similar total energy intake. Thus, if you want to reduce both the amount of fat and the number of calories you consume, you must read the labels of modified-fat foods carefully before you buy.[16]

It is important to recognize that there can be some risk associated with eating large amounts of fish on a regular basis. Depending on the species of fish and the level of pollution in the water in which it is caught, the fish may contain high levels of poisons such as mercury, polychlorinated biphenyls (PCBs), and other environmental contaminants. Types of fish that are currently considered safe to consume include salmon (except from the Great Lakes region), farmed trout, flounder, sole, mahi mahi, and cooked shellfish. Fish more likely to be contaminated are shark, swordfish, golden bass, golden snapper, marlin, bluefish, and largemouth and smallmouth bass. For more information on food safety, see Chapter 15.

Be Aware of Fat Replacers

The rising rates of obesity and its associated health concerns have increased the demand for low-fat versions of our favorite foods, which in turn has created a booming industry for *fat replacers*, substances that mimic the palate-pleasing and flavor-enhancing properties of fats with fewer calories. Snack foods and desserts have been the primary target for fat replacers because it is difficult to simply eliminate all or most of the fat in these products without dramatically changing their taste. In the mid 1990s, both food industry executives and nutritionists thought that fat replacers would be the answer to our growing obesity problem. They reasoned that if we could replace some of the fats in snack and fast foods with these products, we might be able to reduce both energy and fat intake and help Americans manage their weight better.

Snack foods have been the primary target for fat replacers such as Olean, because it is more difficult to significantly reduce the fat in these types of foods without dramatically changing the taste.

Table 5.1 Comparison of Full-Fat, Reduced-Fat, and Low-Fat Foods

Product	Serving Size	Energy (kcal)	Protein (g)	Carbohydrate (g)	Fat (g)
Milk, whole (3.3% fat)	8 oz	150	8.0	11.4	8.2
Milk, 2% fat	8 oz	121	8.1	11.7	4.7
Milk, 1% fat	8 oz	102	8.0	11.7	2.6
Milk, skim (nonfat)	8 oz	86	8.4	11.9	0.5
Cheese, cheddar regular	1 oz	111	7.1	0.5	9.1
Cheese, cheddar low-fat	1 oz	81	9.1	0.0	5.1
Cheese, cheddar nonfat	1 oz	41	6.8	4.0	0.0
Mayonnaise, regular	1 tbsp.	100	0.0	0.0	11.0
Mayonnaise, light	1 tbsp.	50	0.0	1.0	5.0
Mayonnaise, fat-free	1 tbsp.	10	0.0	2.0	0.0
Margarine, regular corn oil	1 tbsp.	100	0.0	0.0	11.0
Margarine, reduced-fat	1 tbsp.	60	0.0	0.0	7.0
Peanut butter, regular	1 tbsp.	95	4.1	3.1	8.2
Peanut butter, reduced-fat	1 tbsp.	81	4.4	5.2	5.4
Cream cheese, soft regular	1 tbsp.	50	1.0	0.5	5.0
Cream cheese, soft light	1 tbsp.	35	1.5	1.0	2.5
Cream cheese, soft nonfat	1 tbsp.	15	2.5	1.0	0.0
Crackers, Wheat Thins regular	18 crackers	158	2.3	21.4	6.8
Crackers, Wheat Thins reduced-fat	18 crackers	120	2.0	21.0	4.0
Cookies, Oreo's regular	3 cookies	160	2.0	23.0	7.0
Cookies, Oreo's reduced-fat	3 cookies	130	2.0	25.0	3.5
Cookies, Fig Newton regular	3 cookies	210	3.0	30.0	4.5
Cookies, Fig Newton fat-free	3 cookies	204	2.4	26.8	0.0
Breakfast bars, regular	1 bar	140	2.0	27.0	2.8
Breakfast bars, fat-free	1 bar	110	2.0	26.0	0.0

The Food and Drug Administration and the U.S. Department of Agriculture have set specific regulations on allowable product descriptions for reduced-fat products. The following claims are defined for one serving:

Fat-free: less than 0.5 g of fat
Low-fat: 3 g or less of fat
Reduced-fat or less fat: at least 25% less fat as compared with a standard serving
Light: one-third fewer calories or 50% less fat as compared with a standard serving size

Data from: Food Processor, Version 7.01 (ESHA Research, Salem, OR).

Products such as olestra (brand name Olean) hit the market in 1996 with a lot of fanfare, but the hype was short lived. Initially, foods containing olestra had to bear a label warning of potential gastrointestinal side effects. In 2003, the U.S. Food and Drug Administration (FDA) announced that this warning was no longer necessary, as recent research indicated that olestra caused only mild, infrequent discomfort. However, even with the new labeling, only limited foods in the marketplace contain olestra. It is also evident from our growing obesity problem that fat replacers such as olestra did not help Americans lose weight or even maintain their current weight.

Recently, a new group of fat replacers has been developed using proteins, such as the whey protein found in milk. Like their predecessors, these new fat replacers lower the fat content of food, but in addition, they improve the food's total nutrient profile and decrease

Table 5.2 Omega-3 Fatty Acid Content of Selected Foods

Food Item	Omega-3 Fatty Acid (grams per serving)
Salmon oil (fish oil) (1 tbsp.)	4.39
Herring, Atlantic, broiled (3 oz)	1.52
Herring oil (1 tbsp.)	1.52
Canola oil (1 tbsp.)	1.27
Shrimp, broiled (3 oz)	1.11
Trout, rainbow fillet, baked (3 oz)	1.05
Halibut, fillet, baked (3 oz)	0.58
Walnuts (1 tbsp.)	0.51
Salmon, Chinook, smoked (3 oz)	0.50
Crab, Dungeness, steamed (3 oz)	0.34
Tuna, light in water (3 oz)	0.23

Data from: Food Processor, Version 7.01 (ESHA Research, Salem, OR).

its calorie content. This means we can have a low-fat ice cream with the mouthfeel, finish, and texture of a full-fat ice cream that is also higher in protein and lower in calories than traditional ice cream. So don't be surprised if you see more products containing protein-based fat replacers on your supermarket shelves in the next few years.

RECaP

The AMDR for total fat is 20% to 35% of total energy. The AI for linoleic acid is 14 to 17 g per day for adult men and 11 to 12 g per day for adult women. The AI for alpha-linolenic acid is 1.6 g per day for adult men and 1.1 g per day for adult women. Because saturated and *trans* fatty acids can increase the risk of heart disease, health professionals recommend that we reduce our intake of saturated fat to less than 10% of our total energy intake and reduce our intake of *trans* fatty acids to the absolute minimum. Visible fats can be easily recognized, but invisible fats are added to our food during manufacturing or cooking, so we are not aware of how much we are consuming. A healthful dietary strategy is to switch from saturated and *trans* fats to MUFAs, PUFAs, and EFAs. Fat replacers are used to reduce the fat content of processed foods and, in some cases, improve the nutrient profile while reducing the number of calories.

What Role Do Lipids Play in Cardiovascular Disease and Cancer?

There appears to be a generally held assumption that if you eat fat-free or low-fat foods, you will lose weight and prevent chronic diseases. Certainly, we know that high-fat diets, especially those high in saturated and *trans* fatty acids, can contribute to chronic diseases, including heart disease and cancer; however, as we have explored in this chapter, unsaturated fatty acids do not have this negative effect and are essential to good health. Thus, a sensible health goal would be to eat the appropriate amounts and types of fat.

Fats Can Protect Against or Promote Cardiovascular Disease

Cardiovascular disease is a general term used to refer to any abnormal condition involving dysfunction of the heart or the body's blood vessels. A common form of this disease is *coronary artery disease* (*CAD*), which occurs when blood vessels supplying the heart (the

cardiovascular disease A general term that refers to abnormal conditions involving dysfunction of the heart and blood vessels; cardiovascular disease can result in heart attack or stroke.

Nutrition Label Activity
How Much Fat Is in This Food?

How do you know how much fat is in a food you buy? One simple way to determine the amount of fat in the food you eat is to read the Nutrition Facts Panel on the label. By becoming a better label reader, you can make more healthful food selections.

Two cracker labels are shown in **Figure 5.14**; one cracker is higher in fat than the other. Let's review how you can read the label so you know what percentage of energy is coming from fat from each product. These calculations are relatively simple.

1. Divide the total calories or kilocalories from fat by the total calories per serving, and multiply the answer by 100.
   - For the Regular Wheat Crackers: 50 kcals/150 kcals = 0.33 × 100 = 33%
     Thus, for the regular crackers, the total energy coming from fat is 33%.
   - For the Reduced-Fat Wheat Crackers: 35 kcals/130 kcals = 0.269 × 100 = 27%
     Thus, for the reduced-fat crackers, the total energy coming from fat is 27%.

You can see that although the total amount of energy per serving is not very different between these two crackers, the amount of fat is quite different.

2. If the total calories per serving from fat are not given on the label, you can quickly calculate this value by multiplying the grams of total fat per serving by 9 (as there are 9 kcal per gram of fat).
   - For the Regular Wheat Crackers: 6 g fat × 9 kcals g = 54 cal of fat
   - To calculate percentage of calories from fat: 54 kcals/150 kcals = 0.36 × 100 = 36%

You can see that this value is not exactly the same as the 50 kcals reported on the label or the 33% of calories from fat calculated in Example 1. The values on food labels are rounded off, so your estimations may not be identical when you do this second calculation.

Refer to Table 5.1, which displays a list of regular, reduced-fat, and fat-free foods. You can quickly calculate the percentage of fat per serving for these foods by following the same series of steps: First multiply the grams of fat per serving by 9 kcals per gram; then divide this number by the total calories per serving; and finally, multiply by 100.

Figure 5.14 Labels for two types of wheat crackers.
(a) Regular wheat crackers. **(b)** Reduced-fat wheat crackers.

Wheat Crackers

- **No Cholesterol**

Nutrition Facts

Serving Size: 16 Crackers (31g)
Servings Per Container: About 9

Amount Per Serving

Calories	150
Calories from Fat	50

% Daily Value*

Total Fat 6g	9%
Saturated Fat 1g	6%
Polyunsaturated Fat 0g	
Monounsaturated Fat 2g	
Trans Fat 0g	
Cholesterol 0mg	0%
Sodium 270mg	11%
Total Carbohydrate 21g	7%
Dietary Fiber 1g	4%
Sugars 3g	
Protein 2g	

Vitamin A	0%
Vitamin C	0%
Calcium	2%
Iron	6%

* Percent Daily Values are based on a 2,000
calorie diet. Your daily values may be higher
or lower depending on your calorie needs:

	Calories	2,000	2,500
Total Fat	Less than	65g	80g
Sat. Fat	Less than	20g	25g
Cholesterol	Less than	300mg	300mg
Sodium	Less than	2,400mg	2,400mg
Total Carbohydrate		300g	375g
Dietary Fiber		25g	30g

INGREDIENTS: Enriched Flour (Wheat Flour,
Niacin, Reduced Iron, Thiamine Mononitrate
(Vitamin B1), Riboflavin (Vitamin B2), Folic
Acid), Partially Hydrogenated Soybean Oil,
Defatted Wheat Germ, Sugar, Cornstarch, High
Fructose Corn Syrup, Salt, Corn Syrup, Malt
Syrup, Leavening (Calcium Phosphate, Baking
Soda), Vegetable Colors (Annatto Extract,
Turmeric Oleoresin), Malted Barley Flour.

(a)

Reduced-Fat Wheat Crackers

- **No Cholesterol**
- **Low Saturated Fat**
  Contains 4g Fat Per Serving

Nutrition Facts

Serving Size: 16 Crackers (29g)
Servings Per Container: About 9

Amount Per Serving

Calories	130
Calories from Fat	35

% Daily Value*

Total Fat 4g	6%
Saturated Fat 1g	4%
Polyunsaturated Fat 0g	
Monounsaturated Fat 1.5g	
Trans Fat 0g	
Cholesterol 0mg	0%
Sodium 260 mg	11%
Total Carbohydrate 21g	7%
Dietary Fiber 1g	4%
Sugars 3g	
Protein 2g	

Vitamin A	0%
Vitamin C	0%
Calcium	2%
Iron	6%

* Percent Daily Values are based on a 2,000
calorie diet. Your daily values may be higher
or lower depending on your calorie needs:

	Calories	2,000	2,500
Total Fat	Less than	65g	80g
Sat. Fat	Less than	20g	25g
Cholesterol	Less than	300mg	300mg
Sodium	Less than	2,400mg	2,400mg
Total Carbohydrate		300g	375g
Dietary Fiber		25g	30g

**Reduced Fat Wheat Crackers have 4 grams of fat
per serving compared to 6 grams in Original Wheat
Crackers.**

INGREDIENTS: Enriched Flour (Wheat Flour,
Niacin, Reduced Iron, Thiamine Mononitrate
(Vitamin B1), Riboflavin (Vitamin B2), Folic
Acid), Partially Hydrogenated Soybean Oil,
Defatted Wheat Germ, Sugar, Cornstarch, High
Fructose Corn Syrup, Corn Syrup, Salt, Malt
Syrup, Leavening (Calcium Phosphate, Baking
Soda), Vegetable Colors (Annatto Extract and
Turmeric Oleoresin), Malted
Barley Flour.

(b)

coronary arteries) become blocked or constricted; such blockage reduces blood flow to the heart and so can result in a heart attack. Similar blockage can occur in the cerebral arteries and impair blood flow to the brain, a condition commonly called a *stroke*. According to the Centers for Disease Control and Prevention, diseases of the heart are the leading cause of death in the United States, and stroke is the third leading cause of death. (See Figure 1.3 in Chapter 1.) Combined, these two disease categories account for more than 35% of all deaths annually.[17] Overall, about 80 million Americans of all ages suffer from cardiovascular disease, and it is estimated that in 2008 the cost of such disease was $448 billion.

Being overweight is associated with higher rates of death from cardiovascular disease.

Risk Factors for Cardiovascular Disease

During the past two decades, researchers have identified a number of factors that contribute to an increased risk for cardiovascular disease. Following is a brief description of each of these major risk factors, many of which have a dietary component.[18]

- *Overweight:* Being overweight is associated with higher rates of death from cardiovascular disease. The risk is due primarily to a greater occurrence of high blood pressure, abnormal blood lipids (discussed in more detail shortly), and higher rates of diabetes in overweight individuals. In general, an overweight condition develops from an energy imbalance from eating too much and exercising too little (see Chapter 13).

- *Physical inactivity:* Numerous research studies have shown that physical activity can reduce your risk of cardiovascular disease by improving blood lipid levels, lowering resting blood pressure, reducing body fat and weight, and improving blood glucose levels both at rest and after eating.

- *Smoking:* There is strong evidence that smoking increases your risk for cardiovascular disease. Research indicates that smokers have a 70% greater chance of developing cardiovascular disease than nonsmokers. Without question, smoking cessation or never starting initially is one of the best ways to reduce your risk of cardiovascular disease. People who stop smoking live longer than those who continue to smoke, and a 15-year cessation period will reduce your risk factors for cardiovascular disease to those of a nonsmoker.

- *High blood pressure:* High blood pressure stresses the heart and increases the chance that blockage or rupture of a blood vessel will occur. Elevated blood pressure is associated with a number of factors, including dietary factors (for example, high sodium intakes, low calcium intakes, or high caffeine intake), elevated blood lipid levels, obesity, smoking, diabetes, and physical inactivity.

- *Diabetes mellitus:* As discussed in Chapter 4, in many individuals with diabetes, the condition is directly related to being overweight or obese, which is also associated with abnormal blood lipids and high blood pressure. The risk for cardiovascular disease is three times higher in women with diabetes and two times higher in men with diabetes compared with individuals without diabetes.

- *Inflammation:* Inflammation is now considered a major initiator of cardiovascular disease.[19] As you many know, inflammation occurs as a response to tissue injury. In arterial walls, this injury may be due to any number of physiologic stresses, such as high blood pressure, smoking, high blood lipids, or poor glucose control. When injury occurs to the arteries, the resulting inflammatory response eventually leads to the deposition of plaque in the arterial walls. Plaque build-up increases the risk of a heart attack or stroke. C-reactive protein (CRP) is a nonspecific marker of inflammation that is associated with cardiovascular disease. Risk of cardiovascular disease appears to be higher in individuals who have high CRP levels in addition to other risk factors such as high blood lipids.[20] Thus, reducing the factors that increase inflammation can reduce your risk of cardiovascular disease.

Calculating Your Risk for Cardiovascular Disease

You can estimate your risk of developing cardiovascular disease if you know your blood pressure and blood lipid levels. Blood lipid levels are a measurement of the cholesterol and some of the lipoproteins in the blood that carry fats to and from the body's cells. The significance of laboratory analysis of blood lipid levels, as well as the types of lipoproteins typically measured, is discussed below. It is especially important for those with a family history of heart disease to try to maintain appropriate blood lipid levels.

After determining blood pressure and blood lipid levels, the next step in assessing risk for cardiovascular disease is to calculate the number of points for each risk factor in **Figure 5.15**, and then compare total points to the points in the 10-year risk column. You can do this quick assessment on yourself, family members, or friends. An online version of this risk calculator is available at http://hin.nhlbi.nih.gov/atpiii/calculator.asp?usertype=prof.

The Role of Dietary Fats in Cardiovascular Disease

Recall that lipids are transported in the blood by lipoproteins made up of a lipid center and a protein outer coat. The names of lipoproteins reflect their proportion of lipid, which is less dense, to protein, which is very dense. For example, very-low-density lipoproteins (VLDLs) have a high ratio of lipid to protein. Because lipoproteins are soluble in blood, they are commonly called *blood lipids.*

Our intake of certain types of dietary fats influences our risk for heart disease by increasing or decreasing certain blood lipids. Research indicates that high intakes of saturated and *trans* fatty acids increase the blood's level of those lipids associated with heart disease, namely, total blood cholesterol and the cholesterol found in very-low-density lipoproteins (VLDLs), and low-density lipoproteins (LDLs). Conversely, omega-3 fatty acids decrease our risk of heart disease in a number of ways, such as by reducing inflammation and blood triglycerides[21] and increasing high-density lipoproteins (HDLs).[22] Let's look at each of these blood lipids in more detail to determine how they are linked to heart disease risk (**Figure 5.16**).

Because foods fried in hydrogenated vegetable oils, such as French fries, are high in *trans* fatty acids, these types of foods should be limited in our diet.

Chylomicrons   Only after a meal does the blood contain chylomicrons, which we learned earlier are produced in the enterocytes to transport dietary fat into the lymph system and from there into the bloodstream. At 85% triglyceride, chylomicrons have the lowest density.

Very-Low-Density Lipoproteins   More than half of the substance of **very-low-density lipoproteins (VLDLs)** is triglyceride. The liver is the primary source of VLDLs, but they are also produced in the intestines. VLDLs are primarily transport vehicles ferrying triglycerides from their source to the body's cells, including to adipose tissues for storage (**Figure 5.17a**). The enzyme lipoprotein lipase frees most of the triglyceride from the VLDL molecules, resulting in its uptake by the body's cells.

Diets high in fat, simple sugars, and extra calories can increase the production of endogenous VLDLs, whereas diets high in omega-3 fatty acids can help reduce their production. In addition, exercise can reduce VLDLs because the fat produced in the body is quickly used for energy instead of remaining to circulate in the blood.

Low-Density Lipoproteins   The molecules resulting when VLDLs release their triglyceride load are much higher in cholesterol, phospholipids, and protein and therefore somewhat more dense. These **low-density lipoproteins (LDLs)** circulate in the blood, delivering their cholesterol to cells with specialized LDL receptors (see Figure 5.17b). Diets high in saturated fat *decrease* the removal of LDLs by body cells, apparently by blocking these receptor sites.

What happens to LDLs not taken up by body cells? As LDLs degrade over time, they release their cholesterol; thus, failure to remove LDLs from the bloodstream results in an increased load of cholesterol in the blood. The more cholesterol circulating in the blood, the

very-low-density lipoprotein (VLDL)   A lipoprotein made in the liver and intestine that functions to transport endogenous lipids, especially triglycerides, to the tissues of the body.

low-density lipoprotein (LDL)   A lipoprotein formed in the blood from VLDLs that transports cholesterol to the cells of the body. Often called the "bad cholesterol."

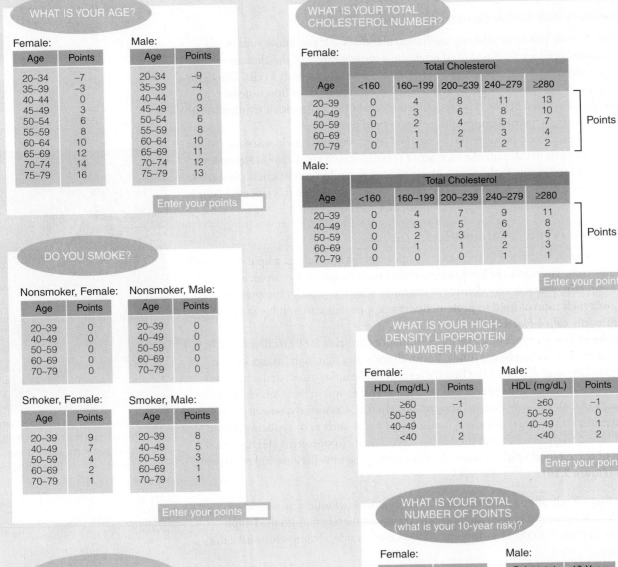

WHAT IS YOUR AGE?

Female:

Age	Points
20–34	–7
35–39	–3
40–44	0
45–49	3
50–54	6
55–59	8
60–64	10
65–69	12
70–74	14
75–79	16

Male:

Age	Points
20–34	–9
35–39	–4
40–44	0
45–49	3
50–54	6
55–59	8
60–64	10
65–69	11
70–74	12
75–79	13

Enter your points ____

WHAT IS YOUR TOTAL CHOLESTEROL NUMBER?

Female:

Age	Total Cholesterol				
	<160	160–199	200–239	240–279	≥280
20–39	0	4	8	11	13
40–49	0	3	6	8	10
50–59	0	2	4	5	7
60–69	0	1	2	3	4
70–79	0	1	1	2	2

Points

Male:

Age	Total Cholesterol				
	<160	160–199	200–239	240–279	≥280
20–39	0	4	7	9	11
40–49	0	3	5	6	8
50–59	0	2	3	4	5
60–69	0	1	1	2	3
70–79	0	0	0	1	1

Points

Enter your points ____

DO YOU SMOKE?

Nonsmoker, Female:

Age	Points
20–39	0
40–49	0
50–59	0
60–69	0
70–79	0

Nonsmoker, Male:

Age	Points
20–39	0
40–49	0
50–59	0
60–69	0
70–79	0

Smoker, Female:

Age	Points
20–39	9
40–49	7
50–59	4
60–69	2
70–79	1

Smoker, Male:

Age	Points
20–39	8
40–49	5
50–59	3
60–69	1
70–79	1

Enter your points ____

WHAT IS YOUR HIGH-DENSITY LIPOPROTEIN NUMBER (HDL)?

Female:

HDL (mg/dL)	Points
≥60	–1
50–59	0
40–49	1
<40	2

Male:

HDL (mg/dL)	Points
≥60	–1
50–59	0
40–49	1
<40	2

Enter your points ____

WHAT IS YOUR TOTAL NUMBER OF POINTS (what is your 10-year risk)?

Female:

Point total	10-Year risk %
<9	<1
9	1
10	1
11	1
12	1
13	2
14	2
15	3
16	4
17	5
18	6
19	8
20	11
21	14
22	17
23	22
24	27
≥25	≥30

Male:

Point total	10-Year risk %
<0	<1
0	1
1	1
2	1
3	1
4	1
5	2
6	2
7	3
8	4
9	5
10	6
11	8
12	10
13	12
14	16
15	20
16	25
≥17	≥30

Enter your 10-year risk percentage ____

WHAT IS YOUR SYSTOLIC BLOOD PRESSURE (the top number)?

Female:

Systolic BP (mmHg)	If untreated	If treated
<120	0	0
120–129	1	3
130–139	2	4
140–159	3	5
≥160	4	6

Male:

Systolic BP (mmHg)	If untreated	If treated
<120	0	0
120–129	0	1
130–139	1	2
140–159	1	2
≥160	2	3

Enter your points ____

Figure 5.15 Calculation matrix to estimate the 10-year risk for cardiovascular disease for men and women. (*Data from:* National Institutes of Health, *Third Report of the National Cholesterol Education Program: Detection, Evaluation and Treatment of High Blood Cholesterol in Adults (ATP:III).* Bethesda, MD: National Cholesterol Education Program, National Heart, Lung, and Blood Institute, NIH, May, 2001. Available online at http://www.nhlbi.nih.gov/guideline/cholesterol/atp3xsum.pdf. Online assessment available at http://hp2010.nhlbihin.net/atpiii/calculator.asp.)

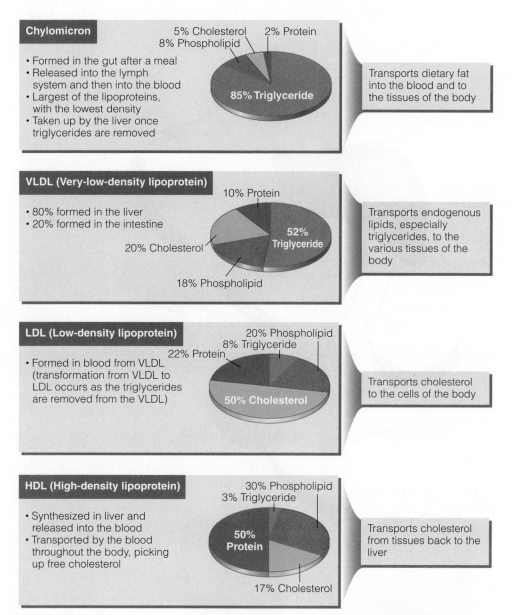

Chylomicron
- Formed in the gut after a meal
- Released into the lymph system and then into the blood
- Largest of the lipoproteins, with the lowest density
- Taken up by the liver once triglycerides are removed

5% Cholesterol 2% Protein
8% Phospholipid
85% Triglyceride

Transports dietary fat into the blood and to the tissues of the body

VLDL (Very-low-density lipoprotein)
- 80% formed in the liver
- 20% formed in the intestine

10% Protein
52% Triglyceride
20% Cholesterol
18% Phospholipid

Transports endogenous lipids, especially triglycerides, to the various tissues of the body

LDL (Low-density lipoprotein)
- Formed in blood from VLDL (transformation from VLDL to LDL occurs as the triglycerides are removed from the VLDL)

20% Phospholipid
8% Triglyceride
22% Protein
50% Cholesterol

Transports cholesterol to the cells of the body

HDL (High-density lipoprotein)
- Synthesized in liver and released into the blood
- Transported by the blood throughout the body, picking up free cholesterol

30% Phospholipid
3% Triglyceride
50% Protein
17% Cholesterol

Transports cholesterol from tissues back to the liver

Figure 5.16 The chemical components of various lipoproteins. Notice that chylomicrons contain the highest proportion of triglycerides, making them the least dense, and high-density lipoproteins (HDLs) have the highest proportion of protein, making them the most dense.

greater the risk that some of it will adhere to the walls of the blood vessels. This adhesion causes "scavenger" white blood cells to rush to the site and bind cholesterol to their receptors. As more and more cholesterol binds to these cells, they burst to form a fatty patch, or *plaque*, that eventually becomes fibrous and calcified, blocking the artery (**Figure 5.18**). Because high blood levels of LDL-cholesterol increase the risk of heart disease, it is often labeled the "bad cholesterol."

High-Density Lipoproteins   As their name indicates, **high-density lipoproteins (HDLs)** are small, dense lipoproteins with a very low cholesterol content and a high protein content. They are released from the liver and intestines to circulate in the blood, picking up cholesterol from dying cells and arterial plaques and transferring it to other lipoproteins, which return it to the liver (see Figure 5.17a). The liver takes up the cholesterol and uses it to synthesize bile, thereby removing it from the circulatory system. High blood levels of HDL-cholesterol are therefore associated with a low risk of coronary artery disease. That's

high-density lipoprotein (HDL)   A lipoprotein made in the liver and released into the blood. HDLs function to transport cholesterol from the tissues back to the liver. Often called the "good cholesterol."

(a)

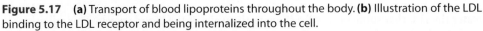

(b)

Figure 5.17 **(a)** Transport of blood lipoproteins throughout the body. **(b)** Illustration of the LDL binding to the LDL receptor and being internalized into the cell.

why HDL-cholesterol is often referred to as the "good cholesterol." There is some evidence that diets high in omega-3 fatty acids and participation in regular physical exercise can modestly increase HDL-cholesterol levels.

Refer to the Highlight box "Blood Lipid Levels: Know Your Numbers!" on the next page to gain more insight into your own blood lipid levels.

Total Serum Cholesterol Normally, as the dietary level of cholesterol increases, the body decreases the amount of cholesterol it makes, which keeps the body's level of cholesterol constant. Unfortunately, this feedback mechanism does not work well in everyone. For some individuals, eating dietary cholesterol doesn't decrease the amount of

Highlight

Blood Lipid Levels: Know Your Numbers!

One of the most important steps you can take to reduce your own risk of heart disease is to know your "numbers"—that is, your blood lipid values. In addition, if you are considering a career in nutrition or healthcare, you'll need to be able to work with your clients to track their blood lipid levels as they change their diet and lifestyle to decrease their risk of heart disease. So it's important to keep a record of blood lipid values and have them checked every 1 to 2 years.

How are blood lipids, such as LDL-cholesterol or HDL-cholesterol, actually measured? First, a blood sample is taken, and the lipoproteins in the blood are extracted. Total cholesterol is determined by breaking apart all the lipoproteins and measuring their combined cholesterol content. You can see from Figure 5.16 that each of the lipoproteins contains some cholesterol and some triglycerides. This same process is used to determine total blood triglyceride level. The next step is to measure the amount of cholesterol in the LDLs and HDLs, because these two lipoproteins can either raise or lower an individual's risk of heart disease. These lipoproteins are separated, and the amount of cholesterol in each one is determined to give an LDL-cholesterol and an HDL-cholesterol value. Once these values are determined, you can compare them to the following "target" levels, which identify healthful ranges for each blood lipid, and see how you measure up.

The target lipid values are as follows:[23]

Total Cholesterol (mg/dl): < 200 mg/dl
LDL-Cholesterol (mg/dl): <130 mg/dl
HDL-Cholesterol (mg/dl): > 40 mg/dl
Triglycerides (mg/dl): > 150 mg/dl

(*Data from:* the National Institutes of Health. 2001. *Third Report of the National Cholesterol Education Program: Detection, Evaluation and Treatment of High Blood Cholesterol in Adults (ATP III)*. Bethesda, MD: National Cholesterol Education Program, National Heart, Lung, and Blood Institute, NIH. Available at www.nhlbi.nih.gov/guidelines/cholesterol/atp3xsum.pdf.)

cholesterol produced in the body, and their total body cholesterol level rises. This also increases the level of cholesterol in the blood. These individuals benefit from reducing their intake of dietary cholesterol. Although this appears somewhat complicated, both dietary cholesterol and saturated fats are found in animal foods; thus, by limiting intake of animal products or selecting low-fat animal products, people reduce their intake of both saturated fat and cholesterol. Based on data collected in 1994–1996, U.S. adults get the majority of their dietary cholesterol from eggs (30%), beef and poultry (28%), and milk and cheese (11%).[24] Selecting low-fat meat, poultry, and dairy products and consuming egg whites without yolks can dramatically reduce the amount of cholesterol in the diet.

(a)   (b)

Artery wall
Interior of the artery
Plaque

Figure 5.18   These light micrographs show a cross section of **(a)** a normal artery containing little cholesterol-rich plaque and allowing adequate blood flow through the heart, and **(b)** an artery that is partially blocked with cholesterol-rich plaque, which can lead to a heart attack.

Invisible and *trans* fats are hidden in processed and prepared foods, such as pies. Without a label, it is impossible to know the amount of fat in each serving of these types of foods, and so their intake should be limited.

The Role of Trans Fatty Acids We have known for a long time that saturated fats increase blood levels of total cholesterol and LDL-cholesterol and increase the risk of heart disease. Because saturated fat is found primarily in the fats of animal products, many people believe that eating low-fat dairy and meat products eliminates this risk. But in vegetable oils converted to solids (for example, corn oil to corn-oil margarine), the level of saturated fat dramatically increases, as does the level of *trans* fatty acids. Recent research indicates that *trans* fatty acids can raise blood LDL-cholesterol levels as much as saturated fat.[25] Thus, to reduce the risk of heart disease, we must reduce our intake of both high-fat animal products and hydrogenated vegetable products. Because many commercially prepared baked goods, as well as foods fried in hydrogenated vegetable oils, such as French fries, are also high in *trans* fatty acids, these types of foods should also be limited in our diet.

The FDA requires that *trans* fatty acid content be listed on labels for conventional foods and some dietary supplements. Based on data collected by the FDA in 2003, approximately 40% of our *trans* fatty acids come from cakes, cookies, crackers, pies, and breads, with 21% coming from animal products, 17% from margarines, and 13% from fried potatoes, potato chips, corn chips, and popcorn.[26] Unfortunately, no federal regulations require restaurants to provide nutrition facts for any of their foods at the present time, although some local ordinances do require restaurants to post this information. Until all restaurants are required to identify the *trans* fatty acid content of their foods, avoid ordering fried foods and baked goods such as cakes, cookies, and pies to limit your intake of *trans* fatty acids.

Lifestyle Changes Can Prevent or Reduce Cardiovascular Disease

Diet and exercise interventions aimed at reducing the risk of cardiovascular disease center on reducing high levels of triglycerides and LDL-cholesterol while raising HDL-cholesterol. The Centers for Disease Control and Prevention (CDC); the Expert Panel on Detection, Evaluation, and Treatment of High Blood Cholesterol in Adults (ATP III), and the American Heart Association have made the following dietary and lifestyle recommendations to improve blood lipid levels and reduce the risk of cardiovascular disease:[17, 19, 21, 27]

Consuming whole fruits and vegetables can reduce your risk for cardiovascular disease.

- Maintain total fat intake to within 20% to 35% of energy.[8] Polyunsaturated fats (for example, soy and canola oil) can comprise up to 10% of total energy intake, and monounsaturated fats (for example, olive oil) can comprise up to 20% of total energy intake. For some people, a lower fat intake may help to maintain a healthful body weight.
- Decrease dietary saturated fat to less than 7% of total energy intake. Decrease cholesterol intake to less than 300 mg per day, and keep *trans* fatty acid intake to an absolute minimum (<1% of energy). Lowering the intakes of these fats will lower your LDL-cholesterol level. Replace saturated and *trans* fats (for example, butter, margarine, vegetable shortening, or lard) with more healthful fats, such as olive oil or canola oil. Select lean meats and vegetable alternatives and use fat-free (skim), 1%-fat, or low-fat dairy products.
- Increase intake of dietary omega-3 fatty acids from dark green, leafy vegetables; fatty fish; soybeans or soybean oil; walnuts or walnut oil; flaxseed meal or oil; or canola oil. Consuming fish, especially oily fish, at least twice a week will increase omega-3 fatty acid intake.
- Increase dietary intakes of whole grains, fruits, and vegetables so that total dietary fiber is 20 to 30 g per day, with 10 to 25 g per day coming from fiber sources such as oat bran, beans, and fruits. Foods high in fiber decrease blood LDL-cholesterol levels.
- Consume 400 μg/day of folate from dietary or supplemental sources to help maintain low blood levels of the amino acid homocysteine. High homocysteine levels in the blood are associated with increased risk of cardiovascular disease. Folate is discussed in Chapter 12.

- Maintain blood glucose and insulin concentrations within normal ranges. High blood glucose levels are associated with high blood triglycerides. Consume whole foods (such as whole-wheat breads and cereals, whole fruits and vegetables, and beans and legumes), and select low-saturated-fat meats and dairy products, while limiting your intake of foods high in refined carbohydrates and saturated and *trans* fats (for example, cookies, high-sugar drinks and snacks, candy, fried foods, and convenience and fast foods).
- Eat throughout the day (for example, smaller meals and snacks) instead of eating most of your calories in the evening before bed.
- Consume no more than two alcoholic drinks per day for men and one drink per day for women. Alcohol consumption is discussed in detail in the In Depth look on pages 154–165.
- Maintain an active lifestyle. Exercise most days of the week for 30 to 60 minutes if possible. Exercise will increase HDL-cholesterol while lowering blood triglyceride levels. Exercise also helps maintain a healthful body weight and a lower blood pressure and reduces your risk for diabetes.
- Balance calorie intake and physical activity to achieve or maintain a healthful body weight. Blood lipids and glucose levels typically improve when obese individuals lose weight and engage in regular physical activity. Obesity promotes inflammation; thus, keeping body weight within a healthy range helps keep inflammation low (Libby et al. 2002).
- Decrease salt intake by selecting and preparing foods with little or no salt to help keep blood pressure normal (<120/80 mm Hg). High blood pressure is an independent risk factor for cardiovascular disease.

The impact of diet on reducing the risk of cardiovascular disease was clearly demonstrated in the Dietary Approaches to Stop Hypertension (DASH) study, which is discussed in detail in Chapter 9. Although this study focused on dietary interventions to reduce hypertension (high blood pressure), the results of the study showed that eating the DASH way could also dramatically improve blood lipids. The DASH diet includes high intakes of fruits, vegetables, whole grains, low-fat dairy products, poultry, fish, and nuts and low intakes of fats, red meat, sweets, and sugar-containing beverages. Combining the DASH dietary approach with an active lifestyle significantly reduces the risk of cardiovascular disease.

Prescription Medications Can Reduce Cardiovascular Disease Risk

Sometimes medications are needed in addition to lifestyle changes to reduce cardiovascular risk. A number of medications on the market help lower LDL-cholesterol. The following are some of the most common:

- Endogenous cholesterol synthesis inhibitors: These types of drugs, typically called *statins,* block an enzyme in the cholesterol synthesis pathway. Thus, these drugs lower blood levels of LDL-cholesterol and VLDL-cholesterol. Statins also have an important anti-inflammatory effect that contributes to the reduction in cardiovascular disease risk independent of their effect on blood lipids.[28]
- Bile acid sequestrants: These types of drugs bind the bile acids, preventing them from being reabsorbed by the intestinal tract. Because bile acids are made from cholesterol, blocking their reabsorption means the liver must use cholesterol already in the body to make new bile acids. Continually eliminating bile acids from the body reduces the total cholesterol pool.
- Nicotinic acid: Therapeutic doses of nicotinic acid, a form of niacin, favorably affect all blood lipids when given pharmacologically. (The form of niacin found in multivitamin supplements does not affect lipids.) Unfortunately, this drug has a number of side effects, such as flushing of the skin, gastrointestinal distress, and liver problems.[23] Because of this, it is used less frequently than the other two drugs just discussed.

Gustavo
Nutri-Case

"Sometimes I wonder where doctors get their funny ideas. Yesterday I had my annual checkup and my doctor says, 'You're doing great! Your weight is fine, your blood sugar's good. . . The only thing that concerns me is that your blood pressure is a little high. So I want you to watch your diet. Choose fish more often. When you eat meat, trim off all the fat. Use one of the new heart-healthy margarines instead of butter, and olive oil instead of lard. And when you have eggs, don't eat the yolks.' I know he means well, but my wife's just managing to get around again after breaking her hip. How am I supposed to go home and tell her she has to learn a whole new way to cook?"

Do you feel that Gustavo's objection to his physician's advice is valid? Why or why not? Identify at least two interventions or resources that might help Gustavo and his wife.

Does a High-Fat Diet Cause Cancer?

Cancer develops as a result of a poorly understood interaction between the environment and genetic factors. In addition, most cancers take years to develop, so examining the impact of diet on cancer development can be a long and difficult process. Diet and lifestyle are two of the most important environmental factors that have been identified in the development of cancer.[29, 30] Of the dietary factors, fat intake has been extensively researched. The relationship between type and amount of fat consumed and increased risk for breast cancer is controversial.[31, 32] Early research showed an association between animal fat intake and increased risk for colon cancer, whereas more recent research indicates that the association is between factors other than fat that are found in red meat. Because we now know that physical activity can reduce the risk of colon cancer, earlier diet and colon cancer studies that did not control for this factor are now being questioned. The strongest association between dietary fat intake and cancer is for prostate cancer. Research shows that there is a consistent link between prostate cancer risk and consumption of animal fats but not other types of fats. The exact mechanism by which animal fats may contribute to prostate cancer has not yet been identified.

RECaP

The types of fats we eat can significantly influence our health and risk of disease. Saturated and *trans* fatty acids increase our risk of heart disease, whereas omega-3 fatty acids can reduce our risk. Other risk factors for heart disease include being overweight, being physically inactive, smoking, having high blood pressure, and having diabetes. You can calculate your 10-year risk of heart disease by knowing a few facts about yourself: your blood cholesterol and HDL-cholesterol levels, blood pressure, age, and smoking status. High levels of LDL-cholesterol and low levels of HDL-cholesterol increase your risk of heart disease. Selecting appropriate types of fat in the diet may also reduce your risk of some cancers, especially prostate cancer.

See for Yourself

Tips for Heart-Healthy Eating

When preparing meals at home, as well as when dining out, try these simple strategies and see for yourself how easy it can be to tip the balance of your diet toward heart-healthy fats.

At Home

☐ Boost the omega-3 profile of your favorite breakfast cereal by adding 1 tablespoon of ground flaxseed meal.

☐ Select whole-grain breads, and try peanut, almond, or walnut butter as a spread for your toast.

☐ If you normally eat two eggs for breakfast, discard the yolk from one egg for half the cholesterol. Do the same in recipes calling for two eggs.

☐ Select low-fat or nonfat milk, coffee creamers, yogurt, cream cheese, cottage cheese, sour cream, mayonnaise, and salad dressings.

☐ Substitute lower-fat cheeses such as parmesan for higher-fat cheeses such as cheddar.

☐ If you use margarine, select one that is made from an oil high in omega-3, such as canola oil, and is *trans*-fat free.

☐ Start meals with a salad dressed with olive oil and vinegar or a fat-free soup.

☐ Select lean cuts of meat. Load your plate with vegetables, and make meat a "condiment."

☐ Instead of frying meats, fish, and vegetables, bake or broil them.

☐ Trim all visible fat from meats and poultry before cooking. Eat poultry without the skin.

☐ Instead of buttering your bread, dip it in a mixture of olive oil and a dribble of balsamic vinegar.

☐ Make sure that any crackers or cookies you buy are low in saturated fats and free of *trans* fatty acids.

☐ Choose ice milk, sorbet, or low-fat or nonfat yogurt and fruit for dessert instead of high-fat ice cream.

☐ For snacks, substitute raw vegetables, whole and dried fruits, pretzels, or air-popped popcorn for potato chips or sweets.

☐ Choose water, skim milk, soy milk, or unsweetened beverages over sugar-sweetened beverages.

☐ Read food labels. Select high-fat foods less often or use them in moderation.

☐ Control your portion size, especially when consuming high-fat foods.

Eating Out

☐ When dining out, select a fish high in omega-3 fatty acid, such as salmon, or try a vegetarian entrée made with tofu or tempeh. If you do choose meat, ask that it be trimmed of fat and broiled rather than fried.

☐ Consider splitting an entrée with your dinner companion and complement it with a side salad.

☐ On your salad, choose olive oil and vinegar instead of a high-fat dressing. Also, use olive oil instead of butter for your bread.

☐ Order a baked potato or rice instead of French fries or potatoes au gratin.

☐ Share or skip dessert or choose a fat-free sorbet.

☐ The next time you order a fast-food meal, either skip the French fries or order the kid's meal for portion control.

☐ Order pizza with vegetable toppings instead of pepperoni or sausage.

☐ Order coffee drinks with skim milk instead of cream or whole milk, and accompany them with a biscotti instead of a brownie.

Chapter Review

Test Yourself | Answers

1 (F) Eating too much fat, or too much of unhealthful fats such as saturated and *trans* fatty acids, can increase our risk for diseases such as cardiovascular disease and obesity. However, fat is an important part of a nutritious diet, and we need to consume a certain minimum amount to provide adequate levels of essential fatty acids and fat-soluble vitamins.

2 (T) Fat is our primary source of energy, both at rest and during low-intensity exercise. Fat is also an important fuel source during prolonged exercise.

3 (F) Even foods fried in vegetable shortening can be unhealthful because they are higher in *trans* fatty acids. In addition, fried foods are high in total fat and energy and can contribute to overweight and obesity.

4 (T) Certain essential fatty acids, including EPA and DHA, reduce inflammation, blood clotting, and plasma triglycerides and thereby reduce an individual's risk of heart disease.

5 (F) Cancer develops as a result of a poorly understood interaction between environmental and genetic factors. Some research indicates an association between high dietary fat consumption and certain cancers, but this research is inconclusive.

Summary

- Fats and oils are forms of a larger and more diverse group of substances called lipids; most lipids are insoluble in water.

- The three types of lipids commonly found in foods are triglycerides, phospholipids, and sterols.

- Most of the fat we eat is in the form of triglycerides; a triglyceride is a molecule that contains three fatty acids attached to a glycerol backbone.

- Short-chain fatty acids are usually less than six carbon atoms in length; medium-chain fatty acids are six to twelve carbons in length, and long-chain fatty acids are fourteen or more carbons in length.

- Saturated fatty acids have no carbons attached together with a double bond, which means that every carbon atom in the fatty acid chain is saturated with hydrogen. They are straight in shape and solid at room temperature.

- Monounsaturated fatty acids contain one double bond between two carbon atoms. Polyunsaturated fatty acids contain more than one double bond between carbon atoms. Unsaturated fatty acids are usually liquid at room temperature.

- A *cis* fatty acid has hydrogen atoms located on the same side of the double bond in an unsaturated fatty acid. This *cis* positioning produces a kink in the unsaturated fatty acid and is the shape found in naturally occurring fatty acids.

- A *trans* fatty acid has hydrogen atoms located on opposite sides of the double carbon bond. This positioning causes *trans* fatty acids to be straighter and more rigid, like saturated fats. This *trans* positioning results when oils are hydrogenated during food processing.

- The essential fatty acids (linoleic acid and alpha-linolenic acid) must be obtained from food. These fatty acids are precursors to important biological compounds called eicosanoids, which are essential for growth and health.

- Linoleic acid is found primarily in vegetable and nut oils, whereas alpha-linolenic acid is found in dark green, leafy vegetables; flaxseeds and oil; walnuts and walnut oil; soybean oil and soy foods; canola oil; and fish products and fish oil.

- Phospholipids consist of a glycerol backbone and two fatty acids with a phosphate group; phospholipids are soluble in water and assist with transporting fats in the bloodstream.

- Sterols have a ring structure; cholesterol is the most common sterol in our diets.

- The majority of fat digestion and absorption occurs in the small intestine. Fat is broken into smaller components by bile, which is produced by the liver and stored in the gallbladder.

- Lipid digestion products are transported to enterocytes by micelles.

- Because fats are not soluble in water, triglycerides are packaged into lipoproteins before being released into the bloodstream for transport to the cells.

- Dietary fat is primarily used either as an energy source for the cells or to make lipid-containing compounds in the body, or it is stored in the muscle and adipose tissue as triglyceride for later use.

- Fats are a primary energy source during rest and exercise, are our major source of stored energy, provide essential fatty acids, enable the transport of fat-soluble vitamins, help maintain cell function, provide protection for body organs, contribute to the texture and flavor of foods, and help us feel satiated after a meal.

- The AMDR for fat is 20% to 35% of total energy intake. Our intake of saturated fats and *trans* fatty acids should be kept to a minimum. Individuals who limit fat intake to less than 15% of energy intake need to make sure that essential fatty acid needs are met, as well as protein and energy needs.

- For the essential fatty acids, 5% to 10% of energy intake should be in the form of linoleic acid and 0.6% to 1.2% as alpha-linolenic acid.

- Watch for invisible fats found in cakes, cookies, marbling in meat, regular-fat dairy products, and fried foods. Select beneficial fats such as UFAs and EFAs.

- Diets high in saturated fat and *trans* fatty acids can increase our risk for cardiovascular disease. Other risk factors for cardiovascular disease are overweight or obesity, physical inactivity, smoking, high blood pressure, and diabetes.

- High levels of circulating low-density lipoproteins, or LDLs, increase total blood cholesterol concentrations and the formation of plaque on arterial walls, leading to an increased risk for cardiovascular disease. This is why LDL-cholesterol is sometimes called the "bad cholesterol."

- High levels of circulating high-density lipoproteins, or HDLs, reduce our blood cholesterol levels and our risk for cardiovascular disease. This is why HDL-cholesterol is sometimes called the "good cholesterol."

- Some studies suggest that diets high in fat may increase our risk for prostate cancer, while the role of dietary fat in breast and colon cancer is still controversial.

Review Questions

1. Omega-3 fatty acids are
   a. a form of *trans* fatty acid.
   b. metabolized in the body to arachidonic acid.
   c. synthesized in the liver and small intestine.
   d. found in flaxseeds, walnuts, and fish.

2. One of the most sensible ways to reduce body fat is to
   a. limit intake of dietary fat to less than 15% of total energy consumed.
   b. exercise regularly.
   c. avoid all consumption of *trans* fatty acids.
   d. restrict total energy to 1,200 kcals per day.

3. Lipids in chylomicrons are taken up by cells with the help of
   a. lipoprotein lipase.
   b. micelles.
   c. sterols.
   d. pancreatic enzymes.

4. The risk of heart disease is reduced in people who have high blood levels of
   a. triglycerides.
   b. very-low-density lipoproteins.
   c. low-density lipoproteins.
   d. high-density lipoproteins.

5. Fatty acids with a double bond at one part of the molecule are referred to as
   a. monounsaturated.
   b. hydrogenated.
   c. saturated.
   d. essential.

6. **True or false?** Lecithin is a protein found in egg whites that assists in the transport of lipids.

7. **True or false?** During exercise, lipids cannot be mobilized from adipose tissue for use as energy.

8. **True or false?** Triglycerides are the same as fatty acids.

9. **True or false?** *Trans* fatty acids are produced by food manufacturers; they do not occur in nature.

10. **True or false?** A serving of food labeled *reduced fat* has at least 25% less fat and 25% fewer calories than a full-fat version of the same food.

11. Explain how the straight, rigid shape of the saturated and *trans* fatty acids we eat affects our health.

12. Explain the contribution of dietary fat to bone health.

13. You have volunteered to participate in a 20-mile walk-a-thon to raise money for a local charity. You have been training for several weeks, and the event is now 2 days away. An athlete friend of yours advises you to "load up on carbohydrates" today and tomorrow and says you should avoid eating any foods that contain fat during the day of the walk-a-thon. Do you take this advice? Why or why not?

14. Caleb's father returns from an appointment with his doctor feeling down. He tells Caleb that his "blood test didn't turn out so good." He then adds, "My doctor told me I can't eat any of my favorite foods anymore. He says red meat and butter have too much fat. I guess I'll have to switch to cottage cheese and margarine!" What type of blood test do you think Caleb's father had? How should Caleb respond to his father's intention to switch to cottage cheese and margarine? Finally, suggest a non-dietary lifestyle choice that might improve his health.

15. Your friend Maria has determined that she needs to consume about 2,000 kcals per day to maintain her healthful weight. Create a chart for Maria showing the recommended maximum number of calories she should consume in each of the following forms: unsaturated fat, saturated fat, linoleic acid, alpha-linolenic acid, and *trans* fatty acids.

Web Links

www.americanheart.org
American Heart Association
Learn the best way to help lower your blood cholesterol level. Access the AHA's online cookbook for heart-healthy recipes and cooking methods.

www.caloriecontrol.org
Calorie Control Council
Go to this site to find out more about fat replacers.

www.nhlbi.nih.gov/chd
Live Healthier, Live Longer
Take a cholesterol quiz, and test your heart disease IQ. Create a diet using the Heart Healthy Diet or the TLC Diet online software.

www.nhlbi.nih.gov
National Heart, Lung, and Blood Institute
Learn how a healthful diet can lower your cholesterol levels. Use the online risk assessment tool to estimate your 10-year risk of having a heart attack.

www.nlm.nih.gov/medlineplus
MEDLINE Plus Health Information
Search for "fats" or "lipids" to obtain additional resources and the latest news on dietary lipids, heart disease, and cholesterol.

www.hsph.harvard.edu/nutritionsource
The Nutrition Source: Knowledge for Healthy Eating
Harvard University's Department of Nutrition
Go to this site and click on "Fats & Cholesterol" to find out how selective fat intake can be part of a healthful diet.

http://ific.org
International Food Information Council Foundation
Access this site to find out more about fats and dietary fat replacers.

References

1. Marieb, E. 2007. *Human Anatomy and Physiology.* 7th ed. San Francisco: Benjamin Cummings, p. 48.
2. Champe, P. C., R. A. Harvey, and D. R. Ferrier. 2008. *Lippincott's Illustrated Reviews: Biochemistry.* 4th ed. Philadelphia: Lippincott Williams & Wilkins.
3. Smith, C., A. D. Marks, and M. Lieberman. 2005. *Mark's Basic Medical Biochemistry: A Clinical Approach.* 2nd ed. Philadelphia: Lippincott Williams & Wilkins.
4. Jebb, S. A., A. M. Prentice, G. R. Goldberg, P. R. Murgatroyd, A. E. Black, and W. A. Coward. 1996. Changes in macronutrient balance during over- and underfeeding assessed by 12-d continuous whole-body calorimetry. *Am. J. Clin. Nutr.* 64:259–266.
5. Institute of Medicine (IOM), Food and Nutrition Board. 2000. *Dietary Reference Intakes for Vitamin C, Vitamin E, Selenium and Carotenoids.* Washington, DC: National Academies Press.

6. Rolls, B. J. 2000. The role of energy density in the overconsumption of fat. *J. Nutr.* 130:268S–271S.

7. Gerstein, D. E., G. Woodward-Lopez, A. E. Evans, K. Kelsey, and A. Drewnowski. 2004. Clarifying concepts about macronutrients' effects on satiation and satiety. *J. Am. Diet. Assoc.* 104:1151–1153.

8. Institute of Medicine (IOM), Food and Nutrition Board. 2002. *Dietary Reference Intakes for Energy, Carbohydrate, Fiber, Fat, Fatty Acids, Cholesterol, Protein, and Amino Acids (Macronutrients).* Washington, DC: National Academies Press.

9. Manore, M. M., S. I. Barr, and G. E. Butterfield. 2000. Position of the American Dietetic Association, Dietitians of Canada, and the American College of Sports Medicine: Nutrition and athletic performance. *J. Am. Diet. Assoc.* 100:1543–1556.

10. Lichtenstein, A. H., and L. Van Horn. 1998. Very low fat diets. *Circulation* 98:935–939.

11. American Dietetic Association (ADA). 2005. Position of the American Dietetic Association: Fat replacers. *J. Am. Diet. Assoc.* 105:266–275; Briefel, R. R., and C. L. Johnson. 2004. Secular trend in dietary intake in the United States. *Ann. Rev. Nutr.* 24:401–431.

12. Harnack, L. J., R. W. Jeffery, and K. N. Boutelle. 2000. Temporal trends in energy intake in the United States: An ecologic perspective. *Am. J. Clin. Nutr.* 71:1478–1484.

13. Expert Panel on Detection, Evaluation, and Treatment of High Blood Cholesterol in Adults, National Institutes of Health. 2002. Third Report of the National Cholesterol Education Program (NCEP) Expert Panel on Detection, Evaluation, and Treatment of High Blood Cholesterol in Adults (Adult Treatment Panel III) final report. *Circulation* 106:3143–3421.

14. Allison, D. B., S. K. Egan, L. M. Barraj, C. Caughman, M. Infante, and J. T. Heimbach. 1999. Estimated intakes of *trans* fatty and other fatty acids in the U.S. population. *J. Am. Diet. Assoc.* 99:166–174.

15. Kennedy, E., and D. Bowman. 2001. Assessment of the effect of fat-modified foods on diet quality in adults, 19–50 years, using data from the Continuing Survey of Food Intake by Individuals. *J. Am. Diet. Assoc.* 101(4):455–460.

16. Calloway, C. W. 1998. The role of fat-modified foods in the American diet. *Nutr. Today* 33:156–163.

17. National Center for Chronic Disease Prevention and Health Promotion (NCCDPHP). 2008. Division for Heart Disease and Stroke Prevention addressing the nation's leading killers. At a glance 2008. Available online at www.cdc.gov/print.do?url=http://www.cdc.gov/nccdphp/publications/AAG/dhdsp.htm.

18. Hahn, R. A., and G. W. Heath. 1998. Cardiovascular disease risk factors and preventive practices among adults—United States, 1994: A behavioral risk factor atlas. *Morb. Mortal. Wkly. Rep.* 47(SS-5):35–69.

19. Wilson, P. W. F. 2004. CDC/AHA workshop on markers of inflammation and cardiovascular disease. Application to clinical and public health practice. Ability of inflammatory markers to predict disease in asymptomatic patients. A background paper. *Circulation* 110:e568–e571.

20. Libby, P., P. M. Ridker, and A. Maseri. 2002. Inflammation and atherosclerosis. *Circulation* 105:1135–1143.

21. Kris-Etherton, P. M., W. S. Harris, L. J. Appel, and the Nutrition Committee of the American Heart Association. 2002. Fish consumption, fish oil, omega-3 fatty acids and cardiovascular disease. *Circulation* 106:2747–2757.

22. Harris, W. S. 1997. n-3 fatty acids and serum lipoproteins: Human studies. *Am. J. Clin. Nutr.* 65(Suppl.):1645S–1654S.

23. National Institutes of Health (NIH). 2001. *Third report of the National Cholesterol Education Program: Detection, evaluation and treatment of high blood cholesterol in adults (ATP III).* National Cholesterol Education Program, National Heart, Lung, and Blood Institute, NIH. Available online at www.nhlbi.nih.gov/guidelines/cholesterol/atp3xsum.pdf.

24. Cotton, P. A., A. F. Subar, J. E. Friday, and A. Cook. 2004. Dietary sources of nutrients among US adults, 1994–1996. *J. Am. Diet. Assoc.* 104:921–931.

25. Oomen, C. M., M. C. Ocké, E. J. Feskens, M. A. van Erp-Baart, F. J. Kok, and D. Kromhout. 2001. Association between *trans* fatty acid intake and 10-year risk of coronary heart disease in the Zutphen Elderly Study: A prospective population-based study. *Lancet* 357(9258):746–751.

26. DHHS/USDA. 2005. Dietary guidelines for Americans. Available online at www.health.gov/dietaryguidelines/dga2005/report/.

27. Lichtenstein A. H., L. J. Appel, M. Brands, M. Carnethon, S. Daniels, H. A. Franch, B. Franklin, P. Kris-Ethergon, W. S. Harris, B. Howard, N. Karanja, M. Lefevre, L. Rudel, F. Sancks, L. Van Horn, M. Winston, and J. Wylie-Rosett. 2006. Diet and lifestyle recommendations revision 2006: A scientific statement from the American Heart Association Nutrition Committee. *Circulation* 114:82–96.

28. Libby, P., Ridker, P. M., Maseri, A. 2002. Inflammation and atherosclerosis. *Circulation* 105;1135-1143.

29. Kim, Y. I. 2001. Nutrition and cancer. In: Bowman, B. A., and R. M. Russell, eds. *Present Knowledge in Nutrition.* 8th ed. Washington, DC: International Life Sciences Institute Press, pp. 573–589.

30. Kris-Etherton, P. M., and S. Innis. 2007. Position of the American Dietetic Association and Dietitians of Canada: Dietary fatty acid. *J. Am. Diet. Assoc.* 107:1599–1611.

31. Willett, W. C. 1999. Diet, nutrition and the prevention of cancer. In: Shils, M. E., J. A. Olsen, M. Shike, and A. C. Ross, eds. *Modern Nutrition in Health and Disease.* 9th ed. Baltimore: Williams & Wilkins.

32. Prentice, R. L., C. Bette, R. Chlebowski, et al. 2006. Low-fat dietary patterns and risk of invasive breast cancer. The Women's Health Initiative Randomized Controlled Dietary Modification Trial. *JAMA* 295:629–642.

33. Variyam, J. N. 2004. The price is right. Economics and the rise of obesity. *Amber Waves. USDA Economic Research Service,* 3(1):20–27.

34. Nestle, M., and L. B. Dixon. 2004. *Taking Sides. Clashing Views on Controversial Issues in Food and Nutrition.* Guilford, CA: McGraw-Hill/Dushin, pp. 24–39.

35. American Dietetic Association. 2002. Position of the American Dietetic Association: Total diet approaches to communicating food and nutrition information. *J. Am. Diet. Assoc.* 102(1):100–108.

Should Nutrition Professionals Speak Out Against "Bad" Foods?

Look around you. How many fast-food restaurants are within walking distance of your home, place of work, or campus? These restaurants are notorious for the high-fat, high-calorie meals they serve. So why do consumers choose them? Fast food has three major advantages over traditional restaurant meals and home-cooked meals: It is quick to obtain, tastes good to a majority of consumers, and is relatively cheap for the number of calories it provides.[33] Many Americans view the large portions served in fast-food restaurants as evidence that they are getting good "value" for their money. It took the movie *Super Size Me* to make many Americans realize how quickly eating these large portions of high-fat foods can pack on the pounds and harm their health.

Several questions are raised by the high-fat, low-cost, fast-food environment in which we live. First, can all foods fit into a healthful diet, or are there certain high-fat foods, like many of those offered at fast-food outlets, that we should avoid entirely? As a nation, how are we going to curb our growing obesity problem? Do populations respond better to guidelines, or proscriptions? What type of food recommendations should nutrition professionals make to government agencies, media, clients, and friends and family members? Fundamentally, these questions all contribute to the same debate—that is, whether or not nutrition professionals should advise their clients to avoid specific foods.

This debate touches on the interaction between science and politics in the matter of nutrition advice. On one side of the debate, we have a growing body of scientific evidence that identifies specific foods that promote health and specific foods that detract from health. Many dietitians and healthcare professionals say that they have an obligation to share this information with their clients.[34] They argue that consumers have a right to know which foods protect against disease and which increase the risk of disease.[34] They point out that most Americans

Fast food can be convenient for students and others with busy lifestyles. Should nutrition professionals tell people not to eat it at all?

are light years away from meeting the 2005 Dietary Guidelines and thus need specific, straightforward advice on what to eat and what to avoid if their diets are to improve and if we are to curb the epidemic of obesity we are facing as a nation.[26]

On the other side of the debate are the politics of food and food preferences. Every nutrition professional knows that quick, good-tasting, and low-cost food sells extremely well even among consumers who know it does not promote their health.[34] Thus, many nutrition professionals attempt to work with clients' food preferences to the extent possible. Many dietitians and professional groups, including the American Dietetic Association, share the philosophy that all foods can fit into a healthful diet.[35] They believe that it is important to look at an individual's total diet and dietary patterns, including portion sizes, and not focus just on "bad" foods. They also argue that you cannot assign "moral" qualities to foods. They believe their responsibility is to communicate positive nutrition messages that inspire people to make better food choices.

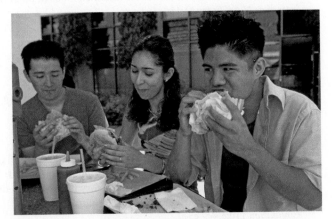

What kind of information will help you make the best dietary choices?

Should some foods be avoided entirely?

Dietitians on this side of the debate believe it is unrealistic to tell people to stop eating their favorite foods, and that change will be achieved by encouraging clients to eat these foods in moderation. They point out that a significant percentage of people advised to make dramatic dietary changes get discouraged and give up. Thus, in working with a client who eats fast food daily, they would not tell the client to stop eating it altogether but rather would suggest the client eat it less often and make better food choices at fast-food restaurants. Their goal is to help individuals set achievable goals and make small steps toward changing their diet.

In controlled environments, when health-promoting food messages are reinforced by increased availability of healthful foods, it appears that study participants improve their diet. But the real world is not a lab. Certainly, more research is needed to determine what kinds of advice and messages are most helpful in producing health-promoting dietary changes in large populations.

Critical Thinking Questions

◼ Prior to taking this class, how frequently did you consider the fat and energy content of the food you ordered?

◼ Did you frequently order high-fat, large-portion meals at fast-food restaurants?

◼ Did you "super-size" your serving?

◼ Now that you know more about nutrition, do you agree that all foods can fit into a healthful diet, or do you think that some foods should be avoided completely?

◼ Should professional nutrition organizations warn people against "bad" foods?

◼ What approach is best in helping Americans make positive dietary changes?

6 Proteins: Crucial Components of All Body Tissues

Test Yourself | True or False?

1. Protein is a primary source of energy for our bodies. **T** *or* **F**
2. We must consume amino acid supplements in order to build muscle tissue. **T** *or* **F**
3. Any protein eaten in excess is excreted in your urine. **T** *or* **F**
4. Vegetarian diets are inadequate in protein. **T** *or* **F**
5. Most people in the United States consume more protein than they need. **T** *or* **F**

Test Yourself answers are located in the Chapter Review.

Chapter Objectives *After reading this chapter, you will be able to:*

1. Describe how proteins differ from carbohydrates and lipids, *p. 210.*

2. Sketch an amino acid molecule and include its five essential components, *p. 211.*

3. Differentiate between essential amino acids, nonessential amino acids, and conditionally essential amino acids, *pp. 211–212.*

4. Explain the relationship between protein shape and function, *pp. 216–217.*

5. Discuss how proteins are digested, absorbed, and synthesized by the body, *pp. 219–221.*

6. Describe four functions of proteins in the body, *pp. 222–225.*

7. Calculate your recommended dietary allowance for protein, *p. 228.*

8. Identify the potential health risks associated with high-protein diets, *p. 229.*

9. List six foods that are good sources of protein, including at least three non-meat sources, *pp. 230–231.*

10. Describe two disorders related to inadequate protein intake or genetic abnormalities, *pp. 237–239.*

Proteins are an integral part of our body tissues, including our muscle tissue.

What do professional skateboarder Forrest Kirby, Olympic figure-skating champion Surya Bonaly, wrestler "Killer" Kowalski, and hundreds of other athletes have in common? They're all vegetarians! Olympic track icon Carl Lewis states: "I've found that a person does not need protein from meat to be a successful athlete. In fact, my best year of track competition was the first year I ate a vegan diet."[1] Although precise statistics on the number of vegetarian American athletes aren't available, a total of 2.3% of all U.S. adults are estimated to be vegetarians.[2]

What is a protein, and what makes it so different from carbohydrates and fats? How much protein do people really need, and do most people get enough in their daily diets? What exactly is a vegetarian, anyway? Do you qualify? If so, how do you plan your diet to include sufficient protein, especially if you play competitive sports? Are there real advantages to eating meat, or is plant protein just as good?

It seems as if everybody has an opinion about protein, both how much you should consume and from what sources. In this chapter, we address these and other questions to clarify the importance of protein in the diet and dispel common myths about this crucial nutrient.

What Are Proteins?

Proteins are large, complex molecules found in the cells of all living things. Although proteins are best known as a part of our muscle mass, they are in fact critical components of all tissues of the human body, including bones, blood, and hormones. Proteins function in metabolism, immunity, fluid balance, and nutrient transport, and they can provide energy in certain circumstances. The functions of proteins will be discussed in detail later in this chapter.

How Do Proteins Differ from Carbohydrates and Lipids?

As we saw in Chapter 1, proteins are one of the three macronutrients. Like carbohydrates and lipids, proteins are found in a wide variety of foods, plus the human body is able to synthesize them. But unlike carbohydrates and lipids, proteins are made according to instructions provided by our genetic material, or DNA. We'll explore how DNA dictates the structure of proteins shortly.

Another key difference between proteins and the other macronutrients lies in their chemical makeup. In addition to the carbon, hydrogen, and oxygen also found in carbohydrates and lipids, proteins contain a special form of nitrogen that the body can readily use. Our bodies are able to break down the proteins in foods and utilize the nitrogen for many important body processes. Carbohydrates and lipids do not provide nitrogen. In addition, two amino acids, cysteine and methionine, also contain sulfur; neither carbohydrates nor lipids contain sulfur.

The Building Blocks of Proteins Are Amino Acids

The proteins in our bodies are made from a combination of building blocks called **amino acids,** molecules composed of a central carbon atom connected to four other groups: an amine group, an acid group, a hydrogen atom, and a side chain (**Figure 6.1a**). The word *amine* means *nitrogen-containing,* and nitrogen is indeed the essential component of the amine portion of the molecule.

As shown in Figure 6.1b, the portion of the amino acid that makes each unique is its side chain. This side chain is referred to as the R group. The amine group, acid group, and carbon and hydrogen atoms do not vary. Variations in the structure of the R group give each amino acid its distinct properties.

The singular term *protein* is misleading, as there are potentially an infinite number of unique types of proteins in living organisms. Most of the body's proteins are made from combinations of just 20 amino acids, identified in Table 6.1. By combining a few dozen to

proteins Large, complex molecules made up of amino acids and found as essential components of all living cells.

amino acids Nitrogen-containing molecules that combine to form proteins.

Figure 6.1   Structure of an amino acid. **(a)** All amino acids contain five parts: a central carbon atom, an amine group around the atom that contains nitrogen, an acid group, a hydrogen atom, and a side chain called the R group. **(b)** Only the side chain differs for each of the twenty amino acids, giving each its unique properties.

Table 6.1 Amino Acids of the Human Body

Essential Amino Acids	Nonessential Amino Acids
These amino acids must be consumed in the diet.	*These amino acids can be manufactured by the body.*
Histidine	Alanine
Isoleucine	Arginine
Leucine	Asparagine
Lysine	Aspartic acid
Methionine	Cysteine
Phenylalanine	Glutamic acid
Threonine	Glutamine
Tryptophan	Glycine
Valine	Proline
	Serine
	Tyrosine

more than 300 of these 20 amino acids in various sequences, the body synthesizes an estimated 10,000 to 50,000 unique proteins. **Figure 6.2** illustrates how the components of a protein differ from that of a carbohydrate such as starch. As you can see, starch is composed of a chain of glucose molecules. In contrast, the protein insulin is composed of 51 amino acids connected in a specific order, or sequence.

We Must Obtain Essential Amino Acids from Food

Of the 20 amino acids in the body, nine are classified as essential. This does not mean that they are more important than the others. Instead, an **essential amino acid** is one that the body cannot produce at all or cannot produce in sufficient quantities to meet physiologic needs. Thus, essential amino acids must be obtained from food. Without the proper amount of essential amino acids in our bodies, we lose our ability to make the proteins and other nitrogen-containing compounds we need.

The Body Can Make Nonessential Amino Acids

Nonessential amino acids are just as important to the body as essential amino acids, but the body can synthesize them in sufficient quantities, so we do not need to consume them in our diet. We make nonessential amino acids by transferring the amine group from an essential amino acid to a different acid group and R group. This process of transferring is called **transamination** and is shown in **Figure 6.3**. The acid groups and R groups can be donated by amino acids, or they can be made from the breakdown products of carbohydrates

essential amino acids   Amino acids not produced by the body or not produced in sufficient amounts so that they must be obtained from food.

nonessential amino acids   Amino acids that can be manufactured by the body in sufficient quantities and therefore do not need to be consumed regularly in our diet.

transamination   The process of transferring the amine group from one amino acid to another in order to manufacture a new amino acid.

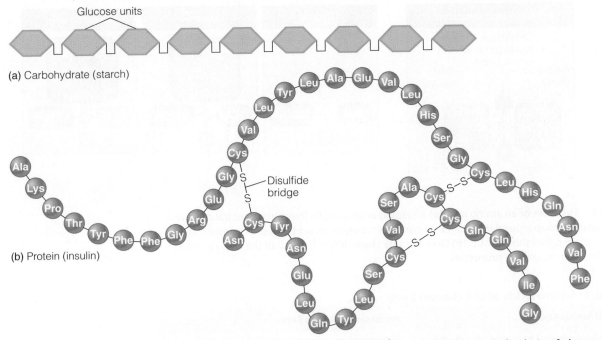

(a) Carbohydrate (starch)

(b) Protein (insulin)

Figure 6.2 How proteins differ from starch. **(a)** Starch is composed of a chain of glucose molecules, whereas proteins are composed of multiple amino acids connected together. **(b)** Insulin is a protein that contains fifty-one amino acids in two chains that are connected by three disulfide bridges—two that connect the two amino acid chains and a third that connects a section of the shortest amino acid chain.

and fats. Thus, by combining parts of different amino acids, the necessary nonessential amino acid can be made.

Under some conditions, a nonessential amino acid can become an essential amino acid. In this case, the amino acid is called a **conditionally essential amino acid.** Consider what occurs in the disease known as phenylketonuria (PKU). As discussed in Chapter 4, someone with PKU cannot metabolize phenylalanine (an essential amino acid). Normally, the body uses phenylalanine to produce the nonessential amino acid tyrosine, so the inability to metabolize phenylalanine results in failure to make tyrosine. If PKU is not diagnosed immediately after birth, it results in irreversible brain damage. In this situation, tyrosine becomes a conditionally essential amino acid that must be provided by the diet. Other conditionally essential amino acids include arginine, cysteine, and glutamine.

conditionally essential amino acids Amino acids that are normally considered nonessential but become essential under certain circumstances when the body's need for them exceeds the ability to produce them.

Figure 6.3 Transamination. Our bodies can make nonessential amino acids by transferring the amine group from an essential amino acid to a different acid group and side chain.

Recap

Proteins are critical components of all tissues of the human body. Like carbohydrates and lipids, they contain carbon, hydrogen, and oxygen. Unlike the other macronutrients, they also contain nitrogen and some contain sulfur, and their structure is dictated by DNA. The building blocks of proteins are amino acids. The amine group of the amino acid contains nitrogen. The portion of the amino acid that changes, giving each amino acid its distinct identity, is the side chain (or R group). The body cannot make essential amino acids, so we must obtain them from our diet. The body can make nonessential amino acids from parts of other amino acids, carbohydrates, and fats.

How Are Proteins Made?

The body can synthesize proteins by selecting the needed amino acids from the "pool" of all amino acids available in the bloodstream at any given time. Let's look more closely at how this occurs.

Amino Acids Bond to Form a Variety of Peptides

Figure 6.4 shows that when two amino acids join together, the amine group of one binds to the acid group of another in a unique type of chemical bond called a **peptide bond.** In the process, a molecule of water is released as a by-product.

Two amino acids joined together form a *dipeptide,* and three amino acids joined together are called a *tripeptide.* The term *oligopeptide* is used to identify a string of four to nine amino acids, and a *polypeptide* is ten or more amino acids bonded together. As a polypeptide chain grows longer, it begins to fold into any of a variety of complex shapes that give proteins their sophisticated structure.

Genes Regulate Amino Acid Binding

Each of us is unique because we inherited a specific set of genes from our parents. Our genes encode a specific sequence of the amino acids for each individual protein molecule in our bodies. Minute differences in amino acid sequences can lead to significant differences in the proteins synthesized. These differences in proteins result in the unique physical and physiologic characteristics each one of us possesses. **Gene expression** (see page 215) is the process by which cells use genes to make proteins.

The Structure of Genes

A *gene* is a segment of deoxyribonucleic acid (DNA) that serves as a template for the synthesis—or expression—of a particular protein.

The building blocks of DNA are **nucleotides,** molecules composed of a "backbone" made up of a phosphate group and a pentose sugar called deoxyribose, to which is attached

peptide bonds   Unique types of chemical bonds in which the amine group of one amino acid binds to the acid group of another in order to manufacture dipeptides and all larger peptide molecules.

gene expression   The process of using a gene to make a protein.

nucleotide   A molecule composed of a phosphate group, a pentose sugar called deoxyribose, and one of four nitrogenous bases: adenine (A), guanine (G), cytosine (C), or thymine (T).

Figure 6.4   Amino acid bonding. Two amino acids join together to form a dipeptide. By combining multiple amino acids, proteins are made.

Figure 6.5 The double helix of DNA. DNA is a complex compound made up of molecules called nucleotides, each of which consists of a deoxyribose sugar and phosphate backbone and a nitrogenous base. Hydrogen bonding of complementary bases holds the two strands of DNA together.

transcription The process through which messenger RNA copies genetic information from DNA in the nucleus.

translation The process that occurs when the genetic information carried by messenger RNA is translated into a chain of amino acids at the ribosome.

one of four nitrogenous bases: adenine (A), guanine (G), cytosine (C), or thymine (T). Within DNA molecules, these nucleotides occur in two long, parallel chains coiled into the shape of a double helix (**Figure 6.5**). Because nucleotides vary only in their nitrogenous bases, the astonishing variability of DNA arises from the precise sequencing of nucleotides along these chains.

Chains of nucleotides are held together by hydrogen bonds that link their nitrogenous bases. Each base can bond only to its *complementary base:* A always bonds to T, and G always bonds to C. The complementary nature of bases guides the transfer of genetic instructions from DNA into the resulting protein.

Transcription and Translation

Proteins are actually manufactured at the site of ribosomes in the cell's cytoplasm. But DNA never leaves the nucleus. So for gene expression to occur (**Figure 6.6**), a gene's DNA has to replicate itself—that is, it must make an exact copy of itself, which can then be carried out to the cytoplasm. DNA replication ensures that the genetic information in the original gene is identical to the genetic information used to build the protein. Through the process of replication, DNA provides the instructions for building every protein in the body (Figure 6.5).

Cells use a special molecule to copy, or transcribe, the information from DNA and carry it to the ribosomes. This molecule is *messenger RNA* (*messenger ribonucleic acid,* or *mRNA*). In contrast with DNA, RNA is a single strand of nucleotides, and its four nitrogenous bases are A, G, C, and U (stands for uracil, which takes the place of the thymine found in DNA). Also, as its name suggests, it contains the pentose sugar ribose instead of deoxyribose. During **transcription**, mRNA copies to its own base sequence the genetic information from DNA's base sequence. The mRNA then detaches from the DNA and leaves the nucleus, carrying its genetic "message" to the ribosomes in the cytoplasm.

Once the genetic information reaches the ribosomes, **translation** occurs; that is, the language of the mRNA nucleotide sequences is translated into the language of amino acid sequences, or proteins (see Figure 6.5). At the ribosomes, mRNA binds with ribosomal RNA (rRNA) and its nucleotide sequences are distributed, somewhat like orders for parts in an assembly plant, to molecules of transfer RNA (tRNA). Now the tRNA molecules roam the cytoplasm until they succeed in binding with the specific amino acid that matches their "order." They then transfer their amino acid to the ribosome, which assembles the amino acids into proteins. Once the amino acids are loaded onto the ribosome, tRNA works to maneuver each amino acid into its proper position. When synthesis of the new protein is completed, it is released from the ribosome and can either go through further modification in the cell or can be functional in its current state.

The proper sequencing of amino acids determines both the shape and function of a particular protein. Genetic abnormalities can occur when the DNA contains errors in proper nucleotide sequencing or when mistakes occur in the translation of this sequencing. Two examples of the consequences of these types of genetic abnormalities, sickle cell anemia and cystic fibrosis, are discussed later in this chapter.

Although the DNA for making every protein in our bodies is contained within each cell nucleus, not all genes are expressed and each cell does not make every type of protein. For example, each cell contains the DNA to manufacture the hormone insulin. However, only the cells of the pancreas *express* the insulin gene to produce insulin. As we explored in the Nutrition Debate in Chapter 1, our physiologic needs alter gene expression, as do various nutrients. For instance, a cut in the skin that causes bleeding will prompt the production of various proteins that clot the blood. Or if we consume more dietary iron than we need, the gene for ferritin (a protein that stores iron) will be expressed so that we can store this excess iron. Our genetic makeup and how appropriately we express our genes are important factors in our health.

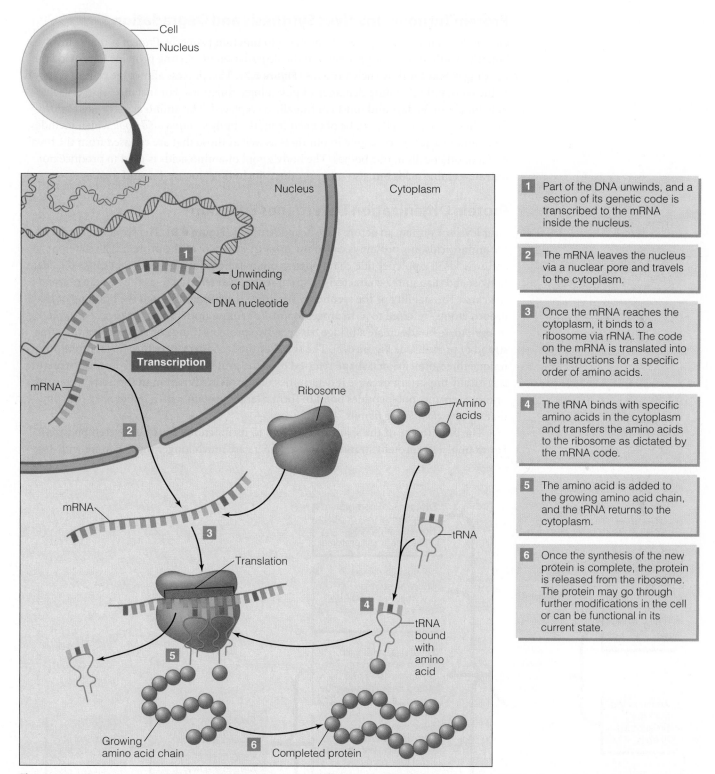

Figure 6.6 Gene expression. Messenger RNA (mRNA) transcribes the genetic information from DNA in the nucleus and carries it to ribosomes in the cytoplasm. At the ribosome, this genetic information is translated into a chain of amino acids that eventually makes a protein.

Protein Turnover Involves Synthesis and Degradation

Our bodies constantly require new proteins to function properly. *Protein turnover* involves both the synthesis of new proteins and the degradation of existing proteins to provide the building blocks for those new proteins (**Figure 6.7**). This process allows the cells to respond to the constantly changing demands of physiologic functions. For instance, skin cells live only for about 30 days and must continually be replaced. The amino acids needed to produce these new skin cells can be obtained from the body's *amino acid pool*, which includes those amino acids we consume in our diets as well as those that are released from the breakdown of other cells in our bodies. The body's pool of amino acids is used to produce not only new amino acids but also other products including glucose, fat, and urea.

Protein Organization Determines Function

Four levels of protein structure have been identified (**Figure 6.8**). The sequential order of the amino acids in a protein is called the *primary structure* of the protein. The different amino acids in a polypeptide chain possess unique chemical attributes that cause the chain to twist and turn into a characteristic spiral shape, also referred to as the protein's *secondary structure*. The stability of the secondary structure is achieved through the bonding of hydrogen atoms (referred to as hydrogen bonds) or sulfur atoms (referred to as a *disulfide bridge*); these bonds create a bridge between two protein strands or two parts of the same strand of protein (see Figure 6.2). The spiral of the secondary structure further folds into a unique three-dimensional shape referred to as the protein's *tertiary structure;* this structure is critically important because it determines that protein's function in the body. Often, two or more separate polypeptides bond to form a larger protein with a *quaternary structure* that may be *globular* or *fibrous.*

The importance of the shape of a protein to its function cannot be overemphasized. For example, the protein strands in muscle fibers are much longer than they are wide (see

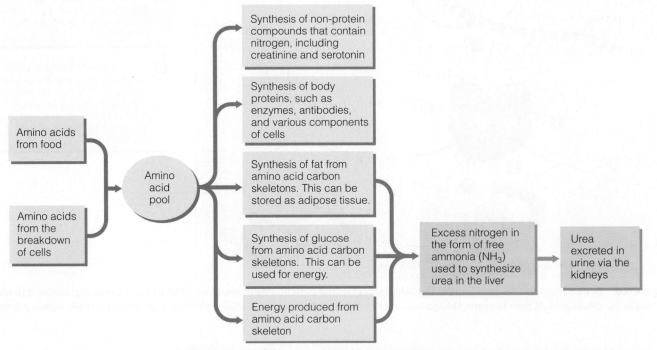

Figure 6.7   Protein turnover involves the synthesis of new proteins and breakdown of existing proteins to provide building blocks for new proteins. Amino acids are drawn from the body's amino acid pool and can be used to build proteins, fat, glucose, and non-protein nitrogen-containing compounds. Urea is produced as a waste product from any excess nitrogen, which is then excreted by the kidneys.

(a) Primary structure (b) Secondary structure (c) Tertiary structure (d) Quaternary structure

Figure 6.8 Levels of protein structure. **(a)** The primary structure of a protein is the sequential order of amino acids. **(b)** The secondary structure of a protein is the folding of the amino acid chain. **(c)** The tertiary structure is a further folding that results in the three-dimensional shape of the protein. **(d)** The quaternary structure of a protein refers to the situation in which two or more polypeptides interact, join together, and form a larger protein such as the actin molecule illustrated here. In this figure, strands of actin molecules intertwine to form contractile elements involved in generating muscle contractions.

Figure 6.8d). This structure plays an essential role in enabling muscle contraction and relaxation. In contrast, the proteins that form red blood cells are globular in shape (see **Figure 6.9**), and they result in the red blood cells being shaped like flattened discs with depressed centers, similar to a miniature doughnut. This structure and the flexibility of the proteins in the red blood cells permit them to change shape and flow freely through even the tiniest capillaries to deliver oxygen and still return to their original shape.

Figure 6.9 Protein shape determines function. **(a)** Hemoglobin, the protein that forms red blood cells, is globular in shape. **(b)** The globular shape of hemoglobin results in red blood cells being shaped like flattened discs.

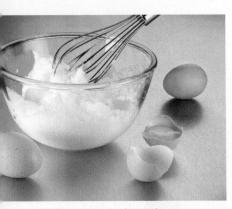

Stiffening egg whites denatures some of the proteins within them.

Protein Denaturation Affects Shape and Function

Proteins can uncoil and lose their shape when they are exposed to heat, acids, bases, heavy metals, alcohol, and other damaging substances. The term used to describe this change in the shape of proteins is **denaturation.** Everyday examples of protein denaturation that we can see are stiffening of egg whites when they are whipped, the curdling of milk when lemon juice or another acid is added, and the solidifying of eggs as they cook.

Denaturation does not affect the primary structure of proteins. However, when a protein is denatured, its function is also lost. For instance, denaturation of a critical enzyme due to exposure to heat or acidity is harmful, because it prevents the enzyme from doing its job. This type of denaturation can occur during times of high fever or when blood pH is out of the normal range. In some cases, denaturation is helpful. For instance, denaturation of proteins during the digestive process allows for their breakdown into amino acids and absorption of these amino acids from the digestive tract into the bloodstream.

Protein Synthesis Can Be Limited by Missing Amino Acids

For protein synthesis to occur, all essential amino acids must be available to the cell. If this is not the case, the amino acid that is missing or in the smallest supply is called the **limiting amino acid.** Without the proper combination and quantity of essential amino acids, synthesis of a particular protein slows and can even halt entirely. For instance, the protein hemoglobin contains the essential amino acid histidine. If we do not consume enough histidine, it becomes the limiting amino acid in hemoglobin production. As no other amino acid can be substituted, the body becomes unable to produce adequate hemoglobin and loses the ability to transport oxygen to cells.

Inadequate energy consumption also limits protein synthesis. If there is not enough energy available from the diet, the body will use any accessible amino acids for energy, thus preventing them from being used to build new proteins.

A protein that does not contain all of the essential amino acids in sufficient quantities to support growth and health is called an **incomplete** (or *low-quality*) **protein.** Proteins that have all nine of the essential amino acids in sufficient quantities are considered **complete** (or *high-quality*) **proteins.** The most complete protein sources are foods derived from animals and include egg whites, meat, poultry, fish, and milk. Soybeans are the most complete source of plant protein. In general, the typical American diet is very high in complete proteins, as we eat proteins from a variety of food sources.

Protein Synthesis Can Be Enhanced by Mutual Supplementation

Many people believe that we must consume meat or dairy products to obtain complete proteins. Not true! Consider a meal of beans and rice. Beans are low in the amino acids methionine and cysteine but have adequate amounts of isoleucine and lysine. Rice is low in isoleucine and lysine but contains sufficient methionine and cysteine. By combining beans and rice, a complete protein source is created.

Mutual supplementation is the process of combining two or more incomplete protein sources to make a complete protein, and the two foods involved are called complementary foods; these foods provide **complementary proteins** (**Figure 6.10**) that, when combined, provide all nine essential amino acids. It is not necessary to eat these foods at the same meal. As previously mentioned, the body maintains a free pool of amino acids in the blood; these amino acids come from food and sloughed-off cells. When we eat one potentially complementary protein, its amino acids join those in the amino acid pool. These free amino acids can then combine to synthesize complete proteins. However, it is wise to eat complementary-protein foods during the same day, as partially completed proteins cannot be stored and saved for a later time. Mutual supplementation is important for people eating a vegetarian diet, particularly if they consume no animal products whatsoever.

denaturation   The process by which proteins uncoil and lose their shape and function when they are exposed to heat, acids, bases, heavy metals, alcohol, and other damaging substances.

limiting amino acid   The essential amino acid that is missing or in the smallest supply in the amino acid pool and is thus responsible for slowing or halting protein synthesis.

incomplete proteins   Foods that do not contain all of the essential amino acids in sufficient amounts to support growth and health.

complete proteins   Foods that contain all nine essential amino acids.

mutual supplementation   The process of combining two or more incomplete protein sources to make a complete protein.

complementary proteins   Proteins contained in two or more foods that together contain all nine essential amino acids necessary for a complete protein. It is not necessary to eat complementary proteins at the same meal.

Food with limiting amino acid	+	Foods high in limiting amino acid	→	Complementary food combination	
Legumes: limited in methionine and cysteine	+	**Grains Nuts and seeds**		• Rice and lentils • Red beans and rice • Rice and black-eyed peas • Hummus (garbanzo beans and sesame seeds)	
Grains: limited in lysine	+	**Legumes**		• Peanut butter and bread • Barley and lentil soup • Corn tortilla and beans	
Vegetables: limited in lysine, methionine, and cysteine	+	**Legumes** (lysine) **Grains** **Nuts and seeds** (methionine and cysteine)		• Tofu and broccoli with almonds • Spinach salad with pine nuts and kidney beans	
Nuts and seeds: limited in lysine and isoleucine	+	**Legumes**		• Sesame seeds with mixed bean salad • Lentil soup with slivered almonds	

Figure 6.10 Complementary food combinations.

Recap

Amino acids bind together to form proteins. Genes regulate the amino acid sequence, and thus the structure, of all proteins. During transcription, mRNA copies to its own base sequence the genetic information from DNA. mRNA carries this information from the cell nucleus to the ribosomes in the cytoplasm, where translation into proteins occurs. Protein turnover involves the synthesis and degradation of proteins so that the body can constantly adapt to a changing environment. The shape of a protein determines its function. When a protein is denatured by heat or damaging substances such as acids, it loses its shape and its function. When a particular amino acid is limiting, protein synthesis cannot occur. A complete protein provides all nine essential amino acids. Mutual supplementation combines two or more complementary-protein sources to make a complete protein.

How Does the Body Break Down Proteins?

The body does not directly use proteins from the diet to make the proteins it needs. Dietary proteins are first digested and broken into amino acids so that they can be absorbed and transported to the cells. In this section, we will review how proteins are digested and absorbed. As you read about each step in this process, refer to **Figure 6.11** for a visual tour through the digestive system.

Stomach Acids and Enzymes Break Proteins into Short Polypeptides

Virtually no enzymatic digestion of proteins occurs in the mouth. As shown in step 1 in Figure 6.11, proteins in food are chewed, crushed, and moistened with saliva to ease

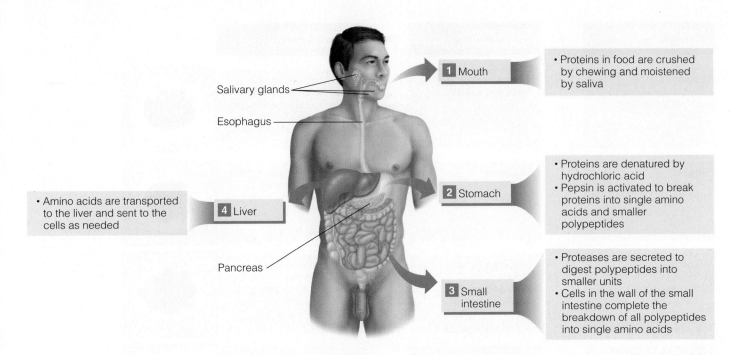

Salivary glands

Esophagus

1 Mouth
- Proteins in food are crushed by chewing and moistened by saliva

2 Stomach
- Proteins are denatured by hydrochloric acid
- Pepsin is activated to break proteins into single amino acids and smaller polypeptides

4 Liver
- Amino acids are transported to the liver and sent to the cells as needed

Pancreas

3 Small intestine
- Proteases are secreted to digest polypeptides into smaller units
- Cells in the wall of the small intestine complete the breakdown of all polypeptides into single amino acids

Figure 6.11 The process of protein digestion.

swallowing and to increase the surface area of the protein for more efficient digestion. There is no further digestive action on proteins in the mouth.

When proteins reach the stomach, hydrochloric acid denatures the protein strands (Figure 6.11, step 2). It also converts the inactive enzyme, *pepsinogen,* into its active form, **pepsin,** which is a protein-digesting enzyme. Although pepsin is itself a protein, it is not denatured by the acid in the stomach because it has evolved to work optimally in an acidic environment. The hormone *gastrin* controls both the production of hydrochloric acid and the release of pepsin; thinking about food or actually chewing food stimulates the gastrin-producing cells located in the stomach. Pepsin begins breaking proteins into single amino acids and shorter polypeptides via hydrolysis; these amino acids and polypeptides then travel to the small intestine for further digestion and absorption.

Enzymes in the Small Intestine Break Polypeptides into Single Amino Acids

As the polypeptides reach the small intestine, the pancreas and the small intestine secrete enzymes that digest them into oligopeptides, tripeptides, dipeptides, and single amino acids (Figure 6.11, step 3). The enzymes that digest polypeptides are called **proteases;** proteases found in the small intestine include trypsin, chymotrypsin, and carboxypeptidase.

The cells in the wall of the small intestine then absorb the single amino acids, dipeptides, and tripeptides. Peptidases, enzymes located in the intestinal cells, break the dipeptides and tripeptides into single amino acids. Dipeptidases break dipeptide bonds, whereas tripeptidases break tripeptide bonds. The amino acids are then transported via the portal vein to the liver. Once in the liver, amino acids may be converted to glucose or fat, combined to build new proteins, used for energy, or released into the bloodstream and transported to other cells as needed (Figure 6.11, step 4).

The cells of the small intestine have different sites that specialize in transporting certain types of amino acids, dipeptides, and tripeptides. This fact has implications for users of amino acid supplements. When very large doses of supplements containing single amino acids are taken on an empty stomach, they typically compete for the same absorption sites. This competition can block the absorption of other amino acids, causing an imbalance of

pepsin An enzyme in the stomach that begins the breakdown of proteins into shorter polypeptide chains and single amino acids.

proteases Enzymes that continue the breakdown of polypeptides in the small intestine.

amino acids and leading to various amino acid deficiencies. Also, taking large amounts of amino acids can lead to toxicity. Park and colleagues found that 3 days of arginine supplementation resulted in a stimulation of cancer growth in breast cancer patients.[3] These results have not been confirmed by other researchers but do suggest that arginine supplementation could cause harmful toxicity symptoms in certain individuals. Although some amino acids are known to cause toxic effects in animals when taken in high doses, the data necessary to establish a tolerable upper intake level (UL) for individual amino acids in humans are considered insufficient at this time.[4] For more information on the use of amino acid supplements to enhance exercise performance, refer to Chapter 14.

Protein Quality Is Affected by Amino Acid Content and Digestibility

Earlier in this chapter, we discussed how various protein sources differ in quality of protein. The quantity of essential amino acids in a protein determines its quality: Higher-protein-quality foods are those that contain more of the essential amino acids in sufficient quantities needed to build proteins, and lower-protein-quality foods contain fewer essential amino acids.

A number of methods are used to estimate a food's protein quality. One method is to calculate a *chemical score*. The **chemical score** is a comparison of the amount of the limiting amino acid in a food with the amount of that same amino acid in a reference food. The amino acid that is found to have the lowest proportion in the test food as compared with the reference food is defined as the limiting amino acid. Thus, the chemical score of a protein gives an indication of the lowest amino acid ratio calculated for any amino acid in a particular food.

An important factor in protein quality is *digestibility*, or how well the body can digest a protein. The **protein digestibility corrected amino acid score (PDCAAS)** uses the chemical score and a correction factor for digestibility to calculate a value for protein quality. Proteins with higher digestibility are more complete. Animal protein sources such as meat and dairy products are highly digestible, as are many soy products; we can absorb more than 90% of these proteins. Legumes are also highly digestible (about 70% to 80%). Grains and many vegetable proteins are less digestible, with PDCAAS values ranging from 60% to 90%.

These measures of protein quality are useful when determining the quality of protein available to populations of people. However, these measures are impractical and are not used for individual diet planning.

Meats are highly digestible sources of dietary protein.

Recap

In the stomach, hydrochloric acid denatures proteins and converts pepsinogen to pepsin; pepsin breaks proteins into smaller polypeptides and individual amino acids. In the small intestine, proteases break polypeptides into smaller fragments and single amino acids. Enzymes in the cells in the wall of the small intestine break the smaller peptide fragments into single amino acids, which are then transported to the liver for distribution to our cells. Taking high doses of individual amino acid supplements can lead to toxicity of those amino acids and deficiencies of others. Protein quality is a function of its digestibility and amino acid content. Methods used to determine protein quality include calculating a chemical score and calculating the protein digestibility corrected amino acid score.

Why Do We Need Proteins?

The functions of proteins in the body are so numerous that only a few can be described in detail in this chapter. Note that proteins function most effectively when we also consume adequate amounts of the other energy nutrients, carbohydrates and fat. When there is not

chemical score A method used to estimate a food's protein quality; it is a comparison of the amount of the limiting amino acid in a food with the amount of that same amino acid in a reference food.

protein digestibility corrected amino acid score (PDCAAS) A measurement of protein quality that considers the balance of amino acids as well as the digestibility of the protein in the food.

enough energy available, the body uses proteins as an energy source, limiting their availability for the functions described in the following sections.

Proteins Contribute to Cell Growth, Repair, and Maintenance

The proteins in the body are dynamic, meaning that they are constantly being broken down, repaired, and replaced. When proteins are broken down, many amino acids are recycled into new proteins. Think about all of the new proteins that are needed to allow an embryo to develop and grow. In this case, an entirely new human body is being made! In fact, a newborn baby has more than 10 trillion body cells.

Even in the mature adult, all cells are constantly turning over, meaning old cells are broken down and parts are used to create new cells. In addition, the cellular damage that occurs on a regular basis must be repaired in order to maintain health. Red blood cells live for only 3 to 4 months and then are replaced by new cells that are produced in bone marrow. The cells lining the intestinal tract are replaced every 3 to 6 days. The "old" intestinal cells are treated just like the proteins in food; they are digested and the amino acids absorbed back into the body. The constant turnover of proteins from our diet is essential for such cell growth, repair, and maintenance.

Proteins Act as Enzymes and Hormones

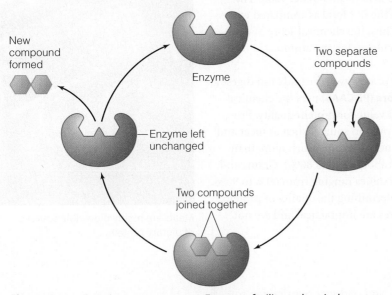

New compound formed

Enzyme

Enzyme left unchanged

Two separate compounds

Two compounds joined together

Figure 6.12 Proteins act as enzymes. Enzymes facilitate chemical reactions such as joining two compounds together.

Recall that enzymes are small chemicals, usually proteins, that speed up chemical reactions, without being changed by the chemical reaction themselves. Enzymes can act to bind substances together or break them apart and can transform one substance into another. **Figure 6.12** shows how an enzyme can bind two substances together.

Each cell contains thousands of enzymes that facilitate specific cellular reactions. For example, the enzyme phosphofructokinase (PFK) is critical to driving the rate at which we break down glucose and use it for energy during exercise. Without PFK, we would be unable to generate energy at a fast enough rate to allow us to be physically active.

Hormones are substances that act as chemical messengers in the body. Some hormones are made from amino acids, whereas others are made from lipids (refer to Chapter 5). Hormones are stored in various glands in the body, which release them in response to changes in the body's environment. They then act on the body's organs and tissues to restore the body to normal conditions. For example, recall that insulin, a hormone made from amino acids, acts on cell membranes to facilitate the transport of glucose into cells. Other examples of amino-acid-containing hormones are glucagon, which responds to conditions of low blood glucose, and thyroid hormone, which helps control our resting metabolic rate.

Proteins Help Maintain Fluid and Electrolyte Balance

Electrolytes are electrically charged particles that assist in maintaining fluid balance. For our bodies to function properly, fluids and electrolytes must be maintained at healthy levels inside and outside cells and within blood vessels. Proteins attract fluids, and the proteins that are in the bloodstream, in the cells, and in the spaces surrounding the cells work together to keep fluids moving across these spaces in the proper quantities to maintain fluid balance and blood pressure. When protein intake is deficient, the concentration of proteins in the bloodstream is insufficient to draw fluid from the tissues and across the blood vessel walls;

(a) Normal fluid balance

(b) Edema caused by insufficient protein in bloodstream

Figure 6.13 The role of proteins in maintaining fluid balance. The heartbeat exerts pressure that continually pushes fluids in the bloodstream through the arterial walls and out into the tissue spaces. By the time blood reaches the veins, the pressure of the heartbeat has greatly decreased. In this environment, proteins in the blood are able to draw fluids out of the tissues and back into the bloodstream. **(a)** This healthy (nonswollen) tissue suggests that body fluids in the bloodstream and in the tissue spaces are in balance. **(b)** When the level of proteins in the blood is insufficient to draw fluids out of the tissues, edema can result. This foot with edema is swollen due to fluid imbalance.

fluid then collects in the tissues, causing **edema** (**Figure 6.13**). In addition to being uncomfortable, edema can lead to serious medical problems.

Sodium (Na^+) and potassium (K^+) are examples of common electrolytes. Under normal conditions, Na^+ is more concentrated outside the cell, and K^+ is more concentrated inside the cell. This proper balance of Na^+ and K^+ is accomplished by the action of **transport proteins** located within the cell membrane. **Figure 6.14** shows how these transport proteins work to pump Na^+ outside and K^+ inside of the cell. Conduction of nerve signals and contraction of muscles depend on a proper balance of electrolytes. If protein intake is deficient, we lose our ability to maintain these functions, resulting in potentially fatal changes in the rhythm of the heart. Other consequences of chronically low protein intakes include muscle weakness and spasms, kidney failure, and, if conditions are severe enough, death.

Proteins Help Maintain Acid–Base Balance

The body's cellular processes result in the constant production of acids and bases. These substances are transported in the blood to be excreted through the kidneys and the lungs. The human body maintains very tight control over the **pH,** or the acid–base balance of the blood. The body goes into a state called **acidosis** when the blood becomes too acidic. **Alkalosis** results if the blood becomes too basic. Both acidosis and alkalosis can be caused

edema A disorder in which fluids build up in the tissue spaces of the body, causing fluid imbalances and a swollen appearance.

transport proteins Protein molecules that help to transport substances throughout the body and across cell membranes.

pH Stands for percentage of hydrogen. It is a measure of the acidity—or level of hydrogen—of any solution, including human blood.

acidosis A disorder in which the blood becomes acidic; that is, the level of hydrogen in the blood is excessive. It can be caused by respiratory or metabolic problems.

alkalosis A disorder in which the blood becomes basic; that is, the level of hydrogen in the blood is deficient. It can be caused by respiratory or metabolic problems.

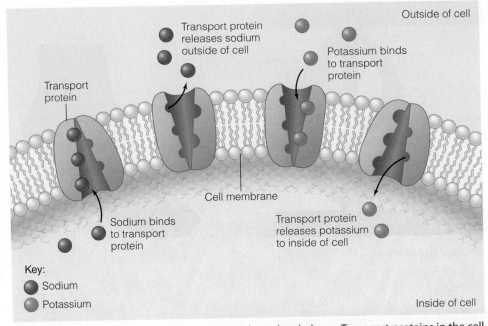

Figure 6.14 Transport proteins help maintain electrolyte balance. Transport proteins in the cell membrane pick up potassium and sodium and transport them across the cell membrane.

by respiratory or metabolic problems. Acidosis and alkalosis can cause coma and death by denaturing body proteins.

Proteins are excellent **buffers,** meaning they help maintain proper acid–base balance. Acids contain hydrogen ions, which are positively charged. The side chains of proteins have negative charges that attract the hydrogen ions and neutralize their detrimental effects on the body. Proteins can release the hydrogen ions when the blood becomes too basic. By buffering acids and bases, proteins maintain acid–base balance and blood pH.

Proteins Help Maintain a Strong Immune System

Antibodies are special proteins that are critical components of the immune system. When a foreign substance attacks the body, the immune system produces antibodies to defend against it. Bacteria, viruses, toxins, and allergens (substances that cause allergic reactions) are examples of antigens that can trigger antibody production. (An *antigen* is any substance—but typically a protein—that our bodies recognize as foreign and that triggers an immune response.)

Each antibody is designed to destroy one specific invader. When that substance invades the body, antibodies are produced to attack and destroy the specific antigen. Once antibodies have been made, the body "remembers" this process and can respond more quickly the next time that particular invader appears. *Immunity* refers to the development of the molecular memory to produce antibodies quickly upon subsequent invasions.

Adequate protein is necessary to support the increased production of antibodies that occurs in response to a cold, flu, or allergic reaction. If we do not consume enough protein, our resistance to illnesses and disease is weakened. On the other hand, eating more protein than we need does not improve immune function.

Proteins Serve as an Energy Source

The body's primary energy sources are carbohydrate and fat. Remember that both carbohydrate and fat have specialized storage forms that can be used for energy—carbohydrate as glycogen and fat as triglycerides. Proteins do not have a specialized storage form for energy. This means that when proteins need to be used for energy, they are taken from the blood and body tissues such as the liver and skeletal muscle. In healthy people, proteins contribute

buffers   Proteins that help maintain proper acid–base balance by attaching to, or releasing, hydrogen ions as conditions change in the body.

antibodies   Defensive proteins of the immune system. Their production is prompted by the presence of bacteria, viruses, toxins, and allergens.

very little to energy needs. Because we are efficient at recycling amino acids, protein needs are relatively low as compared with needs for carbohydrate and fat.

To use proteins for energy, the nitrogen (or amine) group is removed from the amino acid in a process called **deamination.** The nitrogen is converted to ammonia, which is transported to the liver and converted to *urea.* The urea is then transported to the kidneys, where it is excreted in the urine. The remaining fragments of the amino acid contain carbon, hydrogen, and oxygen. The body can directly metabolize these fragments for energy or use them to build carbohydrate. Certain amino acids can be converted into glucose via gluconeogenesis. This is a critical process during times of low carbohydrate intake or starvation. Fat cannot be converted into glucose, but body proteins can be broken down and converted into glucose to provide needed energy to the brain.

To protect the proteins in our body tissues, it is important that we regularly eat an adequate amount of carbohydrate and fat to provide energy. We also need to consume enough dietary protein to perform the required work without using up the proteins that already are playing an active role in our bodies. Unfortunately, the body cannot store excess dietary protein. As a consequence, eating too much protein results in the removal and excretion of the nitrogen in the urine and the use of the remaining components for energy.

Proteins Assist in the Transport and Storage of Nutrients

Proteins act as carriers for many important nutrients in the body. As discussed in Chapter 5, lipoproteins contain lipids bound to proteins, which allows the transport of hydrophobic lipids through the watery medium of blood. Another example of a transport protein is transferrin, which carries iron in the blood. Ferritin, in contrast, is an example of a storage protein: it is the compound in which iron is stored in the liver.

As discussed on page 223, transport proteins are located in cell membranes and allow for the proper transport of many nutrients across the cell membrane. These transport proteins also help in the maintenance of fluid and electrolyte balance and conduction of nerve impulses.

RecaP

Proteins serve many important functions, including (1) enabling growth, repair, and maintenance of body tissues; (2) acting as enzymes and hormones; (3) maintaining fluid and electrolyte balance; (4) maintaining acid–base balance; (5) making antibodies, which strengthen the immune system; (6) providing energy when carbohydrate and fat intake are inadequate; and (7) transport and storage of nutrients. Proteins function best when adequate amounts of carbohydrate and fat are consumed.

How Much Protein Should We Eat?

Consuming adequate protein is a major concern of many people. In fact, one of the most common concerns among active people and athletes is that their diets are deficient in protein (see the Nutrition Myth or Fact? box on page 226 for a discussion of this topic). This concern about dietary protein is generally unnecessary, as we can easily consume the protein our bodies need by eating an adequate and varied diet.

Nitrogen Balance Is a Method Used to Determine Protein Needs

A highly specialized procedure referred to as *nitrogen balance* is used to determine a person's protein needs. Nitrogen is excreted through the body's processes of recycling or using proteins; thus, the balance can be used to estimate if protein intake is adequate to meet protein needs.

Typically performed only in experimental laboratories, the nitrogen-balance procedure involves measuring both nitrogen intake and nitrogen excretion over a 2-week period. A

deamination The process by which an amine group is removed from an amino acid. The nitrogen is then transported to the kidneys for excretion in the urine, and the carbon and other components are metabolized for energy or used to make other compounds.

Nutrition Myth or Fact?
Do Athletes Need More Protein Than Inactive People?

At one time it was believed that the Recommended Dietary Allowance (RDA) for protein, which is 0.8 g/kg body weight, was sufficient for both inactive people and athletes. Recent studies, however, show that athletes' protein needs are higher.

Why do athletes need more protein? Regular exercise increases the transport of oxygen to body tissues, requiring changes in the oxygen-carrying capacity of the blood. To carry more oxygen, we need to produce more of the protein that carries oxygen in the blood (i.e., hemoglobin). During intense exercise, we use a small amount of protein directly for energy. We also use protein to make glucose to maintain adequate blood glucose levels and to prevent hypoglycemia (low blood sugar) during exercise. Regular exercise stimulates tissue growth and causes tissue damage, which must be repaired by additional proteins. Strength athletes (such as bodybuilders and weightlifters) need 1.8 to 2 times more protein than the current RDA, and

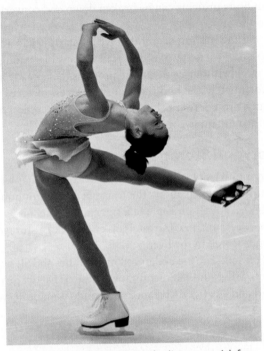

Some athletes who persistently diet are at risk for low protein intake.

endurance athletes (such as distance runners and triathletes) need 1.5 to 1.75 times more protein than the current RDA.[5] Later in this chapter, we will calculate the protein needs for inactive and active people.

If you're active, does this mean you should add more protein to your diet? Not necessarily. Contrary to popular belief, most Americans, including inactive people *and athletes*, already consume more than twice the RDA for protein. For healthy individuals, evidence does not support eating more than two times the RDA for protein to increase strength, build muscle, or improve athletic performance. In fact, eating more protein as food or supplements or taking individual amino acid supplements does not cause muscles to become bigger or stronger. Only regular strength training can achieve these goals. By eating a balanced diet and consuming a variety of foods, both inactive and active people can easily meet their protein requirements.

standardized diet, the nitrogen content of which has been measured and recorded, is fed to the study participant. The person is required to consume all of the foods provided. Because the majority of nitrogen is excreted in the urine and feces, laboratory technicians directly measure the nitrogen content of the subject's urine and fecal samples. Small amounts of nitrogen are excreted in the skin, hair, and body fluids such as mucus and semen, but because of the complexity of collecting nitrogen excreted via these routes, the measurements are estimated. Then, technicians add the estimated nitrogen losses to the nitrogen measured in the subject's urine and feces. Nitrogen balance is then calculated as the difference between nitrogen intake and nitrogen excretion.

People who consume more nitrogen than is excreted are considered to be in positive nitrogen balance (**Figure 6.15**). This state indicates that the body is retaining or adding protein, and it occurs during periods of growth, pregnancy, or recovery from illness or a protein deficiency. People who excrete more nitrogen than is consumed are in negative nitrogen balance. This situation indicates that the body is losing protein, and it occurs during starvation or when people are consuming very-low-energy diets. This is because when energy intake is too low to meet energy demands over a prolonged period of time, the body metabolizes body proteins for energy. The nitrogen from these proteins is excreted in the urine and feces. Negative nitrogen balance also occurs during severe illness, infections, high fever, serious burns, or injuries that cause significant blood loss. People in these situations

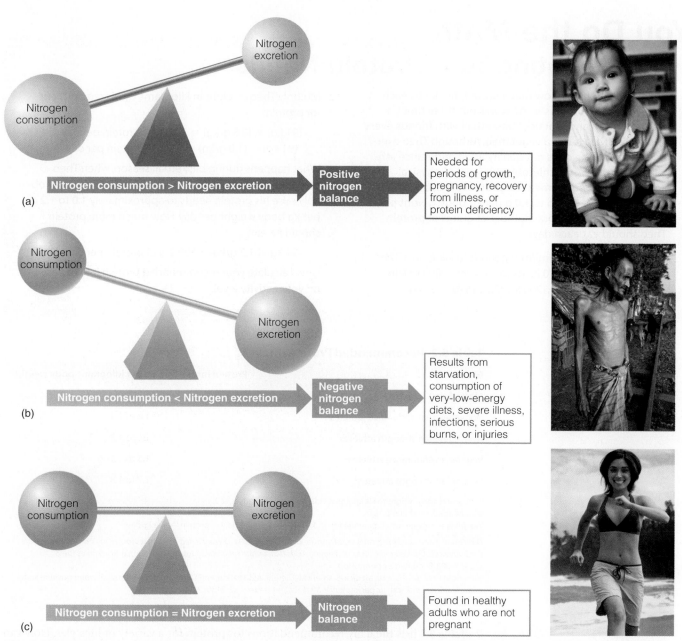

Figure 6.15 Nitrogen balance describes the relationship between how much nitrogen (or protein) we consume and excrete each day. **(a)** Positive nitrogen balance occurs when nitrogen consumption is greater than excretion. **(b)** Negative nitrogen balance occurs when nitrogen consumption is less than excretion. **(c)** Nitrogen balance is maintained when nitrogen consumption equals excretion.

require increased dietary protein. A person is in nitrogen balance when nitrogen intake equals nitrogen excretion. This indicates that protein intake is sufficient to cover protein needs. Healthy adults who are not pregnant are in nitrogen balance.

Recommended Dietary Allowance for Protein

How much protein should we eat? The RDA for protein is 0.8 g per kilogram of body weight per day. The recommended percentage of energy that should come from protein is 10% to 35% of total energy intake. Protein needs are higher for children, adolescents, and pregnant/lactating women because more protein is needed during times of growth and development (refer to Chapters 16 and 17 for details on protein needs during these phases of the life cycle). Protein needs can also be higher for active people and for vegetarians.

You Do the Math

Calculating Your Protein Needs

Theo wants to know how much protein he needs each day. During the off season, he works out three times a week at a gym and practices basketball with friends every Friday night. He is not a vegetarian. Although Theo exercises regularly, he does not qualify as an endurance athlete or as a strength athlete. At this level of physical activity, Theo's requirement for protein probably ranges from the RDA of 0.8 up to 1.0 g per kg body weight per day. To calculate the total number of grams of protein Theo should eat each day:

1. Convert Theo's weight from pounds to kilograms. Theo presently weighs 200 lb. To convert this value to kilograms, divide by 2.2: (200 lb)/(2.2 lb/kg) = 91 kg

2. Multiply Theo's weight in kilograms by his requirement for protein:

(91 kg) $\times$ (0.8 g/kg) = 72.8 g of protein per day
(91 kg) $\times$ (1.0 g/kg) = 91 g of protein per day

What happens during basketball season, when Theo practices or has games 5 to 6 days a week? This will probably raise his protein needs to approximately 1.0 to 1.2 g per kg body weight per day. How much more protein should he eat?

91 kg $\times$ 1.2 g/kg = 109.2 g of protein per day

Now calculate your recommended protein intake based on your activity level.

Table 6.2 Recommended Protein Intakes

Group	Protein Intake (grams per kilogram* body weight)
Most adults[1]	0.8
Nonvegetarian endurance athletes[2]	1.2 to 1.4
Nonvegetarian strength athletes[2]	1.6 to 1.7
Vegetarian endurance athletes[2]	1.3 to 1.5
Vegetarian strength athletes[2]	1.7 to 1.8

*To convert body weight to kilograms, divide weight in pounds by 2.2.
Weight (lb)/2.2 = Weight (kg)
Weight (kg) $\times$ protein recommendation (g/kg body weight per day) = protein intake (g/day)

Data from: [1]Food and Nutrition Board, Institute of Medicine. 2002. *Dietary Reference Intakes for Energy, Carbohydrate, Fiber, Fat, Fatty Acids, Cholesterol, Protein, and Amino Acids (Macronutrients).* Washington, DC: National Academies Press, pp. 465–608. Reprinted by permission.
[2]American College of Sports Medicine, American Dietetic Association, and Dietitians of Canada. 2001. Joint position statement. Nutrition and athletic performance. *Med. Sci. Sports Exerc.* 32: 2130–2145.

Table 6.2 lists the daily recommendations for protein for a variety of lifestyles. How can we convert this recommendation into total grams of protein for the day? Using the You Do the Math box above, let's calculate Theo's protein requirements.

Is it possible for Theo to eat this much protein each day? It may surprise you to discover that most Americans eat 1.5 to 2 times the RDA for protein without any effort!

Most Americans Meet or Exceed the RDA for Protein

Surveys indicate that Americans eat 15% to 17% of their total daily energy intake as protein.[6–8] In these studies, women reported eating about 65 to 70 g of protein each day, and men consumed 88 to 110 g per day. Putting these values into perspective, let's assume that the average man weighs 75 kg (165 lb) and the average woman weighs 65 kg (143 lb). Their protein requirements (assuming they are not athletes or vegetarians) are 60 g and 52 g per day, respectively. As you can see, most adults in the United States appear to have no problems meeting their protein needs each day.

What are the typical protein intakes of active people? Research indicates that the self-reported protein intake of athletes participating in a variety of sports can well exceed current recommendations.[9] For instance, the protein intake for some female distance runners is 1.2.g per kilogram body weight per day, accounting for 15% of their total daily energy intake. In addition, some male bodybuilders consume 3 g per kilogram body weight per day, accounting for almost 38% of their total daily energy intake! However, there are certain groups of athletes who are at risk for low protein intakes. Athletes who consume inadequate energy and limit food choices, such as some distance runners, figure skaters, female gymnasts, and wrestlers who are dieting, are all at risk for low protein intakes. Unlike people who consume adequate energy, individuals who are restricting their total energy intake (kilocalories) need to pay close attention to their protein intake.

Too Much Dietary Protein Can Be Harmful

High protein intake may increase the risk of health problems. Three health conditions that have received particular attention include heart disease, bone loss, and kidney disease.

High Protein Intake Is Associated with High Cholesterol

High-protein diets composed of predominantly animal sources are associated with higher blood cholesterol levels. This is probably due to the saturated fat in animal products, which is known to increase blood cholesterol levels and the risk of heart disease. One study showed that people with heart disease improved their health when they ate a diet that was high in whole grains, fruits, and vegetables and met the RDA for protein.[10] However, some of the people in this study chose to eat a high-protein diet, and their risk factors worsened. In addition, vegetarians have been shown to have a greatly reduced risk of heart disease.[11,12]

High Protein Intake May Contribute to Bone Loss

How might a high-protein diet lead to bone loss? Until recently, nutritionists have been concerned about high-protein diets because they increase calcium excretion. This may be because animal products contain more of the sulfur amino acids (methionine and cysteine). Metabolizing these amino acids makes the blood more acidic, and calcium is pulled from the bone to buffer these acids. Although eating more protein can cause an increased excretion of calcium, it is very controversial whether high protein intakes actually cause bone loss. We do know that eating too little protein causes bone loss, which increases the risk of fractures and osteoporosis. Higher intakes of animal and soy protein have been shown to protect bone in middle-aged and older women.[13, 14] There does not appear to be enough direct evidence at this time to show that higher protein intakes cause bone loss in healthy people.

High Protein Intake Can Increase the Risk for Kidney Disease

A third risk associated with high protein intakes is kidney disease. People with kidney problems are advised to eat a low-protein diet because a high-protein diet can increase the risk of acquiring kidney disease in people who are susceptible. People with diabetes have higher rates of kidney disease and may benefit from a lower-protein diet.[15] The American Diabetes Association states that people with diabetes have a higher protein need than people without diabetes, but a protein intake of 15% to 20% of total energy is adequate to meet these increased protein needs.[16] This level of protein intake is deemed safe for people with diabetes who have normal renal function. There is no evidence, however, that eating more protein causes kidney disease in healthy people who are not susceptible to this condition. In fact, one study found that athletes consuming up to 2.8 g of protein per kilogram body weight per day experienced no unhealthy changes in kidney function.[17] Experts agree that eating no more than 2 g of protein per kilogram body weight each day is safe for healthy people.

It is important for people who consume a lot of protein to drink more water. This is because eating more protein increases protein metabolism and urea production. As mentioned earlier, urea is a waste product that forms when nitrogen is removed during amino acid metabolism. Adequate fluid is needed to flush excess urea from the kidneys. This is particularly important for athletes, who need more fluid due to higher sweat losses.

Liz
Nutri-Case

"One of my dancer friends, Silvie, was always a little pudgy, but now she's tighter than I've ever seen her. Yesterday, even our teacher commented on how great she looks! After class, I asked her secret and she said she's been on a high-protein diet for 2 months. She said it's pretty easy to stick to—you just have to avoid starches like bread and pasta. Oh, and most sweets, too, though you can still have ice cream. She said she never feels hungry anymore, that the meat and eggs and cheese keep her feeling full. I'm thinking to myself, heck, I'm hungry all the time! So I asked her to bring me her book about the diet so I can try it for myself."

One issue that has been a major controversy for many years is the use of high-protein diets for weight loss. What do you think of Liz's idea of trying such a diet? Would your opinion change if you learned that Liz has high LDL-cholesterol and that her father suffered a heart attack last year at age 49? How might you advise Liz to adapt the diet for her unique health concerns?

Good Food Sources of Protein

Table 6.3 compares the protein content of a variety of foods. In general, good sources of protein include meats (beef, pork, poultry, seafood), dairy products (milk-based products and eggs), soy products, legumes, whole grains, and nuts. A new source of non-meat protein that is available on the market is *quorn*, a protein product derived from fermented fungus. It is mixed with a variety of other foods to produce various types of meat substitutes.

Although most people are aware that meats are an excellent source of protein, many people are surprised to learn that the quality of the protein in some legumes is almost equal to that of meat. Legumes include foods such as kidney beans, pinto beans, black beans, soybeans, garbanzo beans (or chickpeas), lentils, green peas, black-eyed peas, and lima beans. Interestingly, the quality of soybean protein is almost identical to that of meat, and the protein quality of other legumes is relatively high. In addition to being excellent sources of protein, legumes are also high in fiber, iron, calcium, and many of the B-vitamins. They are also low in saturated fat and cholesterol. Legumes are not nutritionally complete, however, as they do not contain vitamins B_{12}, C, or A and are deficient in methionine, an essential amino acid. Eating legumes regularly, including foods made from soybeans (such as soy milk, tofu, textured soy protein, and tempeh), may help reduce the risk of heart disease by lowering blood cholesterol levels. Diets high in legumes and soy products are also associated with lower rates of some cancers.

The quality of the protein in some legumes, such as these black-eyed peas, lentils, and garbanzo beans, is almost equal to that of meat.

Nuts are a healthful high-protein food. In the past, the high fat and energy content of nuts was assumed to be harmful, and people were advised to eat nuts only occasionally and in very small amounts. The results from recent epidemiological studies have helped to substantially change the way nutrition experts view nuts. These studies show that consuming about 2 to 5 oz of nuts per week significantly reduced people's risk for cardiovascular disease.[18–21] Although the exact mechanism for the reduction in cardiovascular disease risk with increased nut intake is not known, nuts contain many nutrients and other substances that are associated with health benefits, including fiber, unsaturated fats, potassium, folate, and plant sterols that inhibit cholesterol absorption.

Fruits and many vegetables are not particularly high in protein; however, these foods provide fiber and many vitamins and minerals and are excellent sources of carbohydrates. Thus, eating these foods can help provide the carbohydrates and energy that our bodies need so that we can spare protein for use in building and maintaining our bodies rather than using it for energy. Try the Nutrition Label Activity on page 232 to determine how much protein you typically eat.

Table 6.3 Protein Content of Commonly Consumed Foods

Food	Serving Size	Protein (g)	Food	Serving Size	Protein (g)
Beef:			**Beans:**		
Ground, lean, baked (15% fat)	3 oz	22	Refried	½ cup	7
Prime rib, broiled (⅛-in. fat)	3 oz	18	Kidney, red	½ cup	7.7
Top sirloin, broiled (⅛-in. fat)	3 oz	23	Black	½ cup	7
Poultry:			**Nuts:**		
Chicken breast, broiled with skin (bone removed)	½ breast	29	Peanuts, dry roasted	1 oz	6.7
			Peanut butter, creamy	2 tbsp.	8
Chicken thigh, bone and skin removed	1 thigh	13.5	Almonds, blanched	1 oz	6
Turkey breast, roasted, Louis Rich	3 oz	15	**Cereals, Grains, and Breads:**		
Seafood:			Oatmeal, quick instant	1 cup	5.4
Cod, cooked	3 oz	19	Cheerios	1 cup	3
Salmon, Chinook, baked	3 oz	22	Grape Nuts	½ cup	6
Shrimp, steamed	3 oz	18	Raisin Bran	1 cup	5
Tuna, in water, drained	3 oz	22	Brown rice, cooked	1 cup	5
Pork:			Whole-wheat bread	1 slice	2.7
Pork loin chop, broiled	3 oz	25	Bagel, 3½-in. diameter	1 each	7
Ham, roasted, lean	3 oz	20	**Vegetables:**		
Dairy:			Carrots, raw (7.5 × 1⅛-in.)	1 each	0.7
Whole milk (3.3% fat)	8 fl. oz	7.9	Broccoli, raw, chopped	1 cup	2.6
1% milk	8 fl. oz	8.5	Collards, cooked from frozen	1 cup	5
Skim milk	8 fl. oz	8.8	Spinach, raw	1 cup	0.9
Low-fat, plain yogurt	8 fl. oz	13			
American cheese, processed	1 oz	6			
Cottage cheese, low-fat (2%)	1 cup	27			
Soy Products:					
Tofu	3.3 oz	7			
Tempeh, cooked	3.3 oz	18			
Soy milk beverage	1 cup	7			

Data from: Values obtained from U.S. Department of Agriculture, Agricultural Research Service. 2008. USDA National Nutrient Database for Standard Reference, Release 21. Available online at www.ars.usda.gov/ba/bhnrc/ndl.

RECAP

The RDA for protein for most non-pregnant, non-lactating, nonvegetarian adults is 0.8 g per kg body weight. Children, pregnant women, nursing mothers, vegetarians, and active people need slightly more. Most people who eat enough kilocalories and carbohydrates have no problem meeting their RDA for protein. Eating too much protein may increase a person's risk for heart disease and kidney disease if he or she is already at risk for these diseases. Good sources of protein include meats, eggs, dairy products, soy products, legumes, quorn, whole grains, and nuts.

Can a Vegetarian Diet Provide Adequate Protein?

Vegetarianism is the practice of restricting the diet to food substances of plant origin, including fruits, grains, and nuts. It is currently estimated that almost 7 million adults in the United States are vegetarians; of these, about 4 million are vegans, people who do not eat any kind of animal product, including dairy foods and eggs.[2] Many vegetarians are college students; moving away from home and taking responsibility for one's eating habits appears to influence some young adults to try vegetarianism as a lifestyle choice.

vegetarianism The practice of restricting the diet to food substances of plant origin, including vegetables, fruits, grains, and nuts.

Nutrition Label Activity
How Much Protein Do You Eat?

Theo wants to know if his diet contains enough protein. To calculate his protein intake, he records all foods that he eats for 3 days in a food diary. The foods Theo consumed for 1 of his 3 days are listed below on the left, and the protein content of those foods is listed on the right. Theo recorded the protein content listed on the Nutrition Facts label for those foods with labels. For products without labels, he used the nutrient analysis program that came with this book. There is also a U.S. Department of Agriculture Web site that lists the energy and nutrient content of thousands of foods (go to www.ars.usda.gov/ba/bhnrc/ndl).

Foods Consumed	Protein Content (g)
BREAKFAST:	
Brewed coffee (2 cups) with 2 tbsp. cream	1
1 large bagel (5-in. diameter)	10
Low-fat cream cheese (1.5 oz)	4.5
MID-MORNING SNACK:	
Cola beverage (32 fl. oz)	0
Low-fat strawberry yogurt (1 cup)	10
Snackwells Apple Cinnamon Bars (37 g each bar; 2 bars eaten)	2
LUNCH:	
Ham and cheese sandwich:	
Whole-wheat bread (2 slices)	4
Mayonnaise (1.5 tbsp.)	1
Lean ham (4 oz)	24
Swiss cheese (2 oz)	16
Iceberg lettuce (2 leaves)	0.5
Sliced tomato (3 slices)	0.5
Banana (1 large)	1
Triscuit crackers (20 each)	7
Bottled water (20 fl. oz)	0

Foods Consumed	Protein Content (g)
DINNER:	
Cheeseburger:	
Broiled ground beef (1/2 lb, cooked)	64
American cheese (1 oz)	6
Seeded bun (1 large)	6
Ketchup (2 tbsp.)	1
Mustard (1 tbsp.)	1
Shredded lettuce (1/2 cup)	0.5
Sliced tomato (3 slices)	0.5
French fries (2- to 3-in. strips; 30 each)	6
Baked beans (2 cups)	28
2% low-fat milk (2 cups)	16
EVENING SNACK:	
Chocolate chip cookies (4 each of 3-in. diameter cookie)	3
2% low-fat milk (1 cup)	8
Total Protein Intake for the Day:	**221.5 g**

As calculated in the You Do the Math box on page 228, Theo's RDA is 72.8 to 91 g of protein. He is consuming 2.4 to 3 times that amount! You can see that he does not need to use amino acid or protein supplements, because he has more than adequate amounts of protein to build lean tissue. Now calculate your own protein intake using food labels and a diet analysis program. Do you obtain more protein from animal or non-animal sources? If you consume mostly non-animal sources, are you eating soy products and complementary foods throughout the day? If you eat animal-based products on a regular basis, notice how much protein you consume from even small servings of meat and dairy products.

Soy products are also a good source of dietary protein.

Types of Vegetarian Diets

There are almost as many types of vegetarian diets as there are vegetarians. Some people who consider themselves vegetarians regularly eat poultry and fish. Others avoid the flesh of animals, but consume eggs, milk, and cheese liberally. Still others strictly avoid all products of animal origin, including milk and eggs, and even by-products such as candies and puddings made with gelatin. A type of "vegetarian" diet receiving significant media attention recently is the *flexitarian* diet: Flexitarians are considered semivegetarians who eat mostly plant foods, eggs, and dairy but occasionally eat red meat, poultry, and/or fish.

Table 6.4 identifies the various types of vegetarian diets, ranging from the most inclusive to the most restrictive. Notice that

Table 6.4 Terms and Definitions of a Vegetarian Diet

Type of Diet	Foods Consumed	Comments
Semivegetarian (also called partial vegetarian or flexitarian)	Vegetables, grains, nuts, fruits, legumes; sometimes seafood, poultry, eggs, and dairy products	Typically exclude or limit red meat; may also avoid other meats
Pescovegetarian	Similar to a semivegetarian but excludes poultry	*Pesco* means fish, the only animal source of protein in this diet
Lacto-ovo-vegetarian	Vegetables, grains, nuts, fruits, legumes, dairy products (*lacto*) and eggs (*ovo*)	Excludes animal flesh and seafood
Lactovegetarian	Similar to a lacto-ovo-vegetarian but excludes eggs	Relies on milk and cheese for animal sources of protein
Ovovegetarian	Vegetables, grains, nuts, fruits, legumes, and eggs	Excludes dairy, flesh, and seafood products
Vegan (also called strict vegetarian)	Only plant-based foods (vegetables, grains, nuts, seeds, fruits, legumes)	May not provide adequate vitamin B_{12}, zinc, iron, or calcium
Macrobiotic diet	Vegan type of diet; becomes progressively more strict until almost all foods are eliminated. At the extreme, only brown rice and small amounts of water or herbal tea are consumed.	Taken to the extreme, can cause malnutrition and death
Fruitarian	Only raw or dried fruit, seeds, nuts, honey, and vegetable oil	Very restrictive diet; deficient in protein, calcium, zinc, iron, vitamin B_{12}, riboflavin, and other nutrients

the more restrictive the diet, the more challenging it becomes to achieve an adequate protein intake.

Why Do People Become Vegetarians?

When discussing vegetarianism, one of the most often-asked questions is why people would make this food choice. The most common responses are included here.

Religious, Ethical, and Food-Safety Reasons

Some make the choice for religious or spiritual reasons. Several religions prohibit or restrict the consumption of animal flesh; however, generalizations can be misleading. For example, whereas certain sects within Hinduism forbid the consumption of meat, perusing the menu at any Indian restaurant will reveal that many other Hindus regularly consume small quantities of meat, poultry, and fish. Many Buddhists are vegetarians, as are some Christians, including Seventh Day Adventists.

Many vegetarians are guided by their personal philosophy to choose vegetarianism. These people feel that it is morally and ethically wrong to consume animals and any products from animals (such as dairy or egg products) because they view the practices in the modern animal industries as inhumane. They may consume milk and eggs but choose to purchase them only from family farms where they feel animals are treated humanely.

There is also a great deal of concern about meat-handling practices, because contaminated meat has occasionally made its way into our food supply. For example, in 1982, there was an outbreak of severe bloody diarrhea that was eventually traced to contaminated meat in hamburgers served at a fast-food restaurant. One recent concern surrounding beef that has taken Europe by storm is the epidemic of **mad cow disease.** See the accompanying Highlight box for a review of mad cow disease and its impact on the United States and other countries.

Ecological Benefits

Many people choose vegetarianism because of their concerns about the effect of meat industries on the global environment. Due to the high demand for meat in developed nations, meat production has evolved from small family farming operations into the larger system of agribusiness. Critics point to the environmental costs of agribusiness, including massive uses of water and grain to feed animals, methane gases and other wastes produced

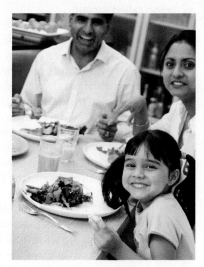

People who follow certain sects of Hinduism refrain from eating meat.

mad cow disease A fatal brain disorder caused by an abnormal form of protein that causes brain damage. Also referred to as bovine spongiform encephalopathy (BSE).

Highlight

Mad Cow Disease—What's the Beef?

Mad cow disease is a fatal brain disorder in cattle. It is caused by a *prion,* which is an abnormally folded, infectious protein. Prions influence other proteins to take on their abnormal shape, and these abnormal proteins cause brain damage. Mad cow disease is also called *bovine spongiform encephalopathy (BSE).* The disease eats away at a cow's brain, leaving it full of sponge-like holes. Eventually, the brain can no longer control vital life functions, and the cow literally "goes mad." Unfortunately, people who ingest contaminated tissue from infected cattle will also be infected. The human form of this disease, called variant Creutzfeldt-Jakob disease (vCJD), has killed at least 200 people, most of them in Great Britain.

Scientists are not certain how the prions are introduced to cattle. They think that cattle become infected by eating feed made with the brains and spinal cords of infected cattle. Using neural tissue in animal feed used to be a common practice in many countries. Even after exposure, it takes years for mad cow disease to manifest itself. Scientists speculate that older cattle are more infectious than younger animals. When cattle are slaughtered at an older age, this increases the risk of passing the disease from one animal to another.

In the late 20th century, the effect of mad cow disease on the European beef market was staggering, with beef consumption dropping 25% to 70% in certain countries; Great Britain, France, and Germany were particularly affected. Millions of cattle, including many that were only potentially infected, had to be slaughtered.

Three cases of mad cow disease were found in Canada from 2003 to early 2005. To date, no person eating Canadian beef has developed symptoms suggestive of infection. However, the occurrence of this disease in Canadian cattle has prompted the United States to temporarily ban the import of Canadian beef.

In December 2003, the first case of mad cow disease was reported in the United States, shocking those who believed the food supply to be safe from this disease. This discovery prompted many countries to immediately ban importation of American beef. As a result of this discovery, the federal government and beef industry took aggressive steps to destroy any potentially infected beef and to reassure the public that American beef is safe for consumption. Additional steps taken to protect beef include feeding U.S. cattle high-protein meal made from soybeans and working to ensure that the banning of the use of animal feed made with animal by-products is strictly enforced. In addition, cattle in the United States have for many years been slaughtered at an early age, reducing the likelihood of advanced infection. Finally, the United States has banned the import of all cattle, sheep, and goats from Europe. It is unclear whether, or for how long, the ban on Canadian beef will continue.

Should Americans fear our beef supply? The U.S. Department of Agriculture, the Food and Drug Administration, the National Institutes of Health, and the Centers for Disease Control and Prevention are working together to ensure enforcement of the ban related to the use of animal-based feed and to enhance technology that can track signs of the disease and act quickly if it reappears in our food supply. In addition, the U.S. beef industry is highly motivated to comply with safety regulations because reduced beef intake translates into millions of dollars in lost income.

Although it is not possible for the United States to be completely immune to mad cow disease, adherence to strict safety standards should minimize our risk and keep our beef safe for human consumption.

by animals themselves, and increased land use to support livestock. For an in-depth discussion of this complex and emotionally charged topic, refer to the Nutrition Debate at the end of this chapter.

Health Benefits

Still others practice vegetarianism because of its health benefits. Research over several years has consistently shown that a varied and balanced vegetarian diet can reduce the risk of many chronic diseases. Health benefits include:[22]

- Reduced intake of fat and total energy, which reduces the risk for obesity. This may in turn lower a person's risk for type 2 diabetes.
- Lower blood pressure, which may be due to a higher intake of fruits and vegetables. People who eat vegetarian diets tend to be nonsmokers, drink little or no alcohol, and exercise more regularly, which are also factors known to reduce blood pressure and help maintain a healthy body weight.
- Reduced risk of heart disease, which may be due to lower saturated fat intake and a higher consumption of *antioxidants* that are found in plant-based foods. Antioxidants, discussed in detail in Chapter 10, are substances that can protect our cells from damage. They are abundant in fruits and vegetables.
- Fewer digestive problems such as constipation and diverticular disease, perhaps due to the higher fiber content of vegetarian diets. Diverticular disease, discussed in Chapter 4, occurs when the wall of the bowel (large intestine) pouches and becomes inflamed.
- Reduced risk of some cancers. Research shows that vegetarians may have lower rates of cancer, particularly colon cancer.[23] Many components of a vegetarian diet could contribute to reducing cancer risks, including higher fiber and antioxidant intakes, lower dietary fat intake, lower consumption of **carcinogens** (cancer-causing agents) that are formed when cooking meat, and higher consumption of soy protein, which may have anticancer properties.[24]
- Reduced risk of kidney disease, kidney stones, and gallstones. The lower protein contents of vegetarian diets, plus the higher intake of legumes and vegetable proteins such as soy, may be protective against these conditions.

A well-balanced vegetarian diet can provide adequate protein.

What Are the Challenges of a Vegetarian Diet?

Although a vegetarian diet can be healthful, it also presents many challenges. Limiting consumption of flesh and dairy products introduces the potential for inadequate intakes of certain nutrients, especially for people consuming a vegan, macrobiotic, or fruitarian diet. Table 6.5 lists the nutrients that can be deficient in a vegan-type of diet plan and describes good non-animal sources that can provide these nutrients. Vegetarians who consume dairy and/or egg products obtain these nutrients more easily.

Research indicates that a sign of disordered eating in some female athletes is the switch to a vegetarian diet.[25] Instead of eating a healthful variety of non-animal foods, people with disordered eating problems may use vegetarianism as an excuse to restrict many foods from their diets.

Can a vegetarian diet provide enough protein? Because non-meat high-quality protein sources are quite easy to obtain in developed countries, a well-balanced vegetarian diet can provide adequate protein. In fact, the American Dietetic Association and the Dietitians of

carcinogens Cancer-causing agents, such as certain pesticides, industrial chemicals, and pollutants.

Table 6.5 Nutrients of Concern in a Vegan Diet

Nutrient	Functions	Non-meat/Nondairy Food Sources
Vitamin B_{12}	Assists with DNA synthesis; protection and growth of nerve fibers	Vitamin B_{12} fortified cereals, yeast, soy products, and other meat analogues; vitamin B_{12} supplements
Vitamin D	Promotes bone growth	Vitamin D fortified cereals, margarines, and soy products; adequate exposure to sunlight; supplementation may be necessary for those who do not get adequate exposure to sunlight
Riboflavin (vitamin B_2)	Promotes release of energy; supports normal vision and skin health	Whole and enriched grains, green leafy vegetables, mushrooms, beans, nuts, and seeds
Iron	Assists with oxygen transport; involved in making amino acids and hormones	Whole-grain products, prune juice, dried fruits, beans, nuts, seeds, leafy vegetables such as spinach
Calcium	Maintains bone health; assists with muscle contraction, blood pressure, and nerve transmission	Fortified soy milk and tofu, almonds, dry beans, leafy vegetables, calcium-fortified juices, fortified breakfast cereals
Zinc	Assists with DNA and RNA synthesis, immune function, and growth	Whole-grain products, wheat germ, beans, nuts, and seeds

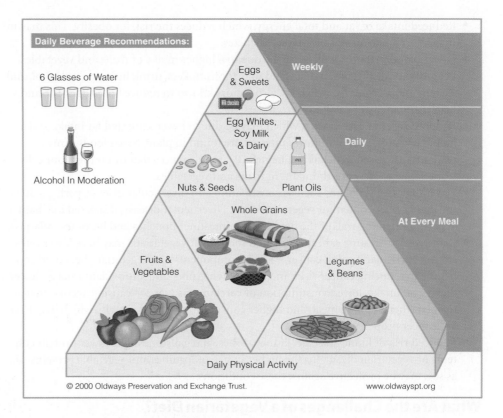

Figure 6.16 The Vegetarian Food Pyramid. This pyramid guides general food choices for vegetarians on a daily basis.

Vegetarians should eat 2 to 3 servings of beans, nuts, seeds, eggs, or meat substitutes, such as tofu, daily.

Canada endorse an appropriately planned vegetarian diet as healthful, nutritionally adequate, and providing many benefits in reducing and preventing various diseases.[23] As you can see, the emphasis is on a *balanced* and *adequate* vegetarian diet; thus, it is important for vegetarians to consume soy products, eat complementary proteins, and obtain enough energy from other macronutrients to spare protein from being used as an energy source. Although the digestibility of a vegetarian diet is potentially lower than that of an animal-based diet, there is no separate protein recommendation for vegetarians who consume complementary plant proteins.[4]

Using the Vegetarian Food Pyramid to Guide Food Choices

An example of a Vegetarian Food Pyramid based on the USDA MyPyramid is illustrated in **Figure 6.16**. This pyramid can be used by vegetarians to design a healthful diet that contains all of the necessary nutrients.

For example, to meet their needs for protein and calcium, lacto-vegetarians can consume low-fat or nonfat dairy products. Vegans and ovovegetarians can consume calcium-fortified soy milk or one of the many protein bars now fortified with calcium.

In addition to protein and calcium, vegans need to pay special attention to consuming foods high in vitamins D, B_{12}, and riboflavin (B_2) and the minerals zinc and iron. Supplementation of these micronutrients may be necessary for certain individuals if they cannot consume adequate amounts in their diet.

RECAP

A balanced vegetarian diet may reduce the risk of obesity, type 2 diabetes, heart disease, digestive problems, some cancers, kidney disease, kidney stones, and gallstones. Whereas varied vegetarian diets can provide enough protein, vegetarians who consume no animal products need to make sure they consume adequate plant sources of protein and supplement their diet with good sources of vitamin B_{12}, vitamin D, riboflavin, iron, calcium, and zinc.

Theo
Nutri-Case

"No way would I ever become a vegetarian! The only way to build up your muscles is to eat meat. I was reading in a bodybuilding magazine last week about some guy who doesn't eat anything from animals, not even milk or eggs, and he looked pretty buff—but I don't believe it. They can do anything to photos these days. Besides, after a game I just crave meat. If I don't have it, I feel sort of like my batteries don't get recharged. It's just not practical for a competitive athlete to go without meat."

What two claims does Theo make here about the role of meat in his diet? Do you think these claims are valid? Why or why not? Without trying to convert Theo to vegetarianism, what facts might you offer him about the nature of plant and animal proteins?

What Disorders Are Related to Protein Intake or Metabolism?

As we have seen, consuming inadequate protein can result in severe illness and death. Typically, this occurs when people do not consume enough total energy, but a diet deficient specifically in protein can have similar effects.

Protein-Energy Malnutrition Can Lead to Debility and Death

When a person consumes too little protein and energy, the result is **protein-energy malnutrition** (also called *protein-calorie malnutrition*). Two diseases that can follow are marasmus and kwashiorkor (**Figure 6.17**).

Marasmus Results from Grossly Inadequate Energy Intake

Marasmus is a disease that results from grossly inadequate intakes of protein, energy, and other nutrients. Essentially, people with marasmus slowly starve to death. It is most common in young children (6 to 18 months of age) who are living in impoverished conditions. These children are fed diluted cereal drinks that are inadequate in energy, protein,

protein-energy malnutrition A disorder caused by inadequate consumption of protein. It is characterized by severe wasting.

marasmus A form of protein-energy malnutrition that results from grossly inadequate intakes of protein, energy, and other nutrients.

(a)

(b)

Figure 6.17 Two forms of protein-energy malnutrition are **(a)** marasmus and **(b)** kwashiorkor.

and most nutrients. People suffering from marasmus have the look of "skin and bones," as their body fat and tissues are wasting. Consequences of marasmus include:

- Wasting and weakening of muscles, including the heart muscle
- Stunted brain development and learning impairment
- Depressed metabolism and little insulation from body fat, causing a dangerously low body temperature
- Stunted physical growth and development
- Deterioration of the intestinal lining, which further inhibits absorption of nutrients
- *Anemia* (abnormally low levels of hemoglobin in the blood)
- Severely weakened immune system
- Fluid and electrolyte imbalances

If marasmus is left untreated, death from dehydration, heart failure, or infection will result. Treating marasmus involves carefully correcting fluid and electrolyte imbalances. Protein and carbohydrates are provided once the body's condition has stabilized. Fat is introduced much later, as the protein levels in the blood must improve to the point at which the body can use them to carry fat (in the form of lipoproteins) so it can be safely metabolized by the body.

Kwashiorkor Results from a Low-Protein Diet

Kwashiorkor often occurs in developing countries when infants are weaned early due to the arrival of a subsequent baby. This deficiency disease is typically seen in young children (1 to 3 years of age) who no longer drink breast milk. Instead, they often are fed a low-protein, starchy cereal. Unlike marasmus, kwashiorkor often develops quickly and causes the person to look swollen, particularly in the belly. This is because the low protein content of the blood is inadequate to keep fluids from seeping into the tissue spaces. Other symptoms of kwashiorkor include:

- Some weight loss and muscle wasting, with some retention of body fat
- Retarded growth and development; less severe than that seen with marasmus
- Edema, which results in extreme distension of the belly and is caused by fluid and electrolyte imbalances
- Fatty degeneration of the liver
- Loss of appetite, sadness, irritability, apathy
- Development of sores and other skin problems; skin pigmentation changes
- Dry, brittle hair that loses its pigment, straightens, and falls out easily

Kwashiorkor can be reversed if adequate protein and energy are given in time. Because of their severely weakened immune systems, many individuals with kwashiorkor die from diseases they contract in their weakened state. Of those who are treated, many return home to the same impoverished conditions, only to develop this deficiency once again.

Many people think that only children in developing countries suffer from these diseases. However, protein-energy malnutrition occurs in all countries and affects both children and adults. In the United States, poor people living in inner cities and isolated rural areas are affected. Others at risk include the elderly, the homeless, people with eating disorders, those addicted to alcohol and drugs, and individuals with wasting diseases such as AIDS and cancer. Despite the fact that the United States produces more than enough food, Americans do experience malnutrition and hunger. Chapter 19 provides a detailed review of malnutrition in the United States and worldwide.

kwashiorkor   A form of protein-energy malnutrition that is typically seen in developing countries in infants and toddlers who are weaned early because of the birth of a subsequent child. Denied breast milk, they are fed a cereal diet that provides adequate energy but inadequate protein.

Disorders Related to Genetic Abnormalities

Numerous disorders are caused by defective DNA. These genetic disorders include phenylketonuria (or PKU), sickle cell anemia, and cystic fibrosis.

As discussed in Chapter 4, *phenylketonuria* is an inherited disease in which a person does not have the ability to break down the amino acid phenylalanine. As a result, phenylalanine and its metabolic by-products build up in tissues and can cause brain damage. Individuals with PKU must eat a diet that is severely limited in phenylalanine.

Sickle cell anemia is an inherited disorder of the red blood cells in which a single amino acid present in hemoglobin is changed. As shown in Figure 6.9, normal hemoglobin is globular, giving red blood cells a round, doughnut-like shape. The genetic alteration that occurs with sickle cell anemia causes the red blood cells to be shaped like a sickle or a crescent (**Figure 6.18**). Because sickled red blood cells are hard and sticky, they cannot flow smoothly through the smallest blood vessels. Instead, they block the vessels, depriving nearby tissues of their oxygen supply and eventually damaging vulnerable organs, particularly the spleen. Sickled cells also have a life span of only about 10 to 20 days, as opposed to the 120-day average for globular red blood cells. The body's greatly increased demand for new red blood cells leads to severe anemia. Other signs and symptoms of sickle cell anemia include impaired vision, headaches, convulsions, bone degeneration, and decreased function of various organs. This disease occurs in any person who inherits the sickle cell gene from both parents.

Cystic fibrosis is an inherited disease that primarily affects the respiratory system and digestive tract. It is caused by a defective gene that causes cells to build and then reject an abnormal version of a protein that normally allows passage of chloride into and out of certain cells. This alteration in chloride transport causes cells to secrete thick, sticky mucus. The linings of the lungs and pancreas are particularly affected, causing breathing difficulties, lung infections, and digestion problems that lead to nutrient deficiencies. Symptoms include wheezing, coughing, and stunted growth. The severity of this disease varies greatly; some individuals with cystic fibrosis live relatively normal lives, whereas others are seriously debilitated and die in childhood.

Figure 6.18 A sickled red blood cell.

sickle cell anemia A genetic disorder that causes red blood cells to be shaped like a sickle or crescent. These cells cannot travel smoothly through blood vessels, causing cell breakage and anemia.

cystic fibrosis A genetic disorder that causes an alteration in chloride transport, leading to the production of thick, sticky mucus that causes life-threatening respiratory and digestive problems.

RECAP

Protein-energy malnutrition can lead to marasmus and kwashiorkor. These diseases primarily affect impoverished children in developing nations. However, residents of developed countries are also at risk, especially the elderly, homeless, people who abuse alcohol or other drugs, and people with AIDS, cancer, and other wasting diseases. Genetic disorders involving abnormal proteins include phenylketonuria, sickle cell anemia, and cystic fibrosis.

See for Yourself
Tips for Adding Legumes to Your Daily Diet

They're high in protein and fiber, low in fat, and fill you up with fewer calories than meat sources of protein. What's more, they taste good! Maybe that's why nutrition experts consider legumes an almost perfect food. From main dishes to snacks, here are some simple ways to add legumes to your daily diet. By the way, some people experience uncomfortable intestinal gas after eating legumes. This is produced when bacteria in the colon break down the starches. If you're one of those people, make sure you soak legumes thoroughly, changing the water once or twice, before cooking. You can also try using Beano, an enzyme supplement available in most grocery stores. Taken before meals, it reduces intestinal gas.

Breakfast

☐ Instead of cereal, eggs, or a muffin, microwave a frozen bean burrito for a quick, portable breakfast.

☐ Make your pancakes with soy milk or pour soy milk on your cereal.

☐ If you normally have a side of bacon, ham, or sausage with your eggs, have a side of black beans.

Lunch and Dinner

☐ Try a sandwich made with hummus (a garbanzo bean spread), cucumbers, tomato, avocado, and/or lettuce in a whole-wheat pocket.

- ☐ Add garbanzo beans, kidney beans, or fresh peas to tossed salads or make a three-bean salad with kidney beans, green beans, and garbanzo beans.
- ☐ Make a side dish using legumes, such as peas with pearl onions or succotash (lima beans, corn, and tomatoes).
- ☐ Make black-bean soup, lentil soup, pea soup, minestrone soup, or a batch of dal (a type of yellow lentil used in Indian cuisine) and serve over brown rice. Top with plain yogurt, a traditional accompaniment in many Asian cuisines.
- ☐ Make burritos with black or pinto beans instead of shredded meat.

- ☐ Make a "meatloaf" using cooked, mashed lentils instead of ground beef.
- ☐ For fast food at home, keep canned beans on hand. Serve over rice with a salad for a complete and hearty meal.

Snacks

- ☐ Instead of potato chips or pretzels, try one of the new bean chips.
- ☐ Dip fresh vegetables in bean dip or hummus.
- ☐ Add roasted soy "nuts" to your trail mix.
- ☐ Keep frozen tofu desserts such as tofu ice cream in your freezer.

Chapter Review

Test Yourself | Answers

1. **F** Although protein can be used for energy in certain circumstances, fats and carbohydrates are the primary sources of energy for our bodies.

2. **F** There is no evidence that consuming amino acid supplements assists in building muscle tissue. Exercising muscles, specifically using weight training, is the stimulus needed to build muscle tissue.

3. **F** Excess protein is broken down and its component parts are either stored as fat or used for energy or tissue building and repair. Only the nitrogen component of protein is excreted in the urine.

4. **F** Vegetarian diets can meet and even exceed an individual's protein needs, assuming that adequate energy-yielding macronutrients, a variety of protein sources, and complementary protein sources are consumed.

5. **T** Most people in the United States consume 1.5 to 2 times more protein than they need.

Summary

- Unlike carbohydrates and fat, the structure of proteins is dictated by DNA, and proteins contain nitrogen.

- Amino acids are the building blocks of proteins; they are composed of an amine group, an acid group, a hydrogen atom, and a unique side chain called the R group.

- There are twenty different amino acids in our bodies: nine are essential amino acids, meaning that our bodies cannot produce them, and we must obtain them from food; eleven are nonessential, meaning our bodies can make them so they do not need to be consumed in the diet.

- Our genetic makeup determines the sequence of amino acids in our proteins. Gene expression refers to using a gene in a cell to make a protein.

- Deoxyribonucleic acid (DNA) is the genetic template for gene expression and protein synthesis. The building blocks of DNA are nucleotides, molecules composed of a phosphate group, a pentose sugar called deoxyribose, and one of four nitrogenous bases.

- Protein turnover involves the synthesis of new proteins and the degradation of existing proteins.

- The three-dimensional shape of proteins determines their function in the body.

- When proteins are exposed to damaging substances such as heat, acids, bases, and alcohol, they are denatured, meaning they lose their shape and function.

- A limiting amino acid is one that is missing or in limited supply, preventing the synthesis of adequate proteins.

- Mutual supplementation is the process of combining two incomplete protein sources to make a complete protein. The two foods involved in this process are called complementary proteins.

- Most digestion of proteins occurs in the small intestine.

- Protein quality is determined by its amino acid content and digestibility. Higher-quality proteins contain more essential amino acids and are more digestible. Animal sources, soy protein, and legumes are highly digestible forms of protein.

- Proteins are needed to promote cell growth, repair, and maintenance. They act as enzymes and hormones; help maintain the balance of fluids, electrolytes, acids, and bases; and support healthy immune function. They are also critical for nutrient transport and storage.

- The RDA for protein for adults is 0.8 g of protein per kilogram of body weight per day; protein should comprise 10% to 35% of total energy intake. Most people in the United States routinely eat 1.5 to 2 times the RDA for protein.

- High protein intakes may be harmful and can lead to increased blood cholesterol levels, increased calcium excretion, and increased risk for kidney disease in people who are susceptible to kidney problems.

- There are many forms of vegetarianism: lacto-ovo-vegetarians eat plant foods plus eggs and dairy products; pescovegetarians consume plant foods and rely on fish as the only meat source; vegans consume only plant foods.

- Consuming a well-planned vegetarian diet may reduce the risk of obesity, heart disease, type 2 diabetes, and some forms of cancer.

- Vegans may need to supplement their diet with vitamins B_{12} and D, riboflavin, iron, calcium, and zinc.

- Marasmus and kwashiorkor are two forms of protein-energy malnutrition that results from grossly inadequate energy and protein intake.

- Phenylketonuria is a genetic disease in which the person cannot break down the amino acid phenylalanine. The build-up of phenylalanine and its by-products leads to brain damage.

- Sickle cell anemia is a genetic disorder of the red blood cells. Because of an alteration of one amino acid in hemoglobin, the red blood cells become sickle-shaped and cannot travel smoothly through blood vessels. This blocks the vessels, causing inadequate oxygenation of nearby tissues, organ damage, and anemia.

- Cystic fibrosis is a genetic disease that causes an alteration in chloride transport that leads to the production of thick, sticky mucus. This mucus causes serious respiratory and digestive problems, which leads to variable levels of debilitation and, in some cases, premature death.

Review Questions

1. The process of combining peanut butter and whole-wheat bread to make a complete protein is called
   a. deamination.
   b. vegetarianism.
   c. transamination.
   d. mutual supplementation.

2. Which of the following meals would be appropriate in a well-planned vegan diet?
   a. Rice, pinto beans, acorn squash, soy butter, and almond milk
   b. Veggie dog, bun, and a banana-yogurt milkshake
   c. Brown rice and green tea
   d. Egg salad on whole-wheat toast, broccoli, carrot sticks, and soy milk

3. The substance that breaks down polypeptides in the small intestine is called
   a. hydrochloric acid.
   b. pepsin.
   c. protease.
   d. ketones.

4. The portion of an amino acid that contains nitrogen is called the
   a. R group.
   b. amine group.
   c. acid group.
   d. nitrate cluster.

5. All proteins contain
   a. carbon, oxygen, iron, and nitrogen.
   b. iron, oxygen, and hydrogen.
   c. carbon, oxygen, hydrogen, and nitrogen.
   d. carbon, oxygen, hydrogen, and sulfur.

6. **True or false?** After leaving the small intestine, amino acids are transported to the liver for distribution throughout the body.

7. **True or false?** When a protein is denatured, its shape is lost but its function is retained.

8. **True or false?** All hormones are proteins.

9. **True or false?** Buffers help the body maintain its fluids in proper balance.

10. **True or false?** Athletes typically require about three times as much protein as nonactive people.

11. Explain the relationship between inadequate protein intake and the swollen bellies of children with kwashiorkor.

12. Explain the relationship between excessive protein intake and an increased risk for kidney disease.

13. Differentiate between the roles of mRNA and tRNA in DNA replication.

14. You've always thought of your dad as a bit of a "health nut," so you're not surprised when you come home on spring break and he offers you a dinner of stir-fried vegetables and something called *quorn*. Over dinner, he announces that he is now a vegetarian and has joined an online vegetarian chat group. "But Dad," you protest, "you still eat meat, don't you?" "Sure I do," he answers, "but only once or twice a week. Lots of the other people in my chat group occasionally eat meat, too!" In your opinion, is your dad really a vegetarian? Defend your position.

15. Draw a sketch showing how amino acids bond to form proteins.

Web Links

References

1. Bennett, J., and C. Lewis. 2001. *Very Vegetarian.* Nashville: Rutledge Hill Press.
2. Vegetarian Resource Group. 2006. *Vegetarian Journal,* Issue 4. Available online at www.vrg.org/journal/vj2006issue4/ vj2006issue4poll.htm.
3. Park, K. G., S. D. Heys, K. Blessing, P. Kelly, M. A. McNurlan, O. Eremin, and P. J. Garlick. 1992. Stimulation of human breast cancers by dietary L-arginine. *Clin. Sci.* 82:413–417.
4. Institute of Medicine, Food and Nutrition Board. 2002. *Dietary Reference Intakes for Energy, Carbohydrate, Fiber, Fat, Fatty Acids, Cholesterol, Protein, and Amino Acids (Macronutrients).* Washington, DC: National Academies Press.
5. Lemon, P. W. 2000. Beyond the zone: Protein needs of active individuals. *J. Am. Coll. Nutr.* 19(5 suppl.):513S–521S.
6. McDowell, M. A., R. R. Briefel, K. Alaimo, A. M. Bischof, C. R. Caughman, M. D. Carroll, C. M. Lona, and C. L. Johnson. 1994. Energy and macronutrient intakes of persons ages 2 months and over in the United States: Third National Health and Nutrition Examination Survey, Phase I 1988–1991. *Advance Data* 255:1–24.
7. Tillotson, J. L., G. E. Bartsch, D. Gorder, G. A. Grandits, and J. Stamler. 1997. Food group and nutrient intakes at baseline in the Multiple Risk Factor Intervention Trial. *Am. J. Clin. Nutr.* 65(suppl.):228S–257S.
8. Smit, E., J. Nieto, C. J. Crespo, and P. Mitchell. 1999. Estimates of animal and plant protein intake in US adults: Results from the Third National Health and Nutrition Examination Survey, 1988–1991. *J. Am. Diet Assoc.* 99:813–820.
9. Manore, M., and J. Thompson. 2000. *Sport Nutrition for Health and Performance.* Champaign, IL: Human Kinetics.
10. Fleming, R. M. 2000. The effect of high-protein diets on coronary blood flow. *Angiology* 51:817–826.
11. Leitzmann, C. 2005. Vegetarian diets: What are the advantages? *Forum Nutr.* 57:147–156.
12. Szeto, Y. T., T. C. Y. Kwok, and I. F. F. Benzie. 2004. Effects of a long-term vegetarian diet on biomarkers of antioxidant status and cardiovascular disease risk. *Nutrition* 20:863–866.
13. Munger, R. G., J. R. Cerhan, and B. C.-H. Chiu. 1999. Prospective study of dietary protein intake and risk of hip fracture in postmenopausal women. *Am. J. Clin. Nutr.* 69:147–152.
14. Alekel, D. L., A. St. Germain, C. T. Peterson, K. B. Hanson, J. W. Stewart, and T. Toda. 2000. Isoflavone-rich soy protein isolate attenuates bone loss in the lumbar spine of perimenopausal women. *Am. J. Clin. Nutr.* 72:844–852.
15. Kontessis, P., I. Bossinakou, L. Sarika, E. Iliopoulou, A. Papantoniou, R. Trevisan, D. Roussi, K. Stipsanelli, S. Grigorakis, and A. Souvatzoglou. 1995. Renal, metabolic, and hormonal responses to proteins of different origin in normotensive, non-proteinuric type 1 diabetic patients. *Diabetes Care* 18:1233–1240.
16. American Diabetes Association (ADA). 2003. Evidence-based nutrition principles and recommendations for the treatment and prevention of diabetes and related complications. *Diabetes Care* 26:S51–S61.
17. Poortmans, J. R., and O. Dellalieux. 2000. Do regular high protein diets have potential health risks on kidney function in athletes? *Int. J. Sport Nutr.* 10:28–38.
18. Fraser, G. E., J. Sabaté, W. L. Beeson, and M. Strahan. 1992. A possible protective effect of nut consumption on risk of coronary heart disease. *Arch. Intern. Med.* 152:1416–1424.
19. Hu, F. B., M. J. Stampfer, J. E. Manson, E. B. Rimm, G. A. Colditz, B. A. Rosner, F. E. Speizer, C. H. Hennekens, and W. C. Willett. 1998. Frequent nut consumption and risk of coronary heart disease in women: Prospective cohort study. *BMJ* 317:1341–1345.
20. Albert, C. M., J. M. Gaziano, W. C. Willett, J. E. Mason, and C. H. Hennekens. 2002. Nut consumption and decreased risk of sudden cardiac death in the Physicians' Health Study. *Arch. Intern. Med.* 162:1382–1387.
21. Centers for Disease Control and Prevention (CDC). 2004. Division of Bacterial and Mycotic Diseases. Disease information. *Escherichia coli* O157:H7. Available online at www.cdc.gov/ncidod/ dbmd/diseaseinfo/escherichiacoli_g.htm.
22. Messina, M., and V. Messina. 1996. *The Dietitian's Guide to Vegetarian Diets.* Gaithersburg, MD: Aspen Publishers.
23. American Dietetic Association; Dietitians of Canada. 2003. Position of the American Dietetic Association and Dietitians of Canada: Vegetarian diets. *J. Am. Diet. Assoc.* 103(6):748–765.
24. Messina, V. K., and K. I. Burke. 1997. Position of the American Dietetic Association: Vegetarian diets. *J. Am. Diet. Assoc.* 97:1317–1321.
25. O'Conner, M. A., S. W. Touyz, S. M. Dunn, and P. J. V. Beaumont. 1987. Vegetarianism in anorexia nervosa? A review of 116 consecutive cases. *Med. J. Aust.* 147:540–542.
26. Food and Agriculture Organization. 2006. Livestock a major threat to environment: Remedies urgently needed. *FAO Newsroom.* 29 November. www.fao.org/newsroom/en/news/2006/ 1000448/index.html. (Accessed March 2009.)
27. Eshel, G., and P. Martin. 2006. Diet, energy and global warming. *Earth Interactions* (March)10:1–17. http://geosci.uchicago.edu/ ~gidon/papers/nutri/nutri.html. (Accessed March 2009.)
28. Jowit, J. 2008. UN says eat less meat to curb global warming. *The Observer* (September 7). www.guardian.co.uk/environment/2008/ sep/07/food.foodanddrink. (Accessed March 2009.)
29. National Cattlemen's Beef Association. November 2003. Beef industry "factoid" fighter. Available online at www.beef.org/documents/ Factoid%20Fighter%20Revisions%2011-03-03.doc.

Meat Consumption and Global Warming: Tofu to the Rescue?

Which causes more greenhouse gas emissions: livestock production or transportation? The answer may surprise you: According to the United Nations Food and Agriculture Organization (FAO), livestock production generates more of the gases responsible for global warming—18%—than transportation.[26] The FAO estimates that livestock production accounts for:

- 9% of all carbon-dioxide (CO_2) production deriving from human activity
- 37% of all human-induced methane, a gas with twenty-three times the global warming potential (GWP) of CO_2
- 64% of ammonia, which contributes to acid rain
- 65% of human-related production of nitrous oxide, a gas with 296 times the GWP of CO_2.

(a) (b)

The difference in greenhouse gas emissions associated with meat-based **(a)** versus vegetarian **(b)** meals is similar to the difference between driving an SUV versus an average sedan.

How does this compare to emissions generated from production of plant foods? A recent study from researchers at the University of Chicago concluded that an adult consuming an average daily number of calories from a typical mixed American diet causes the emission of 1,485 kg of greenhouse gases *above* the emission associated with consuming the same number of calories from plant sources. Far from trivial, nationally, this difference amounts to over 6% of the total U.S. greenhouse gas emissions.[27]

Livestock production is also a major source of land degradation, through both overgrazing and feed production. Livestock now use 30% of the earth's land surface for pasture or feed production. Aggressive deforestation, which has long been linked to global warming, is claiming more and more land for pasture; for example, in Latin America, about 70% of former forests in the Amazon have been cleared for grazing.[26] In

addition, production of feed crops for livestock uses 33% of global arable land—acres that could be cultivated for crops for human consumption. Livestock's presence in vast tracts of land and its demand for feed crops also have contributed significantly to a reduction in biodiversity and decline in ecosystems.[26]

Water use can also be tremendous. It is estimated that in the United States, it takes 430 gallons of water to produce 1 lb of pork. This is in contrast with the 151 gallons of water it takes to produce 1 lb of wheat. Water pollution is another concern: Animal waste, antibiotics, hormones,

(a) (b)

Livestock production **(a)** and aggressive deforestation **(b)** both contribute to increased greenhouse emissions.

and fertilizers and pesticides used on feed crops can run off into surrounding bodies of water, resulting in the pollution of neighboring streams, rivers, and lakes, as well as nearby irrigation fields used to produce crops for human consumption.

Considering the damage that livestock production wreaks on the environment, should you adopt a vegetarian—or semivegetarian—diet? The world's leading authority on global warming thinks you should. In 2008, Dr. Rajendra Pachauri, chair of the United Nations Intergovernmental Panel on Climate Change, which earned a joint share of the Nobel Peace Prize in 2007, released a statement calling upon individuals to have one meat-free day a week if they want to make a personal and effective sacrifice that would help tackle climate change. He went on to advocate that people progressively reduce their meat consumption even further.[28] Pachauri noted that reducing meat consumption is an action that anyone can take immediately, and one that can have a significant impact on global warming in a short period of time.

But not everyone agrees. In response to many of the claims of environmental degradation due to livestock production, meat industry organizations have published information in defense of their practices. In a 2003 fact sheet, the National Cattlemen's Beef Association disputes many of the claims made by critics. It states:[29]

- The waste produced by cattle is very minor. In fact, the primary source of methane emissions is from landfills; only about 2% of the total methane production in the United States comes from domestic livestock.
- Much of the land used to raise livestock is not suitable for growing vegetable or grain crops.
- Although many countries have destroyed significant areas of rainforest to provide grazing land for domestic livestock, less than 1% of the total 2001 beef supply in the United States was imported from rainforest countries, and the largest fast-food chains have policies in place that prohibit the purchase of beef from these same countries.
- Although it does take more water to produce a pound of beef than a pound of vegetables, the amount is much lower than claimed by many activists and is only 11% of the total amount of water used in the United States each year.

In addition, although some individuals choose vegetarianism to protect the environment, it is not practical or realistic to expect every human around the world to adopt this lifestyle. Animal products provide important nutrients for our bodies, and many people on the brink of starvation cannot survive without small amounts of milk and meat.

Still, if people were to significantly reduce their consumption of meat, it might be possible to return to the system of small family farming, which is more environmentally friendly. When animals are raised on smaller farms and/or allowed to range freely, they consume grass, crop wastes, and scraps recycled from the kitchen, which is an efficient means of utilizing food sources that humans do not consume. What's more, the waste produced by these animals can be used for fertilizer and fuel.

Critical Thinking Questions

■ Are the data convincing that meat consumption increases global warming?

■ Given the accelerated pace of climate change, as well as land and water degradation, is adopting a vegetarian or semivegetarian diet our ethical responsibility as citizens of the earth?

■ Would such a diet be practical for you?

■ Whether or not you decide to eat less meat, what other actions could you take to reduce the "carbon footprint" of your diet?

7 Metabolism: From Food to Life

Test Yourself | True or False?

1 Every cell of the body is metabolically active. **T** *or* **F**
2 Certain vitamins are essential for producing energy in the body. **T** *or* **F**
3 All excess energy is stored as body fat. **T** *or* **F**
4 The fatty acids stored in adipose tissue are easily converted to glucose. **T** *or* **F**
5 During a period of extreme starvation, the body will use heart muscle for energy and to help maintain blood glucose levels. **T** *or* **F**

Test Yourself answers are located in the Chapter Review.

Chapter Objectives *After reading this chapter, you will be able to:*

1. Distinguish between metabolism, catabolism, and anabolism, *pp. 248–249.*

2. Illustrate the following types of metabolic reactions: hydrolysis, condensation, oxidation–reduction, and phosphorylation, *pp. 249–253.*

3. Explain the role of enzymes, cofactors, and coenzymes during chemical reactions, *pp. 253–254.*

4. Describe in correct order the three stages by which energy is extracted from glucose, *pp. 254–259.*

5. Describe two conditions that are likely to increase ketone formation in the liver, *pp. 261–262.*

6. Explain how the catabolism of proteins differs from the catabolism of carbohydrates and lipids, *pp. 263–265.*

7. Delineate the process by which alcohol is metabolized, *pp. 266–268.*

8. Identify the body's mechanisms for storing excess glucose, triglycerides, and proteins, *pp. 268–269.*

9. Compare the processes of gluconeogenesis, lipogenesis, and amino acid synthesis, *pp. 269–271.*

10. Explain how the states of feasting and fasting affect metabolism, *pp. 273–275.*

Malia, just 12 hours old, was fussing in her father's arms when the hospital pediatrician and a neonatal nurse entered the room. While the nurse soothed Malia, the pediatrician broke the news: The results of a routine screening test had indicated that Malia was born with maple syrup urine disease (MSUD), a metabolic disorder, and further tests had confirmed the diagnosis. He explained that MSUD occurs when a baby lacks an enzyme necessary to break down certain amino acids. If the disorder is not treated, the unmetabolized amino acids quickly build up in the body's tissues, especially the brain, resulting in severe and sometimes fatal neurologic damage. Malia's parents had never heard of MSUD and immediately asked if their daughter would be okay. The pediatrician assured them that when the disease is detected and dietary treatment initiated in the first days of life, children with MSUD develop normally. He explained that Malia would not be able to breastfeed but would have to be fed a special formula low in the amino acids leucine, isoleucine, and valine. "Are you saying that the only thing we have to do to keep Malia healthy is switch her from breast milk to a special formula?" Malia's father asked. "For now, yes," the pediatrician replied. "But as she grows, you'll have to pay careful and consistent attention to her diet." He then scheduled them to meet with the hospital's registered dietitian that afternoon to discuss Malia's dietary needs.

Metabolic disorders such as MSUD, phenylketonuria (see Chapter 4), galactosemia (an error of carbohydrate metabolism), and others are rare, but because they interrupt the normal processes of metabolism, their consequences can be severe or fatal. Why is metabolism so critical to our health and life, and how does it occur? We explore these and other questions in this chapter.

Why Is Metabolism Essential for Life?

Although some people say they live to eat, we all have to eat to live. The food we eat each day provides the energy and nutrients the body needs to sustain life. **Metabolism** is the sum of all the chemical and physical processes by which the body breaks down and builds up molecules. When nutrition researchers burn food in a **calorimeter** to determine how much energy the food contains, carbon dioxide, water, and thermal energy (heat) are released. In a similar way, when the body uses food for fuel, carbon dioxide, water, and energy, both chemical and thermal, are released. Cells throughout the body require chemical energy to grow, reproduce, repair themselves, and maintain their functions. Indeed, every chemical reaction in the body either requires or releases energy. In addition, energy released as heat helps keep us warm. When cell metabolism functions properly, so too will the body.

Anabolism and Catabolism Require or Release Energy

As you learned in previous chapters, the end products of digestion are absorbed into the small intestine and then circulated to the body's cells. There, they may be broken down even further for energy. Alternatively, the cells may use these small, basic molecules as building blocks to synthesize compounds such as glycogen, cholesterol, hormones, enzymes, or cell membranes, according to the body's needs. The process of making larger, chemically complex molecules from smaller, more basic ones is called **anabolism** (**Figure 7.1**). Because the process of anabolism supports the building of compounds, it is critical for growth, repairing and maintaining the body's tissues, and synthesizing the chemical products essential for human functioning. From a small subset of metabolic "building blocks" including glucose, amino acids, and fatty acids, the body is able to use anabolism to synthesize thousands of chemically complex substances.

Anabolic reactions require energy. If you've studied physics, you know that *energy* can be broadly defined as the capacity to perform work. Mechanical energy is necessary for movement, electrical energy sparks nerve impulses, and thermal energy maintains body temperature. The energy that fuels anabolic reactions is chemical energy. How exactly does the body generate this chemical energy?

The food we eat is converted to fuel and other necessary substances through metabolism.

metabolism   The sum of all the chemical and physical changes that occur in body tissues.

calorimeter   A special instrument in which food can be burned and the amount of heat that is released can be measured; this process demonstrates the energy (caloric) content of the food.

anabolism   The process of making new molecules from smaller ones.

Figure 7.1 Anabolic reactions use energy to convert simple chemical compounds into larger, more complex structures. Catabolic reactions degrade complex compounds and produce energy.

Catabolism is the breakdown or degradation of larger, more complex molecules to smaller, more basic molecules (Figure 7.1). The opposite of anabolism, catabolism releases chemical energy. Catabolism of food begins with digestion, when chemical reactions break down the macronutrients we consume. The thousands of different proteins, lipids, and carbohydrates in the human diet are all broken down into the same small group of end products: amino acids, fatty acids, glycerol, and monosaccharides (usually glucose). After absorption, these basic components are transported to body cells. When a cell needs energy, it can catabolize these components into even smaller molecules. Energy is released as a by-product of this intracellular catabolism. Catabolism is also used to break down old cells or tissues that need to be repaired or replaced. The energy gained via catabolic reactions is used not only to fuel the body's work but also to build new compounds, cells, and tissues via anabolism. Thus, in response to our earlier question, the energy to fuel anabolic reactions comes from the body's catabolic reactions.

Overall, a balance between anabolism and catabolism maintains health and function. However, there are times when one of these two processes dominates. For example, fetal and childhood growth represents a net anabolic state, because more tissue is formed than broken down. However, disease is often dominated by catabolism, with more tissue being broken down than repaired. Of course, one goal of treatment is to stop or minimize these catabolic processes and allow the anabolic phase of recovery to begin.

Energy Stored in Adenosine Triphosphate Fuels the Work of All Body Cells

When cells catabolize nutrients such as glucose, they package the energy that is released during the reaction in a compound called **adenosine triphosphate (ATP).** As you might guess from its name, a molecule of ATP includes an organic compound called adenosine and three phosphate groups (**Figure 7.2a**). The bonds between the phosphate groups store a significant amount of potential energy and are sometimes termed *high-energy phosphate bonds.*[1] When these bonds are broken, their energy is released and can be used to do the

catabolism The breakdown or degradation of larger molecules to smaller molecules.

adenosine triphosphate (ATP) A high-energy compound made up of the purine adenine, the simple sugar ribose, and three phosphate units; it is used by cells as a source of metabolic energy.

(a) Structure of ATP

Figure 7.2 **(a)** Structure of adenosine triphosphate (ATP). **(b)** When one high-energy phosphate group is removed, adenosine diphosphate (ADP) is formed. When two high-energy phosphate groups are removed, adenosine monophosphate (AMP) is formed. **(c)** ATP can be regenerated by adding phosphate groups back to AMP and ADP through the process of phosphorylation.

(b) Conversion of ATP to ADP and AMP

(c) Regeneration of ATP

work of the cell. This explains why ATP is often called the molecular "currency" of the cell: Its phosphate bonds store energy to build new molecules, break down old molecules, and keep the cell functioning optimally.

When one high-energy phosphate bond is broken and a single phosphate group released, **adenosine diphosphate (ADP)** is produced (see Figure 7.2b). When two phosphates are removed, **adenosine monophosphate (AMP)** is produced. ATP can be regenerated by adding phosphate groups back to these molecules (see Figure 7.2c).

A small amount of ATP is stored in every cell for immediate use. When cells need more ATP, they can generate it via the catabolism of glucose, glycerol, fatty acids, and amino acids. Thus, the food we eat each day continues to help the body regenerate the ATP required by the cells.

Recap

All forms of life are dependent upon metabolic pathways for survival. A balance between anabolic and catabolic reactions helps the body achieve growth and repair and maintain health and functioning. The body uses and produces energy in the form of ATP.

What Chemical Reactions Are Fundamental to Metabolism?

Metabolic pathways are clusters of chemical reactions that occur sequentially and achieve a particular goal, such as the breakdown of glucose for energy. Cells use different, yet related, metabolic pathways to release the energy in each of the major energy-containing nutrients—glucose, fatty acids, and amino acids. These pathways typically occur within a specific part of a cell. This is because many metabolic enzymes are restricted to one or a few

adenosine diphosphate (ADP) A metabolic intermediate that results from the removal of one phosphate group from ATP.

adenosine monophosphate (AMP) A low-energy compound that results from the removal of two phosphate groups from ATP.

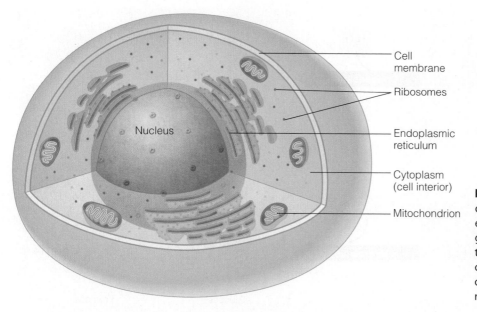

Figure 7.3 Structure of a typical cell. The cell membrane separates the cell from the extracellular fluid. The nucleus contains the genetic information. The cytoplasm contains the organelles, surrounded by a fluid called cytosol. Organelles include mitochondria, endoplasmic reticulum, and ribosomes.

Labels on figure: Cell membrane · Ribosomes · Endoplasmic reticulum · Cytoplasm (cell interior) · Mitochondrion · Nucleus

locations within the cell. As an example, the process of glycolysis, to be discussed shortly, occurs in the cytosol, the liquid portion of the cytoplasm, because all of the enzymes needed for that process can be found in the cytosol. **Figure 7.3** shows the general structure of a cell and its components.

The cell's mitochondria, which might be compared to the furnace in your house, are the location of many other metabolic reactions. The mitochondria contain large numbers of metabolic enzymes and are the primary sites where chemical energy, in the form of ATP, is produced. Cells that lack mitochondria, such as red blood cells, are limited in their ability to produce energy. These cells must rely on less efficient energy-producing processes that can occur in their cytoplasm.

Metabolic pathways are not only limited to certain types of cells and certain cell structures, but they may also be limited to specific body organs or tissues. Glycogen stored in the liver can be catabolized and the resulting glucose released into the bloodstream, yet the catabolism of muscle glycogen does not allow for the release of glucose into the blood. Why the difference? Muscle lacks one enzyme that catalyzes one simple step in the metabolic pathway that is found in the liver.

Although all cells are metabolically active, many nutritionists view liver, muscle, and adipose cells as key locations for the integration of metabolic pathways. As this chapter unfolds, it will be possible to visualize the "networking" of metabolic pathways that occur between these and other body organs.

Before describing each of the unique metabolic pathways involving carbohydrates, fats, and proteins, we will review a few simple chemical reactions common to all of them.

In Condensation and Hydrolysis Reactions, Water Reacts with Molecules

Condensation and **hydrolysis** are chemical reactions involving water. *Condensation* is an anabolic process. It occurs when small, chemically simple units combine to produce a larger, more complex molecule. In the process, water is released as a by-product. Because the water produced is removed from the original molecules, this reaction is also called *dehydration synthesis*. The general formula for condensation reactions is written as follows:

$$A\text{—}OH + H\text{—}B \rightarrow A\text{—}B + H_2O$$

Disaccharides are synthesized from individual monosaccharides via condensation. As discussed in Chapter 4, the formation of a chemical bond between two simple sugars occurs

condensation An anabolic process by which smaller, chemically simple compounds are joined with the removal of water.

hydrolysis A catabolic process by which a large, chemically complex compound is broken apart with the addition of water.

(a) Condensation of glucose and fructose

(b) Hydrolysis of sucrose

Figure 7.4 **(a)** Condensation of glucose and fructose. Glucose and fructose react and, with the release of water, combine through condensation to form sucrose. **(b)** Hydrolysis of sucrose. Sucrose undergoes hydrolysis, with the addition of water, to form glucose and fructose.

when one monosaccharide donates a hydroxyl (OH) group and the other donates a hydrogen (H) group. The condensation of glucose and fructose is shown in **Figure 7.4a**.

Condensation is typically an anabolic process. Its opposite, termed *hydrolysis,* is usually catabolic. In hydrolysis, a large, chemically complex molecule is broken apart with the addition of water. Because the original molecule becomes hydrated, this reaction is also called a *hydration* reaction. Notice that the general formula for hydrolysis reactions is opposite that of condensation reactions:

$$A—B + H_2O \rightarrow A—OH + H—B$$

The disaccharide sucrose, for example, is broken down via hydrolysis to its smaller and chemically simpler components (glucose and fructose). This process is illustrated in Figure 7.4b.

In Phosphorylation Reactions, Molecules Exchange Phosphate

As mentioned, ATP is an energy reservoir within the cell because it contains two high-energy phosphate bonds. When these bonds are broken, energy is released and the inorganic phosphate (P_i) can be transferred to other molecules. The process by which phosphate is transferred is called **phosphorylation**. For example, glucose undergoes phosphorylation when it first enters a cell:

$$C_6H_{12}O_6 + A—P—P—P \rightarrow C_6H_{12}O_6—P + A—P—P$$

Glucose   ATP   Glucose phosphate   ADP

Once glucose is phosphorylated, it can either be stored as glycogen or oxidized for immediate energy (discussed shortly). Another example of phosphorylation is the synthesis of ATP from ADP plus a phosphate group (see Figure 7.2c). The energy required for this reaction comes from the oxidation of energy-containing substrates such as glucose. As you may have guessed, removal of phosphate groups, as in the breakdown of ATP (see Figure 7.2b), is called *dephosphorylation.*

phosphorylation   The addition of one or more phosphate groups to a chemical compound.

In Oxidation–Reduction Reactions, Molecules Exchange Electrons

In **oxidation–reduction reactions,** the molecules involved exchange electrons, often in the form of hydrogen. These reactions always occur together, as electrons gained by one molecule must be donated by another. The molecule that gives up an electron is said to be *oxidized* because typically its electron has been removed by an oxygen atom. The molecule that has acquired an electron is said to be reduced because, in gaining an electron (e^-), it becomes more negatively charged. In the human body, the oxygen needed for oxidation reactions is obtained from the air we breathe. Because they involve the exchange of electrons, oxidation–reduction (or *redox*) reactions are classified as *exchange reactions.*

An example of a redox reaction important to metabolism involves **FAD (flavin adenine dinucleotide)** and FADH$_2$, two forms of riboflavin, one of the B-vitamins involved in energy metabolism. These compounds are required for the enzymes in energy reactions to function. FADH$_2$ is easily oxidized, losing electrons as hydrogen, and forming FAD (**Figure 7.5**). In contrast, FAD is easily reduced back to FADH$_2$ by the simple addition of hydrogen.

The production of energy from the energy-containing nutrients occurs through a series of oxidation–reduction reactions that ultimately yields carbon dioxide (CO_2) and water (H_2O). The oxidation of a fatty acid through this process is illustrated later in this chapter.

Enzymes Mediate Metabolic Reactions

As you know, chemical reactions in living cells are typically mediated by enzymes. During metabolism, one function of enzymes is to channel the energy-containing nutrients into useful pathways. For example, by increasing or decreasing the activity of an enzyme, the body can channel fatty acids toward breakdown for energy or toward storage as adipose tissue. Thus, enzymes are essential to the metabolism of the energy-containing nutrients.

In order to function, enzymes generally require substances called coenzymes and cofactors. **Coenzymes** are non-protein substances (**Figure 7.6**) that provide a functional group that either enhances or is necessary for the action of the enzyme yet is smaller than the enzyme. Both FAD and FADH$_2$ function as coenzymes, as do forms of many other vitamins.[1, 2] **Cofactors** are typically minerals, such as iron, magnesium, or zinc, that are required for enzyme activity. For example, they may help bind different parts of an enzyme together, or they may bind substrates or intermediates of the reaction, thereby helping to speed up the reaction.[1] In short, these non-energy-containing micronutrients are essential to ensure that energy can be extracted from food.

An example of an enzyme-driven metabolic reaction is the phosphorylation of glucose, mentioned earlier. The enzyme that activates this process is **glucokinase.** When glucose concentrations in the liver rise after a meal, the activity of this enzyme increases to handle the increased load, allowing for efficient metabolism of the glucose. Not every metabolic enzyme is as responsive, however. As discussed shortly, the liver enzyme that typically oxidizes alcohol does not increase in response to a sudden increase in alcohol consumption.

oxidation–reduction reactions Reactions in which electrons are lost by one compound (it is oxidized) and simultaneously gained by another compound (it is reduced).

FAD (flavin adenine dinucleotide) A coenzyme derived from the B-vitamin riboflavin; FAD readily accepts electrons (hydrogen) from various donors.

coenzymes The nonprotein component of enzymes; many coenzymes are B-vitamins.

cofactor A small, chemically simple organic or inorganic substance that is required for enzyme activity; trace minerals such as iron, zinc, and copper function as cofactors.

glucokinase An enzyme that adds a phosphate group to a molecule of glucose.

Figure 7.5 Oxidation and reduction of FAD and FADH$_2$. FADH$_2$ is easily oxidized to FAD, which can easily be reduced back to FADH$_2$.

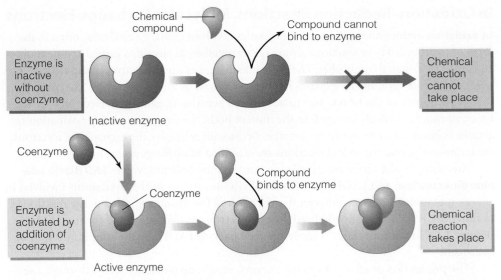

Figure 7.6 Coenzymes combine with enzymes to activate them, ensuring that the chemical reactions that depend upon these enzymes occur.

RECAP

Condensation and hydrolysis are chemical reactions involving water. The reaction in which phosphate is transferred is called phosphorylation. In oxidation–reduction reactions, the molecules involved exchange electrons. Enzymes, coenzymes, and cofactors increase the efficiency of metabolism.

How Is Energy Extracted from Carbohydrates?

As you learned in Chapter 3, most dietary carbohydrate is digested and absorbed as glucose. The glucose is then transported to the liver, where it has a number of metabolic fates:

- The glucose can be phosphorylated, as described earlier, and stored in the liver as glycogen.
- The glucose can be phosphorylated and then metabolized in the liver for energy or used to make other glucose-containing compounds.
- The glucose can be released into circulation for other cells of the body to take up and use as a fuel or, in the case of muscle tissue, store as glycogen.
- The glucose, if consumed in excess of total energy needs, can be converted to fatty acids and stored as triglycerides, primarily in the adipose tissue.

What happens to fructose and galactose, the other dietary monosaccharides? Although there are many other metabolic options for each, both can be (a) converted into glucose through a series of reactions or (b) channeled into the glycolysis pathway (discussed shortly) for energy production. For that reason, and because glucose is the dominant simple sugar in the human diet, this discussion will explore how the body uses glucose as an energy source.

The oxidation of glucose for the production of energy progresses through three distinct stages, each of which takes place in a different part of the cell. The three stages are (1) glycolysis, (2) the tricarboxylic acid (TCA) cycle, also known as the Krebs cycle, and (3) oxidative phosphorylation. Step by step, we will review these metabolic pathways.

In Glycolysis, Glucose Is Broken Down into Pyruvate

The metabolic pathway used by cells to produce energy from glucose begins with a sequence of reactions known as **glycolysis** (**Figure 7.7**). Because glycolysis occurs in the cy-

Most dietary carbohydrate is digested and absorbed as glucose.

glycolysis A sequence of chemical reactions that converts glucose to pyruvate.

tosol, even cells without mitochondria can extract energy from this pathway. Also, because the reactions of glycolysis are anaerobic (that is, do not require oxygen), this short pathway can be completed even when tissues are in an oxygen-deprived state.

During glycolysis, six-carbon glucose is converted into two molecules of three-carbon pyruvate. The first step of glycolysis is the phosphorylation of glucose, which, as described earlier, yields glucose 6-phosphate and ADP. The ATP that fuels this reaction is stored in the cell. Then, several enzyme-driven reactions result in the formation of pyruvate. (These reactions are omitted from Figure 7.7 but included in the complete figure in Appendix A.) Initially the process of glycolysis requires two ATP for the phosphorylation of glucose, but eventually this pathway produces a small amount (four molecules) of ATP, thus yielding a net of two ATP to be used as energy for the cell.

As shown in Figure 7.7, the process of glycolysis is one example of an oxidative pathway, because two hydrogen atoms (with their electrons) are released. These hydrogen atoms are picked up by the coenzyme **NAD (nicotinamide adenine dinucleotide),** derived from the B-vitamin niacin, forming NADH, the reduced form of NAD. The metabolic fate of the newly formed NADH will be explained shortly.

If the pyruvate molecules generated by glycolysis are to be used for the production of energy, they must go through a number of further metabolic steps, which vary depending on whether oxygen is present (*aerobic* environment) or absent (*anaerobic* environment). If energy is not immediately needed by the cell, pyruvate can be used to resynthesize glucose, moving "back up" this stage of the metabolic pathway through a separate series of reactions (see Figure 7.7). This reverse process is known as gluconeogenesis and will be discussed later in this chapter.

In the Absence of Oxygen, Pyruvate Is Converted to Lactic Acid

In the absence of oxygen, the pyruvate produced through glycolysis is anaerobically converted to **lactate (or lactic acid).** This one-step reaction involves a simple transfer of hydrogen. Both pyruvate and lactate are three-carbon compounds, so there is no loss or gain of carbon atoms. In a reversal of the hydrogen transfer that occurred in glycolysis (when NAD$^+$ accepted 2H$^+$ + 2e$^-$ to form NADH + H$^+$), the conversion of pyruvate to lactate involves the transfer of 2e$^-$ + 2H$^+$ from NADH to lactate, leaving NAD$^+$ (**Figure 7.8a**). The production of lactate therefore regenerates the NAD$^+$ required for the continued functioning of the glycolysis pathway.

The anaerobic conversion of pyruvate to lactate occurs in cells with few or no mitochondria, such as the red blood cells and the lens and cornea of the eye. It also occurs in the muscle cells during high-intensity exercise, when oxygen delivery to the muscle is limited. Compared with the entire three-stage oxidation of glucose, the production of energy in this phase of anaerobic glycolysis is not very efficient. The short pathway from pyruvate to lactate does not yield any ATP; therefore, when one molecule of glucose is converted to lactate, the only ATP produced is the two (net) ATP units that were generated when the glucose was initially converted to pyruvate (see Figure 7.8). The anaerobic production of lactate is, however, a way of producing at least a small amount of energy when oxygen is absent or in those cells lacking mitochondria. The production of lactate, also known as lactic acid, also allows the regeneration of NAD$^+$ so that glycolysis can continue. During intense exercise,

Figure 7.7 Overview of glycolysis. In the first stage of glucose oxidation, glucose is converted to pyruvate. A separate pathway provides for the regeneration of glucose via gluconeogenesis, which requires the input of ATP. Net production from glycolysis: two pyruvate molecules, two ATP, and two NADH + H$^+$.

NAD (nicotinamide adenine dinucleotide) A coenzyme form of the B-vitamin niacin; NAD readily accepts electrons (hydrogen) from various donors.

lactate (or lactic acid) A three-carbon compound produced from pyruvate in oxygen-deprived conditions.

Figure 7.8   (a) Anaerobic conversion of pyruvate to lactate. In the absence of oxygen, the body converts pyruvate to lactate. **(b)** Interconversion of lactate and glucose. After the anaerobic production and release of lactate by the muscle, when oxygen becomes available, the liver converts lactate back to glucose. This process, known as the Cori cycle, is discussed in more detail in Chapter 14.

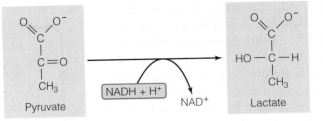

(a) Anaerobic conversion of pyruvate to lactate

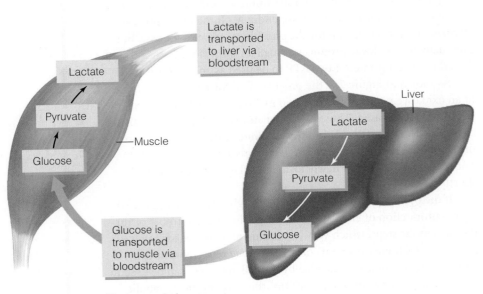

(b) Interconversion of lactate and glucose

Figure 7.9   Aerobic conversion of pyruvate to acetyl CoA. In the presence of oxygen, the body converts pyruvate to acetyl CoA. This reaction links the first and second stages of glucose oxidation. The two pyruvate molecules were generated from glucose through glycolysis.

acetyl CoA (or acetyl coenzyme A) Coenzyme A is derived from the B-vitamin pantothenic acid; it readily reacts with two-carbon acetate to form the metabolic intermediate acetyl CoA.

lactic acid and other acids and metabolic by-products can build up in tissues, especially the muscle tissues, possibly contributing to fatigue and soreness (see Nutrition Myth or Fact? box in Chapter 14, page 555). This is one of the many reasons why individuals cannot sustain high-intensity exercise for long periods of time. After exercise, lactate can diffuse from the muscle cells into the blood, which transports it back to the liver. Then, when oxygen is readily available, it is reconverted to pyruvate, which can be used to synthesize glucose (Figure 7.8b). This cycle of glucose-to-lactate (during oxygen deprivation) followed by lactate-to-glucose (during oxygen availability) will be discussed in more detail in Chapter 14.

In the Presence of Oxygen, Pyruvate Is Converted to Acetyl CoA

In an aerobic environment where oxygen is plentiful, pyruvate is converted to a two-carbon compound known as **acetyl CoA** (**Figure 7.9**). This reaction occurs in the mitochondria and therefore does not occur in red blood cells or other cells that lack mitochondria. The "CoA" is shorthand for *Coenzyme A*, a coenzyme derived from the B-vitamin pantothenic acid. As with the conversion of glucose to pyruvate, the metabolic pathway taking pyruvate to acetyl CoA generates NADH + H$^+$ from the niacin-derived coenzyme NAD$^+$. Pyruvate is a three-carbon compound, whereas acetyl CoA is a two-carbon metabolite. What happens to the other carbon? It ends up within the gas carbon dioxide (CO_2), which the lungs exhale as a waste product.

Unlike the metabolic option to convert lactate to glucose, once pyruvate is metabolized to acetyl CoA, there is no "going back" to glucose synthesis. In other words, there is no metabolic option for the conversion of acetyl CoA to glucose. Once acetyl CoA is produced, it can be further metabolized to produce energy (ATP) or, when the body has adequate ATP, redirected into fatty acid synthesis (discussed shortly).

The conversion of pyruvate to acetyl CoA is a critical step in the oxidation of glucose because it links stage 1 (glycolysis) to stage 2 (the TCA cycle). This reaction also marks the transition of cytosol-based pathways to mitochondria-based pathways. To begin this step, pyruvate moves from the cytosol into the mitochondria, where it is converted to acetyl CoA. Once acetyl CoA is produced in the mitochondria, it cannot be transferred back across the mitochondrial membrane without conversion to another compound called citrate. Thus, acetyl CoA is committed to the TCA cycle for energy production or the conversion to citrate, in which form it can move back out of the mitochondria for fat synthesis.

As this chapter proceeds, it will become clear that acetyl CoA is generated not only from glucose oxidation but also from fatty acid and amino acid catabolism (**Figure 7.10**). You may be familiar with the phrase "All roads lead to Rome." In metabolism, most "roads" (metabolic pathways) lead to acetyl CoA!

The Tricarboxylic Acid Cycle Begins with the Entry of Acetyl CoA

The process of glycolysis has a clear starting point (glucose) and a clear ending point (pyruvate). The linking step (pyruvate to acetyl CoA) also has distinct start and end points. In contrast, the **TCA cycle** is a continuous circle of eight metabolic reactions (**Figure 7.11**). The complete TCA cycle is illustrated in Appendix B, and a condensed version will be used here for simplicity.

Figure 7.10 Metabolic crossroads. Acetyl CoA is generated as a result of carbohydrate, fatty acid, amino acid, and alcohol metabolism.

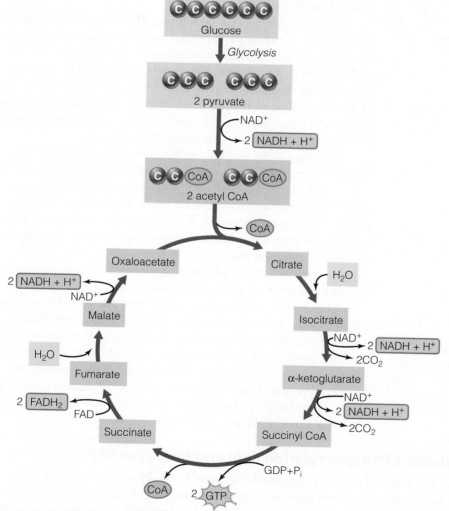

Figure 7.11 Overview of the TCA cycle. In the second stage of glucose oxidation, acetyl CoA enters the TCA cycle, resulting in the release of carbon dioxide, GTP (ATP), and reduced coenzymes NADH and FADH$_2$.

TCA cycle The tricarboxylic acid (TCA) cycle is a repetitive series of eight metabolic reactions, located in cell mitochondria, that metabolizes acetyl CoA for the production of carbon dioxide, high-energy GTP, and reduced coenzymes NADH and FADH$_2$.

The TCA cycle is located in the mitochondria of the cell, which is where all of the necessary metabolic enzymes can be found. The mitochondria are also the location of stage 3 of glucose oxidation (involving the electron transport chain) and ATP synthesis; thus, the transition between stages 2 and 3 is highly efficient.

We think of cycles as self-regenerative, but the acetyl CoA within the TCA cycle does not regenerate. As will be seen, the two carbons that form acetyl CoA end up within two molecules of carbon dioxide. In contrast, the fate of the four-carbon compound oxaloacetate does illustrate the cyclical nature of this stage of glucose oxidation: As shown in Figure 7.11, it is "used up" in the first step of the TCA cycle and is regenerated in the final step. Oxaloacetate and other metabolic intermediates within the TCA cycle are necessary for continued functioning of the TCA cycle; when these compounds are limited, the TCA cycle decreases in activity, and energy production sharply declines.[1]

Although oxaloacetate can be made from some amino acids, dietary carbohydrate is the primary source. The glucose that is derived from dietary carbohydrate can be converted to acetyl CoA (stage 1, Figure 7.11), which can enter the TCA cycle and be converted to oxaloacetate. In contrast, oxaloacetate cannot be synthesized from fatty acids. If a person is following a very-low-carbohydrate diet, such as the Atkins Diet, he or she will have limited ability to produce oxaloacetate, resulting in a slowdown of the TCA cycle.

The first step of the TCA cycle begins with the entry of acetyl CoA into the cycle. As previously explained, pyruvate crosses from the cytosol into the mitochondria, where it is converted into acetyl CoA. The two-carbon acetyl CoA reacts with four-carbon oxaloacetate to form six-carbon citrate (hence the term *citric acid cycle*), and the metabolic cycle begins. By the time all eight metabolic steps are completed, the cycle has produced two molecules of carbon dioxide; this is in addition to the one carbon dioxide produced in the earlier "linking" step.

In addition to the release of carbon dioxide, a high-energy compound known as GTP (guanosine triphosphate), equivalent to one ATP, is produced. Finally, a total of eight hydrogen, with their electrons, are transferred to two coenzymes: NAD$^+$ and FAD, producing NADH and FADH$_2$. These newly formed, hydrogen-rich coenzymes serve as the transition to stage 3, transporting the hydrogen and their electrons to the electron transport chain.

For every molecule of glucose that goes through glycolysis, two pyruvate molecules are generated, leading to two molecules of acetyl CoA. Thus, the TCA cycle must complete two "rotations" for each molecule of glucose. From glycolysis through the TCA cycle, one molecule of glucose produces the following: six molecules of carbon dioxide (including those produced in the "linking step"), two ATP, two GTP, and ten reduced coenzymes (including the NADH from the linking step). Note the low energy output: This small amount will not do much to fuel the activities of the body. The final stage of glucose oxidation is where energy production as ATP assumes a major role.

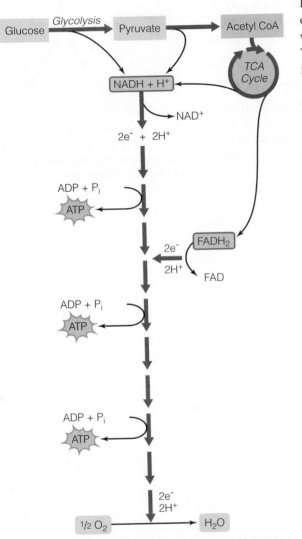

Figure 7.12 Overview of the electron transport chain. In the third and final stage of glucose oxidation, called *oxidative phosphorylation*, additional ATP and water are produced as electrons from NADH and FADH$_2$ and are passed from one carrier to the next along the electron transport chain.

Oxidative Phosphorylation Captures Energy as ATP

The third and final stage of glucose oxidation, termed *oxidative phosphorylation*, occurs in the **electron transport chain** and takes place in the inner membrane of the mitochondria (**Figure 7.12**). The electron transport chain is a series of enzyme-driven reactions or couplings; various proteins, called electron carriers, alternately accept, then donate, electrons. The electrons come from the NADH and FADH$_2$ generated during glycolysis, the linking

electron transport chain A series of metabolic reactions that transports electrons from NAHD or FADH$_2$ through a series of carriers, resulting in ATP production.

step, and the TCA cycle. As summarized in Figure 7.12, as the electrons are passed from one carrier to the next, energy is released. In this process, NADH and $FADH_2$ are oxidized and their electrons are donated to O_2, which is reduced to H_2O (water). The energy released from the reduction of O_2 to water is used to phosphorylate mitochondrial ADP to ATP, thereby capturing the metabolic energy in ATP's high-energy phosphate bonds. Once formed, the ATP can exit the mitochondria for use by all components of the cell.

As mentioned, the final step in the electron transport chain occurs when oxygen accepts the low-energy electrons, reacts with hydrogen, and forms water. If the cell lacks adequate oxygen for this final step, the entire electron transport chain comes to a halt. Oxygen is essential for cellular energy production; without oxygen, cell metabolism stops.

This brings the process of glucose oxidation to a close. The complete process started with glucose and ended with the production of carbon dioxide, water, and ATP. The carbon dioxide was produced in the linking step (pyruvate to acetyl CoA) and the TCA cycle. The water was produced in the final step of the electron transport chain. ATP was produced in various amounts during the three stages.

Finally, the amount of ATP produced by NADH and $FADH_2$ is not exact (about two to three ATP per NADH and one to two for $FADH_2$); thus, different researchers calculate different values. Many biochemistry textbooks report a net of 30 to 32 ATP produced by the complete oxidation of one glucose molecule. Other references (including Appendix A of this textbook) use the range of 36 to 38 ATP per glucose molecule. To the student, this may seem confusing, but the study of nutrient metabolism is rarely an exact science.

RECAP

Glucose oxidation occurs in three well-defined stages: glycolysis, the TCA cycle, and oxidative phosphorylation. The conversion of pyruvate to acetyl CoA is a critical link between glycolysis and the TCA cycle. In the absence of oxygen, the pyruvate is converted to lactate, which can then be "recycled" by liver cells back into glucose. The end products of glucose oxidation are carbon dioxide, water, and ATP.

How Is Energy Extracted from Fats?

The fatty acids used for cellular energy can come from the triglycerides circulating in serum lipoproteins, including the dietary fat in chylomicrons, or from the triglycerides stored in body tissues, including adipose tissue. Because the triglyceride molecule is more complex than that of glucose, there are more steps involved in converting it into energy. Of course, the first step requires that each fatty acid be removed from the glycerol backbone. Through a process called **lipolysis,** dietary and adipocyte triglycerides are broken down by lipases to yield glycerol and three fatty acids. Triglycerides in lipoproteins are broken down through the action of **lipoprotein lipase,** while triglycerides in adipose cells are catabolized by the enzyme **hormone-sensitive lipase.** Whether the glycerol and fatty acids have come from dietary fat or stored body fat, they feed into the same metabolic pathways.

Glycerol Is Converted to Pyruvate

Glycerol, the small three-carbon backbone of triglycerides, does not produce much energy but does serve other important metabolic functions. The liver readily converts glycerol into pyruvate, another three-carbon compound (see **Figure 7.13**). As previously discussed, pyruvate can be converted into acetyl CoA for entry into the TCA cycle (see Figure 7.9) or it can be used for the regeneration of glucose (see Figure 7.7).

Fatty Acids Are Converted to Acetyl CoA

Fatty acids are attached to **albumin,** a blood protein, and transported to working cells in need of energy, such as muscle or liver cells. They are catabolized for energy through a

The first step in breaking down fats, such as fats in the meat and cheese of a taco, is lipolysis.

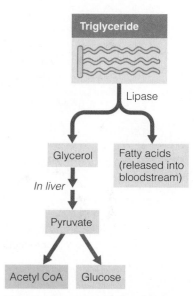

Figure 7.13 Conversion of glycerol to pyruvate. The glycerol derived from the catabolism of fatty acids is readily converted to pyruvate, which can be used for glucose synthesis or be converted to acetyl CoA.

lipolysis   The enzyme-driven catabolism of triglycerides into free fatty acids and glycerol.

lipoprotein lipase   The enzyme that breaks down the triglycerides on chylomicrons, very-low-density lipoproteins (VLDLs), and other lipoproteins.

hormone-sensitive lipase   The enzyme that breaks down the triglycerides stored in adipose tissue.

albumin   A serum protein, made in the liver, that transports free fatty acids from one body tissue to another.

Figure 7.14 Overview of β-oxidation of fatty acids. Fatty acids are sequentially broken down into two-carbon segments that result in the formation of one additional acetyl CoA during each step of the process. A 16-carbon fatty acid yields 8 acetyl CoA units.

process known as **β-oxidation** or **fatty acid oxidation.** This metabolic pathway takes place in the mitochondria, which means that fatty acids must move from the cytosol across the mitochondrial membrane. Before the fatty acids can be transported, however, they must be activated by the addition of Coenzyme A (CoA), the same coenzyme used in the synthesis of acetyl CoA from pyruvate. This reaction requires an "investment" of energy from ATP. The activated fatty acids are then shuttled across the mitochondrial membrane by a compound known as **carnitine.**

Once in the mitochondria, β-oxidation proceeds, systematically breaking down long-chain fatty acids into two-carbon segments that lead to the formation of acetyl-CoA units (**Figure 7.14**). Thus, a sixteen-carbon fatty acid is converted to eight acetyl-CoA units. As the two-carbon segments are cleaved off the fatty acid, high-energy electrons are transferred to the coenzymes NAD^+ and FAD, forming $NADH + H^+$ and $FADH_2$. As with glucose oxidation, the acetyl CoA generated from fatty acid oxidation feeds into the TCA cycle for the production of ATP. The electron-rich coenzymes produced in the TCA cycle feed into the electron transport chain and produce ATP. An overview of β-oxidation is provided in Figure 7.14; a more detailed illustration is provided in Appendix B.

As previously described, the glycerol component of triglycerides also feeds into the TCA cycle after its conversion to pyruvate and acetyl CoA. In summary, the process of extracting energy from triglycerides started with fatty acids and glycerol and ended with the

β-oxidation (or fatty acid oxidation)   A series of metabolic reactions that oxidizes free fatty acids, leading to the end products of water, carbon dioxide, and ATP.

carnitine   A small organic compound that transports free fatty acids from the cytosol into the mitochondria for oxidation.

production of carbon dioxide, water, and ATP (**Figure 7.15**). These are the same three compounds produced during the oxidation of glucose.

As previously noted, because fatty acids almost always have more carbons than the six found in glucose, more acetyl CoA and more ATP are produced during β-oxidation than during glucose catabolism. A single 18-carbon fatty acid yields nearly 3.5 times the ATP than that derived from one 6-carbon molecule of glucose. In addition, fatty acids have relatively few oxygen atoms compared with oxygen-rich glucose (**Figure 7.16**). Fatty acids offer numerous opportunities for oxidation, which results in a higher output of NADH and $FADH_2$, leading to greater production of ATP through the electron transport chain. The result is that fatty acids have a much higher energy potential compared with carbohydrates, approximately 9 kcal/g versus approximately 4 kcal/g.

Fatty Acids Cannot Be Converted to Glucose

Earlier, we noted that the liver is able to convert pyruvate to glucose and that glycerol can feed into glucose production via pyruvate. In contrast, there is no metabolic pathway to convert acetyl CoA into pyruvate for glucose synthesis. Because cells cannot convert acetyl CoA into glucose, it is impossible for fatty acids to feed into glucose production. Again, there is no metabolic pathway that allows for the conversion of fatty acids to glucose.

Ketones Are a By-Product of Fat Catabolism

Recall that the acetyl CoA that enters the TCA cycle can come from glucose or fatty acid catabolism. But the TCA cycle functions only when there is adequate oxaloacetate, a carbohydrate derivative (see Figure 7.11). Thus, if a person is following a very-low-carbohydrate diet, which increases fat catabolism, or has too little functioning insulin to allow glucose to enter cells, oxaloacetate production falls and TCA cycle activity decreases. As fat catabolism continues during this carbohydrate-depleted state, acetyl CoA builds up, exceeding the ability of the TCA cycle to metabolize it, and begins to accumulate in the liver cells.

As the acetyl CoA builds up, liver cells divert it into an alternative metabolic pathway leading to the synthesis of **ketone bodies** (for example, acetoacetate, acetone, and β-hydroxybutyrate or 3-hydroxybutyrate) (**Figure 7.17**). The liver constantly produces low levels of ketone bodies; however, production increases dramatically during times of very low carbohydrate intake, whether from prolonged fasting, starvation,

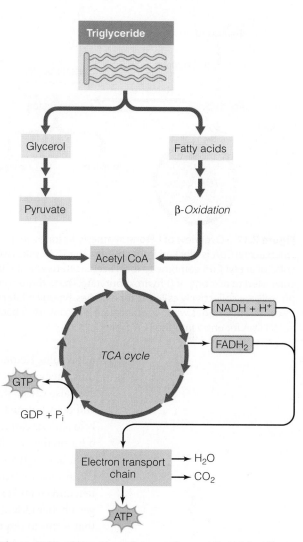

Figure 7.15 Extraction of energy from triglycerides. Glycerol and fatty acids can be metabolized to yield energy as ATP.

Figure 7.16 A comparison of glucose and fatty acid structures. In contrast with glucose, where each carbon is attached to an oxygen, there are many opportunities for oxidation of the carbon-to-hydrogen bonds of a fatty acid.

ketone bodies Three- and four-carbon compounds (acetoacetate, acetone, and β- or 3-hydroxybutyrate) derived when acetyl CoA levels become elevated.

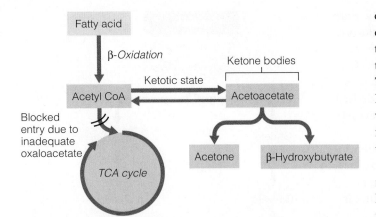

Figure 7.17 Overview of ketone synthesis. Ketones are produced when acetyl CoA is blocked from entering the TCA cycle. Two molecules of acetyl CoA combine to form acetoacetate, which can be converted to acetone or β-hydroxybutyrate. These three compounds are collectively called ketone bodies. Energy is later extracted from ketones when acetoacetate is reconverted back to acetyl CoA for entry into the TCA cycle.

or very-low-carbohydrate diets, as well as in people with type 1 diabetes who require external insulin for glucose transport into the cell. If someone with type 1 diabetes cannot obtain insulin, the body will be unable to maintain oxaloacetate production, the TCA cycle will shut down, and ketone production will increase. Ketone bodies are released from the liver into the bloodstream, where they can be taken up by the cells and used as an alternative fuel by the brain, certain kidney cells, and other body cells when their normal fuel source (glucose) is not available.

The production of energy from ketones is metabolically inefficient because the total number of ATP produced will be lower than what would have been produced through β-oxidation of fatty acids. A little energy, however, is better than none; thus, ketone synthesis provides a backup energy system for carbohydrate-deprived cells.

When the rate of ketone production increases above its use by cells, blood and urine ketone levels rise, a condition known as **ketosis.** Typical blood levels of ketones are < 3 mg/dl in a healthy individual eating a mixed diet but can rise to 90 mg/dl in severe ketosis, as seen in a person with type 1 diabetes without insulin. Ketones are acidic and inappropriately lower blood pH (increasing its acidity); thus, the body attempts to eliminate them by excreting them in the urine. This process, however, also causes dehydration as fluid is lost in the urine. As the pH of the blood falls further and dehydration becomes more severe, **ketoacidosis** occurs. If allowed to persist unchecked, ketoacidosis can result in coma or death. A classic symptom of diabetic ketoacidosis is a fruity odor on the breath that results from increased production of the specific ketone body acetone. Although high amounts of ketone bodies are normally harmful to the body, some medical conditions are treated with ketogenic diets. These medically supervised diets are high in protein and fat and extremely low in carbohydrates (10–20 g/d). See the You Do the Math box to get a better idea of the strict limitations of this medical ketogenic diet. One medical condition that seems to respond to a ketogenic diet is epilepsy, specifically childhood epilepsy that has not responded to other treatments. The ketones produced on this diet appear to reduce the number of severe seizures experienced. The exact mechanism by which the ketogenic diet exerts its antiseizure action is not yet fully understood.[3, 4]

RECAP

Triglycerides are broken down into glycerol and free fatty acids. Glycerol can be (a) converted to glucose via pyruvate or (b) oxidized for energy. Free fatty acids are oxidized to produce acetyl CoA and coenzymes, which can enter the TCA cycle and electron transport chain. The end products of fatty acid oxidation are carbon dioxide, water, and ATP. Fatty acids cannot be converted into glucose. With carbohydrate inadequacy, fat catabolism increases and the excess acetyl CoA is diverted to ketone formation.

Hannah
Nutri-Case

I was walking through the Student Union this morning, minding my own business, when this really attractive guy from biology class comes up to me all friendly, like I'm his long-lost sister or something. "Hannah! Can I walk with you to class?" Now I hardly know this guy, so I just shrugged, "Sure, whatever . . ." Well, before you know it, he's trying to sell me this "awesome"—that's what he kept calling it—weight-loss supplement. He tells me it's full of pyruvate, some kind of chemical that we need to burn fat. He says that if I take it, my body will burn a lot

ketosis Elevated serum levels of ketone bodies.

ketoacidosis A form of metabolic acidosis caused by elevated serum levels of ketone bodies.

more fat, so I'll use up my fat stores and lose weight. By the time we got to class, he had me half-convinced, but the supplements cost $30 a bottle, and I didn't even have that much on me. So I said I'd think about it and maybe buy some next week. But I'm not sure. My mom always says if it sounds too good to be true, it is."

Should Hannah buy the pyruvate supplements? Review the metabolic pathway of β-oxidation and consider whether or not it seems logical that consuming pyruvate supplements would increase the burning of the body's fat stores. Why or why not?

How Is Energy Extracted from Proteins?

As you read in Chapter 6, protein is the preferred substrate for the building and repair of body tissues; however, small amounts of protein can be and are used for energy. The exact amount of protein used for energy will depend on the total energy in the diet and the amount of fat and carbohydrate consumed. The body preferentially uses fat and carbohydrate as fuel sources and prefers to save protein for metabolic functions that cannot be performed by other compounds. Proteins are used as fuel sources primarily when total energy or carbohydrate intake is low.

Dietary proteins are broken down into single amino acids or small peptides.

In Proteolysis, Proteins Are Broken Down to Amino Acids

During protein breakdown, called **proteolysis,** dietary proteins are digested into single amino acids or small peptides that are absorbed into the body; eventually, the small peptides are further catabolized into single amino acids. These amino acids are absorbed then transported to the liver, where they can be made into various proteins or released into the bloodstream for uptake by other cells for their unique building and repair functions. If protein is consumed in excess of what is needed by the cells, some of this protein can be used for energy or converted into fatty acids for storage as triglycerides. Additionally, if we don't eat enough total energy or carbohydrate, the tissues can break down some of the proteins in their cells for energy. This process is explained shortly.

Figure 7.18 The process of deamination. Amino acids are deaminated when the amine group is removed; the remaining structure is known as a keto acid or carbon skeleton.

In Deamination, the Amino Group Is Removed

Under conditions of starvation or extreme dieting, the body must turn to its own tissues for energy, including protein. Amino acids are unique from other energy-containing nutrients in that they contain nitrogen, which must be removed so the remaining carbon skeleton can be used for energy. Thus, the utilization of amino acids for energy begins with **deamination** of the amino acids, which removes their amine (NH_2), or nitrogen, group and leaves a **carbon skeleton** (**Figure 7.18**). The end products of deamination are **ammonia** (NH_3), derived from the amine group, and the remaining carbon skeleton, often classified as a **keto acid.** (Note: Even though the terms *ketone* and *keto acid* appear very similar, they are produced from completely different metabolic pathways and have very different metabolic roles. Be careful not to get the two terms confused!)

After Deamination, the Carbon Skeleton Feeds into Energy Production

The carbon skeleton produced through deamination can be channeled into glycolysis or the TCA pathway to produce energy (**Figure 7.19**). Each of the twenty amino acids identified in Chapter 6 has a different carbon skeleton and is classified into a number of different groups, many of which overlap. We will discuss only two of these groups here:

- The carbon skeletons of **glucogenic amino acids** are converted to pyruvate, which can then be used to synthesize glucose or converted to acetyl CoA for entry into the TCA cycle. The primary glucogenic amino acids are alanine, glycine, serine, cysteine, and tryptophan.
- The carbon skeletons of **ketogenic amino acids** are converted directly to acetyl CoA for entry into the TCA cycle or for use in synthesizing fatty acids. The only totally ketogenic amino acids are leucine and lysine.

proteolysis The breakdown of dietary proteins into single amino acids or small peptides that are absorbed by the body.

deamination The removal of an amine group from an amino acid.

carbon skeleton The unique "side group" that remains after deamination of an amino acid, also referred to as a keto acid.

ammonia A highly toxic compound released during the deamination of amino acids.

keto acid The chemical structure that remains after deamination of an amino acid.

glucogenic amino acid An amino acid that can be converted to glucose via gluconeogenesis.

ketogenic amino acid An amino acid that can be converted to acetyl CoA for the synthesis of free fatty acids.

Figure 7.19   Extraction of energy from amino acids. The carbon skeletons of amino acids can be converted into pyruvate or acetyl CoA or can feed into the TCA cycle at various entry points. The point of entry into the catabolic pathway determines how much energy is extracted from that particular carbon skeleton.

Many of the amino acids can feed into the TCA cycle at various entry points. For example, some amino acids can have both ketogenic and gluconeogenic functions, such as tyrosine, phenylalanine, tryptophan, lysine, and leucine. Because amino acids can have multiple functions, it is difficult to easily fit them into groups. Appendix B shows how the carbon skeletons of the various amino acids can contribute to TCA cycle intermediates, glucose production, and/or ketone body production.

The amount of energy or ATP produced from the catabolism of amino acids depends on where in the metabolic pathway the carbon skeleton enters. The "higher up" the point of entry, such as conversion to pyruvate, the greater the ATP production. No amino acid, however, generates as much ATP as one molecule of glucose or one free fatty acid.

Ammonia Is a By-Product of Protein Catabolism

Whereas some ammonia is useful as a nitrogen source for the synthesis of nonessential amino acids, high levels of ammonia are toxic to the body. Thus, the ammonia generated as the result of the deamination of amino acids must be quickly eliminated. To protect against ammonia toxicity, liver cells combine two molecules of ammonia together with carbon dioxide to form urea, which is much less toxic. **Figure 7.20** illustrates a simplified pathway for urea synthesis; the complete metabolic pathway can be found in Appendix B. The urea produced from amino acid catabolism is released from the liver into the bloodstream, then

You Do the Math
Designing a Ketogenic Diet

As noted in our discussion on ketosis, some children with epilepsy are prescribed a ketogenic diet, in addition to their medication, to reduce the number or severity of their seizures. The benefits of the ketogenic diet for the reduction of epileptic seizures has been known for centuries; accounts of the beneficial effect of fasting on epilepsy are long-standing.[3, 4] American physicians have been using ketogenic diets to treat epilepsy for the past 80 years; however, we still do not know the specific mechanism of how ketones alter brain chemistry to reduce seizures. A medical ketogenic diet is very high in fat and low in both protein and carbohydrate. Although the diet should always be developed and monitored by a registered dietitian and/or physician, you can work through these calculations to get a general idea of the diet plan.

Most children are prescribed a diet providing 4 g of fat (36 kcal) for every 1 g of protein/carbohydrate (4 kcal). A child needing 1,500 kcal/day would be fed 150 g of fat and about 38 g of protein/carbohydrate combined. Estimating the protein requirement at about 20 g per day, that means the child could eat 18 g of carbohydrates each day. In summary, the child's diet would be as follows:

1,500 kcal/day	
150 g of fat	1,350 fat kcal
20 g of protein	80 protein kcal
18 g of carbohydrate	72 carbohydrate kcal

Using the nutrient data from the food composition tables, develop a 1-day menu for this child. High-fat, low-protein/carbohydrate foods include cream, butter, bacon, oils, and so forth. Small amounts of fried chicken or fish would provide fat plus protein, as would nuts and peanut butter.

Obviously, children on a medical ketogenic diet eat very few fruits and vegetables, very little milk/dairy, and few grains/cereals. The dietitian develops a strict plan describing exactly how much of which foods are allowed; a nutrient supplement is also prescribed. Usually, the diet is tried for about 3 months to see how well it works. If there is little or no improvement, the dietitian will usually recommend a return to the normal diet.

Figure 7.20 Overview of urea synthesis. The liver converts highly toxic ammonia, derived from deamination of amino acids, into urea. The urea is then released into the bloodstream for urinary excretion by the kidney.

eliminated by the kidneys in the urine. When the body has to make and excrete a large amount of urea, as occurs with a very high protein intake, the kidney excretes a large volume of urine. This in turn increases the risk of dehydration unless the individual drinks a large amount of water or other fluids.

The processes by which energy is extracted from carbohydrates, triglycerides, and proteins are summarized in Table 7.1.

RECAP

After deamination, the carbon skeletons of amino acids can be used as sources of energy. Glucogenic amino acids are converted into pyruvate, whereas ketogenic amino acids are converted into acetyl CoA. Some amino acids feed into the TCA cycle as various metabolic intermediates. The amine group released as a result of deamination can be transferred onto a keto acid for the synthesis of nonessential amino acids or, via ammonia, converted to and excreted as urea.

Table 7.1 Extraction of Energy from Carbohydrate, Triglycerides, Protein, and Alcohol

Nutrient	Yields Energy as ATP?	Oxidative End Products?	Feeds into Glucose Production?	Feeds into Nonessential Amino Acid Production?	Feeds into Fatty Acid Production and Storage as Triglycerides?
Carbohydrate (Glucose)	Yes	CO_2, H_2O	Yes	Yes, if source of nitrogen is available	Yes, although process is inefficient
Triglycerides: Fatty acids	Yes	CO_2, H_2O	No	No	Yes
Triglycerides: Glycerol	Yes	CO_2, H_2O	Yes, if carbohydrate is unavailable to cells	Yes, if source of nitrogen is available	Yes
Protein (Amino acids)	Yes	CO_2, H_2O, N as urea	Yes, if carbohydrate is unavailable to cells	Yes	Yes
Alcohol	Yes	CO_2, H_2O	No	No	Yes

Alcohol is metabolized in the stomach and liver.

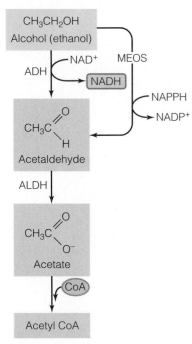

Figure 7.21 Pathways of alcohol metabolism. The primary metabolic by-product of alcohol oxidation is acetyl CoA.

alcohol dehydrogenase (ADH)   An enzyme that converts ethanol to acetaldehyde in the first step of alcohol oxidation.

aldehyde dehydrogenase (ALDH) An enzyme that oxidizes acetaldehyde to acetate.

microsomal ethanol oxidizing system (MEOS)   A liver enzyme system that oxidizes ethanol to acetaldehyde; its activity predominates at higher levels of alcohol intake.

How Is Alcohol Metabolized?

We took an *In Depth* look at alcohol on pages 154–165. Now we're ready to explore how the body metabolizes alcohol. Are there ways to speed up the process? These and other topics are explored here.

Alcohol Is Metabolized Through Oxidation

As with glucose and fatty acids, alcohol is metabolized in a stepwise fashion through a series of oxidation reactions. In people with low to moderate intakes, alcohol is oxidized first into acetaldehyde by the action of **alcohol dehydrogenase (ADH)**, then the acetaldehyde is oxidized by **aldehyde dehydrogenase (ALDH)** into acetate (**Figure 7.21**). Last, acetate is readily converted into acetyl CoA. In people who chronically abuse alcohol, an alternative pathway, the **microsomal ethanol oxidizing system (MEOS)**, becomes important for oxidizing the increased levels of alcohol. Both the ADH and MEOS pathways result in the formation of acetyl CoA. As previously discussed (pages 256–257), acetyl CoA is the primary "fuel" for the TCA cycle and is also generated from the catabolism of carbohydrates, lipids, and amino acids. The oxidation of alcohol into acetaldehyde creates imbalances in two key pairs of coenzymes, NAD^+/NADH and $NADP^+$/NADPH, which contribute to some of the metabolic and health problems associated with chronic alcohol abuse.

The Oxidation of Alcohol Begins in the Stomach

While the oxidation of alcohol occurs primarily in the liver, a small but important amount of alcohol is actually oxidized in the stomach, before it is even absorbed into the bloodstream. This is known as *first-pass metabolism* and occurs via the ADH pathway. The action of gastric (stomach) ADH reduces, rather than simply delaying, the absorption of alcohol by as much as 20%. This enzyme is less active in young women than men; thus, women do not oxidize as much alcohol in their stomach, leaving more alcohol to be absorbed.[5] As a result of this biological difference, women absorb an average of 30% to 35% more alcohol than a similar-sized man consuming the same amount of alcohol. Gastric ADH activity decreases with age in men but apparently not in women, and there also appear to be genetic differences in the amount or activity of this enzyme.[6] Fasting for as little as 1 day prior to alcohol consumption lowers gastric ADH activity, increasing the amount of alcohol absorbed into the bloodstream.

The Oxidation of Alcohol Continues in the Liver

While a small amount is oxidized in the stomach, most of the alcohol consumed by an individual is rapidly absorbed into the bloodstream and transported to the liver, the primary site of alcohol oxidation. In the liver, the ADH pathway dominates at low to moderate intakes of alcohol while the MEOS pathway becomes more important as the amount of alcohol consumed increases. The liver typically oxidizes alcohol at a fairly constant rate, equivalent to approximately one drink per hour. This rate varies somewhat with the individual's genetic profile, state of health, body size, use of medication, and nutritional status. If a person drinks more alcohol than the liver can oxidize over the same period of time, the excess is released back into the bloodstream. The greater the disparity between rate of alcohol intake and rate of alcohol oxidation, the higher the blood alcohol level (**Figure 7.22**).

Despite popular theories, there are no practical interventions that will speed up the breakdown of alcohol: It doesn't help to walk around (skeletal muscles don't oxidize alcohol), consume coffee or caffeinated beverages (caffeine doesn't increase rates of ADH or ALDH activity), or use commercial herbal or nutrient supplements (no impact on rates of ADH or ALDH activity). The key to avoiding the behavioral and physiologic consequences of alcohol is to consume alcohol at the rate of about one drink per hour, which then allows the liver to keep up with intake.

ALCOHOL IMPAIRMENT CHART

FEMALE										MALE								
Approximate blood alcohol concentration										Approximate blood alcohol concentration								
Drinks	Body Weight in Pounds									Drinks	Body Weight in Pounds							
	90	100	120	140	160	180	200	220	240		100	120	140	160	180	200	220	240
0	.00	.00	.00	.00	.00	.00	.00	.00	.00	0	.00	.00	.00	.00	.00	.00	.00	.00
1	.05	.05	.04	.03	.03	.03	.02	.02	.02	1	.04	.03	.03	.02	.02	.02	.02	.02
2	.10	.09	.08	.07	.06	.05	.05	.04	.04	2	.08	.06	.05	.05	.04	.04	.03	.03
3	.15	.14	.11	.10	.09	.08	.07	.06	.06	3	.11	.09	.08	.07	.06	.06	.05	.05
4	.20	.18	.15	.13	.11	.10	.09	.08	.08	4	.15	.12	.11	.09	.08	.08	.07	.06
5	.25	.23	.19	.16	.14	.13	.11	.10	.09	5	.19	.16	.13	.12	.11	.09	.09	.08
6	.30	.27	.23	.19	.17	.15	.14	.12	.11	6	.23	.19	.16	.14	.13	.11	.10	.09
7	.35	.32	.27	.23	.20	.18	.16	.14	.13	7	.26	.22	.19	.16	.15	.13	.12	.11
8	.40	.36	.30	.26	.23	.20	.18	.17	.15	8	.30	.25	.21	.19	.17	.15	.14	.13
9	.45	.41	.34	.29	.26	.23	.20	.19	.17	9	.34	.28	.24	.21	.19	.17	.15	.14
10	.51	.45	.38	.32	.28	.25	.23	.21†	.19	10	.38	.31	.27	.23	.21	.19	.17	.16

FEMALE — ONLY SAFE DRIVING LIMIT: Impairment Begins · Driving Skills Affected · Possible Criminal Penalties · Legally Intoxicated Criminal Penalties

MALE — ONLY SAFE DRIVING LIMIT: Impairment Begins · Driving Skills Affected · Possible Criminal Penalties · Legally Intoxicated Criminal Penalties

Your body can get rid of one drink per hour. Each 1.5 oz of 80 proof liquor, 12 oz of beer or 5 oz of table wine = 1 drink.

Figure 7.22 Effect of alcohol intake on blood alcohol concentration (BAC) and driving behavior. A 180-lb male will experience a BAC of .08 and a significant decline in driving skills after only three drinks.
(*Data from:* Pennsylvania Liquor Control Board and the University of Wisconsin Center for Health Sciences, 1988, and U.S. Department of Transportation Highway Safety Administration, 1992. Available online at http://staff.washington.edu/chudler/alco.html [for female chart]; and Watson P. E., I. D. Watson, and R. D. Batt. 1981. Prediction of blood alcohol concentrations in human subjects—updating the Widmark equation. *Journal of Studies on Alcohol,* 42:545–556 [for male chart].)

Although alcohol itself is a cellular toxin, acetaldehyde also produces specific and damaging effects. The degree to which acetaldehyde accumulates depends on the relative activities of ADH and ALDH. In some ethnic groups, including certain Asian populations, the rate of ADH activity is normal or high and the activity of ALDH is relatively low. When a person with this genetic profile drinks alcohol, acetaldehyde accumulates. This causes a characteristic cluster of signs and symptoms, including facial flushing, headaches, nausea, tachycardia (rapid heartbeat), and hyperventilation (rapid breathing), which are often severe enough to inhibit future intake of alcohol. Researchers have long known that people with this type of enzyme imbalance are at low risk for alcohol abuse because the downside of alcohol intake typically outweighs any pleasurable effect, even at low levels of consumption. Acetaldehyde also contributes to metabolic abnormalities such as inhibition of protein synthesis, increased free-radical production, and increased lipid **peroxidation**.[5]

As an individual's alcohol intake increases over time, the liver's ADH pathway for alcohol oxidation becomes less efficient, and the MEOS pathway becomes more active. As a result of increased MEOS activity, the liver metabolizes alcohol more efficiently, and blood alcohol levels rise more slowly. This condition reflects a metabolic tolerance to alcohol. Compared with light or moderate drinkers, people who chronically abuse alcohol must consume increasingly larger amounts before reaching a state of intoxication. Over time, they may need to consume twice as much alcohol as when they first started to drink in order to reach the same state of euphoria.

People who chronically consume alcohol in more-than-moderate amounts are at significant risk of dangerous drug–alcohol interactions. Thus, a number of pain killers, antidepressants, and other drugs are clearly labeled "not to be consumed with alcohol." What accounts for this risk? The MEOS system is commonly used in the breakdown of many drugs. When an individual is consuming alcohol, however, the MEOS enzymes prioritize alcohol metabolism, leaving the drugs to accumulate. This "metabolic diversion" away from drug detoxification means the medication remains intact, continues to circulate in the blood, and leads to an exaggerated or intensified drug effect. The combination of drugs and alcohol can be fatal, and drug label warnings must be taken very seriously.

Black coffee will not speed the breakdown of alcohol.

peroxidation The continuous oxidation of a compound, such as a lipid, resulting in the formation of a peroxide.

Although the majority of ingested alcohol is oxidized by enzymatic pathways in the stomach and liver, a small amount, typically less than 10% of intake, is excreted through the urine, breath, and sweat. Alcohol is distributed throughout all body fluids and water-based tissue spaces in roughly equivalent concentrations. Increases in blood alcohol concentration are paralleled by increases in breath vapor alcohol levels; this relationship forms the basis of the common Breathalyzer testing done by law enforcement agencies. Some people try to rid themselves of alcohol through saunas and steam rooms, but the amount of alcohol lost through the increased sweat is negligible.

Recap

The majority of ingested alcohol is oxidized in the stomach and liver by pathways involving ADH and ALDH. As an individual's alcohol intake increases over time, these pathways for alcohol oxidation become less efficient and the MEOS pathway becomes more active. The liver oxidizes alcohol at a steady rate of approximately one drink per hour; there is no effective way to speed up the liver's oxidation of alcohol.

How Is Energy Stored?

The body needs stored energy it can use during times of sleep, fasting, or exercise, when energy demands persist but food is not being consumed. The body typically stores extra energy as either fat, in the form of triglycerides, or carbohydrate, in the form of glycogen (discussed in the next section). Although humans appear to have an unlimited ability to store fat, only a limited amount of carbohydrate can be stored as glycogen (Table 7.2). The body has no storage mechanism for amino acids or nitrogen, and the pool of free amino acids in the blood is small. Thus, most of the body's amino acids are bound up in protein molecules. These factors make triglycerides the most useful form of stored energy.

The Energy of Dietary Glucose Is Stored as Muscle and Liver Glycogen

Recall from Chapter 4 that limited amounts of carbohydrate are stored in the body as glycogen, the storage form of glucose synthesized primarily in the liver and muscles. Glucose can easily be stored as glycogen within these tissues, and after an overnight fast, much of the carbohydrate consumed at breakfast is used to replenish the liver glycogen depleted during the night to maintain blood glucose levels.

Overall, the body stores approximately 250 to 500 kcal of carbohydrate as liver glycogen and approximately 800 to 2,000 kcal as muscle glycogen.[7] Of course, the amount of stored glycogen will depend on the adequacy of dietary carbohydrate and the size of the individual: People on a low-carbohydrate diet store very little glycogen, and larger individuals, assuming an adequate dietary carbohydrate intake, can store more glycogen because of the larger size of their muscle tissues and livers. But even in larger individuals, typical body stores of glycogen can be quickly depleted if dietary intake of carbohydrate is low and utilization of glucose as fuel is high. Individuals who participate in endurance exercise are heavy glycogen users. Therefore they need to make sure their glycogen stores are replenished after each workout or competitive event. Chapter 14 explores the process of carbohydrate loading for endurance athletes in detail.

The body needs stored energy during sleep.

Table 7.2 Body Energy Reserves of a Well-Nourished 70-kg Male

	Triglycerides	Glycogen	Protein
Weight	15 kg	0.2 kg	6 kg
Kilocalories	135,000	800	24,000

The Energy of Dietary Triglycerides Is Stored as Adipose Tissue

Whenever we eat in excess of energy needs, the body uses the dietary carbohydrate for energy and preferentially stores the dietary fat as body fat. A number of factors contribute to this preference:

- The conversion of dietary fat to body fat is very efficient and requires little energy.
- Dietary fatty acids can be taken up by adipose tissue cells and converted into stored triglycerides without dramatic changes to the fatty acid structures from their original (dietary) form.
- The conversion of dietary carbohydrates to fatty acids that can be stored within the adipose cells requires a number of metabolic steps and is energy inefficient.
- When dietary carbohydrate is consumed in excess of the body's need, there is an increase in the oxidation of carbohydrate (glucose) over fat for energy, leaving more of the dietary fat available for storage in the adipose tissue.

Thus, when you overeat and consume a large meal, the fat within that meal will probably be converted to body fat and stored, whereas the carbohydrate in the meal will be preferentially used to fuel your body for the next 4 to 5 hours and to replenish glycogen stores.

The Energy of Dietary Proteins Is Found as Circulating Amino Acids

Although the body has no designated storage place for extra protein, some free amino acids circulating within the blood can be quickly broken down for energy if necessary. These free amino acids are either derived from dietary protein or are produced when tissue proteins are broken down. During protein catabolism, cells recycle as many of the amino acids as possible, using them to make new proteins or releasing them into the blood for uptake by other tissues. This process efficiently recycles many of the amino acids within the body, reducing our overall protein requirements from food.

RecaP

The body is able to convert glucose into muscle and liver glycogen, the body's storage form of carbohydrate. Free fatty acids and glycerol are readily reassembled into triglycerides for storage in the adipose tissue, the body's largest energy depot. Technically, there are no protein stores in the human body; a small circulating pool of free amino acids can be used for energy if needed.

How Are Macronutrients Synthesized?

During the process of anabolism, a relatively small number of chemically simple components, including glucose, fatty acids, and amino acids, is used to synthesize a very large number of more complex body proteins, lipids, carbohydrates, and other compounds (recall Figure 7.1). The body also has the ability to synthesize glucose, fatty acids, and some amino acids. The following discussion will explore some of these common anabolic pathways.

Gluconeogenesis Is the Synthesis of Glucose

Glucose is the preferred source of energy for most body tissues and the sole or primary energy source for the brain and other nerve cells. If the supply of glucose is interrupted, loss of consciousness and even death may occur. In the absence of adequate dietary carbohydrate, liver glycogen can sustain blood glucose levels for several hours. Beyond that time, however, if dietary intake is not restored, the body must synthesize glucose from noncarbohydrate substances.

The process of making new glucose from noncarbohydrate substrates is called **gluconeogenesis** (**Figure 7.23**). The primary substrates for gluconeogenesis are the

gluconeogenesis The synthesis of glucose from noncarbohydrate precursors such as glucogenic amino acids and glycerol.

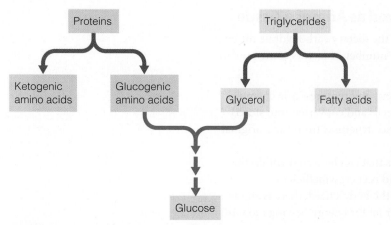

Figure 7.23 Overview of gluconeogenesis. In the absence of dietary carbohydrate and adequate glycogen stores, the body is able to convert glycerol and glucogenic amino acids into glucose.

glucogenic amino acids derived from the catabolism of body proteins or free glucogenic amino acids circulating in the blood. A small amount of glucose can be produced from the glycerol found in triglycerides, although the body cannot make glucose from free fatty acids.

The body relies on gluconeogenesis to maintain blood glucose levels at night when we are sleeping and during times of fasting, trauma, and exercise. Normally, the amount of body protein used for gluconeogenesis is low, but it increases dramatically during times of illness, fasting, or starvation. Protein catabolism for glucose production can draw on vital tissue proteins, such as skeletal and heart muscles and organ proteins. The deadly consequences of this metabolic pathway are described in more detail in the section on starvation.

Lipogenesis Is the Synthesis of Fatty Acids

Lipogenesis is the production of fat from nonfat substances such as carbohydrates, ketogenic amino acids, and alcohol. This process is also called *de novo* **synthesis** of fatty acids, because it is the synthesis of new fatty acids from nonfat compounds. Lipogenesis typically occurs when individuals consume any energy-producing nutrient in excess of energy needs: excess dietary carbohydrate, protein, and alcohol all contribute to lipogenesis.

How does the body convert the six-carbon ring of glucose or the carbon skeleton of an amino acid to a long-chain fatty acid with many carbons? Not surprisingly, the process involves many steps. As shown in **Figure 7.24**, the two-carbon acetyl CoA units derived from glucose, amino acid, and alcohol metabolism are "reassembled" into fatty acid chains. Most lipogenesis occurs in liver cells. The newly synthesized fatty acids are then combined with glycerol to form triglycerides. The liver releases these triglycerides as VLDLs, which then

Consuming an excess amount of carbohydrate, protein, or alcohol will contribute to lipogenesis.

lipogenesis The synthesis of free fatty acids from nonlipid precursors such as ketogenic amino acids or ethanol.

de novo **synthesis** The process of synthesizing a compound "from scratch."

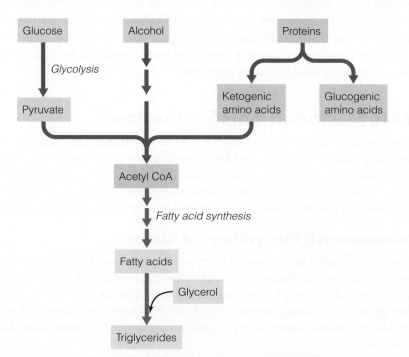

Figure 7.24 Overview of lipogenesis. Acetyl CoA, derived from glucose, ketogenic amino acids, or alcohol, can be converted into fatty acids for eventual storage as adipocyte triglycerides.

circulate in the bloodstream. Eventually, the fatty acids are removed from the VLDLs, taken up into adipose tissue cells, and reassembled into triglycerides for storage as body fat.

The Synthesis of Amino Acids

As discussed in Chapter 6, the human body is capable of synthesizing as many as eleven nonessential amino acids (NEAAs). The body typically makes the carbon skeleton of NEAAs from carbohydrate- or fat-derived metabolites. The amine group can be provided through the process of transamination, where it is donated by one amino acid and accepted by a keto acid (**Figure 7.25**). When the keto acid accepts the donated amine group, it becomes a newly formed amino acid. The synthesis of nonessential amino acids occurs only when the body has enough energy and nitrogen to complete the necessary anabolic steps.

Figure 7.25 Transamination and the synthesis of nonessential amino acids. The amine group of amino acid A is transferred onto keto acid B, resulting in the formation of keto acid A and nonessential amino acid B.

Essential amino acids (EAAs) are distinguished from NEAAs by their carbon skeletons. The carbon skeletons of EAAs cannot be derived from carbohydrate or fat metabolic intermediates; therefore, EAAs must be consumed in their existing form from dietary proteins. Essential amino acids can be degraded or catabolized through several metabolic reactions, but they cannot be synthesized by cellular pathways.

RECAP

The dietary intake of carbohydrates, fats, and protein supplies the body with glucose, fatty acids, and amino acids. If intake is interrupted or inadequate, the body has the ability to endogenously (internally) synthesize glucose, almost all fatty acids, and eleven nonessential amino acids from readily available metabolic intermediates, including pyruvate and acetyl CoA.

What Hormones Regulate Metabolism?

To maintain homeostasis (balanced internal conditions), the body must regulate energy storage and breakdown as needed. A set of anabolic and catabolic hormones helps regulate metabolism (Table 7.3).

The primary anabolic hormone is **insulin,** which increases in the blood after a meal, especially when protein and carbohydrate are consumed. Insulin activates the storage enzymes of the body and signals the cells to take up glucose, fatty acids, and amino acids. These compounds are then converted into glycogen, triglycerides, and body protein. Thus, insulin turns on substrate uptake, emphasizes macronutrient storage, and turns off catabolic processes within the body (see Table 7.3). If endogenous insulin production is inhibited in any way, then exogenous insulin (insulin injections) must be provided.

Conversely, **glucagon, epinephrine,** and **cortisol** are catabolic hormones that trigger the breakdown of stored triglycerides, glycogen, and body proteins for energy. They also turn off the anabolic pathways that store energy (see Table 7.3). As blood glucose drops, glucagon concentrations increase, prompting the body to release glucose from stored glycogen. During exercise, blood levels of epinephrine increase quickly, stimulating the breakdown of stored energy reserves. Cortisol rises during times of energy deprivation and physical stress such as injury or exercise.

A rise in blood cortisol levels also occurs during times of emotional stress and is considered a hallmark of the primitive "fight-or-flight" response. Catabolism of stored energy

insulin A hormone produced by the beta cells of the pancreas that increases cell uptake of glucose and amino acids.

glucagon A hormone produced by the alpha cells of the pancreas that stimulates the release of glucose into the bloodstream.

epinephrine A hormone produced mainly by the adrenal medulla that stimulates the release of glucose from liver glycogen and the release of free fatty acids from stored triglycerides.

cortisol A hormone produced by the adrenal cortex that increases rates of gluconeogenesis and lipolysis.

Table 7.3 Hormonal Regulation of Metabolism

Metabolic State	Hormone	Site of Secretion	Role in Carbohydrate Metabolism	Role in Lipid Metabolism	Role in Protein Metabolism	Overall Metabolic Effect
Fed	Insulin	Pancreatic beta cells	Increases cell uptake of glucose Increases glycogen synthesis	Increases synthesis and storage of triglycerides	Increases cell uptake of amino acids and protein synthesis	Anabolic
Fasted	Glucagon	Pancreatic alpha cells	Increases glycogen degradation Increases gluconeogenesis	Increases lipolysis	Increases degradation of proteins	Catabolic
Exercise	Epinephrine	Adrenal medulla	Increases glycogen degradation	Increases lipolysis	No significant effect	Catabolic
Stress	Cortisol	Adrenal cortex	Decreases cell uptake of glucose Increases gluconeogenesis	Increases lipolysis	Decreases cell uptake of amino acids Increases degradation of proteins	Catabolic

prepares the body to either fight or flee from an enemy, two situations that typically demand high energy. In today's world, we do not typically physically fight or flee from our enemies, so the fatty acids and glucose that are dumped into the bloodstream in response to stress are not utilized as physiologically intended. When day-to-day stresses chronically trigger elevations in blood cortisol levels during physically inactive periods, these metabolically inappropriate responses can increase a person's risk of excessive abdominal fat storage and/or glucose intolerance.

As you can see, a number of catabolic hormones regulate substrate breakdown, and insulin is the major anabolic hormone. Homeostasis requires a balance among these hormones. If one or more of them ceases to regulate properly, normal metabolic controls fail. For example, most people with type 2 diabetes make plenty of insulin, even too much. As described in Chapter 4, however, when the cells of people with type 2 diabetes become insensitive to insulin, they fail to take up glucose for fuel and must turn to glucogenic amino acids. Normally, insulin promotes amino acid uptake and protein synthesis; in people with type 2 diabetes, however, the ineffective insulin response triggers protein catabolism. Thus, normal metabolic controls are lost, and the balance between anabolism and catabolism is disrupted.

RECAP

To maintain homeostasis, the body must regulate energy storage and breakdown as needed. The primary anabolic hormone is insulin, whereas glucagon, epinephrine, and cortisol are catabolic hormones.

Theo
Nutri-Case

"One of the guys on my basketball team just finished a book called the *Pure Protein Path to Power*. The author says if you eat a diet based on pure protein foods, with almost no fat or carbohydrate, you'll gain muscle, but not fat, no matter how much you eat because 'protein makes protein.' He also says it will keep your blood sugar really low, even if you have diabetes, because protein can't be used to make sugar. I think I'll give this diet a try over the next few weeks so I can be in top shape for next season."

What do you think of this author's advice? Are there any foods that are really "pure protein," with no dietary carbohydrate or fat? HINT: Look at the Nutrition Facts labels of high-protein foods such as tuna fish, canned pinto beans, and eggs. Is it true that you can eat as much protein as you want without gaining body fat? And, knowing the definition of *gluconeogenesis*, do you agree with the claim "protein can't be used to make sugar"?

How Do Feeding and Fasting Affect Metabolism?

Although the need for energy is constant, most people eat or fuel their bodies on an intermittent basis. Every night, while we sleep, the body continues its metabolic processes, drawing upon stored energy. In the morning, when we "break our fast," the body receives an infusion of new energy sources. How does the body take advantage of energy when it is available, even if not needed at that moment? And how does it remain metabolically active even in the absence of food intake? The metabolic responses to the cycles of feeding and fasting are explored here.

Metabolic Responses to Feeding

For several hours after the consumption of a meal, food is digested and nutrients are absorbed. The bloodstream is enriched with glucose, fatty acids, and amino acids. Most cells are able to meet their immediate energy needs through glucose oxidation. Only if the meal was very low in carbohydrate would body cells break down fatty acids or amino acids for fuel.

The fed state is generally an anabolic state; after absorption, the end products of digestion are converted into larger, more chemically complex compounds. Glucose in excess of energy needs is converted to and stored as liver and muscle glycogen. Once glycogen stores are saturated, any remaining glucose is converted to fatty acids and eventually stored as triglycerides. Dietary fatty acids are combined with glycerol to form and be stored as triglycerides, largely in the adipose tissue. The liver takes up newly absorbed amino acids and converts some of them to needed proteins. The remaining amino acids are deaminated, and the carbon skeletons are converted to fatty acids for eventual storage as triglycerides. **Figure 7.26** summarizes the interrelated metabolic responses to feeding.

Metabolic Responses to Short-Term Fasting

As the gap between meals lengthens beyond 3 hours or so, the body shifts from its previous anabolic state to a catabolic profile. Without a readily available supply of dietary carbohydrate, the body must turn inward in order to maintain normal blood glucose levels. **Figure 7.27** summarizes these metabolic responses.

Recall from Chapter 4 that muscle glycogen is "reserved" for muscle tissue alone and is not available for normalization of blood glucose levels. Liver glycogen is broken down and glucose is released into the bloodstream; however, the supply of liver glycogen is limited. Most body cells, including muscle cells, are able to switch to the use of fatty acids as fuel, conserving the remaining blood glucose for brain and other cells that rely very heavily on glucose as fuel. As the carbohydrate-deprived state continues, ketone bodies accumulate as fatty-acid-derived acetyl CoA units are blocked from entering the TCA cycle. As the fasted state becomes more prolonged, the process of gluconeogenesis increases in intensity: Glucose is synthesized from glucogenic amino acids (drawn initially from free amino acids in the blood, then largely from the breakdown of muscle protein) and glycerol. These short-term adaptations will provide the glucose and energy needed to meet the body's needs for a few days (see Figure 7.27b).

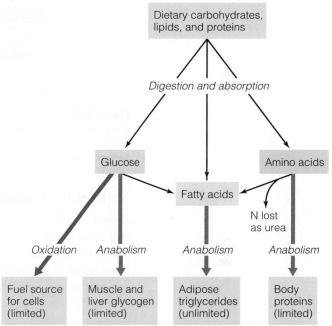

Figure 7.26 Overview of the fed state. Once the energy needs of cells have been met, a limited amount of glucose is converted to and stored as liver and muscle glycogen. Some amino acids are used to synthesize body proteins. Excess glucose and amino acids are converted to fatty acids, which then are used to synthesize triglycerides for storage in the adipose tissue.

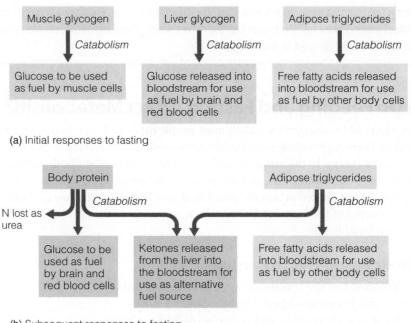

(a) Initial responses to fasting

(b) Subsequent responses to fasting

Figure 7.27 Metabolic responses to short-term fasting. **(a)** In the early stages of a fast, glycogen stores are depleted, and the body increases its use of fatty acids as fuel. **(b)** Subsequent responses to prolonged fasting: Glucogenic amino acids provide some glucose for brain and red blood cells. Ketones and free fatty acids are used as fuel by other body cells.

Metabolic Responses to Prolonged Starvation

After 2 to 3 days of fasting, the body senses an approaching crisis and responds with dramatic changes in its metabolic profile. Whether the starvation is the result of a voluntary action (for example, political protest, religious ritual, or self-defined act) or involuntary circumstances (for example, severe illness, famine, war, extreme poverty), the body shifts into survival mode. There are two overriding problems to be solved: the problem of meeting energy requirements and the problem of maintaining blood glucose levels in support of glucose-dependent cells such as brain and red blood cells. The body must solve these problems while maintaining the integrity of its essential functions, including preservation of skeletal and cardiac muscle, maintenance of the immune system, and continuation of brain function for as long as possible. How, then, does the body meet these challenges?

In response to continued starvation, the body initiates several energy-conserving tactics: As fatigue sets in, there is a sharp decline in voluntary physical activity, core body temperature drops, and resting metabolic rate declines. Overall, the energy needs of the body drop dramatically. In order to meet the remaining energy needs, most cells further increase their use of fatty acids as primary fuel, conserving the limited supply of glucose. Plasma levels of free fatty acids increase sharply as they move from adipose stores to the tissues and cells in need of energy. In addition, the brain shifts away from its normal reliance on glucose and uses ketone bodies for fuel. Plasma ketone levels increase to an even greater extent as they are released from the liver and circulate throughout the body. Yet, even with these adaptations, the need by brain cells for a certain amount of glucose remains.

There are very few options available for solving the body's glucose problem. As stored triglycerides are broken down to provide fatty acids for fuel, the glycerol component is used to provide small amounts of glucose. Glucogenic amino acids, however, remain the major source of glucose for use by the brain. Day after day, the body sacrifices muscle protein in order to maintain a small but essential supply of glucose.

Over time, from weeks to even months later, a new crisis arises: Fat stores become depleted, depriving the body of its most efficient source of fuel. With no other option available, the body turns to its previously protected pools of protein: skeletal muscle, cardiac muscle, protein in organs such as the liver and kidney, and serum proteins such as immune factors and transport proteins. As discussed in Chapter 6, children with marasmus illustrate this final stage of depletion: They have no visible fat stores, their muscles are atrophied, and they lack the reserves to sustain immune, hair, skin, and other protein synthesis. At this final stage, many die of cardiac failure as the heart muscle becomes too wasted to properly function. Others die of infections, lacking normal immune responses.

How long can a person survive complete starvation? Obviously, the need for water is critical; a person will die of dehydration long before reaching these final stages of prolonged starvation. Prior health and nutritional status play an important role: If a person enters starvation with large stores of body fat, his or her survival will be prolonged. If a person has good muscle mass and adequate nutrient stores, he or she is also at a slight advantage. The elderly and young children are more susceptible to the effects of starvation. Most previously healthy adults can survive without food for 1 to 3 months, assuming no illness or trauma and an adequate supply of water. Extreme environmental conditions and increased physical activity shorten survival time.

RecaP

In the fed state, the body assumes an anabolic profile, converting newly absorbed glucose, fatty acids, and amino acids into stored glycogen and triglycerides, and synthesizing some proteins. During short-term fasts, the body mobilizes stored glycogen and triglycerides to meet its need for glucose and energy. If the fasted state persists, more extreme adaptations to glucose and energy deficits occur. The body relies heavily on fatty acids and ketones as fuel sources and catabolizes proteins for gluconeogenesis. Over time, body fat and protein stores are so depleted that death occurs.

See for Yourself
Galactosemia

Galactosemia is a metabolic disorder that develops when one or more enzymes in the pathway to break down galactose are abnormal or missing. If left untreated, galactose builds up in the bloodstream and body tissues, leading to cataracts, enlarged liver, developmental disabilities, and early death. Luckily, strict limitation of dietary galactose lowers the risk of these health problems.

Galactose is one of the two monosaccharides that make up lactose, so greatly reducing dietary intake of lactose will lower galactose intake. Easy enough, you may think: Just avoid milk, cheese, yogurt, ice cream, and other dairy products. You may be surprised, however, at the number of different foods that contain lactose or milk-based ingredients. Each of these foods represents a "hidden" source of galactose that would create problems for a person with galactosemia.

Next time you are at the supermarket, carefully look at the labels of foods such as bologna and other processed meats; cream soups or chowders; breaded frozen fish; and baked goods such as breads, cakes, and cookies. Look for the following milk or milk-based ingredients:

- Nonfat dry milk or milk solids
- Lactose
- Whey protein or whey solids
- Casein, caseinates, or hydrolyzed casein
- Milk chocolate

Every time you find a label with one of those ingredients, you have found a food that is forbidden or strictly limited in the diet of a person with galactosemia. Would you have trouble following this diet?

Chapter Review

Test Yourself | Answers

1 (T) All cells are metabolically active, but liver, muscle, and adipose cells are key locations for integration of metabolic pathways.
2 (T) Two vitamins that help produce energy from the macronutrients are riboflavin and niacin.
3 (F) Carbohydrate is stored in the liver or muscle as glycogen. We also store smaller amounts of glycogen in certain organs, such as the heart.
4 (F) There is no metabolic pathway by which fatty acids can be converted into glucose.
5 (T) During periods of starvation, body proteins are catabolized and their glucogenic

Summary

- Metabolism is the sum of all the chemical and physical processes by which the body breaks down and builds up molecules.

- All forms of life maintain a balance between anabolic and catabolic reactions, which determines if the body achieves growth and repair or if it persists in a state of loss.

- Metabolic pathways are clusters of chemical reactions that occur sequentially and achieve a particular goal, such as the breakdown of glucose for energy. These pathways are carefully controlled, either turned on or off, by hormones released within the body.

- Condensation and hydrolysis are chemical reactions involving water, whereas phosphorylation is a chemical reaction in which phosphate is transferred. In oxidation–reduction reactions, the molecules involved exchange electrons.

- Enzymes, coenzymes, and cofactors increase the efficiency of metabolism.

- Glucose oxidation occurs in three well-defined stages: glycolysis, the TCA cycle, and oxidative phosphorylation via the electron transport chain. The end products of glucose oxidation are carbon dioxide, water, and ATP.

- During glycolysis, six-carbon glucose is converted into two molecules of three-carbon pyruvate. If glycolysis is anaerobic, this pyruvate is converted to lactic acid. If glycolysis is aerobic, this pyruvate is converted to acetyl CoA and enters the TCA cycle.

- During the TCA cycle, acetyl CoA coming from either carbohydrate, fat, or protein metabolism results in the production of

GTP or ATP, NADH, and $FADH_2$. These two final compounds go through oxidative phosphorylation (as part of the electron transport chain) to produce energy.

- During oxidative phosphorylation, the NADH and the $FADH_2$ enter the electron transport chain where, through a series of reactions, ATP is produced.

- Triglycerides are broken down into glycerol and free fatty acids. Glycerol can be (a) converted to glucose or (b) oxidized for energy. Free fatty acids are oxidized for energy but cannot be converted into glucose. In a carbohydrate-depleted state, fatty acids are diverted to ketone formation. The end products of fatty acid oxidation are carbon dioxide, water, and ATP.

- After deamination, the carbon skeletons of amino acids can be oxidized for energy. The carbon skeletons of glucogenic amino acids are converted into pyruvate, whereas those of ketogenic amino acids are converted into acetyl CoA. Some amino acids feed into the TCA cycle as various metabolic intermediates. The end products of amino acid oxidation are carbon dioxide, water, ATP, and urea.

- The amine group released as a result of deamination can be transferred onto a keto acid for the synthesis of nonessential amino acids or, via ammonia, converted to and excreted as urea.

- Alcohol metabolism begins in the stomach, where up to 20% of the alcohol consumed is oxidized. The remainder is oxidized in the liver. At high intakes, some alcohol continues to circulate in the blood because the liver oxidizes alcohol at a steady rate of approximately one drink per hour.

- The body extracts energy from glucose, fatty acids, glycerol, and amino acids. Glycogen is the body's storage form of carbohydrate. Triglycerides in the adipose tissue form the body's largest energy depot. Technically, there are no protein stores in the human body.

- The dietary intake of carbohydrates, fats, and protein supplies the body with glucose, fatty acids, and amino acids. If intake is inadequate, the body synthesizes glucose, almost all fatty acids, and eleven nonessential amino acids from readily available metabolic intermediates.

- The primary substrates for gluconeogenesis are the glucogenic amino acids. A small amount of glucose can be produced from glycerol, but the body cannot make glucose from fatty acids.

- Excess dietary carbohydrate, protein, and alcohol all contribute to lipogenesis and triglyceride storage.

- The body can make the carbon skeleton of NEAAs from carbohydrate- or fat-derived metabolites. The amine group can be provided through the process of transamination. The carbon skeletons of EAAs cannot be derived from carbohydrate or fat metabolic intermediates; therefore, EAAs must be consumed in their existing form from dietary proteins.

- To maintain homeostasis, the body must regulate energy storage and breakdown as needed. The primary anabolic hormone is insulin, whereas glucagon, epinephrine, and cortisol are catabolic hormones.

- In the fed state, the body converts newly absorbed glucose, fatty acids, and amino acids into stored glycogen and triglycerides.

- During short-term fasts, the body uses stored glycogen and triglycerides for glucose and energy. If the fast persists, the body relies heavily on fatty acids and ketones for fuel and initiates gluconeogenesis from glycerol and glucogenic amino acid to meet its glucose requirements. Over time, body fat and protein stores are so depleted that death occurs.

Review Questions

1. One by-product of anaerobic glucose metabolism is
   a. lactic acid.
   b. acetyl CoA.
   c. oxaloacetate.
   d. six molecules of NADH.

2. Mitochondria are often called the cell's
   a. energy currency.
   b. power plant.
   c. fat producer.
   d. fat storage center.

3. In which of the following types of chemical reactions is a molecule catabolized by the addition of a molecule of water?
   a. hydrolysis
   b. condensation
   c. oxidation
   d. phosphorylation

4. Anya skipped breakfast this morning. It is now mid-afternoon, and she has joined a friend for a late lunch. Although she rarely drinks alcohol, while waiting for her food to arrive, she enjoys a glass of wine. Which of the following statements best describes Anya's body's response to the alcohol?
   a. Gastric ADH oxidizes about 30% to 35% of the alcohol Anya consumes; the rest is absorbed into her bloodstream.
   b. When the alcohol enters Anya's bloodstream, her muscles quickly take it up for oxidation before her blood alcohol level increases.
   c. The microsomal ethanol oxidizing system breaks down about 20% of the alcohol Anya consumes before it is absorbed into her bloodstream.
   d. None of the above statements is true.

5. Glucogon, epinephrine, and cortisol are
   a. coenzymes.
   b. cofactors.
   c. anabolic hormones.
   d. catabolic hormones.

6. **True or false?** Liver synthesis of urea increases as dietary protein intake increases.

7. **True or false?** The body stores enough glycogen to last about 5 to 7 days.

8. **True or false?** Glucogenic amino acids can be converted into glucose during prolonged starvation.

9. **True or false?** The body requires energy to catabolize larger molecules into smaller molecules.

10. **True or false?** During glycolysis, glucose, a six-carbon compound, is converted to two molecules of pyruvate, a three-carbon compound.

11. Explain the statement that, within the electron transport chain, energy is captured in ATP.

12. Describe the process of fatty acid oxidation.

13. An elderly patient who has type 1 diabetes is admitted to the hospital in a state of severe ketoacidosis. The patient is comatose, but an elderly friend tells the admitting staff that he thinks his companion is sick because recently she has not had enough money to buy insulin. Describe a possible series of physiologic events that might have led to her ketoacidosis.

14. Review the information you learned about phenylketonuria (PKU) in Chapter 4, then describe the physiologic events likely to occur in a child with phenylketonuria who, unknown to his parents, goes off his diet every day at school and eats whatever his friends are eating.

15. Your Aunt Winifred has been overweight her entire life. Recently, she began a very strict semistarvation diet because it promises that "all the weight you lose will be fat." What information could you share with her that would explain why her weight loss will include loss of body protein, not just body fat?

Web Links

www.nutritionandmetabolism.com
Nutrition and Metabolism
An online, peer-reviewed journal with articles concerning the integration of nutrition, exercise physiology, clinical investigations, and metabolism.

www.msud-support.org
MSUD Family Support Group
This site offers practical advice for families with a child diagnosed with maple syrup urine disease (MSUD). There are updates on dietary products, treatment options, and research projects as well as links to local networks.

www.pkuparents.org
California Coalition for PKU and Allied Disorders
This Web site directs users to support groups within their home state and provides updates on newly developed nutritional products for persons with PKU.

References

1. Champe, P. C., R. A. Harvey, and D. R. Ferrier. 2008. *Lippincott's Illustrated Reviews: Biochemistry.* 4th ed. Philadelphia: Lippincott Williams & Wilkins.
2. *Stedman's Medical Dictionary.* 5th ed. 2005. Philadelphia: Lippincott Williams & Wilkins.
3. Zupec-Kania, B. A., and E. Spellman. 2008. An overview of the ketogenic diet for pediatric epilepsy. *Nutr. Clinic. Pract.* 23(6):589–596.
4. Freeman, J. M., E. H. Kossoff, and A. L. Hartman. 2007. The ketogenic diet: One decade later. *Pediatrics* 119(3):535–543.
5. Caballeria, J. 2003. Current concepts in alcohol metabolism. *Annals Hepatology* 2(2):60–68.
6. Suter, P. M. 2006. Alcohol: The role in health and nutrition. In: B. A. Bowman and R. M. Russell, eds. *Present Knowledge in Nutrition, Volume I.* 9th ed. Washington, DC: ILSI Press, pp. 138–156.
7. Manore, M., N. Meyer, and J. Thompson. 2009. *Sport Nutrition for Health and Performance.* 2nd ed. Champaign, IL: Human Kinetics.
8. Kreider, R. G., A. L. Almada, J. Antonio, C. Broeder, C. Earnest, M. Greenwood, T. Incledon, D. S. Kalman, S. M. Kleiner, B. Leutholtz, L. M. Lowery, R. Mendel, J. R. Stout, D. S. Willoughby, and T. N. Ziegenfuss. 2004. ISSN exercise and sport nutrition review: Research and recommendations. *J. Int. Soc. Sports Nutr.* 1(1):1–44.
9. Brass, E. P. 2004. Carnitine and sports medicine: Use or abuse? *Ann. NY Acad. Sci.* 1033:67–78.
10. Villani R. G., J. Gannon, M. Self, and P. A. Rich. 2000. L-carnitine supplementation combined with aerobic training does not promote weight loss in moderately obese women. *Int. J. Sport. Nutr. Exerc. Metab.* 10:199–207.
11. Stephens, F. B., D. Constantin-Teodosiu, and P. L. Greenhaff. 2007. New insights concerning the role of carnitine in the regulation of fuel metabolism in skeletal muscle. *J. Physiol.* 581(2):431–444.
12. Calvani, M. P. Benatti, A. Mancinelli, S. D'Iddio, V. Giordano, A. Koverech, A. Amato, and E. P. Brass. 2004. Carnitine replacement in end-stage renal disease and hemodialysis. *NY Ann. Acad. Sci.* 1033:52–66.

Carnitine Supplements: A Fat-Burning Miracle?

Product labels, magazine advertisements, and TV infomercials practically shout the term "fat burner" in trying to convince consumers of the value of carnitine supplements; for years, carnitine has been included in many so-called weight-loss products.[8] The appeal of their claim is undeniable: Use this product, and body fat will "melt" away.

As previously explained, carnitine shuttles fatty acids across the mitochondrial membrane. Fatty acids are oxidized along the inside of the mitochondrial membrane because that is where the enzymes of the β-oxidation pathway are found. If fatty acids can't get across the mitochondrial membrane, they will not be oxidized as a fuel and will accumulate. It seems logical, then, that carnitine supplements will increase fat oxidation and decrease body fat stores. But do they? There are two arguments often used in marketing carnitine supplements: (1) Many people are low in carnitine, and so would benefit from carnitine supplements, and (2) even healthy people with normal carnitine levels could lower their body fat by taking extra carnitine. How do these arguments hold up?

Looking at the first issue: Are many people low in carnitine? Two important pieces of information are often left out of advertisements for carnitine supplements: (1) Carnitine is widely available from a large number of foods, and (2) humans synthesize carnitine in amounts that fully meet the needs of healthy people. Food sources of carnitine include meat, poultry, fish, and dairy products; healthy children and adults on a mixed diet get all the carnitine needed from their normal diet. What about vegetarians and vegans? It is true that they *eat* much less dietary carnitine than nonvegetarians, but the body can easily synthesize it from the amino acids lysine and methionine. Lysine is found in legumes, including soybeans, whereas methionine is plentiful in grains, nuts, and seeds. Vegetarians commonly consume these foods in abundant amounts. As long as their diets provide enough of these foods, as well as the iron, niacin, vitamin B_6, and vitamin C used as cofactors, healthy vegetarians and vegans can meet their need for carnitine through endogenous (internal) synthesis. So, well-nourished healthy people—vegetarians and vegans included—are rarely, if ever, low in carnitine.

What about the second claim? Do high doses of carnitine supplements benefit overweight or obese persons? Manufacturers promote carnitine supplements as "fat burners" by implying that high intakes will increase blood levels, then muscle levels, of carnitine. Once in the muscle, the advertisements suggest, the carnitine would trigger fat oxidation and "burn up" body fat. Most studies have shown that taking large doses of carnitine, for up to 2 weeks, does not increase muscle carnitine levels, and so would have no effect on body fat oxidation.[9] In addition, carnitine supplementation had no impact on weight loss in obese women.[10] Overall, well-controlled research has failed to support either of the claims made by those marketing carnitine supplements to healthy persons.

Are there any situations where carnitine supplements are useful? Yes, but they are limited to a small number of unusual situations. Persons with rare genetic metabolic defects must be provided with supplementary carnitine because they are unable to synthesize or utilize it;[11] patients with chronic kidney failure or those on dialysis treatment for kidney failure are often supplemented with carnitine as well.[12] In general, however, there is no evidence to support the claims that carnitine supplements increase the body's rate of fat oxidation or reduce body fat in healthy adults. The only "burning" you might experience when buying carnitine supplements is that of the money in your wallet!

Critical Thinking Questions

- What lessons can we learn from the marketing of carnitine supplements?

- If a label or advertising claim seems logical, does that mean it's necessarily true? What's the difference?

- Even if a substance is necessary for normal body functioning, does that mean consuming extra amounts of it will be beneficial? Why or why not?

- Are supplement manufacturers the most reliable sources of information about human physiology? Why or why not? If not, who or what would be a better source?

Read on.

Have you heard the one about the college student on the junk-food diet who developed scurvy, a disease caused by inadequate intake of vitamin C? This "urban legend" seems to circulate on most college campuses every year, but that might be because there's some truth behind it. Away from their families, many college students do adopt diets that are deficient in one or more micronutrients. For instance, some students adopt a vegan diet with insufficient iron, whereas others stop choosing foods rich in calcium and vitamin D. Why is it important to consume adequate levels of the micronutrients, and exactly what constitutes a micronutrient, anyway? This *In Depth* explores the discovery of micronutrients, their classification and naming, and their impact on our health.

Discovering the "Hidden" Nutrients

As you recall from Chapter 1, there are three general classes of nutrients. Fluids provide water, which is essential for our survival and helps regulate many body functions. Macronutrients, which include carbohydrates, fats, and proteins, provide energy; thus, we need to consume them in relatively large amounts. **Micronutrients,** which include vitamins and minerals, are needed in much smaller amounts. They assist body functions such as energy metabolism and the formation and maintenance of healthy cells and tissues.

Much of our knowledge of vitamins and minerals comes from accidental observations of animals and humans. For instance, in the 1890s, a Dutch physician by the name of C. Eijkman noticed that chickens fed polished rice developed paralysis, which could be reversed by feeding them whole-grain rice. Noting the high incidence of beriberi, which results in extensive nerve damage, among hospital patients fed polished rice, he hypothesized that a highly refined diet was the main cause of beriberi. We now know that whole-grain rice, with its nutrient-rich bran layer, contains the vitamin thiamin and that thiamin deficiency results in beriberi. Similarly, in the early 1900s, it was observed that Japanese children living in fishing villages rarely developed a type of blindness common among Japanese children who did not eat fish. Experiments soon showed that cod liver oil, chicken liver, and eel fat prevented the disorder. We now know that each of

---

micronutrients Nutrients needed in relatively small amounts to support normal health and body functions. Vitamins and minerals are micronutrients.

these foods contains vitamin A, which is essential for healthy vision.

Such observations were followed by years of laboratory research before nutritionists came to fully accept the idea that very small amounts of substances present in food were critical to good health. In 1906, the term *accessory factors* was coined by the English scientist F. G. Hopkins; we now categorize these accessory factors as vitamins and minerals.

How Are Vitamins Classified?

Vitamins are carbon-containing compounds that regulate a wide range of body processes. Of the thirteen vitamins recognized as essential, humans can synthesize only small amounts of vitamins D and K, so we must consume virtually all of the vitamins in our diets. Almost everyone who eats a varied and healthful diet can readily meet their vitamin needs from foods alone. The exceptions to this will be discussed shortly.

Fat-Soluble Vitamins

Vitamins A, D, E, and K are **fat-soluble vitamins** (Table 1). They are found in the fatty portions of foods (butterfat, cod liver oil, corn oil, and so on) and are absorbed along with dietary fat. Fat-containing meats, dairy products, nuts, seeds, vegetable oils, and avocados are all sources of one or more fat-soluble vitamins.

In general, the fat-soluble vitamins are readily stored in the body's adipose tissue; thus, we don't need to consume them every single day. While this may simplify day-to-day menu planning, there is also a disadvantage to our ability to store these nutrients. When we consume more of them than we can use, they build up in the adipose tissue, liver, and other tissues and can reach toxic levels. Symptoms of fat-soluble vitamin toxicity, described in Table 1, include damage to our hair, skin, bones, eyes, and nervous system. Overconsumption of vitamin supplements is the most common cause of vitamin toxicity in the United States; rarely do our dietary choices lead to toxicity. Of the four fat-soluble vitamins, vitamins A and D are the most toxic; **megadosing** with ten or more times the recommended intake of either can result in irreversible organ damage and even death.

---

vitamins   Micronutrients that contain carbon and assist us in regulating our bodies' processes. They are classified as water-soluble or fat-soluble.

fat-soluble vitamins   Vitamins that are not soluble in water but are soluble in fat. These include vitamins A, D, E, and K.

megadosing   Taking a dose of a nutrient that is 10 or more times greater than the recommended amount.

Vitamins and Minerals: Micronutrients with Macro Powers

Want to find out . . .

- how a few fortunate accidents led to the discovery of micronutrients?
- where vitamins and minerals come from?
- why large doses of certain micronutrients could kill you—and which ones?
- whether micronutrient supplements have the same health benefits as nutrients in whole foods?

Fruits contain many vitamins.

Table 1 Fat-Soluble Vitamins

Vitamin Name	Primary Functions	Recommended Intake*	Reliable Food Sources	Toxicity/Deficiency Symptoms
A (retinol, retinal, retinoic acid)	Required for ability of eyes to adjust to changes in light Protects color vision Assists cell differentiation Required for sperm production in men and fertilization in women Contributes to healthy bone Contributes to healthy immune system	RDA: Men = 900 μg/day Women = 700 μg/day UL = 3,000 μg/day	Preformed retinol: Beef and chicken liver, egg yolks, milk Carotenoid precursors: Spinach, carrots, mango, apricots, cantaloupe, pumpkin, yams	*Toxicity:* Fatigue; bone and joint pain; spontaneous abortion and birth defects of fetuses in pregnant women; nausea and diarrhea; liver damage; nervous system damage; blurred vision; hair loss; skin disorders *Deficiency:* Night blindness, xerophthalmia; impaired growth, immunity, and reproductive function
D (cholecalciferol)	Regulates blood calcium levels Maintains bone health Assists cell differentiation	AI (assumes that person does not get adequate sun exposure): Adult aged 19 to 50 = 5 μg/day Adult aged 50 to 70 = 10 μg/day Adult aged > 70 = 15 μg/day UL = 50 μg/day	Canned salmon and mackerel, milk, fortified cereals	*Toxicity:* Hypercalcemia *Deficiency:* Rickets in children; osteomalacia and/or osteoporosis in adults
E (tocopherol)	As a powerful antioxidant, protects cell membranes, polyunsaturated fatty acids, and vitamin A from oxidation Protects white blood cells Enhances immune function Improves absorption of vitamin A	RDA: Men = 15 mg/day Women = 15 mg/day UL = 1,000 mg/day	Sunflower seeds, almonds, vegetable oils, fortified cereals	*Toxicity:* Rare *Deficiency:* Hemolytic anemia; impairment of nerve, muscle, and immune function
K (phylloquinone, menaquinone, menadione)	Serves as a coenzyme during production of specific proteins that assist in blood coagulation and bone metabolism	AI: Men = 120 μg/day Women = 90 μg/day	Kale, spinach, turnip greens, brussels sprouts	*Toxicity:* None known *Deficiency:* Impaired blood clotting; possible effect on bone health

*Abbreviations: RDA, Recommended Dietary Allowance; UL, upper limit; AI, Adequate Intake.

Even though we can store the fat-soluble vitamins, deficiencies can occur, especially in people who have a disorder that reduces their ability to absorb dietary fat. In addition, people who are "fat phobic," or eat very small amounts of dietary fat, are at risk for a deficiency. The consequences of fat-soluble vitamin deficiencies, described in Table 1, include osteoporosis, the loss of night vision, and even death in the most severe cases.

Water-Soluble Vitamins

Vitamin C (ascorbic acid) and the B vitamins (thiamin, riboflavin, niacin, vitamin B$_6$, vitamin B$_{12}$, folate, pantothenic acid, and biotin) are all **water-soluble vitamins** (Table 2). They are found in a wide variety of foods, in-

cluding whole grains, fruits, vegetables, meats, and dairy products. They are easily absorbed through the intestinal tract directly into the bloodstream, where they then travel to target cells.

With the exception of vitamin B$_{12}$, we do not store large amounts of water-soluble vitamins. Instead, our kidneys filter from our bloodstream any excess amounts, and they are excreted in urine. Because we do not store large amounts of these vitamins in our

Avocados are a source of fat-soluble vitamins.

---

water-soluble vitamins Vitamins that are soluble in water. These include vitamin C and the B-vitamins.

Table 2 Water-Soluble Vitamins

Vitamin Name	Primary Functions	Recommended Intake*	Reliable Food Sources	Toxicity/Deficiency Symptoms
Thiamin (vitamin B₁)	Required as enzyme cofactor for carbohydrate and amino acid metabolism	RDA: Men = 1.2 mg/day Women = 1.1 mg/day	Pork, fortified cereals, enriched rice and pasta, peas, tuna, legumes	*Toxicity:* None known *Deficiency:* Beriberi; fatigue, apathy, decreased memory, confusion, irritability, muscle weakness
Riboflavin (vitamin B₂)	Required as enzyme cofactor for carbohydrate and fat metabolism	RDA: Men = 1.3 mg/day Women = 1.1 mg/day	Beef liver, shrimp, milk and dairy foods, fortified cereals, enriched breads and grains	*Toxicity:* None known *Deficiency:* Ariboflavinosis; swollen mouth and throat; seborrheic dermatitis; anemia
Niacin, nicotinamide, nicotinic acid	Required for carbohydrate and fat metabolism Plays role in DNA replication and repair and cell differentiation	RDA: Men = 16 mg/day Women = 14 mg/day UL = 35 mg/day	Beef liver, most cuts of meat/fish/poultry, fortified cereals, enriched breads and grains, canned tomato products	*Toxicity:* Flushing, liver damage, glucose intolerance, blurred vision differentiation *Deficiency:* Pellagra; vomiting, constipation, or diarrhea; apathy
Pyridoxine, pyridoxal, pyridoxamine (vitamin B₆)	Required as enzyme cofactor for carbohydrate and amino acid metabolism Assists synthesis of blood cells	RDA: Men and women aged 19 to 50 = 1.3 mg/day Men aged >50 = 1.7 mg/day Women aged >50 = 1.5 mg/day UL = 100 mg/day	Chickpeas (garbanzo beans), most cuts of meat/fish/poultry, fortified cereals, white potatoes	*Toxicity:* Nerve damage, skin lesions *Deficiency:* Anemia; seborrheic dermatitis; depression, confusion, and convulsions
Folate (folic acid)	Required as enzyme cofactor for amino acid metabolism Required for DNA synthesis Involved in metabolism of homocysteine	RDA: Men = 400 µg/day Women = 400 µg/day UL = 1,000 µg/day	Fortified cereals, enriched breads and grains, spinach, legumes (lentils, chickpeas, pinto beans), greens (spinach, romaine lettuce), liver	*Toxicity:* Masks symptoms of vitamin B₁₂ deficiency, specifically signs of nerve damage *Deficiency:* Macrocytic anemia; neural tube defects in a developing fetus; elevated homocysteine levels
Cobalamin (vitamin B₁₂)	Assists with formation of blood Required for healthy nervous system function Involved as enzyme cofactor in metabolism of homocysteine	RDA: Men = 2.4 µg/day Women = 2.4 µg/day	Shellfish, all cuts of meat/fish/poultry, milk and dairy foods, fortified cereals	*Toxicity:* None known *Deficiency:* Pernicious anemia; tingling and numbness of extremities; nerve damage; memory loss, disorientation, and dementia
Pantothenic acid	Assists with fat metabolism	AI: Men = 5 mg/day Women = 5 mg/day	Meat/fish/poultry, shiitake mushrooms, fortified cereals, egg yolk	*Toxicity:* None known *Deficiency:* Rare
Biotin	Involved as enzyme cofactor in carbohydrate, fat, and protein metabolism	RDA: Men = 30 µg/day Women = 30 µg/day	Nuts, egg yolk	*Toxicity:* None known *Deficiency:* Rare
Ascorbic acid (vitamin C)	Antioxidant in extracellular fluid and lungs Regenerates oxidized vitamin E Assists with collagen synthesis Enhances immune function Assists in synthesis of hormones, neurotransmitters, and DNA Enhances iron absorption	RDA: Men = 90 mg/day Women = 75 mg/day Smokers = 35 mg more per day than RDA UL = 2,000 mg	Sweet peppers, citrus fruits and juices, broccoli, strawberries, kiwi	*Toxicity:* Nausea and diarrhea, nosebleeds, increased oxidative damage, increased formation of kidney stones in people with kidney disease *Deficiency:* Scurvy; bone pain and fractures, depression, and anemia

*Abbreviations: RDA, Recommended Dietary Allowance; UL, upper limit; AI, Adequate Intake.

Water-soluble vitamins can be found in a variety of foods.

tissues, toxicity is rare. When it does occur, however, it is often from overuse of high-potency vitamin supplements. Toxicity can cause nerve damage and skin lesions.

Because most water-soluble vitamins are not stored in large amounts, they need to be consumed on a daily or weekly basis. Deficiency symptoms, including diseases or syndromes, can arise fairly quickly, especially during fetal development and in growing infants and children. The signs of water-soluble vitamin deficiency vary widely and are identified in Table 2.

Same Vitamin, Different Names and Forms

Food and supplement labels, magazine articles, and even nutrition textbooks such as this often use simplified alphabetic (A, D, E, K) names for the fat-soluble vitamins. The letters reflect their order of discovery: Vitamin A was discovered in 1916, whereas vitamin K was not isolated until 1939. These lay terms, however, are more appropriately viewed as "umbrellas" that unify a small cluster of chemically related compounds. For example, the term *vitamin A* refers to the specific compounds retinol, retinal, and retinoic acid. Similarly, *vitamin E* occurs naturally in eight forms, known as tocopherols, of which the primary form is alpha-tocopherol. Compounds with *vitamin D* ac-

---

minerals   Solid, crystalline substances that do not contain carbon and are not changed by natural processes, including digestion.
major minerals   Minerals we need to consume in amounts of at least 100 mg per day and of which the total amount present in the body is at least 5 g (or 5,000 mg).

tivity include cholecalciferol and ergocalciferol, and the *vitamin K* "umbrella" includes phylloquinone and menaquinone. As you can see, most of the individual compounds making up a fat-soluble vitamin cluster have similar chemical designations (tocopherols, calciferols, and so on). Table 1 lists both the alphabetic and chemical terms for the fat-soluble vitamins.

Similarly, there are both alphabetic and chemical designations for water-soluble vitamins. In some cases, such as *vitamin C* and *ascorbic acid*, you may be familiar with both terms. But few people would recognize *cobalamin* as designating the same micronutrient as *vitamin B$_{12}$*. Some of the water-soluble vitamins, such as niacin and vitamin B$_6$, mimic the "umbrella" clustering seen with vitamins A, E, D, and K: The term *vitamin B$_6$* includes pyridoxal, pyridoxine, and pyridoxamine. If you read any of these three terms on a supplement label, you'll know it refers to vitamin B$_6$.

Some vitamins exist in only one form. For example, thiamin is the only chemical compound known as *vitamin B$_1$*. There are no other related chemical compounds. Table 2 lists both the alphabetic and chemical terms for the water-soluble vitamins.

How Are Minerals Classified?

Minerals are naturally occurring inorganic (non-carbon-containing) substances such as calcium, iron, and zinc. All minerals are elements; that is, they are already in the simplest chemical form possible and are not digested or broken down prior to absorption. Furthermore, unlike vitamins, they cannot be synthesized in the laboratory or by any plant or animal, including humans. Minerals are the same wherever they are found, whether in soil, a car part, or the human body. The minerals in our foods ultimately come from the environment; for example, the selenium in soil and water is taken up into plants and then incorporated into the animals that eat the plants. Whether humans eat the plant foods directly or eat the animal products, all of the minerals in our food supply originate from Mother Earth!

Major Minerals

Major minerals are those that are required in amounts of at least 100 mg per day. In addition, these minerals are found in the human body in amounts of 5 g (5,000 mg) or higher. There are seven major minerals: sodium, potassium, phosphorus, chloride, calcium, magnesium, and sulfur. Table 3 summarizes the primary functions, recommended intakes, food sources, and toxicity/deficiency symptoms of these minerals.

Table 3 Major Minerals

Mineral Name	Primary Functions	Recommended Intake*	Reliable Food Sources	Toxicity/Deficiency Symptoms
Sodium	Fluid balance Acid–base balance Transmission of nerve impulses Muscle contraction	AI: Adults = 1.5 g/day (1,500 mg/day)	Table salt, pickles, most canned soups, snack foods, cured luncheon meats, canned tomato products	*Toxicity:* Water retention, high blood pressure, loss of calcium in urine *Deficiency:* Muscle cramps, dizziness, fatigue, nausea, vomiting, mental confusion
Potassium	Fluid balance Transmission of nerve impulses Muscle contraction	AI: Adults = 4.7 g/day (4,700 mg/day)	Most fresh fruits and vegetables: potatoes, bananas, tomato juice, orange juice, melons	*Toxicity:* Muscle weakness, vomiting, irregular heartbeat *Deficiency:* Muscle weakness, paralysis, mental confusion, irregular heartbeat
Phosphorus	Fluid balance Bone formation Component of ATP, which provides energy for our bodies	RDA: Adults = 700 mg/day	Milk/cheese/yogurt, soy milk and tofu, legumes (lentils, black beans), nuts (almonds, peanuts and peanut butter), poultry	*Toxicity:* Muscle spasms, convulsions, low blood calcium *Deficiency:* Muscle weakness, muscle damage, bone pain, dizziness
Chloride	Fluid balance Transmission of nerve impulses Component of stomach acid (HCl) Antibacterial	AI: Adults = 2.3 g/day (2,300 mg/day)	Table salt	*Toxicity:* None known *Deficiency:* Dangerous blood acid–base imbalances, irregular heartbeat
Calcium	Primary component of bone Acid–base balance Transmission of nerve impulses Muscle contraction	AI: Adults aged 19 to 50 = 1,000 mg/day Adults aged >50 = 1,200 mg/day UL = 2,500 mg/day	Milk/yogurt/cheese (best-absorbed form of calcium), sardines, collard greens and spinach, calcium-fortified juices	*Toxicity:* Mineral imbalances, shock, kidney failure, fatigue, mental confusion *Deficiency:* Osteoporosis, convulsions, heart failure
Magnesium	Component of bone Muscle contraction Assists more than 300 enzyme systems	RDA: Men aged 19 to 30 = 400 mg/day Men aged >30 = 420 mg/day Women aged 19 to 30 = 310 mg/day Women aged >30 = 320 mg/day UL = 350 mg/day	Greens (spinach, kale, collard greens), whole grains, seeds, nuts, legumes (navy and black beans)	*Toxicity:* None known *Deficiency:* Low blood calcium, muscle spasms or seizures, nausea, weakness, increased risk of chronic diseases such as heart disease, hypertension, osteoporosis, and type 2 diabetes
Sulfur	Component of certain B-vitamins and amino acids Acid–base balance Detoxification in liver	No DRI	Protein-rich foods	*Toxicity:* None known *Deficiency:* None known

*Abbreviations: RDA, Recommended Dietary Allowance; UL, upper limit; AI, Adequate Intake; DRI, Dietary Reference Intake.

Trace Minerals

Trace minerals are those we need to consume in amounts of less than 100 mg per day. They are found in the human body in amounts of less than 5 g (5,000 mg). Currently, the Dietary Reference Intake (DRI) Committee recognizes eight trace minerals as essential for human health: selenium, fluoride, iodine, chromium, manganese, iron, zinc, and copper.[1] Table 4 identifies the primary functions, recommended intakes, food sources, and toxicity/deficiency symptoms of these minerals.

Same Mineral, Different Forms

Unlike most vitamins, which can be identified by either alphabetic designations or the more complicated chemical terms, minerals are known by one name only. Iron, calcium, sodium, and all other minerals are simply referred to by their chemical name. That said, minerals do often

trace minerals Minerals we need to consume in amounts less than 100 mg per day and of which the total amount present in the body is less than 5 g (or 5,000 mg).

Table 4 Trace Minerals

Mineral Name	Primary Functions	Recommended Intake*	Reliable Food Sources	Toxicity/Deficiency Symptoms
Selenium	Required for carbohydrate and fat metabolism	RDA: Adults = 55 µg/day UL = 400 µg/day	Nuts, shellfish, meat/fish/poultry, whole grains	*Toxicity:* Brittle hair and nails, skin rashes, nausea and vomiting, weakness, liver disease *Deficiency:* Specific forms of heart disease and arthritis, impaired immune function, muscle pain and wasting, depression, hostility
Fluoride	Development and maintenance of healthy teeth and bones	RDA: Men = 4 mg/day Women = 3 mg/day UL = 2.2 mg/day for children aged 4 to 8; 10 mg/day for children aged >8	Fish, seafood, legumes, whole grains, drinking water (variable)	*Toxicity:* Fluorosis of teeth and bones *Deficiency:* Dental caries, low bone density
Iodine	Synthesis of thyroid hormones Temperature regulation Reproduction and growth	RDA: Adults = 150 µg/day UL = 1,100 µg/day	Iodized salt, saltwater seafood	*Toxicity:* Goiter *Deficiency:* Goiter, hypothyroidism, cretinism in infant of mother who is iodine deficient
Chromium	Glucose transport Metabolism of DNA and RNA Immune function and growth	AI: Men aged 19 to 50 = 35 µg/day Men aged >50 = 30 µg/day Women aged 19 to 50 = 25 µg/day Women aged >50 = 20 µg/day	Whole grains, brewers yeast,	*Toxicity:* None known *Deficiency:* Elevated blood glucose and blood lipids, damage to brain and nervous system
Manganese	Assists many enzyme systems Synthesis of protein found in bone and cartilage	AI: Men = 2.3 mg/day Women = 1.8 mg/day UL = 11 mg/day for adults	Whole grains, nuts, leafy vegetables, tea	*Toxicity:* Impairment of neuromuscular system *Deficiency:* Impaired growth and reproductive function, reduced bone density, impaired glucose and lipid metabolism, skin rash
Iron	Component of hemoglobin in blood cells Component of myoglobin in muscle cells Assists many enzyme systems	RDA: Adult men = 8 mg/day Women aged 19 to 50 = 18 mg/day Women aged >50 = 8 mg/day	Meat/fish/poultry (best-absorbed form of iron), fortified cereals, legumes, spinach	*Toxicity:* Nausea, vomiting, and diarrhea; dizziness, confusion; rapid heart beat, organ damage, death *Deficiency:* Iron-deficiency microcytic (small red blood cells), hypochromic anemia
Zinc	Assists more than 100 enzyme systems Immune system function Growth and sexual maturation Gene regulation	RDA: Men 11 mg/day Women = 8 mg/day UL = 40 mg/day	Meat/fish/poultry (best-absorbed form of zinc), fortified cereals, legumes	*Toxicity:* Nausea, vomiting, and diarrhea; headaches, depressed immune function, reduced absorption of copper *Deficiency:* Growth retardation, delayed sexual maturation, eye and skin lesions, hair loss, increased incidence of illness and infection
Copper	Assists many enzyme systems Iron transport	RDA: Adults = 900 µg/day UL = 10 mg/day	Shellfish, organ meats, nuts, legumes	*Toxicity:* Nausea, vomiting, and diarrhea; liver damage *Deficiency:* Anemia, reduced levels of white blood cells, osteoporosis in infants and growing children

*Abbreviations: RDA, Recommended Dietary Allowance; UL, upper limit; AI, Adequate Intake.

exist within different chemical compounds; for example, a supplement label might identify calcium as calcium lactate, calcium gluconate, or calcium citrate. As we will discuss shortly, these different chemical compounds, while all containing the same elemental mineral, may differ in their ability to be absorbed by the body.

How Do Our Bodies Use Micronutrients?

In Chapter 3, we investigated the truth behind the claim that "You are what you eat." We found out that the body has to change food in order to use it. This is also true for foods containing vitamins and minerals, because the micronutrients found in foods and supplements are not always in a chemical form that can be used by our cells. This discussion will highlight some of the ways in which our bodies modify the food forms of vitamins and minerals in order to maximize their absorption and utilization.

What We Eat Differs from What We Absorb

The most healthful diet is of no value to our bodies unless the nutrients can be absorbed and transported to the cells that need them. Unlike carbohydrates, fats, and proteins, which are efficiently absorbed (85–99% of what is eaten makes it into the blood), some micronutrients are so poorly absorbed that only 3% to 10% of what is eaten ever arrives in the bloodstream.

The absorption of many vitamins and minerals depends on their chemical form. Dietary iron, for example, can be in the form of **heme iron** (found only in meats,

The iron in foods is chemically identical to that in a wrought iron fence.

Plants absorb minerals from soil and water.

fish, and poultry) or **non-heme iron** (found in plant and animal foods as well as iron-fortified foods and supplements). Healthy adults absorb about 25% of heme iron but as little as 3% to 5% of non-heme iron.

In addition, the presence of other factors within the same food influences mineral absorption. For example, approximately 30% to 45% of the calcium found in milk and dairy products is absorbed, but the calcium in spinach, Swiss chard, seeds, and nuts is absorbed at a much lower rate because factors in these foods bind the calcium and prevent its absorption. Non-heme iron, zinc, vitamin E, and vitamin B_6 are other micronutrients whose absorption can be reduced by various binding factors in foods.

The absorption of many vitamins and minerals is also influenced by other foods within the meal. For example, the fat-soluble vitamins are much better absorbed when the meal contains some dietary fat. Calcium absorption is increased by the presence of lactose, found in milk, and non-heme iron absorption can be doubled if the meal includes vitamin C–rich foods such as red peppers, oranges, or tomatoes. On the other hand, high-fiber foods such as whole grains and foods high in oxalic acid, such as tea, spinach, and rhubarb, can decrease the absorption of zinc and iron. It may seem an impossible task to correctly balance your food choices to optimize micronutrient absorption, but the best approach, as always, is to eat a variety of healthful foods every day.

heme iron   Iron that is part of hemoglobin and myoglobin; found only in animal-based foods such as meat, fish, and poultry.
non-heme iron   The form of iron that is not a part of hemoglobin or myoglobin; found in animal- and plant-based foods.

What We Eat Differs from What Our Cells Use

Foods high in oxalic acid, like rhubarb, can decrease zinc and iron absorption.

Many vitamins undergo one or more chemical transformations after they are eaten and absorbed into our bodies. For example, before they can go to work for our bodies, the B-complex vitamins must combine with other substances. For thiamin and vitamin B_6, a phosphate group is added. Vitamin D is another example: Before cells can use it, the food form of vitamin D must have two hydroxyl ($-OH$) groups added to its structure. These transformations activate the vitamin; because the reactions don't occur randomly, but only when the active vitamin is needed, they help the body maintain control over its metabolic pathways.

While the basic nature of minerals does not, of course, change, they can undergo minor modifications that change their atomic structure. Iron (Fe) may alternate between Fe^{2+} (ferrous) and Fe^{3+} (ferric); copper (Cu) may exist as Cu^{1+} or Cu^{2+}. These are just two examples of how micronutrients can be modified from one form to another to help the body make the best use of dietary nutrients.

Liz
Nutri-Case

"I used to have dinner in the dorm cafeteria, but not anymore. It's too tempting to see everybody eating all that fattening food and then topping it off with a big dessert. . . . My weight would balloon up in a week if I ate like that! So instead I stay in my dorm room and have a bowl of cereal with skim milk. The cereal box says it provides a full day's supply of all the vitamins and minerals, so I know it's nutritious. And when I eat cereal for dinner, it doesn't matter if I didn't eat all the right things earlier in the day!"

What do you think of Liz's "cereal suppers"? If the cereal provides 100% of the DRI for all vitamins and minerals, then is Liz correct that it doesn't matter what else she eats during the day? If not, why not? What factors besides the percentage of DRI does Liz need to consider?

Controversies in Micronutrient Metabolism

The science of nutrition continues to evolve, and our current understanding of vitamins and minerals will no doubt change over the next several years or decades. While some people interpret the term *controversy* as negative, nutrition controversies are exciting developments, proof of new information, and a sign of continued growth in the field.

Are Supplements Healthful Sources of Micronutrients?

For millions of years, humans relied solely on natural foodstuffs as their source of nutrients. Only within the past 60 years or so has a second option become available: nutrient supplements, including those added to fortified foods. Are the micronutrients in supplements any better or worse than those in foods? Do our bodies use the nutrients from these two sources any differently? These are issues that nutrition scientists and consumers continue to discuss.

As previously noted, the availability or "usefulness" of micronutrients in foods depends in part on the food itself. The iron and calcium in spinach are poorly absorbed,

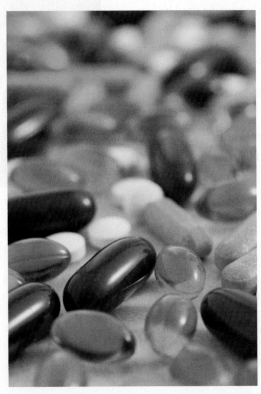

Thousands of supplements are marketed to consumers.

whereas the iron in beef and the calcium in milk are absorbed efficiently. Because of these and other differences in the availability of micronutrients from different sources, it is difficult to generalize about the usefulness of supplements. Nevertheless, we can say a few things about this issue:

- In general, it is much easier to develop a toxic overload of nutrients from supplements than it is from foods. It is very difficult, if not impossible, to develop a vitamin or mineral toxicity through diet (food) alone.
- Some micronutrients consumed as supplements appear to be harmful to the health of certain subgroups of consumers. For example, recent research has shown that use of high-potency supplements of vitamins A, C, and E may actually increase rates of death.[2] Earlier, it had been shown that high-potency beta-carotene supplements increased death rates among male smokers. Alcoholics are more susceptible to the potentially toxic effects of vitamin A supplements and should avoid their use unless specifically prescribed by a healthcare provider. There is also some evidence that a high intake of vitamin A, including supplement use, increases risk of osteoporosis and hip fracture in older adults.[3]
- Most minerals are better absorbed from animal food sources than they are from supplements. The one exception might be calcium citrate-malate, used in calcium-fortified juices. This form is used by the body as effectively as the calcium from milk or yogurt.
- Enriching a low-nutrient food with a few vitamins and/or minerals does not turn it into a healthful food. For example, soda that has been fortified with selected micronutrients is still basically soda.
- Eating a variety of healthful foods provides you with many more nutrients, phytochemicals, and other dietary factors than supplements alone. Nutritionists are not even sure they have identified all essential nutrients; it is possible that the list of essential micronutrients may, in the future, expand. Supplements provide only those nutrients that the manufacturer puts in; foods provide nutrients that have been identified as well as yet-unknown factors.
- Foods often provide a balance of micronutrients and other factors that work in concert with one another. The whole food is more healthful than its isolated individual nutrients, providing benefits not always seen with purified supplements or highly refined, highly enriched food products. As one science reporter recently suggested, "Eat food. Don't eat anything your great-great-grandmother wouldn't recognize as food."[4]

- A healthful diet, built from a wide variety of foods, offers social, emotional, and other benefits that are absent from supplements. Humans eat food, not nutrients.

In certain populations, micronutrient supplements can play an important role in promoting good health. These include pregnant women, children with poor eating habits, and people with certain illnesses. The relative benefits of supplements versus whole foods are discussed further in the Nutrition Debate in Chapter 10 (pages 393–397).

Can Micronutrients Really Prevent or Treat Disease?

Nutritionists and other healthcare professionals clearly accept the role that dietary fat plays in the prevention and treatment of coronary heart disease. The relationship between total carbohydrate intake and the management of diabetes is also firmly established. Less clear, however, are the links between individual vitamins and minerals and certain chronic diseases.

A number of research studies have suggested, but not proven, links between the following vitamins and disease states. In each case, adequate intake of the nutrient has been associated with lower disease risk.

- Vitamin C and cataracts
- Vitamin D and colon cancer
- Vitamin E and complications of diabetes
- Vitamin K and osteoporosis

Other studies have examined relationships between minerals and chronic diseases. Again, in each case, the nutrient seems to be protective against the disease listed.

- Calcium and high blood pressure (hypertension)
- Chromium and type 2 diabetes in older adults
- Magnesium and muscle wasting (sarcopenia) in older adults
- Selenium and certain types of cancer

As consumers, it is important to critically evaluate any claim that might be made regarding the protective or disease-preventing ability of a specific vitamin or mineral. Supplements that provide megadoses of micronutrients are potentially harmful, and vitamin/mineral therapies should never replace more traditional, proven methods of disease treatment. Current, reputable information can provide updates as the research into micronutrients continues.

Do More Essential Micronutrients Exist?

Nutrition researchers continue to explore the potential of a variety of substances to qualify as essential micronutrients. Vitamin-like factors such as carnitine and trace minerals such as boron, nickel, and silicon seem to have beneficial roles in human health, yet additional information is needed in order to fully define their metabolic roles. Until more research is done, we cannot classify such substances as essential micronutrients.

Another subject of controversy is the question, "What is the appropriate intake of each micronutrient?" Contemporary research suggests that the answer to this question is to be found in each individual's genetic profile. As you learned in the Nutrition Debate in Chapter 1, the science of *nutrigenomics* blends the study of human nutrition with that of genetics. It is becoming clear that some individuals, for example, require much higher intakes of folate in order to achieve optimal health. Researchers have identified a specific genetic variation in a subset of the population that increases their need for dietary folate.[5] Future studies may identify other examples of how a person's genetic profile influences his or her individual need for vitamins and minerals.

As explained in Chapter 1, the DRI Committees rely on Adequate Intake (AI) guidelines to suggest appropriate nutrient intake levels when research has not clearly defined an Estimated Average Requirement (EAR). As the science of nutrition continues to evolve, the next 50 years will be an exciting time for micronutrient research. Who knows? Within a few decades, we all might have personalized micronutrient prescriptions matched to our gender, age, and DNA!

Web Links

www.fda.gov
U.S. Food and Drug Administration
Select "Food" and then "Dietary Supplements" on the menu for information on how to evaluate dietary supplements.

www.ars.usda.gov/ba/bhnrc/ndl
Nutrient Data Laboratory Home Page
Click on "Search" and then type "Nutrients Lists" to find information on food sources of selected vitamins and minerals.

www.nal.usda.gov/fnic
The Food and Nutrition Information Center
Click on "Dietary Supplements" to obtain information on vitamin and mineral supplements.

http://dietary-supplements.info.nih.gov
Office of Dietary Supplements
This site provides summaries of current research results and helpful information about use of dietary supplements.

http://lpi.oregonstate.edu
Linus Pauling Institute of Oregon State University
This site provides up-to-date information on vitamins and minerals that promote health and lower disease risk. You can search for individual nutrients (for example, vitamin C) as well as types of nutrients (for example, antioxidants).

References

1. Institute of Medicine, Food and Nutrition Board. 2001. *Dietary Reference Intakes for Vitamin A, Vitamin K, Arsenic, Boron, Chromium, Copper, Iodine, Iron, Manganese, Molybdenum, Nickel, Silicon, Vanadium, and Zinc.* Washington, DC: National Academy Press.
2. Bjelakovic, G., D. Nikolova, L. L. Gluud, R. G. Simonetti, and C. Gluud. 2007. Mortality in randomized trials of antioxidant supplements for primary and secondary prevention. *J. Am. Med. Assoc.* 297:842–857.
3. Penniston, K. L., and S. A. Tanumihardjo. 2006. The acute and chronic toxic effects of vitamin A. *Am. J. Clin. Nutr.* 83:191–201.
4. Pollan, M. 2007. The age of nutritionism. *The New York Times Magazine,* January 28.
5. Stover, P. J. 2006. Influence of human genetic variation on nutritional requirements. *Am. J. Clin. Nutr.* 83:436S–443S.

8 Nutrients Involved in Energy Metabolism

Test Yourself | True or False?

1 The B-vitamins are an important source of energy for our bodies. **T** *or* **F**

2 A severe deficiency of certain B-vitamins active in energy metabolism can be fatal. **T** *or* **F**

3 B-vitamins are water soluble, so there is no risk of toxicity.

4 Chromium supplementation reduces body fat and enhances muscle mass. **T** *or* **F**

5 In the United States, if we use table salt, we consume adequate iodine. **T** *or* **F**

Test Yourself answers are located in the Chapter Review.

Chapter Objectives *After reading this chapter, you will be able to:*

1. Describe how coenzymes enhance the activities of enzymes, *pp. 294–295.*

2. Name the B-vitamins that are primarily involved in energy metabolism and describe their function, *pp. 295–306.*

3. Describe the actions of at least two minerals that function as cofactors in energy metabolism, *pp. 307–309.*

4. Identify the deficiency disorders associated with thiamin, niacin, and riboflavin, *pp. 297–302.*

5. Describe the toxic effects of high doses of niacin and vitamin B_6, *pp. 301–304.*

6. Identify the deficiency disorders associated with poor iodine intake, *pp. 308–309.*

7. Explain why poor B-vitamin intake decreases the ability to do physical activity, *p. 312.*

8. Explain how researchers determine the minimum amount of a vitamin we need to consume for good health, *p. 313.*

In southern Africa, the months of September through December, the season when the rains begin, are known as "the hungry period."[1] In many areas, food stores have been depleted: meat is a rare luxury, and the variety and quantity of fruits and vegetables are extremely limited. The one staple typically available, including through food-aid programs, is maize.[1] It is during the hungry period that physicians begin to see patients suffering from the same constellation of symptoms: a skin rash, diarrhea, depression, apathy, loss of memory, and fatigue. These people suffer from pellagra, a deficiency disease we described in Chapter 1. As you may recall, pellagra is caused by an extreme shortage of niacin, which is not available from maize.

In this chapter, we explore the reasons why certain B-vitamins, including niacin, are essential to the body's breakdown and use of the macronutrients and why severe deficiency of these vitamins is incompatible with life. We also discuss the role of the minerals iodine, chromium, manganese, and sulfur in energy metabolism; and we conclude the chapter with a look at the impact of low B-vitamin intake on our ability to work, play, and exercise.

How Does the Body Regulate Energy Metabolism?

We explored the digestion and metabolism of carbohydrates, lipids, proteins, and alcohol in Chapters 3 through 7 of this text. In those chapters, you learned that the regulation of energy metabolism is a complex process involving numerous biological substances and chemical pathways. Here, we describe how certain micronutrients we consume in our diet assist us in generating energy from the carbohydrates, lipids, and proteins we eat along with them.

The Body Requires Vitamins and Minerals to Produce Energy

Although vitamins and minerals do not contain calories and thus do not directly provide energy, the body is unable to generate energy from the macronutrients without them. The B-vitamins are particularly important in assisting energy metabolism and include thiamin, riboflavin, vitamin B_6, niacin, folate, vitamin B_{12}, pantothenic acid, and biotin. Except for vitamin B_{12}, these water-soluble vitamins need to be consumed regularly, because the body has no storage reservoir for them. Conversely, excess amounts of these vitamins, either from food or supplementation, are easily lost in the urine.

The primary role of the B-vitamins is to act as coenzymes in a number of metabolic processes. As you learned in Chapter 7 (see page 253), a coenzyme is a molecule that combines with an enzyme to activate it and help it do its job. Six of them (thiamin, riboflavin, vitamin B_6, niacin, pantothenic acid, and biotin) function primarily in energy metabolism, whereas the other two (folate and vitamin B_{12}) function primarily in cell regeneration and the synthesis of red blood cells. Although folate and vitamin B_{12} have minor roles in energy metabolism, we discuss them in Chapter 12 with the other blood nutrients.

Figure 8.1 provides a simple overview of how some of the B-vitamins act as coenzymes to promote energy metabolism, and **Figure 8.2** on page 296 shows how these coenzymes participate in the energy metabolism pathways. For instance, thiamin is part of the coenzyme thiamin pyrophosphate, or TPP, which is required for the breakdown of glucose. Riboflavin is a part of two coenzymes, flavin mononucleotide (FMN) and flavin adenine dinucleotide (FAD), which help break down glucose and fatty acids. The specific functions of each B-vitamin primarily involved in energy metabolism are described in detail shortly.

Some Micronutrients Assist with Nutrient Transport and Hormone Production

Some micronutrients promote energy metabolism by facilitating the transport of nutrients into the cells. For instance, the mineral chromium helps improve glucose uptake into cells. Other micronutrients assist in the production of hormones that regulate metabolic

Vitamins do not provide energy directly, but the B-vitamins help the body create the energy that it needs from the foods we eat.

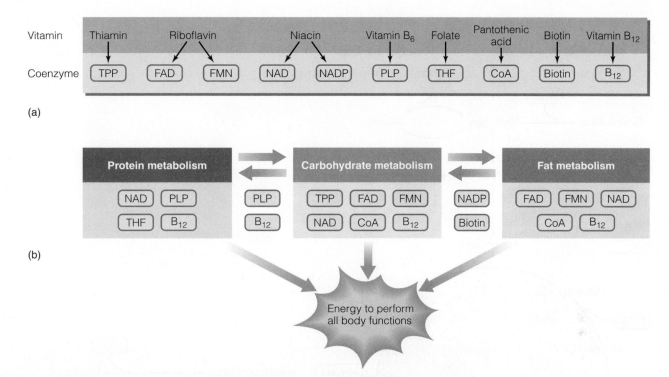

Figure 8.1 The B-vitamins play many important roles in the reactions involved in energy metabolism. **(a)** B-vitamins and the coenzymes they are a part of. **(b)** This chart illustrates many of the coenzymes essential for various metabolic functions; however, this is only a small sample of the thousands of roles that the B-vitamins serve in our bodies. TPP, thiamin pyrophosphate; FAD, flavin adenine dinucleotide; FMN, flavin mononucleotide; NAD, nicotinamide adenine dinucleotide; NADP, nicotinamide adenine dinucleotide phosphate; PLP, pyridoxal phosphate; CoA, coenzyme A.

processes; the mineral iodine, for example, is necessary for synthesis of thyroid hormones, which regulate our metabolic rate and promote growth and development. The details of these processes and their related nutrients are discussed in the following section.

RECAP

Vitamins and minerals are not direct sources of energy, but they help generate energy from carbohydrates, fats, proteins, and alcohol. Acting as coenzymes and cofactors, micronutrients such as the B-vitamins assist enzymes in metabolizing macronutrients to produce energy. Minerals such as chromium and iodine assist with nutrient uptake into the cells and with regulating energy production and cell growth.

A Profile of Nutrients Involved in Energy Metabolism

As we have stated, the primary function of the B-vitamins, except for folate and B_{12}, is to facilitate the production of energy in the body. Other nutrients involved in energy metabolism include a vitamin-like substance called choline and the minerals iodine, chromium, manganese, and sulfur. In this section, we discuss the functions, recommended intakes, toxicity, and deficiency symptoms for these nutrients. A summary of the B-vitamins is provided in Table 2, page 283 in the *In Depth* feature "Vitamins and Minerals: Micronutrients with Macro Powers."

Thiamin (Vitamin B_1)

Thiamin was the first B-vitamin discovered, hence its designation as vitamin B_1. Because this compound was recognized as vital to health and has a functional amine group, it was

Figure 8.2   Example of some metabolic pathways that require B-vitamins for energy production.

initially called "vitamine."[2] Later, this term was applied to several other nonmineral compounds that are essential for health, and the spelling was changed to *vitamin*. Thiamin was given a new name reflecting both its thiazole and amine groups. Thiamin is required for the formation of its coenzyme thiamin pyrophosphate, or TPP. The structures of thiamin and TPP are shown in **Figure 8.3**. Dietary thiamin is converted to TPP by the body.

(a) Thiamin

(b) Thiamin pyrophosphate

Figure 8.3   Structure of **(a)** thiamin and **(b)** thiamin pyrophosphate (TPP).

Functions of Thiamin

Thiamin is important in a number of energy-producing metabolic pathways within the body. As a part of TPP, thiamin plays a critical role in the breakdown of glucose for energy. For example, TPP is required for pyruvate dehydrogenase, the enzyme responsible for the conversion of pyruvate to acetyl-CoA (see Figure 8.2). This is a critical step in the conversion of glucose into a smaller molecule that can enter the TCA cycle for energy production. Thus, when dietary thiamin is inadequate, the body's ability to metabolize carbohydrate is diminished.

Another primary role of TPP is to act as a coenzyme in the metabolism of the branched-chain amino acids, which include leucine, isoleucine, and valine. TPP is a coenzyme for two α-keto acid dehydrogenase complexes. One of these enzyme complexes helps convert the carbon skeletons of the branched-chain amino acids into products that can enter the TCA cycle, whereas the other converts α-ketoglutarate to succinate in the TCA cycle (see Figure 8.2). The highest concentrations of the branched-chain amino acids are found in the muscle, where they make up approximately 25% of the content of the average protein. Thus, these amino acids play a significant role in providing fuel for the working muscle, especially during high-intensity exercise.[3]

TPP also assists in the production of DNA and RNA, making it important for cell regeneration and protein synthesis. Finally, it plays a role in the synthesis of neurotransmitters—chemicals that transmit messages throughout the central nervous system.

How Much Thiamin Should We Consume?

The RDA for thiamin for adults aged 19 years and older is 1.2 mg/day for men and 1.1 mg/day for women. Based on the National Health and Nutrition Examination Survey (NHANES) III data collected in the United States between the years 1988 and 1994, the average dietary intake of thiamin for men and women between the ages of 19 and 70 years was approximately 2 mg/day and approximately 1.5 mg/day, respectively.[4] Thus, it appears that the average adult in the United States gets adequate amounts of thiamin in the diet.

Those at greatest risk of poor thiamin status are the elderly, who typically have reduced total energy intakes, and anyone with malabsorption syndrome or on renal dialysis, as thiamin is easily cleared by the kidney. Also, people who eat a diet high in unenriched processed grains may be at risk for poor thiamin status.

Physically active individuals, especially those who consume high amounts of carbohydrate, may be at risk for poor B-vitamin status, including thiamin. Research indicates that depletion of the B-vitamins can reduce the ability to perform physical activity. This is discussed in more detail at the end of the chapter.

Food Sources of Thiamin

Thiamin is found abundantly in ham and other pork products (**Figure 8.4**). Sunflower seeds, beans, oat bran, mixed dishes that contain whole or enriched grains and meat, tuna fish, soy milk, and soy-based meat substitutes are also good sources. Enriched and whole-grain foods, including fortified ready-to-eat cereals, are rich in several B-vitamins, including thiamin. **Figure 8.5** identifies the B-vitamin content of one popular fortified cereal.

What Happens If We Consume Too Much Thiamin?

Excess thiamin is readily cleared by the kidneys, and to date there have been no reports of adverse effects from consuming high amounts of thiamin from either food or supplements. Thus, the Institute of Medicine (IOM) has not been able to set a tolerable upper intake level (UL) for thiamin.[4]

What Happens If We Don't Consume Enough Thiamin?

As the B-vitamins are involved in most energy-generating processes, the deficiency symptoms include a combination of fatigue, apathy, muscle weakness, and reduced cognitive function. As you learned in Chapter 1, thiamin-deficiency disease is called **beriberi.** In this disease, the body's inability to metabolize energy leads to muscle wasting and nerve damage; in later stages, patients may be unable to move at all. The heart muscle may also be affected, and the patient may die of heart failure. Beriberi is seen in countries in which unenriched, processed grains are a primary food source; for instance, beriberi was widespread in China when rice was processed and refined, and it still occurs in refugee camps and other settlements dependent on poor-quality food supplies.

Thiamin deficiency is also seen in industrialized countries in people with chronic heavy alcohol consumption and limited food intake. This alcohol-related thiamin deficiency is called Wernicke–Korsakoff syndrome. High alcohol intake contributes to thiamin deficiency in three ways: it is generally accompanied by low thiamin intake; at the same time, it increases the need for thiamin to metabolize the alcohol; and it reduces thiamin

Table 8.1 Overview of Nutrients Involved in Energy Metabolism

To see the full profile of nutrients involved in energy metabolism, turn to *In Depth,* Vitamins and Minerals: Micronutrients with Macro Powers, pages 280–291.

Nutrient	Recommended Intake
Thiamin (Vitamin B₁)	RDA for 19 years and older: Women = 1.1 mg/day Men = 1.2 mg/day
Riboflavin (Vitamin B₂)	RDA for 19 years and older: Women = 1.1 mg/day Men = 1.3 mg/day
Niacin (nicotinamide and nicotinic acid)	RDA for 19 years and older: Women = 14 mg/day Men = 16 mg/day
Vitamin B₆ (pyridoxine)	RDA for 19 to 50 years of age: Women and men = 1.3 mg/day RDA for 51 years and older: Women = 1.5 mg/day Men = 1.7 mg/day
Folate (folic acid)	RDA for 19 years and older: Women and men = 400 µg/day
Vitamin B₁₂ (cobalamin)	RDA for 19 years and older: Women and men = 2.4 µg/day
Pantothenic acid	AI for 19 years and older: Women and men = 5 mg/day
Biotin	AI for 19 years and older: Women and men = 30 µg/day
Choline	AI for 19 years and older: Women = 425 mg/day Men = 550 mg/day

beriberi A disease caused by thiamin deficiency.

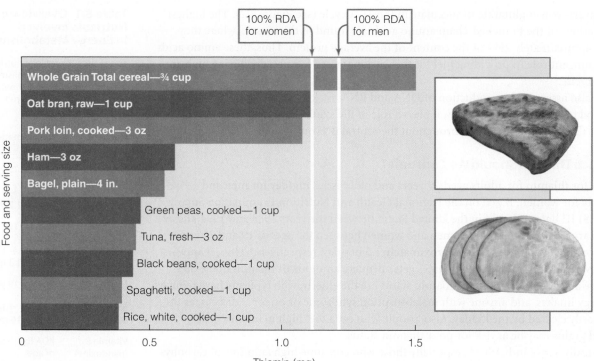

Figure 8.4 Common food sources of thiamin. The RDA for thiamin is 1.2 mg/day for men and 1.1 mg/day for women 19 years and older. (*Data from:* U.S. Department of Agriculture, Agricultural Research Service. 2008. USDA Nutrient Database for Standard Reference, Release 21. Nutrient Data Laboratory Home Page. Available online at www.ars.usda.gov/Services/docs.htm?docid=8964.)

absorption. Together, these factors contribute to thiamin deficiency.[5] The symptoms of Wernicke–Korsakoff syndrome are tremors, confusion, and impairment of memory.[5]

Riboflavin (Vitamin B$_2$)

Riboflavin was the second B-vitamin discovered, thus, its designation as vitamin B$_2$. The term *riboflavin* reflects its structure; *ribo* refers to the carbon-rich ribityl side chain, and *flavin* is associated with the ring-structure portion of the vitamin (**Figure 8.6a**). Riboflavin is water soluble and has a yellow color. It is relatively heat stable but sensitive to light: When exposed to light, the ribityl side chain is cleaved off and the vitamin loses its activity.

Figure 8.5 Many enriched ready-to-eat cereals, like the one in this example, are a consistently good source of B-vitamins. (*Data from:* U.S. Department of Agriculture, Agricultural Research Service. 2008. USDA Nutrient Database for Standard Reference, Release 21. Available online at www.ars.usda.gov/Services/docs.htm?docid=8964.)

(a) Riboflavin

(b) Flavin adenine dinucleotide (FAD) (coenzyme)

Figure 8.6   Structure of **(a)** riboflavin and **(b)** its coenzyme forms flavin mononucleotide (FMN) and flavin adenine dinucleotide (FAD).

Functions of Riboflavin

Riboflavin is an important component of two coenzymes that are involved in oxidation–reduction reactions occurring within the energy-producing metabolic pathways, including the electron transport chain. These coenzymes, flavin mononucleotide (FMN) and flavin adenine dinucleotide (FAD), are involved in the metabolism of carbohydrates, fatty acids, and amino acids for energy. (The structures of FMN and FAD are shown in Figure 8.6b.) For example, you will recall from Chapter 7 that FAD and FMN function as electron acceptors in the electron transport chain, which eventually results in the production of ATP. FAD is also a part of the α-ketoglutarate dehydrogenase complex, which converts α-ketoglutarate to succinate in one step of the TCA cycle (see Figure 8.2). It is also a coenzyme for succinate dehydrogenase, the enzyme involved in the conversion of succinate to fumarate in the next step of the TCA cycle. Finally, riboflavin is a part of the coenzyme required by glutathione peroxidase, which assists in the fight against oxidative damage. Antioxidants are discussed in detail in Chapter 10.

How Much Riboflavin Should We Consume?

The RDA for riboflavin for adults aged 19 years and older is 1.3 mg/day for men and 1.1 mg/day for women. Based on NHANES III data, the average dietary intake of riboflavin from food for men between the ages of 19 and 70 years was approximately 2.0 to 2.3 mg/day (median = 2 mg/day) and for women of the same age the average intake was approximately 1.7 to 1.9 mg/day (median = 1.5 mg/day).[4] Thus, it appears that, on average, adults in the United States get adequate amounts of riboflavin in their diet.

As with thiamin, those at greatest risk of low riboflavin intakes are the elderly, who may have reduced total energy intake; individuals who make poor food selections; those with malabsorption problems; and patients on renal dialysis.[6] People who eliminate milk and

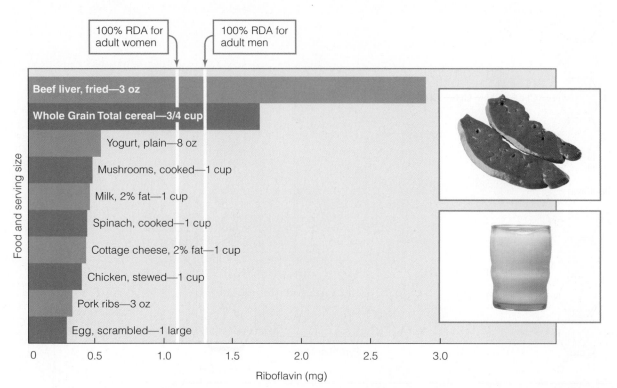

Figure 8.7   Common food sources of riboflavin. The RDA for riboflavin is 1.3 mg/day for men and 1.1 mg/day for women. (*Data from:* U.S. Department of Agriculture, Agricultural Research Service. 2008. USDA Nutrient Database for Standard Reference, Release 21. Available online at www.ars.usda.gov/Services/docs.htm?docid=8964.)

milk products from their diet may also be at risk. Approximately one-third of the RDA for riboflavin is supplied in the American diet by milk and milk products; thus, it is easy to see how individuals who do not consume these foods could have a lower riboflavin intake.[5, 6]

Food Sources of Riboflavin

In addition to dairy products, foods considered good sources of riboflavin include eggs, meats, including organ meats, broccoli, enriched bread and grain products, and ready-to-eat cereals (see Figure 8.5 and **Figure 8.7**). As mentioned, milk is a good source of riboflavin; however, riboflavin is destroyed when it is exposed to light. Thus, milk is generally stored in opaque containers to prevent the destruction of riboflavin.

What Happens If We Consume Too Much Riboflavin?

As with thiamin, there are no reports of adverse effects from consuming high amounts of riboflavin from either food or supplements; thus, the IOM has not been able to set a UL for riboflavin.[4]

What Happens If We Don't Consume Enough Riboflavin?

Riboflavin deficiency is referred to as **ariboflavinosis.** Symptoms of ariboflavinosis include sore throat; swelling of the mucous membranes in the mouth and throat; lips that are dry and scaly; a purple-colored tongue; and inflamed, irritated patches on the skin. Severe riboflavin deficiency can impair the metabolism of vitamin B_6 (or pyridoxine) and niacin.[4]

Niacin

Niacin is a generic name for two specific vitamin compounds, nicotinic acid and nicotinamide, which are shown in **Figure 8.8**. This B-vitamin was previously designated as vitamin B_3, a name you will sometimes still see on vitamin supplement labels. Niacin was first established as an essential nutrient in the treatment of pellagra in 1937.

Milk is a good source of riboflavin and is stored in opaque containers to prevent the destruction of riboflavin by light.

ariboflavinosis   A condition caused by riboflavin deficiency.

Functions of Niacin

The two forms of niacin, nicotinic acid and nicotinamide, are essential for the formation of the two coenzymes nicotinamide adenine dinucleotide (NAD) and nicotinamide adenine dinucleotide phosphate (NADP). These coenzymes, like those formed from riboflavin and thiamin, are required for the oxidation–reduction reactions involved in the catabolism of carbohydrate, fat, and protein for energy. For example, NADP-dependent dehydrogenase enzymes catalyze steps in the β-oxidation of fatty acids, the oxidation of ketone bodies, the degradation of carbohydrates, and the catabolism of amino acids.[5] Some metabolic pathways in which niacin functions are illustrated in Figure 8.2. Niacin is also an important coenzyme in DNA replication and repair and in the process of cell differentiation.

How Much Niacin Should We Consume?

Niacin is a unique vitamin in that the body can synthesize a limited amount from the amino acid tryptophan. However, the ratio reflecting the conversion of tryptophan to niacin is 60:1; thus, the body relies on the diet to provide the majority of niacin necessary for functioning. The term *niacin equivalents (NE)* is used to express niacin intake recommendations, and reflects the amount of niacin in our diet and the amount synthesized from tryptophan within the body.

The RDA for niacin for adults aged 19 and older is 16 mg/day of NE for men and 14 mg/day of NE for women. Based on NHANES III data, the average dietary intake of niacin from food for men and women between the ages of 19 and 70 years was approximately 27 mg/day and approximately 21 mg/day, respectively.[4]

Food Sources of Niacin

Good food sources of niacin include meat, fish, poultry, enriched bread products, and ready-to-eat cereals; however, the availability of this niacin for absorption differs. For example, the niacin in cereal grains is bound to other substances and is only 30% available for absorption, whereas the niacin found in meats is much more available.[4] To calculate the NE in your own diet, see You Do the Math below. See **Figure 8.9** for the niacin content of commonly consumed foods.

What Happens If We Consume Too Much Niacin?

There seem to be no adverse effects from the consumption of naturally occurring niacin in foods; however, niacin can cause toxicity symptoms when taken in supplement form.[4] These symptoms include *flushing*, which is defined as burning, tingling, and itching sensations accompanied by a reddened flush primarily on the face, arms, and chest. Liver

Figure 8.8 Forms of niacin. **(a)** Structure of nicotinic acid. **(b)** Structure of nicotinamide. The generic term *niacin* is used to refer to these two compounds.

Halibut is a good source of niacin.

You Do the Math
Calculating Niacin Equivalents

When you analyze your diet using the nutrient analysis program provided with this book, you will notice that the program calculates your total niacin equivalents (NE). How is this calculation done? How would you calculate your own intake of NE if the computer program was not doing this for you?

To calculate NE, you first need to determine the amount of two components of your diet: (1) total niacin intake from food in mg/day; (2) total intake of tryptophan in mg/day. Now you are ready to do the calculation, using the following formula. Just keep in mind that 1 NE = either 60 mg of tryptophan or 1 mg of niacin.

Total NE = niacin intake from food +
(tryptophan intake/60)

Now calculate the NE intake of an adult male who consumes 18.9 mg/day of niacin and 630 mg/day of tryptophan. What percentage of his total NE intake is coming from tryptophan? Is this person meeting his RDA?

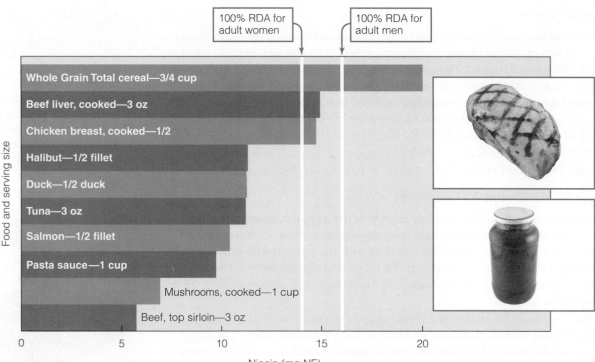

Figure 8.9 Common food sources of niacin. The RDA for niacin is 16 mg NE/day for men and 14 mg NE/day for women. (*Data from:* U.S. Department of Agriculture, Agricultural Research Service. 2008. USDA Nutrient Database for Standard Reference, Release 21. Available online at www.ars.usda.gov/Services/docs.htm?docid=8964.)

damage, glucose intolerance, blurred vision, and edema of the eyes can be seen with very large doses of niacin taken over long periods of time. The UL for niacin is 35 mg/day and was determined based on the level of niacin below which flushing is typically not observed.

What Happens If We Don't Consume Enough Niacin?

Pellagra results from severe niacin deficiency. It commonly occurred in the United States and parts of Europe in the early 20th century in areas where corn, maize, or sorghum was the dietary staple. These foods are low in both niacin and the amino acid tryptophan. Although traditional diets in South America are also high in corn, these diets do not cause pellagra, a fact attributed to the cooking of the corn in lime powder (that is, calcium oxide), which makes niacin more available. At the present time, pellagra is rarely seen in industrialized countries, except in cases of chronic alcoholism. Pellagra is still found in India, China, and Africa. (For more information on this disease, see the Highlight box, "Solving the Mystery of Pellagra," on page 5 in Chapter 1.)

Initial symptoms of pellagra include functional changes in the gastrointestinal tract that decrease the amount of HCl produced and the absorption of nutrients, and lesions in the central nervous system causing weakness, fatigue, and anorexia. These initial symptoms are followed by what have been identified as the classic "three Ds"—dermatitis, diarrhea, and dementia.[5] The name *pellagra* literally means "rough skin": dermatitis occurs on parts of the body more exposed to the elements, such as the face, neck, hands, and feet (see the photograph on page 5). The diarrhea and dementia develop as the disease worsens and further affect the gastrointestinal tract and central nervous system.

Vitamin B₆ (Pyridoxine)

Vitamin B$_6$ is actually a group of three related compounds: pyridoxine (PN), pyridoxal (PL), pyridoxamine (PM), and their phosphate forms, which include pyridoxine phosphate

pellagra A disease that results from severe niacin deficiency.

Figure 8.10   Structure of the vitamin B$_6$ compounds and their interconversions to the phosphorylated forms.

(PNP), pyridoxal phosphate (PLP), and pyridoxamine phosphate (PMP), respectively. The structures of these compounds are shown in **Figure 8.10**.

Functions of Vitamin B$_6$

Some of the metabolic pathways in which vitamin B$_6$ functions are illustrated in Figure 8.2. In the form of PLP, vitamin B$_6$ is a coenzyme for more than 100 enzymes involved in the metabolism of amino acids. It plays a critical role in transamination, which is the key process in making nonessential amino acids; without adequate vitamin B$_6$, all amino acids become essential, as the body cannot make them in sufficient quantities. In addition, PLP is required for synthesis of glycogen phosphorylase, the enzyme responsible for releasing glucose from stored glycogen. Vitamin B$_6$ is also essential for gluconeogenesis and assists in several steps of glucose metabolism.

Vitamin B$_6$ is also important, along with folate and vitamin B$_{12}$, for the metabolism of the amino acid homocysteine, which is described in more detail in Chapter 12. It also plays a role in the synthesis of hemoglobin and in oxygen transport.

How Much Vitamin B$_6$ Should We Consume?

The RDA for vitamin B$_6$ for adult men and women aged 19 to 50 years is 1.3 mg/day. For adults 51 years of age and older, the RDA increases to 1.7 mg/day for men and 1.5 mg/day for women. The increased requirement with aging is based on data indicating that more vitamin B$_6$ is required to maintain normal vitamin B$_6$ status, using blood PLP concentrations as a status indicator, in older individuals. Based on NHANES III data, the average dietary intake of vitamin B$_6$ from food for men and women between the ages of 19 and 70 years was approximately 2 mg/day and approximately 1.5 to 1.6 mg/day, respectively.[4]

Because of the role vitamin B$_6$ plays in protein metabolism, it has been proposed that the requirement for vitamin B$_6$ be based on protein intake. Although the RDAs did not define vitamin B$_6$ intake in terms of protein intake, we do know that as protein intake increases, more vitamin B$_6$ is required.[4] Fortunately, nature has combined vitamin B$_6$ and protein in many of the same foods so that food sources high in protein are also typically high in vitamin B$_6$.

Food Sources of Vitamin B$_6$

Good sources of vitamin B$_6$ include meat, fish (especially tuna), poultry, and organ meats, which are also high in protein (**Figure 8.11**). Thus, protein and vitamin B$_6$ are provided together in the same food, which ensures adequate protein metabolism. Besides meat and fish, good food sources of vitamin B$_6$ include enriched ready-to-eat cereals, white potatoes and other starchy vegetables, bananas, and fortified soy-based meat

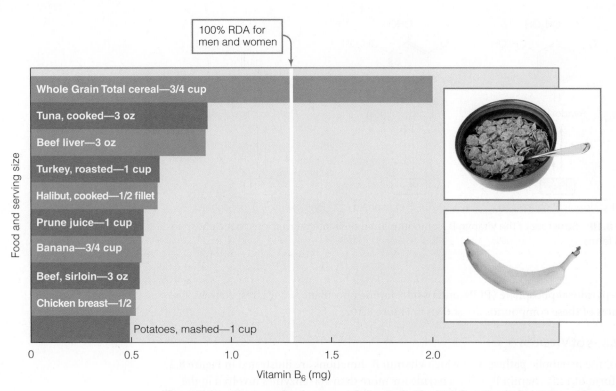

100% RDA for men and women

Whole Grain Total cereal—3/4 cup

Tuna, cooked—3 oz

Beef liver—3 oz

Turkey, roasted—1 cup

Halibut, cooked—1/2 fillet

Prune juice—1 cup

Banana—3/4 cup

Beef, sirloin—3 oz

Chicken breast—1/2

Potatoes, mashed—1 cup

Food and serving size

0   0.5   1.0   1.5   2.0

Vitamin B$_6$ (mg)

Figure 8.11   Common food sources of vitamin B$_6$. The RDA for vitamin B$_6$ is 1.3 mg/day for men and women aged 19 to 50 years. (*Data from:* U.S. Department of Agriculture, Agricultural Research Service. 2008. USDA Nutrient Database for Standard Reference, Release 21. Available online at www.ars.usda.gov/Services/docs.htm?docid=8964.)

substitutes. In the typical American diet, approximately 40% of the dietary vitamin B$_6$ comes from animal sources, while 60% comes from plants. For this reason, individuals who eliminate animal foods from their diet need to make sure they select plant foods high in vitamin B$_6$.

What Happens If We Consume Too Much Vitamin B$_6$?

As with the other B-vitamins discussed earlier, there are no adverse effects associated with high intakes of vitamin B$_6$ from food sources. Vitamin B$_6$ supplements have been used to treat conditions such as premenstrual syndrome and carpal tunnel syndrome. Caution is required, however, when using such supplements. High doses of supplemental vitamin B$_6$ have been associated with sensory neuropathy and dermatological lesions.[4] Thus, the UL for vitamin B$_6$ is set at 100 mg/day. See the Nutrition Debate following this chapter for more discussion of high intakes of vitamin B$_6$ and premenstrual syndrome.

What Happens If We Don't Consume Enough Vitamin B$_6$?

A number of conditions appear to increase the need for vitamin B$_6$. These include alcoholism, certain prescription medications, intense physical activity, and chronic diseases such as arthritis and vascular disease.[4, 7, 8] If we don't get enough vitamin B$_6$ in the diet, the symptoms of vitamin B$_6$ deficiency can develop. These include anemia, convulsions, depression, confusion, and inflamed, irritated patches on the skin. Notice that the symptoms associated with vitamin B$_6$ deficiency involve three tissues: skin, blood, and nervous system. This fact reflects the role of vitamin B$_6$ in protein metabolism, red blood cell development, and the synthesis of neurotransmitters.

As you will read in Chapter 12, vitamin B$_6$, folate, and vitamin B$_{12}$ are important for the metabolism of the amino acid methionine. If the intakes of any of these three vitamins are low, blood levels of homocysteine increase because of incomplete metabolism of

Tuna is a very good source of vitamin B$_6$.

(a) Coenzyme A (CoA)

(b) Acyl carrier protein (ACP)

Figure 8.12 Structure of coenzymes containing pantothenic acid. **(a)** Coenzyme A (CoA).
(b) Acyl carrier protein (ACP).

methionine. High blood homocysteine concentrations are an independent risk factor for cardiovascular disease. There is no specific disease that is solely attributed to vitamin B_6 deficiency.

Pantothenic Acid

Pantothenic acid is an essential vitamin that is metabolized into two major coenzymes: coenzyme A (CoA) and acyl carrier protein (ACP), which are shown in **Figure 8.12**. Both are essential in the synthesis of fatty acids, while CoA is essential for fatty acid oxidation, ketone metabolism, and the metabolism of carbohydrate and protein.[9] For example, in the conversion of pyruvate to acetyl CoA, the enzyme pyruvate dehydrogenase requires CoA. Many of the metabolic reactions that require pantothenic acid for energy production are illustrated in Figure 8.2. Besides its role in energy metabolism, pantothenic acid is required in the synthesis of cholesterol and steroids and in the detoxification of drugs.

Shiitake mushrooms contain ten to twenty times more pantothenic acid than other types of mushrooms.

The AI for pantothenic acid for adult men and women aged 19 years and older is 5 mg/day. Pantothenic acid is widely distributed in foods, with the average daily intake at approximately 5 mg/day and usual intakes ranging from 4 to 7 mg/day.[4, 9] Thus, the AI for pantothenic acid and the average dietary intake are similar. As mentioned, pantothenic acid is available from a variety of foods, including chicken, beef, egg yolk, potatoes, oat cereals, tomato products, whole grains, and organ meats (**Figure 8.13**). There are no known adverse effects from consuming excess amounts of pantothenic acid, and deficiencies of pantothenic acid are very rare.

Biotin

Biotin is a component of four carboxylase enzymes that are present in humans. These enzymes serve as the CO_2 (carbon dioxide) carrier and the carboxyl donor for substrates.[9] **Figure 8.14** shows the structure of biotin.

The enzymes that require biotin as a coenzyme are involved in fatty acid synthesis (for example, lipogenesis), gluconeogenesis, and carbohydrate, fat, and protein metabolism. For example, pyruvate carboxylase catalyzes the synthesis of oxaloacetate from pyruvate in the

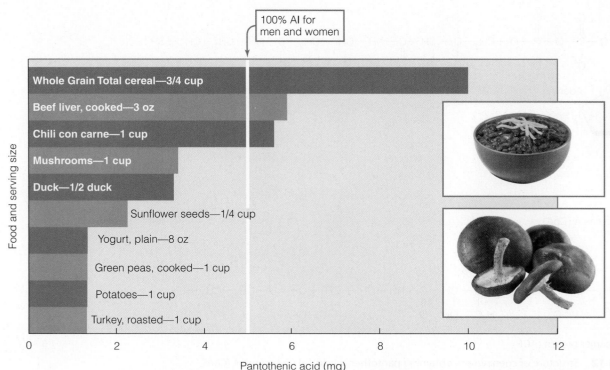

Figure 8.13 shows a bar chart with the y-axis labeled "Food and serving size" and x-axis labeled "Pantothenic acid (mg)" ranging from 0 to 12. A vertical line at 5 mg is labeled "100% AI for men and women."

- Whole Grain Total cereal—3/4 cup
- Beef liver, cooked—3 oz
- Chili con carne—1 cup
- Mushrooms—1 cup
- Duck—1/2 duck
- Sunflower seeds—1/4 cup
- Yogurt, plain—8 oz
- Green peas, cooked—1 cup
- Potatoes—1 cup
- Turkey, roasted—1 cup

Figure 8.13 Common food sources of pantothenic acid. The AI for pantothenic acid is 5 mg/day for men and women. (*Data from:* U.S. Department of Agriculture, Agricultural Research Service. 2008. USDA Nutrient Database for Standard Reference, Release 21. Available online at www.ars.usda.gov/Services/docs.htm?docid=8964.)

Figure 8.14 Structure of biotin.

TCA cycle. Many of the enzyme reactions that require biotin for energy production are illustrated in Figure 8.2.

The AI for biotin for adult men and women aged 19 and older is 30 µg/day. The biotin content has been determined for very few foods, and these values are not reported in food composition tables or dietary analysis programs. In food, biotin exists as free biotin or bound to protein as biocytin, both of which appear to be widespread in foods. The free form of biotin is shown in Figure 8.14; the structure of biocytin is similar to free biotin but has an amino acid attached to the carboxyl end.

There are no known adverse effects from consuming excess amounts of biotin. Biotin deficiencies are typically seen only in people who consume a large number of raw egg whites over long periods of time. This is because raw egg whites contain a protein that binds with biotin and prevents its absorption. Biotin deficiencies are also seen in people fed total parenteral nutrition (nutrients administered by a route other than the GI tract) that is not supplemented with biotin. Symptoms include thinning of hair; loss of hair color; development of a red, scaly rash around the eyes, nose, and mouth; depression; lethargy; and hallucinations.

RECaP

The B-vitamins include thiamin, riboflavin, niacin, vitamin B_6 (pyridoxine), folate, vitamin B_{12} (cobalamin), pantothenic acid, and biotin. The primary action of the B-vitamins, except for folate and B_{12}, is to assist in the metabolism of carbohydrates, fats, protein, and alcohol. They are commonly found in whole grains, enriched breads, ready-to-eat cereals, meats, dairy products, and some fruits and vegetables. B-vitamin toxicity is rare unless a person consumes large doses as supplements. Thiamin deficiency causes beriberi, and niacin deficiency causes pellagra.

Judy
Nutri-Case

"Ever since my doctor put me on this crazy diet, I've been feeling hungry and exhausted. This morning I'm sitting in the lunch room on my break, and I actually doze off and start dreaming about food! Maureen, one of the gals I work with, comes in and has to wake me up! I told her what's been going on with me, and she thinks I should start taking some B-vitamins so I stay healthy while I'm on the diet. She says B-vitamins are the most important because they give you energy. Maybe after work I'll stop off at the mall and buy some. If they give you energy, maybe they'll make it easier to stick to my diet, too."

Is Judy's co-worker correct when she asserts that B-vitamins "give you energy"? Either way, do you think it's likely that Judy needs to take B-vitamin supplements to ensure that she "stays healthy" while she is on her prescribed diet? Why or why not? Finally, could taking B-vitamins help Judy stick to her diet?

Choline

Choline is a vitamin-like substance that is important for metabolism, the structural integrity of cell membranes, and neurotransmission. It is typically grouped with the B-vitamins because of its role in fat digestion and transport and homocysteine metabolism.

Specifically, choline plays an important role in the metabolism and transport of fats and cholesterol. High amounts of the choline-containing compound phosphatidylcholine are found in bile, which aids fat digestion, and in the formation of lipoproteins, which transport endogenous and dietary fat and cholesterol in the blood to the cells. Choline is also necessary for the synthesis of phospholipids and other components of cell membranes; thus, choline plays a critical role in the structural integrity of cell membranes. Finally, choline accelerates the synthesis and release of **acetylcholine,** a neurotransmitter that is involved in many functions, including muscle movement and memory storage.

Although small amounts of choline can be synthesized within the body, the amount made is insufficient for our needs; thus, choline is considered an essential dietary nutrient. Choline has an AI of 550 mg/day for men aged 19 and older and an AI of 425 mg/day for women aged 19 and older. There are limited data on the choline intake of North Americans, because choline intake is not reported in the NHANES or other large surveys done in the United States or Canada. In addition, it is not reported in major nutrient databases. However, it is estimated that choline intakes in the United States and Canada range from 730 to 1,040 mg/day,[4] based on the typical choline content of foods.

Choline is widespread in foods, typically in the form of phosphatidylcholine (see Figure 5.6 on page 175) in the cell membranes of the food. Foods that are high in choline include milk, liver, eggs, and peanuts.[4] Lecithin (another term for phosphatidylcholine) is added to foods during processing as an emulsifying agent, which also increases choline intakes in the diet. Inadequate intakes of choline can lead to increased fat accumulation in the liver, which eventually leads to liver damage. Excessive intake of supplemental choline results in various toxicity symptoms, including a fishy body odor, vomiting, excess salivation, sweating, diarrhea, and low blood pressure. The UL for choline for adults 19 years of age and older is 3.5 g/day.

Iodine

Iodine is the heaviest trace element required for human health and a necessary component of the thyroid hormones, which help regulate human metabolism. In nature, this element is found primarily as inorganic salts in rocks, soil, plants, animals, and water as either iodine

Choline is widespread in foods and can be found in eggs and milk.

acetylcholine A neurotransmitter that is involved in many functions, including muscle movement and memory storage.

(a) Thyroxine (T$_4$)

(b) 3, 5, 3'–Triiodothyronine (T$_3$)

(c) Tyrosine

Figure 8.15 Thyroid hormones contain iodine (I). **(a)** Structure of the thyroid hormone T$_4$. **(b)** Structure of the thyroid hormone T$_3$. Both are derived from the iodination of **(c)** tyrosine, an amino acid.

Figure 8.16 Goiter, or enlargement of the thyroid gland, occurs with both iodine toxicity and deficiency.

goiter Enlargement of the thyroid gland; can be caused by iodine toxicity or deficiency.

or iodide, but once it enters the GI tract, it is broken down to iodide, which is the negative ion of iodine, designated I⁻. Upon absorption, the majority of this iodide is taken up by the thyroid gland.[10]

Functions of Iodine

As just noted, iodine is responsible for a single function within the body: the synthesis of thyroid hormones.[11] Although iodine's function is singular, the multiple actions of thyroid hormones mean that it affects the whole body. Thyroid hormones regulate key metabolic reactions associated with body temperature, resting metabolic rate, macronutrient metabolism, and reproduction and growth.[11]

The structure of the thyroid hormones, thyroxine (T$_4$) and 3, 5, 3'-triiodothyronine (T$_3$), illustrates the placement of iodine (I) in these two hormones (**Figure 8.15**). Both are derived from the iodination of the amino acid tyrosine, shown in Figure 8.15c. Notice that thyroxine has four iodine molecules as part of its structure, whereas triiodothyronine has three—thus, the abbreviated designations T$_4$ and T$_3$. Thyroxine (T$_4$) is the primary circulating thyroid hormone. The removal of one iodine group is required to generate the active form of T$_3$.[11]

How Much Iodine Should We Consume?

The body needs relatively little iodine to maintain health. The RDA for adults 19 years of age and older is 150 µg/day. It is estimated that the iodine intake from food in the United States is approximately 200 to 300 µg/day for men and 190 to 210 µg/day for women.[12]

Very few foods are reliable sources of iodine, because the amount of iodine in foods varies according to the soil, irrigation, and fertilizers used. Saltwater foods, both fish and plants, tend to have higher amounts because marine species concentrate iodine from seawater. Good food sources include saltwater fish, shrimp, seaweed, iodized salt, and white and whole-wheat breads made with iodized salt and bread conditioners. In addition, iodine is added to dairy cattle feed and used in sanitizing solutions in the dairy industry, making dairy foods an important source of iodine.

Iodine has been voluntarily added to salt in the United States since 1924 to combat iodine deficiency resulting from the poor iodine content of soils in this country. For many people, iodized salt is their primary source of iodine, and approximately one-half a teaspoon of iodized salt meets the entire adult RDA for iodine. When you buy salt, look carefully at the package label, because stores carry both iodized and non-iodized salt. If iodine has been added to the salt, it will be clearly marked on the label. Most specialty salts, such as kosher salt or sea salt, do not have iodine added; thus, you need to read the label carefully.

Excess iodine intakes can cause a number of health-related problems, especially related to thyroid gland function. Too much iodine blocks the synthesis of thyroid hormones. As the thyroid gland attempts to produce more hormones, it may enlarge, a condition known as **goiter** (**Figure 8.16**). Goiter refers to the enlargement of the thyroid gland, regardless of its cause. Iodine toxicity generally occurs as a result of excessive supplementation. Thus, the UL for iodine is 1,100 µg/day.

A number of deficiency disorders are associated with low iodine intakes. Paradoxically, goiter is also the most classic disorder of iodine deficiency. An insufficient supply of iodine means there is less iodine for the production of thyroid hormones. The body responds by stimulating the thyroid gland, including increasing the size of the gland, in an attempt to capture more iodine from the blood.

The development of a goiter is only one of many symptoms that result when iodine is insufficient in the diet. A broader term applied to the disorders associated with poor iodine intakes is *iodine deficiency disorders,* or *IDDs,* which include cretinism, growth and developmental disorders, mental deficiencies, neurologic disorders, decreased fertility, congenital abnormalities, and prenatal and infant death.[11-13] The World Health Organization (WHO) considers iodine deficiency to be the "greatest single cause of preventable brain damage and mental retardation" in the world.[13] If a woman experiences iodine deficiency during pregnancy, her infant has a high risk of being born with a unique form of mental retardation referred to as **cretinism.** In addition to mental retardation, these infants may suffer from stunted growth, deafness, and muteness. Among pregnant women, iodine deficiency may also increase the occurrence of spontaneous abortion, stillbirths and congenital abnormalities, and infant mortality.[11] The impact of mild iodine deficiency on the development of the brain and neurologic system of a child is more difficult to determine. Iodine deficiency can also cause **hypothyroidism** (low blood levels of thyroid hormone), which is characterized by decreased body temperature, inability to tolerate cold environmental temperatures, weight gain, fatigue, and sluggishness.

According to the International Council for the Control of IDDs (ICCIDD), 2.2 billion people live in areas of iodine deficiency and are at increased risk for its health complications and consequences.[14] In the United States, large areas of crop-producing lands are low in iodine, and thus foods grown on these lands are low in iodine. At the beginning of the 20th century, IDDs and goiter were considered endemic in the United States. However, the problem was not fully addressed until World War I, when many conscripted men were barred from military service because they had goiters. At this time, treatment of goiters with sodium iodine was shown to be effective, and the search was on for a method of increasing iodine in the food supply from either fortification of processed foods, increasing the level of iodine in the soil through fertilizers, or adding iodine to the feed of animals. After much debate, it was determined that the fortification of salt with iodine was the best solution. This action has reduced the incidence of goiter to <2.8% of individuals in developed countries.[11, 13]

Hyperthyroidism (high blood levels of thyroid hormone) is most commonly caused by Graves' disease, which is an autoimmune disease that causes an overproduction of thyroid hormones. The symptoms include weight loss, increased heat production, muscular tremors, nervousness, racing heart beat, and protrusion of the eyes.

Saltwater fish, fresh or canned, contain iodine.

Chromium

Chromium is a trace mineral that plays an important role in carbohydrate metabolism. You may be interested to learn that the chromium in the body is the same metal used in the chrome plating for cars. Chromium enhances the ability of insulin to transport glucose from the bloodstream into cells.[12] Chromium also plays important roles in the metabolism of RNA and DNA, in immune function, and in growth.

Chromium supplements are marketed to reduce body fat and enhance muscle mass and have become popular with bodybuilders and other athletes interested in improving their body composition. The Nutrition: Myth or Fact? box in this chapter investigates whether taking supplemental chromium is effective in improving body composition.

The body needs only small amounts of chromium. The AI for adults aged 19 to 50 years is 35 μg/day for men and 25 μg/day for women. For adults 51 years of age and older, the AI decreases to 30 μg/day and 20 μg/day for men and women, respectively.[12] The AI for individuals over 50 years was based on the energy intake of older adults, which is typically lower than that of younger individuals.

The question of whether or not the average diet provides adequate chromium is controversial: Chromium is widely distributed in foods, but concentrations in any particular food are not typically high. In addition, determining the chromium content of food is difficult because contamination can easily occur during the laboratory analysis. Thus, we cannot determine average chromium intake from any currently existing nutrient database.

Foods identified as good sources of chromium include mushrooms, prunes, dark chocolate, nuts, whole grains, cereals, asparagus, brewer's yeast, some beers, red wine, and meats, especially processed meats. Dairy products are typically poor sources of chromium.

Our bodies contain very little chromium. Asparagus is a good dietary source of this trace mineral.

cretinism A unique form of mental retardation that occurs in infants when the mother experiences iodine deficiency during pregnancy.

hypothyroidism A condition characterized by low blood levels of thyroid hormone.

hyperthyroidism A condition characterized by high blood levels of thyroid hormone.

Nutrition Myth or Fact?
Can Chromium Supplements Enhance Body Composition?

Chromium supplements, predominantly in the form of chromium picolinate, are popular with bodybuilders and weight lifters. This popularity stems from claims that chromium increases muscle mass and muscle strength and decreases body fat. But are these claims myth or fact?

An early study of chromium supplementation was promising, in that chromium use in both untrained men and football players was found to decrease body fat and increase muscle mass.[15] These findings caused a surge in the popularity of chromium supplements and motivated many scientists across the United States to test the reproducibility of these early findings. The next study of chromium supplementation found no effects of chromium on muscle mass, body fat, or muscle strength.[16]

These contradictory reports led experts to closely examine the two studies. When they did so, they found a number of flaws in the methodology of both. One major concern with the first study was that the chromium status of the research participants prior to the study was not measured or controlled.[15] It was possible that the participants were deficient in chromium; this deficiency could cause a more positive reaction to chromium than would be expected in people with normal chromium status. Thus, subsequent studies were designed to control for participants' pre-study chromium status.

A second major concern was that body composition was measured in these studies using the skinfold technique, in which calipers are used to measure the thickness of the skin and fat at various sites on the body. Although this method gives a good general estimate of body fat in young, lean, healthy people, it is not sensitive to small changes in muscle mass. Thus, subsequent studies of chromium used more sophisticated methods of measuring body composition.

The results of research studies conducted over the past 10 years consistently show that chromium supplementation has no effect on muscle mass, body fat, or muscle strength in a variety of groups, including untrained college males and females, overweight and obese females, collegiate wrestlers, and older men and women.[17–23] Neither have scientists found an effect of chromium on body composition when different types of experimental designs have been used, with varying energy intakes and exercise expenditure.[24, 25] Despite this overwhelming evidence to the contrary, many supplement companies still claim that chromium supplements enhance strength and muscle mass and reduce body fat. These claims result in millions of dollars of sales of supplements to consumers each year. Before you decide to purchase chromium supplements, read some of the studies cited here. The information they provide may help you avoid being one of the many consumers fooled by this costly nutrition myth.

Food-processing methods can also add chromium to foods, especially if the food is processed in stainless steel containers. For example, it is assumed that wine and beer derive some of their chromium content from processing.[12]

There appears to be no toxicity related to consuming chromium in the diet, but there are insufficient data to establish a UL for chromium. Because chromium supplements are widely used in the United States, the Institute of Medicine (IOM) has recommended more research to determine the safety of high-dose chromium supplements. Until this research is available, supplementation with high amounts of chromium is discouraged. Chromium deficiency appears to be uncommon in the United States. When chromium deficiency is induced in a research setting, glucose uptake into the cells is inhibited, causing a rise in blood glucose and insulin levels. Chromium deficiency can also result in elevated blood lipid levels and in damage to the brain and nervous system.[12]

Manganese

A trace mineral, manganese is a cofactor involved in protein, fat, and carbohydrate metabolism, gluconeogenesis, cholesterol synthesis, and the formation of urea, the primary com-

Figure 8.17 Common food sources of manganese. The AI for manganese is 2.3 mg/day for men and 1.8 mg/day for women. (*Data from:* U.S. Department of Agriculture, Agricultural Research Service. 2008. USDA Nutrient Database for Standard Reference, Release 21. Available online at www.ars.usda.gov/Services/docs.htm?docid=8964.)

ponent of urine.[26] It also assists in the synthesis of the protein matrix found in bone tissue and in building cartilage, a tissue supporting joints. Manganese is also an integral component of superoxide dismutase, an antioxidant enzyme. Thus, it assists in the conversion of free radicals to less damaging substances, protecting the body from oxidative damage (see Chapter 10).

The AI for manganese for adults 19 years of age and older is 2.3 mg/day for men and 1.8 mg/day for women. Manganese requirements are easily met, as this mineral is widespread in foods and is readily available in a varied diet. Whole-grain foods such as oat bran, wheat flour, whole-wheat spaghetti, and brown rice are good sources of manganese (**Figure 8.17**). Other sources include pineapple, pine nuts, okra, spinach, and raspberries. Overall, grain products contribute approximately 37% of dietary manganese, and vegetables and beverages, primarily tea, contribute another 18% to 20%.[12]

Manganese toxicity can occur in occupational environments in which people inhale manganese dust. It can also result from drinking water high in manganese. Toxicity results in impairment of the neuromuscular system, causing symptoms similar to those seen in Parkinson's disease, such as muscle spasms and tremors. Elevated blood manganese concentrations and neurotoxicity were the criteria used to determine the UL for manganese, which is 11 mg/day for adults 19 years of age and older.[12]

Manganese deficiency is rare in humans. Symptoms include impaired growth and reproductive function, reduced bone density and impaired skeletal growth, impaired glucose and lipid metabolism, and skin rash.

Okra is one of the many foods that contain manganese.

Sulfur

Sulfur is a major mineral and a component of the B-vitamins thiamin and biotin. As such, it is essential for macronutrient metabolism. In addition, as part of the amino acids methionine and cysteine, sulfur helps stabilize the three-dimensional shapes of proteins in the body. The liver requires sulfur to assist in the detoxification of alcohol and various drugs, and sulfur assists in maintaining acid–base balance.

The body is able to obtain ample sulfur from protein-containing foods; as a result, there is no DRI specifically for sulfur. There are no known toxicity or deficiency symptoms associated with sulfur.

Recap

Choline is a vitamin-like substance that is required for the production of phosphatidyl-choline. Iodine is necessary for the synthesis of thyroid hormones, which regulate metabolic rate and body temperature. Chromium assists the transport of glucose into the cell, the metabolism of RNA and DNA, and immune function and growth. Manganese is involved in energy metabolism, the formation of urea, the synthesis of bone protein matrix and cartilage, and protection against free radicals. Sulfur is part of the B-vitamins thiamin and biotin and the amino acids methionine and cysteine.

What Disorders Can Result from Inadequate B-Vitamin Intake?

We have already discussed the classic deficiency diseases that can result when intake of selected B-vitamins is significantly inadequate, such as beriberi with thiamin deficiency and pellagra with niacin deficiency. However, what happens when intake of the B-vitamins is low, but not low enough to cause one of these deficiency diseases? What happens when the diet provides a minimum level of B-vitamins, but not enough to fully supply the metabolic pathways of the body with the coenzymes they need? Here, we discuss how a low intake of the B-vitamins can affect an individual's ability to perform physical activity.

How Do Researchers Compare Vitamin Status in Active and Sedentary Populations?

As you have learned in this chapter, the B-vitamins, especially thiamin, riboflavin, and vitamin B_6, are coenzymes for many metabolic reactions that produce energy. Thus, it is not surprising that researchers would ask the question: Do individuals who engage in regular physical activity have higher needs for thiamin, riboflavin, and vitamin B_6 than sedentary adults? Researchers have attempted to answer this question in a number of ways.

First, researchers have designed studies in which they identify individuals with poor B-vitamin status and then determine the impact of the low status on the individuals' ability to perform exercise. They can then compare the average performance of low-status individuals to the average performance of individuals with good B-vitamin status.

Second, they have performed controlled metabolic diet studies to determine if athletes need higher levels of B-vitamins than sedentary adults to maintain their vitamin status. For more information on this type of study, see the accompanying Highlight: How Do Scientists Determine Vitamin Requirements?

Third, researchers have conducted cross-sectional studies that compare the nutritional status of trained athletes to sedentary individuals to determine the frequency of poor B-vitamin status in each group. A drawback of cross-sectional studies is that the two groups of people they compare may have other differences besides their fitness level that contribute to their differences in nutritional status. Cross-sectional studies help determine whether or not differences exist between two groups, but more detailed studies are needed to determine if those differences were due to level of physical activity alone.

Perhaps the ideal study of the effect of physical activity on B-vitamin status would be longitudinal, controlling B-vitamin intake over several months in a study group of athletes, while varying their activity level from low to high. Researchers would then be able to monitor any changes in nutritional status and determine whether these changes affect an individual's ability to perform physical activity. Unfortunately, such studies are difficult and expensive to conduct.

Highlight

How Do Scientists Determine Vitamin Requirements?

Throughout this book, we identify the precise amounts of the different vitamins you need to consume each day to maintain good health. But have you ever wondered how researchers determine these recommendations? Of the several methods used, one of the most rigorous is the metabolic diet study.

The goal of a metabolic diet study is to determine how vitamin assessment parameters in the blood, urine, and feces change as the dietary intake of a nutrient, such as vitamin B_6, is closely controlled. In a metabolic diet study, which may last for weeks or months, all foods eaten by study participants are carefully prepared, weighed to within 0.1 g, and recorded. Subjects are usually required to either live at the research facility (where all physical activity is monitored) or come to the research facility for all of their meals. Depending on the nutrient being studied, all fluids, even water, may also be provided to the participant. Throughout the study, each participant's body weight is measured daily to prevent any increase or decrease in weight. If weight does change, energy intake is altered so that the subject returns to the baseline weight. This must be done without altering the intake of the vitamin being studied. Because many of the vitamins we talked about in this chapter help to metabolize protein, fat, and/or carbohydrate, it is important that the body stores of these macronutrients do not change during the metabolic study. This is why monitoring weight and physical activity is so important. At different times during the study, vitamin assessment parameters will be measured in the blood, urine, and feces. This may require that the subject collect all urine and feces throughout the study.

For example, let's say you want to determine whether active and sedentary men have different requirements for vitamin B_6. You know that during physical activity, carbohydrate is burned for fuel, and that protein is necessary for the building and repair of muscle tissue. You also know that vitamin B_6 is very important for glucose and protein metabolism; thus, physical activity might increase the body's need for this B-vitamin.

To compare vitamin B_6 requirements, you might design a study as follows. First you would recruit active young men between the ages of 20 and 35 years (all of equal fitness levels and exercising the same number of hours/week), as well as sedentary males of the same age. You would then feed the participants a succession of three different diets, each lasting 3 weeks, and each providing a different level of vitamin B_6. The diets would be:

1. vitamin B_6 below the RDA (1.0 mg/day)
2. vitamin B_6 at the level of the RDA (1.3 mg/day)
3. vitamin B_6 above the RDA (1.6 mg/day)

Ideally, you would randomly assign these diets so that one individual might be fed diet number 1 while another individual is on diet number 2, and another is on diet number 3. By randomly assigning the diets, you ensure that you do not dictate the order in which they are fed. Because you don't want the effect of one diet to carry over to the next diet you are feeding, you would need to include a "washout" period between diets. How long this washout period lasted would depend on the vitamin you are researching, but for our example, 6 weeks should be long enough because vitamin B_6 is a water-soluble vitamin. During the washout period, all participants would be fed a diet providing the RDA for vitamin B_6 for normal healthy men.

During the study period, you would need to ensure that subjects do not eat any foods except what you feed them. In addition, study participants must be monitored to *make sure they eat all the food*. Throughout the study, the amount of vitamin B_6 in the foods would need to be determined via chemical analysis in a lab, as would the amount of vitamin B_6 in the participants' blood, urine, and fecal samples. You would also need to make sure all subjects maintained baseline body weights.

You would then determine nutritional status for the men when they were on each of the three test diets to determine which diet was able to keep assessment parameters within normal range. You would also compare vitamin status between groups for each of the diets. If the active men have poor status on 1.3 mg/day of vitamin B_6, while the sedentary subjects have adequate status on this level, you would conclude that the RDA is not adequate for the active individuals and they would need more vitamin B_6 to maintain good status.

What Evidence Links Exercise Performance and B-Vitamin Status?

Because of the role B-vitamins play in energy production during exercise, researchers generally assume that individuals with poor B-vitamin status will have a reduced ability to perform physical activity. This hypothesis has been supported in classic studies examining the effect of thiamin, riboflavin, and vitamin B_6 deficiency on work performance.[27–29]

For example, a team of Dutch researchers depleted 24 healthy active men of thiamin, riboflavin, and vitamin B_6 over an 11-week period by feeding them a diet high in processed foods (see the diet below).[26] Specifically, the diet contained only 50% of the RDA for thiamin, riboflavin, and vitamin B_6. Researchers then examined the effect of this B-vitamin deficiency on the men's ability to perform physical activity. They found that B-vitamin depletion significantly decreased the ability to perform maximal work by 7% to 12%, depending on the testing method used. Thus, it took only 11 weeks of eating a low-B-vitamin diet before these men were unable to exercise at the same intensity and duration as they had when they were consuming adequate amounts of these vitamins.

What Types of Diets Are Low in B-Vitamins?

Diets high in unenriched processed foods typically provide inadequate levels of the B-vitamins. In the Dutch study just described, feeding a diet high in processed foods produced poor vitamin status in just 11 weeks.[25, 26] The diet used in this study follows. Does it resemble your own diet or that of someone you know?

Diets high in processed foods and simple carbohydrates are low in B-vitamins.

- Breakfast: white rolls, margarine, cheese, jam
- Lunch: white rolls, margarine, cheese, beef, jam, peanut butter
- Dinner: white rice, carrots, green peas, beans, margarine, applesauce, beef, cream, peaches
- Snacks: soft drinks, honey cake, cookies, tea, coffee, sugar, margarine

As you will notice, it is easy to have low intakes of the B-vitamins if you elect to eat a diet that is low in whole grains, fruits, and vegetables, and high in sugar and fat. To help overcome this problem, in the 1940s the United States Food and Drug Administration mandated the enrichment of refined grains, such as wheat, corn, and rice, with thiamin, riboflavin, niacin, and iron. Thus, some of the nutrients lost in the milling process are replaced by the enrichment process.

RECAP

The hypothesis that individuals with poor B-vitamin status will have a reduced ability to perform physical activity has been supported in studies examining the effect of thiamin, riboflavin, and vitamin B_6 deficiency on work performance. Consuming a diet high in whole grains, fruits, vegetables, and lean meats and dairy will ensure that your body has adequate B-vitamins to fuel physical activity. In the United States, some of the nutrients lost in the milling of grains are replaced by the enrichment process.

Theo
Nutri-Case

"I'm healthy and I eat lots of different kinds of foods. But I use up a lot of fuel playing basketball and working out. So I'm wondering—should I take one of those basic vitamin pills every day—just to make sure I'm getting enough of everything I need?"

What do you think? Should highly active people who eat a balanced diet take a multivitamin–mineral supplement every day? Defend your answer.

See for Yourself

Meeting your RDA for Vitamin B₆

Open up your cupboard and take a look inside. How many processed foods providing B-vitamins do you consume on a typical day? Pull out all such foods, including breads, ready-to-eat cereals, pasta, energy bars, meal replacement drinks, and so forth. Then, if you take any supplements, including vitamins, protein powders, weight loss supplements, and so forth, line those up, too.

Now, let's see if we can determine whether you are meeting or exceeding your RDA for vitamin B₆. We'll limit our analysis to B₆ because it is one of the B vitamins with a UL. Use the template provided below to document your vi-

tamin B₆ intake for a typical day. On food labels, the amount of the vitamin will be given as a percentage of the daily value (%DV). Thus, you will first have to write down the %DV for each serving. Be sure to look at the serving size! If you eat 2 servings, you will need to multiply this value by 2, and so on. Finally, convert the %DV to the amount that you ate. For vitamin B₆, 100% of the DV is 2 mg. The "You Do the Math" box on pages 58–59 in Chapter 2 will also help you with this activity. Notice that we have filled in one line of the template as an example.

Meal	Food	% DV for B₆	Servings	%DV per serving	B₆ consumed (mg)
Breakfast	Wheaties	50%	2	100%	2 mg
Lunch					
Snack					
Dinner					
Supplements					
Total mg B₆/day:					

How much vitamin B₆ did you get each day from processed foods and supplements alone? How much additional vitamin B₆ would you estimate you get in whole foods, such as meat, fish, poultry, starchy vegetables, and ba-

nanas? Are you close to the UL for vitamin B₆ (100 mg for adults age 19–70)? Although this assignment was designed to look at vitamin B₆, you could look at other micronutrients in your diet that have a UL.

Chapter Review

Test Yourself | Answers

1 F B-vitamins do not directly provide energy. However, they play critical roles in ensuring that the body is able to generate energy from carbohydrates, fats, and proteins.

2 T A severe niacin deficiency can cause pellagra, which once killed thousands of people in the United States alone each year; and thiamin deficiency causes beriberi, which can result in heart failure.

3 F The IOM has set ULs for both niacin and vitamin B_6. High intakes of these nutrients can cause adverse effects.

4 F Research studies have failed to show any consistent effects of chromium supplements on reducing body fat or enhancing muscle mass.

5 F Not necessarily! Although much of the salt sold in the United States is iodized, you need to read the label carefully. Some brands of table salt, kosher salt, sea salt, and other specialty salts do not provide iodine.

Summary

- The B-vitamins include thiamin, riboflavin, vitamin B_6, niacin, folate, vitamin B_{12}, pantothenic acid, and biotin.

- The primary role of thiamin, riboflavin, niacin, pantothenic acid, and biotin is to act as coenzymes. In this role, they activate enzymes and assist them in the metabolism of carbohydrates, fats, amino acids, and alcohol for energy; the synthesis of fatty acids and cholesterol; and gluconeogenesis.

- Food sources of the B-vitamins include whole grains, enriched breads, ready-to-eat cereals, meats, dairy products, and some fruits and vegetables.

- A deficiency of thiamin can cause beriberi, and a deficiency of niacin can cause pellagra.

- Toxicity is possible with megadoses of some B-vitamins from supplements.

- Choline is a vitamin-like substance that assists with homocysteine metabolism. Choline also accelerates the synthesis and release of acetylcholine, a neurotransmitter.

- Iodine is a trace mineral needed for the synthesis of thyroid hormones. Thyroid hormones are integral to the regulation of body temperature, maintenance of resting metabolic rate, and healthy reproduction and growth.

- Chromium is a trace mineral that enhances the ability of insulin to transport glucose from the bloodstream into the cell. Chromium is also necessary for the metabolism of RNA and DNA and supports normal growth and immune function.

- Manganese is a trace mineral that acts as a cofactor in energy metabolism and in the formation of urea. Manganese also assists in the synthesis of bone and cartilage and is a component of the superoxide dismutase antioxidant enzyme system.

- Sulfur is a major mineral that is a component of thiamin and biotin and the amino acids methionine and cysteine. Sulfur helps stabilize the three-dimensional shapes of proteins and helps the liver detoxify alcohol and various drugs.

- Inadequate levels of the B-vitamins can reduce an individual's ability to perform physical activity. A diet high in processed foods typically provides inadequate levels of the B-vitamins.

Review Questions

1. The B-vitamins include
   a. niacin, folate, and iodine.
   b. cobalamin, iodine, and chromium.
   c. manganese, riboflavin, and pyridoxine.
   d. thiamin, pantothenic acid, and biotin.

2. Which of the following statements about choline is true?
   a. Choline is found exclusively in foods of animal origin.
   b. Choline is a B-vitamin that assists in homocysteine metabolism.
   c. Choline is a neurotransmitter that is involved in muscle movement and memory storage.
   d. Choline is necessary for the synthesis of phospholipids and other components of cell membranes.

3. According to the World Health Organization (WHO), the greatest single cause of preventable brain damage and mental retardation in the world is
   a. iodine deficiency.
   b. chromium deficiency.
   c. manganese deficiency.
   d. sulfur deficiency.

4. Which of the following lunches provides the highest levels of thiamin, riboflavin, niacin, and vitamin B_6?
   a. cheeseburger on a white bun, French fries, applesauce, diet soda
   b. tuna sandwich on whole-wheat bread, green peas, banana, 1 cup of low-fat milk
   c. yogurt parfait (made with plain low-fat yogurt, canned peaches, and raw, unprocessed oats) and fresh-squeezed orange juice
   d. green salad with olive oil and vinegar dressing, low-fat cottage cheese, a slice of sourdough bread with butter, and water

5. Which of the following statements is true of riboflavin?
   a. It is sensitive to heat.
   b. It is a component of CoA.
   c. It is associated primarily with protein metabolism.
   d. It is water soluble.

6. **True or false?** There is no DRI for sulfur.

7. **True or false?** Biotin is a B-vitamin.

8. **True or false?** Iodine is necessary for the synthesis of thyroid hormones.

9. **True or false?** Wernicke–Korsakoff syndrome is a thiamin deficiency related to chronic alcohol abuse.

10. **True or false?** In the United States, milk is fortified with riboflavin to prevent pellagra.

11. Would you expect goiter to be more common in coastal regions or inland? Explain your answer.

12. Explain the statement that, without vitamin B_6, all amino acids become essential.

13. Aaron eats only whole, unprocessed foods and beverages. He asserts that "we would all be better off if we ate foods fresh off the farm" instead of allowing our food industry to "spray" foods with factory-produced vitamins and minerals. Do you agree with Aaron's position? Why or why not?

14. Your great-aunt is on renal dialysis. Explain the implications, if any, for her B-vitamin status.

15. Sally is 35 years old and has always been energetic; however, lately she has been feeling exhausted. She can hardly get out of bed in the morning even after 8 hours of sleep. She has attributed this fatigue to the fact that she has been dieting for weight loss for the last 6 months and is using a low-sodium, low-calorie vegan diet (1,000 kcal/day) that she also hopes will help reduce her blood pressure. She is eating lots of fruits and vegetables, but little else. Although she knows it is important to exercise for weight loss, she is too tired. What do you think might be contributing to Sally's fatigue? Of the micronutrients discussed in this chapter, which ones might be low in her diet? How might they contribute to fatigue?

Web Links

www.ars.usda.gov/ba/bhnrc/ndl
Nutrient Data Laboratory Home Page
Click on "Reports for Single Nutrients" to find reports listing food sources for selected nutrients.

www.bbc.co.uk/health/healthy_living/ complementary_medicine/index.shtml
BBC Healthy Living: Complementary Medicine: Vitamins
Click on "Vitamins" or "Minerals" under "A to Z of remedies" to find pages that provide information on vitamins and minerals, signs of deficiency, therapeutic uses, and food sources.

www.unicef.org/nutrition/index.html
UNICEF: Nutrition
This site provides information about micronutrient deficiencies in developing countries and UNICEF's efforts and programs to combat them.

www.who.dk
World Health Organization (WHO)
This site provides information on nutrient deficiencies throughout the world, including iodine deficiency disorders (IDDs).

http://ods.od.nih.gov
National Institutes of Health (NIH) Office of Dietary Supplements
This site provides information on vitamins and minerals, safe use of supplements, and the research available on the treatment of health problems and disease with various supplements.

http://lpi.oregonstate.edu
Linus Pauling Institute at Oregon State University
This site provides accurate and current information on vitamins, minerals, and phytochemicals that promote health and prevent disease. Search for information on a micronutrient using the micronutrient information center.

References

1. James, N. 2002. Malnutrition data, food security and the geography of food in a communal area of North West Zimbabwe. *Global Built Environment Review* 2(3):42–53. Available online at www.edgehill.account.uk/gber/pdf/vol2/issue3.

2. Tanphaichiter, V. 1999. Thiamin. In: M. E. Shils, J. A. Olson, M. Shire, and A. C. Ross, eds. *Modern Nutrition in Health and Disease*, 9th ed. Philadelphia: Lippincott Williams & Wilkins, pp. 381–389.

3. Smith, C., A. D. Marks, and M. Lieberman. 2005. *Mark's Basic Medical Biochemistry: A Clinical Approach*. 2nd ed. Philadelphia: Lippincott Williams & Wilkins.

4. Institute of Medicine, Food and Nutrition Board. 1998. *Dietary Reference Intakes for Thiamin, Riboflavin, Niacin, Vitamin B_6, Folate, Vitamin B_{12}, Pantothenic Acid, Biotin, and Choline*. Washington, DC: National Academy Press.

5. McCormick, D. B. 2000. Niacin, riboflavin, and thiamin. In: M. H. Stipanuk, ed. *Biochemical and Physiological Aspects of Human Nutrition*. Philadelphia: W. B. Saunders, pp. 458–482.

6. Powers, H. J. 2003. Riboflavin (vitamin B_2) and health. *Am. J. Clin. Nutr.* 77:1352–1360.

7. Manore, M. M. 2000. Effect of physical activity on thiamin, riboflavin, and vitamin B_6 requirements. *Am. J. Clin. Nutr.* 72:598S–606S.

8. Woolf, K., and M. M. Manore. 1999. Nutrition, exercise and rheumatoid arthritis. *Topics Clin. Nutr.* 14(3):30–42.

9. Sweetman, L. 2000. Pantothenic acid and biotin. In: M. H. Stipanuk, ed. *Biochemical and Physiological Aspects of Human Nutrition*. Philadelphia: W. B. Saunders, pp. 519–540.

10. Dunn, J. T. 2006. Iodine. In: M. E. Shils, M. Shike, A. C. Ross, B. Caballero, and R. Cousins, eds. *Modern Nutrition in Health and Disease*. 10th ed. Philadelphia: Lippincott Williams & Wilkins, pp. 300–311.

11. Freake, H. C. 2000. Iodine. In: M. H. Stipanuk, ed. *Biochemical and Physiological Aspects of Human Nutrition*. Philadelphia: W. B. Saunders, pp. 761–781.

12. Institute of Medicine, Food and Nutrition Board. 2001. *Dietary Reference Intakes for Vitamin A, Vitamin K, Arsenic, Boron, Chromium, Copper, Iodine, Iron, Manganese, Molybdenum, Nickel, Silicon, Vanadium, and Zinc*. Washington, DC: National Academy Press.

13. World Health Organization. 2004. Nutrition. Micronutrient deficiencies. International Council of Control of Iodine Deficiency Disorders. Available online at www.who.dk/eprise/main/WHO/Progs/NUT/Deficiency.

14. International Council for the Control of Iodine Deficiency Disorders (ICCIDD). Iodine deficiency. www.iccidd.org/pages/iodine-deficiency.php. (Accessed February 2009.)

15. Evans, G. W. 1989. The effect of chromium picolinate on insulin controlled parameters in humans. *Int. J. Biosoc. Med. Res.* 11:163–180.

16. Hasten, D. L., E. P. Rome, D. B. Franks, and M. Hegsted. 1992. Effects of chromium picolinate on beginning weight training students. *Int. J. Sports Nutr.* 2:343–350.

17. Lukaski, H. C., W. W. Bolonchuk, W. A. Siders, and D. B. Milne. 1996. Chromium supplementation and resistance training: Effects on body composition, strength, and trace element status of men. *Am. J. Clin. Nutr.* 63:954–965.

18. Hallmark, M. A., T. H. Reynolds, C. A. DeSouza, C. O. Dotson, R. A. Anderson, and M. A. Rogers. 1996. Effects of chromium and resistive training on muscle strength and body composition. *Med. Sci. Sports. Exerc.* 28:139–144.

19. Pasman, W. J., M. S. Westerterp-Plantenga, and W. H. Saris. 1997. The effectiveness of long-term supplementation of carbohydrate, chromium, fiber and caffeine on weight maintenance. *Int. J. Obes. Relat. Metab. Disord.* 21:1143–1151.

20. Walker, L. S., M. G. Bemben, D. A. Bemben, and A. W. Knehans. 1998. Chromium picolinate effects on body composition and muscular performance in wrestlers. *Med. Sci. Sports Exerc.* 30:1730–1737.

21. Campbell, W. W., L. J. Joseph, S. L. Davey, D. Cyr-Campbell, R. A. Anderson, and W. J. Evans. 1999. Effects of resistance training and chromium picolinate on body composition and skeletal muscle in older men. *J. Appl. Physiol.* 86:29–39.

22. Volpe, S. L., H. W. Huang, K. Larpadisorn, and I. I. Lesser 2001. Effect of chromium supplementation and exercise on body composition, resting metabolic rate and selected biochemical parameters in moderately obese women following an exercise program. *J. Am. Coll. Nutr.* 20:293–306.

23. Campbell, W. W., L. J. O. Joseph, R. A. Anderson, S. L. Davey, J. Hinton, and W. J. Evans. 2002. Effects of resistive training and chromium picolinate on body composition and skeletal muscle size in older women. *Int. J. Sports Nutr. Exerc. Metab.* 12:125–135.

24. Diaz, L. D., B. A. Watkin, Y. Li, R. A. Anderson, and W. W. Campbell. 2008. Chromium picolinate and conjugated linoleic acid do not synergistically influence diet- and exercise-induced changes in body composition and health indexes in overweight women. *J Nutr. Biochemistry* 19:61–68.

25. Lukaski, H. C., W. A. Siders, and J. G. Penland. 2007. Chromium picolinate supplementation in women: Effects on body weight, composition and iron status. *Nutr.* 23:187–195.

26. Fleet, J. C. 2000. Zinc, copper and manganese. In: M. H. Stipanuk, ed. *Biochemical and Physiological Aspects of Human Nutrition.* Philadelphia: W.B. Saunders, pp. 741–761.

27. van der Beek, E. J., W. van Dokkum, J. Schrijver, M. Wedel, A. W. K. Gaillard, A. Wesstra, H. van de Weerd, and R. J. J. Hermus. 1988. Thiamin, riboflavin, and vitamins B_6 and C: Impact of combined restricted intake on functional performance in man. *Am. J. Clin. Nutr.* 48:1451–1462.

28. van der Beek, E. J., W. van Dokkum, M. Wedel, J. Schrijver, and H. van den Berg. 1994. Thiamin, riboflavin and vitamin B_6: Impact of restricted intake on physical performance in man. *J. Am. Coll. Nutr.* 13:629–640.

29. Wyatt, K. M., P. W. Dimmock, P. W. Jones, and P. M. Shaughn O'Brien. 1999. Efficacy of vitamin B_6 in the treatment of premenstrual syndrome: Systemic review. *Br. J. Med.* 318:1375–1381.

30. Freeman, E. W. 2003. Premenstrual syndrome and premenstrual dysphoric disorder: Definitions and diagnosis. *Psychoneuroendocrinology* 28:25–37.

31. Rapkin, A. 2003. The review of treatment of premenstrual syndrome & premenstrual dysphoric disorder. *Psychoneuroendocrinology* 28:39–53.

32. Thys-Jacobs, S. 2000. Micronutrients and the premenstrual syndrome: The case for calcium. *J. Am. Coll. Nutr.* 19:220–227.

33. Bendich, A. 2000. The potential for dietary supplements to reduce premenstrual syndrome (PMS) symptoms. *J. Am. Coll. Nutr.* 29(1):3–12.

34. Schaumburg, H., J. Kaplan, A. Winderbank, N. Vick, S. Rasmus, D. Pleasure, and M. J. Brown. 1983. Sensory neuropathy from pyridoxine abuse: A new megavitamin syndrome. *N. Engl. J. Med.* 309:445–448.

35. Connolly, M., 2001. Premenstrual syndrome: An update on definitions, diagnosis and management. *Advances in Psychiatric Treatment* 7:469–477.

36. Fugh-Berman, A., and F. Kronenbertg. 2003. Complementary and alternative medicine (CAM) in reproductive-age women: A review of randomized controlled trials. *Reproductive Toxicology* 17:137–152.

Treating Premenstrual Syndrome with Vitamin B$_6$: Does It Work? Is It Risky?

Perform an Internet search for treatments for premenstrual syndrome (PMS) and you are likely to find many recommendations for supplementing with high doses of vitamin B$_6$. In addition, almost any PMS supplement sold in a pharmacy or health food store will contain 50 to 200 mg of vitamin B$_6$ per capsule or tablet, with the recommendation that the consumer take at least two capsules per day. As you learned in this chapter, the UL of vitamin B$_6$ is 100 mg/day, and high doses of vitamin B$_6$ over an extended period of time can cause neurologic disorders. Is there research to support recommending high levels of vitamin B$_6$ for PMS? Do the benefits of supplementing outweigh the risk of toxicity?

What Is PMS?

PMS is a disorder characterized by a cluster of symptoms triggered by hormonal changes that occur 1 to 2 weeks prior to the start of menstruation. These symptoms typically fall into the three general categories in the following bulleted list.[30, 31] These categories are also used by the American College of Obstetricians and Gynecologists in the diagnosis of PMS.

- Physical symptoms: Fluid retention leading to bloating, breast tenderness, weight gain, abdominal discomfort and pain, and headache pain
- Behavioral symptoms: Appetite changes, especially cravings for sweets, dairy products, and alcohol; sleep disturbances; poor concentration and social withdrawal
- Mood symptoms: Depression and anxiety, including irritability, tension, feeling out of control, crying without reason, rapid mood changes, and/or aggression

For a woman to be diagnosed with PMS, she typically has to complain of at least one moderate to severe mood symptom and one physical symptom.[31] It is estimated that 90% of menstruating women experience at least a mild form of one or more of these symptoms, 30% to 50% experience troublesome symptoms, and 5% have severe symptoms that impact their work and health.[32]

Currently, there is no universally accepted medical treatment for PMS.

Headaches, anxiety, irritability, tension, and depression are common symptoms of PMS.

Not surprisingly, given the diversity of associated symptoms, a wide variety of therapies have been promoted, including megadoses of vitamins (vitamin B$_6$ and vitamin E), minerals (calcium, magnesium), amino acid supplements (L-tryptophan), and herbs (St. John's wort, kava-kava, chaste tree fruit, and *dong quai*).[31, 33] Unfortunately, some of these remedies, such as vitamin B$_6$, have the potential for negative health consequences if taken in excess.

Vitamin B$_6$ Toxicity

In 1983, the *New England Journal of Medicine* first reported the development of sensory neuropathy (a disorder affecting the sensory nerves) in individuals taking high doses of pyridoxine, the most common form of vitamin B$_6$ in supplements.[34] In this report, the researchers described seven individuals, ranging from 20 to 43 years of age, with serious neurotoxicity associated with megadoses of pyridoxine.

Five of the individuals began with 50 to 100 mg/day of vitamin B$_6$ before steadily increasing their dose in an attempt to derive a benefit. In one case, a 27-year-old woman began taking 500 mg/day of vitamin B$_6$ to treat premenstrual edema. Over the course of a year, she gradually increased her dose to 5,000 mg/day (5 g/day), which is 50 times higher than the UL for vitamin B$_6$. She reported a tingling sensation in her neck, legs, and feet; numbness in her hands and feet; impaired walking; and impairment in handling small objects. She also noticed changes in the feeling in her lips and tongue. Within 2 months of stopping her supplement, she began to see improvement in her gait and sensation, but it was 7 months before she could walk without a cane. At the time the report was written, the numbness in her legs and hands had still not improved.

A total of four of the seven individuals became so severely disabled they could not walk or could walk only with a cane. The other individuals experienced less severe symptoms, including "lightning-like" pains in their calves and shins, especially after exercise. Unfortunately, none of the individuals reported that the supplements had improved their premenstrual edema, made them feel better, or improved their mood, the reasons they gave for taking the supplement in the first place.

In summary, four of the seven individuals began feeling better within 6 months after stopping supplementation but still had diminished sensory perception. Two individuals did not experience recovery until 2 to 3 years after supplementation stopped.

Does Research Support the Treatment of PMS with Vitamin B_6?

Does a review of the research literature support the use of high doses of vitamin B_6 for the treatment of PMS? To date, there have been nine randomized clinical trials testing whether vitamin B_6 supplementation improves PMS symptoms. These nine trials, including 940 subjects, were systematically reviewed by researchers in the United Kingdom to determine if there was enough evidence to recommend using vitamin B_6 as a treatment for PMS.[35] Unfortunately, none of the clinical trials met the highest criteria set for research quality. The results show that about half of the studies reported some positive effects of vitamin B_6 supplements on PMS symptoms when compared with the placebo group, but frequently the improvement was only for some of the symptoms. The authors concluded that "there was insufficient evidence of high enough quality to give a confident recommenda-

Vitamin B_6: Do the potential benefits outweigh the risk of toxicity?

tion for using vitamin B_6 in the treatment of PMS."[35]

Some of the problems observed when reviewing these studies reveal why the authors could not give definitive recommendations. For example, one study showed that 58% of the individuals taking vitamin B_6 felt better, but then so did 59% of the individuals taking the placebo; thus, there were no differences between the groups. Many of the studies showed improvement in only some of the symptoms of PMS, such as anxiety and food cravings, but not headaches and depression. Finally, the level of treatment varied in the studies from 50 to 600 mg/day of vitamin B_6. Thus, although some studies suggest a benefit, the evidence for efficacy of treating PMS with vitamin B_6 is not convincing and further research is needed.[31, 33, 35, 36]

Critical Thinking Questions

- Do you think the limited benefits of treating PMS with vitamin B_6 outweigh the risks of vitamin B_6 toxicity?

- What would you do if a friend told you she was taking 100 mg/day of vitamin B_6 for PMS?

- What if she told you she was taking twice that amount and had been doing so for several months?

For more information on the use of vitamin B_6 for PMS, see the National Institutes of Health (NIH) Office of Dietary Supplements in the Web Links section of this chapter.

9 Nutrients Involved in Fluid and Electrolyte Balance

Test Yourself | True or False?

1 About 50% to 70% of body weight is made up of fluid. **T** *or* **F**

2 Sodium is an unhealthful nutrient, and we should avoid consuming it in our diets. **T** *or* **F**

3 Drinking until we are no longer thirsty always ensures that we are properly hydrated. **T** *or* **F**

4 Although more expensive than tap water, bottled water provides additional health and nutritional benefits. **T** *or* **F**

5 Eating a high-sodium diet causes high blood pressure in most individuals. **T** *or* **F**

Test Yourself answers are located in the Chapter Review.

Chapter Objectives *After reading this chapter, you will be able to:*

1. Distinguish between extracellular fluid, intracellular fluid, interstitial fluid, and intravascular fluid, *pp. 324–325.*

2. Identify four nutrients that function as electrolytes in our bodies, *pp. 325–326.*

3. Discuss how the kidneys regulate blood pressure and blood volume, *p. 326.*

4. List three functions of water in our bodies, *pp. 326–327.*

5. Describe how electrolytes assist in the regulation of healthful fluid balance, *pp. 327–329.*

6. Discuss the physical changes that occur to trigger the thirst mechanism, *pp. 330–332.*

7. Describe the avenues of fluid intake and excretion in our bodies, *pp. 331–332.*

8. Define hyponatremia and identify factors that can cause this condition, *pp. 338–339.*

9. Identify four symptoms of dehydration, *pp. 343–344.*

10. Define hypertension and list three lifestyle changes that can reduce it, *pp. 345–348.*

I n April 2002, Cynthia Lucero, a healthy 28-year-old woman who had just completed her doctoral dissertation, was running the Boston Marathon. Although not a professional athlete, Cynthia was running in her second marathon and had trained carefully. While her parents, who had traveled from Ecuador, waited at the finish line, friends in the crowd watched as Cynthia steadily completed mile after mile, drinking large amounts of sports drinks as she progressed through the course. They described her as looking strong until she began to jog up Heartbreak Hill, about 6 miles from the finish. She drank more fluid, but a few minutes later began to visibly falter. One of her friends ran to her side and asked if she was okay. Cynthia replied that she felt dehydrated and rubber-legged, then she fell to the pavement. She was rushed to nearby Brigham and Women's Hospital, but by the time she got there, she was in an irreversible coma. The official cause of her death was hyponatremia, commonly called "low blood sodium." According to a study involving the 488 runners in that 2002 Boston Marathon, 13% had hyponatremia by the end of the race. Hyponatremia continues to cause illness and death in runners, triathletes, and even hikers.[1]

What is hyponatremia, and how does it differ from dehydration? Are you at risk for either condition? Do sports beverages confer any protection against these fluid imbalances? If at the start of football practice on a hot, humid afternoon, a friend confided to you that he had been on a drinking binge the night before and had vomited twice that morning, what would you say to him? Would you urge him to tell his coach, and if so, why?

In this chapter, we explore the role of fluids and electrolytes in keeping the body properly hydrated and maintaining the functions of nerves and muscles. We also discuss how blood pressure is maintained and take a look at some disorders that occur when fluids and electrolytes are out of balance.

What Are Fluids and Electrolytes, and What Are Their Functions?

Of course you know that orange juice, blood, and shampoo are all fluids, but what makes them so? A **fluid** is characterized by its ability to move freely and changeably, adapting to the shape of the container that holds it. This might not seem very important, but as you'll learn in this chapter, the fluid composition of cells and tissues is critical to the body's ability to function.

Body Fluid Is the Liquid Portion of Cells and Tissues

Between about 50% and 70% of a healthy adult's body weight is fluid. When we cut a finger, we can see some of this fluid dripping out as blood, but the fluid in the bloodstream can't account for such a large percentage of one's total body weight. So where is all this fluid hiding?

About two-thirds of the body's fluid is held within the walls of cells and is therefore called **intracellular fluid** (**Figure 9.1a**). Every cell in the body contains fluid. When cells lose their fluid, they quickly shrink and die. On the other hand, when cells take in too much fluid, they swell and burst apart. This is why appropriate fluid balance—which we'll discuss throughout this chapter—is so critical to life.

The remaining third of the body's fluid is referred to as **extracellular fluid** because it flows outside of the cells (see Figure 9.1a). There are two types of extracellular fluid:

1. **Interstitial fluid** flows between the cells that make up a particular tissue or organ, such as muscle fibers or the liver (Figure 9.1b).
2. **Intravascular fluid** is the water in the bloodstream and lymph. *Plasma* is specifically the extracellular fluid portion of blood that transports blood cells within the body's arteries, veins, and capillaries (Figure 9.1c).

Not every tissue in the body contains the same amount of fluid. Lean tissues, such as muscle, are more than 70% fluid, whereas fat tissue is only between 10% and 20% fluid.

fluid A substance composed of molecules that move past one another freely. Fluids are characterized by their ability to conform to the shape of whatever container holds them.

intracellular fluid The fluid held at any given time within the walls of the body's cells.

extracellular fluid The fluid outside of the body's cells, either in the body's tissues (interstitial fluid) or as the liquid portion of the blood or lymph (intravascular fluid).

interstitial fluid The fluid that flows between the cells that make up a particular tissue or organ, such as muscle fibers or the liver.

intravascular fluid The fluid in the bloodstream and lymph.

(a)

(b)

(c)

- Intracellular fluid (inside of cell)
- Extracellular fluid (outside of cell)
- Intracellular fluid
- Extracellular fluid (tissue fluid, or interstitial fluid)
- Extracellular fluid (plasma)
- Intracellular fluid
- Extracellular fluid (interstitial fluid)

Cell

Liver

Capillary network

Blood cell inside capillary

Figure 9.1 The components of body fluid. **(a)** Intracellular fluid is contained within the cells that make up our body tissues. Extracellular fluid is external to cells. **(b)** Interstitial fluid is external to tissue cells, and **(c)** plasma is external to blood cells.

This is not surprising considering the hydrophobic nature of lipid cells, which was discussed in Chapter 5.

Body fluid levels also vary according to gender and age. Males have more lean tissue and thus a higher percentage of body weight as fluid than females. The amount of body fluid as a percentage of total weight decreases with age. About 75% of an infant's body weight is water, whereas the total body water of an elderly person is generally less than 50% of body weight. This decrease in total body water is, in part, a result of the loss of lean tissue that can occur as people age.

Body Fluid Is Composed of Water and Dissolved Substances Called Electrolytes

Water is made up of molecules consisting of two hydrogen atoms bound to one oxygen atom (H_2O). Although water is essential to maintain life, we would quickly die if our cell and tissue fluids contained only water. Instead, within the body fluids are a variety of dissolved substances (called *solutes*) critical to life. These include four major minerals: sodium, potassium, chloride, and phosphorus. We consume these minerals in compounds called *salts*, including table salt, which is made of sodium and chloride.

As we age, our body water content decreases: Approximately 75% of an infant's body weight is composed of water, whereas an elderly adult's is only 50% (or less).

These mineral salts are called **electrolytes,** because when they dissolve in water, the two component minerals separate and form electrically charged particles called **ions.** This electrical charge, which can be positive or negative, is the "spark" that stimulates nerves and causes muscles to contract, making electrolytes critical to body function.

Of the four major minerals just mentioned, sodium (Na^+) and potassium (K^+) are positively charged, whereas chloride (Cl^-) and phosphorus (in the form of hydrogen phosphate, or HPO_4^{2-}) are negatively charged. In the intracellular fluid, potassium and phosphate are the predominant electrolytes. In the extracellular fluid, sodium and chloride predominate. There is a slight difference in electrical charge on either side of the cell's membrane that is needed in order for the cell to perform its normal functions.

Fluids Serve Many Critical Functions

Water not only quenches our thirst; it performs a number of functions that are critical to support life.

Fluids Dissolve and Transport Substances

Water is an excellent **solvent,** which means it is capable of dissolving a wide variety of substances. All water-soluble substances—such as amino acids, glucose, the water-soluble vitamins, minerals, and some medications—are readily transported via the bloodstream. In contrast, fats do not dissolve in water. To overcome this chemical incompatibility, fatty substances such as lipids and the fat-soluble vitamins are either attached to or surrounded by water-soluble proteins so they, too, can be transported in the blood to the cells.

Fluids Account for Blood Volume

Blood volume is the amount of fluid in blood; thus, appropriate body fluid levels are essential to maintaining healthful blood volume. When blood volume rises inappropriately, blood pressure increases; when blood volume decreases inappropriately, blood pressure decreases. As you know, high blood pressure is an important risk factor for heart disease and stroke, whereas low blood pressure can cause people to feel tired, confused, or dizzy. We discuss high blood pressure (called *hypertension*) later in this chapter.

The kidneys play a central role in the regulation of blood volume and blood pressure. While filtering the blood, they reabsorb (retain) water and other nutrients that the body needs and excrete waste products and excess water in the urine. Changes in blood volume, blood pressure, and concentration of solutes in the blood signal the kidneys to adjust the volume and concentration of urine.

Imagine that you have just finished working out for an hour, during which time you did not drink any fluids, but you lost fluid through sweat. In response to the increased concentration of solutes in your blood, **antidiuretic hormone (or ADH)** is released from the pituitary gland (**Figure 9.2**). The action of ADH is appropriately described by its name: It has an antidiuretic effect, stimulating the kidneys to reabsorb water and to reduce the production of urine.

Simultaneously, your reduced blood volume has resulted in a decrease in blood pressure. This drop in blood pressure stimulates pressure receptors in the kidney, which signal the kidney to secrete the enzyme **renin.** Renin then activates a blood protein called angiotensinogen, which is produced in the liver. Angiotensinogen is the precursor of another blood protein, angiotensin I. Angiotensin I is converted to **angiotensin II,** which is a powerful vasoconstrictor; this means it works to constrict the diameter of blood vessels, which results in an increase in blood pressure.

Angiotensin II also signals the release of the hormone **aldosterone** from the adrenal glands. Aldosterone signals the kidneys to retain sodium and chloride. Because water travels with these two minerals, this results in water retention, which increases blood pressure and decreases urine output. These responses help regulate fluid balance and blood pressure.

electrolyte   A substance that disassociates in solution into positively and negatively charged ions and is thus capable of carrying an electrical current.

ion   Any electrically charged particle, either positively or negatively charged.

solvent   A substance that is capable of mixing with and breaking apart a variety of compounds. Water is an excellent solvent.

blood volume   The amount of fluid in blood.

antidiuretic hormone (or ADH)   A hormone released from the pituitary gland in response to an increase in blood solute concentration. ADH stimulates the kidneys to reabsorb water and to reduce the production of urine.

renin   An enzyme secreted by the kidneys in response to a decrease in blood pressure. Renin converts the blood protein angiotensinogen to angiotensin I, which eventually results in an increase in sodium reabsorption.

angiotensin II   A potent vasoconstrictor that constricts the diameter of blood vessels and increases blood pressure; it also signals the release of the hormone aldosterone from the adrenal glands.

aldosterone   A hormone released from the adrenal glands that signals the kidneys to retain sodium and chloride, which in turn results in the retention of water.

Fluids Help Maintain Body Temperature

Just as overheating is disastrous to a car engine, a high internal temperature can cause the body to stop functioning. Fluids are vital to the body's ability to maintain its temperature within a safe range. Two factors account for the cooling power of fluids. First, water has a high capacity for heat: it takes a lot of energy to raise its temperature. Because the body contains a lot of water, only sustained high heat can increase body temperature.

Second, body fluids are our primary coolant. When heat needs to be released from the body, there is an increase in the flow of blood from the warm body core to the vessels lying just under the skin. This action transports heat out to the body periphery, where it can be released from the skin. When we are hot, the sweat glands secrete more sweat from the skin. As this sweat evaporates off of the skin's surface, heat is released and the skin and underlying blood are cooled (**Figure 9.3**). This cooler blood flows back to the body's core and reduces internal body temperature.

Fluids Protect and Lubricate the Tissues

Water is a major part of the fluids that protect and lubricate tissues. The cerebrospinal fluid that surrounds the brain and spinal column protects these vital tissues from damage, and a fetus in a mother's womb is protected by amniotic fluid. Synovial fluid lubricates joints, and tears cleanse and lubricate the eyes. Saliva moistens the food we eat, and the mucus lining the walls of the GI tract helps it move smoothly along. Finally, the pleural fluid covering the lungs allows their friction-free expansion and retraction behind the chest wall.

RECAP

Body fluid consists of water plus a variety of dissolved substances, including electrically charged minerals called electrolytes. Water serves many important functions, including dissolving and transporting substances, accounting for blood volume, regulating body temperature, and cushioning and lubricating body tissues.

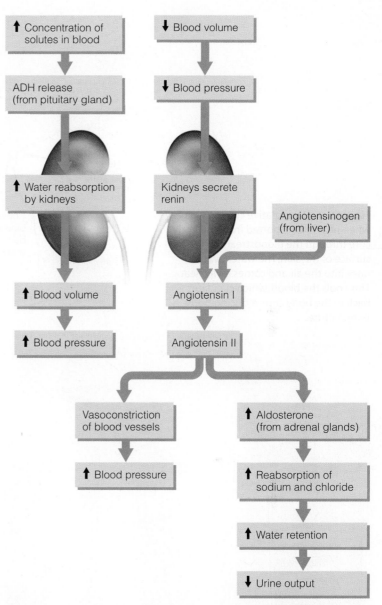

Figure 9.2 Regulation of blood volume and blood pressure by the kidneys.

To prevent illness, hikers need to adjust their fluid intake according to the humidity level and temperature of their environment.

Electrolytes Support Many Body Functions

Now that you know why fluid is so essential to the body's functioning, we're ready to explore the critical role of the minerals within it.

Electrolytes Help Regulate Fluid Balance

Cell membranes are *permeable* to water. This means that water flows easily through them. Cells cannot voluntarily regulate this flow of water and thus have no active control over the balance of fluid between the intracellular and extracellular compartments. In contrast, cell

Figure 9.3 Evaporative cooling occurs when heat is transported from the body core through the bloodstream to the surface of the skin. The water evaporates into the air and carries away heat. This cools the blood, which circulates back to the body core, reducing body temperature.

membranes are *not* freely permeable to electrolytes. Sodium, potassium, and the other electrolytes stay where they are, either inside or outside of a cell, unless they are actively transported elsewhere by special proteins. So how do electrolytes help the cells maintain their fluid balance? To answer this question, we need to review a bit of chemistry.

Imagine that you have a special filter that has the same properties as cell membranes; in other words, this filter is freely permeable to water but not permeable to electrolytes. Now imagine that you insert this filter into a glass of pure distilled water to divide the glass into two separate chambers (**Figure 9.4a**). The level of water on either side of the filter would of course be identical, because it is freely permeable to water. Now imagine that you add a teaspoon of salt (which contains the electrolytes sodium and chloride) to the water on one side of the filter only (Figure 9.4b). You would see the water on the "pure water" side of the glass suddenly begin to flow through the filter to the "salt water" side of the glass (Figure 9.4c). Why would this mysterious movement of water occur? The answer is that water always moves from areas where solutes such as sodium and chloride are in low concentrations to areas where they are highly concentrated. This movement is referred to as **osmosis.** To put it another way, electrolytes attract water toward areas where they are concentrated. This movement of water toward solutes continues until the concentration of solutes is equal on both sides of the cell membrane.

(a)   (b)   (c)

Figure 9.4 Osmosis. **(a)** A filter that is freely permeable to water is placed in a glass of pure water. **(b)** Salt is added to only one side of the glass. **(c)** Drawn by the high concentration of electrolytes, pure water flows to the "salt water" side of the filter. This flow of water into the concentrated solution will continue until the concentration of electrolytes on both sides of the membrane is equal.

osmosis The movement of water (or any solvent) through a semipermeable membrane from an area where solutes are less concentrated to areas where they are highly concentrated.

osmotic pressure The pressure that is needed to keep the particles in a solution from drawing liquid toward them across a semipermeable membrane.

Water follows the movement of electrolytes; this action provides a means to control movement of water into and out of the cells. The pressure that is needed to keep the particles in a solution from drawing liquid toward them across a semipermeable membrane is referred to as **osmotic pressure.** Cells can regulate the osmotic pressure, and thus the balance of fluids between their internal and extracellular environments, by using special transport proteins to actively pump electrolytes across their membranes. An example of how

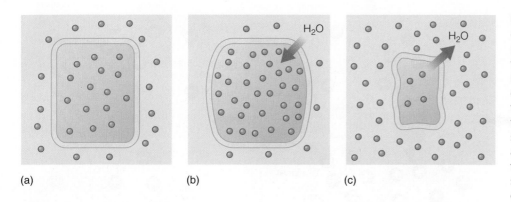

(a)   (b)   (c)

Figure 9.5 The health of our body's cells depends on maintaining the proper balance of fluids and electrolytes on either side of the cell membrane. **(a)** The concentration of electrolytes is the same on either side of the cell membrane. **(b)** The concentration of electrolytes is much greater inside the cell, drawing water into the cell and making it swell. **(c)** The concentration of electrolytes is much greater outside the cell, drawing water out of the cell and making it shrink.

transport proteins pump sodium and potassium across the cell membrane was illustrated in Chapter 6 (see Figure 6.11).

By maintaining the appropriate movement of electrolytes into and out of the cell, the proper balance of fluid and electrolytes is maintained between the intracellular and extracellular compartments (**Figure 9.5a**). If the concentration of electrolytes is much higher inside of the cells as compared with outside, water will flow into the cells in such large amounts that the cells can burst (Figure 9.5b). On the other hand, if the extracellular environment contains too high a concentration of electrolytes, water flows out of the cells, and they can dry up (Figure 9.5c).

Certain illnesses can threaten the delicate balance of fluid inside and outside of the cells. You may have heard of someone being hospitalized because of excessive diarrhea and vomiting. When this happens, the body loses a great deal of fluid from the intestinal tract and extracellular compartment. This heavy fluid loss causes the extracellular electrolyte concentration to become very high. In response, a great deal of intracellular fluid leaves the cells to try to balance this extracellular fluid loss. This imbalance in fluid and electrolytes changes the flow of electrical impulses through the heart, causing an irregular heart rate that can be fatal if left untreated. Food poisoning and eating disorders involving repeated vomiting and diarrhea can also result in death from life-threatening fluid and electrolyte imbalances.

By sprinkling salt on a slice of tomato, you can see for yourself the effects of osmotic pressure.

Electrolytes Enable Nerves to Respond to Stimuli

In addition to their role in maintaining fluid balance, electrolytes are critical in enabling nerves to respond to stimuli. Nerve impulses are initiated at the membrane of a nerve cell in response to a change in the degree of electrical charge across the membrane. An influx of sodium into a nerve cell causes the cell to become slightly less negatively charged. This is called *depolarization* (**Figure 9.6**). If enough sodium enters the cell, the change in electrical charge triggers an *action potential*, an electrical signal that is then propagated along the length of the cell. Once the signal is transmitted, that portion of cell membrane returns to its normal electrical state through the release of potassium to the outside of the cell. This return of the cell to its initial electrical state is termed *repolarization*. Thus, both sodium and potassium play critical roles in ensuring that nerve impulses are generated, transmitted, and completed.

Electrolytes Signal Muscles to Contract

Muscles contract because of a series of complex physiologic changes that we will not describe in detail here. Simply stated, muscles are stimulated to contract in response to stimulation of nerve cells. As described earlier, sodium and potassium play a key role in the generation of nerve impulses, or electrical signals. When a muscle fiber is stimulated by an electrical signal, changes occur in the cell membrane that lead to an increased flow of calcium into the muscle from the extracellular fluid. This release of calcium into the muscle stimulates muscle contraction. The muscles can relax after a contraction once the electrical signal is complete and calcium has been pumped out of the muscle cell.

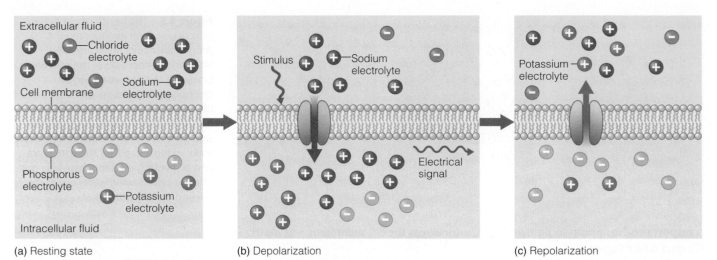

(a) Resting state (b) Depolarization (c) Repolarization

Figure 9.6 The role of electrolytes in conduction of a nerve impulse. **(a)** In the resting state, the intracellular fluid has slightly more electrolytes with a negative charge. **(b)** A stimulus causes changes to occur that prompt the influx of sodium into the interior of the cell. Sodium has a positive charge, so when this happens, the charge inside the cell becomes slightly positive. This is called depolarization. If enough sodium enters the cell, an action potential is transmitted to adjacent regions of the cell membrane. **(c)** Release of potassium to the exterior of the cell allows the first portion of the membrane almost immediately to return to the resting state. This is called repolarization.

Fruits and vegetables are delicious sources of water.

RECAP

Electrolytes help regulate fluid balance by controlling the movement of fluid into and out of cells. Electrolytes, specifically sodium and potassium, play a key role in generating nerve impulses in response to stimuli. Calcium is an electrolyte that stimulates muscle contraction.

How Does the Body Maintain Fluid Balance?

The proper balance of fluid is maintained in the body by a series of mechanisms that prompt us to drink and retain fluid when we are dehydrated and to excrete fluid as urine when we consume more than we need.

The Thirst Mechanism Prompts Us to Drink Fluids

Imagine that, at lunch, you ate a ham sandwich and a bag of salted potato chips. Now it's almost time for your afternoon seminar to end and you are very thirsty. The last 5 minutes of class are a torment, and when the instructor ends the session you dash to the nearest drinking fountain. What prompted you to suddenly feel so thirsty?

The body's command center for fluid intake is a cluster of nerve cells in the same part of the brain we studied in relation to food intake; that is, the *hypothalamus*. Within the hypothalamus is a group of cells, collectively referred to as the **thirst mechanism,** that causes you to consciously desire fluids. The thirst mechanism prompts us to feel thirsty when it is stimulated by:

- Increased concentration of salt and other dissolved substances in the blood. Remember that ham sandwich and those potato chips? Both of these foods are salty, and eating them increased the blood's sodium concentration.
- A reduction in blood volume and blood pressure. This can occur when fluids are lost through profuse sweating, blood loss, vomiting, diarrhea, or simply when fluid intake is too low.
- Dryness in the tissues of the mouth and throat. Tissue dryness reflects a lower amount of fluid in the bloodstream, which causes a reduced production of saliva.

thirst mechanism A cluster of nerve cells in the hypothalamus that stimulates our conscious desire to drink fluids in response to an increase in the concentration of salt in our blood or a decrease in blood pressure and blood volume.

Once the hypothalamus detects such changes, it stimulates the release of ADH to signal the kidneys to reduce urine flow and return more water to the bloodstream. As previously discussed, the kidneys also secrete renin, which eventually results in the production of angiotensin II and the retention of water. Water is drawn out of the salivary glands in the mouth in an attempt to further dilute the concentration of substances in the blood; this causes the mouth and throat to become even drier. Together, these mechanisms prevent a further loss of body fluid and help avoid dehydration.

Although the thirst mechanism can trigger an increase in fluid intake, this mechanism alone is not always sufficient: People tend to drink until they are no longer thirsty, but the amount of fluid consumed may not be enough to achieve fluid balance. This is particularly true when body water is rapidly lost, such as during intense exercise in the heat or high humidity. Because the thirst mechanism has some limitations, it is important that you drink regularly throughout the day and not wait to drink until you become thirsty, especially if you are active.

We Gain Fluids by Consuming Beverages and Foods and Through Metabolism

The fluid needed each day is obtained from three primary sources: beverages, foods, and the production of metabolic water by the body. Of course you know that beverages are mostly water, but it isn't as easy to see the water content in foods. For example, iceberg lettuce is almost 99% water, and even almonds contain a small amount of water (**Figure 9.7**).

Metabolic water is the water formed from the body's metabolic reactions. In the breakdown of fat, carbohydrate, and protein, adenosine triphosphate (ATP), carbon dioxide, and water are produced. The water that is formed during metabolic reactions contributes about 10% to 14% of the water the body needs each day.

We Lose Fluids Through Urine, Sweat, Evaporation, Exhalation, and Feces

Water loss that is noticeable, such as through urine output and sweating, is referred to as **sensible water loss.** Most of the water we consume is excreted through the kidneys in the form of urine. When we consume more water than we need, the kidneys process and excrete it in the form of dilute urine.

metabolic water The water formed as a by-product of the body's metabolic reactions.

sensible water loss Water loss that is noticed by a person, such as through urine output and sweating.

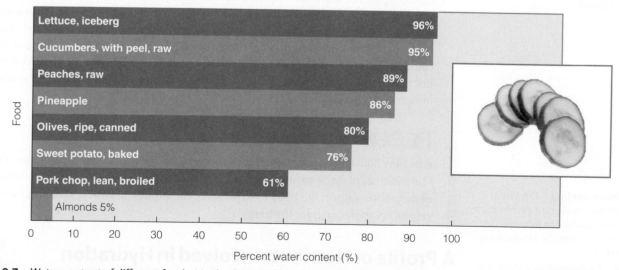

Figure 9.7 Water content of different foods. Much of your daily water intake comes from the foods you eat. (*Data from:* U.S. Department of Agriculture, Agricultural Research Service. 2006. USDA Nutrient Database for Standard Reference, Release 19. Nutrient Data Laboratory Home Page. Available at www.ars.usda.gov/ba/bhnrc/ndl.)

The second type of sensible water loss is via sweat. The sweat glands produce more sweat during exercise or when a person is in a hot environment. The evaporation of sweat from the skin releases heat, which cools the skin and reduces the body's core temperature.

Water is continuously evaporated from the skin even when a person is not consciously sweating, and water is also continuously exhaled from the lungs. Water loss through these avenues is referred to as **insensible water loss,** as it is not perceived by the person. Under normal resting conditions, insensible water loss is less than 1 liter (L) of fluid each day; during heavy exercise or in hot weather, a person can lose up to 2 L of water per hour from insensible water loss.

Under normal conditions, only about 150 to 200 ml of water is lost each day in the feces. The gastrointestinal tract typically reabsorbs much of the large amounts of fluids that pass through it each day. However, when someone suffers from extreme diarrhea due to illness or from consuming excess laxatives, water loss in the feces can be as high as several liters per day.

In addition to these five avenues of regular fluid loss, certain situations can cause a significant loss of fluid from the body:

- Illnesses that involve fever, coughing, vomiting, diarrhea, and a runny nose significantly increase fluid loss. This is why doctors advise people to drink plenty of fluids when they are ill.
- Traumatic injury, internal hemorrhaging, blood donation, and surgery also increase loss of fluid because of the blood loss involved.
- Exercise increases fluid loss via sweat and respiration; although urine production typically decreases during exercise, fluid losses increase through the skin and lungs.
- Environmental conditions that increase fluid loss include high altitudes, cold and hot temperatures, and low humidity such as in a desert or on an airplane. Because the water content of these environments is low, water from the body readily evaporates into the atmosphere. We also breathe faster at higher altitudes due to the lower oxygen pressure; this results in greater fluid loss via the lungs. We sweat more in the heat, thus losing more water. Cold temperatures can trigger hormonal changes that result in an increased fluid loss.
- Pregnancy increases fluid loss for the mother because fluids are continually diverted to the fetus and amniotic fluid.
- Breastfeeding requires a tremendous increase in fluid intake to make up for the loss of fluid.
- Consumption of **diuretics**—substances that increase fluid loss via the urine—can result in dangerously excessive fluid loss. Diuretics include certain prescription medications and alcohol. Many over-the-counter weight-loss remedies are really just diuretics. In the past, it was believed that the caffeine in beverages such as coffee, tea, and cola could cause serious dehydration, but recent research suggests that caffeinated drinks do not have a significant impact on the hydration status of adults.[2, 3] The caffeine content of numerous beverages and foods is listed in Appendix E.

Drinking alcoholic beverages causes an increase in water loss because alcohol is a diuretic.

RecaP

A healthy fluid level is maintained in the body by balancing intake with excretion. Primary sources of fluids include water and other beverages, foods, and the production of metabolic water in the body. Fluid losses occur through urination, sweating, the feces, and evaporation from the lungs.

insensible water loss   The loss of water not noticeable by a person, such as through evaporation from the skin and exhalation from the lungs during breathing.

diuretic   A substance that increases fluid loss via the urine. Common diuretics include alcohol as well as prescription medications for high blood pressure and other disorders.

A Profile of Nutrients Involved in Hydration and Neuromuscular Function

Nutrients that assist in maintaining hydration and neuromuscular function include water and the minerals sodium, potassium, chloride, and phosphorus (see Table 9.1). As discussed in Chapter 1, these minerals are classified as *major minerals,* as the body needs more than 100 mg of each per day.

Calcium and magnesium also function as electrolytes and influence the body's fluid balance and neuromuscular function. However, because of their critical importance to bone health, they are discussed in Chapter 11.

Water

Water is essential for life. Although we can live for weeks without food, we can survive only a few days without water, depending on environmental temperature. We do not have the capacity to store water, so we must continuously replace the water lost each day.

How Much Water Should We Drink?

The need for water varies greatly depending on age, body size, health status, physical activity level, and exposure to environmental conditions. It is important to pay attention to how much the need for water changes under various conditions so that dehydration can be avoided.

Recommended Intake Fluid requirements are very individualized. For example, a highly active male athlete training in a hot environment may require up to 10 L of fluid per day to maintain healthy fluid balance, whereas an inactive, petite woman who lives in a mild climate and works in a temperature-controlled office building may only require about 3 L of fluid per day. The DRI for adult men aged 19 to 50 years is 3.7 L of total water per day. This includes approximately 3.0 L (or 13 cups) as total water, other beverages, and food.[4] The DRI for adult women aged 19 to 50 is 2.7 L of total water per day. This includes about 2.2 (or 9 cups) as total water, other beverages, and food.[4]

Figure 9.8 shows the amount and sources of water intake and output for a woman expending 2,500 kcal per day. Based on current recommendations, this woman needs about 3,000 ml of water per day. As illustrated:

- Water from metabolism provides 300 ml of water.
- The foods she eats provides her with an additional 500 ml of water each day.
- The beverages she drinks provide the remainder of water needed, which is equal to 2,200 ml.

An 8-oz glass of water is equal to 240 ml. In this example, the woman would need to drink 9 glasses of fluid to meet her needs. You may have read or heard that drinking 8 glasses of fluid each day is recommended for most people. Drinking this amount will provide most people with enough fluid to maintain proper fluid balance. Remember, however, that this recommendation of 8 glasses of fluid each day is a general guideline. You may need to drink a different amount to meet your fluid needs.

Athletes or people who are active, especially those working in very hot environments, may require more fluid than the current recommendations. The amount of sweat lost during exercise is very individualized and depends on body size, exercise intensity, level of fitness, environmental temperature, and humidity. We do know that some people can lose as much as 4 lb of fluid (or 1.8 kg) per hour as sweat![5] Thus, these individuals need to drink more to replace the fluid they lose. Sodium is the major electrolyte lost in sweat; we also lose some potassium and small amounts of minerals such as iron and calcium in sweat.[6]

Because of these fluid and electrolyte losses during exercise, some athletes drink sports beverages instead of plain water to help them maintain fluid balance. Recently, sports beverages have also become popular with recreationally active people and non-athletes. Is it really necessary for people to consume these beverages? See the Nutrition Debate on sports beverages at the end of this chapter to learn whether they are right for you.

Table 9.1 Overview of Nutrients Involved in Hydration and Neuromuscular Function

To see the full profile of nutrients involved in hydration and neuromusclar function, turn to *In Depth, Vitamins and Minerals: Micronutrients with Macro Powers,* pages 280–291.

Nutrient	Recommended Intake
Sodium	1.5 g/day*
Potassium	4.7 g/day *
Chloride	2.3 g/day*
Phosphorus	700 mg/day†

* Adequate Intake (AI).

† RDA.

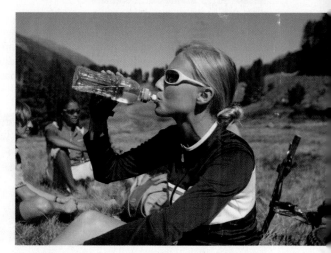

Vigorous exercise causes significant water loss that must be replenished to optimize performance and health.

Figure 9.8 Amounts and categories of water sources and losses for a woman expending 2,500 kcal per day. Water from metabolism provides 300 ml. The foods she eats provide her with an additional 500 ml. The beverages she drinks, including water, provide the remainder of water she needs, about 2,200 ml. The total of 3,000 ml matches her water losses.

Judy
Nutri-Case

"I've seen on the TV news about how important it is to drink at least 8 cups of fluid a day. At first that seemed like an awful lot, but after keeping track of what I drank yesterday, I figure I'm good. I had a mug of coffee when I first got up, a can of soda on my way to work, a coffee mocha on my morning break, another soda with lunch, and a bottle of Gatorade in the afternoon. On my way home, I stopped to pick up a pizza, and they were offering a free 22-ounce bottle of soda, so I went for it. I'm not sure what all that adds up to, but I know it's more than 8 cups. It's not as hard as I thought to get enough fluid!"

What do you think of the nutritional quality of Judy's fluid choices? If one 8-ounce serving of soda provides about 100 kcal, and a can is 12 ounces, how many calories did Judy consume just from her soft drinks? Given what you've learned about Judy so far in this text, could you suggest some other beverages that might be smarter choices for her?

Sources of Drinking Water So many types of drinking water are available in the United States, how can we distinguish among them? Carbonated water contains carbon dioxide gas that either occurs naturally or is added to the water. Mineral water contains 250 to 500 parts per million (ppm) of minerals. Many people prefer the unique taste of mineral water; however, a number of brands contain high amounts of sodium and so should be avoided by people who are trying to reduce their sodium intake. Distilled water is processed in such a way that all dissolved minerals are removed; this type of water is often used in steam irons, as it will not clog the iron with mineral build-up, but it has a flat taste. Purified water has been treated so that all dissolved minerals and contaminants are removed, making this type of water useful in research and medical procedures. Of course, we can also drink the tap water found in our homes and in public places.

One of the major changes in the beverage industry during the past 20 years is the marketing of bottled water.[7] Americans now consume about 29 gallons of bottled water per person, per year. This meteoric rise in bottled water production and consumption is most likely due to the convenience of drinking bottled water, to the health messages related to drinking more water, and to the public's fears related to the safety of tap water. Recent environmental concerns related to disposal of water bottles, however, has blunted the use of bottled water.[8] Is bottled water safer or more healthful than tap water? Refer to the Nutrition Myth or Fact? box on the next page on bottled water to find the answer.

What Happens If We Drink Too Much Water?

Drinking too much water and becoming overhydrated is very rare. Even individuals who regularly consume large quantities of water do not develop major health problems because healthy kidneys are able to process the excess water.

Certain illnesses can cause excessive reabsorption or retention of water by the kidneys. When this occurs, overhydration and dilution of blood sodium result. Also, as described in the introductory story on Cynthia Lucero, marathon runners and other endurance athletes can overhydrate and dangerously dilute their serum sodium concentration. This condition, called *hyponatremia,* is discussed in more detail in the next section.

What Happens If We Don't Drink Enough Water?

Dehydration results when we do not drink enough water or are unable to retain the water we drink. It is one of the leading causes of death around the world. Because an understanding of the physiology of dehydration requires familiarity with the roles and requirements for the major electrolytes, we discuss this condition, along with a related illness called *heat stroke,* later in this chapter.

Sodium

Virtually all of the dietary sodium consumed is absorbed by the body. Most dietary sodium is absorbed from the small intestine, although some can be absorbed in the large intestine. As discussed earlier in this chapter, the kidneys reabsorb sodium when it needs to be retained by the body and excrete excess sodium in the urine.

Over the past 20 years, researchers have linked high sodium intake to an increased risk for high blood pressure among some groups of individuals. Because of this link, many people have come to believe that sodium is harmful to the body. That oversimplification, however, is just not true: sodium is a valuable nutrient that is essential for survival.

Functions of Sodium

Sodium has a variety of functions. As discussed earlier in this chapter, it is the major positively charged electrolyte in the extracellular fluid. Its exchange with potassium across cell membranes allows cells to maintain proper fluid balance; it also helps regulate blood pressure and acid–base balance.

Sodium also assists with the transmission of nerve signals and aids in muscle contraction and relaxation. Finally, sodium assists in the absorption of glucose from the small intestine. Glucose is absorbed via active transport that involves sodium-dependent glucose transporters.

How Much Sodium Should We Consume?

Many people are concerned with consuming too much sodium in the diet, as they believe it causes high blood pressure and bloating. Although this concern may be valid for certain individuals, sodium is an important nutrient that is necessary for maintaining health. Therefore, it should not be completely eliminated from the diet.

Recommended Dietary Intake for Sodium   The AI for sodium is 1.5g/day (or 1,500 mg/day) for adult men and women aged 19 to 50 years, which is equivalent to just over

Nutrition Myth or Fact?

Is Bottled Water Safer or More Healthful than Tap Water?

Bottled water has become increasingly popular during the past 20 years. It is estimated that Americans drank almost 9 billion gallons of bottled water in 2007.[7] Many people prefer the taste of bottled water to that of tap water. They also feel that bottled water is safer and better for them. Is this true?

The water we drink in the United States generally comes from two sources: surface water and groundwater. *Surface water* comes from lakes, rivers, and reservoirs. Common contaminants of surface water include runoff from highways, pesticides, animal wastes, and industrial wastes. Many of the cities across the United States obtain their water from surface-water sources. *Groundwater* comes from underground rock formations called *aquifers*. People who live in rural areas generally pump groundwater from a well as their water source. Hazardous substances leaking from waste sites, dumps, landfills, and oil and gas pipelines can contaminate groundwater. Groundwater can also be contaminated by naturally occurring substances such as arsenic or high levels of iron.

Water treatment plants treat and purify community water supplies, typically with either chlorine or ozone. These chemicals are effective in killing many contaminants. Water treatment plants routinely check our water supplies for hazardous chemicals, minerals, and other contaminants. Because of these efforts, the United States has one of the safest water systems in the world.

The Environmental Protection Agency (EPA) sets and monitors the standards for our city water systems. The EPA does not monitor water from private wells, but it publishes recommendations for well owners to help them maintain a safe water supply. Local water regulatory agencies must provide an annual report on specific water contaminants to all households served by that agency.

In contrast, the Food and Drug Administration (FDA) regulates bottled water. It does not require that bottled water meet higher-quality standards than public water. As with tap water, bottled water is taken from either surface water or groundwater sources. Bottled water is often treated and filtered by different methods than those used for tap water, and thus its taste and appearance may differ. For instance, most bottling plants use an ozone treatment instead of chlorine to disinfect water, and many people feel this process leaves the water tasting better than water treated with chlorine.

Although bottled water may or may not taste better than tap water, there is no evidence that it is safer to drink.[8] For example, there is no strong research to support the use of bottled water by most persons with compromised immune systems. On the other hand, some people do not have access to safe tap water where they live. For these people, bottled water is the safer choice.

Is bottled water more healthful? While some brands may contain more minerals than tap water, bottled water has no other nutritional advantages over tap water. In fact, many bottled waters are labeled "from a public water source," which means the bottles are filled from the tap![8]

As the popularity of bottled water has increased, there are growing concerns about the potential burden drinking bottled water can have on the environment.[9] Specifically, many people have become concerned that the world will be inundated with billions of plastic bottles if people throw them away in landfills in place of recycling. Although plastic bottles can be reused, they do not last forever, and bacterial growth becomes a concern with repeated use. On the other hand, many environmentally conscious consumers using refillable plastic (polycarbonate) water bottles have been faced with recent concerns over the use of BPA (bisphenol A) in certain brands of reusable water bottles. Many manufacturers have removed BPA from their

Numerous varieties of bottled water are available to consumers.

products, so it is important that those who opt for reusable water bottles versus commercial bottled water purchase stainless steel or BPA-free plastic reusable bottles.

Should you spend money on bottled water? Before you decide, consider this simple calculation: Let's say you purchase one bottle 5 days a week from the vending machine at the gym when you finish your workout. It costs you $1.00. Over the course of a single year, you'll have spent over $250, and have added over 250 bottles to recycling centers or landfills!

If, after reading this discussion, you still choose to drink bottled water, look for brands that carry the trademark of the International Bottled Water Association (IBWA). This association follows the regulations of the FDA. If you get your water from a water cooler, make sure the cooler is cleaned once per month by running half a gallon of white vinegar through it, then rinsing thoroughly with about 5 gallons of clean water. For more information on drinking water safety, go to the EPA Web site at www.epa.gov; for information on bottled water, go to www.bottledwater.org.

half a teaspoon of salt.[4] The AI drops to 1.3 g/day for those 51 to 70 years of age and 1.2 g/d for persons over the age of 70 years. Most people in the United States greatly exceed this guideline, consuming between 3 and 6 g of sodium per day. Most health organizations recommend a daily sodium intake of no more than 2.3 g per day, and the 2005 Dietary Guidelines specifically recommend that African Americans (who have a higher risk of hypertension) and persons with hypertension limit their daily sodium intake to no more than 1.5 g.[10]

Food Sources of Sodium Sodium is found naturally in many common foods, and many processed foods contain large amounts of added sodium. Thus, it is easy to consume excess amounts in our daily diets. Try to guess which of the following foods contains the most sodium: 1 cup of tomato juice, 1 oz of potato chips, or 4 saltine crackers? Now look at Table 9.2 to find the answer. This table shows foods that are high in sodium and gives lower-sodium alternatives. Are you surprised to find out that of all of these food items, the tomato juice has the most sodium? When eating processed foods, such as lunch meats, canned soups and beans, vegetable juices, and prepackaged rice and pasta dishes, look for labels with the words "low-sodium" or "no added salt," as these foods are lower in sodium than the original versions.

Many popular snack foods are high in sodium.

What Happens If We Consume Too Much Sodium?

High blood pressure is more common in people who consume high-sodium diets. This strong relationship has prompted many health organizations to recommend lowering sodium intakes. Whether high-sodium diets actually cause high blood pressure is the subject

Table 9.2 High-Sodium Foods and Lower-Sodium Alternatives

High-Sodium Food	Sodium (mg)	Lower-Sodium Food	Sodium (mg)
Dill pickle (1 large, 4 in.)	1731	Low-sodium dill pickle (1 large, 4 in.)	25
Ham, cured, roasted (3 oz)	1177	Pork, loin roast (3 oz)	54
Chipped beef (3 oz)	913	Beef chuck roast, cooked (3 oz)	53
Tomato juice, regular (1 cup)	654	Tomato juice, lower sodium (1 cup)	24
Tomato sauce, canned (1/2 cup)	741	Fresh tomato (1 medium)	11
Canned cream corn (1 cup)	730	Cooked corn, fresh (1 cup)	28
Tomato soup, canned (1 cup)	695	Lower-sodium tomato soup, canned (1 cup)	480
Potato chips, salted (1 oz)	168	Baked potato, unsalted (1 medium)	14
Saltine crackers (4 each)	156	Saltine crackers, unsalted (4 each)	100

Data from: U.S. Department of Agriculture 2005. USDA National Nutrient Database for Standard Reference, Release 18. Nutrient Data Laboratory Home Page. Available at www.ars.usda.gov/ba/bhnrc/ndl.

of some controversy (see pages 345–346). Also controversial is the effect of high sodium intake on bone loss: Consuming excessive sodium has been shown to cause increased urinary excretion of calcium in some people, which in turn may increase the risk for bone loss. Recent studies have shown that a reduction in sodium intake improves bone status,[11] yet the extent to which excess sodium intake affects bone health remains under study.

Hypernatremia refers to an abnormally high blood sodium concentration. It is usually caused by a rapid intake of high amounts of sodium, such as when a shipwrecked sailor drinks seawater. Eating a high-sodium diet does not usually cause hypernatremia in a healthy person, as the kidneys are able to excrete excess sodium in the urine. But people with congestive heart failure or kidney disease are not able to excrete sodium effectively, making them more prone to the condition. Hypernatremia is dangerous because it causes an abnormally high blood volume, leading to edema (swelling) of tissues and raising blood pressure to unhealthy levels.

What Happens If We Don't Consume Enough Sodium?

Because dietary sodium intake is so high in the United States, deficiencies are extremely rare, except in individuals who sweat heavily or consume little or no sodium in the diet. Nevertheless, certain conditions can cause dangerously low blood sodium levels. **Hyponatremia,** abnormally low blood sodium concentration, can occur in active people who drink large volumes of water and fail to replace sodium. This was the subject of the chapter-opening vignette and is also discussed in the Highlight box. Severe diarrhea, vomiting, or excessive prolonged sweating can also cause hyponatremia.

Symptoms of hyponatremia include headaches, dizziness, fatigue, nausea, vomiting, and muscle cramps. If hyponatremia is left untreated, it can lead to seizures, coma, and death. Treatment for hyponatremia includes the ingestion of liquids and foods high in sodium and may even require the administration of electrolyte-rich solutions intravenously if the person has lost consciousness or is not able to consume beverages and foods by mouth.[12–15]

ReCaP

Sodium is the primary positively charged electrolyte in the extracellular fluid. It works to maintain fluid balance and blood pressure, assists in acid–base balance and transmission of nerve signals, aids muscle contraction, and assists in the absorption of some nutrients. The AI for sodium is 1.5 g per day. Deficiencies are rare, because the typical American diet is high in sodium. Excessive sodium intake has been related to high blood pressure and loss of bone density in some, but not all, studies.

Potassium

As we discussed previously, potassium is the major positively charged electrolyte in the intracellular fluid. It is a major constituent of all living cells and is found in both plants and animals. About 85% of dietary potassium is absorbed, and as with sodium, the kidneys regulate reabsorption and urinary excretion of potassium.

Functions of Potassium

Potassium and sodium work together to maintain proper fluid balance and to regulate the contraction of muscles and transmission of nerve impulses. Potassium also assists in maintaining blood pressure. In contrast with a high-sodium diet, eating a diet high in potassium actually helps maintain a lower blood pressure.

How Much Potassium Should We Consume?

We can reduce our risk for high blood pressure by consuming adequate potassium in our diet. The AI for potassium for adult men and women aged 19 to 50 years is 4.7 g/day (or 4,700 mg/day).[4]

Tomato juice is an excellent source of potassium.

hypernatremia   A condition in which blood sodium levels are dangerously high.

hyponatremia   A condition in which blood sodium levels are dangerously low.

Highlight

Can Water Be Too Much of a Good Thing? Hyponatremia in Marathon Runners

At the beginning of this chapter, we described the death of Boston Marathon runner Cynthia Lucero. Her case is only one of several that have gained attention in recent years. How can seemingly healthy, highly fit individuals competing in marathons collapse and even die during or after a race? One common challenge faced by these athletes is maintaining a proper balance of fluid and electrolytes during the race.

It is well known that people participating in distance events such as marathons (26.2 miles) need to drink enough fluid to ensure proper fluid balance. But how much is enough? The winner of the women's marathon in the Athens Olympics, running in 97-degree heat, drank for just 30 seconds of the entire race. Surprisingly, recent research has suggested that runners, particularly novice runners, may be at greater risk from drinking too much water than from drinking too little.

Two recent studies examined exercise-associated hyponatremia among marathon runners after a race.[1, 11] The major contributing factors appeared to be longer race time and drinking large amounts of fluid during the race. Experts observe that elite runners complete a race more quickly and drink as they run; thus, they simply don't have time to overdo the fluids. In contrast, less experienced athletes run more slowly, increasing the total time that they are competing; at the same time, they consume very large amounts of fluid to avoid potential dehydration. The slower and longer these individuals run, the more they drink and the more diluted their blood sodium levels become. About half of the hyponatremic runners in one study had to be hospitalized.[11]

Hyponatremia is a dangerous and potentially fatal condition, but it can be prevented. Recently, a group of international experts on exercise physiology and fluid balance developed guidelines for the prevention and treatment of exercise-associated hyponatremia.[12]

The fear of hyponatremia should not cause athletes to avoid drinking adequate fluids during long-distance activities, as dehydration and subsequent heat illness are as important to prevent as hyponatremia. The key to staying safe during competitive events is to match fluid and sodium intake with sweat loss.[13] Athletes should weigh themselves regularly before and after training to determine average sweat loss and then consume enough fluid to minimize loss of body weight but not enough to cause weight gain. Drinking sports beverages, which contain electrolytes (particularly sodium), and moderating fluid intake during marathons and other long-distance events can help prevent hyponatremia.

Potassium is found in abundance in many fresh foods, particularly fresh fruits and vegetables. **Figure 9.9** identifies foods that are high in potassium. Processing foods generally increases their amount of sodium and decreases their amount of potassium. Thus, you can optimize your potassium intake and reduce your sodium intake by avoiding processed foods and eating more fresh fruits, vegetables, legumes, and whole grains.

What Happens If We Consume Too Much Potassium?

People with healthy kidneys are able to excrete excess potassium effectively. However, people with kidney disease are not able to regulate their blood potassium levels. **Hyperkalemia,** or high blood potassium concentration, occurs when potassium is not efficiently excreted from the body. Because of potassium's role in cardiac muscle contraction, severe hyperkalemia can alter the normal rhythm of the heart, resulting in heart attack and death. People with kidney disease must monitor their potassium intake very carefully, and should avoid consuming salt substitutes, as these products are high in potassium.

hyperkalemia A condition in which blood potassium levels are dangerously high.

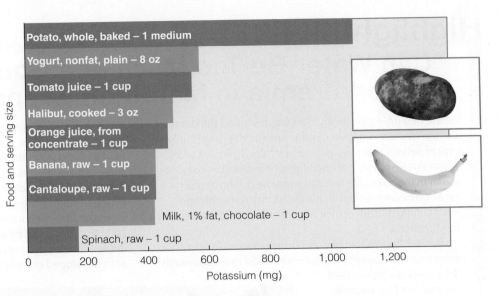

Figure 9.9 Common food sources of potassium. The AI for potassium is 4.7 g/day. (*Data from:* U.S. Department of Agriculture, Agricultural Research Service. 2006. USDA Nutrient Database for Standard Reference, Release 19. Nutrient Data Laboratory Home Page. Available at www.ars.usda.gov/ba/bhnrc/ndl.)

The chart shows food and serving size versus Potassium (mg), with axis ticks at 0, 200, 400, 600, 800, 1,000, 1,200:
- Potato, whole, baked – 1 medium
- Yogurt, nonfat, plain – 8 oz
- Tomato juice – 1 cup
- Halibut, cooked – 3 oz
- Orange juice, from concentrate – 1 cup
- Banana, raw – 1 cup
- Cantaloupe, raw – 1 cup
- Milk, 1% fat, chocolate – 1 cup
- Spinach, raw – 1 cup

What Happens If We Don't Consume Enough Potassium?

Because potassium is widespread in many foods, a dietary potassium deficiency is rare. However, potassium deficiency is not uncommon among people who have serious medical disorders. Kidney disease, diabetic ketoacidosis, and other illnesses can lead to potassium deficiency.

In addition, people with high blood pressure who are prescribed certain diuretic medications to treat their disease are at risk for potassium deficiency. As we noted earlier, diuretics promote the excretion of fluid as urine through the kidneys. Some diuretics also increase the body's urinary excretion of potassium. People who are taking diuretic medications should have their blood potassium monitored regularly and should eat foods that are high in potassium to prevent **hypokalemia,** or low blood potassium concentration. This is not a universal recommendation, however, because some diuretics are specially formulated to spare or retain potassium; therefore, people taking diuretics should consult their physician regarding dietary potassium intake.

Extreme dehydration, vomiting, and diarrhea can also cause hypokalemia, as can long-term consumption of natural licorice, which contains glycyrrhizic acid (GZA), a substance that increases urinary excretion of potassium. Because the majority of foods that contain licorice flavoring in the United States do not contain GZA, licorice-induced hypokalemia is rarely seen here. People who abuse alcohol or laxatives can suffer from hypokalemia. Symptoms include confusion, loss of appetite, and muscle weakness. Severe cases of hypokalemia result in fatal changes in heart rate; many deaths attributed to extreme dehydration or an eating disorder are caused by abnormal heart rhythms due to hypokalemia.

RECAP

Potassium is the major positively charged electrolyte inside of the cell. It regulates fluid balance, blood pressure, and muscle contraction, and it helps in the transmission of nerve impulses. The AI for potassium is 4.7 g per day. Potassium is found in abundance in fresh foods, particularly fruits and vegetables. Both hyperkalemia and hypokalemia can result in heart failure and death.

Chloride

hypokalemia A condition in which blood potassium levels are dangerously low.

Chloride is a negatively charged ion that is obtained almost exclusively from sodium chloride or table salt. It should not be confused with *chlorine*, which is a poisonous gas used to kill germs in our water supply. As with sodium, the majority of dietary chloride is absorbed in the small intestine. The kidneys regulate urinary excretion of chloride.

Functions of Chloride

Coupled with sodium in the extracellular fluid, chloride assists with the maintenance of fluid balance. Chloride is also a part of hydrochloric acid (HCl) in the stomach, which aids in preparing food for further digestion (see Chapter 3). Chloride also works with the white blood cells during an immune response to help kill bacteria, and it assists in the transmission of nerve impulses.

How Much Chloride Should We Consume?

The AI for chloride for adult men and women aged 19 to 50 years is 2.3 g/day (or 2,300 mg/day).[4] As chloride is coupled with sodium to form table salt, our primary dietary source of chloride is salt in our foods. Chloride is also found in some fruits and vegetables. Keep in mind that salt is composed of about 60% chloride; thus, you can calculate the content of chloride in processed foods by multiplying its salt content by 0.60 (or 60%). For instance, a food that contains 500 mg of salt would contain 300 mg of chloride (or 500 mg × 0.60 = 300 mg).

Almost all chloride is consumed through table salt.

What Happens If We Consume Too Much Chloride?

Because we consume virtually all of our dietary chloride in the form of sodium chloride, there is no known toxicity symptom for chloride alone. As noted earlier, consuming excess amounts of sodium chloride over a prolonged period leads to hypertension in salt-sensitive individuals.

What Happens If We Don't Consume Enough Chloride?

Because of our relatively high dietary salt intake in the United States, most people consume more than enough chloride. Even when a person consumes a low-sodium diet, chloride intake is usually adequate. A chloride deficiency can occur, however, during conditions of severe dehydration and frequent vomiting. This is sometimes seen in people with eating disorders who regularly vomit to rid their bodies of unwanted energy.

ReCaP

Chloride is the major negatively charged electrolyte outside of the cell. It assists with fluid balance, digestion, immune responses, and the transmission of nerve impulses. The AI for chloride is 2.3 g per day. Our main dietary source of chloride is sodium chloride. There is no known toxicity for chloride alone. Chloride deficiencies are rare but can occur during severe dehydration and frequent vomiting.

Phosphorus

Phosphorus is the major intracellular negatively charged electrolyte. In the body, phosphorus is most commonly found combined with oxygen in the form of phosphate, PO_4^{-3}. Phosphorus is an essential constituent of all cells and is found in both plants and animals. Adults absorb about 55% to 70% of dietary phosphorus, primarily in the small intestine. The active form of vitamin D (1,25-dihydroxyvitamin D or calcitriol) facilitates the absorption of phosphorus, whereas consumption of aluminum-containing antacids and high doses of calcium carbonate reduce its absorption. The kidneys regulate reabsorption and urinary excretion of phosphorus.

Functions of Phosphorus

Phosphorus works with potassium inside of the cell to maintain proper fluid balance. It also plays a critical role in bone formation, as it is a part of the mineral complex of bone (see Chapter 11). In fact, about 85% of the body's phosphorus is stored in the bones.

Milk is a good source of phosphorus.

As a primary component of ATP, phosphorus plays a key role in creating energy for the body through the reactions in glycolysis and oxidative phosphorylation. It also helps regulate many biochemical reactions by activating and deactivating enzymes during phosphorylation. Phosphorus is a part of both DNA and RNA, and it is a component of cell membranes (as phospholipids) and of lipoproteins.

How Much Phosphorus Should We Consume?

The RDA for phosphorus is 700 mg per day.[16] The average U.S. adult consumes about twice this amount each day, thus phosphorus deficiencies are rare. Phosphorus is widespread in many foods and is found in high amounts in foods that contain protein. Milk, meats, and eggs are good sources of phosphorus (**Figure 9.10**).

It is important to note that phosphorus from animal sources is absorbed more readily than phosphorus from plant sources. Much of the phosphorus in plant foods such as beans, whole-grain cereals, and nuts is found in the form of **phytic acid,** a plant storage form of phosphorus. Our bodies do not produce enzymes that can break down phytic acid, but we are still able to absorb up to 50% of the phosphorus found in plant foods because the bacteria in the large intestine can break down phytic acid. Soft drinks are another common source of phosphorus in the diet; refer to Chapter 11 to learn how heavy consumption of soft drinks may be detrimental to bone health.

phytic acid   The form of phosphorus stored in plants.

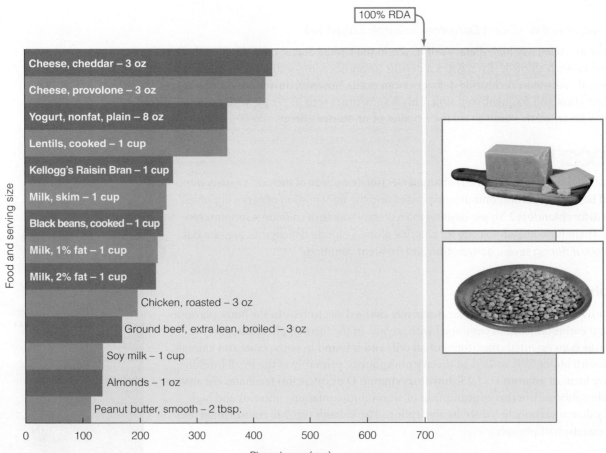

Figure 9.10   Common food sources of phosphorus. The RDA for phosphorus is 700 mg/day. (*Data from:* U.S. Department of Agriculture, Agricultural Research Service. 2006. USDA Nutrient Database for Standard Reference, Release 19. Nutrient Data Laboratory Home Page. Available at www.ars.usda.gov/ba/bhnrc/ndl.)

What Happens If We Consume Too Much Phosphorus?

People suffering from kidney disease and people taking too many vitamin D supplements or too many phosphorus-containing antacids can suffer from high blood phosphorus levels. Severely high levels of blood phosphorus cause muscle spasms and convulsions.

What Happens If We Don't Consume Enough Phosphorus?

As mentioned previously, deficiencies of phosphorus are rare. People who may suffer from low blood phosphorus levels include premature infants, elderly people with poor diets, and people who abuse alcohol. People with vitamin D deficiency, hyperparathyroidism (oversecretion of parathyroid hormone), and those who overuse antacids that bind with phosphorus may also have low blood phosphorus levels.

RECAP

Phosphorus is the major negatively charged electrolyte inside of the cell. It helps maintain fluid balance and bone health. It also assists in making energy available and in regulating chemical reactions, and it is a primary component of genetic materials. The RDA for phosphorus is 700 mg per day, and it is commonly found in high-protein foods. Excess phosphorus can lead to muscle spasms and convulsions, and phosphorus deficiencies are rare.

What Disorders Are Related to Fluid and Electrolyte Imbalances?

A number of serious, and potentially fatal, disorders can result from an imbalance of fluid and electrolytes in the body. We review some of these here.

Dehydration

Dehydration is a serious health problem that results when fluid losses exceed fluid intake. It can occur as a result of heavy exercise or exposure to high environmental temperatures, when the body loses significant amounts of water through increased sweating and breathing. However, elderly people and infants can get dehydrated even when inactive, as their risk for dehydration is much higher than that of healthy young and middle-aged adults. The elderly are at increased risk because they have a lower total amount of body water and their thirst mechanism is less effective than that of a younger person; they are therefore less likely to meet their fluid needs. Infants, on the other hand, excrete urine at a higher rate, cannot tell us when they are thirsty, and have a greater ratio of body surface area to body core, causing them to respond more dramatically to heat and cold and to lose more body water than an older child.

Dehydration is classified in terms of the percentage of weight loss that is exclusively due to the loss of fluid. As indicated in Table 9.3, relatively small losses in body water result in symptoms such as thirst, discomfort, and loss of appetite. More severe water losses result in symptoms that include sleepiness, nausea, flushed skin, and problems with mental concentration. Severe losses of body water can result in delirium, coma, cardiac arrest, and death.

We discussed earlier the importance of fluid replacement when you are exercising. How can you tell whether you are drinking enough fluid before, during, and after your exercise sessions? First, you can measure your body weight before and after each session. If you weighed in at 160 lb before basketball practice, and immediately afterward you weigh 158 lb, then you have lost 2 lb of body weight. This is equal to 1.3% of your body weight prior to practice. As you can see in Table 9.3, you are most likely feeling strong thirst, diminished appetite, and you may even feel generally uncomfortable. Your goal is to consume

Dehydration occurs when fluid excretion exceeds fluid intake.

dehydration Depletion of body fluid that results when fluid excretion exceeds fluid intake.

Table 9.3 Percentages of Body Fluid Loss Correlated with Weight Loss and Symptoms

% Body Water Loss	Weight Lost If You Weigh 160 lb	Weight Lost If You Weigh 130 lb	Symptoms
1–2	1.6 lb–3.2 lb	1.3 lb–2.6 lb	Strong thirst, loss of appetite, feeling uncomfortable
3–5	4.8 lb–8.0 lb	3.9 lb–6.5 lb	Dry mouth, reduced urine output, greater difficulty working and concentrating, flushed skin, tingling extremities, impatience, sleepiness, nausea, emotional instability
6–8	9.6 lb–12.8 lb	7.8 lb–10.4 lb	Increased body temperature that doesn't decrease, increased heart rate and breathing rate, dizziness, difficulty breathing, slurred speech, mental confusion, muscle weakness, blue lips
9–11	14.4 lb–17.6 lb	11.7 lb–14.3 lb	Muscle spasms, delirium, swollen tongue, poor balance and circulation, kidney failure, decreased blood volume and blood pressure

Figure 9.11 Urine color chart. Color variations indicate levels of hydration.

enough water and other fluids to bring your body weight back to 160 lb prior to your next exercise session. This would require drinking about 4 cups of fluid, as 2 lb of body weight is equal to just less than 1 L, or 4 cups.

A simpler method of monitoring your fluid levels is to observe the color of your urine (**Figure 9.11**). If you are properly hydrated, your urine should be clear to pale yellow in color, similar to diluted lemonade. Urine that is medium to dark yellow in color, similar to apple juice, indicates an inadequate fluid intake. Very dark or brown-colored urine, such as the color of a cola beverage, is a sign of severe dehydration and indicates potential muscle breakdown and kidney damage. People should strive to maintain a urine color that is clear or pale yellow.

Gustavo
Nutri-Case

"Something is going on with me this week. Every day at work, I've been feeling weak and like I'm going to be sick to my stomach. It's been really hot, over a hundred degrees out in the fields, but I'm used to that, and besides, I've been drinking lots of water. It's probably just my high blood pressure acting up again."

What do you think might be wrong with Gustavo? If you learned that he was following a low-sodium diet prescribed to manage his high blood pressure, would this information argue for or against your theory, and why? To avoid these symptoms, what could Gustavo do differently at work tomorrow?

Heat Stroke

Heat stroke is a potentially fatal heat illness characterized by failure of the body's heat-regulating mechanisms. Symptoms include rapid pulse; hot, dry skin; high temperature; and loss of consciousness.

Athletes who work out in hot, humid weather are particularly vulnerable to heat stroke. In August 2001, 27-year-old National Football League all-star player Korey Stringer died of complications from heat stroke after working out in a hot and humid environment.[17] Despite having access to ample fluid and excellent medical assistance, Stringer's temperature rose to 108°F. In addition to heat, humidity, and dehydration, Stringer's tightly fitting polyester uniform and helmet, which trapped warm air close to his body, were factors in his death. Stringer's large body size (6'4", 330 lb) also contributed: our ability to dissipate body heat via sweat is extremely limited in a humid environment, and

heat stroke A potentially fatal response to high temperature characterized by failure of the body's heat-regulating mechanisms. Symptoms include rapid pulse, reduced sweating, hot and dry skin, high temperature, headache, weakness, and sudden loss of consciousness. Commonly called sunstroke.

large individuals with a great deal of muscle mass produce a lot of body heat. In addition, excess body fat adds an extra layer of insulation that makes it even more difficult to dissipate body heat.

Similar deaths have occurred in the past with collegiate and high-school football players. These deaths prompted national attention and resulted in strict guidelines encouraging regular fluid breaks and cancellation of events or changing the time of the event to avoid high heat and humidity. In addition, people who are active in a hot environment should stop exercising if they feel dizzy, light-headed, disoriented, or nauseated. Heat illnesses can be avoided by following established guidelines for fluid intake before, during, and after exercise.

Water Intoxication

Is it possible to drink too much water? **Overhydration,** or *water intoxication,* can occur but it is rare. It generally only occurs in people with health problems that cause the kidneys to retain too much water, causing overhydration and hyponatremia, which were discussed earlier. However, there are also documented cases of deaths due to overhydration among college students participating in hazing rituals. In these examples, people were forced to consume very large amounts of water in a short period of time while being prevented from going to the bathroom, resulting in fatalities. Thus, the overconsumption of water can be deadly and should never be thought of as a prank or a joke.

Hypertension

One of the major chronic diseases in the United States is high blood pressure, which healthcare professionals refer to as **hypertension.** A person with hypertension is unable to maintain blood pressure in a healthy range. It was recently estimated that nearly 30% of U.S. adults had hypertension and another 28% had a condition termed prehypertension.[18] Although hypertension itself is often without symptoms, it increases a person's risk for many other serious conditions, including heart disease, stroke, and kidney disease; it can also reduce brain function, impair physical mobility, and cause death.

Blood pressure is measured in two phases: systolic and diastolic. *Systolic blood pressure* represents the pressure exerted in the arteries at the moment that the heart contracts, sending blood into the blood vessels. *Diastolic blood pressure* represents the pressure in the arteries between contractions, when the heart is relaxed. You can also think of diastolic blood pressure as the resistance in the arteries that the heart must pump against every time it beats. Blood pressure is measured in millimeters of mercury (mm Hg). When your blood pressure is measured, the systolic pressure is given first, followed by the diastolic pressure. For example, your reading might be given as "115 (systolic) over 75 (diastolic)."

Optimal systolic blood pressure is *less than* 120 mm Hg, whereas optimal diastolic blood pressure is *less than* 80 mm Hg. Pre-hypertension is defined as a systolic blood pressure between 120 and 139 mm Hg, or a diastolic blood pressure between 80 and 89 mm Hg. You would be diagnosed with hypertension if your systolic blood pressure were greater than or equal to 140 mm Hg or your diastolic blood pressure were greater than or equal to 90 mm Hg.

What Causes Hypertension?

For about 90% to 95% of people who have it, the causes of hypertension are unknown. This type is referred to as *primary* or *essential hypertension.* For the other 5% to 10% of people with hypertension, causes may include kidney disease, sleep apnea (a sleep disorder that affects breathing), or chronic alcohol abuse. It is estimated that over half of all adults with hypertension have a condition known as **salt sensitivity.** These people respond to a high salt intake by experiencing an increase in blood pressure; they also experience a decrease in blood pressure when salt intake is low. People who do not experience changes in blood pressure with changes in salt intake are referred to as **salt resistant.**

National Football League all-star Korey Stringer died in 2001 as a result of heat stroke.

overhydration Dilution of body fluid. It results when water intake or retention is excessive.

hypertension A chronic condition characterized by above-average blood pressure readings; specifically, systolic blood pressure over 140 mm Hg or diastolic blood pressure over 90 mm Hg.

salt sensitivity A condition in which certain people respond to a high salt intake by experiencing an increase in blood pressure; these people also experience a decrease in blood pressure when salt intake is low.

salt resistance A condition in which certain people do not experience changes in blood pressure with changes in salt intake.

Hypertension is a major chronic disease in the United States, affecting more than 50% of adults over 65 years of age.

Losing weight and increasing physical activity can help fight hypertension.

DASH diet Term for the Dietary Approach to Stop Hypertension, this diet plan emphasizes fruits and vegetables, whole grains, low/no-fat milk and dairy, and lean meats.

Five Lifestyle Changes Can Reduce Hypertension

Although we do not know what causes most cases of hypertension, there are five primary lifestyle changes that can help reduce it. These changes include:

- Losing weight. Systolic blood pressure values have been shown to decrease 5 to 20 points in people who were overweight or obese and lost an average of 22 lb of body weight.[19]
- Increasing physical activity. The amount and intensity of exercise needed to improve blood pressure are easily achievable for most people. Regular physical activity, such as brisk walking, lasting at least 30 minutes per day, most days of the week, can help lower blood pressure.[19]
- Reducing alcohol intake. Because alcohol consumption can worsen high blood pressure, it is suggested that people with this disease abstain from drinking alcohol or limit their intake to no more than one (women) or two (men) drinks per day.[19]
- Reducing sodium intake in salt-sensitive individuals. Some people who are not salt sensitive also benefit from eating lower-sodium diets.[19, 20]
- Eating more whole grains, fruits, vegetables, and low-fat dairy foods.[19, 20]

Among nutrition and healthcare professionals, one area of controversy is the impact that sodium intake has on our blood pressure. For years it was believed that the high sodium intakes of the typical American diet led to hypertension. This is because people who live in countries in which sodium intake is high have greater rates of hypertension than people from countries in which sodium intake is low. We have recently learned, however, that not everyone with hypertension is sensitive to sodium. Unfortunately, it is impossible to know who is sensitive to sodium, as there is no definitive test for the condition. Because lowering sodium intake does not reduce blood pressure in all people with hypertension, there is significant debate over whether everyone can benefit from eating a lower-sodium diet. Despite this debate, the leading health organizations, including the American Heart Association, the National High Blood Pressure Education Program, and the National Heart, Lung, and Blood Institute of the National Institutes of Health, continue to support a reduction in dietary sodium to 2,300 mg per day as recommended in the Dietary Guidelines for Americans.[10] Currently, the average sodium intake in the United States is about 3,400 mg per day.[18]

The Role of the DASH Diet Plan

The **DASH diet** plan resulted from a large research study funded by the National Institutes of Health (NIH).[21, 22] DASH stands for "Dietary Approaches to Stop Hypertension"; thus, this study was designed to assess the effects of the DASH diet on high blood pressure. Table 9.4 shows the DASH eating plan for a 2,000-kcal diet. This plan is similar to the goals of MyPyramid in that it is low in fat and high in fiber. The DASH diet also emphasizes foods that are rich in potassium, calcium, and magnesium, including 10 servings of fruits and vegetables each day along with whole-grain foods and low-fat or nonfat milk and dairy products. The sodium content of the DASH diet is about 3 g (or 3,000 mg) of sodium, which is slightly less than the average sodium intake in the United States.

Over the past several years, many research studies have convincingly illustrated that eating the DASH diet has a positive impact on blood pressure. Decreases in blood pressure can occur within the first 2 weeks of following it. Researchers estimated that if all Americans followed the DASH diet plan, heart disease would be reduced by 15% and the number of strokes would be 27% lower.

Another study of the DASH diet has found that blood pressure continues to decrease if sodium intake is reduced below 3,000 mg per day.[20] Participants ate a DASH diet that provided either 3,300 mg (average U.S. intake), 2,400 mg (upper recommended intake), or 1,500 mg of sodium each day. After 1 month on this diet, all people eating the DASH diet saw a significant decrease in their blood pressure; however, those who ate the lowest-

Table 9.4 The DASH Diet Plan

Food Group	Daily Servings	Serving Size
Grains and grain products	7–8	1 slice bread 1 cup ready-to-eat cereal* 1/2 cup cooked rice, pasta, or cereal
Vegetables	4–5	1 cup raw leafy vegetables 1/2 cup cooked vegetable 6 fl. oz vegetable juice
Fruits	4–5	1 medium fruit 1/4 cup dried fruit 1/2 cup fresh, frozen, or canned fruit 6 fl. oz fruit juice
Low-fat or fat-free dairy foods	2–3	8 fl. oz milk 1 cup yogurt 1½ oz cheese
Lean meats, poultry, and fish	2 or less	3 oz cooked lean meats, skinless poultry, or fish
Nuts, seeds, and dry beans	4–5 per week	1/3 cup or 1½ oz nuts 1 tbsp. or 1/2 oz seeds 1/2 cup cooked dry beans
Fats and oils†	2–3	1 tsp. soft margarine 1 tbsp. low-fat mayonnaise 2 tbsp. light salad dressing 1 tsp. vegetable oil
Sweets	5 per week	1 tbsp. sugar 1 tbsp. jelly or jam 1/2 oz jelly beans 8 fl. oz lemonade

Note: The plan is based on 2,000 kcal per day. The number of servings in a food group may differ from the number listed, depending on your own energy needs.

*Serving sizes vary between 1/2 and 1¼ cups. Check the product's nutrition label.

†Fat content changes serving counts for fats and oils: for example, 1 tablespoon of regular salad dressing equals 1 serving; 1 tablespoon of a low-fat dressing equals 1/2 serving; 1 tablespoon of a fat-free dressing equals 0 servings.

Data from: National Institutes of Health. Healthier Eating with DASH. Available at www.nhlbi.nih.gov/health/public/heart/hbp/dash/new_dash.pdf.

sodium version of the DASH diet experienced the largest decrease. These results indicate that eating a diet low in sodium and high in fruits and vegetables reduces blood pressure and decreases the risk for heart disease and stroke.

In addition to its beneficial effects in reducing blood pressure, the DASH diet has also been shown to lower risk for coronary heart disease and stroke among women[23] as well as the risk for metabolic syndrome.[24] Finally, the DASH diet has been shown to be particularly beneficial in hypertensive African Americans, a population group at very high risk for the disease and its complications.[25]

Medications

For some individuals, lifestyle changes are not completely effective in normalizing hypertension. When this is the case, a variety of medications can bring a person's blood pressure into the normal range. Individuals taking medications to control blood pressure should also continue to practice the healthful lifestyle changes identified earlier, as these changes will continue to benefit their long-term health.

Hypertension is called "the silent killer," because often there are no obvious symptoms of this disease. For this reason, it is important that people get their blood pressure checked on a regular basis. Tragically, many people with hypertension fail to take their

The DASH diet emphasizes fruits and vegetables, whole grains, low-fat or nonfat dairy, and lean protein sources.

prescribed medication because they do not feel sick. Some of these people eventually suffer the consequences of their actions by experiencing a heart attack or stroke.

Neuromuscular Disorders

Because nerves synapse with muscles, electrolyte imbalances that alter nervous system function will in turn disturb muscle function. For example, **seizures** are uncontrollable muscle spasms that may be localized to one area of the body, such as the face, or can violently wrack a person's entire body. **Muscle cramps** are involuntary, spasmodic, and painful muscle contractions that last for many seconds or even minutes. Hypernatremia that occurs with dehydration is known to cause cramps, as are other electrolyte imbalances. Muscle weakness and paralysis can also occur with severe electrolyte imbalances such as hypokalemia, hyperkalemia, and low blood phosphorus levels.

Obesity

Until about 50 years ago, beverage choices were fairly limited. The introduction of a very cheap sweetener, high-fructose corn syrup, and dramatic changes in the marketing and sales of beverages led to a surge in the popularity of sodas and other sweetened drinks. Today, Americans take in approximately 21% of their calories from beverages, mostly in the form of sweetened soft drinks and fruit juices. Recently, sweetened bottled waters, bottled teas, and specialty coffee drinks have contributed to the problem: a coffee mocha at one national chain provides 400 calories, which is 20% of an average adult's total daily calorie needs.

It's not surprising, then, that researchers believe that calories from these types of sweetened beverages have contributed to half of the rise in caloric intake among Americans since the late 1970s—and thus are factors in our current obesity epidemic. Beverages with a high calorie content do little to curb appetite, so most people do not compensate for the extra calories they drink by eating less. In addition, sweetened sodas, teas, and other specialty beverages displace more nutritious beverages such as milk, which provides protein, calcium, vitamin D, and other nutrients important for bone health (see Chapter 11).

seizures   Uncontrollable muscle spasms caused by increased nervous system excitability that can result from electrolyte imbalances or a chronic disease such as epilepsy.

muscle cramps   Involuntary, spasmodic, and painful muscle contractions that last for many seconds or even minutes; electrolyte imbalances are often the cause of muscle cramps.

RECaP

Dehydration, heat stroke, and even death can occur when water loss exceeds water intake. Because the thirst mechanism is not always sufficient, it is important to drink water throughout the day to promote adequate fluid intake. Hypertension is a major chronic illness in the United States; it can often be controlled by losing weight if overweight, increasing physical activity, decreasing alcohol intake, and making specific dietary changes such as those in the DASH diet. Electrolyte imbalances can also lead to neuromuscular disorders. Intake of sugary beverages can contribute to obesity.

See for Yourself
How Pure Is Your Favorite Bottled Water?

Next time you reach for your favorite brand of bottled water, check the label. To find out how pure it is, consider the following factors:

1. Find out where it comes from. If no location is identified, even a bottle labeled "spring water" may actually contain tap water with minerals added to improve the taste. What you're looking for are the words "Bottled at the source." Water that comes from a protected groundwater source is less likely to have contaminants such as disease-causing microbes. If the label doesn't identify the water's source, it should at least provide contact information such as a phone number or Web site of the bottled water company so that you can track down the source.

2. Find out how the water in the bottle has been treated. There are several ways of treating water, but what you're looking for are either of the following two methods, which have been proven to be effective against the most common waterborne disease-causing microorganisms:

   ■ *Micron filtration* is a process whereby water is filtered through screens with various-sized microscopic holes. High-quality micron filtration can eliminate most chemical contaminants and microbes.

   ■ *Reverse osmosis* is a process often referred to as *ultrafiltration* because it uses a membrane with microscopic openings that allow water to pass through but not larger compounds. Reverse-osmosis membranes also utilize electrical charges to reject harmful chemicals.

   If the label on your bottle of water says that the water was purified using any of the following methods, you might want to consider switching brands: filtered, carbon-filtered, particle-filtered, ozonated or ozone-treated, ultraviolet light, ion exchange, and deionized. These methods have not been proven to be effective against the most common waterborne disease-causing microorganisms.

Can you tell where the water in each bottle comes from?

3. Check the nutrient content on the label. Ideally, water should be high in magnesium (at least 20 mg/8 fl oz serving) and calcium, but low in sodium (less than 5 mg/8 fl oz serving). Avoid bottled waters with sweeteners, as their "empty calories" can contribute significantly to your energy intake. These products are often promoted as healthful beverage choices, with names including words like *vitamins*, *herbs*, *nature*, and *life*, but they are essentially "liquid candy." Check the Nutrition Facts Panel and don't be fooled!

Chapter Review

Test Yourself | Answers

1 **T** Between approximately 50% and 70% of our body weight consists of fluid.

2 **F** Sodium is a nutrient necessary for health, but we should not consume more than recommended amounts.

3 **F** Our thirst mechanism signals that we need to replenish fluids, but it is not always sufficient to ensure we are completely hydrated.

4 **F** There is no evidence that bottled water consistently offers any additional health or nutrition benefits compared to tap water.

5 **F** We do not know the cause of high blood pressure in most people. A high-sodium diet can cause high blood pressure in a subset of people who are sensitive to sodium.

Summary

- Approximately 50% to 70% of a healthy adult's body weight is fluid. Two-thirds of this fluid is intracellular fluid, and the remainder is extracellular fluid.

- Electrolytes are electrically charged particles found in body fluid that assist in maintaining fluid balance and the normal functioning of cells and the nervous system.

- Water acts as a solvent, provides protection and lubrication for organs and tissues, and acts to maintain blood volume, blood pressure, and body temperature.

- The three primary sources of fluid intake are beverages, foods, and metabolic water produced by chemical reactions during metabolism.

- The primary avenues of fluid excretion are sensible water loss (urine and sweat), insensible water loss (via evaporation and exhalation), and feces.

- Conditions that significantly increase water loss from our bodies include fever, vomiting, diarrhea, hemorrhage, blood donation, heavy exercise, and exposure to heat, cold, and altitude.

- Fluid intake needs are highly variable and depend on body size, age, physical activity, health status, and environmental conditions.

- Drinking too much water can lead to overhydration and hyponatremia, or dilution of blood sodium, whereas drinking too little water leads to dehydration, one of the leading causes of death around the world.

- Sodium assists in maintaining fluid balance, blood pressure, nervous function, and muscle contraction.

- Consuming excess sodium can cause high blood pressure or hypernatremia. Sodium deficiencies are rare, but hyponatremia can occur when excessive fluid intake is not accompanied by adequate sodium intake.

- Potassium assists in maintaining fluid balance, healthy blood pressure, transmission of nerve impulses, and muscle function.

- Hyperkalemia is excess blood potassium, which occurs due to kidney disease or malfunction. Hypokalemia is low blood potassium and can occur as a result of kidney disease, diabetic acidosis, and through the use of some diuretic medications.

- Chloride assists in maintaining fluid balance, normal nerve transmission, and the digestion of food via the action of HCl.

- Phosphorus assists in maintaining fluid balance and transferring energy via ATP. It is also a component of bone, phospholipids, genetic material, and lipoproteins.

- Dehydration occurs when water excretion exceeds water intake. Individuals at risk include the elderly, infants, people exercising heavily for prolonged periods in the heat, and individuals suffering from prolonged vomiting and diarrhea.

- Heat stroke occurs when the body's core temperature rises above 100°F. Heat stroke can lead to death if left untreated.

- Overhydration, or water intoxication, is caused by consuming too much water. Hyponatremia can also result from water intoxication.

- Hypertension, or high blood pressure, increases the risk for heart disease, stroke, and kidney disease. Consuming excess sodium is associated with hypertension in some, but not all, people.

- Lifestyle changes such as normalization of body weight, regular physical activity, reduction in alcohol intake, and dietary modifications such as the DASH diet are effective and low-risk approaches that reduce a person's risk for hypertension.

Review Questions

1. Which of the following is a characteristic of potassium?
   a. It is the major positively charged electrolyte in the extracellular fluid.
   b. It can be found in fresh fruits and vegetables.
   c. It is a critical component of the mineral complex of bone.
   d. It is the major negatively charged electrolyte in the extracellular fluid.

2. Which of the following people probably has the greatest percentage of body fluid?
   a. A female adult who is slightly overweight and vomits nightly after eating dinner
   b. An elderly male of average weight who has low blood pressure
   c. An overweight football player who has just completed a practice session in high heat
   d. A healthy infant of average weight

3. Plasma is one example of
   a. extracellular fluid.
   b. intracellular fluid.
   c. tissue fluid.
   d. metabolic water.

4. Which of the following is true of the cell membrane?
   a. It is freely permeable to water and many solutes.
   b. It is freely permeable only to water.
   c. It is freely permeable only to water and fats.
   d. It is freely permeable only to water and proteins.

5. Which of the following lifestyle changes has been shown to reduce hypertension in all people with high blood pressure?
   a. Consuming a low-sodium diet
   b. Normalizing body weight
   c. Getting at least 8 hours of sleep nightly
   d. Consuming one to two glasses of red wine daily

6. **True or false?** Drinking lots of water throughout a marathon will prevent fluid imbalances.

7. **True or false?** A decreased concentration of electrolytes in our blood stimulates the thirst mechanism.

8. **True or false?** Hypernatremia is commonly caused by a rapid intake of plain water.

9. **True or false?** Absence of thirst is a reliable indicator of adequate hydration.

10. **True or false?** Conditions that increase fluid loss include constipation, blood transfusions, and high humidity.

11. Explain why severe diarrhea in a young child can lead to death from heart failure.

12. After winning a cross-country relay race, you and your teammates celebrate with a trip to the local tavern for a few beers. That evening, you feel shaky and disoriented, and you have a "pins and needles" feeling in your hands and feet. What could be going on that is contributing to these feelings?

13. For lunch today, your choices include (a) chicken soup, a ham sandwich, and a can of tomato juice; or (b) potato salad, a tuna-fish sandwich, and a bottle of mineral water. You have hockey practice in mid-afternoon. Which lunch should you choose, and why?

14. Your cousin, who is breastfeeding her 3-month-old daughter, confesses to you that she has resorted to taking over-the-counter weight-loss pills to help her lose the weight she gained during pregnancy. What concerns might this raise?

15. While visiting your grandmother over the holidays, you notice that she avoids drinking any beverage with her evening meal or in the hours prior to bedtime. You ask her about it, and she explains that she avoids fluids so that she won't have to get up and go to the bathroom during the night. "Though I still don't get a good night's sleep," she sighs. "Many nights I wake up with cramps in my legs and have to get up and walk around anyway!" Is there a link here? If so, explain.

Web Links

www.epa.gov/OW
U.S. Environmental Protection Agency
Go to the EPA's water site for more information about drinking-water quality, standards, and safety.

www.bottledwater.org
International Bottled Water Association
Find current information about bottled water from this trade association that represents the bottled water industry.

www.mayoclinic.com
Mayo Clinic
For specific information on dehydration, use the link

www.mayoclinic.com/health/dehydration/ds00561
to learn more about hyponatremia, use the link

www.mayoclinic.com/health/hyponatremia/DS00974
and to learn how to estimate your personal fluid needs during exercise, use the link

www.mayoclinic.com/health/water/NU00283.

www.nlm.nih.gov/medlineplus
MEDLINE Plus Health Information
Search for "dehydration" and "heat stroke" to obtain additional resources and the latest news about the dangers of these heat-related illnesses.

www.nhlbi.nih.gov
National Heart, Lung, and Blood Institute
Go to this site to learn more about heart disease, including how to prevent high blood pressure and hypertension.

www.americanheart.org
American Heart Association
The American Heart Association provides plenty of tips on how to lower your blood pressure.

www.nih.gov
The National Institutes of Health (NIH)
Search this site to learn more about the DASH diet (Dietary Approaches to Stop Hypertension).

References

1. Almond, C. S. D., A. Y. Shin, E. B. Fortescue, R. C. Mannix, D. Wypij, B. A. Binstadt, C. N. Duncan, D. P. Olson, A. E. Salerno, J. W. Newburger, and D. S. Greenes. 2005. Hyponatremia among runners in the Boston Marathon. *N. Engl. J. Med.* 352:1150–1156.
2. Maughan R. J., and J. Griffin. 2003. Caffeine ingestion and fluid balance: A review. *J. Hum. Nutr. Diet.* 16:411–420.
3. Armstrong, L. E. 2002. Caffeine, body fluid-electrolyte balance, and exercise performance. *International Journal of Sport Nutrition and Exercise Metabolism* 12(2):189–206.
4. Institute of Medicine. 2004. *Dietary Reference Intakes for Water, Potassium, Sodium, Chloride, and Sulfate.* Washington, DC: The National Academies Press.
5. American College of Sports Medicine (ACSM). 1996. Exercise and fluid replacement. *Med. Sci. Sports Exerc.* 28:i–vii.
6. Coyle, E. F. 2004. Fluid and fuel intake during exercise. *J. Sports Sciences* 22:39–55.
7. Bottled water continues as number 2 in 2007. Available at www.bottledwater.org/public/marketin.htm. (Accessed April 2009.)
8. Napier, G. L., and C. M. Kodner. 2008. Health risks and benefits of bottled water. *Prim. Care Clin. Office Pract.* 35:789–802.
9. Marsh, B. 2007. A battle between the bottle and the faucet. *The New York Times*, 15 July 15.
10. U.S. Department of Health and Human Services (USDHHS) and U.S. Department of Agriculture (USDA). 2005. *Dietary Guidelines for Americans, 2005.* 6th ed. Washington, DC: U.S. Government Printing Office. Available at www.healthierus.gov/dietaryguidelines.
11. Lin, P. H., F. Ginty, L. J. Appel, M. Aickin, A. Bohannon, P. Garnero, D. Barclay, and L. P. Svetkey. 2003. The DASH diet and sodium reduction improve markers of bone turnover and calcium metabolism in adults. *J. Nutr.* 133:3130–3136.
12. Kolata, G. 2005. Study cautions runners to limit intake of water. *New York Times* 14 April:A1, A20.
13. Davis D. P., J. S. Videen, A. Marino, G. M. Vilke, J. V. Dunford, S. P. Van Camp, and L. G. Maharam. 2001. Exercise-associated hyponatremia in marathon runners: A two-year experience. *J. Emerg. Med.* 21:47–57.
14. Exercise-Associated Hyponatremia (EAH) Consensus Panel. 2005. Consensus statement of the 1st International Exercise-Associated Hyponatremia Consensus Development Conference, Cape Town, South Africa, 2005. *Clin. J. Sport Med.* 15:208–213.
15. Noakes, T. 2003. Fluid replacement during marathon running. *Clin. J. Sport Med.* 13(5):309–318.
16. Institute of Medicine. Food and Nutrition Board. 1999. *Dietary Reference Intakes for Calcium, Phosphorus, Magnesium, Vitamin D, and Fluoride.* Washington, DC: National Academies Press.
17. George, T. 2001. Pro football. Heat kills a pro football player. N.F.L. orders a training review. *New York Times*, 2 August. Available at www.nytimes.com/2001/08/02/sports/pro-football-heat-kills-a-pro-football-player-nfl-orders-a-training-review.html?scp=1&sq=korey%20stringer%20death&st=cse. (Accessed April 2009.)

18. Centers for Disease Control and Prevention (CDC). 2009. Application of lower sodium intake recommendations to adults–United States, 1999–2006. *Morbidity and Mortality Weekly Report* 58(11):281–283.

19. U.S. Department of Health and Human Services. 2004. *The Seventh Report of the Joint National Committee on Prevention, Detection, Evaluation, and Treatment of High Blood Pressure.* NIH Publication No. 04-5230. Washington, DC: U.S. Government Printing Office.

20. Bray, G. A., W. M. Vollmer, F. M. Sacks, E. Obarzanek, L. P. Svetkey, and L. J. Appel. 2004. A further subgroup analysis of the effects of the DASH diet and three dietary sodium levels on blood pressure: Results of the DASH-sodium trial. *Am. J. Card.* 94:222–227.

21. Appel L. J., T. J. Moore, E. Obarzanek, W. M. Vollmer, L. P. Svetkey, F. M. Sacks, G. A. Bray, T. M. Vogt, J. A. Cutler, M. M. Windhauser, P. H. Lin, and N. Karanja. 1997. A clinical trial of the effects of dietary patterns on blood pressure. *N. Engl. J. Med.* 336:1117–1124.

22. Sacks F. M., L. P. Svetkey, W. M. Vollmer, L. J. Appel, G. A. Bray, D. Harsha, E. Obarzanek, P. R. Conlin, E. R. Miller III, D. G. Simons-Morton, N. Karanja, and P. H. Lin. 2001. Effects on blood pressure of reduced dietary sodium and the Dietary Approaches to Stop Hypertension (DASH) diet. *N. Engl. J. Med.* 344:3–10.

23. Fung T. T., S. E. Chiuve, M. L. McCullough, K. M. Rexrode, G. Logroscino, and F. B. Hu. 2008. Adherence to a DASH-style diet and risk of coronary heart disease and stroke in women. *Archives of Internal Medicine* 168(7):713–720.

24. Azadbakht L., P. Mirmiran, A. Esmaillzadeh, T. Azizi, and F. Azizi. 2005. Beneficial effects of dietary approaches to stop hypertension eating plan on features of the metabolic syndrome. *Diabetes Care* 28:2823–2831.

25. Reusser, M. E., and D. A. McCarron. 2006. Reducing hypertensive cardiovascular disease risk of African Americans with diet: Focus on the facts. *J. Nutr.* 136:1099–1102.

26. Manore, M., and J. Thompson. 2000. *Sport Nutrition for Health and Performance.* Champaign, IL: Human Kinetics.

Sports Beverages: Help or Hype?

Once considered specialty items used exclusively by elite athletes, sports beverages have become popular everyday beverage choices for both active and non-active people. These drinks have become such reliable money makers that most large beverage companies now produce them. This surge in popularity leads us to ask three important questions:

- Do sports beverages benefit highly active athletes?
- Do sports beverages benefit recreationally active people?
- Do non-athletes benefit from the consumption of sports beverages?

The first question is relatively easy to answer. Sports beverages were originally developed to meet the unique fluid, electrolyte, and carbohydrate needs of competitive athletes. They are particularly beneficial for athletes who exercise in the heat and are thus at an even greater risk for loss of water and electrolytes through respiration and sweat. In addition, the carbohydrates in sports beverages provide critical fuel during relatively intense exercise bouts lasting more than 1 hour. Some athletes, such as endurance cyclists, regularly train or compete for 6 to 8 hours a day. With this schedule, it is almost impossible for them to eat enough solid foods to meet their energy needs, and sports beverages can help fill the caloric gap. For all these reasons, in response to the first question, the answer is "yes": endurance athletes are able to exercise longer, maintain a higher intensity, and improve performance times when they drink a sports beverage during exercise.[26]

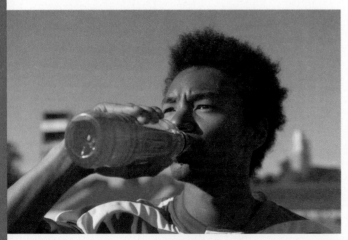

Sports beverages were originally designed to meet the needs of competitive athletes.

Do recreationally active people need to consume sports beverages? The short answer is that most probably do not. The few who exercise for periods longer than 1 hour at an intense level of effort probably can benefit from consuming the carbohydrate and electrolytes in sports beverages during exercise. In general, the duration and intensity of exercise, the environmental conditions, and the characteristics of the individual determine whether or not sports beverages can be more beneficial than plain water. Here are some situations in which drinking a sports beverage is appropriate:[26]

Before exercising in conditions when dehydration can occur, especially if someone is already dehydrated prior to exercise

During exercise or physical work in high heat and/or high humidity, especially for those not accustomed to activity in the heat

During exercise at high altitude and in cold environments

After exercise when rapid rehydration is needed or desired

Between exercise bouts when it is difficult to consume food, such as between multiple soccer matches during a tournament

During exercise sessions that last longer than 60 minutes, when blood glucose levels get low and risk of dehydration increases

During exercise in people who may have poor glycogen stores due to illness or inability to eat enough solid food prior to exercise

Interestingly, sports beverages have become very popular with people who do little or no regular exercise. Do these people benefit from drinking sports beverages? The response to this final questions is "no": there does not appear to be any evidence that people who do not exercise or exercise very little derive any benefits from consuming sports beverages. Even if these individuals live in a hot environment, they should be able to replenish the fluid and electrolytes they lose during sweating by drinking water and other beverages and eating a normal diet.

In addition, negative consequences can result when inactive people drink sports beverages. The primary consequence is weight gain, which could lead to obesity. As you can see in Table 9.5, sports beverages contain not only fluid and electrolytes, but also energy. While some manufacturers are producing "light" sports beverages that are lower in calories than the traditional product, drinking

Table 9.5 Nutrient Content of Sports Beverages and Other Common Beverages*

Beverage	Energy (kcal)	Carbohydrate (g)	Sodium (mg)	Potassium (mg)
Cola, regular	153	39	15	4
Ginger ale	124	32	26	4
Beer, regular	146	9	18	89
Gatorade	90	22.5	144	39
All Sport	80	22.5	55.5	55.5
Beer, light	8	<1	1	5
Coffee, brewed	7.5	1.5	7.5	192
Cola, diet	4	<1	21	0
Tea, brewed	3	<1	7	88
Water, bottled	0	0	2	0
Water, tap	0	0	7	0

*Amounts compared are 12 fl. oz (1.5 cups).

12 fl. oz (1.5 cups) of a traditionally formulated Gatorade adds 90 kcal to a person's daily energy intake. Many inactive people consume two to three times this amount each day. An inactive person has much lower energy needs than someone who is physically active. As with any other food, sports beverages could contribute to excess energy consumption. With obesity rates at an all-time high, it is important that the foods and beverages consumed provide "calories that count"—that is, calories that support our health.

Critical Thinking Questions

■ Are sports beverages smart choices for you? Why or why not?

■ Why do you think sports drinks are so popular among inactive people?

■ Should registered dietitians and other healthcare professionals discourage overweight clients from consuming sports beverages? Why or why not?

10 Nutrients Involved in Antioxidant Function

Test Yourself | True or False?

1   Free radicals are a normal by-product of our bodily functions. **T** *or* **F**

2   Taking large doses of vitamin C supplements reduces our risk of suffering from the common cold. **T** *or* **F**

3   Eating carrots promotes good vision. **T** *or* **F**

4   Smoking is the most preventable cause of death in our society. **T** *or* **F**

5   Consuming a diet high in antioxidant nutrients can help cure cancer. **T** *or* **F**

Test Yourself answers are located in the Chapter Review.

Chapter Objectives *After reading this chapter, you will be able to:*

1. Define free radicals and discuss how they can damage cells, *pp. 358–359*.

2. Describe how antioxidants protect cells from the oxidative damage caused by free radicals, *pp. 359–360*.

3. List three antioxidant enzyme systems and describe how these systems help fight oxidative damage, *p. 360*.

4. List three vitamins that have antioxidant properties, *p. 360*.

5. Describe how vitamin A works to ensure healthy vision, *pp. 372–373*.

6. Identify food sources that are high in nutrients with antioxidant properties, *pp. 361–362, 366–367, 370, 374–375, 377–378*.

7. Describe the relationship between antioxidant nutrients and the risk for cancer, *pp. 383–384*.

8. Discuss how consuming foods with antioxidant nutrients can reduce the risk for cardiovascular disease, *pp. 385–386*.

9. Compare and contrast macular degeneration and cataracts, and discuss how antioxidants may affect these two disorders, *pp. 386–387*.

Mika, a first-year student at a university hundreds of miles from home, just opened another care package from her mom. As usual, it contained an assortment of healthful snacks, a box of chamomile tea, and several types of supplements: echinacea extract to ward off colds, powdered papaya for good digestion, and antioxidant vitamins. "Wow, Mika!" her roommate laughed. "Can you let your mom know I'm available for adoption?"

"I guess she just wants me to stay healthy," Mika sighed. She wondered what her mother would think if she ever found out how much junk food Mika had been eating since she'd started college, or that she'd been binge-drinking every weekend, or that she'd been smoking since high school. "Still," Mika reminded herself, "at least I take the vitamins she sends."

What do you think of Mika's current lifestyle? Can a poor diet, binge-drinking, and smoking cause cancer or other health problems, and can the use of dietary supplements provide some protection? What are antioxidant vitamins, and why do you think Mika's mom included a bottle of these in her care package? If your health food store were promoting an antioxidant supplement, would you buy it?

It isn't easy to sort fact from fiction when it comes to antioxidants—especially when they're in the form of supplements. Internet ads and articles in fitness and health magazines tout their benefits, yet some researchers claim that they don't protect us from diseases and in some cases may even be harmful. In this chapter, you'll learn what antioxidants are and how they work in the body. We'll also profile the antioxidant nutrients and discuss their relationship to health. Finally, you'll learn about the role antioxidants may play in preventing cancer and heart disease and in slowing the aging process.

What Are Antioxidants, and How Does the Body Use Them?

Antioxidants are compounds that protect cells from the damage caused by oxidation. *Anti* means "against," and antioxidants work *against,* or *prevent* oxidation. Before we can go further in our discussion of antioxidants, we need to review what oxidation is and how it damages cells.

Oxidation Is a Chemical Reaction in Which Atoms Lose Electrons

As you recall from Chapter 7, during metabolic reactions, atoms may lose electrons (**Figure 10.1a**). This loss of electrons is called **oxidation,** because it is fueled by oxygen. Atoms are also capable of gaining electrons, through a complementary process called *reduction* (Figure 10.1b). Because oxidation-reduction reactions typically result in an even exchange of electrons, scientists call them *exchange reactions.*

Stable atoms have an even number of electrons orbiting in pairs at successive distances (called *shells* or *rings*) from the nucleus. When a stable atom loses an electron during oxidation, it is left with an odd number of electrons in its outermost shell. In other words, it now has an *unpaired electron.* In most exchange reactions, two atoms with unpaired electrons immediately pair up, making newly stabilized molecules, but in rare cases, atoms with unpaired electrons in their outermost shell remain unpaired. Such atoms are highly unsta-

antioxidant   A compound that has the ability to prevent or repair the damage caused by oxidation.

oxidation   A chemical reaction in which molecules of a substance are broken down into their component atoms. During oxidation, the atoms involved lose electrons.

(a) Oxidation   (b) Reduction

Figure 10.1   The exchange reaction. Exchange reactions consist of two parts. **(a)** During oxidation, molecules *lose* electrons. **(b)** In the second part of the reaction, molecules *gain* electrons, which is called reduction.

ble and are called **free radicals**. When an oxygen molecule becomes a free radical, it is specifically referred to as a **reactive oxygen species (ROS)**.

As you learned in Chapter 7, the body uses oxygen and hydrogen to generate energy (ATP). The process of metabolism sometimes results in the release of single electrons. Occasionally, oxygen accepts one of these single electrons. When it does so, the newly unstable oxygen atom becomes a free radical because of the added unpaired electron. This type of free-radical production is common during metabolism. Free radicals are also formed from other metabolic processes, such as when our immune systems fight infections. Environmental factors that cause free-radical formation include exposure to pollution, excessive sunlight, toxic substances, radiation, tobacco smoke, and asbestos. Continual exposure to these factors leads to uncontrollable free-radical formation and increases the individual's risk for chronic disease, as discussed next.

Free Radicals Can Destabilize Other Molecules and Damage Cells

Why are we concerned with the formation of free radicals? Simply put, it is because of their destabilizing power. If you were to think of paired electrons as a married couple, a free radical would be an extremely seductive outsider. Its unpaired electron exerts a powerful attraction toward all stable molecules around it. In an attempt to stabilize itself, a free radical will "steal" an electron from stable compounds, in turn generating more unstable free radicals. This is a dangerous chain reaction, because the free radicals generated can damage or destroy cells.

One of the most significant sites of free-radical damage is the cell membrane. As shown in **Figure 10.2a,** free radicals that form within the phospholipid bilayer of cell membranes steal electrons from their stable lipid molecules. When the lipid molecules, which are hydrophobic, are destroyed, they no longer repel water. With the cell membrane's integrity lost, the ability to regulate the movement of fluids and nutrients into and out of the cell is also lost. This loss of cell integrity causes damage to the cell and to all systems affected by this cell.

Other sites of free-radical damage include low-density lipoproteins (LDLs), cell proteins, and DNA. Damage to these sites disrupts the transport of substances into and out of cells, alters protein function, and can disrupt cell function because of defective DNA. These changes may increase our risk for chronic diseases such as heart disease, various cancers, diabetes, cataracts, Alzheimer's disease, and Parkinson disease.

Antioxidants Work by Stabilizing Free Radicals or Opposing Oxidation

How does the body fight free radicals and repair the damage they cause? Antioxidant vitamins, minerals, and other compounds accomplish these functions in a variety of ways:

1. Antioxidant *vitamins* work independently by donating their electrons or hydrogen molecules to free radicals to stabilize them and reduce the damage caused by oxidation (see Figure 10.2b).

Exposure to pollution from car exhaust and industrial waste increases our production of free radicals.

free radical A highly unstable atom with an unpaired electron in its outermost shell.

reactive oxygen species (ROS) A specific term used to describe an oxygen molecule that has become a free radical.

(a)　　　　　　　(b)

Figure 10.2 (a) The formation of free radicals in the lipid portion of our cell membranes can cause a dangerous chain reaction that damages the integrity of the membrane and can cause cell death. **(b)** Vitamin E is stored in the lipid portion of our cell membranes. By donating an electron to free radicals, it protects the lipid molecules in our cell membranes from being oxidized and stops the chain reaction of oxidative damage.

2. Antioxidant *minerals*, including selenium, copper, iron, zinc, and manganese, act as cofactors within complex antioxidant enzyme systems that convert free radicals to less damaging substances that are excreted by the body. They also work to break down fatty acids that have become oxidized, thereby destroying the free radicals associated with them. Antioxidant enzyme systems also make more vitamin antioxidants available to fight other free radicals. Examples of antioxidant enzyme systems include the following:
   - Superoxide dismutase converts free radicals to less damaging substances, such as hydrogen peroxide.
   - Catalase removes hydrogen peroxide from the body by converting it to water and oxygen.
   - Glutathione peroxidase also removes hydrogen peroxide from the body and stops the production of free radicals in lipids.
3. Other compounds such as *beta-carotene* and other *phytochemicals* help stabilize free radicals and prevent damage to cells and tissues.

In summary, free-radical formation is generally kept safely under control by certain vitamins, minerals working within antioxidant systems, and phytochemicals. Next, we take a look at the specific vitamins and minerals involved. Phytochemicals are discussed in the *In Depth* immediately following this chapter.

RecaP

Free radicals are formed when a stable atom loses or gains an electron and this electron remains unpaired. They can be produced during the formation of ATP, when our immune system fights infections, and when we are exposed to radiation or toxic substances. Free radicals can damage our cell membranes, low-density lipoproteins (LDLs), cell proteins, and DNA and are associated with many chronic diseases, including heart disease, various cancers, and diabetes. Antioxidant vitamins donate electrons or hydrogen atoms to free radicals to stabilize them. Antioxidant minerals function as part of antioxidant enzyme systems that convert free radicals to less damaging substances. Some phytochemicals also have antioxidant properties.

A Profile of Nutrients That Function as Antioxidants

The body cannot form antioxidants spontaneously. Instead, we must consume them in our diet. Nutrients that appear to have antioxidant properties or are part of our protective antioxidant enzyme systems include vitamins E, C, and A; beta-carotene (a precursor to vitamin A); and the mineral selenium (see Table 1, page 362). The minerals copper, iron, zinc, and manganese play a peripheral role in fighting oxidation and are only mentioned in this chapter. Let's review each of these nutrients now and learn more about their functions in the body.

Vitamin E

Vitamin E is one of the fat-soluble vitamins; thus, dietary fats carry it from the intestines through the lymph system and eventually transport it to the cells. Vitamin E is absorbed with dietary fat and incorporated into the chylomicrons. As the chylomicrons are broken down, most of the vitamin E remains in their remnants and is transported to the liver. There, vitamin E is incorporated into very-low-density lipoproteins (VLDLs) and released into the blood. As described in Chapter 5, VLDLs are transport vehicles that ferry triglycerides from their source to the body's cells. After VLDLs release their triglyceride load, they become LDLs. Vitamin E is a part of both VLDLs and LDLs and is transported to the tissues and cells by both of these lipoproteins.

Vitamin E and the other fat-soluble vitamins are stored in the body. The liver serves as a storage site for vitamins A and D, and about 90% of the vitamin E in the body is stored in our adipose tissue. The remaining vitamin E is found in cell membranes.

Vegetable oils, nuts, seeds, and avocados are good sources of vitamin E.

Forms of Vitamin E

Vitamin E is actually two separate families of compounds, **tocotrienols** and **tocopherols**. None of the four different tocotrienol compounds—alpha, beta, gamma, and delta—appears to play an active role in the body. The tocopherol compounds are the biologically active forms. Four different tocopherol compounds have been discovered; as with tocotrienol, these have been designated alpha, beta, gamma, and delta. Of these, the most active, or potent, vitamin E compound found in food and supplements is *alpha-tocopherol* (**Figure 10.3**). The RDA for vitamin E is expressed as alpha-tocopherol in milligrams per day (α-tocopherol, mg per day). Food labels and vitamin and mineral supplements may express vitamin E in units of alpha-tocopherol equivalents (α-TE), milligrams, and as International Units (IU). For conversion purposes:

- In food, 1α-TE is equal to 1 mg of active vitamin E.
- In supplements containing natural sources of vitamin E, 1 IU is equal to 0.67 mg α-TE.
- In supplements containing synthetic sources of vitamin E, 1 IU is equal to 0.45 mg α-TE.

Functions of Vitamin E

The primary function of vitamin E is as an antioxidant: It donates an electron to free radicals, stabilizing them and preventing them from destabilizing other molecules. Once vitamin E is oxidized, it is either excreted from the body or recycled back into active vitamin E through the help of other antioxidant nutrients, such as vitamin C.

Because vitamin E is prevalent in adipose tissue and cell membranes, its action specifically protects *polyunsaturated fatty acids* (PUFAs) and other fatty components of our cells and cell membranes from being oxidized (see Figure 10.2b). Vitamin E also protects LDLs from being oxidized, thereby lowering the risk for heart disease.[1,2] (The relationship between antioxidants and heart disease is reviewed later in this chapter.) In addition to protecting PUFAs and LDLs, vitamin E protects the membranes of red blood cells from oxidation and plays a critical role in protecting the cells of our lungs, which are constantly exposed to oxygen and the potentially damaging effects of oxidation. Vitamin E's role in protecting PUFAs and other fatty components also explains why it is added to many oil-based foods and skincare products—by preventing oxidation in these products, it reduces rancidity and spoilage.

Vitamin E serves many other roles essential to human health. It is critical for normal fetal and early childhood development of nerves and muscles, as well as for maintenance of their functions. It enhances immune function by protecting white blood cells and other components of the immune system, thereby helping the body to defend against illness and disease. It also improves the absorption of vitamin A if the dietary intake of vitamin A is low.

How Much Vitamin E Should We Consume?

Considering the importance of vitamin E to our health, you might think that you need to consume a huge amount daily. In fact, the RDA is modest and the food sources are plentiful.

Recommended Dietary Allowance for Vitamin E

The RDA for vitamin E for men and women is 15 mg alpha-tocopherol per day. This is the amount determined to be sufficient to prevent **erythrocyte hemolysis,** or the rupturing (*lysis*) of red blood cells (*erythrocytes*). The tolerable upper intake level (UL) is 1,000 mg alpha-tocopherol per day. Remember that one of the primary roles of vitamin E is to protect PUFAs from oxidation. Thus, our need for vitamin E increases as we eat more oils and other foods that contain PUFAs. Fortunately, these foods also contain vitamin E, so we typically consume enough vitamin E within them to protect their PUFAs from oxidation.

Good Food Sources of Vitamin E

Vitamin E is widespread in foods. Much of the vitamin E that we consume comes from vegetable oils and the products made from them (**Figure 10.4**). Safflower oil, sunflower oil, canola oil, and soybean oil are good sources.

Figure 10.3 Chemical structure of α-tocopherol. Note that α-tocopherol is composed of a ring structure and a long carbon tail. Variations in the spatial orientation of the carbon atoms in this tail and in the composition of the tail itself are what result in forming the different tocopherol and tocotrienol compounds.

tocopherols A family of vitamin E that is the active form in our bodies.

tocotrienols A family of vitamin E that does not play an important biological role in our bodies.

erythrocyte hemolysis The rupturing or breakdown of red blood cells, or erythrocytes.

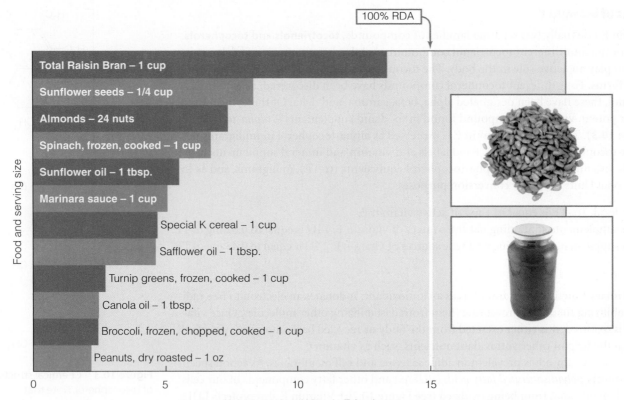

Figure 10.4 Common food sources of vitamin E. The RDA for vitamin E is 15 mg α-tocopherol per day for men and women. (*Data from:* U.S. Department of Agriculture, Agricultural Research Service, 2008. USDA National Nutrient Database for Standard Reference, Release 21. Available at www.ars.usda.gov/ba/bhnrc/ndl.)

Table 10.1 Overview of Nutrients Involved in Antioxidant Function

To see the full profile of nutrients involved in energy metabolism, turn to *In Depth,* Vitamins and Minerals: Micronutrients with Macro Powers, page 280.

Nutrient	Recommended Intake
Vitamin E (fat soluble)	RDA: Women and men = 15 mg alpha-tocopheral
Vitamin C (water soluble)	RDA: Women = 75 mg Men = 90 mg Smokers = 35 mg more per day than RDA
Beta-carotene (fat-soluble provitamin for vitamin A)	None at this time
Vitamin A (fat soluble)	RDA: Women: 700 μg Men: 900 μg
Selenium (trace mineral)	RDA: Women and men = 55 μg

Mayonnaise and salad dressings made from these oils also contain vitamin E. Nuts, seeds, and some vegetables also contribute vitamin E to our diet. Although no single fruit or vegetable contains very high amounts of vitamin E, eating the recommended amounts of fruits and vegetables each day will help ensure adequate intake of this nutrient. Cereals are often fortified with vitamin E, and other grain products contribute modest amounts to our diet. Wheat germ and soybeans are also good sources of vitamin E. Animal and dairy products are poor sources.

Vitamin E is destroyed by exposure to oxygen, metals, ultraviolet light, and heat. Although raw (uncooked) vegetable oils contain vitamin E, heating these oils destroys vitamin E. Thus, foods that are deep-fried and processed contain little vitamin E. This includes most fast foods and convenience foods.

What Happens If We Consume Too Much Vitamin E?

Until recently, standard supplemental doses (1 to 18 times the RDA) of vitamin E were not associated with any adverse health effects. However, among adults 55 years of age or older with vascular disease or diabetes, a daily intake of 268 mg of vitamin E per day (about 18 times the RDA) for approximately 7 years resulted in a significant increase in heart failure.[3] However, these results have not been confirmed by additional research studies. At this time, it is unclear whether these adverse effects are an anomaly or if high supplemental doses of vitamin E may be harmful for certain individuals.

Some individuals report side effects such as nausea, intestinal distress, and diarrhea with vitamin E supplementation. In addition, certain medications interact negatively with vitamin E. The most important of these are the *anticoagulants,* substances that stop blood from clotting excessively. Aspirin is an anticoagulant, as is the prescription drug Coumadin.

Vitamin E supplements can augment the action of these substances, causing uncontrollable bleeding. In addition, new evidence suggests that in some people, long-term use of standard vitamin E supplements may cause hemorrhaging in the brain, leading to a type of stroke called *hemorrhagic stroke.*[4]

What Happens If We Don't Consume Enough Vitamin E?

True vitamin E deficiencies are uncommon in humans. This is primarily because vitamin E is fat soluble, so we typically store adequate amounts in our fatty tissues even when our diets are low in this nutrient. However, it is common for people in the United States to consume suboptimal amounts of vitamin E. Results from the NHANES III survey show that the dietary intake of vitamin E of many Americans is low enough that 27% to 41% of these individuals have blood levels of vitamin E putting them at increased risk for cardiovascular disease.[5]

Despite the rarity of true vitamin E deficiencies, they do occur. One vitamin E deficiency symptom is *erythrocyte hemolysis.* This rupturing of red blood cells leads to *anemia,* a condition in which the red blood cells cannot carry and transport enough oxygen to the tissues, leading to fatigue, weakness, and a diminished ability to perform physical and mental work. We discuss anemia in more detail in Chapter 12. Premature babies can suffer from vitamin E–deficiency anemia; if born too early, the infant does not receive vitamin E from its mother, as the transfer of this vitamin from mother to baby occurs during the last few weeks of the pregnancy.

Other symptoms of vitamin E deficiency include loss of muscle coordination and reflexes, leading to impairments in vision, speech, and movement. As you might expect, vitamin E deficiency can also impair immune function, especially if accompanied by low body stores of the mineral selenium.

In adults, vitamin E deficiencies are usually caused by diseases, particularly diseases that cause malabsorption of fat, such as those that affect the small intestine, liver, gallbladder, and pancreas. As reviewed in Chapter 3, the liver makes bile, which is necessary for the absorption of fat. The gallbladder delivers the bile into our intestines, where it facilitates digestion of fat. The pancreas makes fat-digesting enzymes. Thus, when the liver, gallbladder, or pancreas are not functioning properly, fat and the fat-soluble vitamins, including vitamin E, cannot be absorbed, leading to their deficiency.

RECaP

Vitamin E protects cell membranes from oxidation, enhances immune function, and improves the absorption of vitamin A if dietary intake is low. The RDA for vitamin E is 15 mg alpha-tocopherol per day for men and women. Vitamin E is found primarily in vegetable oils and nuts. Toxicity is uncommon, but taking very high doses can cause excessive bleeding. A genuine deficiency is rare, but symptoms include anemia and impaired vision, speech, and movement.

Vitamin C

Vitamin C is a water-soluble vitamin. We must therefore consume it on a regular basis, as any excess is excreted (primarily in the urine) rather than stored. There are two active forms of vitamin C: ascorbic acid and dehydroascorbic acid (**Figure 10.5**). Interestingly, most animals can make their own vitamin C from glucose. Humans and guinea pigs are two groups that cannot synthesize their own vitamin C and must consume it in the diet.

At low concentrations, vitamin C is absorbed in the intestines via active transport; at high concentrations, it is absorbed via simple diffusion. Between consumptions of 30 to 80 mg/day, about 70% to 90% of dietary vitamin C is absorbed, but absorption falls to less than 50% when more than 1 g per day is consumed.[6] The kidneys regulate excretion of vitamin C, with increased excretion occurring during periods of high dietary intake and decreased excretion when dietary intakes are low.

Donated to free radicals

$2H^+$

$2H^+$

(a) Ascorbic acid   (b) Dehydroascorbic acid

Figure 10.5 Chemical structures of ascorbic acid and dehydroascorbic acid. **(a)** By donating two of its hydrogens to free radicals, ascorbic acid protects against oxidative damage and becomes **(b)** dehydroascorbic acid. In turn, dehydroascorbic acid can accept two hydrogens to become ascorbic acid.

Many fruits, like these yellow tomatoes, are high in vitamin C.

collagen A protein found in all connective tissues in the body.

glutathione A tripeptide composed of glycine, cysteine, and glutamic acid that assists in regenerating vitamin C into its antioxidant form.

Functions of Vitamin C

Vitamin C is probably most well known for its role in preventing scurvy, a disease that ravaged sailors on long sea voyages centuries ago. In fact, the derivation of the term *ascorbic acid* means "a" (without) "scorbic" (having scurvy). Scurvy was characterized by bleeding tissues, especially of the gums, and is thought to have caused more than half of the deaths that occurred at sea. During these long voyages, the crew ate all of the fruits and vegetables early in the trip then had only grain and animal products available until they reached land to resupply. In 1740 in England, Dr. James Lind discovered that citrus fruits could prevent scurvy. This is due to their high vitamin C content. Fifty years after the discovery of the link between citrus fruits and prevention of scurvy, the British Navy finally required all ships to provide daily lemon juice rations for each sailor to prevent the onset of scurvy. A century later, sailors were given lime juice rations, earning them the nickname "limeys." It wasn't until 1930 that vitamin C was discovered and identified as a nutrient.

One reason that vitamin C prevents scurvy is that it assists in the synthesis of **collagen.** Collagen, a protein, is a critical component of all connective tissues in the body, including bone, teeth, skin, tendons, and blood vessels. Collagen assists in preventing bruises, and it ensures proper wound healing, as it is a part of scar tissue and a component of the tissue that mends broken bones. Without adequate vitamin C, the body cannot form collagen, and tissue hemorrhage, or bleeding, occurs. Vitamin C may also be involved in the synthesis of other components of connective tissues, such as elastin and bone matrix.

In addition to connective tissues, vitamin C assists in the synthesis of DNA, bile, neurotransmitters such as serotonin (which helps regulate mood), and carnitine, which transports long-chain fatty acids from the cytosol into the mitochondria for energy production. Vitamin C also helps ensure that appropriate levels of thyroxine, a hormone produced by the thyroid gland, are produced to support basal metabolic rate and to maintain body temperature. Other hormones that are synthesized with assistance from vitamin C include epinephrine, norepinephrine, and steroid hormones.

Vitamin C also acts as an antioxidant. Because it is water soluble, it is an important antioxidant in the extracellular fluid. Like vitamin E, it donates electrons to free radicals, thus preventing the damage of cells and tissues (see Figure 10.5a). It also protects LDL-cholesterol from oxidation, which may reduce the risk for cardiovascular disease. Vitamin C acts as an important antioxidant in the lungs, helping to protect us from the damage caused by ozone and cigarette smoke.[1] It also enhances immune function by protecting the white blood cells from the oxidative damage that occurs in response to fighting illness and infection. But contrary to popular belief, it is not a miracle cure (see the accompanying Nutrition Myth or Fact? box on vitamin C). In the stomach, vitamin C reduces the formation of *nitrosamines,* cancer-causing agents found in foods such as cured and processed meats. We discuss the role of vitamin C and other antioxidants in preventing some forms of cancer later in this chapter (pages 383–384).

Vitamin C also regenerates vitamin E after it has been oxidized. This occurs when ascorbic acid donates electrons to vitamin E radicals, becoming dehydroascorbic acid (**Figure 10.6**). The regenerated vitamin E can now continue to protect cell membranes and other tissues. In turn, dehydroascorbic acid is regenerated as an antioxidant by gaining an electron from the reduced form of **glutathione (GSH),** which is a tripeptide composed of glycine, cysteine, and glutamic acid. Glutathione is then restored to its antioxidant form by the enzyme *glutathione reductase,* in a reaction (not shown in Figure 10.6) that is dependent on the mineral selenium, which is discussed later in this chapter.

Nutrition Myth or Fact?
Can Vitamin C Prevent the Common Cold?

What do you do when you feel a cold coming on? If you are like many people, you drink a lot of orange juice or take vitamin C supplements to ward it off. Do these tactics really help prevent a cold?

It is well known that vitamin C is important for a healthy immune system. A deficiency of vitamin C can seriously weaken the immune cells' ability to detect and destroy invading microbes, increasing susceptibility to many diseases and illnesses—including the common cold. Many people have taken vitamin C supplements to prevent the common cold, basing their behavior on its actions of enhancing our immune function. Interestingly, scientific studies do not support this action. A recent review of many of the studies of vitamin C and the common cold found that people taking vitamin C regularly in an attempt to ward off the common cold experienced as many colds as people who took a placebo. However, the *duration* of their colds was significantly reduced—by 8% in adults and 13.6% in children.[7] Timing appears to be impor-

tant, though: Taking vitamin C after the onset of cold symptoms did not reduce either the duration or severity of the cold. Interestingly, taking vitamin C supplements regularly did reduce the number of colds experienced in marathon runners, skiers, and soldiers participating in exercises done under extreme environmental conditions.

The amount of vitamin C taken in these studies was at least 200 mg per day, with many using doses as high as 4,000 mg per day (more than 40 times the RDA), with no harmful effects noted in those studies that reported adverse events.

In summary, it appears that, for most people, taking vitamin C supplements regularly will not prevent colds, but may reduce their duration. Consuming a healthful diet that includes excellent sources of vitamin C will also help you maintain a strong immune system. Taking vitamin C after the onset of cold symptoms does not appear to help, so next time you feel a cold coming on, you may want to think twice before taking extra vitamin C.

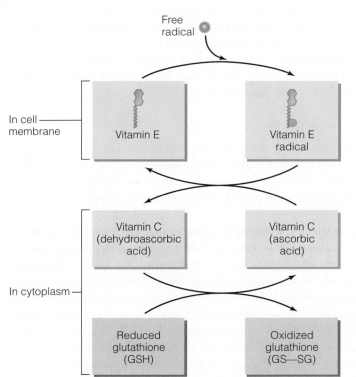

Figure 10.6 Regeneration of vitamin E by vitamin C. Vitamin E neutralizes free radicals in the cell membrane, and vitamin C (in the form of ascorbic acid) regenerates vitamin E from the resulting vitamin E radical. Vitamin C (in the form of dehydroascorbic acid) is regenerated to ascorbic acid by the reduced form of glutathione (GSH).

Vitamin C also enhances the absorption of iron. It is recommended that people with low iron stores consume vitamin C–rich foods along with iron sources to improve absorption. For people with high iron stores, this practice can be dangerous and lead to iron toxicity (discussed on page 453).

How Much Vitamin C Should We Consume?

Although popular opinion suggests our needs for vitamin C are high, we really only require amounts that are easily obtained when we eat the recommended amounts of fruits and vegetables daily.

Recommended Dietary Allowance for Vitamin C   The RDA for vitamin C is 90 mg per day for men and 75 mg per day for women. The Tolerable Upper Intake Level (UL) is 2,000 mg per day for adults. Smoking increases a person's need for vitamin C. Thus, the RDA for smokers is 35 mg more per day than for nonsmokers. This equals 125 mg per day for men and 110 mg per day for women. Other situations that may increase the need for vitamin C include healing from a traumatic injury, surgery, or burns and the use of oral contraceptives among women; there is no consensus as to how much extra vitamin C is needed in these circumstances.

Fresh vegetables are good sources of vitamin C and beta-carotene.

Good Food Sources of Vitamin C   Fruits and vegetables are the best sources of vitamin C. Because heat and oxygen destroy vitamin C, fresh sources of these foods have the highest content. Cooking foods, especially boiling them, leaches their vitamin C, which is then lost when we strain them. Forms of cooking that are least likely to compromise the vitamin C content of foods include steaming, microwaving, and stir-frying.

As indicated in **Figure 10.7,** many fruits and vegetables are high in vitamin C. Citrus fruits (such as oranges, lemons, and limes), potatoes, strawberries, tomatoes, kiwi fruit, broccoli, spinach and other leafy greens, cabbage, green and red peppers, and cauliflower are excellent sources of vitamin C. Fortified beverages and cereals are also good sources. Dairy foods, meats, and nonfortified cereals and grains provide little or no vitamin C. By eating the recommended amounts of fruits and vegetables daily, we can easily meet the body's requirement for vitamin C. Remember that a serving of vegetables is 1/2 cup of cooked or 1 cup of raw vegetables or 6 oz of vegetable juice, and a serving of fruit is one medium fruit, 1 cup of chopped or canned fruit, or 6 oz of fruit juice.

What Happens If We Consume Too Much Vitamin C?

Because vitamin C is water soluble, we usually excrete any excess. Consuming excess amounts in food sources does not lead to toxicity, and only supplements can lead to toxic doses. Taking megadoses of vitamin C is not fatally harmful. However, side effects of doses exceeding 2,000 mg per day for a prolonged period include nausea, diarrhea, nosebleeds, and abdominal cramps.

There are rare instances in which consuming even moderately excessive doses of vitamin C can be harmful. As mentioned earlier, vitamin C enhances the absorption of iron. This action is beneficial to people who need to increase iron absorption. It can be harmful, however, to people with a disease called *hemochromatosis,* which causes an excess accumulation of iron in the body. Such iron toxicity can damage tissues and lead to a heart attack. In people who have preexisting kidney disease, taking excess vitamin C can lead to the formation of kidney stones. This does not appear to occur in healthy individuals. Critics of vitamin C supplementation claim that taking the supplemental form of the vitamin is "unbalanced" nutrition and leads vitamin C to act as a prooxidant. A **prooxidant,** as you might guess, is a nutrient that promotes oxidation. It does this by pushing the balance of

prooxidant   A nutrient that promotes oxidation and oxidative cell and tissue damage.

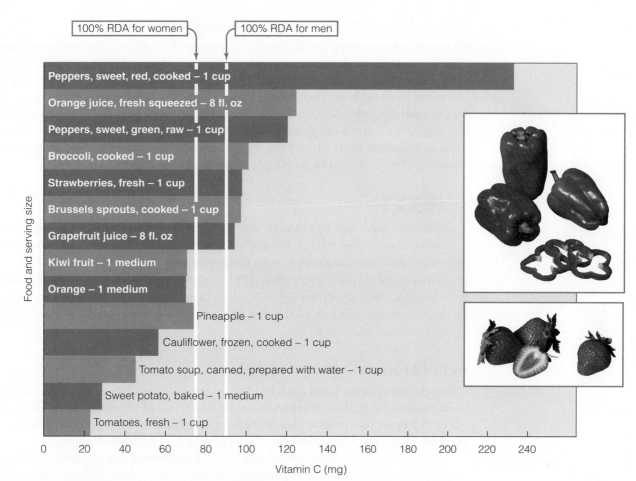

Figure 10.7 Common food sources of vitamin C. The RDA for vitamin C is 90 mg per day for men and 75 mg per day for women. (*Data from:* U.S. Department of Agriculture, Agricultural Research Service, 2008. USDA National Nutrient Database for Standard Reference, Release 21. Available at http://www.ars.usda.gov/ba/bhnrc/ndl.)

exchange reactions toward oxidation, which promotes the production of free radicals. Although the results of a few studies have suggested that vitamin C acts as a prooxidant, these studies were found to be flawed or irrelevant for humans. At the present time, there appears to be no strong scientific evidence that vitamin C, either from food or dietary supplements, acts as a prooxidant in humans.

Hannah
Nutri-Case

"Since I started college in September, I've had one cold after another. I guess it's being around so many different people every day, plus all the stress. Then a few weeks ago I found this cool orange-tasting vitamin C powder at the health food outlet on campus, and I started mixing it into my orange juice every morning. I guess it's working, because I haven't had a cold since I started using it, but this morning I woke up with stomach cramps and diarrhea, so now I guess I have to worry about a stomach flu. I wish there was a vitamin C powder for that!"

Given what you've learned about the effects of vitamin C supplementation, do you think it is possible that Hannah's vitamin C regimen is doing her more harm than good? Explain.

What Happens If We Don't Consume Enough Vitamin C?

Vitamin C deficiencies are rare in developed countries but can occur in developing countries. Scurvy is the most common vitamin C–deficiency disease. The symptoms of scurvy appear after about 1 month of a vitamin C–deficient diet. Symptoms include bleeding gums and joints, loose teeth, weakness, hemorrhages around the hair follicles of the arms and legs, wounds that fail to heal, swollen ankles and wrists, bone pain and fractures, diarrhea, and depression. Anemia can also result from vitamin C deficiency. People most at risk of deficiencies include those who eat few fruits and vegetables, including impoverished or homebound individuals, and people who abuse alcohol and drugs.

> ## RecaP
>
> Vitamin C scavenges free radicals and regenerates vitamin E after it has been oxidized. Vitamin C prevents scurvy and assists in the synthesis of collagen, hormones, neurotransmitters, and DNA. Vitamin C also enhances iron absorption. The RDA for vitamin C is 90 mg per day for men and 75 mg per day for women. Many fruits and vegetables are high in vitamin C. Toxicity is uncommon with dietary intake; symptoms include nausea, diarrhea, and nosebleeds. Deficiency symptoms include scurvy, anemia, diarrhea, and depression.

Beta-Carotene

Although beta-carotene is not considered an essential nutrient, it is a *provitamin* found in many fruits and vegetables. **Provitamins** are inactive forms of vitamins that the body cannot use until they are converted to their active form. Our bodies convert beta-carotene to an active form of vitamin A, or *retinol*; thus, beta-carotene is a precursor of retinol.

Beta-carotene is a phytochemical classified as a **carotenoid,** one of a group of plant pigments that are the basis for the red, orange, and deep-yellow colors of many fruits and vegetables. (Even dark-green leafy vegetables contain plenty of carotenoids, but the green pigment, chlorophyll, masks their color!) Although there are more than 600 carotenoids found in nature, only about 50 are found in the typical human diet. The six most common carotenoids found in human blood are alpha-carotene, beta-carotene, beta-cryptoxanthin, lutein, lycopene, and zeaxanthin. Of these, the body can convert only alpha-carotene, beta-carotene, and beta-cryptoxanthin to retinol. These are referred to as *provitamin A carotenoids.* We are just beginning to learn more about how carotenoids function in our bodies and how they may affect our health (see the Nutrition Myth or Fact? box, next page). Most of our discussion will focus on beta-carotene, as the majority of research on carotenoids to date has focused on this substance.

One molecule of beta-carotene can be split to form two molecules of active vitamin A (**Figure 10.8**). So why are 12 g of beta-carotene considered equivalent to just 1 g of

provitamin An inactive form of a vitamin that the body can convert to an active form. An example is beta-carotene.

carotenoids Fat-soluble plant pigments that the body stores in the liver and adipose tissues. The body is able to convert certain carotenoids to vitamin A.

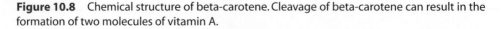

Figure 10.8 Chemical structure of beta-carotene. Cleavage of beta-carotene can result in the formation of two molecules of vitamin A.

vitamin A? Several factors account for this. Sometimes a beta-carotene molecule is cleaved in such a way that only one molecule of vitamin A is produced. In addition, not all of the dietary beta-carotene that is consumed is converted to vitamin A, and the absorption of beta-carotene from the intestines is not as efficient as our absorption of vitamin A. Nutritionists express the units of beta-carotene in a food as Retinol Activity Equivalents, or RAE. This measurement indicates how much active vitamin A is available to the body after it has converted the beta-carotene in the food.

Functions of Beta-Carotene

Beta-carotene and some other carotenoids are nutrients recognized to have antioxidant properties.[8] Like vitamin E, they are fat-soluble and fight the harmful effects of oxidation in the lipid portions of the cell membranes and in LDLs; but, compared with vitamin E, beta-carotene is a relatively weak antioxidant. In fact, other carotenoids, such as lycopene and lutein, may be stronger antioxidants than beta-carotene. Research is currently being conducted to elucidate how many carotenoids are found in foods and which ones are effective antioxidants.

Carotenoids play other important roles in the body through their antioxidant actions. Specifically, they:

- Enhance the immune system and boost the body's ability to fight illness and disease.
- Protect skin from the damage caused by the sun's ultraviolet rays.
- Protect our eyes, preventing or delaying age-related vision impairment.

Carotenoids are also associated with a decreased risk of certain types of cancer. We discuss the roles of carotenoids and other antioxidants in cancer later in this chapter.

Nutrition Myth or Fact?
Can Beta-Carotene Supplements Cause Cancer?

Beta-carotene is one of many carotenoids known to have antioxidant properties. Because there is substantial evidence that people eating foods high in antioxidants have lower rates of cancer, large-scale studies are being conducted to determine whether taking antioxidant supplements can decrease our risk for cancer. In particular, the Alpha-Tocopherol Beta-Carotene (ATBC) Cancer Prevention Study and the Beta-Carotene and Retinol Efficacy Trial (CARET) have shown surprising results.[9,10]

The ATBC Cancer Prevention Study was conducted in Finland from 1985 to 1993 with the purpose of determining the effects of beta-carotene and vitamin E supplements on the rates of lung cancer and other forms of cancer among male smokers between the ages of 50 and 69 years. Almost 30,000 men participated in the study for an average of 6 years. The participants were given daily a beta-carotene supplement, a vitamin E supplement, a supplement containing both beta-carotene and vitamin E, or a placebo.

Contrary to what was expected, the male smokers who took beta-carotene supplements experienced an *increased* number of deaths during the study. More men in this group died of lung cancer, heart disease, and stroke. There was also a trend in this group for higher rates of prostate and stomach cancers. This negative effect appeared to be particularly strong in men who had a higher alcohol intake.[9]

CARET began as a pilot study in the United States in 1985 and included more than 18,000 men and women who were smokers, former smokers, or workers who were exposed to asbestos. The participants were randomly assigned to take daily supplements of beta-carotene and retinol (vitamin A) or a placebo. After a 4-year follow-up period, the incidence of lung cancer was 28% higher among those taking the beta-carotene and retinol supplement. This significant finding, in addition to the results from the ATBC Cancer Prevention Study, prompted researchers to end the CARET study early and recommend that participants discontinue the supplements.[10]

The reasons why beta-carotene increased lung cancer risk in this population are not clear. It is possible that the supplementation period was too brief to benefit these high-risk individuals, although studies of shorter duration have found beneficial effects. There may be other components besides beta-carotene in whole foods that are protective against cancer, making supplementation with an isolated nutrient ineffective. In any case, the results of this study suggest that for certain people, supplementation with beta-carotene may be harmful. There is still much to learn about how people of differing risk levels respond to antioxidant supplementation.

Foods that are high in carotenoids are easy to recognize by their bright colors.

How Much Beta-Carotene Should We Consume?

Nutritional scientists do not consider beta-carotene and other carotenoids to be essential nutrients, as they play no known essential roles in our body and are not associated with any deficiency symptoms. Thus, no RDA for these compounds has been established. It has been suggested that consuming 6 to 10 mg of beta-carotene per day from food sources can increase the beta-carotene levels in the blood to amounts that may reduce the risks for some diseases, such as cancer and heart disease.[8] Supplements containing beta-carotene have become very popular, and supplementation studies have prescribed doses of 15 to 30 mg of beta-carotene. Refer to the accompanying Nutrition Myth or Fact? box on beta-carotene to learn more about how supplementation with this compound may affect the risk for cancer.

Fruits and vegetables that are red, orange, yellow, and deep green are generally high in beta-carotene and other carotenoids such as lutein and lycopene. Eating the recommended amounts of fruits and vegetables each day ensures an adequate intake of carotenoids. Because of its color, beta-carotene is used as a natural coloring agent for many foods, including margarine, yellow cheddar cheese, cereal, cake mixes, gelatins, and soft drinks. However, these foods are not significant sources of beta-carotene. **Figure 10.9** identifies common foods that are high in beta-carotene.

We generally absorb only between 20% and 40% of the carotenoids present in the foods we eat. In contrast to vitamins E and C, carotenoids are absorbed better from cooked foods. Carotenoids are bound in the cells of plants, and the process of lightly cooking these plants breaks chemical bonds and can rupture cell walls, which humans don't digest. These actions result in more of the carotenoids being released from the plant. For instance, 1 cup of raw carrots contains approximately 9 mg of beta-carotene, whereas the same amount of cooked frozen carrots contains approximately 12 mg.[11]

What Happens If We Consume Too Much Beta-Carotene?

Consuming large amounts of beta-carotene or other carotenoids in foods does not appear to cause toxic symptoms. However, your skin can turn yellow or orange if you consume

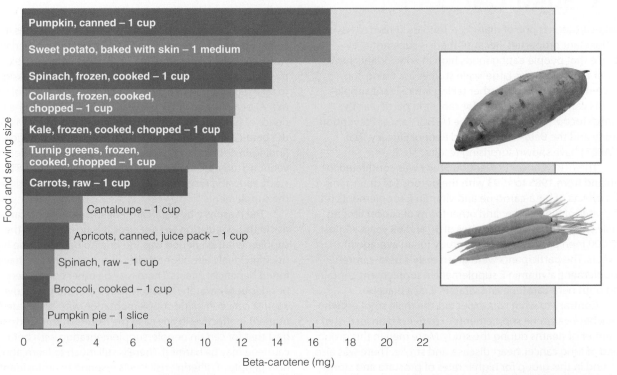

Figure 10.9   Common food sources of beta-carotene. There is no RDA for beta-carotene. (*Data from:* U.S. Department of Agriculture, Agricultural Research Service, 2008. USDA National Nutrient Database for Standard Reference, Release 21. Available at www.ars.usda.gov/ba/bhnrc/ndl.)

large amounts of foods that are high in beta-carotene. This condition is referred to as *carotenosis* or *carotenodermia*, and it appears to be both reversible and harmless. Taking beta-carotene supplements is not generally recommended, because we can get adequate amounts of this nutrient by eating more fruits and vegetables.

What Happens If We Don't Consume Enough Beta-Carotene?

There are no known deficiency symptoms of beta-carotene or other carotenoids apart from beta-carotene's function as a precursor for vitamin A.

> ## Recap
>
> Beta-carotene is a carotenoid and a provitamin of vitamin A. It protects the lipid portions of cell membranes and LDL-cholesterol from oxidative damage. It also enhances immune function and protects vision. There is no RDA for beta-carotene. Orange, red, and deep-green fruits and vegetables are good sources of beta-carotene. There are no known toxicity or deficiency symptoms, but yellowing of the skin can occur if too much beta-carotene is consumed.

Vitamin A: Much More Than an Antioxidant Nutrient

Vitamin A, a fat-soluble vitamin, plays a number of significant roles in the body. Limited research suggests that it has antioxidant properties; thus, it is discussed in this chapter. More important, vitamin A is critical to vision and the growth and differentiation of cells.

There are three active forms of vitamin A in the body: **retinol** is the alcohol form, **retinal** is the aldehyde form, and **retinoic acid** is the acid form. These three forms are collectively referred to as the *retinoids* (**Figure 10.10**). Of the three, retinol has the starring role in maintaining the body's physiologic functions. Remember from the previous section that beta-carotene is a precursor to vitamin A: The beta-carotene in foods is converted to retinol in the wall of the small intestine. Preformed vitamin A is present in foods in the form of retinol and also as *retinyl ester-compounds*, in which retinol is attached to a fatty acid. These retinyl ester-compounds are hydrolyzed in the small intestine, leaving retinol in its free form. Free retinol is then absorbed into the wall of the small intestine, where a fatty acid is attached to form new retinyl ester-compounds. These compounds are then packaged into chylomicrons and enter into the lymph system. The chylomicrons transport vitamin A to the cells as needed or into the liver for storage. About 90% of the vitamin A we absorb is stored in the liver; the remainder is stored in adipose tissue, the kidneys, and the lungs.

Because fat-soluble vitamins cannot dissolve in the blood, they require proteins that can bind with and transport them from their storage sites through the bloodstream to

retinol An active, alcohol form of vitamin A that plays an important role in healthy vision and immune function.

retinal An active, aldehyde form of vitamin A that plays an important role in healthy vision and immune function.

retinoic acid An active, acid form of vitamin A that plays an important role in cell growth and immune function.

Figure 10.10 The three active forms of vitamin A in our bodies are retinol, retinal, and retinoic acid. Retinol and retinal can be converted interchangeably; retinoic acid is formed from retinal, and this process is irreversible. Each form of vitamin A contributes to many of our bodily processes.

target tissues and cells. *Retinol-binding protein* is one such carrier protein for vitamin A. Retinol-binding protein carries retinol from the liver to the cells that require it.

The unit of expression for vitamin A is Retinol Activity Equivalents (RAE). You may still see the expression Retinol Equivalents (RE) or International Units (IU) for vitamin A on food labels or dietary supplements. The conversions to RAE from various forms of retinol and from the units IU and RE are as follows:

- 1 RAE = 1 microgram (μg) retinol
- 1 RAE = 12 μg beta-carotene
- 1 RAE = 24 μg alpha-carotene or beta-cryptoxanthin
- 1 RAE = 1 RE
- 1 RAE = 3.3 IU

Functions of Vitamin A

The known functions of vitamin A are numerous, and researchers speculate that many are still to be discovered.

Vitamin A Acts as an Antioxidant   Limited research indicates that vitamin A may act as an antioxidant.[12, 13] Like vitamins E and C, it appears to scavenge free radicals and protect LDLs from oxidation. As you might expect, adequate vitamin A levels in the blood are associated with lower risks of some forms of cancer and heart disease. However, the role of vitamin A as an antioxidant is not strongly established and is still under investigation.

Vitamin A Is Essential to Sight   A critical role of vitamin A in the body is certainly in the maintenance of healthy vision. Specifically, vitamin A affects our sight in two ways: it enables us to react to changes in the brightness of light, and it enables us to distinguish between different wavelengths of light; in other words, to see different colors. Let's take a closer look at this process.

retina The delicate, light-sensitive membrane lining the inner eyeball and connected to the optic nerve. It contains retinal.

Light enters the eyes through the cornea, travels through the lens, and then hits the **retina,** which is a delicate membrane lining the back of the inner eyeball (see **Figure 10.11**).

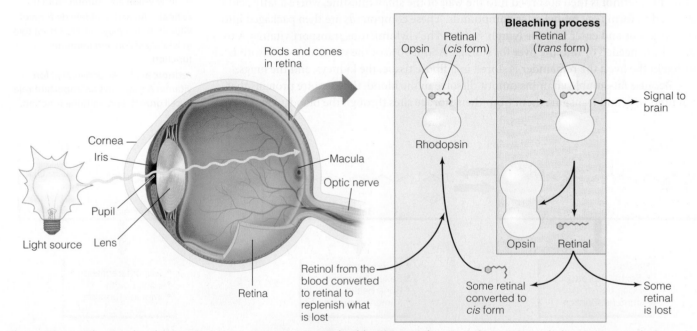

Figure 10.11   The visual cycle. Vitamin A is necessary to maintain healthy vision. Light enters the eye through the cornea, travels through the lens, and hits the retina located in the back of the eye. The light reacts with the retinal stored in the rod cells of the retina, thereby allowing us to see black-and-white images. A similar reaction occurring in the cone cells allows for color vision.

You might already have guessed how *retinal* got its name: It is found in—and integral to—the retina. In the retina, retinal combines with a protein called **opsin** to form **rhodopsin,** a light-sensitive pigment. Rhodopsin is found in the **rod cells,** which are cells that react to dim light and interpret black-and-white images.

When light hits the retina, the rod cells go through a **bleaching process.** In this reaction, rhodopsin is split into retinal and opsin and the rod cells lose their color. The retinal component also changes spatial orientation from a *cis* configuration, which is bent, into a *trans* configuration, which is straight. The opsin component also changes shape. These changes in retinal and opsin during the bleaching process generate a nerve impulse that travels to the brain, resulting in the perception of a black-and-white image. Most of the retinal is converted back to its original *cis* form and binds with opsin to regenerate rhodopsin, allowing the visual cycle to begin again. However, some of the retinal is lost with each cycle and must be replaced by retinol from the bloodstream. This visual cycle goes on continually, allowing our eyes to adjust moment-to-moment to subtle changes in our surroundings or in the level of light.

When levels of vitamin A are deficient, people suffer from a condition referred to as night blindness. **Night blindness** results in the inability of the eyes to adjust to dim light. It can also result in the failure to regain sight quickly after a bright flash of light (**Figure 10.12**).

At the same time that we are interpreting black-and-white images, the **cone cells** of the retina, which are only effective in bright light, use retinal to interpret different wavelengths of light as different colors. The pigment involved in color vision is **iodopsin.** Iodopsin experiences similar changes during the color vision cycle as rhodopsin does during the black-and-white vision cycle. As with the rod cells, the cone cells can also be affected by a deficiency of vitamin A, resulting in color blindness.

In summary, the abilities to adjust to dim light, recover from a bright flash of light, and see in color are all critically dependent on adequate levels of retinal in the eyes.

opsin A protein that combines with retinal in the retina to form rhodopsin.

rhodopsin A light-sensitive pigment found in the rod cells that is formed by retinal and opsin.

rod cells Light-sensitive cells found in the retina that contain rhodopsin and react to dim light and interpret black-and-white images.

bleaching process A reaction in which the rod cells in the retina lose their color when rhodopsin is split into retinal and opsin.

night blindness A vitamin A–deficiency disorder that results in loss of the ability to see in dim light.

cone cells Light-sensitive cells found in the retina that contain the pigment iodopsin and react to bright light and interpret color images.

iodopsin A color-sensitive pigment found in the cone cells of the retina.

(a) Normal vision   Poor night vision

(b) Normal vision   Slow adjustment

Figure 10.12 A deficiency of vitamin A can result in night blindness. This condition results in **(a)** loss of side vision, poor night vision, and **(b)** difficulty in adjusting from bright light to dim light.

(a) Normal vision Poor night vision
(b) Normal vision Slow adjustment

Vitamin A Contributes to Cell Differentiation

Another important role of vitamin A is its contribution to **cell differentiation,** the process by which stem cells mature into highly specialized cells that perform unique functions. The retinoic acid form of vitamin A interacts with the receptor sites on a cell's DNA. This interaction influences gene expression and the determination of the type of cells that the stem cells eventually become. Obviously, this process is critical to the development of healthy organs and effectively functioning body systems.

An example of cell differentiation is the development of epithelial cells such as skin cells and mucus-producing cells of the protective linings of the lungs, vagina, intestines, stomach, bladder, urinary tract, and eyes. The mucus that epithelial cells produce lubricates the tissue and helps to propel microbes, dust particles, foods, and fluids out of the body tissues (for example, when we cough up secretions or empty the bladder). When vitamin A levels are insufficient, the epithelial cells fail to differentiate appropriately and we lose these protective barriers against infectious microbes and irritants.

Vitamin A is also critical to the differentiation of specialized immune cells called *T-lymphocytes,* or *T-cells.* T-cells assist in fighting infections. You can therefore see why vitamin A deficiency can lead to a breakdown of immune responses and to infections and other disorders of the lungs and respiratory tract, urinary tract, vagina, and eyes.

Other Functions of Vitamin A

Vitamin A is involved in reproduction. Although its exact role is unclear, it appears necessary for sperm production in men and for fertilization to occur in women. It also contributes to healthy bone growth by assisting in breaking down old bone so that new, longer, and stronger bone can develop. As a result of a vitamin A deficiency, children suffer from stunted growth and wasting.

Two popular treatments for acne contain derivatives of vitamin A. Retin-A, or tretinoin, is a treatment applied to the skin. Accutane, or isotretinoin, is taken orally. These medications should be used carefully and only under the supervision of a licensed physician. Both medications increase a person's sensitivity to the sun, and it is recommended that exposure to sunlight be limited while using them. They also can cause birth defects in infants if used while a woman is pregnant and can lead to other toxicity problems, depression, and suicide in some individuals. Interestingly, vitamin A itself has no effect on acne; thus, vitamin A supplements are not recommended in its treatment.

How Much Vitamin A Should We Consume?

Vitamin A toxicity can occur readily because it is a fat-soluble vitamin, so it is important to consume only the amount recommended for your gender and age range.

Recommended Dietary Intake for Vitamin A

The RDA for vitamin A is 900 μg per day for men and 700 μg per day for women. The UL is 3,000 μg per day of preformed vitamin A in women (including those pregnant and lactating) and men.

Liver contains vitamin A, and carrots and cantaloupe contain carotenoids that can be converted to vitamin A.

cell differentiation The process by which immature, undifferentiated stem cells develop into highly specialized functional cells of discrete organs and tissues.

Good Food Sources of Vitamin A

Vitamin A is present in both animal and plant sources. To calculate the total RAE in a person's diet, you must take into consideration both the amount of retinol and the amount of provitamin A carotenoids that are present in the foods eaten. Remember that 12 g of beta-carotene yields 1 g of RAE, and 24 g of alpha-carotene or beta-cryptoxanthin yields 1 g of RAE. Thus, if a person consumes 400 g retinol, 1,200 g beta-carotene, and 3,000 g alpha-carotene, the total RAE is equal to 400 g + (1,200 g ÷ 12) + (3,000 g ÷ 24), or 625 g RAE.

The most common sources of dietary preformed vitamin A are animal foods such as beef liver, chicken liver, eggs, and whole-fat dairy products. Vitamin A is also found in fortified reduced-fat milks, margarine, and some breakfast cereals (**Figure 10.13**). The other half of the vitamin A we consume comes from foods high in beta-carotene and other carotenoids that can be converted to vitamin A. As discussed earlier in this chapter, dark-

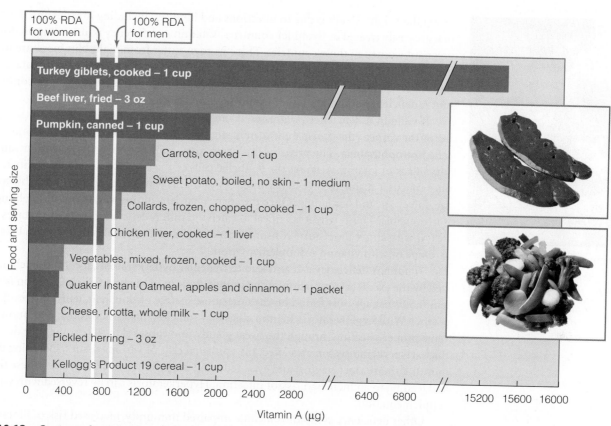

Figure 10.13   Common food sources of vitamin A. The RDA for vitamin A is 900 μg per day for men and 700 μg per day for women. (*Data from:* U.S. Department of Agriculture, Agricultural Research Service, 2008. USDA National Nutrient Database for Standard Reference, Release 21. Available at www.ars.usda.gov/ba/bhnrc/ndl.)

green, orange, and deep-yellow fruits and vegetables are good sources of beta-carotene and thus of vitamin A. Carrots, spinach, mango, cantaloupe, and tomato juice are excellent sources of vitamin A because they contain beta-carotene.

What Happens If We Consume Too Much Vitamin A?

Vitamin A is highly toxic, and toxicity symptoms develop after consuming only three to four times the RDA. Toxicity rarely results from food sources, but vitamin A supplements are known to have caused severe illness and even death. Consuming excess vitamin A while pregnant can cause serious birth defects and spontaneous abortion. Other toxicity symptoms include fatigue, loss of appetite, blurred vision, hair loss, skin disorders, bone and joint pain, abdominal pain, nausea, diarrhea, and damage to the liver and nervous system. If caught in time, many of these symptoms are reversible once vitamin A supplementation is stopped. However, permanent damage can occur to the liver, eyes, and other organs. Because liver contains such a high amount of vitamin A, children and pregnant women should not consume liver on a daily or weekly basis.

What Happens If We Don't Consume Enough Vitamin A?

As discussed earlier, night blindness and color blindness can result from vitamin A deficiency. How severe a problem is night blindness? Although less common among people of developed nations, vitamin A deficiency is a severe public health concern in developing nations. According to the World Health Organization, approximately 250 million preschool children suffer from vitamin A deficiency.[14] Of the children affected, 250,000 to 500,000 become permanently blinded every year. At least half of these children will die within 1 year of

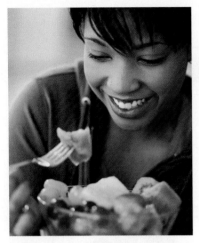

Eating plenty of fruits and vegetables will help prevent vitamin A deficiency.

losing their sight. Death is due to infections and illnesses, including measles and diarrhea, that are easily treated in wealthier countries. Vitamin A deficiency is also a tragedy for pregnant women in these countries. These women suffer from night blindness, are more likely to transmit HIV to their child if HIV-positive, and run a greater risk of maternal mortality. Chapter 19 includes an in-depth discussion of what is being done to combat vitamin A deficiency and night blindness throughout the world.

If vitamin A deficiency progresses, it can result in irreversible blindness due to hardening of the cornea (the transparent membrane covering the front of the eye), a condition called **xerophthalmia.** The prefix of this word, *xero-*, comes from a Greek word meaning "dry." Lack of vitamin A causes the epithelial cells of the cornea to lose their ability to produce mucus, causing the eye to become very dry. This leaves the cornea susceptible to damage, infection, and hardening. Once the cornea hardens in this way, the resulting blindness is irreversible. This is why it is critical to catch vitamin A deficiency in its early stages and treat it with either the regular consumption of fruits and vegetables that contain beta-carotene or with vitamin A supplementation.

Vitamin A deficiency can also lead to follicular **hyperkeratosis,** a condition characterized by the excess accumulation of the protein keratin in the hair follicles. Keratin is a protein that is usually only found on the outermost surface of skin, hair, nails, and tooth enamel. With hyperkeratosis, keratin clogs hair follicles, makes skin rough and bumpy, prevents proper sweating through the sweat glands, and causes skin to become very dry and thick. Hyperkeratosis can also affect the epithelial cells of various tissues, including the mouth, urinary tract, vagina, and eyes, reducing the production of mucus by these tissues and leading to an increased risk of infection. Hyperkeratosis can be reversed with vitamin A supplementation.

Other deficiency symptoms include impaired immunity, increased risk of illness and infections, reproductive system disorders, and failure of normal growth. Individuals who are at risk for vitamin A deficiency include elderly people with poor diets, newborn or premature infants (due to low liver stores of vitamin A), young children with inadequate vegetable and fruit intakes, and alcoholics. Any condition that results in fat malabsorption can also lead to vitamin A deficiency. Children with cystic fibrosis; individuals with Crohn disease, celiac disease, and diseases of the liver, pancreas, or gallbladder; and people who consume large amounts of the fat substitute Olestra are at risk for vitamin A deficiency.

RecaP

The role of vitamin A as an antioxidant is still under investigation. Vitamin A is critical for maintaining our vision. It is also necessary for cell differentiation, reproduction, and growth. The RDA for vitamin A is 900 μg per day for men and 700 μg per day for women. Animal liver, dairy products, and eggs are good animal sources of vitamin A; fruits and vegetables are high in beta-carotene, which is used to synthesize vitamin A. Supplementation can be dangerous, as toxicity is reached at levels of only three to four times the RDA. Toxicity symptoms include birth defects, spontaneous abortion, blurred vision, and liver damage. Deficiency symptoms include night blindness, impaired immune function, and growth failure.

xerophthalmia   An irreversible blindness due to hardening of the cornea and drying of the mucous membranes of the eye.

hyperkeratosis   A condition resulting in the excess accumulation of the protein keratin in the follicles of the skin; this condition can also impair the ability of epithelial tissues to produce mucus.

Selenium

Selenium is a trace mineral, and it is found in varying amounts in soil and thus in the food grown there. Keep in mind that although we need only minute amounts of trace minerals, they are just as important to our health as the vitamins and the major minerals. Selenium is efficiently absorbed, with about 50% to 90% of dietary selenium absorbed from the small intestine.[6]

Figure 10.14 Selenium is part of glutathione peroxidase, which neutralizes peroxide molecules that are formed by the body so they cannot form free radicals; this decrease in the number of free radicals spares vitamin E and prevents oxidative damage.

Functions of Selenium

It is only recently that we have learned about the critical role of selenium as a nutrient in human health. In 1979, Chinese scientists reported an association between a heart disorder called **Keshan disease** and selenium deficiency. This disease occurs in children in the Keshan province of China, where the soil is depleted of selenium. The scientists found that Keshan disease can be prevented with selenium supplementation.

The selenium in our bodies is contained in amino acids. Two amino acid derivatives contain the majority of selenium in our bodies: **selenomethionine** is the storage form for selenium, and **selenocysteine** is the active form of selenium. Selenocysteine is a critical component of the glutathione peroxidase enzyme system mentioned earlier (page 360). As shown in **Figure 10.14**, glutathione peroxidase breaks down the peroxides (such as hydrogen peroxide) that are formed by the body so they cannot form free radicals; this decrease in the number of free radicals spares vitamin E. Thus, selenium and vitamin E work together to prevent oxidative damage to lipids and decrease damage to cell membranes.

Like vitamin C, selenium is needed for the production of *thyroxine,* or thyroid hormone. By this action, selenium is involved in the maintenance of basal metabolism and body temperature. Selenium appears to play a role in immune function, and poor selenium status is associated with higher rates of some forms of cancer.

How Much Selenium Should We Consume?

The content of selenium in foods is highly variable. As it is a trace mineral, we need only minute amounts to maintain health. The RDA for selenium is 55 µg per day for both men and women. The UL is 400 µg per day.

Selenium is present in both plant and animal food sources but in variable amounts. Because it is stored in the tissues of animals, selenium is found in reliably consistent amounts in animal foods. Organ meats, such as liver and kidney, as well as pork and seafood, are particularly good sources (see **Figure 10.15**).

Wheat is a rich source of selenium.

Keshan disease A heart disorder caused by selenium deficiency. It was first identified in children in the Keshan province of China.

selenomethionine An amino acid derivative that is the storage form for selenium in the body.

selenocysteine An amino acid derivative that is the active form of selenium in the body.

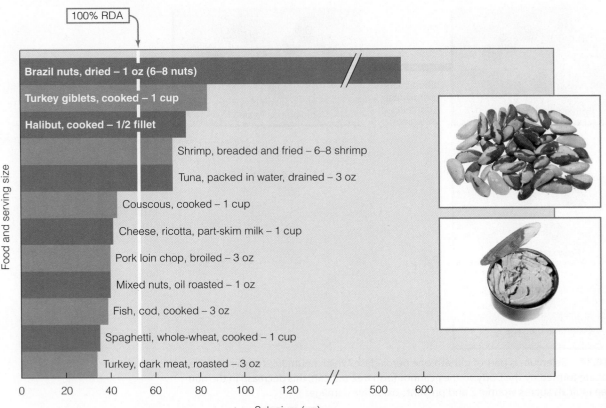

100% RDA

Food and serving size

Brazil nuts, dried – 1 oz (6–8 nuts)

Turkey giblets, cooked – 1 cup

Halibut, cooked – 1/2 fillet

Shrimp, breaded and fried – 6–8 shrimp

Tuna, packed in water, drained – 3 oz

Couscous, cooked – 1 cup

Cheese, ricotta, part-skim milk – 1 cup

Pork loin chop, broiled – 3 oz

Mixed nuts, oil roasted – 1 oz

Fish, cod, cooked – 3 oz

Spaghetti, whole-wheat, cooked – 1 cup

Turkey, dark meat, roasted – 3 oz

0   20   40   60   80   100   120   500   600

Selenium (μg)

Figure 10.15   Common food sources of selenium. The RDA for selenium is 55 μg per day. (*Data from:* U.S. Department of Agriculture, Agricultural Research Service, 2008. USDA National Nutrient Database for Standard Reference, Release 21. Available at www.ars.usda.gov/ba/bhnrc/ndl.)

In contrast, the amount of selenium in plants is dependent on the selenium content of the soil in which the plant is grown. Many companies marketing selenium supplements warn that the agricultural soils in the United States are depleted of selenium and inform us that we need to take selenium supplements. In reality, the selenium content of soil varies greatly across North America, and because we obtain our food from a variety of geographic locations, few people in the United States suffer from selenium deficiency. This is especially true for people who eat even small quantities of meat or seafood.

What Happens If We Consume Too Much Selenium?

Selenium toxicity does not result from eating foods high in selenium. However, supplementation can cause toxicity. Toxicity symptoms include brittle hair and nails that can eventually break and fall off. Other symptoms include skin rashes, nausea, vomiting, weakness, and cirrhosis of the liver.

What Happens If We Don't Consume Enough Selenium?

As discussed previously, selenium deficiency is associated with a form of heart disease called Keshan disease. Selenium deficiency does not cause the disease, but selenium is necessary to help the immune system effectively fight the viral infection or exposure to chemicals that prompt it.[6] Selenium supplements significantly reduce the incidence of Keshan disease, but they cannot reduce the damage to the heart muscle once it occurs.

Another deficiency disease is *Kashin-Beck disease,* a disease of the cartilage that results in deforming arthritis (**Figure 10.16**). Kashin-Beck disease is also found in selenium-depleted areas in China and in Tibet. Other deficiency symptoms include impaired immune responses, infertility, depression, impaired cognitive function, and muscle pain and wasting. Deficiencies

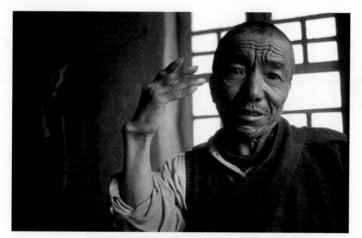

Figure 10.16   Selenium deficiency can lead to a form of deforming arthritis called Kashin-Beck disease.

of both selenium and iodine in pregnant women can cause a form of *cretinism* in the infant. Cretinism was discussed in detail in Chapter 8.

Copper, Iron, Zinc, and Manganese Play a Peripheral Role in Antioxidant Function

As discussed earlier, there are numerous antioxidant enzyme systems in our bodies. Copper, zinc, and manganese are a part of the superoxide dismutase enzyme complex. Iron is part of the structure of catalase. In addition to their role in protecting against oxidative damage, these minerals play major roles in the optimal functioning of many other enzymes in the body. Copper, iron, and zinc help maintain the health of our blood, and manganese is an important cofactor in carbohydrate metabolism. The functions, requirements, food sources, and deficiency and toxicity symptoms of these nutrients are discussed in detail in Chapter 12, which focuses on the nutrients involved in blood health and immunity.

> ## Recap
>
> Selenium is part of the glutathione peroxidase enzyme system. It indirectly spares vitamin E from oxidative damage, and it assists with immune function and the production of thyroid hormone. Organ meats, pork, and seafood are good sources of selenium, as are Brazil nuts. The selenium content of plants is dependent on the amount of selenium in the soil in which they are grown. Toxicity symptoms include brittle hair and nails, nausea, vomiting, and liver cirrhosis. Deficiency can result in Keshan disease, Kashin-Beck disease, impaired immune function, infertility, and muscle wasting. Copper, zinc, and manganese are cofactors for the superoxide dismutase antioxidant enzyme system. Iron is a cofactor for the catalase antioxidant enzyme. These minerals play critical roles in blood health and energy metabolism.

What Disorders Are Related to Free-Radical Damage?

You've probably encountered a plethora of health claims related to the functions of antioxidants—for instance, that they slow the effects of aging or prevent heart disease and cancer. In opposition to these claims, there is some evidence that taking antioxidant supplements may be harmful for certain people (refer back to the Nutrition Myth or Fact? box on beta-carotene, page 369).

In this section, we will review what is currently known about the role of antioxidant nutrients in cancer, heart disease, and aging.

Carcinogen

a Initiation: a carcinogen causes a mutation in the DNA of a normal cell

Normal cell undergoing mutation in DNA

b Promotion: cell with mutation in DNA divides repeatedly.

Rapidly dividing genetically altered cells

c Progression: cancer cells invade surrounding tissues and spread to other sites in body.

Cancer cell transported in blood vessel

Figure 10.17 **(a)** Cancer cells develop as a result of a genetic mutation in the DNA of a normal cell. **(b)** The mutated cell replicates uncontrollably, eventually resulting in a tumor. **(c)** If not destroyed or removed, the cancerous tumor metastasizes (spreads) to other parts of the body.

Cancer

Before we explore how antioxidants affect the risk for cancer, let's take a closer look at precisely what cancer is and how it spreads. **Cancer** is actually a group of diseases that are all characterized by cells that grow "out of control." By this we mean that cancer cells reproduce spontaneously and independently, and they are not inhibited by the boundaries of tissues and organs. Thus, they can aggressively invade tissues and organs far away from those in which they originally formed.

cancer A group of diseases characterized by cells that reproduce spontaneously and independently and may invade other tissues and organs.

Most forms of cancer result in one or more **tumors,** which are newly formed masses of undifferentiated cells that are immature and have no physiologic function. Although the word *tumor* sounds frightening, it is important to note that not every tumor is *malignant,* or cancerous. Many are *benign* (not harmful to us) and are made up of cells that will not spread widely.

Figure 10.17 shows how changes to normal cells prompt a series of other changes that can progress into cancer. There are three primary steps of cancer development: initiation, promotion, and progression. These steps occur as follows:

1. **Initiation:** The initiation of cancer occurs when a cell's DNA is *mutated* (or changed). This mutation causes permanent changes in the cell.
2. **Promotion:** During this phase, the genetically altered cell is stimulated to repeatedly divide. The mutated DNA is locked into each new cell's genetic instructions. Because the enzymes that normally work to repair damaged cells cannot detect alterations in the DNA, the cells can continue to divide uninhibited.
3. **Progression:** During this phase, the cancerous cells grow out of control and invade surrounding tissues. These cells then *metastasize* (spread) to other sites of the body. In the early stages of progression, the immune system can sometimes detect these cancerous cells and destroy them. However, if the cells continue to grow, they develop into malignant tumors, and cancer results.

Heredity, Lifestyle Choices, and Infectious and Environmental Agents Can Increase Cancer Risk

Cancer is the second leading cause of death in the United States, and researchers estimate that about half of all men and one-third of all women will develop cancer during their lifetime. But what factors cause cancer? Are you and your loved ones at risk? The answer depends on several factors, including your family history of cancer, your exposure to environmental agents, and various lifestyle choices.

Heredity can play a role in the development of cancer, because inherited "cancer genes," such as the BRC genes for breast cancer, increase the risk that an individual with those genes will develop cancer. However, it is important to bear in mind that a family history of cancer does not guarantee you will get cancer, too. It just means that you are at an increased risk and should take all preventive actions available to you. While some risk factors are out of your control, others are modifiable, which means that you can take positive steps to reduce your risk.

The American Cancer Society identifies five modifiable risk factors that have been shown to have the greatest impact on an individual's cancer risk; each is discussed next.[15]

Tobacco Use   More than 40 compounds in tobacco and tobacco smoke are **carcinogens,** or substances that can cause cancer. Using tobacco increases the risk for cancers of the lung, larynx, mouth, and esophagus and can also cause heart disease, stroke, and emphysema (**Figure 10.18**). (See the Highlight box on disorders linked to tobacco use, page 382.) The positive news is that tobacco use is a modifiable risk factor. If you smoke or use smokeless tobacco, you can reduce your risk for cancer considerably by quitting.[16,17]

Unhealthful Diet   Consumption of substances such as alcohol, dietary fat, and compounds found in cured and charbroiled meats can increase the risk for cancer (see Highlight on page 384). Nutritional factors that are protective against cancer include antioxidants, fiber, and *phytochemicals* (discussed *In Depth* on pages 389–407). Diets high in saturated fats and low in fruits and vegetables increase the risk of cancers of the esophagus, colon, breast, and prostate.[18] Increasing your intake of whole grains, fruits, and vegetables, decreasing your intake of red meats and fatty meats, and maintaining a healthy weight are keys to cancer prevention.

Using tobacco is a risk factor for cancer.

(a)   (b)

Figure 10.18   Cigarette smoking significantly increases our risk for lung and other types of cancer. The risk of lung cancer is 22.4 times higher in men who smoke and 12 times higher in women who smoke. **(a)** A normal, healthy lung; **(b)** the lung of a smoker. Notice the deposits of tar as well as the areas of tumor growth.

tumor   Any newly formed mass of undifferentiated cells.

carcinogen   Any substance capable of causing the cellular mutations that lead to cancer.

Highlight

Disorders Linked to Tobacco Use

Many people smoke cigarettes or cigars, or use smokeless tobacco. The use of these products can lead to serious health consequences that together reduce life expectancy by more than 13 years in males and 14 years in females.[16] Tobacco use is a risk factor in development of all of the following diseases and health concerns:

1. Cancers:
   - Lung
   - Larynx
   - Mouth (Figure 10.19a)
   - Pharynx
   - Esophagus
   - Bladder
   - Pancreas
   - Uterus
   - Kidney
   - Stomach
   - Some leukemias
2. Heart disease
3. Bronchitis
4. Emphysema
5. Stroke
6. Erectile dysfunction
7. Conditions related to maternal smoking:
   - Miscarriage
   - Preterm delivery
   - Stillbirth
   - Infant death
   - Low birth weight

(a)

(b)

Figure 10.19 Effects of tobacco use. In addition to increasing your risk for lung cancer and cardiovascular disease, **(a)** using tobacco increases your risk of mouth cancer, and **(b)** smoking results in premature wrinkling of the skin, especially around the mouth.

In addition, smoking causes a variety of other problems, such as the premature wrinkling and coarsening of the skin shown in **Figure 10.19b**. Smoking also causes bad breath, yellowing of the fingernails and hair, and bad-smelling clothes, hair, and living quarters. Sidestream smoke is another concern, especially for those who live or work with smokers. Nonsmokers who are exposed to smoke at home or work increase their risk of developing heart disease by 25% to 30% and increase their risk of developing lung cancer by 20% to 30%. Research indicates that there is no risk-free level of exposure to sidestream smoke.[17]

Figure 10.20 Human papillomavirus (HPV) is an infectious agent that can cause cancer.

Infectious Agents Infectious agents account for 18% of cancers worldwide. For example, infection of the female cervix with the sexually transmitted virus *Human papillomavirus* is linked to cervical cancer (**Figure 10.20**), and infection with the bacterium *Helicobacter pylori* is linked not only to ulcers but also to stomach cancer. As microbial research advances, it is thought that more cancers will be linked to infectious agents.

Ultraviolet Radiation Skin cancer is the most common form of cancer in the United States and accounts for over half of all cancers diagnosed each year. Most cases of skin cancer are linked to exposure to ultraviolet (UV) rays from the sun and indoor tanning beds. UV rays damage the DNA of immature skin cells, which then reproduce uncontrollably. Research has shown that a person's risk for skin cancer doubles if he or she has had five or more sunburns; however, your risk for skin cancer still increases with UV exposure even if you do not get sunburned.[19] Exposure to tanning beds before age 35 increases by 75% your risk of developing the most invasive form of skin cancer.[20]

Skin cancer includes the nonmelanoma cancers (basal cell and squamous cell cancers), which are not typically invasive, and malignant melanoma, which is one of the most deadly of all types of cancer (**Figure 10.21**). Limiting exposure to sunlight to no more than

20 minutes between 10 AM and 4 PM can help reduce your risk for skin cancer while allowing your body to synthesize adequate vitamin D. After that, wear sunscreen with at least a 15 SPF (sun protection factor) rating and protective clothing.

Physical Inactivity   A sedentary lifestyle increases the risk of colon cancer and may increase the risk for other forms of cancer.[18] At the same time, a recent review of several studies has found that moderately intense and vigorous physical activity are associated with a 20% to 30% reduction in our overall risk for cancer.[21] A clear protective effect of exercise was found specifically for breast and colon cancers. At this time, we do not know how exercise reduces the overall risk for cancer or for certain types of cancers. However, these findings have prompted the American Cancer Society and the National Cancer Institute to promote increased physical activity as a way to reduce our risk for cancer.

Antioxidants Play a Role in Preventing Cancer

There is a large and growing body of evidence that antioxidants play an important role in cancer prevention. But how? Some proposed mechanisms include:

Arctic explorers wear special clothing to protect themselves from the cold as well as the high levels of ultraviolet rays from the sun.

- Enhancing the immune system, which assists in the destruction and removal of pre-cancerous cells from the body
- Inhibiting the growth of cancer cells and tumors
- Preventing oxidative damage to the cells' DNA by scavenging free radicals and stopping the formation and subsequent chain reaction of oxidized molecules

Eating whole foods that are high in antioxidants—especially fruits, vegetables, and whole grains—is consistently shown to be associated with decreased cancer risk.[22] In addition, populations eating diets low in antioxidant nutrients have a higher risk for cancer. These studies show a strong association between level of dietary antioxidants and cancer risk, but they do not prove cause and effect. Nutrition experts agree that there are important interactions between antioxidant nutrients and other substances in foods, such as fiber and phytochemicals, which work together to reduce the risk for many types of cancers. Studies are now being conducted to determine whether eating foods high in antioxidants directly causes lower rates of cancer.

The link between taking antioxidant supplements and reducing cancer risk is not clear. Laboratory animal and test tube studies show that the individual nutrients reviewed in this chapter act as antioxidants in various situations. However, supplementation studies in humans do not consistently show benefits of taking antioxidant supplements in the prevention of cancer and other diseases. For example:

Figure 10.21   A lesion associated with malignant melanoma is characterized by asymmetry, uneven or blurred borders, mixed shades of tan, brown, black, and sometimes red or blue, and a diameter larger than a pencil eraser (6 mm).

- In the Alpha-Tocopherol Beta-Carotene Cancer Prevention Study discussed earlier, supplementation with vitamin E resulted in a lower risk for cancers of the prostate, colon, and rectum but was related to more cancers of the stomach.[9] In this same study, beta-carotene supplements increased risk for cancers of the lung, prostate, and stomach in current and former smokers.[23]
- In the Nutritional Prevention of Cancer Trial, selenium supplementation was found to reduce the risk of prostate, colon, and lung cancers, but it did not reduce the risk of nonmelanoma skin cancers.[24]
- The Linxian intervention trials, named for the region of China where the studies were conducted, found that a supplement containing beta-carotene, vitamin E, and selenium reduced mortality from overall cancer, specifically reducing the risk for cancers of the esophagus and stomach.[25]
- More recent trials such as the Physician's Health Study II,[26] the SELECT trial,[27] and the Women's Health Study[28] have shown that taking vitamin C, vitamin E, and selenium supplements does not reduce the risk for total cancer or the risk for many site-specific cancers such as prostate, breast, colo-rectal, and lung.

Staying physically active may help reduce our risk for some cancers.

Highlight

Nutritional Factors That Influence Our Risk for Cancer

Nutritional factors that may increase our cancer risk include the following:

■ Heterocyclic amines in cooked meat: carcinogenic chemicals formed when meat is cooked at high temperatures, such as during broiling, barbecuing, and frying.

■ Nitrates in drinking water: a carcinogenic chemical found in fertilizers that is proven to increase the risk of non-Hodgkin's lymphoma. People drinking contaminated tap water in agricultural areas may be at risk.

■ Nitrites and nitrates in cured meats: compounds found in some sausages, hams, bacon, and lunch meats. These compounds bind with amino acids to form nitrosamines, which are potent carcinogens.

■ Obesity: appears to increase the risk of cancers of the breast, colon, prostate, endometrium (the lining of the uterus), cervix, ovary, kidney, gallbladder, liver, pancreas, rectum, and esophagus. The exact link between obesity and increased cancer risk is not clear but may be linked with hormonal changes that occur in people with excess body fat.

■ High-saturated-fat diet: diets high in saturated fat have been associated with increased risk of many cancers, including prostate and breast. However, not all studies support this association.

■ Alcohol: excessive use is linked with an increased risk of cancers of the esophagus, pharynx, and mouth. May also increase the risk for cancers of the liver, breast, colon, and rectum. Alcohol may impair cells' ability to repair damaged DNA, increasing the possibility of cancer initiation.

Factors that may protect against cancer include the following:

■ Antioxidant-rich foods: includes vitamins E, C, A, beta-carotene, and other

These vegetables provide antioxidant nutrients, fiber, and phytochemicals, all of which reduce the risk of some cancers.

carotenoids and minerals such as selenium. Supplementation with individual antioxidants does not show consistent benefits.

■ Dietary fiber: some studies show reduced risks for breast, colon, and rectal cancer with increased fiber intake, although findings are not consistent.

■ Phytoestrogens: compounds found in soy-based foods and some vegetables and grains that may decrease the risk for breast, endometrial, and prostate cancers.

■ Omega-3 fatty acids: includes alpha-linolenic acid, eicosapentaenoic acid (EPA), and docosahexaenoic acid (DHA). These fatty acids are found in fish and fish oils. Consuming foods high in omega-3 fatty acids is associated with reduced rates of breast, colon, and rectal cancers.

Factors falsely claimed to cause cancer include the following:

■ Artificial sweeteners: there are claims that aspartame (brand name Nutrasweet) is carcinogenic. There is no evidence to support these claims; however, they continue to resurface on the Internet.

■ Coffee: no studies support the claim that drinking coffee increases the risk for cancer. Some of the chemicals used to make decaffeinated coffee are known to be carcinogenic; most companies now use safer chemicals for this process.

■ Fluoridated water: studies conducted over the past 40 years show no association between drinking fluoridated water and increased cancer risk.

■ Food additives: it is estimated that more than 15,000 substances are added to our foods during growth, processing, and packaging. To date, there is no evidence that food additives contribute significantly to cancer risk.

Why do antioxidant supplements appear to work in some studies and for some cancers but not in others? The human body is very complex, as is the development and progression of the numerous forms of cancer. People differ substantially in their susceptibility and response to carcinogens, as well as to protective factors. These complexities cloud the relationship between nutrition and cancer. In any research study, it is impossible to control all factors that may increase the risk for cancer. Thus, many unknown factors can affect study outcomes. It has also been speculated that antioxidants taken in supplemental form may act as prooxidants in some situations, whereas antioxidants consumed in foods may be more balanced. Many studies currently being conducted are examining the impact of whole foods and antioxidant supplements on the risk for various forms of cancer. The results of these studies will provide important insights into the link between whole foods, individual nutrients, and cancer. Refer to the Nutrition Debate at the end of the chapter to gain a better understanding of situations that may warrant vitamin and mineral supplementation.

Gustavo
Nutri-Case

"Last night, there was an actress on TV talking about having colon cancer and saying everybody over age 50 should get tested. It brought back all the memories of my father's cancer, how thin and weak he got before he went to the doctor, so that by the time they found the cancer it had already spread too far. But I don't think I'm at risk. I only eat red meat two or three times a week, and I eat a piece of fruit or a vegetable at every meal. I don't smoke, and I get plenty of exercise, sunshine, and fresh air working in the vineyard."

What lifestyle factors reduce Gustavo's risk for cancer? What factors increase his risk? Think especially about possible occupational risk factors. Would you recommend he increase his consumption of fruits and vegetables? Why or why not? If Gustavo were your father, would you ask him to have the screening test for colon cancer that the actress on television recommended?

Cardiovascular Disease

The details of *cardiovascular disease* (*CVD*) and its relationship to cholesterol and lipoproteins were presented in Chapter 5. A brief review of CVD is presented in this section, which focuses on the question of how antioxidants may reduce the risk for CVD.

CVD is the leading cause of death for adults in the United States. CVD encompasses all diseases of the heart and blood vessels, including coronary heart disease, hypertension (or high blood pressure), and atherosclerosis (or hardening of the arteries). The two primary manifestations of CVD are heart attack and stroke. Almost 1 million people die each year from CVD, and it is estimated that CVD costs the United States $448 billion in healthcare costs and lost work revenue.[29]

Remember that the major risks for CVD are smoking, hypertension (high blood pressure), high blood levels of LDL-cholesterol, obesity, and a sedentary lifestyle. Other risk factors include a low level of high-density lipoprotein (HDL) cholesterol, diabetes, family history (CVD in males younger than 55 years of age and females younger than 65 years of age), being a male older than 45 years of age, and being a postmenopausal woman. Although we cannot alter our gender, family history, or age, we can change our nutrition and physical activity habits to reduce our risk for CVD.

Research has recently identified a risk factor for CVD that may be even more important than elevated cholesterol levels. This risk factor is a condition called *low-grade inflammation*.[30] This condition weakens the plaque in the blood vessels, making it more fragile. You may remember from Chapter 5 that plaque is the fatty material that builds up on the lining of arteries and causes atherosclerosis. As the plaque becomes more fragile, it is more likely to burst, breaking away from the arterial lining and traveling freely in the bloodstream. It may then lodge in the blood vessels of the heart or brain, closing them off and leading to a heart attack or stroke, respectively.

In laboratory blood tests, the marker that indicates the degree of inflammation is C-reactive protein. Having higher levels of C-reactive protein increases the risk for a heart attack even if people do not have elevated cholesterol levels. For people with high levels of C-reactive protein and cholesterol, the risk of a heart attack is almost nine times higher than that of someone with normal cholesterol and C-reactive protein levels. These findings have prompted the medical community to develop standards for measuring C-reactive protein along with cholesterol as a test for CVD risk.

How can antioxidants decrease the risk for CVD? There is growing evidence that certain antioxidants, specifically vitamin E and lycopene, work in a variety of ways that reduce the damage to the vessels, which in turn reduces the risk for a heart attack or stroke. Some of the ways these nutrients decrease the risk for CVD include scavenging free radicals, reducing low-grade inflammation, and reducing blood coagulation and the formation of blood clots.

As with the research conducted on cancer, the studies of antioxidants and CVD show inconsistent results. Two large-scale surveys conducted in the United States show that men and women who eat more fruits and vegetables have a significantly reduced risk of CVD.[31, 32] However, few intervention studies have been conducted to determine the effect of antioxidant supplements on risk for CVD. Vitamin E was found to lower the number of heart disease deaths in smokers in the Alpha-Tocopherol Beta-Carotene Cancer Prevention Study, but had no overall effect on the risk of stroke.[33] In the HOPE study, vitamin E had no impact on the risk for CVD in people who are at high risk for heart attack and stroke.[3] Recently published results of large intervention studies in the United States indicate no reductions in major cardiovascular events in men and women taking vitamins E or C.[4, 28] Thus, there is growing evidence that antioxidant supplements do not reduce our risk for CVD.

It is important to note that other compounds (besides antioxidants) found in fruits, vegetables, and whole grains can reduce our risk for CVD. For instance, soluble fiber has been shown to reduce elevated LDL-cholesterol and total cholesterol. The most successful effects have been found in people eating oatmeal and oat-bran cereals. Dietary fiber in general has been shown to reduce blood pressure, lower total cholesterol levels, and improve blood glucose and insulin levels. Folate, a B-vitamin, is found in fortified cereals, green leafy vegetables, bananas, legumes, and orange juice. Folate is known to reduce homocysteine levels in the blood, and a high concentration of homocysteine in the blood is a known risk factor for CVD. A recent study from the Netherlands showed that individuals who drank more than three cups of black tea (which is high in flavonoids) per day had a lower rate of heart attacks than non–tea drinkers.[34] Thus, it appears that there are a plethora of nutrients and other components in fruits, vegetables, and whole-grain foods that may be protective against CVD.

The flavonoids in black tea might reduce the risk of CVD.

Age-Related Vision Impairment

Some diseases associated with aging may be preventable by consuming antioxidants. Two of these diseases are macular degeneration and cataracts, both of which impair vision in older adults.

Macular degeneration is the leading cause of blindness of adults 55 years and older in the United States. The macula is the central part of the retina, and it is responsible for our central vision and our ability to see details. A person with macular degeneration loses the ability to see details, such as small print, small objects, and facial features. Objects seem to fade or disappear, straight lines or edges appear wavy, and the ability to read standard printed material is lost (**Figure 10.22a**). Macular degeneration does not affect peripheral vision. There is no known cure for macular degeneration. The causes of this disease are unknown.

A **cataract** is a damaged portion of the eye's lens, the portion of the eye through which we focus entering light. Cataracts cause cloudiness in the lens that impairs vision (Figure 10.22b). People with cataracts have a very difficult time seeing in bright light; for

macular degeneration   A vision disorder caused by deterioration of the central portion of the retina and marked by loss or distortion of the central field of vision.

cataract   A damaged portion of the eye's lens, which causes cloudiness that impairs vision.

(a)   (b)

Figure 10.22 These photos simulate two forms of vision loss common in older adults. **(a)** Macular degeneration results in a loss of central vision. **(b)** Cataracts impair vision across the visual field. (*Data from:* National Eye Institute, National Institutes of Health. November 2003. Photos, Images, and Videos. Ref. no. EDS05. Available at www.nei.nih.gov/photo/search/keyword.asp? keyword=macular; and National Eye Institute, National Institutes of Health. November 2003. Photos, Images, and Videos. Ref. no. EDS03. Available at www.nei.nih.gov/photo/search/ keyword.asp?keyword=cataract.)

instance, they see halos around lights, glare, and scattering of light. Having cataracts also impairs a person's ability to adjust from dark to bright light. It is estimated that more than one-half of all people over the age of 65 years in the United States have some cataract development. Cataracts can be treated with surgery. As with macular degeneration, the causes of cataracts are unknown.

Current research findings are showing some promise of reducing the risk for macular degeneration and cataracts through the use of antioxidant supplements. A recent study conducted with individuals who had early signs of macular degeneration found that consuming a supplement containing vitamins C and E, beta-carotene, and zinc reduced the progression of this disease.[35] Earlier studies have also shown that higher blood levels of antioxidants and consuming more antioxidants in the diet are associated with a lower risk of macular degeneration.[36, 37] The effects of antioxidant supplements and cataracts are mixed, with some studies showing a reduced rate of cataract development in people taking vitamin C and E and beta-carotene supplements or having higher blood levels of antioxidants, but other studies show no benefit of antioxidants.[38–40] At this time, it is not possible to reach a conclusion regarding the effectiveness of antioxidant supplements to prevent these two diseases of aging. However, there is enough evidence that consuming a healthful diet that includes fruits, vegetables, and whole grains is associated with improved quality of life as we age.

RECAP

Cancer is a group of diseases in which genetically mutated cells grow out of control. Tobacco use, nutritional factors, environmental exposures, UV radiation, and low physical activity levels are related to a higher risk for some cancers. Eating foods high in antioxidants is associated with lower rates of cancer, but studies of antioxidant supplements and cancer are equivocal. Cardiovascular disease (CVD) is the leading cause of death in the United States. Antioxidants may help reduce the risk by preventing oxidative damage to LDL-cholesterol, reducing inflammation in the vessels, and reducing the formation of blood clots. Macular degeneration and cataracts are two diseases of vision that are associated with aging. Antioxidant nutrients have been found to reduce the risk of these diseases in some studies.

See for Yourself
What's Your Cancer Risk?

Cancer often seems to strike apparently healthy people "out of the blue." Because genetic and certain environmental factors are beyond your control, you may be wondering how your diet and lifestyle choices might be influencing your risk. If so, take the following quiz and see for yourself! Answer each question True or False.

1. I eat a variety of colorful fruits and vegetables daily.	True	False
2. I choose whole grains in preference to refined grains.	True	False
3. I limit my consumption of saturated and *trans* fats.	True	False
4. I eat meatless meals several times a week.	True	False
5. I rarely eat cured meats containing nitrates and nitrites.	True	False

6. I rarely eat broiled, fried, or barbecued meats.	True	False
7. I maintain a healthful weight.	True	False
8. I do not smoke.	True	False
9. I limit my exposure to sidestream smoke and air pollution.	True	False
10. I do not drink more than 1 alcoholic beverage per day (for women) or 2 alcoholic beverages per day (for men).	True	False
11. I limit my sun exposure to no more than 20 minutes per day.	True	False
12. I engage in moderate or vigorous physical activity for 30 minutes or more on 5 or more days of the week.	True	False

Data adapted from: American Cancer Society. ACS Recommendations for Nutrition and Physical Activity for Cancer Prevention. Available at www.cancer.org.

Chapter Review

Test Yourself | Answers

1 **(T)** Free radicals are highly unstable atoms that can destabilize neighboring atoms or molecules and harm our cells; however, they are produced as a normal by-product of human physiology.

2 **(F)** Overall, the research on vitamin C and colds does not show strong evidence that taking vitamin C supplements reduces our risk of suffering from the common cold.

3 **(T)** Carrots are an excellent source of beta-carotene, a precursor for vitamin A, which helps maintain good vision.

4 **(T)** According to the American Cancer Society, smoking is the most preventable cause of death in our society. In addition, tobacco use accounts for about 30% of all cancer deaths and is the primary modifiable risk factor for cancer. Among other factors known to significantly influence cancer risk are nutrition, sun exposure, and level of physical activity.

5 **(F)** Currently, there is no known dietary cure for cancer. However, eating a diet that is plentiful in fruits and vegetables and exercising regularly may help reduce our risk for some forms of cancer.

Summary

- Antioxidants are compounds that protect our cells from oxidative damage.

- Free radicals are produced under many situations, including when the body generates ATP, when the immune system fights infection, and when we are exposed to environmental toxins such as pollution, overexposure to sunlight, radiation, and tobacco smoke.

- Free radicals are dangerous because they can damage the lipid portion of our cell membranes, destroying the integrity of our cell membranes. Free radicals also damage LDLs, cell proteins, and DNA.

- Antioxidant vitamins donate their electrons or hydrogen molecules to free radicals to neutralize them. Antioxidant minerals are cofactors in antioxidant enzyme systems, which convert free radicals to less damaging substances that our bodies excrete.

- Vitamin E is an antioxidant that protects the fatty components of cell membranes from oxidation. It also protects LDLs, vitamin A, and our lungs from oxidative damage. Other functions of vitamin E are the development of nerves and muscles, enhancement of the immune function, and improvement of the absorption of vitamin A if intake of vitamin A is low.

- Vitamin C is an antioxidant that is oxidized by free radicals and prevents the damage of cells and tissues. Vitamin C also regenerates vitamin E after it has been oxidized. Other functions of vitamin C include helping the synthesis of collagen, carnitine, various hormones, neurotransmitters, and DNA; enhancing immune function; and increasing the absorption of iron.

- Beta-carotene is one of about 600 carotenoids identified to date. Beta-carotene is a provitamin, or precursor, to vitamin A, meaning it is an inactive form of vitamin A that is converted to vitamin A in the body.

- Beta-carotene protects the lipid portions of our membranes and the LDL-cholesterol from oxidative damage. Other functions of beta-carotene include enhancing our immune systems, protecting our skin from sun damage, and protecting our eyes from oxidative damage. The carotenoids may help reduce our risk for some forms of cancer.

- Vitamin A is a fat-soluble vitamin. The three active forms of vitamin A are retinol, retinal, and retinoic acid. Beta-carotene is converted to vitamin A in the small intestine.

- Vitamin A is extremely important for healthy vision. It ensures our ability to adjust to changes in the brightness of light, and it also helps us maintain color vision. Vitamin A may also act as an antioxidant, as it protects LDL-cholesterol from oxidative damage. Other functions of vitamin A include assistance in cell differentiation, maintaining healthy immune function, sexual reproduction, and proper bone growth.

- Selenium is a trace mineral that is part of the structure of glutathione peroxidases, a family of antioxidant enzymes. Other functions of selenium include assisting in the production of thyroid hormone and enhancing immune function.

- Copper, iron, zinc, and manganese are minerals that act as cofactors for antioxidant enzyme systems. Copper, zinc, and manganese are part of the superoxide dismustase complex, whereas iron is part of catalase. These minerals also play critical roles in energy metabolism and blood formation.

- Antioxidants play a role in cancer prevention. Eating foods high in antioxidants results in lower rates of some cancers, but supplementing with antioxidants can cause cancer in some situations.

- Antioxidants may help reduce our risk for CVD by scavenging free radicals and preventing oxidative damage to LDL-cholesterol, reducing low-grade inflammation (which, in turn, prevents the rupture of plaque in our blood vessels), and preventing the formation of blood clots.

- Antioxidants may help prevent two age-related diseases of vision: macular degeneration and cataracts. Macular degeneration causes us to lose the ability to see details, small print, and facial features. A cataract is a damaged portion of the eye's lens that causes cloudiness and impairs vision. Cataracts impair our ability to adjust from dark to bright light.

Review Questions

1. Which of the following is a characteristic of vitamin E?
   a. It enhances the absorption of iron.
   b. It can be manufactured from beta-carotene.
   c. It is a critical component of the glutathione peroxidase system.
   d. It is destroyed by exposure to high heat.

2. Oxidation is best described as a process in which
   a. a carcinogen causes a mutation in a stem cell's DNA.
   b. an atom loses an electron.
   c. an element loses an atom of oxygen.
   d. a compound loses a molecule of water.

3. Which of the following disorders is linked with the production of free radicals?
   a. cardiovascular disease
   b. carotenosis
   c. ulcers
   d. malaria

4. Which of the following are known carcinogens?
   a. phytochemicals
   b. antioxidants
   c. carotenoids
   d. nitrates

5. Taking daily doses of three to four times the RDA of which of the following nutrients may cause death?
   a. vitamin A
   b. vitamin C
   c. vitamin E
   d. selenium

6. **True or false?** Tocopherol is the biologically active form of vitamin E in our bodies.

7. **True or false?** Free-radical formation can occur as a result of normal cellular metabolism.

8. **True or false?** Vitamin C helps regenerate vitamin A.

9. **True or false?** Reliable food sources of selenium include beef liver, pork, and seafood.

10. **True or false?** Pregnant women are advised to consume plentiful quantities of beef liver.

11. Explain how free radicals damage cell membranes and lead to cell death.

12. Describe the process by which cancer occurs, beginning with initiation and ending with metastasis of the cancer to widespread body tissues.

13. Explain how vitamin E reduces our risk for heart disease.

14. Discuss the contribution of trace minerals such as selenium to the prevention of oxidation.

15. Your mother has a heart condition that requires her to take the prescription drug Coumadin, an anticoagulant. While chatting with you over lunch one day, she mentions that she has started taking an antioxidant supplement that is supposed to "boost cardiovascular health." You ask to see the supplement and note that it contains 500 mg vitamin E as alpha-tocopherol, 500 mg of vitamin C, and 100 µg of selenium. Should you be concerned? Why or why not?

Web Links

www.who.int
World Health Organization
Click on "Health Topics" and select "deficiency diseases" to find out more about vitamin A deficiency around the world.

www.americanheart.org
American Heart Association
Discover the best way to lower your risk for cardiovascular disease.

www.cancer.org
The American Cancer Society
Get ACS recommendations for nutrition and physical activity for cancer prevention.

www.cancer.gov
The National Cancer Institute
Learn more about the nutritional factors that can influence your risk for cancer.

www.nei.nih.gov
National Eye Institute
Visit this site to find out more about how macular degeneration and cataracts can impair vision.

www.fda.gov
U.S. Food and Drug Administration
Select "Dietary Supplements" on the pull-down menu for more information on how to make informed decisions and evaluate information related to dietary supplements.

www.nal.usda.gov/fnic
The Food and Nutrition Information Council
Click on the "Dietary Supplements" button to obtain information on vitamin and mineral supplements, including consumer reports and industry regulations.

http://dietary-supplements.info.nih.gov
Office of Dietary Supplements
Go to this site to obtain current research results and reliable information about dietary supplements.

References

1. Yeomans, V. C., J. Linseisen, and G. Wolfram. 2005. Interactive effects of polyphenols, tocopherol, and ascorbic acid on the Cu2+-mediated oxidative modification of human low density lipoproteins. *Eur. J. Nutr.* (April 15), Epub DO: 10.1007/s00394–005–0546–y.

2. Winklhofer-Roob, B. M., A. Meinitzer, M. Maritschnegg, J. M. Roob, G. Khoschsorur, J. Fibalta, I. Sundl, S. Wuga, W. Wonisch, B. Tiran, and E. Rock. 2004. Effects of vitamin E depletion/repletion on biomarkers of oxidative stress in healthy aging. *Ann. N.Y. Acad. Sci.* 1031:361–364.

3. The HOPE and HOPE-TOO Trial Investigators. 2005. Effects of long-term vitamin E supplementation on cardiovascular events and cancer. A randomized controlled trial. *JAMA* 293:1338–1347.

4. Sesso, H. D., J. E. Buring, W. G. Christen, T. Kurth, C. Belanger, J. MacFadyn, V. Bubes, J. E. Manson, R. J. Glynn, and J. M. Gaziano. 2008. Vitamins E and C in the prevention of cardiovascular disease in men: The Physicians' Health Study II randomized controlled trial. *JAMA* 300(18):2123–2133.

5. Ford, E. S., and A. Sowell. 1999. Serum alpha-tocopherol status in the United States population: Findings from the Third National Health and Nutrition Examination Survey. *Am. J. Epidemiol.* 150(3):290–300.

6. Institute of Medicine, Food and Nutrition Board. 2000. *Dietary Reference Intakes for Vitamin C, Vitamin E, Selenium, and Carotenoids.* Washington, DC: The National Academy of Sciences.

7. Hemilä, H., E. Chalker, B. Treacy, and B. Douglas. 2007. Vitamin C for preventing and treating the common cold. *Cochrane Database of Systematic Reviews.* Issue 3. Art. No. CD000980. DOI: 10.1002/14651858.CD000980.pub3.

8. Burri, B. J. 1997. Beta-carotene and human health: A review of current research. *Nutr. Res.* 17:547–580.

9. Albanes D., O. P. Heinonen, J. K. Huttunen, P. R. Taylor, J. Virtamo, B. K. Edwards, J. Haapakoski, M. Rautalahti, A. M. Hartman, J. Palmgren, and P. Greenwald. 1995. Effects of α-tocopherol and β-carotene supplements on cancer incidence in the Alpha-Tocopherol Beta-Carotene Cancer Prevention Study. *Am. J. Clin. Nutr.* 62(suppl.):1427S–1430S.

10. Omenn G. S., G. E. Goodman, M. D. Thornquist, J. Balmes, M. R. Cullen, A. Glass, J. P. Keogh, F. L. Meyskens Jr., B. Valanis, J. H. Williams Jr., S. Barnhart, and S. Hammar. 1996. Effects of a combination of beta carotene and vitamin A on lung cancer and cardiovascular disease. *N. Engl. J. Med.* 334:1150–1155.

11. U.S. Department of Agriculture (USDA), Agricultural Research Service. 2008. USDA National Nutrient Database for Standard Reference, Release 21. Available at www.ars.usda.gov/ba/bhnrc/ndl.

12. Livrea, M. A., L. Tesoriere, A. Bongiorno, A. M. Pintaudi, M. Ciaccio, and A. Riccio. 1995. Contribution of vitamin A to the oxidation resistance of human low density lipoproteins. *Free Radic. Biol. Med.* 18:401–409.

13. Gutteridge, J. M. C., and B. Halliwell. 1994. *Antioxidants in Nutrition, Health, and Disease.* Oxford, UK: Oxford University Press.

14. World Health Organization (WHO). 2009. Micronutrient deficiencies. Vitamin A deficiency. Available at www.who.int/nutrition/topics/vad/en/.

15. American Cancer Society. 2008. Prevention and early detection. At a glance—nutrition and physical activity. Available at www.cancer.org/docroot/PED/content/PED_3_2X_Recommendations.asp?sitearea=PED.

16. American Cancer Society. 2009. ACS guide to quitting smoking. Available at www.cancer.org/docroot/PED/content/PED_10_13X_Guide_for_Quitting_Smoking.asp?sitearea=PED.

17. U.S. Department of Health and Human Services (USDHHS). 2004. *The Health Consequences of Smoking: A Report of the Surgeon General.* Washington, DC: U.S. Department of Health and Human Services, Centers for Disease Control and Prevention, National Center for Chronic Disease Prevention and Health Promotion, Office on Smoking and Health.

18. American Cancer Society. 2007. Cancer atlas. Available at www.cancer.org/downloads/AA/CancerAtlas02.pdf.

19. Pfahlberg, A., K. F. Kolmel, and O. Gefeller. 2002. Adult vs. childhood susceptibility to melanoma. Is there a difference? *Arch. Dermatol.* 138:1234–1235.

20. Heinonen, O. P., D. Albanes, J. Virtamo, P. R. Taylor, J. K. Huttunen, A. M. Hartman, J. Haapakoski, N. Malila, M. Rautalahti, S. Ripatti, H. Maepaa, and International Agency for Research on Cancer (IARC). 2007. The association of use of sunbeds with cutaneous malignant melanoma and other skin cancers: A systematic review. *Intl. J. Cancer* 120:1116–1122.

21. Thune, I., and A. S. Furberg. 2001. Physical activity and cancer risk: Dose-response and cancer, all sites and site-specific. *Med. Sci. Sports Exerc.* 33(suppl.):S530–S550.

22. Greenwald P., C. K. Clifford, and J. A. Milner. 2001. Diet and cancer prevention. *Eur. J. Cancer* 37:948–965.

23. Heinonen O. P., D. Albanes, J. Virtamo, P. R. Taylor, J. K. Huttunen, A. M. Hartman, J. Haapakoski, N. Malila, M. Rautalahti, S. Ripatti, H. Maepaa, L. Teerenhovi, L. Koss, M. Virolainen, and B. K. Edwards. 1998. Prostate cancer and supplementation with α-tocopherol and β-carotene: Incidence and mortality in a controlled trial. *J. Natl. Cancer Inst.* 90:440–446.

24. Clark, L. C., B. Dalkin, A. Krongrad, G. F. Combs Jr., B. W. Turnbull, E. H. Slate, R. Witherington, J. H. Herlong, E. Janosko, D. Carpenter, C. Borosso, S. Falk, and J. Rounder. 1998. Decreased incidence of prostate cancer with selenium supplementation: Results of a double-blind cancer prevention trial. *Br. J. Urol.* 81:730–734.

25. Blot, W. J., J.-Y. Li, P. R. Taylor, W. Guo, S. M. Dawsey, and B. Li. 1995. The Linxian trials: Mortality rates by vitamin-mineral intervention group. *Am. J. Clin. Nutr.* 62(suppl.):1424S–1426S.

26. Gaziano, J. M., R. J. Glynn, W. G. Christen, T. Kurth, C. Belanger, J. MacFadyen, V. Bubes, J. E. Manson, H. D. Sesso, and J. E. Buring. 2009. Vitamins E and C in the prevention of prostate and total cancer in men: The Physicians' Health Study II Randomized Controlled Trial. *JAMA* 301(1):52–62.

27. Lippman, S. M., E. A. Klein, P. J. Goodman, M. S. Lucia, I. M. Thompson, L. G. Ford, H. L. Parnes, L. M. Minasian, J. M. Gaziano, J. A. Hartline, J. Kellogg Parsons, J. D. Bearden III, E. D. Crawford, G. E. Goodman, J. Claudio, E. Winquist, E. D. Cook, D. D. Karp, P. Walther, M. M. Lieber, A. R. Kristal, A. K. Darke, K. B. Arnold, P. A. Ganz, R. M. Santella, D. Albanes, P. R. Taylor, J. L. Probstfield, T. J. Jagpal, J. J. Crowley, F. L. Meyskens Jr., L. H. Baker, and C. A. Coltman Jr. 2009. Effect of selenium and vitamin E on risk of prostate cancer and other cancers: The

Selenium and Vitamin E Cancer Prevention Trial (SELECT). *JAMA* 301(1):39–51.

28. Lee, I. M., N. R. Cook, J. M. Gaziano, D. Gordon, P. M. Ridker, J. E. Manson, C. H. Hennekens, and J. E. Buring. 2005. Vitamin E in the primary prevention of cardiovascular disease and cancer: The Women's Health Study: A randomized controlled trial. *JAMA* 294(1):56–65.

29. National Center for Chronic Disease Prevention and Health Promotion (NCCDPHP). 2008. Chronic disease prevention. Chronic disease overview. Available at www.cdc.gov/nccdphp/overview.htm.

30. de Ferranti S., and N. Rifai. 2002. C-reactive protein and cardiovascular disease: A review of risk prediction and interventions. *Clinica Chimica Acta* 317:1–15.

31. Joshipura, K. J., F. B. Hu, J. E. Manson, M. J. Stampfer, E. B. Rimm, F. E. Speizer, G. Colditz, A. Ascherio, B. Rosner, D. Spiegelman, and W. C. Willett. 2001. The effect of fruit and vegetable intake on risk for coronary heart disease. *Ann. Intern. Med.* 134:1106–1114.

32. Liu, S., I.-M. Lee, U. Ajani, S. R. Cole, J. E. Buring, and J. E. Manson. 2001. Intake of vegetables rich in carotenoids and risk of coronary heart disease in men: The Physicians' Health Study. *Intl. J. Epidemiol.* 30:130–135.

33. The Alpha-Tocopherol, Beta-Carotene Cancer Prevention Study Group (The ATBC Study Group). 1994. The effect of vitamin E and beta carotene on the incidence of lung cancer and other cancers in male smokers. *N. Engl. J. Med.* 330:1029–1035.

34. Geleijnse, J. M., L. J. Launer, D. A. M. van der Kuip, A. Hofman, and J. C. M. Witteman. 2002. Inverse association of tea and flavonoid intakes with incident myocardial infarction: The Rotterdam Study. *Am. J. Clin. Nutr.* 75:880–886.

35. Age-Related Eye Disease Study Research Group. 2001. A randomized, placebo-controlled, clinical trial of high-dose supplementation with vitamins C and E, beta-carotene, and zinc for age-related macular degeneration and vision loss: AREDS Report No. 8. *Arch. Ophthalmol.* 119:1417–1436.

36. Delcourt C., J. P. Cristol, F. Tessier, C. L. Léger, B. Descomps, and L. Papoz. 1999. Age-related macular degeneration and antioxidant status in the POLA study. POLA Study Group. Pathologies Oculaires Liées à l'Age. *Arch. Ophthalmol.* 117:1384–1390.

37. West S., S. Vitale, J. Hallfrisch, B. Munoz, D. Muller, S. Bressler, and N. M. Bressler. 1994. Are antioxidants or supplements protective for age-related macular degeneration? *Arch. Ophthalmol.* 112:222–227.

38. Chylack, L. T. Jr., N. P. Brown, A. Bron, M. Hurst, W. Kopcke, U. Thien, and W. Schalch. 2002. The Roche European American Cataract Trial (REACT): A randomized clinical trial to investigate the efficacy of an oral antioxidant micronutrient mixture to slow progression of age-related cataract. *Ophthalmic Epidemiol.* 9:49–80.

39. Gale, C. R., N. F. Hall, D. I. Phillips, and C. N. Martyn. 2001. Plasma antioxidant vitamins and carotenoids and age-related cataract. *Ophthalmology* 108:1992–1998.

40. Age-Related Eye Disease Study Research Group. 2001. A randomized, placebo-controlled, clinical trial of high-dose supplementation with vitamins C and E and beta-carotene for age-related cataract and vision loss: AREDS Report No. 9. *Arch. Ophthalmol.* 119:1439–1452.

41. Nutrition Business Journal. 2006. *NBJ's Supplement Business Report 2006.* ©Penton Media, Inc.

42. Blendon, R. J., C. M. DesRoches, J. M. Benson, M. Brodie, and D. E. Altman. 2001. Americans' views on the use and regulation of dietary supplements. *Arch. Intern. Med.* 26:805–810.

43. U.S. Food and Drug Administration (FDA). Center for Food Safety and Applied Nutrition. 2008. Overview of dietary supplements. Available at www.cfsan.fda.gov/~dms/supplmnt.html.

44. U.S. Food and Drug Administration (FDA). Center for Food Safety and Applied Nutrition. 2002. Dietary supplements. Tips for the savvy supplement user: Making informed decisions and evaluating information. Available at www.cfsan.fda.gov/~dms/ds-savvy.html.

45. Dancho, C., and M. M. Manore. 2001. Dietary supplement information on the World Wide Web. Sorting fact from fiction. *ACSM's Health and Fitness Journal* 5:7–12.

46. American Dietetic Association. 2005. Dietary supplements. *J. Am. Diet. Assoc.* 102:460–470.

Vitamin and Mineral Supplementation: Necessity or Waste?

Marcus has type 2 diabetes and high blood cholesterol and is worried about his health. He attended a nutrition seminar in which the health benefits of various vitamin and mineral supplements were touted. After attending this seminar, Marcus was convinced that he needed to take a series of supplements that contain more than 200% of the RDA for many vitamins and minerals. After a few months of taking these supplements on a daily basis, Marcus started to experience headaches, nausea, diarrhea, and tingling in his hands and feet. Although Marcus was not an expert in nutrition, he suspected that he might be experiencing side effects related to nutrient toxicity. He decided to talk to his doctor about the supplements he was taking to determine whether they could be causing his symptoms.

Marcus's story is not unique. The use of dietary supplements in the United States has skyrocketed in recent years. One industry source cites annual sales of supplements in the United States at $21.3 billion.[41] A recent review of national opinion surveys found that a significant number of Americans regularly take dietary supplements, but they do not report the use of these products to their physicians because they feel their physicians have little knowledge of these products and may harbor a bias toward their use.[42] Interestingly, many supplement users stated that they would continue to use these products even if scientific studies found them to be ineffective!

Why do so many people take dietary supplements? Many people believe they cannot consume adequate nutrients in their diet, and they take a supplement as extra nutritional insurance. Others have been advised by their healthcare provider to take a supplement to address a given health concern. There are people, like Marcus, who believe that they can use certain supplements to treat their disease. There are also people who believe supplements are necessary to enhance their appearance or athletic performance.

Are such uses wise? Who should be taking supplements? These questions are not easy to answer. Before deciding whether you might benefit from taking dietary supplements, read on.

Dietary Supplements Include Vitamins, Minerals, and Other Products

According to the U.S. Food and Drug Administration (FDA), a dietary supplement is "a product taken by mouth that contains a 'dietary ingredient' intended to supplement the diet."[43] Ingredients in supplements may include vitamins, minerals, herbs or other botanicals, amino acids, enzymes, tissues from animal organs or glands, or a concentrate, metabolite, constituent, or extract. Supplements come in many forms, including pills, capsules, liquids, and powders.

How Are Dietary Supplements Regulated?

As presented in the Dietary Supplement Health and Education Act (DSHEA) of 1994, dietary supplements are categorized within the general group of foods, not drugs. This means that the regulation of supplements is much less rigorous than the regulation of drugs. Currently, the FDA is reconsidering how it regulates food and supplements that are marketed with health claims, but no changes have been finalized at this time. As an informed consumer, you should know that:

- Supplements do not need approval from the FDA before they are marketed.
- The company that manufactures the supplements is responsible for determining that the supplement is safe; the FDA does not test any supplement for safety prior to marketing.
- Supplement companies do not have to provide the FDA with any evidence that their supplements are safe unless the company is marketing a new dietary ingredient that was not sold in the United States prior to 1994.

Supplements can be powders, pills, or liquid.

- There are at present no federal guidelines on practices to ensure the purity, quality, safety, and composition of dietary supplements.
- There are no rules to limit the serving size or amount of a nutrient in any dietary supplement.
- Once a supplement is marketed, the FDA must prove it unsafe before the product will be removed from the market.

Despite these limitations in supplement regulations, supplement manufacturers are required to follow dietary supplement labeling guidelines. The figure in this box shows a label from a multivitamin and mineral supplement. As you can see, there are specific requirements for the information that must be included on the supplement label. Federal advertising regulations also require that any advertising on the label must be truthful and not misleading and that advertisers must have adequate substantiation of all product claims before disseminating the advertisement. Any products not meeting these labeling and advertising guidelines can be removed from the market.

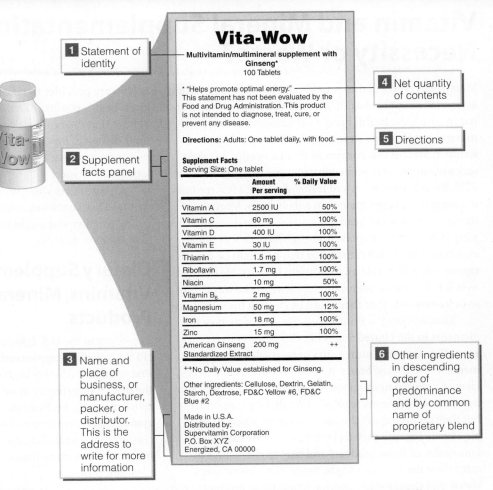

A multivitamin-mineral supplement label highlighting the dietary supplement guidelines.

1 Statement of identity

2 Supplement facts panel

3 Name and place of business, or manufacturer, packer, or distributor. This is the address to write for more information

4 Net quantity of contents

5 Directions

6 Other ingredients in descending order of predominance and by common name of proprietary blend

Vita-Wow

Multivitamin/multimineral supplement with Ginseng*
100 Tablets

* "Helps promote optimal energy." This statement has not been evaluated by the Food and Drug Administration. This product is not intended to diagnose, treat, cure, or prevent any disease.

Directions: Adults: One tablet daily, with food.

Supplement Facts
Serving Size: One tablet

	Amount Per serving	% Daily Value
Vitamin A	2500 IU	50%
Vitamin C	60 mg	100%
Vitamin D	400 IU	100%
Vitamin E	30 IU	100%
Thiamin	1.5 mg	100%
Riboflavin	1.7 mg	100%
Niacin	10 mg	50%
Vitamin B$_6$	2 mg	100%
Magnesium	50 mg	12%
Iron	18 mg	100%
Zinc	15 mg	100%
American Ginseng Standardized Extract	200 mg	++

++No Daily Value established for Ginseng.

Other ingredients: Cellulose, Dextrin, Gelatin, Starch, Dextrose, FD&C Yellow #6, FD&C Blue #2

Made in U.S.A.
Distributed by:
Supervitamin Corporation
P.O. Box XYZ
Energized, CA 00000

How Can We Protect Ourselves from Fraudulent or Dangerous Supplements?

Although many of the supplement products sold today are safe, some are not. In addition, some companies are less than forthright about the true content of ingredients in their supplements. How can you avoid purchasing fraudulent or dangerous supplements? The FDA suggests that consumers can do the following to protect themselves from fraudulent or dangerous supplements:[44]

1. Look for the U.S.P. (U.S. Pharmacopoeia) symbol or notation on the label. This symbol indicates that the manufacturer followed the standards established by the U.S.P. for drugs for features such as purity, strength, quality, packaging, labeling, and acceptable length of storage.

2. Consider buying recognized brands of supplements. Although not guaranteed, products made by nationally recognized companies more likely have well-established manufacturing standards.

3. Do not assume that the word "natural" on the label means that the product is safe. Arsenic, lead, and mercury are all natural substances that can kill you if consumed in large enough quantities.

4. Do not hesitate to question a company about how it makes its products. Reputable companies have nothing to hide and are more than happy to inform their customers about the safety and quality of their products.

Many supplements are also sold today over the Internet. Dancho and Manore suggest six criteria that can be used to evaluate dietary supplement Web sites.[45] Keep

these criteria in mind each time you consider buying a dietary supplement over the Web:

1. What is the purpose of the site? Is the Web site trying to sell a product or educate the consumer? Keep in mind that the primary purpose of supplement companies is to make money. Look for sites that provide educational information about a specific nutrient or product and don't just focus on selling the products.

2. Does the site contain accurate information? Accuracy of the information on the Web site is the most difficult thing for a consumer to determine. Testimonials (claims by athletes or other famous people) are *not* reliable and accurate; claims supported by scientific research are most desirable. If what the company claims about its product sounds too good to be true, it probably is.

3. Does the site contain reputable references? References should be from articles published in peer-reviewed scientific journals. The reference should be complete and contain author names, title of article, journal title, date, volume, and page numbers. This information allows the consumer to check original research for the validity of a company's claims about its product. Be cautious of sites that refer to claims that are "proven by research studies" but fail to provide a complete reference.

4. Who owns or sponsors the site? Full disclosure regarding sponsorship and possible sources of bias or conflict of interest should be included in the site's information.

5. Who wrote the information? Web sites should clearly identify the author of the article and include the credentials of the author. Recognized experts include individuals with relevant health-related credentials such as RD, Ph.D., M.D., or M.S. Keep in mind that this person is responsible for the information posted in the article but may not be the creator of the Web site.

6. Is the information current and updated regularly? As information about supplements changes regularly, Web sites should be updated regularly, and the date should be clearly posted. All Web sites should also include contact information to allow consumers to ask questions about the information posted.

For more information on how to make informed deci-

Always research supplements and supplement manufacturers before purchasing.

sions and evaluate information related to dietary supplements, go to the Dietary Supplements Web site of the U.S. FDA Center for Food Safety and Applied Nutrition at www.cfsan.fda.gov/~dms/supplmnt.html. Other Web sites that contain reliable information about dietary supplements include The National Institutes of Health (NIH) Office of Dietary Supplements at http://dietary-supplements.info.nih.gov, and The Food and Nutrition Information Council (FNIC) at www.nal.usda.gov/fnic/.

Dietary Supplements Can Be Both Helpful and Harmful

Contrary to what some people believe, the U.S. food supply is not void of nutrients, and all people do not need to supplement all of the time. In fact, we now know that foods contain a diverse combination of compounds that are critical to our health, and vitamin and mineral supplements do not contain the same amount or variety of substances found in foods. Thus, dietary supplements are not substitutes for whole foods. However, our nutritional needs change throughout our life span, and some of us may need to take supplements at certain times for certain reasons. For instance, some athletes can benefit from consuming foods or beverages formulated to provide carbohydrate and other nutrients necessary to support intense exercise. Dietary supplements include hundreds of thousands of products sold for many purposes, and it is impossible to discuss here all of the various situations in which their use may be advisable. So to simplify this discussion, let's focus on identifying the groups of people who may or may not benefit from taking vitamin and mineral supplements.

Who Might Benefit from Taking Vitamin and Mineral Supplements?

Table 10.2 lists groups of people who may benefit from supplementation. But even if you fall within one of these groups, it's still important to analyze your total diet to determine whether you might need to take the vitamin or mineral supplement indicated. It is also a good idea to check with your healthcare provider or a registered dietitian (RD) before taking any supplements, as supplements can interfere with some prescription and over-the-counter medications.

Table 10.2 Individuals Who May Benefit from Dietary Supplementation

Type of Individual	Specific Supplements That May Help
Newborns	Routinely given a single dose of vitamin K at birth
Infants	Depends on age and nutrition; may need iron, vitamin D, or other nutrients
Children not drinking fluoridated water	Fluoride supplements
Children on strict vegetarian diets	Vitamin B$_{12}$, iron, zinc, vitamin D (if not exposed to sunlight)
Children with poor eating habits or overweight children on an energy-restricted diet	Multivitamin/multimineral supplement that does not exceed the RDA for the nutrients it contains
Pregnant teenagers	Iron and folic acid; other nutrients may be necessary if diet is very poor
Women who may become pregnant	Multivitamin or multivitamin/multimineral supplement that contains 0.4 mg of folic acid
Pregnant or lactating women	Multivitamin/multimineral supplement that contains iron, folic acid, zinc, copper, calcium, vitamin B$_6$, vitamin C, vitamin D
People on prolonged weight-reduction diets	Multivitamin/multimineral supplement
People recovering from serious illness or surgery	Multivitamin/multimineral supplement
People with HIV/AIDS or other wasting diseases; people addicted to drugs or alcohol	Multivitamin/multimineral supplement or single-nutrient supplements
People who do not consume adequate calcium	Calcium supplements: for example, women need to consume 1,000 to 1,300 mg of dietary calcium per day; thus, supplements may be necessary
People whose exposure to sunlight is inadequate to allow synthesis of adequate vitamin D	Vitamin D
People eating a vegan diet	Vitamin B$_{12}$, riboflavin, calcium, vitamin D, iron, and zinc
People who have had portions of the intestinal tract removed; people who have a malabsorptive disease	Depends on the exact condition; may include various fat-soluble and/or water-soluble vitamins and other nutrients
People with lactose intolerance	Calcium supplements
Elderly people	Multivitamin/multimineral supplement, vitamin B$_{12}$

When Can Taking a Vitamin and Mineral Supplement Be Harmful?

You can see from the table that there are many people who can benefit from taking vitamin and mineral supplements in certain situations. There are also many people who do not need to take supplements but do so anyway. Instances in which taking vitamin and mineral supplements is unnecessary or harmful include:

1. Providing fluoride supplements to children who already drink fluoridated water.
2. Taking supplements in the belief that they will cure a disease such as cancer, diabetes, or heart disease.
3. Taking supplements with certain medications. For instance, people who take the blood-thinning drug Coumadin should not take vitamin E supplements, as this can cause excessive bleeding. People who take aspirin daily should check with their physician before taking vitamin E supplements, as aspirin also thins the blood.
4. Taking nonprescribed supplements if you have liver or kidney diseases. Physicians may prescribe vitamin and mineral supplements for their patients because many nutrients are lost during treatment for these diseases. However, these individuals cannot properly metabolize certain supplements and should not take any that are not prescribed by their physicians because of a high risk for toxicity.
5. Taking beta-carotene supplements if you are a smoker. As already mentioned, there is evidence that beta-carotene supplementation increases the risk of lung and other cancers in smokers.
6. Taking vitamins and minerals in an attempt to improve physical appearance or athletic performance. There is no evidence that vitamin and mineral supplements enhance appearance or athletic performance in healthy adults who consume a varied diet with adequate energy.
7. Taking supplements to increase your energy level. Vitamin and mineral supplements do not provide en-

Table 10.3 Ingredients Found in Supplements That Are Associated with Illnesses and Injuries

Ingredient	Potential Risks
Herbal Ingredients	
Chaparral	Liver disease
Kava (also known as kava kava)	Severe liver toxicity
Comfrey	Obstruction of blood flow to liver, possible death
Slimming/dieter's teas	Nausea, diarrhea, vomiting, stomach cramps, constipation, fainting, possible death
Ephedra (also known as ma huang, Chinese ephedra, and epitonin)	High blood pressure, irregular heartbeat, nerve damage, insomnia, tremors, headaches, seizures, heart attack, stroke, possible death
Germander	Liver disease, possible death
Lobelia	Breathing problems, excessive sweating, rapid heartbeat, low blood pressure, coma, possible death
Magnolia-Stephania preparation	Kidney disease, can lead to permanent kidney failure
Willow bark	Reyes syndrome (a potentially fatal disease that may occur when children take aspirin), allergic reaction in adults
Wormwood	Numbness of legs and arms, loss of intellectual processing, delirium, paralysis
Vitamins and Essential Minerals	
Vitamin A (when taking 25,000 IU or more per day)	Birth defects, bone abnormalities, severe liver disease
Vitamin B_6 (when taking more than 100 mg per day)	Loss of balance, injuries to nerves that alter touch sensation
Niacin (when taking slow-release doses of 500 mg or more per day, or when taking immediate-release doses of 750 mg or more per day)	Stomach pain, nausea, vomiting, bloating, cramping, diarrhea, liver disease, damage to the muscles, eyes, and heart
Selenium (when taking 800 to 1,000 µg per day)	Tissue damage
Other Ingredients	
Germanium (a nonessential mineral)	Kidney damage
L-tryptophan (an amino acid)	Eosinophilia-myalgia syndrome (a potentially fatal blood disorder that causes high fever)

Data from: U.S. Food and Drug Administration. 2007. Dietary supplements. Warnings and safety information. Available at www.cfsan.fda.gov/~dms/ds-warn.html; and U.S. Food and Drug Administration. 1998. Supplements associated with illnesses and injuries. *FDA Consumer Magazine.* September/October. Available at http://www.fda.gov/fdac/features/1998/dietchrt.html.

ergy, because they do not contain fat, carbohydrate, or protein (sources of calories). Although many vitamins and minerals are necessary for us to produce energy, taking dietary supplements in place of eating food will not provide us with the energy necessary to live a healthy and productive life.

8. Taking single-nutrient supplements, unless a qualified healthcare practitioner prescribes a single-nutrient supplement for a diagnosed medical condition (for example, prescribing iron supplements for someone with anemia). These products contain very high amounts of the given nutrient, and taking these types of products can quickly lead to toxicity.

The American Dietetic Association advises that the ideal nutritional strategy for optimizing health is to eat a healthful diet that contains a variety of whole foods.[46] This way, you will not need to take vitamin and mineral supplements. And if you do use a supplement, select one that contains no more than 100% of the recommended levels for the nutrients it contains. Avoid taking single-nutrient supplements unless advised to do so by your healthcare practitioner. Finally, avoid taking supplements that contain substances that are known to cause illness or injuries. Some of these substances are listed in Table 10.3.

Critical Thinking Questions

- Do you think that the FDA should more closely regulate supplement manufacturers? If so, how?

- Have you decided whether or not taking a supplement is right for you? Why or why not?

Read on.

Imagine a patient seeing his physician for a minor problem: "sluggish" bowel movements. The physician asks him several questions and performs an exam. At the close of the visit, he hands the patient a prescription: *One apple, two servings of dark-green leafy vegetables, 1 cup of yogurt, and 2 cups of green tea daily.* The patient accepts the prescription gratefully, assuring his physician as he says goodbye, "I'll stop at the market on my way home!"

Sound unreal? As researchers provide more and more evidence on the link between nutrition and health, it's possible that scenarios like this might become familiar. Here, we explore *In Depth* some of the reasons why the chemicals naturally occurring in plant foods, called *phytochemicals*, are thought to promote our health. We'll also examine the claims made for so-called *functional foods* like special yogurts, eggs, chocolate, and beverages that their manufacturers say have health benefits beyond

Apricots contain carotenoids, a type of phytochemical.

their basic nutritional function. Who knows? When you finish reading, you might find yourself writing up your own health-promoting grocery list!

What Are Phytochemicals?

Phyto- means plant, so **phytochemicals** are literally plant chemicals. These naturally occurring compounds are believed to protect plants from a variety of injurious agents, including insects, microbes, the oxygen they produce, and the UV light they capture and transform into the nutrients we need. Although more than 5,000 different phytochemicals have already been identified, researchers believe there are thousands more.[1] Any one food can contain hundreds. **Figure 1** on page 400 shows some groups of only a few of the most common.

Phytochemicals are not considered nutrients, that is, substances necessary for sustaining life. Even for

---

phytochemicals Compounds found in plants that are believed to have health-promoting effects in humans.

carotenoids, a well-studied class of phytochemicals, the Food and Nutrition Board of the Institute of Medicine concluded in 2000 that there was not enough evidence to establish a daily recommended intake.[2] So whereas a total lack of vitamin C or iron is incompatible with life, a total lack of lutein or allylic sulfur compounds is not known to be fatal. On the other hand, eating an abundance of phytochemical-rich foods has been shown to reduce the risk of cardiovascular disease, cancer, diabetes, Alzheimer's disease, cataracts, and age-related functional decline.[1, 3]

The evidence supporting this observation of a reduced disease risk stems mainly from large epidemiologic studies in which people report their usual food intake to researchers who then look for relationships between specific dietary patterns and common diseases. These large studies often find that the reduced disease risk from high intakes of plant foods cannot be attributed solely to differences in intake of macronutrients and micronutrients. This suggests that other compounds in plant foods may be reducing the risk for disease.

As we noted in Chapter 1, epidemiologic studies can only reveal *associations* between general patterns of food intake and health conditions; they cannot prove that a food or dietary pattern directly *causes* a health outcome. To better understand how phytochemicals influence health and disease, researchers have turned to biochemical, cellular, and animal studies.

How Do Phytochemicals Reduce Our Risk of Disease?

For decades, laboratory experiments have shown that, at least in the test tube, many phytochemicals have antioxidant properties. Recall from Chapter 10 that antioxidants can neutralize free radicals, those unstable, highly reactive compounds that damage proteins, lipids, and DNA in our cells. Free radicals are an unavoidable by-product of normal metabolism, but are also produced in response to x-rays, air pollution, industrial chemicals, tobacco smoke, infections, and even intense exercise.

The health effects of this damage, also known as oxidative damage, typically don't arise until later in life. Many **diseases of aging,** such as cardiovascular disease, cancer, cataracts, arthritis, and certain neurologic disorders, have been linked to oxidative damage that accumulates over years. It's no surprise, therefore, that antioxidant-rich foods would reduce the risk of these conditions.

---

diseases of aging Conditions that typically occur later in life as a result of lifelong accumulated risk, such as exposure to high-fat diets, lack of physical activity, and excess sun exposure.

Phytochemicals and Functional Foods

Want to find out . . .

- what's behind all the fuss about phytochemicals?
- why you can't put fruits and veggies in a pill?
- whether yogurt can boost your immune system?
- whether "calorie-burning" drinks could help you lose weight?

Phytochemical	Health Claims	Food Source
Carotenoids: alpha-carotene, beta-carotene, lutein, lycopene, zeaxanthin, etc.	Diets with foods rich in these phytochemicals may reduce the risk of cardiovascular disease, certain cancers (e.g., prostate), and age-related eye diseases (cataracts, macular degeneration).	Red, orange, and deep-green vegetables and fruits such as carrots, cantaloupe, sweet potatoes, apricots, kale, spinach, pumpkin, and tomatoes
Flavonoids:[1] flavones, flavonols (e.g., quercetin), catechins (e.g., epigallocatechin gallate or EGCG), anthocyanidins, isoflavonoids, etc.	Diets with foods rich in these phytochemicals are associated with lower risk of cardiovascular disease and cancer, possibly because of reduced inflammation, blood clotting, and blood pressure, and increased detoxification of carcinogens or reduction in replication of cancerous cells.	Berries, black and green tea, chocolate, purple grapes and juice, citrus fruits, olives, soybeans and soy products (soy milk, tofu, soy flour, textured vegetable protein), flaxseed, whole wheat
Phenolic acids:[1] ellagic acid, ferulic acid, caffeic acid, curcumin, etc.	Similar benefits as flavonoids.	Coffee beans, fruits (apples, pears, berries, grapes, oranges, prunes, strawberries), potatoes, mustard, oats, soy
Phytoestrogens:[2] genistein, diadzein, lignans	Foods rich in these phytochemicals may provide benefits to bones and reduce the risk of cardiovascular disease and cancers of reproductive tissues (e.g., breast, prostate).	Soybeans and soy products (soy milk, tofu, soy flour, textured vegetable protein), flaxseed, whole grains
Organosulfur compounds: allylic sulfur compounds, indoles, isothiocyanates, etc.	Foods rich in these phytochemicals may protect against a wide variety of cancers.	Garlic, leeks, onions, chives, cruciferous vegetables (broccoli, cabbage, cauliflower), horseradish, mustard greens

[1] Flavonoids, phenolic acids, and stilbenes are three groups of phytochemicals called phenolics. Resveratrol, the phytochemical discussed in the Highlight "Will a PB&J Keep the Doctor Away?" on page 402, is a stilbene. Flavonoids and phenolic acids are the most abundant phenolics in our diet.

[2] Phytoestrogens include phytochemicals that have mild or anti-estrogenic action in our body. They are grouped together based on this similarity in biologic function, but they also can be classified into other phytochemical groups, such as isoflavonoids.

Figure 1   Health claims and food sources of phytochemicals.

Unfortunately, biology is not fully explained by a few simple chemical reactions. In fact, the latest research evidence on phytochemicals suggests that their health-promoting properties are largely unrelated to the antioxidant activity measured in the test tube.[4, 5] This is in part because phytochemicals can be modified during digestion and also after absorption so that cells are exposed to **metabolites** that are structurally different from the phytochemicals found in foods.[5] Clearly, the test tube cannot explain what is happening inside the body.

Fortunately, researchers have also employed cellular and animal studies, which have revealed that phytochemicals have many health-promoting functions independent of their antioxidant properties. These functions of phytochemicals include the following:

- Reduce inflammation,[6] which is linked to the development of Alzheimer's disease and cardiovascular disease and is symptomatic of arthritis.
- Enhance the activity of certain enzymes throughout the body that function to detoxify carcinogens.[7]
- Protect against cancer by slowing tumor cell growth and instructing cancer cells to die.[7]
- Protect against infections indirectly by enhancing our immune function and directly by acting as antibacterial and antiviral agents.[7]
- Reduce the risk of cardiovascular disease by lowering blood lipids, blood pressure, and blood clotting.[1]

Which of these roles is most important in reducing disease risk is not yet known. Many other issues are also not well understood yet, such as which phytochemicals are needed and how much.

Is There an RDA for Phytochemicals?

Most well-controlled studies in cells, animals, or people typically research only one phytochemical or food. When the results are published, we read about them in the popular press: one day we're advised to eat tomatoes, another day blueberries, then pomegranates. But these findings are only the tip of the iceberg that must be explored before we can make precise recommendations about phytochemicals and health. As scientists begin to "map" more and more phytochemical "icebergs," they're making the following discoveries:

- Phytochemicals interact with each other in the body to produce a synergistic effect that is greater than the sum

of the effects of individual phytochemicals.[1] This may explain why whole tomatoes were found to reduce prostate cancer in rats, whereas a phytochemical called lycopene that is present in tomatoes, when given alone, did not.[8]

- Phytochemicals interact with macronutrients and vitamins and minerals. For example, the anticancer effect of garlic is enhanced by vitamin A, selenium, and certain fats.[9]
- Phytochemicals can act in different ways under different circumstances in the body. For example, phytoestrogens in soy appear to reduce the incidence of breast cancer in healthy women, but they may enhance cancer development when the disease is already present.[10]

For these reasons, no RDA for phytochemicals can safely be established for any life stage group.

In addition, although epidemiological studies suggest that the more phytochemicals we consume, the better our health, this benefit appears to be limited to phytochemicals found in foods. That is, phytochemicals appear to be protective in the low doses commonly provided by foods, but may have very different effects as supplements. This may be due to their mode of action: scientists now believe that, instead of *protecting* our cells, phytochemicals might benefit our health by *stressing* our cells, causing them to rev up their internal defense systems.[4] Cells are very well equipped to deal with minor stresses, but not with excessive stress, which may explain why clinical trials with phytochemical supplements rarely show the same benefits as high intakes of plant foods.[4, 11]

So are phytochemical supplements harmful? Generally speaking, taking high doses of anything is risky. A basic principle of toxicology is that any compound can be toxic if the dose is high enough. Dietary supplements are no exception to this rule. For example, clinical trials found that supplementing with 20 to 30 mg/day of beta-carotene for 4 to 6 years increased lung cancer risk by 16% to 28% in smokers.[12, 13] Based on these and other results, experts from the U.S. Preventive Health Services Task Force recommend against beta-carotene supplementation.[14]

Avoid phytochemical supplements in favor of whole foods.

---

metabolites The form that nutrients take when they have been used by the body. For example, lactate is a metabolite of carbohydrate that is produced when we use carbohydrate for energy.

Highlight

Will a PB&J Keep the Doctor Away?

Whole-grain bread, natural peanut butter, and grape jelly: how could a food that tastes so good be good for the body, too? We've known for decades about some of the healthful nutrients in peanut butter and jelly sandwiches, including the fiber and micronutrients in whole-grain bread and the plant protein, fiber, monounsaturated fat, and minerals in peanuts. But recently, research has revealed that the comforting PB&J also appears to be a good source of resveratrol, a phytochemical that is being studied in labs across the world because of its health-promoting potential.[15, 16] A flavonoid found in the skins of dark grapes, resveratrol

is plentiful both in the raw fruit, in dark grape juice, and in most red wines, which are fermented with the grape skins still in the vat. It is also present to a lesser extent in dark berries such as blueberries and cranberries. But fruits are not the only source: resveratrol just happens to also be plentiful in peanuts, including peanut butter.

But what does resveratrol do, and does a PB&J contain enough of the stuff to make a difference? Researchers have linked resveratrol to protective effects against cancer, heart disease, obesity, viral infections, and neurologic diseases like Alzheimer's; however, so far, the effects have been demonstrated only in mice. What's more, no one yet knows what an effective "dose" of resveratrol looks like, nor whether the amounts in a peanut butter and jelly sandwich could possibly confer health benefits. More disturbingly, we don't yet know whether high doses, such as those found in supplements, could be harmful. Unfortunately, these facts have not stopped supplements manufacturers from marketing hundreds of different resveratrol supplements to humans.

If you do decide to add resveratrol to your diet, we hope you'll bypass supplements in favor of the humble PB&J. Although the jury is still out on the benefits of its resveratrol content, it still makes a highly nutritious meal or snack, doesn't need refrigeration, is inexpensive, and tastes great.

In short, whereas there is ample evidence to support the health benefits of diets rich in fruits, vegetables, legumes, whole grains, and nuts, no recommendation for precise amounts can be given, and phytochemical supplements should be avoided. The best advice for optimal health is to consume a plant-based diet consisting of as many whole foods as possible.

What Are Functional Foods?

The Institute of Food Technologists defines a **functional food** as a food or food component that provides a health benefit beyond basic nutrition. Examples include conventional foods, fortified, enriched, or enhanced foods,

and dietary supplements.[17] Functional foods (also called *nutraceuticals*) may contain naturally occurring phytochemicals, helpful bacteria required for production of the food, or a level of micronutrients higher than what would be provided by the same food in an unprocessed form.[18]

Most commonly, the health-promoting substances are added to an existing food. For example, iodine is added to salt, grains are enriched with iron and B-vitamins, orange juice is fortified with calcium, or milk is enriched with *extra* calcium. Alternatively, the health-promoting substances are caused to develop in a functional food by altering the way in which the food is produced. For example, eggs with higher levels of omega-3 fatty acids result from feeding chickens a diet rich in this nutrient. Also, tomatoes can be genetically engineered to contain higher levels of phytochemicals. These qualify as functional foods.

functional food A food that provides a health benefit beyond basic nutrition.

Are Functional Foods Safe?

The U.S. Food and Drug Administration (FDA) is responsible for ensuring that all foods are safe and properly labeled. Currently, the FDA has no official definition or regulatory category for functional foods; it regulates them in the same way as conventional foods. This means that in order for a food to be allowed on the market, any "functional" ingredient added to that food must be generally recognized as safe.

Recently, other federal agencies and consumer advocacy groups have petitioned the FDA to reevaluate the way it ensures the safety of ingredients in functional foods and the truthfulness of health claims on functional food labels.[19] Their concern is twofold. First, they contend that by making unsubstantiated health claims for their products, companies are misleading consumers into wasting billions of dollars annually. Second, they point to dozens of products currently sold as foods that contain ingredients such as herbs that are not FDA approved for use in foods. They caution that such products could have adverse health effects on vulnerable consumers, including pregnant women, children, and the frail elderly, as well as consumers with chronic disease, in whom the ingredients could exacerbate symptoms or interfere with prescription medications.

In response to these and other concerns, the FDA is currently considering a new regulatory system by which any product bearing health claims would be subject to FDA oversight. Thus, not only herbs, but even conventional food ingredients promoted for use in the treatment or prevention of disease in humans would be subject to FDA control.[20] But until such a system is in effect, consumers should remain skeptical about the safety and effectiveness of the functional foods they see on the shelves.

Are Functional Foods Effective?

Is there any research to support the claims of health benefits made by manufacturers of functional foods? That depends on the product. So if you're considering regular consumption of a functional food, do your homework. To give you some practice, let's consider a few currently on the market.

Designer Yogurts

People have been consuming yogurt and other fermented milk products for thousands of years. But interest in their health benefits began only about 100 years ago, when a

Grains enriched with iron and B-vitamins are an example of a functional food.

Russian microbiologist named Ilya Metchnikov linked the long, healthy lives of Bulgarian peasants with their consumption of such foods. Subsequent research identified bacteria in fermented milk products as responsible for their healthful effects, and the probiotics industry was born.

Probiotics means "pro-life." Probiotics are live microorganisms found in, or added to, fermented dairy foods such as yogurt, buttermilk, sour cream, and kefir (a yogurt-style liquid beverage) and fermented vegetable foods such as sauerkraut, miso, and tempeh (fermented tofu). Probiotics are also available in supplement form.

Our intestines contain an amazing number and variety of bacteria and other microorganisms. Many of these are vital to maintaining our health and supporting digestive function, but some can be harmful. The correct balance between beneficial and harmful microbes can be disturbed by medications and illness. The main symptoms of an unbalanced microbial environment are digestive, such as diarrhea or constipation, but other conditions may also be related to inadequate intestinal bacteria.

---

probiotics Live beneficial microorganisms in foods that can colonize the intestine and optimize the intestinal bacterial environment. There is promising research suggesting various health benefits from consuming probiotics.

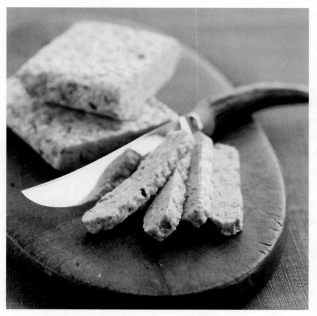

Fermented foods such as tempeh contain probiotics.

How do probiotics work? When a person consumes a product containing probiotics, these bacteria adhere to the intestinal wall for a few days. Once attached to the intestinal wall, the bacteria can exert their beneficial actions. The activity of these bacteria is short lived, and they probably need to be consumed on a daily basis to benefit human health. The exact mechanism of how probiotics work is currently being researched. It is believed that different types of bacteria provide benefits in different ways: some crowd out harmful bacterial, viral, and fungal species; some produce nutrients and other substances that influence nutrition and health; and others appear to influence our immune system.[21] Although there is still limited research on whether probiotics can really improve immune function and overall health in humans, there is promising evidence that probiotics may be beneficial in the following conditions:[21–23]

Consuming Activia yogurt may improve bowel function.

- Diarrhea caused by certain infectious microorganisms (rotavirus, *Clostridium difficile*, and so on) or associated with use of antibiotic medications
- Infections in infants and children in day care
- Irritable bowel syndrome and inflammatory bowel diseases
- Infection from *Helicobacter pylori*, the bacteria associated with peptic ulcers, gastritis, and gastric cancer
- Urinary and genital tract infections in women
- Atopic dermatitis (eczema) in children
- Lactose intolerance
- Reducing the risk of allergies in infants

It is important to remember that in order to be effective, foods must provide a minimum number of bacteria. While the exact number of bacteria is not known, it is estimated that a daily dose of at least 1 billion to 10 billion bacteria is needed to be effective.[24] Because these live cultures can survive only for a limited period of time, foods and supplements containing probiotics have a limited shelf life, and these products must be properly stored and consumed within a relatively brief period of time to receive maximal benefit.

At this time, there are no national standards for identifying the level of active bacteria in foods or supplements.

prebiotics Types of fiber that beneficial intestinal bacteria thrive on.

In the United States, the National Yogurt Association has established a "Live Active Culture" seal, which indicates that the yogurt contains an adequate amount of active bacteria per gram.

Prebiotics are food components related to probiotics. These are types of fiber naturally found in fruits, vegetables, and whole grains that promote the growth of friendly bacteria. Inulin and oligofructose are the most widely studied. Prebiotics can be added to functional foods, typically to those that contain probiotics. For example, yogurt manufacturer Stonyfield Farm states that the prebiotic inulin in its yogurt "increases calcium absorption . . . by as much as 20%," and its Web site lists numerous studies to support this claim.

Some food manufacturers are employing researchers to find and cultivate strains of probiotic bacteria that have specific health benefits. For example, Activia, a yogurt recently introduced by Dannon, contains a probiotic species called *Bifidus regularis*. The company states that this species promotes regular bowel movements by reducing the time stool stays in the colon. As you learned in Chapter 3, the longer fecal matter remains in the colon, the more water is removed from it, so reduced transit time means softer bowel movements. Is this claim valid?

If you check out the research cited on Dannon's Web site (www.activia.com), you'll discover that four studies on Activia and *Bifidus regularis* have been published in peer-reviewed journals. The studies found that consuming three 4-oz servings of Activia a day for 10 to 14 days sped up stool transit time by 10% to 40%. This effect was seen in men and women, and in both young (mid-20s) and older (up to 75 years) subjects. Although benefits were seen with just one 4-oz serving a day, the biggest benefits were seen with 2 or 3 daily servings. Convinced? If constipation were a problem for you, what further questions might you want to ask to determine whether or not this product would be worth purchasing?

Extraordinary Eggs

In the Nutrition Debate in Chapter 1, you learned that the diet fed to agouti mice could influence the constitution of their offspring. Similarly, the diet fed to hens can influence the nutrients present in their eggs. Feeding chickens a diet rich in omega-3 fatty acids, vitamin E, or lutein results in eggs that contain these substances. Such eggs can cost twice as much per dozen as conventional eggs. Are they worth the cost?

It is unclear whether eggs enriched with omega-3s or vitamin E are better for us, but there's no question that they are more expensive.

"I've always bought the store brand of eggs—or whatever is on sale. But yesterday, Hannah told me that we should be buying these new so-called healthy eggs. She says they feed the hens some kind of fish oil that's good for heart disease, and it gets into the eggs the hens lay. I asked her what these fancy eggs cost and she said she wasn't sure, so I checked them out at the store today. I couldn't believe my eyes! They're more than twice as much as the store brand! I told Hannah that, until they put their price down, they can keep their fishy eggs."

Do you think Judy should switch from local eggs to the new "functional food" eggs? Why or why not? What else could Judy do to reduce her risk of heart disease?

As you learned in Chapter 5, increased intake of omega-3 fatty acids may be important in reducing the risk of cardiovascular disease.[25–27] Typically, the positive effects are seen in clinical trials with a precisely controlled high omega-3 intake. Would the level of omega-3s in these eggs confer health benefits? We simply don't have the research to answer this question. Nevertheless, small doses of omega-3s via foods can certainly add up.

What about vitamin E? We know that diets with plenty of vitamin E–rich foods (nuts and dark-green leafy vegetables) are associated with better health, but research on vitamin E supplements has found no benefits at all.[4, 28] Thus, there is no evidence to support recommending vitamin E–enriched eggs for disease prevention.

Lutein is a phytochemical found in many green and yellow plants. Lutein and zeaxanthin are the only carotenoids found in the retina and lens of the eye. Epidemiological studies suggest that diets rich in lutein and zeaxanthin (providing about 6 mg/day) may help slow the development of age-related macular degeneration. However, it is not known whether consuming eggs with lutein has the same effect.[5]

Extra Dark Chocolate

You've just finished lunch when a friend offers you a piece of her extra dark chocolate bar. Should you, or shouldn't you? Recently, the results from a number of laboratory and clinical studies have suggested you *should*. Here's why.

Certain fruits, vegetables, tea, and red wine have long been associated with lower cardiovascular disease (CVD) risk. These foods are especially rich in a class of antioxidant phytochemicals called flavonoids. Cocoa has been found to have

Chocolate is high in flavonoids.

greater amounts of flavonoids per serving than teas and red wines, as well as many fruits and vegetables.[29] The darker the chocolate, the more flavonoids per serving. Thus, research interest in the potential effects of chocolate—especially dark chocolate—on CVD risk has grown.

Dozens of human feeding trials have been conducted since 2000. Most have shown that daily doses of cocoa have positive effects on one or more CVD risk factors, including improvements in blood lipids and blood pressure.[29] Several studies have shown benefits from consuming as little as 30 calories of dark chocolate daily.[30] In response, some chocolate manufacturers have produced specialty brands of "extra dark chocolate" with increased amounts of "antioxidant-rich cocoa."

So what's the hitch? One is that not all studies show the same effects. The variability in response is likely due to differences in the subjects' health and age and in the dose they consumed. And we can't ignore the fact that chocolate contains sugar and fat: some studies have fed subjects about 100 grams (3 oz) of chocolate per day, which can deliver over 400 extra calories to the diet!

Which raises a question that chocolate lovers would probably prefer to ignore: to reduce our risk of CVD, do we need to eat chocolate at all? Why not apples, for example, which contain 50% more flavonoids than a comparable serving of dark chocolate, only about 60 calories each, and no fat?[29]

For now, it seems likely that cocoa has positive health effects mediated by phytochemicals. So when debating whether or not to indulge in a small dose of extra dark chocolate, consider your diet as a whole: do you consume a wide variety of unrefined plant foods each day? If you do, then a little chocolate might be a sensible indulgence.

Calorie-Burning Beverages

Enviga is one of several so-called "calorie-burning beverages" recently brought onto the market. The manufacturers of these beverages claim that they increase the consumer's metabolic rate, causing the body to burn additional calories, and that the effect lasts for several hours after consuming the beverage. The Enviga Web site (www.enviga.com/#Science) states that a clinical trial found that, on average, participants expended 106 more calories per day after consuming 3 servings of Enviga for 3 days. The study was conducted in 2004 and has now been published in a peer-reviewed journal.[31] Although the Enviga study has not been repeated, allowing it to be reviewed suggests it is sound.

Why, then, does the Center for Science in the Public Interest (CSPI), a consumer advocacy group, contend in a lawsuit that the claims made for Enviga are fraudulent?[32] Here are some of the claims challenged by the CSPI: Enviga is "much smarter than fads, quick-fixes, and crash diets." It keeps "those extra calories from building up," and there is a "calorie burning effect from a single can." The CSPI is challenging these claims because not one of them was substantiated by the clinical trial.

Is it safe? Enviga contains caffeine and *epigallocatechin gallate* (*EGCG*), a phytochemical that occurs in green tea. No negative effects have been seen with EGCG. The ingredient of concern is caffeine. Three cans of Enviga provide 300 mg of caffeine, which is the caffeine equivalent of nine cans of Coke. This level of caffeine intake is generally not recommended.[33] (Caffeine is discussed in more detail in Chapters 13 and 14.)

Is Enviga worth the cost? The Web site states that three cans would boost one's metabolism by 60 to 100 calories per day. At an average cost of about $1.39 per 12-oz can, drinking the effective dose of Enviga would cost about

Enviga claims to burn extra calories.

$130 a month! In comparison, you could brew coffee containing the same amount of caffeine for less than $10 a month. Even better, you could burn more calories free of charge by running 1 mile a day (about 106 calories for a 132-pound person), and you'd get all of the other health benefits of exercise to boot!

Are You Ready to Choose Functional Foods?

As these examples show, when it comes to functional foods, "Let the buyer beware." If you're considering specific products, do you know enough about their safety and effectiveness to feel confident adding them to your daily diet? Do you support the FDA proposal to more strictly regulate the health claims and safety of functional foods? How do you think food labels could be improved to assist you in identifying foods that might be beneficial for your specific health concerns? As the number of functional foods increases in the U.S. market, these are just some of the questions that consumers need to answer.

Web Links

http://nccam.nih.gov/health/probiotics
National Center for Complementary and Alternative Medicine
This brochure, called "An Introduction to Probiotics," provides additional info on probiotics.

www.aicr.org
American Institute for Cancer Research
Search for "phytochemicals" to learn about the AICR's stance and recommendations about phytochemicals and their roles in cancer prevention.

http://lpi.oregonstate.edu
Linus Pauling Institute
This extensive Web site covers not only phytochemicals but also nutrients and other cutting-edge health and nutrition topics.

References

1. Liu, R. H. 2003. Health benefits of fruit and vegetables are from additive and synergistic combinations of phytochemicals. *Am. J. Clin. Nutr.* 78(suppl.):517S–520S.
2. Panel on Dietary Antioxidants and Related Compounds. Subcommittee on Upper Reference Levels of Nutrients and

Interpretation and Uses of Dietary Reference Intakes. Standing Committee on the Scientific Evaluation of Dietary Reference Intakes. Food and Nutrition Board. Institute of Medicine. 2000. *Dietary Reference Intakes for Vitamin C, Vitamin E, Selenium, and Carotenoids.* Washington, DC: National Academies Press.

3. Chun, O. K., et al. 2007. Estimated dietary flavonoid intake and major food sources of US adults. *J. Nutr.* 137:1244–1252.

4. Melton, L. 2006. The antioxidant myth: A medical fairy tale. *New Sci.* 2563:40–43.

5. Linus Pauling Institute, Oregon State University. 2005. Micronutrient information center: Flavonoids. Available at http://lpi.oregonstate.edu/infocenter/phytochemicals/flavonoids/. (Accessed July 2007.)

6. Beauchamp, G. K., R. S. Keast, D. Morel, J. Lin, J. Pika, Q. Han, C. H. Lee, A. B. Smith, and P. A. Breslin. 2005. Ibuprofen-like activity in extra virgin olive oil. *Nature* 437:45–46.

7. Liu, R. H. 2004. Potential synergy of phytochemicals in cancer prevention: Mechanism of action. *J. Nutr.* 134:3479S–3485S.

8. Boileau, T. W.-M., et al. 2003. Prostate carcinogenesis in N-methyl-N-nitrosurea (NMU)-testosterone-treated rats fed tomato powder, lycopene, and energy-restricted diets. *J. Natl. Cancer Inst.* 95:1578–1586.

9. Milner, J. A. 2001. A historical perspective on garlic and cancer. *J. Nutr.* 131:1027S–1031S.

10. Rice S., and S. A. Whitehead. 2006. Phytoestrogens and breast cancer—promoters or protectors? *Endocr. Relat. Cancer* 13(4):995–1015.

11. Meyskens, F. L., and E. Szabo. 2005. Diet and cancer: The disconnect between epidemiology and randomized clinical trials. *Cancer Epidemiol. Biomarkers Prev.* 14(6):1366–1369.

12. The Alpha-Tocopherol, Beta-Carotene Cancer Prevention Study Group. 1994. The effect of vitamin E and beta carotene on the incidence of lung cancer and other cancers in male smokers. *N. Engl. J. Med.* 330(15):1029–1035.

13. Omenn, G. S., et al. 1996. Risk factors for lung cancer and for intervention effects in CARET, the Beta-Carotene and Retinol Efficacy Trial. *J. Natl. Cancer Inst.* 88(21):1550–1559.

14. U.S. Preventive Services Task Force. 2003. Routine vitamin supplementation to prevent cancer and cardiovascular disease: Recommendations and rationale. *Ann. Intern. Med.* 139(1):51–55.

15. Baur, J. A., et al. 2006. Resveratrol improves health and survival of mice on a high-calorie diet. *Nature* 444:337–342.

16. Lagouge, M., et al. 2006. Resveratrol improves mitochondrial function and protects against metabolic disease by activating SIRT1 and PGC-1alpha. *Cell* 27(6):1109–1122.

17. Institute of Food Technologists. Functional foods: Opportunities and challenges. *IFT Expert Report.* Available at http://members.ift.org/NR/rdonlyres/4D40132D-B06B-4F2B-9753-CE18B73E187E/0/OnePagerIntro.pdf.

18. Committee on Opportunities in the Nutrition and Food Sciences, Food and Nutrition Board, Institute of Medicine, Thomas, P. R., and R. Earl (eds.). 1994. *Opportunities in the Nutrition and Food Sciences: Research, Challenges and the Next Generation of Investigators.* Washington, DC: National Academies Press.

19. *Federal Register*, October 25, 2006 (Volume 71, Number 206). From the Federal Register Online via GPO Access [wais.access.gpo.gov] [DOCID:fr25oc06-12] Food and Drug Administration, HHS; 21 CFR Parts 101 and 170 [Docket No. 2002P-0122] (formerly 02P-0122). Conventional Foods Being Marketed as "Functional Foods"; Public Hearing; Request for Comments.

20. U.S. Food and Drug Administration (FDA). 2006. Docket No. 2006D-0480. Draft Guidance for Industry on Complementary and Alternative Medicine Products and Their Regulation by the Food and Drug Administration.

21. Saier, M. H., Jr., and N. M. Mansour. 2005. Probiotics and prebiotics in human health. *J. Mol. Microbiol. Biotechnol.* 10(1):22–25.

22. Doron, S., and S. L. Gorbach. 2006. Probiotics: Their role in the treatment and prevention of diseases. *Expert Rev. Anti-Infect. Ther.* 4(2):261–275.

23. Ezendam, J., and H. van Loveren. 2006. Probiotics: Immunomodulation and evaluation of safety and efficacy. *Nutr. Rev.* 64(1):1–14.

24. Sanders, M. E., D. C. Walker, K. M. Walker, K. Aoyama, and T. R. Klaenhammer. 1996. Performance of commercial cultures in fluid milk applications. *J. Dairy Sci.* 79:943–955.

25. American Heart Association. 2007. Fish and omega-3 fatty acids: AHA recommendation. Available at www.americanheart.org/presenter.jhtml?identifier=4632. (Accessed July 2007.)

26. Center for Food Safety and Applied Nutrition. 2004. Questions and answers: Qualified health claims for omega-3 fatty acids, eicosapentaenoic acid (EPA) and docosahexaenoic acid (DHA). CFSAN/Office of Nutritional Products, Labeling, and Dietary Supplements. Available at /www.cfsan.fda.gov/~dms/labo3qa.html. (Accessed July 2007.)

27. National Heart, Lung, and Blood Institute, NIH, DHHS. 2005. Your guide to lowering cholesterol with therapeutic lifestyle changes (TLC). Available at www.nhlbi.nih.gov/health/public/heart/chol/chol_tlc.pdf. (Accessed July 2007.)

28. Friedrich, M. J. 2004. To "E" or not to "E," vitamin E's role in health and disease is the question. *JAMA* 292(6):671–673.

29. Ding, E. L., S. M. Hutfless, X. Ding, and S. Girotra. 2006. Chocolate and prevention of cardiovascular disease: A systematic review. *Nutr. Metab.* 3:2. Available at www.nutritionandmetabolism.com/content/3/1/2.

30. Taubert, D., et al. 2007. Effects of low habitual cocoa intake on blood pressure and bioactive nitric oxide: A randomized controlled trial. *JAMA* 298(1):49–60.

31. Rudelle, S., et al. 2007. Effect of a thermogenic beverage on 24-hour energy metabolism in humans. *Obesity* 15(2):349–355.

32. Center for Science in the Public Interest. 2006. "Calorie burning" Enviga tea drink a fraud, group says. CSPI to sue Coke, Nestlé if weight loss claims persist. Press release: December 4, 2006. Available at www.cspinet.org/new/200612041.html. (Accessed July 2007.)

33. McGee, W. 2005. Caffeine in the diet. Medline Plus Medical Encyclopedia. Available at www.nlm.nih.gov/medlineplus/ency/article/002445.htm. (Accessed July 2007.)

11 Nutrients Involved in Bone Health

Test Yourself | True or False?

1 Most people are unable to consume enough calcium in their diets; therefore, they must take calcium supplements. **T** *or* **F**

2 Osteoporosis is a disease that affects only elderly women. **T** *or* **F**

3 We are capable of making vitamin D within our bodies by using energy obtained from exposure to sunlight. **T** *or* **F**

4 Dairy products must be consumed to meet the current dietary recommendations for calcium. **T** *or* **F**

5 Being overweight or obese may increase a person's risk for osteoporosis. **T** *or* **F**

Test Yourself answers are located in the Chapter Review.

Chapter Objectives *After reading this chapter, you will be able to:*

1. Discuss the processes of bone growth, modeling, and remodeling, *pp. 411–412.*

2. Describe three methods used to measure bone density, *pp. 413–414.*

3. List and describe the functions of two vitamins and three minerals that play important roles in maintaining bone health, *pp. 414–432.*

4. Identify foods that are good sources of calcium, *pp. 417–418.*

5. Delineate the process by which the body synthesizes vitamin D from exposure to sunlight, and explain why the geographic region where people live affects their ability to do so, *pp. 421–423.*

6. Describe how vitamin D assists in regulating blood calcium levels, *pp. 415, 421.*

7. Explain why consumption of soft drinks may be detrimental to bone health, *p. 428.*

8. Define osteoporosis, discuss how it affects a person's health, and list three reasons women are at greater risk than men for this disease, *pp. 432–434.*

As a young woman, Erika Goodman leapt across the stage in leading roles with the Joffrey Ballet, one of the premier dance companies in the world. But at the age of 59, she died after falling in her Manhattan apartment. Goodman had a disease called *osteoporosis*, which means "porous bone." As you might suspect, the less dense the bone, the more likely it is to break; indeed, osteoporosis can cause bones to break during even minor weight-bearing activities, such as carrying groceries. In advanced cases, bones in the hip and spine fracture spontaneously, merely from the effort of holding the body erect.

If you are age 20 or older, your bones are already at or close to their peak density. But just how dense are your bones, and what changes can you make right now, no matter what your age, to keep them as strong as possible? What foods build bone? Are there foods that accelerate its breakdown? In this chapter, we discuss the nutrients and lifestyle factors that play a critical role in maintaining bone health.

How Does the Body Maintain Bone Health?

Contrary to what most people think, the skeleton is not an inactive collection of bones that simply holds the body together. Bones are living organs that contain several tissues, including bone tissue, nerves, cartilage, and connective tissue. Blood vessels supply nutrients to bone to support its activities. Bones have many important functions in the body, some of which might surprise you (Table 11.1). For instance, did you know that most blood cells are formed deep within the bones?

Given the importance of bones, it is critical that we maintain their health. Bone health is achieved through complex interactions among nutrients, hormones, and environmental factors. To better understand these interactions, we first need to learn about bone structure and the constant activity of bone cells.

The Composition of Bone Provides Strength and Flexibility

We tend to think of bones as totally rigid, but if they were, how could we play basketball or even carry an armload of books up a flight of stairs? Bones need to be both strong and flexible so they can resist the compression, stretching, and twisting that occur throughout our daily activities. Fortunately, the composition of bone is ideally suited for its complex job: About 65% of bone tissue is made up of an assortment of minerals (mostly calcium and phosphorus) that provide hardness, but the remaining 35% is a mixture of organic substances that provide strength, durability, and flexibility. The most important of these substances is a fibrous protein called **collagen.** You might be surprised to learn that collagen fibers are actually stronger than steel fibers of similar size. Within bones, the minerals form tiny crystals (called *hydroxyapatite*) that cluster around the collagen fibers. This design enables bones to bear weight while responding to demands for movement.

Bone strength and flexibility are also affected by its structure. If you examine a bone very closely, you will notice two distinct types of tissue (**Figure 11.1**): cortical bone and trabecular bone. **Cortical bone,** which is also called *compact bone*, is very dense. It comprises approximately 80% of the skeleton. The outer surface of all bones is cortical; plus many small bones of the body are made entirely of cortical bone. Although cortical bone looks

collagen A protein that forms strong fibers in bone and connective tissue.

cortical bone (compact bone) A dense bone tissue that makes up the outer surface of all bones, as well as the entirety of most small bones of the body.

Table 11.1 Functions of Bone in the Human Body

Functions Related to Structure and Support	Functions Related to Metabolic Processes
Bones provide physical support for our organs and body segments.	Bone tissue acts as a storage reservoir for many minerals, including calcium, phosphorus, and fluoride. The body draws upon such deposits when these minerals are needed for various body processes; however, this can reduce bone mass.
Bones protect our vital organs; for example, the rib cage protects our lungs, the skull protects our brains, and the vertebrae in the spine protect the spinal cord.	Most of the blood cells needed by our bodies are produced in the marrow of our bones.
Bones provide support for muscles that allow movement—muscles attach to bones via tendons, and we are able to move all of our joints because of the connections between our muscles and our bones.	

solid to the naked eye, it actually contains many microscopic openings that serve as passageways for blood vessels and nerves.

In contrast, **trabecular bone** makes up only 20% of the skeleton. It is found within the ends of the long bones (such as the bones of the arms and legs), and inside the spinal vertebrae, the breastbone, ribs, most bones of the skull, and the bones of the pelvis. Trabecular bone is sometimes referred to as *spongy bone* because to the naked eye it looks like a sponge, with no clear organization. The microscope reveals that trabecular bone is in fact aligned in a precise network of columns that protects the bone from stress. You can think of trabecular bone as the scaffolding of the inside of the bone that supports the outer cortical bone.

Cortical and trabecular bone also differ in their rate of turnover—that is, in how quickly the bone tissue is broken down and replenished. Trabecular bone has a faster turnover rate than cortical bone. This makes trabecular bone more sensitive to changes in hormones and nutritional deficiencies. It also accounts for the much higher rate of age-related fractures in the spine and pelvis (including the hip)—all of which contain a significant amount of trabecular bone. Let's now investigate how bone turnover, or the constant activity of bone, influences bone health.

Figure 11.1   The structure of bone. Notice the difference in density between the trabecular (spongy) bone and the cortical (compact) bone.

The Constant Activity of Bone Tissue Promotes Bone Health

Bones develop through a series of three processes: bone growth, bone modeling, and bone remodeling (**Figure 11.2**). Bone growth and modeling begin during the early months of fetal life when the skeleton is forming and continue until early adulthood Bone remodeling predominates during adulthood; this process helps to maintain a healthy skeleton as one ages.

Bone Growth and Modeling Determine the Size and Shape of Our Bones

Through the process of *bone growth,* the size of bones increases. The first period of rapid bone growth is from birth to age 2, but growth continues in spurts throughout childhood and into adolescence. Most girls reach their adult height by age 14, and boys generally reach adult height by age 17.[1] In the later decades of life, some loss in height usually occurs because of decreased bone density in the spine, as will be discussed shortly.

Bone modeling is the process by which the shape of bones is determined, from the round "pebble" bones that make up the wrists, to the uniquely shaped bones of the face, to the long bones of the arms and legs. Even after bones stop growing in length, they can still increase in thickness if they are stressed by repetitive exercise such as weight training or by being overweight or obese.

Bone Remodeling Maintains a Balance Between Breakdown and Repair

Although the shape and size of bones do not significantly change after puberty, **bone density,** or the compactness of bones, continues to develop into early adulthood. *Peak bone density* is the point at which bones are strongest because they are at their highest density. Factors associated with a lower peak bone density include: late pubertal age in

trabecular bone   (spongy or cancellous bone) A porous bone tissue that makes up only 20% of the skeleton and is found within the ends of the long bones, inside the spinal vertebrae, inside the flat bones (breastbone, ribs, and most bones of the skull), and inside the bones of the pelvis.

bone density   The degree of compactness of bone tissue, reflecting the strength of the bones. Peak bone density is the point at which a bone is strongest.

Figure 11.2   Bone develops through three processes: bone growth, bone modeling, and bone remodeling.

boys and late onset of menstruation in girls; inadequate calcium intake; low body weight; and physical inactivity during the pubertal years.[2–4] About 90% of a woman's bone density is built by 17 years of age, whereas the majority of a man's bone density is built during his twenties. However, male or female, before we reach the age of 30 years, our bodies have reached peak bone mass, and we can no longer significantly add to our bone density. In our thirties, our bone density remains relatively stable, but by age 40, it begins its irreversible decline.

Although bones cannot increase in density after our twenties without medication, bone cells remain very active throughout adulthood, balancing the breakdown of older bone tissue and the formation of new bone tissue. This bone recycling process is called **remodeling.** Remodeling is also used to repair fractures and to strengthen bone regions that are exposed to higher physical stress. The process of remodeling involves two steps: resorption and formation.

Bone is broken down through a process referred to as **resorption** (**Figure 11.3a**). During resorption, cells called **osteoclasts** erode the bone surface by secreting enzymes and acids that dig grooves into the bone matrix. Their ruffled surface also acts somewhat like a scrubbing brush to assist in the erosion process. One of the primary reasons the body regularly breaks down bone is to release calcium into the bloodstream. As discussed in more detail later in this chapter, calcium is critical for many physiologic processes, and bone is an important calcium reservoir. The body also breaks down bone that is fractured and needs to be repaired. Resorption at the injury site smooths the rough edges created by the break. Bone may also be broken down in areas away from the fracture site to obtain the minerals that are needed to repair the damage. Regardless of the reason, once bone is broken down, the resulting products are transported into the bloodstream and utilized for various body functions.

New bone is formed through the action of cells called **osteoblasts,** or "bone builders" (see Figure 11.3b). These cells work to synthesize new bone matrix by laying down the collagen-containing organic component of bone. Within this substance, the hydroxyapatite crystallizes and packs together to create new bone where it is needed.

In young healthy adults, the processes of bone resorption and formation are equal, so that just as much bone is broken down as is built, resulting in bone mass being maintained. Around 40 years of age, bone resorption begins to occur more rapidly than bone formation, and this imbalance results in an overall loss in bone density. Because this affects the vertebrae of the spine, people tend to lose height as they age. As discussed shortly, achieving a high peak bone mass through proper nutrition and exercise when one is young provides for a stronger skeleton before the loss of bone begins, and it can be protective against the debilitating effects of osteoporosis.

remodeling   The two-step process by which bone tissue is recycled; includes the breakdown of existing bone and the formation of new bone.

resorption   The process by which the surface of bone is broken down by cells called osteoclasts.

osteoclasts   Cells that erode the surface of bones by secreting enzymes and acids that dig grooves into the bone matrix.

osteoblasts   Cells that prompt the formation of new bone matrix by laying down the collagen-containing component of bone that is then mineralized.

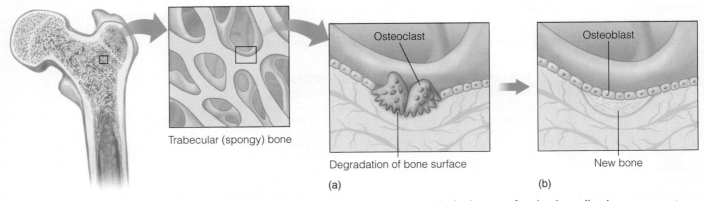

Trabecular (spongy) bone

Osteoclast

Degradation of bone surface

(a)

Osteoblast

New bone

(b)

Figure 11.3   Bone remodeling involves resorption and formation. **(a)** Osteoclasts erode the bone surface by degrading its components, including calcium, other minerals, and collagen; these components are then transported to the bloodstream. **(b)** Osteoblasts work to build new bone by filling the pit formed by the resorption process with new bone.

Recap

Bones are organs that contain metabolically active tissues composed primarily of minerals and a fibrous protein called collagen. Of the two types of bone, cortical bone is more dense and trabecular bone is more porous. Trabecular bone is also more sensitive to hormonal and nutritional factors and turns over more rapidly than cortical bone. The three types of bone activity are growth, modeling, and remodeling. Bones reach their peak bone mass by the late teenage years into the twenties; bone mass begins to decline around age 40.

How Do We Assess Bone Health?

Over the past 30 years, technological advancements have led to the development of a number of affordable methods for measuring bone health. **Dual energy x-ray absorptiometry,** also referred to as DXA (or DEXA), is considered the most accurate assessment tool for measuring bone density. This method can measure the density of the bone mass over the entire body. Special software is also available that provides an estimation of percentage of body fat.

The DXA procedure is simple, painless, noninvasive, and considered to be of minimal risk to humans. It takes only 15 to 30 minutes to complete. The person participating in the test remains fully clothed but must remove all jewelry or other metal objects. The participant lies quietly on a table, and bone density is assessed through the use of a very low level of x-ray (**Figure 11.4**).

DXA is a very important tool to determine a person's risk for osteoporosis. It generates a bone density score that is compared to the average peak bone density of a 30-year-old healthy adult. Doctors use this comparison, which is known as the **T-score,** to assess the risk of fracture and determine whether or not the person has osteoporosis. If bone density is normal, the T-score will range between $+1$ and -1 of the value for a 30-year-old healthy adult. A negative T-score between -1 and -2.5 indicates low bone mass and an increased risk for fractures. If the T-score is more negative than -2.5, the person has osteoporosis.

dual energy x-ray absorptiometry (DXA, or DEXA) Currently the most accurate tool for measuring bone density.
T-score A comparison of an individual's bone density to the average peak bone density of a 30-year-old healthy adult.

Figure 11.4 Dual energy x-ray absorptiometry is a safe and simple procedure that assesses bone density.

DXA tests are generally recommended for postmenopausal women because they are at highest risk for osteoporosis and fracture. Men and younger women may also be recommended for a DXA test if they have significant risk factors for osteoporosis (see pages 433–435).

Other technologies have been developed to measure bone density. The quantitative ultrasound technique uses sound waves to measure the density of bone in the heel, shin, and kneecap. Peripheral dual energy x-ray absorptiometry, or pDXA, is a form of DXA that measures bone density in the peripheral regions of our bodies, including the wrist, heel, or finger. Single energy x-ray absorptiometry is a method that measures bone density at the wrist or heel. These technologies are frequently used at health fairs because the machines are portable and provide scores faster than the traditional DXA.

RecaP

Dual energy x-ray absorptiometry (DXA or DEXA) is the gold-standard measurement of bone mass. It is a simple, painless, and minimal-risk procedure. The results of a DXA include a T-score, which is a comparison of the person's bone density with that of a 30-year-old healthy adult. A T-score between +1 and −1 is normal; a score between −1 and −2.5 indicates poor bone density; and a score more negative than −2.5 indicates osteoporosis. Quantitative ultrasound, peripheral dual energy x-ray absorptiometry, and single energy x-ray absorptiometry are additional methods that can be used to measure bone density.

A Profile of Nutrients That Maintain Bone Health

Calcium is the most recognized nutrient associated with bone health; however, vitamins D and K, phosphorus, magnesium, and fluoride are also essential for strong bones, and the roles of other vitamins, minerals, and phytochemicals are currently being researched.

Calcium

One major role of calcium is to form and maintain bones and teeth.

Dietary calcium is absorbed in the intestines via active transport and passive diffusion across the intestinal mucosal membrane. The majority of calcium consumed in the diet is absorbed from the duodenum, as this area of the small intestine is slightly more acidic than the more distal regions, and calcium absorption is enhanced in an acidic environment. Active transport of calcium is dependent upon the active form of vitamin D, or 1,25-dihydroxyvitamin D; most of the absorption of calcium at low to moderate intake levels is accounted for by this vitamin D–enhanced active transport. Passive diffusion of calcium across the intestinal mucosal membrane is a function of the calcium concentration gradient in the intestines, and this mechanism becomes a more important means of calcium absorption at high calcium intakes.[5]

Calcium is by far the most abundant major mineral in the body, comprising about 2% of our entire body weight! Not surprisingly, it plays many critical roles in maintaining overall function and health.

Functions of Calcium

One of the primary roles of calcium is to provide structure to the bones and teeth. About 99% of the calcium found in the body is stored in the hydroxyapatite crystals built up on the collagen foundation of bone. As noted earlier, the combination of crystals and collagen provides both the characteristic hardness of bone and the flexibility needed to support various activities.

The remaining 1% of calcium in the body is found in the blood and soft tissues. Calcium is alkaline, or basic, and plays a critical role in assisting with acid–base balance. We cannot survive for long if our blood calcium level rises above or falls below a very narrow range; therefore, the body maintains the appropriate blood calcium level at all costs.

(a)   (b)

Figure 11.5 Regulation of blood calcium levels by various organs and hormones. **(a)** Low blood calcium levels stimulate the production of parathyroid hormone and activation of vitamin D, which in turn causes an increase in blood calcium levels. **(b)** High blood calcium levels stimulate the secretion of calcitonin, which in turn causes a decrease in blood calcium levels.

Figure 11.5 illustrates how various organ systems and hormones work together to maintain blood calcium levels. When blood calcium levels fall (Figure 11.5a), the parathyroid glands are stimulated to produce **parathyroid hormone (PTH).** Also known as parathormone, PTH stimulates the activation of vitamin D. Together, PTH and vitamin D stimulate the kidneys to reabsorb calcium. They also stimulate osteoclasts to break down bone, releasing more calcium into the bloodstream. In addition, vitamin D increases the absorption of calcium from the intestines. Through these three mechanisms, blood calcium levels increase.

When blood calcium levels are too high, the thyroid gland secretes a hormone called **calcitonin,** which inhibits the actions of vitamin D (Figure 11.5b). Thus, calcitonin prevents reabsorption of calcium in the kidneys, limits calcium absorption in the intestines, and inhibits the osteoclasts from breaking down bone.

As just noted, the body must maintain blood calcium levels within a very narrow range. Thus, when an individual does not consume or absorb enough calcium from the diet, osteoclasts erode bone so that calcium can be released into the blood. To maintain healthy bone density, we need to consume and absorb enough calcium to balance the calcium taken from our bones.

Calcium is also critical for the normal transmission of nerve impulses. Calcium flows into nerve cells and stimulates the release of molecules called neurotransmitters, which transfer the nerve impulses from one nerve cell (neuron) to another. Without adequate calcium, the nerves' ability to transmit messages is inhibited. Not surprisingly, when blood calcium levels fall dangerously low, a person can experience convulsions.

A fourth role of calcium is to assist in muscle contraction. Muscles are relaxed when calcium levels in the muscle are low. Contraction is stimulated by calcium flowing into the muscle cell; conversely, muscles relax when calcium is pumped back outside of the muscle cell. If calcium levels are inadequate, normal muscle contraction and relaxation is inhibited, and the person may suffer from twitching and spasms. This is referred to as **calcium tetany.**

parathyroid hormone (PTH) A hormone secreted by the parathyroid gland when blood calcium levels fall. It is also known as parathormone, and it increases blood calcium levels by stimulating the activation of vitamin D, increasing reabsorption of calcium from the kidneys, and stimulating osteoclasts to break down bone, which releases more calcium into the bloodstream.

calcitonin A hormone secreted by the thyroid gland when blood calcium levels are too high. Calcitonin inhibits the actions of vitamin D, preventing reabsorption of calcium in the kidneys, limiting calcium absorption in the intestines, and inhibiting the osteoclasts from breaking down bone.

calcium tetany A condition in which muscles experience twitching and spasms due to inadequate blood calcium levels.

Table 11.2 Overview of Nutrients Essential to Bone Health

To see the full profile of nutrients essential to bone health, turn to *In Depth*, Vitamins and Minerals: Micronutrients with Macro Powers, page 280.

Nutrient	Recommended Intake
Calcium (major mineral)	Adequate Intake (AI): Women and men aged 19 to 50 years = 1,000 mg/day Women and men aged >50 years = 1,200 mg/day
Vitamin D (fat-soluble vitamin)	AI:* Women and men aged 19 to 50 years = 5 µg /day Women and men aged 50 to 70 years = 10 µg /day Women and men aged >70 years = 15 µg /day
Vitamin K (fat-soluble vitamin)	AI: Women: 90 µg/day Men: 120 µg/day
Phosphorous (major mineral)	Recommended Dietary Allowance (RDA): Women and men = 700 mg/day
Magnesium (major mineral)	RDA: Women aged 19 to 30 years = 310 mg/day Women aged >30 years = 320 mg/day Men aged 19 to 30 years = 400 mg/day Men aged >30 years = 420 mg/day
Fluoride (trace mineral)	AI: Women: 3 mg/day Men: 4 mg/day

Based on the assumption that a person does not get adequate sun exposure.

calcium rigor A failure of muscles to relax, which leads to a hardening or stiffening of the muscles; caused by high levels of blood calcium.

bioavailability The degree to which our bodies can absorb and utilize any given nutrient.

High levels of blood calcium can cause **calcium rigor,** which results in a failure of muscles to relax and leads to a hardening or stiffening of the muscles. These problems affect the function not only of skeletal muscles but also of heart muscle and can cause heart failure.

A recent research study has suggested that a weight-loss diet high in calcium-rich foods may help people lose more weight than if they reduce their energy intake but do not consume enough dietary calcium.[6] This research has led to a major advertising campaign by the dairy industry, called the "3-A-Day" campaign. This campaign encourages people who want to lose weight to eat at least 3 servings of dairy foods per day, as study participants who ate calcium-rich foods experienced significantly more weight loss than those who consumed calcium supplements. Interestingly, Bowen and colleagues published a study that failed to replicate these findings.[7] Until more research is published on this topic, the question of whether dietary calcium can enhance weight loss in people who are dieting remains unanswered.

Other roles of calcium include the maintenance of healthy blood pressure, the initiation of blood clotting, and the regulation of various hormones and enzymes.

How Much Calcium Should We Consume?

Calcium requirements, and thus recommended intakes, vary according to age and gender. Many people, particularly adolescents and postmenopausal women, do not consume enough calcium to maintain bone health (Table 11.2).

Recommended Dietary Intake for Calcium There are no RDA values for calcium. The Adequate Intake (AI) value for adult men and women aged 19 to 50 years is 1,000 mg of calcium per day. For men and women older than 50 years of age, the AI increases to 1,200 mg of calcium per day. At 1,300 mg per day, the AI for boys and girls aged 15 to 18 years is even higher, reflecting their developing bone mass. The Upper Limit (UL) for calcium is 2,500 mg for all age groups.

The term **bioavailability** refers to the degree to which the body can absorb and utilize any given nutrient. The bioavailability of calcium depends in part on a person's age and his or her need for calcium. For example, infants, children, and adolescents can absorb more than 60% of the calcium they consume, as calcium needs are very high during these stages of life. In addition, pregnant and lactating women can absorb about 50% of dietary calcium. In contrast, healthy young adults only absorb about 30% of the calcium consumed in the diet. When calcium needs are high, the body can generally increase its absorption of calcium from the small intestine. Although older adults have a high need for calcium, their ability to absorb calcium from the small intestine diminishes with age and can be as low as 25%. These variations in bioavailability and absorption capacity were taken into account when calcium recommendations were determined.

The bioavailability of calcium also depends on how much calcium is consumed throughout the day or at any one time. When diets are generally high in calcium, absorption of calcium is reduced. In addition, the body cannot absorb more than 500 mg of calcium at any one time, and as the amount of calcium in a single meal or supplement goes up, the fraction that is absorbed goes down. This explains why it is critical to consume calcium-rich foods throughout the day rather than relying on a single high-dose supplement. Conversely, when dietary intake of calcium is low, the absorption of calcium is increased.

Dietary factors can also affect the absorption of calcium. Binding factors such as phytates and oxalates occur naturally in some calcium-rich seeds, nuts, grains, and vegetables such as spinach and Swiss chard. Such factors bind to the calcium in these foods and prevent its absorption from the intestine. Additionally, consuming calcium at the same time as iron, zinc, magnesium, or phosphorus has the potential to interfere with the absorption and utilization of all of these minerals. Despite these potential interactions, the Institute of Medicine concluded that at the present time, there is not sufficient evidence to suggest that these interactions cause deficiencies of calcium or other minerals in healthy individuals.[5]

However, there are people who are vulnerable to mineral deficiencies, such as the elderly or people consuming very low mineral intakes, and more research needs to be done in these populations to determine the health risks associated with interactions between calcium and other minerals.

Finally, because vitamin D is necessary for the absorption of calcium, lack of vitamin D severely limits the bioavailability of calcium. We discuss this and other contributions of vitamin D to bone health shortly.

Food Sources of Calcium Dairy products are among the most common sources of calcium in the U.S. diet. Skim milk, low-fat cheeses, and nonfat yogurt are excellent sources of calcium, and they are low in fat and calories (**Figure 11.6**). Ice cream, regular cheese, and whole milk also contain a relatively high amount of calcium, but these foods should be eaten in moderation because of their high saturated fat and energy content. Cottage cheese is one dairy product that is a relatively poor source of calcium, as the processing of this food removes a great deal of the calcium. One cup of low-fat cottage cheese contains approximately 150 mg of calcium, whereas the same serving of low-fat milk contains almost 300 mg. However, calcium-fortified cottage cheese has recently become available. One cup of calcium-fortified cottage cheese contains 400 mg of calcium.

Other good sources of calcium are green leafy vegetables such as kale, collard greens, turnip greens, broccoli, cauliflower, green cabbage, brussels sprouts, and Chinese cabbage (bok choy). The bioavailability of the calcium in these vegetables is relatively high compared with spinach, as they contain low levels of oxalates. Many packaged foods are now available fortified with calcium. For example, you can buy calcium-fortified orange juice,

Although spinach contains high levels of calcium, binding factors in the plant prevent much of its absorption.

Kale is a good source of calcium.

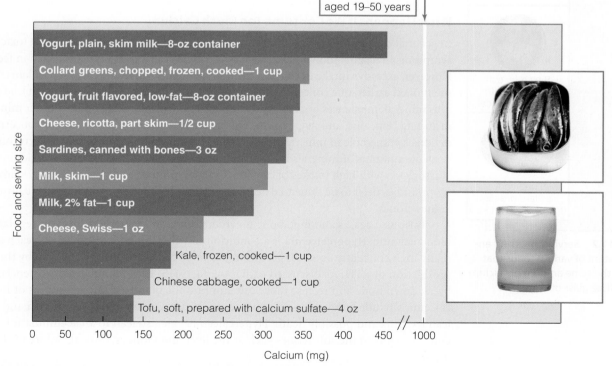

Figure 11.6 Common food sources of calcium. The AI for adult men and women aged 19 to 50 years is 1,000 mg of calcium per day. For men and women older than 50 years of age, the AI increases to 1,200 mg of calcium per day. (*Data from:* U.S. Department of Agriculture, Agricultural Research Service, 2008, USDA Nutrient Database for Standard Reference, Release 21. Nutrient Data Laboratory Home Page, www.ars.usda.gov/ba/bhnrc/ndl.)

6 cups lima beans
1255 kcal

5.4 oz plain,
skim milk yogurt
86 kcal

1.4 oz Swiss cheese
151 kcal

2.8 oz canned
sardines 165 kcal

9 oz tofu, soft
prepared with
calcium 165 kcal

7/8 cup cooked
collard greens
(from frozen) 54 kcal

8 fl. oz
skim milk
306 mg Ca
83 kcal

Figure 11.7 Serving sizes and energy content of various foods that contain the same amount of calcium as an 8-fl. oz glass of skim milk.

hypercalcemia A condition marked by an abnormally high concentration of calcium in the blood.

soy milk, rice milk, and tofu processed with calcium. Some dairies have even boosted the amount of calcium in their brand of milk!

Figure 11.7 illustrates serving sizes of various calcium-rich foods that contain the equivalent amount of calcium as one glass (8 fl. oz) of skim milk. As you can see from this figure, a wide variety of foods can be consumed each day to contribute to adequate calcium intakes. When you are selecting foods that are good sources of calcium, it is important to remember that we do not absorb 100% of the calcium contained in our foods.[8] For example, although a serving of milk contains approximately 300 mg of calcium, we do not actually absorb this entire amount into our bodies. To learn more about how calcium absorption rates vary for select foods, see the Nutrition Label Activity.

In general, meats and fish are not good sources of calcium. An exception is canned fish with bones (for example, sardines or salmon), providing you eat the bones. Fruits (except dried figs) and nonfortified grain products are also poor sources of calcium.

Although many foods in the U.S. diet are good sources of calcium, many Americans do not have adequate intakes because they consume very few dairy-based foods and calcium-rich vegetables. At particular risk are women and young girls. For example, a large national survey conducted by the U.S. Department of Agriculture found that teenage girls consumed less than 60% of the recommended amount of calcium.[9]

There are now quick, simple tools available to assist individuals in determining their daily calcium intake. Most of these tools are designed to estimate a calcium intake score or to calculate calcium intake based on the types and amounts of calcium-rich foods a person consumes. To estimate your calcium intake, go to the Calcium Quiz at www.dairycouncilofca.org/Tools/CalciumQuiz/Default.aspx.

If you do not consume enough dietary calcium, you will probably benefit from taking calcium supplements. Refer to the Highlight, "Calcium Supplements: Which Ones Are Best?" to learn how to choose a calcium supplement that is right for you.

What Happens If We Consume Too Much Calcium?

In general, consuming too much calcium in the diet does not lead to significant toxicity symptoms in healthy individuals. Much of the excess calcium is simply excreted in feces. However, excessive intake of calcium from supplements can lead to health problems.[10] As mentioned earlier, one concern with consuming too much calcium is that it can lead to various mineral imbalances because calcium interferes with the absorption of other minerals, including iron, zinc, and magnesium. This interference may only be of major concern in individuals vulnerable to mineral imbalance, such as the elderly and people who consume very low amounts of minerals in their diets. In some people, the formation of kidney stones is associated with high intakes of calcium, oxalates, protein, and vegetable fiber.[11] However, more studies need to be done to determine whether high intakes of calcium actually cause kidney stones.

Various diseases and metabolic disorders can alter the body's ability to regulate blood calcium. **Hypercalcemia** is a condition in which blood calcium levels reach abnormally high concentrations. Hypercalcemia can be caused by cancer and also by the overproduction of PTH. As discussed earlier on page 415, PTH stimulates the osteoclasts to break down bone and release more calcium into the bloodstream. Symptoms of hypercalcemia include fatigue, loss of appetite, constipation, and mental confusion and can lead to coma and possibly death. Hypercalcemia can also lead to an accumulation of calcium deposits in the soft tissues such as the liver and kidneys, causing failure of these organs.

What Happens If We Don't Consume Enough Calcium?

There are no short-term symptoms associated with consuming too little calcium. Even when a person does not consume enough dietary calcium, the body continues to tightly

Nutrition Label Activity
How Much Calcium Am I Really Consuming?

As you have learned in this chapter, we do not absorb 100% of the calcium contained in our foods. This is particularly true for individuals who eat a diet predominated by foods that are high in fiber, oxalates, and phytates, such as whole grains and certain vegetables. Thus, it is important to understand how the rate of calcium absorption differs for various foods as you design an eating plan that contains adequate calcium to optimize bone health.

How do you determine the amount of calcium you are absorbing from various foods? Unfortunately, the absorption rate of calcium has not been determined for most foods. However, estimates have been established for a variety of common foods that are considered good sources of calcium. The table in the next column shows some of these foods, their calcium content per serving, the calcium absorption rate, and the estimated amount of calcium absorbed from each food.

As you can see from this table, many dairy products have a similar calcium absorption rate, just over 30%. Interestingly, many green leafy vegetables have a higher absorption rate of around 60%; however, because a typical serving of these foods contains less calcium than dairy foods, you would have to eat more vegetables to get the same calcium as you would from a standard serving of dairy foods. Note the relatively low calcium absorption rate for spinach, even though it contains a relatively high amount of calcium. This is due to the high levels of oxalates in spinach, which bind with calcium and reduce its bioavailability.

Remember that the DRIs for calcium take these differences in absorption rate into account. Thus, the 300 mg of calcium in a glass of milk counts as 300 mg toward your daily calcium goal. In general, you can trust that dairy products such as milk and yogurt (but not cottage cheese) are good, absorbable sources of calcium, as are most dark-green, leafy vegetables. Other dietary sources of calcium with good absorption rates include calcium-fortified orange juice, soy milk, and rice milk, tofu processed with calcium, and fortified breakfast cereals such as Total and Special K.[8] Armed with this knowledge, you will be better able to select food sources that can optimize your calcium intake and support bone health.

Food	Serving Size	Calcium per Serving (mg)*	Absorption Rate (%)†	Estimated Amount of Calcium Absorbed (mg)
Yogurt, plain skim milk	8 fl. oz	452	32	145
Milk, skim	1 cup	306	32	98
Milk, 2%	1 cup	285	32	91
Kale, frozen, cooked	1 cup	179	59	106
Turnip greens, boiled	1 cup	197	52	103
Broccoli, frozen, chopped, cooked	1 cup	61	61	37
Cauliflower, boiled	1 cup	20	69	14
Spinach, frozen, cooked	1 cup	291	5	14

Data from: *U.S. Department of Agriculture, Agricultural Research Service. 2008. USDA National Nutrient Database for Standard Reference, Release 21. Available at www.ars.usda.gov/ba/bhnrc/ndl.† Weaver, C. M., W. R. Proulx, and R. Heaney. 1999. Choices for achieving adequate dietary calcium with a vegetarian diet. *Am. J. Clin. Nutr.* 70(suppl.):543S–548S; Weaver, C. M., and K. L. Plawecki. 1994. Dietary calcium: Adequacy of a vegetarian diet. *Am. J. Clin. Nutr.* 59(suppl.):1238S–1241S.

regulate blood calcium levels by taking the calcium from bone. A long-term repercussion of inadequate calcium intake is osteoporosis. But because other nutrients may be involved, we discuss this disease later in the chapter.

Hypocalcemia is a term that describes an abnormally low level of calcium in the blood. Hypocalcemia does not result from consuming too little dietary calcium but is caused by various diseases. Some of the causes of hypocalcemia include kidney disease, vitamin D deficiency, and diseases that inhibit the production of PTH. Symptoms of hypocalcemia include muscle spasms and convulsions.

hypocalcemia A condition characterized by an abnormally low concentration of calcium in the blood.

Highlight

Calcium Supplements: Which Ones Are Best?

We know that calcium is a critical nutrient for bone health. Now that so many products are fortified with calcium, from cereals and energy bars to orange juice and soy milk, it is not difficult for many people, even vegans, to get sufficient calcium from the diet. Still, small or inactive people who eat less to maintain a healthful weight may not be able to consume enough food to provide adequate calcium, and elderly people may need more calcium than they can obtain in their normal diets. In these circumstances, calcium supplements may be warranted.

Numerous calcium supplements are available to consumers, but which are best? Most supplements come in the form of calcium carbonate, calcium citrate, calcium lactate, or calcium phosphate. Our bodies are able to absorb about 30% of the calcium from these various forms. Calcium citrate malate, which is the form of calcium used in fortified juices, is slightly more absorbable at 35%. Many antacids are also good sources of calcium, and it appears these are safe to take as long as you only consume enough to get the recommended level of calcium.

What is the most cost-effective form of calcium? In general, supplements that contain calcium carbonate tend to have more calcium per pill than other types. Thus, you are getting more calcium for your money when you buy this type. However, be sure to read the label of any calcium supplement you are considering taking to determine just how much calcium it contains. Some very expensive calcium supplements do not contain a lot of calcium per pill, and you could be wasting your money.

The lead content of calcium supplements is an important public health concern. Those made from "natural" sources such as oyster shell, bone meal, and dolomite are known to be higher in lead, and some of these products can contain dangerously high levels. One study of 22 calcium supplements found that 8 (or 36%) of the supplements tested were unacceptably high in lead, including both oyster shell supplements and refined calcium carbonate.[10] Shockingly, the supplement with the highest lead content was a popular, nationally recognized brand-name supplement! To avoid taking supplements that contain too much lead, look for supplements claiming to be lead-free,[7] and make sure the word "purified" is on the label in addition to the U.S.P. (U.S. Pharmacopeia) symbol.

If you decide to use a calcium supplement, how should you take it? Remember that the body cannot absorb more than 500 mg of calcium at any given time. Thus, taking a supplement that contains 1,000 mg calcium will be no more effective than taking one that contains 500 mg calcium. If at all possible, try to consume calcium supplements in small doses throughout the day. In addition, calcium is absorbed better with meals, as the calcium stays in the intestinal tract longer during a meal and more calcium can be absorbed.

By consuming foods high in calcium throughout the day, you can avoid the need for calcium supplements. But if you cannot consume enough calcium in your diet, many inexpensive, safe, and effective supplements are available. The best supplement for you is the one that you can tolerate, is affordable, is lead-free, and is readily available when you need it.

Recap

Calcium is the most abundant mineral in the body and a significant component of bones. It is also necessary for normal nerve and muscle function. Blood calcium is maintained within a very narrow range, and bone calcium is used to maintain normal blood calcium if dietary intake is inadequate. The AI for calcium is 1,000 mg per day for adults aged 19 to 50; the AI increases to 1,200 mg per day for older adults and to 1,300 mg per day for adolescents. Dairy products, canned fish with bones, and some green leafy vegetables are good sources of calcium. The most common long-term effect of inadequate calcium consumption is osteoporosis.

Vitamin D

Vitamin D is like other fat-soluble vitamins in that excess amounts are stored in the liver and adipose tissue. But vitamin D is different from other nutrients in two ways. First, vitamin D does not always need to come from the diet. This is because the body can synthesize vitamin D using energy from exposure to sunlight. However, when we do not get enough sunlight, we must consume vitamin D in our diet. Second, in addition to being a nutrient, vitamin D is considered a *hormone* because it is made in one part of the body, yet regulates various activities in other parts of the body.

Figure 11.8 illustrates how the body makes vitamin D. When the ultraviolet rays of the sun hit the skin, they react with 7-dehydrocholesterol. This cholesterol compound is converted into a precursor of vitamin D, cholecalciferol, which is also called provitamin D_3. This inactive form is then converted to calcidiol in the liver, where it is stored. When needed, calcidiol travels to the kidneys where it is converted into **calcitriol,** which is considered the primary active form of vitamin D in the body. Calcitriol then circulates to various parts of the body, performing its many functions. Excess calcitriol can also be stored in adipose tissue for later use.

Functions of Vitamin D

As discussed on page 415, vitamin D, PTH, and calcitonin all work together continuously to regulate blood calcium levels, which in turn maintains bone health. They do this by regulating the absorption of calcium and phosphorus from the small intestine, causing more to be absorbed when the need for them is higher and less when the need is lower. They also decrease or increase blood calcium levels by signaling the kidneys to excrete more or less calcium in the urine. Finally, vitamin D works with PTH to stimulate osteoclasts to break down bone when calcium is needed elsewhere in the body.

Vitamin D is also necessary for the normal calcification of bone; this means it assists the process by which minerals such as calcium and phosphorus are crystallized. Vitamin D

calcitriol The primary active form of vitamin D in the body.

Figure 11.8 The process of converting sunlight into vitamin D in our skin. When the ultraviolet rays of the sun hit the skin, they react with 7-dehydrocholesterol. This compound is converted to cholecalciferol, an inactive form of vitamin D that is also called provitamin D_3. Cholecalciferol is then converted to calcidiol in the liver. Calcidiol travels to the kidneys, where it is converted into calcitriol, which is considered the primary active form of vitamin D in our bodies.

Vitamin D synthesis from the sun is not possible during most of the winter months for people living in high latitudes. Therefore, many people around the world, such as this couple in Russia, need to consume vitamin D in their diets, particularly during the winter.

may also play a role in decreasing the formation of some cancerous tumors, as it can prevent certain types of cells from growing out of control. Similar to vitamin A, vitamin D appears to play a role in cell differentiation in various tissues.

How Much Vitamin D Should We Consume?

If your exposure to the sun is adequate, then you do not need to consume any vitamin D in your diet. But how do you know whether or not you are getting enough sun?

Recommended Dietary Intake for Vitamin D   As with calcium, there is no RDA for vitamin D. The AI is based on the assumption that an individual does not get adequate sun exposure. Of the many factors that affect the ability to synthesize vitamin D from sunlight, latitude and time of year are most significant (Table 11.3). Individuals living in very sunny climates relatively close to the Equator, such as the southern United States and Mexico, may synthesize enough vitamin D from the sun to meet their needs throughout the year—as long as they spend time outdoors. However, vitamin D synthesis from the sun is not possible during most of the winter months for people living in places located at a latitude of more than 40°N or more than 40°S. This is because at these latitudes, the sun never rises high enough in the sky during the winter to provide the direct sunlight needed. The 40°N latitude runs like a belt across the United States from northern Pennsylvania in the East to northern California in the West (**Figure 11.9**). In addition, entire countries such as Canada and the United Kingdom are affected, as of course are countries in the far Southern Hemisphere. Thus, there are many people around the world who need to consume vitamin D in their diets, particularly during the winter months.

Other factors influencing vitamin D synthesis include time of day, skin color, age, and obesity status:

- More vitamin D can be synthesized during the time of day when the sun's rays are strongest, generally between 9 AM and 3 PM. Vitamin D synthesis is severely limited or may be nonexistent on overcast days.
- Darker skin contains more melanin pigment, which reduces the penetration of sunlight. Thus, people with dark skin have a more difficult time synthesizing vitamin D from the sun than do light-skinned people.
- People 65 years of age or older experience a fourfold decrease in their capacity to synthesize vitamin D from the sun.[12, 13]
- Obesity is associated with lower levels of circulating vitamin D, possibly because of lower bioavailability of cholecalciferol from adipose tissue, decreased exposure to sunlight due to limited mobility or time spent outdoors with skin exposed, and alterations in vitamin D metabolism in the liver.[14, 15]

Table 11.3 Factors Affecting Sunlight-Mediated Synthesis of Vitamin D in the Skin

Factors That Enhance Synthesis of Vitamin D	Factors That Inhibit Synthesis of Vitamin D
Season—Most vitamin D is produced during summer months, particularly June and July	Season—Winter months (October through February) result in little or no vitamin D production
Latitude—Locations closer to the Equator get more sunlight throughout the year	Latitude—Regions that are north of 40°N and south of 40°S get inadequate sun
Time of Day—Generally the hours between 9:00 AM and 3:00 PM (depending on latitude and time of year)	Time of Day—Early morning, late afternoon, and evening hours
Age—Younger	Age—Older, due to reduced skin thickness with age
Limited or no use of sunscreen	Use of sunscreen with SPF 8 or greater
Sunny weather	Cloudy weather
Exposed skin	Protective clothing
Lighter skin pigmentation	Darker skin pigmentation
	Glass and plastics—Windows or other barriers made of glass or plastic (such as Plexiglas) block the sun's rays
	Obesity—May negatively affect metabolism and storage of vitamin D

Wearing protective clothing and sunscreen (with an SPF greater than 8) limits sun exposure, so it is suggested that we expose our hands, face, and arms to the sun two to three times per week for a period of time that is one-third to one-half of the amount needed to get sunburned.[16] This means that if you normally sunburn in 1 hour, you should expose yourself to the sun for 20 to 30 minutes two to three times per week to synthesize adequate amounts of vitamin D. Again, this guideline does not apply to people living in more northern climates during the winter months; they can only get enough vitamin D by consuming it in their diet.

Because not everyone is able to get adequate sun exposure throughout the year, an AI has been established for vitamin D. For men and women aged 19 to 50 years, the AI for vitamin D is 5 µg per day. The AI for vitamin D for men and women aged 50 to 70 years is 10 µg per day, and the AI increases to 15 µg per day for adults over the age of 70 years. The UL for vitamin D is 50 µg per day for all age groups. Recent evidence suggests that the current AI for vitamin D is not sufficient to maintain optimal bone health and reduce the risks for diseases such as cancer; the controversy surrounding the current recommendations for vitamin D intake are discussed in more detail in the Nutrition Debate at the end of this chapter.

When reading labels, you will see the amount of vitamin D expressed on food and supplement labels in units of either µg or IU. For conversion purposes, 1 µg of vitamin D is equal to 40 IU of vitamin D.

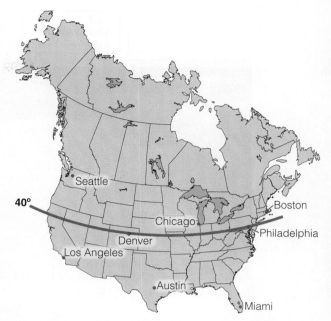

Figure 11.9 This map illustrates the geographical location of 40° latitude in the United States. In southern cities below 40° latitude such as Los Angeles, Austin, and Miami, the sunlight is strong enough to allow for vitamin D synthesis throughout the year. In northern cities above 40° latitude such as Seattle, Chicago, and Boston, the sunlight is too weak from about mid-October to mid-March to allow for adequate vitamin D synthesis.

Food Sources of Vitamin D

There are many forms of vitamin D, but only two are active in the body. These two forms are vitamin D$_2$, also called **ergocalciferol,** and vitamin D$_3$, or **cholecalciferol.** Vitamin D$_2$ is found exclusively in plant foods and may also be used in vitamin D supplements, whereas vitamin D$_3$ is found in animal foods and is also the form of vitamin D we synthesize from the sun.

Most foods naturally contain very little vitamin D, and those foods that do, such as cod liver oil and canned mackerel, are not typically consumed in the American diet. Thus, the primary source of vitamin D in the diet is from fortified foods such as milk (**Figure 11.10**). In the United States, milk is fortified with 10 µg of vitamin D per quart. Because earlier studies examining the actual vitamin D content of fortified milk found that the amount of vitamin D varied widely, the USDA now monitors dairies to make sure they meet the mandated vitamin D fortification guidelines.

Other foods that contain high amounts of vitamin D include cod liver oil, fatty fish (such as salmon, mackerel, and sardines), and certain fortified cereals. Eggs, butter, some margarines, and liver contain small amounts of vitamin D, but one would have to eat very large amounts of these foods to consume enough vitamin D. In addition, because plants contain very little vitamin D, vegetarians who consume no dairy products need to obtain their vitamin D from sun exposure, fortified soy or cereal products, or supplements.

Fatty fish contain vitamin D.

What Happens If We Consume Too Much Vitamin D?

A person cannot get too much vitamin D from sun exposure, as the skin has the ability to limit its production. In addition, foods contain little natural vitamin D. Thus, the only way a person can consume too much vitamin D is through supplementation.

Consuming too much vitamin D causes hypercalcemia, or high blood calcium concentrations. As discussed in the section on calcium, symptoms of hypercalcemia include weakness, loss of appetite, diarrhea, mental confusion, vomiting, excessive urine output, and extreme thirst. Hypercalcemia also leads to the formation of calcium deposits in soft tissues such as the kidney, liver, and heart. In addition, toxic levels of vitamin D lead to increased bone loss because calcium is then pulled from the bones and excreted more readily from the kidneys.

ergocalciferol Vitamin D$_2$, a form of vitamin D found exclusively in plant foods.

cholecalciferol Vitamin D$_3$, a form of vitamin D found in animal foods and the form we synthesize from the sun.

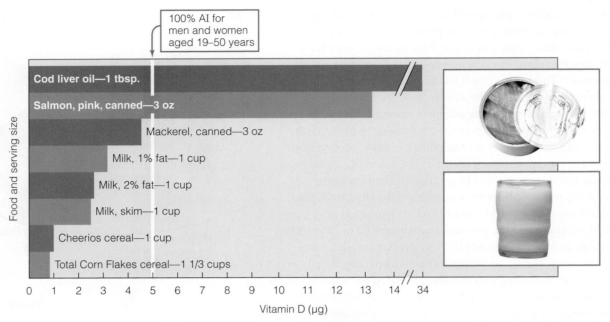

Food and serving size

100% AI for men and women aged 19–50 years

Cod liver oil—1 tbsp.

Salmon, pink, canned—3 oz

Mackerel, canned—3 oz

Milk, 1% fat—1 cup

Milk, 2% fat—1 cup

Milk, skim—1 cup

Cheerios cereal—1 cup

Total Corn Flakes cereal—1 1/3 cups

0 1 2 3 4 5 6 7 8 9 10 11 12 13 14 34

Vitamin D (µg)

Figure 11.10 Common food sources of vitamin D. For men and women aged 19 to 50 years, the AI for vitamin D is 5 µg per day. The AI for vitamin D for men and women aged 50 to 70 years is 10 µg per day, and the AI increases to 15 µg per day for adults over the age of 70 years. (*Data from:* U.S. Department of Agriculture, Agricultural Research Service, 2008, USDA Nutrient Database for Standard Reference, Release 21. Nutrient Data Laboratory Home Page, www.ars.usda.gov/ba/bhnrc/ndl.)

Figure 11.11 A vitamin D deficiency causes a bone-deforming disease in children called rickets.

rickets Vitamin D–deficiency disease in children. Symptoms include deformities of the skeleton such as bowed legs and knocked knees.

osteomalacia Vitamin D–deficiency disease in adults, in which bones become weak and prone to fractures.

What Happens If We Don't Consume Enough Vitamin D?

The primary deficiency associated with inadequate vitamin D is loss of bone mass. In fact, when vitamin D levels are inadequate, the intestines can only absorb 10% to 15% of the calcium consumed. Vitamin D deficiencies occur most often in individuals who have diseases that cause intestinal malabsorption of fat and thus the fat-soluble vitamins. People with liver disease, kidney disease, Crohn's disease, celiac disease, cystic fibrosis, or Whipple disease suffer from vitamin D deficiencies and require supplements.

Vitamin D–deficiency disease in children, called **rickets,** results in inadequate mineralization or demineralization of the skeleton. The symptoms of rickets include deformities of the skeleton such as bowed legs, knocked knees, and an enlarged head and rib cage (**Figure 11.11**). Rickets is not common in the United States because of fortification of milk products with vitamin D, but children with illnesses that cause fat malabsorption or who drink no milk and get limited sun exposure are at increased risk. A recent review of reported cases of rickets among children in the United States found that approximately 83% of children with rickets were African American, and 96% were breast-fed.[17] Breast milk contains very little vitamin D, and fewer than 5% of the breast-fed children were reported to have received vitamin D supplementation. Thus, rickets appears to occur more commonly in children with darker skin, as their need for adequate sun exposure is higher than that for light-skinned children, and in breast-fed children who do not receive adequate vitamin D supplementation. In addition, rickets is still a significant nutritional problem for children outside of the United States.

Vitamin D–deficiency disease in adults is called **osteomalacia,** a term meaning "soft bones." With osteomalacia, bones become weak and prone to malformations and fractures. Osteoporosis, discussed in detail later in this chapter, can also result from a vitamin D deficiency.

Vitamin D deficiencies have recently been found to be more common among American adults than previously thought. This may be partly due to jobs and lifestyle choices that keep people indoors for most of the day. Not surprisingly, the population at greatest risk is older institutionalized individuals who get little or no sun exposure.

Various medications can also alter the metabolism and activity of vitamin D. For instance, glucocorticoids, which are medications used to reduce inflammation, can cause bone loss by inhibiting the ability to absorb calcium through the actions of vitamin D. Antiseizure medications such as phenobarbital and Dilantin alter vitamin D metabolism. Thus, people who are taking such medications may need to increase their vitamin D intake.

RecaP

Vitamin D is a fat-soluble vitamin and a hormone. It can be made in the skin using energy from sunlight. Vitamin D regulates blood calcium levels and maintains bone health. The AI for vitamin D is 5 µg per day for adult men and women aged 19 to 50 years; the AI increases to 15 µg per day for adults over the age of 70 years. Foods contain little vitamin D, with fortified milk being the primary source. Vitamin D toxicity causes hypercalcemia. Vitamin D deficiency can result in osteoporosis; rickets is vitamin D deficiency in children, whereas osteomalacia describes vitamin D deficiency in adults.

Theo
Nutri-Case

"The health center here on campus is running a study on vitamin D levels among students, and the instructor in my nutrition class invited everybody to participate. I don't think I need to be worried about it, though, 'cause I exercise outdoors a lot—at least, whenever Wisconsin weather allows it! It's true I don't drink much milk, and I hate fish, but otherwise I eat right, and besides, I'm a guy, so I don't have to worry about my bone density."

Should Theo have his vitamin D levels checked? Why or why not? Before you answer, take another look at Table 11.2. Also, consider Theo's assertion that because he is male, he doesn't have to worry about his bone density. Is he right? And is calcium regulation the only significant role of vitamin D?

Vitamin K

Vitamin K, a fat-soluble vitamin stored primarily in the liver, is actually a family of compounds known as quinones. **Phylloquinone,** which is the primary dietary form of vitamin K, is also the form found in plants; **menaquinone** is the animal form of vitamin K produced by bacteria in the large intestine (**Figure 11.12**).

The absorption of phylloquinone occurs in the jejunum and ileum of the small intestine, and its absorption is dependent upon the normal flow of bile and pancreatic juice. Dietary fat enhances its absorption. The absorption of phylloquinone has been reported to be as low as 10% from boiled spinach eaten with butter to as high as 80% when given in its free form.[18] It is transported through the lymph as a component of chylomicrons, and it circulates to the liver, where most of the vitamin K in the body is stored. Small amounts of vitamin K are also stored in adipose tissue and bone.[18] The absorption of menaquinone is not well understood, and its contribution to the maintenance of vitamin K status has been difficult to assess.[19]

(a) Phylloquinone

(b) Menaquinone

Figure 11.12 The chemical structure of **(a)** phylloquinone, the plant form of vitamin K, and **(b)** menaquinone, the animal form of vitamin K.

phylloquinone The form of vitamin K found in plants.
menaquinone The form of vitamin K produced by bacteria in the large intestine.

Functions of Vitamin K

The primary function of vitamin K is to serve as a coenzyme during the production of specific proteins that play important roles in the coagulation of blood and in bone metabolism. Refer to Chapter 12 for an in-depth description of the role of vitamin K in maintaining blood health.

Here, we limit our discussion to vitamin K's role in the production of two bone proteins, referred to as "Gla" proteins: **Osteocalcin** is a Gla protein that is secreted by osteoblasts and is associated with bone remodeling. **Matrix Gla protein** is located in the protein matrix of bone and is also found in cartilage, blood vessel walls, and other soft tissues.[18] The specific role of vitamin K in maintaining bone health is still under study, but there is growing evidence that vitamin K supplementation may increase bone density in people with osteoporosis and that diets rich in vitamin K are associated with reduced fracture rates.[20] Matrix Gla protein also appears to play a role in preventing the calcification of arteries, which may reduce the risk for cardiovascular disease.[21]

How Much Vitamin K Should We Consume?

We can obtain vitamin K from our diets, and we also absorb the vitamin K produced by bacteria in the large intestine. These two sources of vitamin K usually provide adequate amounts of this nutrient to maintain health, and there is no RDA for vitamin K. AI recommendations for adult men and adult women are 120 μg per day and 90 μg per day, respectively. No UL has been set.

Only a few foods contribute substantially to our dietary intake of vitamin K. Green leafy vegetables including kale, spinach, collard greens, turnip greens, and lettuce are good sources, as are broccoli, Brussels sprouts, and cabbage. Vegetable oils, such as soybean oil and canola oil, are also good sources. **Figure 11.13** identifies the micrograms per serving for these foods. The action of vitamin K is inhibited in laboratory animals given large doses of vitamin A and vitamin E; however, these vitamins do not appear to have the same effect on vitamin K in healthy humans.[19]

osteocalcin   A vitamin K–dependent protein that is secreted by osteoblasts and is associated with bone turnover.

matrix Gla protein   A vitamin K–dependent protein that is located in the protein matrix of bone and also found in cartilage, blood vessel walls, and other soft tissues.

Figure 11.13   Common food sources of vitamin K. The AIs for adult men and adult women are 120 μg per day and 90 μg per day, respectively. (*Data from:* U.S. Department of Agriculture, Agricultural Research Service, 2008, USDA Nutrient Database for Standard Reference, Release 21. Nutrient Data Laboratory Home Page, www.ars.usda.gov/ba/bhnrc/ndl.)

What Happens If We Consume Too Much Vitamin K?

Based on our current knowledge, for healthy individuals there appear to be no side effects associated with consuming large amounts of vitamin K.[19] This seems to be true for both supplements and food sources. In the past, a synthetic form of vitamin K was used for therapeutic purposes and was shown to cause liver damage; thus, this form is no longer used.

What Happens If We Don't Consume Enough Vitamin K?

Vitamin K deficiency is associated with a reduced ability to form blood clots, leading to excessive bleeding; however, primary vitamin K deficiency is rare in humans. People with diseases that cause malabsorption of fat, such as celiac disease, Crohn's disease, and cystic fibrosis, can suffer secondarily from a deficiency of vitamin K. Long-term use of antibiotics, which typically reduce bacterial populations in the colon, combined with limited dietary intake of vitamin K–rich food sources can also lead to vitamin K deficiency. Newborns are typically given an injection of vitamin K at birth, as they lack the intestinal bacteria necessary to produce this nutrient.

The impact of vitamin K deficiency on bone health is controversial. A recent study of vitamin K intake and risk of hip fractures found that women who consumed the least amount of vitamin K had a higher risk of bone fractures than women who consumed relatively more vitamin K.[22] Despite the results of this study, there is not enough scientific evidence to support the contention that vitamin K deficiency directly causes osteoporosis.[19] In fact, there is no significant impact on overall bone density in people who take anticoagulant medications that result in a relative state of vitamin K deficiency.

Green leafy vegetables, including Brussels sprouts and turnip greens, are good sources of vitamin K.

RECaP

Vitamin K is a fat-soluble vitamin and coenzyme that is important for blood clotting and bone metabolism. We obtain vitamin K largely from bacteria in the large intestine. The AIs for adult men and adult women are 120 μg per day and 90 μg per day, respectively. Green leafy vegetables and vegetable oils contain vitamin K. There are no known toxicity symptoms for vitamin K in healthy individuals. Vitamin K deficiency is rare and may lead to excessive bleeding.

Phosphorus

As discussed in Chapter 9, phosphorus is the major intracellular negatively charged electrolyte. In the body, phosphorus is most commonly found combined with oxygen in the form of phosphate (or PO_4^{3-}). Phosphorus is an essential constituent of all cells and is found in both plants and animals.

Functions of Phosphorus

Phosphorus plays a critical role in bone formation, as it is a part of the mineral complex of bone. As discussed earlier in this chapter, calcium and phosphorus crystallize to form hydroxyapatite crystals, which provide the hardness of bone. About 85% of the body's phosphorus is stored in bones, with the rest stored in soft tissues such as muscles and organs.

The role of phosphorus in maintaining proper fluid balance was discussed in detail in Chapter 9. Phosphorus is also a primary component of several energy molecules including adenosine triphosphate (ATP). It helps activate and deactivate enzymes, is a component of the genetic material in the nuclei of the cells (including both DNA and RNA), and is a component of cell membranes and lipoproteins.

How Much Phosphorus Should We Consume?

The details of phosphorus recommendations, food sources, and deficiency and toxicity symptoms were discussed in Chapter 9 (pages 341–343). In general, phosphorus is

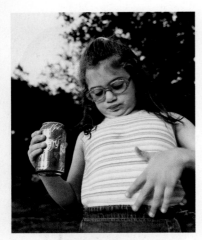

Phosphorus, in the form of phosphoric acid, is a major component of soft drinks.

widespread in many foods and is found in high amounts in foods that contain protein. Milk, meats, and eggs are good sources. Refer to Figure 9.10 (page 342) for a review of the phosphorus content of various foods.

Phosphorus is found in many processed foods as a food additive, where it enhances smoothness, binding, and moisture retention. In the form of phosphoric acid, it is also a major component of soft drinks. Phosphoric acid is added to soft drinks to give them a sharper, or more tart, flavor and to slow the growth of molds and bacteria. Our society has increased its consumption of processed foods and soft drinks substantially during the past 20 years, resulting in an estimated 10% to 15% increase in phosphorus consumption.[5]

Nutrition and medical professionals have become increasingly concerned that the heavy consumption of soft drinks may be detrimental to bone health. Studies have shown that consuming soft drinks is associated with reduced bone mass or an increased risk of fractures in both youth and adults.[23–25] Researchers have proposed three theories to explain why consumption of soft drinks may be detrimental to bone health. These include the following:

- consuming soft drinks in place of calcium-containing beverages, such as milk, leads to a deficient intake of calcium;
- the acidic properties and high phosphorus content of soft drinks cause an increased loss of calcium because calcium is drawn from bone into the blood to neutralize the excess acid; and
- the caffeine found in many soft drinks causes increased calcium loss through the urine.

A recent study of this problem tried to tease out which component of soft drinks may be detrimental to bone health.[26] Four different carbonated soft drinks were tested: two that contained phosphoric acid and two that contained citric acid. Two of these drinks also contained caffeine and two did not. Calcium loss was measured as the amount of calcium excreted in the participants' urine. Interestingly, the results showed that the contents of soft drinks had little effect on calcium status. Although the two beverages that contained caffeine caused some loss of calcium during the 5-hour testing period, this effect of caffeine on calcium tends to taper off throughout the day and night, leading to no overall impact on calcium status over a 24-hour period. The researchers concluded that the most likely explanation for the link between soft drink consumption and poor bone health is the *milk-displacement effect;* that is, soft drinks take the place of milk in our diets, depriving us of calcium and vitamin D. Additional nutritional and lifestyle factors that affect bone health are discussed later in this chapter.

What Happens If We Consume Too Much Phosphorus?

As discussed in Chapter 9, people with kidney disease and those who take too many vitamin D supplements or too many phosphorus-containing antacids can suffer from high blood phosphorus levels; severely high levels of blood phosphorus can cause muscle spasms and convulsions.

What Happens If We Don't Consume Enough Phosphorus?

Phosphorus deficiencies are rare but can occur in people who abuse alcohol, in premature infants, and in elderly people with poor diets. People with vitamin D deficiency, hyperparathyroidism (oversecretion of parathyroid hormone), and those who overuse antacids that bind with phosphorus may also have low blood phosphorus levels.

RECAP

Phosphorus is the major negatively charged electrolyte inside of the cell. It helps maintain fluid balance and bone health. It also assists in regulating chemical reactions, and it is a primary component of ATP, DNA, and RNA. Phosphorus is commonly found in high-protein foods. Excess phosphorus can lead to muscle spasms and convulsion, whereas phosphorus deficiencies are rare.

Magnesium

Magnesium is a major mineral. Approximately 50% of dietary magnesium is absorbed via both passive and active transport mechanisms; maximal absorption of magnesium occurs in the distal jejunum and ileum of the small intestine. The absorption of magnesium decreases with higher dietary intakes. The kidneys are responsible for the regulation of blood magnesium levels. Two forms of vitamin D, 25-hydroxyvitamin D and 1,25-dihydroxyvitamin D, can enhance the intestinal absorption of magnesium to a limited extent. Excessive alcohol intake can cause magnesium depletion, and some diuretic medications can lead to increased excretion of magnesium in the urine. Dietary fiber and phytates decrease intestinal absorption of magnesium.

Total body magnesium content is approximately 25 g. About 50% to 60% of the magnesium in the body is found in bones, with the rest located in soft tissues.

Functions of Magnesium

Magnesium is one of the minerals that make up the structure of bone. It is also important in the regulation of bone and mineral status. Specifically, magnesium influences the formation of hydroxyapatite crystals through its regulation of calcium balance and its interactions with vitamin D and parathyroid hormone.

Magnesium is a critical cofactor for more than 300 enzyme systems. Magnesium is necessary for the production of ATP, and it plays an important role in DNA and protein synthesis and repair. Magnesium supplementation has been shown to improve insulin sensitivity, and there is epidemiological evidence that a high magnesium intake is associated with a decrease in the risk for colorectal cancer.[27, 28] Magnesium supports normal vitamin D metabolism and action and is necessary for normal muscle contraction and blood clotting.

How Much Magnesium Should We Consume?

As magnesium is found in a wide variety of foods, people who are adequately nourished generally consume adequate magnesium in their diets. The RDA for magnesium changes across age groups and genders. For adult men 19 to 30 years of age, the RDA for magnesium is 400 mg per day; the RDA increases to 420 mg per day for men 31 years of age and older. For adult women 19 to 30 years of age, the RDA for magnesium is 310 mg per day; this value increases to 320 mg per day for women 31 years of age and older. There is no UL for magnesium for food and water; the UL for magnesium from pharmacologic sources is 350 mg per day.

Magnesium is found in green leafy vegetables such as spinach. It is also found in whole grains, seeds, and nuts. Other good food sources of magnesium include seafood, beans, and some dairy products. Refined and processed foods are low in magnesium. **Figure 11.14** shows many foods that are good sources of magnesium.

The magnesium content of drinking water varies considerably. The "harder" the water, the higher its content of magnesium. This large variability in the magnesium content of water makes it impossible to estimate how much our drinking water may contribute to the magnesium content of our diets.

The ability of the small intestine to absorb magnesium is reduced when one consumes a diet that is extremely high in fiber and phytates, because these substances bind with magnesium. Even though seeds and nuts are relatively high in fiber, they are excellent sources of absorbable magnesium. Overall, our absorption of magnesium should be sufficient if we consume the recommended amount of fiber each day (20 to 35 g per day). In contrast, higher dietary protein intakes enhance the absorption and retention of magnesium.

Trail mix with chocolate chips, nuts, and seeds is one common food source of magnesium.

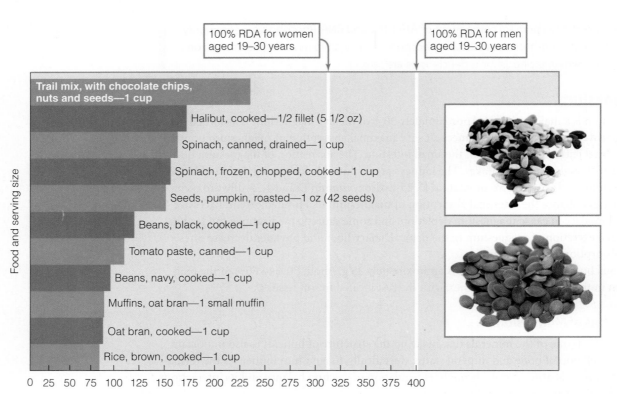

Figure 11.14   Common food sources of magnesium. For adult men 19 to 30 years of age, the RDA for magnesium is 400 mg per day; the RDA increases to 420 mg per day for men 31 years of age and older. For adult women 19 to 30 years of age, the RDA for magnesium is 310 mg per day; this value increases to 320 mg per day for women 31 years of age and older. (*Data from:* U.S. Department of Agriculture, Agricultural Research Service, 2008, USDA Nutrient Database for Standard Reference, Release 21. Nutrient Data Laboratory Home Page, www.ars.usda.gov/ba/bhnrc/ndl.)

What Happens If We Consume Too Much Magnesium?

There are no known toxicity symptoms related to consuming excess magnesium in the diet. The toxicity symptoms that result from pharmacologic use of magnesium include diarrhea, nausea, and abdominal cramps. In extreme cases, large doses can result in acid–base imbalances, massive dehydration, cardiac arrest, and death. High blood magnesium, or **hypermagnesemia,** occurs in individuals with impaired kidney function who consume large amounts of nondietary magnesium, such as antacids. Side effects include impairment of nerve, muscle, and heart function.

What Happens If We Don't Consume Enough Magnesium?

Hypomagnesemia, or low blood magnesium, results from magnesium deficiency. This condition may result from kidney disease, chronic diarrhea, or chronic alcohol abuse. Elderly people seem to be at particularly high risk of low dietary intakes of magnesium because they have a reduced appetite and blunted senses of taste and smell. In addition, the elderly face challenges related to shopping and preparing meals that contain foods high in magnesium, and their ability to absorb magnesium is reduced.

Low blood calcium levels are a side effect of hypomagnesemia. Other symptoms of magnesium deficiency include muscle cramps, spasms or seizures, nausea, weakness, irritability, and confusion. Considering magnesium's role in bone formation, it is not surprising that long-term magnesium deficiency is associated with osteoporosis. Magnesium deficiency is also associated with many other chronic diseases, including heart disease, high blood pressure, and type 2 diabetes.[5]

hypermagnesemia   A condition marked by an abnormally high concentration of magnesium in the blood.
hypomagnesemia   A condition characterized by an abnormally low concentration of magnesium in the blood.

Recap

Magnesium is a major mineral found in fresh foods, including spinach, nuts, seeds, whole grains, and meats. Magnesium is important for bone health, energy production, and muscle function. The RDA for magnesium is a function of age and gender. Hypermagnesemia can result in diarrhea, muscle cramps, and cardiac arrest. Hypomagnesemia causes hypocalcemia, muscle cramps, spasms, and weakness. Magnesium deficiencies are also associated with osteoporosis, heart disease, high blood pressure, and type 2 diabetes.

Fluoride

Fluoride is the ionic form of the element fluorine, and it is also a trace mineral. About 99% of the fluoride in the body is stored in teeth and bones.

Functions of Fluoride

Fluoride assists in the development and maintenance of teeth and bones. During the development of both baby teeth and permanent teeth, fluoride combines with calcium and phosphorus to form **fluorohydroxyapatite,** which is more resistant to destruction by acids and bacteria than hydroxyapatite. Even after all of our permanent teeth are in, treating them with fluoride, whether at the dentist's office or by using fluoridated toothpaste, gives them more protection against dental caries (cavities) than teeth that have not been treated. That's because fluoride enhances tooth mineralization, decreases and reverses tooth demineralization, and inhibits the metabolism of acid-producing bacteria that cause tooth decay.

Fluoride also stimulates new bone growth, and it is currently being researched as a potential treatment for osteoporosis both alone and in combination with other medications.[29–31] While early results are promising, more research needs to be conducted to determine if fluoride is an effective treatment for osteoporosis.[32]

How Much Fluoride Should We Consume?

Our need for fluoride is relatively small. There is no RDA for fluoride. The AI for children aged 4 to 8 years is 1 mg per day; this value increases to 2 mg per day for boys and girls aged 9 to 13 years. The AI for boys and girls aged 14 to 18 years is 3 mg per day. The AI for adults is 4 mg per day for adult men and 3 mg per day for adult women. The UL for fluoride is 2.2 mg per day for children aged 4 to 8 years; the UL for everyone older than 8 years of age is 10 mg per day.

Fluoride is readily available in many communities in the United States through fluoridated water and dental products. Fluoride is absorbed directly in the mouth into the teeth and gums and can also be absorbed from the gastrointestinal tract once it is ingested. In the early 1990s, there was considerable concern that our intake of fluoride was too high due to the consumption of fluoridated water and fluoride-containing toothpastes and mouthwashes; it was speculated that this high intake of fluoride could be contributing to an increased risk for cancer, bone fractures, kidney and other organ damage, infertility, and Alzheimer's disease. After reviewing the potential health hazards of fluoride, the U.S. Department of Health and Human Services found that there is no reliable scientific evidence available to indicate that fluoride increases our risks for these illnesses.[33]

Currently, there are concerns that individuals who consume bottled water exclusively may be consuming too little fluoride and increasing their risk for dental caries, as most bottled waters do not contain fluoride. However, these individuals may still consume fluoride through other beverages that contain fluoridated water and through fluoridated dental products. Toothpastes and mouthwashes that contain fluoride are widely marketed and used by the majority of consumers in the United States, and these products can contribute as much if not more fluoride to our diets than fluoridated water. Fluoride supplements are available only by prescription, and these are generally only given to children who do not

fluorohydroxyapatite A mineral compound in human teeth that contains fluoride, calcium, and phosphorus and is more resistant to destruction by acids and bacteria than hydroxyapatite.

Fluoride is readily available in many communities in the United States through fluoridated water and dental products.

have access to fluoridated water. Incidentally, tea is a good source of fluoride: one 8-oz cup provides about 20% to 25% of the AI.

What Happens If We Consume Too Much Fluoride?

Consuming too much fluoride increases the protein content of tooth enamel, resulting in a condition called **fluorosis.** Because increased protein makes the enamel more porous, the teeth become stained and pitted (**Figure 11.15**). Teeth seem to be at highest risk for fluorosis during the first 8 years of life, when the permanent teeth are developing. To reduce the risk of fluorosis, children should not swallow oral care products that are meant for topical use only, and children under the age of 6 years should be supervised while using fluoride-containing products.[32] Mild fluorosis generally causes white patches on the teeth, and it has no effect on tooth function. Although moderate and severe fluorosis causes greater discoloration of the teeth, there appears to be no adverse effect on tooth function.[5]

Excess consumption of fluoride can also cause fluorosis of the skeleton. Mild skeletal fluorosis results in an increased bone mass and stiffness and pain in the joints. Moderate and severe skeletal fluorosis can be crippling, but it is extremely rare in the United States, with only five confirmed cases in the past 35 years.[5]

What Happens If We Don't Consume Enough Fluoride?

The primary result of fluoride deficiency is dental caries. Adequate fluoride intake appears necessary at an early age and throughout adult life to reduce the risk for tooth decay. Inadequate fluoride intake may also be associated with lower bone density, but there is not enough research currently available to support the widespread use of fluoride to prevent osteoporosis. Studies are currently being done to determine the role fluoride might play in reducing the risk for osteoporosis and fractures.

Figure 11.15 Consuming too much fluoride causes fluorosis, leading to staining and pitting of the teeth.

RECaP

Fluoride is a trace mineral whose primary function is to support the health of teeth and bones. The AI for fluoride is 4 and 3 mg per day for adult men and women, respectively. Primary sources of fluoride are fluoridated dental products and fluoridated water. Fluoride toxicity causes fluorosis of the teeth and skeleton, and fluoride deficiency causes an increase in tooth decay.

Osteoporosis Is the Most Prevalent Disorder Affecting Bone Health

Of the many disorders associated with poor bone health, the most prevalent in the United States is osteoporosis. **Osteoporosis** is a disease characterized by low bone mass and deterioration of bone tissue, leading to enhanced bone fragility and increase in fracture risk. The bone tissue of a person with osteoporosis is more porous and thinner than that of a person with healthy bone. These structural changes weaken the bone, leading to a significantly reduced ability of the bone to bear weight (**Figure 11.16**).

As mentioned earlier in this chapter, the hip and the vertebrae of the spinal column are common sites of osteoporosis; thus, it is not surprising that osteoporosis is the single most important cause of fractures of the hip and spine in older adults. These fractures are extremely painful and can be debilitating, with many individuals requiring nursing home care. In addition, they cause an increased risk of infection and other related illnesses that can lead to premature death. In fact, about 20% of older adults who suffer a hip fracture die within 1 year after the fracture occurs, and death rates are higher for men than for women.[34] Osteoporosis of the spine also causes a generalized loss of height and can be disfiguring: Gradual compression fractures in the vertebrae of the upper back lead to a shortening and hunching of the spine called *kyphosis,* commonly referred to as *dowager's hump* (**Figure 11.17**).

fluorosis   A condition marked by staining and pitting of the teeth; caused by an abnormally high intake of fluoride.

osteoporosis   A disease characterized by low bone mass and deterioration of bone tissue, leading to increased bone fragility and fracture risk.

Figure 11.16 The vertebrae of a person with osteoporosis (right) are thinner and more collapsed than the vertebrae of a healthy person, in which the bone is more dense and uniform (left).

Osteoporosis is a common disease: Worldwide, one in three women and one in five men over the age of 50 are affected, and in the United States, more than 10 million people have been diagnosed.[34, 35] Factors that influence the risk for osteoporosis include age, gender, genetics, nutrition, and physical activity (Table 11.4). Let's review these factors and identify lifestyle changes that reduce the risk for osteoporosis.

The Impact of Aging on Osteoporosis Risk

Because bone density declines with age, low bone mass and osteoporosis are significant health concerns for both older men and women. The prevalence of osteoporosis and low bone mass are predicted to increase in the United States during the next 20 years, primarily because of increased longevity; as the U.S. population ages, more people will live long enough to suffer from osteoporosis.

Hormonal changes that occur with aging have a significant impact on bone loss. Average bone loss approximates 0.3% to 0.5% per year after 30 years of age; however, during menopause in women, levels of the hormone estrogen decrease dramatically and cause bone loss to increase to about 3% per year during the first 5 years of menopause. Both estrogen and testosterone play important roles in promoting the deposition of new bone and limiting the activity of osteoclasts. Thus, men can also suffer from osteoporosis caused by age-related decreases in testosterone. In addition, reduced levels of physical activity in older people and a decreased ability to metabolize vitamin D with age exacerbate the hormone-related bone loss.

Figure 11.17 Osteoporosis of the spine causes kyphosis, a shortening and hunching of the spine.

Table 11.4 Risk Factors for Osteoporosis

Modifiable Risk Factors	Nonmodifiable Risk Factors
Smoking	Older age (elderly)
Low body weight	Caucasian or Asian race
Low calcium intake	History of fractures as an adult
Low sun exposure	Family history of osteoporosis
Alcohol abuse	Gender (female)
History of amenorrhea (failure to menstruate) in women with inadequate nutrition	History of amenorrhea (failure to menstruate) in women with no recognizable cause
Estrogen deficiency (females)	
Testosterone deficiency (males)	
Repeated falls	
Sedentary lifestyle	

Data adapted from: Milott, J. L., S. S. Green, and M. M. Schapira. 2000. Osteoporosis: Evaluation and treatment. *Comp. Ther.* 26:183–189. Copyright © 2000 American Society of Contemporary Medicine and Surgery. Reprinted with permission of Humana Press.

Gender and Genetics Affect Osteoporosis Risk

Approximately 80% of Americans with osteoporosis are women. There are three primary reasons for this:

- Adult women have a lower absolute bone density than men. From birth through puberty, bone mass is the same in girls as in boys. But during puberty, bone mass increases more in boys, probably because of their prolonged period of accelerated growth. This means that when bone loss begins around age 40, women have less bone stored in their skeleton than men; thus, the loss of bone that occurs with aging causes osteoporosis sooner and to a greater extent in women than in men.
- The hormonal changes that occur in men as they age do not have as dramatic an effect on bone density as those in women.
- On average, women live longer than men, and because risk increases with age, more elderly women suffer from this disease.

Secondary factors that are gender-specific include social pressure on girls to be thin. Extreme dieting is particularly harmful in adolescence, when bone mass is building and adequate consumption of calcium and other nutrients is critical. In many girls, weight loss causes both a loss of estrogen and reduced weight-bearing stress on the bones. In contrast, men experience pressure to "bulk up," typically by lifting weights. This puts healthful stress on the bones, resulting in increased density.

Some individuals have a family history of osteoporosis, which increases their risk for this disease. Particularly at risk are Caucasian women of low body weight who have a first-degree relative (mother or sister) with osteoporosis. Asian women are also at higher risk than other non-Caucasian groups. Although we cannot change our gender or genetics, we can modify various lifestyle factors that affect our risk for osteoporosis.

Smoking and Poor Nutrition Increase Osteoporosis Risk

Cigarette smoking is known to decrease bone density because of its effects on hormones that influence bone formation and resorption; thus, cigarette smoking increases the risk for osteoporosis and resulting fractures.

Smoking increases our risk for osteoporosis and resulting fractures.

Chronic alcoholism is detrimental to bone health and is associated with high rates of fractures. In contrast, numerous research studies have shown that bone density is higher in people who are *moderate* drinkers.[22, 36–39] Despite the fact that moderate alcohol intake may be protective for bone, the dangers of alcohol abuse on overall health warrant caution in making any dietary recommendations. As is consistent with the alcohol recommendations related to heart disease, it is recommended that people should not start drinking if they are nondrinkers, and people who do drink should do so in moderation. That means no more than two drinks per day for men and one drink per day for women.

Some researchers consider excess caffeine consumption to be detrimental to bone health. Caffeine is known to increase calcium loss in the urine, at least over a brief period of time. Younger people are able to compensate for this calcium loss by increasing absorption of calcium from the intestine. However, older people are not always capable of compensating to the same degree. Although the findings have been inconsistent, recent research now indicates that the relative amounts of caffeine and calcium consumed are critical factors affecting bone health. In general, elderly women do not appear to be at risk for increased bone loss if they consume adequate amounts of calcium and moderate amounts of caffeine (equal to less than 2 cups of coffee, 4 cups of tea, or six 12-oz cans of caffeine-containing soft drinks per day).[40] Elderly women who consume high levels of caffeine (more than 3 cups of coffee per day) have much higher rates of bone loss than women with low intakes.[41] Thus, it appears important to bone health that we moderate our caffeine intake and ensure adequate consumption of calcium in the diet.

The excretion of sodium and calcium by the kidneys are linked; thus, higher intakes of sodium are known to increase the excretion of calcium in the urine. One study found an association between high urinary sodium excretion and increased bone loss from the hip in postmenopausal women.[42] However, there is no direct evidence that a high-sodium diet causes osteoporosis. At this time, the Institute of Medicine states that there is insufficient evidence to warrant different calcium recommendations based on dietary salt intake.[5]

The effect of high dietary protein intake on bone health is controversial. Whereas it is well established that high protein intakes increase calcium loss, protein is a critical component of bone tissue and is necessary for bone health. High protein intakes have been shown to have both a negative and positive impact on bone health. Similar to caffeine, the key to this mystery appears to be adequate calcium intake. Elderly individuals taking calcium and vitamin D supplements and eating higher-protein diets were able to significantly increase bone mass over a 3-year period, whereas those eating more protein and not taking supplements lost bone mass over this same time period.[43] Low protein intakes are also associated with bone loss and increased risk for osteoporosis and fractures in elderly people. Thus, there appears to be an interaction between dietary calcium and protein, in that adequate amounts of each nutrient are needed together to support bone health.

Of the many nutrients that help maintain bone health, calcium and vitamin D have received the most attention for their role in the prevention of osteoporosis. Research studies conducted with older individuals have shown that these individuals reduce their bone loss and fracture risk by taking calcium and vitamin D supplements. We know that if people do not consume enough of these two nutrients over a prolonged period of time, their bone density is lower and they have a higher risk of bone fractures. Because bones reach peak density when people are young, it is very important that children and adolescents consume a high-quality diet that contains the proper balance of calcium, vitamin D, protein, and other nutrients to allow for optimal bone growth. Young adults also require a proper balance of these nutrients to maintain bone mass. In older adults, diets rich in calcium and vitamin D can help minimize bone loss.

In addition to their role in reducing the risk for heart disease and cancer, diets high in fruits and vegetables are also associated with improved bone health.[44, 45] This is most likely due to the fact that fruits and vegetables are good sources of nutrients that play a role in bone and collagen health, including magnesium, vitamin C, and vitamin K.

The Impact of Physical Activity on Osteoporosis Risk

Regular exercise is highly protective against bone loss and osteoporosis. Athletes are consistently shown to have more dense bones than nonathletes, and regular participation in weight-bearing exercises such as walking, jogging, tennis, and strength training can help increase and maintain bone mass. When we exercise, our muscles contract and pull on our bones; this stresses bone tissue in a healthful way that stimulates increases in bone density. In addition, carrying weight during activities such as walking and jogging stresses the bones of the legs, hips, and lower back, resulting in a healthier bone mass in these areas. It appears that people of all ages can improve and maintain bone health by consistent physical activity.

Can exercise ever be detrimental to bone health? Yes, when the body is not receiving the nutrients it needs to rebuild the hydroxyapatite and collagen broken down in response to physical activity. Thus, active people who are chronically malnourished, including people who are impoverished and those who suffer from eating disorders, are at increased fracture risk. Research has confirmed this association between nutrition, physical activity, and bone loss in the **female athlete triad,** a condition characterized by the coexistence of three (or a *triad* of) clinical conditions in some physically active females: low energy availability (with or without eating disorders), amenorrhea, and osteoporosis. In the female athlete triad, inadequate food intake and regular strenuous exercise together result in a state of severe energy drain that causes a multitude of hormonal changes, including a reduction in estrogen production. These hormonal changes can result in the complete loss of menstrual function, called *amenorrhea*. Estrogen is important to maintaining healthy bone in women, so the loss of estrogen leads to osteoporosis in young women. The female athlete triad is discussed *In Depth* on pages 537–538.

Regular weight-bearing exercises such as jogging can help us increase and maintain our bone mass.

female athlete triad A condition characterized by the coexistence of three disorders in some athletic females: an eating disorder, amenorrhea, and osteoporosis.

Gustavo
Nutri-Case

"When my wife, Antonia, fell and broke her hip, I was shocked. You see, the same thing happened to her mother, but she was an old lady by then! Antonia's only 68, and she still seems young and beautiful—at least to me! As soon as she's better, her doctor wants to do some kind of scan to see how thick her bones are. But I don't think she has that disease everyone talks about! She's always watched her weight and keeps active with our kids and grandchildren. It's true she likes her coffee and diet colas, and doesn't drink milk, but that's not enough to make a person's bones fall apart, is it?"

Study Table 11.4. What risk factors do not apply to Antonia? What risk factors do? Given what Gustavo has said about his wife's nutrition and lifestyle, would you suggest he encourage her to have a DXA test? Why or why not?

Treatments for Osteoporosis

Although there is no cure for osteoporosis, a variety of treatments can slow and even reverse bone loss. First, individuals with osteoporosis are encouraged to consume adequate calcium and vitamin D and to exercise regularly. Studies have shown that the most effective exercise programs include weight-bearing exercises such as jogging, stair climbing, and resistance training.[46]

In addition, several medications are available:

- Bisphosphonates, such as alendronate (brand name Fosamax), which decrease bone loss and can increase bone density and reduce the risk of spinal and nonspinal fractures
- Selective estrogen receptor modulators, such as raloxifene (brand name Evista), which have an estrogen-like effect on bone tissue, slowing the rate of bone loss and prompting some increase in bone mass
- Calcitonin (brand name Calcimar or Miacalcin), a pharmacologic preparation of the same thyroid hormone mentioned earlier, which can reduce the rate of bone loss
- Hormone replacement therapy (HRT), which combines estrogen with a hormone called progestin, and can reduce bone loss, increase bone density, and reduce the risk of hip and spinal fractures

All of these drugs can prompt side effects. For example, bisphosphonates are associated with several gastrointestinal side effects, including abdominal pain, constipation, diarrhea, heartburn, irritation of the esophagus, and difficulty swallowing. Side effects of HRT include breast tenderness, changes in mood, vaginal bleeding, and an increased risk for gallbladder disease.

Until recently, it was believed that HRT protected women against heart disease. A recent study found that one type of HRT actually increases a woman's risk for heart disease, stroke, and breast cancer.[47] As a result, hundreds of thousands of women in the United States have stopped taking HRT as a means to prevent or treat osteoporosis. However, despite the associated risks, it is recognized that HRT is still an

Hormone replacement medications come in a variety of forms.

effective treatment and prevention option for osteoporosis. It also reduces risk of colorectal cancer. Thus, women should work with their physicians to weigh these benefits against the increased risks of breast cancer and heart disease when considering HRT as a treatment option for osteoporosis.

Recap

Osteoporosis is a major disease of concern for elderly men and women in the United States. Osteoporosis increases the risk for fractures and premature death from subsequent illness. Factors that increase the risk for osteoporosis include genetics, being female, being of the Caucasian or Asian race, low levels of estrogen, cigarette smoking, alcohol abuse, sedentary lifestyle, and diets low in calcium and vitamin D. Medications are available for the prevention and treatment of osteoporosis.

A healthy diet and regular physical activity can reduce your risk of osteoporosis.

See for Yourself
Calculate Your Risk for Osteoporosis

One in three women and one in eight men will develop osteoporosis in their lifetimes.[22] But if you know you're at risk, you can take the steps identified in this chapter, such as increasing your amount of weight-bearing exercise and making sure you get enough calcium and vitamin D, to maintain the maximum amount of bone mass possible. That's why it's important to assess your risk. Below is the International Osteoporosis Foundation's One-Minute Osteoporosis Risk Test. The more "yes" answers you have, the greater the likelihood that you're in a higher risk group than the general population.

If you answered yes to any of these questions, it does not mean you have osteoporosis.[22] Positive answers simply mean that you have clinically-proven risk factors which may lead to osteoporosis and fractures. Discuss your results with your doctor, who can advise you on whether a bone density test is recommended.

1. Have either of your parents broken a hip after a minor bump or fall?	Yes	No
2. Have you broken a bone after a minor bump or fall?	Yes	No
3. Have you taken corticosteroid tablets (cortisone, prednisone, etc.) for more than 3 months?	Yes	No
4. Have you lost more than 3 cm (just over 1 in.) in height?	Yes	No
5. Do you regularly drink heavily (in excess of safe drinking limits)?	Yes	No
6. Do you smoke more than 20 cigarettes a day?	Yes	No
7. Do you suffer frequently from diarrhea (caused by problems such as celiac disease or Crohn disease)?	Yes	No
For women:		
8. Did you undergo menopause before the age of 45?	Yes	No
9. Have your periods stopped for 12 months or more (other than because of pregnancy)?	Yes	No
For men:		
10. Have you ever suffered from impotence, lack of libido, or other symptoms related to low testosterone levels?	Yes	No

Data adapted from: International Osteoporosis Foundation's *Are you at risk of osteoporosis? Take the One-Minute Osteoporosis Risk Test.* Available at www.osteofound.org.

Chapter Review

Test Yourself | Answers

1 (F) By selecting foods that are good sources of calcium each day, most people can consume enough calcium in their diets to meet the DRI. People at risk for low calcium intakes include elderly people, people who do not consume enough minerals in their diets, and people who do not consume enough food to maintain a healthful weight.

2 (F) Osteoporosis is more common among elderly women, but elderly men are also at increased risk for osteoporosis. Young women who suffer from an eating disorder and menstrual cycle irregularity, referred to as the female athlete triad, may also have osteoporosis.

3 (T) When exposed to sunlight, our bodies can convert a cholesterol compound in our skin to vitamin D.

4 (F) There are many good sources of calcium besides dairy foods, including calcium-fortified juices and soy/rice beverages and green leafy vegetables such as kale, broccoli, and collard greens.

5 (T) Recent studies indicate that overweight and obese people are more likely to have poor vitamin D status than people of normal weight. Poor vitamin D status increases the risk for osteoporosis.

Summary

- Bone develops through three processes: growth, modeling, and remodeling. Bone size is determined during growth, bone shape is determined during modeling and remodeling, and bone remodeling also affects the density of bone.

- Dual energy x-ray absorptiometry (DXA) is the most accurate tool for measuring bone density.

- Calcium is a major mineral that is an integral component of bones and teeth. Calcium levels are maintained in the blood at all times; calcium is also necessary for normal nerve transmission, muscle contraction, healthy blood pressure, and blood clotting.

- The AI for calcium is 1,000 mg per day for adult men and women aged 19 to 50 years and 1,200 mg per day for adult men and women older than 50 years of age.

- Consuming excess calcium leads to mineral imbalance, and consuming inadequate calcium causes osteoporosis.

- Vitamin D is a fat-soluble vitamin that can be produced from a cholesterol compound in skin using energy from sunlight. Vitamin D regulates blood calcium levels, regulates absorption of calcium and phosphorus from the intestines, and helps maintain bone health.

- The AI for vitamin D is 5 μg per day for adult men and women aged 19 to 50 years; the AI increases to 10 μg per day for men and women aged 51 to 70 years and to 15 μg per day for adults over the age of 70 years.

- Hypercalcemia results from consuming too much vitamin D, causing weakness, loss of appetite, diarrhea, vomiting, and formation of calcium deposits in soft tissues. Vitamin D deficiency leads to loss of bone mass, causing rickets in children or osteomalacia and osteoporosis in adults.

- Vitamin K is a fat-soluble vitamin that is obtained in the diet and is also produced in the large intestine by normal bacteria.

Vitamin K serves as a coenzyme for blood clotting and bone metabolism.

- Phosphorus is a major mineral that is an important part of the structure of bone; phosphorus is also a component of ATP, DNA, RNA, cell membranes, and lipoproteins.

- Magnesium is a major mineral that is part of the structure of bone, influences the formation of hydroxyapatite crystals and bone health through its regulation of calcium balance and the actions of vitamin D and parathyroid hormone, and is a cofactor for more than 300 enzyme systems.

- Fluoride is a trace mineral that strengthens teeth and bones and reduces the risk for dental caries.

- Osteoporosis is a major bone disease in the United States, affecting more than 10 million Americans. About 80% of people with this disease are women.

- Osteoporosis leads to increased risk of bone fractures and premature disability and death due to subsequent illness.

- Factors that increase the risk for osteoporosis include increased age, being female, being of the Caucasian or Asian race, cigarette smoking, alcohol abuse, low calcium and vitamin D intakes, and a sedentary lifestyle.

Review Questions

1. Hydroxyapatite crystals are predominantly made up of
   a. calcium and phosphorus.
   b. hydrogen, oxygen, and titanium.
   c. calcium and vitamin D.
   d. calcium and magnesium.

2. On a DXA test, a T-score of +1.0 indicates that the patient
   a. has osteoporosis.
   b. is at greater risk of fractures than an average, healthy person of the same age.
   c. has normal bone density as compared with an average, healthy 30-year-old.
   d. has slightly lower bone density than an average, healthy person of the same age.

3. Which of the following statements about trabecular bone is true?
   a. It accounts for about 80% of the skeleton.
   b. It forms the core of all bones of the skeleton.
   c. It is also called compact bone.
   d. It provides the scaffolding for cortical bone.

4. Which of the following individuals is most likely to require vitamin D supplements?
   a. a dark-skinned child living in Hawaii
   b. a fair-skinned construction worker living in Florida
   c. a dark-skinned retiree living in Illinois
   d. a fair-skinned college student living in Oklahoma

5. Calcium is necessary for several body functions, including
   a. demineralization of bone, nerve transmission, and immune responses.
   b. cartilage structure, nerve transmission, and muscle contraction.
   c. structure of bone, nerve, and muscle tissue, immune responses, and muscle contraction.
   d. structure of bone, nerve transmission, and muscle contraction.

6. **True or false?** The process by which bone is formed through the action of osteoblasts and resorbed through the action of osteoclasts is called remodeling.

7. **True or false?** Moderate consumption of alcohol has been associated with increased bone density.

8. **True or false?** Although osteoporosis can lead to painful and debilitating fractures, it is not associated with an increased risk of premature death.

9. **True or false?** The amount of calcium we absorb depends on our age, our calcium intake, the types of calcium-rich foods we eat, and the body's supply of vitamin D.

10. **True or false?** The body absorbs vitamin D from sunlight.

11. Explain why people with diseases that cause a malabsorption of fat may suffer from deficiency of vitamins D and K.

12. Most people reach their peak height by the end of adolescence, maintain that height for several decades, and then start to lose height in their later years. Describe the two processes behind this phenomenon.

13. The morning after reading this chapter, you are eating your usual breakfast cereal when you notice that the Nutrition Facts Panel on the box states that 1 serving contains 100% of your DRI for calcium. In addition, you're eating the cereal with about 1/2 cup of skim milk. Does this meal ensure that your calcium needs for the day are met? Why or why not?

14. Bert has light skin and lives in Buffalo, New York. How much time does Bert need to spend out of doors with exposed skin on winter days to avoid the need for consuming vitamin D in the diet or from supplements?

15. Look back at the information you learned about Liz in the Nutri-Case introductions, as well as in Chapters 1, 5, and 6. Identify aspects of Liz's nutrition and lifestyle that put her at increased risk for osteoporosis.

Web Links

www.nlm.nih.gov/medlineplus
Medline Plus Health Information
Search for rickets or osteomalacia to learn more about these vitamin D–deficiency diseases.

www.ada.org
American Dental Association
Look under "oral health topics" to learn more about the fluoridation of community water supplies and the use of fluoride-containing products.

www.nof.org
National Osteoporosis Foundation

Learn more about the causes, prevention, detection, and treatment of osteoporosis.

www.osteofound.org
International Osteoporosis Foundation
Find out more about this foundation and its mission to increase awareness and understanding of osteoporosis worldwide.

www.osteo.org
National Institutes of Health
Osteoporosis and Related Bone Diseases—National Resource Center
Access this site for additional resources and information on metabolic bone diseases, including osteoporosis.

References

1. Ball, J. W., and R. C. Bindler. 2003. *Pediatric Nursing: Caring for Children.* Upper Saddle River, NJ: Pearson Education.
2. Ho, A. Y. Y., and A. W. C. Kung. 2005. Determinants of peak bone mineral density and bone area in young women. *J. Bone Miner. Metab.* 23:470–475.
3. Chevalley, T., R. Rizzoli, D. Hans, S. Ferrari, and J. P. Bonjour. 2005. Interaction between calcium intake and menarcheal age on bone mass gain: An eight-year follow-up study from prepuberty to postmenarche. *J. Clin. Endocrinol. Metab.* 90:44–51.
4. Kindblom, J. M., M. Lorentzon, E. Norjavaara, A. Hellqvist, S. Nilsson, D. Mellström, and C. Ohlsson. 2006. Pubertal timing predicts previous fractures and BMD in young adult men: The GOOD study. *J. Bone Min. Res.* 21:790–795.
5. Institute of Medicine, Food and Nutrition Board. 1997. *Dietary Reference Intakes for Calcium, Phosphorus, Magnesium, Vitamin D, and Fluoride.* Washington, DC: National Academy Press.
6. Zemel, M. B., W. Thompson, A. Milstead, K. Morris, and P. Campbell. 2004. Calcium and dairy acceleration of weight and fat loss during energy restriction in obese adults. *Obes. Res.* 12:582–590.
7. Bowen J., M. Noakes, and P. M. Clifton. 2005. Effect of calcium and dairy foods in high protein, energy-restricted diets on weight loss and metabolic parameters in overweight adults. *Int. J. Obes.* 29:957–965.
8. Keller, J. L., A. J. Lanou, and N. D. Barnard. 2002. The consumer cost of calcium from food and supplements. *J. Am. Diet. Assoc.* 102:1669–1671.
9. Nusser, S. M., A. L. Carriquiry, K. W. Dodd, and W. A. Fuller. 1996. A semiparametric transformation approach to estimating usual daily intake distributions. *J. Am. Stat. Assoc.* 91:1440–1449.
10. Ross, E. A., N. J. Szabo, and I. R. Tebbett. 2000. Lead content of calcium supplements. *JAMA* 284:1425–1433.
11. Massey, L. K., H. Roman-Smith, and R. A. Sutton. 1993. Effect of dietary oxalate and calcium on urinary oxalate and risk of formation of calcium oxalate kidney stones. *J. Am. Diet. Assoc.* 93:901–906.
12. Holick, M. F., L. Y. Matsuoka, and J. Wortsman. 1989. Age, vitamin D, and solar ultraviolet. *Lancet* 2:1104–1105.
13. Need, A. G., H. A. Morris, M. Horowitz, and C. Nordin. 1993. Effects of skin thickness, age, body fat, and sunlight on serum 25-hydroxyvitamin D. *Am. J. Clin. Nutr.* 58:882–885.
14. Florez, H., R. Martinez, W. Chacra, N. Strickman-Stein, and S. Levis. 2007. Outdoor exercise reduces the risk of hypovitaminosis D in the obese. *J. Steroid Biochem. Mol. Biol.* 103:679–681.
15. Holick, M. F. 2005. The vitamin D epidemic and its health consequences. *J. Nutr.* 135:2739S–2748S.
16. Holick, M. F. 1994. McCollum Award Lecture, 1994: Vitamin D: New horizons for the 21st century. *Am. J. Clin. Nutr.* 60:619–630.
17. Weisberg, P., K. S. Scanlon, R. Li, and M. E. Cogswell. 2004. Nutritional rickets among children in the United States: Review of cases reported between 1986 and 2003. *Am. J. Clin. Nutr.* 80(suppl.):1697S–1705S.
18. FAO and WHO. 2002. Vitamin K. In: Human vitamin and mineral requirements. Report of a joint FAO/WHO expert consultation. Available at www.micronutrient.org/idpas/pdf/846.10-CHAPTER10.pdf.
19. Institute of Medicine, Food and Nutrition Board. 2002. *Dietary Reference Intakes for Vitamin A, Vitamin K, Arsenic, Boron, Chromium, Copper, Iodine, Iron, Manganese, Molybdenum, Nickel, Silicon, Vanadium, and Zinc.* Washington, DC: National Academy Press.
20. Weber, P. 2001. Vitamin K and bone health. *Nutrition* 17:880–887.
21. Shearer, M. J. 2000. Role of vitamin K and Gla proteins in the pathophysiology of osteoporosis and vascular calcification. *Curr. Opin. Clin. Nutr. Metab. Care* 3:433–438.
22. Feskanich, D., S. A. Korrick, S. L. Greenspan, H. N. Rosen, and G. A. Colditz. 1999. Moderate alcohol consumption and bone density among post-menopausal women. *J. Women's Health* 8:65–73.
23. Wyshak, G., R. E. Frisch, T. E. Albright, N. L. Albright, I. Schiff, and J. Witschi. 1989. Nonalcoholic carbonated beverage consumption and bone fractures among women former college athletes. *J. Orthop. Res.* 7:91–99.

24. Wyshak, G., and R. E. Frisch. 1994. Carbonated beverages, dietary calcium, the dietary calcium/phosphorus ratio, and bone fractures in girls and boys. *J. Adolesc. Health* 15:210–215.

25. Wyshak, G. 2000. Teenaged girls, carbonated beverage consumption, and bone fractures. *Arch. Pediatr. Adolesc. Med.* 154:610–613.

26. Heaney, R. P., and K. Rafferty. 2001. Carbonated beverages and urinary calcium excretion. *Am. J. Clin. Nutr.* 74:343–347.

27. Paolisso G., S. Sgambato, A. Gambardella, G. Pizza, P. Tesauro, M. Varricchio, and F. D'Onofrio. 1992. Daily magnesium supplements improve glucose handling in elderly subjects. *Am. J. Clin. Nutr.* 55:1161–1167.

28. Larsson, S. C., L. Bergkvist, and A. Wolk. 2005. Magnesium intake in relation to risk of colorectal cancer in women. *JAMA* 293:86–89.

29. Pak, C. Y., K. Sakhaee, B. Adams-Huet, V. Piziak, R. D. Peterson, and J. R. Poindexter. 1995. Treatment of postmenopausal osteoporosis with slow-release sodium fluoride. Final report of a randomized controlled trial. *Ann. Int. Med.* 123:401–408.

30. Reginster, J. Y., D. Felsenberg, I. Pavo, J. Stepan, J. Payer, H. Resch, C. C. Glüer, D. Mühlenbacher, D. Quail, H. Schmitt, and T. Nickelsen. 2003. Effect of raloxifene combined with monofluorophosphate as compared with monofluorophosphate alone in postmenopausal women with low bone mass: A randomized, controlled trial. *Osteoporosis Int.* 14:741–749.

31. Ringe, J. D., A. Dorst, H. Faber, C. Kipshoven, L. C. Rovati, and I. Setnikar. 2005. Efficacy of etidronate and sequential monofluorophosphate in severe postmenopausal osteoporosis: a pilot study. *Rheumatol. Int.* 25:296–300.

32. American Dietetic Association. 2005. Position of the American Dietetic Association: The impact of fluoride on health. *J. Am. Diet. Assoc.* 105:1620–1628.

33. U.S. Department of Health and Human Services. Public Health Service. 1991. Review of fluoride: Benefits and risks. Report of the Ad Hoc Subcommittee on Fluoride of the Committee to Coordinate Environmental Health and Related Programs. Available at www.health.gov/environment/ReviewofFluoride/default.htm.

34. International Osteoporosis Foundation. 2007. Facts and statistics about osteoporosis and its impact. Available at www.iofbonehealth.org/facts-and-statistics.html.

35. National Osteoporosis Foundation. 2008. Fast facts on osteoporosis. Available at www.nof.org/osteoporosis/diseasefacts.htm.

36. Laitinen, K., M. Valimaki, and P. Keto. 1991. Bone mineral density measured by dual-energy x-ray absorptiometry in healthy Finnish women. *Calcif. Tissue Int.* 48:224–231.

37. Holbrook, T. L., and E. Barrett-Connor. 1993. A prospective study of alcohol consumption and bone mineral density. *BMJ* 306:1506–1509.

38. Felson, D. T., Y. Zhang, M. T. Hannan, W. B. Kannel, and D. P. Kiel. 1995. Alcohol intake and bone mineral density in elderly men and women. The Framingham Study. *Am. J. Epidemiol.* 142:485–492.

39. Rapuri, P. B., J. C. Gallagher, K. E. Balhorn, and K. L. Ryschon. 2000. Alcohol intake and bone metabolism in elderly women. *Am. J. Clin. Nutr.* 72:1206–1213.

40. Massey, L. K. 2001. Is caffeine a risk factor for bone loss in the elderly? *Am. J. Clin. Nutr.* 74:569–570.

41. Rapuri, P. B., J. C. Gallagher, H. K. Kinyamu, and K. L. Ryschon. 2001. Caffeine intake increases the rate of bone loss in elderly women and interacts with vitamin D receptor genotypes. *Am. J. Clin. Nutr.* 74:694–700.

42. Devine A., R. A. Criddle, I. M. Dick, D. A. Kerr, and R. L. Prince. 1995. A longitudinal study of the effect of sodium and calcium intakes on regional bone density in post-menopausal women. *Am. J. Clin. Nutr.* 62:740–745.

43. Dawson-Hughes, B., and S. S. Harris. 2002. Calcium intake influences the association of protein intake with rates of bone loss in elderly men and women. *Am. J. Clin. Nutr.* 75:773–779.

44. Tucker, K. L., M. T. Hannan, H. Chen, L. A. Cupples, P. W. F. Wilson, and D. P. Kiel. 1999. Potassium, magnesium, and fruit and vegetable intakes are associated with greater bone mineral density in elderly men and women. *Am. J. Clin. Nutr.* 69:727–736.

45. Tucker, K. L., H. Chen, M. T. Hannan, L. A. Cupples, P. W. F. Wilson, D. Felson, and D. P. Kiel. 2002. Bone mineral density and dietary patterns in older adults: The Framingham Osteoporosis Study. *Am. J. Clin. Nutr.* 76:245–252.

46. South-Pal, J. E. 2001. Osteoporosis: Part II. Nonpharmacologic and pharmacologic treatment. *Am. Fam. Physician* 63:1121–1128.

47. Writing Group for the Women's Health Initiative Investigators. 2002. Risks and benefits of estrogen plus progestin in healthy postmenopausal women. Principal results from the Women's Health Initiative randomized control trial. *JAMA* 288:321–332.

48. Weaver, C. M. and J. C. Fleet. 2004. Vitamin D requirements: Current and future. *Am. J. Clin. Nutr.* 80(suppl):1735S–1739S.

49. Hollis, B. W. 2005. Circulating 25-hydroxyvitamin D levels indicative of vitamin D sufficiency: Implications for establishing a new effective dietary intake recommendation for vitamin D. *J. Nutr.* 135:317–322.

50. Yetley, E. A., B. Brulé, M. C. Cheney, C. D. Davis, K. A. Esslinger, P. W. F. Fischer, K. E. Friedl, L. S. Greene-Finestone, P. M. Guenther, D. M. Klurfeld, M. R. L'Abbe, and K. Y. McMurry. 2009. Dietary reference intakes for vitamin D: Justification for a review of the 1997 values. *Am. J. Clin. Nutr.* 89:719–727.

51. Brannon, P. M., E. A. Yetley, R. L. Bailey, and M. F. Picciano. 2008. Overview of the conference "Vitamin D and Health in the 21st Century: An Update." *Am. J. Clin. Nutr.* 88(suppl):483S–490S.

52. Koutkia, P., T. C. Chen, and M. F. Holick. 2001. Vitamin D intoxication associated with an over-the-counter supplement. *N. Engl. J. Med.* 345(1):66–67.

53. Jackson, R. D., A. Z. LaCroix, M. Gass, R. B. Wallace, J. Robbins, C. E. Lewis, T. Bassford, S. A. A. Beresford, H. R. Black, P. Blanchette, D. E. Bonds, R. L. Brunner, R. G. Brzyski, B. Caan, J. A. Cauley, R. T. Chlebowski, S. R. Cummings, I. Granek, J. Hays, G. Heiss, S. L. Hendrix, B. V. Howard, J. Hsia, F. A. Hubbell, K. C. Johnson, H. Judd, J. Morley Kotchen, L. H. Kuller, R. D. Langer, N. L. Lasser, M. C. Limacher, S. Ludlam, J. E. Manson, K. L. Margolis, J. McGowan, J. K. Ockene, M. J. O'Sullivan, L. Phillips, R. L. Prentice, G. E. Sarto, M. L. Stefanick, L. Van Horn, J. Wactawski-Wende, E. Whitlock, G. L. Anderson, A. R. Assaf, and D. Barad. 2006. Calcium plus vitamin D supplementation and the risk of fractures. *N. Engl. J. Med.* 354:669–683.

54. Stolzenberg-Solomon, R. Z., R. Vieth, A. Azad, P. Pietinen, P. R. Taylor, J. Virtamo, and D. Albanes. 2006. A prospective nested case-control study of vitamin D status and pancreatic cancer risk in male smokers. *Cancer Res.* 66:10213–10219.

Vitamin D Recommendations: Time for a Boost?

No doubt about it: unless you live at a latitude within 40° of the equator and spend time outdoors without sunscreen, it's tough to get enough vitamin D. That's because, as you learned in this chapter, there are very few natural food sources of vitamin D, and even fortified food sources are limited to milk and a handful of other products. But if meeting the Institute of Medicine's current AI for vitamin D is already posing a challenge to many Americans, why are some researchers calling for an even higher intake recommendation?

An individual's vitamin D status is assessed by measuring circulating levels of 25-dihydroxy vitamin D. These measurements in a variety of population studies in recent years have led to a growing concern about widespread vitamin D deficiency and its associated diseases, including rickets in children and osteomalacia and osteoporosis in adults. In addition, since the Institute of Medicine set its vitamin D recommendations in 1997, new information has been published about vitamin D metabolism and its potential role in reducing the risks for diseases such as type 1 diabetes, some cancers, and multiple sclerosis.[48] This new information has led some researchers to argue that our current definition of what constitutes a "normal" circulating level of 25-dihydroxy vitamin D is seriously flawed, and that our blood levels should be much higher than what we can achieve by consuming the current AI values.[49] These discussions have resulted in some nutrition and bone health experts calling for a full review of the recent research on vitamin D and a reevaluation of the current recommendations.[50]

However, there are valid concerns about increasing the current vitamin D recommendations. Recall that vitamin D is fat-soluble, so the body readily stores it. Thus, excess amounts can build up in adipose and other tissues. Increasing current recommendations could therefore increase the population's risk for vitamin D toxicity and its damaging side effects, such as hypercalcemia, increased bone loss, kidney stones, and calcification of other soft tissues such as the heart and liver.

What do we really know about vitamin D metabolism and the role of vitamin D in human health? Is there sufficient evidence to support increasing the current AI recommendations?

In 2008, *The American Journal of Clinical Nutrition* published a special supplement that reported findings from an evidence-based review and conference on vitamin D and health.[51] Articles published in this supplement explored many important issues surrounding vitamin D and its role in optimizing our health. These issues included:

- **Whether circulating vitamin D levels are associated with bone health across the life span.** While the evidence is relatively strong that circulating levels of vitamin D are associated with falls, hip fractures, and poor bone mineral density (BMD) in elderly and postmenopausal white women, there is little evidence of this association in infants, young children, or ethnic minority groups.

- **The effect (if any) of dietary intake of fortified foods and supplements or sun exposure on circulating levels of vitamin D.** It appears that responses to fortified foods, supplements, or sun exposure vary depending on a person's baseline circulating levels of vitamin D, and some people (for example, postmenopausal African American women) may have no response or a limited response to vitamin D from fortified foods and supplements.

- **The evidence that exists on the efficacy of supplementary doses of vitamin D on bone health.** The poor quality of our food composition databases limits our ability to analyze how much vitamin D is in food.[48] At the same time, the amount of vitamin D in supplements can be highly variable and significantly greater than what is listed on the label. This erroneous labeling has been reported to lead to toxicity.[52] Furthermore, although there is good evidence that combined calcium and vitamin D supplementation increases BMD and reduces the risk for bone fractures, vitamin D alone does not have this beneficial effect.

- **Whether consuming vitamin D in amounts greater than recommendations results in toxicities.** Although some evidence suggests that people can tolerate up to 10,000 IU per day of vitamin D (which is five times the current tolerable upper limit), recent studies have indicated increased kidney stones with modest supplementation of 400 IU vitamin D_3 and 1000 mg calcium daily.[53] Also, smokers with relatively high circulating levels of vitamin D have a three-fold increased risk of pancreatic cancer than smokers with lower levels.[54]

- **Whether there is a level of sun exposure adequate to maintain healthy vitamin D levels that does not increase a person's risk for skin cancer.** There does not appear to be a threshold for sun exposure below which people do not increase their risk for skin cancer. At the same time, numerous factors affect a person's ability to produce vitamin D from exposure to sunlight. Thus, it is not possible to recommend a uniform amount of sunlight exposure for the general population.

In addition, the journal supplement concluded that there is very little published evidence related to the impact of vitamin D on our risks for chronic diseases such as diabetes, some cancers, and autoimmune diseases.

Critical Thinking Questions

- Now that you've read this debate about what is presently known about vitamin D and its role in our health, do you believe that the current recommendations are too low and should be increased?

- Do you think you would benefit from vitamin D supplementation? Why or why not?

- If you think you do need to improve your vitamin D status, what method(s) would you choose?

- Would you prefer to try to increase your circulating levels of vitamin D through natural foods, fortified foods, supplements, or increased sun exposure?

- What are your reasons for your preference(s)?

12

Nutrients Involved in Blood Health and Immunity

Test Yourself | True or False?

1 Iron deficiency is the most common nutrient deficiency in the world. **T** or **F**

2 To reduce their risk of having a baby with a serious central nervous system defect, women should begin taking folate supplements when they are planning a pregnancy or as soon as they learn they are pregnant. **T** or **F**

3 People consuming a vegan diet are at greater risk for micronutrient deficiencies than are people who eat foods of animal origin. **T** or **F**

4 *Anemia* is the clinical term for iron deficiency. **T** or **F**

5 Fever, vomiting, and diarrhea all play a role in protecting the body from infectious disease. **T** or **F**

Test Yourself answers are located in the Chapter Review.

Chapter Objectives *After reading this chapter, you will be able to:*

1. Describe the four components of blood, *p. 446.*

2. Discuss the role that iron plays in oxygen transport, *pp. 447–448.*

3. Discuss the functions of zinc and copper and the contributions of these minerals to blood health, *pp. 455–459.*

4. Compare and contrast the functions of two B vitamins associated with blood health, *pp. 462–467.*

5. Describe the association of folate and vitamin B_{12} with vascular disease, *pp. 468–469.*

6. Distinguish between microcytic anemia, pernicious anemia, and macrocytic anemia, *pp. 469–470.*

7. Discuss common malfunctions of the immune system, *p. 473.*

8. Describe how nutrient deficiencies affect immunity, *pp. 473–475.*

D r. Leslie Bernstein looked in astonishment at the 80-year-old man in his office. A leading gastroenterologist and professor of medicine at Albert Einstein College of Medicine in New York City, he had admired Pop Katz for years as one of his most healthy patients, a strict vegetarian and athlete who just weeks before had been going on 3-mile runs as if he were 40 years younger. Now, he could barely stand. He was confused, cried easily, was wandering away from the house partially clothed, and had lost control of his bladder. Tests showed that he was not suffering from Alzheimer's disease, had not had a stroke, did not have a tumor or infection, and had no evidence of exposure to pesticides, metals, drugs, or other toxins. Blood tests were normal except for one important clue: his red blood cells were slightly enlarged. Bernstein consulted with a neurologist, who diagnosed "rapidly progressive dementia of unknown origin."

Bernstein was unconvinced: "In a matter of weeks, a man who hadn't been sick for eighty years suddenly became demented. . . . 'Holy smoke!,' I thought, 'I'm an idiot! The man's been a vegetarian for thirty-eight years. No meat. No fish. No eggs. No milk. He hasn't had any animal protein for decades. He has to be vitamin B_{12} deficient!'"[1]

Bernstein immediately tested Katz's blood, then gave him an injection of vitamin B_{12}. The blood test confirmed Bernstein's hunch: The level of vitamin B_{12} in Katz's blood was too low to measure. The morning after his injection, Katz could sit up without help. Within a week of continuing treatment, he could read, play card games, and hold his own in conversations. Unfortunately, the delay in diagnosis left some permanent neurologic damage, including alterations in his personality and an inability to concentrate. Bernstein notes, "A diet free of animal protein can be healthful and safe, but it should be supplemented periodically with vitamin B_{12} by mouth or by injection."[1]

It was not until 1906, when English biochemist F. G. Hopkins discovered what he called *accessory factors*, that scientists began to appreciate the many critical roles of micronutrients in maintaining human health. Vitamin B_{12}, for instance, was not even isolated until 1948! In Chapters 8 through 11, we explored several key roles of vitamins and minerals, including energy metabolism, the regulation of fluids and nerve-impulse transmission, protection against the damage caused by oxidation, and maintenance of healthy bones. In this chapter, we conclude our exploration of the micronutrients with a discussion of two final roles: their contributions to the formation and maintenance of blood and to the production of the cells and chemicals of the immune system.

What Is the Role of Blood in Maintaining Health?

Blood transports to body cells virtually all the components necessary for life. No matter how much carbohydrate, fat, and protein we eat, we could not survive without healthy blood to transport these nutrients, and the oxygen to metabolize them, to our cells. In addition to transporting nutrients and oxygen, blood removes the waste products generated from metabolism so that they can be properly excreted. Our health and our ability to perform daily activities are compromised if the quantity and quality of our blood is diminished.

Blood is actually a tissue, the only fluid tissue in the body. It is composed of four components (**Figure 12.1**). **Erythrocytes,** or red blood cells, are the cells that transport oxygen. **Leukocytes,** or white blood cells, are the key to our immune function and protect us from infection and illness. **Platelets** are cell fragments that assist in the formation of blood clots and help stop bleeding. **Plasma** is the fluid portion of the blood, and it is needed to maintain adequate blood volume so that blood can flow easily throughout the body.

Certain micronutrients play important roles in the maintenance of blood health through their actions as **coenzymes** and **cofactors** and as regulators of oxygen transport. These nutrients are discussed in detail in the following section.

A Profile of Nutrients That Maintain Healthy Blood

The nutrients recognized as playing a critical role in maintaining blood health include iron, zinc, copper, vitamin K, folate, and vitamin B_{12} (Table 12.1). Because blood is a tissue, ade-

erythrocytes   Red blood cells; they transport oxygen in the blood.

leukocytes   White blood cells; they protect the body from infection and illness.

platelets   Cell fragments that assist in the formation of blood clots and help stop bleeding.

plasma   The fluid portion of the blood; it is needed to maintain adequate blood volume so that the blood can flow easily throughout the body.

coenzyme   The nonprotein component of enzymes; many coenzymes are B-vitamins.

cofactor   A small, chemically simple organic or inorganic substance that is required for enzyme activity; trace minerals such as iron, zinc, and copper function as cofactors.

Figure 12.1 Blood has four components, which are visible when the blood is drawn into a test tube and spun in a centrifuge. The bottom layer is the erythrocytes, or red blood cells. The milky layer above the erythrocytes contains the leukocytes and platelets. The yellow fluid on top is the plasma.

quate protein intake is also important for good blood health (see Chapter 6 for more on protein and its requirements).

Iron

Iron (Fe) is a trace mineral found in very small amounts in the body. Despite our relatively small need for iron, the World Health Organization lists iron deficiency as the most common nutrient deficiency in the world, including industrialized countries.[2] Iron is a unique mineral with a positive charge that can easily give up and/or gain an electron, thereby changing its state from ferrous iron (Fe^{+2}) to ferric iron (Fe^{+3}) and back again. Although other forms of iron exist, ferrous and ferric iron are the two most common forms in our diet. Iron also binds easily to negatively charged elements such as oxygen, nitrogen, and sulfur, a capacity that is important for the various functions iron plays in the body. We will discuss more about the various oxidative states of iron shortly.

Functions of Iron

Iron is a component of numerous proteins in the body, including enzymes and other proteins involved in energy production and both hemoglobin and myoglobin, the proteins involved in the transport and metabolism of oxygen. **Hemoglobin** is the oxygen-carrying protein found in the erythrocytes. It transports oxygen to tissues and accounts for almost two-thirds of all of the body's iron. Every day, within the bone marrow, the body produces approximately 200 billion erythrocytes that require more than 24 mg of iron.[3] Thus, it is easy to see that hemoglobin synthesis for the formation of red blood cells is a primary factor in iron homeostasis. **Myoglobin,** another oxygen-carrying protein that is similar to hemoglobin, transports and stores oxygen within the muscles, accounting for approximately 10% of total iron in the body.

We cannot survive for more than a few minutes without oxygen; thus, hemoglobin's ability to transport oxygen throughout the body is absolutely critical to life. To carry oxygen, hemoglobin depends on the iron in its **heme** groups. As shown in **Figure 12.2,** the hemoglobin molecule consists of four polypeptide chains studded with four iron-containing heme groups. Iron is able to bind with and release oxygen easily. It does this by transferring electrons to and from the other atoms as it moves between various oxidation states. In the bloodstream, iron acts as a shuttle, picking up oxygen from the

Table 12.1 Overview of Nutrients Essential to Blood Health

To see the full profile of nutrients essential to bone health, turn to *In Depth*, Vitamins and Minerals: Micronutrients with Macro Powers, pages 282–286.

Nutrient	Recommended Intake (RDA or AI and UL)
Iron	RDA: Women aged 19 to 50 years = 18 mg/day Men aged 19 to 50 years = 8 mg/day UL = 45 mg/day
Zinc	RDA: Women aged 19 to 50 years = 8 mg/day Men aged 19 to 50 years =11 mg/day UL = 40 mg/day
Copper	RDA for all people 19–50 years = 90 µg/day UL = 10,000 µg/day
Vitamin K	AI: Women 19–50 years = 90 µg/day Men 19–50 years = 120 µg/day UL = none determined
Folate (folic acid)	RDA for all people 19–50 years = 400 µg/day UL = 1,000 µg/day
Vitamin B12 (cyanocobalamin)	RDA for all people 19–50 years = 2.4 µg/day UL = not determined (ND)

*Based on the assumption that a person does not get adequate sun exposure.

hemoglobin The oxygen-carrying protein found in red blood cells; almost two-thirds of all of the iron in the body is found in hemoglobin.

myoglobin An iron-containing protein similar to hemoglobin except that it is found in muscle cells.

heme The iron-containing molecule found in hemoglobin.

Figure 12.2 Iron is contained in the heme portion of hemoglobin and myoglobin.

environment, binding it during its transport in the bloodstream, and then dropping it off again in our tissues.

As just noted, iron is also important in energy metabolism. It is a component of the cytochromes, electron carriers within the metabolic pathways that result in the production of energy from carbohydrates, fats, and protein. Cytochromes contain heme and thus require iron. If iron is not available to form them, the production of energy is limited, especially during times of high energy demand, such as during physical activity. Iron is also involved in some of the key enzymes in the tricarboxylic acid (TCA) cycle and for enzymes required in amino acid and lipid metabolism. As presented in Chapter 10, iron is a part of the antioxidant enzyme system that assists in fighting free radicals. Interestingly, excess iron can also act as a prooxidant and promote the production of free radicals. Finally, iron is necessary for enzymes involved in DNA synthesis and plays an important role in cognitive development and immune health (discussed later in this chapter).[3, 4]

How Does the Body Regulate Iron Homeostasis?

As mentioned earlier, the body contains relatively little iron; men have less than 4 g of iron in their bodies, and women have just over 2 g. Iron is necessary for life, yet too much iron is toxic; therefore, the body maintains iron homeostasis primarily through regulating iron digestion, absorption, transport, storage, and excretion. **Figure 12.3** provides an overview of iron digestion, absorption, and transport.

Iron Digestion and Absorption The body's ability to digest and absorb dietary iron is influenced by a number of factors. The most important of these are: the individual's iron status; the level of dietary iron consumption; the type of iron present in the foods consumed; the amount of stomach acid present to digest the foods; and the presence of dietary factors that can either enhance or inhibit the absorption of iron.

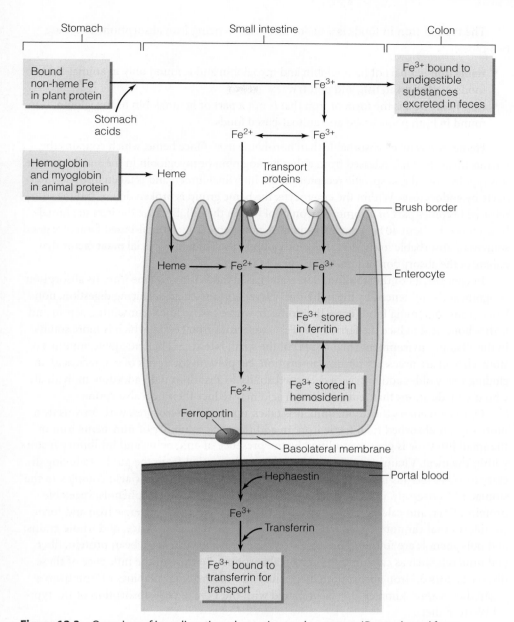

Figure 12.3 Overview of iron digestion, absorption, and transport. (*Data adapted from:* Figure 12.2 in Gropper, S., J. L. Smith, and J. L. Groff. 2005. *Advanced Nutrition and Human Metabolism,* 4th ed. © 2005. Reprinted with permission of Brooks Cole, a division of Thomson Learning.)

Typically, the amount of iron absorbed from the diet is low, from 14% to 18% depending on the way iron absorption is measured; however, if iron status is poor, absorption can increase to as high as 40%.[3, 4] Thus, people with poor iron status, such as those with iron deficiency, pregnant women, or people who have recently experienced blood loss (including menstruation), generally have the highest iron absorption rates. The typical Western diet of 2,000 kcal/day would contain about 12 mg of iron. In an individual with good iron status, only about 1.9 mg of this would be absorbed. However, in an individual with poor iron status, a maximum of 4.8 mg would be absorbed. By altering absorption rate, the body can improve iron status without dramatic increases in dietary iron intake.

Similarly, the total amount of iron consumed in the diet influences an individual's iron absorption rate. People who consume low levels of dietary iron absorb more iron from their foods than those with higher dietary iron intakes. If the gut mucosal cells have a high iron pool, less iron is absorbed from the next meal.

The type of iron in foods is a major factor influencing iron absorption. There are two types:

- **Heme iron** is a part of hemoglobin and myoglobin and is found only in animal-based foods such as meat, fish, and poultry.
- **Non-heme iron** is the form of iron that is not a part of hemoglobin or myoglobin. It is found in both plant-based and animal-based foods.

Heme iron is more absorbable than non-heme iron. Once heme, which contains the ferrous form (Fe^{2+}), is released from either hemoglobin or myoglobin in the small intestine, it is rapidly bound to a specific receptor on the intestinal lumen and is taken into the enterocyte by endocytosis. Within the enterocyte, the heme group is broken down, and the iron released becomes part of a common iron pool within the cell. Because the iron in animal-based foods is about 40% heme iron and 60% non-heme iron, animal-based foods are good sources of absorbable iron. Meat, fish, and poultry also contain a special **meat factor** that enhances the absorption of non-heme iron in the diet.[3]

In contrast, all of the iron found in plant-based foods is non-heme iron. Its absorption is significantly influenced by the individual's level of stomach acid. During digestion, non-heme iron–containing foods enter the stomach, where gastric juices containing pepsin and hydrocholic acid reduce the ferric iron (Fe^{3+}) to ferrous iron (Fe^{2+}), which is more soluble in the alkaline environment (higher pH) of the small intestine. Thus, adequate amounts of stomach acid are necessary for iron absorption. People with low levels of stomach acid, including many older adults, have a decreased ability to absorb iron. In addition, individuals who use medications that reduce stomach acid may reduce their iron absorption.

Once iron enters the duodenum, it is taken up by the enterocytes, with ferrous iron more rapidly absorbed than ferric iron. In addition, the solubility of non-heme iron in the small intestine is greatly modified by the presence of enhancing and inhibitory factors within the meal. Vitamin C enhances non-heme absorption from the gut by reducing dietary ferric to ferrous iron, which then forms a soluble iron–ascorbic acid complex in the stomach.[4] Conversely, iron absorption is impaired by phytates, polyphenols, vegetable proteins, fiber, and calcium. Typically, these substances bind to the ferric iron and form complexes that cannot be digested. Phytates are found in legumes, rice, and whole grains; and polyphenols are found in oregano, red wine, tea, and coffee. Soybean protein, fiber, and minerals such as calcium inhibit iron absorption. Because of the influence of these dietary factors on iron absorption, it is estimated that the bioavailability of iron from a vegan diet is approximately 10%, compared with the 14% to 18% absorption of the typical Western diet.

To optimize absorption of the non-heme iron in plant foods, consume these foods either with foods rich in heme iron or in combination with foods high in vitamin C. For instance, eating meat with beans or vegetables enhances the absorption of the non-heme iron found in the beans and vegetables. Drinking a glass of orange juice with breakfast cereal will increase the absorption of the non-heme iron in the cereal. Avoid taking zinc or calcium supplements or drinking milk when eating iron-rich foods, as iron absorption will be impaired.

Finally, cooking foods in cast-iron pans will significantly increase the iron content of any meal. That's because the iron in the pan is released and combines with food during the cooking process.

Iron Transport   Regardless of the form, iron taken into the enterocytes becomes part of the total iron pool. From this pool the iron can be stored within the enterocytes or it can be transported across the membrane of the enterocytes by **ferroportin** into the interstitial fluid, from which it can enter the circulation. Ferroportin is an iron transporter that helps regulate intestinal iron absorption and release.[5] Iron crossing into the interstitial fluid is in the ferrous form (Fe^{2+}) but it is quickly converted to ferric iron (Fe^{3+}) by either **hephaestin** in the intestinal basal cell membrane (see Figure 12.3) or **ceruloplasmin** in the blood, two

Cooking foods in cast-iron pans significantly increases their iron content.

heme iron   Iron that is a part of hemoglobin and myoglobin; found only in animal-based foods such as meat, fish, and poultry.

non-heme iron   The form of iron that is not a part of hemoglobin or myoglobin; found in animal-based and plant-based foods.

meat factor   A special factor found in meat, fish, and poultry that enhances the absorption of non-heme iron.

ferroportin   An iron transporter that helps regulate intestinal iron absorption and the release of iron from the enterocyte into the general circulation.

hephaestin   A copper-containing protein that oxidizes Fe^{2+} to Fe^{3+} once iron is transported across the basolateral membrane by ferroportin.

ceruloplasmin   A copper-containing protein that transports copper in the body. It also plays a role in oxidizing ferric to ferrous iron (Fe^{2+} to Fe^{3+}).

copper-containing plasma proteins capable of oxidizing iron. This Fe^{3+} is rapidly bound to **transferrin,** the primary iron-transport protein in the blood, which transports the Fe^{3+} to cells of the body. Transferrin receptors on the cells increase and decrease in number depending on the cells' need for iron. In this way, cells can regulate the amount of iron they take in from the blood.

Iron Storage   The body is capable of storing small amounts of iron in two storage forms: **ferritin** and **hemosiderin.** These storage forms of iron provide us with iron when our diets are inadequate or when our needs are high. Both ferritin and hemosiderin can be mobilized if the body needs iron.

Figure 12.3 shows iron storage in the enterocytes as ferritin or hemosiderin. Other common areas of iron storage are the liver, bone marrow, and spleen. Ferritin is the normal storage form, whereas hemosiderin storage occurs predominately in conditions of iron overload. However, if an iron overload occurs, and excess iron is stored as hemosiderin in the heart and liver, organ damage can occur.

The amount of iron stored can vary dramatically between men and women, with women at greater risk for having low iron stores (from 300 to 1,000 mg). Average iron stores for men are estimated to be 500 to 1,500 mg. Women of childbearing age have one of the highest rates of iron deficiency, which is attributed to increased iron losses in menstrual blood, poor intakes of iron, and the additional iron requirements that accompany pregnancy. The iron "cost" of pregnancy is high; thus, a woman of childbearing age should have good iron stores prior to pregnancy and consume iron-rich foods during pregnancy. Iron supplements are routinely prescribed during the last two trimesters to ensure that there is adequate iron for the woman and her developing fetus. The iron needs of pregnancy are covered in more detail in Chapter 16.

Regulation of Total Body Iron   The body regulates iron balance and homeostasis through three mechanisms:

- *Iron absorption.* As discussed earlier, the change in iron absorption rate is based on the amount of iron consumed, the amount needed by the body, and the dietary factors that affect absorption.
- *Iron losses.* One of the major routes of iron loss is through the turnover of the gut enterocytes. Every 3 to 6 days, the gut cells are shed and lost into the lumen of the intestine. In this way, the iron stored as ferritin within the enterocytes is returned to the lumen, from which it is lost in the feces. The regulation of iron absorption in this way dramatically reduces the possibility of too much iron entering the system, regardless of the iron source. Iron can also be lost in blood (menses, blood donations, injury), sweat, semen, and passively from cells that are shed from the skin and urinary tract. Depending on body size, iron losses range from 0.75 to 1 mg of iron/day in nonmenstruating women and in men.[4] Active individuals can also have increased iron losses due to iron lost in urine, sweat, and increased red cell turnover.[4] A recent study showed that iron deficiency was prevalent in 29% to 36% and 4% to 6% of recreationally active women and men, respectively.[6]
- *Storage and recycling of iron.* Stored iron gives the body access to iron to maintain health when intakes of dietary iron are low or losses are great. Conversely, once iron balance has been restored, the body will gradually increase the amount of iron stored so that reserves are again available in times of need. The body is also efficient at recycling iron already within the system. The majority of the body's iron is bound to hemoglobin within the red blood cells, which have a life of 120 days. In order to prevent the body from losing this valuable source of iron, as old red cells are broken down, the iron is recycled and returned to the body's iron pool. The iron supplied through recycling is approximately twenty times greater than the amount of iron absorbed from the diet.[5] Thus, the ability of the body to recycle iron is extremely important in maintaining iron homeostasis.

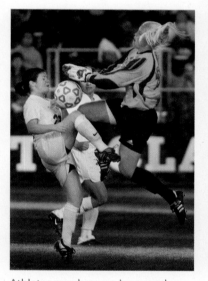

Athletes may have an increased need for iron.

transferrin   The transport protein for iron.

ferritin   A storage form of iron found primarily in the intestinal mucosa, spleen, bone marrow, and liver.

hemosiderin   A storage form of iron found primarily in the intestinal mucosa, spleen, bone marrow, and liver.

How Much Iron Should We Consume?

In determining the RDA for iron, researchers took into account the bioavailability of iron from food and absorption rates.[7]

Recommended Dietary Intakes for Iron   The RDA for iron for men aged 19 years and older is 8 mg/day. The RDA for iron for women aged 19 to 50 years is 18 mg/day and decreases to 8 mg/day for women 51 years of age and older. The higher iron requirement for younger women is due to the excess iron and blood lost during menstruation. Pregnancy is a time of very high iron needs, and the RDA for pregnant women is 27 mg/day. The UL for iron for adults aged 19 and older is 45 mg/day. Although it is difficult to get too much iron from whole foods, it is easy to get high doses of iron from supplements and/or the use of highly fortified processed foods such as meal-replacement drinks, energy bars, and protein powders. Special circumstances that significantly affect iron status and may increases requirements are identified in Table 12.2.

Good Food Sources of Iron   Good food sources of heme iron include meats, poultry, and fish (**Figure 12.4**). Clams, oysters, and beef liver are particularly good sources of iron. Many breakfast cereals and breads are enriched or fortified with iron; although this iron is the non-heme type and less absorbable, it is still significant because these foods are a major part of the Western diet. Some vegetables and legumes are also good sources of iron, and the absorption of their non-heme iron can be enhanced by eating them with animal foods that contain the meat factor and heme iron or with vitamin C–rich foods. People who avoid animal products need to pay special attention to their diet to ensure adequate iron intake, because heme iron sources are eliminated.

What Happens If We Consume Too Much Iron?

Accidental iron overdose is the most common cause of poisoning deaths in children younger than 6 years of age in the United States.[7] It is important for parents to take the same precautions with dietary supplements as they would with other drugs, keeping them in a locked cabinet or well out of reach of children. Symptoms of iron toxicity include nausea, vomiting, diarrhea, dizziness, confusion, and rapid heart beat. If iron toxicity is not treated quickly, significant damage to the heart, central nervous system, liver, and kidneys can result in death.

Many adults who take iron supplements, even at prescribed doses, commonly experience constipation and gastrointestinal distress.[4] High doses of iron supplements can also cause nausea, vomiting, and diarrhea. Taking iron supplements with food can reduce these adverse effects in most, but not all, people.

Table 12.2 Special Circumstances Affecting Iron Status

Circumstances That Improve Iron Status	Circumstances That Diminish Iron Status
Use of oral contraceptives—reduces menstrual blood loss in women.	**Use of hormone replacement therapy**—can cause uterine bleeding.
Breast-feeding—delays resumption of menstruation in new mothers and thereby reduces blood loss. It is therefore an important health measure, especially in developing nations.	**Eating a vegetarian diet**—reduces or eliminates sources of heme iron.
Consumption of iron-containing foods and supplements	**Intestinal parasite infection**—causes intestinal bleeding. Iron-deficiency anemia is common in people with intestinal parasite infection. **Blood donation**—reduces iron stores; people who donate frequently, particularly premenopausal women, may require iron supplementation. **Intense endurance exercise training**—appears to increase the risk for poor iron status because of many factors, including inflammation, suboptimal iron intake and increased iron loss due to rupture of red blood cells and increased fecal losses.

Data from: Institute of Medicine, Food and Nutrition Board. 2000. *Dietary Reference Intakes for Vitamin A, Vitamin K, Arsenic, Boron, Chromium, Copper, Iodine, Iron, Manganese, Molybdenum, Nickel, Silicon, Vanadium, and Zinc.* Washington, DC: National Academies Press. © 2000 by the National Academy of Sciences.

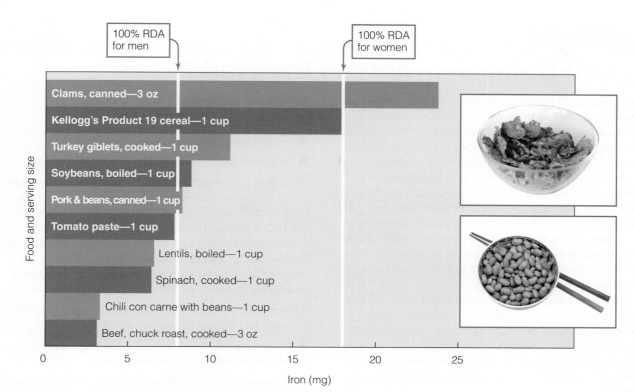

Figure 12.4 Common food sources of iron. The RDA for iron is 8 mg/day for men and 18 mg/day for women aged 19 to 50 years. (*Data from:* U.S. Department of Agriculture, Agricultural Research Service. 2005. USDA Nutrient Database for Standard Reference, Release 21. Available at www.ars.usda.gov/Services/docs.htm?docid=8964.)

As mentioned in Chapter 10, some individuals suffer from a hereditary disorder called hemochromatosis. This disorder affects between 1 in 200 and 1 in 400 individuals of northern European descent.[8] Hemochromatosis is characterized by excessive absorption of dietary iron and altered iron storage. In this disease, the transport of iron from the enterocytes into the circulation is not regulated appropriately and iron transport continues even when it is not needed.[5] Because the body has no homeostatic mechanism for eliminating high amounts of iron from the system, iron accumulates in body tissues over many years, causing organ damage and other disease. Treatment includes reducing dietary intake of iron, avoiding high intakes of vitamin C, and blood removal, a process similar to the donation of blood, except the blood is not reused.

What Happens If We Don't Consume Enough Iron?

Iron deficiency is the most common nutrient deficiency in the world and can have a number of health consequences that will be discussed here. People at particularly high risk for iron deficiency include infants and young children, adolescent girls, premenopausal women, and pregnant women. Refer to the Highlight box to learn more about the impact of iron deficiency on people around the world.

Many Factors Contribute to Iron Deficiency   For some individuals, iron deficiency is simply due to poor dietary intakes of iron. Other factors can include high iron losses in blood and sweat, diets high in fiber or phytates that bind iron, low stomach acid, or poor iron absorption due to poor gut health or the consumption of dietary supplements containing high levels of minerals such as calcium that compete with iron-absorption binding sites. Significant blood losses through blood donations, surgery, or heavy menstrual periods can contribute to poor iron status. For example, the typical menstruating female loses approximately 14 mg of iron per menstrual cycle.[4] Thus, the causes of iron deficiency and/or depletion can be numerous and may involve a number of issues that need to be addressed before iron status can be improved.

Highlight

Iron Deficiency Around the World

Iron deficiency is the most common nutritional deficiency in the world. According to the World Health Organization, approximately 4 to 5 billion people, or 66% to 80% of the world's population, are iron deficient.[9] Because of its high prevalence worldwide, iron deficiency is considered an epidemic.

As you have learned in this chapter, severe iron deficiency results in a type of anemia. Other factors that can cause anemia include deficiencies of folate, vitamin B_{12}, and vitamin A, as well as diseases that cause inflammation and infections such as hookworm and malarial parasites. In fact, it is estimated that 2 billion people worldwide suffer from worm infections, while 300 to 500 million people suffer from malaria.

Those who are particularly susceptible to iron deficiency include people living in developing countries, pregnant women, and young children. But iron deficiency not only hurts individuals. Because it results in increased healthcare needs, premature death, resultant family breakdown, and lost work productivity, it also damages communities and entire nations.

Among children, the health consequences of iron-deficiency anemia are particularly devastating. They include:

■ Premature birth

■ Low birth weight

■ Increased risk of infections

■ Increased risk of premature death

■ Impaired cognitive and physical development

■ Behavioral problems and poor school performance

To date, it is still unclear whether iron supplementation in children already suffering from iron-deficiency anemia can effectively and consistently reverse the cognitive and behavioral damage that has occurred.[10]

The World Health Organization has developed a comprehensive plan to address all aspects of iron deficiency and anemia.[9] This plan, which is being implemented in several developing countries, involves the following initiatives:

1. Increasing iron intake with iron supplements, iron-rich foods, and foods that enhance iron absorption;

2. Controlling infections that cause anemia, including hookworm infections and malaria; and

3. Improving overall nutritional status by controlling major nutrient deficiencies and improving the quality and diversity of people's diets.

By implementing this plan around the world, it is hoped that the devastating effects of iron deficiency can be reduced and potentially even eliminated.

Iron Deficiency Progresses Through Three Stages   As shown in **Figure 12.5, stage I** of iron deficiency is called **iron depletion.**[11] It is caused by a decrease in iron *stores*, resulting in reduced levels of circulating ferritin in the blood. As discussed earlier, ferritin is one form of stored iron. Small amounts of ferritin circulate in the blood, and these concentrations are highly correlated with iron stores.

During iron depletion, there are generally no physical symptoms because hemoglobin levels are not yet affected. However, when iron stores are low, the amount of iron available to mitochondrial proteins and enzymes appears to be depleted. This reduces the individual's ability to produce energy during periods of high demand. For example, research has shown that when sedentary women with poor ferritin levels participated in an exercise-training program, they did not experience the same improvements in fitness compared with women who had adequate ferritin levels.[12]

The second stage of iron deficiency causes a decrease in the *transport* of iron and is called **iron-deficiency erythropoiesis (stage II).** This stage is manifested by a reduction in the saturation of transferrin with iron. Transferrin, the transport protein for iron, has the ability to bind two iron molecules and transport them to the cells of the body. During this stage, the iron binding sites on transferrin are left empty, because there is no iron available for binding. This results in transferrin having an increased ability to bind iron, which is called *total iron binding capacity (TIBC)*. Overall, then, individuals with iron-deficiency erythropoiesis will have low serum ferritin and iron concentrations, a low level of iron saturation, and a high TIBC. The production of heme and the ability to make new red blood cells (for example, erythropoiesis) starts to decline during this

iron depletion (stage I)   The first phase of iron deficiency characterized by a decrease in stored iron, which results in a decrease in blood ferritin levels.

iron-deficiency erythropoiesis (stage II)   The second stage of iron deficiency characterized by a decrease in the transport of iron in the blood.

stage, leading to symptoms of reduced work capacity, because fewer red blood cells are being made.

During the third and final stage of iron deficiency, **iron-deficiency anemia (stage III)** results. In iron-deficiency anemia, the production of normal, healthy red blood cells has decreased, the size decreases as much as a third, and hemoglobin levels are inadequate. Thus, too few red blood cells are made, and those that are made cannot bind and transport oxygen adequately. Individuals with stage III iron-deficiency anemia will still have abnormal values for all the assessment parameters measured in stages I and II. The symptoms of iron-deficiency anemia are discussed in detail on page 469 under "Microcytic Anemia."

Stage I, iron depletion
- Decreased iron stores
- Reduced ferritin level
- No physical symptoms

Stage II, iron-deficiency erythropoiesis
- Decreased iron transport
- Reduced transferrin
- Reduced production of heme
- Physical symptoms include reduced work capacity

Stage III, iron-deficiency anemia
- Decreased production of normal red blood cells
- Reduced production of heme
- Inadequate hemoglobin to transport oxygen
- Symptoms include pale skin, fatigue, reduced work performance, impaired immune and cognitive functions

Figure 12.5 Iron deficiency passes through three stages. The first stage is identified by decreased iron stores and reduced ferritin levels. The second stage is identified by decreased iron transport and a reduction in transferrin. The final stage is iron-deficiency anemia, which is identified by decreased production of normal, healthy red blood cells and inadequate hemoglobin levels.

Recap

Iron is a trace mineral that, as part of the hemoglobin and myoglobin proteins, plays a major role in the transport of oxygen in the body. Iron is also a coenzyme in many metabolic pathways involved in energy production. The RDA for adult men aged 19 years and older is 8 mg/day. The RDA for adult women aged 19 to 50 years is 18 mg/day. Meat, fish, and poultry are good sources of heme iron, which is more absorbable than non-heme iron. Toxicity symptoms for iron range from nausea and vomiting to organ damage and potentially death. If left untreated, iron depletion can eventually lead to iron-deficiency anemia.

Zinc

Zinc (Zn^{2+}) is a positively charged trace mineral that, like iron, is found in very small amounts within the body (1.5–2.5 g). Most of the zinc found in the body is concentrated in the muscles and bone. However, in contrast with iron and other minerals, zinc has no dedicated storage sites within the body. Instead a small, exchangeable pool of zinc is found within the bone, liver, and blood.[11] Loss of zinc from this pool, if not replaced, leads to zinc deficiency.

Functions of Zinc

Zinc has multiple functions within nearly every body system. As a component of various enzymes, zinc helps to maintain the structural integrity of proteins and assists in the regulation of gene expression.[4] Without zinc, the body cannot grow, develop, or function properly. It is easiest to review the many roles of zinc within the body by dividing them into three categories: enzymatic, structural, and regulatory.

Enzymatic Functions   It is estimated that more than one hundred different enzymes within the body require zinc for their functioning.[4] If zinc is not present, these enzymes cannot function properly and lose their activity. For example, we require zinc to metabolize alcohol, digest our food, help form bone, provide the body with energy through glycolysis, and synthesize the heme structure in hemoglobin. Thus, zinc, like iron, is required to make the oxygen-carrying component of hemoglobin. In this way, zinc contributes to the maintenance of blood health.

iron-deficiency anemia (stage III)   A form of anemia that results from severe iron deficiency.

Structural Functions   Zinc helps maintain the structural integrity and shape of proteins. If proteins lose their shape, they lose their function, much like a plastic spoon that has melted into a ball. Zinc helps stabilize the structure of certain DNA-binding proteins, called *zinc fingers*, which help regulate gene expression by facilitating the folding of proteins into biologically active molecules used in gene regulation.[11] Zinc fingers also help stabilize vitamin A receptors in the retina of the eye, thereby facilitating night vision. Other functions associated with zinc fingers include the sequencing of hormone receptors for vitamin D and thyroid hormone.

Zinc's ability to help maintain protein structures also includes maintaining the integrity of some enzymes. For example, zinc helps to maintain the integrity of copper–zinc superoxide dismutase, which is important in helping to prevent oxidative damage caused by free radicals. Zinc also helps to maintain the integrity of enzymes involved in the development and activation of certain immune cells (discussed on page 475). In fact, zinc has received so much attention for its contribution to immune system health that zinc lozenges have been formulated to fight the common cold. The Nutrition Debate at the end of this chapter explores the question of whether or not these lozenges are effective in combating the common cold.

Regulatory Functions   As a regulator of gene expression, zinc helps to turn genes "on" and "off," thus regulating the body functions these genes control. For example, in humans, if zinc is not available to activate certain genes related to cellular growth during the development of the fetus and after the child is born, growth is stunted. Zinc also plays a role in cell signaling. For example, zinc helps maintain blood glucose levels by interacting with insulin and influencing the way fat cells take up glucose. Zinc also helps regulate the activity of a number of other hormones, such as human growth hormone, sex hormones, and corticosteroids.[11]

A number of biological actions require zinc in all three of the functions just covered. The major example of this is in reproduction. Zinc is critical for cell replication and normal growth. In fact, zinc deficiency was discovered in the early 1960s when researchers were trying to determine the cause of severe growth retardation, anemia, and poorly developed testicles in a group of Middle Eastern men. These symptoms of zinc deficiency illustrate its critical role in normal growth and sexual maturation.

What Factors Alter Zinc Digestion, Absorption, and Balance?

Overall, zinc absorption is similar to that of iron, ranging from 10% to 35% of dietary zinc. People with poor zinc status absorb more zinc than individuals with optimal zinc status, and zinc absorption increases during times of growth, sexual development, and pregnancy. See **Figure 12.6** for an overview of zinc digestion, absorption, and transport.

Zinc is absorbed from the lumen of the intestine into the enterocytes through both active transport by carriers and simple diffusion, with the efficiency of absorption decreasing as the amount of zinc in the diet increases. Once inside the enterocytes, zinc can be released into the interstitial fluid (as discussed shortly) or bound to a protein called **metallothionein,** which prevents zinc from moving out of the enterocyte into the system. In this way, the body can regulate the amount of absorbed zinc that actually enters the total zinc pool of the body. When the enterocytes are sloughed off into the intestine, the zinc bound to metallothionein is lost in the feces. In this way, the body can maintain total zinc homeostasis.

Several dietary factors influence zinc absorption. High non-heme iron intakes can inhibit zinc absorption, which is a primary concern with iron supplementation, particularly during pregnancy and lactation. (Iron supplements contain non-heme iron.) High intakes of heme iron, however, appear to have no effect on zinc absorption. Although calcium is known to inhibit zinc absorption in animals, this effect has not been demonstrated in humans. The phytates and fiber found in whole grains and beans strongly inhibit zinc absorp-

metallothionein   A zinc-containing protein within the enterocyte; it assists in the regulation of zinc homeostasis.

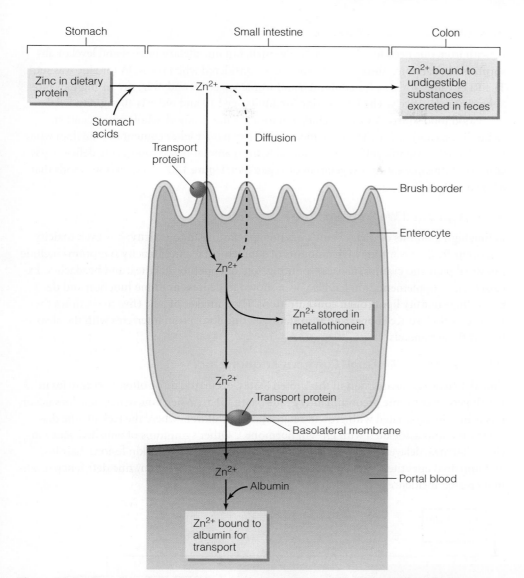

Figure 12.6 Overview of zinc digestion, absorption, and transport. (*Data adapted from:* Figure 12.8 in Gropper, S., J. L. Smith, and J. L. Groff. 2005. *Advanced Nutrition and Human Metabolism,* 4th ed. Reprinted with permission of Brooks Cole, a division of Thomson Learning.)

tion. In contrast, dietary protein enhances zinc absorption, with animal-based proteins increasing the absorption of zinc to a much greater extent than plant-based proteins. It's not surprising, then, that the primary cause of the zinc deficiency in the Middle Eastern men just mentioned was their low consumption of meat and high consumption of beans and unleavened breads (also called *flat breads*). In leavening bread, the baker adds yeast to the dough. This not only makes the bread rise but also helps reduce the phytate content of the bread.

How Is Zinc Transported in the Body?

Zinc is absorbed from the lumen of the intestine and moves into the enterocyte. It then crosses the basolateral enterocyte membrane via a process of active transport using both a zinc transporter and energy (ATP). Upon reaching the interstitial fluid, zinc is picked up by albumin, a transport protein in the plasma, and carried via the portal vein to the liver. Once in the liver, some of the zinc is repackaged and released back into the blood, bound to either albumin (about 60%) or other transport proteins (about 40%). The bound zinc can then be delivered to the cells, where it is taken up by energy-dependent carriers.

Zinc can be found in pork and beans.

How Much Zinc Should We Consume?

As with iron, our need for zinc is relatively small, but our dietary intakes and level of absorption are variable. Absorption factors were considered when the RDA for zinc was set.[4] The RDA values for zinc for adult men and women aged 19 and older are 11 mg/day and 8 mg/day, respectively. The UL for zinc for adults aged 19 and older is 40 mg/day.

Good food sources of zinc include red meats, some seafood, whole grains, and enriched grains and cereals. The dark meat of poultry has a higher content of zinc than white meat. As zinc is significantly more absorbable from animal-based foods, zinc deficiency is a concern for people eating a vegetarian or vegan diet. **Figure 12.7** shows various foods that are relatively high in zinc.

What Happens If We Consume Too Much Zinc?

Eating high amounts of dietary zinc does not appear to lead to toxicity; however, toxicity can occur from consuming high amounts of supplemental zinc. Toxicity symptoms include intestinal pain and cramps, nausea, vomiting, loss of appetite, diarrhea, and headaches. Excessive zinc supplementation has also been shown to depress immune function and decrease high-density lipoprotein concentrations. High intakes of zinc (five to six times the RDA) can also reduce copper and iron status, as zinc absorption interferes with the absorption of these minerals.[4]

What Happens If We Don't Consume Enough Zinc?

Zinc deficiency is uncommon in the United States, occurring more often in countries in which people consume predominantly grain-based foods. When zinc deficiency does occur, it is primarily associated with growth retardation in children, where the lack of zinc disrupts functions associated with growth hormone.[13] Other symptoms of zinc deficiency include diarrhea, delayed sexual maturation and impotence, eye and skin lesions, hair loss, and impaired appetite. As zinc is critical to a healthy immune system, zinc deficiency results in increased incidence of infections and illnesses.

Figure 12.7 Common food sources of zinc. The RDA for zinc is 11 mg/day for men and 8 mg/day for women. (*Data from:* U.S. Department of Agriculture, Agricultural Research Service. 2005. USDA Nutrient Database for Standard Reference, Release 21. Available at www.ars.usda.gov/Services/docs.htm?docid=8964.)

Because we do not have good assessment parameters for zinc, we have no way of recognizing poor zinc status until deficiency symptoms occur. In developed countries, those at greatest risk of zinc deficiencies are individuals with malabsorption syndromes and adults and children who eliminate high-zinc foods from their diet while consuming diets high in fiber. For example, recent research has shown that low-income Hispanic children who were in lower growth percentiles than predicted respond to zinc supplementation by growing closer to the predicted rate.[13]

Copper

Copper is a trace mineral that is required for a number of enzymes that have oxidative functions. Fortunately, copper is widely distributed in foods and deficiency is rare.

Functions of Copper

In the body, copper is primarily found as a component of ceruloplasmin, a protein that is critical for its transport. Indeed, an individual's copper status is typically assessed by measuring plasma levels of ceruloplasmin. As we mentioned in the discussion of iron, ceruloplasmin is important for the oxidation of ferrous to ferric iron ($Fe^{2+} \rightarrow Fe^{3+}$), which is necessary before iron can bind to transferrin and be transported in the plasma.[4] Because of ceruloplasmin's role in iron metabolism, it is also called ferroxidase I. When ceruloplasmin is inadequate, the transport of iron for heme formation is impaired and anemia can result. Because iron cannot be transported properly, iron accumulates in the tissues, causing symptoms similar to those described with the genetic disorder hemochromatosis (page 453).

Copper also functions as a cofactor in the metabolic pathways that produce energy, in the production of the connective tissues collagen and elastin, and as part of the superoxide dismutase enzyme system that fights the damage caused by free radicals. Copper is also necessary for the regulation of certain neurotransmitters, especially serotonin, important to brain function.

Lobster is a food that contains copper.

What Factors Alter Copper Absorption and Balance?

The major site of copper absorption is in the small intestine, with small amounts also absorbed in the stomach. As with zinc and iron, the amount of copper absorbed is related to the amount of copper in the diet, with absorption decreasing on high-copper diets and increasing on low-copper diets. Thus, regulation of copper absorption is one of the primary ways the body maintains good copper balance.

Copper is transported across the enterocytes by both carrier-mediated transport and simple diffusion.[13] Once absorbed, copper is bound to albumin (as with zinc), then transported in the portal blood to the liver. In the liver, about 60% to 95% of the copper is incorporated into ceruloplasmin, where it is then released into the plasma for general circulation and distribution to other tissues.[11] Copper is lost from the system in the feces when enterocytes are sloughed off into the lumen. When the copper in bile is not reabsorbed, it, too, is lost in the feces.

How Much Copper Should We Consume?

As with iron and zinc, our need for copper is small, but our dietary intakes are variable and, as we have seen, absorption is influenced by a number of factors. People who eat a varied diet can easily meet their requirements for copper. High zinc intakes can reduce copper absorption and, subsequently, copper status. In fact, zinc supplementation is used as a treatment for a rare genetic disorder called Wilson disease, in which copper toxicity occurs. High iron intakes can also interfere with copper absorption. The RDA for copper for men and women aged 19 years and older is 900 μg/day. The UL for adults ages 19 years and older is 10 mg/day.

Good food sources of copper include organ meats, seafood, nuts, and seeds. Whole-grain foods are also relatively good sources. **Figure 12.8** reviews some foods relatively high in copper.

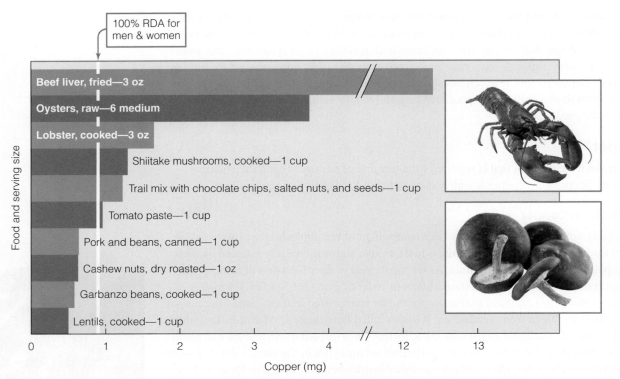

Figure 12.8 Common food sources of copper. The RDA for copper is 900 μg/day for men and women. (*Data from:* U.S. Department of Agriculture, Agricultural Research Service. 2005. USDA Nutrient Database for Standard Reference, Release 21. Available at www.ars.usda.gov/Services/docs.htm?docid=8964.)

What Happens If We Consume Too Much Copper?

The long-term effects of copper toxicity are not well studied in humans. However, accidental copper toxicity has occurred by drinking beverages that have come into contact with copper.[11] Toxicity symptoms include abdominal pain and cramps, nausea, diarrhea, and vomiting. Liver damage occurs in the extreme cases of copper toxicity that occur with Wilson disease and other health conditions associated with excessive copper levels. In Wilson disease, the copper accumulates in the liver because the liver cells cannot incorporate the copper into ceruloplasmin or eliminate it in the bile.[11]

What Happens If We Don't Consume Enough Copper?

Copper deficiency is rare but can occur in premature infants fed milk-based formulas and in adults fed prolonged formulated diets that are deficient in copper. Deficiency symptoms include anemia, reduced levels of white blood cells, and osteoporosis in infants and growing children, in whom the lack of copper contributes to bone demineralization.

ReCap

Zinc is a trace mineral that is a part of almost one hundred enzymes that affect virtually every body system. It plays a critical role in hemoglobin synthesis, physical growth and sexual maturation, and immune function and assists in fighting the oxidative damage caused by free radicals. For adults, the RDA for zinc is 8 mg/d. Copper is a component of ceruloplasmin, a protein that is critical for the proper transport of iron. This trace mineral is also a cofactor in the metabolic pathways that produce energy, in the production of the connective tissues collagen and elastin, and as part of the superoxide dismutase enzyme system that fights the damage caused by free radicals. For adults, the RDA for copper is 900 μg/day.

Vitamin K

Vitamin K is a fat-soluble vitamin important for both bone and blood health. Although a number of compounds exhibit vitamin K activity, the primary forms are phylloquinones and menaquinones. Phylloquinones are the form of vitamin K found in green plants and the primary form of vitamin K in our diet, whereas menaquinones are synthesized in the intestine from bacteria. The role of vitamin K in the synthesis of proteins involved in maintaining bone density was discussed in detail on page 426 in Chapter 11. In this section, we focus primarily on its role in blood health.

Blood clotting. Without enough vitamin K, the blood will not clot properly.

Functions of Vitamin K

Vitamin K acts as a coenzyme that assists in the synthesis of a number of proteins that are involved in the coagulation of blood, including *prothrombin* and the *procoagulants, factors VII, IX,* and *X*. Without adequate vitamin K, the blood does not clot properly: Clotting time can be delayed or clotting may even fail to occur. The failure of the blood to clot can lead to increased bleeding from even minor wounds, as well as internal hemorrhaging.

What Factors Alter Vitamin K Absorption and Balance?

Vitamin K is not only found in food but also is synthesized in the intestine; thus, the amount of vitamin K needed from the diet will depend on intestinal health. Factors that reduce the ability of the gastrointestinal bacteria to produce vitamin K will also reduce our total vitamin K status.

Because vitamin K is a fat-soluble vitamin, it is absorbed into the enterocyte, incorporated into chylomicrons, and then released into the lymphatic system with other dietary fats and fat-soluble vitamins. Any factors, either dietary or intestinal, that disrupt fat absorption will also disrupt vitamin K absorption.

Vitamin K is found in all the circulating lipoproteins, and assessment of plasma phylloquinone is a good measure of recent vitamin K intake.[14] Although both forms of vitamin K are found in the liver, the phylloquinones are rapidly turned over and lost in the urine and bile. The liver does not store vitamin K as it does other fat-soluble vitamins.

How Much Vitamin K Should We Consume?

Our needs for vitamin K are relatively small, but intakes of this nutrient in the United States are highly variable because vitamin K is found in relatively few foods.[4, 15] Healthful intestinal bacteria produce vitamin K in the large intestine, providing us with an important nondietary source. The AI for vitamin K for adults 19 years of age and older is 120 µg/day and 90 µg/day for men and women, respectively. There is no UL established for vitamin K at this time.[4]

Green, leafy vegetables are a good source of vitamin K.

In general, green, leafy vegetables are the major sources of vitamin K in our diets. Good sources include collard greens, kale, spinach, broccoli, brussels sprouts, and cabbage. Soybean and canola oils are also good sources. Refer to Figure 11.13 on page 426 for other common food sources of vitamin K.

What Happens If We Consume Too Much Vitamin K?

There are no known side effects associated with consuming large amounts of vitamin K from supplements or from food.[4] In the past, a synthetic form of vitamin K was used for therapeutic purposes and was shown to cause liver damage; this form is no longer used.

What Happens If We Don't Consume Enough Vitamin K?

Vitamin K deficiency inhibits the blood's ability to clot, resulting in excessive bleeding and even severe hemorrhaging in some cases. Fortunately, vitamin K deficiency is rare in humans. People with diseases that cause malabsorption of fat, such as celiac disease, Crohn's disease, and cystic fibrosis, can suffer secondarily from a deficiency of vitamin K. Newborns are typically given an injection of vitamin K at birth, as they lack the intestinal bacteria necessary to produce this nutrient.

As discussed in Chapter 11, the impact of vitamin K deficiency on bone health is controversial. Although a recent study found that low intakes of vitamin K were associated with a higher risk of bone fractures in women, there is not enough scientific evidence to indicate that vitamin K deficiency causes osteoporosis.[4, 16]

Recap

Vitamin K is a fat-soluble vitamin and coenzyme that is important for blood clotting and bone metabolism. Bacteria manufacture vitamin K in the large intestine. The AIs for adult men and adult women are 120 µg per day and 90 µg per day, respectively.

Figure 12.9   Structure of folic acid.

Folate

Folate is a water-soluble vitamin and one of the B-vitamins introduced in Chapter 8. The generic term *folate* is used for all the various forms of food folate that demonstrate biological activity. Folic acid (pteroylglutamate; see **Figure 12.9**) is the form of folate found in most supplements and used in the enrichment and fortification of foods. Folate was originally identified as a growth factor in green, leafy vegetables (foliage), and hence the name.[17]

Functions of Folate and Folic Acid

Within the body, folate functions primarily in association with folate-dependent coenzymes that act as acceptors and donors of one-carbon units. These enzymes are critical for DNA synthesis, cell differentiation, and amino acid metabolism, which occur within the cytosol, nucleus, and mitochondria of the cells. Folate's role in assisting with cell division makes it a critical nutrient during the first few weeks of pregnancy when the combined sperm–egg cell multiplies rapidly to form the primitive tissues and structures of the human body. Without adequate folate, the embryo cannot develop properly. Folate is also essential in the synthesis of new cells, such as the red blood cells, and for the repair of damaged cells.

Folate, vitamin B_{12}, and vitamin B_6 are closely interrelated in some metabolic functions, including the metabolism of methionine, an essential amino acid. If these nutrients are not available, methionine cannot be metabolized completely, and a compound called **homocysteine** builds up in the body. High levels of homocysteine have been associated with an increased risk of cardiovascular disease and as a measure of poor intakes of folate, vitamin B_{12}, and vitamin B_6 in the diet. In this chapter, we will focus on the roles of vitamin B_{12} and folate in the metabolism of homocysteine.

What Factors Alter Folate Digestion, Absorption, and Balance?

Dietary folates are hydrolyzed by the brush border of the lumen and then absorbed into the enterocytes. This process is typically achieved through a carrier-mediated process, but some folates can cross the mucosal cell membrane by diffusion. Folates are then released from the enterocytes into the portal circulation, in which they are transported to the liver.[17]

The bioavailability of folate varies depending on its source. When folic acid is given as a supplement or in a fortified food, such as breakfast cereal, the amount absorbed is high—nearly 85% to 100%.[18] However, the bioavailability of food folate is less than 50%.[17] When large doses of folic acid are given as supplements, they are well absorbed, but the body has no mechanism for retaining this folate, so it is easily lost in the urine.

Because dietary folate is only half as bioavailable as synthetic folic acid, the amount of food folate in the diet is expressed as dietary folate equivalents, or DFE. In order to calculate the amount of DFE, you need to know that 1 µg of food folate is equal to 0.5 µg of folic acid

homocysteine   An amino acid that requires adequate levels of folate, vitamin B_6, and vitamin B_{12} for its metabolism. High levels of homocysteine in the blood are associated with an increased risk for vascular diseases such as cardiovascular disease.

taken on an empty stomach or 0.6 µg of folic acid taken with a meal.[18] Thus, to calculate the total DFEs in an individual's diet, use the following equation:

$$\mu g \text{ of DFE provided in diet} = \mu g \text{ of food folate per day} +$$
$$(1.7 \times \mu g \text{ of synthetic folic acid/day})$$

Because this calculation can be time consuming, most nutrient databases calculate the DFEs automatically so that the total micrograms per day of folate provided in the nutrient analysis printout has already taken into account the bioavailability of the different types of folate in the diet.

Much of the folate circulating in the blood is attached to transport proteins, especially albumin, for transport to cells of the body. The red blood cells also contain folate attached to hemoglobin. Because this folate is not transferred out of the red blood cell to other tissues, it may be a good measure of folate status over the past 3 months—the life of the red blood cell.[17] If red blood cell folate levels begin to drop, this indicates that when the red blood cells were being formed, folate was inadequate in the body.

Alterations in total body folate status mimic those seen with iron.[11, 19] As the body has less and less folate available to it, the serum levels of folate begin to decline. This level of folate deficiency is called **negative folate balance (stage I).** If folate is not increased in the diet or through supplementation, then **folate depletion (stage II)** occurs. This stage of folate deficiency is characterized by both low serum and red blood cell folate, with slightly elevated serum homocysteine concentrations. In **folate-deficiency erythropoiesis (stage III),** the folate levels in the body are low enough that the ability to synthesize new red blood cells is inhibited. Finally, in **folate-deficiency anemia (stage IV),** the number of red blood cells has declined because folate is not available for DNA synthesis, and macrocytic anemia develops. This condition is discussed in more detail later in this chapter.

How Much Folate Should We Consume?

Folate is so important for good health and the prevention of birth defects that in 1998, the U.S. Department of Agriculture (USDA) mandated the fortification with folic acid of enriched breads, flours, corn meals, rice, pastas, and other grain products. Because folic acid is highly available for absorption, the goal of this fortification was to increase folate intake in all Americans and thus decrease the risk of birth defects and chronic diseases associated with low folate intakes.

The RDA for folate for adult men and women aged 19 years and older is 400 µg/day, with 600 µg/day required for pregnant women.[18] These higher levels of folate were set to minimize the risk of birth defects. The UL for folate is 1,000 µg/day.

Ready-to-eat cereals, bread, and other grain products are among the primary sources of folate in the United States; however, you need to read the label of processed grain products to make sure they contain folate. Other good food sources include liver, spinach, lentils, oatmeal, asparagus, and romaine lettuce. **Figure 12.10** shows some foods relatively high in folate. Losses of folate can occur when food is heated or when folate leaches out of cooked foods and the liquid from these foods is discarded. For this reason, cook green vegetables in a minimal amount of water and limit the time foods are exposed to high temperatures. These actions will help preserve the folate in the food.

What Happens If We Consume Too Much Folate?

There have been no studies suggesting toxic effects of consuming high amounts of folate in food; however; toxicity can occur with high amounts of supplemental folate.[17] One especially frustrating problem with folate toxicity is that it can mask a simultaneous vitamin B_{12} deficiency. This often results in failure to detect the B_{12} deficiency and, as described in the chapter-opening case, a delay in diagnosis of B_{12} deficiency can contribute to severe damage to the nervous system. There do not appear to be any clear symptoms of folate toxicity independent from its interaction with vitamin B_{12} deficiency.

Ready-to-eat grain products, such as pasta, are often fortified with folic acid.

negative folate balance (stage I) The first stage of folate depletion in which the body has less folate available to it and serum levels of folate begin to decline.

folate depletion (stage II) The second stage of folate depletion in which both serum and red blood cell folate are low.

folate-deficiency erythropoiesis (stage III) The third stage of folate depletion in which body levels of folate are so low that the ability to make new red blood cells is impaired.

folate-deficiency anemia (stage IV) A state of severe folate depletion in which there is inadequate folate for a long enough time that the number of red blood cells has declined.

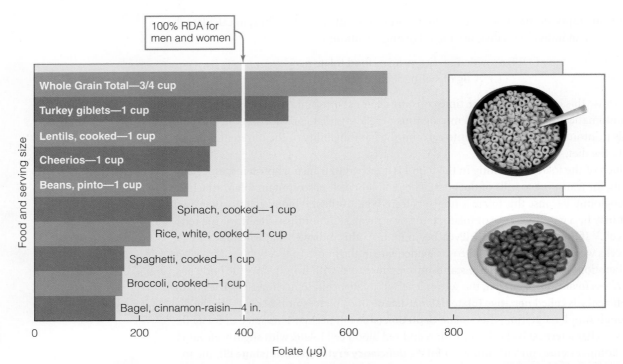

Figure 12.10 Common food sources of folate and folic acid. The RDA for folate is 400 μg/day for men and women. (*Data from:* U.S. Department of Agriculture, Agricultural Research Service. 2005. USDA Nutrient Database for Standard Reference, Release 21. Available at www.ars.usda.gov/Services/docs.htm?docid=8964.)

What Happens If We Consume Too Little Folate?

A folate deficiency can cause many adverse health effects, including *macrocytic anemia*. Folate and vitamin B_{12} deficiencies can cause elevated levels of homocysteine in the blood, a condition that is associated with heart disease. When folate intake is inadequate in pregnant women, *neural tube defects* (major malformations of the central nervous system that occur during the growth and development of the fetus) can occur. All of these conditions are discussed in more detail later in this chapter.

RECaP

Folate is a water-soluble vitamin and coenzyme critical for the synthesis of DNA, cell differentiation, and amino acid metabolism. Because folate is essential in the synthesis of new cells, such as red blood cells, anemia can develop if folate is deficient. Folate is also important for normal development of the central nervous system of the fetus and, thus, the prevention of neural tube defects. In addition to plant foods, ready-to-eat cereals, breads, and many other grain products are good sources of folate or folic acid. The RDA for folate for adult men and women aged 19 years and older is 400 μg, with 600 μg/day required for pregnant women. The UL for folate is 1,000 μg/day.

Vitamin B_{12} (Cyanocobalamin)

As with folate, the generic terms *vitamin B_{12}* or *cyanocobalamin* are used to describe a number of compounds that exhibit vitamin B_{12} biological activity. These compounds have cobalt in their center and are surrounded by ring structures. See **Figure 12.11** for a diagram of the structure of cyanocobalamin, which is derived when vitamin B_{12} is purified from natural sources.[17] As you can see, vitamin B_{12} is a complex molecule, and the Nobel Prize was awarded for the delineation of its structure.

Functions of Vitamin B$_{12}$

Vitamin B$_{12}$ is part of coenzymes that assist with DNA synthesis, which is necessary for the proper formation of red blood cells.[11] As described in the chapter-opening scenario, vitamin B$_{12}$ is essential for healthy functioning of the nervous system because it helps maintain the myelin sheath that coats nerve fibers. When this sheath is damaged or absent, the conduction of nerve signals is altered, causing numerous neurologic problems.

Adequate levels of vitamin B$_{12}$ and folate, as well as B$_6$, are also necessary for the metabolism of the amino acid homocysteine, which we discussed earlier. We discuss the relationship between homocysteine and heart disease in more detail on pages 468–469.

What Factors Alter Vitamin B$_{12}$ Absorption, Metabolism, and Balance?

Vitamin B$_{12}$ is synthesized almost entirely by bacteria in animals. For this reason, plant sources generally do not contain vitamin B$_{12}$. Thus, the vitamin B$_{12}$ in our diet comes almost exclusively from meat, eggs, dairy products, and some seafood, and is approximately 50% bioavailable.[17]

Figure 12.11 Structure of vitamin B$_{12}$ (cyanocobalamin). As you can see, this is a highly complex molecule, and the Nobel Prize was awarded for the delineation of its structure.

The absorption of vitamin B$_{12}$ is complex (**Figure 12.12**). In food, vitamin B$_{12}$ is bound to protein. It is released from this protein in the acidic environment of the stomach, where it is then attached to another group of proteins called R-binders. The stomach also secretes **intrinsic factor,** a protein necessary for vitamin B$_{12}$ absorption in the small intestine. The intrinsic factor and vitamin B$_{12}$–R-binder complexes formed in the stomach pass into the small intestine, where the R-binder protein is hydrolyzed by pancreatic proteolytic enzymes, after which free vitamin B$_{12}$ binds to the intrinsic factor. The vitamin B$_{12}$–intrinsic factor complexes are then recognized by receptors on the enterocytes and internalized. These receptors do not recognize vitamin B$_{12}$ alone but only when it is bound to intrinsic factor. Within the enterocytes, vitamin B$_{12}$ is released into the cytosol. The vitamin B$_{12}$ is then released from the enterocyte, bound to a protein called transcobalamin II, and then transported to the cells of the body. The body stores vitamin B$_{12}$ in the liver, approximately 2 to 3 mg, which means we can probably survive for months without vitamin B$_{12}$ in our diet.[18] Vitamin B$_{12}$ is lost from the system in the urine and the bile.

Alterations in total body vitamin B$_{12}$ status mimic those seen with iron and folate, with states of deficiency developing as the amount of vitamin B$_{12}$ decreases in the body.[11] The states of vitamin B$_{12}$ deficiency are as follows:

- *Stage I or negative vitamin B$_{12}$ balance.* A decline in the blood level of cobalamin attached to its transport protein. This occurs as vitamin B$_{12}$ absorption declines, decreasing the amount of total vitamin B$_{12}$ available to the body.
- *Stage II or vitamin B$_{12}$ depletion.* If vitamin B$_{12}$ absorption is not increased or B$_{12}$ supplementation provided, then blood levels of cobalamin attached to its transport protein continue to decline, resulting in a decreased saturation of the transport protein with cobalamin.
- *Stage III or vitamin B$_{12}$–deficiency erythropoiesis.* The body's level of vitamin B$_{12}$ is so low that the ability to synthesize new red blood cells is inhibited.
- *Stage IV, called vitamin B$_{12}$–deficiency anemia.* The number of red blood cells has declined because vitamin B$_{12}$ is not available for DNA synthesis, and macrocytic anemia develops.

intrinsic factor   A protein secreted by cells of the stomach that binds to vitamin B$_{12}$ and aids its absorption in the small intestine.

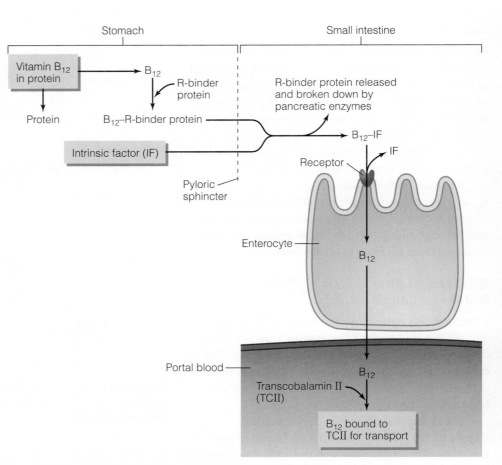

Figure 12.12 Digestion and absorption of vitamin B_{12}. (*Data adapted from:* Figure 9.36 in Gropper, S., J. L. Smith, and J. L. Groff. 2005. *Advanced Nutrition and Human Metabolism,* 4th ed. Reprinted with permission of Brooks Cole, a division of Thomson Learning.)

How Much Vitamin B_{12} Should We Consume?

Vitamin B_{12} has two unique features. First, it is found almost exclusively in animal foods; thus, the elimination of animal foods from the diet increases the risk of deficiency. Second, it is a water-soluble vitamin that is stored in the liver. This storage is important for anyone consuming very little vitamin B_{12} in the diet.

The RDA for vitamin B_{12} for adult men and women aged 19 and older is 2.4 µg/day. Vitamin B_{12} is found primarily in dairy products, eggs, meats, and poultry. **Figure 12.13** reviews some foods relatively high in vitamin B_{12}. Individuals consuming a vegan diet need to eat vegetable-based foods that are fortified with vitamin B_{12} or take vitamin B_{12} supplements or injections to ensure that they maintain adequate blood levels of this nutrient.

As we age, our sources of vitamin B_{12} may need to change. Nonvegan individuals younger than 51 years are generally able to meet the RDA for vitamin B_{12} by consuming it in foods. However, it is estimated that about 10% to 30% of adults older than 50 years have a condition referred to as **atrophic gastritis,** which results in low stomach-acid secretion. Because stomach acid separates food-bound vitamin B_{12} from dietary proteins, if the acid content of the stomach is inadequate, then we cannot free up enough vitamin B_{12} from food sources alone.[18] Because atrophic gastritis can affect almost one-third of the older adult population, it is recommended that people older than 50 years of age consume foods fortified with vitamin B_{12}, take a vitamin B_{12}–containing supplement, or have periodic vitamin B_{12} injections.

atrophic gastritis A condition, frequently seen in individuals over the age of 50 years, in which stomach-acid secretion is low.

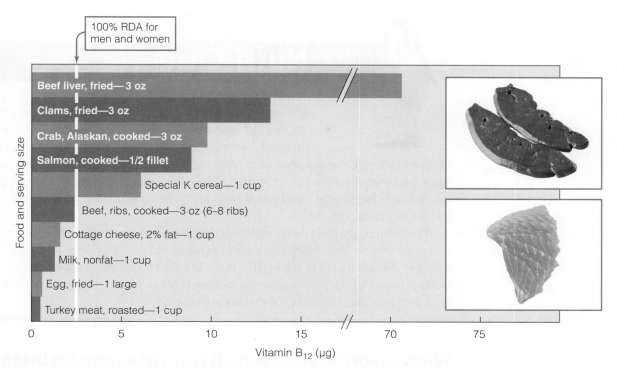

100% RDA for men and women

Food and serving size

Beef liver, fried—3 oz
Clams, fried—3 oz
Crab, Alaskan, cooked—3 oz
Salmon, cooked—1/2 fillet
Special K cereal—1 cup
Beef, ribs, cooked—3 oz (6–8 ribs)
Cottage cheese, 2% fat—1 cup
Milk, nonfat—1 cup
Egg, fried—1 large
Turkey meat, roasted—1 cup

0   5   10   15   70   75

Vitamin B$_{12}$ (µg)

Figure 12.13 Common food sources of vitamin B$_{12}$. The RDA for vitamin B$_{12}$ is 2.4 µg/day for men and women. (*Data from:* U.S. Department of Agriculture, Agricultural Research Service. 2005. USDA Nutrient Database for Standard Reference, Release 21. Available at www.ars.usda.gov/Services/docs.htm?docid=8964.)

What Happens If We Consume Too Much Vitamin B$_{12}$?

There are no known adverse effects from consuming excess amounts of vitamin B$_{12}$ from food. Data are not available on the effects of excess amounts of vitamin B$_{12}$ from supplements.

What Happens If We Consume Too Little Vitamin B$_{12}$?

Vitamin B$_{12}$ deficiency is rare but is generally associated with either dietary insufficiency or reduced absorption. Deficiency symptoms generally include those associated with anemia, as well as gastrointestinal and neurologic effects.[11] The symptoms of anemia include pale skin, diminished energy and exercise tolerance, fatigue, and shortness of breath. Gastrointestinal symptoms include loss of appetite, constipation, excessive gas, and changes in the tongue.[11] Neurologic symptoms include tingling and numbness of extremities, abnormal gait, memory loss, dementia, disorientation, visual disturbances, insomnia, and impaired bladder and bowel control. A deficiency of vitamin B$_{12}$, as with folate, has been linked to cardiovascular disease due to high levels of homocysteine.

As just noted, an important cause of vitamin B$_{12}$ deficiency is reduced absorption. A common culprit in reduced absorption is a condition called pernicious anemia, which is caused by inadequate secretion of intrinsic factor by parietal cells of the stomach. Pernicious anemia is discussed in more detail in the following section.

Turkey contains vitamin B$_{12}$.

Recap

Vitamin B$_{12}$ is a water-soluble vitamin and functions as a coenzyme for enzymes involved with DNA synthesis, which is necessary for formation of red blood cells. Vitamin B$_{12}$ is found exclusively in animal foods or foods fortified with vitamin B$_{12}$, such as ready-to-eat cereals. The RDA for vitamin B$_{12}$ for adult men and women aged 19 years and older is 2.4 µg/d. There is no UL for vitamin B$_{12}$.

Liz

Nutri-Case

"It was really hard spending last summer with my parents, because we kept arguing over food! Even though I'd told them that I'm a vegetarian, they kept serving meals with meat! Then they'd get mad when I'd fix myself a hummus sandwich! When it was my turn to cook, I made lentils with brown rice, whole-wheat pasta primavera, vegetarian curries, and lots of other yummy meals, but my father still complained. He kept insisting, "You have to eat meat or you won't get enough iron!" I told him that plant foods have lots of iron, but he wouldn't listen. Was I ever glad to get back onto campus this fall!"

Recall that Liz is a ballet dancer who trains daily. If she eats a vegetarian diet including meals such as the ones she describes here, will she be at risk for iron deficiency? Why or why not? Are there any other micronutrients that might be low in Liz's diet because she avoids meat? If so, what are they? Overall, will Liz get enough energy to support her high level of physical activity on a vegetarian diet? How would she know if she were low on energy?

What Disorders Can Result from Inadequate Intakes of Nutrients Involved in Blood Health?

We have mentioned a number of illnesses and disorders that can occur if our intake of the nutrients related to blood health is inadequate. Following is a more detailed discussion of some of these disorders.

Neural Tube Defects

A woman's requirement for folate substantially increases during pregnancy. This is because of the high rates of cell development needed for enlargement of the uterus, development of the placenta, expansion of the mother's red blood cells, and growth of the fetus. Inadequate folate intake during pregnancy can not only cause macrocytic anemia but is also associated with major malformations in the fetus that are classified as neural tube defects.

Neural tube defects are the most common malformations of the central nervous system that occur during fetal development. The neural tube, which is formed by the fourth week of pregnancy, is a primitive structure that eventually develops into the brain and the spinal cord of the fetus. In a folate-deficient environment, the tube will fail to fold and close properly. The resultant defect in the newborn depends on the degree of failure and can range from protrusion of the spinal cord outside of the vertebral column to an absence of brain tissue. Some neural tube defects are minor and can be surgically repaired; others result in paralysis, and still others are fatal. Neural tube defects are described in more detail in Chapter 16 and shown in Figure 16.7.

The nutritional challenge with neural tube defects is that they occur very early in a woman's pregnancy, almost always before a woman knows she is pregnant. Thus, adequate folate intake is extremely important for all sexually active women of childbearing age, whether or not they intend to become pregnant. To prevent neural tube defects, it is recommended that all women capable of becoming pregnant consume 400 µg of folate daily from supplements, fortified foods, or both in addition to the folate they consume in their standard diet.[18]

Vascular Disease and Homocysteine

Folate and vitamin B_{12} are necessary for the metabolism of the amino acid methionine. Vitamin B_6 is also involved, but we will focus only on vitamin B_{12} and folate here. If intakes

neural tube defects The most common malformations of the central nervous system that occur during fetal development. A folate deficiency can cause neural tube defects.

of these nutrients are insufficient, methionine cannot be metabolized properly, and blood levels of homocysteine, a by-product of incomplete methionine metabolism, begin to increase (**Figure 12.14**). A systematic review of the research on this topic showed that elevated levels of homocysteine are associated with a 1.5 to 2 times greater risk for cardiovascular, cerebrovascular, and peripheral vascular diseases.[20] These diseases substantially increase a person's risk for a heart attack or stroke.

The exact mechanism by which elevated homocysteine levels increase the risk for vascular diseases is currently unknown. It has been speculated that homocysteine may damage the lining of blood vessels and stimulate the accumulation of plaque, which can lead to hardening of the arteries.[21] Homocysteine also increases blood clotting, which could lead to an increased risk of blocked arteries. Thus, by eating foods that contain ample amounts of folate, vitamin B_6, and vitamin B_{12}, we may decrease our risk for a heart attack or stroke.

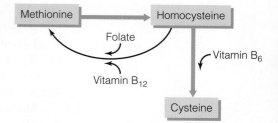

Figure 12.14 The metabolism of methionine, an essential amino acid, to homocysteine. Homocysteine can then be converted back to methionine through a vitamin B_{12}– and folate-dependent reaction or to cysteine through a vitamin B_6–dependent reaction. Cysteine is a nonessential amino acid important for making other biological compounds. Without these B vitamins, blood levels of homocysteine can increase. High levels of homocysteine are a risk factor for cardiovascular disease.

Anemia

The term *anemia* literally means "without blood"; it is used to refer to any condition in which hemoglobin levels are low, regardless of the cause. Some anemias are caused by genetic problems. For instance, you've probably heard of *sickle cell anemia*, a genetic disorder in which the red blood cells have a sickle shape. Another inherited anemia is *thalassemia*, a condition characterized by red blood cells that are small and short-lived. Here, we discuss anemias due to deficiencies of iron, vitamin B_6, vitamin B_{12}, or folate.

Microcytic Anemias

Microcytic anemias are a group of anemias characterized by red blood cells that are smaller than normal (*micro-* means small, and *–cyte* means cell). Red blood cells that are synthesized in an iron-deficient environment will be microcytic, and will not contain enough hemoglobin to transport adequate oxygen or to allow the proper transfer of electrons to produce energy. Microcytic anemia is sometimes referred to as *microcytic hypochromic anemia*, because reduced levels of hemoglobin deprive the cells of their bright-red color (*hypo-* means low and *–chromic* refers to color). As normal red blood cell death occurs over time, more and more healthy red blood cells are replaced by these abnormally small cells. At the same time, fewer total red blood cells are made. These changes prompt classic symptoms of oxygen and energy deprivation, including general fatigue, pale skin, depressed immune function, and impaired cognitive and nerve function, work performance, and memory. Pregnant women with severe anemia are at higher risk for low-birth-weight infants, premature delivery, and increased infant mortality.

Although we associate microcytic anemia with iron deficiency, a deficiency in vitamin B_6 can also cause it. Vitamin B_6 is required for the formation of the porphyrin rings that surround iron (see the gold area in Figure 12.2) and comprise an integral part of the heme complex. Without vitamin B_6, heme synthesis is impaired, just as it is with iron deficiency. Thus, either iron or vitamin B_6 deficiency can cause microcytic hypochromic anemia; however, iron deficiency is the more common cause.

Macrocytic Anemias

Macrocytic anemias are characterized by the production of larger-than-normal red blood cells (macrocytes) containing insufficient hemoglobin, thus inhibiting adequate transport of oxygen. Symptoms of macrocytic anemia are similar to the symptoms that occur with microcytic anemias, and include weakness, fatigue, difficulty concentrating, irritability, headache, shortness of breath, and reduced work tolerance. Deficiencies of two micronutrients are associated with macrocytic anemias: vitamin B_{12} and folate.

Pernicious anemia is classified as a type of macrocytic anemia, and is associated with vitamin B_{12} deficiency. Pernicious anemia occurs at the end stage of an **autoimmune**

microcytic anemia A form of anemia manifested as the production of smaller-than-normal red blood cells containing insufficient hemoglobin, which reduces the ability of the red blood cell to transport oxygen; it can result from iron deficiency or vitamin B_6 deficiency.

macrocytic anemia A form of anemia manifested as the production of larger-than-normal red blood cells containing insufficient hemoglobin, which inhibits adequate transport of oxygen; also called megaloblastic anemia. Macrocytic anemia can be caused by a severe folate deficiency or by vitamin B_{12} deficiency.

pernicious anemia A special form of macrocytic anemia that is the primary cause of a vitamin B_{12} deficiency; occurs at the end stage of an autoimmune disorder that causes the loss of various cells in the stomach.

autoimmune A destructive immune response directed toward the individual's own tissues.

disorder that causes the loss of various cells in the stomach, including the parietal cells that produce intrinsic factor. As you know, intrinsic factor binds to vitamin B_{12} in the small intestine and aids its absorption into the enterocyte. Without intrinsic factor, vitamin B_{12} cannot be absorbed from the gut. It is estimated that approximately 3% of elderly individuals test positive for intrinsic factor antibodies, suggesting that they do not make intrinsic factor.[17]

Macrocytic anemia can also occur in people who consume little or no vitamin B_{12} in their diets, such as people following a vegan diet. It is also commonly seen in people with malabsorption disorders, such as people with tapeworm infestation of the gut, as the worms take up the vitamin B_{12} before it can be absorbed by the intestines.

In addition to the symptoms associated with all anemias—such as pale skin, reduced energy and exercise tolerance, fatigue, and shortness of breath—lack of B_{12} also causes the destruction of nerve cells. Thus, patients lose the ability to perform coordinated movements and to maintain body positioning. Central nervous system involvement can lead to irritability, confusion, depression, and even paranoia. As we saw in the case of Mr. Katz in the chapter opener, after onset of central nervous system–involved symptoms, even prompt intramuscular injections of vitamin B_{12} can only partially reverse the deficits.

A severe folate deficiency is another common cause of macrocytic anemia. Folate deficiency impairs DNA synthesis, which impairs the normal production of red blood cells. Because a deficiency of folate or vitamin B_{12} causes similar symptoms, it is important to determine if the macrocytic anemia observed is due to a folate or a vitamin B_{12} deficiency. As mentioned earlier, high doses of folate supplements can mask the physical symptoms of vitamin B_{12} deficiency so that this deficiency progresses unchecked and causes neurologic damage.[18] Thus, before treatment for macrocytic anemia can occur, the cause must be identified.

RecaP

Neural tube defects are potentially serious and even fatal malformations of the central nervous system in a developing fetus that can result from folate deficiency in the first few weeks of pregnancy. Low intakes of folate, vitamin B_6, or vitamin B_{12} are associated with elevated blood homocysteine levels, which increase the risk of cardiovascular, cerebrovascular, and peripheral vascular disease. Anemia refers to any condition in which hemoglobin levels are low. Inadequate intake of iron or vitamin B_6 can lead to microcytic anemia, whereas deficiency of either vitamin B_{12} or folate causes macrocytic anemia.

What Is the Immune System, and How Does It Function?

A healthy immune system protects the body from infectious diseases, helps heal wounds, and guards against the development of cancers. Made up of cells and tissues throughout the body, the immune system acts as an integrated network to carry out surveillance against invaders and destroy them before they can cause significant tissue damage. Although immune cells communicate with one another extensively, each cell has a specialized protective function in either nonspecific or specific immunity.

Nonspecific Immune Function Protects Against All Potential Invaders

nonspecific immune function   Generalized body defense mechanisms that protect against the entry of foreign agents such as microorganisms and allergens; also called innate immunity.

Nonspecific immune function is the body's primary defense against microbes, airborne particles, venom, and ingested toxins. Nonspecific immunity is active even if you are encountering the invader for the first time. Because even infants have all of the cells and tissues required for it to operate effectively, it is also called *innate immunity*.

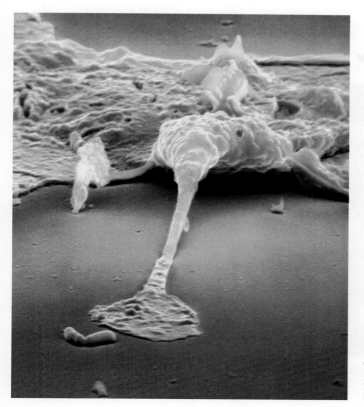

A macrophage is a type of nonspecific immune cell. The one shown here is about to engulf an invading microbe.

Nonspecific defenses include intact skin and healthy mucous membranes, which block invaders from entering the blood, lungs, and other deeper tissues. Coughing, sneezing, vomiting, and diarrhea all serve to expel harmful agents before they can take hold. Food-borne microbes can also be destroyed by stomach acid.

In addition, a variety of immune cells, including macrophages, neutrophils, and natural killer (NK) cells, work together to kill a wide variety of harmful microorganisms, even if they never have been encountered before.

Finally, our nonspecific defenses include the release of inflammatory chemicals that cause discomfort, loss of appetite, fatigue, and fever: Most disease-causing microbes thrive at normal body temperature, whereas a high temperature inhibits their growth. Fever also facilitates the actions of cells and chemicals involved in repair.

Together, our nonspecific defenses can inhibit the penetration and reproduction of invaders until the slower-acting, but more effective, specific immune system is activated.

Specific Immune Function Protects Against Identified Antigens

Specific immune function is directed against recognized **antigens**—that is, portions of microorganisms, allergens, or other foes that the immune system has encountered before and recognizes as foreign, or *non-self*. But how does this recognition occur?

The first time the immune system encounters a substance with an antigen that is detected as non-self, it produces a primary immune response. This response takes several days to peak, but eventually, in most cases, it destroys the invader. A key process within that primary immune response is the production of **memory cells** dedicated to the task of seeking out and destroying any substance bearing that particular antigen. Memory cells remain in circulation (in some cases, for life) so that any subsequent encounter with the same antigen causes a faster and stronger response. Often, the response is so fast that the person does not even feel sick.

specific immune function The strongest defense against pathogens. Requires adaptation of white blood cells that recognize antigens and that multiply to protect against the pathogens carrying those antigens. Also called *adaptive immunity* or *acquired immunity*.

antigens Parts of a molecule, usually large proteins, from microbes, toxins, or other substances that are recognized by immune cells and activate an immune response.

memory cells White blood cells that recognize a particular antigen and circulate in the body, ready to respond if the antigen is encountered again. The purpose of vaccination is to create memory cells.

Natural killer (NK) cells are part of our nonspecific defenses. Here, an NK cell attacks two cancer cells.

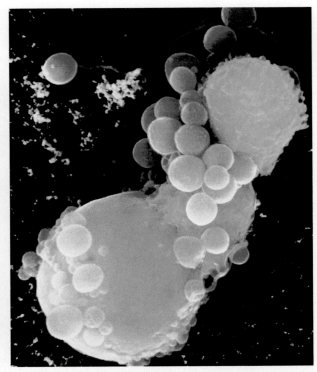

Two cytotoxic T cells (orange) killing another cell (mauve).

Two Main Types of Cells Provide Specific Immunity

In specific immune responses, two primary types of immune cells are activated:

- **B cells** are a type of white blood cell. During a primary immune response, B cells differentiate into two types: the memory cells just described and **plasma cells.** The job of plasma cells is to produce thousands of **antibodies,** proteins that attach to recognized antigens on invaders and flag them for destruction.
- **T cells** are also white blood cells. They differentiate into several types, the most important of which are cytotoxic T cells and helper T cells. As their name suggests, **cytotoxic T cells** are toxic to body cells harboring microbes or any other non-self substances. For instance, by killing body cells that have been infected by a flu virus, they keep the virus from multiplying and spreading. **Helper T cells** don't kill directly. Rather, they manufacture chemicals that activate B cells and cytotoxic T cells.

Specific Immunity Can Be Acquired in a Variety of Ways

There are four primary ways in which humans acquire immunity to specific invaders:

- One natural way is to have a disease once. For example, if you had mumps as a child, you will never get it again because memory cells against mumps are continuously circulating throughout your body.
- **Vaccinations** (also called *immunizations*) are another way to develop immunity. When you are vaccinated, a small amount of antigen from a particular microbe is injected into your body. Your plasma cells produce antibodies against the antigen, and memory cells begin to circulate. If you encounter the microbe later, your immune response will protect you from getting sick.
- When a woman is pregnant, antibodies from her blood pass into the bloodstream of her fetus. These maternal antibodies protect a newborn during the first few months of life while the specific immune system is maturing. In addition, breast milk contains antibodies that protect the infant for as long as he or she nurses.

B cells   White blood cells that can become either antibody-producing plasma cells or memory cells.

plasma cells   White blood cells that have differentiated from activated B cells and produce millions of antibodies to an antigen during an infection.

antibodies   Circulating proteins produced by plasma cells to a particular antigen in response to a disease or vaccination or acquired passively.

T cells   White blood cells that are of several varieties, including cytotoxic T cells and helper T cells.

cytotoxic T cells   Activated T cells that kill infected body cells.

helper T cells   Activated T cells that secrete chemicals needed to activate other immune cells.

vaccination   Administering a small amount of antigen to elicit an immune response for the purpose of developing memory cells that will protect against the disease at a later time.

- The injection of **antiserum** can provide immediate protection from a specific foe—for instance, to snake venom in the bloodstream of a victim of a snakebite. Antiserum is a pharmacologic preparation containing antibodies to specific antigens, such as those in snake venom. Injection of this antibody-rich serum provides immediate protection. Without it, the snake venom would be fatal before the victim's immune system could produce antibodies.

Immune System Malfunction Can Cause Chronic Inflammation and Infection

A malfunctioning immune system can damage body tissues or prevent resolution of infection. For example, during allergic reactions, harmless proteins in the environment or in food are mistaken for pathogens, producing a hypersensitivity immune response (see Chapter 3). Autoimmune responses occur when the body's own proteins are mistaken for pathogens. This occurs, for example, in rheumatoid arthritis and lupus and results in a chronic inflammatory state.

In some people, infections cannot be resolved and become chronic. Chronic infection is commonly seen in malnourished individuals, as well as in people with immune deficiency diseases. Cancer patients and transplant recipients also are more susceptible to infection when they are taking immunosuppressive drugs.

Vaccinations provide active immunity.

RECAP

The main function of the immune system is to protect the body against foreign agents. Nonspecific defenses include skin, mucous membranes, enzymes, inflammatory chemicals, and certain defensive cells. Specific immunity is provided by B cells and T cells. B cells include plasma cells, which produce antibodies, and memory cells, which circulate throughout the body seeking antigens to which they are sensitized. Cytotoxic T cells kill infected body cells, and helper T cells help B cells and cytotoxic T cells to proliferate. We gain immunity through previous infection, vaccination, maternal antibodies, or the administration of antiserum. Immune system malfunction can result in chronic inflammation or chronic infection.

How Does Nutrition Affect the Immune System?

A nourishing diet provides all the nutrients the immune system needs to carry out its defense of the body. Single-nutrient deficiencies or subclinical deficiencies can cause subtle, but important, abnormalities in immune function, even in apparently healthy people. This type of malnutrition is common in hospitalized individuals and the elderly.[22] Recent studies have demonstrated that viruses multiplying in malnourished hosts actually become more infective and destructive than viruses multiplying in well-nourished hosts.[23] Moreover, protein/energy malnutrition and severe deficiencies of several micronutrients reduce immune function. This problem is a leading cause of death in children in developing countries.[24]

Protein/Energy Malnutrition Impairs Immune Function

Malnutrition and infection participate in a vicious cycle: Malnutrition increases the risk for infection; infection depresses appetite and often causes vomiting and diarrhea; decreased appetite, vomiting, and/or diarrhea cause malnutrition, which increases vulnerability to infection. Specifically, protein/energy malnutrition (see Chapter 6) is known to severely diminish the ability of the immune system to respond to antigens. Malnourished children show reduced production of antibodies and diminished capacity of their immune cells to kill bacteria.[25] In addition, a healthy immune response requires energy and amino acids, two things that are in short supply in a malnourished individual. The synergistic effect of

antiserum Human or animal serum that contains antibodies to a particular antigen because of previous exposure to the disease or to a vaccine containing antigens from that infectious agent.

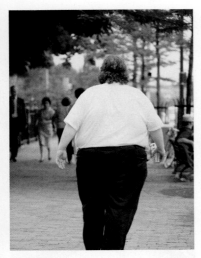

Obesity has been linked to disorders involving chronic inflammation, such as asthma, hypertension, heart disease, and type 2 diabetes.

protein/energy malnutrition and infection in diminishing both the capacity of the immune response and nutritional status is now widely recognized. Because even moderate nutrient deficiencies impair immune function, it has been suggested that decreased **immunocompetence** is a sensitive indicator of reduced nutritional status.

Obesity Increases Incidence and Severity of Infections

Obesity has become a public health issue much more recently than the problem of protein/energy malnutrition. Therefore, fewer studies have been done on the effects of obesity on immune function. However, obesity has been associated with increased incidence of infection, delayed wound healing, and poor antibody response to vaccination.[26]

The mechanisms underlying lower immune function in obese individuals are unclear. Most, but not all, studies show a lower ability of B and T cells from obese individuals to multiply in response to stimulation. This inhibition is resolved after weight loss.[27] Short-term fasting by obese individuals appears to improve the killing capacity of macrophages and increase serum concentrations of antibodies.[26] More consistent are the data documenting elevated levels of macrophages, inflammatory chemicals, and immune proteins in obese individuals, suggesting the existence of a low-grade inflammatory state.[28] This inflammatory state is currently thought to increase the likelihood that obese individuals will develop asthma, hypertension, cardiovascular disease, and type 2 diabetes.[28]

Essential Fatty Acids Make Signaling Molecules for the Immune System

As noted in Chapter 5, the essential fatty acids are precursors for important signaling molecules called **eicosanoids.** The immune system requires certain eicosanoids to respond appropriately to threatening agents. Experimental dietary deficiency of essential fatty acids impairs aspects of the immune response. On the other hand, excess amounts given by supplementation can also diminish immune function.[29]

This may be due in part to the importance of the *ratio* of omega-6 and omega-3 fatty acids in modulating the immune response. For example, omega-6 fatty acids are thought to promote the inflammatory response, which helps contain infection. In contrast, clinical trials have shown that omega-3 fatty acids diminish inflammation, including within blood vessels, and thus provide protection against heart disease. Indeed, the potential health benefits of omega-3 fatty acids in fish oils were first observed in Greenland Eskimos who had low levels of heart disease. However, their high incidence of tuberculosis raised the question of whether omega-3 fatty acids might diminish immune response to infections.

For these reasons, caution against both deficient and excessive intake of omega-3 fatty acids is prudent for maintaining appropriate immune response.[30] Both the absolute amount of omega-6 and omega-3 fatty acids and their ratio are considered important for health. The dietary reference intakes for adults over age 19 are 17 g omega-6 (linoleic acid) and 1.6 g omega-3 (linolenic acid) for men and 12 g omega-6 (linoleic acid) and 1.1 g omega-3 (linolenic acid) for women.[31]

Certain Vitamins and Minerals Are Critical to a Strong Immune Response

Although all essential nutrients are likely needed in some measure for effective immune function, certain micronutrient deficiencies and excesses have been recognized as particularly important. These include the following:

- *Vitamin A.* As early as the 1920s, vitamin A was called "the anti-infective vitamin" because it is needed to maintain the mucosal surfaces of the respiratory, gastrointestinal, and genitourinary tracts and for differentiation of immune system cells. More than one hundred clinical trials have shown that vitamin A supplementation in populations with

immunocompetence Adequate ability to produce an effective immune response to an antigen.

eicosanoids Physiologically active signaling molecules, including prostaglandins, thromboxanes, and leukotrienes, derived from the twenty-carbon fatty acids arachidonic acid and eicosapentaenoic acid.

low vitamin A status reduces incidence and fatality of infections of measles, malaria, and diarrheal diseases.[32] However, animal studies suggest that excessive vitamin A can actually suppress immune response and increase susceptibility to pathogens.[33] Thus, screening for vitamin A status before administering supplements has been recommended as part of public health efforts to combat deficiency.[34]

Vitamins E and C can be found in fruits and vegetables, and can contribute to immune system health.

- *Vitamins C and E.* The immune activities of defensive cells such as macrophages require oxygen and generate a highly reactive molecule, called a *reactive oxygen species*, that can damage the cell membrane if there is insufficient antioxidant protection. Both vitamin C and vitamin E provide this protection.

- *Zinc.* The importance of zinc to immune function was suggested by the observation that zinc-deficient dwarves in the Middle East died of infections by their early twenties.[35] Zinc is now known to be necessary for gene expression and enzyme activation for B and T cell proliferation. Even marginal zinc deficiency impairs immune response. However, excessive zinc supplementation depresses immunity, possibly by causing copper deficiency.

- *Copper.* Even a marginal copper deficiency reduces a growth factor needed for immune cells to multiply.[36] Lack of circulating neutrophils is a classic sign of copper deficiency in humans. Lack of copper also impairs the ability of both the neutrophils and macrophages to kill pathogens.

- *Iron.* Iron has a complicated relationship with immune function. It is now clear that a mild iron deficiency impairs immune function, perhaps because activated T cells produce a receptor on their surface that can take up the iron they need for multiplication.[33] However, severe deficiency does impair the function of T and B cells, as well as neutrophils. Macrophages take up and store iron during an infection and seem unaffected by deficiency. This storage is thought to be beneficial because it keeps iron away from invading microbes, which require iron to multiply. This may explain why some studies show that iron supplementation given to children during infection is detrimental, and why iron toxicity increases the rate of infections.[37] In addition, excessive iron is a potent oxidant that can damage immune-cell membranes.

- *Selenium.* In trace amounts, selenium is necessary for the synthesis of thirty-five body proteins, many of which are important enzymes.[38] Selenium has two roles in immune function. It is a required coenzyme for glutathione peroxidase, an important antioxidant enzyme in neutrophils and other immune cells. It also promotes proper B and T cell proliferation and antibody production. Selenium deficiency in an infected host also permits viruses to multiply over a longer time period and to mutate into more pathogenic strains.[23] However, selenium excess also impairs immune cell activity.[39] Thus, as with iron and vitamin A, both excess and deficiency of selenium compromise the ability to resolve infection.

RECAP

A nourishing diet is important in optimizing immune response. Protein/energy malnutrition increases the frequency and severity of infection. Obesity compromises immune response, exacerbating infection and inflammation. Balanced consumption of omega-6 and omega-3 essential fatty acids is needed for production of signaling molecules important in immune function. Vitamin A is critically important for maintenance of the skin and mucosal barrier to infection as well as for development of immune cells. Both vitamins C and E function as antioxidants to protect cell membranes from destruction during an immune response. The minerals zinc, copper, iron, and selenium are all necessary for appropriate immune function. In general, adequate micronutrients are critical for immune function, but excessive amounts impair immune response.

Hannah
Nutri-Case

"I can't believe how tough things are right now. I've got three mid-terms next week, an assignment to turn in for my lab, plus somebody at work quit, so my boss made everybody take on extra hours. This morning when I woke up, I could feel another cold coming on, plus I just got over a stomach flu! I guess that doesn't say much for the vitamin C powder I've been taking. My friend Kristi says I should drink veggie juices to boost my immune system—she owns a juice machine and starts every day with weird stuff like liquid parsley and kale. My mom says I should start taking iron pills. But I eat meat or chicken almost every day, so I think I'm getting all the iron I need. And besides, I ate pretty much the same way all through high school, and I almost never got sick, so I don't think it's got anything to do with my diet!"

Do you think Hannah should try veggie juices, iron pills, or any other specific foods or supplements to prevent colds and flu? Why or why not? What non-nutritional factors might be contributing to her illnesses?

See for Yourself

Adequate intake of micronutrients is important for healthy blood and for healthy immune function, but excessive intakes of vitamin A, zinc, copper, iron, and selenium may impair immune response and be toxic. In addition, too much folic acid can mask low vitamin B_{12} deficiency. It is very easy to buy supplements online.

Check out a few supplements Web sites, and see how variable the amounts of vitamins and minerals are in numerous products. Would it be likely that someone might easily oversupplement one or more of these micronutrients? Did you find any supplements with more than the RDA for folic acid? Did these same supplements also include vitamin B_{12}?

Chapter Review

Test Yourself | Answers

1. **T** This deficiency is particularly common in infants, children, and women of childbearing age.

2. **F** To reduce their risk of having a baby with serious central nervous system defects, all women capable of becoming pregnant should take folate supplements. Beginning folate supplementation after recognizing a pregnancy, typically following the first missed menstrual period, may be too late to prevent a neural tube defect.

3. **T** People who consume a vegan diet need to pay particularly close attention to consuming enough vitamin B_{12}, iron, and zinc. In some cases, these individuals may need to take supplements to consume adequate amounts of these nutrients.

4. **F** The term *anemia* means "without blood" and can refer to any condition in which hemoglobin levels are low. Iron-deficiency anemia is just one type.

5. **T** Fever increases the body temperature, making the internal environment inhospitable to microbes, and increasing the rate of protective immune reactions. Vomiting and diarrhea serve to expel microbes and toxins from the GI tract before they can cause widespread tissue damage.

Summary

- Blood is the only fluid tissue in the body. It has four components: erythrocytes, or red blood cells; leukocytes, or white blood cells; platelets; and plasma, or the fluid portion of blood.

- Blood is critical for transporting oxygen and nutrients to cells and for removing waste products from cells so these products can be properly excreted.

- Iron is a trace mineral. Almost two-thirds of the iron in the body is found in hemoglobin, the oxygen-carrying protein in blood. One of the primary functions of iron is to assist with the transportation of oxygen in blood. Iron is a cofactor for many of the enzymes involved in the metabolism of carbohydrates, fats, and protein. It is also a part of the antioxidant enzyme system that fights free radicals.

- Zinc is a trace mineral that acts as a cofactor in the production of hemoglobin; in the superoxide dismutase antioxidant enzyme system; in the metabolism of carbohydrates, fats, and proteins; and in activating vitamin A in the retina. Zinc is also critical for cell reproduction and growth and for proper development and functioning of the immune system.

- Copper is a trace mineral that functions as a cofactor in the metabolic pathways that produce energy, in the production of collagen and elastin, and as part of the superoxide dismutase antioxidant enzyme system. Copper is also a component of ceruloplasmin, a protein needed for the proper transport of iron.

- Vitamin K is a fat-soluble vitamin that acts as a coenzyme assisting in the coagulation of blood. Vitamin K is also a coenzyme in the synthesis of proteins that assist in maintaining bone density.

- The B-vitamins primarily involved in blood health are folate and vitamin B_{12}.

- Neural tube defects, which can result from inadequate folate intake during the first 4 weeks of pregnancy, are the most common malformations of the fetal central nervous system. Some neural tube defects are minor and can be treated with surgery; other neural tube defects are fatal.

- Inadequate intakes of folate and vitamin B_{12} are associated with elevated homocysteine levels. Elevated homocysteine levels are associated with a greater risk of cardiovascular, cerebrovascular, and peripheral vascular disease. These diseases significantly increase one's risk for a heart attack or stroke.

- *Anemia* is a term that means "without blood." Severe iron deficiency results in microcytic anemia, in which the production of normal, healthy red blood cells decreases and hemoglobin levels are inadequate. Deficiency of vitamin B_6 can also cause microcytic anemia.

- Macrocytic anemia results from folate or vitamin B_{12} deficiency and causes the formation of excessively large red blood cells that have reduced hemoglobin. Symptoms are similar to those of microcytic anemia. One form of macrocytic anemia, called pernicious anemia, is caused by a deficit of intrinsic factor, which in turn results in vitamin B_{12} deficiency.

- A healthy immune system is a network of cells and tissues that protects us from harmful agents.

- Nonspecific defenses include the skin and mucosal membranes, as well as protective molecules such as mucus, stomach acid, and enzymes, and immune cells like macrophages, neutrophils, and NK cells that destroy invaders.

- Specific immune function is directed against specific antigens. An initial encounter with a foreign agent triggers development of immune cells that recognize that agent. On subsequent encounters with the same agent, these cells mount a faster, stronger immune response.

- The two primary types of cells involved in specific immunity are B cells and T cells.

- Plasma cells are B cells that produce antibodies that mark antigens for destruction. Memory cells are another type of B cell that, after becoming sensitized to a specific antigen, circulate in the body, seeking that antigen.

- Cytotoxic T cells destroy body cells harboring foreign agents, and helper T cells signal other immune cells to respond.

- Human beings can acquire immunity by experiencing an infection, being vaccinated, receiving maternal antibodies, or receiving an injection of antiserum.

- Malfunctions of the immune system include allergies, autoimmune diseases, chronic inflammation, and immunodeficiencies.

- Both protein/energy malnutrition and obesity impair immune responses.

- A balanced intake of omega-6 and omega-3 essential fatty acids is important for regulating immune function.

- Critically important to immune function are vitamins A, C, and E and the minerals zinc, copper, iron, and selenium. In general, both deficiency and excess of these micronutrients can impair immune response.

Review Questions

1. The micronutrient most closely associated with blood clotting is
   a. iron.
   b. vitamin K.
   c. zinc.
   d. vitamin B_{12}.

2. Which of the following statements about iron is true?
   a. Iron is stored primarily in the liver, the blood vessel walls, and the heart muscle.
   b. Iron is a component of hemoglobin, myoglobin, and certain enzymes.
   c. Iron is a component of red blood cells, platelets, and plasma.
   d. Excess iron is stored primarily in the form of ferritin, cytochromes, and intrinsic factor.

3. Homocysteine is a
   a. by-product of glycolysis.
   b. trace mineral.
   c. by-product of incomplete methionine metabolism.
   d. B-vitamin.

4. Which of the following cells produce antibodies?
   a. plasma cells.
   b. antigens.
   c. macrophages.
   d. helper T cells.

5. Breastfeeding promotes infant health because breast milk contains
   a. antiserum.
   b. ceruloplasmin.
   c. intrinsic factor.
   d. antibodies.

6. **True or false?** Blood has four components: erythrocytes, leukocytes, platelets, and plasma.

7. **True or false?** Iron deficiency causes pernicious anemia.

8. **True or false?** Wilson disease occurs when copper deficiency allows accumulation of iron in the body.

9. **True or false?** Studies suggest that excessive vitamin A, iron, or selenium can impair immune function.

10. **True or false?** Macrocytic anemias can result from deficiencies of either folate or vitamin B_{12}.

11. In the chapter-opening story, Mr. Katz was given an injection of vitamin B_{12}. Why didn't his physician simply give him the vitamin in pill form?

12. Jessica is 11 years old and has just begun menstruating. She and her family members are vegans (that is, they consume only plant-based foods). Explain why Jessica's parents should be careful that their daughter consumes not only adequate iron and zinc but also adequate vitamin C.

13. Robert is a lacto-ovo-vegetarian. His typical daily diet includes milk, yogurt, cheese, eggs, nuts, seeds, legumes, whole grains, and a wide variety of fruits and vegetables. He does not take any supplements. What, if any, micronutrients are likely to be inadequate in his diet?

14. Janine is 23 years old and engaged to be married. She is 40 lb overweight, has hypertension, and her mother suffered a mild stroke recently, at age 45. For all these reasons, Janine is highly motivated to lose weight and has put herself on a strict low-carbohydrate diet recommended by a friend. She now scrupulously avoids breads, cereals, pastries, pasta, rice, and "starchy" fruits and vegetables. Identify two reasons why Janine should begin taking a folate supplement.

15. What health risk do people who are emaciated and people who are obese have in common? Why?

Web Links

www.ars.usda.gov/ba/bhnrc/ndl
Nutrient Data Laboratory Home Page
Click on "Reports for Single Nutrients" to find reports listing food sources for selected nutrients.

**www.bbc.co.uk/health/healthy_living/
complementary_medicine/remedies_vitamins.shtml**
BBC Healthy Living: Complementary Medicine: Vitamins
This page provides information on vitamins and minerals, signs of deficiency, therapeutic uses, and food sources.

www.anemia.com
Anemia Lifeline
Visit this site to learn about anemia and its various treatments.

www.unicef.org/nutrition/index.html
UNICEF-Nutrition
This site provides information about micronutrient deficiencies in developing countries and the efforts to combat them.

www.thearc.org
The Arc
Search this site for "neural tube defects" and find a wealth of information on the development and prevention of these conditions.

www.kidshealth.org/parent
Kidshealth.org
Search for "immune system" to find a good overview of the immune system.

http://fitness.gov/June2001Digest.pdf
President's Council of Physical Fitness and Sports Research Digest
This article discusses the effects of exercise on immune function and respiratory infections.

www.crnusa.org
Council for Responsible Nutrition
Search for "immune function" for articles on vitamin E, zinc, nutritional supplements, and other practices and substances that may improve immune function.

www.fda.gov
U.S. Food and Drug Administration (FDA)
Click on "Food" and then "Dietary Supplements" for a wealth of information about various dietary supplements and the FDA's regulation of them.

http://dietary-supplements.info.nih.gov
Office of Dietary Supplements (ODS)
Go to this site to obtain current research results and reliable information about dietary supplements.

References

1. Bernstein, L. 2000. Dementia without a cause: Lack of vitamin B12 can cause dementia. *Discover*. Available at www.discover.com/issues/feb-00/departments/featdementia.

2. World Health Organization. 2003. Nutrition. Micronutrient deficiencies. Battling iron deficiency anemia. Available at www.who.int/nut/ida.htm.

3. Crichton, R. R., 2006. Iron. In: M. H. Stipanuk, ed. *Biochemical, Physiological, and Molecular Aspects of Human Nutrition*. Philadelphia: W. B. Saunders, pp. 1001–1042.

4. Institute of Medicine, Food and Nutrition Board. 2001. *Dietary Reference Intakes for Vitamin A, Vitamin K, Arsenic, Boron, Chromium, Copper, Iodine, Iron, Manganese, Molybdenum, Nickel, Silicon, Vanadium, and Zinc.* Washington, DC: National Academy Press.

5. Donovan, A., C. A. Lima, J. L. Pinkus, G. S. Pinkus, L. I. Zon, S. Robine, and N. C. Andrews. 2005. The iron exporter ferroportin/Sic40a1 is essential for iron homeostasis. *Cell Metab.* 1:191–200.

6. Sinclair, L. M., and P. S. Hinton. 2005. Prevalence of iron deficiency with and without anemia in recreationally active men and women. *J. Am. Diet. Assoc.* 105:975–978.

7. U.S. Food and Drug Administration. 1997. Preventing iron poisoning in children. FDA backgrounder. Available at www.fda.gov/opacom/backgrounders/ironbg.html.

8. Bacon, B. R., J. K. Olynyk, E. M. Brunt, R. S. Britton, and R. K. Wolff. 1999. HFE genotype in patients with hemochromatosis and other liver diseases. *Ann. Intern. Med.* 130:953–962.

9. Baltussen, R., C. Knai, and M. Sharan. 2004. Iron fortification and iron supplementation are cost-effective interventions to reduce iron deficiency in four subregions of the world. *J. Nut.* 134:2678–2684.

10. Grantham-McGregor, S., and C. Ani. 2001. A review of studies on the effect of iron deficiency on cognitive development in children. *J. Nutr.* 131:649S–668S.

11. Gibson, S. R. 2005. *Principles of Nutritional Assessment*, 2nd ed. New York: Oxford University Press.

12. Hinton, P. S., C. Giordano, T. Brownlie, and J. D. Hass. 2000. Iron supplementation improves endurance after training in iron-depleted, nonanemic women. *J. Appl. Physiol.* 88:1103–1111.

13. Grider, A.. 2006. Zinc, copper, and manganese. In: M. H. Stipanuk, ed. *Biochemical, Physiological, and Molecular Aspects of Human Nutrition*. Philadelphia: W. B. Saunders, pp. 1043–1067.

14. Wallin, R., and S. M Huston . 2006. Vitamin K. In: M. H. Stipanuk, ed. *Biochemical, Physiological and MolecularAspects of Human Nutrition*. Philadelphia: W. B. Saunders, pp. 797–818.

15. Booth, S. L., and J. W. Suttie. 1998. Dietary intake and adequacy of vitamin K. *J. Nutr.* 128:785–788.

16. Feskanich, D., S. A. Korrick, S. L. Greenspan, H. N. Rosen, and G. A. Colditz. 1999. Moderate alcohol consumption and bone density among post-menopausal women. *J. Women's Health* 8:65–73.

17. Shane, B. 2006. Folic acid, vitamin B_{12}, and vitamin B_6. In: M. H. Stipanuk, ed. *Biochemical, Physiological, and Molecular Aspects of Human Nutrition*. Philadelphia: W. B. Saunders, pp. 693–732.

18. Institute of Medicine, Food and Nutrition Board. 1998. *Dietary Reference Intakes for Thiamin, Riboflavin, Niacin, Vitamin B_6, Folate, Vitamin B_{12}, Pantothenic Acid, Biotin, and Choline*. Washington, DC: National Academy Press.

19. Herbert, V. 1999. Folic acid. In: M. E. Shils, J. A. Olsen, M. Shike, and A. C. Ross, eds. *Modern Nutrition in Health and Disease*, 9th ed. Philadelphia: Lippincott Williams & Wilkins, pp. 433–446.

20. Beresford, S. A., and C. J. Boushey. 1997. Homocysteine, folic acid, and cardiovascular disease risk. In: A. Bendich and R. J. Deckelbaum, eds. *Preventive Nutrition: The Comprehensive Guide for Health Professionals*. Totowa, NJ: Humana Press.

21. Mayer, E. L., D. W. Jacobsen, and K. Robinson. 1996. Homocysteine and coronary atherosclerosis. *J. Am. Coll. Cardiol.* 27:517–527.

22. Keusch, G. T. 2003. The history of nutrition: malnutrition, infection and immunity. *J. Nutr.* 133:336S–340S.

23. Beck, M. A., J. Handy, and O. A. Levander. 2004. Host nutritional status: The neglected virulence factor. *Trends Microbiol.* 12:417–423.

24. Brundtland, G. H. 2000. Nutrition and infection: Malnutrition and mortality in public health. *Nutr. Rev.* 58:S1–4.

25. Scrimshaw, N. S. 2003. Historical concepts of interactions, synergism and antagonism between nutrition and infection. *J. Nutr.* 133:316S–321S.

26. Marti, A., A. Marcos, and J. A. Martinez. 2001. Obesity and immune function relationships. *Obesity Rev.* 2:131–140.

27. Lamas, O., A. Marti, and J. A. Martinez. 2002. Obesity and immunocompetence. *Eur. J. Cin. Nutr.* 56(suppl):S42–45.

28. Fantuzzi, G. 2005. Adipose tissue, adipokines, and inflammation. *J. Allergy Clin. Immunol.* 115:911–919.

29. Calder, P. C., and C. J. Field. 2002. Fatty acids, inflammation and immunity. In: P. C. Calder, C. J. Field, and H. S. Gill, eds. *Nutrition and Immune Function*. New York: CABI Publishing, pp. 57–92.

30. Wu, D. 2004. Modulation of immune and inflammatory responses by dietary lipids. *Curr. Opin. Lipidol.* 15:43–47.

31. Institute of Medicine, Food and Nutrition Board. 2005. *Dietary Reference Intakes for Energy, Carbohydrate, Fiber, Fat, Fatty Acids, Cholesterol, Protein, and Amino Acids (Macronutrients)*. Washington, DC: National Academy Press.

32. Semba, R. D. 2002. Vitamin A, infection and immune function. In: P. C. Calder, C. J. Field, and H. S. Gill, eds. *Nutrition and Immune Function*. New York: CABI Publishing, pp. 151–169.

33. Field, C. J., I. R. Johnson, and P. D. Schley. 2002. Nutrients and their role in host resistance to infection. *J. Leukoc. Biol.* 71:16–32.

34. Griffiths, J. K. 2000. The vitamin A paradox. *J. Pediatr.* 137:604–607.

35. Prasad, A. Zinc, infection and immune function. In: P. C. Calder, C. J. Field, and H. S. Gill, eds. *Nutrition and Immune Function.* New York: CABI Publishing, pp. 193–207.

36. Bonham, M., J. M. O'Connor, B. M. Hannigan, and J. J. Strain. 2002. The immune system as a physiological indicator of marginal copper status? *Br. J. Nutr.* 87:393–403.

37. Kuvibidila, S., and B. S. Baliga. 2002. Role of iron in immunity and infection. In: P. C. Calder, C. J. Field, and H. S. Gill, eds. *Nutrition and Immune Function.* New York: CABI Publishing, pp. 209–228.

38. McKenzie, R. C., J. R. Arthur, S. M. Miller, T. S. Rafferty, and G. J. Beckett. 2002. Selenium and the immune system. In: P. C. Calder, C. J. Field, and H. S. Gill, eds. *Nutrition and Immune Function.* New York: CABI Publishing, pp. 229–250.

39. Nair, M. P., and S. A. Schwartz. 1990. Immunoregulation of natural and lymphokine-activated killer cells by selenium. *Immunopharmacology.* 19:177–183.

40. National Institute of Allergy and Infectious Diseases. National Institutes of Health. 2007. The common cold. Available at www3.niaid.nih.gov/topics/commonCold/.

41. Prasad, A. 1996. Zinc: The biology and therapeutics of an ion. *Ann. Intern. Med.* 125:142–143.

42. Jackson, J. L., E. Lesho, and C. Peterson. 2000. Zinc and the common cold: A meta-analysis revisited. *J. Nutr.* 130:1512S–1515S.

43. Caruso, T. J., C. G. Prober, and J. M Gwaltney. 2007. Treatment of naturally acquired common colds with zinc: a structured review. *Clin. Infect Dis.* 45(5):569–574.

44. Chandra, R. K. 1984. Excessive intake of zinc impairs immune responses. *JAMA.* 252:1443–1446.

Do Zinc Lozenges Help Fight the Common Cold?

The common cold has plagued human beings since the beginning of time. It is estimated that approximately 1 billion colds occur in the United States each year.[40] Children suffer from six to ten colds each year, and adults average two to four per year. Although colds are typically benign, they result in significant absenteeism from work and cause discomfort and stress. Finding a cure for the common cold has been at the forefront of modern medicine for many years.

It is estimated that more than two hundred different viruses can cause a cold. The most frequent causes of adult colds are a group of viruses called coronaviruses; rhinoviruses are another group that causes about one-third of all adult colds. Because of this variety, finding treatments or potential cures for a cold is extremely challenging.

The role of zinc in the overall health of our immune system is well known, but zinc has also been shown to inhibit the replication of rhinoviruses and other viruses that cause the common cold. These specific findings have led to speculation that taking zinc supplements may reduce the length and severity of colds.[41, 42] Consequently, zinc lozenges were formulated as a means of providing potential relief from cold symptoms. These lozenges are readily found in a variety of formulations and dosages in most drugstores.

Does taking zinc in lozenge form actually reduce the length and severity of a cold? During the past 20 years, numerous research studies have been conducted to try to answer this question. Unfortunately, the results of these studies are inconclusive: about half have found that zinc lozenges do reduce the length and severity of a cold, whereas about half have found that zinc lozenges have no effect on cold symptoms or duration.[43] Some reasons that researchers have proposed to explain the different findings of these various studies include the following:

- Inability to truly "blind" participants to the treatment: Because zinc lozenges have a unique taste, it may be difficult to keep the research participants uninformed about whether they are getting zinc lozenges or a placebo. Knowing which lozenge they are taking could lead participants to report biased results.

- Self-reported symptoms are subject to inaccuracy: Many studies had the research participants self-report changes in symptoms. Such self-reports may be inaccurate and influenced by mood and other emotional factors.

- Wide variety of viruses that cause a cold: We noted that more than two hundred different viruses can cause a cold, and it is highly unlikely that zinc can combat all of these. It is possible that people who do not respond favorably to zinc lozenges are suffering from a cold virus that cannot be treated with zinc.

- Differences in zinc formulations and dosages: The type of zinc formulation, the dosages of zinc consumed, and the timing of consumption differed across studies. For example, it is estimated that for zinc to be effective, at least 80 mg of zinc should be consumed each day and that people should begin using zinc lozenges within 48 hours of onset of cold symptoms. Yet studies followed a variety of dosing and timing protocols. These differences most likely contributed to the wide variety of responses. Also, sweeteners and flavorings found in many zinc lozenges, such as citric acid, sorbitol, and mannitol, may bind the zinc and inhibit its ability to be absorbed into the body, limiting its effectiveness.

- Another consideration is that supplements may provide excessive zinc and actually impair immune function. The level of zinc noted earlier as the effective

Zinc lozenges come in different formulations and dosages.

The congestion, fatigue, and other symptoms of the common cold cause absenteeism from work or school as well as personal discomfort.

dose—80 mg—is nearly ten times the RDA and can decrease the absorption of copper and iron if continued for long periods of time. In addition, one experimental study showed that 300 mg/day of supplemental zinc reduced immune cell response and decreased destruction of bacteria by neutrophils.[44] This amount is about six tablets of a zinc gluconate pill that has 50 mg of elemental zinc.

- Measurement of subject compliance: Typically participants need to take the zinc lozenges every 2 to 3 hours while they are awake (5–8 lozenges/day) for the duration of the study, which can last 6 to 10 days. Unless the participants are monitored by research staff, researchers have to rely on the participants to self-report their compliance to the study protocol. Of course, different compliance rates could alter the outcomes of different studies.

Because there is no conclusive evidence supporting or refuting the effectiveness of zinc lozenges on the common cold, the debate on whether people should take them to treat their colds will most likely continue for many years.

Critical Thinking Questions

- Based on what you have learned here, do you think taking zinc lozenges can be an effective means of fighting the common cold?

- Have you ever tried them, and did you find them effective?

- Even if you have only about a 50% chance of reducing the length and severity of your cold by taking zinc lozenges, do you think they're worth a try?

A word of caution: If you decide to use zinc lozenges, more is not necessarily better. Excessive or prolonged zinc supplementation can cause other mineral imbalances. Check the label of the product you are using, and do not exceed its recommended dosage or duration of use.

13 Achieving and Maintaining a Healthful Body Weight

Chapter Objectives *After reading this chapter, you will be able to:*

1. Define what is meant by a healthful weight, *p. 486.*

2. Define the terms *underweight, overweight, obesity,* and *morbid obesity* and discuss the potential health risks of each of these weight classifications, *pp. 486–487, 513–516.*

3. List at least three methods that can be used to assess your body composition or risk for obesity, *pp. 487–491.*

4. Define *direct calorimetry, indirect calorimetry,* and *doubly labeled water* and list one strength and one limitation of each of these methods, *pp. 493–494.*

5. Identify and discuss the three components of energy expenditure, *pp. 493–496.*

6. Discuss three factors that can increase BMR and three factors that can decrease BMR, *p. 494.*

7. List and describe at least two theories that link genetic influences to control of body weight, *pp. 498–499.*

8. Discuss at least two societal factors that influence body weight, *pp. 501–504.*

9. Develop an action plan for healthful weight loss, *pp. 505–511.*

10. List and describe three treatment options for obesity, *pp. 511–512, 518–519.*

A healthful body weight varies from person to person. Fashion model Emme's body weight is healthful for her.

underweight Having too little body fat to maintain health, causing a person to have a weight that is below an acceptable defined standard for a given height.

overweight Having a moderate amount of excess body fat, resulting in a person having a weight that is greater than some accepted standard for a given height but is not considered obese.

obesity Having an excess body fat that adversely affects health, resulting in a person having a weight that is substantially greater than some accepted standard for a given height.

A s a teenager, she won a full athletic scholarship to Syracuse University, where she was honored for her "significant contribution to women's athletics and to the sport of rowing." After graduating, she became a television reporter and news anchor in Flagstaff, Arizona. Then she went into modeling, and soon her face smiled out from the covers of fashion magazines, cosmetics ads, even a billboard in Times Square. Now considered a "supermodel," she has her own Web site, her own clothing line, and even a collection of dolls. *People* magazine has twice selected her as one of the "50 Most Beautiful People," and *Glamour* magazine named her "Woman of the Year." So who is she? Her name is Emme Aronson . . . and by the way, at 5'11" tall, her average weight is 190 lb.

Emme describes herself as "very well-proportioned." She focuses not on maintaining a certain weight but instead on keeping healthy and fit. A cancer survivor, she follows a nutritious diet and works out regularly. Observing that "We live in a society that is based on the attainment of unrealistic beauty," Emme works hard to get out the message that self-esteem should not be contingent on size. On news programs and talk shows, at high schools, and on college campuses, she speaks out against weight-based discrimination and promotes acceptance of body diversity. Citing reports that 80% of women and many men are unhappy with their bodies, she encourages people of all sizes to celebrate their individuality.[1, 2]

Are you happy with your weight, shape, body composition, and fitness? If not, what needs to change—your diet, your level of physical activity, or maybe just your attitude? What role do diet and physical activity play in maintaining a healthful body weight? How much of your body size and shape is due to genetics? What influence does society—including food advertising—have on your weight? And if you decide that you do need to lose weight, what's the best way to do it? In this chapter, we will explore these questions and provide some answers.

What Is a Healthful Body Weight?

As you begin to think about achieving and maintaining a healthful weight, it's important to understand what a healthful body weight actually means. A healthful weight can be defined as all of the following:[3]

- A weight that is appropriate for your age and physical development
- A weight that you can achieve and sustain without severely curtailing your food intake or constantly dieting
- A weight that is based on your genetic background and family history of body shape and weight
- A weight that is compatible with normal blood pressure, lipid levels, and glucose tolerance
- A weight that promotes good eating habits and allows you to participate in regular physical activity
- A weight that is acceptable to you

As you can see, a healthful weight is not necessarily identified by thinness or extreme muscularity. In truth, there is no one particular body type that can be defined as healthful. Thus, achieving a healthful body weight should not be dictated by the latest fad or current societal expectations of what is acceptable.

Now that we know what a healthful body weight is, let's look at some terms applying to underweight and overweight. Physicians, nutritionists, and other scientists define **underweight** as having too little body fat to maintain health; having too little body fat causes a person to have a weight that is below an acceptably defined standard for a given height. **Overweight** is defined as having a moderate amount of excess body fat; this moderate amount of excess fat results in a person having a weight that is greater than some accepted standard for a given height but is not considered obese. **Obesity** is defined as having an excess body fat that adversely affects health, resulting in a person having a weight that is substantially greater than some accepted standard for a given height. People can also suffer from **morbid obesity;** in this case, their body weights exceed 100% of normal, putting them at very high risk for serious health consequences. In the next section, we discuss how these terms are defined using certain indicators of body weight and body composition.

How Can You Evaluate Your Body Weight?

Various methods are available to help you determine whether or not you are currently maintaining a healthful body weight. Let's review a few of these methods.

Determine Your Body Mass Index (BMI)

Body mass index (**BMI,** or *Quetelet's index*) is a commonly used index representing the ratio of a person's body weight to the square of his or her height. A person's BMI can be calculated using the following equation:

$$BMI\ (kg/m^2) = weight\ (kg)/height\ (m)^2$$

For those less familiar with the metric system, there is an equation to calculate BMI using weight in pounds and height in inches:

$$BMI\ (kg/m^2) = [weight\ (lb)/height\ (inches)^2] \times 703$$

A less exact but often useful method is to use the graph in **Figure 13.1**, which shows approximate BMIs for a person's height and weight and whether a given BMI is in a healthful range. BMI can also be calculated on the Internet using the BMI calculator found at www.nhlbisupport.com/bmi.

morbid obesity A condition in which a person's body weight exceeds 100% of normal, putting him or her at very high risk for serious health consequences.

body mass index (BMI) A measurement representing the ratio of a person's body weight to his or her height.

Figure 13.1 Measure your body mass index (BMI) using this graph. To determine your BMI, find the value for your height on the left and follow this line to the right until it intersects with the value for your weight on the bottom axis. The area on the graph where these two points intersect is your BMI.

Figure 13.2 shows relative risk on the y-axis and Body Mass Index (BMI; kg/m²) on the x-axis with categories <18.5, 18.5 to <25, 25 to <30, 30 to <35, ≥35, and a dashed line labeled Normal risk.

Figure 13.2 Having a body mass index value below 18.5 kg/m² or above 30 kg/m² is significantly associated with an increased risk for premature mortality.

Why Is BMI Important?

BMI provides an important clue to a person's overall health. Research studies show that a person's risk for type 2 diabetes, high blood pressure, heart disease, and other diseases largely increases when BMI is above a value of 30. On the other hand, having a very low BMI, defined as a value below 18.5, is also associated with increased risk of health problems and death.

Figure 13.2 shows how the *mortality rate,* or death rate, from all diseases increases significantly with a BMI value below 18.5 kg/m² or above a BMI value of 30 kg/m². Having a BMI value within the healthful range means that the risk of dying prematurely is within the expected average. If a person's BMI value falls outside of this range, either higher or lower, the risk of dying prematurely becomes greater than the average risk. For example, men with a BMI equal to or greater than 35 kg/m² have a risk of dying prematurely that is more than twice that of men with a BMI value in the range of 22 to 25 kg/m².

Theo always worries about being too thin, and he wonders if he is underweight. Theo calculates his BMI (see the calculations in the You Do the Math box below) and is surprised to find that it is 22 kg/m², which falls within the normal range.

Limitations of BMI

While calculating your BMI can be very helpful in estimating your health risk, this method has a number of limitations that should be taken into consideration. BMI cannot tell us how much of a person's body mass is composed of fat, nor can it give us an indication of where on the body excess fat is stored. As we'll discuss shortly, upper-body fat stores increase the risk of chronic disease more than fat stores in the lower body. A person's age affects his or her BMI; BMI does not give a fair indication of overweight or obesity in people over the age of 65 years, as the BMI standards are based on data from younger people, and BMI does not accurately reflect the differential rates of bone and muscle loss in older people. BMI also cannot reflect differences in bone and muscle growth in children. Recent research indicates that BMI is more strongly associated with height in young people; thus, taller children are more likely to be identified as overweight or obese, even though they may not have higher levels of body fat.[4]

You Do the Math

Calculating Your Body Mass Index

Calculate your personal BMI value based on your height and weight. Let's use Theo's values as an example:

$$BMI = weight\ (kg)/height\ (m)^2$$

1. Theo's weight is 200 lb. To convert his weight to kilograms, divide his weight in pounds by 2.2 lb per kg:

$$200\ lb/2.2\ lb\ per\ kg = 90.91\ kg$$

2. Theo's height is 6 feet 8 inches, or 80 inches. To convert his height to meters, multiply his height in inches by 0.0254 meters/inch:

$$80\ in. \times 0.0254\ m/in. = 2.03\ m$$

3. Find the square of his height in meters:

$$2.03\ m \times 2.03\ m = 4.13\ m^2$$

4. Then, divide his weight in kilograms by his height in square meters to get his BMI value:

$$90.91\ kg/4.13\ m^2 = 22.01\ kg/m^2$$

Is Theo underweight according to this BMI value? As you can see in Figure 13.1, this value shows that he is maintaining a normal, healthful weight!

BMI also does not take into account physical and metabolic differences between people of different ethnic backgrounds. At the same BMI, people from different ethnic backgrounds will have different levels of body fat. For instance, African American and Polynesian people have less body fat than white people at the same BMI value, while Indonesian, Thai, and Ethiopian people have more body fat than white people at the same BMI value.[5] There is also evidence that, even at the same BMI level, Asian, Hispanic, and African American women have a higher risk for diabetes than white women.[6] The same study also found that when Asian and Hispanic women gained weight, their risk of developing diabetes over a 20-year period was approximately twice as high as it was for white and African American women who gained the same amount of weight.

Finally, BMI is limited when used with people who have a disproportionately higher muscle mass for a given height, such as certain types of athletes, and with pregnant and lactating women. For example, one of Theo's friends, Randy, is a 23-year-old weight lifter who is 5′ 7″ and weighs 210 pounds. According to our BMI calculations, Randy's BMI is 32.9, placing him in the obese and high-risk category for many diseases. Is Randy really obese? In cases such as his, an assessment of body composition is necessary.

Measuring Your Body Composition

There are many methods available to assess your **body composition,** or the amount of **body fat** (or *adipose tissue*) and **lean body mass** (or *lean tissue*) you have. **Figure 13.3** lists and describes some of the more common methods. It is important to remember that tools for measuring body composition can provide only an *estimate* of your body fat and lean body mass; they cannot determine your exact level of these tissues. Because the range of error of these methods can be from 3% to more than 20%, body composition results should not be used as the only indicator of health status.

Let's return to Randy, whose BMI of 32.9 kg/m² places him in the obese category. But is he obese? Randy trains with weights 4 days per week, rides the exercise bike for about 30 minutes per session three times per week, and does not take drugs, smoke cigarettes, or drink alcohol. Through his local gym, Randy contacted a trained technician who assesses body composition. The results of his skinfold measurements show that his body fat is 9%. This value is within the healthful range for men. Randy is an example of a person whose BMI appears very high but who is not actually obese.

Assess Your Fat Distribution Patterns

To evaluate the health of your current body weight, it is also helpful to consider the way fat is distributed throughout your body. This is because your fat distribution pattern is known to affect your risk for various diseases. **Figure 13.4** on page 491 shows two types of fat patterning. *Apple-shaped fat patterning*, or upper-body obesity, is known to significantly increase a person's risk for many chronic diseases, such as type 2 diabetes, heart disease, and high blood pressure. It is thought that the apple-shaped patterning causes problems with the metabolism of fat and carbohydrate, leading to unhealthful changes in blood cholesterol, insulin, glucose, and blood pressure. In contrast, *pear-shaped fat patterning*, or lower-body obesity, does not seem to significantly increase your risk for chronic diseases. Women tend to store fat in their lower body, and men in their abdominal region. In 2004, a study involving more than 10,000 people found that 64% of women are pear-shaped and 38% of men are apple-shaped.[7]

You can use the following three-step method to determine your type of fat patterning:

1. Ask a friend to measure the circumference of your natural waist, that is, the narrowest part of your torso as observed from the front (**Figure 13.5a** on page 491).
2. Now have that friend measure your hip circumference at the maximal width of the buttocks as observed from the side (Figure 13.5b).
3. Now divide the waist value by the hip value. This measurement is called your *waist-to-hip ratio*. For example, if your natural waist is 30 inches and your hips are 40 inches, then your waist-to-hip ratio is 30 divided by 40, which equals 0.75.

BMI is not an accurate indicator of overweight for certain populations, including heavily muscled people.

body composition The ratio of a person's body fat to lean body mass.
body fat mass The amount of body fat, or adipose tissue, a person has.
lean body mass The amount of fat-free tissue, or bone, muscle, and internal organs, a person has.

Method		Limitations

Underwater weighing:
Considered the most accurate method. Estimates body fat within a 2–3% margin of error. This means that if your underwater weighing test shows you have 20% body fat, this value could be no lower than 17% and no higher than 23%. Used primarily for research purposes.

- Must be comfortable in water.
- Requires trained technician and specialized equipment.
- Does not work well with obese people.
- Must abstain from food for at least 8 hours and from exercise for at least 12 hours prior to testing.

Skinfolds:
Involves "pinching" a person's fold of skin (with its underlying layer of fat) at various locations of the body. The fold is measured using a specially designed caliper. When performed by a skilled technician, it can estimate body fat with an error of 3–4%. This means that if your skinfold test shows you have 20% body fat, your actual value could be as low as 16% or as high as 24%.

- Less accurate unless technician is well trained.
- Proper prediction equation must be used to improve accuracy.
- Person being measured may not want to be touched or may not want to expose their skin.
- Cannot be used to measure obese people, as their skinfolds are too large for the caliper.

Bioelectrical impedance analysis (BIA):
Involves sending a very low level of electrical current through a person's body. As water is a good conductor of electricity and lean body mass is made up of mostly water, the rate at which the electricity is conducted gives an indication of a person's lean body mass and body fat. This method can be done while lying down, with electrodes attached to the feet, hands, and the BIA machine. Hand-held and standing models (that look like bathroom scales) are now available. Under the best of circumstances, BIA can estimate body fat with an error of 3–4%.

- Less accurate.
- Body fluid levels must be normal.
- Proper prediction equation must be used to improve accuracy.
- Should not eat for 4 hours and should not exercise for 12 hours prior to the test.
- No alcohol should be consumed within 48 hours of the test.
- Females should not be measured if they are retaining water because of menstrual cycle changes.

Dual-energy X-ray absorptiometry (DXA):
The technology is based on using very low level x-ray to differentiate between bone tissue, soft (or lean) tissue, and fat (or adipose) tissue. It involves lying for about 30 minutes on a specialized bed fully clothed, with all metal objects removed. The margin of error for predicting body fat ranges from 2% to 4%.

- Expensive; requires trained technician with specialized equipment.
- Cannot be used to measure extremely tall, short, or obese people, as they do not fit properly within the scanning area.

Bod Pod:
A machine that uses air displacement to measure body compostition. This machine is a large, egg-shaped chamber made from fiberglass. The person being measured sits in the machine wearing a swimsuit. The door is closed and the machine measures how much air is displaced. This value is used to calculate body composition. It appears promising as an easier and equally accurate alternative to underwater weighing in many populations, but it may overestimate body fat in some African American men.

- Expensive.
- Less accurate in some populations.

Figure 13.3   Overview of various body composition assessment methods.

(a) Apple-shaped fat patterning **(b)** Pear-shaped fat patterning

Figure 13.4 Fat distribution patterns. **(a)** An apple-shaped fat-distribution pattern increases an individual's risk for many chronic diseases. **(b)** A pear-shaped fat-distribution pattern does not seem to be associated with an increased risk for chronic disease.

(a)

(b)

Figure 13.5 Determining your type of fat patterning. **(a)** Measure the circumference of your natural waist. **(b)** Measure the circumference of your hips at the maximal width of the buttocks as observed from the side. Dividing the waist value by the hip value gives you your waist-to-hip ratio.

Once you figure out your ratio, how do you interpret it? An increased risk for chronic disease is associated with the following waist-to-hip ratios:

- In men, a ratio higher than 0.90
- In women, a ratio higher than 0.80

These ratios suggest an apple-shaped fat distribution pattern. In addition, waist circumference alone can indicate your risk for chronic disease. For males, your risk of chronic disease is increased if your waist circumference is above 40 inches (or 102 cm). For females, your risk is increased at measurements above 35 inches (or 88 cm).

Recap

Body mass index, body composition, and the waist-to-hip ratio and waist circumference are tools that can help assess the risk of disease associated with a person's current body weight. None of these methods is completely accurate, but most may be used appropriately as general health indicators.

What Makes Us Gain and Lose Weight?

Have you ever wondered why some people are thin and others are overweight, even though they seem to eat about the same diet? If so, you're not alone. For hundreds of years, researchers have puzzled over what makes us gain and lose weight. In this section, we explore some information and current theories that may shed light on this complex question.

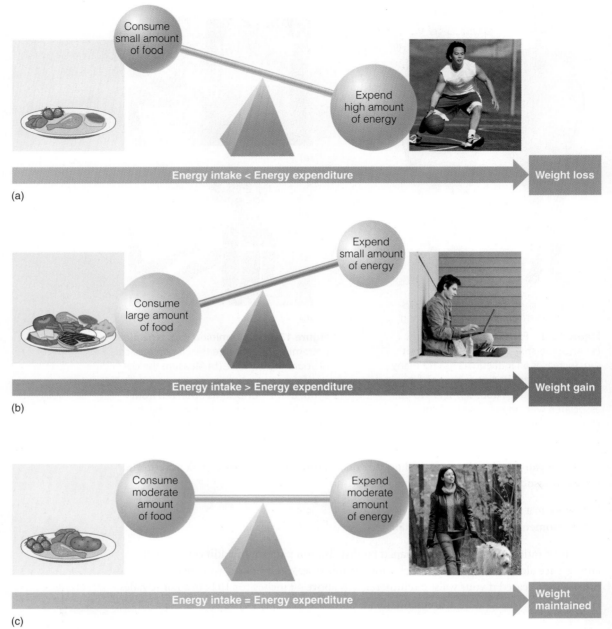

(a)   Energy intake < Energy expenditure   Weight loss

(b)   Energy intake > Energy expenditure   Weight gain

(c)   Energy intake = Energy expenditure   Weight maintained

Figure 13.6   Energy balance describes the relationship between the food we eat and the energy we expend each day. **(a)** Weight loss occurs when food intake is less than energy output. **(b)** Weight gain occurs when food intake is greater than energy output. **(c)** We maintain our body weight when food intake equals energy output.

We Gain or Lose Weight When Energy Intake and Expenditure Are Out of Balance

Fluctuations in body weight are a result of changes in **energy intake** (the food and beverages consumed) and **energy expenditure** (or the amount of energy expended at rest and during physical activity). This relationship between what we eat and what we do is defined by the energy balance equation:

Energy balance occurs when energy intake = energy expenditure

This means that energy is balanced when we consume the same amount of energy that we expend each day. **Figure 13.6** shows how our weight changes when we change either side of this equation. From this figure, you can see that in order to lose body weight, we must

energy intake   The amount of energy a person consumes; in other words, it is the number of kilocalories consumed from food and beverages.

energy expenditure   The energy the body expends to maintain its basic functions and to perform all levels of movement and activity.

expend more energy than we consume. In contrast, to gain weight, we must consume more energy than we expend. Finding the proper balance between energy intake and expenditure allows someone to maintain a healthful body weight.

Energy Intake Is the Food We Eat Each Day

Energy intake is equal to the amount of energy in the food we eat each day. This value includes all foods and beverages. Daily energy intake is expressed as *kilocalories per day* (*kcal/day*, or *kcal/d*). Energy intake can be estimated manually by using food composition tables or computerized dietary analysis programs. The energy content of each food is a function of the amount of carbohydrate, fat, protein, and alcohol that each food contains; vitamins and minerals have no energy value, so they contribute zero kilocalories to our energy intake.

Remember that the energy value of carbohydrate and protein is 4 kcal/g and the energy value of fat is 9 kcal/g. The energy value of alcohol is 7 kcal/g. By multiplying the energy value (in kcal/g) by the amount of the nutrient (in grams), you can calculate how much energy is in a particular food. For instance, 1 cup of quick oatmeal has an energy value of 142 kcal. How is this energy value derived? One cup of oatmeal contains 6 g of protein, 25 g of carbohydrate, and 2 g of fat. Using the energy values for each nutrient, you can calculate the total energy content of oatmeal:

$$6 \text{ g protein} \times 4 \text{ kcal/g} = 24 \text{ kcal from protein}$$
$$25 \text{ g carbohydrate} \times 4 \text{ kcal/g} = 100 \text{ kcal from carbohydrate}$$
$$2 \text{ g fat} \times 9 \text{ kcal/g} = 18 \text{ kcal from fat}$$
$$\text{Total kcal for 1 cup oatmeal} = 24 \text{ kcal} + 100 \text{ kcal} + 18 \text{ kcal} = 142 \text{ kcal}$$

When someone's total daily energy intake exceeds the amount of energy that person expends, then weight gain results. An excess intake of approximately 3,500 kcal will result in a gain of 1 pound. Without exercise, this gain will likely be fat.

Energy Expenditure Includes More Than Just Physical Activity

Energy expenditure (also known as energy output) is the energy the body expends to maintain its basic functions and to perform all levels of movement and activity. Total 24-hour energy expenditure is calculated by estimating the energy used during rest and as a result of physical activity. There are three components of energy expenditure: basal metabolic rate (BMR), thermic effect of food (TEF), and energy cost of physical activity (**Figure 13.7**). We discuss these components in detail shortly.

Energy Expenditure Can Be Measured Using Direct or Indirect Calorimetry

Energy expenditure can be measured using direct or indirect calorimetry. **Direct calorimetry** is a method that measures the amount of heat the body releases. This method is done using an air-tight chamber in which the heat produced by the body warms the water that surrounds the chamber. The amount of energy a person expends is calculated from the changes in water temperature. The minimum period of time that a person must stay in a direct calorimetry chamber is 24 hours; because of the burden to the individual, the high cost, and complexity of this method, it is rarely used to measure energy expenditure in humans.

Indirect calorimetry estimates energy expenditure by measuring oxygen consumption and carbon dioxide production. Because there is a predictable relationship between the amount of heat produced (or energy expended) by the body and the amount of oxygen consumed and carbon dioxide produced, this method can be used to indirectly determine energy expenditure. This method involves the use of a whole-body chamber, mask, hood, or mouthpiece to collect expired air over a specified period of time. The expired air is analyzed for oxygen and carbon dioxide content (**Figure 13.8**). This method is much less expensive and more accessible than direct calorimetry, so it is most commonly used to measure energy expenditure under both resting and physically active conditions.

The energy provided by a bowl of oatmeal is derived from its protein, carbohydrate, and fat content.

Components of energy expenditure

Figure 13.7 The components of energy expenditure include basal metabolic rate (BMR), the thermic effect of food (TEF), and the energy cost of physical activity. BMR accounts for 60% to 75% of our total energy output, whereas TEF and physical activity together account for 25% to 40%.

direct calorimetry   A method used to determine energy expenditure by measuring the amount of heat released by the body.

indirect calorimetry   A method used to estimate energy expenditure by measuring oxygen consumption and carbon dioxide production.

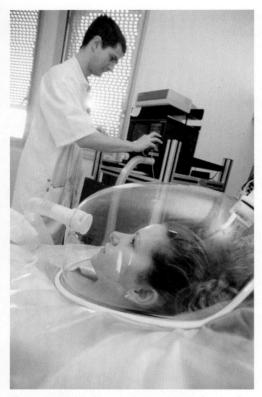

Figure 13.8 Indirect calorimetry can be used to measure the components of energy expenditure.

doubly labeled water A form of indirect calorimetry that measures total daily energy expenditure through the rate of carbon dioxide production. It requires the consumption of water that is labeled with nonradioactive isotopes of hydrogen (deuterium, or ^{2}H) and oxygen (^{18}O).

basal metabolic rate (BMR) The energy the body expends to maintain its fundamental physiologic functions.

Both direct and indirect calorimetry require a person to be confined to a laboratory setting or special metabolic chamber, which limits the ability to determine a person's energy expenditure in a free-living environment. This limitation is overcome in a technique using **doubly labeled water,** that is, water labeled with isotopes of hydrogen (deuterium, or ^{2}H) and oxygen (^{18}O). In this method, the research subject consumes controlled amounts of doubly labeled water. Both the labeled hydrogen and oxygen are used during metabolism; the ^{2}H is eliminated in water, and the ^{18}O is eliminated in both water and carbon dioxide. Thus, the difference between the elimination rates of these labeled isotopes measures carbon dioxide production, which in turn can be used to estimate energy expenditure. The advantages of this method are that it measures energy expenditure in free-living situations over periods of 3 days to 3 weeks, requires only periodic collection of urine, and requires little inconvenience to the person being measured. The primary disadvantages of the method are that it is expensive, the doubly labeled water is difficult to acquire, and it only measures total 24-hour energy expenditure. This method cannot separately measure the three components of energy expenditure discussed next: BMR, TEF, or the energy cost of physical activity.

Our Basal Metabolic Rate Is Our Energy Expenditure at Rest   Basal metabolic rate, or BMR, is the energy expended just to maintain the body's *basal,* or *resting,* functions. These functions include respiration, circulation, maintaining body temperature, synthesis of new cells and tissues, secretion of hormones, and nervous system activity. The majority of our energy output each day (about 60% to 75%) is a result of our BMR. This means that 60% to 75% of our energy output goes to fuel the basic activities of staying alive, aside from any physical activity.

BMR varies widely among people. The primary determinant of our BMR is the amount of lean body mass we have. People with a higher lean body mass have a higher BMR, as lean body mass is more metabolically active than body fat. Thus, it takes more energy to support this active tissue. One common assumption is that obese people have a depressed BMR. This is usually not the case. Most studies of obese people show that the amount of energy they expend for every kilogram of lean body mass is similar to that of a non-obese person. In general, people who weigh more also have more lean body mass and consequently have a *higher* BMR. See **Figure 13.9** for an example of how lean body mass can vary for people with different body weights and body fat levels.

BMR decreases with age, approximately 3% to 5% per decade after age 30. This age-related decrease results partly from hormonal changes, but much of this change is due to the loss of lean body mass resulting from physical inactivity. Thus, a large proportion of this decrease may be prevented with regular physical activity. There are other factors that can affect a person's BMR, and some of these are listed in Table 13.1.

Table 13.1 Factors Affecting Basal Metabolic Rate (BMR)

Factors That Increase BMR	Factors That Decrease BMR
Higher lean body mass	Lower lean body mass
Greater height (more surface area)	Lower height
Younger age	Older age
Elevated levels of thyroid hormone	Depressed levels of thyroid hormone
Stress, fever, illness	Starvation or fasting
Male gender	Female gender
Pregnancy and lactation	
Certain drugs such as stimulants, caffeine, and tobacco	

Figure 13.9 Lean body mass varies in people with different body weights and body fat levels. **(a)** The person on the left has a higher body weight, body fat, and lean body mass than the person on the right. **(b)** The two people are the same weight but the person on the right has more body fat and less lean body mass than the person on the left.

How can you estimate the amount of energy you expend for your BMR? Of the many methods that can be used, one of the simplest is to multiply your body weight in kilograms by 1.0 kcal per kilogram of body weight per hour for men or by 0.9 kcal per kilogram of body weight per hour for women. A little later in this chapter, you will have an opportunity to calculate your BMR and determine your total daily energy needs.

The Thermic Effect of Food Is the Energy Expended to Process Food   The **thermic effect of food (TEF)** is the energy we expend as a result of processing the food we eat. A certain amount of energy is needed to digest, absorb, transport, metabolize, and store the nutrients we need. The TEF is equal to about 5% to 10% of the energy content of a meal, a relatively small amount. Thus, if a meal contains 500 kcal, the thermic effect of processing that meal is about 25 to 50 kcal. These values apply to eating what is referred to as a mixed diet, or a diet containing a mixture of carbohydrate, fat, and protein. Most of us eat some combination of these nutrients throughout the day. Individually, the processing of each nutrient takes a different amount of energy. Whereas fat requires very little energy to digest, transport, and store in our cells, protein and carbohydrate require relatively more energy to process.

At one time, it was thought that obese people had a blunted (or reduced) TEF, which was thought to contribute to their obesity. We now know that errors associated with measuring the TEF make our previous assumptions about its link to obesity questionable. One of the most important contributors to obesity in industrialized countries is having an inactive lifestyle, which significantly reduces the energy output due to physical activity, our next topic.

The Energy Cost of Physical Activity Is Highly Variable   The **energy cost of physical activity** represents about 15% to 35% of our total energy output each day. This is the energy we expend due to any movement or work above basal levels. This includes lower-intensity activities such as sitting, standing, and walking, and higher-intensity activities such as running, skiing, and bicycling. One of the most obvious ways to increase how much energy we expend as a result of physical activity is to do more activities for a longer period of time.

Brisk walking expends energy.

thermic effect of food (TEF)   The energy expended as a result of processing food consumed.

energy cost of physical activity   The energy that is expended on body movement and muscular work above basal levels.

Table 13.2 Energy Costs of Various Physical Activities

Activity	Intensity	Energy Cost (kcal/kg body weight/min)
Sitting, knitting/sewing	Light	0.026
Cooking or food preparation (standing or sitting)	Light	0.035
Walking, shopping	Light	0.04
Walking, 2 mph (slow pace)	Light	0.044
Cleaning (dusting, straightening up, vacuuming, changing linen, carrying out trash)	Moderate	0.044
Stretching—Hatha yoga	Moderate	0.044
Weight lifting (free weights, Nautilus, or universal type)	Light or moderate	0.052
Bicycling <10 mph	Leisure (work or pleasure)	0.07
Walking, 4 mph (brisk pace)	Moderate	0.088
Aerobics	Low impact	0.088
Weight lifting (free weights, Nautilus, or universal type)	Vigorous	0.105
Bicycling, 12 to 13.9 mph	Moderate	0.14
Running, 5 mph (12 minutes per mile)	Moderate	0.14
Running, 6 mph (10 minutes per mile)	Moderate	0.175
Running, 8.6 mph (7 minutes per mile)	Vigorous	0.245

Data from: Ainsworth B. E., W. L. Haskell, M. C. Whitt, M. L. Irwin, A. M. Swartz, S. J. Strath, W. L. O'Brien, D. R. Bassett, Jr., K. H. Schmitz, P. O. Emplaincourt, D. R. Jacobs, Jr., and A. S. Leon. 2000. Compendium of physical activities: An update of activity codes and MET intensities. *Med. Sci. Sports Exerc.* 32:S498–S516. Used with permission of Lippincott Williams & Wilkins.

Table 13.2 lists the energy costs for certain activities. As you can see, activities such as running, swimming and cross-country skiing that involve moving our larger muscle groups (or more parts of the body) require more energy. The amount of energy we expend during activities is also affected by our body size, the intensity of the activity, and how long we perform the activity. This is why the values in Table 13.2 are expressed as kilocalories of energy per kilogram of body weight per minute.

Using the energy value for running at 6 miles per hour (or a 10-minute-per-mile running pace) for 30 minutes, let's calculate how much energy Theo would expend doing this activity:

- Theo's body weight (in kg) = 200 lb/2.2 lb/kg = 90.91 kg
- Energy cost of running at 6 mph = 0.175 kcal/kg body weight/min
- At Theo's weight, the energy cost of running per minute = 0.175 kcal/kg body weight/min × 90.91 kg = 15.91 kcal/min
- If Theo runs at this pace for 30 minutes, his total energy output = 15.91 kcal/min × 30 min = 477 kcal

Given everything we've discussed so far, you're probably asking yourself, "How many kilocalories do I need each day to maintain my current weight?" This question is not always easy to answer, as our energy needs fluctuate from day to day according to our activity level, environmental conditions, and other factors such as the amount and type of food we eat and our intake of caffeine, which temporarily increases our BMR. However, you can get a general estimate of how much energy your body needs to maintain your present weight. The You Do the Math box describes how you can estimate your total daily energy needs.

RECAP

The energy balance equation relates food intake to energy expenditure. Eating more energy than you expend causes weight gain, while eating less energy than you expend causes weight loss. Energy expenditure can be measured using direct calorimetry, indirect calorimetry, and doubly labeled water. The three components of energy expenditure are basal metabolic rate, the thermic effect of food, and the energy cost of physical activity.

You Do the Math

Calculating BMR and Total Daily Energy Needs

One potential way to estimate how much energy you need each day is to record your total food and beverage intake for a defined period of time, such as 3 or 7 days. You can then use a food composition table or computer dietary assessment program to estimate the amount of energy you eat each day. Assuming that your body weight is stable over this period of time, your average daily energy intake should represent how much energy you need to maintain your present weight.

Unfortunately, many studies of energy intake in humans have shown that dietary records estimating energy needs are not very accurate. Most studies show that humans underestimate the amount of energy they eat by 10% to 30%. Overweight people tend to underestimate by an even higher margin, at the same time overestimating the amount of activity they do. This means that someone who really eats about 2,000 kcal/day may record eating only 1,400 to 1,800 kcal/day. So one reason many people are confused about their ability to lose weight is that they are eating more than they realize.

A simpler and more accurate way to estimate your total daily energy needs is to calculate your BMR, and then add the amount of energy you expend as a result of your activity level. Refer to the example below to learn how to do this. As the energy cost for the thermic effect of food is very small, you don't need to include it in your calculations.

1. *Calculate your BMR:* If you are a man, you will need to multiply your body weight in kilograms by 1 kcal per kilogram body weight per hour. Assuming you weigh 175 pounds, your body weight in kilograms would be 175 lb/2.2 lb/kg = 79.5 kg. Next, multiply your weight in kilograms by 1 kcal per kilogram body weight per hour:

   1 kcal/kg body weight/hour × 79.5 kg = 79.5 kcal/hour

   Calculate your BMR for the total day (or 24 hours):

   79.5 kcal/hour × 24 hours/day = 1,909 kcal/day

If you are a woman, multiply your body weight in kg by 0.9 kcal/kg body weight/hour.

2. *Estimate your activity level by selecting the description that most closely fits your general lifestyle.* The energy cost of activities is expressed as a percentage of your BMR. Refer to the values in the following table when estimating your own energy output.

3. *Multiply your BMR by the decimal equivalent of the lower and higher percentage values for your activity level.* Let's use the man referred to in step 1. He is a college student who lives on campus. He walks to classes located throughout campus, carries his book bag, and spends most of his time reading and writing. He does not exercise on a regular basis. His lifestyle would be defined as lightly active, meaning he expends 50% to 70% of his BMR each day in activities. You want to calculate how much energy he expends at both ends of this activity level. How many kcal does this equal?

   1,909 kcal/day × 0.50 (or 50%) = 955 kcal/day

   1,909 kcal/day × 0.70 (or 70%) = 1,336 kcal/day

   These calculations show that this man expends about 955 to 1,336 kcal/day doing daily activities.

4. *Calculate total daily energy output by adding together BMR and the energy needed to perform daily activities.* In this man's case, his total daily energy output is:

   1,909 kcal/day + 955 kcal/day = 2,864 kcal/day

   or

   1,909 kcal/day + 1,336 kcal/day = 3,245 kcal/day

   Assuming this man is maintaining his present weight, he requires between 2,864 and 3,245 kcal/day to stay in energy balance!

	Men	**Women**
Sedentary/Inactive	25–40%	25–35%
Involves mostly sitting, driving, or very low levels of activity.		
Lightly Active	50–70%	40–60%
Involves a lot of sitting; may also involve some walking, moving around, and light lifting.		
Moderately Active	65–80%	50–70%
Involves work plus intentional exercise such as an hour of walking or walking 4 to 5 days per week; may have a job requiring some physical labor.		
Heavily Active	90–120%	80–100%
Involves a great deal of physical labor, such as roofing, carpentry work, and/or regular heavy lifting and digging.		
Exceptionally Active	130–145%	110–130%
Involves a lot of physical activities for work and intentional exercise. Also applies to athletes who train for many hours each day, such as triathletes and marathon runners or other competitive athletes performing heavy, regular training.		

Percent (%) contribution to body fat

Figure 13.10   Research indicates that about 25% of body fat is accounted for by genetic heritage. However, nongenetic factors such as diet and exercise play a much larger role.

Genetic Factors Affect Body Weight

Our genetic background influences our height, weight, body shape, and metabolic rate. A classic study shows that the body weights of adults who were adopted as children are similar to the weights of their biological parents, not their adoptive parents.[8] **Figure 13.10** shows that about 25% of our body fat is accounted for by genetic influences. Two theories linking genetics with our body weight are the thrifty gene theory and the set-point theory.

The Thrifty Gene Theory

The **thrifty gene theory** suggests that some people possess a gene (or genes) that causes them to be energetically thrifty. This means that at rest and even during active times, these individuals expend less energy than people who do not possess this gene. The proposed purpose of this gene is to protect a person from starving to death during times of extreme food shortages. This theory has been applied to some Native American tribes, as these societies were exposed to centuries of feast and famine. Those with a thrifty metabolism survived when little food was available, and this trait was passed on to future generations. Although an actual thrifty gene (or genes) has not yet been identified, researchers continue to study this explanation as a potential cause of obesity.

If this theory is true, think about how people who possess this thrifty gene might respond to today's environment. Low levels of physical activity, inexpensive food sources that are high in fat and energy, and excessively large serving sizes are the norm in our society. People with a thrifty metabolism would experience a great amount of weight gain, and their bodies would be more resistant to weight loss. Theoretically, having thrifty genetics would be advantageous during times of minimal food resources; however, this state could lead to very high levels of obesity in times of plenty.

The Set-Point Theory

The **set-point theory** suggests that our bodies are designed to maintain our weight within a narrow range, or at a "set point." In many cases, the body appears to respond in such a way as to maintain a person's current weight. When we dramatically reduce energy intake (such as with fasting or strict diets), the body responds with physiologic changes that cause BMR to drop. This causes a significant slowing of our energy output. In addition, being physically active while fasting or starving is difficult because a person just doesn't have the energy for it. These two mechanisms of energy conservation may contribute to some of the rebound weight gain many dieters experience after they quit dieting.

Conversely, overeating in some people may cause an increase in BMR and is thought to be associated with an increased thermic effect of food as well as an increase in spontaneous movements, or fidgeting. This in turn increases energy output and prevents weight gain. These changes may explain how some people fail to gain all of the weight expected from eating excess food. We don't eat the exact same amount of food each day; some days we overeat, other days we eat less. When you think about how much our daily energy intake fluctuates (about 20% above and below our average monthly intake), our ability to maintain a certain weight over long periods of time suggests that there is some evidence to support the set-point theory.

Can we change our weight set point? It appears that when we maintain changes in our diet and activity level over a long period of time, weight change does occur. This is obvious in the case of obesity, since many people become obese during middle adulthood, and they are not able to maintain the lower body weight they had as a younger adult. Also, many people do successfully lose weight and maintain that weight loss over long periods of time. Thus, the set-point theory cannot entirely account for the body's resistance to weight loss. An interesting study on weight gain in twins demonstrates how genetics may affect our tendency to maintain a set point; this study is reviewed in the accompanying Highlight box.

thrifty gene theory   A theory that suggests that some people possess a gene (or genes) that causes them to be energetically thrifty, resulting in them expending less energy at rest and during physical activity.

set-point theory   A theory suggesting that the body raises or lowers energy expenditure in response to increased and decreased food intake and physical activity. This action serves to maintain an individual's body weight within a narrow range.

Highlight

Overfeeding Responses of Identical Twins

A classic study done by researchers at Laval University in Quebec, Canada, shows how genetics may play a role in our responses to overeating.[9] Twelve pairs of male identical twins volunteered to stay in a dormitory where they were supervised 24 hours a day for 120 consecutive days. Researchers measured how much energy each man needed to maintain his body weight at the beginning of the study. For 100 days, the subjects were fed 1,000 kcal more per day than they needed to maintain body weight. Daily physical activity was limited, but each person was allowed to walk outdoors for 30 minutes each day, read, watch television and videos, and play cards and video games. The research staff stayed with these men to ensure that they did not stray from the study protocol.

The average weight gain experienced by this group of men was almost 18 pounds. Although they were all overfed enough energy to gain about 26 pounds, the average weight gain was 8 pounds less than expected. These men

Identical twins tend to maintain a similar weight throughout life.

gained mostly fat but also gained about 6 pounds of lean body mass. Interestingly, there was a very wide range of weight gained. One man only gained about 9.5 pounds, whereas another man gained more than 29 pounds! Keep in mind that the food these men ate and the activities they performed were tightly controlled.

This study shows that when people overeat by the same amount of food, they can gain very different amounts of weight and body fat. Whereas each twin gained a similar amount of weight to his twin pair, there was a lot of difference in how each set of twins responded. It is suggested that those more resistant to weight gain when they overeat have the ability to increase BMR, store more excess energy as lean body mass instead of fat, and increase spontaneous movements such as fidgeting. Thus, genetic differences may explain why some people have a better ability to maintain a certain weight set point than others.

Composition of the Diet Affects Fat Storage

As previously discussed, when we eat more energy than we expend, we gain weight. Most people eat what is referred to as a "mixed" diet, meaning it contains a mix of carbohydrate, fat, and protein. Scientists used to think that people would gain the same amount of weight if they ate too much food of any type, but now there is evidence to support the theory that when we overeat dietary fat, we store it more easily as adipose tissue than we do either carbohydrate or protein.[10] This may be due to the fact that eating fat doesn't cause much of an increase in metabolic rate, and the body stores fat in the form of adipose tissue quite easily. In contrast, when we overeat protein or carbohydrate, our body's initial response is to use this extra food for energy, storage, or the building of tissues, with a smaller amount of the excess stored as fat. This does not mean, however, that you can eat as many low-fat foods as you want and not gain weight! Consistently overeating protein or carbohydrate will also lead to weight gain. Instead, maintain a balanced diet combining fat, carbohydrate, and protein, and reduce dietary fat to less than 35% of total energy. This strategy may help reduce the storage of fat energy as adipose tissue.

A balanced diet contains protein, carbohydrate, and fat.

Physiologic Factors Influence Body Weight

Numerous physiologic factors affect body weight, including hunger, specific proteins, hormones, and blood glucose levels. These various factors contribute to the complexities of weight regulation.

Hunger and Satiety

As introduced in Chapter 3, *hunger* is the innate, physiological drive or need to eat. Physical signals such as a growling stomach and lightheadedness indicate when one is hungry. This drive for food is triggered by physiologic changes such as low blood glucose that affect chemicals in the brain. The hypothalamus plays an important role in hunger regulation. Special hypothalamic cells referred to as *feeding cells* respond to conditions of low blood glucose, causing hunger and driving a person to eat. Once one has eaten and the body has responded accordingly, other centers in the hypothalamus are triggered, and the desire to eat is reduced. The state reached in which there is no longer a desire to eat is referred to as *satiety*. It may be that some people have an insufficient satiety mechanism, which prevents them from feeling full after a meal, allowing them to overeat.

Proteins

Leptin is a protein that is produced by adipose cells and functions as a hormone. First discovered in mice, leptin acts to reduce food intake and cause a decrease in body weight and body fat. A gene called the *ob* gene (obesity gene) codes for the production of leptin. Obese mice were found to have a genetic mutation in the *ob* gene. This mutation reduces the ability of adipose cells to synthesize leptin in sufficient amounts; therefore, food intake increases dramatically, energy output is reduced, and weight gain occurs.

When these findings were first published, a great deal of excitement was generated about how leptin might decrease obesity in humans. Unfortunately, studies have shown that although obese mice respond positively to leptin injections, obese humans do not. Instead, they tend to have very high amounts of leptin in their bodies and are insensitive to leptin's effects. In truth, we have just begun to learn about leptin and its role in the human body. Researchers are currently studying its role in starvation and overeating, and it appears it might play a role in cardiovascular and kidney complications that result from obesity and related diseases.

In addition to leptin, numerous proteins affect the regulation of appetite and storage of body fat. Primary among these is **ghrelin,** a protein synthesized in the stomach. It acts as a hormone and plays an important role in appetite regulation through its actions in the hypothalamus. Ghrelin stimulates appetite and increases the amount of food one eats. Ghrelin levels increase before a meal and fall within about 1 hour after a meal. This action indicates that ghrelin may be a primary contributor to both hunger and satiety. Ghrelin levels appear to increase after weight loss, and researchers speculate that this factor could help to explain why people who have lost weight have difficulty keeping it off.[11] We noted earlier that obese people seem to lose their sensitivity to leptin, but this is not true for ghrelin: obese people are just as sensitive to the effects of ghrelin as non-obese people.[12] For this reason, potential mechanisms that can block the actions of ghrelin are currently a prime target of research into the treatment of obesity.

Peptide YY, or **PYY,** is a protein produced in the gastrointestinal tract. It is released after a meal, in amounts proportional to the energy content of the meal. In contrast with ghrelin, PYY decreases appetite and inhibits food intake in animals and humans.[13] Interestingly, obese individuals have lower levels of PYY when they are fasting and also show less of an increase in PYY after a meal as compared with non-obese individuals, which suggests that PYY may be important in the manifestation and maintenance of obesity.[14]

Recall that mitochondria are organelles found abundantly within cells that generate ATP, including skeletal muscle cells and adipose cells. Some research suggests that

leptin   A hormone that is produced by body fat that acts to reduce food intake and to decrease body weight and body fat.

ghrelin   A protein synthesized in the stomach that acts as a hormone and plays an important role in appetite regulation by stimulating appetite.

peptide YY (PYY)   A protein produced in the gastrointestinal tract that is released after a meal in amounts proportional to the energy content of the meal; it decreases appetite and inhibits food intake.

uncoupling proteins present in the inner mitochondrial membrane may influence body weight. These proteins uncouple the oxidation of fat from ATP formation; when this occurs, the oxidation of fat produces heat instead of ATP. This production of heat increases energy expenditure and results in less storage of excess energy. Thus, a person with more uncoupling proteins or a higher activity of these proteins would be more resistant to weight gain and obesity.

Three forms of uncoupling proteins have been identified: UCP1 is found exclusively in **brown adipose tissue,** a type of adipose tissue that has more mitochondria than white adipose tissue. It is found in significant amounts in animals and newborn humans. It was traditionally thought that adult humans have very little brown adipose tissue. However, recent evidence suggests that humans may have substantially more brown adipose tissue than previously assumed,[15] and that people with higher BMI values have lower amounts of brown adipose tissue.[16] These findings suggest a possible role of brown adipose tissue in obesity. Two other uncoupling proteins, UCP2 and UCP3, are known to be important to energy expenditure and resistance to weight gain. These proteins are found in various tissues, including white adipose tissue and skeletal muscle. The roles of brown adipose tissue and uncoupling proteins in human obesity are currently being researched.

Other Physiologic Factors

Various other physiologic factors known to increase satiety (or decrease food intake) include:

- Hormones such as serotonin and cholecystokinin (CCK). Serotonin is made from the amino acid tryptophan; and CCK is produced by the intestinal cells and stimulates the gallbladder to secrete bile.
- An increase in blood glucose levels, such as that normally seen after the consumption of a meal.
- Stomach expansion.
- Nutrient absorption from the small intestine.

Other physiologic factors that can decrease satiety (or increase food intake) include:

- Hormones such as beta-endorphins. Beta-endorphins increase a sense of pleasure while eating, which can increase food intake.
- Neuropeptide Y, an amino-acid-containing compound produced in the hypothalamus, stimulates appetite.
- Decreased blood glucose levels, such as the decrease that occurs after an overnight fast.

Cultural and Economic Factors Affect Food Choices and Body Weight

Both cultural and economic factors can contribute to obesity. As discussed in detail in Chapter 1, cultural factors (including religious beliefs and learned food preferences) affect our food choices and eating patterns. In addition, the customs of many cultures put food at the center of celebrations of festivals and holidays, and overeating is tacitly encouraged. In addition, as both parents now work outside the home in most American families, more people are embracing the "fast-food culture," preferring and almost exclusively choosing highly processed and highly caloric fast foods from restaurants and grocery stores to lower-kilocalorie, home-cooked meals.

Coinciding with these cultural influences on food intake are cultural factors that promote an inactive life. Research with sedentary ethnic minority women in the United States indicates that other common barriers to increasing physical activity include lack of personal motivation, no physically active role models to emulate, acceptance of larger body size, exercise being considered culturally unacceptable, and fear for personal safety in both rural and urban settings.[17, 18] In short, cultural factors influence both food consumption and levels of physical activity, and can contribute to weight gain.

brown adipose tissue A type of adipose tissue that has more mitochondria than white adipose tissue and can increase energy expenditure by uncoupling oxidation from ATP production. It is found in significant amounts in animals and newborn humans.

Food preferences often depend on culture. Some cultures enjoy foods such as frogs' legs, whereas others do not.

Economic status is known to be related to health status, particularly in developed countries such as the United States: people of lower economic status have higher rates of obesity and related chronic diseases than people of higher incomes.[19] In addition to the impact of one's income on access to healthcare, economic factors strongly impact our food choices and eating behaviors. It is a common belief that healthful foods are expensive, and that only wealthy people can afford to purchase them. While it is true that certain foods considered more healthful, such as organic foods, imported fruits and vegetables, many fish, and leaner selections of some meats, can be costly, does healthful eating always have to be expensive? Refer to the Nutrition Myth or Fact? box to learn more about whether a healthful diet can also be an affordable diet.

Psychologic and Social Factors Influence Behavior and Body Weight

We explored in Chapter 3 the concept that *appetite* can be experienced in the absence of hunger. Appetite may therefore be considered a psychological drive to eat, being stimulated by learned preferences for food and particular situations that promote eating. For instance, some people learn as children to love or hate certain foods. This may explain why foods such as frogs' legs, cactus, and cultured yeast extract (Marmite) appeal to people in certain cultures who were raised on them but are almost never adopted into the diet as new foods by an adult. Others may follow learned behaviors related to timing and size of meals. In addition, the sight and fragrance of certain foods stimulate the pleasure centers of the brain, whether or not we happen to be hungry at the time. Mood can also affect appetite, as some people will eat more or less if they feel depressed or happy. As you can imagine, appetite leads many people to overeat.

Some Social Factors Promote Overeating

Social factors can encourage people to overeat or choose high-energy foods. For example, pressure from family and friends to eat the way they do and easy access to large servings of inexpensive and high-fat foods contribute to overeating. Think about how you might eat differently when you attend a birthday celebration with family or friends. Perhaps you are offered hot dogs, pizza, birthday cake, ice cream, or other dishes that are relatively high in fat and energy. The pressure to overeat on holidays is also high, as family members or friends offer extra servings of favorite holiday foods and follow a very large meal with a rich dessert.

Americans also have numerous opportunities to overeat because of easy access throughout the day to foods high in fat and energy. Vending machines selling junk foods are everywhere: on campus, in business offices, and even at fitness centers. Shopping malls are filled with fast-food restaurants, where inexpensive, large serving sizes are the norm. Food manufacturers are producing products in ever-larger serving sizes: For instance, in 2005, the Mars candy company introduced a supersize version of M&M's candy, with each piece about 55% larger than the standard-size M&M's. Other supersize examples include the Monster Thickburger from Hardee's restaurant, the Full House XL pizza from Pizza Hut, and the Enormous Omelet Sandwich from Burger King.[20] Serving sizes have become so large that many Americans are suffering from "portion distortion." To test your understanding of a serving size, take the "Portion Distortion" interactive quiz from the National Institutes of Health at http://hin.nhlbi.nih.gov/portion/. Even foods traditionally considered healthful, such as some brands of peanut butter, yogurt, chicken soup, and milk, are often filled with added sugars and other ingredients that are high in energy. This easy access to large servings of high-energy meals and snacks leads many people to consume excess energy.

Some Social Factors Promote Inactivity

Social factors can also cause people to be less physically active. For instance, we don't even have to spend time or energy preparing food anymore, as everything is either ready-

Easy-access foods and fast foods may be inexpensive and filling but are often high in fat and sugar.

Nutrition Myth or Fact?
Does It Cost More to Eat Right?

The shelves of American supermarkets are filled with an abundance of healthful food options: organic meats and produce, exotic fish, out-of-season fresh fruits and vegetables that are flown in from warmer climates, whole-grain breads and cereals, and low-fat and low-sodium options of traditional foods. With all of this choice, it would seem easy for anyone to consume healthful foods throughout the year. But a closer look at the prices of these foods suggests that, for many, they simply are not affordable. This raises the question: Does eating right have to be expensive?

It is a fact that organic foods are more expensive than non-organic options. However, as we'll explore in detail in Chapter 15, there is little evidence indicating that organic foods are actually more healthful choices than non-organic foods. In addition, some of the lowest-cost foods currently available in stores are also some of the most nutritious: these include beans, lentils, and other legumes, seasonal fruits, root vegetables such as potatoes and winter squashes, frozen fruits and vegetables, and cooking oils high in mono- and polyunsaturated fats. In fact, frozen as well as canned fruits and vegetables are generally just as nutritious as fresh options, and may be more so depending on how long the fresh produce has been transported and stored, and how long it has been sitting on the supermarket shelves. Thus, with some knowledge, skills, and focused attention, people can still eat healthfully on a tight budget.

Here are some more tips to help you save money when shopping for healthful foods:

■ Buy whole grains such as cereals, brown rice, and pastas in bulk—they store well for longer periods and provide a good base for meals and snacks.

■ Buy frozen vegetables on sale and stock up—these are just as healthful as fresh vegetables, require less preparation, and are many times cheaper.

■ If lower-sodium options of canned vegetables are too expensive, buy the less expensive regular option and drain the juice from the vegetables before cooking.

■ Consume smaller amounts of leaner meats—by eating less you'll not only save money but reduce your total intake of energy and fat while still providing the nutrients that support good health.

■ Choose frozen fish or canned salmon or tuna packed in water as an alternative to fresh fish.

■ Avoid frozen or dehydrated prepared meals. These are usually expensive, high in sodium, saturated fats, and energy, and low in fiber and other important nutrients.

■ Buy generic or store brands of foods—be careful to check the labels to ensure the foods are similar in nutrient value as the higher-priced options.

■ Cut coupons from local newspapers and magazines, and watch the sale circulars so that you can stock up on healthful foods you can store.

■ Consider cooking more meals at home; you'll have more control over what goes into your meals and will also be able to cook larger amounts and freeze leftovers for future meals.

As you can see, eating healthfully does not have to be expensive. However, it helps to become a savvy consumer by reading food labels, comparing prices, and gaining the skills and confidence to cook at home. The information shared throughout this text should help you acquire these skills so that you can eat healthfully, even on a limited budget!

Although specialty foods (such as organic or imported products) can be expensive, lower-cost alternatives can be just as nutritious.

Behaviors learned as a child can affect adult weight and physical activity patterns.

to-serve or requires just a few minutes to cook in a microwave oven. Other social factors restricting physical activity include living in an unsafe community; coping with family, community, and work responsibilities that do not involve physical activity; and living in an area with harsh weather conditions. Many overweight people identify such factors as major barriers to maintaining a healthful body weight, and research seems to confirm their influence.

Certainly, social factors are contributing to decreased physical activity among children. There was a time when children played outdoors regularly and when physical education was offered daily in school. In today's society, many children cannot play outdoors due to safety concerns and lack of recreational facilities, and few schools have the resources to regularly offer physical education to children.

Another social factor promoting inactivity in both children and adults is our increasingly technological lifestyle. Watching television, surfing the Internet, and playing with video games and other hand-held devices is occupying more and more of our time, both as children and adults. By reducing energy expenditure, these behaviors contribute to weight gain. For instance, a study of 11- to 13-year-old schoolchildren found that children who watched more than 2 hours of television per night were more likely to be overweight or obese than children who watched less than 2 hours of television per night. Similarly, adults who reported an increase in television watching of 20 hours per week (approximately 3 hours per day) over a 9-year period had a significant increase in waist circumference, indicating significant weight gain.[21]

Social Pressures Can Promote Underweight

On the other hand, social pressures to maintain a lean body are great enough to encourage many people to undereat or to avoid foods that are perceived as "bad," especially fats. Our society ridicules and often ostracizes overweight people, many of whom face discrimination in many areas of their lives, including employment. Media images of waiflike fashion models and men in tight jeans with muscular chests and abdomens encourage many people—especially adolescents and young adults—to skip meals, resort to crash diets, and exercise obsessively. Even some people of normal body weight push themselves to achieve an unrealistic and unattainable weight goal, in the process threatening their health and even their lives (see the following *In Depth* for information on the consequences of disordered eating).

It should be clear that how a person gains, loses, and maintains body weight is a complex matter. Most people who are overweight have tried several weight-loss programs but have been unsuccessful in maintaining long-term weight loss. A significant number of these people have consequently given up all weight-loss attempts. Some even suffer from severe depression related to their body weight. Should we condemn these people as failures and continue to pressure them to lose weight? Should people who are overweight but otherwise healthy (for example, low blood pressure, cholesterol, triglycerides, and glucose levels) be advised to lose weight? As we continue to search for ways to help people achieve and maintain a healthful body weight, our society must take measures to reduce the social pressures facing people who are overweight or obese.

RECaP

Many factors affect our ability to gain and lose weight. Our genetic background influences our height, weight, body shape, and metabolic rate. The thrifty gene theory suggests that some people possess a gene or set of genes that causes them to expend less energy. The set-point theory suggests that the body is designed to maintain weight within a narrow range. The macronutrient composition of the diet influences the storage of body fat, and physiologic factors such as hunger, leptin, ghrelin, peptide YY, uncoupling proteins, and various hormones impact body weight by their effects on satiety, appetite, and energy expenditure. A person's diet and activity patterns as a child influence his or her body weight as an adult. Cultural and economic factors can significantly influence the amounts and types of foods we eat. Psychological and social factors influencing weight include ready availability of large portions of high-energy foods and lack of physical activity. Social pressures facing those who are overweight can drive people to use harmful methods to achieve an unrealistic body weight.

Hannah
Nutri-Case

"I wonder what it would be like to be able to look in the mirror and not feel fat. Like my friend Kristi—she's been skinny since we were kids. I'm just the opposite: I've felt bad about my weight ever since I can remember. One of my worst memories is from the YMCA swim camp the summer I was 10 years old. Of course we had to wear a swimsuit, and the other kids picked on me so bad I'll never forget it. One of the boys called me "fatso," and the girls were even meaner, especially when I was changing in the locker room. That was the last year I was in the swim camp, and I've never owned a swimsuit since."

Think back to your own childhood. Were you ever teased for some aspect of yourself that you felt unable to change? How might organizations that work with children, such as schools, YMCAs, scout troops, and church-based groups, increase their leaders' awareness of social stigmatization of overweight children and reduce incidents of teasing, bullying, and other insensitivity?

How Can You Achieve and Maintain a Healthful Body Weight?

Achieving and maintaining a healthful body weight involve three primary strategies (Table 13.3):

- Gradual changes in energy intake
- Incorporation of regular and appropriate physical activity
- Application of behavior modification techniques

In this section, we first discuss popular diet plans, which may or may not incorporate these strategies. We then explain how to design a personalized weight-loss plan that includes all three of them. Finally, we review the use of prescribed medications and dietary supplements in losing weight.

If You Decide to Follow a Popular Diet Plan, Choose One Based on the Three Strategies

With the assistance of the USDA Food Guide and the information in this book, you are ready to design your own personalized diet plan. If you'd feel more comfortable following an established plan, however, many are available. How can you know whether or not it is based on sound dietary principles, and whether its promise of long-term weight loss will prove true for *you*? Look to the three strategies just identified: Does the plan promote gradual reductions in energy intake? Does it advocate increased physical activity? Does it include strategies for modifying your eating and activity-related behaviors? Reputable diet plans incorporate all of these strategies. Unfortunately, many dieters are drawn to fad diets, which do not.

Table 13.3 Recommendations for a Sound Weight-Loss Plan

Dietary Recommendations	Physical Activity Recommendations	Behavior Modification Recommendations
Reasonable weight loss is defined as 0.5 to 2 pounds per week. To achieve this, energy intake should be reduced from 250 to no more than 1,000 kcal/day of present intake. A weight-loss plan should never provide less than a total of 1,200 kcal/day.	A long-term goal for physical activity should be a minimum of 30 minutes of moderate physical activity most, or preferably all, days of the week. Doing 45 minutes or more of an activity such as walking at least 5 days per week is ideal.	Shop only when you are not hungry, eat only at set times in one location, refuse to buy problem foods, and avoid vending machines, convenience stores, and fast-food restaurants.
Total fat intake should be 15–25% of total energy intake.		Suppress inappropriate behaviors by taking small food portions, eating foods on smaller serving dishes so they appear larger, and avoiding feelings of deprivation by eating regular meals throughout the day.
Saturated fat intake should be 5–10% of total energy intake.		Strengthen appropriate behaviors by sharing food with others, learning appropriate serving sizes, planning healthful snacks, scheduling walks and other physical activities with friends, and keeping clothes and equipment for physical activity in convenient places.
Monounsaturated fat intake should be 10–15% of total energy intake.		
Polyunsaturated fat intake should be no more than 10% of total energy intake.		Repeat desired behaviors by slowing down eating, always using utensils, leaving food on your plate, moving more throughout the day, and joining groups that are physically active.
Cholesterol intake should be less than 300 mg/day.		
Protein intake should be approximately 15–20% of total energy intake.		Reward yourself for positive behaviors by getting a massage, buying new clothes or tickets to nonfood amusements, taking a walk, or reading a book (for fun).
Carbohydrate intake should be around 55% of total energy intake, with less than 10% of energy intake coming from simple sugars.		Use the "buddy" system by exercising with a friend or relative and/or calling this support person when you need an extra boost to stay motivated.
Fiber intake should be 25 to 35 g/day.		Don't punish yourself if you deviate from your plan (and you will—everyone does). Ask others to avoid responding to any slips you make.
Calcium intake should be 1,000 to 1,500 mg/day.		

Data adapted from: National Heart, Lung, and Blood Institute Expert Panel, National Institutes of Health. 1998. *Clinical Guidelines on the Identification, Evaluation, and Treatment of Overweight and Obesity in Adults.* Washington, DC: U.S. Government Printing Office.

Avoid Fad Diets

Beware of fad diets! They are simply what their name implies—fads that do not result in long-term, healthful weight changes. To be precise, fad diets are programs that enjoy short-term popularity and are sold based on a marketing gimmick that appeals to the public's desires and fears. Of the hundreds of such diets on the market today, most will "die" within a year, only to be born again as a "new and improved" fad diet. The goal of the person or company designing and marketing a fad diet is to make money. How can you tell if the program you are interested in qualifies as a fad diet? Here are some pointers to help you:

- The promoters of the diet claim that the program is new, improved, or based on some new discovery; however, no scientific data are available to support these claims.
- The program is touted for its ability to promote rapid weight loss or body fat loss, usually more than 2 pounds per week, and may include the claim that weight loss can be achieved with little or no physical exercise.
- The diet includes special foods and supplements, many of which are expensive and/or difficult to find or can be purchased only from the diet promoter. Common recommendations for these diets include avoiding certain foods, eating only a special combination of certain foods, or including "magic" foods in the diet that "burn fat" and "speed up metabolism."
- The diet may include a rigid menu that must be followed daily or may limit participants to eating a few select foods each day. Variety and balance are discouraged, and restriction of certain foods (such as fruits and vegetables) is encouraged.
- Many programs promote supplemental foods and/or nutritional supplements that are described as critical to the success of the diet. They usually include claims that these supplements can cure or prevent a variety of health ailments or that the diet can stop the aging process.

In a world where many of us feel we have to meet a certain physical standard to be attractive and "good enough," fad diets flourish: it is estimated that we currently spend more than $33 billion on fad diets each year.[22] Unfortunately, the only people who usually benefit from them are their marketers, who can become very wealthy promoting programs that are highly ineffectual.

Diets Focusing on Macronutrient Composition May or May Not Work for You

A comprehensive review of the currently available evidence shows that achieving a negative energy balance is the major factor in successful weight loss.[23] The macronutrient composition of a diet does not appear to affect the amount of weight lost. However, the three main types of weight-loss diets that have been most seriously and comprehensively researched all encourage increased consumption of certain macronutrients and restrict the consumption of others. Provided here is a brief review of these three main types and their general effects on weight loss and health parameters.[23]

Moderate-Fat, High-Carbohydrate, Moderate-Protein Diets
Moderate-fat, high-carbohydrate, moderate-protein diets that are balanced in nutrients typically contain 20% to 30% of total energy intake as fat, 55% to 60% of total energy intake as carbohydrate, and 15% to 20% of energy intake as protein. These diets include Weight Watchers, Jenny Craig, and others that follow the general guidelines of the DASH diet and the USDA Food Guide. All of these diet plans emphasize that weight loss occurs when energy intake is lower than energy expenditure. The goal is gradual weight loss, or about 1 to 2 lb of body weight per week. Typical energy deficits are between 500 and 1,000 kcal/day. It is recommended that women eat no less than 1,000 to 1,200 kcal/day and that men consume no less than 1,200 to 1,400 kcal/day. Regular physical activity is encouraged.

To date, these types of low-energy diets have been researched more than any others. A substantial amount of high-quality scientific evidence (from randomized controlled trials) indicates that they are effective in decreasing body weight. In addition, the people who lose weight on these diets also decrease their LDL-cholesterol, reduce their blood triglyceride levels, and decrease their blood pressure. The diets are nutritionally adequate if the individual's food choices follow the USDA Food Guide. If the individual's food choices are not varied and balanced, the diets may be low in nutrients such as fiber, zinc, calcium, iron, and vitamin B_{12}. Under these circumstances, supplementation is needed.

High-Fat, Low-Carbohydrate, High-Protein Diets
High-fat, low-carbohydrate, high-protein diets cycle in and out of popularity on a regular basis. By definition, these types of diets generally contain about 55% to 65% of total energy intake as fat and less than 100 g of carbohydrate per day, with the balance of daily energy intake as protein. Examples of these types of diets include Dr. Atkins' Diet Revolution, the Carbohydrate Addict's Diet, Life Without Bread, Sugar Busters, and Protein Power. These diets minimize the role of restricting total energy intake on weight loss. They instead advise participants to restrict carbohydrate intake, proposing that carbohydrates are addictive and that they cause significant overeating, insulin surges leading to excessive fat storage, and an overall metabolic imbalance that leads to obesity. The goal is to reduce carbohydrates enough to cause ketosis, which will decrease blood glucose and insulin levels and can reduce appetite.

Countless people claim to have lost substantial weight on high-fat, low-carbohydrate, high-protein diets; however, reputable scientific studies of their effectiveness are only just beginning to be conducted. The current limited evidence suggests that individuals in both free-living and experimental conditions do lose weight by following these types of diets. In addition, it appears that those people who lose weight may also experience positive metabolic changes such as decreased blood lipid levels, decreased blood pressure, and decreased blood glucose and insulin. However, the amount of weight loss and the improvements in metabolic health measured with these diets are no greater than those seen with higher-

"Low-carb" diets may lead to weight loss but are nutritionally inadequate and can cause negative side effects.

Low-fat and very-low-fat diets emphasize eating foods higher in complex carbohydrates and fiber.

carbohydrate diets. Our current limited evidence of the effectiveness, along with concerns about long-term compliance, potential health risks, and side effects, has made these diets controversial. Refer to the Nutrition Debate at the end of this chapter to learn more about high-fat, low-carbohydrate, high-protein diets.

Low-Fat and Very-Low-Fat Diets   Low-fat diets contain 11% to 19% of total energy as fat, whereas very-low-fat diets contain less than 10% of total energy as fat. Both of these types of diets are high in carbohydrate and moderate in protein. Examples include Dr. Dean Ornish's Program for Reversing Heart Disease and the New Pritikin Program. These diets do not focus on total energy intake but emphasize eating foods higher in complex carbohydrates and fiber. Consumption of sugar and white flour is very limited. The Ornish diet is vegetarian, whereas the Pritikin diet allows 3.5 oz of lean meat per day. Regular physical activity is a key component.

These programs were not originally designed for weight loss but rather were developed to decrease or reverse heart disease. Also, these diets are not popular with consumers, who view them as too restrictive and difficult to follow. Thus, there are limited data on their effects. However, high-quality evidence suggests that people following these diets do lose weight, and some data suggest that these diets may also decrease LDL-cholesterol, blood triglyceride levels, glucose, insulin levels, and blood pressure. Few side effects have been reported on these diets; the most common is flatus that typically decreases over time. Low-fat diets are low in vitamin B_{12}, and very-low-fat diets are low in essential fatty acids, vitamins B_{12} and E, and zinc. Thus, supplementation is needed. These types of diets are not considered safe for people with diabetes who are insulin dependent (either type 1 or type 2) or for people with carbohydrate-malabsorption illnesses.

If You Decide to Design Your Own Diet Plan, Include the Three Strategies

As we noted earlier, a healthful and effective weight-loss plan involves a modest reduction in energy intake, incorporating physical activity into each day, and practicing changes in behavior that can assist you in reducing your energy intake and increasing your energy expenditure. Following are some guidelines for designing your own personalized diet plan that incorporates these strategies.

Set Realistic Goals

The first key to safe and effective weight loss is setting realistic goals related to how much weight to lose and how quickly (or slowly) to lose it. Although making gradual changes in body weight is frustrating for most people, this slower change is much more effective in maintaining weight loss over the long term. Ask yourself the question, "How long did it take me to gain this extra weight?" If you are like most people, your answer is that it took 1 or more years, not just a few months. A fair expectation for weight loss is similarly gradual: experts recommend a pace of about 0.5 to 2 pounds per week. Your weight-loss goals should also take into consideration any health-related concerns you may have. After checking with your physician, you may decide initially to set a goal of simply maintaining your current weight and preventing additional weight gain. After your weight has remained stable for several weeks, you might then write down realistic goals for weight loss.

Goals that are more likely to be realistic and achievable share the following characteristics:

- *They are specific.* Telling yourself "I will eat less this week" is not helpful because the goal is not specific. An example of a specific goal is "I will eat only half of my restaurant entrée tonight and take the rest home and eat it tomorrow for lunch."
- *They are reasonable.* If you are not presently physically active, it would be unreasonable to set of a goal of exercising for 30 minutes every day. A more reasonable goal would be to exercise for 15 minutes per day, 3 days per week. Once you've achieved that goal, you

can increase the frequency, intensity, and time of exercise according to the improvements in fitness that you have experienced.

- *They are measurable.* Effective goals are ones you can measure. An example is "I will lose at least one pound by May 1st," or "I will substitute drinking water for my regular soft drink at lunch each day this week." Recording your specific, measurable goals will help you to better determine whether you are achieving them.

By monitoring your progress regularly you can determine whether you are meeting your goals or whether you need to revise them based on accomplishments or challenges that arise.

Eat Smaller Portions of Lower-Fat Foods

The portion sizes of foods offered and sold in restaurants and grocery stores have expanded considerably over the past 40 years. One of the most challenging issues related to food is understanding what a healthful portion size is and how to reduce the portion sizes of foods that we eat.

Recent studies indicate that when children and adults are presented with large portion sizes of foods and beverages, they eat more energy overall and do not respond to cues of fullness.[24, 25] Thus, it has been suggested that effective weight-loss strategies include reducing both the portion size and energy density of foods consumed, and replacing energy-dense beverages with low-calorie or noncalorie beverages.[25]

What specific changes can you make to reduce your energy intake and stay healthy? Here are some helpful suggestions:

1. Follow the serving sizes recommended in the USDA Food Guide (pages 55–56). Making this change involves understanding what constitutes a serving size and measuring foods to determine whether they meet or exceed the recommended serving size.
2. Reduce your consumption of foods that are high in fat and energy. People trying to lose weight should aim for a total fat intake of 15% to 25% of total energy intake. This goal can be achieved by eliminating extra fats such as butter, margarine, and mayonnaise and snack foods such as ice cream, doughnuts, and cakes. Save these foods as occasional special treats. Select lower-fat versions of the foods listed in the USDA Food Guide. This means selecting leaner cuts of meat (such as the white meat of poultry and extra-lean ground beef) and reduced-fat or skim dairy products, and selecting lower-fat preparation methods (such as baking and broiling instead of frying). It also means switching from a sugar-filled beverage to a low-calorie or noncalorie beverage during and between meals.
3. Consume foods that are relatively low in energy density. This includes foods such as salads (with low- or nonfat dressings), fruits, vegetables, and soups (broth-based). These foods are low in energy and high in fiber, water, and nutrients. Because they contain relatively more water and fiber than more energy-dense foods, they allow a person to feel satiated without having to consume large amounts of energy.

Figure 13.11 illustrates two sets of meals, one higher in energy and one lower in energy. You can see from this figure that simple changes to a meal, such as choosing lower-fat dairy products, smaller portion sizes, and foods that are relatively less dense in energy, can reduce energy intake without sacrificing taste, pleasure, or nutritional quality!

Participate in Regular Physical Activity

As compared to the previous version of the USDA Food Guide Pyramid, MyPyramid places far greater emphasis on the role of physical activity in maintaining a healthful weight. Why is being physically active so important for achieving changes in body weight and for maintaining a healthful body weight? Of course, we expend extra energy during physical activity, but there's more to it than that because exercise alone (without a reduction of energy intake) does not result in dramatic decreases in body weight. Instead, one of

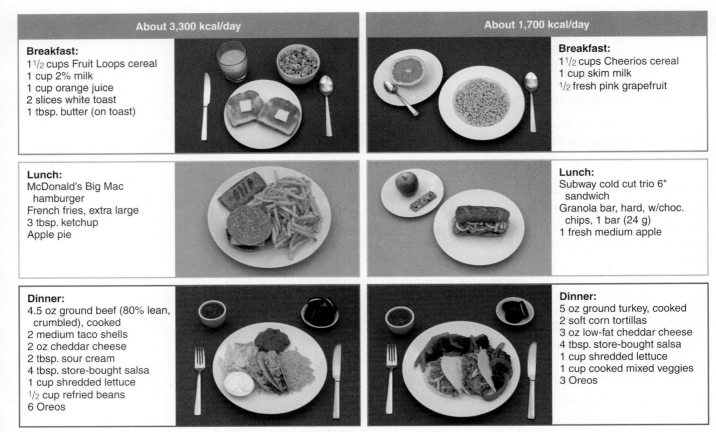

About 3,300 kcal/day	About 1,700 kcal/day
Breakfast: 1¹/₂ cups Fruit Loops cereal 1 cup 2% milk 1 cup orange juice 2 slices white toast 1 tbsp. butter (on toast)	**Breakfast:** 1¹/₂ cups Cheerios cereal 1 cup skim milk ¹/₂ fresh pink grapefruit

Lunch:
McDonald's Big Mac
  hamburger
French fries, extra large
3 tbsp. ketchup
Apple pie
	Lunch:
	Subway cold cut trio 6"
	  sandwich
	Granola bar, hard, w/choc.
	  chips, 1 bar (24 g)
	1 fresh medium apple

Dinner: 4.5 oz ground beef (80% lean, crumbled), cooked 2 medium taco shells 2 oz cheddar cheese 2 tbsp. sour cream 4 tbsp. store-bought salsa 1 cup shredded lettuce ¹/₂ cup refried beans 6 Oreos	**Dinner:** 5 oz ground turkey, cooked 2 soft corn tortillas 3 oz low-fat cheddar cheese 4 tbsp. store-bought salsa 1 cup shredded lettuce 1 cup cooked mixed veggies 3 Oreos

Figure 13.11   The energy density of two sets of meals. The set on the left is higher in energy density, while the set on the right is lower in energy density and the preferred choice for a person trying to lose weight.

the most important reasons for being regularly active is that it helps us maintain or increase our lean body mass and our BMR. In contrast, energy restriction alone causes us to lose lean body mass. As you've learned, the more lean body mass we have, the more energy we expend over the long term.

The National Weight Control Registry is an ongoing project documenting the habits of people who have lost at least 30 pounds and kept their weight off for at least 1 year. Of the 784 people studied thus far, the average weight loss was 66 pounds, and the group maintained the minimum weight-loss criteria of 30 pounds for more than 5 years.[26] Almost all of the people (89%) reported changing both physical activity and dietary intake to lose weight and maintain weight loss. No one form of exercise seems to be most effective, but many people report doing some form of aerobic exercise (such as bicycling, walking, running, aerobic dance, step aerobics, or hiking) and weight lifting at least 45 minutes most days of the week. In fact, on average, this group expended more than 2,800 kcal each week through physical activity! While very few weight-loss studies have documented long-term maintenance of weight loss, those that have find that only people who are regularly active are able to maintain most of their weight loss.

In addition to expending energy and maintaining lean body mass and BMR, regular physical activity improves our mood, results in a higher quality of sleep, increases self-esteem, and gives us a sense of accomplishment (see Chapter 14 for more benefits of regular physical activity). All of these changes enhance our ability to engage in long-term healthful lifestyle behaviors.

Incorporate Appropriate Behavior Modifications into Daily Life

Successful weight loss and long-term maintenance of a healthful weight require people to modify their behaviors. Some of the behavior modifications related to food and physical activity have been discussed in the previous sections. Here are a few more tips on modifying behavior that will assist you in losing weight and maintaining a healthful weight:

- Eat only at set times in one location. Do not eat while studying, working, driving, watching television, and so forth.
- Keep a log of what you eat, when, and why. Try to identify social or emotional cues that cause you to overeat, such as getting a poor grade on an exam or feeling lonely. Then strategize about non-food-related ways to cope, such as phoning a sympathetic friend.
- Save high-fat, high-kilocalorie snack foods such as ice cream, donuts, and cakes for occasional special treats.
- Avoid buying problem foods—that is, foods that you may have difficulty eating in moderate amounts.
- Avoid purchasing high-fat, high-sugar foods from vending machines and convenience stores.
- Serve your food portions on smaller dishes so they appear larger.
- Avoid feelings of deprivation by eating small, regular meals throughout the day.
- Whether at home or dining out, share food with others.
- Prepare healthful snacks to take along with you so that you won't be tempted by foods from vending machines, fast-food restaurants, and so forth.
- Chew food slowly, taking at least 20 minutes to eat a full meal, and stopping at once if you begin to feel full.
- Always use appropriate utensils.
- Leave food on your plate or store it for the next meal.

Weight Loss Can Be Enhanced with Prescribed Medications

The biggest complaint about the recommendations for healthful weight loss is that they are difficult to maintain. Many people are looking for a "magic bullet" that will allow them to lose weight quickly and easily, requiring little sustained effort on their part to achieve their weight goals. Other people have tried to follow healthful weight-loss suggestions for years and have not been successful. In response to these challenges, prescription drugs have been developed to assist people with weight loss. These drugs typically act as appetite suppressants and may also increase satiety.

Weight-loss medications should be used only with proper supervision from a physician. One reason physician involvement is so critical is that many drugs developed for weight loss have side effects. Some have even proven deadly. Fenfluramine (brand name Pondimin), dexfenfluramine (brand name Redux), and a combination of phentermine and fenfluramine (called "phen-fen") are appetite-suppressing drugs that were banned from the market in 1996. These drugs, while resulting in more weight loss than diet alone, were found to cause two life-threatening conditions: primary pulmonary hypertension and valvular heart disease. Although these drugs were banned many years ago, they still serve as examples illustrating that the treatment of obesity through pharmacological means is neither simple nor risk-free.

Two Prescribed Medications Are Available   Two prescription weight-loss drugs are currently available: sibutramine and orlistat. Their long-term safety and efficacy are still being explored.

Sibutramine (brand name Meridia) is an appetite suppressant that can cause increased heart rate and blood pressure in some people. Because many people who are overweight or obese have high blood pressure and are at increased risk for heart disease, these side effects could limit the widespread use of this drug. However, in one study, combining sibutramine therapy with medically supervised aerobic exercise and a low-fat diet resulted in significant weight loss and a significant decrease in heart rate and blood pressure.[27] In addition to increased blood pressure, side effects of sibutramine include dry mouth, anorexia, constipation, insomnia, dizziness, and nausea.

Orlistat (brand name Xenical) is a drug that acts to inhibit the absorption of dietary fat from the intestinal tract, which can result in weight loss in some people. Recent research shows that orlistat results in significant weight loss in obese adolescents, and adults experience significant weight loss and improved blood lipid profiles when orlistat is combined with an energy-restricted diet.[28, 29] The side effects of orlistat include abdominal pain, fatty and loose stools, leaky stools, flatulence, and decreased absorption of fat-soluble nutrients such as vitamins E and D.

For Whom Are Prescription Weight-Loss Medications Prescribed? Although the use of prescribed weight-loss medications is associated with side effects and a certain level of risk, they are justified for people who are obese. That's because the health risks of obesity override the risks of the medications. Specifically, prescription weight-loss medications are advised for people who have:

- a BMI greater than or equal to 30 kg/m^2
- a BMI greater than or equal to 27 kg/m^2 who also have other significant health risk factors such as heart disease, high blood pressure, and type 2 diabetes

These medications should be used only while under a physician's supervision so that progress and health risks can be closely monitored. They are most effective when combined with a program that supports energy restriction, regular exercise, and increasing physical activity throughout the day.

Using Dietary Supplements to Lose Weight Is Controversial

Over-the-counter medications and dietary supplements are also marketed for weight loss. It is important to remember that the Food and Drug Administration (FDA) requires prescription drugs and over-the-counter medications to undergo rigorous testing for safety and effectiveness before they can be released onto the market, but the FDA does not have a similar level of control over the development of dietary supplements. Thus, dangerous or ineffective supplements can be marketed and sold without meeting the FDA's strict safety and quality standards. Moreover, the FDA can pull a dietary supplement from the shelves only if it can prove that the supplement is dangerous. The FDA cannot force the makers of an ineffective but harmless supplement to stop selling it. Recently, two reviews of various supplements and alternative treatments for weight loss were published.[30, 31] Both concluded that there is insufficient evidence to support the use of the following products widely marketed to enhance weight loss: chromium, spirulina (or blue-green algae), ginseng, chitosan (derived from the exoskeleton of crustaceans), green tea, and psyllium (a source of fiber). Yet these products continue their brisk sales to people desperate to lose weight.

Many products marketed for weight loss do indeed increase metabolic rate and decrease appetite; however, they prompt these effects because they contain *stimulants*, substances that speed up physiologic processes. Stimulants commonly found in weight-loss supplements include caffeine, phenylpropanolamine (PPA), and ephedra. Use of these substances is controversial and may be dangerous, as abnormal increases in heart rate and blood pressure can occur.

Caffeine In addition to being a stimulant, caffeine is addictive; nevertheless, it is legal and unregulated in most countries and is considered safe when consumed in moderate amounts (up to the equivalent of 3 to 4 cups of coffee). The extent to which it affects people is influenced by their tolerance for caffeine, the amount consumed, and their body weight. In most adults, a moderate amount of caffeine causes positive mood changes and increased alertness. Its effects on the body include increased heart rate, blood pressure, and urine output. Adverse effects of high doses of caffeine include nervousness, irritability, anxiety, muscle twitching and tremors, headaches, elevated blood pressure, and irregular or rapid heartbeat. Long-term overuse of high doses of caffeine can lead to sleep and anxiety disorders that require clinical attention. Caffeine overdose can be fatal; however, the lethal dose of caffeine is estimated to be about 150 to 200 mg/kg body weight, which is about equivalent to the amount of caffeine contained in 80 to 100 cups of coffee. As this volume of coffee is very difficult to consume, deaths due to caffeine have occurred primarily as a result of taking caffeine tablets.

Phenylpropanolamine (PPA)   In the year 2000, the FDA banned over-the-counter medications containing phenylpropanolamine (PPA), an ingredient that had been used in many cough and cold medications as well as in weight-loss formulas. The FDA acted in response to the deaths of several women who experienced brain hemorrhage after taking prescribed doses of such medications. Consumers were instructed to throw away any medications in their homes that contained PPA. However, PPA may still be present in dietary supplements marketed for weight loss, as these are beyond FDA control.

Ephedra   The use of ephedra has been associated with dangerous elevations in heart rate, blood pressure, and death. Ephedra has been banned by the International Olympic Committee for many years, and the FDA banned the manufacture and sale of ephedra in the United States in 2004 because of its potentially fatal side effects. In April 2005, a federal judge in Utah struck down this FDA ban. The judge's ruling stated that the FDA had failed to prove that low doses of ephedra were dangerous. The FDA appealed this ruling, and the U.S. Court of Appeals eventually ruled in favor of the FDA's original ban. As a result of this ruling it is illegal to sell ephedra-containing supplements in the United States. Some herbal supplement producers still include *ma huang,* the so-called herbal ephedra, in their weight-loss products; however, *ma huang* is simply the Chinese name for ephedra. Some herbal weight-loss supplements contain a combination of *ma huang,* caffeine, and aspirin. As you can see, using weight-loss dietary supplements entails serious health risks.

RECaP

Achieving and maintaining a healthful body weight involve gradual reductions in energy intake, such as by eating smaller portion sizes and limiting dietary fat, incorporating regular physical activity, and applying appropriate behavioral modification techniques. Fad diets do not incorporate these strategies and do not result in long-term, healthful weight change. Diets based on macronutrient composition may promote long-term weight loss, but some have unhealthful side effects. When necessary, drugs can be used to reduce obesity with a doctor's prescription and supervision. Using dietary supplements to lose weight is controversial and can be dangerous in some instances.

What Disorders Are Related to Energy Intake?

At the beginning of this chapter, we provided some definitions of underweight, overweight, obesity, and morbid obesity. Let's take a closer look at these disorders.

Underweight

As defined earlier in this chapter, underweight occurs when a person has too little body fat to maintain health. People with a BMI of less than 18.5 kg/m² are typically considered underweight. Being underweight can be just as unhealthful as being obese, because it increases the risk for infections and illness and impairs the body's ability to recover. Some people are healthy but underweight because of their genetics and/or because they are very physically active and consume adequate energy to maintain their underweight status, but not enough to gain weight. In others, underweight is due to heavy smoking, an underlying disease such as cancer or HIV infection, or an eating disorder such as anorexia nervosa (see the *In Depth* on eating disorders on pages 528–541).

Eating frequent nutrient-dense snacks can help promote weight gain.

Safe and Effective Weight Gain

With so much emphasis in the United States on obesity and weight loss, some find it surprising that many people are trying to gain weight. People looking to gain weight include those who are underweight to the extent that it is compromising their health and many athletes who are attempting to increase strength and power for competition.

To gain weight, people must eat more energy than they expend. While overeating large amounts of foods high in saturated fats (such as bacon, sausage, and cheese) can cause weight gain, doing this without exercising is not considered healthful because most of the weight gained is fat, and high-fat diets increase our risks for cardiovascular and other diseases. Unless there are medical reasons to eat a high-fat diet, it is recommended that people trying to gain weight eat a diet that is relatively low in dietary fat (less than 30% of total calories) and relatively high in complex carbohydrates (55% of total calories). Recommendations for weight gain include:

- Eat a diet that includes about 500 to 1,000 kcal/day more than is needed to maintain present body weight. Although we don't know exactly how much extra energy is needed to gain 1 pound, estimates range from 3,000 to 3,500 kcal. Thus, eating 500 to 1,000 kcal/day in excess should result in a gain of 1 to 2 pounds of weight each week.
- Eat frequently, including meals and numerous snacks throughout the day. Many underweight people do not take the time to eat often enough.
- Avoid the use of tobacco products, as they depress appetite and increase metabolic rate, and both of these effects oppose weight gain. Tobacco use also causes lung, mouth, and esophageal cancers.
- Exercise regularly and incorporate weight lifting or some other form of resistance training into your exercise routine. This form of exercise is most effective in increasing muscle mass. Performing aerobic exercise (such as walking, running, bicycling, or swimming) at least 30 minutes for 3 days per week will help maintain a healthy cardiovascular system.

The key to gaining weight is to eat frequent meals throughout the day and to select energy-dense foods. When selecting foods that are higher in fat, make sure you select foods higher in polyunsaturated and monounsaturated fats (such as peanut butter, olive and canola oils, and avocados). For instance, smoothies and milkshakes made with low-fat milk or yogurt are a great way to take in a lot of energy. Eating peanut butter with fruit or celery and including salad dressings on your salad are other ways to increase the energy density of foods. The biggest challenge to weight gain is setting aside time to eat; by packing a lot of foods to take with you throughout the day, you can enhance your opportunities to eat more.

Theo
Nutri-Case

"I'm sick and tired of everybody everywhere complaining about how they can't lose weight even though they're starving themselves and feel hungry all the time. Nobody talks about people like me, who have exactly the opposite problem. I keep super-busy, I'm almost never hungry, and I can't keep weight on! It's especially bad right now because it's basketball season: no matter what I do, the pounds peel off! For breakfast this morning, I had bacon and eggs. For lunch, I'll probably eat a couple of ham sandwiches. Then a protein bar after practice, and for dinner, I'll probably go out for burgers with my friends. What more can I do? Don't tell me to eat between meals because, like I said, I'm just not that hungry."

Given what you've learned about energy balance and weight management, what, if any, problems do you perceive with Theo's food intake today? What changes might make his diet more healthful? Finally, should Theo focus on gaining weight, or on maintaining his current weight? Hint: Review the You Do the Math box on page 488.

Protein Supplements Do Not Increase Muscle Growth or Strength

As with weight loss, there are many products marketed for weight gain. One of the most common claims is that these products are *anabolic,* that is, that they increase muscle mass. These products include amino acid and protein supplements, anabolic steroids, and *androstenedione,* a substance that became very popular after baseball player Mark McGwire claimed he used this product during the time he was breaking home run records. Do these substances really work?

A growing body of evidence exists to show that amino acid and protein supplements do not enhance muscle gain or result in improvements in strength.[32] Anabolic steroids can increase body weight and muscle mass, but are known to cause major health problems. Although the case of Mark McGwire may seem to suggest that androstenedione is an extremely effective product for building muscle mass, gaining strength, and improving performance, several studies report that this product did not have any benefits.[33–35] Protein supplements and androstenedione are legal to sell in the United States, but these and other potentially anabolic substances are banned by the National Football League, the National Collegiate Athletic Association, and the International Olympic Committee.

The health consequences of using protein supplements are unknown. As just noted, the health consequences of using anabolic steroids are severe. They include unhealthful changes in blood cholesterol, mood disturbances (such as anger leading to violence), testicular shrinkage and breast enlargement in men, and irreversible clitoral enlargement in women (see Chapter 14 for a more detailed discussion of anabolic steroid use). Androstenedione causes unhealthful changes in high-density and low-density lipoprotein (HDL and LDL) levels in middle-aged men, potentially increasing their risk for heart disease.[34] We also know that buying these substances can have a substantial slenderizing effect—on your wallet!

Protein powders or amino acid supplements will not enhance muscle growth or make you stronger.

RECaP

Weight gain can be achieved by eating more and performing weight-lifting and aerobic exercise. Protein and amino acid supplements and androstenedione do not increase muscle growth or strength, and their potential side effects are unknown. Anabolic steroid use can increase body weight and muscle mass but is known to cause major health problems.

Overweight

Overweight is defined as having a moderate amount of excess body fat, resulting in a person having a weight for a given height that is greater than some accepted standard but is not considered obese. People with a BMI between 25 and 29.9 kg/m² are considered overweight. Being overweight does not appear to be as detrimental to our health as being obese, but some of the health risks of overweight include an increased risk for high blood pressure, heart disease, type 2 diabetes, sleep disorders, osteoarthritis, gallstones, and gynecological abnormalities.[36] It is also more likely that overweight people will become obese, and obesity confers an even higher risk for these diseases and for premature death. Because of these concerns, health professionals recommend that overweight individuals adopt a lifestyle that incorporates healthful eating and regular physical activity in an attempt to prevent additional weight gain, to reduce body weight to a normal level, and/or to support long-term health even if body weight is not significantly reduced.

Obesity and Morbid Obesity

Obesity is defined as having an excess body fat that adversely affects health, resulting in a person having a weight for a given height that is substantially greater than some accepted standard. People with a BMI between 30 and 39.9 kg/m² are considered obese. Morbid obesity occurs when a person's body weight exceeds 100% of normal; people who are morbidly obese have a BMI greater than or equal to 40 kg/m².

Health Effects of Obesity

Both overweight and obesity are now considered an epidemic in the United States. Obesity rates have increased more than 50% during the past 20 years, and it is now estimated that about 34% of adults in the United States are obese.[37] This alarming rise in obesity is a major health concern because it is linked to many chronic diseases and adverse health conditions. These include:

- Hypertension
- Dyslipidemia, including elevated total cholesterol, triglycerides, and LDL-cholesterol and decreased HDL-cholesterol
- Type 2 diabetes
- Heart disease
- Stroke
- Gallbladder disease
- Osteoarthritis
- Sleep apnea
- Certain cancers such as colon, breast, endometrial, and gallbladder
- Menstrual irregularities and infertility
- Gestational diabetes, premature fetal deaths, neural tube defects, and complications during labor and delivery
- Depression

Both overweight and obesity can also contribute to a condition referred to as the **metabolic syndrome.** The metabolic syndrome is a clustering of risks factors that increase one's risk for heart disease, type 2 diabetes, and stroke. These risk factors include:

- abdominal obesity (defined as a waist circumference greater than or equal to 40 inches for men and 35 inches for women)
- higher-than-normal triglyceride levels (greater than or equal to 150 mg/dL)
- lower-than-normal HDL cholesterol levels (less than 40 mg/dL in men and 50 mg/dL in women)
- higher-than-normal blood pressure (greater than or equal to 130/85 mm Hg)
- fasting blood glucose levels greater than or equal to 100 mg/dL, including people with diabetes[38]

People with the metabolic syndrome are twice as likely to develop heart disease and five times as likely to develop type 2 diabetes than people without the metabolic syndrome. It is estimated that about 25% of adults in the United States have the metabolic syndrome, and rising obesity rates are contributing to increased rates.[39]

Obesity is also associated with an increased risk of premature death: Mortality rates for people with a BMI of 30 kg/m² or higher are 50% to 100% above the rates for those with a BMI between 20 and 25 kg/m². As discussed in Chapter 1, several of the leading causes of death in the United States are associated with obesity (see page 8).

Ironically, up to 40% of women and 25% of men are dieting at any given time. How can obesity rates be so high when there are so many people dieting? Certainly, some people who are dieting are actually at a normal or even below-normal weight, and these people account for a small percentage of this total. However, a telephone survey of American adults with a history of obesity found that approximately 20% had been successful in achieving and maintaining at least a 10% weight loss for a minimum of 1 year.[40] These results suggest that while some obese individuals are able to lose weight and maintain weight loss, about 80% of obese people who are dieting are somehow failing to lose weight or to maintain long-term weight loss. Why?

Obesity Is a Multifactorial Disease

Obesity is known as a **multifactorial disease,** meaning that there are many factors that cause it. This makes it extremely difficult to treat. Although it is certainly true that obesity, like

metabolic syndrome   A clustering of risks factors that increase one's risk for heart disease, type 2 diabetes, and stroke, including abdominal obesity, higher-than-normal triglyceride levels, lower-than-normal HDL cholesterol levels, higher-than-normal blood pressure (greater than or equal to 130/85 mm Hg), and elevated fasting blood glucose levels.

multifactorial disease   Any disease that may be attributable to one or more of a variety of causes.

overweight, is caused by eating more energy than is expended, it is also true that some people are more susceptible to becoming obese than others. In addition, as we saw with the twin study, some people are more resistant than others to losing weight and keeping it off. Research on the causes and best treatments of obesity is ongoing, but let's explore some current theories.

Genetic and Physiologic Factors   Because a person's genetic background influences his or her height, weight, body shape, and metabolic rate, it can also affect a person's risk for obesity. Some obesity experts point out that, if proved, the existence of a thrifty gene or genes (discussed earlier) would show that obese people have a genetic tendency to expend less energy both at rest and during physical activity. Other researchers are working to determine whether the set-point theory can partially explain why many obese people are very resistant to weight loss. As we learn more about genetics, we will gain a greater understanding of the role it plays in the development and treatment of obesity.

We also discussed earlier several physiologic factors that may influence an individual's experience of hunger and satiation. These include the proteins leptin, ghrelin, PYY, and uncoupling proteins. Other physiologic factors such as beta-endorphins, neuropeptide Y, and decreased blood glucose can reduce satiety or increase hunger, theoretically promoting overeating and weight gain.

Childhood Obesity Is Linked to Adult Obesity   The prevalence of overweight in children and adolescents is increasing at an alarming rate in the United States (**Figure 13.12**). There was a time when having extra "baby fat" was considered good for the child. We assumed that childhood overweight and obesity were temporary and that the child would grow out of it. While it is important for children to have a certain minimum level of body fat to maintain health and to grow properly, researchers are now concerned that overweight and obesity are harming children's health and increasing their risk of overweight and obesity in adulthood.

Adequate physical activity is instrumental in preventing childhood obesity.

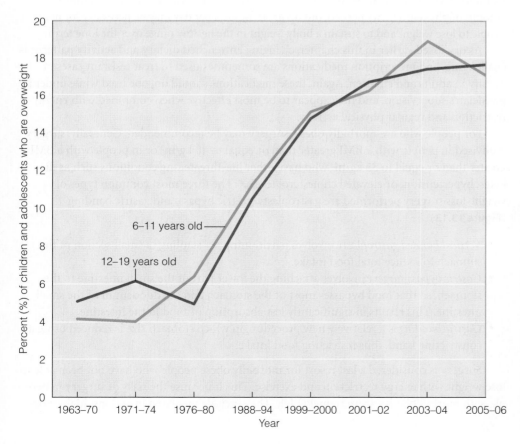

Figure 13.12   Increases in childhood and adolescent overweight from 1963 to 2006. (*Data adapted from:* Centers for Disease Control and Prevention. National Center for Health Statistics. 2005. Prevalence of overweight among children and adolescents: United States, 1999–2002. Available at www.cdc.gov/nchs/products/pubs/pubd/hestats/overwght99.htm; and Ogden, C. L., M. D. Carroll, and K. M. Flegal. 2008. High body mass index for age among U.S. children and adolescents, 2003–2006. *JAMA* 299[20]:2401–2405.)

Health data demonstrate that obese children are already showing signs of chronic disease while they are young, including elevated blood pressure, high cholesterol levels, and changes in insulin and glucose metabolism that may increase the risk for type 2 diabetes (formerly known as *adult-onset diabetes*). In some communities, children as young as 5 years of age have been diagnosed with type 2 diabetes. Unfortunately, many of these children will maintain these disease risk factors into adulthood.

Does being an obese child guarantee that obesity will be maintained during adulthood? Although some children who are obese grow up to have a normal body weight, it has been estimated that about 70% of children who are obese maintain their higher weight as adults.[41] Obviously, this has important consequences for their health.

It has been suggested that there are three critical periods in childhood during which substantial weight gain can increase the risk of obesity and related diseases in adulthood:

- Gestation and early infancy
- The period of weight gain (called *adiposity rebound*) that occurs between 5 and 7 years of age
- Adolescence (or puberty)

Having either one or two overweight parents increases the risk of obesity two to four times.[42] This may be explained in part by genetics or by unhealthful eating patterns or lack of physical activity within the family.

Obesity Treatment Is Challenging

The first line of defense in treating obesity in adults is a low-energy diet and regular physical activity. Overweight and obese individuals should work with a healthcare practitioner to design and maintain a low-fat diet (less than 30% of total energy from fat) that has a deficit of 500 to 1,000 kcal/day.[36] Physical activity should be increased gradually so that the person can build a program in which he or she is exercising at least 30 minutes per day, five times per week. The Institute of Medicine[43] concurs that 30 minutes a day, five times a week is the minimum amount of physical activity needed, but up to 60 minutes per day may be necessary for many people to lose weight and to sustain a body weight in the healthy range over the long term.

As discussed earlier in this chapter, changing entrenched dietary and activity patterns is challenging, and prescription medications are sometimes used to treat resistant cases of obesity in adults and children. Again, these medications should only be used while under a physician's supervision, and they appear to be most effective when combined with energy restriction and regular physical activity.

For people who are morbidly obese, surgery may be recommended. Generally, surgery is advised in people with a BMI greater than or equal to 40 kg/m^2 or in people with a BMI greater than or equal to 35 kg/m^2 who have other life-threatening conditions such as diabetes, hypertension, or elevated cholesterol levels.[36] The three most common types of weight-loss surgery performed are gastroplasty, gastric bypass, and gastric banding (**Figure 13.13**).

- *Vertical banded gastroplasty* involves partitioning or "stapling" a small section of the stomach to reduce total food intake.
- *Gastric bypass surgery* involves attaching the lower part of the small intestine to the stomach, so that food bypasses most of the stomach and the duodenum of the small intestine. This results in significantly less absorption of food in the intestine.
- *Gastric banding* is a relatively new procedure in which stomach size is reduced using a constricting band, thus restricting food intake.

Surgery is considered a last resort for morbidly obese people who have not been able to lose weight with energy restriction and exercise. This is because the risks of surgery in people with morbid obesity are extremely high. They include increased infections, higher for-

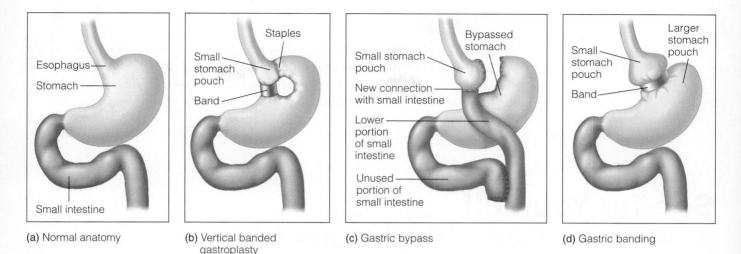

(a) Normal anatomy

(b) Vertical banded gastroplasty

(c) Gastric bypass

(d) Gastric banding

Figure 13.13 Three forms of surgery alter the **(a)** normal anatomy of the gastrointestinal tract to result in weight loss in morbid obesity: **(b)** vertical banded gastroplasty **(c)**, gastric bypass, and **(d)** gastric banding.

mation of blood clots, and more adverse reactions to anesthesia. After the surgery, many recipients face a lifetime of problems with chronic diarrhea, vomiting, intolerance to dairy products and other foods, dehydration, and nutritional deficiencies resulting from alterations in nutrient digestion and absorption. Thus, the potential benefits of the procedure must outweigh the risks. It is critical that each surgery candidate is carefully screened by a trained physician. If the immediate threat of serious disease and death is more dangerous than the risks associated with surgery, then the procedure is justified.

Are these surgical procedures successful in reducing obesity? About one-third to one-half of people who received obesity surgery lose significant amounts of weight and keep this weight off for at least 5 years. The reasons that one-half to two-thirds do not experience long-term success include:

- inability to eat less over time, even with a smaller stomach
- loosening of staples and gastric bands and enlargement of stomach pouch
- failure to survive the surgery or the postoperative recovery period

Although these surgical procedures may seem extremely risky, many of those who survive the surgery lose weight, maintain much of this weight loss over time, reduce their risk for type 2 diabetes and cardiovascular disease, and may even improve their ability to stay physically active over a prolonged period of time.[44]

Liposuction is a cosmetic surgical procedure that removes fat cells from localized areas in the body. It is not recommended or typically used to treat obesity or morbid obesity. Instead, it is often used by normal or mildly overweight people to "spot reduce" fat from various areas of the body. This procedure is not without risks; blood clots, skin and nerve damage, adverse drug reactions, and perforation injuries can and do occur as a result of liposuction. It can also result in deformations in the area where the fat is removed. This procedure is not the solution to long-term weight loss, as the millions of fat cells that remain in the body after liposuction enlarge if the person continues to overeat. In addition, although liposuction may reduce the fat content of a localized area, it does not reduce a person's risk for the diseases that are more common among overweight or obese people. Only traditional weight loss with diet and exercise can reduce body fat and the risks for chronic diseases.

Liposuction removes fat cells from specific areas of the body.

> ## ReCaP
> Obesity is a multifactorial disease, and genetics, physiology, and lifestyle choices are all thought to contribute. In addition, childhood obesity is strongly associated with adult obesity. Treatments for overweight, obesity, and morbid obesity include low-calorie, low-fat diets in combination with regular physical activity, weight-loss prescription medications, and/or surgery.

See for Yourself

Rate the Latest Weight-Loss Craze

Quick: Name the latest weight-loss craze on your campus! Is it sound, or just another fad? To find out, go to your local library, bookstore, or search the Internet to find a description of its components. Evaluate the plan using the recommendations in Table 13.3. For example, is the total fat intake 15% to 25% of total energy? Does the plan recommend a minimum of 30 minutes of daily physical activity? Does the plan include behavior modification strategies, and if so, do they seem effective? After completing your evaluation, rate the plan on a 1-to-10 scale, with 1 indicating that the plan fails to meet any of the recommendations and 10 indicating that the plan meets all of the recommendations. If you rated the plan lower than 5, check it out against the bulleted points on page 506. Does it meet the criteria for a fad diet? If so, consider submitting your evaluation to your campus newspaper or Web site. Publishing your results could help other students avoid wasting their time and money—and possibly harming their health.

Chapter Review

Test Yourself | Answers

1. **F** Being underweight increases our risk for illness and premature death and in many cases can be just as unhealthful as being obese.

2. **F** Obesity is a multifactorial disease with many contributing factors. Although eating too much food and not getting enough exercise can lead to being overweight and obese, the disease of obesity is complex and is not simply caused by overeating.

3. **T** Body composition assessments can help give us a general idea of body fat levels, but most methods are not extremely accurate.

4. **F** According to the Centers for Disease Control and Prevention, in 2005–2006, approximately 34% of all adults in the United States were considered obese.

5. **T** Health can be defined in many ways. An individual who is overweight, but who exercises regularly and has no additional risk factors for various disease such as heart disease and type 2 diabetes is considered a healthy person.

Summary

- Definitions of a healthful body weight include one that is appropriate for someone's age and level of development, promotes healthful blood lipids and glucose, can be achieved and sustained without constant dieting, promotes good eating habits, and allows for regular physical activity.

- Body mass index (BMI) is an index of weight per height squared. It is useful to indicate health risks associated with overweight and obesity in groups of people.

- Underweight is defined as having too little body fat to maintain health, causing a person to have a weight for a given height that is below an acceptably defined standard. A BMI below 18.5 is considered underweight.

- Overweight is defined as having a moderate amount of excess body fat, resulting in a person having a weight for a given height that is greater than some accepted standard but is not considered obese. A BMI of 25 to 29.9 is considered overweight.

- Obesity is defined as having excess body fat that adversely affects health, resulting in a person having a weight for a given height that is substantially greater than some accepted standard. A BMI of 30 to 39.9 is considered obese. Morbid obesity occurs when a person's body weight exceeds 100% of normal, which puts him or her at very high risk for serious health consequences. A BMI of 40 or above is considered morbidly obese.

- The waist-to-hip ratio and waist circumference are used to determine patterns of fat storage. People with large waists (as compared to the hips) have an apple-shaped fat pattern. People with large hips (as compared to the waist) have a pear-shaped fat pattern. Having an apple-shaped pattern increases your risk for heart disease, type 2 diabetes, and other chronic diseases.

- We lose or gain weight based on changes in our energy intake, the food we eat, and our energy expenditure (both at rest and when physically active).

- Basal metabolic rate (BMR) is the energy needed to maintain the body's resting functions. BMR accounts for 60% to 75% of our total daily energy needs.

- The thermic effect of food is the energy we expend to process the food we eat. It accounts for 5% to 10% of the energy content of a meal and is higher for processing proteins and carbohydrates than for fats.

- The energy cost of physical activity represents energy that we expend for physical movement or work we do above basal levels. It accounts for 15% to 35% of our total daily energy output.

- Our genetic heritage influences the risk for obesity, and factors such as possessing a thrifty gene (or genes) or maintaining a weight set point may affect a person's risk for obesity.

- Eating a diet proportionally higher in fat may increase the risk for obesity, as dietary fat is stored more easily as adipose tissue than is dietary carbohydrate or protein.

- Physiologic factors that contribute to obesity include alterations in various proteins and hormones that influence hunger and satiety, including leptin, ghrelin, peptide YY, uncoupling proteins, beta-endorphins, serotonin, and cholecystokinin.

- Cultural and social factors, such as easy access to large portions of inexpensive and high-fat foods and excessive use of electronic devices for entertainment, also contribute to obesity. Mood and emotional state also affect appetite.

- Fad diets are weight-loss programs that enjoy short-term popularity and are sold based on a marketing gimmick that appeals to the public's desires and fears. They typically promise rapid weight loss, often without increased physical activity or long-term behavioral modification, and rarely result in long-term maintenance of weight loss.

- Diet plans that restrict intake of certain macronutrients can help many people lose weight, but some have unhealthful side effects.

- A sound weight-loss plan involves gradual reduction in energy intake, incorporating physical activity into each day, and practicing changes in behavior that can assist in meeting realistic weight-change goals.

- Prescription drugs can be used to assist with weight loss when the risks of obesity override the risks associated with the medications.

- Various dietary supplements are marketed as weight-loss products. Many of these products cause dangerous changes in heart rate and blood pressure. Unlike prescription drugs, these products are not strictly regulated by the FDA.

- Being underweight can be detrimental to one's health. Most of the products marketed for weight gain have been shown to be ineffective. Healthful weight gain involves consuming more energy than expended by selecting ample servings of nutritious, high-energy foods and exercising regularly by including resistance training and aerobic exercise.

- Overweight is not as detrimental to health as obesity, but it is associated with an increased risk for high blood pressure, heart disease, type 2 diabetes, sleep disorders, osteoarthritis, gallstones, and gynecological abnormalities.

- Obesity and morbid obesity are associated with significantly increased risks for many diseases and for premature death. Obesity can be treated with low-energy diets and regular physical activity, prescription medications, and surgery when necessary.

Review Questions

1. The ratio of a person's body weight to height is represented as his or her
   a. body composition.
   b. basal metabolic rate.
   c. bioelectrical impedance.
   d. body mass index.

2. The body's total daily energy expenditure includes
   a. basal metabolic rate, thermal effect of food, and effect of physical activity.
   b. basal metabolic rate, movement, standing, and sleeping.
   c. effect of physical activity, standing, and sleeping.
   d. body mass index, thermal effect of food, and effect of physical activity.

3. All people gain weight when they
   a. eat a high-fat diet ($>$35% fat).
   b. take in more energy than they expend.
   c. fail to exercise.
   d. take in less energy than they expend.

4. The set-point theory proposes that
   a. obese people have a gene not found in slender people that regulates their weight so that it always hovers near a given set point.
   b. obese people have a gene that causes them to be energetically thrifty.
   c. all people have a genetic set point for their body weight.
   d. all people have a hormone that regulates their weight so that it always hovers near a given set point.

5. A body protein that increases appetite is
   a. leptin.
   b. ghrelin.
   c. PYY.
   d. orlistat.

6. **True or false?** Pear-shaped fat patterning is known to increase a person's risk for many chronic diseases, including diabetes and heart disease.

7. **True or false?** One pound of fat is equal to about 3,500 kcal.

8. **True or false?** Weight-loss medications are typically prescribed for people who have a body mass index greater than or equal to 18.5 kg/m^2.

9. **True or false?** Recommendations for weight gain include avoiding both aerobic and resistance exercise for the duration of the weight-gain program.

10. **True or false?** More than half of American adults are currently either overweight or obese.

11. Identify at least four characteristics of a healthful weight.

12. Describe a sound weight-loss program, including recommendations for diet, physical activity, and behavioral modifications.

13. Can you increase your basal metabolic rate? Is it wise to try? Defend your answer.

14. Identify at least four societal factors that may have influenced the rise in obesity rates in the United States since 1963.

15. Your friend Misty joins you for lunch and confesses that she is discouraged about her weight. She says that she has been trying "really hard" for 3 months to lose weight but that no matter what she does, she cannot drop below 148 lb. Based on her height, you know Misty is not overweight, and she exercises regularly. What questions would you suggest she think about? How would you advise her?

Web Links

www.nhlbisupport.com/bmi
National Heart, Blood, and Lung Institute BMI calculator
Calculate your body mass index (BMI) on the Internet.

www.ftc.gov
Federal Trade Commission
Click on "For Consumers" and then "Diet, Health and Fitness" to find how to avoid false weight-loss claims.

www.consumer.gov/weightloss
Partnership for Healthy Weight Management
Visit this site to learn about successful strategies for achieving and maintaining a healthy weight.

http://hp2010.nhlbihin.net/portion/
National Institutes of Health Portion Distortion site
Visit this site and take the interactive "Portion Distortion" quiz to challenge your understanding of portion sizes. For instance, how does a standard restaurant cup of coffee compare with a coffee mocha from a national-chain coffeehouse? Find out, and then guess how long you'd have to walk to burn off that mocha!

www.eatright.org

American Dietetic Association

Go to this site to learn more about fad diets and nutrition facts.

www.niddk.nih.gov/health/nutrit/nutrit.htm

National Institute of Diabetes and Digestive and Kidney Diseases

Find out more about healthy weight loss and how it pertains to diabetes and digestive and kidney diseases.

www.sne.org

Society for Nutrition Education

Click on "Resources and Relationships" and then "Weight Realities Resources" for additional resources related to positive attitudes about body image and healthful alternatives to dieting.

www.oa.org

Overeaters Anonymous

Visit this site to learn about ways to reduce compulsive overeating.

References

1. Emme. 2009. Bio profile. Available at www.emmestyle.com/about.

2. Stoynoff, N. 2008. Emme's cancer battle. *People,* January 21, pp. 99–101.

3. Manore, M. M., N. L. Meyer, and J. L. Thompson. 2009. *Sport Nutrition for Health and Performance,* 2nd ed. Champaign, IL: Human Kinetics.

4. Wang, Y. 2004. Epidemiology of childhood obesity—methodological aspects and guidelines: What is new?*Int. J. Obes.* 23:S21–S28.

5. Deurenberg, P., M. Yap, and W. A. van Staveren. 1998. Body mass index and percent body fat: A meta analysis among different ethnic groups. *Int. J. Obes.* 22:1164–1171.

6. Shai, I., R. Jiang, J. E. Manson, M. J. Stampfer, W. C. Willett, G. A. Colditz, and F. B. Hu. 2006. Ethnicity, obesity, and risk of type 2 diabetes in women. *Diab. Care* 29:1585–1590.

7. Zernike, K. 2004. U.S. body survey, head to toe, finds signs of expansion. *New York Times,* March 1: pp. 1, 12.

8. Stunkard, A. J., T. I. A. Sørensen, C. Hanis, T. W. Teasdale, R. Chakraborty, W. J. Schull, and F. Schulsinger. 1986. An adoption study of human obesity. *N. Engl. J. Med.* 314:193–198.

9. Bouchard, C., A. Tremblay, J. P. Després, A. Nadeau, P. J. Lupien, G. Thériault, J. Dussault, S. Moorjani, S. Pinault, and G. Fournier. 1990. The response to long-term overfeeding in identical twins. *N. Engl. J. Med.* 322:1477–1482.

10. Hellerstein, M. 2001. No common energy currency: De novo lipogenesis as the road less traveled. *Am. J. Clin. Nutr.* 74:707–708.

11. Cummings, D. E., D. S. Weigle, R. S. Frayo, P. A. Breen, M. K. Ma, E. P. Dellinger, and J. Q. Purnell. 2002. Plasma ghrelin levels after diet-induced weight loss or gastric bypass surgery. *N. Engl. J. Med.* 346:1623–1630.

12. Druce, M. R., A. M. Wren, A. J. Park, J. E. Milton, M. Patterson, G. Frost, M. A. Ghatei, C. Small, and S. R. Bloom. 2005. Ghrelin increases food intake in obese as well as lean subjects. *Int. J. Obes.* 29:1130–1136.

13. Batterham, R. L., M. A. Cowley, C. J. Small, H. Herzog, M. A. Cohen, C. L. Dakin, A. M. Wren, A. E. Brynes, M. J. Low, M. A. Ghatei, R. D. Cone, and S. R. Bloom. 2002. Gut hormone PYY[3-36] physiologically inhibits food intake. *Nature* 418:650–664.

14. Batterham, R. L., M. A. Cohen, S. M. Ellis, C. W. Le Roux, D. J. Withers, G. S. Frost, M. A. Ghatei, and S. R. Bloom. 2003. Inhibition of food intake in obese subjects by peptide YY[3-36]. *N. Engl. J. Med.* 349:941–948.

15. Virtanen, K. A., M. E. Lidell, J. Orava, M. Heglind, R. Westergren, T. Niemi, M. Taittonen, J. Laine, N-J. Savito, S. Enerbäck, and P. Nuutila. 2009. Functional brown adipose tissue in healthy adults. *N. Engl. J. Med.* 360(15):1518–1525.

16. Cypess, A. M., S. Lehman, G. Williams, I. Tal, D. Rodman, A. B. Goldfine, F. C. Kuo, E. L. Palmer, Y-H. Tseng, A. Doria, G. M. Kolodny, and C. R. Kahn. 2009. Identification and importance of brown adipose tissue in adult humans. *N. Engl. J. Med.* 360(15):1509–1517.

17. Eyler, A. E., D. Matson-Koffman, D. Rohm-Young, S. Wilcox, J. Wilbur, J. L. Thompson, B. Sanderson, and K. R. Evenson. 2003. Quantitative study of correlates of physical activity in women from diverse racial/ethnic groups: The Women's Cardiovascular Health Network Project. *Am. J. Prev. Med.* 25(3Si):93–103.

18. Eyler, A. E., D. Matson-Koffman, J. R. Vest, K. R. Evenson, B. Sanderson, J. L. Thompson, J. Wilbur, S. Wilcox, and D. Rohm-Young. 2002. Environmental, policy, and cultural factors related to physical activity in a diverse sample of women: The Women's Cardiovascular Health Network Project—Summary and Discussion. *Women and Health.* 36:123–134.

19. Pickett, K. E., S. Kelly, E. Brunner, T. Lobstein, and R. G. Wilkinson. 2005. Wider income gaps, wider waistbands? An ecological study of obesity and income inequality. *J. Epidemiol. Community Health* 59:670–674.

20. Elliott, S. 2005. Calories? Hah! Munch Some Mega M&M's. *New York Times,* August 5. p. C5.

21. Koh-Banerjee, P., N. F. Chu, D. Spiegelman, B. Rosner, G. Colditz, W. Willett, and E. Rimm. 2003. Prospective study of the association of changes in dietary intake, physical activity, alcohol consumption, and smoking with 9-y gain in waist circumference among 16,587 U.S. men. *Am. J. Clin. Nutr.* 78:719–727.

22. American Dietetic Association. 2002. Position of the American Dietetic Association: Food and nutrition misinformation. *J. Am. Diet. Assoc.* 102(2):260–266.

23. Freedman, M. R., J. King, and E. Kennedy. 2001. Popular diets: A scientific review. *Obes. Res.* 9(suppl. 1):1S–40S.

24. Ello-Martin, J. A., J. H. Ledikwe, and B. J. Rolls. 2005. The influence of food portion size and energy density on energy intake: Implications for weight management. *Am. J. Clin. Nutr.* 82(suppl.):236S–241S.

25. Flood, J. E., L. S. Roe, and B. J. Rolls. 2006. The effect of increased beverage portion size on energy intake at a meal. *J. Am. Diet. Assoc.* 106:1984–1990.

26. Klem, M. L., R. R. Wing, M. T. McGuire, H. M. Seagle, and J. O. Hill. 1997. A descriptive study of individuals successful at long-term maintenance of substantial weight loss. *Am. J. Clin. Nutr.* 66:239–246.

27. Bérubé-Parent, S., D. Prud'homme, S. St-Pierre, E. Doucet, and A. Tremblay. 2001. Obesity treatment with a progressive clinical tri-therapy combining sibutramine and a supervised diet-exercise intervention. *Int. J. Obes.* 25:1144–1153.

28. Chanoine, J.-P., S. Hampl, C. Jensen, M. Boldrin, and J. Hauptman. 2005. Effect of orlistat on weight and body composition in obese adolescents. A randomized controlled trial. *JAMA* 293(23):2873–2883.

29. Hutton, B., and D. Fergusson. 2004. Changes in body weight and serum lipid profile in obese patients treated with orlistat in addition to a hypocaloric diet: A systemic review of randomized clinical trials. *Am. J. Clin. Nutr.* 80:1461–1468.

30. Saper, R. B., D. M. Eisenberg, and R. S. Phillips. 2004. Common dietary supplements for weight loss. *Am. Fam. Phys.* 70(9):1731–1738.

31. Allison, D. B., K. R. Fontaine, S. Heshka, J. L. Mentore, and S. B. Heymsfield. 2001. Alternative treatments for weight loss: a critical review. *Crit. Rev. Food Sci. Nutr.* 41(1):1–28.

32. Kreider, R. B., V. Miriel, and E. Bertun. 1993. Amino acid supplementation and exercise performance. *Sports Med.* 16:190–209.

33. Joyner, M. J. 2000. Over-the-counter supplements and strength training. *Exerc. Sport Sci. Rev.* 28:2–3.

34. Broeder, C. E., J. Quindry, K. Brittingham, L. Panton, J. Thomson, S. Appakondu, K. Breuel, R. Byrd, J. Douglas, C. Earnest, C. Mitchell, M. Olson, T. Roy, and C. Yarlagadda. 2000. The Andro Project: physiological and hormonal influences of androstenedione supplementation in men 35 to 65 years old participating in a high-intensity resistance training program. *Arch. Int. Med.* 160:3093–3104.

35. Brown, G. A., M. D. Vukovich, T. A. Reifenrath, N. L. Uhl, K. A. Parsons, R. L. Sharp, and D. S. King. 2000. Effects of anabolic precursors on serum testosterone concentrations and adaptations to resistance training in young men. *Intl. J. Sport Nutr. Ex. Metab.* 10:340–359.

36. National Institutes of Health. National Heart, Lung, and Blood Institute. 1998. Clinical guidelines on the identification, evaluation, and treatment of overweight and obesity in adults. The Evidence Report. Available at www.nhlbi.nih.gov/guidelines/obesity/ob_gdlns.htm.

37. Ogden, C. L., M. D. Carroll, M. A. McDowell, and K. M. Flegal. 2007. Obesity among adults in the United States—no change since 2003–2004. NCHS data brief no 1. Hyattsville, MD: National Center for Health Statistics. Available at www.cdc.gov/nchs/data/databriefs/db01.pdf.

38. Grundy, S. M., B. Hansen, S. C. Smith, J. I. Cleeman, and R. A. Kahn. 2004. Clinical management of metabolic syndrome: Report of the American Heart Association/National Heart, Lung, and Blood Institute/American Diabetes Association Conference on Scientific Issues Related to Management. *Circulation* 109:551–556.

39. Department of Health and Human Services. National Institutes of Health. National Heart, Lung and Blood Institute. Diseases and conditions index. Metabolic syndrome. What is metabolic syndrome? Available at www.nhlbi.nih.gov/health/dci/Diseases/ms/ms_whatis.html.

40. McGuire, M. T., R. R. Wing, and J. O. Hill. 1999. The prevalence of weight loss maintenance among American adults. *Int. J. Obes.* 23:1314–1319.

41. Torgan, C. 2002. Childhood obesity on the rise. The NIH Word on Health. Available at http://www.nih.gov/news/WordonHealth/jun2002/childhoodobesity.htm.

42. Dietz, W. H. 1994. Critical periods in childhood for the development of obesity. *Am. J. Clin. Nutr.* 59:955–959.

43. Institute of Medicine. Food and Nutrition Board. 2002. *Dietary Reference Intakes for Energy, Carbohydrate, Fiber, Fat, Fatty Acids, Cholesterol, Protein, and Amino Acids (Macronutrients).* Washington, DC: The National Academies Press.

44. Sjöström, L., A-K. Lindroos, M. Peltonen, J. Torgerson, C. Bouchard, B. Carlsson, S. Dahlgren, B. Larsson, K. Narbro, C. D. Sjöström, M. Sullivan, and H. Wedel. 2004. Lifestyle, diabetes, and cardiovascular risk factors 10 years after bariatric surgery. *N. Engl. J. Med.* 351(26):2683–2693.

45. Taubes, G. 2002. What if fat doesn't make you fat? *New York Times Magazine,* July 7, section 6.

46. Liebman, B. 2002. Big fat lies: The truth about the Atkins Diet. *Center Sci. Public Interest Nutr. Action Health Letter* 29(9):1–7.

47. Stern, L., N. Iqbal, P. Seshadri, K. L. Chicano, D. A. Daily, J. McGrory, M. Williams, E. J. Gracely, and F. F. Samaha. 2004. The effects of low-carbohydrate versus conventional weight loss diets in severely obese adults: One-year follow-up of a randomized trial. *Ann. Intern. Med.* 140:778–785.

48. Samaha, F. F., N. Iqbal, P. Seshadri, K. L. Chicano, D. A. Daily, J. McGrory, T. Williams, M. Williams, E. J. Gracely, and L. Stern. 2003. A low-carbohydrate as compared with a low-fat diet in severe obesity. *N. Engl. J. Med.* 348:2074–2081.

49. Foster, G. D., H. R. Wyatt, J. O. Hill, B. G. McGuckin, C. Brill, B. S. Mohammed, P. O. Szapary, D. J. Rader, J. S. Edman, and S. Klein. 2003. A randomized trial of a low-carbohydrate diet for obesity. *N. Engl. J. Med.* 348:2082–2090.

50. Boden, G., K. Sargrad, C. Homko, M. Mozzoli, and T. P. Stein. 2005. Effect of a low-carbohydrate diet on appetite, blood glucose levels, and insulin resistance in obese patients with type 2 diabetes. *Ann. Intern. Med.* 142:403–411.

51. Bravata, D. M., L. Sanders, J. Huang, H. M. Krumholz, I. Olkin, C. D. Gardner, and D. M. Bravata. 2003. Efficacy and safety of low-carbohydrate diets. A systematic review. *JAMA* 289:1837–1850.

High-Protein Diets—Are They the Key to Weight Loss?

High-protein diets have been popular over the last 40 years. Very-low-energy, high-protein programs (200 to 400 kcal per day, 1.5 g of protein per kg body weight) were very popular in the 1970s. Many of these diets consisted of low-quality protein, however, and at least fifty-eight people died from heart problems while following them. As a result of these deaths, we now know that these extreme diets are only appropriate for severely obese people under medical supervision, and must include high-quality protein sources.

Proponents of high-protein diets claim that you can eat all your favorite foods and still lose weight. Is this possible? This chapter provides a detailed explanation of weight loss, and you can now see that the key to weight loss is eating less energy than you expend. If you eat more energy than you expend, you can gain weight. Thus, any type of diet, even high-protein diets, must contain fewer kilocalories than a person expends to result in weight loss.

It is important to recognize that high-protein diets are synonymous with low-carbohydrate diets, because high-protein foods typically replace those high in carbohydrates. In addition, many high-protein diets are also high in fat. It is well established that reducing carbohydrate intake causes the body to break down its stored carbohydrate (or glycogen) in the liver and muscle; this is necessary to maintain blood glucose levels and provide energy to the brain. As water is stored along with glycogen, using stored carbohydrate for energy results in the loss of water from the body, which registers on the scale as rapid weight loss.

Among high-protein diets, probably the Atkins Diet is the best known. This diet plan advocates consumption of a diet very low in starches (including potatoes, white bread, pasta, and refined sugars) and very high in protein. A highly controversial article in support of the Atkins Diet was published in 2002 in the *New York Times Magazine*.[45] In this article, supporters of the diet emphasize that eating a high-carbohydrate diet has caused obesity in the United States. They contend that the Atkins Diet results in substantial weight loss, but does not cause unhealthy changes in blood cholesterol despite its high saturated-fat content.

Detractors of the Atkins Diet tell a different story. According to many nutrition and obesity experts, the U.S. population is substantially overweight because we eat too many calories, not because we eat too much carbohydrate or fat per se. They also assert that numerous potential health risks are associated with eating a low-carbohydrate (and high-fat) diet, including the following:

- Low blood glucose levels, or hypoglycemia, leading to low energy levels, diminished cognitive functioning, and elevated ketones. Some high-protein diets are so low in carbohydrate that the body does not receive enough glucose to maintain brain function. As you know, when blood glucose levels are not sufficient to support brain function, the body produces ketones from body fat, as ketones are an alternative energy source for the central nervous system. High ketone levels in the blood can be toxic, as they increase blood acidity. This state is called *ketoacidosis*, and it can be dangerous if maintained over a prolonged period of time. Left untreated, increased blood acidity causes disorientation, eventual loss of consciousness, coma, and even death. Despite this often-cited concern, there is no evidence that following the Atkins Diet has resulted in any serious disability or death due to ketoacidosis. However, low glucose levels can prompt feelings of low energy, which could prevent some people from exercising regularly, as well as detrimental changes in memory and cognitive function.

- Increased risk of heart disease caused by eating foods high in saturated fat. Until recently the Atkins Diet promoted the consumption of foods that are high in protein and saturated fat. For instance, daily intakes of cheese, whole-fat dairy products, and fatty meats such as bacon, sausage, and regular ground beef were encouraged. It is well established that eating a diet high in saturated fat increases a person's LDL-cholesterol, which in turn increases the risk for heart disease.

Low blood glucose levels often result in feelings of low energy and confusion, and may lead to more serious negative effects.

- Increased risk of some forms of cancer due to eating a diet that is high in fat and low in fiber. Historically the Atkins Diet recommended few, if any, foods that contain fiber and antioxidants; as a result, many nutrition experts have expressed concern that eating this type of a diet over many years will increase a person's risk for some forms of cancer. However, currently the Atkins Diet has been modified to address some of these concerns and now promotes the consumption of many

foods that are higher in fiber and antioxidants and lower in saturated fat than earlier published versions of the diet.

It appears that the Atkins Diet will continue to be controversial for many years. After the publication of the article in the *New York Times Magazine,* the Center for Science in the Public Interest (CSPI) published a response that claimed irresponsible and inaccurate reporting.[46] The CSPI interviewed many of the experts quoted in the article as supporting the Atkins Diet. These experts state they were misquoted or quoted out of context and that the information they shared that was contrary to supporting the Atkins Diet was ignored.

Are there any research studies to support the contention that the Atkins Diet is effective for weight loss? Until recently, most reports of substantial weight loss on this diet were anecdotal, meaning they came from individuals who were not participants in a controlled, scientific study. However, a few randomized controlled trials conducted over 1 year have recently shed light on the effects low-carbohydrate diets have on weight loss in obese individuals. Stern and colleagues placed participants on either the Atkins Diet or a low-fat diet plan recommended by the American Heart Association.[47] Participants consuming the Atkins Diet lost significantly more weight than those on the low-fat diet during the first 6 months, but weight loss between the two groups was no longer different after 1 year.[48] However, people consuming the Atkins Diet had lower triglyceride levels and had less of a decrease in HDL-cholesterol (the "good" cholesterol) as compared with people eating the low-fat diet. In another study conducted over a 1-year period using similar diet plans, the results were quite similar.[49]

Few of these trials have included participants with type 2 diabetes, which is a group that could benefit from both weight loss and a decreased intake of refined carbohydrate foods. Boden and colleagues studied how ten people with type 2 diabetes responded after following the Atkins diet for 2 weeks.[50] Unlike the relatively larger randomized controlled trials done previously, the researchers in this study controlled food intake by having the participants select approved foods through a modified hospital diet. All foods consumed were weighed and recorded daily. Participants were found to lose an average of 1.65 kg (or 3.63 lb) of body weight during the 2-week study period. Surprisingly, this rapid loss of body weight was not exclusively due to the loss of body water in all participants. In fact, six participants lost body water, three participants gained body water, and one had no change in body water during the diet period. Positive changes in the health of these individuals included normalization of blood glucose levels, an increase in insulin sensitivity, and significant decreases in blood triglyceride and cholesterol levels. The participants were able to lose weight because they spontaneously reduced their energy intake by 1,000 kcal per day. It is important to emphasize that this study is of a very short duration and included only ten people. The researchers concluded that this diet was beneficial in the short term, but they recognized that we cannot speculate about its long-term implications.

A recent review of all of the published studies of low-carbohydrate diets resulted in the conclusion that there are not enough data to currently make recommendations for or against their use.[51] The authors of this review state that the weight loss that occurs with low-carbohydrate diets appears to be associated with a decreased energy intake and longer diet duration and is not necessarily due to the reduced carbohydrate content of the diet per se. Thus, at this time, it is not possible to state with any certainty that the Atkins Diet is better than other diet plans recommending higher carbohydrate intakes. The long-term health implications of this type of a diet are also unknown at this time, and more research must be conducted in this area.

Critical Thinking Questions

- Should you adopt a low-carb, high-protein diet?

- Is this type of diet compatible with your personal needs, preferences, health risks, and lifestyle?

- Do you think the Atkins Diet or other high-protein diets are better or worse alternatives to higher-carbohydrate, lower-fat diets? Why or why not?

- What diet do you think would work best to help you maintain a healthful weight and muscle mass and provide enough energy and nutrients to maintain your lifestyle and your long-term health?

Read on.

On August 2, 2006, Uruguayan fashion model Luisel Ramos collapsed during a fashion show. Just 22 years old, she was pronounced dead of heart failure brought on by anorexia nervosa, a condition of self-imposed starvation. Family members say that, in the months prior to her death, she had adopted a diet of lettuce leaves and Diet Coke, and at 5'9" tall, her weight had dropped to just 98 pounds. The following month, Madrid's "Fashion Week" responded to Ramos' death by banning from its runway fashion models who could not meet a minimum weight–height standard. A similar ruling was quickly adopted by the Milan fashion show, and several modeling agencies began to require prospective models to present medical records certifying that they are healthy. Although promising, such measures alone are clearly inadequate, as at least three more fashion models had died from self-starvation by the summer of 2008.

Do only fashion models develop eating disorders, or do they occur in people like you? When does normal dieting cross the line into disordered eating? What early warning signs might tip you off that a friend was crossing that line? If you noticed the signs in a friend or family member, would you confront him or her? If so, what would you say? In the following pages, we explore *In Depth* some answers to these important questions.

Ana Carolina Reston, one of a string of models who have died due to eating disorders.

Eating Behaviors Occur on a Continuum

Disordered eating is a general term used to describe a variety of atypical eating behaviors that people use to

---

disordered eating   Disordered eating is a general term used to describe a variety of abnormal or atypical eating behaviors that are used to keep or maintain a lower body weight.

achieve or maintain a lower body weight. These behaviors may be as simple as going on and off diets or as extreme as refusing to eat any fat. Such behaviors don't usually continue for long enough to make the person seriously ill, nor do they significantly disrupt the person's normal routine.

In contrast, some people restrict their eating so much or for so long that they become dangerously underweight. These people have an **eating disorder,** a psychiatric condition that involves extreme body dissatisfaction and long-term eating patterns that negatively affect body functioning. The two more commonly diagnosed eating disorders are anorexia nervosa and bulimia nervosa. **Anorexia nervosa** is a potentially life-threatening eating disorder that is characterized by self-starvation, which eventually leads to a severe nutrient deficiency. In contrast, **bulimia nervosa** is characterized by recurrent episodes of extreme overeating and compensatory behaviors to prevent weight gain, such as self-induced vomiting, misuse of laxatives, fasting, or excessive exercise. Both disorders will be discussed in more detail shortly.

When does normal dieting cross the line into disordered eating? Eating behaviors occur on a *continuum*, a spectrum that can't be divided neatly into parts. An example is a rainbow—where exactly does the red end and the orange begin? Thinking about eating behaviors as a continuum makes it easier to understand how a person could progress from relatively normal eating behaviors to a pattern that is disordered. For instance, let's say that for several years you've skipped breakfast in favor of a midmorning snack, but now you find yourself avoiding the cafeteria until early afternoon. Is this normal? To answer that question, you'd need to consider your feelings about food and your **body image**—the way you perceive your body.

Take a moment to study the Eating Issues and Body Image Continuum (**Figure 1**). Which of the five columns best describes your feelings about food and your body? If

---

eating disorder   An eating disorder is a clinically diagnosed psychiatric disorder characterized by severe disturbances in body image and eating behaviors.

anorexia nervosa   A serious, potentially life-threatening eating disorder that is characterized by self-starvation, which eventually leads to a deficiency in energy and essential nutrients that are required by the body to function normally.

bulimia nervosa   A serious eating disorder characterized by recurrent episodes of binge eating and recurrent inappropriate compensatory behaviors in order to prevent weight gain, such as self-induced vomiting, fasting, excessive exercise, or misuse of laxatives, diuretics, enemas, or other medications.

body image   A person's perception of his or her body's appearance and functioning.

Disordered Eating

Want to find out . . .

- if constant dieting is normal?
- the leading cause of death in females age 15 through 24?
- if males experience disordered eating?
- how to talk to someone who might have an eating disorder?

Hectic schedules often force us to grab a quick meal "on the go."

• I am not concerned about what others think regarding what and how much I eat. • When I am upset or depressed I eat whatever I am hungry for without any guilt or shame. • I feel no guilt or shame no matter how much I eat or what I eat. • Food is an important part of my life but only occupies a small part of my time. • I trust my body to tell me what and how much to eat.	• I pay attention to what I eat in order to maintain a healthy body. • I may weigh more than what I like, but I enjoy eating and balance my pleasure with eating with my concern for a healthy body. • I am moderate and flexible in goals for eating well. • I try to follow Dietary Guidelines for healthy eating.	• I think about food a lot. • I feel I don't eat well most of the time. • It's hard for me to enjoy eating with others. • I feel ashamed when I eat more than others or more than what I feel I should be eating. • I am afraid of getting fat. • I wish I could change how much I want to eat and what I am hungry for.	• I have tried diet pills, laxatives, vomiting, or extra time exercising in order to lose or maintain my weight. • I have fasted or avoided eating for long periods of time in order to lose or maintain my weight. • I feel strong when I can restrict how much I eat. • Eating more than I wanted to makes me feel out of control.	• I regularly stuff myself and then exercise, vomit, or use diet pills or laxatives to get rid of the food or calories. • My friends/family tell me I am too thin. • I am terrified of eating fat. • When I let myself eat, I have a hard time controlling the amount of food I eat. • I am afraid to eat in front of others.
FOOD IS NOT AN ISSUE	CONCERNED WELL	FOOD PREOCCUPIED/ OBSESSED	DISRUPTIVE EATING PATTERNS	DISORDERED EATING
BODY OWNERSHIP	BODY ACCEPTANCE	BODY PREOCCUPIED/ OBSESSED	DISTORTED BODY IMAGE	BODY HATE/ DISASSOCIATION
• Body image is not an issue for me. • My body is beautiful to me. • My feelings about my body are not influenced by society's concept of an ideal body shape. • I know that the significant others in my life will always find me attractive. • I trust my body to find the weight it needs to be at so I can move and feel confident of my physical body.	• I base my body image equally on social norms and my own self-concept. • I pay attention to my body and my appearance because it is important to me, but it only occupies a small part of my day. • I nourish my body so it has the strength and energy to achieve my physical goals. • I am able to assert myself and maintain a healthy body without losing my self-esteem.	• I spend a significant time viewing my body in the mirror. • I spend a significant time comparing my body to others. • I have days when I feel fat. • I am preoccupied with my body. • I accept society's ideal body shape and size as the best body shape and size. • I'd be more attractive if I was thinner, more muscular, etc....	• I spend a significant amount of time exercising and dieting to change my body. • My body shape and size keep me from dating or finding someone who will treat me the way I want to be treated. • I have considered changing or have changed my body shape and size through surgical means so I can accept myself. • I wish I could change the way I look in the mirror.	• I often feel separated and distant from my body—as if it belongs to someone else. • I hate my body and I often isolate myself from others. • I don't see anything positive or even neutral about my body shape and size. • I don't believe others when they tell me I look OK. • I hate the way I look in the mirror.

Figure 1 The Eating Issues and Body Image Continuum. The progression from normal eating (far left) to disordered eating (far right) occurs on a continuum. (*Data from:* Smiley, L., L. King, and H. Avery. University of Arizona Campus Health Service. Original Continuum, C. Shlaalak. Preventive Medicine and Public Health. Copyright © 1997 Arizona Board of Regents. Used with permission.)

you find yourself identifying with the statements on the left side of the continuum, you probably have few issues with food or body image. Most likely you accept your body size and view food as a normal part of maintaining your health and fueling your daily physical activity. As you progress to the right side of the continuum, food and body image become bigger issues, with food restriction becoming the norm. If you identify with the statements on the far right, you are probably afraid of eating and dislike your body. If so, what can you do to begin to move toward the left side of the continuum? How can you begin to develop a more healthful approach to food selection and to view your body in a more positive light? Before you can begin to find solutions, you need to understand the many complex factors that contribute to eating disorders and disordered eating and the differences between these terms.

Many Factors Contribute to Disordered Eating Behaviors

The factors that result in the development of disordered eating are very complex, but research indicates that a number of psychological, interpersonal, social, and biological factors may contribute in any particular individual.

Influence of Family

Research suggests that family conditioning, structure, and patterns of interaction can influence the development of an eating disorder. Based on observational studies, compared to families without a member with an eating disorder, families with an anorexic member show more rigidity in their family structure, less clear interpersonal boundaries, and tend to avoid open discussions on topics of disagreement. Conversely, families with a member diagnosed with bulimia nervosa tend to have a less stable family organization and to be less nurturing, more angry, and more disruptive.[1] In addition, childhood physical or sexual abuse can increase the risk of an eating disorder.[2]

Influence of Media

As media saturation has increased over the last century, so has the incidence of eating disorders among white women.[3] Every day, we are confronted with advertisements in which computer-enhanced images of lean, beautiful women promote everything from beer to cars (**Figure 2**). Most adult men and women understand that these images are unrealistic, but adolescents, who are still developing a sense of their identity and body image, lack the same ability to distance themselves from what they see.[4] Because body image influences eating behaviors, it is not unlikely that the barrage of media models may be contributing to the increase in eating disorders. However, scientific evidence demonstrating that the media is *causing* increased eating disorders is difficult to obtain.

Influence of Social and Cultural Values

Eating disorders are significantly more common in white females in Western societies than in other women world-

Figure 2 Photos of celebrities or models are often airbrushed or altered to "enhance" physical appearance. Unfortunately, many people believe that these are accurate portrayals and strive to reach an unrealistic level of physical beauty.

wide. This may be due in part to the white Western culture's association of slenderness with health, wealth, and high fashion (**Figure 3**). In contrast, until recently, the prevailing view in developing societies has been that excess body fat is desirable as a sign of health and material abundance.

The members of society with whom we most often interact—our family members, friends, classmates, and co-workers—also influence the way we see ourselves. Their comments related to our body weight or shape can be particularly hurtful—enough so to cause some people to start down the path of disordered eating. For example, individuals with bulimia nervosa report that they perceived greater pressure from their peers to be thin than controls, while

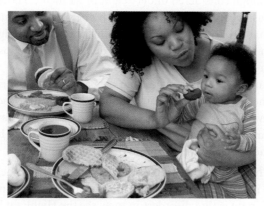

Family environment influences when, what, and how much we eat.

Figure 3 Until recently, the preferred look among runway models required extreme emaciation, often achieved by self-starvation and/or drug abuse.

research shows that peer teasing about weight increases body dissatisfaction and eating disturbances.[5] Thus, our comments to others regarding their weight do count.

Influence of Personality

A number of studies suggest that people with anorexia nervosa exhibit increased rates of obsessive-compulsive behaviors and perfectionism. They also tend to be socially inhibited, compliant, and emotionally restrained.[6] Unfortunately, many studies observe these behaviors only in individuals who are very ill and in a state of starvation, which may affect personality. Thus, it is difficult to determine if personality is the cause or effect of the disorder.

In contrast to people with anorexia nervosa, people with bulimia nervosa tend to be more impulsive, have low self-esteem, and demonstrate an extroverted, erratic personality style that seeks attention and admiration. In these people, negative moods are more likely to cause overeating than food restriction.[6]

Influence of Genetic Factors

Overall, the diagnosis of anorexia nervosa and bulimia nervosa is several times more common in siblings and other blood relatives who also have the diagnosis than in the general population.[7] This observation might imply the existence of an "eating disorder gene"; however, it is difficult to separate the contribution of genetic and environmental factors within families.

Anorexia Nervosa Is a Potentially Deadly Eating Disorder

According to the American Psychiatric Association, 90% to 95% of individuals with anorexia nervosa are young girls or women.[7] Approximately 0.5% to 1% of American females develops anorexia, and between 5% and 20% of these will die from complications of the disorder within 10 years of initial diagnosis.[2] These statis-

Figure 4   People with anorexia nervosa experience an extreme drive for thinness, resulting in potentially fatal weight loss.

tics make anorexia nervosa the most common and deadly psychiatric disorder diagnosed in women and the leading cause of death in females between the ages of 15 and 24 years.[2] As the statistics indicate, anorexia nervosa also occurs in males, but the prevalence is much lower than in females.[8]

Signs and Symptoms of Anorexia Nervosa

The classic sign of anorexia nervosa is an extremely restrictive eating pattern that leads to self-starvation (**Figure 4**). These individuals may fast completely, restrict energy intake to only a few kilocalories per day, or eliminate all but one or two food groups from their diet. They also have an intense fear of weight gain, and even small amounts (for example, 1–2 lb.) trigger high stress and anxiety.

In females, **amenorrhea** (no menstrual periods for at least 3 months) is a common feature of anorexia nervosa. It occurs when a young woman consumes insufficient energy to maintain normal body functions.

The American Psychiatric Association identifies the following conditions of anorexia nervosa (reprinted with permission from the *Diagnostic and Statistical Manual of Mental Disorders, Text Revision*, © 2000 American Psychiatric Association):

- Refusal to maintain body weight at or above a minimally normal weight for age and height
- Intense fear of gaining weight or becoming fat, even though considered underweight by all medical criteria
- Disturbance in the way in which one's body weight or shape is experienced, undue influence of body weight or shape on self-evaluation, or denial of the seriousness of the current low body weight
- Amenorrhea in females who are past puberty. Amenorrhea is defined as the absence of at least three consecutive menstrual cycles. A woman is considered to have amenorrhea if her periods occur only when given hormones, such as estrogen or oral contraceptives.

The signs of an eating disorder such as anorexia nervosa may be somewhat different in males. For more information on eating disorders in men, see the Highlight box: Eating Disorders in Men: Are They Different? on pages 534–535.

---

amenorrhea   Amenorrhea is the absence of menstruation. In females who had previously been menstruating, it is defined as the absence of menstrual periods for 3 or more months.

Skin/hair/nails:
- Hair becomes thin, dry, and brittle; hair loss occurs
- Skin is dry, easily bruised, and discolored
- Nails turn brittle

Brain:
- Altered levels of serotonin and other neurotransmitters
- Alteration in glucose metabolism
- Mood changes

Blood and immune system:
- Anemia
- Compromised immune system increases risk of infection

Thyroid gland:
- Abnormal thyroid levels due to starvation

Kidneys:
- Dehydration
- Electrolyte abnormalities that can be life-threatening
- Chronic renal failure

Heart:
- Low blood pressure and abnormal heart rate contribute to dizziness and fainting
- Abnormal electrocardiogram (ECG)
- Sudden death due to ventricular arrhythmias

Reproductive function:
- Disruption of sex hormone production, resulting in menstrual dysfunction and amenorrhea in females
- Infertility

Gastrointestinal system:
- Abdominal pain and bloating caused by slowed gastric emptying and intestinal motility
- Acute pancreatitis
- Constipation

Bone:
- Decreased bone mineral density (osteopenia)
- Decreased ability to absorb calcium due to low estrogen levels
- Decreased intake of bone-building nutrients due to starvation
- Increased loss of bone due to elevated cortisol levels

Muscle:
- Loss of muscle tissue as the body uses the muscles as an energy source

Figure 5 Impact of anorexia nervosa on the body.

Health Risks of Anorexia Nervosa

Left untreated, anorexia nervosa eventually leads to a deficiency in energy and other nutrients that are required by the body to function normally. The body will then use stored fat and lean tissue (for example, organ and muscle tissue) as an energy source to maintain brain tissue and vital body functions. The body will also shut down or reduce nonvital body functions to conserve energy. Electrolyte imbalances can lead to heart failure and death. **Figure 5** highlights many of the health problems that occur in people with anorexia nervosa.

Because the best chances for recovery occur when an individual receives intensive treatment early, it is important to recognize the signs of anorexia nervosa. Use these signs as a guide to help identify those at risk and to encourage them to seek help.

Bulimia Nervosa Is Characterized by Binging and Purging

Bulimia nervosa is an eating disorder characterized by repeated episodes of **binge eating** followed by some form of **purging.** While binge eating, the person feels a loss of self-control, including an inability to end the binge once it has started. At the same time, the person feels a sense of euphoria not unlike a drug-induced high. A "binge" is

binge eating Consumption of a large amount of food in a short period of time, usually accompanied by a feeling of loss of self-control.

purging An attempt to rid the body of unwanted food by vomiting or other compensatory means, such as excessive exercise, fasting, or laxative abuse.

Highlight
Eating Disorders in Men: Are They Different?

Like many people, you might find it hard to believe that men develop eating disorders . . . or if they do, their disorders must be somehow "different," right? Let's explore this question.

Comparing Men and Women with Eating Disorders

Until about a decade ago, little research was conducted on eating disorders in males. Recently, however, eating disorder experts have begun to study males. They've discovered that although eating disorders are similar in males and females, some differences *do* exist.

Females with eating disorders say they *feel* fat even though they typically are normal weight or even underweight before they develop the disorder. In contrast, males who develop eating disorders are more likely to have actually *been* overweight or

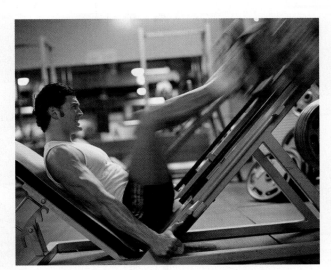

Men are more likely than women to exercise excessively in an effort to control their weight.

even obese.[8, 9] Thus, the male's fear of "getting fat again" is based on reality. In addition, males with disordered eating are less concerned with actual body weight (that is, scale weight) than females but are more concerned with body composition (that is, percentage of muscle mass compared to fat mass).

The methods that men and women use to achieve weight loss also appear to differ. Males are more likely to use excessive exercise as a means of weight control, whereas females tend to use severe energy restriction, vomiting, and laxative abuse. These weight control differences may stem from sociocultural biases; that is, dieting is considered to be more acceptable for women whereas the overwhelming sociocultural belief is that "real men don't diet."[9]

usually defined as a quantity of food that is large for the person and for the amount of time in which it is eaten (**Figure 6**). For example, a person may eat a dozen brownies with two quarts of ice cream in 30 minutes.

The prevalence of bulimia nervosa is higher than anorexia nervosa and is estimated to affect 1% to 4% of women. Like anorexia nervosa, bulimia nervosa is found predominately in women: six to ten females are diagnosed for every one male. The mortality rate is lower than for anorexia nervosa, with 1% of patients dying within 10 years of diagnosis.[2]

Although the prevalence of bulimia nervosa is much higher in women, rates for men are significant in some predominately "thin-build" sports in which par-

Figure 6 People with bulimia nervosa can consume relatively large amounts of food in brief periods of time.

ticipants are encouraged to maintain a low body weight (for example, horse racing, wrestling, crew, and gymnastics). Individuals in these sports typically do not have all the characteristics of bulimia nervosa, however, and the purging behaviors they practice typically stop once the sport is discontinued.

An individual with bulimia nervosa typically purges after most episodes, but not necessarily on every occasion, and weight gain as a result of binge eating can be significant. Methods of purging include vomiting, laxative or diuretic abuse, enemas, fasting, or excessive exercise. For example, after a binge, a runner may increase her daily mileage to equal the "calculated" energy content of the binge.

Muscle Dysmorphia: The Male Eating Disorder?

Is there an eating disorder unique to men? Recently, some eating disorder experts who work with men have suggested that there is. Observing men who are distressed by the idea that they are not sufficiently lean and muscular, who spend long hours lifting weights, and who follow an extremely restrictive diet, they have defined a disorder called *muscle dysmorphia*. (The disorder is also called *reverse anorexia nervosa*.) Men with muscle dysmorphia perceive themselves as small and frail even though they may actually be quite large and muscular. Thus, like men with anorexia nervosa, they suffer from a body image distortion, but it is reversed. No matter how "buff" or "chiseled" they become, their biology cannot match their idealized body size and shape.[10]

A common behavior of men with muscle dysmorphia is abuse of performance-enhancing drugs. Additionally, whereas people with anorexia eat little of anything, men with muscle dysmorphia tend to consume excessive high-protein foods and dietary supplements like protein powders.

On the other hand, men with muscle dysmorphia share some characteristics with men and women with other eating disorders. For instance, they too report "feeling fat" and engage in the same behaviors indicating an obsession with appearance (such as looking in the mirror). They also express significant discomfort with the idea of having to expose their bodies to others (for example, take off their clothes in the locker room) and have increased rates of mental illness.[11]

There are some outward indications that someone may be struggling with muscle dysmorphia. Not all of them apply to all men with the disorder. If you notice any of these behaviors in a friend or relative, talk about it with him and let him know that help is available.

- Rigid and excessive schedule of weight training
- Strict adherence to a high-protein, muscle-enhancing diet
- Use of anabolic steroids, protein powders, or other muscle-enhancing drugs or supplements
- Poor attendance at work, school, or sports activities because of interference with rigid weight-training schedule
- Avoidance of social engagements in which the person will not be able to follow his strict diet
- Avoidance of situations in which the person would have to expose his body to others
- Frequent and critical self-evaluation of body composition

Whereas muscle dysmorphia isn't typically life-threatening, it can cause distress and despair. Therapy—especially participation in an all-male support group—can help.

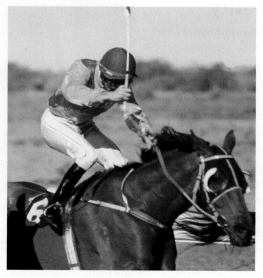

Men who participate in "thin-build" sports, such as jockeys, have a higher risk for bulimia nervosa than men who do not.

Symptoms of Bulimia Nervosa

As with anorexia nervosa, the American Psychiatric Association has identified conditions of bulimia nervosa (reprinted with permission from the Diagnostic and Statistical Manual of Mental Disorders, Text Revision, © 2000 American Psychiatric Association):

- Recurrent episodes of binge eating (for example, eating a large amount of food in a short period of time, such as within 2 hours)
- Recurrent inappropriate compensatory behavior in order to prevent weight gain, such as self-induced vomiting, misuse of laxatives, diuretics, enemas, or other medications, fasting, or excessive exercise
- Binge eating occurs on average at least twice a week for 3 months
- Body shape and weight unduly influence self-evaluation
- The disturbance does not occur exclusively during episodes of anorexia nervosa. Some individuals will

have periods of binge eating and then periods of starvation, which makes classification of their disorder difficult.

How can you tell if someone has bulimia nervosa?[12] In addition to the recurrent and frequent binge eating and purging episodes, the National Institutes of Health have identified the following symptoms of bulimia nervosa:

- chronically inflamed and sore throat
- swollen glands in the neck and below the jaw
- worn tooth enamel and increasingly sensitive and decaying teeth as a result of exposure to stomach acids
- gastroesophageal reflux disorder
- intestinal distress and irritation from laxative abuse
- kidney problems from diuretic abuse
- severe dehydration from purging of fluids

Health Risks of Bulimia Nervosa

The destructive behaviors of bulimia nervosa can lead to illness and even death. The most common health consequences associated with bulimia nervosa are:

- Electrolyte imbalance typically caused by dehydration and the loss of potassium and sodium from the body with frequent vomiting. This can lead to irregular heartbeat and even heart failure and death.
- Gastrointestinal problems: inflammation, ulceration, and possible rupture of the esophagus and stomach from frequent bingeing and vomiting. Chronic irregular bowel movements and constipation may result in people with bulimia who chronically abuse laxatives.
- Dental problems: tooth decay and staining from stomach acids released during frequent vomiting.

As with anorexia nervosa, the chance of recovery from bulimia nervosa increases, and the negative effects on health decrease, if the disorder is detected at an early stage. Familiarity with the warning signs of bulimia nervosa can help you identify friends and family members who might be at risk.

Binge-Eating Disorder Can Cause Significant Weight Gain

When was the last time a friend or relative confessed to you about "going on an eating binge"? Most likely, they

---

binge-eating disorder   A disorder characterized by binge eating an average of twice a week or more, typically without compensatory purging.

night-eating syndrome   Disorder characterized by intake of the majority of the day's energy between 8:00 PM and 6:00 AM. Individuals with this disorder also experience mood and sleep disorders.

explained that the behavior followed some sort of stressful event, such as a problem at work, the breakup of a relationship, or a poor grade on an exam. Many people have one or two binge episodes every year or so, in response to stress. But in people with **binge-eating disorder,** the behavior occurs an average of twice a week or more and is not usually followed by purging. This lack of compensation for the binge distinguishes binge-eating disorder from bulimia nervosa and explains why the person tends to gain a lot of weight.

The prevalence of binge-eating disorder is estimated to be 2% to 3% of the adult population and 8% of the obese population. In contrast to anorexia and bulimia, binge-eating disorder is also common in men. Our current food environment, which offers an abundance of good-tasting, cheap food any time of the day, makes it difficult for people with binge-eating disorder to avoid food triggers.

As you would expect, the increased energy intake associated with binge eating significantly increases a person's risk of being overweight or obese. In addition, the types of foods individuals typically consume during a binge episode are high in fat and sugar, which can increase blood lipids. Finally, the stress associated with binge eating can have psychological consequences, such as low self-esteem, avoidance of social contact, depression, and negative thoughts related to body size.

Night-Eating Syndrome Can Lead to Obesity

Night-eating syndrome was first described in a group of patients who were not hungry in the morning, but spent the evening and night eating and also reported insomnia. Like binge-eating disorder, it is associated with obesity because although night eaters don't binge, they do consume significant energy in their frequent snacks, and they don't compensate for the excess energy intake.

Someone with night-eating syndrome consumes most of his or her daily energy between 8 PM and 6 AM.

Symptoms of Night-Eating Syndrome

The distinguishing characteristic of night-eating syndrome is the time during which most of the day's energy intake occurs. Night eaters eat relatively little during the day, consuming the majority of their energy between 8:00 PM and 6:00 AM. They even get up in the night to eat. Night eating is also characterized by a depressed mood and by insomnia. In short, night eaters appear to have a unique combination of three disorders: an eating disorder, a sleep disorder, and a mood disorder.[13]

Health Risks of Night-Eating Syndrome

Night-eating syndrome is important clinically because of its association with obesity, which increases the risk for several chronic diseases, including heart disease, high blood pressure, stroke, type 2 diabetes, and arthritis. Obesity also increases the risk for sleep apnea, which can further disrupt the night eater's already abnormal sleeping pattern.

The Female Athlete Triad Consists of Three Disorders

The **female athlete triad** is a term used to describe a serious syndrome that consists of three clinical conditions in some physically active females: low energy availability (with or without eating disorders), amenorrhea, and osteoporosis (**Figure 7**).[14] Sports that emphasize leanness or a thin body build may place a young girl or a woman at risk for the female athlete triad. These include figure skating, gymnastics, diving, and others. Classical ballet dancers are also at increased risk for the disorder.

Components of the Female Athlete Triad

Active women experience the general social and cultural demands placed on women to be thin, as well as pressure from their coach, teammates, judges, and/or spectators to meet weight standards or body-size expectations for their sport. Failure to meet these standards can result in severe consequences, such as be-

ing cut from the team, losing an athletic scholarship, or decreased participation with the team.

As the pressure to be thin mounts, active women may restrict their energy intake, typically by engaging in disordered eating behaviors. Energy restriction combined with high levels of physical activity can disrupt the menstrual cycle and result in amenorrhea. Menstrual dysfunction can also occur in active women who are not dieting and don't have an eating disorder. These women are just not eating enough to cover the energy costs of their exercise training and all the other energy demands of the

Former gymnast Christy Henrich and her fiancé, a year before she died.

---

female athlete triad A serious syndrome that consists of three clinical conditions in some physically active females: low energy availability (with or without eating disorders), amenorrhea, and osteoporosis.

Figure 7 The female athlete triad is a syndrome composed of three coexisting disorders: low energy availability (with or without eating disorders), menstrual dysfunction such as amenorrhea, and osteoporosis. Energy availability is defined as dietary energy intake minus exercise energy expenditure.

body and daily living. Female athletes with menstrual dysfunction, regardless of the cause, typically have reduced levels of the reproductive hormones estrogen and progesterone. When estrogen levels in the body are low, it is difficult for bone to retain calcium, and gradual loss of bone mass occurs. Thus, many female athletes develop premature bone loss (osteoporosis) and are at increased risk for fractures.

Recognizing and Treating the Female Athlete Triad

Recognition of an athlete with one or more of the components of the female athlete triad can be difficult, especially if the athlete is reluctant to be honest when

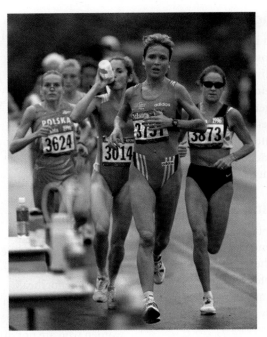

Sports that emphasize leanness or require the athlete to wear body-contouring clothing increase the risk for female athlete triad.

questioned about the symptoms. For this reason, familiarity with the early warning signs is critical. These include excessive dieting and/or weight loss, excessive exercise, stress fractures, and self-esteem that appears to be dictated by body weight and shape. You may not know whether a female friend or teammate is experiencing irregular periods, but you might overhear her commenting negatively on her body or see her head off to the gym after eating only a lettuce salad for lunch.

Treating an athlete requires a multidisciplinary approach. This means that the sports medicine team, sports dietitian, exercise physiologist, psychologist, coach, trainer, parents, friends of the athlete, and the athlete all must work together. As with any health problem, prevention is the best treatment. Thus, recognition of the risk factors by the sports medicine team and education of athletes, coaches, and parents are imperative, as all causes of menstrual dysfunction need to be examined. If the athlete is having trouble with weight and body shape issues, care should be taken to deal with these issues before they develop into something more serious.

Treatment for Disordered Eating Requires a Multidisciplinary Approach

As with any health problem, prevention is the best treatment for disordered eating. People having trouble with eating and body image issues need help to deal with these issues before they develop into something more serious.

Treating anyone with disordered eating requires a multidisciplinary approach. In addition to a physician and psychologist, a nutritionist, the person's coach (if an athlete), and family members and friends all must work together. Patients who are severely underweight, display signs of malnutrition, are medically unstable, or are suicidal may require immediate hospitalization. Conversely, patients who are underweight but are still medically stable may enter an outpatient program designed to meet

Liz
Nutri-Case

"I used to dance with a really cool modern company, where everybody looked sort of healthy and 'real.' No waifs! When they folded after Christmas, I was really bummed, but this spring, I'm planning to audition for the City Ballet. My best friend dances with them, and she told me that they won't even look at anybody over 100 pounds. So I've just put myself on a strict diet. Most days, I come in under 1,200 calories, though some days I cheat and then I feel so out of control. Last week, my dance teacher stopped me after class and asked me whether or not I was menstruating. I thought that was a pretty weird question, so I just said sure, but then when I thought about it, I realized that I've been so focused and stressed out lately that I really don't know! The audition is only a week away, so I'm going on a juice fast this weekend. I've just got to make it into the City Ballet!"

What factors increase Liz's risk for the female athlete triad? What, if anything, do you think Liz's dance teacher should do? Is intervention even necessary, since the audition is only a week away?

their specific needs. Some outpatient programs are extremely intensive, requiring patients to come in each day for treatment, whereas others are less rigorous, requiring only weekly visits for meetings with a psychiatrist or eating disorder specialist.

A Variety of Nutritional Therapies Are Important in Treating Anorexia Nervosa

The goals of nutritional therapies are to restore the individual to a healthy body weight and resolve the nutrition-related eating issues. For hospitalized patients, the expected weight gain per week ranges from 1 to 3 pounds. For outpatient settings, the expected weight gain is much lower (0.5 to 1 pound/week). During the weight-gain phase of a treatment program, energy intake goals may be set at 1,000 to 1,600 kcal/day, depending on body size, severity of the disease, and achievable levels of intake.

Patients frequently try a variety of methods to avoid consuming the food presented to them. They may discard the food, vomit, exercise excessively, or engage in a high level of non-exercise motor activity to eliminate the calories they just consumed. For this reason, patients are carefully watched by hospital staff or parents to make sure they swallow all their food. In addition to increasing amounts of food, patients may be given vitamin and mineral supplements to ensure that adequate micronutrients are consumed.

Nutrition counseling is an important aspect of the treatment to deal with the body image issues that occur as weight is regained. Once the patient reaches an acceptable body weight, nutrition counseling will address issues such as acceptability of certain foods, dealing with food situations such as family gatherings and eating out, and learning to put together a healthful food plan for weight maintenance.

Nutrition Counseling Is Important in Treating Bulimia Nervosa

Most individuals with bulimia nervosa are of normal weight or overweight, so restoring body weight is generally not the focus of treatment as it is with anorexia nervosa. Instead, nutrition counseling generally focuses on identifying and dealing with events and feelings that trigger binging, reducing purging, and establishing eating behaviors that can maintain a healthful body weight. In addition, nutrition counseling will address negative feelings about foods and the fear associated with uncontrolled binge eating of foods.

Talking to Someone About Disordered Eating

Discussing a friend's eating behaviors can be difficult. It is important to choose an appropriate time and place to raise your concerns and to listen closely and with great sensitivity to your friend's feelings. Here, we outline an approach you might use.

Background

Before approaching a friend or family member you suspect of having an eating disorder, learn as much as you possibly can about the eating disorder. Make sure you know the difference between the facts and myths about eating disorders. Locate a health professional specializing in eating disorders to whom you can refer your friend, and be ready to go with your friend if he or she does not want to go alone. If you are at a university or college, check with your local health center to see if it has an eating disorder team or can recommend someone to you. Set the stage for your discussion by finding a relaxed and private setting.[15]

Discussion

The National Eating Disorders Association recommends the following steps to take during your discussion:[15]

- Schedule a time to talk. Set aside a time and place for a private discussion in which you can share your concerns openly and honestly in a caring and supportive way. Make sure the setting is quiet and away from other distractions.
- Communicate your concerns. Share your memories of specific times when you felt concerned about your friend's eating or exercise behaviors. Explain that you think these things may indicate that there could be a problem that needs professional attention.
- Ask your friend to explore these concerns with a counselor, doctor, nutritionist, or other health professional who is knowledgeable about eating issues. If you feel comfortable doing so, offer to help your friend make an appointment or accompany your friend on the first visit.
- Avoid conflicts or a "battle of the wills" with your friend. If your friend refuses to acknowledge that there is a problem, or any reason for you to be concerned, restate your feelings and the reasons for them and leave yourself open and available as a supportive listener.
- Avoid placing shame, blame, or guilt on your friend regarding his or her actions or attitudes. Do not use accusatory "you" statements such as, "You just need to

eat" or "You are acting irresponsibly." Instead, use "I" statements. For example, "I'm concerned about you because I never see you in the cafeteria anymore," or "It makes me afraid when I hear you vomit."

- Avoid giving simple solutions. For example, "If you would just stop, everything would be fine."
- Express your continued support. Remind your friend that you care and want your friend to be healthy and happy.

Web Links

www.harriscentermgh.org
Harris Center, Massachusetts General Hospital
This site provides information about current eating disorder research, as well as sections on understanding eating disorders and resources for those with eating disorders.

www.nimh.nih.gov
National Institute of Mental Health (NIMH) Office of Communications and Public Liaison
Search this site for "disordered eating" or "eating disorders" to find numerous articles on the subject.

www.anad.org
National Association of Anorexia Nervosa and Associated Disorders
Visit this site for information and resources about eating disorders.

www.nationaleatingdisorders.org
National Eating Disorders Association
This site is dedicated to expanding public understanding of eating disorders and promoting access to treatment for those affected and support for their families.

References

1. Vandereycken, W. 2002. Families of patients with eating disorders. In: Fairburn, D. G., and K. D. Brownell, eds. *Eating Disorders and Obesity: A Comprehensive Handbook,* 2nd ed. New York: Guilford Press, pp. 215–220.
2. Patrick, L. 2002. Eating disorders: A review of the literature with emphasis on medical complication and clinical nutrition. *Altern. Med. Rev.* 7(3):184–202.
3. Striegel-Moore, R. H., and L. Smolak. 2002. Gender, ethnicity, and eating disorders. In: Fairburn, D. G., and K. D. Brownell, eds. *Eating Disorders and Obesity: A Comprehensive Handbook,* 2nd ed. New York: Guilford Press, pp. 251–255.
4. Steinberg, L. 2002. *Adolescence,* 6th ed. New York: McGraw-Hill.
5. Stice, E., 2002. Sociocultural influences on body image and eating disturbances. In: Fairburn, D. G., and K. D. Brownell, eds. *Eating Disorders and Obesity: A Comprehensive Handbook,* 2nd ed. New York: Guilford Press, pp. 103–107.
6. Wonderlich, S. A. 2002. Personality and eating disorders. In: Fairburn, D. G., and K. D. Brownell, eds. *Eating Disorders and Obesity: A Comprehensive Handbook,* 2nd ed. New York: Guilford Press, pp. 204–209.
7. American Psychiatric Association. 1994. *Diagnostic and Statistical Manual of Mental Disorders (DSM-IV),* 4th ed. Washington, DC: Author.
8. Robb, A. S., and M. J. Dadson. 2002. Eating disorders in males. *Child Adolesc. Psychiatric. Clin. N. Am.* 11:399–418.
9. Beals, K. A. 2004. *Disordered Eating in Athletes: A Comprehensive Guide for Health Professionals.* Champaign, IL: Human Kinetics Publishers.
10. Andersen, A. E. 2001. Eating disorders in males: Gender divergence management. *Currents* 2(2). University of Iowa Health Care. Available at www.uihealthcare.com/news/currents/vol2issue2/eatingdisordersinmen.html.
11. Pope H. G., K. A. Phillips, and R. Olivardia. 2000. *The Adonis Complex: The Secret Crisis of Male Body Obsession.* New York: The Free Press.

12. Garfinkel, P. E. 2002. Classification and diagnosis of eating disorders. In: Fairburn, D. G., and K. D. Brownell, eds. *Eating Disorders and Obesity: A Comprehensive Handbook,* 2nd ed. New York: Guilford Press, pp. 155–161.

13. Stunkard, A. J. 2002. Night eating syndrome. In: D. G. Fairburn, and K. D. Brownell, eds. *Eating Disorders and Obesity: A Comprehensive Handbook,* 2nd ed. New York: Guilford Press, pp. 183–187.

14. Nattiv A., A. B. Loucks, M. M. Manore, C. F. Sanborn, J. Sundgot-Borgen, and M. P. Warren. 2007. The female athlete triad. *Medicine and Science in Sport and Exercise.* 39(10):1867–1882.

15. National Eating Disorders Association. 2005.What should I say? Tips for talking to a friend who may be struggling with an eating disorder. Available at www.nationaleatingdisorders.org/p.asp?WebPage_ID 5322&Profile_ID541174.

14 Nutrition and Physical Activity: Keys to Good Health

Test Yourself | True or False

1 More than half of all Americans are not sufficiently active. **T** *or* **F**

2 To achieve fitness, a person needs to exercise at least 1 hour each day. **T** *or* **F**

3 Carbohydrate loading before a 1,500-meter run can improve performance. **T** *or* **F**

4 Eating extra protein beyond our requirements helps us to build muscle. **T** *or* **F**

5 Most ergogenic aids are not effective, and some can be dangerous or cause serious health consequences. **T** *or* **F**

Test Yourself answers are located in the Chapter Review.

Chapter Objectives *After reading this chapter, you will be able to:*

1. Compare and contrast the concepts of physical activity, leisure-time physical activity, exercise, and physical fitness, *p. 544*.

2. Define the four components of fitness, *pp. 544–545*.

3. List at least four health benefits of being physically active on a regular basis, *pp. 544–545*.

4. Describe the FIT principle and calculate your maximal and training heart rate range, *pp. 548–550*.

5. List and describe at least three processes we use to break down fuels to support physical activity, *pp. 552–556*.

6. Explain why lactic acid is not simply a waste product of exercise metabolism, *pp. 554–555*.

7. Discuss at least three changes in nutrient needs that can occur in response to an increase in physical activity or vigorous exercise training, *pp. 557–567*.

8. Describe the concept of carbohydrate loading, and discuss situations in which this practice may be beneficial to athletic performance, *pp. 561–562*.

9. Define the heat illnesses, including heat syncope, heat cramps, heat exhaustion, and heatstroke, *p. 565*.

10. Define the term *ergogenic aids*, and discuss the potential benefits and risks of at least four ergogenic aids that are currently on the market, *pp. 568–572*.

n June 2007, Bill Finch of North Carolina won two gold medals in track and field at the National Senior Games. In the 800-meter dash, he clocked 6:34.25, and in the 1,500-meter dash, he made 13:07.12. If his performance times don't impress you, perhaps they will when you consider his age: At the time he gave these winning performances, Bill Finch was 95 years old!

There's no doubt about it: Regular physical activity dramatically improves a person's strength, stamina, health, and longevity. But what qualifies as "regular physical activity"? In other words, how much does a person need to do to reap the benefits? And if people do become more active, does their diet have to change, too?

A healthful diet and regular physical activity are like two sides of the same coin, interacting in a variety of ways to improve strength and stamina and to increase resistance to many chronic diseases and acute illnesses. In fact, the nutrition and physical activity recommendations for reducing the risks for heart disease also reduce the risks for high blood pressure, type 2 diabetes, obesity, and some forms of cancer! In this chapter, we define physical activity, identify its many benefits, and discuss the nutrients needed to maintain an active life.

Hiking is a leisure-time physical activity that can contribute to your physical fitness.

physical activity   Any movement produced by muscles that increases energy expenditure; includes occupational, household, leisure-time, and transportation activities.

leisure-time physical activity   Any activity not related to a person's occupation; includes competitive sports, recreational activities, and planned exercise training.

exercise   A subcategory of leisure-time physical activity; any activity that is purposeful, planned, and structured.

physical fitness   The ability to carry out daily tasks with vigor and alertness, without undue fatigue, and with ample energy to enjoy leisure-time pursuits and meet unforeseen emergencies.

cardiorespiratory fitness   Fitness of the heart and lungs; achieved through regular participation in aerobic-type activities.

musculoskeletal fitness   Fitness of the muscles and bones.

flexibility   The ability to move a joint through its full range of motion.

body composition   The amount of bone, muscle, and fat tissue in the body.

Why Engage in Physical Activity?

A lot of people are looking for a "magic pill" that would help them maintain weight loss, reduce their risk of diseases, make them feel better, and improve their quality of sleep. Although many people are not aware of it, regular physical activity is this magic pill. **Physical activity** describes any movement produced by muscles that increases energy expenditure. Different categories of physical activity include occupational, household, leisure-time, and transportation.[1] **Leisure-time physical activity** is any activity not related to a person's occupation and includes competitive sports, planned exercise training, and recreational activities such as hiking, walking, and bicycling. **Exercise** is therefore considered a subcategory of leisure-time physical activity and refers to activity that is purposeful, planned, and structured.[2]

One of the most important benefits of regular physical activity is that it increases our physical fitness. **Physical fitness** is a state of being that arises largely from the interaction between nutrition and physical activity. It is defined as the ability to carry out daily tasks with vigor and alertness, without undue fatigue, and with ample energy to enjoy leisure-time pursuits and meet unforeseen emergencies.[1] Physical fitness has many components (Table 14.1).[3] These include the following:

- **Cardiorespiratory fitness** is defined as the ability of the heart, lungs, and circulatory system to efficiently supply oxygen and nutrients to working muscles.
- **Musculoskeletal fitness** involves fitness of both the muscles and bones. It includes *muscular strength*, the maximal force or tension level that can be produced by a muscle group, and *muscular endurance*, the ability of a muscle to maintain submaximal force levels for extended periods of time.
- **Flexibility** is the ability to move a joint fluidly through the complete range of motion, and **body composition** is the amount of bone, muscle, and fat tissue in the body.

Although many people are interested in improving their physical fitness, some are more interested in maintaining general fitness, while others are interested in achieving higher levels of fitness to optimize their athletic performance.

Other benefits of regular physical activity include the following:

- *Reduces our risks for, and complications of, heart disease, stroke, and high blood pressure:* Regular physical activity increases high-density lipoprotein cholesterol (HDL, the "good" cholesterol) and lowers triglycerides in the blood, improves the strength of the

Table 14.1 The Components of Fitness

Fitness Component	Examples of Activities for Achieving Fitness in Each Component
Cardiorespiratory	Aerobic-type activities such as walking, running, swimming, cross-country skiing
Musculoskeletal fitness:	Resistance training, weight lifting, calisthenics, sit-ups, push-ups
Muscular strength	Weight lifting or related activities using heavier weights with fewer repetitions
Muscular endurance	Weight lifting or related activities using lighter weights with greater number of repetitions
Flexibility	Stretching exercises, yoga
Body composition	Aerobic exercise and resistance training

heart, helps maintain healthy blood pressure, and limits the progression of atherosclerosis (or hardening of the arteries).

- *Reduces our risk for obesity:* Regular physical activity maintains lean body mass and promotes more healthful levels of body fat, may help in appetite control, and increases energy expenditure and the use of fat as an energy source.
- *Reduces our risk for type 2 diabetes:* Regular physical activity enhances the action of insulin, which improves the cells' uptake of glucose from the blood, and can improve blood glucose control in people with diabetes, which in turn reduces the risk for, or delays the onset of, diabetes-related complications.
- *Potential reduction in our risk for colon cancer:* Although the exact role that physical activity may play in reducing colon cancer risk is still unknown, we do know that regular physical activity enhances gastric motility, which reduces transit time of potential cancer-causing agents through the gut.
- *Reduces our risk for osteoporosis:* Regular physical activity strengthens bones and enhances muscular strength and flexibility, thereby reducing the likelihood of falls and the incidence of fractures and other injuries when falls occur.

Regular physical activity is also known to improve our sleep patterns, reduce our risk for upper respiratory infections by improving immune function, and reduce anxiety and mental stress. It also can be effective in treating mild and moderate depression.

Despite the plethora of benefits derived from regular physical activity, most people find that this magic pill is not easy to swallow. In fact, most people in the United States are physically inactive. The Centers for Disease Control and Prevention report that over half of all U.S. adults do not do enough physical activity to meet national health recommendations, and almost 16% of adults in the United States admit to doing no leisure-time physical activity at all (**Figure 14.1**).[4,5] These statistics mirror the reported increases in obesity, heart disease, and type 2 diabetes in industrialized countries.

This trend toward inadequate physical activity levels is also occurring in young people. Only 17% of middle and junior high schools and only 2% of senior high schools require daily physical activity for all students.[6] Low rates of voluntary participation in physical education (PE) compound this problem, as less than 30% of high school students participate in daily PE. Since our habits related to eating and physical activity are formed early in life, it is imperative that we provide opportunities for children and adolescents to engage in regular, enjoyable physical activity. An active lifestyle during childhood increases the likelihood of a healthier life as an adult.

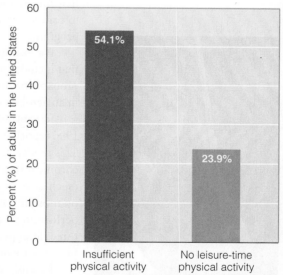

Figure 14.1 Rates of physical inactivity in the United States. Over 50% of the U.S. population does not do enough physical activity to meet national health recommendations, and almost 24% reports doing no leisure-time physical activity. (*Data from:* Centers for Disease Control and Prevention (CDC). 2005. Adult participation in recommended levels of physical activity—United States, 2001 and 2003. *Morb. Mortal. Wkly. Rep.* 54[47]:1208–1212; CDC. 2008. 1988–2007 No leisure-time physical activity trend chart. Available at www.cdc.gov/nccdphp/dnpa/physical/stats/leisure_time.htm.)

RecaP

Physical activity is any movement produced by muscles that increases energy expenditure. Physical fitness is the ability to carry out daily tasks with vigor and alertness, without undue fatigue, and with ample energy to enjoy leisure-time pursuits and meet unforeseen emergencies. Physical activity provides a multitude of health benefits, including reducing our risk for obesity and other chronic diseases and relieving anxiety and stress. Most people in the United States, including many children, are insufficiently active.

What Is a Sound Fitness Program?

There are several widely recognized qualities of a sound fitness program, as well as guidelines to help people design one that is right for them. These are explored here. Keep in mind that people with heart disease, high blood pressure, diabetes, osteoporosis, or arthritis should get approval to exercise from their healthcare practitioner prior to starting a fitness program. In addition, a medical evaluation should be conducted before starting an exercise program for an apparently healthy but currently inactive man 40 years or older or woman 50 years or older.

A Sound Fitness Program Meets Your Personal Goals

A fitness program that may be ideal for you is not necessarily right for everyone. Before designing or evaluating any program, it is important that each person define his or her personal fitness goals. Is the goal to prevent osteoporosis, diabetes, or another chronic disease that runs in the family? Is the goal simply to increase energy and stamina? Or is the intent to compete in athletic events? Each of these scenarios would require a very different fitness program.

For example, if a person wants to train for athletic competition, a traditional approach that includes planned exercise sessions under the guidance of a trainer or coach would probably be most beneficial. If the goal is to achieve cardiorespiratory fitness, participating in an aerobics class at least three times per week may be recommended.

In contrast, if the goal is to maintain overall health, one might do better to follow the 1996 report of the Surgeon General on achieving health through regular physical activity.[1] This report emphasizes that significant health benefits, including reducing the risk for chronic diseases, can be achieved by participating in a moderate amount of physical activity (such as 45 minutes of gardening, 20 minutes of brisk walking, or 30 minutes of basketball) on most, if not all, days of the week. These health benefits occur even when the time spent performing the physical activities is cumulative (for example, brisk walking for 10 minutes three times per day). Although these guidelines are appropriate for achieving health benefits, they are not necessarily of sufficient intensity and duration to improve physical fitness.

Recently, the Institute of Medicine published guidelines stating that the minimum amount of physical activity that should be done each day to maintain health and fitness is 60 minutes, not 30 minutes as recommended in the Surgeon General's report.[1, 7] This discrepancy in fitness guidelines has caused some confusion among consumers and even among some educators and scientists. Refer to the Nutrition Debate at the end of this chapter to learn more about this controversy.

A Sound Fitness Program Is Varied, Consistent . . . and Fun!

One of the most important goals for everyone is fun; unless you enjoy being active, you will find it very difficult to maintain your physical fitness. What activities do you consider fun? If you enjoy the outdoors, hiking, camping, fishing, and rock climbing are potential activities for you. If you would rather exercise with friends on your lunch break, walking, climbing stairs, and bicycle riding may be more appropriate. Or you may find it more enjoyable

Moderate physical activity, such as gardening, helps maintain overall health.

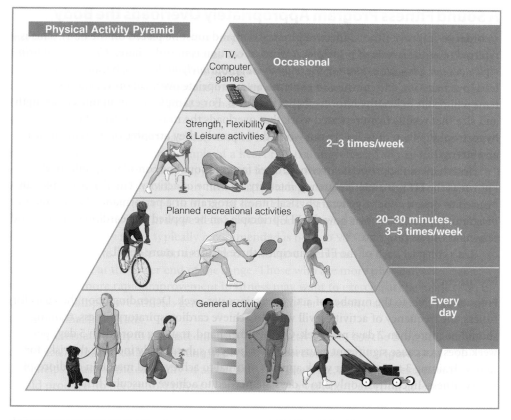

Physical Activity Pyramid

TV, Computer games — Occasional

Strength, Flexibility & Leisure activities — 2–3 times/week

Planned recreational activities — 20–30 minutes, 3–5 times/week

General activity — Every day

Figure 14.2 You can use this Physical Activity Pyramid as a guide to increase your level of physical activity. (*Data from:* Corbin, C. B., and R. D. Pangrazi. 1998. Physical Activity Pyramid rebuffs peak experience. *ACSM Health Fitness J. 2*[1]. © 1998. Used with permission.)

Watching television or reading can provide variety while running on a treadmill.

to stay indoors and use the programs and equipment at your local fitness club . . . or purchase your own treadmill and free weights.

Variety is critical to maintaining your fitness. While some people enjoy doing similar activities day after day, most of us get bored with the same fitness routine. Variety can be achieved by combining indoor and outdoor activities throughout the week, taking a different route when you walk each day, watching a movie or reading a book while you ride a stationary bicycle or walk on a treadmill, or participating in different activities each week such as walking, bicycling, and gardening. This smorgasbord of activities can increase your activity level without leading to monotony and boredom.

A fun and useful tool has been developed to help you increase the variety of your physical activity choices (**Figure 14.2**). The **Physical Activity Pyramid** makes recommendations for the type and amount of activity that should be done weekly to increase your physical activity level. The bottom of the pyramid describes activities that should be done every day, including walking more, taking the stairs instead of the elevator, and working in your garden. Aerobic types of exercises (such as bicycling and brisk walking) and recreational activities (such as soccer, tennis, and basketball) should be done three to five times each week, for at least 20 or 30 minutes. Flexibility, strength, and leisure activities should be done two to three times each week. The top of the pyramid emphasizes things we should do less of, including watching TV, playing computer games, or sitting for more than 30 minutes at one time.

It is important to understand that you cannot do just one activity to achieve overall fitness because every activity is specific to a certain fitness component. Refer back to Table 14.1, and notice the different activities listed as examples for the various components. For instance, participating in aerobic-type activities will improve our cardiorespiratory fitness but will do little to improve muscular strength. To achieve that goal, we must participate in some form of **resistance training,** or exercises in which our muscles work against resistance. Flexibility is achieved by participating in stretching activities. By following the recommendations put forth in the Physical Activity Pyramid, you can achieve physical fitness in all components.

Physical Activity Pyramid   A pyramid similar to the Food Guide Pyramid that makes recommendations for the type and amount of activity that should be done weekly to increase physical activity levels.

resistance training   Exercises in which our muscles work against resistance.

You Do the Math

Calculating Your Maximal and Training Heart Rate Range

Judy was recently diagnosed with type 2 diabetes, and her healthcare provider has recommended she begin an exercise program. She is considered obese according to her body mass index, and she has not been regularly active since she was a teenager. Judy's goals are to improve her cardiorespiratory fitness and achieve and maintain a more healthful weight. Fortunately, Valley Hospital, where she works as a nurse's aide, recently opened a small fitness center for its employees. Judy plans to begin by either walking on the treadmill or riding the stationary bicycle at the fitness center during her lunch break.

Judy needs to exercise at an intensity that will help her improve her cardiorespiratory fitness and lose weight. She is 38 years of age, is obese, has type 2 diabetes, and has been approved to do moderate-intensity activity by her healthcare provider. Even though she does a lot of walking and lifting in her work as a nurse's aide, her doctor has recommended that she set her exercise intensity range to begin at a heart rate that is slightly lower than the currently recommended minimal intensity of 64%. Based on this information, Judy should set her training heart rate range between 50% and 75% of her maximal heart rate.

Let's calculate Judy's maximal heart rate values:

- Maximal heart rate: 220 − age = 220 − 38 = 182 beats per minute (bpm)

- Lower end of intensity range: 50% of 182 bpm = 0.50 × 182 bpm = 91 bpm

- Higher end of intensity range: 75% of 182 bpm = 0.75 × 182 bpm = 137 bpm

Because Judy is a trained nurse's aide, she is skilled at measuring a heart rate, or pulse. To measure your own pulse:

- Place your second (index) and third (middle) finger on the inside of your wrist, just below the wrist crease and near the thumb. Press lightly to feel your pulse. Don't press too hard, or you will occlude the artery and be unable to feel its pulsation.

- If you can't feel your pulse at your wrist, try the carotid artery at the neck. This is located below your ear, on the side of your neck directly below your jaw. Press lightly against your neck under the jaw bone to find your pulse.

- Begin counting your pulse with the count of "zero," then count each beat for 15 seconds.

- Multiply that value by 4 to estimate heart rate over 1 minute.

- Do not take your pulse with your thumb, as it has its own pulse, which would prevent you from getting an accurate estimate of your heart rate.

As you can see from these calculations, when Judy walks on the treadmill or rides the bicycle, her heart rate should be between 91 and 137 bpm; this will put her in her aerobic training zone and allow her to achieve cardiorespiratory fitness. It will also assist in weight loss.

Stretching should be included in the warm-up and the cool-down for exercise.

warm-up   Also called preliminary exercise; includes activities that prepare you for an exercise bout, including stretching, calisthenics, and movements specific to the exercise bout.

cool-down   Activities done after an exercise session is completed; should be gradual and allow your body to slowly recover from exercise.

achieve higher levels of fitness, it is important that the activities be done for at least 20 to 30 consecutive minutes.

For example, let's say you want to compete in triathlons. To be successful during the running segment of the triathlon, you will need to be able to run quickly for at least 5 miles. Thus, it is appropriate for you to train so that you can complete 5 miles during one session and still have enough energy to swim and bicycle during the race. You will need to consistently train at a distance of 5 miles; you will also benefit from running longer distances.

A Sound Fitness Plan Includes a Warm-up and a Cool-down Period

To properly prepare for and recover from an exercise session, warm-up and cool-down activities should be performed. **Warm-up** properly prepares muscles for exertion by increasing blood flow and temperature, and includes general activities (such as stretching and calisthenics) and specific activities that prepare a person for the actual activity (such as jogging or swinging a golf club). The warm-up should be brief (5 to 10 minutes), gradual, and sufficient to increase muscle and body temperature, but should not cause fatigue or deplete energy stores.

Cool-down activities are done after the exercise session is completed. The cool-down should be gradual, allowing the body to slowly recover, and should include ample stretching

Rating of Perceived Exertion (RPE)

Scale	Perceived Exertion	Physical Signs
6	No exertion at all	No perceptible sign
7	Extremely light	No perceptible sign
8		
9	Very light	No perceptible sign
10		
11	Light	Feeling of motion
12		
13	Somewhat hard	Warmth on cold day, slight sweat on warm days
14		
15	Hard (heavy)	Sweating but can still talk without difficulty
16		
17	Very hard	Heavy sweating, difficulty talking
18		
19	Extremely hard	Feeling of near exhaustion
20	Maximal exertion	Feeling of near exhaustion

Figure 14.5 Rating of perceived exertion (RPE) scale to estimate exercise intensity. An intensity of 12 to 15, or somewhat hard to hard, is recommended to achieve physical fitness. (*Data from:* The Borg RPE Scale ®. Copyright © 1985, 1994 by Gunnar Borg.)

as well as a lower-intensity version of some of the same activities that were performed during the exercise session. Cooling down after exercise assists in the prevention of injury and may help reduce muscle soreness.

Recap

A sound fitness program must meet your personal fitness goals. It should be fun and include variety and consistency to help you maintain interest and achieve fitness in all components. It must also place an extra physical demand, or an overload, on your body. To achieve appropriate overload, follow the FIT principle: Frequency refers to the number of activity sessions per week. Intensity refers to how difficult the activity is to perform. Time refers to how long each activity session lasts. Warm-up exercises prepare the muscles for exertion by increasing blood flow and temperature. Cool-down activities assist in the prevention of injury and may help reduce muscle soreness.

Judy
Nutri-Case

"I can't remember a time in my life when I wasn't trying to lose weight. But nothing ever works, and when I go off a diet, I always end up fatter than I started out! These last couple of years I'd sort of given up, but last week I had my annual check-up and my doctor confirmed what I already knew—I'm obese! Being a nurse's aide, I know all about the health problems caused by obesity. Still, like I told my doctor, knowing how bad it is doesn't help me lose the weight and keep it off. So we talked about some slow-and-steady strategies for losing weight: I promised I'd do a better job of watching my diet, take my medications, and start working out at the new fitness center here at the hospital. I checked it out on my lunch break today, and I guess it's okay. They have a couple of treadmills and stationary bikes right in front of a big TV so you can watch the soaps while you work out. Still, I'm not really sure what I'm supposed to do or how many times a week or how long. I mean, if I only had to lose 5 pounds, that would be easy. But I've got to lose 50! And I only get half an hour for lunch!"

Imagine that you were a trainer at the Valley Hospital employee fitness center, and Judy told you about her weight-loss and fitness goals. Applying the FIT principle, recommend a physical activity program that includes an appropriate:

- number of times per 5-day work week
- intensity
- duration of activity
- variety of activity

If you get stuck, revisit the You Do the Math box on page 550.

What Fuels Our Activities?

In order to perform exercise, or muscular work, we must be able to generate energy. **Figure 14.6** provides an overview of all of the metabolic pathways that result in the generation of energy to support exercise. As this figure shows, the body can use carbohydrates, fats, and even relatively small amounts of proteins to fuel physical activity.

As you learned in Chapter 7, the common currency of energy for virtually all cells in the body is ATP, or adenosine triphosphate (refer to Figure 7.2, page 250). Remember that when one of the three phosphates in ATP is cleaved, energy is released. The products remaining after this reaction are adenosine diphosphate (ADP) and an independent inorganic phosphate group (Pi). In a mirror image of this reaction, the body regenerates ATP by

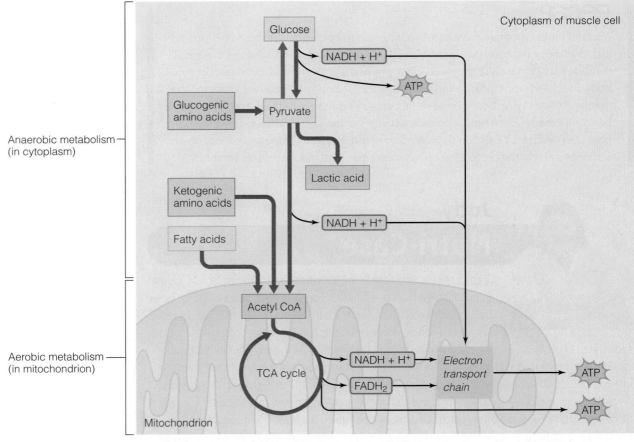

Figure 14.6   An overview of the metabolic pathways that result in ATP production during exercise. Carbohydrate, in the form of glucose, and proteins, in the form of amino acids, can be metabolized via anaerobic and aerobic pathways, whereas fatty acids are predominantly metabolized via aerobic pathways.

adding a phosphate group back to ADP. In this way, energy is continually provided to the cells both at rest and during exercise.

The amount of ATP stored in a muscle cell is very limited; it can keep the muscle active for only about 1 to 3 seconds. Thus, we need to generate ATP from other sources to fuel activities for longer periods of time. Fortunately, we are able to generate ATP from the breakdown of carbohydrate, fat, and protein, providing the cells with a variety of sources from which to receive energy. The primary energy systems that provide energy for physical activities are the adenosine triphosphate–creatine phosphate (ATP-CP) energy system and the anaerobic and aerobic breakdown of carbohydrates. Our bodies also generate energy from the breakdown of fats. As you will see, the type, intensity, and duration of the activities performed determine the amount of ATP needed and therefore the energy system that is used.

The ATP-CP Energy System Uses Creatine Phosphate to Regenerate ATP

As previously mentioned, muscle cells store only enough ATP to maintain activity for 1 to 3 seconds. When more energy is needed, a high-energy compound called **creatine phosphate (CP)** (also called phosphocreatine, or PCr) can be broken down to support the regeneration of ATP (**Figure 14.7**). Because this reaction can occur in the absence of oxygen, it is referred to as an anaerobic reaction (meaning "without oxygen").

Muscle tissue contains about four to six times as much CP as ATP, but there is still not enough CP available to fuel long-term activity. CP is used the most during very intense, short bouts of activity such as lifting, jumping, and sprinting (**Figure 14.8**). Together, the stores of ATP and CP can only support a *maximal* physical effort for about 3 to 15 seconds. The body must rely on other energy sources, such as carbohydrate and fat, to support activities of longer duration.

The Breakdown of Carbohydrates Provides Energy for Both Brief and Long-Term Exercise

During activities lasting about 30 seconds to 3 minutes, the body needs an energy source that can be used quickly to produce ATP. The breakdown of carbohydrates, specifically glucose, provides this quick energy through glycolysis. The most common source of glucose during exercise comes from glycogen stored in the muscles and glucose found in the blood. As shown in Figure 7.7 (page 255), for every glucose molecule that goes through glycolysis, two ATP molecules are produced. The primary end product of glycolysis is pyruvate.

creatine phosphate (CP) A high-energy compound that can be broken down for energy and used to regenerate ATP.

Figure 14.7 When the compound creatine phosphate (CP) is broken down into a molecule of creatine and an independent phosphate molecule, energy is released. This energy, along with the independent phosphate molecule, can then be used to regenerate ATP.

Activity	Percent (%) contribution to energy to perform activity
Sprint start (0–3 sec)	100% ATP/CP
100-m dash (10–12 sec)	50% ATP/CP 50% Carbohydrate
1500-m race (4–6 min)	6% ATP/CP 94% Carbohydrate
10-km race (32–40 min)	100% Carbohydrate
Marathon (2.5–3 hr)	5% Other 20% Fat 75% Carbohydrate
Day-long hike (5.5–7 hr)	65% Fat 35% Carbohydrate

Figure 14.8 The relative contributions of ATP-CP, carbohydrate, and fat to activities of various durations and intensities.

As shown in Figure 7.8, pyruvate is converted to lactic acid (or lactate) when oxygen availability is limited in the cell. For years it was assumed that lactic acid was a useless, even potentially toxic, by-product of high-intensity exercise. We now know that lactic acid is an important intermediate of glucose breakdown and that it plays a critical role in supplying fuel for working muscles, the heart, and resting tissues (see the Nutrition Myth or Fact? box, "Does Lactic Acid Cause Muscle Fatigue and Soreness?"). Any excess lactic acid that is not used by the muscles is transported in the blood back to the liver, where it is converted back into glucose via the Cori cycle (**Figure 14.9**). The glucose produced in the liver via the Cori cycle can recirculate to the muscles and provide energy as needed.

The major advantage of glycolysis is that it is the fastest way to generate ATP for exercise, other than the ATP-CP system. However, this high rate of ATP production can be sustained only for a brief period of time, generally less than 3 minutes. To perform exercise that lasts longer than 3 minutes, the body relies on the aerobic energy system.

In the aerobic energy system, pyruvate goes through the additional metabolic pathways of the TCA cycle and the electron transport chain in the presence of oxygen (see Figure 7.12). Although this process is slower than glycolysis occurring under anaerobic conditions, the breakdown of one glucose molecule going through aerobic metabolism yields 36 to 38 ATP molecules for energy, whereas the anaerobic process yields only 2 ATP molecules. Thus, this aerobic process supplies 18 times more energy! Another advantage of the aerobic process is that it does not result in the significant production of acids and other compounds that contribute to muscle fatigue, which means that a low-intensity activity can be performed for hours. Aerobic metabolism of glucose is the primary source of fuel for our muscles during activities lasting from 3 minutes to 4 hours (see Figure 14.8).

As you learned in Chapter 4, the body can store only a limited amount of glycogen. An average, well-nourished

Figure 14.9 The Cori cycle is the metabolic pathway by which excess lactic acid can be converted into glucose in the liver.

Nutrition Myth or Fact?
Does Lactic Acid Cause Muscle Fatigue and Soreness?

Theo and his teammates won their basketball game last night, but just barely. With two of the players sick, Theo got more court time than usual, and when he got back to the dorm, he could hardly get his legs to carry him up the stairs. This morning, Theo's muscles ache all over, and he wonders if a build-up of lactic acid is to blame.

Lactic acid is a by-product of glycolysis. For many years, both scientists and athletes believed that lactic acid causes muscle fatigue and soreness. Does recent scientific evidence support this belief?

The exact causes of muscle fatigue are not known, and there appear to be many contributing factors. Recent evidence suggests that fatigue may be due not only to the accumulation of many acids and other metabolic by-products but also to the depletion of creatine phosphate and changes in calcium in the cells that affect muscle contraction. Depletion of muscle glycogen, liver glycogen, and blood glucose, as well as psychological factors, can all contribute to fatigue.[9] Thus, it appears that lactic acid only contributes to fatigue and does not cause fatigue independently.

So what factors cause muscle soreness? As with fatigue, there are probably many contributors. It is hypothesized

that soreness usually results from microscopic tears in the muscle fibers as a result of strenuous exercise. This damage triggers an inflammatory reaction that causes an influx of fluid and various chemicals to the damaged area. These substances work to remove damaged tissue and initiate tissue repair, but they may also stimulate pain.[9] However, it appears highly unlikely that lactic acid is an independent cause of muscle soreness.

Recent studies indicate that lactic acid is produced even under aerobic conditions! This means it is produced at rest as well as during any intensity of exercise. The reasons for this constant production of lactic acid are still being studied. What we do know is that lactic acid is an important fuel for resting tissues and for working cardiac and skeletal muscles. That's right—skeletal muscles not only *produce* lactic acid, but they also *use* it for energy, both directly and after it is converted into glucose and glycogen in the liver.[9, 10] We also know that endurance training improves the muscle's ability to use lactic acid for energy. Thus, contrary to being a waste product of glucose metabolism, lactic acid is actually an important energy source for muscle cells during rest and exercise.

man who weighs about 154 lb (70 kg) can store about 200 to 500 g of muscle glycogen, which is equal to 800 to 2,000 kcal of energy. Although trained athletes can store more muscle glycogen than the average person, even their bodies do not have enough stored glycogen to provide an unlimited energy supply for long-term activities. Thus, we also need a fuel source that is abundant and can be broken down under aerobic conditions so that it can support activities of lower intensity and longer duration. This fuel source is fat.

Aerobic Breakdown of Fats Supports Exercise of Low Intensity and Long Duration

When we refer to fat as a fuel source, we mean stored triglycerides. Their fatty acid chains provide much of the energy needed to support long-term activity. The longer the fatty acid, the more ATP that can be generated from its breakdown. For instance, palmitic acid is a fatty acid with 16 carbons. If palmitic acid is broken down completely, it yields 129 ATP molecules! Obviously, far more energy is produced from this one fatty acid molecule than from the aerobic breakdown of a glucose molecule.

There are two major advantages of using fat as a fuel. First, fat is an abundant energy source, even in lean people. For example, a man who weighs 154 lb (70 kg) who has a body fat level of 10% has approximately 15 lb of body fat, which is equivalent to more than 50,000 kcal of energy! This is significantly more energy than can be provided by his stored

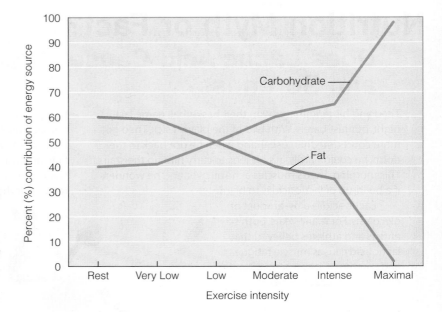

Figure 14.10 For most daily activities, including exercise, we use a mixture of carbohydrate and fat for energy. At lower exercise intensities, we rely more on fat as a fuel source. As exercise intensity increases, we rely more on carbohydrate for energy. (*Data adapted from:* Brooks, G. A., and J. Mercier. 1994. Balance of carbohydrate and lipid utilization during exercise: The "crossover" concept. *J. Appl Physiol.* 76[6]: 2253–2261.)

muscle glycogen (800 to 2,000 kcal). Second, fat provides 9 kcal of energy per gram, more than twice as much energy per gram as carbohydrate. The primary disadvantage of using fat as a fuel is that the breakdown process is relatively slow; thus, fat is used predominantly as a fuel source during activities of lower intensity and longer duration. Fat is also our primary energy source during rest, sitting, and standing in place.

What specific activities are fueled by fat? Walking long distances uses fat stores, as does hiking, long-distance cycling, and other low- to moderate-intensity forms of exercise. Fat is also an important fuel source during endurance events such as marathons (26.2 miles) and ultra-marathon races (49.9 miles). Endurance exercise training improves our ability to use fat for energy, which may be one reason that people who exercise regularly tend to have lower body fat levels than people who do not exercise.

It is important to remember that we are almost always using some combination of carbohydrate and fat for energy. At rest, very little carbohydrate is used, and the body relies mostly on fat. During maximal exercise (at 100% effort), the body uses mostly carbohydrate and very little fat. However, most activities done each day involve some use of both fuels (**Figure 14.10**).

When it comes to eating properly to support regular physical activity or exercise training, the nutrient to focus on is carbohydrate. This is because most people store more than enough fat to support exercise, whereas our storage of carbohydrate is limited. It is especially important that adequate stores of glycogen are maintained for moderate to intense exercise. Dietary recommendations for fat, carbohydrate, and protein are reviewed later in this chapter (pages 558–564).

Amino Acids Are Not Major Sources of Fuel During Exercise

Proteins, or more specifically, amino acids—are not major energy sources during exercise. As discussed in Chapters 6 and 7, amino acids can be used directly for energy if necessary, but they are more often used to make glucose to maintain blood glucose levels during exercise. The carbon skeletons of amino acids can be converted into pyruvate or acetyl CoA, or they can feed directly into the TCA cycle to provide energy during exercise if necessary (see Figure 7.19). Amino acids also help build and repair tissues after exercise. Depending upon the intensity and duration of the activity, amino acids may contribute about 3% to 6% of the energy needed.[11]

Given this, why is it that so many people are concerned about their protein intakes? As you learned in Chapter 6, muscles are not stimulated to grow by consuming extra dietary protein. Only appropriate physical training can stimulate muscles to grow and strengthen. Thus, while adequate dietary protein is needed to support activity and recovery, consuming very high amounts does not provide an added benefit. The protein needs of athletes are only slightly higher than the needs of nonathletes, and most people eat more than enough protein to support even the highest requirements for competitive athletes! Thus, there is generally no need for recreationally active people or even competitive athletes to consume protein or amino acid supplements.

RecaP

The amount of ATP stored in a muscle cell is limited and can only keep a muscle active for about 1 to 3 seconds. For intense activities lasting about 3 to 15 seconds, creatine phosphate can be broken down to provide energy and support the regeneration of ATP. To support activities that last from 30 seconds to 2 minutes, energy is produced from glycolysis. Fatty acids can be broken down aerobically to support activities of low intensity and longer duration. The two major advantages of using fat as a fuel are that it is an abundant energy source and it provides more than twice the energy per gram as compared with carbohydrate. Amino acids may contribute from 3% to 6% of the energy needed during exercise, depending upon the intensity and duration of the activity. Amino acids help build and repair tissues after exercise.

What Kind of Diet Supports Physical Activity?

Lots of people wonder, "Do my nutrient needs change if I become more physically active?" The answer to this question depends upon the type, intensity, and duration of the chosen activities. It is not necessarily true that our requirement for every nutrient is greater if we are physically active.

People who are performing moderate-intensity daily activities for health can follow the general guidelines put forth in the USDA Food Guide. For smaller or less active people, the lower end of the range of recommendations for each food group may be appropriate. For larger or more active people, the higher end of the range is suggested. Modifications may be necessary for people who exercise vigorously every day, and particularly for athletes training for competition. Table 14.2 provides an overview of the nutrients that can be affected by regular, vigorous exercise training. Each of these nutrients is described in more detail in the following sections.[12]

Vigorous Exercise Increases Energy Needs

Athletes generally have higher energy needs than moderately active or sedentary people. The amount of extra energy needed to support regular training is determined by the type, intensity, and duration of the activity. In addition, the energy needs of male athletes are higher than those of female athletes because male athletes weigh more, have more muscle mass, and will expend more energy during activity than female athletes. This is relative, of course: A large woman who trains 3 to 5 hours each day will probably need more energy than a small man who trains 1 hour each day. The energy needs of athletes can range from only 1,500 to 1,800 kcal per day for a small female gymnast to more than 7,500 kcal per day for a male cyclist competing in the Tour de France cross-country cycling race!

Figure 14.11 on page 559 shows a sample of meals that total 1,800 kcal per day and 4,000 kcal per day, with the carbohydrate content of these meals meeting more than 60% of total energy intake. As you can see, athletes who need more than 4,000 kcal per day need to consume very large quantities of food. However, the heavy demands of daily physical

Small snacks can be helpful to meet daily energy demands.

Table 14.2 Suggested Intakes of Nutrients to Support Vigorous Exercise

Nutrient	Functions	Suggested Intake
Energy	Supports exercise, activities of daily living, and basic body functions	Depends upon body size and the type, intensity, and duration of activity. For many female athletes: 1,800 to 3,500 kcal/day For many male athletes: 2,500 to 7,500 kcal/day
Carbohydrate	Provides energy, maintains adequate muscle glycogen and blood glucose; high complex carbohydrate foods provide vitamins and minerals	45–65% of total energy intake Depending upon sport and gender, should consume 6–10 g of carbohydrate per kg body weight per day
Fat	Provides energy, fat-soluble vitamins, and essential fatty acids; supports production of hormones and transport of nutrients	20–35% of total energy intake
Protein	Helps build and maintain muscle; provides building material for glucose; energy source during endurance exercise; aids recovery from exercise	10–35% of total energy intake Endurance athletes: 1.2–1.4 g per kg body weight Strength athletes: 1.2–1.7 g per kg body weight
Water	Maintains temperature regulation (adequate cooling); maintains blood volume and blood pressure; supports all cell functions	Consume fluid before, during, and after exercise Consume enough to maintain body weight Consume at least 8 cups (or 64 fl. oz) of water daily to maintain regular health and activity Athletes may need up to 10 liters (or 170 fl. oz) every day; more is required if exercising in a hot environment
B-vitamins	Critical for energy production from carbohydrate, fat, and protein	May need slightly more (1–2 times the RDA) for thiamin, riboflavin, and vitamin B_6
Calcium	Builds and maintains bone mass; assists with nervous system function, muscle contraction, hormone function, and transport of nutrients across cell membrane	Meet the current AI: 14–18 yr: 1,300 mg/day 19–50 yr: 1,000 mg/day 51 and older: 1,200 mg/day
Iron	Primarily responsible for the transport of oxygen in blood to cells; assists with energy production	Consume at least the RDA: Males: 14–18 yr: 11 mg/day 19 and older: 8 mg/day Females: 14–18 yr: 15 mg/day 19–50 yr: 18 mg/day 51 and older: 8 mg/day

training, work, school, and family responsibilities often leave these athletes with little time to eat adequately. Thus, many athletes meet their energy demands by planning regular meals and snacks and **grazing** (eating small meals throughout the day) consistently. They may also take advantage of the energy-dense snack foods and meal replacements specifically designed for athletes participating in vigorous training. These steps help athletes to maintain their blood glucose and energy stores.

If an athlete is losing body weight, then his or her energy intake is inadequate. Conversely, weight gain may indicate that energy intake is too high. Weight maintenance is generally recommended to maximize performance. If weight loss is warranted, food intake should be lowered no more than 200 to 500 kcal per day, and athletes should try to lose weight prior to the competitive season if at all possible. Weight gain may be necessary for some athletes and can usually be accomplished by consuming 500 to 700 kcal per day more than needed for weight maintenance. The extra energy should come from a healthy balance of carbohydrate (45% to 65% of total energy intake), fat (20% to 35% of total energy intake), and protein (10% to 35% of total energy intake).

Many athletes are concerned about their weight. Jockeys, boxers, wrestlers, judo athletes, and others are required to "make weight," or meet a predefined weight category. Others, such as distance runners, gymnasts, figure skaters, and dancers, are required to maintain a very lean figure for performance and aesthetic reasons. These athletes tend to eat less energy than they need to support vigorous training, which puts them at risk for inadequate

grazing Consistently eating small meals throughout the day; done by many athletes to meet their high energy demands.

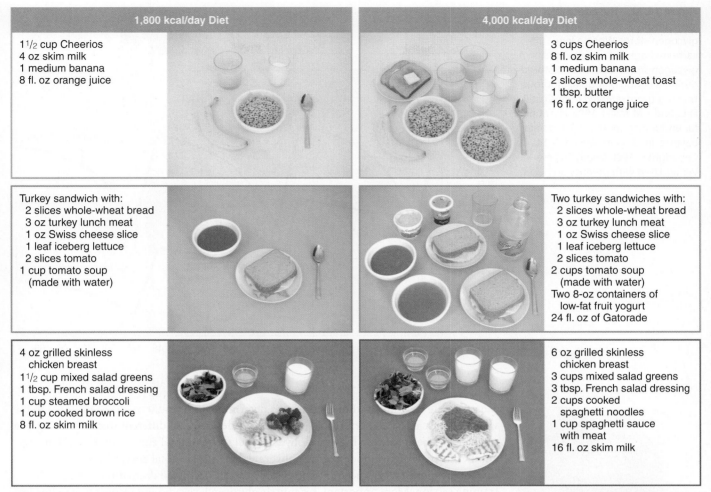

1,800 kcal/day Diet	4,000 kcal/day Diet
1¹/₂ cup Cheerios 4 oz skim milk 1 medium banana 8 fl. oz orange juice	3 cups Cheerios 8 fl. oz skim milk 1 medium banana 2 slices whole-wheat toast 1 tbsp. butter 16 fl. oz orange juice

Turkey sandwich with:
  2 slices whole-wheat bread
  3 oz turkey lunch meat
  1 oz Swiss cheese slice
  1 leaf iceberg lettuce
  2 slices tomato
  1 cup tomato soup
   (made with water)
	Two turkey sandwiches with:
	  2 slices whole-wheat bread
	  3 oz turkey lunch meat
	  1 oz Swiss cheese slice
	  1 leaf iceberg lettuce
	  2 slices tomato
	  2 cups tomato soup
	   (made with water)
	Two 8-oz containers of
	  low-fat fruit yogurt
	24 fl. oz of Gatorade

4 oz grilled skinless
  chicken breast
1¹/₂ cup mixed salad greens
1 tbsp. French salad dressing
1 cup steamed broccoli
1 cup cooked brown rice
8 fl. oz skim milk
	6 oz grilled skinless
	  chicken breast
	3 cups mixed salad greens
	3 tbsp. French salad dressing
	2 cups cooked
	  spaghetti noodles
	1 cup spaghetti sauce
	  with meat
	16 fl. oz skim milk

Figure 14.11 High-carbohydrate (approximately 60% of total energy) meals that contain approximately 1,800 kcal per day (on left) and 4,000 kcal per day (on right). Athletes must plan their meals carefully to meet energy demands, particularly those with very high energy needs.

intakes of all nutrients. They are also at a higher risk of suffering from health consequences resulting from poor energy and nutrient intake, including eating disorders, osteoporosis, menstrual disturbances, dehydration, heat illnesses, physical injuries, and even death.

Carbohydrate Needs Increase for Many Active People

As you know, carbohydrate (in the form of glucose) is one of the primary sources of energy needed to support exercise. Both endurance athletes and strength athletes require adequate carbohydrate to maintain their glycogen stores and provide quick energy.

How Much of an Athlete's Diet Should Be Composed of Carbohydrate?

You may recall from Chapter 4 that the AMDR for carbohydrate is 45% to 65% of total energy intake. Athletes should consume carbohydrate intakes within this same recommended range. Although high-carbohydrate diets (greater than 60% of total energy intake) have been recommended in the past, this percentage value may not be appropriate for all athletes.

To illustrate the importance of carbohydrate intake for athletes, let's see what happens to Theo when he participates in a study designed to determine how carbohydrate intake affects glycogen stores during a period of heavy training. Theo was asked to come to the exercise laboratory at the university and ride a stationary bicycle for 2 hours a day for 3 consecutive days at 75% of his maximal heart rate. Before and after each ride, samples of

Some athletes may diet to meet a predefined weight category.

Figure 14.12 The effects of a low-carbohydrate diet on muscle glycogen stores. When a low-carbohydrate diet is consumed, glycogen stores cannot be restored during a period of regular vigorous training. (*Data adapted from:* Costill, D. L., and J. M. Miller. 1980. Nutrition for endurance sport: CHO and fluid balance. *Int. J. Sports Med.* 1:2–14. Copyright © 1980 Georg Thieme Verlag. Used with permission.)

Fruit and vegetable juices can be a good source of carbohydrates.

muscle tissue were taken from his thighs to determine the amount of glycogen stored in the working muscles. Theo performed this series of rides twice, in different weeks—during one week he had been eating a high-carbohydrate diet (80% of total energy intake) and during another he had eaten a moderate-carbohydrate diet (40% of total energy intake). As you can see in **Figure 14.12**, Theo's muscle glycogen levels decreased dramatically after each training session. More important, his muscle glycogen levels did not recover to baseline levels over the 3 days when Theo ate the lower-carbohydrate diet. He was able to maintain his muscle glycogen levels only when he was eating the higher-carbohydrate diet. Theo also told the researchers that completing the 2-hour rides was much more difficult when he had eaten the moderate-carbohydrate diet as compared to when he was eating the diet that was higher in carbohydrate. In fact, athletes use the term "hitting the wall" or "bonking" to refer to the physical and mental fatigue they experience once glycogen stores are depleted; their ability to work typically drops below 50% of their maximum capacity.

When Should Carbohydrates Be Consumed?

It is important for athletes not only to consume enough carbohydrate to maintain glycogen stores but also to time their intake optimally. The body stores glycogen very rapidly during the first 24 hours of recovery from exercise, with the highest storage rates occurring during the first few hours.[13] Higher carbohydrate intakes during the first 24 hours of recovery from exercise are associated with higher amounts of glucose being stored as muscle glycogen. Experts recommend a daily carbohydrate intake of approximately 6 to 10 g of carbohydrate per kg body weight to optimize muscle glycogen stores in athletes. However, this need could be much greater in athletes who are training heavily daily, as they have less time to recover and require more carbohydrate to support both training and storage needs.

If an athlete has to perform or participate in training bouts that are scheduled less than 8 hours apart, then he or she should try to consume enough carbohydrate in the few hours after training to allow for ample glycogen storage. However, with a longer recovery time (generally 12 hours or more), the athlete can eat when he or she chooses, and glycogen levels should be restored as long as the total carbohydrate eaten is sufficient.

Interestingly, studies have shown that muscle glycogen can be restored to adequate levels in the muscle whether the food is eaten in small, multiple snacks or in larger meals,[13, 14] although some studies show enhanced muscle glycogen storage during the first 4 to 6 hours of recovery when athletes are fed large amounts of carbohydrate every 15 to 30 minutes.[15, 16]

What Food Sources of Carbohydrates Are Good for Athletes?

What are good carbohydrate sources to support vigorous training? In general, complex, less-processed carbohydrate foods such as whole grains and cereals, fruits, vegetables, and juices are excellent sources that also supply fiber, vitamins, and minerals. Guidelines for intake of simple sugars is less than 10% of total energy intake, but some athletes who need very large energy intakes to support training may need to consume more. In addition, there is evidence that consuming high-glycemic-index foods during the immediate post-recovery period results in higher glycogen storage than is achieved as a result of eating low-glycemic-index foods. This may be due to a greater malabsorption of the carbohydrate in low-glycemic-index foods, as these foods contain more indigestible forms of carbohydrate.[13] Thus, there are advantages to consuming a wide variety of carbohydrate sources.

As a result of time constraints, many athletes have difficulties consuming enough food to meet carbohydrate demands. Many beverages and snack bars have therefore been designed to assist athletes with increasing carbohydrate intake. Some of these are listed in Table 14.3, along with other simple, inexpensive foods that contain 50 to 100 g of carbohydrate.

When Does Carbohydrate Loading Make Sense?

As you know, carbohydrate is a critical energy source to support exercise, particularly endurance-type activities. Because of the importance of carbohydrates as an exercise fuel

Table 14.3 Nutrient Composition of Various Foods and Sport Bars

Food	Amount	Carbohydrate (grams)	Energy from Carbohydrate (%)	Total Energy (kcal)
Sweetened applesauce	1 cup	50	97	207
Large apple and	1 each	50	82	248
Saltine crackers	8 each			
Whole-wheat bread and	1 oz slice	50	71	282
Jelly and	4 tsp			
Skim milk	12 fl. oz			
Spaghetti noodles (cooked) and	1 cup	50	75	268
Tomato sauce	1/4 cup			
Brown rice (cooked) and	1 cup	100	88	450
Mixed vegetables and	1/2 cup			
Apple juice	12 fl. oz			
Grape Nuts cereal and	1/2 cup	100	84	473
Raisins and	3/8 cup			
Skim milk	8 fl. oz			
Clif Bar (chocolate chip)	2.4 oz	45	72	250
Meta-Rx (fudge brownie)	3.53 oz	48	60	320
Power Bar (chocolate)	2.25 oz	42	75	225
PR Bar Ironman	2 oz	24	42	230

Data adapted from: Manore, M. M., N. L. Meyer, and J. L. Thompson. 2009. *Sport Nutrition for Health and Performance,* 2nd ed. Champaign, IL: Human Kinetics.

Table 14.4 Recommended Carbohydrate Loading Guidelines for Endurance Athletes

Days Prior to Event	Exercise Duration (minutes) at 70% Maximal Effort	Carbohydrate Content of Diet (grams per kg of body weight)
6	90	5
5	40	5
4	40	5
3	20	10
2	20	10
1	Rest	10
Day of race	Competition	Precompetition food and fluid

Data adapted from: Coleman, E. 2006. Carbohydrate and exercise. In: Marie Dunford, ed. *Sports Nutrition,* 4th ed. Chicago, IL. The American Dietetic Association. Used with permission.

Carbohydrate loading may benefit endurance athletes, such as cross-country skiers.

and our limited capacity to store them, discovering ways to maximize the body's storage of carbohydrates has been at the forefront of sports nutrition research for many years. The practice of **carbohydrate loading,** also called *glycogen loading,* involves altering both exercise duration and carbohydrate intake such that it maximizes the amount of muscle glycogen. Table 14.4 reviews a schedule for carbohydrate loading for an endurance athlete. Athletes who may benefit from maximizing muscle glycogen stores are those competing in marathons, ultra-marathons, long-distance swimming, cross-country skiing, and triathlons. Athletes who compete in baseball, American football, 10-kilometer runs, walking, hiking, weight lifting, and most swimming events will not gain any performance benefits from this practice, nor will people who regularly participate in moderately intense physical activities to maintain fitness.

It is important to emphasize that carbohydrate loading does not always improve performance. There are many adverse side effects of this practice, including extreme gastrointestinal distress, particularly diarrhea. We store water along with the extra glycogen in the muscles, which leaves many athletes feeling heavy, bloated, and sluggish. Athletes who want to try carbohydrate loading should experiment prior to competition to determine if it is an acceptable and beneficial approach for them.

Moderate Fat Consumption Is Enough to Support Most Activities

As you have learned, fat is an important energy source for both moderate physical activity and vigorous endurance training. When athletes reach a physically trained state, they are able to use more fat for energy; in other words, they become better "fat burners." This can also occur in people who are not athletes but who regularly participate in aerobic-type fitness activities. This training effect occurs for a number of reasons, including an increase in the number and activity of various enzymes involved in fat metabolism, improved ability of the muscles to store fat, and improved ability to extract fat from the blood for use during exercise. By using fat as a fuel, athletes can spare carbohydrate so they can use it during prolonged, intense training or competition.

Many athletes concerned with body weight and physical appearance believe they should eat less than 15% of their total energy intake as fat, but this is inadequate for vigorous activity and good health. Instead, a fat intake of 20% to 35% of total energy intake is generally recommended for athletes, with less than 10% of total energy intake as saturated fat. These same recommendations are put forth for non-athletes. Recall from Chapter 5 that fat provides not only energy but also fat-soluble vitamins and essential fatty acids that are critical to maintaining general health. If fat consumption is too low, inadequate levels of these can eventually prove detrimental to training and performance. Athletes who have chronic disease risk factors such as high blood lipids, high blood pressure, or unhealthful blood glucose levels should work with a physician to adjust their intake of fat and carbohydrate according to their health risks.

carbohydrate loading   Also known as glycogen loading. A process that involves altering training and carbohydrate intake so that muscle glycogen storage is maximized.

Many Athletes Have Increased Protein Needs

The protein intakes suggested for competitive athletes and moderately active people are given in Table 14.5. Let's pause a moment to explain the terminology used in the table:

- Competitive male and female endurance athletes are those individuals who train 5 to 7 days per week for more than an hour each day; many of these individuals may train for 3 to 6 hours per day. These athletes need significantly more protein than the current RDA of 0.8 g of protein per kg body weight.

- Resistance athletes focus on building and maintaining muscle mass and strength. Those who are already trained need less protein than those who are initiating training. Studies do not support the claim that consuming more than 2 g of protein per kilogram body weight improves protein synthesis, muscle strength, or performance.[12]

- Moderate-intensity endurance athletes are people exercising four to five times per week for 45 to 60 minutes each time; these individuals may compete in community races and other activities. Their protein needs are only modestly increased above the RDA.

- Recreational endurance athletes are people who exercise four to five times per week for 30 minutes at less than 60% of their maximal effort. These individuals have a protein need that is equal to or only slightly higher than the RDA.

As we mentioned earlier, most inactive people and many athletes in the United States consume more than enough protein to support their needs.[17] However, some athletes do not consume enough protein; these typically include individuals with very low energy intakes, vegetarians or vegans who do not consume high-protein food sources, and young athletes who are growing and are not aware of their higher protein needs.

In 1995, Dr. Barry Sears published *The Zone: A Dietary Road Map*, a book that claims numerous benefits of a high-protein, low-carbohydrate diet for athletes.[18] Although this book was published a number of years ago, many of the principles it espoused are still being recommended to both athletes and non-athletes today. As you learned in Chapter 6, low-carbohydrate, high-protein diets are quite popular, especially among people who want to lose weight (see Nutrition Debate in Chapter 13, pages 525–527). Unlike many of the current high-protein diets, the Zone Diet was developed and marketed specifically for competitive athletes. It recommends that athletes eat a 40–30–30 diet, or one composed of 40% carbohydrate, 30% fat, and 30% protein. Dr. Sears claims that high-carbohydrate diets impair athletic performance because of unhealthy effects of insulin. These claims have never been supported by research—in fact, many of Dr. Sears' claims are not consistent with human physiology. The primary problem with the Zone Diet for athletes is that it is too low in both energy and carbohydrate to support training and performance.

As described in Chapter 6, high-quality protein sources include lean meats, poultry, fish, eggs and egg whites, low-fat dairy products, legumes, and soy products. By following the Dietary Guidelines for Americans and meeting energy needs, people of all fitness levels

Table 14.5 Estimated Protein Requirements for Athletes

Group	Protein Requirements (grams per kg body weight)
Competitive male and female athletes	1.4–1.6
Moderate-intensity endurance athletes	1.2
Recreational endurance athletes	0.8–1.0
Football, power sports	1.4–1.7
Resistance athletes, weightlifters (early training)	1.5–1.7
Resistance athletes, weightlifters (steady-state training)	1.0–1.2

Data from: Tarnopolsky, M. 2006. Protein and amino acid needs for training and bulking up. In: Burke, L., and V. Deakin, eds. *Clinical Sports Nutrition,* 3rd ed. Sydney, Australia: McGraw-Hill, p. 109.

can consume more than enough protein without the use of supplements or specially formulated foods.

> ## Recap
>
> The type, intensity, and duration of activities a person participates in determine his or her nutrient needs. Carbohydrate needs may increase for some active people. In general, athletes should consume 45% to 65% of their total energy as carbohydrate. Carbohydrate loading involves altering physical training and the diet such that the storage of muscle glycogen is maximized. Active people use more fat than carbohydrates for energy because they experience an increase in the number and activity of the enzymes involved in fat metabolism, and they have an improved ability to store fat and extract it from the blood for use during exercise. A dietary fat intake of 20% to 35% is recommended for athletes, with less than 10% of total energy intake as saturated fat. Although protein needs can be higher for athletes, most people in the United States already consume more than twice their daily needs for protein.

Regular Exercise Increases Our Need for Fluids

A detailed discussion of fluid and electrolyte balance is provided in Chapter 9. In this chapter, we will briefly review some of the basic functions of water and its role during exercise.

Functions of Water

Water serves many important functions in the body. It is:

- A lubricant that bathes the tissues and cells
- A transport medium for nutrients, hormones, and waste products
- An important component of many chemical reactions, particularly those related to energy production
- A structural part of body tissues such as proteins and glycogen
- A vital component in temperature regulation; without adequate water, the body cannot cool properly through sweating, which can result in severe heat illness and even death.

Cooling Mechanisms

Heat production can increase fifteen to twenty times during heavy exercise! The primary way in which heat is dissipated is through sweating, which is also called **evaporative cooling.** When body temperature rises, more blood (which contains water) flows to the surface of the skin. Heat is carried in this way from the core of the body to the surface of the skin. By sweating, the water (and body heat) leaves our bodies and the air around us picks up the evaporating water from our skin, cooling our bodies.

Dehydration and Heat-Related Illnesses

Heat illnesses occur because when we exercise in the heat, our muscles and skin constantly compete for blood flow. When there is no longer enough blood flow to simultaneously provide adequate blood to our muscles and our skin, muscle blood flow takes priority and evaporative cooling is inhibited. Exercising in heat plus humidity is especially dangerous because whereas the heat dramatically raises body temperature, the high humidity inhibits evaporative cooling; that is, the environmental air is already so saturated with water that it is unable to absorb the water in sweat. Body temperature becomes dangerously high, and heat illness is likely. Exercise in environmental temperatures at or above 90°F is commonly associated with heat illnesses; heatstroke, a potentially fatal form of heat illness, is highly likely in environmental temperatures at or above 130°F.[19]

It is important to remember that dehydration significantly increases our risk for heat illnesses. The signs and symptoms of dehydration were introduced in Table 3.3 (page 100). In **Figure 14.13,** specific signs of dehydration during heavy exercise are listed.

Water is essential for maintaining fluid balance and preventing dehydration.

evaporative cooling Another term for sweating, which is the primary way in which we dissipate heat.

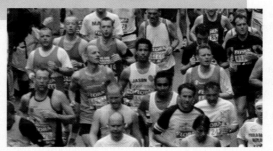

Symptoms of Dehydration During Heavy Exercise:

- Decreased exercise performance
- Increased level in perceived exertion
- Dark yellow or brown urine color
- Increased heart rate at a given exercise intensity
- Decreased appetite
- Decreased ability to concentrate
- Decreased urine output
- Fatigue and weakness
- Headache and dizziness

Figure 14.13 Symptoms of dehydration during heavy exercise.

Heat illnesses include heat syncope, heat cramps, heat exhaustion, and heatstroke. **Heat syncope** is dizziness that occurs when people stand for too long in the heat, and the blood pools in their lower extremities rather than fully supplying their brains. It can also occur when people stop suddenly after a race or stand suddenly from a lying position. **Heat cramps** are muscle spasms that occur during exercise or even several hours after strenuous exercise. They occur during times when sweat losses and fluid intakes are high, sodium intake is inadequate to replace these losses, and urine volume is low. These cramps generally are felt in the legs, arms, or abdomen after a person cools down from exercise. **Heat exhaustion** and **heatstroke** occur on a continuum, with unchecked heat exhaustion leading to heatstroke. Early signs of heat exhaustion include excessive sweating, weakness, nausea, dizziness, headache, and difficulty concentrating. As this condition progresses, the sweat response fails entirely. Thus, a cardinal sign that a person is progressing to heatstroke is hot, dry skin. Other signs include a rapid heart rate, vomiting, diarrhea, and a body temperature greater than or equal to 104°F. As consciousness becomes impaired, hallucinations and coma occur. It is critical that the person get proper medical care, or death can result.

Guidelines for Proper Fluid Replacement

How can we prevent dehydration and heat illnesses? Obviously, adequate fluid intake is critical before, during, and after exercise. Unfortunately, our thirst mechanism cannot be relied upon to signal when we need to drink. If we rely on our feelings of thirst, we will not consume enough fluid to support exercise.

General fluid replacement recommendations are based on maintaining body weight. As discussed in Chapter 9, athletes who are training and competing in hot environments should weigh themselves before and after the training session or event and should regain the weight lost over the subsequent 24-hour period. They should avoid losing more than 2% to 3% of body weight during exercise, as performance can be impaired with fluid losses as small as 1% of body weight.

Table 14.6 reviews guidelines for proper fluid replacement. For activities lasting less than 1 hour, plain water is generally adequate to replace fluid losses. However, for training and competition lasting longer than 1 hour in any weather, sports beverages containing carbohydrates and electrolytes are recommended. These beverages are also recommended for people who will not drink enough water because they don't like the taste. If drinking these beverages will guarantee adequate hydration, they are appropriate to use. For more specific information about sports beverages, refer to pages 354–355.

Drinking sports beverages during training and competition lasting more than 1 hour replaces fluid, carbohydrates, and electrolytes.

heat syncope Dizziness that occurs when people stand for too long in the heat or when they stop suddenly after a race or stand suddenly from a lying position; results from blood pooling in the lower extremities.

heat cramps Muscle spasms that occur several hours after strenuous exercise; most often occur when sweat losses and fluid intakes are high, urine volume is low, and sodium intake is inadequate.

heat exhaustion A heat illness that is characterized by excessive sweating, weakness, nausea, dizziness, headache, and difficulty concentrating. Unchecked heat exhaustion can lead to heatstroke.

heatstroke A potentially fatal heat illness that is characterized by hot, dry skin, rapid heart rate, vomiting, diarrhea, an increase in body temperature greater than or equal to 104°F, hallucinations, and coma.

Table 14.6 Guidelines for Fluid Replacement

Activity Level	Environment	Fluid Requirements (liters per day)
Sedentary	Cool	2–3
Active	Cool	3–6
Sedentary	Warm	3–5
Active	Warm	5–10

Before Exercise or Competition:

- Drink adequate fluids during the 24 hours before event; should be able to maintain body weight
- Slowly drink about 0.17 to 0.24 fl. oz per kg body weight of water or a sports drink at least 4 hours prior to exercise or event to allow time for excretion of excess fluid prior to event
- Slowly drink another 0.10 to 0.17 fl. oz per kg body weight about 2 hours before the event
- Consuming beverages with sodium and/or small amounts of salted snacks at a meal will help stimulate thirst and retain fluids consumed

During Exercise or Competition:

- Drink early and regularly throughout event to sufficiently replace all water lost through sweating
- Amount and rate of fluid replacement depend on individual sweating rate, exercise duration, weather conditions, and opportunities to drink
- Fluids should be cooler than the environmental temperature and flavored to enhance taste and promote fluid replacement

During Exercise or Competition That Lasts More Than 1 Hour:

- Fluid replacement beverage should contain 5–10% carbohydrate to maintain blood glucose levels; sodium and other electrolytes should be included in the beverage in amounts of 0.5–0.7 g of sodium per liter of water to replace the sodium lost by sweating

Following Exercise or Competition:

- Consume about 3 cups of fluid for each pound of body weight lost
- Fluids after exercise should contain water to restore hydration status, carbohydrates to replenish glycogen stores, and electrolytes (for example, sodium and potassium) to speed rehydration
- Consume enough fluid to permit regular urination and to ensure the urine color is very light or light yellow in color; drinking about 125–150% of fluid loss is usually sufficient to ensure complete rehydration

In General:

- Products that contain fructose should be limited, as these may cause gastrointestinal distress
- Caffeine and alcohol should be avoided, as these products increase urine output and reduce fluid retention
- Carbonated beverages should be avoided, as they reduce the desire for fluid intake due to stomach fullness

Data adapted from: Murray, R. 1997. Drink more! Advice from a world class expert. *ACSM's Health and Fitness Journal* 1:19–23; American College of Sports Medicine Position Stand. 2007. Exercise and fluid replacement. *Med. Sci. Sports Exerc.* 39(2):377–390; Casa, D. J., L. E. Armstrong, S. K. Hillman, S. J. Montain, R. V. Reiff, B. S. E. Rich, W. O. Roberts, and J. A. Stone. 2000. National Athletic Trainers' Association position statement: fluid replacement for athletes. *J. Athlet. Train.* 35:212–224.

Inadequate Intakes of Some Vitamins and Minerals Can Diminish Health and Performance

When individuals train vigorously for athletic events, their requirements for certain vitamins and minerals may be altered. Many highly active people do not eat enough food or a variety of foods that allows them to consume enough of these nutrients, yet it is imperative that active people do their very best to eat an adequate, varied, and balanced diet to try to meet the increased needs associated with vigorous training.

B-Vitamins

The B-complex vitamins are directly involved in energy metabolism (see pages 294–295). There is reliable evidence that the requirements of active people for thiamin, riboflavin, and vitamin B_6 may be slightly higher than the current RDA.[12, 17] However, these increased needs are easily met by consuming adequate energy and a lot of complex carbohydrates, fruits, and vegetables. Athletes and physically active people at risk for poor B-complex vitamin status are those who consume inadequate energy or who consume mostly refined carbohydrate foods such as soda pop and sugary snacks. Vegan athletes and active individuals may be at risk for inadequate intake of vitamin B_{12}; food sources enriched with this nutrient include soy and cereal products.

Calcium and the Female Athlete Triad

Calcium supports proper muscle contraction and ensures bone health (see pages 414–416). Calcium intakes are inadequate for most women in the United States, including both sedentary and active women. This is most likely due to the failure to consume foods that are high in calcium, particularly dairy products. Although vigorous training does not appear to directly increase our need for calcium, we need to consume enough calcium to support bone health. If we do not, stress fractures and severe loss of bone can result.

Some female athletes suffer from what is referred to as the female athlete triad (see Chapter 11, page 435 for more details). In this triad, nutritional inadequacies from insufficient energy intake and/or disordered eating cause irregularities in the menstrual cycle; these in turn cause hormonal disturbances that lead to a significant loss of bone mass. Thus, for female athletes, consuming the recommended amounts of calcium is critical. For female athletes who are physically small and consume lower energy intakes, calcium supplementation may be needed to meet current recommendations.

Iron

Iron is a part of the hemoglobin molecule and is critical for the transport of oxygen in the blood to the cells and working muscles. Iron also is involved in energy production. Research has shown that active individuals lose more iron in their sweat, feces, and urine than do inactive individuals, and that endurance runners lose iron when their red blood cells break down in their feet in response to the impact of running.[20] Female athletes and non-athletes lose more iron than male athletes because of menstrual blood losses, and females in general tend to eat less iron in their diet. Vegetarian athletes may also consume less iron. Thus, many athletes and active people are at higher risk of iron deficiency. Depending upon its severity, poor iron status can impair athletic performance and the ability to maintain regular physical activity.

Not all athletes suffer from iron deficiency. A phenomenon known as *sports anemia* was identified in the 1960s. Sports anemia is not true anemia, but a transient decrease in iron stores that occurs in some people at the start of an exercise program. It is also seen in some athletes who increase their training intensity. Exercise training increases the amount of water in the blood (called *plasma volume*); however, the amount of hemoglobin does not increase until later into the training period. Thus, the iron content in the blood appears to be low, but it is falsely depressed due to increases in plasma volume. Sports anemia, since it is not true anemia, does not affect performance.

The stages of iron deficiency are described on page 455. In general, it appears that physically active females are at relatively high risk of suffering from the first stage of iron depletion, in which iron stores are low.[21, 22] Because of this, it is suggested that blood tests of iron stores and monitoring of dietary iron intakes be part of routine healthcare for active females.[17] In some cases, iron needs cannot be met through the diet, and supplementation is necessary. Iron supplementation should be done with a physician's approval and proper medical supervision.

RECAP

Regular exercise increases fluid needs. Fluid is critical to cool internal body temperature and prevent heat illnesses. Dehydration is a serious threat during exercise in extreme heat and high humidity. Heat illnesses include heat syncope, heat cramps, heat exhaustion, and heatstroke. Active people may need more thiamin, riboflavin, and vitamin B_6 than inactive people. Exercise itself does not increase calcium needs, but most women, including active women, do not consume enough calcium. Some female athletes suffer from the female athlete triad, a condition that involves the interaction of low energy availability, osteoporosis, and amenorrhea. Many active individuals require more iron, particularly female athletes and vegetarian athletes.

Theo
Nutri-Case

"Ever since I did that cycling test in the fitness lab, I've been watching my carbohydrates. Lately, I've been topping 500 grams of carbs a day. But now I'm beginning to wonder, am I getting enough protein? I'm starting to feel really wiped out, especially after games. We've won four out of the last five games, and I'm giving it everything I've got, but today I was really dragging myself through practice. I'm eating about 180 grams of protein a day, but I think I'm going to try one of those protein powders they sell at my gym. I guess I just feel like, when I'm competing, I need some added insurance."

Theo's weight averages about 200 lb. Given what you've learned about the role of the energy nutrients in vigorous physical activity, what do you think might be causing Theo to feel "wiped out"? Would you recommend that Theo try the protein supplement? What other strategies might be helpful for him to consider?

Are Ergogenic Aids Necessary for Active People?

Many competitive athletes and even some recreationally active people continually search for that something extra that will enhance their performance. **Ergogenic aids** are substances used to improve exercise and athletic performance. For example, nutrition supplements can be classified as ergogenic aids, as can anabolic steroids and other pharmaceuticals. Interestingly, people report using ergogenic aids not only to enhance athletic performance but also to improve their physical appearance, prevent or treat injuries, treat diseases, and help them cope with stress. Some people even report using them because of peer pressure!

As you have learned in this chapter, adequate nutrition is critical to athletic performance and to regular physical activity, and products such as sports bars and beverages can assist athletes with maintaining their competitive edge. However, as we will explore shortly, many ergogenic aids are not effective, some are dangerous, and most are very expensive. For the average consumer, it is virtually impossible to track the latest research findings for these products. In addition, many have not been adequately studied, and unsubstantiated false claims surrounding them are rampant. How can you become a more educated consumer about ergogenic aids?

Lightsey and Attaway describe the most common deceptive practices used to sell ergogenic aids.[23] Although this article was published more than 15 years ago, the practices reviewed are still commonly used, and the article is as timely today as it was when it was published. These practices are identified and discussed in the accompanying Highlight box. You should also know that, in many cases, research done on a product is conducted by an inexperienced investigator. It is important that experienced, independent laboratories conduct some of the research, as they are more likely to be unbiased.

New ergogenic aids are available virtually every month, and keeping track of these substances is a daunting task. It is therefore not possible to discuss every available product in this chapter. However, a brief review of a number of currently popular ergogenic aids is provided.

Anabolic Products Are Touted as Muscle and Strength Enhancers

Many ergogenic aids are said to be **anabolic,** meaning that they build muscle and increase strength. Most anabolic substances promise to increase testosterone, which is the hormone associated with male sex characteristics and that increases muscle size and strength. Although some anabolic substances are effective, they are generally associated with harmful side effects.

ergogenic aids   Substances used to improve exercise and athletic performance.

anabolic   Refers to a substance that builds muscle and increases strength.

Highlight

Nine Deceptive Practices Used to Market Ergogenic Aids

1. **General misrepresentation of research:**
   - Published research is taken out of context or findings are applied in an unproven manner.
   - Claims that the product is university-tested may be true, but the investigator may be inexperienced or the manufacturer may control all aspects of the study.
   - Research may not have been done, but the company falsely claims it has been conducted.

2. **Company claims that research is currently being done:** Although many companies claim they are currently conducting properly controlled research, most are unable to provide specific information about this research.

3. **Company claims that research is not available for public review:** Consumers have a right to obtain proof about performance claims, and there is no rationale to support hiding research findings.

4. **Testimonials:** Celebrities who endorse a product may be doing so only for the money. Testimonials can also be faked and exaggerated. If the product does work for that person, the success may be due to the placebo effect. The placebo effect means that even though a product

has been proven to have no physiologic benefits, a person believes so strongly in the product that his or her performance improves. It is estimated that there is a 40% chance that any substance will enhance mental or physical performance through the placebo effect.

5. **Patents:** These are granted to indicate distinguishable differences among products. Patents do not indicate effectiveness or safety of a product and can be given without any research being done on a product.

6. **Inappropriately referenced research:**
   - References may include poorly designed and inadequately controlled studies.
   - The company may refer to research that was published in another country and is not accessible in the United States or may base claims on unsubstantiated rumors or unconfirmed reports.
   - The company may cite outdated research that has been proven wrong or fail to quote studies that do not support its claims.

7. **Media approaches:** Advertising modes include infomercials and mass-media marketing videos. Although the Federal Trade Commission (FTC) regulates false claims in advertising, products are generally investigated only if they pose significant danger to the public.

8. **Mail-order fitness evaluations:** Used to attract consumers to a company's products, most of these evaluations are not specific enough to be useful to the consumer, and their accuracy is highly questionable.

9. **Anabolic measurements:** Some companies perform in-house tests of hair and blood to give consumers information on protein balance. These tests are often provided only to sell their ergogenic products. The test results may be inaccurate or may indicate nutritional deficiencies that can be remedied with proper nutrition.

Data from: All information adapted from Lightsey, D. M., and J. R. Attaway. 1992. Deceptive tactics used in marketing purported ergogenic aids. *National Strength and Conditioning Association Journal* 14(2):26–31. Reprinted by permission of Alliance Communications Group, a division of Allen Press, Inc.

Anabolic Steroids

Anabolic steroids are testosterone-based drugs that have been used extensively by strength and power athletes. Anabolic steroids are known to be effective in increasing muscle size, strength, power, and speed. However, these products are illegal in the United States, and their use is banned by all major collegiate and professional sports organizations, in addition to both the U.S. and the International Olympic Committees. Proven long-term and irreversible effects of steroid use include infertility; early closure of the plates of the long bones resulting in permanent shortened stature; shriveled testicles, enlarged breast tissue (that can only be surgically removed), and other signs of "feminization" in men; enlarged clitoris, facial hair growth, and other signs of "masculinization" in women; increased risk of certain forms of cancer; liver damage; unhealthful changes in blood lipids; hypertension; severe acne; hair thinning or baldness; and depression, delusions, sleep disturbances, and extreme anger (so-called "roid rage").

Androstenedione and Dehydroepiandrosterone

Androstenedione ("andro") and dehydroepiandrosterone (DHEA) are precursors of testosterone. Manufacturers of these products claim that taking them will increase testosterone levels and muscle strength. Androstenedione became very popular after baseball player Mark McGuire claimed he used it during the time he was breaking home run records. A national survey found that, in 2002, about one of every forty high school seniors had used "andro" in the past year.[24] Contrary to popular claims, recent studies have found that neither androstenedione nor DHEA increases testosterone levels, and androstenedione has been shown to increase the risk of heart disease in men aged 35 to 65 years.[25] There are no studies that support the products' claims of improving strength or increasing muscle mass.

Gamma-Hydroxybutyric Acid

Gamma-hydroxybutyric acid, or GHB, has been promoted as an alternative to anabolic steroids for building muscle. The production and sale of GHB have never been approved in the United States; however, it was illegally produced and sold on the black market. For many users, GHB caused only dizziness, tremors, or vomiting, but others experienced severe side effects, including seizures. Many people were hospitalized and some died.

After GHB was banned, a similar product (gamma-butyrolactone, or GBL) was marketed in its place. This product was also found to be dangerous and was removed from the market. Recently, another replacement product called BD, or 1,4-butanediol, was banned because it has caused at least seventy-one deaths, with forty more under investigation. BD is an industrial solvent and is listed on ingredient labels as tetramethylene glycol, butylene glycol, or sucol-B. Side effects include wild, aggressive behavior; nausea; incontinence; and sudden loss of consciousness.

Creatine

Creatine is a supplement that has become wildly popular with strength and power athletes. Creatine, or creatine phosphate, is found in meat and fish and stored in our muscles. As described earlier in this chapter, we use creatine phosphate (or CP) to regenerate ATP. By taking creatine supplements, it is hypothesized that more CP is available to replenish ATP, which will prolong a person's ability to train and perform in short-term, explosive activities such as weight lifting and sprinting. Between 1994 and 2009, more than 1,700 research articles related to creatine and exercise in humans were published. Studies have shown that creatine does not enhance performance in aerobic-type events, but does enhance sprint performance in swimming, running, and cycling.[26–30] Other studies have shown that creatine increases the work performed and the amount of strength gained during resistance exercise.[28, 30, 31] Currently, creatine is not banned by any sports governing bodies, and many collegiate sports programs readily provide creatine supplements for their athletes.

In January 2001, the *New York Times* reported that the French government claimed that creatine use could lead to cancer.[32] The news spread quickly across national and international news organizations and over the Internet. These claims were found to be false, as there are absolutely no studies in humans that suggest an increased risk of cancer with creatine use. In fact, there are numerous studies that show an anticancer effect of creatine.[33, 34] Although side effects such as dehydration, muscle cramps, and gastrointestinal disturbances have been reported with creatine use, we have very little information on how long-term use of creatine impacts health. A recent study by Schilling and colleagues found that the incidence of muscle cramps, injuries, or other side effects was similar for athletes who had never used creatine as compared with those using creatine for up to 4 years.[35] Further research is needed to determine the effectiveness and safety of creatine use over prolonged periods of time.

Anabolic substances are often marketed to people wishing to increase muscle size, but many cause harmful side effects.

11. Write a plan for a weekly activity/exercise routine that does the following:
- meets your personal fitness goals
- is fun for you to do
- includes variety and consistency
- uses all components of the FIT principle
- includes a warm-up and cool-down period

12. Determine how many grams of carbohydrate, protein, and fat you need to consume daily to support the activity/exercise routine you described in the previous question.

13. You decide to start training for your school's annual marathon. After studying this chapter, which of the following preparation strategies would you pursue, and why?
- use of B-vitamin supplements
- use of creatine supplements
- use of sports beverages
- carbohydrate loading

14. Given what you have learned about Gustavo in the Nutri-Cases in previous chapters, would you advise him to begin a planned exercise program of low to moderate intensity? Why or why not? If so, what steps should he take before starting an exercise program?

15. Marisa and Conrad are students at the same city college. Marisa walks to and from school each morning from her home 7 blocks away. Conrad lives in a suburb 12 miles away and drives to school. Marisa, an early childhood education major, covers the lunch shift, 2 hours a day, at the college's day care center, cleaning up the lunchroom and supervising the children on the playground. Conrad, an accounting major, works in his department office 2 hours a day, entering data into computer spreadsheets. On weekends, Marisa and her sister walk downtown and go shopping. Conrad goes to the movies with his friends. Neither Marisa nor Conrad participates in sports or scheduled exercise sessions. Marisa has maintained a normal, healthful weight throughout the school year, but in the same period of time, Conrad has gained several pounds. Identify at least two factors that might play a role in Marisa's and Conrad's current weights.

Web Links

www.americanheart.org
American Heart Association
The "Healthy Lifestyle" section of this site has sections on health tools, exercise and fitness, healthy diet, managing your lifestyle, and more.

www.acsm.org
American College of Sports Medicine
Click on "Fit Society Page" under the "Inform" section for guidelines on healthy aerobic activity, calculating your exercise heart rate range, and the ACSM's Fit Society Page newsletter.

www.mypyramid.gov/pyramid/physical_activity.html
USDA MyPyramid Steps to a Healthier You
Visit this site to learn more about physical activity and how to find ways to incorporate more physical activity into your daily life.

www.webmd.com
WebMD Health
Visit this site to learn about a variety of lifestyle topics, including fitness and exercise.

www.hhs.gov
U.S. Department of Health and Human Services
Review this site for multiple statistics on health, exercise, and weight as well as information on supplements, wellness, and more.

http://win.niddk.nih.gov/publications/physical.htm
Weight-Control Information Network
Find out more about healthy fitness programs.

http://dietary-supplements.info.nih.gov/
NIH Office of Dietary Supplements
Look on this National Institutes of Health site to learn more about the health effects of specific nutritional supplements.

www.nal.usda.gov/fnic/etext/ds_ergogenic.html
Food and Nutrition Information Center
Visit this page for links to detailed information about ergogenic aids and sports nutrition.

http://nutrition.arizona.edu/new/
Nutrition Exercise Wellness
Check this University of Arizona site for information for athletes on nutrition, fluid intake, and ergogenic aids.

References

1. U.S. Department of Health and Human Services. 1996. *Physical Activity and Health: A Report of the Surgeon General.* Atlanta, GA: U.S. Department of Health and Human Services, Centers for Disease Control and Prevention, National Centers for Chronic Disease Prevention and Health Promotion.

2. Caspersen, C. J., K. E. Powell, and G. M. Christensen. 1985. Physical activity, exercise, and physical fitness: definitions and distinctions for heath-related research. *Public Health Rep.* 100:126–131.

3. Heyward, V. H. 2006. *Advanced Fitness Assessment and Exercise Prescription,* 5th ed. Champaign, IL: Human Kinetics.

4. Centers for Disease Control and Prevention. 2005. Adult participation in recommended levels of physical activity—United States, 2001 and 2003. *Morb. Mortal. Wkly. Rep.* 54(47):1208–1212.

5. Centers for Disease Control and Prevention. 2008. 1988–2007 No Leisure-Time Physical Activity Trend Chart. Available at www.cdc.gov/nccdphp/dnpa/physical/stats/leisure_time.htm.

6. U.S. Department of Health and Human Services. 2000. *Healthy People 2010* (Conference Edition, in Two Volumes). Washington, DC: U.S. Department of Health and Human Services.

7. Institute of Medicine, Food and Nutrition Board. 2002. *Dietary Reference Intakes for Energy, Carbohydrates, Fiber, Fat, Protein and Amino Acids (Macronutrients).* Washington, DC: The National Academy of Sciences.

8. Ettinger, W. H., B. S. Wright, and S. N. Blair. 2006. *Fitness After 50.* Champaign, IL: Human Kinetics.

9. Brooks, G. A. 2000. Intra- and extra-cellular lactate shuttles. *Med. Sci. Sports Exerc.* 32:790–799.

10. Gladden, L. B. 2000. Muscle as a consumer of lactate. *Med. Sci. Sports Exerc.* 32:764–771.

11. Tarnopolsky, M. 2006. Protein and amino acid needs for training and bulking up. In: Burke, L., and V. Deakin, eds. *Clinical Sports Nutrition,* 3rd ed. Sydney, Australia: McGraw-Hill, pp. 73–98.

12. American College of Sports Medicine, American Dietetic Association, and Dietitians of Canada. 2009. Nutrition and athletic performance. Joint position statement. *Med. Sci. Sports Exerc.* 41:709–731.

13. Burke, L. 2006. Nutrition for recovery after competition and training. In: Burke, L., and V. Deakin, eds. *Clinical Sports Nutrition,* 3rd ed. Sydney, Australia: McGraw-Hill, pp. 415–440.

14. Costill, D. L., W. M. Sherman, W. J. Fink, C. Maresh, M. Witten, and J. M. Miller. 1981. The role of dietary carbohydrates in muscle glycogen resynthesis after strenuous running. *Am. J. Clin. Nutr.* 34:1831–1836.

15. van Hall, G., S. M. Shirreffs, and J. A. L. Calbert. 2000. Muscle glycogen resynthesis during recovery from cycle exercise: No effect of additional protein ingestion. *J. Appl. Physiol.* 88:1631–1636.

16. Jentjens, R. L., L. J. C. van Loon, C. H. Mann, A. J. M. Wagenmakers, and A. E. Jeukendrup. 2001. Addition of protein and amino acids to carbohydrates does not enhance postexercise muscle glycogen synthesis. *J. Appl. Physiol.* 91:839–846.

17. Manore, M. M, N. L. Meyer, and J. L. Thompson. 2009. *Sports Nutrition for Health and Performance,* 2nd ed. Champaign, IL: Human Kinetics.

18. Sears, B. 1995. *The Zone: A Dietary Road Map.* New York: HarperCollins.

19. National Weather Service Forecast Office. 2006. Heat index. Available at www.crh.noaa.gov/pub/heat.php.

20. Weaver, C. M., and S. Rajaram. 1992. Exercise and iron status. *J. Nutr.* 122:782–787.

21. Haymes, E. M. 1998. Trace minerals and exercise. In: Wolinsky, I., ed. *Nutrition and Exercise and Sport.* Boca Raton, FL: CRC Press, pp. 1997–2218.

22. Haymes, E. M., and P. M. Clarkson. 1998. Minerals and trace minerals. In: Berning, J. R., and S. N. Steen, eds. *Nutrition and Sport and Exercise.* Gaithersburg, MD: Aspen Publishers, pp. 77–107.

23. Lightsey, D. M., and J. R. Attaway. 1992. Deceptive tactics used in marketing purported ergogenic aids. *Natl. Strength Cond. Assoc. J.* 14:26–31.

24. U.S. Department of Health and Human Services (HHS). 2004. News release. HHS launches crackdown on products containing andro. Available at www.hhs.gov/news/press/2004pres/20040311.html.

25. Broeder, C. E., J. Quindry, K. Brittingham, L. Panton, J. Thomson, S. Appakondu, K. Breuel, R. Byrd, J. Douglas, C. Earnest, C. Mitchell, M. Olson, T. Roy, and C. Yarlagadda. 2000. The Andro Project: Physiological and hormonal influences of androstenedione supplementation in men 35 to 65 years old participating in a high-intensity resistance training program. *Arch. Intern. Med.* 160:3093–3104.

26. Balsom, P. D., K. Söderlund, B. Sjödin, and B. Ekblom. 1995. Skeletal muscle metabolism during short duration high-intensity exercise: Influence of creatine supplementation. *Acta Physiol. Scand.* 1154:303–310.

27. Grindstaff, P. D., R. Kreider, R. Bishop, M. Wilson, L. Wood, C. Alexander, and A. Almada. 1997. Effects of creatine supplementation on repetitive sprint performance and body composition in competitive swimmers. *Int. J. Sport Nutr.* 7:330–346.

28. Kreider, R. B., M. Ferreira, M. Wilson, P. Grindstaff, S. Plisk, J. Reinardy, E. Cantler, and A. L. Almada. 1998. Effects of creatine supplementation on body composition, strength, and sprint performance. *Med. Sci. Sports Exerc.* 30:73–82.

29. Tarnopolsky, M. A., and D. P. MacLennan. 2000. Creatine monohydrate supplementation enhances high-intensity exercise performance in males and females. *Int. J. Sport Nutr. Exerc. Metab.* 10:452–463.

30. Kreider R., M. Ferreira, M. Wilson, and A. L. Almada. 1999. Effects of calcium beta-hydroxy-beta methylbutyrate (HMB) supplementation during resistance-training on markers of catabolism, body composition and strength. *Int. J. Sports Med.* 20(8):503–509.

31. Volek, J. S., N. D. Duncan, S. A. Mazzetti, R. S. Staron, M. Putukian, A. L. Gomez, D. R. Pearson, W. J. Fink, and W. J. Kraemer. 1999. Performance and muscle fiber adaptations to creatine supplementation and heavy resistance training. *Med. Sci. Sports Exerc.* 31:1147–1156.

32. Reuters. 2001. Creatine use could lead to cancer, French government reports. *New York Times,* January 25, www.nytimes.com.

33. Jeong, K. S., S. J. Park, C. S. Lee, T. W. Kim, S. H. Kim, S. Y. Ryu, B. H. Williams, R. L. Veech, and Y. S. Lee. 2000. Effects of cyclocreatine in rat hepatocarcinogenesis model. *Anticancer Res.* 20(3A):1627–1633.

34. Ara, G., L. M. Gravelin, R. Kaddurah-Daouk, and B. A. Teicher. 1998. Antitumor activity of creatine analogs produced by alterations in pancreatic hormones and glucose metabolism. *In Vivo* 12:223–231.

35. Schilling, B. K., M. H. Stone, A. Utter, J. T. Kearney, M. Johnson, R. Coglianese, L. Smith, H. S. O'Bryant, A. C. Fry, M. Starks, R. Keith, and M. E. Stone. 2001. Creatine supplementation and health variable: A retrospective study. *Med. Sci. Sports Exerc.* 33:183–188.

36. Anderson, M. E., C. R. Bruce, S. F. Fraser, N. K. Stepto, R. Klein, W. G. Hopkins, and J. A. Hawley. 2000. Improved 2000-meter rowing performance in competitive oarswomen after caffeine ingestion. *Int. J. Sport Nutr. Exerc. Metab.* 10:464–475.

37. Spriet, L. L., and R. A. Howlett. 2000. Caffeine. In: Maughan, R. J., ed. *Nutrition in Sport.* Oxford: Blackwell Science, pp. 379–392.

38. Bucci, L. 2000. Selected herbals and human exercise performance. *Am. J. Clin. Nutr.* 72:624S–636S.

39. Williams, M. H. 1998. *The Ergogenics Edge.* Champaign, IL: Human Kinetics.

40. Hawley, J. A. 2002. Effect of increased fat availability on metabolism and exercise capacity. *Med. Sci. Sports Exerc.* 34(9):1485–1491.

41. Heinonen, O. J. 1996. Carnitine and physical exercise. *Sports Med.* 22:109–132.

42. Vincent, J. B. 2003. The potential value and toxicity of chromium picolinate as a nutritional supplement, weight loss agent and muscle development agent. *Sports Med.* 33(3):213–230.

43. Pliml, W., T. von Arnim, A. Stablein, H. Hofmann, H. G. Zimmer, and E. Erdmann. 1992. Effects of ribose on exercise-induced ischaemia in stable coronary artery disease. *Lancet* 340(8818):507–510.

44. Earnest, C. P., G. M. Morss, F. Wyatt, A. N. Jordan, S. Colson, T. S. Church, Y. Fitzgerald, L. Autrey, R. Jurca, and A. Lucia. 2004. Effects of a commercial herbal-based formula on exercise performance in cyclists. *Med. Sci. Sports Exerc.* 36(3):504–509.

45. Hellsten, Y., L. Skadhauge, and J. Bangsbo. 2004. Effect of ribose supplementation on resynthesis of adenine nucleotides after intense intermittent training in humans. *Am. J. Physiol. Regul. Integr. Comp. Physiol.* 286:R182–R188.

46. Kreider, R. B., C. Melton, M. Greenwood, C. Rasmussen, J. Lundberg, C. Earnest, and A. Almada. 2003. Effects of oral D-ribose supplementation on anaerobic capacity and selected metabolic markers in healthy males. *Int. J. Sport Nutr. Exerc. Metab.* 13(1):76–86.

47. King, A. C., W. L. Haskell, C. B. Taylor, H. C. Kraemer, and R. F. DeBusk. 1991. Group- vs. home-based exercise training in healthy older men and women: A community-based clinical trial. *JAMA* 266:1535–1542.

48. Kohrt, W. M., M. T. Malley, A. R. Coggan, R. J. Spina, T. Ogawa, A. A. Ehsani, R. E. Bourey, W. H. Martin III, and J. O. Holloszy. 1991. Effects of gender, age, and fitness level on response of VO_{2max} to training in 60–71 yr olds. *J. Appl. Physiol.* 71:2004–2011.

49. LaCroix, A. Z., S. G. Leveille, J. A. Hecht, L. C. Grothaus, and E. H. Wagner. 1996. Does walking decrease the risk of cardiovascular disease hospitalizations and death in older adults? *J. Am. Geriatr. Soc.* 44:113–120.

50. Blair, S. N., H. W. Kohl III, C. E. Barlow, R. S. Paffenbarger Jr., L. W. Gibbons, and C. A. Macera. 1995. Changes in physical fitness and all-cause mortality: A prospective study of healthy and unhealthy men. *JAMA* 273:1093–1098.

51. Paffenbarger, R. S. Jr., R. T. Hyde, A. L. Wing, and C.-C. Hsieh. 1986. Physical activity, all-cause mortality, and longevity of college alumni. *N. Engl. J. Med.* 314:605–613.

52. Leon, A. S., J. Connett, D. R. Jacobs Jr., and R. Rauramaa. 1987. Leisure-time physical activity levels and risk of coronary heart disease and death: The Multiple Risk Factor Intervention Trial. *JAMA* 258:2388–2395.

53. Slattery, M. L., D. R. Jacobs Jr., and M. Z. Nichaman. 1989. Leisure-time physical activity and coronary heart disease death: The U.S. Railroad Study. *Circulation* 79:304–311.

54. Helmrich, S. P., D. R. Ragland, R. W. Leung, and R. S. Paffenbarger Jr. 1991. Physical activity and reduced occurrence of non-insulin-dependent diabetes mellitus. *N. Engl. J. Med.* 325:147–152.

How Much Physical Activity Is Enough?

Your aerobics instructor tells you to work out at your target heart rate for 20 minutes a day, whereas your doctor tells you to walk for half an hour three or four times a week. A magazine article exhorts you to work out to the point of exhaustion, while a new weight-loss book claims that you can be perfectly healthy without ever breaking a sweat. And as if these mixed messages about what constitutes "regular physical activity" weren't enough, a report from the Institute of Medicine (IOM), which contributed to the 2005 revision of the Dietary Guidelines for Americans, has inadvertently added to the confusion. In this report, it is recommended that Americans should be active 60 minutes per day to optimize health.[7] This message appears contradictory to the Surgeon General's report published in 1996, in which it was recommended that Americans need to accumulate 30 minutes of physical activity on most, if not all, days of the week to optimize health.[1]

The publication of the report by the Institute of Medicine resulted in an immediate firestorm of responses from various health organizations condemning the recommendations. A similar response greeted the publication in 2005 of the revised Dietary Guidelines for Americans, which included some of the Institute of Medicine recommendations. The primary concern of these organizations was that consumers would be confused about how much physical activity was enough and that this confusion would result in frustration and lead to people giving up on participating in any physical activity. Another concern was that 60 minutes of physical activity each day is too much to ask a population in which over half are already insufficiently active.

So how much activity is really enough? To try to answer this question, let's take a closer look at how the reports of the Surgeon General and Institute of Medicine differ. First, the Surgeon General's report considered data derived from two types of studies not used by the IOM: exercise training studies and population-based epidemiological studies. *Exercise training studies* involve taking individuals, putting them through a clearly defined training program, and assessing fitness and health outcomes. These studies consistently show that less fit and older individuals can significantly improve their cardiorespiratory fitness and reduce their risk for chronic diseases by participating in moderate levels of physical activity.[47, 48] In contrast, *population-based epidemiological studies* compare self-reports of physical activity and/or fitness to rates of illness and mortality.[49, 50] In other words, the direct effect of exercise training is not being assessed in these studies; instead, they assess only the relationship between level of physical activity/fitness and rates of disease and premature death. These studies show that unfit, sedentary people suffer from the highest rates of disease and premature mortality and that increased physical activity significantly correlates to decreased risks for chronic diseases and premature mortality.

One challenge highlighted in the Surgeon General's report was how to determine the exact dose of exercise needed to improve physical fitness and health. Although the authors of this report acknowledged that using epidemiological studies to determine this dose was problematic, they point to those studies indicating that expending an average of 150 kcal/day, which is equivalent to about

Older and less fit individuals can improve their health and physical fitness with moderate daily activity.

30 minutes of moderate physical activity per day, is associated with significant reductions in disease risk and premature mortality.[51–54] They therefore used this information to shape the recommendations put forth in the Surgeon General's report. It is important to emphasize that these recommendations were intended for individuals who are currently inactive. They were not intended to apply to individuals who are already doing more than 30 minutes of activity a day. In fact, the Surgeon General's report emphasizes that additional health and fitness benefits will result by doing more moderate-intensity physical activity or by substituting vigorous physical activities for those that are moderate in intensity.

In contrast, the Institute of Medicine based its physical activity recommendations on data derived from *doubly-labeled water studies*. These studies used doubly-labeled water to determine the energy expenditure associated with maintaining a healthful body weight, which was defined as a BMI of 18.5 to 25 kg/m^2. After reviewing a large number of studies that assessed energy expenditure and BMI, the Institute of Medicine concluded that participating in about 60 minutes of moderately intense physical activity per day will move people from a very sedentary to an active lifestyle and will allow them to maintain a healthful body weight.

Although this recommendation appears to be very different from that from the Surgeon General's report, and may seem unrealistic, the Institute of Medicine emphasizes that this recommendation includes all activities a person does above resting levels, including gardening, dog walking, housekeeping, and shopping.

So are these two recommendations really that different? Probably not. The Surgeon General's recommendation is based on associations among self-reported physical activity levels, physical fitness levels, and disease and mortality rates. Its report clearly states that 30 minutes per day,

There is no single exercise recommendation for everyone. The amount of daily physical activity you should participate in will be determined by your personal fitness goals.

most days of the week, is the minimum amount of physical activity recommended to improve physical fitness and optimize health. The Institute of Medicine's recommendation is based on studies that precisely determined an energy expenditure associated with a healthful body weight. Its report more clearly defines how much physical activity is needed to maintain a healthful weight and does not focus specifically on disease risk or premature mortality. Nutrition experts, exercise physiologists, and other healthcare professionals all recognize that weight loss and healthful weight maintenance are easier to achieve in people who do more physical activity each day, not less.

Critical Thinking Questions

- Do you think national health recommendations should advise average Americans to get 30 minutes of activity a day, or 60?

- Why or why not?

- Are population-wide recommendations even useful? For instance, how much physical activity is right for you?

To answer the last question, you should first identify your main goal.

- Do you want to improve your health?

- Are you interested in losing weight and keeping it off?

- Or is your goal to train for athletic competition?

Then consider your current state of health and fitness, present level of physical activity, personal interests, and the time you have available.

- Now, do you feel confident that you could identify the right amount of physical activity to meet your goal? Why or why not?

15 Food Safety and Technology: Impact on Consumers

Test Yourself | True or False?

1 | Each year, about 100,000 Americans are sickened and about 500 die as a direct result of eating food contaminated with germs or their toxins. **T** *or* **F**

2 | Freezing destroys any microorganisms that might be lurking in your food. **T** *or* **F**

3 | Mold is the most common cause of food poisoning. **T** *or* **F**

4 | Research has failed to show any nutritional advantage of organic foods. **T** *or* **F**

5 | Every food additive approved for use by food companies in the United States has been tested and proved safe. **T** *or* **F**

Test Yourself answers are located in the Chapter Review.

Chapter Objectives *After reading this chapter, you will be able to:*

1. Identify the types of microorganisms involved in food-borne illness, *pp. 583–588.*

2. Describe strategies for preventing food-borne illness at home, while eating out, and when traveling to other countries, *pp. 589–596.*

3. Explain the advantages and disadvantages of canning, pasteurization, use of preservatives, aseptic packaging, and irradiation to preserve foods, *pp. 597–600.*

4. Describe the process of genetic modification and discuss the potential risks and benefits as-

sociated with genetically modified organisms, *pp. 600–601* and *615–617.*

5. Debate the safety of food additives, including the role of the GRAS list, *pp. 602–604.*

6. Describe the process by which persistent organic pollutants accumulate in foods, *pp. 604–606.*

7. Discuss the benefits and safety concerns related to pesticides, *pp. 606–607.*

8. Explain the current system of labeling for organic foods, *p. 609.*

A nationwide food recall in early 2009 as a result of *Salmonella* contamination included hundreds of products made from peanuts.

I n late 2008, the United States Centers for Disease Control and Prevention (CDC) began conducting an epidemiologic assessment of a growing cluster of cases of food-borne illness due to infection with a microorganism called *Salmonella*. By early 2009, the total number of people infected had grown to 691 in forty-six states, plus a handful of individuals in Canada and other countries. Of these, more than 150 had to be hospitalized, and the infection was thought to have contributed to nine deaths. Detailed interviews conducted by the CDC revealed a likely association with consumption of peanut butter or peanut paste, granules, or meal produced by Peanut Corporation of America (PCA). Testing of samples of PCA's peanut butter revealed *Salmonella* contamination, and the United States Food and Drug Administration (FDA) issued an immediate advisory calling upon consumers to destroy any of over 400 recalled food products, including cookies, crackers, ice cream, snack bars, and even pet foods, that contained peanut products from PCA facilities. By spring of 2009, this had become one of the largest food recalls ever undertaken in the United States, yet within a few weeks, another nation-wide recall had begun, this time because of pistachios contaminated with *Salmonella*. As in the PCA case, the tainted pistachios has been used to manufacture a wide variety of products, including ice cream, cakes, cookies, and snack products at dozens of food companies. As news of the second outbreak broke, the CDC reported that, after decades of steady progress, the safety of the nation's food supply was no longer improving and, in the case of *Salmonella*, infections may be creeping upward.[1]

Every year in the United States, *Salmonella* infection, called salmonellosis, causes more than 40,000 reported illnesses, perhaps thirty times more unreported illnesses, and 400 deaths.[2] What's worse, *Salmonella* is just one of several microbial culprits responsible for millions of cases of food-borne illness in the United States annually.

Food-borne illness is a term generally used to encompass any symptom or illness that arises from ingesting food or water that contains an infectious agent or toxic substance. Food-borne illness is commonly called *food poisoning*. According to the CDC, approximately 76 million Americans report experiencing food-borne illness each year. It is estimated that over half the population of the United States have had symptoms of food-borne illness without ever knowing or reporting it. The people most at risk of serious consequences from food-borne illness include:

- Developing fetuses, infants, and young children, whose immune systems are still immature
- The very old and the frail elderly, whose immune systems may be compromised
- People with chronic illnesses such as diabetes
- People with acquired immunodeficiency syndrome (AIDS)
- People who are receiving immune-system suppressing drugs, such as transplant recipients and cancer patients

Of those afflicted by food-borne illness, 300,000 are hospitalized and 5,000 die each year.[3] Although these statistics may seem frightening, most experts consider our food supply safe. That's partly because not all cases of food contamination make all people sick; in fact, even virulent strains cause illness in only a small percentage of people. In the PCA *Salmonella* case, although more than 500 people became ill, thousands are assumed to have eaten the tainted products. Moreover, modern science and technology have given us a wide array of techniques to preserve foods. We discuss these later in this chapter. Finally, food safety in the United States is monitored by several government agencies. In addition to the CDC and the FDA mentioned earlier, the United States Department of Agriculture (USDA) and the Environmental Protection Agency (EPA) monitor and regulate food production and preservation. Together, these agencies help to set standards to ensure the safety of our food supply. Information about these agencies and how to access them is given in Table 15.1.

Despite these safeguards, food-borne illness is emerging as a major public health issue for two key reasons. First, more foods are mass-produced than ever before, with a combination of ingredients from a much greater number of sources, including fields, feedlots, and a

food-borne illness   An illness transmitted through food or water, either by an infectious agent, a poisonous substance, or a protein that causes an immune reaction.

Table 15.1 Government Agencies That Regulate Food Safety

Name of Agency	Year Established	Role in Food Regulations	Web Site
U.S. Department of Agriculture (USDA)	1785	Oversees safety of meat, poultry, and eggs sold across state lines. Also regulates which drugs can be used to treat sick cattle and poultry.	www.usda.gov
U.S. Food and Drug Administration (FDA)	1862	Regulates food standards of all food products (except meat, poultry, and eggs) and bottled water. Regulates food labeling and enforces pesticide use as established by EPA.	www.fda.gov
Centers for Disease Control and Prevention (CDC)	1946	Works with public health officials to promote and educate the public about health and safety. Able to track information needed in identifying food-borne illness outbreaks.	www.cdc.gov
Environmental Protection Agency (EPA)	1970	Regulates use of pesticides and which crops they can be applied to. Establishes standards for water quality.	www.epa.gov

variety of processing facilities all over the world. These various sources can remain hidden not only to consumers but even to food companies using the ingredients. Contamination can occur at any point, and when it does, it can be difficult to trace. For example, in the PCA outbreak, many of the manufacturers of the recalled cookies and other products could not identify the source of their peanut ingredients.

Second, federal oversight has decreased: 35 years ago, the FDA inspected about half of the nation's food-processing facilities annually. By 2008, the inspection rate had dropped below 5%. Not surprisingly, in the same year, the CDC reported that there had been little progress in reducing the incidence of food-borne illness during the previous 4 years.[4] In 2009, calling the government's failure to inspect 95% of food-processing plants "a hazard to public health," President Barack Obama announced the creation of a Food Safety Working Group to foster coordination across federal agencies, sponsor changes in food-safety laws, improve enforcement of these laws, and increase inspections.[5]

In this chapter, we discuss how contaminants enter our food supply and describe some simple ways to protect yourself from getting sick. We also provide information about food spoilage and food preservation, including information on new techniques such as aseptic packaging and irradiation that increase the shelf life of many foods. Finally, we discuss the effect of various chemicals commonly used in food production, from food additives to pesticides to growth hormones. Whether your food comes from South America, a corporate farm, a local organic grower, or your own backyard, you'll learn about the safeguards that must be in place at every step from field to table to ensure food safety.

What Causes Food-Borne Illness?

Microorganisms (commonly called microbes) or their toxic by-products cause most cases of food-borne illness. However, as discussed later in the chapter (page 604), chemical residues in foods can also cause illness.

Food-Borne Illness Is Commonly Caused by Microorganisms or Their Toxins

Two types of food-borne illness are common: *Food infections* result from the consumption of food containing living microorganisms, whereas *food intoxications* result from consuming food in which microbes have secreted poisonous substances called *toxins*.[6]

Several Types of Microorganisms Contaminate Foods

The microbes that most commonly cause food infections are bacteria and viruses; however, other tiny organisms and non-living particles can also contaminate foods.

According to the CDC, the majority of food infections are caused by **bacteria** (Table 15.2).[3] Bacteria are microorganisms that lack a true nucleus and have a chemical

bacteria Microorganisms that lack a true nucleus and have a chemical called peptidoglycan in their cell walls.

Table 15.2 Common Bacterial Causes of Food-Borne Illness

Bacteria	Incubation Period	Duration	Symptoms	Foods Most Commonly Affected	Usual Source of Contamination	Steps for Prevention
Campylobacter jejuni	1–7 days	7–10 days	Fever Headache and muscle pain followed by diarrhea (sometimes bloody) Nausea Abdominal cramps	Raw and under-cooked meat, poultry, or shellfish Raw eggs Cake icing Untreated water Unpasteurized milk	Intestinal tracts of animals and birds Raw milk Untreated water and sewage sludge	Only drink pasteurized milk Cook foods properly Avoid cross-contamination
Salmonella (more than 2,300 types)	12–24 hours	4–7 days	Diarrhea Abdominal pain Chills Fever Vomiting Dehydration	Raw or undercooked eggs Undercooked poultry and meat Raw milk and dairy products Seafood Fruits and vegetables	Intestinal tract and feces of poultry *Salmonella enteritidis* in raw shell eggs	Cook foods thoroughly Avoid cross-contamination Use sanitary practices
Escherichia coli (0157:H7 and other strains that can cause human illness)	2–4 days	5–10 days	Diarrhea (may be bloody) Abdominal cramps Nausea Can lead to kidney and blood complications	Contaminated water Raw milk Raw or rare ground beef, sausages Unpasteurized apple juice or cider Uncooked fruits and vegetables	Intestinal tracts of cattle Raw milk Unchlorinated water	Thoroughly cook meat Avoid cross-contamination
Clostridium botulinum	12–36 hours	1–8 days	Nausea Vomiting Diarrhea Fatigue Headache Dry mouth Double vision Muscle paralysis (droopy eyelids) Difficulty speaking and swallowing Difficulty breathing	Improperly canned or vacuum-packed food Meats Sausage Fish Garlic in oil Honey	Widely distributed in nature Soil, water, on plants and in intestinal tracts of animals and fish Grows only in little or no oxygen	Properly can foods following recommended procedures Cook foods properly Children under 16 months should not consume raw honey
Staphylococcus	1–6 hours	2–3 days	Severe nausea and vomiting Abdominal cramps Diarrhea	Custard- or cream-filled baked goods Ham Poultry Dressing Gravy Eggs Mayonnaise-based salads and sandwiches Cream sauces	Human skin Infected cuts Pimples Noses and throats	Refrigerate foods Use sanitary practices
Shigella (more than 30 types)	12–50 hours	2 days–2 weeks	Bloody and mucus-containing diarrhea Fever Abdominal cramps Chills Vomiting	Contaminated water Salads Milk and dairy products	Human intestinal tract Rarely found in other animals	Use sanitary practices

Table 15.2 Common Bacterial Causes of Food-Borne Illness

Bacteria	Incubation Period	Duration	Symptoms	Foods Most Commonly Affected	Usual Source of Contamination	Steps for Prevention
Listeria monocytogenes	2 days–3 weeks	None reported	Fever Muscle aches Nausea Diarrhea Headache, stiff neck, confusion, loss of balance, or convulsions can occur if infection spreads to nervous system Infections during pregnancy can lead to miscarriage or stillbirth, premature delivery, or infection of newborn	Uncooked meats and vegetables Soft cheeses Lunch meats and hot dogs Unpasteurized milk	Intestinal tract and feces of animals Soil and manure used as fertilizer Raw milk	Thoroughly cook all meats Wash raw vegetables before eating Keep uncooked meats separate from vegetables and cooked foods Avoid unpasteurized milk or foods made from unpasteurized milk People at high risk should: • not eat hot dogs or lunch meats unless they are reheated until steaming hot • avoid getting fluid from hot dog packages on foods, utensils, and surfaces • wash hands after handling hot dogs or lunch meats • avoid eating soft cheeses such as feta, Brie, and Camembert • avoid eating refrigerated smoked seafood unless it is cooked

Data from: Iowa State University Extension, Food Safety and Quality Project. 2000. Safe food: It's your job too! Available at www.extension.iastate.edu/foodsafety/Lesson/?CFID=2587460&CFTOKEN=69223455. U.S. Food and Drug Administration (FDA). How can I prevent foodborne illness? Available at www.cfsan.fda.gov/~dms/qa-topfd.html. Centers for Disease Control and Prevention (CDC), Division of Bacterial and Mycotic Diseases. Disease information, foodborne illness. Available at www.cdc.gov/ncidod/dbmd/diseaseinfo/foodborneinfections_g.htm.

called peptidoglycan in their cell walls. Of the several species involved, *Campylobacter jejuni* and *Salmonella* are thought to be the most common culprits, causing millions of cases each year in the United States (**Figure 15.1**). Most cases result from eating foods or drinking milk or water contaminated with infected animal feces. Infection with *Campylobacter jejuni* causes fever, cramping, abdominal pain, and diarrhea that may be bloody.[7] Salmonellosis, the disease caused by eating food contaminated by *Salmonella*, causes diarrhea, nausea, and vomiting, and cells of some strains of *Salmonella* can perforate the intestines and infect the blood.[2] The Highlight box on page 587 discusses a particular strain of *Salmonella* that causes a food-borne disease called *typhoid fever* and its most famous host.

Although bacteria are the primary cause of food infections, some food-borne **viruses** also cause disease. Viruses are infectious agents that are much smaller than bacteria, lack independent metabolism, and are incapable of growth or reproduction apart from living cells. The hepatitis A virus can contaminate raw produce and cause liver damage. Hepatitis E also damages the liver and is fatal in about 20% of pregnant women. The hepatitis A and E viruses typically contaminate foods during harvesting, production, or preparation if work areas are unclean or workers have poor personal hygiene. In terms of sheer numbers, the rotaviruses are among the most serious: In the United States, they cause about 50,000 cases of severe diarrhea in children each year, and in developing nations, they are responsible for about 1 million childhood deaths. The Norwalk virus, which was identified after an epidemic in Norwalk, Ohio, can contaminate water supplies and food in contact with the contaminated water, causing diarrhea, nausea, and vomiting.

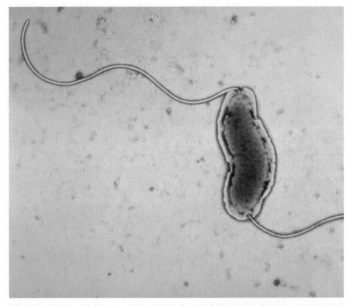

Figure 15.1 The bacteria called *Campylobacter jejuni* causes more than 2 million cases of food infection each year in the United States.

viruses A group of infectious agents that are much smaller than bacteria, lack independent metabolism, and are incapable of growth or reproduction apart from living cells.

Hooks   Sucker

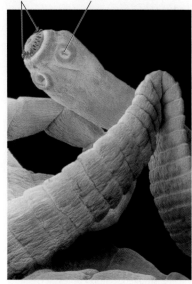

Figure 15.2 Tapeworms have long, worm-like bodies and hooks and suckers, which help them to attach to human tissues.

Figure 15.3 Molds rarely cause human illness, in part because they look so unappealing that we throw the food away.

helminth Multicellular microscopic worm.

parasite A microorganism that simultaneously derives benefit from and harms its host.

fungi Plant-like spore-forming organisms that can grow either as single cells or multicellular colonies.

prion An infectious, self-replicating protein.

toxin Any harmful substance; specifically, a chemical produced by a microorganism that harms tissues or causes harmful immune responses.

Helminths, commonly called worms, include tapeworms, flukes, and roundworms (**Figure 15.2**). These microbes release their eggs into the environment, such as in vegetation or water. Animals, most commonly cattle, pigs, or fish, then consume the contaminated matter. The eggs hatch inside their host, and larvae develop in the host's tissue. The larvae can survive in the flesh long after the host is killed for food. Thoroughly cooking beef, pork, or fish destroys the larvae. In contrast, people who eat contaminated meat or fish either raw or undercooked consume living larvae, which then mature into adult worms in their small intestine. Some worms cause mild symptoms such as nausea and diarrhea, but others can grow large enough to cause intestinal obstruction and some can even cause death.

A **parasite** is a microorganism that simultaneously derives benefit from and harms its host. A parasite known as *Giardia intestinalis* (or *Giardia lamblia*) causes a diarrheal illness called *giardiasis. Giardia* lives in the intestines of infected animals and humans, and it is passed into the environment from their stools. It is one of the most common causes of waterborne disease in humans in the United States. People typically consume *Giardia* by putting something in their mouth that has come into contact with the stool of an infected person or animal, by swallowing contaminated water (this includes water in lakes, streams, rivers, swimming pools, hot tubs, or fountains), or by eating uncooked food contaminated with *Giardia.* Symptoms include diarrhea, loose or watery stools, stomach cramps, and upset stomach, but some people show no symptoms. The symptoms usually begin within 1 to 2 weeks of being infected and generally last 2 to 6 weeks. Symptoms may last longer in some people.

Fungi are plant-like spore-forming organisms that can grow either as single cells or multicellular colonies. Two types of fungi are yeasts, which are globular, and molds, which are long and thin. Growths of these microbes on foods rarely cause food infection. This is due in part to the fact that very few species of fungi cause serious disease in people with healthy immune systems, and those that do cause disease in humans are not typically food-borne.[6] In addition, unlike bacterial growth, which is invisible and often tasteless, fungal growth typically makes food look and taste so unappealing that we immediately discard it (**Figure 15.3**).

A food-borne illness that has had front-page exposure in recent years is mad cow disease, or *bovine spongiform encephalopathy* (*BSE*). Cattle contract this disease from eating feed contaminated with tissue and blood from other infected animals. First discovered in the early 1980s in Britain, this neurologic disorder is caused by a **prion,** a proteinaceous infectious particle that is self-replicating. Prions are normal proteins of animal tissues that can misfold and become infectious. When they do, they can transform other normal proteins into abnormally shaped prions until they eventually cause illness. The human form of BSE can develop in people who consume contaminated meat or tissue. For more information, check out the Highlight "Mad Cow Disease—What's the Beef?" on page 234.

Some Microorganisms Release Toxins

The microbes just discussed cause illness by directly infecting and destroying body cells. In contrast, other bacteria and fungi secrete chemicals called **toxins** that are responsible for serious and even life-threatening illnesses. These toxins bind to body cells and can cause a variety of symptoms such as diarrhea, vomiting, organ damage, convulsions, and paralysis. Toxins can be categorized depending on the type of cell they bind to; the two primary types of toxins associated with food-borne illness are neurotoxins, which damage the nervous system and can cause paralysis, and enterotoxins, which target the gastrointestinal system and generally cause severe diarrhea and vomiting.

One of the most common and deadly toxins is produced by the bacteria *Clostridium botulinum.* The botulism toxin blocks nerve transmission to muscle cells and causes paralysis, including of the muscles required for breathing. Common sources of contamination are split or pierced bulging cans, foods improperly canned at home, and raw honey.

Some fungi produce poisonous chemicals called *mycotoxins.* (The prefix *myco-* means "fungus.") These toxins are typically found in grains stored in moist environments. In some

Highlight

How Typhoid Mary Earned Her Place in History

"Typhoid Mary" is a name commonly given to someone who has a contagious disease, but not many people know much about the real Typhoid Mary, an Irish immigrant named Mary Mallon. In 1868, Mallon came to the United States and found work as a cook. She first came to the attention of health officials after working for the Warren family at their summer home on Oyster Bay, Long Island. Soon after settling in for a summer vacation, one of the children became ill with typhoid fever, followed by her mother, a sister, and three of the hired help.

Typhoid fever's symptoms include a high fever (104°F) and continuous headaches, followed by diarrhea. It is caused by *Salmonella typhi* and is passed through food and water contaminated by an infected person's feces. An examination of the Warren family's outbreaks caused the public health investigator to stumble across Mary Mallon's employment history, which revealed that she had worked at seven previous jobs in which twenty-two people had contracted typhoid fever, with one death, after Mary began cooking for them.[8] Mary was apprehended and taken to a local hospital where samples from her stool and gallbladder tested positive for *S. typhi*. She had no symptoms; and so she became the United States' first "healthy carrier," a person who seems healthy but carries a contagious form of a disease that

Working as a cook, Mary Mallon, also known as Typhoid Mary, caused more than fifty outbreaks of typhoid.

can infect others. Indeed, some people can have such a weak case of typhoid fever that they never know they were infected. Unfortunately, no one ever explained to Mary how she could be a "healthy carrier," and all her life she resisted the designation.

Mary was then sent to North Brother Island, part of the Riverside Hospital's facilities, in the East River, New York, to live in isolation. Mary believed she was unfairly persecuted and sued the health department. The judgment was found in favor of the health department, and Mary stayed on North Brother Island for another year, until a new health commissioner decided to release Mary on the condition that she never work as a cook again. Now using the pseudonym Mrs. Brown, Mary violated the conditions of her parole and returned to employment as a cook. Five years after her release from North Brother Island, she caused another outbreak of typhoid fever at the Sloan Maternity Hospital in Manhattan. This time, twenty-five people became ill, two of whom died. When it was discovered that Mrs. Brown was really Mary Mallon, she was immediately sent back to confinement where she lived out the remainder of her life. In all, it is believed that Typhoid Mary was the cause of fifty-three outbreaks, including the 1903 Ithaca, New York, epidemic in which 1,400 people were infected, including three deaths.[9]

instances, moist conditions in the field encourage fungi to reproduce and release their toxins on the surface of growing crops. Long-term consumption of mycotoxins can cause organ damage or cancer, and they can be fatal if consumed in large doses. A mycotoxin called *aflatoxin* is produced by the mold *Aspergillus flavus*. Aflatoxin has been associated with peanuts and other crops and, if ingested, can cause illness in livestock and humans.

Some Toxins Occur Independently of Microorganisms

Some toxins develop in foods independently of microorganisms. For example, a highly visible fungus that causes food intoxication is the poisonous mushroom. Most mushrooms are not toxic, but a few, such as the deathcap mushroom (*Amanita phalloides*), can be fatal.

Figure 15.4   Some mushrooms, such as this fly agaric, contain toxins that can cause illness or even death.

Sea bass may look appealing, but like several other large predatory tropical fish, it can be contaminated with a high concentration of marine toxins.

Some poisonous mushrooms are quite colorful (**Figure 15.4**), a fact that helps to explain why the victims of mushroom poisoning are often children.[6]

Marine toxins are naturally occurring chemicals that can contaminate certain seafood. When humans consume the seafood, which typically looks, smells, and tastes normal, illness results.[10] Ciguatoxins are among the most common marine toxins. They are produced by microscopic sea plants called *dinoflagellates*, which are consumed by small fish. The toxins become progressively more concentrated as larger fish eat these small fish, and high concentrations can be present in grouper, sea bass, snapper, and a number of other large fish from tropical regions. Symptoms of ciguatoxin poisoning include nausea, vomiting, diarrhea, headache, itching, a "pins-and-needles" feeling, and even nightmares or hallucinations, but the illness is rarely fatal and typically resolves within a few weeks.[10]

Potatoes that have turned green contain the toxin solanine, which forms during the greening process. The green color is actually due to the pigment chlorophyll, which forms when the potatoes are exposed to light and is harmless. Although the production of solanine occurs simultaneously with the production of chlorophyll, the two processes are separate and unrelated.[11] There is the potential for toxicity from consuming potatoes with a very high solanine content. Because solanine formation occurs near the potato's skin, the green areas can be cut away to remove any toxins. A good guide is to taste a small piece of the potato after the green areas have been removed. If the potato tastes bitter, then throw it away. If in doubt, or if serving the potato to someone with allergies or compromised immunity, you should also discard the potato. You can avoid the greening of potatoes by storing them for only short periods in a dark cupboard or brown paper bag in a cool area. Wash the potato to expose its color, and cut away and discard any green areas. Cooked potatoes cannot turn green or produce solanine, but cooking green potatoes does not remove the chlorophyll or solanine that is formed prior to cooking.

The Body Responds to Contaminated Foods with Acute Illness

Many food-borne microbes are killed in the mouth by antimicrobial enzymes in saliva or in the stomach by hydrochloric acid. Any microbe that survives these chemical assaults will usually trigger vomiting and/or diarrhea as the gastrointestinal tract attempts to expel the offender. Simultaneously, the white blood cells of the immune system will be activated, and a generalized inflammatory response will cause the person to experience nausea, fatigue, fever, and muscle cramps. Depending on the state of one's health, the precise microbe involved, and the number of microbes ingested, the symptoms can range from mild to severe, including double vision, loss of muscle control, and excessive or bloody diarrhea. As noted earlier, some cases, if left untreated, can result in death.

To diagnose a food-borne illness, a specimen must be obtained and cultured. This means the specimen is analyzed in a laboratory setting in which the offending microorganisms are grown in a specific chemical medium. Stool (fecal) cultures are usually analyzed, especially if diarrhea is a symptom. Blood is cultured if the patient has a high fever. A physician who suspects that a patient is suffering from a food-borne illness will take a detailed history including a 24-hour dietary recall. Treatment usually involves keeping the person hydrated and comfortable, as most food-borne illness tends to be self-limiting; the person's vomiting and/or diarrhea, though unpleasant, serve to rid the body of the offending microbe. In severe illnesses such as botulism, the patient's intestinal tract will be flushed repeatedly to remove the microbe, and antibodies will be injected to neutralize its deadly toxin.

In the United States, all confirmed cases of food-borne illness must be reported to the state health department, which in turn reports these illnesses to the CDC in Atlanta, Georgia. The CDC monitors its reports for indications of epidemics of food-borne illness and assists local and state agencies in controlling such outbreaks.

Certain Conditions Help Microorganisms Multiply in Foods

Given the correct environmental conditions, microorganisms can thrive in many types of food. Four factors affect the survival and reproduction of food microorganisms:

- *Temperature.* Many microorganisms capable of causing human illness thrive at warm temperatures, from about 40°F to 140°F (4°C to 60°C). You can think of this range of temperatures as the **danger zone.** These microorganisms can be destroyed by thoroughly heating or cooking foods, and their reproduction can be slowed by refrigeration and freezing. We identify safe cooking and food-storage temperatures later in this chapter.
- *Humidity.* Many microorganisms require a high level of moisture, and thus foods like boxed dried pasta do not make suitable microbial homes, though cooked pasta left at room temperature would prove hospitable.
- *Acidity.* Most microorganisms have a preferred range of acidity, or pH, in which they thrive. For instance, *Clostridium botulinum* thrives in alkaline environments. It cannot grow or produce its toxin in acidic environments, so the risk of botulism is decreased in citrus fruits, pickles, and tomato-based foods. In contrast, alkaline foods such as fish and low-acid vegetables are a magnet for *C. botulinum.*
- *Oxygen content.* Many microorganisms require oxygen to function; thus, food-preservation techniques that remove oxygen, such as industrial canning and bottling, keep foods safe for consumption. Because *C. botulinum* thrives in an oxygen-free environment, the canning process heats foods to an extremely high temperature to destroy this organism.

In addition, microorganisms need an entryway into a food. Just as our skin protects our bodies from microbial invasion, the peels, rinds, and shells of many foods seal off access to the nutrients within. Eggshells are a good example of a natural food barrier. Once such a barrier is removed, however, the food loses its primary defense against contamination.

Peels protect foods against microbes.

RecaP

Food infections result from the consumption of food containing living microorganisms, such as bacteria, whereas food intoxications result from consuming food in which microbes have secreted toxins. Some foods develop toxins independently of microbes. The body has several defense mechanisms, such as saliva, stomach acid, vomiting, diarrhea, and the inflammatory response, that help rid us of offending microorganisms or their toxins. In order to reproduce in foods, microbes require a precise range of temperature, humidity, acidity, and oxygen content.

How Can Food-Borne Illness Be Prevented?

Foods of animal origin are most commonly associated with food-borne illness. These include not only raw meat, poultry, and fish, but also eggs, shellfish, and unpasteurized milk. Fruits and vegetables can also cause problems when they are consumed unwashed and raw. For example, in 2006, more than 200 people became ill and three died after eating raw spinach contaminated with *E. coli*, and this was quickly followed by an outbreak of salmonellosis traced to fresh tomatoes.[12] So how can you protect yourself when eating foods of animal origin and fresh fruits and vegetables? Here, we discuss food safety tips for when you're preparing foods at home, eating out, or traveling to other countries.

When preparing foods at home, you can prevent food-borne illness by following four basic rules: clean, separate, chill, and cook (**Figure 15.5**):

1. Clean. Wash your hands and kitchen surfaces often.
2. Separate. Keep foods separated to prevent **cross-contamination**—that is, the spread of bacteria or other microbes from one food to another. This commonly occurs when

Spinach was pulled from supermarket shelves during an *E. coli* outbreak in 2006.

danger zone Range of temperature at which many microorganisms capable of causing human illness thrive; about 40°F to 140°F (4°C to 60°C).

cross-contamination Contamination of one food by another via the unintended transfer of microbes through physical contact.

FIGHT BAC!

CLEAN
Wash hands
and surfaces
often.

SEPARATE
Don't cross-contaminate.

CHILL
Refrigerate promptly.

COOK
Cook to proper
temperatures.

Keep Food Safe From Bacteria™

Figure 15.5   The FightBAC! logo is the food safety logo of the U.S. Department of Agriculture.

Washing dishes, utensils, and cutting boards with hot soapy water and sanitizing with a bleach solution reduces the chances for food contamination.

raw, unwashed foods are cut on the same cutting board or served together on the same plate.

3. Chill. Refrigerate or freeze foods to prevent microbes from growing.

4. Cook. Cook foods to their proper temperatures.

Each of these rules is discussed in detail in the following sections.

Wash Your Hands and Kitchen Surfaces Often

One of the easiest and most effective ways to prevent food-borne illness is to wash your hands both before and after preparing food. Scrub for at least 20 seconds with gentle soap under warm running water (sing "Happy Birthday" or say the ABC's to time yourself). Hot water is too harsh: It causes the surface layer of the skin to break down, increasing the risk that microbes will be able to penetrate your skin. Pay special attention to the areas underneath your fingernails and between your fingers. Also, it's a good idea to remove rings and bracelets while cooking, as they can harbor bacteria. To prevent cross-contamination, always wash your hands after working with each raw food and before progressing to the next one.

A clean area and tools are also essential in reducing cross-contamination. Wash utensils, containers, and cutting boards in the dishwasher or with hot soapy water before and after contact with food. If a cutting board, plate, countertop, or other surface has held raw meat, poultry, or seafood, sanitize it with a solution of 1 teaspoon of chlorine bleach to 1 quart of water, or use a commercial kitchen cleaning agent.[13] It's also important to wash utensils, faucets, cabinet knobs, countertops, or other areas you have touched. Rinse, then air dry or dry with fresh paper towels. For cutting foods, use a nonporous, smooth plastic or stone cutting board because porous wood and scratched plastic can hold juices and harbor bacteria.

Dishtowels, cloths, and aprons should be washed in hot water often. It's a good idea to wash sponges in the dishwasher each time you run it and to replace them regularly. If you don't have a dishwasher, put sponges in boiling water for 3 minutes to sterilize them.

Separate Foods to Prevent Cross-Contamination

Raw meat, poultry, and seafood harbor an array of microbes and can easily contaminate other foods through direct contact, as well as by the juices they leave behind on surfaces (including hands). Avoid contact between foods that have already been cooked or that won't be cooked, like salad ingredients, and raw foods or their juices. Also avoid placing cooked or ready-to-eat foods on a plate or other surface that previously held raw meat, seafood, or poultry. When preparing meals with a marinade, reserve some of the fresh marinade in a clean container, then add the raw ingredients to the remainder. In this way, some noncontaminated marinade will be available if needed later in the cooking process. Raw food should always be marinated in the refrigerator.

Store Foods in the Refrigerator or Freezer

Different microbes thrive in different environmental temperatures. The majority of bacteria that cause food-borne illness grow best in temperatures at or above 40°F.[14] Because of this, refrigeration (keep your refrigerator at or below 40°F) and freezing (keep your freezer at 0°F) are two of the most reliable methods of diminishing the ability of bacteria to cause illness.[14] Not all bacteria in cool environments are killed, but the rate at which they reproduce is drastically reduced. Also, naturally occurring enzymes that cause food decomposition are stopped at freezing temperatures.

Shopping for Perishable Foods

When shopping for food, purchase refrigerated and frozen foods last. Many grocery stores are actually designed so that these foods are in the last aisles. Put packaged meat, poultry, or fish into a plastic bag before placing it in your shopping cart.[15] This prevents food drippings from coming into contact with other foods in your cart.

When buying perishable foods, look for the "sell by" or "use by" date on their packaging. The "sell by" date indicates the last day a product can be sold and still maintain its quality during normal home storage and consumption. It is generally best to purchase foods prior to this date. The "use by" date indicates how long a product will maintain optimum quality.[16] It is best to avoid consuming foods after the "use by" date, even though they are generally still safe to eat. For nonperishable foods such as cereal and baking mixes, the "best if used by (or before)" dates indicate the shelf-life of the product or the date at which the product is no longer at peak flavor, texture, and appearance. These foods can be safely eaten past the listed date if they have been stored properly, but they may not taste as good or be as nutritious as they were before this date. Proper storage for nonperishable items includes storage in a dry, clean, cool (less than 85°F) cabinet or pantry.

Do not purchase foods with punctured or otherwise damaged packaging. Dented or bulging cans are especially dangerous, as they could harbor potentially deadly bacteria. Report any damaged packaging to the store manager.

Watch for unsanitary practices and conditions inside the store. For example, the unsafe displaying of food products, such as cooked shrimp on the same bed of ice as raw seafood, is illegal, as is trimming raw meat with the same knife used to slice cold cuts. Report such unsanitary practices or conditions to your local health authorities.[15]

After purchasing perishable foods, get them home and into the refrigerator or freezer within 1 hour. If your trip home will take longer than an hour, bring along a cooler to transport them in.

The "sell by" date tells the store how long to display the product for sale.

Refrigerating Foods

Once you get home, put meat, poultry, and seafood in the coldest part of the refrigerator. Keep them wrapped in plastic so their juices do not drip onto any other foods. If you are not going to use them within 48 hours, store them in the freezer.[17] Remember that eggs are also perishable and should be kept refrigerated. Avoid overstocking your refrigerator or freezer, as air needs to circulate around food to cool it quickly and discourage microbial growth. Purchase a refrigerator thermometer and check it regularly to ensure your refrigerator is at or below 40°F.

After a meal, leftovers should be promptly refrigerated—even if still hot—to discourage microbial growth. The standard rule for storing leftovers is *2 hours/2 inches/4 days*. Food should be refrigerated *within 2 hours* of serving. If the environmental temperature is 90°F or higher, such as at a picnic, then foods should be refrigerated within 1 hour.[18] Because a larger quantity of food takes longer to cool and will allow more microbes to thrive, food should be stored at a depth of no greater than *2 inches*. The interior of deeper containers of foods can remain warm long enough to allow bacteria to multiply rapidly even when the surface of the food has cooled. Leftovers should only be refrigerated for *up to 4 days*. If you don't plan on using the food within 4 days, freeze it. A guide for storing foods in your refrigerator is provided in **Figure 15.6**.

Freezing and Thawing Foods

The temperature in your freezer should be set at 0°F.[14] Use a thermometer to check periodically that a freezing temperature is being maintained. If your electricity goes out, avoid opening the freezer until the power is restored. When the power does come back on, check to make sure the temperature on the top shelf of the freezer compartment is no warmer than 40°F (5°C). If it is warmer, you should inspect your freezer's contents and discard any items that are not firmly frozen.

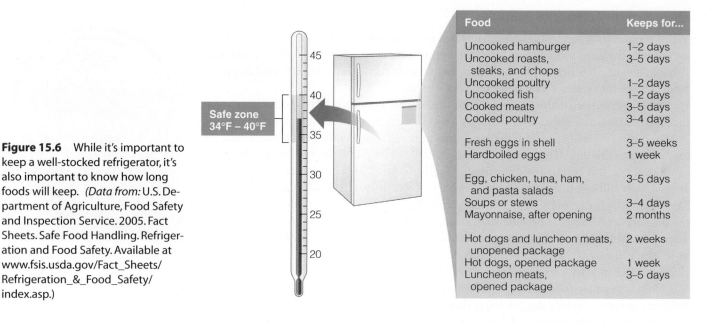

Food	Keeps for...
Uncooked hamburger	1–2 days
Uncooked roasts, steaks, and chops	3–5 days
Uncooked poultry	1–2 days
Uncooked fish	1–2 days
Cooked meats	3–5 days
Cooked poultry	3–4 days
Fresh eggs in shell	3–5 weeks
Hardboiled eggs	1 week
Egg, chicken, tuna, ham, and pasta salads	3–5 days
Soups or stews	3–4 days
Mayonnaise, after opening	2 months
Hot dogs and luncheon meats, unopened package	2 weeks
Hot dogs, opened package	1 week
Luncheon meats, opened package	3–5 days

Safe zone 34°F – 40°F

Figure 15.6 While it's important to keep a well-stocked refrigerator, it's also important to know how long foods will keep. *(Data from:* U.S. Department of Agriculture, Food Safety and Inspection Service. 2005. Fact Sheets. Safe Food Handling. Refrigeration and Food Safety. Available at www.fsis.usda.gov/Fact_Sheets/Refrigeration_&_Food_Safety/index.asp.)

When freezing items, remember that smaller packages will freeze more quickly. So rather than attempting to freeze an entire casserole or a whole batch of homemade spaghetti sauce, divide the food into multiple portions in freezer-safe containers, then freeze.

Sufficient thawing will ensure adequate cooking throughout, which is essential to preventing food-borne illness. Raw poultry is a good example of a food item that needs to be carefully contained as it thaws, so its juices don't contaminate other foods. The perfect place to thaw poultry is on the bottom shelf of the refrigerator in a large bowl to catch any of its juices. Table 15.3 shows recommended poultry thawing times based on weight. Never thaw frozen meat, poultry, or seafood on a kitchen counter or in a basin of warm water. Room temperatures allow growth of bacteria on the surface of food, although the inside may still be frozen.[17] A microwave is also useful for thawing if the food is to be cooked immediately afterward, but be sure to follow your microwave's instructions carefully.

Dealing with Molds in Refrigerated Foods

Have you ever taken cheese out of the refrigerator and noticed that it had a fuzzy blue growth on it? This is mold, one of the two types of fungus. Interestingly, cool temperatures

Table 15.3 A Guide to Thawing Poultry

Method Needed	Size of Poultry	Approximate Length of Time
Refrigerator	1–3 lb, small chickens, pieces	1 day
	3–6 lb, large chickens, ducks, small turkeys	2 days
	4–12 lb, large turkeys	1–3 days
	12–16 lb, whole turkey	3–4 days
	16–20 lb, whole turkey	4–5 days
	20–24 lb, whole turkey	5–6 days
Microwave (read instructions)	1–3 lb, small chickens, pieces	8–15 minutes* (standing time 10 minutes)
	3–6 lb, large chickens, ducks, small turkeys	15–30 minutes* (standing time 20 minutes)

*Approximate; read microwave's instructions.

Note: Turkeys purchased stuffed and frozen with the USDA or state mark of inspection on the packaging are safe because they have been processed under controlled conditions. These turkeys *should not* be thawed before cooking. Follow package directions for handling.

Data from: Lacey, R. W., 1994. *Hard to Swallow: A Brief History of Food.* Cambridge: Cambridge University Press, pp. 85–187. U.S. Department of Agriculture, Food Safety and Inspection Service. 2005. Poultry preparation. Available at www.fsis.usda.gov/Fact_Sheets/Poultry_Preparation_Fact_Sheets/index.asp#talk_turkey.

and high acidity do not slow the growth of some molds; in fact, some prefer these conditions. For instance, when acidic foods such as applesauce, yogurt, and spaghetti sauce are refrigerated, they readily support the growth of mold. But how does mold get into a closed, refrigerated container? Mold spores are common in the atmosphere, and they randomly land on food either in the processing plant or in open containers at your home. If the temperature and acidity of the food is hospitable, they will grow.

Most people throw away moldy foods because they are so unappealing, but as we noted earlier, food-borne illnesses aren't commonly caused by fungi. If the surface of a small portion of a solid food such as hard cheese becomes moldy, it is generally safe to cut off that section down to about an inch and eat the unspoiled portion. If soft cheese, sour cream, yogurt, tomato sauce, applesauce, or another soft or fluid product becomes moldy, discard it.

Some fungi are actually used in the food industry to create popular foods and beverages. The distinct flavor of Roquefort and blue cheeses can be attributed to the molds used in their ripening process. Yeast, the globular form of fungi, gives a distinct flavor to fermented foods such as sourdough bread, miso, soy sauce, beer, wine, and distilled spirits. Even the production of chocolate requires the help of yeasts, which ferment the cacao seeds, causing them to lose their bitter taste.

Cook Foods Thoroughly

Thoroughly cooking food is a sure way to kill the intestinal worms discussed earlier and many other microbes. The proper internal temperatures for doneness of meat, poultry, seafood, and eggs vary, as shown in **Figure 15.7**.

Tips for Cooking Meat, Poultry, Fish, and Eggs

The color of cooked meat can be deceiving. Grilled meat and poultry often brown very quickly on the outside but may not be thoroughly cooked on the inside. The only way to be sure meat is thoroughly cooked is with a food thermometer. Test the food in several places

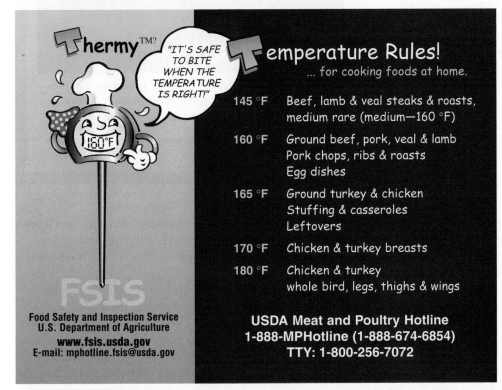

Figure 15.7   The U.S. Department of Agriculture's "Thermy" provides temperature rules for safely cooking foods at home.

Highlight
Food Safety Tips for Your Next Barbecue

It's the end of the term, and you and your friends are planning a lakeside barbecue to celebrate! Here are some tips for preventing food-borne illness at any outdoor gathering.

1. **Wash your hands, utensils, and food preparation surfaces.**   Even in outdoor settings, food safety begins with hand washing. Bring along a water jug, some soap, and paper towels, or a box of moist disposable towelettes. Keep all utensils and platters clean when preparing foods.

2. **Keep foods cold during transport.**   Use coolers with ice or frozen gel packs to keep food at or below 40°F. It's easier to maintain a cold temperature in small coolers. Consider packing three: put beverages in one cooler; washed fruits and vegetables and containers of potato salad, chicken salad, and so forth in another; and meat, poultry, and seafood in another. Meat, poultry, and seafood may be packed while still frozen so that they stay colder longer. Be sure they are wrapped securely so that juices don't leak inside the cooler. Keep coolers in the air-conditioned passenger compartment of your car rather than in a hot trunk.

3. **Grill foods thoroughly.**   Use a food thermometer to be sure the food has reached an adequate internal temperature before serving. For example:
   - Steaks should reach 145°F for medium rare, 160°F for medium, and 170°F for well done.
   - Ground beef should reach 160°F.
   - Poultry breasts should reach 170°F.
   - Fish should reach 145°F, or be cooked until the flesh is opaque and separates easily with a fork.

   When bringing food from the grill to the table, never use the same platter or utensils that previously held raw meat or seafood!

4. **Keep hot foods hot and cold foods cold.**   Keep grilled food hot until it is served by moving it to the side of the grill, just away from the coals, so that it stays at or above 140°F. If grilled food isn't going to be eaten right away, wrap it well and place it in an insulated container. Cold foods like chicken salad should be kept in a bowl of ice during your barbecue. Drain off water as the ice melts and replace the ice frequently. Don't let any perishable food sit out longer than 2 hours. In temperatures above 90°F, don't let food sit out for more than 1 hour.

When barbecuing, grill foods thoroughly, making sure they have reached an adequate internal temperature before serving.

Data from: U.S. Department of Agriculture, Food Safety and Inspection Service. 2003. Fact Sheets. Safe Food Handling. Barbecue and Food Safety. Available at www.fsis.usda.gov/fact_ sheets/Barbecue_Food_Safety/index.asp.

to be sure it's cooked evenly, and remember to wash the thermometer after each use. If you don't have a thermometer available, do not eat hamburger that is still pink inside.[18] For more information on safe grilling or barbecuing, see the Highlight box above, Food Safety Tips for Your Next Barbecue.

Microwave cooking is convenient, but you need to be sure your food is thoroughly cooked and that there are no cold spots in the food where bacteria can thrive. For best results when microwaving, remember to cover food, stir often, and rotate for even cooking.[18] If you are microwaving meat or poultry, use a thermometer to check internal temperatures in several spots, because temperatures vary in different parts of food more in microwave cooking than in conventional ovens.[17] The USDA has published a helpful fact sheet describing how to cook safely in the microwave; see the Web Links at the end of this chapter.

Raw and semiraw (such as marinated or partly cooked) fish delicacies, including sushi, sashimi, and so forth, may be tempting, but their safety cannot be guaranteed. Always cook fish thoroughly. When done, fish should be opaque and flake easily with a fork. It is important to recognize that sushi restaurants cannot guarantee the safety of their food. All fish to be used for sushi must be flash frozen at −31°F (−35°C) or below for 15 hours, or be regularly frozen to −4°F (−20°C) or below for 7 days.[19] Although this effectively kills any parasites that might be in the fish, it does not kill bacteria or viruses. Thus, eating raw seafood remains risky, and the FDA advises that people with compromised immunity, children, pregnant women, and the elderly avoid it.[15]

You may have memories of licking the cake batter off a spoon when you were a kid, but such practices are no longer safe. That's because most cake batters contain raw eggs, and an estimated one-third of chicken eggs in the United States are contaminated with *Salmonella*. For this reason, the USDA recommends that you cook eggs until the yolk and whites are firm. For example, hard-boiled eggs should be boiled for 7 minutes, and fried eggs should be cooked for 3 minutes on one side, 1 minute on the other. Scrambled eggs should not be runny. If you are using eggs in a casserole or custard, make sure that the internal temperature reaches at least 160°F.[20]

Protect Yourself from Toxins in Foods

Killing microorganisms with heat is an important step in keeping food safe, but it won't protect people against their toxins. That's because toxins are unaffected by heat and are capable of causing severe illness even when the microbes that produced them have been destroyed.

For example, let's say you prepare a casserole for a team picnic. Too bad you forget to wash your hands before serving it to your teammates because you contaminate the casserole with the bacteria *Staphylococcus aureus*, which is commonly found on moist skin folds.[6] You and your friends go off and play soccer, leaving the food in the sun, and a few hours later, you take the rest of the casserole home. At supper, you heat the leftovers thoroughly, thinking as you do so that this will kill any bacteria that might have multiplied while it was left out. That night you wake up with nausea, severe vomiting, and abdominal pain. What happened? While your food was left out, the bacteria from your hands multiplied in the casserole and produced a toxin (**Figure 15.8**). When the food was reheated, the microorganisms were killed, but their toxin was unaffected by the heat. When you then ate the food, the toxin made you sick. Fortunately, in the case of *S. aureus*, symptoms typically resolve on their own in healthy people in about 24 hours.

When Eating Out

When choosing a place to eat out, avoid restaurants that don't look clean. Grimy tabletops and dirty restrooms indicate indifference to hygiene. On the other hand, cleanliness of areas used by the public doesn't guarantee that the kitchen is clean. That is why health inspections are important. Public health inspectors randomly visit and inspect the food preparation areas of all businesses that serve food, whether eaten in or taken out. The results of these inspections can usually be found in the local newspaper, by contacting your local health department, or by checking the inspection results posted in the restaurant.

Another way to protect yourself when dining out is by ordering foods to be cooked thoroughly. If you order a hamburger that arrives pink in the middle, send it back and ask for it to be cooked longer. If you order scrambled eggs that arrive runny, send them back to be cooked thoroughly or order something else.

When Traveling to Other Countries

When planning your trip, tell your physician your travel plans and ask about vaccinations needed or any medications that should be taken along in case you get sick. Also pack a waterless antibacterial hand cleanser, and use it frequently during the trip. When dining, select foods and beverages carefully. All raw food has the potential for contamination, especially in areas where hygiene and sanitation are inadequate. See the Highlight on traveler's diarrhea on page 102 for more information. If fish is a local delicacy, be aware that some tropical species can contain marine toxins, even when well cooked.

1 Cooked food is contaminated with bacteria, *Staphylococcus aureus*, when served by a person with unwashed hands.

2 Food is left unrefrigerated.

3 Bacteria multiply in unrefrigerated food and produce toxin.

4 Later, leftover food is reheated. Reheating destroys bacteria but not toxin.

5 Reheated food is eaten.

Food poisoning

6 After 1–6 hours, nausea, vomiting, diarrhea, and stomach pain occur.

Figure 15.8   Food intoxication can occur long after the microbe itself has been destroyed.

Tap water is seldom a safe option, even if chlorinated, as chlorine doesn't kill all organisms that can cause disease. If you think the local water may be contaminated, don't even brush your teeth with it: Use bottled water or boil the water for 1 minute, then allow it to return to room temperature before brushing. You can find more information about food and water safety when traveling by visiting the CDC's Web site (see the Web Links at the end of this chapter) or by contacting your local health department.

RECAP

Food-borne illness can be prevented at home by following four tips: *Clean*: wash your hands and kitchen surfaces often. *Separate*: isolate foods to prevent cross-contamination. *Chill*: store foods in the refrigerator or freezer. *Cook*: heat foods long enough and at proper temperatures to ensure proper cooking. When eating out, avoid restaurants that don't look clean, and ask that all food be cooked thoroughly. When traveling, avoid all raw foods unless thoroughly washed in bottled or boiled water, and choose beverages that are boiled, bottled, or canned, without ice.

Theo
Nutri-Case

"I got really sick yesterday after eating lunch in the cafeteria. I had a turkey sandwich, potato salad, and a cola. I remember thinking that the potato salad looked a little off, as if it had been sitting around too long, but I was late for lunch and the cafeteria was about to close, so I had to make my choices fast. Anyway, around five o'clock, in the middle of basketball practice, I started to shake and sweat. I got really nauseated, and barely made it to the bathroom before vomiting. Then I went back to my dorm room and crawled into bed. This morning I still feel a little nauseated, and sort of weak. I asked some of my friends who ate in the cafeteria yesterday if they got sick, and none of them did, but I still think it was the food. I'm going off-campus for lunch from now on!"

Do you think that Theo's illness was food-borne? If so, what food and/or ingredient(s) do you most suspect, and why? What microbe? (Hint: See Table 15.2.) What do you think of his plan to go off-campus for lunch? Any other actions he might take?

How Is Food Spoilage Prevented?

Any food that has been harvested and that people aren't ready to eat must be preserved in some way or, before long, it will degrade enzymatically and become home to a variety of microorganisms. Even **processed foods**—foods that are manipulated mechanically or chemically—have the potential to spoil.

Spoilage makes food unsafe to eat: because decomposition of foods is accomplished in part by microorganisms, if you eat a food that has spoiled, you risk developing a food-borne illness. Fortunately, spoilage usually degrades the appearance, texture, and smell of food so much that we throw it away uneaten. Would you eat fish with a strong odor or a tomato that has turned to "mush"?

Modern science and technology have given us a wide array of techniques to produce, preserve, and transport food. But these advances have not eliminated the threat of food spoilage, which can occur at any point on the journey from farm to table. Any food that has been harvested and that people aren't ready to eat must be preserved in some way, or before long it will spoil. Here, we look at some techniques that people have used for centuries to preserve food, as well as more modern techniques used in the food industry.

Natural Methods Are Effective in Preserving Foods

Some methods of preserving foods have been used for thousands of years and employ naturally derived substances such as salt, sugars, and smoke or techniques such as drying and cooling.

A worker salting a Parma ham.

- *Salting.* Salt preserves food by drawing the water out of the plant or animal cells by osmosis. This dehydrates the food, making it inhospitable to microbes. Dehydration also dramatically slows the action of enzymes that would otherwise degrade the food. Salt is especially good at drawing water from meats and seafood, but because of current concerns about sodium intake and hypertension, this method is not used as much as it was in the past. Some meats are still preserved with salt: a good example is the Parma ham from Italy, which is dry-salted with sea salt for about a month.[21]
- *Sugaring.* Sugar has an osmotic effect similar to salt. However, foods preserved with sugar retain much of their shape, color, and texture because some of the sugar is absorbed into the cells, replacing the water drawn out. The downside to using sugar is that fungi tend to flourish in sweet, acidic environments such as jams.
- *Drying.* Drying is an ancient method of preserving food that, like salting and sugaring, works by drawing water out of the food. There is evidence that the Egyptians dried fish

processed foods Foods that are manipulated mechanically or chemically during their production or packaging. Processed foods may or may not resemble the original ingredients in their final form.

Before the modern refrigerator, an "iceman" would deliver ice to homes and businesses.

and poultry in the hot desert sun as early as 12,000 BC.[21] Beans, peas, and fruits are also commonly preserved by drying. One drawback to drying is that it can change a food's color, texture, and flavor, and decrease its vitamin content. A modern version called *freeze-drying* preserves color, texture, and flavor: The food is first flash-frozen, so any water within it converts to fine ice crystals. These are evaporated in a vacuum and the product is immediately packaged. Freeze-dried foods have a shelf life of several years as long as the package seal is not broken.

- *Smoking.* Smoking has been used for centuries for preservation of meats, poultry, and fish. If food was not drying well, it would be hung near the campfire or chimney so the smoke of the fire would permeate the food, further drying it. A commercial version of smoking is still used for pork, beef, trout, and other animal foods. Unfortunately, smoking does not guarantee that a food is safe to eat. For example, *Listeria monocytogenes* is a type of bacteria that can survive in smoked fish. Infection causes short-term gastrointestinal distress in healthy people but can cause miscarriage among infected pregnant women and death in young children, frail elderly, and others with compromised immunity.

- *Cooling.* As the temperature of its environment is lowered, a bacteria's metabolism is slowed, and it becomes less able to multiply or produce toxins. Before the advent of electric refrigerators, people stored foods in underground cellars, caves, running streams, and even "cold pantries," north-facing rooms of the house that were kept dark and unheated and often were stocked with ice. The forerunner of our refrigerator, the miniature icehouse, was developed in the early 1800s, and in cities and towns, the local iceman would make rounds delivering ice to homes.

Modern Techniques Improve Food Safety

To be successful, food producers have had to find ways to preserve the integrity of their products during the days, weeks, or months between harvesting and consumption. By the mid-20th century, technological advances in food preservation had given us canning, pasteurization, and the addition of preservative chemicals. However, in the past few decades, modern packaging techniques, irradiation, and genetic modification have greatly expanded our food choices.

Industrial Canning

Canning food involves several steps to ensure all microorganisms in the food are killed.

The French inventor Nicolas-François Appert first developed the canning process in the late 1700s, and modern techniques have contributed to the retention of flavor, texture, and nutrients in canned foods. In the United States, 20 million canned foods are consumed per day.[21]

Producers of canned foods are required by law to ensure that all endospores of *Clostridium botulinum* are eliminated from their goods. As you recall, if the spores of this bacteria were to germinate inside a can of food, the food would soon become saturated with the deadly botulism toxin. The same process that destroys *C. botulinum* endospores also kills other microorganisms that could contaminate the food. This process involves several steps:

1. The food to be canned is sorted and washed.
2. The food is blanched. Blanching involves the use of hot water or steam to parboil or scald the food, thereby stopping enzymatic processes and killing microorganisms on the food's surface.
3. Cans are filled and heated, air is siphoned out, and they are sealed.
4. The sealed cans are heated to a very high temperature and then cooled.

Canned food has an average shelf life of at least 2 years from the date of purchase. In fact, the U.S. Army has found canned meats, vegetables, and jam in "excellent states of preservation" after 46 years.

Pasteurization

Pasteurization was developed in 1864 by Louis Pasteur to destroy microorganisms that spoiled wine. The technique involves a quick use of heat—for example, 162°F (72°C) for 15 seconds pasteurizes milk—to eliminate pathogens, typically in fluids. This barely alters the taste or quality of the product, making pasteurization particularly useful in the dairy and juice industries.

Innovations in Packaging Techniques

Many different packaging techniques have arisen over the past several decades. These include the following:

- *Aseptic packaging* is probably most easily recognized as "juice boxes." Aseptic packaging was first introduced in the United States in the 1980s. Foods and beverages are first sterilized in a flash-heating and cooling process, then placed in the sterile container, which is formulated to provide a unique barrier against light and oxygen. Nutrient quality as well as overall food quality remain high as long as the package seals are not broken. The process uses less energy than traditional canning.[22]
- *Modified atmosphere packaging* is a process in which the oxygen in a package of food is replaced with an inert gas such as nitrogen or carbon dioxide. This slows the growth of bacteria that require oxygen, as well as the oxidation reactions that commonly spoil foods. The process can be used with a variety of foods, including meats, fish, vegetables, and fruits.
- *High-pressure processing* is a technique that subjects food to extremely high pressure. This inactivates most bacteria while retaining the food's quality and freshness.

Addition of Preservatives

Food preservatives are substances added to a variety of foods to prevent or slow food spoilage. There are many natural and synthetically derived preservatives used in our food supply. One of the most commonly used natural preservatives is vitamin C. This nutrient is a powerful antioxidant and helps protect foods from damage due to oxygen exposure. EDTA (ethylenediaminetetraacetic acid) is a commonly used synthetic preservative. It is used to trap trace amounts of metal impurities that can get into foods from containers and processing machinery.

Most processed foods contain preservatives, unless the package touts that it is "preservative free." All preservatives must be listed in the ingredients, but a person must know their chemical names to recognize them. Table 15.4 on page 602 identifies some common preservatives and the types of foods in which they are typically found. A few of these are discussed in more detail here.

Antioxidants In addition to certain vitamins, two antioxidants commonly used in foods are BHT (butylated hydroxytoluene) and BHA (butylated hydroxyanisole). They keep oils and fats in packaged foods from going rancid. BHT is frequently added to breakfast cereals to decrease spoilage. BHA is stable at high temperatures and is often used in products such as soup bases, ice cream, potato flakes, gelatin desserts, dry mixes for desserts, unsmoked dry sausage, and chewing gum.

Propyl gallate, another antioxidant, works synergistically with both BHA and BHT to enhance their effectiveness. Propyl gallate is used in products such as mayonnaise, mashed potato flakes, fruits, chewing gum, ice cream, baked goods, and gelatin desserts.

Mold Inhibitors The bread you bought, left on the counter, and finally got around to eating a week later would have become moldy if it hadn't been treated with mold inhibitors. *Propionic acid* occurs naturally in apples, strawberries, and tea and is used to prevent mold growth in baked goods and processed cheese. *Sodium propionate* and *calcium propionate* are salts synthesized from propionic acid and are used as mold inhibitors in a variety of foods.

Louis Pasteur.

Aseptic packaging allows foods to be stored unrefrigerated for several months without spoilage.

pasteurization A form of sterilization using high temperatures for short periods of time.

food preservatives Chemicals that help prevent microbial spoilage and enzymatic deterioration.

Sulfites   Sodium bisulfite and sulfur dioxide are **sulfites,** sulfur-containing compounds used as preservatives, antioxidants, bleaching agents, and antibrowning agents. Sulfites also have antibacterial and antifungal properties. They are widely used in the beer and wine industry as well as in dehydrated foods, Maraschino cherries, and processed potatoes. Sulfites are not used in enriched grain products because of their capacity to bind with thiamin (vitamin B_1), making it unavailable for absorption.

Sulfur dioxide is used to control mold growth on fresh fruits and vegetables. For example, it has become standard commercial practice to fumigate stored grapes every 10 days with this chemical. Because of such procedures, it's important to remember to wash all fresh fruits and vegetables before eating.

The FDA has banned the use of sulfites as a preservative in salad bars because some people have had adverse asthmatic reactions. All foods that contain added sulfites must be labeled to warn those with sensitivities.

Nitrates and Nitrites   The processed meat industry has long relied on **nitrates** and **nitrites** as antibacterial agents and color enhancers. They give ham, hot dogs, and bologna their familiar pink color. They also inhibit microbial growth and rancidity. However, nitrites can easily be converted to *nitrosamines* during the cooking process. Nitrosamines have been found to be carcinogenic in animals, so the FDA has required all foods with nitrites to contain additional antioxidants to decrease the formation of nitrosamines.

Irradiation

Irradiation eliminates harmful food-borne bacteria in meats and poultry, and inhibits spoilage by fungus. In the United States, the process typically involves exposing food and its packaging to the energy of gamma rays from radioactive metals. Most of this energy simply passes through the food, leaving no residue. While the food remains relatively unchanged, bacteria and fungi are killed or left unable to reproduce.

Irradiation has been approved for use by fifty countries and endorsed by the World Health Organization (WHO), the Food and Agricultural Organization of the United Nations (FAO), and the International Atomic Energy Agency (IAEA). In the United States, many foods are preserved using irradiation; among them are spices, grains, fruits, pork products, beef, and poultry. The U.S. National Aeronautics and Space Administration (NASA) uses irradiated foods for space flights.[23] Although irradiation rids foods of most pathogenic microbes, frozen foods remain frozen and raw foods stay raw through the process. Although many foods can safely be irradiated without any noticeable changes, the flavor of milk and other dairy products becomes unpalatable after irradiation, making them inappropriate for this process. A recent consumer report on irradiated meat did note that the flavor of both beef and chicken had a subtle off-taste and smell, but one that many consumers might not notice.[24] Only a few nutrients, including vitamins A, E, K, and thiamin, seem to be affected by irradiation. Losses of these nutrients are comparable to what would be lost in conventional processing and preparation.

Although irradiated food has been shown to be safe to consume, the FDA requires that all irradiated foods be labeled with a "radura" symbol. The words "treated by irradiation, do not irradiate again" or "treated with radiation, do not irradiate again" must accompany the symbol (**Figure 15.9**). Irradiated foods can be contaminated by improper handling and preparation, so consumers still need to store, clean, prepare, and cook them appropriately.

Genetic Modification

In **genetic modification,** also referred to as *genetic engineering*, the genetic material, or DNA, of an organism is altered to bring about specific changes in its seeds or offspring. Selective breeding is one example of genetic modification; for example, Brahman cattle that have poor-quality meat but high resistance to heat and humidity are bred with English shorthorn cattle that have good meat but low resistance to heat and humidity. The outcome

Figure 15.9   Radura—the international symbol of irradiated food—is required by the Food and Drug Administration to be displayed on all irradiated food sold in the United States.

sulfites   Compounds containing sulfur and used as preservatives and antioxidants. Sulfites also have antibacterial properties, and are used to prevent browning, bleach flour, and inhibit mold growth.

nitrates and nitrites   Chemicals used in meat curing to develop and stabilize the pink color associated with cured meat; also function as antibacterial agents.

irradiation   A sterilization process using gamma rays or other forms of radiation but that does not impart any radiation to the food being treated.

genetic modification   Changing an organism by manipulating its genetic material.

1. Gene that expresses desired trait is extracted from cell.

2. Gene is combined with DNA of host cell that lacks this gene.

3. Host cell containing recombinant DNA is cultured, resulting in many copies of the gene.

4. Gene is extracted and inserted into DNA of cells of an organism that lacks this gene.

5. Cells produce organism that expresses the desired trait.

DNA of host cell — 1

Desired gene — 2

3

4

5 Genetically modified organism

Figure 15.10 Recombinant DNA technology involves producing plants and other organisms that contain modified DNA that enables them to express desirable traits that are not present in the original organism.

of this selective breeding process is Santa Gertrudis cattle, which have the desired characteristics of higher-quality meat and resistance to heat and humidity. Although selective breeding is effective and has helped increase crop yields and improve the quality and quantity of our food supply, it is a relatively slow and imprecise process, as a great deal of trial and error typically occurs before the desired characteristics are achieved.

Recently, technical advances have moved genetic modification beyond selective breeding. These advances include the manipulation of the DNA of living cells of one organism to produce the desired characteristics of a different organism. Called **recombinant DNA technology,** the process commonly begins when scientists isolate from an animal, plant, or microbial cell a particular segment of DNA that codes for a protein conferring a desirable trait, such as salt tolerance. Scientists extract and copy the DNA segment, then splice copies into cells of organisms normally lacking that trait, such as traditional tomato plants. The modified DNA causes the plant's cells to build the protein of interest, and the plant expresses the desired trait (**Figure 15.10**).

The term **genetically modified organism (GMO)** refers to an organism in which the DNA has been altered using recombinant DNA technology. A common use of this technology is to induce resistance to herbicides and pesticides. For example, genetically modified soybean, corn, and cotton crops can be sprayed with chemicals that kill weeds without harming the plants. Another use is to increase the nutritional value of a crop. For instance, researchers have modified soybeans and canola to increase their content of monounsaturated fatty acids. Scientists have also inserted a gene for salt tolerance into tomato and canola plants, enabling these GMOs to grow in soil so salty it would poison normal crops.[6] In addition, these crops remove salt from the soil, making it hospitable to unmodified plants. The most common genetically modified crops are soybeans and corn.

The relative benefits and harm of genetic modification have been debated worldwide. For instance, some environmentalists have raised the concern that seeds from genetically modified crops disrupt other crops through cross-pollination, even those many miles from where the altered ones are growing. Another concern is the long-term effect of genetically modified crops on the plants, insects, and animals that consume them or use them for their habitat. For more information about the debate surrounding genetic modification, see the Nutrition Debate at the end of this chapter.

recombinant DNA technology Type of genetic modification in which scientists combine DNA from different sources to produce a transgenic organism that expresses a desired trait.

genetically modified organism (GMO) An organism in which the genetic material, or DNA, has been altered using recombinant DNA technology.

RecaP

Natural food preservation techniques include salting, sugaring, drying, and smoking, all of which draw water out of foods, making them inhospitable to microbes. Storage in cellars and other cold areas has been used for centuries to preserve food. The canning process was developed in the late 18th century and pasteurization in the 19th century. Aseptic packaging, modified atmosphere packaging, and high-pressure processing are relatively new techniques that increase shelf life. Preservatives are often added to keep foods fresher longer. Irradiation typically involves the use of gamma rays to destroy microbes in foods. The DNA of plants and animals can be genetically modified to enhance certain qualities of the food.

What Are Food Additives, and Are They Safe?

Have you ever picked up a loaf of bread and started reading its ingredients? You'd expect to see flour, yeast, water, and some sugar, but what are all those other items? And why does it feel as if you have to have a degree in chemistry to understand what they are? They are collectively called **food additives,** and they are in almost every processed food. Without additives, that loaf of bread would go stale within a day or two.

Although their use is regulated by the FDA, food additives have been a source of controversy for the past 50 years. Nevertheless, their use has steadily increased, allowing food producers to offer consumers a greater variety of foods at lower costs.

Additives Can Enhance a Food's Taste, Appearance, Safety, or Nutrition

It's estimated that more than 3,000 different additives are currently used in the United States. A few of these are identified in Table 15.4, and this section discusses some of the most common.

Additives Can Be Natural or Synthetic

food additives   Substances intentionally put into food to enhance appearance, palatability, and quality.

Many of the additives used by the food industry come from natural sources. Beet juice (a natural food coloring), salt, and citric acid are common, naturally derived food additives.

Table 15.4 Examples of Common Food Additives

Preservative	Foods Found in
α-tocopherol (vitamin E)	Vegetable oils
Ascorbic acid (vitamin C)	Breakfast cereal, cured meat, fruit drinks
BHA	Breakfast cereal, chewing gum, oil, potato chips
BHT	Breakfast cereal, chewing gum, oil, potato chips
Calcium proprionate/ sodium proprionate	Breads, cakes, pies, rolls
EDTA	Canned shellfish, margarine, mayonnaise, processed fruits and vegetables, salad dressings, sandwich spreads, soft drinks
Propyl gallate	Mayonnaise, chewing gum, chicken soup base, vegetable oil, meat products, potato sticks, mashed potato flakes, fruits, ice cream
Sodium benzoate	Carbonated drinks, fruit juice, pickles, preserves
Sodium chloride (salt)	Most processed foods
Sodium nitrate/sodium nitrite	Bacon, corned beef, ham, luncheon meat, hot dogs, smoked fish
Sorbic acid/potassium sorbate	Cakes, cheese, dried fruit, jelly, syrup, wine
Sulfites (sodium bisulfite, sulfur dioxide)	Dried fruit, processed potatoes, wine

Often, supply or cost prohibits using naturally derived additives. In such cases, additives are synthesized. For instance, vanillin, the main flavoring substance in vanilla beans, is synthesized at a cost considerably lower than the cost of extracting it from the natural beans. Even if the costs were comparable, it is doubtful that natural sources of vanillin could meet consumer demands.

Flavorings

Flavoring agents can be obtained from natural or synthetic sources. Essential oils, extracts, and spices supply most of the naturally derived flavorings.

Flavor enhancers are also widely used. These additives have little or no flavor of their own but accentuate the natural flavor of foods. They are often added when very little of a natural ingredient is used.[25] The most common flavor enhancers used are maltol and MSG (monosodium glutamate). MSG is the sodium salt of glutamic acid, one of the nonessential amino acids, which also serves as a neurotransmitter. It is found in many processed foods; however, the glutamate portion of MSG can cross the blood–brain barrier and, in susceptible people, can cause symptoms such as headaches, difficulty breathing, and heart palpitations. A review of the research conducted in this area indicates that most individuals who report sensitivity to MSG do not show adverse reactions when they are fed MSG in controlled studies, particularly when MSG is given with food.[26]

Colorings

Food colorings, derived from both natural and synthetic sources, are used extensively in processed foods. In the past, many food colorings were made from **coaltar,** a thick or semisolid tar derived from bituminous coal. Derivatives of coaltar have been found to cause cancer in animals, and most have been banned by the FDA from use in foods. Natural colorings such as beet juice (which gives a red color), beta-carotene (which gives a yellow color), and caramel (which adds brown color) are now used instead and do not need to be tested for safety. The coloring tartrazine (FD&C yellow #5) causes an allergic reaction in some people, and its use must be indicated on the product packaging.

Many foods, such as ice cream, contain colorings.

Vitamins and Other Nutrients

Vitamin E is usually added to fat-based products to keep them from going rancid, and vitamin C (or ascorbic acid) is commonly added to foods such as frozen fruit, dry milk, apple juice, soft drinks, candy, and meat products containing sodium nitrates. Sodium ascorbate, a form of vitamin C with sodium added to produce a salt, is used as an antioxidant in foods such as concentrated milk products, cereals, and cured meats.

Iodine, calcium, vitamin D, and folate are examples of purely nutritive additives. Their function in foods is to promote health and prevent disease. Iodine is added to table salt to help decrease the incidence of goiter, a condition that causes the thyroid gland to enlarge. As you learned in Chapter 11, calcium and vitamin D are important for bone health. Folate is added to many breads and ready-to-eat cereals to decrease the incidence of neural tube defects during fetal development.

Additives That Improve Texture or Moisture Content

Certain chemicals are added to foods to improve their texture. For instance, **texturizers** such as calcium chloride are added to canned tomatoes and potatoes so they don't fall apart. **Stabilizers** are added to products to give them "body" and help them maintain a desired texture or color. **Emulsifiers** help to keep fats evenly dispersed within foods.

Thickening agents are used to absorb water and keep the complex mixtures of oils, water, acids, and solids in foods balanced.[25] Natural thickeners include pectin, alginate, and carrageenan. **Humectants** maintain the correct moisture levels, keeping foods like marshmallows soft and stretchy. Common humectants are glycerin, sorbitol, and propylene glycol. Waxes used on produce also help maintain moisture content. The best way to remove wax is

flavoring agents Obtained from either natural or synthetic sources; allow manufacturers to maintain a consistent flavor from batch to batch.

coaltar A food additive made from thick or semisolid tar derived from bituminous coal, the by-products of which have been found to cause cancer in animals.

texturizers A chemical used to improve the texture of various foods.

stabilizers Help maintain smooth texture and uniform color and flavor in some foods.

emulsifiers Chemicals that improve texture and smoothness in foods; stabilizes oil-water mixtures.

thickening agents Natural or chemically modified carbohydrates that absorb some of the water present in food, making the food thicker while keeping food components balanced.

humectants Chemicals that help retain moisture in foods, keeping them soft and pliable.

Mayonnaise contains emulsifiers to prevent separation of fats.

to peel the outer layer off or scrub it with hot, soapy water and rinse well. **Desiccants** prevent moisture absorption from the air; for example, they are used to prevent table salt from forming clumps.

Are Food Additives Considered Safe?

Federal legislation was passed in 1958 to regulate food additives. The Delaney Clause, also enacted in 1958, states that "No additive may be permitted in any amount if tests show that it produces cancer when fed to man or animals or by other appropriate tests." Before a new food additive can be marketed or used in food, the producer of the additive must submit data on its reasonable safety to the FDA. The FDA then makes a determination of the additive's safety based on these data.

During this same year, the U.S. Congress recognized that many substances added to foods would not require a formal safety review by the FDA prior to marketing and use, as their safety had already been established through long-term use or recognized by qualified experts through scientific studies. These substances are exempt from the more stringent testing criteria for new food additives and are referred to as substances that are **Generally Recognized as Safe (GRAS).** The GRAS list identifies substances that either have been tested in the past and determined by the FDA to be safe and approved for use in the food industry, or are deemed safe as a result of consensus among experts qualified by scientific training and experience.

In 1985, the FDA established the Adverse Reaction Monitoring System (ARMS). Under this system, the FDA investigates complaints from consumers, physicians, or food companies. Many of the complaints are about sulfite preservatives causing headaches, asthmatic reactions, and in some cases anaphylactic shock. Because of these complaints and the investigations that followed, the FDA has banned the use of sulfites on raw fruit and vegetables, with the exception of potatoes, while continuing to monitor sulfite use on other foods.

RECAP

Food additives are chemicals intentionally added to foods to enhance their color, flavor, texture, nutrient density, moisture level, or shelf life. Although there is continuing controversy over food additives, they are considered safe based on testing and use in the food industry or as a result of consensus among experts qualified by scientific training and experience.

desiccants   Chemicals that prevent foods from absorbing moisture from the air.

Generally Recognized as Safe (GRAS) list   A list established by Congress that identifies several hundred substances that have either been tested and found to be safe and approved by the FDA for use in the food industry, or are deemed safe as a result of consensus among experts qualified by scientific training and experience.

residues   Chemicals that remain in the foods we eat despite cleaning and processing.

persistent organic pollutants (POPs)   Chemicals released into the environment as a result of industry, agriculture, or improper waste disposal; automobile emissions also are considered POPs.

Do Residues Harm Our Food Supply?

Food **residues** are chemicals that remain in foods despite cleaning and processing. Two residues of global concern are pollutants and pesticides.

Persistent Organic Pollutants Can Cause Illness

Many different organic chemicals are released into the atmosphere as a result of industry, agriculture, automobile emissions, and improper waste disposal. These chemicals, collectively referred to as **persistent organic pollutants (POPs),** eventually enter the food supply through the soil or water. If a pollutant gets into the soil, a plant can absorb the chemical into its structure and can pass it on as part of the food chain. Fish and land animals can also absorb the pollutants into their tissues or can consume them when feeding on plants in the polluted water or soil. Fat-soluble pollutants are especially problematic, as they tend to accumulate in the animal's body tissues and are then absorbed by humans when the animal is used as a food source. *Bioaccumulation*, the process by which increasing concentrations of pollutants are seen in species higher up the food chain, is illustrated in **Figure 15.11**.

POP residues have been found in virtually all categories of foods, including baked goods, fruits, vegetables, meat, poultry, and dairy products. The chemicals can travel long

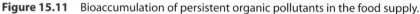

Figure 15.11 Bioaccumulation of persistent organic pollutants in the food supply.

distances in trade winds and water currents, moving from tropical and temperate regions to concentrate in the northern latitudes. It is believed that all living organisms on Earth carry a measurable level of POPs in their tissues.[27]

Mercury and Lead Are Nerve Toxins Found in the Environment

Mercury, a naturally occurring element, is found in soil and rocks, lakes, streams, and oceans. It is also released into the environment by pulp and paper processing and the burning of garbage and fossil fuels. As mercury is released into the environment, it falls from the air, eventually finding its way to streams, lakes, and the ocean, where it accumulates. Fish absorb mercury as they feed on aquatic organisms. This mercury is passed on to humans when they consume the fish. As mercury accumulates in the body, it has a toxic effect on the nervous system.

Large predatory fish, such as swordfish, shark, king mackerel, and tilefish, tend to contain the highest levels of mercury.[28] Because mercury is especially toxic to the developing nervous system of fetuses and growing children, pregnant and breastfeeding women and young children are advised to avoid eating these types of fish. Canned tuna, salmon, cod, pollock, sole, shrimp, mussels, and scallops do not contain high levels of mercury and are safe to consume; however, the FDA advises against eating any one type of fish more often than once a week.[28] Freshwater fish caught in local lakes and rivers have variable levels of mercury; thus, local and state governments routinely monitor mercury levels and post advisories when levels are too high. To learn more about the risks of mercury in seafood, visit the FDA's food safety Web site (see the Web Links at the end of this chapter) or call its 24-hour information line (at 1-888-SAFEFOOD).

Lead, another naturally occurring element, can be found in the soil, water, and even the air. It also occurs as industrial waste from leaded gasolines, lead-based paints, and

One of the ways mercury is released into the environment is by burning fossil fuels.

Antique porcelain is often coated with lead-based glaze.

lead-soldered cans, now outlawed but decomposing in landfills. Some ceramic mugs and other dishes are fired with lead-based glaze. Thus, residues can build up in foods. Excessive lead exposure can cause learning and behavioral impediments in children and cardiovascular and kidney disease in adults. It is impossible to avoid lead residues completely, but because of the health implications, everyone should try to limit their exposure. To find out how to limit lead exposure, visit the Environmental Protection Agency's Web site (see the Web Links at the end of this chapter).

Industrial Pollutants Also Create Residues

Polychlorinated biphenyls (PCBs) and dioxins are two industrial pollutants that enter the soil and can persist in the environment for years, easily accumulating in fatty tissues of animals. They have been found in food worldwide. PCBs and dioxins, along with other POPs, have been linked to cancer, learning disorders, impaired immune function, and infertility.[27]

Pesticides Protect Against Crop Losses

Pesticides are a family of chemicals used in both the field and storage areas to help protect crops from weeds, insects, fungi, and other organisms, including birds and mammals. Rodents, for example, in addition to consuming food, also contaminate large quantities of food with their excreta. Pesticides also help reduce the number of microorganisms on crops, and increase overall crop yield and crop diversity. The three most common types of pesticides used in food production are insecticides, herbicides, and fungicides. Insecticides are used to control insects that can infest crops; herbicides are used to control weeds and other unwanted plant growth; and fungicides are used to control plant-destroying fungal growth.

Pesticides Can Be Natural or Synthetic

Bt bacteria produce crystals, shown here, that are a widely used microbial biopesticide.

Many pesticides used today are **biopesticides,** species-specific chemicals or microorganisms that work to suppress a pest's population, not eliminate it. Biopesticides do not leave residues on crops—most degrade rapidly and are easily washed away with water. Synthetic pheromones are a type of chemical biopesticide. In nature, insects use pheromones, chemicals that act as signals, to attract mates. Synthetic pheromones are used to disrupt insect mating by attracting males into traps. Microbial biopesticides are derived from naturally occurring or genetically altered bacteria, viruses, or fungi. A widely used microbial biopesticide is *Bacillus thuringiensis*, or *Bt*. This is a common soil bacterium that is genetically altered to be toxic to several species of insects.

Aside from biopesticides, many natural products such as salt, boric acid, dried blood, crushed egg shells, or diatomaceous earth (soil made up of a type of algae called diatoms) are used as pesticides. Ladybugs are bred and sold commercially to reduce aphids, and marigolds, mint, sage, garlic, chives, onion, and other strong-smelling plants can be placed among crops to deter a variety of insect pests.

Many synthetic pesticides are made from petroleum-based products. Examples of commonly used synthetic pesticides include thiabendazole (a fungicide used on potatoes) and fungicides commonly used to prevent apple diseases (such as dithane, manzate, and polyram).

Synthetic Pesticides Are Potential Toxins

Years of studies show that synthetic pesticides can remain on food and pose a risk to human health. The liver is responsible for detoxifying chemicals that enter the body; however, if diseases such as cancer or AIDS or toxins such as alcohol already stress the liver, it may be unable to effectively remove pesticide residues. When pesticide residues are not effectively removed, they can build up and damage body tissues. The health effects depend on the type of pesticide. Some affect the nervous system, others the endocrine system, and still others

pesticides Chemicals used either in the field or in storage to destroy plant, fungal, and animal pests.

biopesticides Primarily insecticides, these chemicals use natural methods to reduce damage to crops.

are potential carcinogens.[29] These effects depend on how toxic the pesticide is and how much of it is consumed.[30]

Children may be especially sensitive to pesticides for several reasons: First, their internal organs are still developing and maturing.[31] Second, they consume more food and water per unit of body weight than adults, possibly increasing their exposure. If a child's excretory system is not fully developed, the child may have a limited ability to remove pesticide residues. Also, pesticides may harm a developing fetus or child by blocking the absorption of important food nutrients necessary for normal healthy growth.[31] Because of the potential risks from pesticides to a developing child, pregnant and breastfeeding women should peel fruit and vegetable rinds to decrease their exposure to residues. This is also a sensible precaution when preparing fruits or vegetables for small children.

Government Regulations Control the Use of Pesticides

The EPA is the government agency responsible for regulating the labeling, sale, distribution, use, and disposal of all pesticides in the United States. The EPA also sets a tolerance level, which is the maximum residue level of a pesticide permitted in or on food or feed grown in the United States or imported into the United States from other countries.[32] The EPA reviews every registered pesticide on a 15-year cycle.[32]

Before a pesticide can be accepted by the EPA for use, it must be determined that it performs its intended function with minimal impact to the environment. Once the EPA has certified a pesticide, states may set their own regulations for its use. Canadian regulation of pesticides closely resembles U.S. laws, with provinces and territories given free range to limit pesticide use.

The EPA provides these food-related tips to reduce a person's exposure to pesticides:[33]

- Wash and scrub all fresh fruits and vegetables thoroughly under running water. Using running water instead of soaking fruits and vegetables is more effective in removing pesticides, as running water is more abrasive than soaking. It is important to understand that all pesticide residues cannot be removed by washing.
- Peel fruits and vegetables whenever possible, and discard the outer leaves of leafy vegetables such as cabbage and lettuce. Trim the excess fat from meat and remove the skin from poultry and fish because some pesticide residues collect in the fat.
- Eat a variety of foods from various sources, as this can reduce the risk of exposure to a single pesticide.
- Consume more organically grown foods.

Gustavo
Nutri-Case

"My wife used to make her own corn tortillas from scratch. They were so good! But since she had her fall, she's been using more store-bought foods. Last night we ate tortillas made in New Jersey! Just like I thought, they tasted funny, so I checked the package to see what was in them besides corn. Well, I couldn't read it! I asked my daughter what all the words meant, and even she didn't know. There were three different kinds of acid listed, but why should tortillas need acid? Plus there was some kind of strange-sounding gum, but who ever heard of gum in tortillas? I can't wait for my wife to start home-cooking again, before all those chemicals make us sick."

What do you think of Gustavo's suspicion that the "chemicals" in processed foods will make him and his family sick? Can you guess what the "three different kinds of acid" might be? And the gum? Check Table 15.4 to see if you can determine why the food manufacturer might have included these additives in its packaged tortillas.

RECAP

Persistent organic pollutants (POPs) have been found in virtually all categories of foods. Mercury contaminates certain fish, and lead contaminates many foods. Both are toxic to the nervous system. Polychlorinated biphenyls (PCBs) and dioxins are two industrial pollutants that have been found in food worldwide. Pesticides are substances used to prevent or reduce food crop losses due to weeds, insects, fungi, and other organisms, including birds and mammals. They are potential toxins. The EPA regulates the labeling, sale, distribution, use, and disposal of all pesticides in the United States.

Growth Hormones and Antibiotics Are Used in Animals

Introduced in the U.S. food supply in 1994, **recombinant bovine growth hormone (rBGH)**, also known as *recombinant bovine somatotropin* (*rBST*), is a genetically engineered growth hormone. It is used in beef herds to induce animals to grow more muscle tissue and less fat. It is also injected into a third of U.S. dairy cows to increase milk output. Currently, there are no labeling requirements for products containing rBGH.

Although the FDA has allowed the use of rBGH in the United States, both Canada and the European Union have banned its use because of studies showing an increased risk of mastitis (inflamed udders), infertility, and lameness in dairy cows injected with rBGH.[34] In addition, the milk of cows receiving this hormone has higher levels of insulin-like growth factor (IGF-1). This protein can pass into the bloodstream of humans who drink milk from cows who receive rBGH, and some studies have shown that an elevated level of IGF-1 in humans may increase the risk of breast and prostate cancers.[35, 36] However, there are no studies directly linking increased risk of these cancers with eating products from animals injected with rBGH.

Advocates of rBGH say that its use allows farmers to use less feed for the same yield, reducing resource use by each ranch or farm. In addition, they argue that approximately 90% of the hormone in milk is destroyed during pasteurization and that the remaining percentage is destroyed during digestion in the human gastrointestinal tract.

A related concern is the use of antibiotics, not only in dairy cows, but also in other animals raised for food. As just noted, dairy cows subjected to rBGH are known to have an increased tendency to develop mastitis, which is treated via administration of antibiotics. In addition, antibiotics are routinely added to the feed of swine, in part to reduce the number of disease outbreaks in overcrowded pork-production facilities. Many researchers are concerned that cows, pigs, and other animals treated with antibiotics are becoming significant reservoirs for the development of a particularly virulent antibiotic-resistant strain of bacteria known as methicillin-resistant *Staphylococcus aureus* (MRSA).[37] Infection with MRSA can cause symptoms ranging from a "flesh-eating" skin rash to death: the CDC reports that in 2005, MRSA was responsible for more than 18,000 deaths in the United States.[38] In a recent study conducted on hog farms in Illinois and Iowa, 100% of swine aged 9 and 12 weeks tested positive for MRSA, and the prevalence among their workers was 64%.[37] MRSA appears to spread from animals to humans via contact, not consumption of animal foods; however, because the microorganism resists methicillin and other conventional antibiotics, it can rapidly spread through communities.

The resistant strain of bacteria known as methicillin-resistant *Staphlococcus aureus* (MRSA).

recombinant bovine growth hormone (rBGH) A genetically engineered hormone injected into dairy cows to enhance their milk output.

Are Organic Foods More Healthful?

The term *organic* is commonly used to describe foods that are grown without the use of synthetic pesticides. The thought of organic food used to conjure up images of hippies and bean sprouts. Now organic food has become part of the mainstream food supply. Recent national surveys indicate that approximately 27% of U.S. consumers use organic foods on a daily or weekly basis, and it is predicted that by 2025, 14% of the average household budget in the United States will be spent on organic products.[39, 40] Many small organic companies have been acquired by large corporations, resulting in many processed and snack foods carrying an organic label.

To Be Labeled Organic, Foods Must Meet Federal Standards

The National Organic Program (NOP) of the USDA came into law in October 2002. The organic industry itself had asked for national standards on organic labeling, as different U.S. states had different requirements for organic food labels and some had no rules at all. The European Union enforced a common standard for organic plant produce in 1991. Without a national standard, it was feared that European countries might seek to exclude U.S. organic exports.

The new Organic Standards established uniform definitions for all organic products. Any label or product claiming to be organic must comply with the following definitions:

- *100% organic:* Products containing only organically produced ingredients, excluding water and salt
- *Organic:* Products containing 95% organically produced ingredients by weight, excluding water and salt, with the remaining ingredients consisting of those products not commercially available in organic form
- *Made with organic ingredients:* A product containing more than 70% organic ingredients

If a processed product contains less than 70% organically produced ingredients, it cannot use the term *organic* in the principal display panel, but ingredients that are organically produced can be specified on the ingredients statement on the information panel.

Products that are "100% organic" and "organic" may display the USDA seal (**Figure 15.12**) or mark of certifying agents. Any product that is labeled as organic must identify each organically produced item in the ingredient statement of the label. The name and address of the certifying agency must also be on the label.

Figure 15.12 The USDA organic seal identifies foods that are at least 95% organic.

The USDA Regulates Organic Farming

The USDA regulates organic farming standards, and farms must be certified as organic by a government-approved certifier who inspects the farm and verifies that the farmer is following all USDA organic standards. Companies that handle or process organic food before it arrives at your local supermarket or restaurant must also be certified.[41] Organic farming methods are strict and require farmers to find natural alternatives to many common problems, such as weeds and insects. Contrary to common belief, organic farmers can use pesticides as a final option for pest control when all other methods have failed or are known to be ineffective, but they are restricted to a limited number that have been approved for use based on their origin, environmental impact, and potential to persist as residues.[42] Organic farmers emphasize the use of renewable resources and the conservation of soil and water to enhance environmental and nutritional quality. Once a crop is harvested, a winter crop (usually of a legume origin) is planted to help fix nitrogen in the soil and decrease erosion, which also lessens the need for fertilizers.

Organic meat, poultry, eggs, and dairy products come from animals fed only organic feed, and if the animals become ill, they are removed from the others until well again. None of these animals are given growth hormones to increase their size or ability to produce milk. Irradiation is also prohibited in organic production.

Studies Comparing Organic and Conventionally Grown Foods Are Limited

Recent studies at the University of California, Davis, and other institutions indicate that some organically grown fruits and vegetables are higher in vitamins E and C and in certain antioxidant phytochemicals than their non-organic counterparts.[43–45] Although these studies appear promising, they do not prove that organic foods are more nutritious than non-organic foods. To date, there are very few studies that have assessed the nutritional content of organically grown foods and compared them with the same foods grown non-organically. Thus, no consensus can be reached whether organic foods are more healthful than conventionally grown foods. What's more, an organic seal does not guarantee food safety: the company responsible for the *Salmonella* outbreak described at the beginning of this chapter had federal organic certification.[46]

RECaP

Recombinant bovine growth hormone (rBGH) is injected into meat and dairy cows to increase meat production and milk output. Concerns about rBGH include possible health problems as well as increased administration of antibiotics to dairy cows receiving the hormone. Antibiotics are also used in pork production, and researchers are concerned that both cows and swine are becoming reservoirs for a particularly virulent strain of antibiotic-resistant bacteria called MRSA. Organic Standards in 2002 established uniform definitions for all organic products sold in the United States. The USDA regulates organic farming standards and inspects and certifies farms. Although a few recent studies indicate that some organic foods have higher levels of some nutrients than non-organic foods, there is insufficient evidence to support the claim that organic foods are more nutritious than non-organic foods. Moreover, organic certification does not guarantee food safety.

See for Yourself

Although obtaining fresh produce from the farmers' market, washing it in clean water, cooking it as needed, and storing the leftovers in the refrigerator is a tasty, nutritious, safe way of eating most of the time, processed foods can also serve as welcome nourishment. Imagine that you are a survivor of Hurricane Katrina. You lost all of your belongings, but someone gave you money to travel by bus to stay for a few days in a motel in a nearby town. You share the room with four others. It has no stove and no refrigerator, and you are not sure if the tap water in the bathroom is safe to drink.

What would you buy at a grocery store so that you could eat a safe and balanced diet for 3 days without washing, cooking, or refrigeration?

Chapter Review

Test Yourself | Answers

1 (F) The actual number is much larger. Each year, about 76 million Americans are sickened and about 5,000 die as a direct result of eating food contaminated with germs or their toxins.

2 (F) False. Freezing inhibits the ability of most microbes to reproduce, but when the food is thawed, reproduction can resume.

3 (F) Bacteria cause the vast majority of cases of food-borne illness.

4 **F** Some recent studies have found higher levels of some micronutrients and antioxidant phytochemicals in organic foods as compared with non-organic foods. However, there are not enough studies published on this topic to state with confidence that organic foods are consistently more nutritious than non-organic foods.

5 **T** Before a new food additive can be used in food, the producer of the additive must demonstrate its safety to the FDA. The producer of the additive is required to submit data on its reasonable safety prior to the marketing or use of the additive, and the FDA makes a determination of the additive's safety based on these data. The Delaney Clause, enacted in 1958, states that "No additive may be permitted in any amount if tests show that it produces cancer when fed to man or animals or by other appropriate tests."

Summary

- Approximately 76 million Americans report experiencing food-borne illness each year.

- Food infections result from the consumption of food containing living microorganisms, such as bacteria, whereas food intoxications result from consuming food contaminated with toxins.

- The body has several defense mechanisms, such as saliva, stomach acid, vomiting, diarrhea, and the inflammatory response, that help rid us of offending microorganisms and toxins.

- In order to reproduce in foods, microbes require a precise range of temperature, humidity, acidity, and oxygen content.

- You can prevent food-borne illness at home by following these tips: Clean: wash your hands and kitchen surfaces often. Separate: Isolate foods to prevent cross-contamination. Chill: refrigerate or freeze perishable foods. Cook: heat foods long enough and at the required temperature to ensure proper cooking.

- Some natural techniques for food preservation include salting and sugaring, drying, smoking, and cooling.

- Synthetic food preservation techniques include canning, pasteurization, special packaging, addition of preservatives, irradiation, and genetic modification.

- Food additives are natural or synthetic ingredients added to foods during processing to enhance them in some way. They include flavorings, colorings, nutrients, texturizers, and other additives.

- The GRAS list identifies several hundred substances that have either been tested and found to be safe and approved for use in the food industry or are deemed safe as a result of consensus among experts qualified by scientific training and experience.

- Persistent organic pollutants (POPs) are chemicals released into the atmosphere as a result of industry, agriculture, automobile emissions, and improper waste disposal. Plants, animals, and fish absorb the chemicals from contaminated soil or water and pass them on as part of the food chain.

- Large predatory fish, such as swordfish, shark, king mackerel, and tilefish, tend to contain high levels of mercury, which is toxic to the nervous system.

- Although pesticides prevent or reduce crop losses, they are potential toxins; thus, their use is regulated by the EPA.

- Recombinant bovine growth hormone (rBGH) is injected into beef and dairy cows to increase their yield.

- Cows and pigs administered antibiotics have become significant reservoirs for the development of MRSA, an antibiotic-resistant strain of bacteria.

- Organic Standards in 2002 established uniform definitions for all organic products sold in the United States.

- A few recent research studies indicate that some organic foods may have higher levels of some nutrients than non-organic foods, but there is insufficient evidence to claim that organic foods are generally more nutritious than non-organic foods.

Review Questions

1. The three factors most often responsible for spoilage of foods are
   a. oxygen, heat, and light.
   b. carbon dioxide, heat, and light.
   c. moisture, heat, and cold.
   d. oxygen, cold, and light.

2. Yeasts are a type of
   a. mold used to make bread rise.
   b. bacteria that can cause food intoxication.
   c. fungus used to ferment foods.
   d. mold inhibitor used as a food preservative.

3. Monosodium glutamate (MSG) is a(n)
   a. thickening agent used in baby foods.
   b. flavor enhancer used in a variety of foods.
   c. mold inhibitor used on grapes and other foods.
   d. amino acid added as a nutrient to some foods.

4. Foods that are labeled *100% organic*
   a. contain only organically produced ingredients, excluding water and salt.
   b. may display the EPA's organic seal.
   c. were produced without the use of pesticides.
   d. contain no discernible level of toxic metals.

5. The potential spread of MRSA is a public health concern because
   a. MRSA is a strain of bacteria resistant to conventional antibiotics.
   b. MRSA readily spreads from animal populations to humans.
   c. MRSA can be fatal.
   d. All of the above.

6. **True or false?** Heating foods to at least 160°F guarantees that a food will not cause food-borne illness.

7. **True or false?** The CDC has established an Adverse Reaction Monitoring System (ARMS) to investigate complaints of adverse reactions to food additives.

8. **True or false?** In the United States, farms certified as organic are allowed to use pesticides under certain conditions.

9. **True or false?** Recombinant bovine growth hormone (rBGH) is used to increase the amount and quality of meat in beef herds and milk production in dairy cows.

10. **True or false?** Some colorings used as food additives do not need to be tested for safety.

11. A box of macaroni and cheese has the words *Certified Organic* on the front and the following ingredients listed on the side: "Organic durum semolina pasta (organic durum semolina, water), organic cheddar cheese (organic cultured pasteurized milk, salt, enzymes), whey, salt." Is this food 100% organic? Why or why not? Does it contain any food additives? If so, identify them.

12. Steven and Dante go to a convenience store after a tennis match looking for something to quench their thirst. Steven chooses a national brand of pasteurized orange juice, and Dante chooses a bottle of locally produced, organic, unpasteurized apple juice. Steven points out to Dante that his juice is not pasteurized, but he shrugs and says, "I'm more afraid of the pesticides they used on the oranges in your juice than I am about microorganisms in mine!" Which juice would *you* choose, and why?

13. Pickling is a food-preservation technique that involves soaking foods such as cucumbers in a solution containing vinegar (acetic acid). Why would pickling be effective in preventing food spoilage?

14. In the 1950s and 1960s in Minamata, Japan, more than 100 cases of a similar illness were recorded: Patients, many of whom were infants or young children, suffered irreversible damage to the nervous system. A total of forty-six people died. Adults with the disease and mothers of afflicted young children had one thing in common: They had frequently eaten fish caught in Minamata Bay. What do you think might have been the cause of this disease? Using key words from this description, research the event on the Internet and identify the culprit(s).

15. Your sister Joy, who attends a culinary arts school, is visiting you for dinner. You want to impress her, so you've decided to make chicken marsala. You begin that afternoon by removing two chicken breasts from the freezer and putting them in a bowl in the refrigerator to thaw. Then you go shopping for fresh salad ingredients. When you get home from the market, you take the chicken breasts from the refrigerator and set them on a clean cutting board. You then take the lettuce, red pepper, and scallions you just bought, put them in a colander, and rinse them. Next, you slice them with a clean knife on your marble countertop and toss them together in a salad. You put the chicken breasts in a frying pan and cook them until they lose their pink color. In a separate pan, you prepare the sauce. Finally, using a clean knife, you slice some freshly baked bread on the countertop. You then wash the knives and the cutting board you used for the chicken. Joy arrives and admires your skill in cooking. Later that night, you both wake up vomiting. Identify *at least two* aspects of your food preparation that might have contributed to your illness.

Web Links

www.cdc.gov/travel/foodwater.htm
Centers for Disease Control and Prevention
Check out this Web page before your next trip for information on food safety when traveling.

www.foodsafety.gov
Foodsafety.gov
Use this Web site as a gateway to government food safety information; it contains news and safety alerts, an area to report illnesses and product complaints, information on food-borne pathogens, and much more.

www.fsis.usda.gov
The USDA Food Safety and Inspection Service
A comprehensive site providing information on all aspects of food safety. Click on "Publications" for links to informative publications about food preparation, storage, handling, and other specific safety issues.

www.fsis.usda.gov/Fact_Sheets/ Cooking_Safely_in_the_Microwave/index.asp
USDA Food Fact Sheet on Cooking Safely in the Microwave
This fact sheet provides information on safe cooking and reheating of foods using a microwave oven.

www.cspinet.org/foodsafety/index.html
Center for Science in the Public Interest: Food Safety

Visit this Web site for summaries of food additives and their safety, alerts and other information, and interactive quizzes.

www.cfsan.fda.gov
The USDA Center for Food Safety and Applied Nutrition
This site contains thorough information on topics such as national food safety programs, recent news, and food labeling. It also contains links to special program areas, such as regulation of mercury levels in fish, food colorings, and biotechnology.

www.extension.iastate.edu/foodsafety
Food Safety Project
The Food Safety Project compiles educational materials about food safety for consumer use. Provided on the site are links for food safety from farm to table.

www.epa.gov/pesticides
The U.S. Environmental Protection Agency: Pesticides
This site provides information about agricultural and home-use pesticides, pesticide health and safety issues, environmental effects, and government regulation.

www.ams.usda.gov
The USDA National Organic Program
Click on "National Organic Program" to find the Web site describing the NOP's standards and labeling program, consumer information, and publications.

References

1. Centers for Disease Control and Prevention (CDC). March 17, 2009. Investigation update: Outbreak of *Salmonella typhimurium* infections, 2008–2009. Available at www.cdc.gov/salmonella/typhimurium/update.html. (Accessed April 2009.); U.S. Food and Drug Administration (FDA). FDA urges consumers not to eat hundreds of products recalled because of contaminated peanuts and peanut ingredients. *FDA Hot Topics*. Available at www.fda.gov/oc/opacom/hottopics/salmonellatyph/article.html. (Accessed March 2009.); U.S. Food and Drug Administration (FDA). April 10, 2009. Pistachio product recalls: Salmonella. Available at www.fda.gov/pistachios/. (Accessed April 2009.); Centers for Disease Control and Prevention (CDC). April 9, 2009. Annual report indicates salmonella continues to show least improvement. Available at www.cdc.gov/media/pressrel/2009/r090409.htm. (Accessed April 2009.)

2. Centers for Disease Control and Prevention (CDC), Division of Bacterial and Mycotic Diseases (DFBMD). May 21, 2008. *Salmonellosis*. Available at www.cdc.gov/nczved/dfbmd/disease_listing/salmonellosis_gi.html#8. (Accessed March 2009.)

3. Centers for Disease Control and Prevention (CDC), Division of Bacterial and Mycotic Diseases (DFBMD). 2005. Disease listing. Foodborne illness. Available at www.cdc.gov/ncidod/dbmd/diseaseinfo/foodborneinfections_g.htm.

4. Centers for Disease Control and Prevention (CDC). April 10, 2008. CDC report points to need for new foodborne illness strategies. Available at www.cdc.gov/media/pressrel/2008/r080410.htm.

5. Harris, G., March 15, 2009. President promises to bolster food safety. *The New York Times*. Available at www.nytimes.com/2009/03/15/us/politics/15address.html.

6. Bauman, R. W. 2004. *Microbiology*. San Francisco: Pearson Benjamin Cummings.

7. Centers for Disease Control and Prevention (CDC), Division of Bacterial and Mycotic Diseases (DFBMD). May 21, 2008. *Campylobacter*. Available at www.cdc.gov/nczved/dfbmd/disease_listing/campylobacter_gi.html.

8. Leavitt, J. W. 1996. *Typhoid Mary: Captive to the Public's Health*. Boston: Beacon Press.

9. Cunningham, A., ed. 2000. *Guinness World Records 2002*. Guinness World Records, Ltd. New York: Bantam.

10. Centers for Disease Control and Prevention (CDC), Division of Bacterial and Mycotic Diseases (DFBMD). October 12, 2005. Marine toxins. Available at www.cdc.gov/ncidod/dbmd/diseaseinfo/marinetoxins_g.htm.

11. Pavlista, A. D. 2001. Green potatoes: The problem and solution. NebGuide. The University of Nebraska-Lincoln Cooperative Extension. Available at http://ianrpubs.unl.edu/horticulture/g1437.htm.

12. Food and Drug Administration (FDA). March 23, 2007. FDA finalizes report on 2006 spinach outbreak. *FDA News*. Available at www.fda.gov/bbs/topics/NEWS/2007/NEW01593.html.

13. Food and Drug Administration (FDA). 2000. The unwelcome dinner guest: Preventing foodborne illness, Jan–Feb 1991. *FDA Consumer*. Available at www.cfsan.fda.gov/~dms/qa-prp6.html.

14. National Digestive Diseases Information Clearinghouse (NDDIC). May 2007. Bacteria and foodborne illness. NIH Publication No. 07-4730. Available at http://digestive.niddk.nih.gov/ddiseases/pubs/bacteria/index.htm.

15. Food and Drug Administration (FDA). 2005. Eating defensively: Food safety advice for persons with AIDS. Available at www.cfsan.fda.gov/~dms/aidseat.html.

16. U.S. Department of Agriculture (USDA). February 8, 2007. Food product dating. Fact sheets: Food labeling. Available at www.fsis.usda/gov/Factsheets/Food_Product_Dating/index.asp.

17. Food Marketing Institute. 2003. *A Consumer Guide to Food Quality and Safe Handling: Meat, Poultry, Seafood, Eggs* [pamphlet]. Washington, DC: Food Marketing Institute, pp. 1–5.

18. U.S. Department of Agriculture (USDA). 2003. Safe food handling. Barbecue food safety. Available at www.fsis.usda.gov/Fact_Sheets/Barbecue_Food_Safety/index.asp.

19. Food and Drug Administration (FDA). 2003. *Anisakis simplex* and related worms. *Foodborne Pathogenic Microorganisms and Natural Toxins Handbook*. Available at www.cfsan.fda.gov/~mow/chap25.html.

20. Center for Science in the Public Interest (CSPI). 2006. Tips to prevent food poisoning: CSPI's "eggspert" egg advice. Available at www.cspinet.org/foodsafety/eggspert_advice.html.

21. Shephard, S. 2000. *Pickled, Potted and Canned: The Story of Food Preserving*. London: Headline Publishing.

22. Aseptic Packaging Council. 2005. The award-winning, Earth smart packaging for a healthy lifestyle. Available at www.aseptic.org/main.shtml.

23. Loaharanu, P. 2003. *Irradiated Foods*. New York: American Council on Science & Health Booklets.

24. Consumer Reports. 2003. The truth about irradiated meat. Available at www.consumerreports.org/cro/food/irradiated-meat-803/overview.htm.

25. Center for Science in the Public Interest (CSPI). 2006. Food safety. Chemical cuisine. CSPI's guide to food additives. Available at www.cspinet.org/reports/chemcuisine.htm.

26. Geha, R. S., A. Beiser, C. Ren, R. Patterson, P. A. Greenberger, L. C. Grammer, A. M. Ditto, K. E. Harris, M. A. Shaughnessy, P. R. Yarnold, et al. 2000. Review of alleged reaction to monosodium glutamate and outcome of a multicenter double-blind placebo-controlled study. *J. Nutr.* 130(4S Suppl):1058S–1062S.

27. Schafer, K. S., and S. E. Kegley. 2002. Persistent toxic chemicals in the US food supply. *J. Epidemiol. Community Health* 56:813–817.

28. Food and Drug Administration (FDA). 2004. Mercury in fish: Cause for concern? Available at www. fda.gov/fdac/reprints mercury.html.

29. Environmental Protection Agency (EPA). 2005. Pesticides: Health and safety: Human health issues. Available at www.epa.gov/pesticides/health/human.htm.

30. Environmental Protection Agency (EPA). 2005. Pesticides: Health and safety: Pesticides and food: Health problems pesticides may pose. Available at www.epa.gov/pesticides/food/risks.htm.

31. Environmental Protection Agency (EPA). 2005. Pesticides: Health and safety: Pesticides and food: Why children may be especially sensitive to pesticides. Available at www.epa.gov/pesticides/food/pest.htm.

32. Environmental Protection Agency (EPA). 2005. About pesticides. Available at www.epa.gov/pesticides/about/index.htm.

33. Environmental Protection Agency (EPA). 2005. Pesticides and food: Healthy, sensible food practices. Available at www.epa.gov/pesticides/food/tips.htm.

34. LeSage, L. 1999. News release. Health Canada rejects bovine growth hormone in Canada. Health Canada Online. Available at www.hc-sc.gc.ca/ahc-asc/media/nr-cp/1999/1999_03_e.html.

35. Hankinson, S. E., W. C. Willett, G. A. Colditz, D. J. Hunter, D. S. Michaud, B. Deroo, B. Rosner, F. E. Speizer, and M. Pollak. 1998. Circulating concentrations of insulin-like growth factor-I and risk of breast cancer. *Lancet* 351(9113):1393–1396.

36. Chan, J. M., M. J. Stampfer, E. Giovannucci, P. H. Gann, J. Ma, P. Wilkinson, C. H. Hennekens, and M. Pollak. 1998. Plasma insulin-like growth factor-I and prostate cancer risk: A prospective study. *Science* 279(5350):563–566.

37. Smith, T. C., M. J. Male, A. L. Harper, J. S. Kroeger, G. P. Tinkler, et al. 2009. Methicillin-resistant *Staphylococcus aureus* (MRSA) strain ST398 is present in midwestern U.S. swine and swine workers. PLoS ONE 4(1): e4258. Doi: 10.1371/journal.pone.0004258.

38. Centers for Disease Control and Prevention (CDC). October 17, 2007. Invasive MRSA. Available at www.cdc.gov/ncidod/dhqp/ar_mrsa_Invasive_FS.html.

39. Organic Trade Association. 2004. OTA Survey: U.S. organic sales reach $10.8 billion. *What's News in Organic*. Issue 28. Available at www.ota.com/pics/documents/WhatsNews28.pdf.

40. Organic Trade Association. 2005. News release. Trends: Organic Trade Association envisions organic industry of the future. Available at www.ota.com/news/press/183.html.

41. Aiyana, J. 2002. What consumers should know about the new USDA organic labeling standard. The pulse of oriental medicine. Available at www.pulsemed.org/usdaorganic.htm.

42. Heaton, S. 2003. *Organic Farming, Food Quality and Human Health: A Review of the Evidence*. Soil Association. Bristol: Briston House.

43. Asami, D. K., Y. J. Hong, D. M. Barrett, and A. E. Mitchell. 2003. Comparison of the total phenolic and ascorbic acid content of freeze-dried and air-dried marionberry, strawberry, and corn grown using conventional, organic, and sustainable agricultural practices. *J. Agric. Food Chem.* 51(5):1237–1241.

44. Carbonaro, M., M. Mattera, S. Nicoli, P. Bergamo, and M. Cappelloni. 2002. Modulation of antioxidant compounds in organic vs. conventional fruit (peach, *Prunus persica L.*, and pear, *Pyrus communis L.*). *J. Agric. Food Chem.* 50(19):5458–5462.

45. Grinder-Pedersen, L., S. E. Rasmussen, S. Bügel, L. O. Jørgensen, D. Vagn Gundersen, and B. Sandström. 2003. Effect of diets based on foods from conventional versus organic production on intake and excretion of flavonoids and markers of antioxidative defense in humans. *Agric. Food Chem.* 51(19):5671–5676.

46. Severson, K., and A. Martin. March 4, 2009. It's organic, but does that mean it's safer? *The New York Times*. Available at www.nytimes.com/2009/03/04/dining/04cert.html.

47. U.S. Department of Agriculture (USDA), Economic Research Service. 2005. Data. Adoption of genetically engineered crops in the U.S. Available at www.ers.usda.gov/Data/BiotechCrops/.

48. McHughen, A. 2000. *Pandora's Picnic Basket: The Potential and Hazards of Genetically Modified Foods*. Oxford: Oxford University Press, pp. 17–45.

49. James, C. 2004. P*review: Global Status of Commercialized Biotech/GM Crops: 2004*. ISAAA Briefs No. 32. Ithaca, NY: ISAAA.

NUTRITION DEBATE

Genetically Modified Organisms: A Blessing or a Curse?

Current advances in biotechnology have opened the door to one of the most controversial topics in food science: genetically modified organisms (GMOs). GMOs are organisms that are created through *genetic engineering*, the standard U.S. term for a process in which foreign genes are spliced into a nonrelated species, creating an entirely new (*transgenic*) organism. Biotech foods, gene foods, bioengineered food, gene-altered foods, and transgenic foods are other terms used to describe foods that have been created through genetic engineering.

Developing GMOs is a lengthy, tedious, and costly process requiring years of research and testing. After carefully selecting and cultivating cells from an organism with a desired trait, the DNA is removed and scientists identify, isolate, and extract individual genes that code for the desired functions. Using bacteria to transfer these genes, scientists incorporate them into new cells where the introduced genes trigger the synthesis of proteins that accomplish the chosen functions. By using bacteria as the selected medium, DNA can be easily and efficiently produced and incorporated into any cell. Any plant, animal, or microorganism (such as bacteria or yeast) that has had its DNA altered in a laboratory to enhance or change certain characteristics is considered genetically engineered. For example, *Bacillus thuringiensis* is a genetically engineered bacterium that is used as a pesticide.

In the United States, companies are not required to list whether ingredients are genetically modified. This label from England indicates the genetically modified content of the food.

Golden rice (on right) is a genetically engineered variety of rice that synthesizes precursors of beta-carotene in the edible portions of rice. It was originally developed as a fortified food to be consumed in regions where vitamin A food sources are inadequate. Due to controversy surrounding its use, it is currently not available for human consumption.

Since 1994, hundreds of plants and animals have been genetically modified and incorporated into our current food market. In the United States, soy, corn, canola, and cotton crops make up the majority of the genetically modified crop acreage. The U.S. Department of Agriculture reports that 52% of all corn crops, 79% of all cotton crops, and 87% of all soybean crops grown in the United States are genetically engineered varieties.[47] In addition, several important medical therapeutics have been developed using this process, including human insulin, human growth factor, and factor VIII (a protein needed for blood clotting in people with hemophilia). Many scientists are working on *gene therapy*—that is, replacing defective genes in patients with genetic diseases such as sickle cell anemia with genes from people without the disease. Currently, research labs around the world are devoted to expanding the capabilities and applications of genetic engineering.

However, in genetic engineering, commercial success is not guaranteed: In 1994, the FlavrSavr tomato became the first commercially sold GMO. Developing this tomato involved identifying the gene that codes for an enzyme called polygalacturonase, which causes ripening in the tomato. This gene was removed and inserted back in reverse orientation. As a result, polygalacturonase was not synthesized, and ripening slowed dramatically—making

615

the tomato appear "fresh" longer and enabling it to maintain a longer shelf life.[48] Unfortunately, consumers felt the FlavrSavr tomato had poor flavor, and it was taken off the market in 1997.

Many people envision an ever-expanding role for genetic engineering in food production. They base their support on the numerous potential benefits resulting from the application of this technology. These benefits include:

- Enhanced taste and nutritional quality of food
- Crops that grow faster, have higher yields, can be grown in inhospitable soils, and have increased resistance to pests, disease, herbicides, and spoilage
- Increased production of high-quality meat, eggs, and milk
- Improved animal health due to increased disease resistance and overall hardiness
- Environmentally responsible outcomes such as use of less harmful herbicides and insecticides, conservation of soil, water, and energy, and more efficient food processing
- Increased food security for countries struggling with food insecurity and starvation

Despite these benefits, there is significant opposition to genetic engineering due to concerns related to environmental hazards, human health risks, and economic concerns. The concerns and potential problems of genetic engineering include:

- Gene transfer to nontarget species through cross-pollination, which could result in undesirable plants such as a superweed that is tolerant to herbicides and thus requires newer and stronger chemicals to destroy it
- Loss of biodiversity of plants and animals
- Increased risk of allergens, by either creating a new allergen or causing an allergic reaction in susceptible individuals
- Development of new diseases that can attack plants, animals, and humans
- Production of bacteria that are resistant to all antibiotics
- Potential for only a few food companies and countries to control the majority of world food production
- Inadequate or nonexistent labeling laws that prevent consumers from knowing if they are consuming foods that are genetically modified
- Creation of biological weapons and increased risk of bioterrorism

Some who oppose genetic engineering believe that it is unnatural and unethical to alter the genes of any organism. Most opponents base their concern on the fact that the potential long-term risks and dangers are unknown and may far outweigh the potential short-term benefits.

Genetically modified organisms are welcomed in some countries and outlawed in others. Six countries grow almost 100% of the world's genetically modified crops: the United States (59%), Argentina (20%), Canada (6%), Brazil (6%), China (5%), and Paraguay (2%).[49] Even though the United States and Canada are among the top global producers of genetically modified crops, there is a movement within these countries to ban the production of GMOs. Some counties in California have banned the production of GMOs, including Mendocino, Trinity, and Marin; and the Canadian province of Prince Edward Island has also proposed a ban on GMOs.

The European Union (EU) has strict regulations regarding GMOs, including having mechanisms in place for the tracking of GMO products through production and distribution chains and also monitoring any effect of GMOs on the environment. All foods produced for human consumption and all animal feed products that contain GMOs must be clearly labeled. In addition, any foods that are produced from GMO ingredients must be clearly labeled, even if the final food product does not contain DNA or protein of the original GMO. Currently only eighteen GMOs and fifteen genetically modified foods are marketed in the EU. Companies that wish to market GMOs and genetically modified foods in the EU must submit an ap-

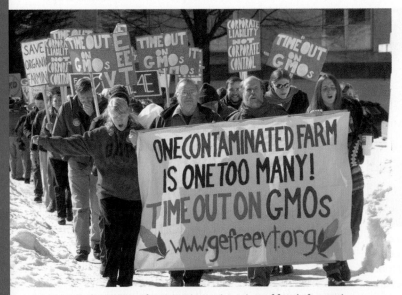

Many people oppose the genetic engineering of foods for environmental, health, or economic reasons.

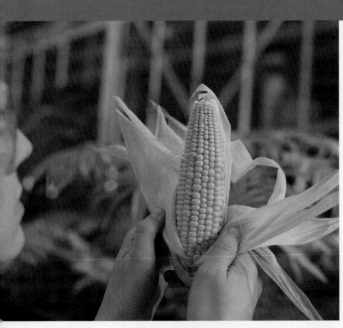

Genetically modified corn is widely cultivated in the United States.

plication that includes a full environmental risk assessment for GMOs and a safety assessment of genetically modified foods. This report is then reviewed by the designated government agencies and a decision is made regarding the application.

As GMOs and genetically modified foods have been available for only a few years, it will take more time to understand their impact on the world.

Critical Thinking Questions

■ What's your view of the controversy around the genetic engineering of food?

■ Based on your current knowledge of GMOs and genetically modified foods, do you support their use and mass distribution both within the United States and around the world?

■ Do you think that genetically modified foods should be clearly labeled for consumers?

■ Do you have any reservations about buying and consuming genetically modified foods? If so, what are they?

16

Nutrition Through the Life Cycle: Pregnancy and the First Year of Life

Test Yourself | True or False?

1   A pregnant woman needs to consume twice as many calories as she did prior to the pregnancy. **T** *or* **F**

2   Despite popular belief, very few pregnant women actually experience morning sickness, food cravings, or food aversions. **T** *or* **F**

3   Breast-fed infants tend to have fewer infections and allergies than formula-fed infants. **T** *or* **F**

4   When a breastfeeding woman drinks caffeinated beverages such as coffee, the caffeine enters the breast milk. **T** *or* **F**

5   Most infants begin to require solid foods by about 3 months (12 weeks) of age. **T** *or* **F**

Test Yourself answers are located in the Chapter Review.

Chapter Objectives   *After reading this chapter, you will be able to:*

1. List four reasons why maintaining a nutritious diet is important for a woman of childbearing age even prior to conception, *pp. 620–621.*

2. Explore the relationship between fetal development, physiologic changes in the pregnant woman, and increasing nutrient requirements during the course of a pregnancy, *pp. 621–623.*

3. Identify the ranges of optimal weight gain for pregnant women, including adolescent and adult pregnancies, singleton and multiple pregnancies, and normal, underweight, and overweight/obese women, *pp. 625–626.*

4. Describe the physiologic basis of lactation, *pp. 638–639.*

5. Compare and contrast the nutrient requirements of pregnant and lactating women, *pp. 639–641.*

6. Identify the primary advantages and most common challenges of breastfeeding, *pp. 642–645.*

7. Relate the growth and activity patterns of infants to their nutrient needs, *pp. 646–650.*

8. Discuss the timing and sequencing of introducing solid foods to infants, *pp. 651–653.*

9. Identify those factors that increase the risk of food allergies in infants, *pp. 653–654.*

When she was a baby, Theresa showed poor coordination, was slow to walk and start talking, and was what her grandmother called "a real handful." Now an energetic 12-year-old, she still struggles every day to learn new information and keep up with her classmates physically and academically. Even though she tries hard, Theresa has a poor attention span and is often in trouble for misbehaving in class. Unfortunately, Theresa's physical, mental, and behavioral problems are likely to persist, and new ones may develop. That's because Theresa was born with fetal alcohol syndrome (FAS). During her pregnancy, Theresa's mother consumed beer and hard alcohol several times a week, causing lifelong health problems for her daughter.

What role does prenatal diet play in determining the future health and well-being of the child? What is the link between alcohol and birth defects? Why is inadequate iron or folate intake especially dangerous to a pregnant woman and her fetus? What roles do protein, zinc, calcium, and other nutrients play in maternal and fetal health? In this chapter, we discuss how adequate nutrition supports fetal development, maintains the pregnant woman's health, and contributes to lactation. We then explore the nutrient needs of breastfeeding and formula-feeding infants.

Starting Out Right: Healthful Nutrition in Pregnancy

At no stage of life is nutrition more crucial than during fetal development and infancy. From conception through the end of the first year of life, adequate nutrition is essential for tissue formation, neurologic development, and bone growth, modeling, and remodeling. The ability to reach peak physical and intellectual potential in adult life is in part determined by the nutrition received during fetal development and the first year of life. Public health officials view pregnancy-related nutrition as so important to the health of the nation that several *Healthy People 2010* goals are specific to prenatal and postnatal nutrition.[1] These goals will be identified throughout the chapter.

Is Nutrition Important Before Conception?

Several factors make adequate nutrition important even before **conception,** the point at which a woman's ovum (egg) is fertilized with a man's sperm. First, some problems related to nutrient deficiency develop extremely early in the pregnancy, typically before the mother even realizes she is pregnant. An adequate and varied preconception diet reduces the risk of such problems, providing "insurance" during those first few weeks of pregnancy.

For example, failure of the spinal cord to close results in *neural tube defects;* these defects are closely related to inadequate folate status during the first few weeks after conception. For this reason, all women capable of becoming pregnant are encouraged to consume 400 μg of folic acid from fortified foods such as cereals or supplements daily, in addition to natural sources of folate from a varied, healthful diet. This recommendation should be followed by all women of childbearing age whether or not they plan to become pregnant.

Second, adopting a healthful diet and lifestyle prior to conception requires women to avoid alcohol, illegal drugs, and other known **teratogens** (substances that cause birth defects). Women should also consult their healthcare provider about their consumption of caffeine, medications, herbs, and supplements; and if they smoke, they should attempt to quit.

Third, a healthful diet and appropriate levels of physical activity can help women achieve and maintain an optimal body weight prior to pregnancy. Women with a prepregnancy body mass index (BMI) between 19.8 and 26.0 have the best chance of an uncomplicated pregnancy and delivery, with low risk of negative outcomes such as prolonged labor and cesarean section.[2] As we will discuss in greater detail shortly, women with a BMI below or above this range prior to conception are at greater risk for pregnancy-related complications.

Finally, maintaining a balanced and nourishing diet before conception reduces a woman's risk of developing a nutrition-related disorder during her pregnancy. These disor-

During conception, a sperm fertilizes an egg, creating a zygote.

conception   (also called *fertilization*) The uniting of an ovum (egg) and sperm to create a fertilized egg, or zygote.

teratogen   Any substance that can cause a birth defect.

ders, which we discuss later in the chapter, include gestational diabetes and hypertensive disorders. Although genetic and metabolic abnormalities are beyond the woman's control, following a healthful diet prior to conception is something a woman can do to help her fetus develop into a healthy baby.

The man's nutrition prior to pregnancy is important as well, because malnutrition contributes to abnormalities in sperm.[3] Both sperm number and motility (ability to move) are reduced by alcohol consumption, as well as the use of certain prescription and illegal drugs. Finally, infections accompanied by a high fever can destroy sperm; so, to the extent that adequate nutrition keeps the immune system strong, it also promotes a man's fertility.

Why Is Nutrition Important During Pregnancy?

A balanced, nourishing diet throughout pregnancy provides the nutrients needed to support fetal growth and development without depriving the mother of nutrients she needs to maintain her own health. It also minimizes the risks of excess energy intake. A full-term pregnancy, also called the period of **gestation,** lasts 38 to 42 weeks and is divided into three **trimesters,** with each trimester lasting about 13 to 14 weeks.

The First Trimester

About once each month, a non-pregnant woman of childbearing age experiences *ovulation,* the release of an ovum (egg cell) from an ovary. The ovum is then drawn into the uterine (fallopian) tube. The first trimester (approximately weeks 1 through 13) begins when the ovum and sperm unite to form a single, fertilized cell called a **zygote.** As the zygote travels through the uterine tube, it further divides into a ball of 12 to 16 cells that, at about day 4, arrives in the uterus (**Figure 16.1**). By day 10, the inner portion of the zygote, called the *blastocyst,* implants into the uterine lining. The outer portion becomes part of the placenta, which is discussed shortly.

Further cell growth, multiplication, and differentiation occurs, resulting in the formation of an **embryo.** Over the next 6 weeks, embryonic tissues fold into a primitive tubelike

gestation   The period of intrauterine development from conception to birth.

trimester   Any one of three stages of pregnancy, each lasting 13 to 14 weeks.

zygote   A fertilized egg (ovum) consisting of a single cell.

embryo   Human growth and developmental stage lasting from the third week to the end of the eighth week after fertilization.

Figure 16.1   Ovulation, conception, and implantation.

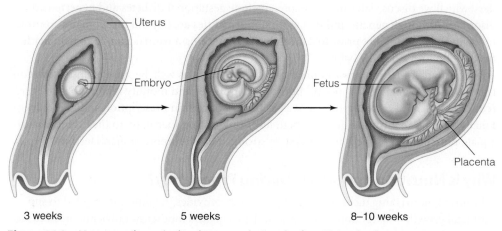

3 weeks   5 weeks   8–10 weeks

Figure 16.2 Human embryonic development during the first 10 weeks. Organ systems are most vulnerable to teratogens during this time, when cells are dividing and differentiating.

spontaneous abortion (also called *miscarriage*) Natural termination of a pregnancy and expulsion of pregnancy tissues because of a genetic, developmental, or physiologic abnormality that is so severe that the pregnancy cannot be maintained.

placenta A pregnancy-specific organ formed from both maternal and embryonic tissues. It is responsible for oxygen, nutrient, and waste exchange between mother and fetus.

structure with limb buds, organs, and facial features recognizable as human (**Figure 16.2**). It isn't surprising, then, that the embryo is most vulnerable to teratogens during this time. Not only alcohol and illegal drugs but also prescription and over-the-counter medications, megadoses of supplements such as vitamin A, certain herbs, viruses, cigarette smoking, and radiation can interfere with embryonic development and cause birth defects.[3] In some cases, the damage is so severe that the pregnancy is naturally terminated in a **spontaneous abortion** (*miscarriage*), which occurs most often in the first trimester.

During the first weeks of pregnancy, the embryo obtains its nutrients from cells lining the uterus. But by the fourth week, a primitive **placenta** has formed in the uterus from both embryonic and maternal tissue. Within a few more weeks, the placenta will be a fully functioning organ through which the mother will provide nutrients and remove fetal wastes (see **Figure 16.3**).

By the end of the embryonic stage, about 8 weeks postconception, the embryo's tissues and organs have differentiated dramatically. A primitive skeleton, including fingers and toes, has formed. Muscles have begun to develop in the trunk and limbs, and some move-

Figure 16.3 Placental development. The placenta is formed from both embryonic and maternal tissues. When the placenta is fully functional, fetal blood vessels and maternal blood vessels are intimately intertwined, allowing the exchange of nutrients and wastes between the two. The mother transfers nutrients and oxygen to the fetus, and the fetus transfers wastes to the mother for disposal.

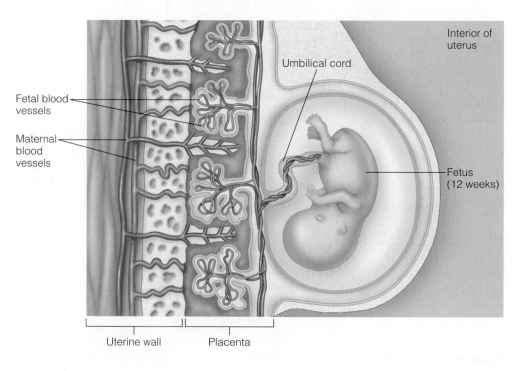

ment is now possible. A primitive heart has also formed and begun to beat, and the digestive system is differentiating into distinct organs (stomach, liver, and so forth). The brain and cranial nerves have differentiated, and the head has a mouth, eyespots with eyelids, and primitive ears.[3]

The third month of pregnancy marks the transition from embryo to **fetus.** The fetus requires abundant nutrients from the mother's body to support its dramatic growth during this period. The placenta is now a mature organ that can provide these nutrients. It is connected to the fetal circulatory system via the **umbilical cord,** an extension of fetal blood vessels emerging from the fetus's navel (called the *umbilicus*). Blood rich in oxygen and nutrients flows through the placenta and into the umbilical vein (Figure 16.3). Once inside the fetus's body, the blood travels to the fetal liver and heart. Wastes are excreted in blood returning from the fetus to the placenta via the umbilical arteries. Although many people think there is a mixing of blood from the fetus and the mother, the two blood supplies remain separate; the placenta is the "go-between" that allows the transfer of nutrients and wastes.

Because the formation of body limbs, eyes and ears, and organs occurs during the first trimester, nutrient deficiencies during this time can lead to irreversible structural or functional damage. At the same time, nutrient toxicities as well as exposure to drugs, alcohol, certain medications, or microbes during this trimester can also result in fetal malformation. The consequences of specific nutrient deficiencies and toxicities are discussed shortly.

The Second Trimester

During the second trimester (approximately weeks 14 to 27 of pregnancy), the fetus continues to grow and mature (**Figure 16.4**). The fetus can suck its thumb, its ears begin to hear, and its eyes can open and close and react to light. The placenta is now fully functional. At the beginning of the second trimester, the fetus is about 3 inches long and weighs about 1.5 lb. By the end of the second trimester, the fetus is generally more than a foot long and weighs more than 2 lb. Some babies born prematurely in the last weeks of the second trimester survive with intensive **neonatal** care.

The Third Trimester

The third trimester (approximately weeks 28 to birth) is a time of remarkable growth for the fetus. During three short months, the fetus gains nearly half its body length and three-quarters of its body weight! At the time of birth, an average baby will be approximately 18 to 22 inches long and about 7.5 lb in weight (see Figure 16.4). Brain growth (which continues to be rapid for the first 2 years of life) is also quite remarkable, and the lungs become fully mature. Because of the intense growth and maturation of the fetus during the third trimester, it continues to be critical that the mother eat an adequate and balanced diet.

Impact of Nutrition on Newborn Maturity and Birth Weight

An adequate, nourishing diet is one of the most important modifiable variables increasing the chances for birth of a mature newborn. Proper nutrition also increases the likelihood that the newborn's weight will be appropriate for his or her gestational age. Generally, a birth weight of at least 5.5 lb is considered a marker of a successful pregnancy.

An undernourished mother is likely to give birth to a **low-birth-weight** infant.[4] Any infant weighing less than 5.5 lb at birth is considered to be of low birth weight and is at increased risk of infection, learning disabilities, impaired physical development, and death in the first year of life (**Figure 16.5** on page 625). Many low-birth-weight infants are born **preterm**—that is, before 38 weeks of gestation. Others are born at term but weigh less than would be expected for their gestational age; this condition is called **small for gestational age (SGA).** Although nutrition is not the only factor contributing to maturity and birth weight, its role cannot be overstated.

fetus Human growth and developmental stage lasting from the beginning of the ninth week after conception to birth.

umbilical cord The cord containing arteries and veins that connects the baby (from the navel) to the mother via the placenta.

neonatal Referring to a newborn.

low birth weight A weight of less than 5.5 lb at birth.

preterm Birth of a baby prior to 38 weeks of gestation.

small for gestational age (SGA) Infants whose birth weight for gestational age falls below the 10th percentile.

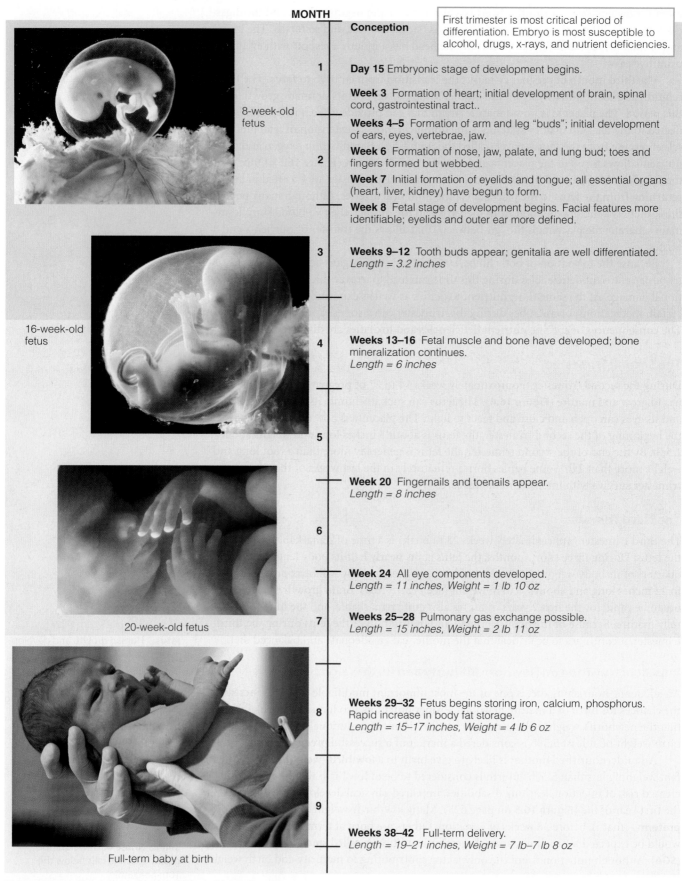

MONTH

Conception

First trimester is most critical period of differentiation. Embryo is most susceptible to alcohol, drugs, x-rays, and nutrient deficiencies.

8-week-old fetus

1

Day 15 Embryonic stage of development begins.

Week 3 Formation of heart; initial development of brain, spinal cord, gastrointestinal tract..

Weeks 4–5 Formation of arm and leg "buds"; initial development of ears, eyes, vertebrae, jaw.

2

Week 6 Formation of nose, jaw, palate, and lung bud; toes and fingers formed but webbed.

Week 7 Initial formation of eyelids and tongue; all essential organs (heart, liver, kidney) have begun to form.

Week 8 Fetal stage of development begins. Facial features more identifiable; eyelids and outer ear more defined.

3

Weeks 9–12 Tooth buds appear; genitalia are well differentiated. *Length = 3.2 inches*

16-week-old fetus

4

Weeks 13–16 Fetal muscle and bone have developed; bone mineralization continues. *Length = 6 inches*

5

Week 20 Fingernails and toenails appear. *Length = 8 inches*

6

Week 24 All eye components developed. *Length = 11 inches, Weight = 1 lb 10 oz*

20-week-old fetus

7

Weeks 25–28 Pulmonary gas exchange possible. *Length = 15 inches, Weight = 2 lb 11 oz*

8

Weeks 29–32 Fetus begins storing iron, calcium, phosphorus. Rapid increase in body fat storage. *Length = 15–17 inches, Weight = 4 lb 6 oz*

9

Weeks 38–42 Full-term delivery. *Length = 19–21 inches, Weight = 7 lb–7 lb 8 oz*

Full-term baby at birth

Figure 16.4   A timeline of embryonic and fetal development.

RECAP

A full-term pregnancy lasts from 38 to 42 weeks and is traditionally divided into trimesters lasting 13 to 14 weeks. During the first trimester, cells differentiate and divide rapidly to form the various tissues of the human body. The fetus is especially susceptible to nutrient deficiencies, toxicities, and teratogens during this time. The second and third trimesters are characterized by continued growth and maturation. Nutrition is important before and throughout pregnancy to support fetal development without depleting the mother's reserves. An adequate, nourishing diet increases the chance that a baby will be born after 37 weeks and will weigh at least 5.5 lb.

How Much Weight Should a Pregnant Woman Gain?

Recommendations for weight gain vary according to a woman's weight *before* she became pregnant (Table 16.1) and whether the pregnancy is singleton (one fetus) or multiple (two or more fetuses). As you can see in Table 16.1, the average recommended weight gain for women of normal prepregnancy weight is 25 to 35 lb; underweight women should gain a little more than this amount, and overweight and obese women should gain somewhat less.[5] Adolescents should follow the same recommendations as those for adults. Women of normal prepregnancy weight who are pregnant with twins are advised to gain 37 to 54 lb.[5]

Women who have a low prepregnancy BMI (<18.5) or gain too little weight during their pregnancy increase their risk of having a preterm or low-birth-weight baby and of dangerously depleting their own nutrient reserves. Gaining *too much* weight during pregnancy or being overweight (BMI ⩾25) or obese (BMI ⩾30) prior to conception is also risky. Excessive prepregnancy weight or prenatal gain increases the risk that the fetus will be large for his or her gestational age, and large babies have an increased risk of trauma during vaginal delivery and of cesarean birth. Also, children born to overweight or obese mothers have higher rates of childhood obesity[6] and childhood metabolic syndrome.[7] A high birth weight has also been linked to increased risk of adolescent obesity. In addition, the more weight gained during pregnancy, the more difficult it is for the mother to return to her prepregnancy weight and the more likely it is that her weight gain will be permanent. This weight retention can become especially problematic if the woman has two or more children; the extra weight also increases her long-term risk for type 2 diabetes and high blood pressure. One goal of *Healthy People 2010* is to increase the proportion of mothers who achieve a recommended weight gain during their pregnancies, thus avoiding excessive and inadequate weight gains.[1]

In addition to the amount of weight, the *pattern* of weight gain is important. During the first trimester, a woman of normal weight should gain no more than 3 to 5 lb. During the second and third trimester, an average of about 1 lb a week is considered healthful for normal-weight women. For overweight women, a gain of 0.6 lb/week is appropriate, and obese women should gain 0.5 lb/week.[5] If weight gain is excessive in a single week, month, or trimester, the woman should not attempt to lose weight. Dieting during pregnancy can harm the health of both mother and fetus by depriving them of critical nutrients. Instead, the woman should merely attempt to slow the rate of weight gain. On the other hand, if a woman has not gained sufficient weight in the early months of her pregnancy, she should gradually increase her energy and nutrient intake. The newborns of women who lose

Figure 16.5 A healthy 2-day-old infant (right) compared with two low-birth-weight infants.

Table 16.1 Recommended Weight Gain for Women During Pregnancy[5]

Prepregnancy Weight Status	Body Mass Index (kg/m²)	Recommended Total Weight Gain (lb)
Normal	18.5–24.9	25–35
Underweight	<18.5	28–40
Overweight	25.0–29.9	15–25

Following a physician-approved exercise program helps pregnant women maintain a positive body image and prevent excess weight gain.

weight during the first trimester, due to severe nausea and vomiting, for example, are likely to be of lower birth weight than newborns of women with appropriate weight gain.[8] If inappropriately low maternal weight gain occurs, the woman should not attempt to "catch up" all at once; rather, she should gradually increase her rate of weight gain. In short, weight gain throughout pregnancy should be slow and steady.

In a society obsessed with thinness, it is easy for pregnant women to worry about weight gain. Focusing on the quality of food consumed, rather than the quantity, can help women feel more in control. In addition, following a physician-approved exercise program helps women maintain a positive body image and prevent excessive weight gain. The 2005 Dietary Guidelines for Americans advises pregnant women to ensure an appropriate weight gain as specified by a qualified healthcare provider.[9]

A pregnant woman may also feel less anxious about her weight gain if she understands how that weight is distributed. Of the total weight gained in pregnancy, 10 to 12 lb are accounted for by the fetus itself, the amniotic fluid, and the placenta (**Figure 16.6**). Another 3 to 4 lb represents an increase of 40% to 50% in maternal blood volume. A woman can expect to be about 10 to 12 lb lighter immediately after the birth and, within about 2 weeks, another 5 to 8 lb lighter because of fluid loss (from plasma and interstitial fluid).

After the first 2 weeks, losing the remainder of pregnancy weight requires that more energy be expended than is taken in. Appropriate physical activity can help women lose those extra pounds. Also, because production of breast milk requires significant energy, breastfeeding helps many new mothers lose the remaining weight. Moderate weight reduction is safe while breastfeeding and will not compromise the weight gain of the nursing infant.[9] We discuss breastfeeding on pages 637–645.

RECaP

Sufficient calories should be consumed so that a pregnant woman gains an appropriate amount of weight, typically 25 to 35 lb, to ensure adequate growth of the fetus. The calories consumed during pregnancy should be nutrient-dense so that both the mother and the fetus obtain the nutrients they need from food.

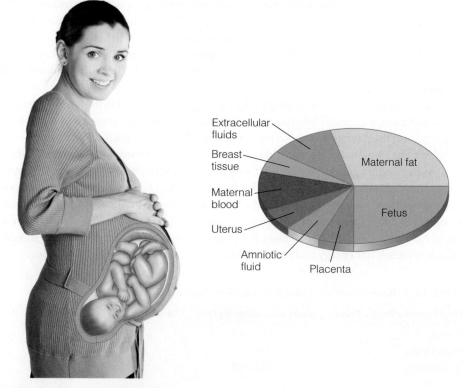

Figure 16.6 The weight gained during pregnancy is distributed between the mother's own tissues and the pregnancy-specific tissues.

(a)   (b)

Figure 16.7   Spina bifida, a common neural tube defect. **(a)** An external view of an infant with spina bifida. **(b)** An internal view of the protruding spinal membrane and fluid-filled sac.

Folate   Because folate is necessary for cell division, it follows that during a time when both maternal and fetal cells are dividing rapidly, the requirement for this vitamin would be increased. Adequate folate is especially critical during the first 28 days after conception, when it is required for the formation and closure of the **neural tube,** an embryonic structure that eventually becomes the brain and spinal cord. Folate deficiency is associated with neural tube defects such as **spina bifida** (**Figure 16.7**) and **anencephaly,** a fatal defect in which there is partial absence of brain tissue.[12] Adequate folate intake does not guarantee normal neural tube development, as the precise cause of neural tube defects is unknown, and, in some cases, there is a genetic component. It is estimated, however, that up to 70% of all neural tube defects could be prevented by simply improving maternal intake of folic acid or folate.[13] One goal of *Healthy People 2010* is to reduce the occurrence of spina bifida and other neural tube defects by increasing the proportion of pregnancies begun with an optimum folate level.[1]

To reduce the risk of a neural tube defect, all women capable of becoming pregnant are encouraged to consume 400 µg of folic acid per day from supplements, fortified foods, or both in addition to a variety of foods naturally high in folates. The emphasis on obtaining folic acid from supplements and fortified foods is due to the higher bioavailability of these sources. Of course, folate remains very important even after the neural tube has closed. The RDA for folate for pregnant women is therefore 600 µg/day, a full 50% increase over the RDA for a non-pregnant female.[12] A deficiency of folate during pregnancy can result in macrocytic anemia (a condition in which blood cells do not mature properly) and has been associated with low birth weight, preterm delivery, and failure of the fetus to grow properly. Sources of food folate are discussed on page 283 and include orange juice, green leafy vegetables such as spinach and broccoli, and lentils. For more than a decade, the Food and Drug Administration (FDA) has mandated that all enriched grain products such as cereals, breads, and pastas be fortified with folic acid; thus, including these foods, ideally as whole grains, in the daily diet can further increase folate intake.

Vitamin B₁₂   Vitamin B_{12} (cobalamin) is vital during pregnancy because it regenerates the active form of folate. Not surprisingly, deficiencies of vitamin B_{12} can also result in macrocytic anemia. Yet the RDA for vitamin B_{12} for pregnant women is only 2.6 µg/day, a mere 8% increase over the RDA of 2.4 µg/day for non-pregnant women.[12] How can this be? One reason is that during pregnancy, absorption of vitamin B_{12} is more efficient. The required amount of vitamin B_{12} can easily be obtained from animal food sources such as meats, dairy products, and eggs. However, deficiencies have been observed in women who have followed a vegan diet for several years; these deficiencies have also been observed in the infants of some mothers who follow a vegan diet. Fortified foods or supplementation provides these women with the needed amounts of vitamin B_{12}.

Spinach is an excellent source of folate.

neural tube   Embryonic tissue that forms a tube, which eventually becomes the brain and spinal cord.

spina bifida   Embryonic neural tube defect that occurs when the spinal vertebrae fail to completely enclose the spinal cord, allowing it to protrude.

anencephaly   A fatal neural tube defect in which there is partial absence of brain tissue most likely caused by failure of the neural tube to close.

Vitamin C Because blood plasma volume increases during pregnancy, and because vitamin C is being transferred to the fetus, the concentration of vitamin C in maternal blood decreases. Vitamin C deficiency during pregnancy has been associated with an increased risk of premature birth and other complications. The RDA for vitamin C during pregnancy is increased by a little more than 10% over the RDA for non-pregnant women (from 75 mg to 85 mg per day for adult pregnant women; 80 mg per day for pregnant adolescents). Women who smoke during pregnancy should consume even higher levels of vitamin C, because smoking lowers both serum and amniotic fluid levels. As described on page 283, many foods are rich sources of vitamin C, such as citrus fruits and juices, peppers, and numerous other fruits and vegetables.

Vitamin A Vitamin A needs increase during pregnancy by about 10%, to 770 μg per day for adult pregnant women and 750 μg per day for pregnant adolescents. Vitamin A deficiency during pregnancy has been linked to an increased risk of low birth weight, growth problems, and preterm delivery. However, excess preformed vitamin A exerts teratogenic effects. Consumption of excessive preformed vitamin A, particularly during the first trimester, increases the risk for birth of an infant with craniofacial malformations, including cleft lip or palate, heart defects, and abnormalities of the central nervous system.[14] A well-balanced diet supplies sufficient vitamin A, so supplementation during pregnancy is not recommended. Note that provitamin A, in the form of beta-carotene (which is converted to vitamin A in the body), has not been associated with birth defects.

Vitamin D Despite the role of vitamin D in calcium absorption, the AI for this nutrient does not increase during pregnancy. According to the Institute of Medicine, the amount of vitamin D transferred from the mother to the fetus is relatively small and does not appear to affect overall vitamin D status.[15] Pregnant women who receive adequate exposure to sunlight do not need vitamin D supplements. However, pregnant women with darkly pigmented skin and/or limited sun exposure who do not regularly drink milk will benefit from vitamin D supplementation. It has been estimated that almost 30% of dark-skinned pregnant women living in the northeastern U.S. are in a state of vitamin D deficiency, which may result in impaired fetal growth, preeclampsia, fetal bone defects, and increased risk for diabetes and asthma later in the offspring's life.[16] Most prenatal vitamin supplements contain 10 μg/day of vitamin D, which is considered safe and acceptable, although some researchers view that level as inadequate for maintaining normal serum levels of vitamin D.[15] Because vitamin D is fat-soluble, pregnant women should avoid consuming excessive vitamin D from supplements, as toxicity can cause developmental disability in the newborn.

Calcium Growth of the fetal skeleton requires as much as 30 g of calcium, most during the last trimester. However, the AI for calcium does not change during pregnancy; it remains at 1,300 mg/day for pregnant adolescents and 1,000 mg/day for adult pregnant women for two reasons. First, pregnant women absorb calcium from the diet more efficiently than do non-pregnant women, assuming adequate vitamin D status. Second, the extra demand for calcium has not been found to cause permanent demineralization of the mother's bones or to increase fracture risk; thus, there is no justification for recommending higher intakes.[15] Sources of calcium are discussed on page 285. Pregnant women who are lactose intolerant can meet their calcium requirements by consuming calcium-fortified soy milk, rice milk, juices, cereals, reduced-lactose milk, and low-lactose dairy foods such as yogurt and aged cheeses.

Iron Recall from Chapter 12 the importance of iron in the formation of red blood cells, which transport oxygen throughout the body so that cells can produce ATP. During pregnancy, the demand for red blood cells increases to accommodate the needs of the expanded maternal blood volume, growing uterus, placenta, and the fetus itself. Thus, more iron is needed. Fetal demand for iron increases even further during the last trimester, when

Meats provide complete protein, which is essential for building and maintaining maternal and fetal tissues.

the fetus stores iron in the liver for use during the first few months of life. This iron storage is protective because breast milk is low in iron. The Dietary Guidelines for Americans specifically advises women of childbearing age who may become pregnant to eat foods high in heme iron, such as meat, fish, and poultry, and/or consume iron-rich plant foods, such as legumes, or iron-fortified foods with vitamin C–rich foods.[9]

Severely inadequate iron intake certainly has the potential to harm the fetus, resulting in an increased rate of low birth weight, preterm birth, stillbirth, and death of the newborn in the first weeks after birth. However, in most cases, the iron-deprived fetus builds adequate stores by "robbing" maternal iron, resulting in iron-deficiency anemia in the mother. During pregnancy, maternal iron deficiency causes extreme paleness and exhaustion, but at birth it endangers the mother's life: Anemic women are more likely to die during or shortly after childbirth because they are less able to tolerate blood loss and fight infection. Two goals of *Healthy People 2010* in relation to iron and pregnancy are to reduce iron deficiency among pregnant females and reduce anemia among low-income pregnant females in their third trimester.[1]

The RDA for iron during pregnancy is 27 mg per day, compared with 18 mg per day for non-pregnant women and 15 mg per day for non-pregnant adolescents.[14] This represents a 50% to 80% increase, despite the fact that iron loss is minimized during pregnancy because menstruation ceases. Typically, women of childbearing age have poor iron stores, and the demands of pregnancy are likely to produce deficiency. To ensure adequate iron stores during pregnancy, an iron supplement (as part of, or separate from, a total prenatal supplement) is routinely prescribed during the last two trimesters. Vitamin C enhances iron absorption, as do dietary sources of heme iron, whereas substances in coffee, tea, milk, bran, and oxalate-rich foods decrease absorption. Therefore, many healthcare providers recommend taking iron supplements with foods high in vitamin C and/or heme iron. Sources of iron are discussed on page 286.

Zinc   The RDA for zinc for adult pregnant women increases by about 38% over the RDA for non-pregnant adult women, from 8 mg per day to 11 mg per day, and the RDA increases from 9 mg per day to 12 mg per day for pregnant adolescents.[14] Because zinc has critical roles in DNA, RNA, and protein synthesis, it is extremely important that adequate zinc status be maintained during pregnancy to ensure proper growth and development of both maternal and fetal tissues. Inadequate zinc can lead to fetal malformations, premature birth, decreased birth size, and extended labor. It should be noted that the absorption of zinc from supplements is inhibited by high intakes of non-heme iron, such as those found in iron supplements, when these two minerals are taken with water.[17] However, when food sources of iron and zinc are consumed together in a meal, absorption of zinc is not affected, largely because the amount of iron in the meal is not high enough to block zinc uptake. Good dietary sources of zinc include red meats, shellfish, and fortified cereals; other sources of zinc are discussed on page 286.

Sodium and Iodine   During pregnancy, the AI for sodium is the same for a non-pregnant adult woman, or 1,500 mg (1.5 g) per day.[18] Although too much sodium is associated with fluid retention and bloating, as well as high blood pressure, increased body fluids are a normal and necessary part of pregnancy, so some sodium is necessary to maintain fluid balance.

Iodine needs increase significantly during pregnancy, but the RDA of 220 µg per day is easy to achieve by using a modest amount of iodized salt (sodium chloride) during cooking.[14] Sprinkling salt onto food at the table is unnecessary; a balanced, healthful diet will provide all the iodine needed during pregnancy.

Do Pregnant Women Need Supplements?

Prenatal multivitamin and mineral supplements are not strictly necessary during pregnancy, but most healthcare providers recommend them. Meeting all the nutrient needs would otherwise take careful and somewhat complex dietary planning. Prenatal

It is important that pregnant women drink about 10 cups of fluid a day.

supplements are especially good insurance for vegans, adolescents, and others whose diets might normally be low in one or more micronutrients. It is important that pregnant women understand, however, that supplements are to be taken *in addition to,* not as a substitute for, a nutrient-rich diet.

Fluid Needs of Pregnant Women

Fluid plays many vital roles during pregnancy. It allows for the necessary increase in the mother's blood volume, acts as a lubricant, aids in regulating body temperature, and is necessary for many metabolic reactions. Fluid that the mother consumes also helps maintain the **amniotic fluid** that surrounds, cushions, and protects the fetus in the uterus. The AI for total fluid intake, which includes drinking water, beverages, and food, is 3 liters per day (or about 12.7 cups). This recommendation includes approximately 2.3 liters (10 cups) of fluid as total beverages, including drinking water.[18]

Drinking adequate fluid helps combat two common discomforts of pregnancy: fluid retention and, possibly, constipation. Drinking lots of fluids (and going to the bathroom as soon as the need is felt) will also help prevent **urinary tract infections,** which are common in pregnancy. Fluids also combat dehydration, which can develop if a woman with morning sickness has frequent bouts of vomiting. For these women, fluids such as soups, juices, and sports beverages are usually well tolerated and can help prevent dehydration.

ReCaP

Protein, carbohydrates, and fats provide the building blocks for fetal growth. Folate deficiency has been associated with neural tube defects. Most healthcare providers recommend prenatal supplements for pregnant women to ensure that sufficient micronutrients such as iron are consumed. Fluid provides for increased maternal blood volume and amniotic fluid.

Nutrition-Related Concerns for Pregnant Women

Pregnancy-related conditions involving a particular nutrient, such as iron-deficiency anemia, have already been discussed. The following sections describe some of the most common discomforts and disorders of pregnant women that are related to their general nutrition.

Morning Sickness

Morning sickness, or *nausea and vomiting of pregnancy* (*NVP*), is gaining recognition as a potentially serious medical condition.[19] It can vary from occasional mild queasiness to constant nausea with bouts of vomiting. In truth, "morning sickness" is not an appropriate name because the nausea and vomiting can begin at any time of the day and may last all day. NVP usually resolves by week 12 to 16 and the mother and fetus do not suffer lasting harm. However, some women experience such frequent vomiting that they require hospitalization or in-home intravenous (IV) therapy. There is no cure for morning sickness. However, here are some practical tips for reducing the severity:

amniotic fluid   The watery fluid contained within the innermost membrane of the sac containing the fetus. It cushions and protects the growing fetus.

urinary tract infection   A bacterial infection of the urethra, the tube leading from the bladder to the body exterior.

morning sickness   Varying degrees of nausea and vomiting associated with pregnancy, most commonly in the first trimester.

- Eat small, frequent meals and snacks throughout the day. An empty stomach can trigger nausea.
- Consume most of the day's fluids between meals. Frozen ice pops, watermelon, gelatin desserts, and mild broths are often well-tolerated sources of fluid.
- Keep snacks such as crackers at the bedside to ease nighttime queasiness or to eat before rising.
- Prenatal supplements should be taken at a time of day when vomiting is least likely.
- Avoid sights, sounds, smells, and tastes that bring on or worsen queasiness. Cold or room-temperature foods are often better tolerated than hot foods.

- For some women, alternative therapies such as acupuncture, acupressure wrist bands, biofeedback, meditation, and hypnosis help. Women should always check with their healthcare provider to ensure that the therapy they are using is safe and does not interact with other medications or supplements.

Cravings and Aversions

It seems as if nothing is more stereotypical about pregnancy than the image of a frazzled husband getting up in the middle of the night to run to the convenience store to get his pregnant wife some pickles and ice cream. This image, although humorous, is far from reality. Although some women have specific cravings, most crave a particular type of food (such as "something sweet" or "something salty") rather than a particular food.

Why do pregnant women crave certain tastes? Does a desire for salty foods mean that the woman is experiencing a sodium deficit? Although there may be some truth to the assertion that we crave what we need, scientific evidence for this claim is lacking.

Most cravings are, of course, for edible substances. But a surprising number of pregnant women crave nonfoods like laundry starch, chalk, and clay. This craving, called **pica,** may result in nutritional or health problems for the mother and fetus.

Food aversions are also common during pregnancy and may originate from social, cultural, or religious beliefs. In some cultures, for example, women would traditionally avoid shellfish ("it causes allergies") or duck ("child will be born with webbed feet"). Such aversions and taboos are often strongly woven into the family's belief system.[20]

Deep-fried foods are often unappealing to pregnant women.

Heartburn

Heartburn, along with indigestion, is common during pregnancy. Pregnancy-related hormones relax lower esophageal smooth muscle, increasing the incidence of heartburn. During the last two trimesters, the enlarging uterus pushes up on the stomach, compounding the problem. Practical tips for minimizing heartburn during pregnancy include the following:

- Avoid excessive weight gain.
- Eat small, frequent meals and chew food slowly.
- Don't wear tight clothing.
- Wait for at least 1 hour after eating before lying down.
- Sleep with your head elevated.
- Ask your healthcare provider to recommend an antacid that is safe for use during pregnancy.

Constipation

Hormone production during pregnancy causes the smooth muscles to relax, including the muscles of the large intestine, slowing colonic movement of food residue. In addition, pressure exerted by the growing uterus on the colon can slow movement even further, making elimination difficult. Practical hints that may help a woman avoid constipation include the following:

Consuming foods high in fiber, such as dried fruits, may reduce the chances of constipation.

- Include 25 to 35 g of fiber in the daily diet, concentrating on fresh fruits and vegetables, dried fruits, legumes, and whole grains.
- Keep fluid intake high as fiber intake increases. Drink plenty of water and eat water-rich fruits and vegetables such as melons, citrus, and lettuce.
- Keep physically active, as exercise is one of many factors that help increase motility of the large intestine.

Pregnant women should use over-the-counter fiber supplements only as a last resort and should not use any laxative product without first discussing it with their healthcare provider.

pica An abnormal craving to eat something not fit for food, such as clay, paint, and so forth.

Gestational Diabetes

Gestational diabetes, diagnosed in approximately 7% of all U.S. pregnancies, is usually a temporary condition in which a pregnant woman is unable to produce sufficient insulin or becomes insulin resistant, and thus develops elevated levels of blood glucose. Fortunately, gestational diabetes has no ill effects on either the mother or the fetus if blood glucose levels are strictly controlled through diet, physical activity, and/or medication. Screening for gestational diabetes is routine for almost all healthcare practitioners and is necessary because several of the symptoms, which include frequent urination, fatigue, and an increase in thirst and appetite, can be indistinguishable from normal pregnancy symptoms. If uncontrolled, gestational diabetes can result in a baby who is too large as a result of receiving too much glucose across the placenta during fetal life. Infants who are overly large are at risk for early birth and trauma during vaginal birth, and may need to be born by cesarean section. There is also evidence that exposing a fetus to maternal diabetes significantly increases the risk for type 2 diabetes and overweight later in life.[21, 22]

Women who are obese, women who are age 35 years or older, women who have a family history of diabetes, and women who are of Native American, African American, or Hispanic origin have a greater risk of developing gestational diabetes, as do women who previously delivered a large-for-gestational-age infant. Any woman who develops gestational diabetes has a 40% to 60% risk of developing type 2 diabetes within the next 5 to 10 years—particularly if she is obese to begin with or fails to maintain normal body weight after pregnancy.[23] As with any type of diabetes, attention to diet, weight control, and physical activity reduces the risk of gestational diabetes.

Hypertensive Disorders in Pregnancy

About 6% to 8% of U.S. pregnancies are complicated by some form of hypertension, or high blood pressure.[24] The term *hypertensive disorders in pregnancy* encompasses several different conditions.[24] A woman who develops high blood pressure, with no other symptoms, during the pregnancy is said to have *gestational hypertension.* **Preeclampsia** is characterized by a sudden increase in maternal blood pressure during pregnancy with the presence of swelling, excessive and rapid weight gain unrelated to food intake, and protein in the urine. If left untreated, it can progress to eclampsia, a condition characterized by seizures and kidney failure and, if untreated, fetal and/or maternal death.

No one knows exactly what causes the various hypertensive disorders in pregnancy, but women who are pregnant for the first time, adolescents, over the age of 35 to 40 years, African American, diabetic, or from a low-income background, as well as those who have a family history of eclampsia, are at greater risk.[25] Deficiencies in dietary protein, vitamin C, vitamin E, calcium, and magnesium also seem to increase the risk. Management of preeclampsia focuses mainly on blood pressure control. Typical treatment includes bed rest and medical oversight. Ultimately, the only thing that will cure the condition is childbirth. Today, with good prenatal care, gestational hypertension is nearly always detected early and can be appropriately managed, and prospects for both mother and fetus are usually very good. In nearly all women without prior chronic high blood pressure, blood pressure returns to normal within about a day or so after the birth.

Adolescent Pregnancy

Throughout the adolescent years, a girl's body is still changing and growing. Peak bone mass has not yet been reached. Full physical stature may not have been attained, and teens are more likely to be underweight than are young adult women. Thus, pregnant adolescents have higher nutrient needs for calories and bone-related nutrients such as calcium, phosphorus, and magnesium. In addition, many adolescents have not established healthful nutritional patterns. Inadequate maternal weight gain, poor prenatal care, and higher rates of prenatal alcohol and drug use contribute to higher rates of preterm births, low-birth-weight babies, and other complications.[26]

Pregnant women have their blood pressure measured to screen for pregnancy-related hypertension.

gestational diabetes   Insufficient insulin production or insulin resistance that results in consistently high blood glucose levels, specifically during pregnancy; condition typically resolves after birth occurs.

preeclampsia   High blood pressure that is pregnancy-specific and accompanied by protein in the urine, edema, and unexpected weight gain.

One of the goals of *Healthy People 2010* is to reduce pregnancies among adolescent females.[1] With adequate and thorough prenatal care and close attention to proper nutrition and other healthful behaviors, the likelihood of a positive outcome for both the adolescent mother and infant is greatly increased.

Vegetarianism

With the possible exception of iron and zinc, vegetarian women who consume dairy products and eggs (lacto-ovo-vegetarians) have no nutritional concerns beyond those encountered by every pregnant woman. In contrast, women who are totally vegetarian (vegan) need to be more vigilant than usual about their intake of nutrients that are derived primarily or wholly from animal products. These include vitamin D (unless regularly exposed to sunlight throughout the pregnancy), vitamin B_6, vitamin B_{12}, calcium, iron, and zinc. Supplements containing these nutrients are usually necessary.[27, 28] A regular prenatal supplement will fully meet the vitamin, iron, and zinc needs of a vegan woman but does not fulfill calcium needs, so a separate calcium supplement, or consumption of calcium-fortified soy milk or orange juice, is usually required.

Consumption of Caffeine

Caffeine, a stimulant found in coffee, tea, soft drinks, and some foods, crosses the placenta and thus reaches the fetus. Current thinking holds that women who consume less than about 200 mg of caffeine per day (the equivalent of 1 to 2 cups of coffee) are very likely doing no harm to the fetus. Evidence suggests that consuming higher daily doses of caffeine (the higher the dose, the more compelling the evidence) may slightly increase the risk of miscarriage and impair fetal growth.[29–31] It is sensible, then, for pregnant women to limit daily caffeine intake to no more than the equivalent of 2 cups of coffee.

Another reason for avoiding coffee and soft drinks during pregnancy is that they can make one feel full and provide considerable calories (if sweetened). If a pregnant woman retains a very strong desire for coffee, she might try a low- or nonfat decaf café latte, known to Latinas as *café con leche*, which offers a healthier nutrient profile than coffee alone.

Consumption of Alcohol

Alcohol is a known teratogen that readily crosses the placenta and accumulates in the fetal bloodstream. The immature fetal liver cannot readily metabolize alcohol, and its presence in fetal blood and tissues is associated with a variety of birth defects. These effects are dose-dependent: The more the mother drinks, the greater the potential harm to the fetus.

As we discussed *In Depth* on pages 154–165, heavy drinking (greater than three to four drinks per day) throughout pregnancy can result in the birth of a baby with fetal alcohol syndrome (FAS). These infants have a high mortality rate, and, as we saw with Theresa in our opening vignette, those who survive typically face lifelong emotional, behavioral, social, and learning problems. Another consequence is fetal alcohol effects (FAE), a milder set of alcohol-related abnormalities. These include developmental and behavioral problems (for example, hyperactivity, attention deficit disorder, and impaired cognition) and possibly physical abnormalities.[32]

In addition to FAS and FAE, frequent drinking (more than seven drinks per week) or occasional binge drinking (more than four to five drinks on one occasion) during pregnancy increases the risk for spontaneous abortion, complications during delivery, low birth weight, and sudden infant death syndrome.

Although some pregnant women do have the occasional alcoholic drink with no apparent ill effects, there is no amount of alcohol that is known to be safe. The best advice regarding alcohol during pregnancy is to abstain, if not from before conception, then as soon as pregnancy is suspected.[32, 33] As with other critical national health concerns, *Healthy People 2010* directly addresses this issue with the stated goals of increasing abstinence from alcohol among pregnant women and reducing the incidence of FAS.[1]

Maternal smoking is extremely harmful to the fetus.

Smoking

Despite the well-known consequences of cigarette smoking and the growing social stigma associated with smoking during pregnancy, more than 10% of pregnant women smoke, and the rate is even higher among adolescents.[34]

Maternal smoking exposes the fetus to toxins such as lead, cadmium, cyanide, nicotine, and carbon monoxide. Fetal blood flow is reduced, which limits the delivery of oxygen and nutrients, resulting in impaired fetal growth and development. Maternal smoking greatly increases risk of miscarriage, stillbirth, placental abnormalities, intrauterine growth retardation, preterm delivery, and low birth weight. Rates of sudden infant death syndrome, overall neonatal mortality (within the first 28 days of life), respiratory illnesses, and allergies are higher in the infants and children of smokers compared with nonsmokers.

Healthy People 2010 has the goal of reducing tobacco use so that no more than 1% of pregnant women smoke.[1] It has been estimated that the potential exists to save almost $900 in neonatal intensive care expenses for every woman who stops smoking during pregnancy.[35]

Illegal Drugs

Despite the fact that the use of illegal drugs during pregnancy is unquestionably harmful to the fetus, more than 5% of U.S. pregnant women report using illicit drugs.[36] Most drugs pass through the placenta into the fetal blood, where they accumulate in fetal tissues and organs, including the liver and brain.

Drugs such as marijuana, cocaine, heroin, ecstasy, and amphetamines all pose similar risks: impaired placental blood flow (thus, reduced transfer of oxygen and nutrients to the fetus) and higher rates of low birth weight, premature delivery, placental defects, and miscarriage. Newborns suffer signs of withdrawal including tremors, excessive crying, sleeplessness, and poor feeding. Even after several years, children born to women who used illicit drugs during pregnancy are at greater risk for developmental delays, impaired learning, and behavioral problems.[37]

All women are strongly advised to stop taking drugs before becoming pregnant. There is no safe level of use for illegal drugs during pregnancy.

Food Safety

The U.S. Departments of Health and Human Services and of Agriculture recommend that pregnant women avoid raw or partially cooked eggs, raw or undercooked meat/fish/poultry, raw sprouts, and unpasteurized juices and milk.[9] Soft cheeses such as Brie, feta, Camembert, Roquefort, and Mexican-style cheeses, also called *queso blanco* or *queso fresco,* should be avoided unless the label specifically states the product is made with pasteurized milk. Unpasteurized milk and cheeses may be contaminated with the bacterium *Listeria monocytogenes* which triggers miscarriage, premature birth, or fetal infection.

Women who are or could become pregnant, as well as breastfeeding mothers, are also advised to avoid eating large fish such as shark, swordfish, and king mackerel and to limit their intake of canned albacore tuna because of the high mercury content of these fish.

All safe food-handling practices discussed in Chapter 15 should be rigorously followed by pregnant women to ensure a healthy pregnancy outcome.

Exercise

Physical activity during pregnancy is recommended for women experiencing normal pregnancies.[9, 38] Exercise can help keep a woman physically fit during pregnancy, enhance mood, and help women feel more in control of their changing bodies. Moderate exercise during pregnancy will reduce the risk of gestational diabetes, help keep blood pressure down, and reduce the risks for preeclampsia.[39, 40] Regular exercise can also lessen lower back pain[41] and shorten the duration of active labor.

If a woman was not active prior to pregnancy, she should begin an exercise program slowly and progress gradually under the guidance of her healthcare provider. If a woman was physically active before pregnancy, she can continue to be physically active during pregnancy, within comfort and reason. Walking, the most common activity among pregnant women, is an excellent low-impact exercise.[42] Hiking, swimming, and water aerobics are also excellent choices. Women who have been avid runners before pregnancy can often continue to run, as long as they feel comfortable. However, they should probably limit the distance and intensity of their runs as the pregnancy progresses.

During pregnancy, women should adjust their physical activity to comfortable low-impact exercises.

ReCap

About half of all pregnant women experience morning sickness, and many crave or feel aversions to specific types of foods. Heartburn and constipation in pregnancy are related to hormonal relaxation of smooth muscle. Gestational diabetes and hypertensive disorders can seriously affect maternal and fetal well-being. The nutrient needs of pregnant adolescents are so high that adequate nourishment becomes difficult. Women who follow a vegan diet usually need to consume multivitamin and mineral supplements, plus supplemental calcium, during pregnancy. Caffeine intake should be limited; and use of alcohol, cigarettes, and illegal drugs should be completely avoided during pregnancy. Safe food-handling practices are especially important during pregnancy. Exercise (provided the mother has no contraindications) can enhance the health of a pregnant woman.

Judy
Nutri-Case

"Back when I was pregnant with Hannah, the doctor told me I had gestational diabetes but I shouldn't worry about it. He said I didn't need any medication, and I don't remember changing my diet. In fact, I just kept eating whatever I wanted, and by the time Hannah was born, I had gained almost 60 pounds. I never did lose all that extra weight."

Review what you learned about diabetes in Chapter 4. What information would have been important for Judy to learn while she was pregnant? Is it common that women with gestational diabetes develop type 2 diabetes years later? What are some things Judy could have done to lower her risk of type 2 diabetes?

Lactation: Nutrition for Breastfeeding Mothers

Throughout most of human history, infants have thrived on only one food: breast milk. During the first half of the 20th century, commercially prepared infant formulas slowly began to replace breast milk as the mother's preferred feeding method. Aggressive marketing campaigns promoting formula as more nutritious than breast milk convinced many families, even in developing nations, to switch. Soon formula-feeding had become a status symbol, proof of the family's wealth and modern thinking.

In the 1970s, this trend began to reverse with a renewed appreciation for the natural simplicity of breastfeeding. At the same time, several international organizations, including the World Health Organization, UNICEF, and La Leche League, began to promote the nutritional, immunologic, financial, and emotional advantages of breastfeeding and developed programs to encourage and support breastfeeding worldwide.

These efforts have paid off. In 2005, almost 75% of new mothers initiated breast-feeding in the hospital, an all-time high, and more than 43% of mothers were still breastfeeding their babies at 6 months of age.[43] Worldwide, slightly more than half of all women breastfeed *exclusively* for at least 6 months; however, this value is significantly lower in the United States, where only 12% of children are breastfed exclusively at 6 months of age.[43] One goal of *Healthy People 2010* is to increase early postpartum breast-feeding to 75% of U.S. mothers, with 50% of women still breastfeeding at 6 months and 25% at 12 months postpartum.[1] Although U.S. mothers have nearly achieved the early postpartum goal, they still fall well below the 6- and 12-month goals.[44, 45]

How Does Lactation Occur?

Lactation, the production of breast milk, is a process that is set in motion during pregnancy in response to several hormones. Once established, lactation can be sustained as long as the mammary glands continue to receive the proper stimuli.

The Body Prepares During Pregnancy

Throughout pregnancy, the placenta produces estrogen and progesterone. In addition to performing various functions to maintain the pregnancy, these hormones physically prepare the breasts for lactation. The breasts increase in size, and milk-producing glands (alveoli) and milk ducts are formed (**Figure 16.8**). Toward the end of pregnancy, the hormone *prolactin* increases. Prolactin is released by the anterior pituitary gland and is responsible for milk synthesis. However, estrogen and progesterone suppress the effects of prolactin during pregnancy.

What Happens After Childbirth

By the time a pregnancy has come to full term, the level of prolactin is about ten times higher than it was at the beginning of pregnancy. At birth, the suppressive effect of estrogen and progesterone ends, and prolactin is free to stimulate milk production. The first substance to be released from the breasts for intake by the newborn is **colostrum,** sometimes called premilk or first milk. It is thick, yellowish in color, rich in protein, and includes antibodies that help protect the newborn from infection. It is also relatively high in vitamins and minerals. Colostrum also contains a factor that fosters the growth of "friendly" bacteria in the infant's GI tract. These bacteria in turn prevent the growth of other bacteria that could potentially be harmful. Finally, colostrum has a laxative effect in infants, helping the infant to expel *meconium,* the sticky "first stool."

Within 2 to 4 days, colostrum is fully replaced by mature milk. Mature breast milk contains protein, fat, and carbohydrate (as the sugar lactose).

Mother–Infant Interaction Maintains Milk Production

Continued, sustained breast milk production depends entirely on infant suckling (or a similar stimulus like a mechanical pump). Infant suckling stimulates the continued production of prolactin, which in turn stimulates more milk production. The longer and more vigorous the feeding, the more milk will be produced. Thus, even twins and triplets can be successfully breastfed.

Prolactin allows for milk to be produced, but that milk has to move through the milk ducts to the nipple in order to reach the baby's mouth. The hormone responsible for this

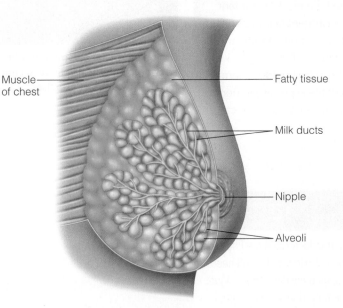

Muscle of chest — Fatty tissue — Milk ducts — Nipple — Alveoli

Figure 16.8 Anatomy of the breast. During pregnancy, estrogen and progesterone secreted by the placenta foster the preparation of breast tissue for lactation. This process includes breast enlargement and development of the milk-producing glands, or alveoli.

lactation The production of breast milk.

colostrum The first fluid made and secreted by the breasts from late in pregnancy to about a week after birth. It is rich in immune factors and protein.

3 Hypothalamus sends message to pituitary gland.

2 Nerves send message to hypothalamus.

4 Pituitary gland releases prolactin, which stimulates milk production, and oxytocin, which stimulates milk release.

1 Suckling stimulates nerves in nipple.

Figure 16.9 Sustained milk production depends on the mother–child interaction during breastfeeding, specifically the suckling of the infant. Suckling stimulates the continued production of prolactin, which is responsible for milk production, and also oxytocin, which is responsible for the let-down response.

"let-down" of milk is *oxytocin*. Like prolactin, oxytocin is produced by the pituitary gland and its production is dependent on the suckling stimulus at the beginning of a feeding (**Figure 16.9**). This response usually occurs within 10 to 30 seconds but can be inhibited by stress. Finding a relaxed environment in which to breastfeed is therefore important. Many women experience let-down in response to other cues, such as hearing a baby cry, or even thinking about their infant.

What Are a Breastfeeding Woman's Nutrient Needs?

You might be surprised to learn that breastfeeding requires even more energy and nutrients than pregnancy! This is because breast milk has to supply an adequate amount of all of the nutrients an infant needs to grow and develop.

Energy and Macronutrient Recommendations for Breastfeeding Women

It is estimated that milk production requires about 700 to 800 kcal/day. It is generally recommended that lactating women aged 19 years and above consume 330 kcal/day above their prepregnancy energy needs during the first 6 months of breastfeeding and 400 additional kcal/day during the second 6 months.[10] This additional energy is sufficient to support adequate milk production. At the same time, the remaining energy deficit will assist in the gradual loss of excess body weight gained during pregnancy. It is critical that lactating women avoid severe energy restriction, as this practice can result in decreased milk production.

The weight loss that occurs during breastfeeding should be gradual, approximately 1 to 4 lb per month. Participating in regular physical activity can assist with weight loss;

the 2005 Dietary Guidelines for Americans confirm that neither occasional nor regular exercise negatively affect a woman's ability to successfully breastfeed.[9] There are, however, some active women who may lose too much weight during breastfeeding and must either increase their energy intake or reduce their activity level to maintain health and milk production.

A lactating woman's needs for carbohydrate and protein increase over pregnancy requirements. Increases of 15 to 20 g of protein per day and 80 g of carbohydrate per day above prepregnancy requirements are recommended.[10] Women who breastfeed also need good dietary sources of DHA to support the rapid brain growth that occurs during the first 3 months of life. The DHA in the mother's diet is incorporated into the breast milk, to the benefit of the infant.

Micronutrient Recommendations for Breastfeeding Women

Micronutrient requirements for several vitamins and minerals increase over the requirements of pregnancy. These include vitamins A, C, E, riboflavin, vitamin B_{12}, biotin, and choline, and the minerals copper, chromium, manganese, iodine, selenium, and zinc. The requirement for folate during lactation is 500 μg/day, which is decreased from the 600 μg/day required during pregnancy but is higher than prepregnancy needs (400 μg/day).[12]

Requirements for iron decrease significantly during lactation, to a mere 9 mg/day. This is because iron is not a significant component of breast milk and breastfeeding usually suppresses menstruation for at least a few months, minimizing iron losses.[14]

Calcium is a significant component of breast milk; however, as in pregnancy, calcium absorption is enhanced during lactation and urinary loss of calcium is decreased. In addition, some calcium appears to come from the demineralization of the mother's bones, and increased dietary calcium does not prevent this. Thus, the recommended intake for calcium for a lactating woman is unchanged from pregnancy and non-pregnant guidelines: 1,000 mg/day. Because of their own continuing growth, however, teen mothers who are breastfeeding should continue to consume 1,300 mg/day.[15] Typically, if calcium intake is adequate, a woman's bone density returns to normal shortly after lactation ends.

Do Breastfeeding Women Need Supplements?

If a breastfeeding woman appropriately increases her energy intake, and does so with nutrient-dense foods, her nutrient needs can usually be met without supplements. The USDA has developed the MyPyramid Plan for Moms, which provides recommendations for food choices for women who are exclusively or partially breastfeeding their infants (see the Web Links at the end of this chapter). However, there is nothing wrong with taking a basic multivitamin, as long as it is not considered a substitute for proper nutrition. Lactating women should consume omega-3 fatty acids either in fish or supplements to increase breast-milk levels of DHA. Women who do not consume dairy products should monitor their calcium intake carefully and may need supplements.

Fluid Recommendations for Breastfeeding Women

Because extra fluid is expended with every feeding, lactating women need to consume about an extra quart (about 1 liter) of fluid per day. The AI for total water is 3.8 liters per day for breastfeeding women, including about 13 cups of beverages.[18] This extra fluid enhances milk production and reduces the risk of dehydration. Many women report that within a minute or two of beginning to nurse their baby, they become intensely thirsty. To prevent this thirst and achieve the recommended fluid intake, women are encouraged to drink a nutritious beverage (water, juice, milk, and so forth) each time they nurse their baby. However, it is not good practice to drink hot beverages while nursing because accidental spills could burn the infant.

MyPyramid.gov

MyPyramid for Moms has specific dietary advice for women who are exclusively or partially breastfeeding their infants.

Highlight
Finding Support for Breastfeeding Moms

Although a natural process, the art of breastfeeding for many women takes a fair amount of education, support, and practice. Fortunately, women today have more opportunities to learn "the art of breastfeeding" than ever before.

Prenatal classes—that is, classes held before the birth—are one such opportunity. Typically taught by certified nurse practitioners, midwives, or other childbirth specialists, these classes provide essential information—including information about breastfeeding—to parents-to-be. In many communities, special breastfeeding classes are offered by certified lactation consultants or other maternity healthcare providers, to help women who plan to breastfeed for the first time or who want to improve upon a previous breastfeeding experience.

Many hospitals and birthing centers also now provide breastfeeding support. Hospitals can seek the designation "Baby Friendly" based on the World Health Organization/UNICEF Baby-Friendly Hospital Initiative, meaning their facilities have shown that they have adopted certain practices to support successful breastfeeding. Some of those practices include:[46]

- Having a written breastfeeding policy communicated to all healthcare staff

- Informing all pregnant women about the benefits and management of breastfeeding

- Helping mothers initiate breastfeeding within a half-hour of birth and helping them to maintain lactation

- Giving newborn infants no food or drink other than breast milk, unless medically indicated

- Practicing rooming-in to encourage breastfeeding on demand

- Fostering the establishment of breastfeeding support groups and referring mothers to them on discharge from the hospital or clinic

Unfortunately, as of 2009, there were fewer than 100 Baby Friendly hospitals and clinics in the United States, a discouragingly low number. A current list can be found at www.babyfriendlyusa.org. Even without this credential, however, many hospitals and clinics are much more proactive in supporting breastfeeding than in years past.

La Leche League International (see the end-of-chapter Web Links) is a worldwide organization dedicated to supporting breastfeeding mothers. La Leche League offers local meetings and conferences, as well as books, CDs, podcasts, online forums, and other materials to help pregnant women and new moms succeed in breastfeeding. However, its most significant contribution may be the free in-home visits offered by experienced members to help women establish or maintain breastfeeding and troubleshoot problems. La Leche League also offers resources for moms of multiples (twins, triplets, and so on), premature infants, or special-healthcare-need babies, as well as materials for working mothers and those who want to provide their infants with breast milk even though they themselves can't nurse. Resources are now available in dozens of different languages, providing education and support to millions of women in the United States and across the globe. Other grassroots organizations provide additional assistance to breastfeeding women and their babies.

To help families identify qualified lactation consultants, groups such as IBLCE, the International Board of Lactation Consultant Examiners, develop and administer certification examinations. When searching for a qualified lactation consultant, parents-to-be can thus confirm a candidate's professional qualifications.

In some communities, local mothers serve as *doulas*, knowledgeable, experienced lay companions who stay with the new mom and family through labor, birth, and beyond, often supporting the breastfeeding process. While these women may not have academic or professional credentials, they are typically well known and respected within the local community.

RECAP

Lactation is the result of the coordinated effort of several hormones. Breasts are prepared for lactation during pregnancy, and infant suckling provides the stimulus that sustains the production of prolactin and oxytocin needed to maintain the milk supply. It is recommended that lactating women consume extra energy above prepregnancy guidelines, including increased protein, certain vitamins and minerals, and fluids. The requirements for folate and iron decrease from pregnancy levels, while the requirement for calcium remains the same. If nutrient intake is inadequate, milk production will decline and the woman will produce a smaller volume of breast milk.

Breastfeeding has benefits for the mother and infant.

Getting Real About Breastfeeding: Advantages and Challenges

Breastfeeding is recognized as the preferred method of infant feeding because of the nutritional value and health benefits of human milk.[47] However, the technique does require patience and practice, and teaching from an experienced mother or certified lactation consultant is important. La Leche League International is an advocacy group for breastfeeding: Its Web site (www.lalecheleague.org), publications, and local meetings are all valuable resources for breastfeeding mothers and their families. Many HMOs offer lactation classes for their members, and some U.S. hospitals, designated as "Baby Friendly," have adopted policies that enhance lactation success.[48]

Advantages of Breastfeeding

As adept as formula manufacturers have been at simulating components of breast milk, an exact replica has never been produced. In addition, there are other benefits that mother and baby can access only through breastfeeding.

Nutritional Superiority of Breast Milk The amount and types of proteins in breast milk are ideally suited to the human infant. The main protein in breast milk, lactalbumin, is easily digested in infants' immature GI tracts, reducing the risk of gastric distress. Other proteins in breast milk bind iron and prevent the growth of harmful bacteria that require iron. Antibodies from the mother are additional proteins that help prevent infection while the infant's immune system is still immature. Certain proteins in human milk improve the absorption of iron; this is important because breast milk is low in iron. Cow's milk contains too much protein for infants, and the types of protein in cow's milk are harder for the infant to digest.

The primary carbohydrate in breast milk is lactose; it's galactose component is important in nervous system development. Lactose provides energy and prevents ketosis in the infant, promotes the growth of beneficial bacteria, and increases the absorption of calcium. Breast milk has more lactose than cow's milk.

The amounts and types of fat in breast milk are ideally suited to the human infant. DHA and arachidonic acid (ARA) have been shown to be essential for the growth and development of the infant's nervous system and for development of the retina of the eyes. Until 2002, these fatty acids were omitted from commercial infant formulas in the United States, although they have been available in formulas in other parts of the world for the better part of a decade. Interestingly, the concentration of DHA in breast milk varies considerably, is sensitive to maternal diet, and is highest in women who consume large quantities of fish.[49]

The fat content of breast milk, which is higher than that of whole cow's milk, changes according to the gestational age of the infant and during the course of every feeding: The milk that is initially released (called *foremilk*) is watery and low in fat, somewhat like skim milk. This milk is thought to satisfy the infant's initial thirst. As the feeding progresses, the milk acquires more fat and becomes more like whole milk. Finally, the very last 5% or so of the milk produced during a feeding (called the *hindmilk*) is very high in fat, similar to cream. This milk is thought to satiate the infant. It is important to let infants suckle for at least 20 minutes at each feeding so that they get this hindmilk. Breast milk is also relatively high in cholesterol, which supports the rapid growth and development of the brain and nervous system.

Another important aspect of breastfeeding (or any type of feeding) is the fluid it provides the infant. Because of their small size, infants are at risk of dehydration, which is one reason why feedings must be consistent and frequent. This topic will be discussed at greater length in the section on infant nutrition.

In terms of micronutrients, breast milk is a good source of readily absorbed calcium and magnesium. It is low in iron, but the iron it does contain is easily absorbed. Because healthy full-term infants store iron in preparation for the first few months of life, most experts agree that their iron needs can be met by breast milk alone for the first 6 months, after which iron-rich foods are needed. Although breast milk has some vitamin D, the American Academy of Pediatrics recommends that all breastfed infants be provided with a vitamin D supplement.[47]

Breast milk composition continues to change as the infant grows and develops. Because of this ability to change as the baby changes, breast milk alone is entirely sufficient to sustain infant growth for the first 6 months of life. Throughout the next 6 months of infancy, as solid foods are gradually introduced, breast milk remains the baby's primary source of superior-quality nutrition. The American Academy of Pediatrics encourages exclusive breastfeeding (no food or other source of sustenance) for the first 6 months of life, continuing breastfeeding for at least the first year of life and, if acceptable within the family unit, into the second year of life.[47]

Some breastfed babies refuse to take a bottle.

Protection from Infections and Allergies   Immune factors from the mother, including antibodies and immune cells, are passed directly from the mother to the newborn through breast milk. These factors provide important disease protection for the infant while its immune system is still immature. It has been shown that breastfed infants have a lower incidence of respiratory tract, gastrointestinal tract, and ear infections than formula-fed infants.[50] Even a few weeks of breastfeeding is beneficial, but the longer a child is breastfed, the greater the level of passive immunity from the mother. In the United States, breastfeeding has the potential to lower healthcare costs by as much as $3.6 billion per year, in part due to a 20% reduction in infant mortality rates in breastfed infants.[47, 51]

In addition, breast milk is nonallergenic, and breastfeeding is associated with a reduced risk of allergies during childhood and adulthood. Breastfed babies also die less frequently from **sudden infant death syndrome (SIDS)** and have a decreased chance of developing diabetes, overweight and obesity, hypercholesterolemia, and chronic digestive disorders.[47]

Physiologic Benefits for Mother   Breastfeeding causes uterine contractions that quicken the return of the uterus to prepregnancy size and reduce bleeding. Many women also find that breastfeeding helps them lose the weight they gained during pregnancy, particularly if it continues for more than 6 months. In addition, breastfeeding appears to be associated with a decreased risk for breast cancer.[50, 52] The relationship between breastfeeding and osteoporosis is still unclear and more research on this topic is needed.[50, 53, 54]

Breastfeeding also suppresses ovulation, lengthening the time between pregnancies and giving a mother's body the chance to recover before she conceives again. This benefit can be life-saving for malnourished women living in countries that discourage or outlaw the use of contraceptives. Ovulation may not cease completely, however, so it is still possible to become pregnant while breastfeeding. Healthcare providers typically recommend use of additional birth control methods while breastfeeding to avoid another conception occurring too soon to allow a mother's body to recover from the earlier pregnancy.

Mother–Infant Bonding   Breastfeeding is among the most intimate of human interactions. Ideally, it is a quiet time away from distractions when mother and baby begin to develop an enduring bond of affection known as *attachment*. Breastfeeding enhances attachment by providing the opportunity for frequent, direct skin-to-skin contact, which stimulates the baby's sense of touch and is a primary means of communication.[3] The cuddling and intense watching that occur during breastfeeding begin to teach the mother and baby about the other's behavioral cues. Breastfeeding also reassures the mother that she is providing the best possible nutrition for her baby. Healthcare providers now recommend that hospitals permit continuous rooming-in of breastfed infants throughout the day and night in order to enhance the initiation and continuation of breastfeeding.[47, 48]

Undoubtedly, bottle-feeding does not preclude parent–infant attachment! As long as attention is paid to closeness, cuddling, and skin contact, bottle-feeding can foster bonding as well.

sudden infant death syndrome (SIDS)   The sudden death of a previously healthy infant; the most common cause of death in infants older than 1 month of age.

Convenience and Cost Breast milk is always ready, clean, at the right temperature, and available on demand, whenever and wherever it's needed. In the middle of the night, when the baby wakes up hungry, a breastfeeding mother can respond almost instantaneously, and both are soon back to sleep. In contrast, formula-feeding is a time-consuming process: parents have to continually wash and sterilize bottles, and each batch of formula must be mixed and heated to the proper temperature.

In addition, breastfeeding costs nothing other than the price of a modest amount of additional food for the mother. In contrast, formula can be relatively expensive, and there are the additional costs of bottles and other supplies, as well as the cost of energy used for washing and sterilization. A hidden cost of formula-feeding is its effect on the environment: the energy used and waste produced during formula manufacturing, marketing, shipping and distribution, preparation, and disposal of used packaging. In contrast, breastfeeding is environmentally responsible, using no external energy and producing no external wastes.

Challenges Associated with Breastfeeding

For some women and infants, breastfeeding is easy from the very first day. Others experience some initial difficulty, but with support from an experienced nurse, lactation consultant, or volunteer mother from La Leche League, the experience becomes successful and pleasurable. Some families, however, encounter difficulties that make formula-feeding their best choice. This section discusses some challenges that may impede the success of breastfeeding.

Effects of Drugs and Other Substances on Breast Milk Many substances, including illegal, prescription, and over-the-counter drugs, pass into breast milk. Breastfeeding mothers should inform their physicians that they are breastfeeding. If a safe and effective form of the necessary medication cannot be found, the mother will have to avoid breastfeeding while she is taking the drug. During this time, she can pump and discard her breast milk so that her milk supply will be adequate when she resumes breastfeeding.

Caffeine and alcohol also enter breast milk. Caffeine can make the baby agitated and fussy, whereas alcohol can make the baby sleepy, depress the central nervous system, and slow motor development, in addition to inhibiting the mother's milk supply. Breastfeeding women should abstain from alcohol in the early stages of lactation since it easily passes into the breast milk at levels equal to blood alcohol concentrations. Nicotine also passes into breast milk; therefore, it is best for the woman to quit smoking altogether.

Environmental contaminants, including pesticides, industrial solvents, and heavy metals such as lead and mercury, can pass into breast milk when breastfeeding mothers are exposed to these chemicals.[55] Mothers can limit their infants' exposure to these harmful substances by controlling their environment. Fresh fruits and vegetables should be thoroughly washed and peeled to minimize exposure to pesticides and fertilizer residues. Exposure to solvents, paints, gasoline fumes, furniture strippers, and similar products should also be limited. Even with some exposure to these environmental contaminants, U.S. and international health agencies all agree that the benefits of breastfeeding almost always outweigh potential concerns.[56, 57]

Food components that pass into the breast milk may seem innocuous; however, some substances, such as those found in garlic, onions, peppers, broccoli, and cabbage, are distasteful enough to the infant to prevent proper feeding. Some babies have allergic reactions to foods the mother ate, such as wheat, cow's milk, eggs, or citrus, and suffer gastrointestinal upset, diaper rash, or another reaction. The offending foods must then be identified and avoided.

Maternal HIV Infection and Other Diseases HIV, which causes AIDS, can be transmitted from mother to baby through breast milk. Thus, HIV-positive women in the United States and Canada are encouraged to feed their infants formula.[58] This

Working moms can be discouraged from breastfeeding in various ways.

recommendation does not apply to all women worldwide, however, because the low cost and sanitary nature of breast milk, as compared to the high cost and potential for waterborne diseases with formula-feeding, often make exclusive breastfeeding the best choice for women in developing countries.[58]

Conflict Between Breastfeeding and the Mother's Employment   Breast milk is absorbed more readily than formula, making more frequent feedings necessary. Newborns commonly require breastfeedings every 1 to 3 hours versus every 2 to 4 hours for formula-feedings. Mothers who are exclusively breastfeeding and return to work within the first 6 months after the baby's birth must leave several bottles of pumped breast milk for others to feed the baby in their absence each day. This means that working women have to pump their breasts to express the breast milk during the work day. This can be a challenge in companies that do not provide the time, space, and privacy required.

Work-related travel is also a concern: if the mother needs to be away from home for longer than 24 to 48 hours, she can typically pump and freeze enough breast milk for others to give the baby in her absence. When longer business trips are required, some mothers bring the baby with them and arrange for childcare at their destination. Others resort to pumping, freezing, and shipping breast milk home via overnight mail. Understandably, many women cite returning to work as the reason they switch to formula-feeding.[59]

Some working women successfully combine breastfeeding with commercial formula. For example, a woman might breastfeed in the morning before she leaves for work, as soon as she returns home, and once again before retiring at night. The remainder of the feedings are formula given by the infant's father or a childcare provider. Women who choose supplemental formula feedings usually find that their bodies adapt quickly to the change and produce ample milk for the remaining breastfeedings.

Although a much more common practice today than in the past, many people still consider it inappropriate to breastfeed in public.

Social Concerns   In North America, women have occasionally been insulted or otherwise harassed for breastfeeding in public. In the past decade, however, both social customs and state laws have become more accommodating for nursing mothers. For example, separate nursing rooms can often be found adjacent to, but not within, public restrooms. Some states have passed legislation preserving a woman's right to breastfeed in public. When women feel free to breastfeed in public, the baby's feeding schedule becomes much less confining.

What About Bonding for Fathers and Siblings?

With all the attention given to attachment between a breastfeeding mother and infant, it is easy for fathers and siblings to feel left out. One option that allows other family members to participate in infant feeding is to supplement breastfeedings with bottle-feedings of stored breast milk or formula. If a family decides to share infant feeding in this manner, bottle-feedings can begin as soon as breastfeeding has become well established. That way, the mother's milk supply will be established, and the infant will not become confused by the artificial nipple. Fathers and other family members can also bond with the infant when bathing and/or dressing the infant as well as through everyday cuddling and play.

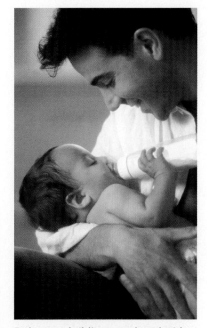

Fathers and siblings can bond with infants through bottle-feeding.

RECAP

Breastfeeding provides many benefits to both mother and newborn, including superior nutrition, heightened immunity, mother–infant bonding, convenience, and cost. However, breastfeeding may not be the best option for every family. The mother may need to use a medication that enters the breast milk and makes it unsafe for consumption. A mother's job may interfere with the baby's requirement for frequent feedings. The infant's father and siblings can participate in feedings using a bottle filled with either pumped breast milk or formula.

Infant Nutrition: From Birth to 1 Year

Most first-time parents are amazed at how rapidly their infant grows and develops. Optimal nutrition is extremely important during the first year, as the baby's organs and nervous system continue to develop and mature and as the baby grows physically and acquires new skills. In fact, physicians use length and weight measurements as the main tools for assessing an infant's nutritional status. These measurements are plotted on growth charts (there are separate charts for boys and girls), which track an infant's growth over time (**Figure 16.10**).

During the first year of life, breast milk remains the food of choice; however, iron-fortified formula is an acceptable substitute for those families who have decided that breastfeeding is not an option. After approximately 6 months, most infants are ready for *complementary* foods such as baby cereals and strained vegetables, which provide key nutrients and introduce the infant to new tastes and textures. An infant who is lovingly and consistently fed when hungry will feel secure and well cared for. A relaxed, consistent feeding

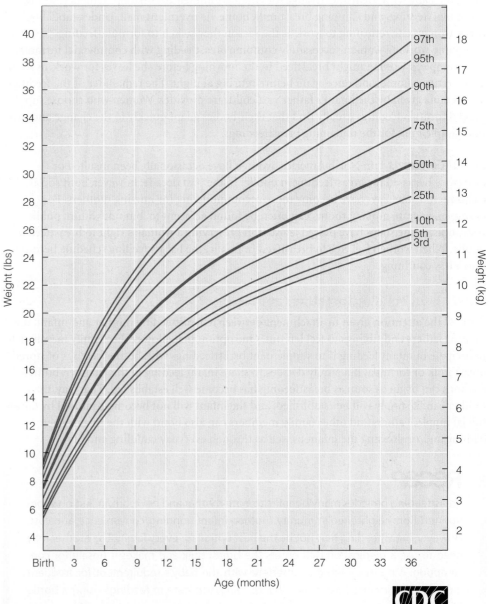

Figure 16.10   This weight-for-age growth chart is a much smaller version of charts used by healthcare practitioners to monitor and assess the growth of an infant/toddler from birth to 36 months. This example shows the growth curves of girls over time, each at different percentiles. (*Data from:* The National Center for Health Statistics in collaboration with the National Center for Chronic Disease Prevention and Health Promotion [2000].)

relationship between parent and child fosters a positive and healthy outlook toward food. In many ways, an infant's diet during his or her first year of life "sets the stage" for future health and development.

Typical Infant Growth and Activity Patterns

In the first year of life, an infant generally grows about 10 inches in length and triples in weight—a growth rate more rapid than will ever occur again. To support this phenomenal growth, energy needs per unit body weight are also the highest they will ever be, approximately triple that of adults. Energy needs are also very high because the basal metabolic rates of babies are high (**Figure 16.11**). This is in part because the body surface area of a baby is large compared with its body size, increasing its loss of body heat. Still, the limited physical activity of a baby keeps total energy expenditure relatively low.

For the first few months of life, an infant's activities consist mainly of eating and sleeping. As the first year progresses, the range of activities gradually expands to include rolling over, sitting up, crawling, standing, and finally taking the first few wobbly steps. As shown in Figure 16.11, the relative need for energy to support growth slows during the second 6 months of life, just as activity begins to increase.

Growth charts, one set for girls and one set for boys, are routinely used by healthcare providers and parents to track growth. They are available from the Centers for Disease Control and Prevention (CDC) free of charge. Charts for children birth to 36 months assess length-for-age, weight-for-age, and weight-for-length, all expressed as percentiles. If an infant is in the 90th percentile for length, he or she is longer than 89% of U.S. infants of that age and gender and thus is considered very long. If an infant is in the 10th percentile for weight, only 10% of U.S. infants of the same age and gender weigh less than he or she does, so that baby can be viewed as relatively underweight compared with other infants. Although every infant is unique, in general, healthcare providers look for a close correlation between length and weight rankings. In other words, an infant who is in the 60th percentile for length is usually in about the 50th to 70th percentile for weight. A child in the 50th percentile for length but the 5th percentile for weight may be malnourished. Consistency over time is also a consideration: For example, an infant who suddenly drops well below her established profile for weight might be underfed or ill. The CDC has also developed BMI-for-age charts for children over 24 months of age.

Although growth charts are effective tools for assessing an infant's nutrition status, there are some limitations. For example, it is important to consider the physical stature of the baby's parents. If both parents are tall, you would expect the infant to remain close to the upper percentiles for length. Exclusively breastfed infants often track at a lower percentile weight-for-age compared with formula-fed infants, although no differences in length-for-age or head circumference are noted.[2] Families need to know that this slower rate of weight gain has not been associated with any negative outcomes. Indeed, many healthcare providers believe that the slower growth rate of breastfed infants should be considered the norm, not the exception, because formula-feeding is a relatively recent cultural phenomenon.

The growth of the brain is more rapid during the first year than at any other time, and infants' heads are typically large in proportion to the rest of their bodies, approximately one-fourth of their total length. Pediatricians use head circumference as an additional tool for the assessment of growth and nutritional status; CDC growth charts for head-circumference-for-age are available for infants and toddlers birth to 36 months of age. After around 18 months of age, the rate of brain growth slows, and gradually the body "catches up" to head size, resulting in body proportions that are closer to those of a child.

As infants grow and develop, their proportion of muscle, fat, and bone evolve. Body fat, as a percentage of total body weight, increases after birth and peaks around 9 months of age. Muscle tissue increases slowly but steadily, and body calcium, a marker for skeletal growth, more than doubles during the first year of life.[15] Body water, as a percentage of total body weight, is highest in newborns and gradually decreases through and beyond early childhood.[18]

0–6 months

6–12 months

Key:
■ Growth
■ Metabolic reactions
■ Physical activity

Figure 16.11 Energy expenditure during infancy. During the first 6 months of life, infants expend more energy to support growth and less energy on physical activity than in the second 6 months of life.

The proportions of muscle, fat, and bone in the bodies of infants change as they grow and become more active.

Nutrient Needs for Infants

Three characteristics of infants combine to make their nutritional needs unique. These are (1) their high energy needs per unit body weight to support rapid growth, (2) their immature digestive tracts and kidneys, and (3) their small size.

Macronutrient Needs of Infants

An infant needs to consume about 40 to 50 kcal/lb of body weight per day, with newborns at the higher end of the range, and infants 6 to 12 months old at the lower end. This amounts to about 600 (girls) to 650 (boys) kcal/day at around 6 months of age.[10] Given the immature digestive tracts and kidneys of infants, as well as their high fluid needs, providing this much energy may seem difficult. Fortunately, breast milk and commercial formulas are energy-dense, providing about 650 kcal/L of fluid.[10] When complementary (solid) foods are introduced, they provide even more energy in addition to the breast milk or formula.

Infants are not small versions of adults; they are growing rapidly compared with the typically stable adult phase of life. The proportions of macronutrients they require differ from adult proportions, as do the types of food they can tolerate. It is generally agreed that about 40% to 50% of an infant's diet should come from fat during the first year of life (30–31 g/day) and that fat intakes below this level can be harmful before the age of 2 years. Given the high energy needs of infants, it makes sense to take advantage of the energy density of fat (9 kcal/g). Breast milk and commercial formulas are both high in fat (about 50% of total energy).

Specific fatty acids are essential for the rapid brain growth, maturation of the retina of the eye, and nervous system development that happens in the first 1 to 2 years of life. The Adequate Intake (AI) fatty acid guidelines for infants are based on the composition of breast milk, which is always the standard for infant nutrient guidelines. For infants 7 to 12 months of age, the contributions of complementary foods are considered. The infant AI for omega-6 fatty acids is 4.4 to 4.6 g/day, about 6% to 8% of total calories, whereas the infant AI for omega-3 fatty acids is 0.5 g/day, approximately 1% of total calories.[10] Breast milk is an excellent source of the fatty acids arachidonic acid (AA) and docosahexaenoic acid (DHA), although levels of DHA vary widely with the mother's diet. Both of these fats have been associated with short-term improvements in visual function and, possibly, cognitive development.[2] Many formula manufacturers are now adding AA and DHA to their products.

The recommended carbohydrate intake for infants 0 to 6 months of age is based on the lactose content of human milk.[10] The AI for infants 0 to 6 months of age is 60 g/day of carbohydrate. The carbohydrate AI for older infants 7 to 12 months of age reflects the intake of human milk and complementary foods and is set at 95 g/day.

The recommended intake of protein for infants 0 to 6 months of age is 9.1 g/day or about 1.5 g/kg body weight per day.[10] Again, this value is based on the protein content of human milk. Formula-fed infants typically consume higher amounts of protein compared with breastfed infants; however, the proteins in commercial formulas are less efficiently digested and absorbed. The protein guideline for infants 7 to 12 months of age is 9.9 g/day or 1.1 g/kg body weight per day.[10] Recall that the adult RDA for protein is 0.8 g/day. The relatively higher intake for infants is to accommodate their rapid growth. However, no more than 20% of an infant's daily energy requirement should come from protein. Immature infant kidneys are not able to process and excrete the excess amine groups from higher-protein diets. Breast milk and commercial formulas both provide adequate total protein and appropriate essential amino acids to support growth and development.

Micronutrient Needs of Infants

An infant's micronutrient needs are also high to accommodate rapid growth and development. Micronutrients of particular note include iron, vitamin D, zinc, fluoride, and, for infants of breastfeeding vegans, vitamin B_{12}. Fortunately, breast milk and commercial formulas provide most of the micronutrients needed for infant growth and development, with some special considerations discussed later in this chapter.

In addition, all infants are routinely given an injection of vitamin K shortly after birth. This provides vitamin K until the infant's intestine can develop its own healthful bacteria, which provide vitamin K thereafter.

Do Infants Need Supplements?

Breast milk and commercial formulas provide most of the vitamins and minerals infants need. However, breast milk is low in vitamin D, and deficiencies of this nutrient have been detected in breastfed infants with dark skin and in those with limited sunlight exposure.[2] Breastfed infants are commonly prescribed a supplement containing vitamin D.[47]

Breastfed infants also require additional iron beginning no later than 6 months of age because the infant's iron stores become depleted and breast milk is a poor source of iron. Iron is extremely important for cognitive development and prevention of iron-deficiency anemia. Infant rice cereal fortified with iron can serve as an additional iron source and is an excellent first solid food.

Fluoride is important for strong tooth development, but fluoride supplementation is not recommended during the first 6 months of life. Depending on the fluoride content of the household water supply, breastfed infants over the age of 6 months may need a fluoride supplement. Most brands of bottled water have low levels of fluoride and many home water treatment systems remove fluoride as well. On the other hand, fluoride toxicity may be a risk for infants simultaneously exposed to fluoridated toothpaste and rinses, fluoridated water, and fluoride supplements.

There are special conditions in which additional supplements may be needed for breastfed infants. For example, if a woman is a vegan, her breast milk may be low in vitamin B_{12}, and a supplement of this vitamin should be given to the baby.

For formula-fed infants, the need for supplementation depends on the formula composition and other factors. Many formulas are already fortified with iron, for example; thus, no additional iron supplement is necessary. If the baby is getting adequate vitamin D through either the ingestion of at least 2 cups of vitamin D–fortified formula or via regular sun exposure, then an extra supplement may not be necessary.

If a supplement is given, careful consideration should be given to dose. The supplement should be formulated specifically for infants, and the recommended daily dose should not be exceeded. High doses of micronutrients can be dangerous. For example, too much iron can be fatal, and too much fluoride can cause mottling, pitting, and staining of the teeth. Excessive vitamin D can cause abnormally high levels of serum calcium and calcification of soft tissues such as the kidney.

Fluid Recommendations for Infants

Fluid is critical for everyone, but for infants the balance is more delicate for two reasons. First, they proportionally lose more water through evaporation from the skin surface area than adults. Second, their kidneys are immature and unable to concentrate urine. Hence, they are at even greater risk of dehydration. An infant needs about 2 oz of fluid per pound of body weight, and either breast milk or formula is almost always adequate in providing this amount. Experts recently confirmed that "infants exclusively fed human milk do not require supplemental water."[18] This is true for infants living in hot and humid climates as well as more moderate environments. Parents can be reassured that their infant's fluid intake is appropriate if the infant produces six to eight wet diapers per day.

Certain conditions, such as diarrhea, vomiting, fever, or extreme hot weather, can accelerate fluid loss. In these instances, supplemental fluid, ideally as water, may be needed. Because too much fluid can be dangerous for an infant, supplemental fluids (whether water or an infant electrolyte formula) should be given only under the advice of a physician. Generally, it is advised that supplemental fluids not exceed 4 oz per day. Parents should avoid giving breastfed or formula-fed infants sugar water, fruit juices, or sweetened beverages in a bottle, especially at bedtime, as the practice can cause decay of developing teeth.

Infants are at high risk for dehydration and should be offered water and other nutritious beverages on a regular basis.

RECaP

Infancy is characterized by the most rapid rate of growth a human being will ever experience, and an infant's energy needs are correspondingly high. Assessment of the infant's growth pattern can provide important clues to his or her nutritional state.

Breast milk is the ideal infant food for the first 6 months of life; iron-fortified formula also provides the necessary nutrients for young infants. Vitamin D supplements are recommended for exclusively breastfed infants; iron and fluoride supplements may be prescribed for infants older than 6 months of age.

What Types of Formula Are Available?

We discussed the advantages of breastfeeding earlier in this chapter, and indeed both national and international healthcare organizations consider breastfeeding the best choice for infant nutrition, when possible. However, if breastfeeding is not feasible, several types of commercial formulas provide nutritious alternatives. In the United States, as many as 80% to 85% of infants are fed commercial formula by the age of 1 year. Formula manufacturers must comply with the Infant Formula Act of 1980 (revised in 1986), which established minimum and maximum levels for twenty-nine different nutrients. Although most formula manufacturers try to mimic the nutritional value of breast milk, these formulas still cannot completely duplicate the immune factors, enzymes, and other unique components of human milk.

Most formulas are based on cow's milk that is modified to make it more appropriate for human infants. The amount of total protein is reduced and levels of milk proteins are altered in order to mirror the types of proteins in breast milk. In addition, the product is heated to denature the proteins and make them more digestible. The naturally occurring lactose may be supplemented with sucrose to provide adequate carbohydrate. Vegetable oils and/or microbiologically produced fatty acids replace the naturally occurring butterfat. A range of vitamins and minerals such as iron is added to meet national standards. Recently, some manufacturers have added compounds such as taurine, carnitine, and the fatty acids AA and DHA to more closely mimic the nutrient profile of breast milk. This chapter's Nutrition Label Activity gives you the opportunity to review some of these ingredients.

Soy-based formulas are effective alternatives for infants who are lactose intolerant (although this is rare in infants) or cannot tolerate the proteins in cow's milk–based formulas. Soy formulas may also satisfy the requirements of families who are strict vegans. However, soy-based formulas are not without controversy.[60] Because soy contains isoflavones, or plant forms of estrogens, there is some concern over the effects these compounds have on growing infants. Babies can also have allergic reactions to soy-based formulas.[61] Currently, it is believed that soy formulas are safe, but they should only be used when breast milk or cow's milk–based formulas are contraindicated. Soy-based formulas are not the same as soy milk, which is not suitable for infant feeding.

Finally, there are specialized formulas for specific medical conditions. Some contain proteins that have been predigested, for example, or have nutrient compositions designed to accommodate certain genetic abnormalities. Others have been developed to meet the unique nutritional needs of preterm infants. Many of these specialized or medical formulas are available only through a physician.

Commercial formulas provide infants with a nutritious alternative to breast milk. Cow's milk, including fresh, evaporated, condensed, and dried milks, should not be introduced to infants until after 1 year of age. Cow's milk is too high in protein, the protein is difficult to digest, and the poor digestibility may contribute to gastrointestinal bleeding. In addition, cow's milk has too much sodium, too little iron, and a poor balance of other vitamins and minerals. Goat's milk is also inappropriate for infants and should not be used as a substitute for breast milk or formula.

Nutrition Label Activity
Reading Infant Food Labels

Imagine that you are a new parent shopping for infant formula. **Figure 16.12** shows the label from a typical can of formula. As you can see, the ingredients list is long and has many technical terms. Even well-informed parents would probably be stumped by many of them. Fortunately, with the information you learned in previous chapters, you can probably answer the following questions.

■ The first ingredient listed is a modified form of *whey protein.* What common food is the source of *whey*?

■ The fourth ingredient

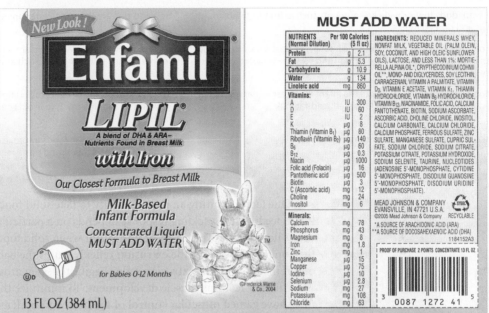

Figure 16.12 An infant formula label. Notice that there is a long list of ingredients and no % Daily Value.

listed is *lactose.* Is lactose a form of protein, fat, or carbohydrate? Why is lactose important for infants?

■ The front label states the formula has a blend of *DHA* (docosahexaenoic acid) and *ARA* (arachidonic acid). Are DHA and ARA forms of protein, fat, or carbohydrate? Why are these two nutrients thought to be important for infants?

The label also claims that this formula is *"Our Closest Formula to Breast Milk."* Can you think of some differences between breast milk and this formula that still exist? Look at the list of nutrients on the label. You'll notice that there is no "% Daily Value" column that you see on most food labels. Next time you are at the grocery store, look at other baby food items, such as baby cereal or pureed fruits. Do their labels simply list the nutrient content or is the "% Daily Value" column used? Why do you think infant formula has a different label format?

Let's say you are feeding a 6-month-old infant who needs about 500 kcal/day. Using the information from the nutrition section of the label, you can calculate the number of fluid ounces of formula the baby needs (this assumes that no cereal or other foods are eaten):

There are 100 kcal (calories) per 5 fl. oz:

100 kcal ÷ 5 fl. oz = 20 kcal/fl. oz

500 kcal ÷ 20 kcal/fl. oz = 25 fl. oz of formula per day to meet this baby's energy needs

A 6-month-old infant needs about 210 mg calcium per day. Based on an intake of 25 fl. oz of formula per day, as just calculated, you can use the label nutrition information to calculate the amount of calcium that is provided:

There are 78 mg calcium per 5 fl. oz serving of formula:

78 mg ÷ 5 fl. oz = 15.6 mg calcium per fl. oz

15.6 mg calcium per fl. oz × 25 fl. oz = 390 mg calcium per day

You can see that the infant's need for calcium is easily met by the formula alone.

When Do Infants Begin to Need Solid Foods?

As the result of declining nutrient stores, particularly iron, and continued growth, infants begin to need complementary, or solid, foods at around 6 months of age (Table 16.3). As previously noted, the American Academy of Pediatrics recommends exclusive breastfeeding for the first 6 months of life, but also recognizes that there is no evidence of significant harm if complementary foods are offered no earlier than 4 months of age.[2]

Table 16.3 Guidelines for the Introduction of Solid Foods to Infants

Guideline	Explanation
Introduce single-item foods, one at a time, at 3- to 5-day intervals. Avoid multigrain cereals and mixed dishes.	Makes it easier to identify possible food allergies.
Start with foods that provide key nutrients such as iron-fortified infant cereals and pureed meats.	Iron and zinc are the most common nutrient deficiencies in infants. Meat provides both.
Do not introduce fruit juices until the infant is at least 6 months of age. When introduced, limit to 4 to 6 oz/day and vary the types of juice offered.	High juice intake displaces calcium- and protein-rich breast milk and formula. Many popular juices, such as apple juice, offer limited nutritional value.
Do not introduce cow's milk until the infant is at least 1 year old. When introduced, provide whole milk, not reduced-fat milk.	The nutrient profile of cow's milk is not optimal to meet the needs of the growing infant. Healthy 1-year-olds need the energy provided by whole milk.
Introduce a variety of foods by the age of 1 year.	Variety and diversity in foods improve nutrient intake, stimulate the senses of taste, odor, and touch, and positively influence future eating habits.

The extrusion reflex will push solid food out of an infant's mouth.

One factor limiting an infant's ability to take solid foods is the *extrusion reflex*. During infant feeding, the suckling response depends on a particular movement of the tongue that draws liquid out of the breast or bottle. But when solid foods are introduced with a spoon, this tongue movement (the extrusion reflex), causes the baby to push most of the food back out of the mouth. The extrusion reflex begins to lessen around 4 to 5 months of age.

Another factor is muscle development. To minimize the risk of choking, the infant must have gained muscular control of the head and neck and must be able to sit up (with or without support).

Still another part of being ready for solid foods is sufficient maturity of the digestive and kidney systems. Infants can digest and absorb lactose from birth; however, the ability to digest starch does not fully develop until the age of 3 to 4 months. If an infant is fed cereal, for example, before he can digest the starch, diarrhea and discomfort may develop. In addition, early introduction of solid foods can lead to improper absorption of intact, undigested proteins, setting the stage for allergies. Finally, the kidneys must have matured so that they are better able to process nitrogen wastes from proteins and concentrate urine.

The need for solid foods is also related to nutrient needs. At about 6 months of age, infant iron stores become depleted; thus, iron-fortified infant cereals are often the first foods introduced. Rice cereal rarely provokes an allergic response and is easy to digest. If all goes well with the rice cereal, another single-grain cereal (other than wheat, which is highly allergenic) can be introduced, or the family may choose to gradually introduce different single-item foods such as strained vegetables, meats, or fruits. Some nutritionists recommend meat as a good source of iron and zinc, and others encourage the introduction of vitamin C–rich fruits and vegetables.

Commercial baby foods are convenient and are typically made without added salt; some are made only with organic ingredients. Dessert items and dinner-type foods are not recommended because they contain added sugars and starches. Parents can use an inexpensive food grinder to prepare home-made baby foods that cost little and reflect the cultural diversity of the family.

Throughout the first year, solid foods should only be a supplement to, not a substitute for, breast milk or iron-fortified formula. Infants still need the nutrient density and energy that breast milk and formula provide.

What *Not* to Feed an Infant

The following foods should never be offered to an infant:

- *Foods that could cause choking.* Foods such as grapes, hot dogs, nuts, popcorn, raw carrots, raisins, and hard candies cannot be chewed adequately by infants and can cause choking.

- *Corn syrup and honey.* These may contain spores of the bacterium *Clostridium botulinum.* These spores can germinate and grow into viable bacteria in the immature digestive tracts of infants, where they produce a potent toxin that can be fatal. Children older than 1 year can safely consume these substances because their digestive tracts are mature enough to kill any *C. botulinum* bacteria.

- *Goat's milk.* Goat's milk is notoriously low in many nutrients that infants need, such as folate, vitamin C, vitamin D, and iron.

- *Cow's milk.* For children under 1 year, cow's milk is too concentrated in minerals and protein and contains too few carbohydrates to meet infant energy needs. Infants can begin to consume whole cow's milk after the age of 1 year. Infants and toddlers should not be given reduced-fat cow's milk before the age of 2 years, as it does not contain enough fat and is too high in mineral content for the kidneys to handle effectively. Infants should not be given evaporated milk or sweetened condensed milk.

- *Large quantities of fruit juices.* Fruit juices are poorly absorbed in the infant digestive tract, causing diarrhea if consumed in excess. Large quantities of fruit juice can make an infant feel full and reject breast milk or formula at feeding time, thus causing him or her to miss out on essential nutrients. Plain water will also effectively quench an infant's thirst.

- *Too much salt and sugar.* Infant foods should not be seasoned with salt or other seasonings, or sweetened. Cookies, cakes, and other excessively sweet, processed foods also should be avoided.

- *Too much breast milk or formula.* As nutritious as breast milk and formula are, once infants reach the age of 6 months, solid foods should be introduced gradually. Six months of age is a critical time, as that is when a baby's iron stores begin to be depleted. In addition, infants are physically and psychologically ready to incorporate solid foods at this time, and solid foods can help appease their increasing appetites. Between 6 months and the time of weaning (from breast or bottle), solid foods should gradually make up an increasing proportion of the infant's diet. Overreliance on breast milk or formula, to the exclusion or displacement of iron-rich foods, can result in a condition known as *milk anemia.*

RECAP

In the absence of breastfeeding, iron-fortified formulas provide adequate nutrition for infants. Solid foods can gradually be introduced into an infant's diet at 4 to 6 months of age beginning with rice cereal, other non-wheat cereals, then moving to single-item vegetables and fruits. Parents should carefully select and prepare the foods to be given to their infants, avoiding those that represent a choking hazard and limiting high-sugar foods and beverages. Solid foods expand the infant's exposure to tastes and textures and represent an important developmental milestone.

Nutrition-Related Concerns for Infants

Nutrition is one of the biggest concerns of new parents. Infants cannot speak, and their cries are sometimes indecipherable. Feeding time can be very frustrating for parents, especially if the child is not eating, not growing appropriately, or has problems like diarrhea, vomiting, or persistent skin rashes. Following are some nutrition-related concerns for infants.

Allergies

Many foods have the potential to stimulate an allergic reaction. Breastfeeding reduces the risk of allergy development, as does delaying the introduction of solid foods until the age of 6 months. One of the most common allergies in infants is to the proteins in cow's milk–based formulas. Egg whites, peanuts, and wheat are other common triggers to allergic

Early introduction of solid foods may play a role in the development of food allergies, especially if infants are introduced to highly allergenic foods early on.

reactions. Every food should be introduced in isolation, so that any allergic reaction can be identified and the particular food avoided.

Symptoms of an allergic reaction vary but may include gastrointestinal distress such as diarrhea or vomiting, rashes or hives, runny nose or sneezing, or even difficulty breathing. Peanut allergy is the leading cause of fatal food reactions in the United States.[2] While about 85% of infants who are allergic to cow's milk and eggs develop a tolerance for them by the age of 5 years, only about 20% of infants allergic to peanuts are able to safely tolerate them by age 5 years.

Colic

Colicky babies will begin crying for no apparent reason even if they otherwise appear well nourished and happy.

Perhaps nothing is more frustrating to new parents than the relentless crying spells of some infants, typically referred to as **colic.** In this condition, newborns and young infants who appear happy, healthy, and well nourished suddenly begin to cry or even shriek and continue no matter what their caregiver does to console them. The spells tend to occur at the same time of day, typically late in the afternoon or early in the evening, and often occur daily for a period of several weeks. Crying lasts for hours at a time. Overstimulation of the nervous system, feeding too rapidly, swallowing of air, and intestinal gas pain are considered possible culprits, but the precise cause is unknown.

As with allergies, if a colicky infant is breastfed, breastfeeding should be continued, but the mother should try to determine whether eating certain foods seems to prompt crying and, if so, eliminate the offending food(s) from her diet. Avoidance of spicy or other strongly flavored foods may also help. Formula-fed infants may benefit from a change in type of formula. In the worst cases of colic, a physician may prescribe medication. Fortunately, most cases disappear spontaneously, possibly because of maturity of the GI tract, around 3 months of age.

Gastroesophageal Reflux

The regurgitation, or reflux, of stomach contents into the esophagus often results in the all too familiar "spitting up" of young infants. Particularly common in preterm infants, gastroesophageal reflux occurs in about 3% of newborns. Typically, as the gastrointestinal tract matures within the first 12 months of life, this condition resolves. Caretakers should avoid overfeeding the infant, keep the infant upright after each feeding, and watch for choking or gagging.

Failure to Thrive

At times, seemingly healthy infants reach an inappropriate plateau or decline in their growth. Pediatric healthcare providers describe **failure to thrive (FTT)** as a condition in which, in the absence of disease or physical abnormalities, the infant's weight or weight-for-height is below the 3rd percentile, or the infant has fallen more than two percentile lines on the NCHS growth charts after a previously stable pattern of growth.[2] Acute malnutrition often results in *wasting*, or low weight-for-height, and chronic malnutrition typically produces growth *stunting*, in which the child has low height-for-age.

Psychosocial factors that increase the risk for FTT include poverty, inadequate knowledge, extreme nutritional beliefs, social isolation, domestic violence, and/or substance abuse. If not corrected in a timely manner, FTT may result in developmental, motor, and cognitive delays typically associated with infants in developing nations.

Anemia

As stated earlier, full-term infants are born with sufficient iron stores to last for approximately the first 6 months of life. In older infants and toddlers, however, iron is the min-

colic Unconsolable infant crying of unknown origin that lasts for hours at a time.

failure to thrive (FTT) An unexplained condition in which the infant's weight gain and growth are far below usual levels for age and previous pattern of growth.

eral most likely to be deficient. Iron-deficiency anemia causes pallor, lethargy, and impaired growth. Iron-fortified formula is a good source for formula-fed infants. Some pediatricians prescribe a supplement containing iron especially formulated for infants. Iron for older infants is typically supplied by iron-fortified rice cereal or pureed meats. Overconsumption of cow's milk remains a common cause of anemia among U.S. infants and children.

Dehydration

Whether the cause is diarrhea, vomiting, prolonged fever, or inadequate fluid intake, dehydration is extremely dangerous to infants, and if left untreated can quickly result in death. The factors behind infants' increased risk of dehydration were discussed on page 649. Treatment includes providing fluids, a task that is difficult if vomiting is occurring. In some cases, the physician may recommend that a pediatric electrolyte solution, readily available at most grocery and drug stores, be administered on a temporary basis. In more severe cases, hospitalization may be necessary. If possible, breastfeeding should continue throughout an illness. A physician or other healthcare provider should be consulted on decisions related to the use of formula and solid foods.

Nursing Bottle Syndrome

Infants should never be left alone with a bottle, whether lying down or sitting up. As infants manipulate the nipple of the bottle, the high-carbohydrate fluid (whether breast milk, formula, or fruit juice) drips out, coming into prolonged contact with the developing teeth. This high-carbohydrate fluid provides an optimal food source for bacteria that are the underlying cause of dental caries (cavities). Severe tooth decay can result (**Figure 16.13**). Encouraging the use of a cup around the age of 8 months helps prevent nursing bottle syndrome, as does weaning the baby from a bottle entirely by the age of 15 to 18 months.

Figure 16.13 Leaving a baby alone with a bottle can result in the tooth decay of nursing bottle syndrome.

Lead Poisoning

Lead is especially toxic to infants and children because their brains and central nervous systems are still developing. Lead poisoning can result in decreased mental capacity, behavioral problems, anemia, impaired growth, impaired hearing, and other problems. Unfortunately, lead in old pipes and lead paint can still be found in older homes and buildings. Measures to reduce lead exposure include:

- Allowing tap water to run for a minute or so before use, to clear the pipes of any lead-contaminated water
- Using only cold tap water for drinking, cooking, and infant formula preparation, as hot tap water is more likely to leach lead
- Professionally removing lead-based paint or painting it over with latex paint

RECaP

Risk for food allergies can be reduced by delaying the introduction of solid foods until the infant is at least 6 months of age. Infants with colic or gastroesophageal reflux present special challenges, but both conditions generally improve over time. Infants who present with failure to thrive require close monitoring by healthcare providers, as do infants experiencing severe dehydration. Anemia is easily prevented through the use of iron-fortified formulas and cereals. Nursing bottle syndrome is characterized by dental caries in infants left lying down or sitting up with a bottle. Lead poisoning can result in cognitive, behavioral, and other problems.

See for Yourself

Planning a Nutrient-Packed Snack

We said earlier in this chapter that, during the last two trimesters of pregnancy, energy needs increase by about 350 to 450 kcal/day. At the same time, a pregnant woman's need for protein increases by 25 g per day. To help you appreciate how important it is for pregnant women to choose nutrient-dense foods, here's a two-part challenge:

Part 1.   Design a healthful mid-morning snack that provides a woman with 350 to 450 kcal and also fulfills at least half of her increased protein needs (that is, 12.5 g). List

each food item, the amount, the kcals, and the g protein provided.

Part 2.   Let's "flip" the assignment: Write out your own favorite mid-morning snack that totals about 350 to 450 kcal, identifying the amount of protein just as you did for the snack in part 1. How much protein does your favorite snack provide? Would you recommend it to a pregnant woman? Is it a healthful snack for *you*?

Chapter Review

Test Yourself | Answers

1   (F) Energy needs increase by only 20% or less above non-pregnant needs. This translates to an extra 350 to 400 additional calories per day, not a doubling of calories.

2   (F) More than half of all pregnant women experience morning sickness, and food cravings or aversions are also common.

3   (T) Breast milk contains various immune factors (antibodies and immune system cells) from the mother that protect the infant against infection. The nutrients in breast milk are structured to be easily digested by an infant, resulting in fewer symptoms of gastrointestinal distress and fewer allergies.

4   (T) Caffeine quickly passes into breast milk, as do alcohol and most prescription and over-the-counter medications.

5   (F) Most infants do not have a physiologic need for solid food until about 6 months of age.

Summary

- Nutrition is important before conception because critical stages of cell division, tissue differentiation, and organ development occur in the early weeks of pregnancy, often before a woman even knows she is pregnant.

- A plentiful, nourishing diet is important throughout pregnancy to provide the nutrients needed to support fetal development without depriving the mother of nutrients she needs to maintain her own health.

- A normal pregnancy progresses over the course of 38 to 42 weeks. This time is divided into three trimesters of 13 to 14 weeks. Each trimester is associated with particular developmental phases of the embryo/fetus.

- Pregnant women of normal weight should consume adequate energy to gain 25 to 35 lb during pregnancy. Women who are underweight should gain slightly more, and women who are overweight or obese should gain less.

- Pregnant women need to be especially careful to consume adequate amounts of folate, vitamin B_{12}, vitamin C, vitamin D, calcium, iron, and zinc. A supplement is often prescribed to ensure adequate intake of these nutrients.

- Many pregnant women experience nausea and/or vomiting during pregnancy, and many crave or feel aversions to specific types of foods and nonfood substances.

- Heartburn and constipation in pregnancy are related to the relaxation of smooth muscle caused by certain pregnancy-related hormones.

- Gestational diabetes and preeclampsia are nutrition-related disorders that can seriously affect maternal and fetal health.

- The bodies of adolescents are still growing and developing; thus, their nutrient needs during pregnancy are higher than those of older pregnant women.

- Dieting during pregnancy can lead to inadequate nutrition for mother and fetus.

- Alcohol is a teratogen and should not be consumed in any amount during pregnancy.

- Cigarette smoking reduces placental transfer of oxygen and nutrients, limiting fetal growth and development.

- Successful breastfeeding requires the coordination of several hormones, including estrogen, progesterone, prolactin, and oxytocin. These hormones govern the preparation of the breasts, as well as actual milk production and the let-down response.

- Breastfeeding women require more energy than is needed during pregnancy. Protein needs increase, and an overall nutritious diet with plentiful fluids is important in maintaining milk quality and quantity, as well as preserving the mother's health.

- The advantages of breastfeeding include nutritional superiority of breast milk, protection from infections and allergies, promotion of attachment, convenience, and lower cost.

- Breastfeeding exclusively for the first 6 months of a baby's life is recommended by North American and international healthcare organizations.

- Challenges that might be encountered with breastfeeding include effect of medications on breast milk, concerns related to transmission of HIV to a breastfeeding infant, scheduling conflicts for mothers who return to work, and social concerns.

- Infants are characterized by their extremely rapid growth and brain development.

- Physicians use length and weight measurements as the main tools for assessing an infant's nutritional status.

- Because infant stores of iron become depleted after about 6 months, an iron supplement is sometimes prescribed for breastfeeding infants.

- Breast milk or formula is entirely sufficient for the first 6 months of life. After that, solid foods can be introduced (for example, rice cereal fortified with iron) and expanded gradually, with breast milk or formula remaining very important throughout the first year.

- Infants need to be monitored carefully for appropriate growth and appropriate number of wet diapers every day to assess adequate nutrient intake and hydration.

- Nutrition-related concerns for infants include the potential for allergies, colic, gastroesophageal reflux, dehydration, failure to thrive, anemia, nursing bottle syndrome, and ingestion of lead.

Review Questions

1. Folate deficiency in the first weeks after conception has been linked with which of the following problems in the newborn?
   a. Anemia
   b. Neural tube defects
   c. Low birth weight
   d. Preterm delivery

2. Which of the following hormones is responsible for the let-down response?
   a. Progesterone
   b. Estrogen
   c. Oxytocin
   d. Prolactin

3. Which of the following nutrients should be added to the diet of breastfed infants when they are around 6 months of age?
   a. Protein
   b. Fat
   c. Iron
   d. Vitamin A

4. A pregnancy weight gain of 28 to 40 lb is recommended for
   a. all women.
   b. women who begin their pregnancy underweight.
   c. women who begin their pregnancy overweight.
   d. women who begin their pregnancy at a normal weight.

5. One of the best solid foods to introduce first to infants is
   a. Cream of Wheat cereal.
   b. applesauce.
   c. teething biscuits.
   d. iron-fortified rice cereal.

6. **True or false?** Major developmental errors and birth defects are most likely to occur in the third trimester of pregnancy.

7. **True or false?** Infant suckling is a critical component of successful and continued lactation.

8. **True or false?** Growth is a key indicator of adequate infant nutrition.

9. **True or false?** Alcohol easily passes from the mother's blood-stream into fetal blood and, in breastfeeding women, into the breast milk.

10. **True or false?** If gestational diabetes is not well controlled, the fetus may not receive enough glucose and is at high risk for low birth weight.

11. Identify five advantages and five disadvantages of breastfeeding. Can you think of others?

12. You are a Registered Dietitian in a public health clinic. A pregnant 15-year-old is referred to you for nutrition-related counseling and services. Identify at least three topics that you would discuss with this client.

13. Your cousin, who is pregnant with her first child, tells you that her physician prescribed supplemental iron tablets for her but that she decided not to take them. "You know me," she says, "I'm a natural food nut! I'm absolutely certain that my careful diet is providing all the nutrients my baby needs!" Is it possible that your cousin is partly right and partly wrong? Explain.

14. You visit your neighbors one afternoon to congratulate them on the birth of their new daughter, Katie. While you are there, 2-week-old Katie suddenly starts crying as if she is in terrible pain. "Oh, no," Katie's dad says to his wife. "Here we go again!" He turns to you and explains, "She's been like this every afternoon for the past week, and it goes on until sunset. I just wish we could figure out what we're doing wrong." What would you say?

15. You are on a picnic with your sister at a park, who drapes a shawl over her shoulders and breastfeeds her 11-month-old son. A woman walking by stops and says, "Isn't that child getting too old for that?" What information could you share with the woman in response to her question?

Web Links

www.aap.org
American Academy of Pediatrics
Visit this Web site for information on infants' and children's health. Clinical information as well as guidelines for parents and caregivers can be found. Searches can be performed for topics such as "neural tube defects" or "infant formulas."

www.mypyramid.gov/mypyramidmoms/
MyPyramid Plan for Moms
This Web site is designed for pregnant and breastfeeding women and provides meal plans that can be personalized to address the
needs of women across the three trimesters of pregnancy, women who are exclusively breastfeeding, and women who are partially breastfeeding.

http://fnic.nal.usda.gov
Food and Nutrition Information Center of the USDA
Click on "Lifecycle Nutrition." This page provides links to topics on pregnancy, breastfeeding, and infant nutrition.

www.emedicine.com/ped
eMedicine: Pediatrics
This site provides references for numerous infant health and nutrition issues. Select "Toxicology" and then "Toxicity, Iron" to learn about accidental iron poisoning and its signs in children and infants.

www.marchofdimes.com
March of Dimes
Click on "Pregnancy & Newborn" to find links on nutrition during pregnancy, breastfeeding, and baby care.

www.lalecheleague.org
La Leche League
This site provides information about breastfeeding; search or browse to find multiple articles on the health effects of breastfeeding for mother and infant.

www.nofas.org
National Organization on Fetal Alcohol Syndrome
This site provides news and information relating to fetal alcohol syndrome.

www.helppregnantsmokersquit.org
The National Partnership to Help Pregnant Smokers Quit
A site created for healthcare providers and smokers with the purpose of educating about the dangers of smoking while pregnant and providing tools to help pregnant smokers quit.

http://smokefreefamilies.tobacco-cessation.org/
National Partnership for Smoke Free Families
This site provides information to help pregnant women quit smoking.

References

1. U.S. Department of Health and Human Services. November 2000. *Healthy People 2010,* 2nd ed. With understanding and improving Health and Objectives for improving health. 2 vols. Washington, DC: U.S. Government Printing Office.
2. Kleinman, R.E., ed. American Academy of Pediatrics, Committee on Nutrition. 2009. *Pediatric Nutrition Handbook.* 6th ed. Elk Grove Village, IL: American Academy of Pediatrics.
3. Davidson, M. R., M. L. London, and P. W. Ladewig. 2008. *Olds' Maternal-Newborn Nursing and Women's Health Across the Lifespan,* 8th ed. Upper Saddle River, NJ: Prentice Hall Health.
4. UNICEF (United Nations Children's Fund). 2004. Maternal nutrition and low birth weight. Available at www.unicef.org/nutrition/index_lowbirthweight.html.
5. Rasmussen, K. M., and A. L. Yaktine, eds. 2009. *Weight Gain During Pregnancy: Reexamining the Guidelines.* Institute of Medicine; National Research Council. Washington, DC: National Academy Press.
6. Wrotniak, B. H., J. Shults, S. Butts, and N. Stettler. 2008. Gestational weight gain and risk of overweight in the offspring at age 7 y in a multicenter, multiethnic cohort study. *Am. J. Clin. Nutr.* 87:1818–1824.
7. Boney, C. M., A. Verma, R. Tucker, and B. R. Vohr. 2005. Metabolic syndrome in childhood: Association with birth weight, maternal obesity, and gestational diabetes mellitus. *Pediatrics* 115:e290–e296.
8. Brown, J. E., M. A. Murtaugh, D. R. Jacobs, and H. C. Margellos. 2002. Variation in newborn size according to pregnancy weight change by trimester. *Am. J. Clin. Nutr.* 76:205–209.
9. U.S. Department of Health and Human Services and U.S. Department of Agriculture. 2005. *Dietary Guidelines for Americans 2005,* 6th ed. Washington, DC: U.S. Government Printing Office. Available at www.healthierus.gov/dietaryguidelines.
10. Institute of Medicine, Food and Nutrition Board. 2002. *Dietary Reference Intakes for Energy, Carbohydrate, Fiber, Fat, Fatty Acids, Cholesterol, Protein, and Amino Acids.* Washington, DC: National Academy Press.
11. U.S. Department of Health and Human Services and U.S. Environmental Protection Agency. November 2008. What you need to know about mercury in fish and shellfish. Available at www.epa.gov/waterscience/fish/advice/. (Accessed May 2009.)
12. Institute of Medicine, Food and Nutrition Board. 1998. *Dietary Reference Intakes for Thiamin, Riboflavin, Niacin, Vitamin B$_6$, Folate, Vitamin B$_{12}$, Pantothenic Acid, Biotin, and Choline.* Washington, DC: National Academy Press.
13. Centers for Disease Control and Prevention (CDC). 2009. Facts about folic acid: Folic acid home page. Available at www.cdc.gov/ncbddd/folicacid/about.html. (Accessed May 2009.)
14. Institute of Medicine, Food and Nutrition Board. 2001. *Dietary Reference Intakes for Vitamin A, Vitamin K, Arsenic, Boron, Chromium, Copper, Iodine, Iron, Manganese, Molybdenum, Nickel, Silicon, Vanadium, and Zinc.* Washington, DC: National Academy Press.
15. Institute of Medicine, Food and Nutrition Board. 1997. *Dietary Reference Intakes for Calcium, Phosphorus, Magnesium, Vitamin D, and Fluoride.* Washington, DC: National Academy Press.
16. Bodnar, L. M., J. M. Catov, H. N. Simhan, M. F. Holick, R. W. Powers, and J. M. Roberts. 2007. Maternal vitamin D deficiency increases the risk of preeclampsia. *J. Clin. Endocrinology & Metab.* 92:3517–3522.
17. Office of Dietary Supplements. 2007. Dietary supplement fact sheet: Iron. National Institutes of Health. Available at http://dietary-supplements.info.nih.gov/factsheets/Iron_pf.asp. (Accessed May 2009.)
18. Institute of Medicine, Food and Nutrition Board. 2004. *Dietary Reference Intakes for Water, Potassium, Sodium, Chloride, and Sulfate.* Washington, DC: National Academy Press.
19. Gordon, M. C. 2007. Maternal physiology. In: Gabbe, S. G., J. R. Niebyl, and J. L. Simpson, eds. *Obstetrics: Normal and Problem Pregnancies,* 5th ed. Philadelphia: Elsevier Churchill Livingstone.
20. Kittler, P. G., and K. P. Sucher. 2001. *Food and Culture.* Belmont, CA: Wadsworth Thomson Learning.
21. Keely, E. J., J. C. Malcolm, S. Hadjiyannakis, I. Gaboury, G. Lough, and M. L. Lawson. 2008. Prevalence of metabolic markers of insulin resistance in offspring of gestational diabetes pregnancies. *Pediatr. Diabetes* 9:53–59.

22. Vääräsmäki, M. A., P. Pouta, P. Elliot, U. Tapanainen, A. Sovio, A. L. Ruokonen, M. Hartikainen, M. McCarthy, and M. R. Järvelin. 2009. Adolescent manifestations of metabolic syndrome among children born to women with gestational diabetes in a general-population birth cohort. *Am. J. Epidemiol.* 169:1209–1215.

23. Damm, P. 2009. Future risk of diabetes in mother and child after gestational diabetes mellitus. *International J. Gynec. Obstetrics* 104:S25–S26; National Institute of Diabetes and Digestive and Kidney Diseases (NIDDK). June 2008. National diabetes statistics, 2007. Available at http://diabetes.niddk.nih.gov/dm/pubs/statistics/DM_Statistics.pdf.

24. Leeman, L., and P. Fontaine. 2008. Hypertensive disorders of pregnancy. *Am. Fam. Physician.* 78:93–100.

25. Solomon, C., G. and E. W. Seely. 2006. Hypertension in pregnancy. *Endocrin. Metab. Clinics. N. Amer.* 35:157–171.

26. Markovitz, B. P., R. Cook, L. H. Flick, and T. L. Leet. 2005. Socioeconomic factors and adolescent pregnancy outcomes: Distinctions between neonatal and post-neonatal deaths? *BMC Public Health* 5:79–85.

27. Koebnick, C., I. Hoffmann, P. C. Dagnelie, U. A. Heins, S. N. Wickramasinghe, I. D. Ratnayaka, S. Gruendel, J. Landemans, and C. Leitzmann. 2004. Long-term ovo-lacto vegetarian diet impairs vitamin B$_{12}$ status in pregnant women. *J. Nutr.* 134:3319–3326.

28. Weiss, R., Y. Fogelman, and M. Bennett. 2004. Severe vitamin B$_{12}$ deficiency in an infant associated with a maternal deficiency and a strict vegetarian diet. *J. Pediatr. Hematol. Oncol.* 26:270–271.

29. Weng, X., R. Odouli, and D. Li. 2008. Maternal caffeine consumption during pregnancy and the risk of miscarriage: a prospective cohort study. *Am. J. Obstet. Gynecol.* 198:279.e1–279.e8.

30. Vik, T., L. S. Bakketeig, K. U. Trygg, K. Lund-Larsen, and G. Jacobsen. 2003. High caffeine consumption in the third trimester of pregnancy: Gender-specific effects on fetal growth. *Pediatric and Perinatal Epidemiology* 17:324–331.

31. CARE Study group. 2008. Maternal caffeine intake during pregnancy and risk of fetal growth restriction: a large prospective observational study. British Medical Journal 337:a2332.

32. March of Dimes. 2008. Drinking alcohol during pregnancy. Available at www.marchofdimes.com/professionals/14332_1170.asp.

33. Atrash, H. K., K. Johnson, M. Adams, J. F. Cordero, and J. Howse. 2006. Preconception care for improving perinatal outcomes: The time to act. *Matern. Child. Health. J.* 10:S3–S11.

34. National Center for Health Statistics. 2009. *Health, United States, 2008 with Chartbooks.* Hyattsville, MD: U.S. Government Printing Office.

35. Ayadi, M. F., E. K. Adams, C. L. Melvin, C. C. Rivera, C. A. Gaffney, J. Pike, V. Rabius, and J. N. Ferguson. 2006. *Pub. Health Reports* 121:120–126.

36. Substance Abuse and Mental Health Services Administration. 2008. *Results from the 2007 National Survey on Drug Use and Health: National Findings.* NSDUH Series H-34, DHHS Publication No. SMA 08-4343. Rockville, MD.

37. March of Dimes. 2006. Illicit drug use during pregnancy. Available at www.marchofdimes.com/professionals/14332_1169.asp. (Accessed May 2009.)

38. American College of Obstetrics and Gynecology Committee on Obstetric Practice. 2002. Committee opinion #267: Exercise during pregnancy and the postpartum period. *Obstet. Gynecol.* 99:171–173.

39. Lewis, B. M. Avery, E. Jennings, N. Sherwood, B. Martinson, and A. L. Crain. 2008. The effect of exercise during pregnancy on maternal outcomes: Practical implications for practice. *Am. J. Lifestyle Med.* 2:441–455.

40. Dempsey, J. C., T. K. Sorensen, M. A. Williams, I. M. Lee, R. S. Miller, E. E. Dashow, and D. A. Luthy. 2004. Prospective study of gestational diabetes mellitus risk in relation to maternal recreational physical activity before and during pregnancy. *Am. J. Epidemiol.* 159:663–670.

41. Garshasbi, A., and S. F. Zadeh. 2004. The effect of exercise on the intensity of low back pain in pregnant women. *Intern. J. Gynec. Obstetr.* 88:271–275.

42. Petersen, A. M., T. L. Leet, and R. C. Brownson. 2005. Correlates of physical activity among pregnant women in the United States. *Med. Sci. Sports Exerc.* 37:1748–1753.

43. Centers for Disease Control and Prevention. 2008. Breastfeeding among U.S. children born 1999–2005, DCD National Immunization Survey. Available at www.cdc.gov/breastfeeding/data/NIS_data/. (Accessed May 2009.)

44. Forste, R., and J. P. Hoffmann. 2008. Are US mothers meeting the Healthy People 2010 breastfeeding targets for initiation, duration, and exclusivity? The 2003 and 2004 National Immunization Surveys. *J. Hum. Lact.* 24(3):278–288.

45. McDowell, M. M., C-Y. Wang, and J. Kennedy-Stephenson. 2008. Breastfeeding in the United States: Findings from the National Health and Nutrition Examination Survey, 1999–2006. *NCHS Data Brief.* Number 5, April 2008. Available at www.cdc.gov/nchs/data/databriefs/db05.htm. (Accessed May 2009.)

46. UNICEF/WHO. 2006. Baby Friendly Hospital Initiative, revised, updated and expanded for integrated care. Available at www.who.int/nutrition/topics/bfhi/en/index.html. (Accessed May 2009.)

47. American Academy of Pediatrics, Section on Breastfeeding. 2005. Breastfeeding and the use of human milk policy statement. *Pediatrics* 115:496–506.

48. Merewood, A., S. D. Mehta, L. B. Chamberlain, B. L. Philipp, and H. Bauchner. 2005. Breastfeeding rates in US baby-friendly hospitals: Results of a national survey. *Ped.* 116:628–634.

49. Brenna, J. T., B. Varamini, R. G. Jensen, D. A. Diersen-Schade, J. A. Boettcher, and L. M. Arterburn. 2007. Docosahexaenoic and arachidonic acid concentrations in human breast milk worldwide. *Am. J. Clin. Nutr.* 85:1457–1464.

50. Agency for Healthcare Research and Quality. 2007. *Breastfeeding and Maternal and Infant Health Outcomes in Developed Countries.* U.S. Department of Health and Human Services. Rockville, MD. AHRQ Publication No. 07-E007.

51. UNICEF (United Nations Children's Fund). 2003. Protecting, promoting and supporting breastfeeding. Available at www.unicef.org/nutrition/index_breastfeeding.html. (Accessed May 2009.)

52. Collaborative Group on Hormonal Factors in Breast Cancer. 2003. Breast cancer and breastfeeding: Collaborative reanalysis of individual data from 47 epidemiological studies in 30 countries, including 50302 women with breast cancer and 96,973 women without the disease. *Lancet* 360:187–195.

53. Grimes, J. P., and S. J. Wimalawansa. 2003. Breastfeeding and postmenopausal osteoporosis. *Curr. Women's Health Rep.* 3(3):193–198.

54. Paton, L. M., J. L. Alexander, C. A. Nowson, C. Margerison, M. G. Frame, B. Kaymakci, and J. D. Wark. 2003. Pregnancy and lactation have no long-term deleterious effect on measures of bone mineral in healthy women: A twin study. *Am. J. Clin. Nutr.* 77:707–714.

55. Nickerson, K. 2006. Environmental contaminants in breast milk. *J. Midwifery Women's Health* 51:26–34.

56. Berlin, C. M., J. S. LaKind, B. R. Sonawane, S. Kacew, C. J. Borgert, M. N. Bates, N. Birnbach, R. Campbell, A. Dermer, K. G. Dewey, S. M. Ellerbee, P. Furst, G. P. Giacoia, L. Gartner, M. Groer, S. G. Haynes, S. S. Humerick, R. A. Lawrence, M. Lorber, C. Lovelady, A. Mason, L. L. Needham, M. F. Picciano, J. Plautz, J. J. Ryan, S. G. Selevan, C. V. Sumaya, M. R. Tully, K. Uhl, E. Vessel, and J. T Wilson. 2002. Conclusions, research needs, and recommendations of the expert panel: Technical workshop on human milk surveillance and research for environmental chemicals in the United States. *Journal of Toxicology and Environmental Health, Part A,* 65(22):1929–35.

57. Bauchner, E. 2004. Environmental contaminants and human milk. *LEAVEN* 39:123–125.

58. Coovadia, H. M., N. C. Rollins, R. M. Bland, K. Little, A. Coutsoudis, M. L. Bennish, and M. L. Newell. 2007. Mother-to-child transmission of HIV-1 infection during exclusive breastfeeding in the first 6 months of life: An intervention cohort study. *Lancet* 369:1107–1116.

59. Adams, C., R. Berger, P. Conning, L. Cruikshank, and K. Dore. 2001. Breastfeeding trends at a community breastfeeding center: An evaluative survey. *J. Obstet. Gynecol. Neonatal Nurs.* 30(4):392–400.

60. Merritt, R. J., and B. H. Jenks. 2004. Safety of soy-based infant formulas containing isoflavones: The clinical evidence. *J. Nutr.* 134:1220S–1224S.

61. ESPGHAN Committee on Nutrition: C. Agostoni, I. Axelsson, O. Goulet, B. Koletzko, K. F. Michaelsen, J. Puntis, D. Rieu, J. Rigo, R. Shamir, H. Szajewska, and D. Turck. 2006. Soy protein infant formulae and follow-on formulae: a commentary by the ESPGHAN committee on nutrition. *J. Ped. Gastroenterol. Nutr.* 42:352–361.

62. Grummer-Strawn, L. M., and M. Zuguo. 2004. Does breastfeeding protect against pediatric overweight? Analysis of longitudinal data from the Centers for Disease Control and Prevention Pediatric Nutrition Surveillance System. *Pediatrics* 113e:e81–e86.

63. Weyermann, M., D. Rothenbacher, and H. Brenner. 2006. Duration of breastfeeding and risk of overweight in childhood: A prospective birth cohort study from Germany. *Int. J. Obesity. (London)* 30:1281–1287.

64. Koletzko, B., R. von Kries, R. Closa Monasterolo, J. Excribano Subias, S. Scaglioni, M. Giovannini, J. Beyer, et al., for the European Childhood Obesity Trial Study Group. 2009. Can infant feeding choices modulate later obesity risk? *Am. J. Clin. Nutr.* 89(suppl):1502S–1508S.

65. Gillman, M. W., S. L. Rifas-Shiman, C. A. Camargo Jr., C. S. Berkey, A. L. Frazier, H. R. Rockett, A. E. Field, and G. A. Colditz. 2001. Risk of overweight among adolescents who were breastfed as infants. *JAMA* 285:2461–1467.

66. Owen, C. G., R. M. Martin, P. H. Whincup, D. Smith, and D. G. Cook. 2005. Effect of infant feeding on the risk of obesity across the life course: A quantitative review of published evidence. *Pediatrics* 115:1367–1377.

67. O'Tierney, P. F., D. J. P. Barker, C. Osmond, E. Kajantie, and J. G. Eriksson. 2009. Duration of breast-feeding and adiposity in adult life. *J. Nutr.* 139:422S–425S.

68. Ludwig, D. S., and H. A. Pollack. 2009. Obesity and the economy: From crisis to opportunity. *JAMA* 301:533–535.

Should Breastfeeding Throughout Infancy Be Mandatory?

The year is 2021. In the United States, obesity rates have continued to skyrocket—especially among children. Type 2 diabetes is increasingly being diagnosed in elementary school children, and schools have begun screening third graders for high blood glucose levels, high blood pressure, unhealthful blood lipids, and other indicators of metabolic syndrome. In this climate, Marcy goes shopping for infant formula. She has been breastfeeding her daughter Sidney exclusively, but next week she returns to work full-time and wants to switch 4-month-old Sidney to formula. Marcy picks up a large can of powdered formula and takes it to the check-out. When the clerk at the register announces the price, she gasps. "There must be some mistake! This is only enough formula to feed my daughter for a week!"

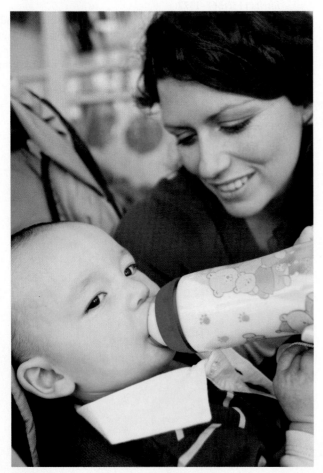

Formula-feeding has been associated with an increased risk of obesity in childhood and adulthood.

"It's not our fault," the clerk replies. "Only half that cost is for the formula. The rest is the new state surcharge to discourage you from buying it! Took effect last month—didn't you hear about it?" Marcy shakes her head as she digs back into her wallet for the extra cash. The clerk offers a sympathetic smile. "I guess it's just one more reason why breast is best!"

If this scenario sounds like bad fiction, you might be interested to learn that some healthcare providers are actually proposing that states implement a system of rewards for breastfeeding and penalties for formula-feeding—and a surcharge like the one just described is among the various proposals. Why? What's behind these recommendations, and could they ever really become law? Let's have a look.

As rates of pediatric and adult obesity have continued to climb, more and more researchers have been asking the question: "Do breastfed infants have lower rates of obesity as children, adolescents, and adult compared to people who were formula-fed as infants?"[62–67] These researchers point to the theory of *metabolic programming,* which states that nutritional and other factors in early postnatal life greatly influence one's physiology and subsequent risk of adult-onset, chronic diseases. Specifically, researchers have been investigating the hypothesis that infant feeding practices (breast- vs. formula-feeding) modify patterns of infant growth and development, which then influence the individual's future health, including risk of obesity. Supporting this theory is the established fact that breastfed infants grow in length and weight at a slower rate than formula-fed infants. But does this lower weight persist into childhood and adulthood?

While some studies show no protective effect, most have concluded that breastfeeding for longer than 3 to 6 months does, in fact, lower rates of child and adult overweight and obesity.[62–65] One researcher estimated that early breastfeeding reduced risk of childhood (school age) obesity by 15% to 25%.[64] Others concluded exclusive breastfeeding provides greater protection than partial breastfeeding, and that the longer breastfeeding persists, the greater the protection against obesity.[62, 66] At least one study reported that the most benefit was seen among Caucasian infants, with less of a protective effect in Hispanic and African-American breastfed infants.[62]

While researchers continue to investigate possible mechanisms, it has been suggested that the obesity risk reduction associated with breastfeeding may stem from the

One proposed disincentive for formula-feeding is a surcharge on purchases of formula similar to the taxes on alcohol and tobacco products in many states.

lower protein and energy intakes of breastfed infants, alterations in their regulation of insulin secretion, and/or differences in adipocyte metabolism.[66] Rapid weight gain during infancy, which is more common among formula-fed infants, is associated with a higher risk of obesity later in life.[62] Some scientists have suggested the differences in feeding patterns between breast- and formula-fed infants impacts risk of obesity: formula-fed infants suck at a faster and more powerful rate, have fewer "meals" per day, consume a larger volume at each meal, and have longer intervals between feedings compared to breastfed infants.[64] It is possible that these feeding differences translate into different eating habits as the infant transitions to child and adult diets.

In light of the convincing data from these studies, a new question arises: Does this difference in weight gain suggest that our society should do more to encourage or even require prolonged breastfeeding? Before you answer, consider the costs of obesity and its related chronic diseases: As you have learned in previous chapters of this book, obesity is a well-established risk factor for heart disease, stroke, type 2 diabetes, and some forms of cancer. As such, it is one of the primary underlying causes of preventable death in the United States. What's more, obesity-related costs account for 5% to 7% of annual U.S. healthcare expenditures, an estimated $100 billion annually, with additional costs related to lost productivity, reduced longevity, and impaired quality of life.[67, 68]

Given this staggering financial burden of obesity, and the fact that much of it is borne by the public in the form of higher healthcare costs and insurance premiums, not to mention reduced tax revenues (from lost productivity) and increased disability payments, does the public have a right to legislate actions that could possibly reduce obesity rates? Let's look at some precedents: By law, most municipal water supplies are fluoridated to reduce incidence of tooth decay. By law, all grain products sold across state lines are fortified with folic acid to reduce incidence of neural tube defects. By law, sales of alcohol and tobacco are restricted to adults, and carry heavy taxes in most states, to reduce the incidence of alcohol abuse, smoking, and substance-related diseases. All of these laws were enacted not only to improve the public health, but also to reduce the financial burden of disease on the American public. Although some would argue that such regulations take away our "personal freedoms," others point out that they primarily protect children and adolescents, either from the poor choices of their parents, or from the harmful consequences of their own choices, which they are too young to fully understand.

Critical Thinking Questions

■ If breastfeeding were shown to significantly lower the rates of child, adolescent, and adult obesity, do you think it should be highly encouraged, or even required? If so, how?

■ Would be fair to impose a surcharge on all infant formula sales? If so, should the money be spent to fund obesity prevention and treatment programs, lactation education and support, or similar measures?

■ Or should the revenues be used to offset income tax relief or other types of "reward" for families who choose breastfeeding? If the latter, who would monitor compliance, and would there be penalties for "cheating"?

■ Or, do you think the decision to breast- or formula-feed an infant should rest only with the family? At what point does "public good" override personal freedoms, especially in an area such as infant-feeding practices?

17 Nutrition Through the Life Cycle: Childhood and Adolescence

Test Yourself | True or False?

1 After their first birthday, all children should be fed nonfat milk products to reduce their risk for obesity. **T** *or* **F**

2 The nutrient needs of boys do not differ from those of girls for the first 8 or 9 years of life. **T** *or* **F**

3 Millions of American children live in households without a dependable supply of food. **T** *or* **F**

4 Adolescents experience an average 10% to 15% increase in height during the pubertal years. **T** *or* **F**

5 It is now believed that diet has virtually no role in the development of acne. **T** *or* **F**

Test Yourself answers are located in the Chapter Review.

Chapter Objectives *After reading this chapter, you will be able to:*

1. Compare and contrast the growth and activity patterns of toddlers and children, *pp. 666–672, 674–678.*

2. List at least three nutrients of concern when feeding a vegan diet to young children, *p. 673.*

3. Describe how micronutrient needs change as a child matures to adolescence, *p. 674.*

4. Describe the consequences of iron-deficiency anemia in young children, *pp. 678–679.*

5. Explain how a community nutritionist might assist a family faced with food insecurity, *p. 679.*

6. List three actions schools have taken to improve the nutrient quality of foods served to their students, *pp. 688, 690.*

7. Define puberty and describe how it influences changes in body composition, *pp. 681–682.*

8. Identify the most common nutrient deficiencies and excesses of the typical adolescent diet, *pp. 684–686.*

9. List at least two factors that increase risk of obesity during childhood and adolescence, *pp. 687–688.*

The Williams children are growing up in a typical time-pressed American household. Breakfast often means grabbing a doughnut or granola bar, lunch is supplied by their school or preschool, and dinners are usually eaten in the car on the way to a music lesson, sports practice, Boy Scouts meeting, or community event. Six-year-old Kimberly is often rewarded by her piano instructor with a piece of candy for a job well done. Eight-year-old Chris typically ends soccer practice with a soda and a fistful of chips, and 11-year-old Sam looks forward to scout meetings mainly for the cupcakes and cookies that are served. Even when the family finds time for a "home-cooked dinner," parents Bill and Emily often serve frozen fried chicken or fish sticks to avoid arguments over carrot sticks or green vegetables. Neither parent will go to the grocery store with the children: The constant food advertising on children's TV programs has led to relentless nagging by the kids for one high-sugar/high-fat food after another.

What are the consequences of this type of haphazard approach to family eating? Are families like the Williams able to meet the changing nutrient needs of their children as they grow and develop? How does the current "epidemic" of childhood obesity relate to the haphazard eating practices of many American families? This chapter will help you answer these and related questions. Although most topics are discussed within specific age groupings (toddlers, children, and adolescents), the chapter closes with an in-depth review of pediatric obesity, a critically important issue that affects children of all ages.

Many families typically grab quick meals "on the go."

Nutrition for Toddlers

When babies celebrate their first birthday, they transition out of infancy and into the active world of toddlers. Personality and behavioral changes introduce potential conflict into mealtimes, and parents who have been accustomed to making all decisions about their child's diet must now begin to consider the child's preferences. In addition, toddlers attending day care may be exposed to foods that may be more or less nutritious than the foods served at home. These and other circumstances add new challenges to the feeding process.

Toddler Growth and Activity Patterns

The rapid growth rate of infancy begins to slow during toddlerhood, the second and third years of life. A toddler will grow a total of about 5.5 to 7.5 inches and gain an average of 9 to 11 lb. Toddlers expend more energy to fuel increasing levels of activity as they explore their ever-expanding world and develop new skills. They progress from taking a few wobbly steps to running, jumping, and climbing with confidence, and they begin to dress, feed, and toilet themselves. Thus, their diet should provide an appropriate quantity and quality of nutrients to fuel their growth and activity.

Toddlers expend significant amounts of energy actively exploring their world.

What Are a Toddler's Nutrient Needs?

Nutrient needs increase as a child progresses from infancy to toddlerhood. Although their rate of growth has slowed, toddlers' increased nutrient needs are based on their larger body size. Refer to Table 17.1 on page 669 for a review of specific nutrient recommendations.

Energy and Macronutrient Recommendations for Toddlers

Although the energy requirement per kilogram of body weight for toddlers is just slightly less than for infants, *total* energy requirements are higher because toddlers are larger and much more active than infants. The **estimated energy requirement (EER),** or the total energy needed per day, varies according to the toddler's age, body weight, and level of activity.

Although there is currently insufficient evidence available to set a DRI for fat for toddlers, healthy toddlers of appropriate body weight need to consume 30% to 40% of their total daily energy intake as fat.[1] That's because fat provides a concentrated source of energy in a relatively small amount of food, and this is important for toddlers, especially those who are fussy eaters or have little appetite. Fat is also necessary during the toddler years to support the continuously developing nervous system.

estimated energy requirement (EER)   The total amount of energy needed per day for any age group.

Toddlers' protein needs increase modestly because they weigh more than infants and are still growing rapidly. The RDA for protein for toddlers is 1.1 g/kg body weight per day, or approximately 13 g of protein daily.[1] Recall that 2 cups of milk alone provide 16 g of protein; thus, most toddlers have little trouble meeting their protein needs.

The RDA for carbohydrate for toddlers is 130 g/day, and carbohydrate intake should be about 45% to 65% of total energy intake.[1] As is the case for older children and adults, most of the carbohydrates eaten should be complex, and refined carbohydrates from high-fat/high-energy foods such as cookies and candy should be kept to a minimum. Fruits and many fruit juices are nutritious sources of simple carbohydrates that can also be included. Keep in mind, however, that too much fruit juice can displace other foods and nutrients and can cause diarrhea. If consumed at bedtime or between meals, the sugars in fruit juice may also contribute to tooth decay. The American Academy of Pediatrics (AAP) recommends that the intake of fruit juice be limited to 4 to 6 fl. oz per day for children 1 to 6 years of age.[2]

Adequate fiber is important for toddlers to maintain regularity. The AI is 14 g of fiber per 1,000 kcal of energy, or, based on the average energy intake of this age group, 19 g/day.[1] In one study, 98% of young children (1–4 years) failed to meet this AI for fiber.[3] Whole-grain cereals, fresh fruits and vegetables, and whole-grain breads are healthful choices for toddlers' meals and snacks. Too much fiber, however, can inhibit the absorption of several nutrients such as iron and zinc, harm toddlers' small digestive tracts, and cause them to feel too full to consume adequate nutrients.

Determining the macronutrient requirements of toddlers can be challenging. See the upcoming box, You Do the Math, for analysis of the macronutrient levels in one toddler's daily diet.

Micronutrient Recommendations for Toddlers

As toddlers grow, their micronutrient needs increase. Of particular concern with toddlers are adequate intakes of the micronutrients associated with fruits and vegetables. In addition, calcium and iron have been identified as "priority nutrients" for children aged 2 to 4 years.[3]

Calcium is necessary for children to promote optimal bone mass, which continues to accumulate until early adulthood. For toddlers, the AI for calcium is 500 mg/day.[4] Dairy products are excellent sources of calcium. When a child reaches the age of 1 year, whole cow's milk can be given; however, reduced-fat milk (2% or less) should *not* be given until age 2. If dairy products are not feasible, calcium-fortified orange juice, soy milk, or rice milk can supply calcium, or children's calcium supplements can be given. Toddlers generally cannot consume enough food to depend on alternate calcium sources such as dark-green vegetables.

Iron-deficiency anemia is the most common nutrient deficiency in young children in the United States and around the world. Iron-deficiency anemia can affect a child's energy level, attention span, and ability to learn. The RDA for iron for toddlers is 7 mg/day.[5] Good sources of well-absorbed heme iron include lean meats, fish, and poultry; non-heme iron is provided by eggs, legumes, greens, and fortified foods such as breakfast cereals. When toddlers consume non-heme sources of iron, such as beans or greens, a source of vitamin C at the same meal will enhance the absorption of iron from these sources.

Fluid Recommendations for Toddlers

Toddlers lose less fluid from evaporation than infants, and their more mature kidneys are able to concentrate urine, conserving the body's fluid. However, as toddlers become active, they start to lose significant fluid through sweat, especially in hot weather. Parents need to make sure an active toddler is drinking adequately. The recommended fluid intake for toddlers is listed in Table 17.1 and includes about 4 cups as beverages, including water.[6] Suggested beverages include plain water, milk, calcium-fortified soy milk or rice milk, and foods high in water content, such as vegetables and fruits.

You Do the Math
Is This Menu Good for a Toddler?

A dedicated mother and father want to provide the best nutrition for their young son, Ethan, who is now 1½ years old and has just been completely weaned from breast milk. Ethan weighs about 26 lb (or 11.8 kg). Following is a typical day's menu for Ethan. Grams of protein, fat, and carbohydrate are given for each food. The day's total energy intake is 1,168 kcal. Calculate the percent of Ethan's calories that come from protein, fat, and carbohydrate (numbers may not add up to exactly 100% because of rounding). Where are Ethan's parents doing well, and where could they use some advice for improvement?

Meal	Foods	Protein (g)	Fat (g)	Carbo-hydrate (g)
Breakfast	Oatmeal (1/2 cup, cooked)	2.5	1.5	13.5
	Brown sugar (1 tsp.)	0	0	4
	Milk (1%, 4 fl. oz)	4	1.25	5.5
	Grape juice (4 fl. oz)	0	0	20
Mid-morning Snack	Banana slices (1 small banana)	0	0	16
	Yogurt (nonfat fruit flavored, 3 fl. oz)	5.5	0	15.5
	Orange juice (4 fl. oz)	1	0	13
Lunch	Whole-wheat bread (1 slice)	1.5	0.5	10
	Peanut butter (1 tbsp.)	4	8	3.5
	Strawberry jam (1 tbsp.)	0	0	13
	Carrots (cooked, 1/8 cup)	0	0	2
	Applesauce (sweetened, 1/4 cup)	0	0	12
	Milk (1%, 4 fl. oz)	4	1.25	5.5
Afternoon Snack	Bagel (1/2)	3	1	20
	American cheese product (1 slice)	3	5	1
	Water	0	0	0
Dinner	Scrambled egg (1)	11	5	1
	Baby food spinach (3 oz)	2	0.5	5.5
	Whole-wheat toast (1 slice)	1.5	0.5	10
	Mandarin orange slices (1/4 cup)	0.5	0	10
	Milk (1%, 4 fl. oz)	4	1.25	5.5

Note: This activity focuses on the macronutrients. It does not ask you to consider Ethan's intake of micronutrients or fluids.

Calculations:

There is a total of 47.5 g protein in Ethan's menu.

$$47.5 \text{ g} \times 4 \text{ kcal/g} = 190 \text{ kcal}$$
$$190 \text{ kcal protein}/1{,}168 \text{ total kcal} \times 100 = 16\% \text{ protein}$$

There is a total of 25.75 g fat in Ethan's menu.

$$25.75 \text{ g} \times 9 \text{ kcal/g} = 232 \text{ kcal}$$
$$232 \text{ kcal fat}/1{,}168 \text{ total kcal} \times 100 = 20\% \text{ fat}$$

There is a total of 186.5 g carbohydrate in Ethan's menu.

$$186.5 \text{ g} \times 4 \text{ cal/g} = 746 \text{ kcal}$$
$$746 \text{ kcal carbohydrate}/1{,}168 \text{ total kcal} \times 100 = 64\% \text{ carbohydrate}$$

Analysis: Ethan's parents are doing very well at offering a wide variety of foods from various food groups; they are especially doing well with fruits and vegetables. Also, according to his EER, Ethan requires about 970 kcal/day, and he is consuming 1,168 kcal/day, thus meeting his energy needs.

Ethan's total carbohydrate intake for the day is 186.5 g, which is higher than the RDA of 130 g per day; however, this value falls within the recommended 45% to 65% of total energy intake that should come from carbohydrates. Thus, high carbohydrate intake is adequate to meet his energy needs.

However, Ethan is being offered far more than enough protein. The DRI for protein for toddlers is about 13 g per day, and Ethan is being offered more than three times that much!

It is also readily apparent that Ethan is being offered too little fat for his age. Toddlers need at least 30% to 40% of their total energy intake from fat, and Ethan is only consuming about 20% of his calories from fat. He should be drinking whole milk, not 1% milk. He should occasionally be offered higher-fat foods like cheese for his snacks or macaroni and cheese for a meal. Yogurt is fine, but it shouldn't be nonfat at Ethan's age.

In conclusion, Ethan's parents should be commended for offering a variety of nutritious foods but should be counseled that a little more fat is critical for toddlers' growth and development. Some of the energy currently being consumed as protein and carbohydrate should be shifted to fat.

Do Toddlers Need Nutritional Supplements?

Toddlers can be well nourished by consuming a balanced, varied diet. But given their typically erratic eating habits, the child's physician may recommend a multivitamin and mineral supplement as a precaution against deficiencies. The toddler's physician or dentist may also prescribe a fluoride supplement, if the community water supply is not fluoridated. Supplements should also be considered for children in vegan families, children from fami-

Table 17.1 Nutrient Recommendations for Children and Adolescents

Nutrient	Children Age 1–3 Years	Children Age 4–8 Years	Children Age 9–13 Years	Adolescents (14–18 Years)
Fat	No DRI	No DRI	No DRI	No DRI
Protein	1.10 g/kg body weight per day	0.95 g/kg body weight per day	0.95 g/kg body weight per day	0.85 g/kg body weight per day
Carbohydrate	130 g/day	130 g/day	130 g/day	130 g/day
Vitamin A	300 µg/day	400 µg/day	600 µg/day	Boys = 900 µg/day Girls = 700 µg/day
Vitamin C	15 mg/day	25 mg/day	45 mg/day	Boys = 75 mg/day Girls = 65 mg/day
Vitamin E	6 mg/day	7 mg/day	11 mg/day	15 mg/day
Calcium	500 mg/day	800 mg/day	1,300 mg/day	1,300 mg/day
Iron	7 mg/day	10 mg/day	8 mg/day	Boys = 11 mg/day Girls = 15 mg/day
Zinc	3 mg/day	5 mg/day	8 mg/day	Boys = 11 mg/day Girls = 9 mg/day
Fluid	1.3 L/day	1.7 L/day	Boys = 2.4 L/day Girls = 2.1 L/day	Boys = 3.3 L/day Girls = 2.3 L/day

lies who cannot afford adequate amounts of nourishing foods, children with certain medical conditions or dietary restrictions, or very picky or erratic eaters.

As always, if a supplement is given, it should be formulated especially for toddlers and the recommended dose should not be exceeded. A supplement should not contain more than 100% of the Daily Value of any nutrient per dose.

Many parents choose special cereals, snack foods, and packaged dinners for their young children. How do the nutrient values of these foods compare to those of similar versions for adults? See the Nutrition Label Activity, next page, to find out.

Encouraging Nutritious Food Choices with Toddlers

Parents and pediatricians have long known that toddlers tend to be choosy about what they eat. Some avoid entire foods groups, such as all meats or vegetables. Others refuse all but one or two favorite foods (such as peanut butter on crackers) for several days or longer. Still others eat in extremely small amounts, seemingly satisfied by a single slice of apple or two bites of toast. These behaviors frustrate and worry many parents, but in fact, as long as a variety of healthful food is available, most normal-weight toddlers are able to match their food intake with their needs. A toddler will most likely make up for one day's nutrient or energy deficiency later in the week. Parents who offer only nutritious foods can feel confident that their children are being well fed, even if a child's choices seem odd or erratic on any particular day. Food should never be "forced" on a child, as doing so sets the stage for eating and control issues later in life.

Toddlers' stomachs are still very small, and they cannot consume all of the energy they need in three meals. They need small meals, interspersed with nutritious snacks, every 2 to 3 hours. A successful technique is to create a snack tray filled with small portions of nutritious food choices, such as one-third of a banana, two pieces of cheese, and two whole-grain crackers, and leave it within reach of the child's play area. The child can then "graze" on these healthful foods while he or she plays. A snack tray, plus a spill-proof cup of milk or water, is particularly useful on car trips.

Foods prepared for toddlers should be developmentally appropriate. Nuts, carrots, grapes, raisins, and cherry tomatoes are difficult for a toddler to chew and pose a choking hazard. Foods should be soft and sliced into strips or wedges that are easy for children to grasp. As the child develops more teeth and becomes more coordinated, the foods offered can become more varied. Though certainly not necessary, several food companies now

Nutrition Label Activity
Comparing Foods for Children and Adults

Parents who purchase foods such as "junior dinners" for their toddlers often check the Nutrition Facts panel for information on the ingredients and nutrient value of the products. Many of these parents may not realize that the FDA and USDA have specific label requirements for products aimed at children less than 2 years old and for those who are 2 to 4 years old. Food products designed for children under 2 years of age cannot list the amount of saturated, polyunsaturated, or monounsaturated fat, the amount of cholesterol, or the calories from fat on the label. This is to avoid the impression that fat is bad for young children; recall that dietary fat should not be restricted in children under the age of 2 years.

Compare the labels of the infant "Chicken Noodle Dinner" (**Figure 17.1a**) and the adult "Noodle Chicken Dinner" (Figure 17.1b). What other differences in the Nutrition Facts Panel do you see? Compare the ingredient list for the two products.

(a)

Figure 17.1 Label guidelines for foods targeting infants and children under the age of 2 years differ from the labeling regulations for other foods. **(a)** Label from infant chicken noodle dinner. **(b)** Label from an adult chicken noodle meal. Note the listing of *trans* and saturated fat contents, among other differences. **(c)** Label from oatmeal cereal for infants and young children.

Chicken Noodle Dinner

INSPECTED FOR U.S. DEPARTMENT OF AGRICULTURE

NET WT 4 OZ (113g)

Nutrition Facts

Serv Size: 1 jar
Calories 80

Amount Per Serving			
Total Fat	3g	Total Carb	11g
Trans Fat	1g	Fiber	2g
Sodium	40mg	Sugars	4g
Potassium	200mg	Protein	3g

% Daily Value • Protein 16% • Vitamin A 270%
Vitamin C 0% • Calcium 2% • Iron 4% • Zinc 10%

★ CONTAINS NATURAL VEGETABLE SUGARS ONLY

INGREDIENTS: WATER, CARROTS, FINELY GROUND CHICKEN, GREEN SPLIT PEAS, ENRICHED EGG NOODLES (DURUM WHEAT FLOUR, EGG SOLIDS, NIACIN, FERROUS SULFATE, THIAMIN MONONITRATE, RIBOFLAVIN, FOLIC ★ ACID), RICE FLOUR, CHICKEN FAT, ONION POWDER, SOYBEAN OIL AND EXTRACTIVES OF CELERY.

• Unsalted
• No artificial flavors, colors or preservatives

Nutrition Facts
Serving Size 2/3 cup mix (60g) Makes 1 cup prepared
Servings Per Container 2

Amount Per Serving	Mix	Prepared as Directed
Calories	220	260
Calories from Fat	30	80

	% Daily Value**	
Total Fat 3.5g*	**5%**	**13%**
Saturated Fat 1g	**4%**	**10%**
Trans Fat 0g		
Cholesterol 50mg	**17%**	**17%**
Sodium 860mg	**36%**	**38%**
Total Carbohydrate 40mg	**13%**	**13%**
Dietary Fiber 2g	**6%**	**6%**
Sugars 2g		
Protein 8g		

Vitamin A	6%	10%
Vitamin C	10%	10%
Calcium	2%	2%
Iron	10%	10%
Thiamin	30%	30%
Riboflavin	15%	15%
Niacin	15%	15%
Folate	25%	25%

*Amount in Mix. 1/2 tbsp. of margarine add 40 calories, 5g fat (1g saturated), and 50mg sodium.

**Percent Daily Values are based on a 2,000 calorie diet. Your daily values may be higher or lower depending on your calorie needs.

	Calories:	2,000	2,500
Total Fat	Less than	65g	80g
Sat. Fat	Less than	20g	25g
Cholesterol	Less than	300mg	300mg
Sodium	Less than	2,400mg	2,400mg
Total Carbohydrate		300g	375g
Dietary Fiber		25g	30g

INGREDIENTS: ENRICHED EGG NOODLES (WHEAT FLOUR, EGGS, NIACIN, FERROUS SULFATE, THIAMIN MONONITRATE, RIBOFLAVIN, FOLIC ACID), CORN STARCH, SALT, CORN SYRUP*, ONION*, MALTODEXTRIN, CHICKEN FAT*, CHICKEN BROTH*, NATURAL FLAVORS, HYDROLYZED PROTEIN (SOY, CORN), AUTOLYZED YEAST EXTRACT, BELL PEPPER*, GARLIC*, PARTIALLY HYDROGENATED SOYBEAN OIL, PARSLEY*, SPICES (INCLUDING PAPRIKA), XANTHAN AND GUAR GUMS, GUM ARABIC, WHEY, SODIUM CASEINATE, DISODIUM PHOSPHATE, DISODIUM INOSINATE, DISODIUM GUANYLATE, ANNATTO AND OLEORESIN TURMERIC (FOR COLOR).
*DEHYDRATED
CONTAINS: EGG, WHEAT, SOY, MILK

(b)

Oatmeal
CEREAL FOR BABY

Nutrition Facts
Serving Size 1/4 cup (15g)
Servings Per Container About 15

Amount Per Serving

Calories 60	
Total Fat	1g
Trans Fat	0g
Sodium	0mg
Potassium	50mg
Total Carbohydrate	10g
Fiber	1g
Sugars	2g
Protein	2g

% Daily Value	Infants 0–1	Children 1–4
Protein	10%	9%
Vitamin A	0%	0%
Vitamin C	0%	0%
Calcium	15%	10%
Iron	45%	60%
Vitamin E	15%	8%
Thiamin	25%	15%
Riboflavin	25%	20%
Niacin	25%	20%
Vitamin B$_6$	25%	10%
Folate	25%	10%
Vitamin B$_{12}$	25%	15%
Phosphorus	15%	10%
Zinc	20%	10%

INGREDIENTS: OAT FLOUR, TRI- AND DICALCIUM PHOSPHATE, SOY OIL-LECITHIN, TOCOPHEROLS (VITAMIN E), ELECTROLYTIC IRON, ZINC SULFATE, NIACINAMIDE (A B VITAMIN), RIBOFLAVIN (VITAMIN B-2), PYRIDOXINE HYDROCHLORIDE (VITAMIN B-6), THIAMIN (VITAMIN B-1), FOLIC ACID (A B VITAMIN) AND VITAMIN B-12 (CYANOCOBALAMIN).

(c)

What is the most prevalent ingredient in the toddler food? Does the toddler food contain all or any of the food additives listed in the adult product? Why do you believe there is a difference?

Foods for children under 2 years of age cannot be labeled with nutrient claims ("low-fat") or health claims that often appear on food labels. Labels of foods for children under the age of 2 years are, however, allowed to make statements such as "Provides 100% of the Daily Value for vitamin C." They can also describe the product as *unsweetened* or *unsalted* because those terms describe taste features more than nutrient value. Terms such as "no sugar added" or "sugar free" cannot be used on foods for children 2 years and under, although they are permitted on dietary supplements for children.

The small size of children 4 years and under means they have lower nutrient needs than adults. Nutrition Facts information for products marketed to young children is therefore based on smaller serving sizes and age-appropriate Daily Values. Some products, such as infant cereal, have nutrient information both for infants up to 1 year and for children 1 to 4 years (Figure 17.1c). This approach provides families with nutrient guidelines for all young children. Because there are no Daily Values (DVs) for fat (total or saturated), cholesterol, sodium, or fiber for children under the age of 4 years, there are also no percent daily value figures for those nutrients on the labels of foods aimed at these children. Use the baby cereal label (Figure 17.1c) to identify the one nutrient for which the DV is actually *higher* for infants than for children 1 to 4 years of age. (Hint: It is a mineral!).

market "toddler foods" geared specifically to their developmental stage. The Nutrition Label Activity provides the opportunity to compare labeling practices for toddler and adult foods.

Foods prepared for toddlers should also be fun. Parents can use cookie cutters to turn a peanut-butter sandwich into a pumpkin face or arrange cooked peas or carrot slices to look like a smiling face on top of mashed potatoes. Juice and yogurt can be frozen into "popsicles" or blended into "milkshakes."

A positive environment helps toddlers develop good mealtime habits as well. Parents should consistently seat the toddler in the same place at the table and make sure that the child is served first. Television and other distractions should be turned off, and pleasant conversation should include the toddler, even if the toddler hasn't begun to speak. Toddlers should not be forced to sit still until they finish every bite, as they still have short attention spans.

Even at mealtime, portion sizes should be small. One tablespoon of a food for each year of age constitutes a serving throughout the toddler and preschool years (**Figure 17.2**). Realistic portion sizes can give toddlers a sense of accomplishment when they "eat it all up" and reduce parents' fears that their child is not eating enough.

New foods should be introduced gradually. Most toddlers are leery of new foods, spicy foods, hot (temperature) foods, mixed foods such as casseroles, and foods with strange textures. A helpful rule is to encourage the child to eat at least one bite of a new food: If the child does not want the rest, nothing negative should be said, and the child should be praised just for the willingness to try. The same food should be reintroduced a few weeks later. Eventually, after several tries, the child might accept the food. Some foods, however, won't be accepted until well into adulthood as tastes expand and develop. Parents should never bribe with food—for example, promising dessert if the child finishes her squash. Bribing teaches children that food can be used to reward and manipulate. Instead, parents should try to positively reinforce good behaviors; for example, "Wow! You ate every bite of your squash! That's going to help you grow big and strong!"

Role modeling is important because toddlers mimic older children and adults: If they see their parents eating a variety of healthful foods, toddlers will be likely to do so as well. Limiting the alternatives can also help toddlers to make nutritious food choices. For example, parents might say, "It's snack time! Would you like apples and cheese, or bananas and yogurt?" Finally, toddlers are more likely to eat food they help prepare: Encourage them to assist in the preparation of simple foods, such as helping pour a bowl of cereal or helping to arrange the raw vegetables on a plate.

Most toddlers are delighted by food prepared in a "fun" way.

Figure 17.2 Portion sizes for toddlers and preschoolers are much smaller than for older children. Use the following guideline: 1 tablespoon of the food for each year of age equals 1 serving. For example, the meal shown here—2 tablespoons of rice, 2 tablespoons of black beans, and 2 tablespoons of chopped tomatoes—is appropriate for a 2-year-old toddler.

Foods that may cause allergies, such as peanuts and citrus fruits, should be introduced to toddlers one at a time.

Soy milk can be a part of a healthy vegan diet for toddlers.

Nutrition-Related Concerns for Toddlers

Just as toddlers have their own specific nutrient needs, they also have toddler-specific nutrition concerns.

Continued Allergy Watch

As during infancy, wheat, peanuts, cow's milk, soy, citrus, egg whites, and seafood remain common food allergens. New foods should be presented one at a time, and the toddler should be monitored for allergic reactions for a week before additional new foods are introduced. To prevent the development of food allergies, even foods that are established in the diet should be rotated rather than served every day.

Vegetarian Families

For toddlers, an ovo-lacto-vegetarian diet in which eggs and dairy foods are included can be as wholesome as a diet including meats and fish.[7] However, because meat, fish, and poultry are excellent sources of zinc and heme iron, the most bioavailable form of iron, vegetarian families must be careful to include enough zinc and iron from other sources in their child's diet.

In contrast, a vegan diet, in which no foods of animal origin are consumed, poses several potential nutritional risks for toddlers:

- Protein: Vegan diets can be too low in protein for toddlers, who need protein for growth and increasing activity. Few toddlers can consume enough legumes and whole grains to provide sufficient protein. The high-fiber content of these foods quickly produces a sense of fullness for the toddler, decreasing total food intake.
- Calcium, iron, and zinc: Calcium is a concern because of the avoidance of milk, yogurt, and cheese. As with protein, few toddlers can consume enough calcium from plant sources to meet their daily requirement, and supplementation is advised. Iron and zinc are also commonly low in vegan diets due to the absence of meat, fish, and poultry. They need to be provided by fortified cereals, legumes, and possibly supplements.
- Vitamins D and B_{12}: Both vitamins are typically lower in strict vegan diets. Some cereals and soy milks are now fortified with vitamin D; however, some toddlers may still need a vitamin D–containing supplement. Vitamin B_{12}, though found in many fortified breakfast cereals, is not available naturally in any amount from plant foods and must be supplemented.
- Fiber: Vegan diets often contain a higher amount of fiber than is recommended for toddlers, resulting in lowered absorption of iron and zinc as well as a premature sense of fullness or satiety at mealtimes.

The practice of feeding a vegan diet to infants and young children is highly controversial. See the Nutrition Myth or Fact? box, next page, for more information about this controversy.

Recap

Growth during toddlerhood is slower than during infancy; however, toddlers are highly active, and total energy, fat, and protein requirements are higher than for infants. Toddlers require small, frequent, nutritious meals and snacks. Until age 2, toddlers should drink whole milk rather than reduced-fat (2% or lower) milk. Iron deficiency is a concern and can be avoided by feeding toddlers lean meats, fish, poultry, eggs, and iron-fortified foods. Toddlers need to drink about 4 cups of beverages, including water. Role modeling by parents and access to ample healthful foods can help toddlers make nutritious choices. Feeding vegan diets to toddlers is controversial and poses potential deficiencies for calcium, iron, zinc, vitamin D, and vitamin B_{12}.

Nutrition Myth or Fact?
Are Vegan Diets Appropriate for Young Children?

According to a poll of U.S. youth, approximately 1% of 8- to 18-year olds follow a vegan diet.[8] Whereas the adoption of a vegan diet among older children and teens is rarely viewed with concern, it only takes an online search in the archives of any major news outlet to realize that feeding a vegan diet to very young children is a controversial practice. Proponents of the vegan diet assert that feeding animal products to children is forcing them into a life of obesity, clogged arteries, and chronic diet-related diseases. In addition, many people who consume a vegan diet feel that consumption of animal products wastes natural resources and contributes to environmental damage and is therefore morally wrong. In contrast, opponents emphasize that feeding a vegan diet to young children deprives them of essential nutrients that can only be found in animal products. Some people even suggest that veganism for young children is, in essence, a form of child abuse.

As with many controversies, there are truths on both sides. For example, there have been documented cases of children failing to thrive, and even dying, on extreme vegan diets.[9, 10] Some research studies document deficiencies of vitamin B_{12}, vitamin D, iron, calcium, and protein in vegan children and infants.[11, 12] These nutrients are found primarily in animal products and are often better utilized from animal vs. plant sources. Deficiencies of these nutrients can have serious and lifelong consequences. For example, not all of the neurologic impairments caused by vitamin B_{12} deficiency can be reversed by timely B_{12} supplement intervention. In addition, inadequate zinc, calcium, and vitamin D can result in impaired bone growth and strength, failure to reach peak bone mass, and retarded growth in general.

However, close inspection of published reports of nutrition-related illness in children, including protein-energy malnutrition, that cite veganism as the culprit reveals that lack of education, fanaticism, and/or extremism is usually at the root of the problem. Informed parents following responsible vegan diets are rarely involved.[13] On the other hand, such cases do point out that veganism is not a lifestyle one can safely undertake without thorough education regarding the necessity of supplementation of those nutrients not available in plant products. Parents also need to understand that typical vegan diets are high in fiber and low in fat, a combination that can be dangerous for very young children.[13] Moreover, certain staples of the vegan diet, such as wheat, soy, and nuts, commonly provoke allergic reactions in children; when this happens, finding a plant-based substitute that contains adequate nutrients can be challenging.

Most nutrition experts recommend a more moderate diet—one that includes fish, dairy products, and eggs—rather than a vegan diet for young children. This snack of peanut-butter sandwiches and milk is a healthful choice.

Both the American Dietetic Association, in conjunction with Dieticians of Canada,[14] and the American Academy of Pediatrics[2] have stated that a balanced vegan diet can promote normal childhood growth and development—*provided* that adequate supplements and/or fortified foods are consumed to account for the nutrients that are normally obtained from animal products. However, most healthcare organizations stop short of outright endorsement of a vegan diet for young children. Instead, many advocate a more moderate approach during the early childhood years. Reasons for this level of caution include acknowledgment of several factors:

- Some vegan parents are not adequately educated on the planning of meals, the balancing of foods, and the inclusion of supplements to ensure adequate levels of all nutrients.

- Most young children are picky eaters and are hesitant to eat certain food groups, particularly vegetables, a staple in the vegan diet.

- The high fiber content of vegan diets may not be appropriate for very young children.

- Young children have small stomachs, and they are not able to consume enough plant-based foods to ensure adequate intakes of all nutrients and energy.

Because of these concerns, most nutrition experts advise parents to take a more moderate dietary approach, one that emphasizes plant foods but also includes some animal-based foods, such as fish, dairy, and/or eggs.

Once children reach school age, the low fat, abundant fiber, antioxidants, and many micronutrients in a vegan diet will promote their health as they progress into adulthood. However, those who consume animal products can also live a healthful life and reduce their risk for chronic diseases by choosing low-fat, nutrient-dense foods such as lean meats, nonfat dairy products, whole grains, and fruits and vegetables. Because animal products are consumed, there are fewer worries about consuming adequate amounts of micronutrients such as vitamin B_{12}, calcium, vitamin D, iron, and zinc.

In summary, the appropriateness of a vegan diet varies according to several factors. Although the potential for malnutrition is ever present, well-educated parents of school-age children can ensure a healthful vegan diet with careful meal planning, including appropriate use of fortified foods and beverages, and supplements.

Nutrition for Preschool and School-Age Children

Children develop increased language fluency, improved decision-making skills, and greater physical coordination and dexterity as they progress through the preschool and school-age years. The nutrient requirements and nutrition issues of importance to children are discussed in this section.

Childhood Growth and Activity Patterns

Growth rate slows and activity ideally increases. Children experience a slow and steady rate of growth, averaging 2 to 4 inches per year, until the rapid growth of adolescence begins. Activity levels among children vary dramatically—some love sports and physical activity, whereas others prefer quieter activities like reading and drawing. Television, computer-based activity, and electronic games often tempt children into a sedentary lifestyle. All children can be encouraged to enjoy walking, to appreciate nature and exploration, and to have fun using their minds and their muscles in various ways that suit their interests. Activity-based interactive DVD games are ideal for children who must remain indoors for extended periods of time. For children ages 6 to 11 years, the USDA has developed a MyPyramid for Kids plan that advises children to "Eat Right. Exercise. Have Fun" (**Figure 17.3**).

What Are a Child's Nutrient Needs?

Three-year-olds have the same set of nutrient recommendations that apply to toddlers (see Table 17.1). From age 4 through 8, the values for most nutrients increase. Until age 9, the nutrient needs of young boys do not differ significantly from those of girls; because of this, the DRI values for macronutrients, fiber, and micronutrients are grouped together for boys and girls aged 4 to 8 years. The onset of sexual maturation, however, has a dramatic effect on the nutrient needs of children. Boys' and girls' bodies develop differently in response to gender-specific hormones. Because the process of sexual maturation begins subtly between the ages of 8 and 9, the DRI values are separately defined for boys and girls beginning at age 9.[1,3–6] (See Table 17.1.)

Energy and Macronutrient Recommendations for Children

Total energy requirements continue to increase throughout childhood because of increasing body size and, for some children, higher levels of physical activity. The EER varies according to the child's age, body weight, and level of activity. Parents should provide diets that support normal growth and appropriate physical activity while minimizing risk of excess weight gain.

Fat.   Although dietary fat remains a key macronutrient in the preschool years, as the child ages, total fat should gradually be reduced to a level closer to that of an adult,

School-aged children grow an average of 2 to 3 inches per year.

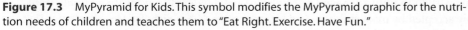

Figure 17.3 MyPyramid for Kids. This symbol modifies the MyPyramid graphic for the nutrition needs of children and teaches them to "Eat Right. Exercise. Have Fun."

around 25% to 35% of total energy.[1] One easy way to start reducing dietary fat is to slowly introduce lower-fat dairy products such as 2% or 1% milk, low-fat yogurt, and low-fat mozzarella cheese sticks while minimizing the intake of fried foods. A diet providing fewer than 25% of calories from fat is not recommended for children, as they are still growing, developing, and maturing. In fact, unless the child is overweight or has specific health concerns, parents should avoid putting too much emphasis on fat restriction during this age span. Impressionable and peer-influenced children may be prone to categorizing foods as "good" or "bad." This may lead to skewed views of food and inappropriate dietary restrictions.

Carbohydrate.   The RDA for carbohydrate for children is 130 g/day, which is about 45% to 65% of total daily energy intake.[1] Complex carbohydrates from whole grains, fruits, vegetables, and legumes should be emphasized. Simple sugars should come from fruits and fruit juices, with foods high in refined sugars, such as such as cakes, cookies, and candies, saved for occasional indulgences. The AI for fiber for children is 14 g/1,000 kcal, which can be met by the consumption of fresh fruits, vegetables, legumes, and whole grains.[1] As was the case with toddlers, too much fiber can be detrimental because it can make a child feel full and interfere with adequate food intake and lower the absorption of certain nutrients such as iron and zinc.

Protein.   Total need for protein (shown in Table 17.1) increases for children because of their larger size, even though their growth rate has slowed. The RDA for protein is 0.95 g/kg body weight per day.[1] This protein requirement is easily met by portions such as one chicken drumstick and two glasses of milk or 1/2 cup pinto beans, 1 oz of cheese, and half a peanut-butter sandwich. Lean meats, fish, poultry, lower-fat dairy products, soy-based foods, and legumes are nutritious sources of protein that can be provided to children of all ages. Children who follow a vegetarian diet can meet their protein needs by following dietary guidelines such as those in the Vegetarian Diet Pyramid for Children.[7]

Micronutrient Recommendations for Children

The need for most micronutrients increases slightly for children up to age 8 because of their increasing size. A sharper increase occurs during the transition years approaching adolescence; this increase is due to the impending adolescent growth spurt and the early phases of sexual maturation. Children who fail to consume the recommended amount of fruits and vegetables each day may become deficient in vitamins A, C, and E. Offering fruits and fresh vegetables as snacks as well as during mealtimes can increase intakes of these vitamins as well as fiber and potassium, two priority nutrients found lacking in the diets of low-income children.[3]

Children's multivitamins often appear in shapes or bright colors.

Minerals of concern continue to be calcium, iron, and zinc, which come primarily from animal-based foods. The AI for calcium is 800 mg/day for children aged 4 to 8 years and 1,300 mg/day for children aged 9 to 13 years.[4] As you learned in Chapter 11, peak bone mass is achieved in the late teens or early 20s, and childhood and adolescence are critical times to ensure adequate deposition of bone tissue. Inadequate calcium intake during childhood and adolescence leads to poor bone health and potential osteoporosis in later years.

Low-fat milk, yogurt, cheese, and fortified fruit juices are child-friendly and convenient sources of calcium. The problem of "milk displacement," when children stop drinking milk in favor of soda, punch, energy drinks, and juice, is a recognized factor in low calcium intake.[15] Diets that are low in calcium also tend to be low in other nutrients, so attention to calcium intake can help ensure a more healthful overall diet for children.

The RDAs for children aged 4 to 8 years for iron and zinc increase slightly to 10 mg/day and 5 mg/day, respectively.[5] The RDA for iron drops to 8 mg/day for boys and girls aged 9 to 13 years. These recommendations are based on the assumption that most girls do not begin menstruation until after age 13.[5] Mild-flavored, tender cuts of meat and poultry are readily accepted by most children, and legumes offer a fiber-rich, fat-free alternative that will also add iron and zinc to the diet. Refer again to Table 17.1 for a review of the micronutrient needs of children.

If there is any concern that a child's nutrient needs are not being met for any reason, such as missed meals or inadequate family resources, vitamin and mineral supplements may help correct any deficit. If used, the supplement should be age-specific and the recommended dose (not more than 100% DV) should not be exceeded.

Fluid Recommendations for Children

The fluid recommendations for children are summarized in Table 17.1 and average about 5 to 8 cups of beverages per day, including water.[6] The exact amount of fluid needed varies according to the child's level of physical activity and weather conditions. At this point in their lives, children are mostly in control of their own fluid intake. However, as they become more active during school, in sports, and while playing, young children in particular may need reminders to drink in order to stay properly hydrated, especially if the weather is hot. Most, if not all, of the beverages offered should be caffeine free.

Although reminders to drink help keep school-aged children hydrated, they mostly control their own fluid intake.

Encouraging Nutritious Food Choices in Children

Peer pressure can be extremely difficult for both parents and their children to deal with during this stage of life. Most children want to feel that they "belong" and will mirror the actions of children they view as popular. Some children have their own spending money, and most are very susceptible to TV and other messages encouraging unhealthful food choices. Children also spend more time visiting friends and eating more meals and snacks without their parents' supervision. The impact of this increasing autonomy on the health of children can be profound, yet parents remain important role models.

Parents and children can work together to find compromises by planning and talking about healthful foods. Families who plan, prepare, and eat meals together are more successful at promoting good food choices. The "Eat Better, Eat Together" nutrition education program promotes family mealtime (**Figure 17.4**). Parents should continue to demonstrate healthy eating and physical activity patterns to maintain a consistent message to their children.

What Is the Effect of School Attendance on Nutrition?

School attendance can affect a child's nutrition in several ways. First, hectic schedules and long bus rides cause many children to minimize or skip breakfast completely. School-aged children who don't eat breakfast may not get a chance to eat until lunch. If the entire morning is spent in a state of hunger, children are more likely to do poorly on schoolwork, have decreased attention spans, and have more behavioral problems than their peers who do eat breakfast.[16] For this reason, many schools now offer low-cost school breakfasts (they are free of charge to low-income families). These breakfasts help children to optimize their nutrient intake and avoid the behavioral and learning problems associated with hunger in the classroom.

Another consequence of attending school is that with no one monitoring what they eat, children do not always consume adequate amounts of food. They may spend their lunch time talking or playing with friends rather than eating. If a school lunch is purchased, they might not like the foods being served, or their peers might influence them to skip certain foods with comments such as, "This broccoli is nasty!" Even nutritious homemade lunches may be left uneaten or traded for less nutritious fare. Many children rush through lunch in order to spend more time on the playground; as a result, some schools now send students to the playground first, allowing the children time to burn off their pent-up energy as well as build their hunger and thirst.

Figure 17.4   "Eat Better, Eat Together" promotes family mealtimes as a way to improve children's diets. (*Data from:* © Washington State University, Cooperative Extension, the Nutrition Education Network of Washington, and the USDA Food and Nutrition Service.)

Finally, many schools accept revenues from soft drink and snack food companies in exchange for the right to advertise and sell their products to children. Although increasing numbers of states and school districts are strictly limiting sales of foods low in nutrient value during the school day, many schools still provide vending machines filled with snacks that are high in energy, sugar, and fat. Eating too many of these foods, either in place of or in addition to lunch, can lead to overweight and potential nutrient deficiencies.

Do School Lunches Improve Child Health and Nutrition?

The impact of the National School Lunch Program (NSLP) on children's diets is enormous: 99% of public schools participate, serving over 30 million children.[17] On the surface, it would appear that school lunches would be expected to improve children's diets, because they must meet the fat, saturated fat, and sodium standards of the Dietary Guidelines for Americans. In addition, every lunch must provide one-third of the 1989 Recommended Dietary Allowances for protein, vitamin A, vitamin C, iron, calcium, and energy and comply with the Healthy Meals for Healthy Americans Act.

School-aged children may receive a standard school lunch, but many choose less healthful foods when given the opportunity.

However, when delving into this question a little more deeply, we discover that the answer is not clear. First of all, very few school lunch programs actually meet all of the dietary guidelines: Virtually none meet the sodium guideline; about 60% meet the total fat guideline (no more than 30% of total energy); and only 30% meet the saturated fat guideline (no more than 10% of total energy).[17] Second, the actual amount of nutrients a student *gets* depends on what the student actually *eats*. School lunch programs do not have to meet the federal guidelines every day but only over the course of a week's meals. Thus, the school lunches that students actually eat (not necessarily those planned or served to the student) tend to be higher in fat because students choose to eat the foods they like the best, such as pizza, hamburgers, hot dogs, and other higher-fat entrees. Children typically prefer to eat French fries instead of other vegetables offered, such as green beans or carrots. Third, keep in mind that children in many schools can still buy high-fat and high-sugar snacks and beverages from vending machines or bring them from home, and some schools actually have fast-food restaurants selling their food in competition with the school lunch program!

The good news is that many schools are working to ensure a more healthful food environment. Almost thirty states have adopted policies that restrict the types of competitive (non-NSLP) foods and beverages that can be sold on school campuses.[17] School districts are required to develop wellness policies that address nutrition. Increased attention to nutrition has resulted in the offering of healthful options such as salad bars, fresh fruit bowls, baked potato bars, and soup stations to entice students into more healthful choices. Many schools now cultivate a garden on school grounds or even on the school rooftop where children help to grow the vegetables that will be used in their lunches. Over 85% of schools in the NSLP now offer lunches that meet the standards for vitamins A and C, iron, calcium, and protein, which means that school lunches are higher in dietary quality and nutrient density compared to lunches brought from home or bought from a la carte menus or vending machines.[17] In addition, participation in the School Breakfast Program is associated with lower BMI, an important finding in light of the epidemic of childhood obesity.[18]

The School Nutrition Association promotes "nutrition integrity" for all schools, promoting healthy diets, appropriate physical activity, and school-based nutrition education. As nutritionists, school foodservice directors, educators, and parents continue to work together to improve the school meal programs, efforts will focus on increasing the use and consumption of fruits, vegetables, and whole grains in order to meet the nutrient needs of the children while minimizing risk of hunger and obesity.[19]

Nutrition-Related Concerns During Childhood

In addition to potential nutrient deficiencies that have already been discussed, new concerns arise during childhood. The issue of childhood obesity is discussed in more detail at the end of this chapter.

Iron-Deficiency Anemia

Despite the best efforts of public health nutritionists and other healthcare providers, iron-deficiency anemia remains a significant problem for many children. Rates of iron-deficiency anemia are higher among children from Mexican American and low-income families, emphasizing the need to evaluate each child in light of his or her family's unique risk factors.[3] Meat, fish, and poultry provide well-absorbed sources of heme iron, and child-friendly foods such as iron-fortified cereals, dried fruits, and legumes can provide additional iron. Children who have very poor appetites or erratic eating habits may need to use an iron-containing supplement, although parents must provide careful supervision because of iron's high potential for childhood toxicity.

If left untreated, iron deficiency with or without anemia can lead to behavioral, cognitive, and motor deficits, developmental delays, and impaired immune response. In those children exposed to lead, iron deficiency increases the rate of lead absorption and severity of lead toxicity.[2] Iron-deficiency anemia reduces the child's energy level and contributes to passivity and lethargy. The cognitive and behavioral consequences of iron deficiency in young children can be long-standing, making prevention a critical goal. Early detection through dietary assessments and simple blood tests, followed by effective treatment, ensures all children will enter school healthy and ready to learn.

Dental Caries

As discussed in Chapter 4, *dental caries,* or cavities, occur when bacteria in the mouth feed on carbohydrates deposited on teeth. As a result of metabolizing the carbohydrates, the bacteria secrete acid that begins to erode tooth enamel, leading to tooth decay. The occurrence of dental caries can be minimized by limiting between-meal sweets, especially jelly beans, caramels, and others that stick to teeth. Frequent brushing helps to eliminate the sugars on teeth, as well as the bacteria that feed on them.

Fluoride, either through a municipal water supply or through supplements, will also help deter the development of dental caries. Because "baby teeth" make room for and guide the permanent teeth into position, preschoolers need regular dental care as much as older children. Children should start having regular dental visits at the age of 3 years.

Body-Image Concerns

As children approach puberty, appearance and body image play increasingly important roles in food choices by both girls and boys. These concerns are not necessarily detrimental to health, particularly if they result in children making more healthful food choices, such as eating more whole grains, fruits, and vegetables. However, it is important for children to understand that being thin does not guarantee health, popularity, or happiness and that a healthy body image includes accepting our own individual body type and recognizing that we can be physically fit and healthy at a variety of weights, shapes, and sizes (**Figure 17.5**). Excessive concern with thinness can lead children to experiment with fad diets, food restriction, and other behaviors that can result in undernutrition and perhaps even trigger a clinical eating disorder.

Childhood Food Insecurity

Although most children in the United States grow up with an abundant and healthful supply of food, millions of American children are faced with food insecurity and hunger.[20] Food insecurity occurs when a family is not able to ensure a consistent, dependable supply of safe and nutritious food. [20] "Very low food security" is a more severe economic state in which the family actually experiences reduced food intake and disruption of normal eating patterns. Approximately 16% of U.S. households with children can be classified as food insecure, meaning over 12 million children are at risk for hunger. Just under 1% of households with children experience very low food security.[20] These statistics are definitely at odds with America's image as "the land of plenty."

The effects of food insecurity and hunger can be very harmful to children. Without an adequate breakfast, they will not be able to concentrate or pay attention to their parents, teachers, or other caretakers. Impaired nutrient status can blunt children's immune responses, making them more susceptible to common childhood illnesses.

Options for families facing food insecurity include a number of government and privately funded programs, including school breakfast and lunch programs and the Supplementary Nutrition Assistance Program (previously termed the Food Stamp program). Families who face economic difficulties should be referred to public health or social service agencies and encouraged to apply for available nutrition benefits. Private and church-based food pantries and kitchens can provide a narrow range of foods for a limited period of time but cannot be relied on to meet the nutritional needs of children and their families over an extended period of time.

Figure 17.5 Normal, healthy school-aged children come in a variety of shapes and sizes.

RECAP

Children have a slower growth rate than toddlers, yet their larger body size and greater level of physical activity increase total energy and nutrient needs. Children need a lower percentage of energy from fat than toddlers but slightly more than adults. Among highly active children, fluid intake should be monitored and encouraged.

Peer pressure has a strong influence on nutritional choices in school-aged children, but parents can encourage healthful eating and act as role models. Calcium needs increase as children mature but intake often declines. Iron deficiency is a common problem and can lead to severe behavioral, learning, and motor deficits. School lunch programs are designed to improve children's nutrient intake, but not all children take full advantage of the program. Body-image concerns arise in both boys and girls as they approach the adolescent years. Families facing economic challenges can be assisted by a number of government and privately funded programs.

Hannah
Nutri-Case

"When I was a kid, I always dreaded gym class, especially when we were playing games with teams. The three of us who were overweight always got picked last—for kickball, relay races, you name it. What made it even more humiliating was overhearing my teammates complain about having me on their team. I remember that the summer before I started middle school, I was so determined to lose weight that I just plain stopped eating. My mom had to leave early to work at the hospital and didn't get home until evening, so it was easy to get around her by telling her

I'd been eating all day and wasn't hungry for dinner. But then, after an entire week of this, it was Saturday, and raining, and my mom had just gone out to run some errands, so I was home alone with nothing to do, and without even thinking about it, I opened up the fridge and spied half of a pizza my mom had left from the night before. I ate a slice. I'll never forget how good it tasted. Then I ate another slice, and another, until it was gone, and then I started in on some cookies. I would have finished those, too, if my mom hadn't come home. She was pretty sharp with me about eating all of the leftover pizza, but then I told her how hungry I'd been because I'd been fasting all week, and she sat down and started to cry. She said she'd been through the same teasing as a kid. After that, we tried to eat better for a while, but it didn't last. I'm really glad I've been taking a nutrition course, because now I know how to make better choices to get down to a weight that's right for me. And maybe I can use what I've learned to help my mom!"

Given what you know about Hannah and her mother, why do you think their initial attempts "to eat better" didn't last? What advice would you give her about talking with her mom about nutrition? Have you shared anything you've learned in this course with family members? If so, how did they respond to the information?

Nutrition for Adolescents

The adolescent years are typically defined as beginning with the onset of **puberty,** the period in life in which secondary sexual characteristics develop and there is the capacity for reproducing. Adolescence continues through age 18. This is a physically and emotionally tumultuous time.

Adolescent Psychosocial Development

Adolescence is a period when emotions and behaviors often seem unpredictable and confusing. It is characterized by increasing independence as the adolescent establishes a personal sense of identity and works toward greater self-reliance. Adolescents may, for example, decide to follow a vegetarian or vegan diet as a means of setting themselves apart from the family unit. Whereas younger adolescents tend to be self-centered, living for the present, older teens typically focus on defining their role in life. All teens deal with their emerging sexuality and many experiment with lifestyle choices, such as use of drugs, alcohol, or cigarettes, that lie outside their traditional cultural or social boundaries. During this developmental phase, they may be unresponsive to parental guidance and may ignore attempts to improve their diet and/or activity patterns. Most adolescents, however, successfully navigate the challenges of this life stage and mature into emotionally stable, self-reliant, productive adults.

Adolescent Growth and Activity Patterns

Growth during adolescence is primarily driven by hormonal changes, including increased levels of testosterone for boys and estrogen for girls. Both boys and girls experience *growth spurts,* or periods of accelerated growth, during later childhood and adolescence. Growth spurts for girls tend to begin around 10 to 11 years of age, and growth spurts for boys begin around 12 to 13 years of age. These growth periods last about 2 years.

Adolescents experience an average 20% to 25% increase in height during the pubertal years. During an average 1-year spurt, girls tend to grow 3.5 inches and boys tend to grow 4 inches.[21] The average girl reaches almost full height by the onset of menstruation (called **menarche**). Boys typically experience continual growth throughout adolescence, and some may even grow slightly taller during early adulthood.

Skeletal growth ceases once closure of the *epiphyseal plates* occurs (**Figure 17.6**). The **epiphyseal plates** are plates of cartilage located toward the end of the long bones (that is, the bones of the arms and legs) that provide for growth in length. In some circumstances,

Figure 17.6 Skeletal growth ceases once closure of the epiphyseal plates occurs.

puberty The period in life in which secondary sexual characteristics develop and people are biologically capable of reproducing.

menarche The beginning of menstruation, or the menstrual period.

epiphyseal plates Plates of cartilage located toward the end of long bones that provide for growth in the length of long bones.

Because of rapid growth and the active lifestyle of many adolescents, their energy needs can be quite high.

such as malnutrition or use of anabolic steroids, the epiphyseal plates can close early in adolescents and result in a failure to reach full stature.

Weight and body composition also change dramatically during adolescence. Weight gain is extremely variable during this time and reflects the adolescent's energy intake, physical activity level, and genetics. The average weight gained by girls and boys during these years is 35 and 45 lb, respectively. The weight gained by girls and boys is dramatically different in terms of its composition. Girls tend to gain significantly more body fat than boys, with this fat accumulating around the buttocks, hips, breasts, thighs, and upper arms. Although many girls are uncomfortable or embarrassed by these changes, they are a natural result of maturation. Boys gain significantly more muscle mass than girls, and they experience an increase in muscle definition. Other changes that occur with sexual maturation include a deepening of the voice in boys and growth of pubic hair in both boys and girls.

The physical activity levels of adolescents are highly variable. Many are physically active in sports, dance, or other organized activities, whereas others become more interested in intellectual or artistic pursuits. This variability in activity levels of adolescents results in highly individual energy needs. Although the rapid growth and sexual maturation that occur during puberty require a significant amount of energy, adolescence is often a time in which overweight begins.

Table 17.2 Examples of Physical Activities for Children and Adolescents

Type of Physical Activity	Age Group: Children	Age Group: Adolescents
Moderate-intensity aerobic	• Active recreation, such as hiking, skateboarding, rollerblading • Bicycle riding • Brisk walking	• Active recreation, such as canoeing, hiking, skateboarding, rollerblading • Brisk walking • Bicycle riding (stationary or road bike) • Housework and yard work, such as sweeping or pushing a lawn mower • Games that require catching and throwing, such as baseball and softball
Vigorous-intensity aerobic	• Active games involving running and chasing, such as tag • Bicycle riding • Jumping rope • Martial arts, such as karate • Running • Sports such as soccer, ice or field hockey, basketball, swimming, tennis • Cross-country skiing	• Active games involving running and chasing, such as flag football • Bicycle riding • Jumping rope • Martial arts, such as karate • Running • Sports such as soccer, ice or field hockey, basketball, swimming, tennis • Vigorous dancing • Cross-country skiing
Muscle-strengthening	• Games such as tug-of-war • Modified push-ups (with knees on the floor) • Resistance exercises using body weight or resistance bands • Rope or tree climbing • Sit-ups (curl-ups or crunches) • Swinging on playground equipment/bars	• Games such as tug-of-war • Push-ups and pull-ups • Resistance exercises with exercise bands, weight machines, hand-held weights • Climbing wall • Sit-ups (curl-ups or crunches)
Bone-strengthening	• Games such as hopscotch • Hopping, skipping, jumping • Jumping rope • Running • Sports such as gymnastics, basketball, volleyball, tennis	• Hopping, skipping, jumping • Jumping rope • Running • Sports such as gymnastics, basketball, volleyball, tennis

Note: Some activities, such as bicycling, can be moderate or vigorous intensity, depending upon level of effort.

Data from: *2008 Physical Activity Guidelines for Americans*, U.S. Department of Health and Human Services. Available at www.health.gov/paguidelines.

What Are an Adolescent's Nutrient Needs?

The nutrient needs of adolescents are influenced by rapid growth, weight gain, and sexual maturation, in addition to the demands of physical activity.

Energy and Macronutrient Recommendations for Adolescents

Adequate energy intake is necessary to maintain adolescents' health, support their dramatic growth and maturation, and fuel their physical activity. Because of these competing demands, the energy needs of adolescents can be quite high. To calculate the EER for this life stage, you must know the person's age, physical activity level, weight, and height.[1]

As with the younger age groups, there is no DRI for fat for adolescents.[1] However, adolescents are at risk for the same chronic diseases as adults, including type 2 diabetes, obesity, coronary heart disease, and various cancers. Thus, it is prudent for adolescents to consume 25% to 35% of total energy from fat and to consume no more than 10% of total energy from saturated fat sources.

The RDA for carbohydrate for adolescents is 130 g/day.[1] As with adults, this amount of carbohydrate covers what is needed to supply adequate glucose to the brain, but it does not cover the amount of carbohydrate needed to support daily activities. Thus, it is recommended that adolescents consume more than the RDA, or about 45% to 65% of their total energy as carbohydrate, and most carbohydrate should come from complex carbohydrate sources. The AI for fiber for adolescent girls is 26 g/day and for adolescent boys is 38 g/day. These levels are virtually the same as for adult women and men.

The RDA for protein for adolescents, at 0.85 g of protein per kilogram body weight per day, is similar to that of adults, which is 0.80 g per kilogram body weight.[1] This amount is assumed to be sufficient to support health and to cover the additional needs of growth and development during the adolescent stage. As with adults, most U.S. adolescents consume protein in amounts that far exceed the RDA.

Micronutrient Recommendations for Adolescents

Micronutrients of particular concern for adolescents include calcium, iron, and vitamin A. Adequate calcium intake is critical to achieve peak bone density, and the AI for calcium for adolescents is 1,300 mg/day.[4] This amount of calcium can be difficult for many adolescents to consume because the quality of foods they select is often less than optimal to meet their nutrient needs. To achieve this level of calcium intake, adolescents need to eat at least 4 servings of dairy foods or calcium-fortified products daily.

The iron needs of adolescents are relatively high; this is because iron is needed to replace the blood lost during menstruation in girls and to support the growth of muscle mass in boys. The RDA for iron for boys is 11 mg/day, and the RDA for girls is 15 mg/day.[5] If energy intake is adequate and adolescents consume heme-iron food sources such as animal products each day, they should be able to meet the RDA for iron. However, some young people adopt a vegetarian lifestyle during this life stage, or they consume foods that have limited nutrient density. Both of these situations can prevent adolescents from meeting the RDA for iron.

Vitamin A is critical to support the rapid growth and development that occurs during adolescence. The RDA for vitamin A is 900 μg per day for boys and 700 μg per day for girls,[5] which can be met by consuming 5 to 9 servings of fruits and vegetables each day. As with iron and calcium, meeting the RDA for vitamin A can be a challenging goal in this age group due to their potential to make less healthful food choices.

If an adolescent is unable or unwilling to eat adequate amounts of nutrient-dense foods, then a multivitamin and mineral supplement that provides no more than 100% of the Daily Value for the micronutrients could be beneficial as a safety net. As with younger children and adults, a supplement should not be considered a substitute for a balanced, healthful diet.

Fluid Recommendations for Adolescents

The fluid needs of adolescents are higher than those for children because of their higher physical activity levels and the extensive growth and development that occur during this phase of life. The recommended daily fluid intakes for adolescents are summarized in

Table 17.1 and average about 11 cups of beverages, including water, for boys and 10 cups for girls.[6] Boys are generally more active than girls and have more lean tissue; thus, they require a higher fluid intake to maintain fluid balance. Very active adolescents who are exercising in the heat may have higher fluid needs than the AI, and these individuals should be encouraged to drink often to quench their thirst and avoid dehydration.

Encouraging Nutritious Food Choices with Adolescents

Adolescents make many of their own food choices and buy and prepare a significant amount of the foods they consume. Although parents can still be effective role models, adolescents are generally strongly influenced by their peers, mass media, personal preferences, and their own developing sense of what foods make up a healthful and adequate diet.

Areas of particular concern in the adolescent diet are the lack of vegetables, fruits, and whole grains. Many teens eat on the run, skip meals, and select fast foods and convenience foods because they are inexpensive, accessible, and taste good. Parents, caretakers, and school food-service programs can capitalize on adolescents' preferences for pizza, burgers, spaghetti, and sandwiches by providing more healthful meat and cheese alternatives, whole-grain breads, and plenty of appealing vegetable-based sides or additions to these foods. In addition, keeping healthful snacks such as fruits and vegetables that are already cleaned and prepared in easy-to-eat pieces may encourage adolescents to consume more of these foods as between-meal snacks. Teens should also be encouraged to consume adequate milk and other calcium-enriched beverages.

Many teens move out of their family home when they attend college or get their first full-time job. The upcoming Highlight box, "On Your Own: Stocking Your First Kitchen," identifies staples to keep on hand for healthful snacks and meals.

Nutrition-Related Concerns for Adolescents

Nutrition-related concerns for adolescents continue to include bone density and body-image issues as well as the health of their skin and hair. Additional concerns include cigarette smoking and the use of alcohol and illegal drugs.

Bone Density Watch

Early adolescence, 13 to 15 years of age, is a crucial time for ensuring adequate dietary calcium in order to maximize bone calcium uptake and bone mineral density over the next several years.[5] Achieving and maintaining optimal bone density during adolescence and into young adulthood is critical for delaying or preventing the onset of osteoporosis.

As previously noted, meeting the adolescent DRI for calcium (1,300 mg/day) is challenging. One of the most reliable sources of calcium is dairy foods, yet by age 18, average fluid milk consumption has fallen by more than 25% compared to intake at age 8 years, whereas soda intake has tripled.[15] Although not the only factor, milk consumption during adolescence is strongly linked to higher bone mineral content and lower risk of adult bone fractures.[22] A national "Milk Matters" campaign, coordinated by the National Institute of Child Health and Human Development in conjunction with the U.S. Department of Health and Human Services, distributes teen-friendly materials to encourage greater intakes of milk and other dairy foods (**Figure 17.7**). Campaign materials are available free of charge from its Web site (see the Web Links at the end of this chapter).

Disordered Eating and Eating Disorders

An initially healthful concern about body image and weight can turn into a dangerous obsession during this emotionally challenging life stage. Clinical eating disorders frequently begin during adolescence and can occur in boys as well as girls. Warning signs include rapid and excessive weight loss, a preoccupation with weight and body image, going to the bathroom regularly after meals, and signs of frequent vomiting or laxative use. Disordered eating is discussed *In Depth* on pages 528–540.

(a)

(b)

Figure 17.7 Milk Matters/Salud con Leche. These logos are part of a new government program to encourage milk consumption in children and adolescents. They are provided **(a)** in English and **(b)** in Spanish.

Highlight

On Your Own: Stocking Your First Kitchen

Many teens move out of the house around age 18 or 19 and settle into apartments, college or university housing, or shared housing. One question teens often have is how to stock their first kitchen. What basic foods—or staples—do they need to always have on hand, so that they can quickly and easily assemble healthful meals and snacks? The following checklist includes the foods that many Americans consider staples. It can be modified to include items that are staples in non-Western cultures and to address vegetarian, vegan, low-fat, low-sodium, or other diets. By stocking healthful foods like the ones listed here, you'll be much more likely to make healthful food choices every day!

Keep your refrigerator stocked with:

- Low-fat or skim milk and/or soy milk
- Calcium-enriched orange juice
- Hard cheeses
- Eggs
- Lean deli meats
- Tofu
- Hummus, peanut butter, low-fat cream cheese, and/or other perishable spreads
- Two- to 3-day supply of dark-green lettuce and other salad fixings or ready-to-eat salads
- Two- to 3-day supply of other veggies
- Two- to 3-day supply of fresh fruits
- Low-fat salad dressings, mustards, salsas, and so forth
- Whole-grain breads, rolls, bagels, pizza crusts
- Tortillas: corn, whole-wheat flour

Stock your freezer with:

- Individual portions of chicken breast, extra lean ground beef, pork loin chops, fish fillets, or soy alternatives

- Lower-fat frozen entrees ("boost" with salad, whole-grain roll, and extra veggies)
- Frozen veggies (no sauce)
- Frozen cheese or veggie pizza ("boost" with added mushrooms, green peppers, and so forth)
- Low-fat ice cream, sherbet, or sorbet

Stock your kitchen cupboards with:

- Potatoes, sweet potatoes, onions, garlic, and so forth, as desired
- Canned or vacuum-packed tuna, salmon, crab (in water, not oil)
- Canned veggies: corn, tomatoes, mushrooms, and so forth
- Canned legumes: black beans, refried beans, pinto/kidney beans, garbanzo beans
- Canned soups that are low in sodium and fat and high in fiber—read the Nutrition Facts panels!
- Dried beans and/or lentils, if desired
- Pasta and rice, preferably whole grain
- Bottled tomato-based pasta sauces
- Canned fruit in juice
- Dried fruits, including golden raisins, dried cranberries, dried apricots
- Nuts, including peanuts, almonds, walnuts, and so forth
- Whole-grain ready-to-eat cereals for breakfast and snacking; whole-grain cooked cereals like oatmeal
- Whole-grain, lower-fat crackers
- Pretzels, low-fat tortilla/corn chips, low/no-fat microwave popcorn
- Salt, pepper, balsamic vinegar, soy sauce, other condiments and spices as desired
- Olive oil, canola oil, and so forth, as desired

Adolescent Acne and Diet

Acne flare-ups plague many adolescents. Acne is an inflammation of the sebaceous (oil) glands associated with hair follicles. These glands produce an oily secretion called *sebum* that normally flows out onto the skin surface, keeping skin soft and moist and repelling microbes. In acne, excessive sebum collects in and plugs up hair follicles. "Blackheads" occur when follicles are exposed to air, and the top layer of sebum oxidizes. They are not caused by dirt! "Whiteheads" are collections of sebum in follicles not exposed to air.

The hormonal changes that occur during puberty are largely responsible for the sudden appearance of acne in many adolescents. Emotional stress, genetic factors, and personal hygiene are most likely secondary contributors. But what about foods? For decades, chocolate, fried foods, fatty foods, sweets, and other foods have been wrongfully linked to acne; it is now believed that diet plays virtually no role in its development. On the other hand, a healthful diet, rich in fruits, vegetables, whole grains, and lean meats, can provide vitamin A, vitamin C, zinc, and other nutrients to optimize skin health and maintain an effective immune system.

Prescription medications, including a vitamin A derivative 13-*cis*-retinoic acid (Accutane), effectively control severe forms of acne. Neither Accutane nor any other prescription vitamin A derivative should be used by women who are pregnant, planning a pregnancy, or may become pregnant. Accutane is a known teratogen, causing severe fetal malformations. The teratogenic effect is so severe that the FDA now requires all women of childbearing age who use Accutane to register in a risk-management program, iPLEDGE, to ensure that pregnancies do not occur while under treatment. Incidentally, vitamin A taken in supplement form is not effective in acne treatment and, due to its own risk for toxicity, should not be used in amounts that exceed 100% of the Daily Value.

Other Nutrition-Related Concerns

Cigarette smoking and use of alcohol and illegal drugs are additional nutrition-related concerns that face adolescents. Adolescents are naturally curious, and many are open to experimenting with tobacco, illegal drugs, and alcohol.

Cigarette smoking may interfere with nutrient metabolism.

Cigarette smoking diminishes appetite; indeed, it is frequently used by adolescent girls to maintain a low body weight. Smoking can also interfere with the metabolism of some nutrients, including calcium, vitamins C, E, and B$_6$, and beta-carotene.[23, 24] Short-term effects of smoking include reduced physical fitness, impaired health, and higher rates of alcohol and drug abuse. Most people who begin smoking during adolescence continue to smoke throughout adulthood, increasing their long-term risks for lung cancer, other cancers, heart disease, osteoporosis, and emphysema. Unfortunately, many adolescents do not accurately perceive smoking-related risks.[25]

Alcohol and drug use can start at early ages, even in school-aged children. Alcohol can interfere with nutrient absorption and metabolism, and it can take the place of foods in an adolescent's diet, putting adolescents at risk for nutrient deficiencies. Alcohol and marijuana use is also associated with getting "the munchies," a food craving that usually results in people eating large quantities of high-fat, high-sugar, nutrient-poor foods. This behavior can result in overweight or obesity and also increases the risk of nutrient deficiencies. Teens who use drugs and alcohol are typically in poor condition, are either underweight or overweight, have poor appetites, and perform poorly in school. For *In Depth* information on alcohol, see pages 154–164.

RECaP

Adolescents experience rapid increases in height, weight, and lean body mass and fat mass. Adequate energy is needed to support growth, maturation, and physical activity. Fat intake should be 25% to 35% of total energy, and carbohydrate intake should be 45% to 65% of total energy intake. Calcium is needed to optimize bone growth and to achieve peak bone density, and iron needs are increased due to increased muscle mass in boys and to menstruation in girls. Adolescents' food choices are influenced by peer pressure and personal preferences. They may select fast foods and high-fat/high-energy snack foods in place of whole grains, fruits, and vegetables. Adolescents with lower levels of physical activity may therefore experience overweight for the first time during this period. Suboptimal bone density, disordered eating behaviors, acne, cigarette smoking, and use of alcohol and illegal drugs are also concerns for this age group.

Pediatric Obesity Watch: A Concern for Children and Adolescents

During the past 30 years, the rate of obesity has doubled or even tripled for U.S children. Currently, about 12% of preschoolers, 17% of children 6 to 11years old, and 18% of youth 12 to 19 years old are classified as obese.[26] Using the CDC (Centers for Disease Control and Prevention) classification system, children are **overweight** when their BMI is at or above the 85th percentile and lower than the 95th percentile; that is, the child's body mass index is higher than that of 85% of U.S. children of the same age and gender. A child is considered by the CDC to be **obese** if his or her BMI is at or above the 95th percentile.[27]

Overweight and obese children are at higher risk of numerous short- and long-term health problems. Even in early childhood, significant overweight can worsen asthma, cause sleep apnea, impair the child's mobility, and lead to intense teasing, low self-esteem, and social isolation. Among children and adolescents who are overweight, rates of type 2 diabetes have increased tenfold over the past 20 years. Fatty liver is diagnosed in one-third of obese children, and increasing numbers of obese children are experiencing high blood lipids, high blood pressure, gallstones, depression, and other medical problems.[28] Obese children are at much higher risk of becoming overweight adults than are normal-weight children, so preventing childhood overweight is important for long-term health and happiness. While there is some evidence that the prevalence rates of childhood obesity and overweight may have leveled off,[29] reversal of the epidemic of pediatric obesity can be accomplished only through an aggressive, comprehensive nationwide health campaign.

The Seeds of Pediatric Obesity

Believe it or not, early signs indicating a tendency toward overweight can occur as early as the toddler years. Toddlers should *not* be denied nutritious food; however, they should not be force-fed nor should they be encouraged to eat when they say or take actions that indicate they are full. In the toddler years, a child who is above the 80th percentile for weight should be monitored. The preschool years are also an important time for parents to be watchful of potential overweight and obesity. Preschoolers should be encouraged and supported in increasing their physical activity, and as for all children, foods with low nutrient density, such as sodas, cookies, and candies, should be limited. Parents should not be offended if the child's pediatrician or other healthcare provider expresses concern over the child's weight status; early intervention is often the most effective measure against lifelong obesity.

Pediatric Obesity: Prevention Through a Healthful Diet

Nutrition and healthcare experts agree that the main contributors to childhood obesity are similar to those involved in adult obesity: eating and drinking too many calories and moving around too little. Parental overweight, low parental concern about the child's weight, and tantrums over food are additional factors contributing to childhood overweight.[30] The introduction and retention of healthful eating habits are key interventions in the fight against pediatric obesity.

The Role of the Family in Healthful Eating

Rather than singling out overweight children and placing them on restrictive diets, experts encourage family-wide improvements in food choices and mealtime habits.[31] Parents should strive to consistently provide nutritious food choices, encourage children to eat a healthful breakfast every morning, and sit down to a shared family meal each evening or as often as possible.[32] The television should be off throughout mealtimes to encourage attentive eating and true enjoyment of the food. Children typically mimic their parents, especially at the younger ages, so parents have many opportunities to improve the dietary patterns of their children.

overweight (childhood) Having a body mass index (BMI) at or above the 85th percentile but below the 95th percentile.

obese (childhood) Having a body mass index (BMI) at or above the 95th percentile.

Parents should try to have shared family meals with their children whenever possible.

Parents should retain control over the purchasing and preparation of foods until older children and teens are responsible and knowledgeable enough to make healthful decisions. Parents can keep a selection of fruits, vegetables, whole-grain products, and low-fat dairy foods readily available as healthful alternatives to high-fat, high-sugar snacks. For children "on the run," parents can keep a supply of nonperishable snacks such as granola bars, dried fruits, and nuts, along with kid-friendly fruits such as apples, bananas, and oranges, to grab as everyone dashes out the door. Mealtimes, especially dinner, should offer a colorful variety of foods with the emphasis on green, yellow, orange, and red vegetables and deep-brown grains.

Whenever possible, parents should minimize the number of meals eaten in restaurants, especially fast-food franchises. Although there is some evidence that children are ordering fewer cheeseburgers, fries, and sodas, many still opt for high-fat, high-sugar foods and larger portion sizes. When families do eat out, large portion sizes can be shared, and grilled, broiled, or baked foods substituted for fried foods.

Many children and adolescents resent parental oversight and involvement in their weight-control program. Parents should not allow the dinner table to turn into a battleground; instead, parents should model healthful eating behaviors, provide a diverse array of healthful foods, and encourage healthful lifestyle choices, including physical activity.[33] Even if the child's weight stabilizes rather than declines, parents should praise the absence of additional weight gain as a positive step.

The Role of the School in Healthful Eating

As previously noted, the federal school lunch program is designed to limit the amount of fat, sugar, and sodium served to students. Many schools, however, fail to meet those guidelines and also sell foods and beverages that exceed federal guidelines. Parents can work with local school boards to eliminate or restrict the sales of soda, candy, and pastries. Several states now ban vending machines at elementary and middle schools; efforts at high schools have generally been less successful. Many schools take advantage of nutrition education programs offered through agencies such as state or county health departments, local Dairy Councils, and the Produce for Better Health Foundation (www.fruitsandveggiesmorematters.org/). Consistent and repeated school-based messages on good nutrition can reinforce the efforts of parents and healthcare providers.

Pediatric Obesity: Prevention Through an Active Lifestyle

Increased energy expenditure through increased physical activity is essential for successful weight management among children. The Institute of Medicine now recommends that children participate in daily physical activity and exercise for at least an hour each day;[1] the 2008 Physical Activity Guidelines for Americans also advises bone- and muscle-strengthening activities at least three days each week.[33] For younger children, this can be divided into two or three shorter sessions, allowing them to regroup, recoup, and refocus between activity sessions. Older children should be able to be active for an hour without stopping. Overweight children are more likely to engage in physical activities that are noncompetitive, fun, and structured in a way that allows them to proceed at their own pace. Children should be exposed to a variety of activities so that they move different muscles, play at various intensities, avoid boredom, and find out what they like and don't like to do. The American Dietetic Association has designed a Fitness Pyramid for Kids to help guide children toward a physically active lifestyle (**Figure 17.8**).

The Role of the Family in Physical Activity

As with healthful eating, parental and adult role models are vitally important in any effort to increase the physical activity level of children and adolescents. When parents and children are active together, healthful activity patterns are established early. To encourage activity throughout the day, parents should encourage shared activities such as ball games,

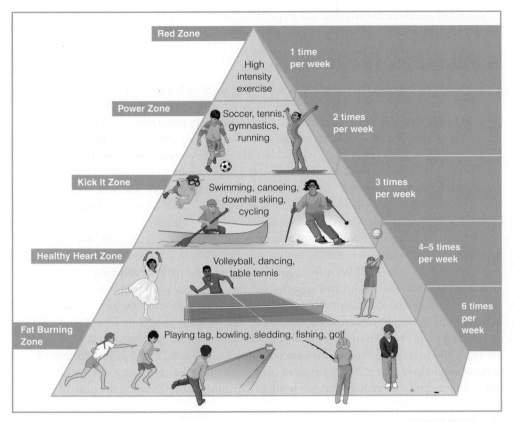

Red Zone — High intensity exercise — 1 time per week

Power Zone — Soccer, tennis, gymnastics, running — 2 times per week

Kick It Zone — Swimming, canoeing, downhill skiing, cycling — 3 times per week

Healthy Heart Zone — Volleyball, dancing, table tennis — 4–5 times per week

Fat Burning Zone — Playing tag, bowling, sledding, fishing, golf — 6 times per week

Figure 17.8 The American Dietetic Association's Fitness Pyramid for Kids gives guidelines for the duration, intensity, and frequency of various types of activities that are appropriate for children aged 2 to 11 years. (Reprinted with permission from Journal of the American Dietetic Association, vol. 104, pp. 660–667. © 2004 American Dietetic Association.)

bicycle rides, hikes, skating outings, and so forth. In addition, community organizations such as the YMCA and municipal recreational centers also have supervised youth-oriented weight-training programs, climbing walls, skateboard parks, and other nontraditional activity options that are typically open to the whole family.

In the past, children played freely outdoors and even kept active indoors in times of bad weather. In recent years, however, several factors have prompted childhood activities to become increasingly sedentary. One such factor is simply the availability of sedentary entertainment technologies, including television, video games, and computer games. The American Academy of Pediatrics recommends no more than 2 hours per day of TV viewing for preschoolers; children who watch more than that are at increased risk for overweight.[34] Too much television can also interfere with the acquisition of physical skills and can hinder children's use of their own imaginations, dampening creativity. Moreover, an abundance of television commercials during children's programs advertise less healthful foods, such as sweetened breakfast cereals made with refined grains, candies, pastries, and high-fat snacks. Even parents who limit television watching should sit with their younger children during several commercials and explain to them, in age-appropriate language, that these foods are made to look appealing to kids but are not healthful choices.

Another factor contributing to low levels of physical activity among America's youth is the high number of households in which no adult is home after school, either because of single-parent families or because both parents have to work to support the family. Safety concerns cause working parents to forbid their children, when they are home alone after school, to venture out of the house. If this is the case, the family may consider investing in some of the new electronic game systems that offer virtual tennis, step aerobics, dancing, and other active simulations.

By increasing their physical activity, many overweight children are able to "catch up" to their weight as they grow taller without restricting their food (and thus nutrient) intake. Increased activity also helps young children acquire motor skills and muscle strength, establish good sleep patterns, and develop self-esteem as they feel themselves becoming faster, stronger, and more skilled. Regular physical activity also optimizes bone mass, strengthens

Encouraging physical play with friends is a good way to combat childhood obesity.

muscles, enhances cardiovascular and respiratory function, and lowers emotional stress in overweight children.

The Role of the School in Physical Activity

As academic standards increase across the country, many schools are reducing or eliminating physical education classes and, in elementary schools, recess periods. Budget cuts have also led to the reduction or elimination of physical activity programs, including high school sports programs. Unfortunately, these decisions are short sighted because daily physical activity not only helps regulate body weight, but also improves academic performance. Researchers have noted that when children have the opportunity to take part in recess, classroom behavior improves,[35] children are more attentive to their teachers, and students are more focused on assigned tasks. In addition, children classified as physically fit have higher levels of academic achievement compared to unfit children.[36]

Parents, healthcare providers, and other community members can join forces to work with local school boards to optimize opportunities for physical activity within the schools. A program called *We Can!* (Ways to Enhance Children's Activity & Nutrition), a collaboration of several national health and government agencies, provides resources for parents, healthcare providers, schools, and communities so they can develop their own local physical activity and nutrition programs. *We Can!* is just one of many programs schools can use in developing their own action plans. Daily physical education in schools, continued funding for team and individual sports, and noncompetitive physical activity options outside of schools can help reduce the prevalence of overweight and obesity among U.S. children and adolescents, slowly reversing what has been an alarming health issue for the past 30 years.[37]

RECAP

Obesity is an important concern for children of all ages, their families, and their communities. Parents should model healthy eating and activity behaviors. Schools play an important role in providing nutritious breakfasts and lunches and varied opportunities for daily physical activity.

See for Yourself

Is Your Local School Committed to Children's Nutrition?

Contact your local elementary school, middle school, or high school and request permission to visit the school's cafeteria. While there, ask for a weekly or monthly breakfast and lunch menu. Also ask how the nutritional value of each meal is determined, including portion sizes, levels of nutrients, and so forth. Ask if there is an RD at the school or district level; if not, ask who is responsible for menu development. In addition to the meals on the menu, what snacks or meal alternatives, if any, are available for purchase? Does the school have vending machines, and if so, what foods and beverages are available? Are vending machine sales restricted during lunch hours or at any other time during the school day? Finally, within the cafeteria setting, what behavioral strategies, if any, are used to promote healthful food choices—for example, serving healthful foods in a fun way, decorating the cafeteria with nutrition-related posters, personnel encouraging children to finish meals, and so forth?

Write up your findings and report them to your classmates. When discussing the school's level of commitment to its students' nutrition, use the following criteria:

- Meals served provide appropriate energy, macronutrients, and micronutrients for population served.
- Available snacks provide appropriate energy, macronutrients, and micronutrients for population served.
- Vending machine choices provide appropriate energy, macronutrients, and micronutrients for population served.
- Cafeteria environment and personnel demonstrate strategies to encourage healthful eating.

Chapter Review

Test Yourself | Answers

1 **F** Children under the age of 2 years have a higher need for fat than do older children or adults, so they should consume foods that are higher in fat, including full-fat milk.

2 **T** The DRI guidelines do not differentiate between girls and boys until the age of 9 years.

3 **T** In 2007, 12.4 million children experienced food insecurity; that is, they lived in households that lacked dependable access to enough food for all members.

4 **F** Adolescents experience an average 20% to 25% increase in height during the pubertal years.

5 **T** Hormonal changes, emotional stress, genetic factors, and personal hygiene are the most likely contributors to adolescent acne.

Summary

- Toddlers grow more slowly than infants but are far more active. They require small, frequent, nutritious snacks and meals, and food should be cut in small pieces so it is easy to handle and swallow.

- For toddlers and young children, a serving of food equals 1 tablespoon for each year of age. For example, 4 tablespoons of yogurt is a full serving for a 4-year-old child.

- Energy, fat, and protein requirements are higher for toddlers than for infants. Many toddlers will not eat vegetables, so micronutrients of concern include vitamins A, C, and E.

- Until age 2, toddlers should drink whole milk rather than reduced-fat milk to meet calcium requirements. Iron deficiency is a concern in the toddler years and can be minimized by the consumption of foods naturally high in iron and iron-fortified foods.

- Feeding vegan diets to toddlers is controversial and poses potential deficiencies for protein, iron, calcium, zinc, vitamin D, and vitamin B_{12}.

- School-aged children are more independent and can make more of their own food choices. Physical activity levels can vary dramatically.

- Sexual maturation begins during the early school-age years. School-aged children should eat 25% to 35% of their total energy as fat and 45% to 65% of their total energy as carbohydrate. Calcium needs increase as children mature, whereas iron needs decrease slightly.

- Although relatively rare, iron-deficiency anemia occurs in some children. Healthful food choices and, if appropriate, use of an iron supplement can prevent the fatigue, illness, and impaired learning that often accompany childhood iron deficiency. Consuming adequate calcium to support the development of peak bone mass is a primary concern for school-aged children.

- Many school-aged children skip breakfast and do not choose healthful foods during school lunch. Peer pressure and popularity are strong influences on food choices. School lunches are nutritious and meet federal guidelines, but the foods that children choose to eat at school, both during and outside of the lunch break, can be high in fat, sugar, and energy and low in nutrients.

- Families experiencing food insecurity should be referred to appropriate government and social service agencies; short-term solutions such as emergency food boxes must be supported with long-term, multidimensional support.

- Puberty is the period in life in which secondary sexual characteristics develop and the physical capability to reproduce begins. Puberty results in rapid increases in height, weight, and lean body mass and fat mass.

- Energy needs for adolescents are variable and can be quite high, and adequate energy is needed to support growth, maturation, and physical activity. Fat intake should be 25% to 35% of total energy, and carbohydrate intake should be 45% to 65% of total energy intake.

- Many adolescents replace whole grains, fruits, and vegetables with fast foods and high-fat/high-energy snack foods, placing them at risk for deficiencies for calcium, iron, and vitamin A. Calcium is needed to optimize bone growth and to achieve peak bone density, and iron needs are increased because of increased muscle mass in boys and menstruation in girls.

- Disordered eating behaviors, eating disorders, personal appearance, cigarette smoking, and use of alcohol and illegal drugs are concerns for adolescents.

- Overweight and obesity can begin to develop at any time from toddlerhood through adolescence if energy intake exceeds energy spent in physical activity. Both families and schools can play important roles in encouraging smart food choices and increased physical activity.

Review Questions

1. The AI for calcium for adolescents is
   a. less than that for young children.
   b. less than that for adults.
   c. less than that for pregnant adults.
   d. greater than that for young children, adults, and pregnant adults.

2. Carbohydrate should make up what percentage of total energy for school-aged children?
   a. 25% to 40%
   b. 35% to 50%
   c. 45% to 60%
   d. 45% to 70%

3. Which of the following is a common nutrition-related concern for school-aged children?
   a. inappropriately low fat intake
   b. skipping breakfast
   c. botulism
   d. protein deficiency

4. Which of the following breakfasts would be most appropriate to serve a 22-month-old child?
   a. 1 cup of iron-fortified cooked oat cereal, 2 tablespoons of mashed pineapple, and 1 cup of skim milk
   b. 2 tablespoons of plain yogurt, 2 tablespoons of applesauce, 2 tablespoons of fortified whole-grain oat cereal, and 1/2 cup of calcium-fortified orange juice
   c. 1/2 cup of iron-fortified cooked oat cereal, 1/2 cup of cubed pineapple, and 1 cup of low-fat milk
   d. 2 small link sausages cut in 1-inch pieces, 2 scrambled eggs, 1 slice of whole-wheat toast, 4 cherry tomatoes, 1/2 cup of applesauce, and 1 cup of whole milk

5. Which of the following statements about cigarette smoking is true?
   a. Cigarette smoking can interfere with the metabolism of nutrients.
   b. Cigarette smoking commonly causes food cravings such as "getting the munchies."

   c. iPLEDGE is a program from the National Institutes of Health that encourages adolescents to stop smoking.
   d. All of the above statements are true.

6. **True or False?** Toddlers need 30% to 40% of their total energy intake as fat.

7. **True or False?** Children are too young to understand and be influenced by the examples of their parents.

8. **True or false?** Among both males and females, the need for calcium decreases after the age of 16 due to the completion of bone growth.

9. **True or false?** National guidelines advise that all children and adolescents get 30 minutes of exercise 3 to 4 days each week.

10. **True or false?** Weight gain during adolescence is expected and healthful.

11. Identify some advantages and disadvantages of modern technology (such as television and computers) in terms of its impact on lifestyle and nutrition.

12. Explain why a toddler in a vegan family might be at risk for protein deficiency.

13. Imagine that you are taking care of four 5-year-old children for an afternoon. Design a menu for the children's lunch that is nutritious and that will be fun for them to eat.

14. Imagine that you plan meals for a high school cafeteria. Design a menu with three lunch choices that are nutritious and that are likely to be popular with teens.

15. Your classmate Lydia is a bit eccentric. An engineering major, she spends an average of 6 hours a day at her computer, drinking diet colas and eating pretzels. She is unusually slender, even though she admits to getting no regular exercise. Your university is in upstate New York, and Lydia is from Vermont. If you were a registered dietitian (RD) and Lydia were your client, what nutrition-related health concern(s) might you discuss with her? Identify *at least* three elements in Lydia's story that are known risk factors for the health problem(s) you identify.

Web Links

www.wecan.nhlbi.nih.gov

We Can!

We Can! (Ways to Enhance Children's Activity & Nutrition) provides materials for families, schools, and healthcare providers to use to help children increase their physical activity, make healthy food choices, and achieve healthy weights.

www.keepkidshealthy.com

Keep Kids Healthy.com

Find information about nutrition and health for toddlers, children, and adolescents on this Web site.

www.cdc.gov

The Centers for Disease Control

Click on "Health Promotion," then select topics such as "Adolescent Health," "Project VERB™," plus many others.

www.vrg.org

The Vegetarian Resource Group

Visit this Web site to learn more about vegetarianism for all ages. Included on the site are special sections for teens and kids, as well as recipes and guides for vegetarian and vegan eating in all kinds of situations.

www.health.gov/dietaryguidelines

Dietary Guidelines for Americans

Visit this site to read the 2005 edition of Dietary Guidelines for Americans and to learn about their development.

www.fns.usda.gov

USDA Food & Nutrition Services

Read about governmental programs to provide food to all ages, including school meal programs, the Child and Adult Care Food Program, and the Women, Infants, and Children Program.

www.eatright.org

American Dietetic Association

Visit this Web site to learn about healthy eating habits for all stages of life.

www.nichd.nih.gov/milk

Milk Matters

Need ideas on how to increase milk and dairy foods intakes? This Web site provides practical tips and menus for children and adolescents.

References

1. Institute of Medicine, Food and Nutrition Board. 2002. *Dietary Reference Intakes for Energy, Carbohydrates, Fiber, Fat, Protein and Amino Acids (Macronutrients).* Washington, DC: The National Academy of Sciences.

2. Kleinman, R. E., ed. 2009. *Pediatric Nutrition Handbook,* 6th ed. Elk Grove Village, IL: American Academy of Pediatrics.

3. Institute of Medicine, Committee to Review the WIC Food Packages. 2005. *Proposed Criteria for Selecting the WIC Food Packages.* Washington, DC: National Academy Press.

4. Institute of Medicine, Food and Nutrition Board. 1997. *Dietary Reference Intakes for Calcium, Phosphorus, Magnesium, Vitamin D, and Fluoride.* Washington, DC: National Academy Press.

5. Institute of Medicine, Food and Nutrition Board. 2001. *Dietary Reference Intakes for Vitamin A, Vitamin K, Arsenic, Boron, Chromium, Copper, Iodine, Iron, Manganese, Molybdenum, Nickel, Silicon, Vanadium, and Zinc.* Washington, DC: National Academy Press.

6. Institute of Medicine, Food and Nutrition Board. 2004. *Dietary Reference Intakes for Water, Potassium, Sodium, Chloride, and Sulfate.* Washington, DC: National Academy Press.

7. Oldways. 2000. The Vegetarian Diet Pyramid for Children. Available at http://oldwayspt.org/vegetarian_pyramid.html. (Accessed June 2009.)

8. Stahler, C. 2005. How many youth are vegetarian? *Vegetarian Journal.* Available at http://www.vrg.org/journal/vj2005issue4/vj2005issue4youth.htm. (Accessed June 2009.)

9. Stern, R. 2007. Diet from hell. *Phoenix New Times,* May 10. Available at www.phoenixnewtimes.com/2007-05-10/news/diet-from-hell/.

10. Second Opinions. 2002. Vegan child abuse. Available at www.second-opinions.co.uk/child_abuse.html.

11. Doron, D., K. Hershkop, and E. Granot. 2001. Nutritional deficits resulting from an almond-based infant diet. *Clinical Nutrition* 20:259–261.

12. Giannini, A., N. Mirra, and M. F. Patria. 2006. Health risks for children raised on vegan or vegetarian diets (Letter to the editor). *Pediatr. Crit. Care Med.* 7:188.

13. Messina, V. and A. R. Mangels. 2001. Considerations in planning vegan diets: Children. *J. Am. Diet. Assoc.* 101:661–669.

14. American Dietetic Association and Dieticians of Canada. 2003. Position statement: Vegetarian diets. *J. Am. Diet. Assoc.* 103:748–756.

15. Striegel-Moore, R. H., D. Thompson, S. G. Affenito, D. L. Franko, E. Obarzanek, B. A. Barton, G. B. Schreiber, S. R. Daniels, M. Schmidt, and P. B. Crawford. 2006. Correlates of beverage intake in adolescent girls: The National Heart, Lung, and Blood Institute growth and health study. *J. Pediatr.* 148:183–187.

16. Rampersaud, G. C., M. A. Pereira, B. L. Girard, J. Adams, and J. D. Metzl. 2005. Breakfast habits, nutritional status, body weight, and academic performance in children and adolescents. *J. Am. Diet. Assoc.* 105:743–760.

17. Story, M. 2009. The Third School Nutrition Dietary Assessment Study: Findings and policy implications for improving the health of US children. *J. Am. Diet. Assoc.* 109: S7–S13.

18. Gleason, P. M., and A. H. Dodd. 2009. School breakfast program but not school lunch program participation is associated with lower body mass index. *J. Am. Diet. Assoc.* 109:S118–S128.

19. Miller, C. H. 2009. A practice perspective on the third School Nutrition Dietary Assessment Study. *J. Am. Diet. Assoc.* 109:S14–S17.

20. Nord, M., M. Andrews, and S. Carlson 2008. *Household Food Security in the United States, 2007.* U.S.D.A. Economic Research Service Report No. (ERR-66). Available at http://www.ers.usda.gov/publications/err66/

21. Steinberg, L. 2007. *Adolescence,* 8th ed. New York: McGraw-Hill.

22. Kalkwarf, H. J., J. C. Khoury, and B. P. Lanphear. 2003. Milk intake during childhood and adolescence, adult bone density, and osteoporotic fractures in US women. *Am. J. Clin. Nutr.* 77:257–265.

23. Bruno, R. S., R. Ramakrishnan, T. J. Montine, T. M. Bray, and M. G. Traber. 2005. α-Tocopherol disappearance is faster in cigarette smokers and is inversely related to their ascorbic acid status. *Am. J. Clin. Nutr.* 81:95–103.

24. Preston, A. M., C. Rodriguez, C. E. Rivera, and H. Sahai. 2003. Influence of environmental tobacco smoke on vitamin C status in children. *Am. J. Clin. Nutr.* 77:167–172.

25. Song, A. V., H. E. R. Morrell, J. L. Cornell, M. E. Ramos, M. Biehl, R. Y. Kropp, and B. L. Halpern-Felsher. 2009. Perceptions of smoking-related risks and benefits as predictors of adolescent smoking initiation. *Am. J. Public Health* 99:487–492.

26. Centers for Disease Control and Prevention. 2009. Childhood overweight and obesity: prevalence. Available at www.cdc.gov/obesity/childhood/prevalence.html. (Accessed June 2009.)

27. Centers for Disease Control and Prevention. 2009. Childhood overweight and obesity: Use of BMI to screen for overweight and obesity in children. Available at www.cdc.gov/obesity/childhood/defining.html. (Accessed June 2009.)

28. Ludwig, D. S. 2007. Childhood obesity—the shape of things to come. *New Engl. J. Med.* 357:2325–2327.

29. Ogden, C. L., M. D. Carroll, and K. M. Flegal. 2008. High body mass index for age among US children and adolescents, 2003–2006. *JAMA* 299:2401–2405.

30. Agras, W. S., L. D. Hammer, F. McNicholas, and H. C. Kraemer. 2004. Risk factors for childhood overweight: A prospective study from birth to 9.5 years. *J. Pediatr.* 145:19–24.

31. Zeller, M., and S. Daniels. 2004. The obesity epidemic: Family matters. *J. Pediatr.* 145:3–4.

32. Ritchie, L. D., G. Welk, D. Styne, D. E. Gerstein, and P. B. Crawford. 2005. Family environment and pediatric overweight: What is a parent to do? *J. Am. Diet. Assoc.* 105:S70–S79.

33. U.S. Department of Health and Human Services. 2008. *2008 Physical Activity Guidelines for Americans.* Washington, DC: Author.

34. Mendoza, J. A., F. J. Zimmermann, and D. A. Christakis. 2007. Television viewing, computer use, obesity, and adiposity in US preschool children. *Int. J. Behav. Nutr. Physical Activity* 4:44. Available at www.ijbnpa.org/content/4/1/44. (Accessed June 2009.)

35. Barros, R. M., E. J. Silver, and R. E. K. Stein. 2009. School recess and group classroom behavior. *Pediatrics* 123:431–436.

36. Chomitz, V. R., M. M. Slining, R. J. McGowan, S. E. Mitchell, G. F. Dawson, and K. A. Hacker. 2009. Is there a relationship between physical fitness and academic achievement? Positive results from public school children in the northeastern United States. *J. School Health* 79:30–37.

37. Levi, J., S. Vinter, L. Richardson, R. St. Laurent, and L. M. Segal. 2009. *F as in Fat: How Obesity Policies Are Failing in America, 2009.* Washington, DC: Trust for America's Health.

38. Huh, S. Y., and C. M. Gordon. 2008. Vitamin D deficiency in children and adolescents: Epidemiology, impact and treatment. *Rev. Endocr. Metab. Disord.* 9:161–170.

39. Smolders, J., J. Damoiseaux, P. Menheere, and R. Hupperts. 2008. Vitamin D as an immune modulator in multiple sclerosis, a review. *J. Neuroimmunology* 194:7–17.

40. Lee, J. H., J. H. O'Keefe, D. Bell, D. D. Hensrud, and M. F. Holick. 2008. Vitamin D deficiency: An important, common, and easily treatable cardiovascular risk factor? *J. Am. Coll. Cardiol.* 52:1949–1956.

41. Lucas, R. M., and A. L. Ponsonby. 2006. Considering the potential benefits as well as adverse effects of sun exposure: Can all the potential benefits be provided by oral vitamin D supplementation? *Prog. Biophys. Molec. Biol.* 92:140–149.

42. Reichrath, J. 2006. The challenge resulting from positive and negative effects of sunlight: How much solar UV exposure is appropriate to balance between risks of vitamin D deficiency and skin cancer? *Prog. Biophys. Molec. Biol.* 92:9–16.

43. Wagner, C. L., F. R. Greer, and the Section on Breastfeeding and Committee on Nutrition. 2008. Prevention of rickets and vitamin D deficiency in infants, children, and adolescents. *Pediatrics* 122:1142–1152.

44. Wolpowitz, D., and B. A. Gilchrest. 2006. The vitamin D question: How much do you need and how should you get it? *J. Am. Acad. Dermatol.* 54:301–307.

45. Mohr, S. B., C. F. Garland, E. D. Gorham, and F. C. Garland. 2008. The association between ultraviolet B irradiance, vitamin D status and incidence rates of type 1 diabetes in 51 regions worldwide. *Diabetologia* 51:1391–1398.

The Vitamin D Dilemma: Supplements Versus Sunshine

Since Lani's birth, her parents have conscientiously followed the healthcare advice they've received. So when Lani's pediatrician phones them shortly after her 18-month check-up to report that she is deficient in vitamin D, they are stunned. Fighting back tears, Lani's mother asks how her daughter could have developed a vitamin deficiency. "I still breastfeed Lani, and she eats a very healthy diet! I take good care of my daughter!"

Lani's pediatrician assures her mother that she is not to blame. He points out that children with dark skin, like Lani, are at increased risk for vitamin D deficiency, then asks how much time Lani spends outdoors in the sun. "Oh, we're very careful!" her mother exclaims. "Before we take her outside, we always put on her sunscreen. She's never been burned—but even if she had been, what does that have to do with her vitamin problem?"

A surprisingly high number of U.S. children are at risk for vitamin D deficiency.[38] As discussed in Chapter 11, vitamin D is essential for normal bone growth and development. It also protects against autoimmune diseases, internal cancers, and cardiovascular disease.[39-42] Recall that vitamin D is referred to as the "sunshine vitamin" because it is synthesized by skin cells exposed to sunlight. Thus, unlike most nutrients, not only can we meet our need for vitamin D by consuming it from foods or supplements, we can also synthesize it following exposure to the sun. In the Nutrition Debate at the end of Chapter 11, we discussed the current controversy over increasing the Institute of Medicine's recommendations for vitamin D intake, which were set in 1997. Here, we explore another angle in the vitamin D dilemma: Should public health authorities advise Americans, especially children and adolescents, to spend more time in the sun?

Historically, the discovery of vitamin D was sparked by researchers' attempts to combat rickets, a disfiguring and potentially fatal bone disorder due to vitamin D deficiency. Around the turn of the 20th century in the United States, several hundred children died each year, especially in polluted cities in northern regions, from rickets. African Americans were affected at higher rates than European Americans. A series of careful studies in the early 20th century led scientists to identify vitamin D as the "anti-rickets" factor present in cod liver oil, a common folk remedy for rickets, and to the recognition of the role of ultraviolet radiation in the body's natural synthesis of vitamin D. Once vitamin D–fortification of milk began in the 1930s, U.S. death rates of infants and children from rickets began to drop. Still, rickets continues to be reported among U.S. infants, children, and adolescents, particularly among those, like Lani, with darker skin pigmentation.[43] A recent study documented that 42% of healthy adolescents and 12% of toddlers from the Boston area were deficient in vitamin D; an even higher number were found to have suboptimal levels of serum vitamin D.[38]

Why has the rate of pediatric vitamin D deficiency increased, and what can families and healthcare providers do to improve vitamin D status in children and adolescents? Remember, humans have three sources of vitamin D: foods, supplements, and sun exposure. For reasons that will be discussed shortly, a number of researchers are now promoting what was previously shunned: increased sunlight exposure. They claim that a lack of exposure to ultraviolet radiation is increasing vitamin D deficiency, and that increased, but prudent, sun exposure is necessary to improve vitamin D status.[41, 42] Let's take a look at the facts behind these assertions.

Historically, humans have obtained most of their vitamin D from internal synthesis following sunlight exposure.[38] During summer months, adults with light skin pigmentation can easily meet their daily vitamin D needs with as little as 10 to 15 minutes of full-body exposure.[44] People with darker pigmentation require a significantly longer exposure. However, as discussed in Chapter 11, no amount of exposure is sufficient to enable vitamin D synthesis for people of any skin tone in winter months in northern latitudes. And, due in part to recent lifestyle changes, it is not clear that children and adolescents are obtaining even 10 to 15 minutes of full-body sun exposure in the summertime.[43]

In addition to increasingly popular indoor activities for children and adolescents, parents have been heeding warnings from the Centers for Disease Control and Prevention, the American Cancer Society, the American Academy of Pediatrics, and the Environmental Protection Agency, which have all aggressively publicized the dangers of excessive sunlight exposure and the risk of skin cancer in youth. Parents are advised to limit children's exposure to full sunlight, to provide hats and sunglasses, and to use high-potency sunscreen, all of which greatly impair the ability of the body to produce adequate vitamin D. Lately, even makers of children's summer clothing advertise its ability to "Block the sun, not the fun" with special UV-protective fabrics. Thus, children's natural ability to synthesize vitamin D through their skin appears to be as constrained as it was in polluted cities a hundred years ago.

696

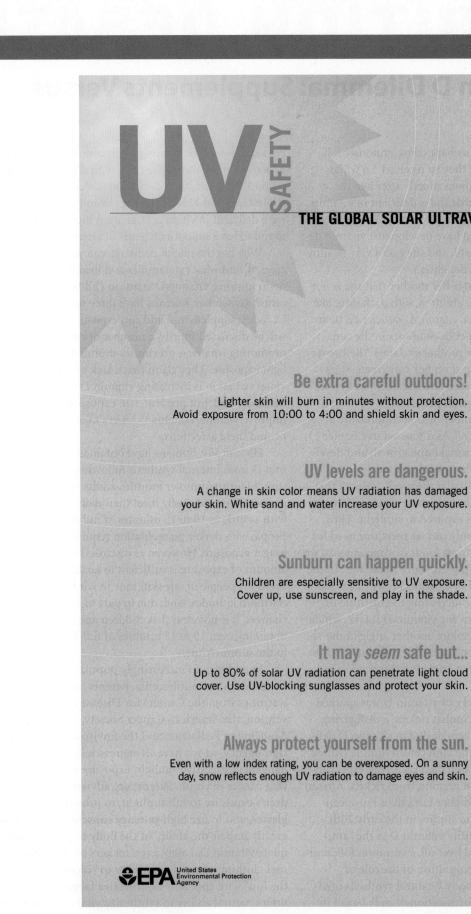

The Environmental Protection Agency is just one of many public health agencies that warn Americans about the danger of exposure to even low levels of sun.

In opposition to these advisories to restrict sun exposure in children and adolescents, a number of researchers are actively *promoting* moderate sun exposure as an inexpensive and effective means of optimizing vitamin D status.[41, 42] They claim that increased sun exposure will help reduce rates of rickets and possibly lower long-term risk for multiple sclerosis, type 1 diabetes, non-skin cancers, and other chronic diseases. Research strongly supports an inverse relationship between UVB exposure and incidence of type 1 diabetes: regions with intense and prolonged sun exposure had the lowest rates of type 1 diabetes.[45]

As noted, vitamin D status can be maintained through appropriate intake from foods and/or supplements. In fact, the American Academy of Dermatology recommends that we "Get vitamin D safely through a healthy diet that may include vitamin supplements." Newly revised vitamin D intake guidelines for healthy children and adolescents are double that of previous recommendations: the

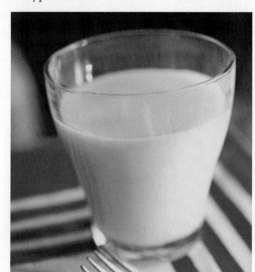

American Academy of Pediatrics now advises a daily intake of 400 IU/day.[43] One 8-ounce glass of vitamin D–fortified milk or orange juice provides 100 IU; therefore, children and teens would have to drink a full quart of milk or fortified orange juice each day to meet the new recommendation.[44] Milk intake among adolescent girls has decreased by almost 40% over the past three decades, so it is very unlikely that the typical teenager will consume that much milk on a regular basis. Children and teens are also unlikely to eat salmon or mackerel—other rich sources—three times a week, as would be required to meet these newly revised vitamin D guidelines. While fortified cereals and egg yolk can add small amounts to the diet (about 50 IU per serving), it would be difficult for most children and adolescents to meet the increased recommendations from these sources either. Thus, dietary sources alone are unlikely to meet the vitamin D requirements of American youth. So, what about supplements?

Many healthcare providers now recommend that most children and adolescents who do not or cannot get adequate sun exposure should take a supplement that provides up to 400 IU of vitamin D per day. Supplementation with vitamin D is efficient, inexpensive, and effective. Used correctly, it is also very safe. Vitamin D toxicity is rare, but is more likely to occur as the result of inappropriate supplementation as compared to excessive consumption of food sources. Thus, parents must monitor their child's intake of vitamin D supplements to ensure a safe as well as adequate intake.

As just noted, supplements are highly effective but do carry some risk of toxicity when used inappropriately. That leads us back to the issue of sun exposure. Responsible, safe exposure to sunlight offers many advantages: it will never lead to vitamin D toxicity, it is easy and virtually cost-free, and sun exposure may offer benefits beyond that of improved vitamin D status.[41] Most advocates of moderate sun exposure simply want to soften the "sun avoidance" campaigns of recent years; they would like to see "well-balanced" recommendations that promote brief (15 minutes or so) periods of sun exposure, two to three times a week, with avoidance of mid-day sun during summer months.[42]

Critical Thinking Questions

There is no debate over the need to maintain appropriate vitamin D status, especially in children and adolescents. But the debate over appropriate sun exposure as a means of achieving this status will likely rage on as scientists continue to explore the pros and cons.

- Do you think the benefits of regular sun exposure outweigh the increased risk of skin cancer? Why or why not?

- As a parent, would you encourage greater sun exposure in order to enhance your child's vitamin D status and possibly promote long-term health benefits; or would you discourage sun exposure in order to protect your child against skin cancer and other skin disorders?

18 Nutrition Through the Life Cycle: The Later Years

Test Yourself | True or False?

1 Experts agree that within the next 20 to 30 years, the human life span will exceed 150 years. T *or* F

2 Loss of odor perception is more common among older adults than is loss of taste perception. T *or* F

3 Older adults have a specific need for vitamin B$_{12}$ supplements even if they are consistently eating a healthful diet. T *or* F

4 The need for iron increases with aging. T *or* F

5 Approximately 7% of older Americans experience food insecurity. T *or* F

Test Yourself answers are located in the Chapter Review.

Chapter Objectives *After reading this chapter, you will be able to:*

1. Describe the demographic changes related to the aging of America, *pp. 700–701.*

2. Identify current theories of human aging and how each relates to nutrient intake and/or status of older adults, *pp. 701–703.*

3. Describe the most common changes in sensory perception and organ function that occur as we age, *pp. 703–707.*

4. Explain how lifestyle choices can influence the rate at which we age, *p. 707.*

5. Compare and contrast the nutrient requirements of older adults to those of younger or middle-aged adults, *pp. 708–711.*

6. Explain the various factors that contribute to inappropriate weight loss in the elderly, *pp. 713–714.*

7. Describe what role, if any, dietary choices play in the prevention and/or treatment of age-related diseases such as osteoporosis, arthritis, dementia, and macular degeneration, *pp. 714–716.*

8. Identify the social and environmental factors that can contribute to food insecurity and malnutrition in older adults, *pp. 718–719.*

9. Discuss the various community nutrition programs available to U.S. elderly, *pp. 719–720.*

10. Evaluate the options for "end-of-life care" that relate to diet and nutritional support, *p. 720.*

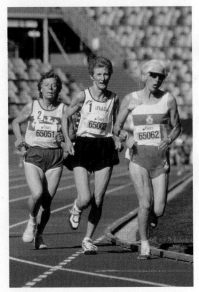

Many adults can remain highly active in their later years with the help of a nutritious diet and regular activity during aging.

I t was a sunny day and hundreds of spectators sat in the bleachers cheering on their favorite athletes competing in a variety of swimming, track, and other events. Strong and fit bodies, laughing companionship, and discussions about future competitions filled the stadium. A typical high school or college competition? Guess again: The competitors were world-class Masters Athletes, all over the age of 40 and a surprisingly high proportion over the age of 60. Were these participants always so athletic or did they come to their sport late in life? Was it genetics or lifestyle that allowed them to maintain such high levels of fitness into middle and late adulthood? Specifically, did they follow a rigid diet and supplement plan or choose the same types of foods as others their age?

Decades of research confirms the importance of a nutritious diet and regular physical activity in helping to prevent chronic disease, enhance productivity, and improve quality of life as we age. What are the unique nutritional needs and concerns of older adults? How can diet and lifestyle affect the aging process? These and other questions will be addressed in this chapter.

What Are the Demographics of Aging?

Before we can discuss meaningfully the nutrient needs and concerns of older adults, it's essential that we understand who makes up the older adult population in America—both their numbers and their characteristics.

The American Population Is Aging

The U.S. population is getting older each year. In 2003, over 36 million people aged 65 and older lived in the United States, representing about 12% of the population.[1] Around the year 2011, the aging of the baby boom generation will begin sharply increasing the number and percentage of older Americans. It is estimated that by the year 2030, the elderly will account for about 20% of Americans, or more than 71 million adults (**Figure 18.1**).

The quality of life of older Americans is also increasing. Older Americans are now healthier, more socially and physically active, and less likely to be confined to bed or have functional limitations than older adults living several decades ago.[2] Ideally, this trend will continue for future generations of elderly as well.

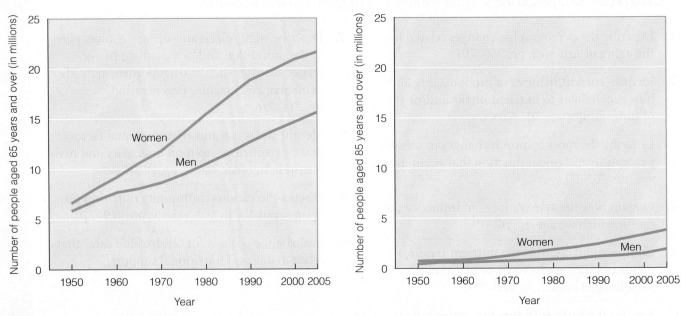

(a) Population growth of older adults

(b) Population growth of very elderly adults

Figure 18.1   In the United States, the population of older **(a)** (age 65 and over), and very elderly **(b)** (age 85 and over) people has grown steadily for several decades. (*Data from:* Robinson, K. 2007. Trends in health status and health care use among older women. *Aging Trends, No. 7.* Hyattsville, MD: National Center for Health Statistics. Available at www.cdc.gov/nchs/data/ahcd/agingtrends/07olderwomen.pdf. Accessed July 2009.)

The racial and ethnic profile of U.S. elderly is changing as well. The proportion of non-Hispanic whites will sharply decline over the next several decades, whereas the older Hispanic population will grow at the fastest rate. The percentage of older Native Americans and African Americans will grow to a lesser extent. As we discuss later in this chapter, the growing diversity of the elderly population and its unique cultural needs will present a significant challenge to the medical and social service communities.

Those 85 years and over, known as the "very elderly" or "oldest of the old," currently represent the fastest growing U.S. population subgroup, projected to grow from 4.2 million in 2000 to more than 20 million by the year 2050. The number of *centenarians,* persons over the age of 100 years, and *super-centenarians,* over 110 years, continues to grow as well. Together, these very elderly account for the majority of healthcare expenditures and nursing home admissions in the United States.

The racial and ethnic profile of U.S. elderly will change over the next several decades.

Life Span Differs from Life Expectancy

Celebrating one's 60th birthday is common today. Yet when George Washington turned 60 years old in 1792, he had outlived most of his peers by about 15 years. U.S. **life expectancy,** about 47 years in the year 1900, has increased dramatically during the past century due largely to medical advances, better nutrition, and improved sanitation.

In 2006, the average U.S. life expectancy reached 78.1 years.[3] Women live longer on average than men and racial disparities in life expectancy exist. African American males live an average of 6 fewer years than white males and African American women 4 years less than white women.[3] Whereas some researchers have argued that the growing rate of obesity and its medical consequences will drive down U.S. life expectancy during the next several decades, others refute this claim, noting the likely impact of future advances in healthcare.[4]

For most older adults, the goal is not to live as long as possible but to live a life free of disability and disease for as long as possible. This concept of healthy longevity is often referred to as *active life expectancy, successful aging,* or *compression of morbidity.*

Life span is the age to which the longest-living member of the species has lived. Madame Jeanne Calment, born in France in 1875, survived to the age of 122 and is generally viewed as achieving the oldest age in the world. There are also dozens of documented cases of people surviving to the ages of 114 to 116 years. Though very difficult to authenticate, one international volunteer organization estimates that there are currently about 75 super-centenarians living around the world, over 90% of them female.[5] Although some researchers have sought ways of extending human life span (see the Nutrition Debate on energy restriction at the end of this chapter), most agree that a life span beyond 125 to 130 years is unlikely.

Centenarians represent the future of U.S. elderly.

Why and How Do We Age?

The process of aging is natural and inevitable, influenced by genetic and environmental factors. Researchers have made great progress toward understanding the aging of humans, but much remains unknown.[6] Scientists can't even agree when the aging process begins: Some believe it starts at birth, whereas others argue it begins after peak reproductive age. While the debate continues, however, gerontologists agree that humans can positively influence the aging process through specific lifestyle and environmental choices.

Many Mechanisms Are Thought to Contribute to Aging

Aging occurs at the molecular, cellular, and tissue levels. Some signs of aging, such as the graying of hair, do not impair function or health. Other age-related changes, however, contribute to declines in functionality, health, and well-being. Scientists use the term **senescence** to describe those age-related processes that increase risk of disability, disease, and death.

Theories attempting to explain the mechanisms of aging can be categorized into two lines of research (see Table 18.1). First are the **programmed theories of aging,** proposing

life expectancy   The expected number of years remaining in one's life; typically stated from the time of birth. Children born in the United States in 2003 could expect to live, on average, 77.6 years.

life span   The highest age reached by any member of a species; currently, the human life span is 122 years.

senescence   The progressive deterioration of bodily functions over time, resulting in increased risk of disability, disease, and death.

programmed theories of aging   Aging is biologically determined, following a predictable pattern of physiologic changes, although the timing may vary from one person to another.

Table 18.1 Theories of Aging

Model	Description	Nutrition Interface
Programmed theories of aging	Aging follows a biologically driven time line, similar to that of adolescence	None evident
Hayflick theory of aging	Cells have a limited reproductive life span; in essence, cells can divide only so many times before they are no longer able to proliferate	None evident
Theory of programmed longevity	Aging occurs when certain genes are turned on or off; the activation or suppression of these genes then triggers age-related loss of function	Indirectly, a diet rich in antioxidants such as vitamins C and E could lower free-radical damage to DNA
Endocrine theory of aging	Senescence is due to hormonal changes such as declines in growth hormone, DHEA, estrogen, and/or testosterone	None directly evident
Immunologic theory of aging	Aging is linked to loss of immune system activity and/or an increase in autoimmune diseases	Adequate protein, zinc, iron, and vitamins A, C, and E help preserve remaining immune function
Error theories of aging	Senescence occurs as the result of cell and tissue damage caused largely by environmental insults	Several theoretical benefits of nutrient adequacy or supplementation
Wear-and-tear theory	Over time, cells simply wear out and eventually die. The greater the exposure to toxins and stressors, the more rapid the rate of decline	Protein, zinc, and vitamins A and C could theoretically delay the aging process by improving cellular repair and recovery
Cross-linkage theory	Abnormal cross-linkages of proteins such as collagen damage cells and tissues, impairing the function of organs	Glycosylation, the abnormal attachment of glucose to proteins, can be limited by controlling blood glucose levels. Adequate intakes of vitamin C, selenium, and copper may reduce other types of protein cross-linkages
Free-radical theory	Senescence is due to the cumulative damage caused by various free radicals	Diets and/or supplements rich in vitamins C and E, selenium, and antioxidant phytochemicals may limit the cellular accumulation of free radicals
Rate-of-living theory	In general, the higher the species' average basal metabolic rate (BMR), the shorter its life span	Theoretically, energy restriction would lower BMR and prolong life (see the Nutrition Debate on pages 726–727)

that aging follows a biologically driven time line, similar to that of adolescence. In programmed theories of aging, nutrition has little, if any, potential or practical impact on senescence. For example, there is no doubt that genes exert tremendous influence on the aging process. Siblings of centenarians are four times more likely to live into their 90s than others. Researchers have even found a genetic mutation dubbed the "I'm Not Dead Yet" gene, which prolongs the life span of certain laboratory animals. Although researchers may never develop a "fountain of youth," they are well on their way to understanding how genetics contributes to cell senescence and human aging.

The second category includes the **error theories of aging,** which argue that senescence occurs as a result of cell and tissue damage caused largely by environmental insults. These mechanisms include the following:

- As cells age, cell membrane function declines, allowing waste products to accumulate within the cell and decreasing normal uptake of nutrients and oxygen.[6]
- Gerontologists have also linked the aging process to a progressive accumulation of free radicals, which are known to damage DNA and various cell proteins.
- Cellular aging has also been linked to a progressive failure in DNA repair.[6] Throughout the life cycle, human DNA is subjected to various insults including free radicals, toxins, and random coding errors. Normally, the cell detects and repairs damaged DNA. With aging, however, the repair process becomes less efficient, leading to abnormal protein synthesis, which then results in cell, tissue, and organ senescence.
- Tissue and organ senescence has been linked to the process of **glycosylation.** This abnormal attachment of glucose to proteins results in loss of protein structure and function. As a result, lung tissue, blood vessels, and tendons become rigid and inflexible.

error theories of aging   Aging is a cumulative process determined largely by exposure to environmental insults; the fewer the environmental insults, the slower the aging process.

glycosylation   Addition of glucose to blood and tissue proteins; typically impairs protein structure and function.

Changes identified by the error theories of aging are directly or indirectly linked to nutrient or energy status. Thus, consumption of adequate levels of antioxidant nutrients could theoretically delay some of these changes.

In truth, the programmed and error theories of aging are not mutually exclusive: It is likely that aging stems from a complex interplay of the factors identified in Table 18.1.

Characteristic Physiologic Changes Accompany Aging

Older adulthood is a time in which growth is complete and body systems begin to slow and degenerate. If the following discussion of this degeneration seems disturbing or depressing, remember that the changes described are at least partly within an individual's control. For instance, some of the decrease seen in muscle mass, bone mass, and muscle strength is due to low physical activity levels. Older adults who regularly participate in strengthening exercises and aerobic-type activities reduce their risks for low bone mass and muscle atrophy and weakness, which in turn reduces their risk for falls.

Age-Related Changes in Sensory Perception

For most individuals, eating is a social and pleasurable process; the sights, sounds, odors, and textures associated with food are closely linked to appetite. Odor, taste, tactile, and visual perception all decline with age; as they do, an older adult's food intake and nutritional status can decline as well.

As people age, their ability to smell foods can decrease.

More than half of elderly adults experience significant loss of olfactory (odor) perception, a condition more common than loss of taste perception.[7] The enjoyment of food relies heavily on the sense of smell: Think of your own response to the smell of bread baking in the oven or the aroma of grilled meat or poultry. Older adults who cannot adequately appreciate the appealing aromas of food may be unable to fully enjoy the foods offered within the meal. Loss of olfaction also restricts the ability to detect spoiled food, increasing the risk of food poisoning. Although often a simple consequence of aging, loss of odor perception can also be caused by zinc deficiency or occur as a side effect of medication. If this is the case, a zinc supplement or change of medication may be a simple solution.

With increasing age, taste perception dims as well, which is one reason why older adults seem to add so much salt to their foods or complain about the blandness of their foods. The ability to perceive sweetness and sourness also declines, but to a lesser extent. Some elderly experience **dysgeusia,** or abnormal taste perception, which can be caused by disease or medication use. For example, an elderly person might experience the sensation of bitterness from a freshly cooked piece of chicken that others would find perfectly enjoyable.

Loss of visual acuity has unexpected consequences for the nutritional health of the elderly. Many older adults have difficulty reading food labels, including nutrient information. Driving skills decline, limiting the ability of some older Americans to acquire healthy, affordable foods. Older adults with vision loss may not be able to see the temperature knobs on stoves or the controls on microwave ovens and may therefore choose cold meals, such as sandwiches, rather than meals that require heating. The visual appeal of a colorful, attractively arranged plate of food is also lost to visually impaired elderly, further reducing their desire to eat healthful meals.

Friends and family members can help older adults adjust to these sensory losses by encouraging appropriate food selections and preparation techniques. Flavor enhancers such as herbs and spices, meat concentrates, and sauces can increase the desirability of otherwise bland foods. Visual enhancements such as brightly colored garnishes and an array of different shapes and textures on the plate can compensate for diminished olfaction. Some older adults experience an increase in appetite from sipping a small glass of wine, which can be healthful if the person has no disease or medication restrictions or history of alcohol abuse.

Age-Related Changes in Gastrointestinal Function

Significant changes in the mouth and gastrointestinal tract occur with aging.[8] Some of these changes have the potential to increase the risk of nutrient deficiency.

dysgeusia Abnormal taste perception.

With increasing age, salivary production declines. In older adults with **xerostomia,** teeth are more susceptible to decay, chewing and swallowing become more difficult, and taste perception declines. A diet rich in moist foods including fruits and vegetables, sauces or gravies on meats, and high-fluid desserts such as puddings is well tolerated by older adults with xerostomia. In the most severe cases, older adults can use an artificial saliva, which is sprayed into the mouth.

Some older adults, including those with Parkinson disease, experience **dysphagia** (difficulty swallowing foods). Smooth, thick foods such as cream soups or applesauce are easy to swallow but foods with mixed textures, such as gelatin with fruit pieces, should be avoided. Milkshakes, fruit nectars, and other thick or viscous beverages are better tolerated than thin liquids such as water and coffee. Dysphagia requires professional assessment and treatment, drawing upon the expertise of an occupational therapist, a physician, and a dietitian. If not accurately diagnosed and treated, dysphagia could lead to malnutrition, inappropriate weight loss, aspiration of food or fluid into the lungs, and pneumonia.

Older adults are at risk for a reduced secretion of gastric acid, intrinsic factor, pepsin, and mucus.[9] **Atrophic gastritis** contributes to bacterial overgrowth and gastric inflammation. **Achlorhydria,** a severe reduction in gastric hydrochloric acid production, limits the absorption of minerals such as calcium, iron, and zinc and food sources of folic acid and vitamin B_{12}. Lack of intrinsic factor, produced by the same cells that secrete gastric hydrochloric acid, reduces the absorption of vitamin B_{12} (see Chapter 12). These elderly, therefore, benefit from vitamin B_{12} supplements. Older adults may also experience a delay in gastric emptying, resulting in a prolonged sense of fullness and a reduced appetite. Although this may be viewed as a positive factor in people who are overweight or obese, it can lead to inappropriate weight loss.

Compared with younger adults, healthy elderly demonstrate no significant loss in digestive enzyme activity, the ability to absorb nutrients, or intestinal motility. Therefore, healthy elderly generally digest and absorb protein, fat, and carbohydrate as efficiently as younger adults. The one exception is the digestion of lactose: Only about 30% of older adults retain an "adequate" level of lactase enzyme activity. African American, Hispanic, Native American, and Asian elderly are at very high risk for lactose intolerance and may need to restrict their fluid milk intake to 1/2-cup servings, use lactose-reduced milk or lactase enzyme supplements, or eliminate milk from their diet entirely. Although tolerance for dairy foods may decrease with aging, the need for calcium does not. Older adults may need to turn to calcium-fortified fruit juices and cereals, calcium-enriched tofu, and other sources to ensure an adequate intake. Finally, although gastrointestinal (GI) function remains largely unaffected by aging, nutrient availability may be severely compromised if an older adult has a disease of the liver, pancreas, or GI tract that impairs digestion of food and absorption of nutrients.

Age-Related Changes in Body Composition

With aging, body fat increases and muscle mass declines. It has been estimated that women and men lose 20% to 25% of their lean body mass, respectively, as they age from 35 to 70 years. Decreased production of certain hormones, including testosterone and growth hormone, and chronic diseases contribute to this loss of muscle, as does poor diet and an inactive lifestyle. Older adults with **sarcopenia** are often so weak that they are unable to rise from a seated position, climb stairs, or carry a bag of groceries. Along with adequate dietary intake, regular physical activity, including strength or resistance training, can help older adults maintain their muscle mass and strength, delaying or preventing the need for institutionalization.

Body fat increases from young adulthood through middle age, peaking at approximately 55 to 65 years of age. Females experience a sharper increase in percent body fat compared with males. Percent body fat tends to decline in persons over the age of 70 years. With aging, body fat shifts from subcutaneous stores, just below the skin, to internal or visceral fat stores.[10] Older women tend to deposit more fat in their abdominal region compared with younger women; this shift in body fat stores is most dramatic after the onset of

A variety of gastrointestinal and other physiologic changes can lead to weight loss in older adults.

xerostomia   Dry mouth due to decreased saliva production.

dysphagia   Abnormal swallowing.

atrophic gastritis   Destruction of gastric (stomach) secretory glands, resulting in decreased production of mucus, hydrochloric acid, pepsin, and intrinsic factor.

achlorhydria   Lack of gastric acid secretion.

sarcopenia   Age-related progressive loss of muscle mass, muscle strength, and muscle function.

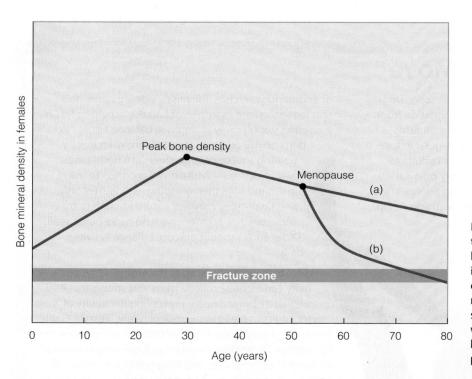

Figure 18.2 Bone mineral density in women tends to decline with aging. **(a)** A healthful lifestyle including optimal diet, physical activity, and possible use of medication slows loss of bone. **(b)** The rapid loss of estrogen with menopause can cause a decrease in bone density and increased risk of bone fracture for women who do not adhere to a regimen of healthful lifestyle, diet, physical activity, and possibly medication.

menopause and coincides with an increased risk for heart disease, diabetes, and metabolic syndrome. Older men are also at higher risk for increases in abdominal fat as they age. Maintaining an appropriate energy intake and remaining physically active can help keep body fat to a healthful level.

An increasing number of elderly are at risk for **sarcopenic obesity,** which is strongly associated with frailty, disability, and inability to perform normal activities of daily living.[11] While total body weight and body fat are increased in these persons, their underlying muscle mass is not adequate in amount or strength to support normal mobility and health.

Bone mineral density declines with age and may eventually drop to the critical fracture zone. Among older women, the onset of menopause leads to a sudden and dramatic loss of bone due to the lack of estrogen (**Figure 18.2**). Although less dramatic, elderly males also experience loss of bone due in part to decreasing levels of testosterone. The nutrients recognized as essential to optimal bone health are identified in Chapter 11. As noted in the Highlight box, "Seniors on the Move" on page 706, bone health can be promoted through regular weight-bearing activity in adults well into their nineties and beyond.

Age-Related Changes in Organ Function

Aged organs are less adaptable to environmental or physiologic stressors. Young adults, for example, readily adapt to varying levels of fluid and sodium intakes because of the kidney's ability to maintain fluid balance. With increasing age, however, the kidneys lose their ability to concentrate waste products, leading to an increase in urine output and greater risk of dehydration. The aging liver is less efficient at breaking down drugs or alcohol, and the aging heart lacks the endurance to sustain a sudden increase in physical activity. The pancreas is less precise in regulating blood glucose levels, and bladder control may decline with aging. In most instances, older adults can adapt to these age-related changes through minor lifestyle adjustments such as eating meals and snacks on a regular basis and ensuring an adequate fluid intake.

As a result of abnormal protein cross-linkages, connective tissues and blood vessels become increasingly stiff. Joint pain, elevated blood pressure, and impaired blood flow are typical consequences. The skin of older adults can become thin, dry, and fragile. Bruises and skin tears are very common and are slow to heal. The growth of nails slows and hair loss is common among elderly males and females. Although some of these consequences are

sarcopenic obesity A condition in which increased body weight and body fat mass coexist with inappropriately low muscle mass and strength.

Highlight

Seniors on the Move

Although this chapter began with an optimistic scene from a competition for Masters Athletes, recent information from the Centers for Disease Control and Prevention confirms that relatively few older adults participate in regular leisure-time physical activity.[12] On average, only 21% of adults 65 years and older maintain a routine of voluntary physical activity, while only 13% engage in strengthening activity, such as resistance training. Participation declines with advancing age, with fewer than 10% of very elderly (85 years and older) engaging in regular physical activity.[12]

For a minor investment of time and energy, older adults reap benefits worth literally thousands of dollars in reduced healthcare costs. A regular program of physical activity lowers the risk of heart disease, hypertension, type 2 diabetes, obesity, depression, and cognitive decline or dementia.[13] The complications of arthritis can also be reduced with appropriate exercise, as can the risk of falls and bone fractures. The need for healthcare visits, diagnostics, medication, and other treatments to control blood glucose, serum cholesterol, blood pressure, and other factors in chronic illness can be reduced or eliminated with regular exercise.

Physically active elders live longer and enjoy better health while they live. Muscular strength and total daily energy expenditure are independently associated with lower risk of death among the elderly.[14, 15] The level of activity needed to improve health is not even that great: both moderate- and even light-intensity activity greatly reduce risk of type 2 diabetes, and as little as 72 minutes of activity per week enhances fitness levels in older women.[16–18] Older adults should plan an activity program that includes four basic types of exercises:

■ **Flexibility exercises:** These activities "set the stage" for other forms of exercise by stretching the muscles and improving range of motion. Gentle arm swings, ankle circles, and torso twists are examples of moves that can slowly increase flexibility. Such exercises can be done while sitting in a chair, standing, or even while in a shallow pool. Ideally, older adults should stretch every day of the week.

■ **Balance exercises:** Balance is important in reducing the risk of falls. Older adults should also have confidence in their ability to maintain balance before starting strength or endurance exercises. Toe raises, side leg raises, and rear leg swings are examples of balance activities; *Tai Chi* is another popular way to improve balance. Fitness experts advise adults to start balance exercises by holding a table or large chair with both hands; with practice, individuals will progress to using one hand only, then grasping with fingers only, and finally they may feel secure enough to try some balance activities with no hand-holds at all. Older adults should practice balance activities daily.

■ **Strength or resistance training:** This type of activity can increase muscle mass and strength as well as enhance bone density, preserving the ability of older adults to maintain an independent lifestyle. Gains in muscle strength also improve balance and provide the foundation for endurance exercise. A growing number of retirement communities and long-term care centers offer "weight rooms" where strength training equipment is available. Community centers, including congregate meal sites, offer strength training using cans of food, gallon bottles of water, and other common items; the exercises are designed for mobile and chair-bound elders. Ideally, older adults should engage in resistance training 2 to 3 days a week.

■ **Endurance or aerobic exercise:** Activities such as brisk walking, bicycle riding, swimming, and dancing increase heart rate and improve cardiorespiratory function. These activities should be low impact (no jump ropes or high-impact aerobics classes!) to minimize risk to aging bones, joints, and muscles. Older adults should aim for an intensity perceived as "fairly light" to "somewhat hard"—a level that is challenging but not exhausting. As with resistance training, older adults should check with their healthcare provider before starting on a program of endurance exercise. Once given approval, they should try to take part in aerobic activities at least 3 days each week for 30 or more minutes a day.

Some seniors may be vulnerable to exercise-related complications such as dehydration, heat stress, fractures, or falls. Exercise rooms should offer appropriate temperature, ventilation, and lighting; participants should wear appropri-

ate clothing and comfortable shoes; and supervised warm-up and cool-down periods should be incorporated into each activity. As always, a thorough medical exam is advised prior to the start of programmed exercise.

The benefits of regular physical activity by older adults almost always far outweigh potential risks—the payoff is better health, more independence, less disability, and a longer, happier life!

---

simply cosmetic and represent no disease risk, the skin's tendency to bruise and tear may increase the risk of infection. A diet rich in vitamins C and A, zinc, copper, and protein may reduce the severity of bruising in some elderly.

The number of neurons in the brain decreases with age, impairing memory, reflexes, coordination, and learning ability. Whereas some believe that dementia is an inevitable part of the aging process, a healthful diet, regular physical activity, and other lifestyle choices can promote cognitive functioning.

What Lifestyle Factors Accelerate Aging?

The way we live greatly influences the way we age. Whereas chronologic age is immovable, **biologic age** can be greatly influenced by personal choices and decisions. It is now possible to predict one's biologic age through a series of scored questions related to smoking habits, alcohol consumption, sun exposure, weight status, level of physical activity, and other factors. A similar approach is used to estimate potential longevity.[19]

In addition to causing a variety of cancers, direct or secondhand exposure to cigarette and cigar smoke accelerates the aging process; inhalation of the thousands of toxins found in smoke impairs lung function, damages the cardiovascular system, increases the risk for osteoporosis, and impairs taste and odor perception. Smoking also causes premature facial wrinkling and impairs dental health. Older adults should be reminded that it is never too late to quit; improvements in taste perception, physical endurance, and lung function can be detected within weeks of smoking cessation.

Excessive consumption of alcohol also speeds up the aging process by interfering with nutrient intake and utilization, injuring the liver, increasing risk for osteoporosis, and contributing to accidental injuries and deaths (see the *In Depth* discussion on alcohol, pages 154–164). These effects are cumulative over the years, so the earlier the alcohol abuse begins, the greater the damage to body systems.

Sunlight exposure is the primary risk factor for age-related discoloration and thinning of the skin as well as skin cancer. Although its use decreases skin production of vitamin D, most healthcare providers recommend lifelong use of sunscreen in order to limit sun-induced skin damage. See the Nutrition Debate in Chapter 17 for more information.

Maintaining a normal weight is associated with healthy and successful aging. Excess body weight, at any age, speeds up the deterioration of joints, increasing the risk of osteoarthritis and contributing to functional limitations.[20] In addition, successful control of blood glucose—in part through weight management—can delay the glycosylation of blood and tissue proteins. When people with diabetes fail to control their blood glucose levels, they experience chronic hyperglycemia and develop complications that seem to mimic the aging process. Obesity also accelerates age-related declines in cardiovascular health. For more information, see Chapter 13.

Lack of physical activity accelerates loss of muscle mass and bone density, increases risk of falls, and impairs the ability to perform simple activities of daily living.[13] The Highlight box "Seniors on the Move" describes the benefits of regular physical activity in the elderly.

Sunlight exposure over a lifetime can lead to discoloration and thinning of the skin in old age.

biologic age Physiologic age as determined by health and functional status; often estimated by scored questionnaires.

Recap

The U.S. population continues to age at an unprecedented rate. The very elderly, 85 years and above, represent the fastest-growing segment of the U.S. population. Scientists are beginning to understand some of the basic cellular changes that contribute to aging and how diet and nutrition might influence the aging process. With aging, sensory perception declines, muscle mass is lost, fat mass increases, bone density decreases, and nutrient metabolism is impaired. Body organs can lose functional capacity and are less tolerant of stressors. These age-related changes influence the nutritional needs of older adults and their ability to consume a healthful diet. Tobacco use, alcohol abuse, excessive sun exposure, overweight, and inactivity accelerate the aging process.

What Are an Older Adult's Nutrient Needs?

As you can see by reviewing the DRI tables in the back of the book, the requirements for many nutrients are the same for older adults as for young and middle-aged adults. A few nutrient requirements increase, and a few are actually lower. Table 18.2, page 710, identifies nutrient recommendations that change with age, as well as the physiologic reason behind these changes.

Energy Needs of Older Adults

The energy needs of older adults are lower than those of younger adults because loss of muscle mass and lean tissue results in a lower basal metabolic rate, and most older adults have a less physically active lifestyle. It is estimated that total daily energy expenditure decreases approximately 10 kcal each year for men and 7 kcal each year for women ages 19 and older.[21] This means that a woman who needed 2,000 kcal at age 20 needs just 1,650 kcal at age 70. Some of this decrease in energy expenditure is an inevitable response to aging, but some of the decrease can be delayed or minimized by staying physically active.

Because their total daily energy needs are lower, older adults need to pay particularly close attention to consuming a diet high in nutrient-dense foods but not too high in energy in order to avoid weight gain. The Tufts Modified MyPyramid for Older Adults is a helpful guide to food choices for this population (**Figure 18.3**).

Benjamin Franklin once noted, "To lengthen thy life, lessen thy meals." Refer to the Nutrition Debate at the end of this chapter to learn more about the theory of energy restriction, which proposes that energy-restricted diets may significantly prolong the human life span.

Macronutrient Recommendations for Older Adults

Because there is no evidence suggesting a minimal amount of dietary fat needed to maintain health, there is no DRI for total fat intake for older adults.[21] However, to reduce the risk for heart disease and other chronic diseases, it is recommended that total fat intake remain within 20% to 35% of total daily energy intake, with no more than 10% of total energy intake coming from saturated fat. Dietary sources of *trans* fatty acids should be kept to a minimum.

The RDA for carbohydrate for older adults is 130 g/day.[21] As with all other age groups, this level of carbohydrate is sufficient to support glucose utilization by the brain. There is no evidence to indicate what percentage of carbohydrate should come from sugars or starches. However, it is recommended that older individuals consume a diet that contains no more than 25% of total energy intake as sugars.[21] The fiber recommendations are slightly lower for older adults than for younger adults because older adults consume less energy. After age 50, 30 g of fiber per day for men and 21 g per day for women is assumed sufficient to reduce the risks for constipation and diverticular disease, maintain

Modified MyPyramid for Older Adults

Figure 18.3 The Tufts Modified MyPyramid for Older Adults highlights the need for fluids, physical activity, and supplemental calcium and vitamins B$_{12}$ and D by the elderly. (*Data from:* © Tufts University.)

healthful blood levels of glucose and lipids, and provide good sources of nutrient-dense, low-energy foods.

The DRI for protein is the same for adults of all ages: 0.8 g of protein per kilogram body weight per day.[21] Although some researchers have argued for a higher protein allowance for older adults in order to optimize protein status, a recent study confirmed no apparent difference in the protein requirement between healthy elderly and younger adults.[22] Protein is critically important in helping reduce the loss of muscle and lean tissue,[23] maintaining immunity, enhancing wound healing and disease recovery, and helping to prevent excessive loss of bone. Protein-rich foods are also important sources of vitamins and minerals that are typically low in the diets of older adults.

Micronutrient Recommendations for Older Adults

The vitamins and minerals of particular concern for older adults are identified in Table 18.2. Preventing or minimizing the consequences of osteoporosis is a top priority for older adults. The requirements for both calcium and vitamin D are higher than for younger adults because of a reduced absorption of calcium from the gut, along with an age-related reduction in the production of vitamin D in the skin. An increasing number of older adults are at risk for vitamin D deficiency because they are institutionalized and are not exposed to adequate amounts of sunlight. Others may limit intake of milk and dairy products due to lactose intolerance or perceived concerns over the fat content of these foods. Older adults

A less physically active lifestyle leads to lower total energy requirements in older adults.

Table 18.2 Nutrient Recommendations That Change with Increased Age

Changes in Nutrient Recommendations	Rationale for Changes
Increased need for vitamin D from 5 µg/day for young adults to 10 µg/day for adults 51 to 70 years and to 15 µg/day for adults over age 70 years.	• Decreased bone density • Decreased ability to synthesize vitamin D in the skin
Increased need for calcium from 1,000 mg/day for young adults to 1,200 mg/day for adults 51 years of age and older.	• Decreased absorption of dietary calcium • Decreased bone density
Decreased need for fiber from 38 g/day for young men to 30 g/day for men 51 years and older. Decreases for women are from 25 g/day for young women to 21 g/day for women 51 years and older.	• Decreased energy intake
Increased need for vitamin B_6. Need for vitamin B_{12} *from fortified foods or supplements*, as opposed to foods of animal origin.	• Lower levels of stomach acid • Decreased absorption of food B_{12} from gastrointestinal tract • Increased need to reduce homocysteine levels and to optimize immune function
Decreased need for iron from 18 mg/day for young women to 8 mg/day for women 51 years and older. No change in iron recommendations for men 51 years and older.	• Cessation of menstruation in women; some loss of muscle and lean tissue in men and women

living in the community are also at risk for vitamin D deficiency due to the widespread use of sunscreen; these creams and lotions are important to prevent skin cancer, but they block the sunlight needed for vitamin D synthesis in the skin. It is critical that older adults consume foods that are high in calcium and vitamin D and, when needed, use vitamin D supplements.

Iron needs decrease with aging as a result of reduced muscle mass in both men and women and the cessation of menstruation in women. The decreased need for iron in older men is not significant enough to change the recommendations for iron intake in this group; thus, the RDA for iron is the same for older men as for younger, 8 mg/day. The RDA for iron in older women is also 8 mg/day, but this represents a significant decrease from the 18 mg/day RDA for younger women. Although zinc recommendations are the same for all adults, zinc is especially critical for optimizing immune function and wound healing in older adults. Intakes of both zinc and iron can be inadequate in older adults if they do not regularly eat red meats, poultry, and fish. These foods are relatively expensive, and older adults on a limited income cannot afford to eat them regularly. Also, the loss of teeth and/or use of dentures may increase the difficulty of chewing meats.

Although it is speculated that older adults have increased oxidative stress, the recommendations for vitamin C and vitamin E are the same as for younger adults because there is insufficient evidence that consuming amounts higher than the current RDA has any additional health benefits.[24] Researchers continue, however, to investigate the potential benefits of dietary or supplemental antioxidants, including vitamins C and E, and the roles they may play in lowering the risk of cataracts and age-related macular degeneration (see Chapter 10).[25]

Older adults need to pay close attention to consuming adequate amounts of the B-vitamins, specifically vitamin B_{12}, vitamin B_6, and folate. As discussed in detail in Chapters 8 and 10, inadequate intakes of these nutrients increases the level of the amino acid homocysteine in the blood, a state that has been linked to elevated risk of age-related dementia, including Alzheimer's disease, and loss of cognitive function in the elderly.[26] The RDA for vitamin B_{12} is the same for younger and older adults; however, up to 30% of older adults cannot absorb enough vitamin B_{12} from foods due to atrophic gastritis (see page 712). It is recommended that older adults consume foods that are fortified with vitamin B_{12} or take B_{12} supplements, because the vitamin B_{12} in these products is absorbed more readily. Vitamin B_6 recommendations are slightly higher for older adults, as these higher levels appear necessary to reduce homocysteine levels and optimize immune function in this population.[27]

Vitamin A requirements are the same for adults of all ages; however, older adults should be careful not to consume more than the RDA, as absorption of vitamin A is actually greater in older adults. The elderly are at greater risk for vitamin A toxicity, which can cause liver damage and neurologic problems. However, consuming foods high in beta-carotene or other carotenoids is safe and does not lead to vitamin A toxicity.

A variety of factors may limit an older adult's ability to eat healthfully. Limited financial resources may prevent some older people from buying nutrient-dense foods on a regular basis; others may experience a reduced appetite, social isolation, inability to prepare foods, or illnesses that limit nutrient absorption and metabolism. Thus, some older adults benefit from taking a multivitamin and multimineral supplement that contains no more than the RDA for each nutrient. Additional supplementation may be necessary for nutrients such as calcium, vitamin D, and vitamin B_{12}. However, supplementation with individual nutrients should be done only under the supervision of the individual's primary healthcare provider, as the risk of nutrient toxicity is high in this population. The accompanying Highlight box, "Supplements for Seniors," reviews the advantages and potential disadvantages of selecting a commercial product designed specifically for older adults.

Fluid Recommendations for Older Adults

The AI for fluid is the same for all adults. Men should consume 3.7 L (about 15.5 cups) of total water per day, which includes 3.0 L (about 13 cups) as total beverages, including drinking water. Women should consume 2.7 L (about 12.7 cups) of total water per day, which includes 2.2 L (about 9 cups) as total beverages, including drinking water. In general, the elderly do not perceive thirst as effectively as do younger adults. Thus, they are at increased risk for chronic dehydration and hypernatremia (elevated blood sodium levels). Some older adults will intentionally limit their beverage intake because they have urinary incontinence or do not want to be awakened for nighttime urination. This practice can endanger their health, so it is important for these individuals to seek treatment for the incontinence and continue to drink adequate fluids.

Older adults need the same amount of fluid as other adults.

RECAP

Older adults have lower energy needs due to their loss of lean tissue and lower physical activity levels. They should consume 20% to 35% of total energy as fat and 45% to 65% as carbohydrate. Protein recommendations are currently the same as for younger adults, although some research suggests the need for slightly higher intakes. Micronutrients of concern for older adults include calcium, vitamin D, the B-vitamins, and the antioxidants. Older adults are at risk for chronic dehydration and hypernatremia, so ample fluid intake should be encouraged.

Gustavo
Nutri-Case

"I don't believe in taking vitamins. If you eat good food, you get everything you need and it's the way nature intended it. My daughter kept nagging at my wife and me to start taking B-vitamins. She said when people get to be our age, they have problems with their nerves if they don't. I didn't fall for it, but my wife did, and then her doctor told her she needed calcium pills and vitamin D, too. The kitchen counter is starting to look like a medicine chest! You know what I think? I think this whole vitamin thing is just a hoax to get you to empty your wallet."

Would you support Gustavo's decision to avoid taking a B-vitamin supplement? Given what you have learned in previous Nutri-Cases about Gustavo's wife, would you support or oppose her taking a B-vitamin, calcium, or vitamin D supplement? Explain your choices.

Highlight

Supplements for Seniors

Consumers have thousands of different options when shopping for nutritional supplements. Even if looking for a "simple" multivitamin/multimineral (MVMM) supplement, there are many targeted products, including those formulated specifically for seniors. How do these senior (or "silver") products differ from other MVMM products? Are they actually better for seniors or just a marketing ploy? A close look at such products yields some interesting information.

Although every product line has its own unique formulation, a side-by-side comparison of the nutrients in a typical "adult" MVMM supplement with those in a "senior" MVMM product from the same manufacturer reveal very few differences. Of the thirty-three nutrients in the adult product, two (iron and tin) are omitted from the senior supplement, one (vitamin K) is provided at a lower dosage, three (calcium and vitamins E and B$_6$) are included at slightly higher levels, and one (vitamin B$_{12}$) is four times higher in the senior supplement. Although not all of these product modifications reflect age-specific DRI values (see the inside cover of this book for DRI values), there are good reasons for most of these product adjustments. As you compare the product labels, remember that the U.S. Food and Drug Administration (FDA) uses "% Daily Value" to describe nutrient levels, not the newer DRI recommendations.

Although the DRI for vitamin E does not change for males or females ages 19 to 70 years or above, there is good evidence that older adults are often in a state of "oxidative stress." Chronic inflammation, as occurs with arthritis and other conditions, is more common among older adults than younger populations and may increase the need for antioxidants such as vitamin E. In addition, as previously discussed, there is preliminary, but inconsistent, research supporting the use of vitamin E in lowering the risk of age-associated eye disorders and dementia. Knowing that vitamin E has a relatively low risk of toxicity, the small increase provided in the senior supplement certainly poses no harm.

As with vitamin E, the DRI for vitamin K does not change with increased age. Why then, does the senior supplement provide a lower dose? Persons on anticoagulant drugs, many of them elderly, are advised to tightly regulate vitamin K intake. By minimizing the amount of vitamin K in the senior supplement, there would be less risk of a negative drug–nutrient interaction among seniors taking both the MVMM supplement and anticoagulant drugs. Some physicians might consider even 13% of the vitamin K Daily Value to be too much, so it would be important for each senior to

Many supplements are targeted for the elderly.

check with his or her doctor before using a MVMM with any vitamin K.

Although the senior supplement provides about 40 mg more calcium than the more general adult product, that amount does not go very far toward satisfying the DRI guideline of an additional 200 mg calcium per day for adults 51 years and above. Calcium is too "bulky" for most MVMM supplements, so all adults, regardless of their stage of life, should choose a specific calcium supplement (possibly one with vitamin D and/or vitamin K) if their food choices do not provide adequate dietary calcium.

The DRI for vitamin B$_6$ for adults 51 years and older is slightly higher than that for younger adults, and the senior supplement reflects that increase by providing 50% more vitamin B$_6$ than the MVMM product targeting the general adult population. This higher intake may provide additional protection against elevated serum homocysteine, a possible risk factor for heart disease.

As discussed earlier, adults over the age of 50 years often poorly absorb vitamin B$_{12}$ from food sources. Older adults are advised to consume foods that are fortified with vitamin B$_{12}$ or supplements, because the vitamin B$_{12}$ in these sources is absorbed more readily than food sources of vitamin B$_{12}$. Although the DRI recommends a change in the *source* of vitamin B$_{12}$ not in the *amount,* the higher dosage in the senior supplement poses no harm.

What about the omission of iron from the senior supplement? Certainly, iron is a nutrient essential for good health; why would a manufacturer totally omit it from the product? Recall from Chapter 12 that a woman's need for iron decreases dramatically after menopause; most women can easily meet that need from food alone. In addition, risk of iron overload increases with age, particularly in older men; thus, eliminating iron from senior supplements actually lowers the risk of inappropriate iron loading. If an older adult has a specific need for supplemental iron, for example following significant blood loss, his or her physician can recommend an iron-only supplement. Tin is the other mineral eliminated from the senior product; because tin has no Daily Value or DRI, there is no strong justification for including it in the senior supplement.

Each age-specific MVMM product line should be evaluated carefully to determine if the nutrient balance is appropriate for seniors. When consumed with a well-balanced diet, the small but important differences between supplements designed for seniors and supplements designed for middle adults can help seniors obtain the appropriate amounts of all the nutrients that they need.

What Nutritional Concerns Threaten the Health of Older Adults?

In this section, we discuss several common nutrition-related concerns of older adults. As we explore each concern, we will attempt to answer two questions: (1) What, if any, nutrient concerns develop as a result of a specific medical disorder? (2) What, if any, effect does nutrition have on the risk of developing that disorder?

Overweight and Underweight

Not surprisingly, overweight and obesity are of concern to older adults. Over the past decade, forty-nine states reported a significant increase in the number of older adults who were obese.[28] Over the past 20 years, rates of obesity among the elderly have doubled, tripled, or even, for the state of New Mexico, increased four-fold (Table 18.3). The elderly population as a whole has a high risk for heart disease, hypertension, type 2 diabetes, and cancer, and these diseases are more prevalent in older adults who are overweight or obese. Obesity increases the severity and consequences of osteoarthritis, limits the mobility of elderly adults, and is associated with functional declines in daily activities.[20] In contrast, overweight can be protective against osteoporosis and fall-related fractures in older adults.

Although some healthcare providers may question the necessity or value of attempting treatment at the age of 70 or 75 years, even moderate weight loss in obese elderly can improve functional status.[29] The interventions for obese elderly are the same as for younger and middle-aged adults: use of dietary modifications to achieve an energy deficit while retaining adequate nutrient intakes; gradual and medically appropriate initiation of physical activity; and culturally appropriate behavior modification. The benefit of bariatric (weight-loss) surgery for this population is not clear. Obese elderly experience more complications, remain in the hospital longer, and have a higher rate of in-hospital deaths following bariatric surgery compared to younger adults.[30]

As we noted in Chapter 13, mortality rates are higher in adults who are underweight (BMI below 18.5) compared with people who are overweight (see Figure 13.2 on page 488). Significantly underweight older adults have fewer protein reserves to call upon during periods of catabolic stress, such as after surgery or after trauma, and are more susceptible to infection. Inappropriate weight loss suggests inadequate intake of both energy and nutrients.

Table 18.3 Change in Rates of Obesity Among Elderly (age 65 and up) over 20 Years: Selected States

State	1985–1987 Rate (%)	2005–2007 Rate (%)
Alabama	8.1	22.4
California	7.3	20.0
Florida	6.8	19.6
Georgia	13.1	23.1
Hawaii	6.6	13.6
Massachusetts	9.0	18.3
Minnesota	10.5	23.6
Montana	7.5	20.4
New Hampshire	5.9	21.5
New Mexico	3.9	17.2
New York	10.0	23.6
South Dakota	17.5	22.1
Texas	9.6	21.7
Utah	7.7	21.9
Washington	14.3	21.6

Data adapted from: Levi, J., S. Vinter, L. Richardson, R. St. Laurent, and L. M. Segal. 2009. *F as in Fat: How Obesity Policies Are Failing in America, 2009.* Washington, DC: Trust for America's Health.

Figure 18.4   The nine Ds of geriatric weight loss: Many factors contribute to inappropriate weight loss in the elderly.

Chronic deficiencies of protein, vitamins, and minerals leave older adults at risk for poor wound healing and a depressed immune response.

Because underweight is so risky for elders, geriatric weight loss is an important healthcare concern. Gerontologists have identified nine "Ds" that account for most cases of geriatric weight loss (**Figure 18.4**). Several of these factors promote weight loss by reducing energy intake. They include drugs that decrease appetite, and eating impairments such as dementia, poor dentition, dysgeusia, dysphagia, and dysfunction. Depression, which is common after the death of family members and friends or when adult children move out of the area, also contributes to reduced food intake. Treatment of inappropriate weight loss in the elderly is often a complex and lengthy process, relying on behavioral, medical, and psychological interventions.

In summary, any of the nine Ds can promote underweight, nutrient deficiencies, and frailty, significantly increasing the risk of serious illnesses, injuries, and death. A condition known as **geriatric failure-to-thrive,** also called "the dwindles," characterizes the complexity of age-related weight loss.

Osteoporosis

Osteoporosis was discussed in detail in Chapter 11. It is estimated that about 10 million U.S. adults have osteoporosis.[31] Among women, it is typically diagnosed within a few years of menopause as estrogen levels sharply decline. Due in part to a higher peak bone density, the onset in males is usually delayed until their 70s or 80s and is linked to declining testosterone levels, steroid therapy, and alcohol abuse.[32] Men with osteoporosis are less likely to be diagnosed or treated for osteoporosis compared to women, although the medical community is now more aware of and responsive to the problem in men.

One of the most serious risks associated with osteoporosis is that of hip fracture; about 30% of all hip fractures now occur in men.[32] Close to 20% of elderly women and almost 40% of elderly men will die within 1 year of their hip fracture; males have a higher mortality rate due to the fact that they are typically much older at the time of fracture.[32]

Many options are available for the treatment of osteoporosis, including a combination of vitamin D and calcium supplementation, strength or resistance training, and medications (see Chapter 11). In addition, it is important to minimize an older adult's risk of a fall-induced fracture by assessing vision and balance, evaluating the need for a cane or walker, surveying the home environment for hazards, and reviewing medications.

Arthritis

Arthritis is one of the most prevalent chronic diseases among the elderly, affecting as many as half of all adults over the age of 65. It can affect one or multiple joints, cause pain on a daily or intermittent basis, and limit range of motion of one or more joints. The two most common forms of arthritis among the elderly are osteoarthritis and rheumatoid arthritis.

Osteoarthritis has been called a disease of "wear and tear." People with arthritis who are overweight or obese are strongly advised to lose weight and to participate in water exercise or other acceptable forms of physical activity. Pain medications and anti-inflammatory drugs may be prescribed. In extreme cases, hip or knee replacement surgery is required in order to reestablish normal mobility and function.

geriatric failure-to-thrive   Inappropriate, unexplained loss of body weight and muscle mass; usually results from a combination of environmental and health factors.

Rheumatoid arthritis (RA) typically strikes younger adults and is not associated with obesity or overuse syndromes. It often affects both hands, wrists, or knees. Because many people with RA are underweight, the nutritional goals focus on appropriate weight gain and a healthful, balanced intake of all nutrients. A wide range of medications is used to treat RA, but some of these interfere with nutrient utilization.

Arthritic adults may turn to nontraditional treatments. Glucosamine has shown some promise in relieving the symptoms of osteoarthritis;[33] however, the majority of herbs, oils, and other dietary products touted as cures for arthritis are ineffective and can be very expensive. An appropriate balance of physical activity and rest, a healthful diet, and use of physician-monitored medications are the most effective and safest treatments currently available.

Rheumatoid arthritis often affects the hands.

Constipation

Although constipation is four to eight times more common in older adults than in younger adults, elderly who are healthy and physically active are not at greater risk.[9] Certain medications, chronic diseases, laxative abuse, and possibly low fiber and fluid intakes contribute to risk of constipation, as does immobility, for instance with wheelchair- or bed-bound elderly. Initial treatment usually revolves around dietary intervention: increased fluid intake and an emphasis on insoluble fiber from foods such as wheat bran. However, medication may be necessary, especially in patients with underlying disease. Use of laxatives by older adults should be monitored by a healthcare provider.

Dental Health Issues

Diet and nutritional status play important roles in the maintenance of dental health in the elderly. A lack of adequate calcium, vitamin D, protein, vitamin C, and the B-vitamins all worsen dental health. As described earlier, saliva production decreases with age, increasing the risk of dental decay. Older adults should be counseled on the importance of a healthful diet in maintaining good oral health.

Despite great advances in dental health over the past several decades, older adults remain at high risk for losing some or all of their teeth, suffering from gum disease, or having poorly fitting dentures, which cause mouth pain and make chewing difficult. Thus, older adults may avoid eating healthful foods such as meats and firm fruits and vegetables. Older adults can select soft protein-rich foods such as eggs, peanut butter, cheese, yogurt, ground meat, fish, and well-cooked legumes. Red meats and poultry can be stewed or cooked in liquid for a long period of time. Oatmeal and other whole-grain cooked cereals can provide needed fiber as will berries, canned corn, bananas, and ripened melons. Shredded and minced raw vegetables can be added to dishes. With planning, older adults with oral health problems can maintain a varied, healthful diet.

Age-Related Eye Diseases

As discussed in Chapter 10, cataracts cause cloudiness in the lens that impairs vision. The condition affects 20% of adults in their 60s and almost 70% of those in their 80s. Another eye disorder, called age-related macular degeneration (AMD), is the most common cause of blindness in U.S. elderly (see Figure 10.22 on page 387). Although these are different conditions, sunlight exposure and smoking are lifestyle practices that increase the risk of each.

Recent research suggests, but does not definitively prove, that dietary choices may slow the progress of these two degenerative eye diseases, saving millions of dollars and preventing or delaying the functional losses associated with impaired vision. Several studies have shown beneficial effects of antioxidants, including vitamins C and E, on cataract formation, whereas others reported no significant benefit.[25] Two phytochemicals, lutein and zeaxanthin, have also been identified as protective by some, but not all, studies.[34] These four antioxidants, as well as zinc, may also provide protection against AMD. Although the research is not yet conclusive, older adults can benefit by consuming foods rich in these nutrients,

Older adults can benefit from the antioxidants and phytochemicals available in colorful fruits and vegetables.

Medications taken by older adults can interact with nutrients.

primarily colorful fruits and vegetables, nuts, and whole grains. Vision-enhancing nutrient supplements remain an unproved therapy.

Dementia

Between 20% and 40% of very elderly adults (85 years and older) have Alzheimer's disease, a slow yet progressive form of dementia. An unknown number of very elderly are afflicted by other forms of dementia and cognitive impairment. As with other age-related disorders, lifelong dietary choices may influence risk and, once in place, the conditions have a significant effect on food intake and nutrient status.

Some research suggests that long-term intake of antioxidants such as vitamin E and certain unsaturated fatty acids may lower risk of dementia and cognitive decline.[35] Elevated serum homocysteine, linked to deficiencies of folate and vitamin B_{12}, has also been linked to Alzheimer's disease and dementia.[36] Mid-life obesity also increases the risk of cognitive decline.[37] These studies emphasize the critical importance of consuming a balanced, healthful diet throughout life.

Dementia is one of the "nine Ds" of geriatric weight loss. Odor and taste perception are often significantly impaired, and many people with dementia refuse to eat. Alzheimer's disease can trigger agitation and pacing, increasing energy expenditure. As the disease progresses, the person loses the ability to manipulate utensils and eventually even to swallow.

Helping people with dementia to eat adequately can be challenging. Finger foods, such as cut-up fruit, cheese or meat cubes, vegetable slices, and small pieces of bread, can be eaten without utensils. Between-meal snacks and liquid nutritional supplements can also improve dietary intake. A multivitamin, multimineral supplement may be necessary.

Interactions Between Medications and Nutrition

Although the elderly account for less than 15% of the U.S. population, they buy 30% of all prescription medication. A recent survey concluded that 30% of U.S. elderly used more than five prescription medications at once, a condition termed **polypharmacy**.[38]

Prescription drugs interact not only with each other but also with nutrients (Table 18.4). Some medications affect appetite, either increasing or decreasing food intake, and others alter nutrient digestion and absorption. Several drugs negatively affect the activation or metabolism of nutrients such as vitamin D, folate, and vitamin B_6, and others increase the kidney's excretion of nutrients. For example, older adults taking the blood-thinning drug warfarin (Coumadin) should avoid consuming excess vitamin E, as vitamin E magnifies the effects of this drug. Both ibuprofen (Advil or Motrin) and acetaminophen (Tylenol) are commonly prescribed for muscle, joint, and headache pain, but taking these drugs with alcohol increases the risk for liver damage and bleeding, so alcohol should not be consumed with these medications.

Some medications should be taken before or between meals, whereas others are best utilized when taken with meals. Foods as diverse as grapefruit juice, spinach, and aged cheese are known to react negatively with specific drugs. Pharmacists and registered dietitians are able to provide information on such drug–food interactions and can give recommendations on dietary choices and the potential need for nutrient supplements. All older adults should be counseled on the potential for drug–food, drug–nutrient, and drug–supplement interactions.

Use of Supplements

Should older adults use supplements? If so, what types? Are there risks associated with supplement use?

In establishing the DRI for vitamin B_{12} for men and women over the age of 50 years, the Institute of Medicine stated, "It is advisable for most of this amount to be obtained by consuming foods fortified with B_{12} or a B_{12} containing supplement."[27] This is the first time

polypharmacy Concurrent use of five or more medications.

Table 18.4 Examples of Common Drug–Nutrient Interactions

Category of Drug	Common Nutrient/Food Interactions
Antacids	May decrease the absorption of iron, calcium, folate, vitamin B_{12}
Antibiotics	May reduce the absorption of calcium, fat-soluble vitamins; reduce the production of vitamin K by gut bacteria
Anticonvulsants	Interfere with the activation of vitamin D
Anticoagulants ("blood thinners")	Oppose the clotting activity of vitamin K
Antidepressants	May cause weight gain as a result of increased appetite
Antiretroviral agents (treatment of HIV/AIDS)	Reduce the absorption of most nutrients
Aspirin	Decrease blood folate levels; increase loss of iron due to gastric bleeding
Diuretics	Some types may increase urinary loss of potassium, sodium, calcium, magnesium; others cause retention of potassium and other electrolytes
Laxatives	Increase fecal excretion of dietary fat, fat-soluble vitamins, calcium, and other minerals

that this agency specifically acknowledged and supported the use of a nutrient supplement as an adjunct to a healthful diet. The Tufts Modified MyPyramid for Older Adults (see Figure 18.3 on page 709) recommends routine use of vitamin B_{12} supplements, along with supplements of calcium and vitamin D. Beyond these guidelines, use of nutrient supplements by the elderly should be encouraged under the following conditions:

- When the amount and/or variety of food is so restricted that nutrient intake is probably deficient
- If the older adult eats fewer than two meals per day or limits food choices because of dental problems
- Whenever there are lifestyle or functional limitations that prevent adequate food intake
- If the older adult suffers from depression, dementia, social isolation, or extreme poverty
- If the older adult has a disease that impairs nutrient status or could be relieved by nutrient supplementation
- If the older adult has osteoporosis, gastrointestinal diseases, or anemia

While there is little risk associated with a broad-spectrum supplement (see the Highlight box, "Supplements for Seniors"), high-potency nutrient supplements can pose real risks to the elderly. Older adults are more vulnerable to high-potency vitamin A supplements than younger adults, especially if they abuse alcohol. Vitamin D is also extremely toxic at high levels of intake, and megadoses of vitamin C can produce diarrhea and cramping. Inappropriate supplementation with iron leads to its accumulation in the liver, pancreas, and other soft tissues, particularly in middle-aged and older men.

Nontraditional supplements such as herbs (e.g., *Ginkgo biloba*, St. John's wort, black cohosh, evening primrose), food derivatives (e.g., flaxseed oil, grapeseed extract, garlic, lecithin), and metabolic compounds (e.g., lipoic acid, coenzyme Q-10, dehydroepiandrosterone [DHEA]) have grown in popularity during the past decade. More than 20% of adults on prescription medication also use nontraditional dietary supplements,[39] and are therefore at risk for potentially harmful drug–supplement interactions.

Up to 70% of older adults do not tell their healthcare providers about their use of nontraditional dietary supplements, even when scheduled for surgery.[39] All healthcare providers should ask their clients about supplement use, discuss possible advantages and potential risks, and refer them to reliable sources of information on supplement use.

Osteoporosis, dental problems, arthritis, vision disorders, GI distress, and age-related dementia are examples of "two-way streets" in which nutritional status influences an older adult's risk for the condition, and the condition itself has the potential to influence nutritional status. An older adult's nutritional status and intake can also influence the effectiveness of certain medications, and many of the drugs used by the elderly contribute to nutrient deficiencies. Appropriate use of nutrient supplements can enhance the nutritional status of older adults; however, use of herbal and other nontraditional supplements, including high-potency vitamin or mineral supplements, should be discussed with a healthcare provider.

Isolation and other social problems can affect an older adult's nutritional status.

What Social Concerns Affect the Nutrition of Older Adults?

We have explored the physical conditions that affect an older adult's nutritional status and needs, but social factors play a role as well. These include elder abuse and neglect, food insecurity, and social isolation.

Elder Abuse and Neglect

It has been estimated that up to 2 million U.S. elderly are abused by their spouse, children, neighbors, or paid caretakers each year.[40] Elder abuse can be physical, sexual, emotional, financial, neglectful, or unintentional. Denial of healthful food and adequate fluid falls within the scope of elder abuse and neglect. Although it may be difficult to detect, possible signs of such abuse include fear of the caregiver, anxiety, increased depression, and a desire for death. Home-bound elderly may demonstrate new health problems, unexplained weight loss, dehydration and malnutrition, poor personal hygiene, and suspicious physical injuries. Older adults without a trusted relative or friend may need to turn to a healthcare provider, court representative, or social service agency for protection. Every state and local municipality has laws against elder abuse and can offer assistance if abuse or neglect is suspected. More information is available from the National Center on Elder Abuse (www. ncea.aoa.gov).

Food Insecurity Among the Elderly

Food insecurity occurs when a family is not able to ensure a consistent, dependable supply of safe and nutritious food.[41] "Very low food security" is a more severe economic state in which the family actually experiences reduced food intake and disruption of normal eating patterns. It is estimated that approximately 7% of elderly men and women in the United States experience some form of food insecurity at least once during the course of a year.

Older adults cope with food insecurity in several ways. Some make use of federal or local food assistance programs such as the Supplemental Nutrition Assessment Program (formerly termed *Food Stamp Program*), discussed shortly. A small number turn to food banks or food pantries for short-term assistance. Elderly adults can be embarrassed by their inability to provide for themselves and may resort to stealing food or going without adequate food.

The most common cause of food insecurity and hunger among older adults is lack of income and poverty. Older adults in poverty often live in areas with few or no supermarkets, may not be able to afford transportation to buy healthful food, and may fear leaving their home to shop for groceries. Their homes may lack working refrigerators and/or stoves, limiting the types of foods that can be bought, stored, and prepared. Healthcare and social service providers should carefully probe for information on the ability of low-income elders to afford an adequate and healthful food supply.

The Impact of Social Isolation

Older adults may become socially isolated for many reasons. Those who are restricted to bed or wheelchairs, have impaired walking, or are in poor health are prone to isolation even if they live in a household with others. The death of a spouse can precipitate isolation, especially among the very old who have also lost siblings and friends.

Lack of adequate transportation also increases the risk of isolation. Family members or friends may not always be able to offer rides, and even where public transportation is available, older adults may be concerned about cost and personal safety. Even if government-funded vans or buses are available for the elderly, transportation may be limited to weekdays and certain hours of the day.

Among minority elderly, particularly recent immigrants with language barriers, isolation can occur after the death of a bilingual spouse or as bilingual children move out of the household. These adults may lack the communication skills to navigate public transportation, shop, and secure social services. Ideally, communities with large immigrant populations can provide translators to help integrate these elderly into the community at large.

Social isolation increases the risk for alcohol and substance abuse, depression, and malnutrition. Personal healthcare habits decline, household maintenance is put off, and behavior becomes increasingly erratic. Isolated older adults are at high risk for victimization, such as telephone scams, and premature institutionalization. Religious, neighborhood, and social service agencies offer many programs to ensure that older adults are not forgotten within their homes.

Community Services Can Help Meet the Nutritional Needs of Older Adults

As the American population continues to age, greater demands are placed on social service agencies. This section identifies several programs available for older adults in need.

Community Nutrition Programs for Older Adults

The federal government has developed an extensive network of food and nutrition services for older Americans. Some are open to people of all ages, whereas others are restricted to people 60 years of age and up. Many are coordinated with state or local governments and community organizations. They include the following:

- *Supplemental Nutrition Assistance Program(SNAP):* This U.S. Department of Agriculture (USDA) program, formerly known as the *Food Stamp Program,* provides food assistance for low-income households. Participants are provided with a monthly allotment, typically as a prepaid debit card. There are very few restrictions on the foods that can be purchased under this plan.
- *Child and Adult Care Program:* This program provides healthy meals and snacks to older and functionally impaired adults in qualified adult day-care settings.
- *Commodity Supplemental Food Program:* This program targets low-income pregnant women, infants and young children, and older adults. Income guidelines must be met. Specific commodity foods are distributed, including cereals, peanut butter, dry beans, rice or pasta, and canned juice, fruits, vegetables, meat, poultry, and tuna. Unlike SNAP, this program is not intended to provide a complete array of foods.
- *Nutrition Services Incentive Program:* The Administration on Aging provides cash and commodity foods to state agencies for meals for senior citizens. There is no income criteria; any person 60 years or above (plus their spouse, even if younger) can take part in this program. Although free, participants are encouraged to contribute what they can to cover meal costs. Lunch meals, designed to provide one-third of the RDA for key nutrients, are served at senior centers, churches, and other sites. Some provide "bag dinners" for evening meals, and others send home meals on Fridays for weekend use.

For home-bound disabled and older adults, community programs such as Meals on Wheels provide nourishing, balanced meals as well as vital social contact.

Meals also can be delivered to the homes of qualified elders through the Meals on Wheels Association of America program.

- *The Emergency Food Assistance Program:* The USDA distributes commodity foods to state agencies for use by food banks, food pantries, and soup kitchens. Each state or agency establishes eligibility criteria, if any. The elderly are more likely to use the services of food banks and local food pantries while avoiding soup kitchens.

Participation in these community programs improves the dietary quality and nutrient intakes of older adults. Unfortunately, many programs have long waiting lists and are unable to meet current demands. As the number of elderly adults grows, the demand and need for these essential services will continue to increase.

Serving Minority Elderly

In 2006, approximately 20% of U.S. elderly were classified as racial or ethnic minorities, a ratio that will increase to 40% by 2050.[42] The changing profile of the U.S. elderly population will require adaptations in current medical and social service interventions. For example, members of certain minority groups are at a greater risk for nutrition-related chronic diseases and their complications compared with non-Hispanic whites: Hispanics have higher rates of diabetes; African Americans experience greater rates of stroke, kidney failure, high blood pressure, colon cancer, and glaucoma; and Native Americans are at higher risk for diabetes, obesity, and alcohol abuse. Dietary counseling and other therapies can be used to lower the risk of such chronic diseases and for their treatment. In order to meet the needs of minority elderly, nutrition professionals must develop an awareness of the cultures they serve, maintain flexibility in foods/meals provided or prescribed, and work toward effective communication with their minority clients.

End-of-Life Care

End-of-life care can be provided to elderly individuals who are terminally ill.

Advances in medical care can prolong the lives of seriously ill persons, resulting in challenging legal and ethical issues. Healthcare providers must be well informed on end-of-life issues, including the provision of food and fluids, in order to help elderly clients and families make difficult decisions that honor the client's personal wishes. Ideally, an advance directive such as a living will is available to guide decision making.

The legalities surrounding end-of-life care are in continual flux as courts and legislative bodies enact, then modify, decisions on enteral nutrition (tube feeding), hydration, and other nutritional issues. Religious and cultural considerations often overlay legal issues, contributing to their complexity.

Healthcare providers, with agreement from the patient and/or appropriate legal authority, can provide **palliative care** to terminally ill individuals. With palliative care, no attempt is made to cure or treat the underlying condition; the care provided is designed primarily to minimize patient discomfort, offer social and spiritual support, and extend assistance to family and friends. Individuals who are facing imminent death rarely express hunger and have little or no thirst. If requested, specific foods or fluids are provided, even if they have no nutritional value, to comfort the patient. Hospice organizations are growing in number and availability and can provide palliative care to terminally ill individuals, either in their own home or in a care facility.

palliative care Reducing an individual's pain and discomfort without any attempts at treatment or cure.

RECAP

Approximately 7% of U.S. elderly experience food insecurity. Disease, disability, death of a spouse, lack of transportation, and language barriers increase the risk for social isolation, which in turn increases the risk for malnutrition. Many social service agencies and programs exist to help older Americans with nutritional needs.

Minority elderly present additional challenges, such as overcoming language barriers and providing culturally appropriate foods. As older adults face end-of-life decisions, healthcare providers must be ready to assist them and their families with difficult decisions related to the provision of food and fluid.

See for Yourself

Are Meal Supplement Drinks Appropriate for Everyone?

You've probably seen the ad on TV: an animated bottle displaying the name of a national brand of a meal supplement beverage struts his stuff among the fruits and veggies inside a fridge. But are his boasts about boosting our health on the level?

For decades, meal supplement drinks have been important in providing adequate energy and nutrients to frail elders and others who are unable to obtain sufficient nutrition via solid foods. But now, manufacturers of these beverages are marketing them to the general public. Do such drinks provide benefits to average consumers beyond the benefits of traditional foods and drinks costing less? Or are they a waste of money? See for yourself by taking the following steps:

1. Go to your local grocer and check out the Nutrition Facts Panel of either the Ensure or Boost brands of nutritional drinks. Or check out the nutrition information provided on their Web sites. Note the kcals, grams of protein, and micronutrients per serving that the drink provides. Focus on the micronutrients discussed in this chapter as important for older adults, such as calcium, vitamin D, and so on.

2. Now take a look at the ingredients list. Specifically, note the first four ingredients listed. Bear in mind that, as you learned in Chapter 2, ingredients must be listed in order of quantity, with the ingredient of greatest quantity first. Does anything about the composition of the beverage surprise you? If so, what?

3. Next, jot down the cost per serving of the beverage.

4. Finally, list the corresponding nutrient data, and the cost, for the same serving size of skim milk.

Summarize your research findings, addressing the following questions: Are meal supplement beverages cost-effective ways of improving our nutrient intake? Would you feel comfortable recommending that your older relatives consume such beverages regularly instead of a glass of milk or a small snack containing some of their favorite foods? Why or why not?

Chapter Review

Test Yourself | Answers

1 (F) Experts agree it is unlikely that the human life span will increase much beyond 125 to 130 years.

2 (T) Older adults are more likely to lose their sense of smell than their sense of taste; however, loss of smell reduces the sense of taste.

3 (T) Because of an age-related decrease in gastric acid production, older adults are advised to get most of their vitamin B_{12} from supplements or fortified foods.

4 (F) Older men and women need less iron due to their loss of muscle mass, and older women require less iron due to the cessation of menstruation.

5 (T) On average, 7% of older Americans experience food insecurity at least once each year.

Summary

- The U.S. population is aging at an unprecedented rate, including minority elderly. The very elderly, 85 and above, are the fastest-growing segment of the U.S. population; the numbers of centenarians and super-centenarians (over age 110) also continue to climb.

- The physiological changes of aging include sensory declines, loss of muscle, increased fat mass, decreased bone density, and impaired ability to absorb and metabolize nutrients. Body organs lose functional capacity. These changes influence the nutritional needs of older adults and their ability to consume a healthful diet.

- Scientists are learning about various genetic and biochemical factors that contribute to senescence. Tobacco use, alcohol abuse, excessive sun exposure, overweight, and inactivity accelerate the aging process.

- Older adults need less energy, but some research suggests the need for slightly higher intakes of protein.

- Micronutrients of concern for older adults include calcium, vitamin D, the B-vitamins, and the antioxidants. Iron needs decrease.

- Older adults are at risk for chronic dehydration, so ample fluid intake should be encouraged.

- Nutritional status influences an older adult's risk for osteoporosis, dental problems, arthritis, vision problems, GI distress, and dementia; these conditions have the potential to influence nutritional status as well.

- An older adult's nutritional status and intake can alter the effectiveness of medications; many drugs used by the elderly contribute to nutrient deficiencies. Appropriate use of supplements can enhance the nutritional status of older adults; however, certain herbal and other nontraditional supplements, including high-dose single supplements, can be dangerous.

- Social issues affecting the nutrition of older adults include elder abuse and neglect, food insecurity, and social isolation.

- Demands on social service agencies increase as the population ages. As older adults face end-of-life decisions, healthcare providers must be ready to assist them and their families with difficult decisions related to the provision of food and fluid.

Review Questions

1. Which of the following nutrients is needed in increased amounts in older adulthood?
   a. Fiber
   b. Vitamin D
   c. Vitamin A
   d. Iron

2. Abnormal taste perception is clinically known as
   a. dysgeusia.
   b. dysphagia.
   c. dysphasia.
   d. dysphonia.

3. Currently, the human life span is
   a. about 74 years.
   b. about 78 years.
   c. 114 years.
   d. 122 years.

4. Which of the following conditions results in defective protein cross-linkages and loss of tissue structure and function?
   a. Xerostomia
   b. Macular degeneration
   c. Glycosylation
   d. Achlorhydria

5. Providing cookies and lemonade to a terminally ill patient is an example of
   a. long-term care.
   b. geriatric care.
   c. palliative care.
   d. inappropriate care.

6. **True or false?** According to programmed theories of aging, nutrition has little, if any, potential or practical impact on disease, disability, or mortality.

7. **True or false?** Percentage of body fat typically continues to increase throughout an individual's entire life span.

8. **True or false?** Mortality rates are higher in underweight elderly than in overweight elderly.

9. **True or false?** The Institute of Medicine recommends that older adults obtain the DRI for vitamin B_{12} by consuming foods fortified with B_{12} or a B_{12}-containing supplement.

10. **True or false?** Older adults who regularly participate in strengthening and aerobic exercises have a reduced risk for fractures.

11. Identify four nutrient deficiencies that may arise from atrophic gastritis.

12. State two reasons why a recent elderly immigrant from Southeast Asia may experience nutrient deficiencies after the death of her husband.

13. Identify several factors that increase the risk of dehydration in older adults.

14. Describe the nutritional counseling you would provide to a male client who is 86 years old and
    - eats only two meals per day: cold cereal with milk for breakfast and canned soup, crackers, and canned peaches or pears for dinner;
    - takes a daily antioxidant supplement containing levels of vitamins A, E, and C and selenium about five times higher than the DRI for these micronutrients;
    - drinks three beers every night so he can "sleep better."

15. Marta and her parents live in Dallas. A year ago, her maternal grandmother, who lives in Boston, stayed with them for several weeks after the death of Marta's grandfather. She seemed fit at the time, going for walks and cooking large meals for the family throughout her stay. Last night, Marta's mother received a phone call from a Boston hospital saying that her mother had been admitted after a hip fracture suffered in a fall at home and was battling significant dehydration and some cognitive impairment as well. Identify several factors that might have contributed to Marta's grandmother's condition.

Web Links

www.aarp.org
AARP
A national advocacy group for the elderly; adults 50 years and above can join this organization of 35 million older Americans. The Web site has links to articles focusing on all aspects of health, finances, housing, and legal issues that are of importance to the elderly.

www.aoa.gov
Administration on Aging
Follow legislative updates on this Web site for information related to Congregate Meal and Meals on Wheels programs. Also provided are resources on Alzheimer's disease, elder rights and resources, housing, and elder nutrition.

www.cdc.gov
The Centers for Disease Control and Prevention
Select "Health Promotion" and choose topics such as "Aging & Elderly Health" for accurate information on the health of America's seniors.

http://familydoctor.org
The American Academy of Family Physicians
By selecting the "seniors" tab on the site's homepage, readers can find a thorough discussion of advance directives, living wills, and "do not resuscitate" orders.

www.fns.usda.gov/fns
Food & Nutrition Service, U.S. Department of Agriculture
This site provides information on federal programs for low-income elderly such as the Nutrition Services Incentive Program.

www.nia.nih.gov
The National Institute on Aging
The National Institute on Aging provides information about how older adults can benefit from physical activity and good diet.

www.nihseniorhealth.gov
NIH Senior Health
This Web site, written in large print, was developed for older adults and offers up-to-date information on popular health topics for older Americans.

References

1. U.S. Census Bureau. 2008. Population by age and sex: 2008. Available at www.census.gov/population/www/socdemo/age/general-age.html#older. (Accessed July 2009.)

2. Lubitz, J., L. Cai, E. Kramarow, and H. Lentzner. 2003. Health, life expectancy, and health care spending among the elderly. *NEJM* 349:1048–11055.

3. Centers for Disease Control and Prevention. 2008. Deaths: Preliminary data for 2006. *National Vital Statistics Report,* Volume 56, No. 16.

4. Olshansky, S. J. 2005. A potential decline in life expectancy in the United States in the 21st century. *N. Engl. J. Med.* 352:1138–1145.

5. Young, R. D. 2009. GRG Tables on Supercentenarians. Available at www.grg.org/calment.html (Accessed July 2009.)

6. Weinert, B. T., and P. S. Timiras. 2003. Physiology of aging: Invited review: Theories of aging. *J. Appl. Physiol.* 95:1706–1716.

7. Duffy, V. B., and A. K. Chapo. 2006. Smell, taste, and somatosensation in the elderly. In: R. Chernoff, ed., *Geriatric Nutrition: The Health Professional's Handbook* (pp. 115–162), 3rd ed. Sudbury, MA: Jones and Bartlett Publishers.

8. Moskovitz, D. N., J. Saltzman, and Y. I. Kim. 2006. The aging gut. In: R. Chernoff, ed., *Geriatric Nutrition: The Health Professional's Handbook* (pp. 233–272), 3rd ed. Sudbury, MA: Jones and Bartlett Publishers.

9. Dryden, G. W., and S. A. McClave. 2004. Gastrointestinal senescence and digestive diseases of the elderly. In: C. W. Bales and C. S. Ritchie, eds. *Handbook of Clinical Nutrition and Aging* (pp. 569–582). Totowa, NJ: Humana Press.

10. Zamboni, M., G. Mazzali, F. Fantin, A. Rossi, and V. DiFrancesco. 2007. Sarcopenic obesity: A new category of obesity in the elderly. *Nutr., Metab., Cardiovascular Dis.* 18:388–395.

11. Jarosz, P. A., and A. Bellar. 2008. Sarcopenic obesity: An emerging cause of frailty in older adults. *Ger. Nursing* 30:64–70.

12. Schoenborn, C. A., and K. M. Heyman. 2009. Health characteristics of adults aged 55 years and over: United States 2004–2007. *National Health Statistics Reports,* Number 16. Hyattsville, MD: National Center for Health Statistics.

13. Chodzko-Zajko, W. 2009. Successful aging: The role of physical activity. *Am. J. Lifestyle Med.* 3:20–28.

14. Ruiz, J. R., X. Sui, F. Lobelo, J. R. Morrow Jr., A. W. Jackson, M. Sjostrom, and S. N. Blair. 2008. Association between muscular strength and mortality in men: Prospective cohort study. *Brit. Med. J.* 337:a439.

15. Manini, T. M., J. E. Everhart, K. V. Patel, D. A. Schoeller, L. H. Colbert, M. Visser, F. Tylavsky, D. C. Bauer, B. H. Goodpaster, and T. B. Harris. 2006. Daily activity energy expenditure and mortality among older adults. *JAMA* 296:171–179.

16. Jeon, C. Y., R. P. Lokken, F. B. Hu, and R. M. van Dam. 2007. Physical activity of moderate intensity and risk of type 2 diabetes: A systematic review. *Diabetes Care* 30:744–752.

17. Healy G. N., D. W. Dunstan, J. Salmon, E. Cerin, J. E. Shaw, P. Z. Zimmet, and N. Owen. 2007. Objectively measured light-intensity physical activity is independently associated with 2-h plasma glucose. *Diabetes Care* 30:1384–1389.

18. Church, T. S., C. P. Earnest, J. S. Skinner, and S. N. Blair. 2007. Effects of different doses of physical activity on cardiorespiratory fitness among sedentary, overweight or obese postmenopausal women with elevated blood pressure: A randomized controlled trial. *JAMA* 297:2081–2091.

19. Life Expectancy Calculator. Available at http://moneycentral.msn.com/investor/calcs/n_expect/main.asp. (Accessed July 2009.)

20. Zoico, E., V. DiFrancesco, J. M. Guralnik, G. Mazzali, A. Bortolani, S. Guariento, G. Sergi, O. Bosello, and M. Zamboni. 2004. Physical disability and muscular strength in relation to obesity and different body composition indexes in a sample of healthy elderly women. *International J. Obesity* 28:234–241.

21. Institute of Medicine, Food and Nutrition Board. 2002. *Dietary Reference Intakes for Energy, Carbohydrates, Fiber, Fat, Protein and Amino Acids (Macronutrients).* Washington, DC: The National Academy of Sciences.

22. Campbell, W. W., C. A. Johnson, G. P. McCabe, and N. S. Carnell. 2008. Dietary protein requirements of younger and older adults. *Am. J. Clin. Nutr.* 88:1322–1329.

23. Houston, D. K., B. J. Nicklas, J. Ding, T. B. Harris, F. A. Tylavsky, A. B. Newman, J. Sun Lee, N. R. Sahyoun, M. Visser, and S. B. Kritchevsky for the Health ABC Study. 2008. Dietary protein intake is associated with lean mass change in older, community-dwelling adults: The Health, Aging, and Body Composition (Health ABC) Study. *Am. J. Clin. Nutr.* 87:150–155.

24. Institute of Medicine, Food and Nutrition Board. 2000. *Dietary Reference Intakes for Vitamin C, Vitamin E, Selenium, and Carotenoids.* Washington, DC: National Academy Press.

25. Chiu, C. J., and A. Taylor. 2007. Nutritional antioxidants and age-related cataract and maculopathy. *Experimental Eye Research* 84:229–245.

26. Haan, M. N., J. W. Miller, A. E. Aiello, R. A. Whitmer, W. J. Jagust, D. M. Mungas, L. H. Allen, and R. Green. 2007. Homocysteine, B-vitamins, and the incidence of dementia and cognitive impairment: Results from the Sacramento Area Latino Study on Aging. *Am. J. Clin. Nutr.* 85:511–517.

27. Institute of Medicine, Food and Nutrition Board. 1998. *Dietary Reference Intakes for Thiamin, Riboflavin, Niacin, Vitamin B_6, Folate, Vitamin B_{12}, Pantothenic Acid, Biotin, and Choline.* Washington, DC: National Academy Press.

28. Levi, J., S. Vinter, L. Richardson, R. St. Laurent, and L. M. Segal. 2009. *F as in Fat: How Obesity Policies Are Failing in America, 2009.* Washington, DC: Trust for America's Health.

29. Villareal, D. T., M. Banks, D. R. Sinacore, C. Siener, and S. Klein. 2006. Effect of weight loss and exercise on frailty in obese older adults. *Arch. Intern. Med.* 166: 860–866.

30. Varela, J. E., S. E. Wilson, and N. T. Nguyen. 2006. Outcomes of bariatric surgery in the elderly. *Am. Surg.* 72:865–869.

31. Burge, R., B. Dawson-Hughes, D. H. Solomon, J. B. Wong, A. King, and A. Tosteson. 2007. Incidence and economic burden of osteoporosis-related fractures in the United States, 2005–2025. *J. Bone Mineral Res.* 22:465–475.

32. Ebeling, P. R. 2008. Osteoporosis in men. *NEJM* 358:1474–1482.

33. Thakral, R., U. K. Debnath, and C. Dent. 2007. Role of glucosamine in osteoarthritis. *Current Orthopaedics* 21:386–389.

34. Bartlett, H. E., and F. Eperjesi. 2008. A randomized controlled trial investigating the effect of lutein and antioxidant dietary supplementation on visual function in healthy eyes. *Clinical Nutr.* 27:218–227.

35. Del Parigi, A., F. Panza, C. Capurso, and V. Solfrizzi. 2006. Nutritional factors, cognitive decline, and dementia. *Brain Res. Bull.* 69:1–19.

36. Clarke, R. 2008. B-vitamins and prevention of dementia. *Proc. Nutr. Soc.* 67:75–81.

37. Whitmer, R. A., E. P. Gunderson, E. Barrett-Connor, C. P. Quesenberry Jr., and K. Yaffe. 2005. Obesity in middle age and future risk of dementia: A 27-year longitudinal population based study. *Brit. Med.* Cited as doi:10.1136/bmj.38446.466238.EO.

38. Qato, D. M., G. C. Alexander, R. M. Conti, M. Johnson, P. Schumm, and S. T. Lindau. 2008. Use of prescription and over-the-counter medications and dietary supplements among older adults in the United States. *JAMA* 300:2867–2878.

39. Gardiner, P., R. E. Graham, A. T. R. Legedza, D. M. Eisengerg, and R. S. Phillips. 2006. Factors associated with dietary supplement use among prescription medication users. *Arch. Intern. Med.* 166:1968–1974.

40. McNamee, C. C., and M. B. Murphy. 2006. Elder abuse in the United States. *National Institute of Justice Journal* 255:16–21.

41. Nord, M., M. Andrews, and S. Carlson. 2008. Household Food Security in the United States, 2007. U.S.D.A. Economic Research Service Report No. (ERR-66). Available at www.ers.usda.gov/publications/err66/. (Accessed July 2009.)

42. Federal Interagency Forum on Aging-Related Statistics. 2008. *Older Americans 2008: Key Indicators of Well Being.* Federal Interagency Forum on Aging-Related Statistics. Washington, DC: U.S. Government Printing Office.

43. Speakman, J. R., and C. Hambly. 2007. Starving for life: What animal studies can and cannot tell us about the use of caloric restriction to prolong human lifespan. *J. Nutr.* 137:1078–1086.

44. Masoro, E. J. 2005. Overview of caloric restriction and aging. *Mechanisms of Ageing and Development* 126:913–922.

45. Wang, C., R. Weindruch, J. R. Fernández, C. S. Coffey, P. Patel, and D. B. Allison. 2004. Caloric restriction and body weight independently affect longevity in Wistar rats. *Int. J. Obesity* 28(3):357–362.

46. Heilbronn, L. K., and E. Ravussin. 2003. Calorie restriction and aging: Review of the literature and implications for studies in humans. *Am. J. Clin. Nutr.* 78(3):361–369.

47. Heilbronn, L. K., L. de Jonge, M. I. Frisard, J. P. DeLany, D. E. Larson-Meyer, J. Rood, T. Nguyen, C. K. Martin, J. Volaufova, M. M. Most, F. L. Greenway, S. R. Smith, W. A. Deutsch, D. A. Williamson, and E. Ravussin. 2006. Effect of 6-month calorie restriction on biomarkers of longevity, metabolic adaptation, and oxidative stress in overweight individuals: A randomized controlled trial. *JAMA* 295:1539–1548.

48. Holloszy, J. O., and L. Fontana. 2007. Caloric restriction in humans. *Experimental Gerontology* 42:709–712.

49. Varady, K. A., and M. K. Hellerstein. 2007. Alternate-day fasting and chronic disease prevention: A review of human and animal trials. *Am. J. Clin. Nutr.* 86:7–13.

Can We Live Longer by Eating a Low-Energy Diet?

How old do you want to live to be—80 years, 100 years, 120 years? If you were to discover that you could live to be 150 years of age by eating a little more than half of your current energy intake and still be healthy as you age, would you do it? Believe it or not, a growing number of people are already severely limiting their caloric intake in response to studies indicating that low-energy diets can significantly increase the life span of animals.

Current research shows that consuming low-energy diets, a practice known as *caloric restriction* (CR), can significantly extend the life span of small species; until recently, however, most of this research had been done in rats, mice, fish, flies, and yeast cells.[43–45] Primate studies followed, with similar results. Only in the past few years have studies of CR been conducted in humans. The results of these preliminary studies suggest that CR can also improve metabolic measures of health in humans, and thus may be able to extend the human life span.[46, 47]

How might CR prolong life span? The answer to this question is not fully understood, but it is speculated that the reduction in metabolic rate that occurs with restricting energy intake results in a much lower production of free radicals, also known as reactive oxygen species (ROS), which in turn significantly reduces oxidative damage and can prolong life. Caloric restriction also causes marked improvements in insulin sensitivity and results in hormonal changes that contribute to a lower incidence of chronic diseases such as heart disease and diabetes. There is also evidence that CR can alter gene expression, which can reduce the effects of aging and prevent diseases such as cancer. Some of the metabolic effects of CR noted in several, but not all, human studies include:[43, 47, 48]

- Decreased fat mass and lean body mass
- Decreased insulin levels and improved insulin sensitivity; decreased fasting serum glucose
- Decreased core body temperature and blood pressure
- Decreased serum LDL and total cholesterol; increased serum HDL cholesterol
- Decreased energy expenditure, beyond that expected for the weight loss that occurred

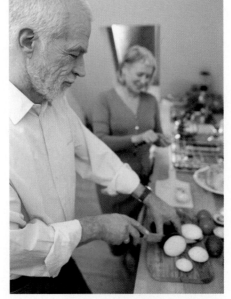

Maintaining a calorically restricted diet that is also highly nutritious requires significant planning and the preparation of most of your own meals.

- Decreased oxidative stress, reduced levels of DNA damage, lower levels of chronic inflammation
- Protective changes in various hormone levels

It is important to emphasize that species that live longer with caloric restriction are fed highly nutritious diets. Unhealthful energy-restriction situations such as starvation, wasting caused by diseases such as cancer, and eating disorders such as anorexia nervosa do not result in prolonged life. In fact, these situations are associated with increased risks for illness and premature death.

Although CR is successful in extending the lives of some animal species, we have at this time only preliminary evidence that this same effect will occur in humans. Studies that can definitively answer this question in humans might never be conducted because of ethical and logistical concerns. Finding enough people to participate in any research study over their entire lifetime would be extremely difficult. In addition, most people find it challenging to follow a caloric-restricted diet for just a few months; compliance with this type of diet for 80 years or more could be almost impossible.[43] Institutional committees that review research studies are hesitant to approve CR research in humans not only because of these logistical problems but also because of the potential risks of malnutrition that could occur. The formation of several voluntary CR groups, including a Caloric Restriction Society, has provided researchers with some data,[48] but there is still very little information on how well and for how long free-living adults actually follow the rigid and extensive demands of CR protocols.[43]

You may be wondering how much less energy you would have to consume to meet the caloric-restriction levels studied in animals. Most studies have found a significant extension of life span when animals are fed 30% to 40% less energy than control animals. A recent assessment estimated that humans would need to restrict their typical caloric intake by at least 20% for 40 years or more in order to gain an additional 4 to 5 years of healthy living. If you are a woman who normally eats about 2,000 kcal/day, a 20% reduction would result in an energy intake of about 1,600 kcal per day. Although this amount of energy reduction does not seem excessive, it is very difficult to achieve this reduction every day over a lifetime—particularly if you live to be 130 years of age!

You must also keep in mind that this diet must be of very high nutritional quality, a requirement that presents a huge number of challenges, including meticulous planning of meals, preparation of most, if not all, of your own foods, limited options for eating meals outside of your home, and the challenge of working the demands of your special diet around the eating behaviors of family members and friends. In addition to the practical barriers of following the CR protocol, there is concern that this type of long-term restriction, initiated in early adulthood, would increase the individual's risk of osteoporosis and prompt inappropriate loss of lean body mass, as well as impair a woman's fertility. Interestingly, most of the mem-

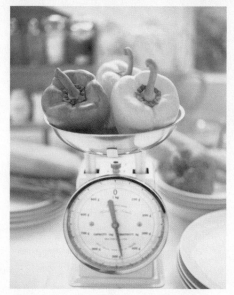

All food must be carefully measured and weighed in a calorie-restricted diet.

bers of the Caloric Restriction Society are men with an average age of 50 years.[48]

An interesting alternative to caloric restriction is the practice of intermittent fasting (IF), also known as every-other-day-feeding (EODF) or alternate-day fasting (ADF). This approach, which does *not* reduce average caloric intake but simply alters the pattern of food intake, has also been shown, in animals, to prolong life span and improve a range of metabolic measures of health.[49] Although not as well studied as caloric restriction, IF has produced beneficial changes in insulin and glucose status, blood lipid levels, and blood pressure in at least some studies.

The debate over the effectiveness of CR in humans will continue as more research is conducted. In the meantime, some people are already consuming diets that are low in energy in the hope that they will live much longer, healthier lives.

A calorie-restricted diet can make family meals challenging.

Critical Thinking Questions

◼ Given the pros and cons noted above, do you think it's advisable to follow a restricted calorie diet? Why or why not?

◼ Are you willing to make the sacrifices necessary to try to prolong your life, even though you can't be sure that CR works in humans?

◼ If research were to eventually show that CR substantially improves health and prolongs life, would you support recommending it on a large-scale basis? Explain your reasoning.

19 Global Nutrition

Test Yourself | True or False?

1   In the United States, more than 10% of the population experiences food insecurity. **T** *or* **F**

2   The major cause of undernutrition in the world is famine. **T** *or* **F**

3   The world is overpopulated. **T** *or* **F**

4   Research suggests that inadequate nourishment during fetal life increases the risk of obesity in adulthood. **T** *or* **F**

5   Once considered a problem affecting only the affluent, obesity is increasingly prevalent worldwide in the poor. **T** *or* **F**

Test Yourself answers are located in the Chapter Review.

Chapter Objectives *After reading this chapter, you will be able to:*

1. Delineate the acute and long-term health problems caused by the three types of malnutrition, *pp. 730–732.*

2. Identify the major global nutrient deficiencies, *pp. 732–734.*

3. Explain how natural disasters and wars can lead to famine, *pp. 735–736.*

4. Describe the nutritional challenges facing transitioning nations, *pp. 735–736.*

5. Discuss several factors that commonly contribute to chronic food shortages, *pp. 736–738.*

6. Discuss the extent of food insecurity in the United States, and identify the populations most affected, *pp. 739–740.*

7. Discuss the achievements of the Green Revolution and the importance of sustainable agriculture in global nutrition, *pp. 742–743.*

8. Discuss the effect of individual actions on the global food supply, *pp. 743–745.*

Hunger and malnutrition are still felt by many in the world today.

I n Sierra Leone, West Africa, a child and her father beg for food. He is blind, and she leads him by the hand through the crowded streets with assurance. Though she looks no more than 5 years old, when asked her age, she says, "I'm 8 or 9. Maybe 10." Her father searches with his hand to stroke his daughter's head. He calls her the strong one. "Her two brothers died, then her mother. Now she takes care of me."

Despite abundant natural resources, including diamonds, gold, and iron, Sierra Leone is one of the poorest countries on earth. Now emerging from a decade of civil war, its physical infrastructure is barely developed, corruption is endemic, and income disparity is extreme. Life expectancy hovers around 40 years, and in 2007 a staggering 262 out of every 1,000 children died before reaching their 5th birthday.[1] Of those who survive, more than one in three will be abnormally small for their age.[2] Tragically, Sierra Leone is not alone in these sobering statistics: throughout West and Central Africa, undernutrition is the cause of more than half of all deaths of children,[3] and from 20% to more than 40% of the total population is hungry.[4]

Despite the advances in food production and preservation you learned about in Chapter 15, many of the world's people still experience hunger and other forms of malnutrition. Why is this so? What causes malnutrition, and what are some solutions? Is there anything you can do in your day-to-day life to combat malnutrition, not only locally but throughout the world? We explore these questions in this chapter.

Why Is Malnutrition a Global Concern?

Throughout this book, you've learned how a nourishing diet contributes to human health and wellness. Adequate nutrient intake helps children to grow at an optimal rate, young adults to be strong and productive, and the elderly to experience less disease and live independently. When adequate and nourishing food either is not available or is not chosen, malnutrition occurs.

Increasingly today, malnutrition is a fiend with two faces. In developing nations, it typically appears in the form of *undernutrition*; that is, people simply don't have enough to eat. In addition, for about the past decade, *overnutrition* has been emerging all over the world, causing rising rates of obesity, and threatening its victims with chronic diseases such as heart disease and type 2 diabetes. Overnutrition is now common not only in developed regions like North America and Western Europe, but also in nations transitioning from the very poorest to the middle range of gross national income, including Brazil, India, and China.

In this chapter, we explore these two forms of malnutrition and explain how they're linked. And if what you read and see on the next few pages spurs you to action, we'll give you plenty of suggestions about how you can fight malnutrition, both globally and in your community.

Undernutrition Causes Acute and Long-Term Health Problems

The Food and Agriculture Organization (FAO) of the United Nations estimates that one in five people in the developing world is chronically undernourished.[5] The prevalence of undernutrition is greatest in sub-Saharan Africa and Southeast Asia, in countries ranging from Liberia to Ethiopia and India to Laos (**Figure 19.1**). Closer to home, parts of Central and South America also experience undernutrition at rates ranging from 16% to 25% of the population (see Figure 19.1).

People who are undernourished suffer more acute and long-term health problems than those who are adequately nourished. Here, we discuss the acute and long-term effects of undernutrition throughout the life cycle (**Figure 19.2**).

Wasting and Stunting

Undernutrition results in **wasting,** a condition of very-low-body-weight-for-height or extreme thinness (**Figure 19.3**). Wasting is a hallmark of **severe acute malnutrition** (SAM), which causes approximately one million preventable deaths annually.[6] Children who are

wasting   A condition of very low body-weight-for-height or extreme thinness.

severe acute malnutrition   A state of extreme energy deficit defined as a weight for height more than 3 standard deviations below the mean or the presence of nutrition-related edema, and associated with a risk of death five to twenty times higher than that of well-nourished individuals.

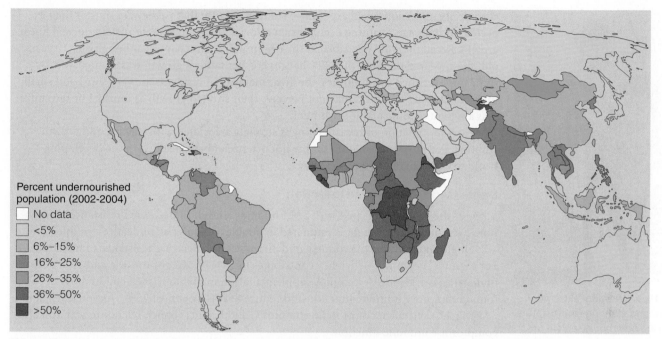

Figure 19.1 Undernutrition occurs throughout the world but is more prevalent in parts of sub-Saharan Africa and Southeast Asia. (*Data from:* Food and Agriculture Organization. Undernourished Population, 2003–2005. Available at www.fao.org/es/ess/faostat/foodsecurity/FSMap/map14.htm. © FAO, 2008.)

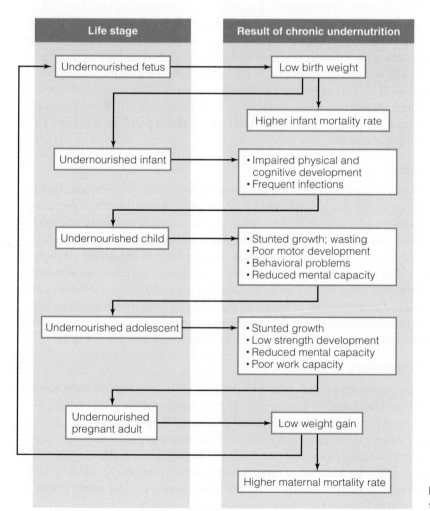

Figure 19.2 Acute and long-term effects of undernutrition throughout the life cycle.

Figure 19.3 Wasting (extreme thinness) and stunting (short stature for age) are commonly seen in undernourished children.

chronically undernourished experience **stunted growth;** that is, they are shorter than expected for their age. Stunting occurs when calories are inadequate to sustain normal linear growth. Recall the child described at the beginning of this chapter: although 8 to 10 years old, she appeared no more than 5. Chances are, her father's growth was stunted, too. In some impoverished communities, the great majority of residents are very short and small; thus, community members may not perceive their stunted growth as unusual or recognize it as a sign of chronic malnourishment.

Early termination of breastfeeding is strongly associated with wasting and growth stunting. For more information on the importance of breastfeeding in the developing world, see the Highlight box, next page.

Decreased Resistance to Infection

Many of the deaths associated with SAM occur as a result of decreased resistance to infection. Even mild underweight is estimated to double a child's risk of death from infection.[7]

Single and multiple micronutrient deficiencies also decrease resistance to infection. For example, vitamin A deficiency contributes to 16% of cases of malaria and 18% of cases of diarrhea worldwide.[7] Vitamin A supplementation in malnourished children has been found to improve immune function and reduce deaths by almost 25%.[8] As you learned in Chapter 12, deficiencies of protein, vitamins C and E, zinc, copper, selenium, and iron also compromise immune function.

Undernutrition and nutrient deficiencies are thought to make individuals more vulnerable to infection by reducing energy reserves and weakening the immune response. Therefore, infections occur more frequently and take longer to resolve. These prolonged infections exacerbate malnutrition by decreasing appetite, causing vomiting and diarrhea, producing weight loss, and further weakening the immune system. A vicious cycle of malnutrition, infection, worsening malnutrition, and increased vulnerability to infection develops.[9] Traditionally, this cycle has been observed with childhood diseases such as measles, diarrheal diseases, and respiratory infections. Today, adults infected with the human immunodeficiency virus (HIV) are more likely to develop acquired immunodeficiency syndrome (AIDS) if they are malnourished, and having AIDS (originally called "thin disease" in Africa) worsens malnutrition.[10] Although HIV/AIDS is a global problem, it is most severe in undernourished populations.

Increased Mortality

We have seen how severe acute malnutrition and its associated vulnerability to infection together increase the mortality rate among children under age 5. In addition, these two interrelated conditions increase by close to 50% the likelihood of **neonatal mortality** (the death of newborns between birth and 28 days of life) and **infant mortality** (the death of infants between birth and 1 year).[11] For example, the infant mortality rate in industrialized countries of Western Europe ranges from about 3 to 5 per 1,000, whereas in countries where malnutrition is endemic, the infant mortality rate can top 100 per 1,000.[12] Not only infants and children, but childbearing women are at increased risk of death from undernutrition. For example, **maternal mortality** (the rate of deaths of women from pregnancy-related causes) in industrialized nations is about 1 in 6,000. In sub-Saharan Africa, the rate is 1 in 22.[13]

Micronutrient Deficiency Diseases

Micronutrient deficiency diseases, such as scurvy, pellagra, goiter, rickets, and night blindness, have largely been eliminated in developed countries because of the great variety of foods available to most people and the fortification of selected foods to prevent a particular deficiency disease. When nutrient deficiency does occur in developed nations, it is usually caused by inadequate selection from available foods and supplements, as, for example, when poverty encourages the selection of inexpensive, nutrient-poor, energy-dense foods.

In impoverished nations, deficiencies of five micronutrients are major public health concerns. These are iron, iodine, zinc, and vitamins A and B_{12}.

stunted growth A condition of shorter stature than expected for chronological age.

neonatal mortality Death rate of newborns between birth and 28 days.

infant mortality Death rate of infants between birth and 1 year.

maternal mortality Death rate of women from pregnancy-related causes, including in the immediate post-partum period.

Highlight

Encouraging Breastfeeding in the Developing World

In the United States and other industrialized nations, the benefits of breast-feeding include its precise correspondence with the infant's nutritional needs, protection of the infant from infections and allergies, promotion of mother–infant bonding, low cost, and convenience. In developing countries, however, breast-feeding may also save the newborn's or mother's life. Here are some reasons why.

It is estimated that a quarter of the earth's population may lack sanitary drinking water. Breast-feeding protects newborns from contaminated water supplies. The least expensive form of infant formula is a packaged powder that must be carefully measured and mixed with a precise quantity of sterilized water. If the water is not sterilized and is contaminated with disease-causing organisms, the baby will become ill.

At the same time, a baby who is fed formula instead of breast milk receives none of the mother's beneficial antibodies; this means that when formula-fed infants do contract an infection, whether from contaminated water or any other source, they are not as well-prepared to fight it off as breast-fed infants would be. As we discuss in this chapter, reduced resistance to infection is extremely dangerous for infants and children throughout the developing world.

In addition, in an attempt to make their supply of formula last longer, some impoverished parents add more water than the amount specified by the manufacturer. In this case, even when the water is sterilized, the child is at risk of

Breastfeeding is highly recommended for developing countries.

malnutrition because the nutrients in the formula are being diluted.

These factors explain why breast-feeding is protective of the infant, but why does it help the mother? First, breast-feeding stimulates the uterus to contract vigorously after childbirth. This reduces the woman's risk of prolonged or excessive postpartum bleeding, a common cause of maternal mortality in developing nations. Second, breastfeeding reduces a woman's risk of developing ovarian and breast cancer. Third, breast-feeding is a natural form of birth control; although not 100% effective as a contraceptive, prolonged, exclusive breast-feeding does delay the onset of ovulation. In regions where access to contraceptives may be lacking, breastfeeding can help a woman to put space between births, giving her body a chance to recover from the physical and metabolic changes of pregnancy, and to nourish her baby adequately without also having to support the development of a growing fetus.

The human immunodeficiency virus (HIV), which causes AIDS, can be transmitted from mother to child via breast milk. For this reason, in areas where sanitary water is available, women with HIV or AIDS may be advised against breastfeeding.*

In summary, international organizations like the World Health Organization and UNICEF encourage all HIV-negative women to breast-feed exclusively until their baby is 6 months of age and to continue supplemented breast-feeding until at least the age of 2.

*World Health Organization. 2007. HIV and infant feeding: Update based on the technical consultation held on behalf of the Inter-agency Task Team (IATT) on Prevention of HIV Infection in Pregnant Women, Mothers and Their Infants, Geneva, October 25–27, 2006. Available at http://whqlibdoc.who.int/publications/2007/9789241595964_eng.pdf.

Iron   Iron deficiency is the most common micronutrient deficiency in the world. Although iron deficiency occurs in both males and females of all ages, it is more prevalent in pregnant women and young children because of their high needs for iron during growth. Contributing factors to low iron intake are poor availability of the non-heme iron in staple foods and the high cost of animal products, the source of highly absorbable heme iron. In addition, blood loss from intestinal worms and other parasites in developing countries increases the need for iron.

Iodine   As noted in Chapter 16, prenatal iodine intake is particularly important for fetal brain development. Severe deficiency leads to irreversible neurological deficits, physical

Meals comprised of adequate, nourishing food are important to avoid nutrient deficiency.

In developing nations, providing vitamin A supplements twice a year to children under age 5 has significantly reduced mortality.

deformities, and mental retardation, a condition known as cretinism. Mild deficits in school-age children lead to impaired cognitive performance and retarded physical development. In 2004, the World Health Organization (WHO) estimated insufficient iodine intake at just over 35% of the general population worldwide.[14] Iodine deficiency disorders have largely been eliminated in areas of the world with access to iodized salt or oil and areas where iodine is added to irrigation water.

Zinc Mild to severe zinc deficiency is estimated to affect about 2.2 billion people worldwide.[7] As we discussed in Chapter 12, severe zinc deficiency impairs growth and sexual maturation and is associated with reduced resistance to infectious diseases such as respiratory tract infections, malaria, and diarrheal diseases. Deficiency is common in populations with low consumption of zinc-rich meats and seafoods and high consumption of either plant foods containing high levels of phytates and fibers, which inhibit zinc absorption, or refined grains and polished rice, which are poor sources of zinc.

Vitamin A Vitamin A deficiency, which affects more than 40% of children under age 5 in West and Central Africa, is the leading cause of blindness in children.[15] In addition, because of greater vulnerability to severe infection, these children are at high risk of death. As noted earlier, international initiatives to supplement vitamin A in deficient children can bring about an average of nearly 25% reduction in deaths of children under age 5—saving the lives of more than 300,000 children annually.[15]

Vitamin B$_{12}$ We noted in Chapter 12 that deficiency of vitamin B$_{12}$ can result in significant cognitive impairments, including deficits in learning and memory. Unfortunately, the prevalence of vitamin B$_{12}$ deficiency in children breast-fed by mothers with lifelong limited access to animal products may be very high. Because meat, fish, and poultry are rich sources of iron, zinc, and vitamin B$_{12}$, it is possible that multiple subclinical deficiencies occur in children with limited access to these foods and impair their development.[16]

Poor Work Capacity of Adults

Undernutrition has long been known to diminish work capacity. The debilitating weakness from undernutrition affects the productivity of adults in developing nations throughout the world today and is especially detrimental when manual labor involved in subsistence farming is the main source of food and income.

Micronutrient deficiency also contributes to poor work capacity; for example, the World Bank estimates that a loss of 5% of the gross domestic product worldwide is attributable specifically to micronutrient deficiencies.[17] Iron-deficiency anemia is particularly debilitating because of iron's role in oxygen transport. Because iron deficiency is a problem among women of childbearing age in both developed and developing countries, it is a global drain on work capacity and productivity.

Susceptibility to Chronic Disease as Undernutrition Is Relieved

A team of scientists in England observed that stunted children, particularly if they were undernourished in the womb and were born at term with low birth weight during war-related famines, were susceptible to obesity and its related chronic diseases as adults. These observations gave rise in the early 1990s to the hypothesis known as "fetal origins of adult disease," which states that adaptations to poor maternal nutrition made by a malnourished fetus as organs are developing help the child during times of food shortages but make the child susceptible to obesity and chronic disease when food is plentiful.[18] For example, when the mother is malnourished during the pregnancy, the baby will tend to have a low birth weight but be relatively fat. This may occur because the fetal body has preserved growth of the brain, which is more than 50% fat, at the expense of muscle tissue. There is now significant evidence supporting this hypothesis.

Overnutrition Causes Overweight, Obesity, and Chronic Disease

As you learned in Chapter 13, overconsumption of energy in excess of energy use increases weight in everyone, to a larger or lesser degree depending on their metabolic efficiency. Chronic overconsumption in any individual leads to obesity, and obesity increases the risk for chronic diseases.

The Prevalence of Obesity and Chronic Disease Is Increasing Worldwide

Throughout the world, the prevalence of obesity and its associated chronic diseases is increasing at an alarming rate. The WHO estimated that more than 1.6 billion adults were overweight in 2005, with 400 million of them clinically obese.[19] As alarming as these statistics are, the predictions for the future are even higher: the WHO estimates that by 2015, 2.3 billion adults will be overweight and more than 700 million will be obese.[19] As we have pointed out throughout this text, overweight and obesity increase the risk of cardiovascular disease, type 2 diabetes, and some cancers. Of these, type 2 diabetes is fast becoming an especially significant burden in the developing world. The WHO predicts that by 2020, deaths due to diabetes will increase worldwide by more than 50%.[19] We'll identify the factors contributing to the increase in global obesity later in this chapter.

Increasing Global Economic Burden of Chronic Disease Management

Management of chronic disease is costly. For example, in 2007, the cost of healthcare for people with diabetes in the United States exceeded $174 billion. People with diagnosed diabetes have medical expenditures that average 2.3 times higher than those of people without diabetes. Approximately $1 in every $10 spent on healthcare goes to diabetes care. In addition, indirect costs include factors such as absenteeism from work, reduced productivity, and lost productive capacity due to early death.[20] As diabetes and other chronic diseases increase in countries without the resources of the United States, lack of access to effective healthcare will increase the indirect economic costs. Families and communities will experience more lost work time, increased disability, and earlier death of adults who would have contributed to the family's resources and local economy.

Recap

Worldwide, malnutrition is increasingly becoming a problem with two very different manifestations: undernutrition, the most serious manifestation of which is severe acute malnutrition, and overnutrition. Undernutrition causes wasting and stunting, increased susceptibility to infection, high mortality rates, micronutrient deficiency diseases, and poor work capacity. The theory called "fetal origins of adult disease" suggests that undernutrition during fetal and childhood development contributes to obesity and chronic disease in adulthood. Overnutrition causes overweight and obesity and underlies the rising prevalence of chronic diseases throughout the world.

What Causes Undernutrition in the Developing World?

Any situation that results in inadequate food for an individual or community will prompt undernutrition. Natural disasters, wars, overpopulation, poor farming practices, disease, inequities in resource distribution, and other factors can result in a food supply that is inadequate to support the needs of all of the people in a particular place.

Famines Are Acute, Widespread Shortages of Food

Famines are severe food shortages affecting a large percentage of the population in a limited geographic area at a particular time. Famines have occurred throughout human history and typically cause significant loss of life. For example, an estimated 30 million people died in

An Indian farmer inspects what is left of his crop during a drought.

famines Widespread, acute food shortages that affect a substantial portion of a population, often associated with starvation and death.

the so-called "great famine" in China from 1958–1961 when disastrous governmental land-use policies combined with both floods and droughts to dramatically limit crop yields.

Natural disasters like floods and droughts are often to blame for widespread famine. The drought that occurred in summer 2004 in western Africa brought life-threatening undernutrition to about 20% of the population of Niger and Mali.[21] Other natural disasters that can destroy substantial amounts of local crops in a short time are tsunamis, high winds, hurricanes, frosts, pest infestations, and plant diseases.

Wars can induce famine when they interfere with planting or harvest times or destroy standing crops. Abandonment of farmland in war-torn areas or takeover of farmland by military forces can lead to widespread shortages. In addition, military actions or policies may unintentionally or deliberately disrupt production, distribution, or sale of foods in regions affected by the conflict. Civil wars in Ethiopia led to a severe famine in the 1980s that killed over a million people. Wars can also contribute to famine when they interfere with food relief assistance by other nations.

Both natural disasters and wars often cause migrations of large populations who are forced to flee their homes and means of livelihood. Refugees may live in hastily erected camps with little access to sanitary water, medical care, or adequate food. Food safety is compromised by rodents and lack of refrigeration. Relief assistance by other countries or areas is vital for survival in these emergencies because infection and malnutrition act synergistically in the crowded camps to erode health. Women, children, and the elderly in refugee camps are especially vulnerable when food supplies are delayed by damaged roads, poor transportation, political embargoes, or active conflict.

Multiple Factors Contribute to Chronic Food Shortages

Less dramatic than famines, but affecting more people over time, are chronic food shortages that lead to **food insecurity,** a condition in which individuals are unable to obtain enough energy and nutrients to meet their physical needs every day. **Food shortages** occur in areas where food production and import are not sufficient to meet the needs of the population in that area. Direct food aid in these situations must be carefully considered. If wealthy nations send food to a developing country in time of need, it provides more food for hungry people in the short term but can also decrease the price that local farmers receive for their products, with the possible effect of increasing poverty in the area in the long run. Food aid is more detrimental if it floods the market at harvest and less detrimental if it is available only when local foods are absent from the market in very lean years.

Several factors contribute to food shortages and food insecurity in different parts of the world. The most common include overpopulation, poor farming practices, use of agricultural land for cash crops, lack of infrastructure, disease, and unequal distribution of limited food supplies. These are discussed briefly here.

Overpopulation

An area is said to be **overpopulated** when its resources are insufficient to support the number of people living there. In parts of the world with fertile land and adequate rainfall or irrigation systems to support abundant harvests, food shortages rarely happen. However, in more arid climates, especially in areas with high birth rates and poor access to imported foods, seasonal and chronic food shortages are common. Slowing population growth is one way of improving an area's **food/population ratio.**

Likely the most effective method of reducing birth rates is to improve the education of women and girls.[22] Their increased earning potential, access to information about contraception, and better health practices lead to smaller, healthier, more economically stable families. Other methods of improving the food/population ratio are to increase food production and the importation of foods into the area.

The population of the earth was about 6.7 billion in 2008, and the Population Reference Bureau projects that world population will reach 7 billion by 2012.[23] So is the earth it-

Hungry children living in refugee camps are highly susceptible to death from infectious disease. The skeletal limbs and swollen bellies of these toddlers suggest severe acute malnutrition.

food insecurity Condition in which the individual is unable to regularly obtain enough food to provide sufficient energy and nutrients to meet physical needs.

food shortage Condition in which food production and import in an area are not sufficient to meet the needs of the population in that area.

overpopulated Characteristic used to describe a region that has insufficient resources to support the number of people living there.

food/population ratio The amount of food available for each individual; also food availability per capita.

self overpopulated? Or will it soon become so? In other words, will we soon suffer worldwide food insufficiency? Unfortunately, no one can answer these questions precisely because we cannot predict how advances in technology will affect our depletion of the earth's natural resources or our ability to produce more food with fewer resources. We do know that, currently, the greatest population growth is occurring in the areas of the world least able to support increased population. For example, whereas the birthrate in Japan and many European countries has fallen below replacement rate (considered to be two births per woman), the birthrate in some impoverished African countries is six births per woman. Although many more of these impoverished children die before their fifth birthday, the net effect is population growth.

Cotton is a cash crop that farmers often grow instead of local food crops.

Agricultural Practices

Some traditional farming practices have the potential to destroy useable land. Deforestation by burning or any other means and overgrazing pastures and croplands destroy the trees and grass roots that preserve soils from wind and water erosion. Growing the same crop year after year on the same plot of ground can deplete the soil of nutrients and reduce crop yield. Some modern agricultural practices, such as avoiding overgrazing and using **crop rotation** to renew the nutrients in a parcel of ground, have benefited small farmers and increased the employment of agricultural workers.

Use of agricultural land for **cash crops** such as cotton, coffee, and tobacco may replace land use for local food crops such as sorghum and corn, also called **subsistence crops.** The end result may be detrimental if less local production of subsistence crops means less food available for local consumption. Another problem with cash crops is that they are likely to be produced by large landholders who pay insufficient wages to their hired laborers. However, if political trade policies result in imports of nutritious foods and effective distribution systems are in place, then the greater variety of available foods will improve nutrition status.

Lack of Infrastructure

Exacerbating the scarcity of food production in some areas is a lack of infrastructure. For example, many developing countries lack roads and transportation into the areas of the country away from ports and major cities. This limits available food to whatever can be produced locally. In addition, lack of electricity and refrigeration can limit storage of perishable foods before they can be used.

Water management is a second aspect of infrastructure that influences nutrition. In dry areas, irrigation can improve food production, but it must be managed carefully to prevent increasing the numbers of mosquitoes and other pests, which can spread infectious diseases such as malaria. The provision of safe drinking water and sewage systems is another aspect of water management that help prevent disease.

Other critically important aspects of infrastructure are sanitation services, communication systems, an adequate healthcare delivery system, and adequate public education. In summary, public health depends on public policies that support the development of personnel, physical structures, and technological innovations that promote health and prevent disease.

Millet is a common subsistence crop.

Impact of Disease

Disease and lack of healthcare resources to fight disease reduce the work capacity of individuals, and this in turn reduces their ability to ward off poverty and malnutrition. This economic phenomenon is demonstrated by the AIDS epidemic. There are now 33 million people living with HIV, and 2 million people died from AIDS in 2007.[24] HIV is most likely to affect young, sexually active adults who are the primary wage earners in their families.

crop rotation   The practice of alternating crops in a particular field to prevent nutrient depletion and erosion of the soil and to help with control of crop-specific pests.

cash crops   Crops grown to be sold rather than eaten, such as cotton, tobacco, jute, and sugar cane.

subsistence crops   Crops grown to be eaten by a family or community such as rice, millet, and garden vegetables. Surpluses may be sold locally.

Thus, their illness or death can impoverish their children, younger siblings, and/or elderly parents. In Africa, AIDS is the leading cause of death, and the death of both parents to AIDS has made orphans of millions of children. By creating populations in which children and the elderly predominate, the AIDS epidemic has exacerbated the risk of undernutrition in many developing countries.[25]

Unequal Distribution of Food

Overpopulation, poor agricultural practices, lack of infrastructure, and diseases like AIDS all can contribute to chronic food shortages, but the major cause of undernutrition in the world is unequal distribution of food because of poverty. In the developing world, more than three-fourths of malnourished children live in countries with food surpluses.[26] The most at-risk populations are the rural poor. Lacking sufficient land to grow their own foods, the rural poor must work for others to earn money to buy food, but because they live in rural areas, employment opportunities are limited.

Unequal distribution also occurs because of cultural biases. In many countries, limited food is distributed first to men and boys and only secondarily to women and girls.[26] In such situations, pregnant women and growing girls are the most vulnerable because of their increased needs. Food distribution to the elderly is sometimes also limited, particularly in developing countries where nutrition services are primarily directed toward pregnant and lactating women, infants, and young children.[27] Access to food also can differ by ethnicity and religion. For example, officials in authority may order that food aid be distributed preferentially to areas where their own ethnic group dominates.

RecaP

Famines are widespread, severe food shortages that can result in starvation and death. They are most commonly caused by natural disasters or wars. Less severe but chronic food shortages can be influenced by regional overpopulation, poor agricultural practices, and the burden of disease; however, unequal distribution of food due to poverty is the major cause of food shortages—and resulting undernutrition—in the world.

What Causes Overnutrition in the Developing World?

Parallel to the ancient, and as yet unsolved, problem of underweight in the developing world is a growing obesity problem that is straining public health resources in a new way. Called the **nutrition paradox,** this new public health problem is characterized by the coexistence of underweight and obesity in the same region and even in the same family. The nutrition paradox is especially common in countries transitioning from the very poorest to the middle range of gross national income, such as Mexico, Brazil, Egypt, India, China, and Thailand.

Changes in Diet and Activity Underlie the Nutrition Paradox

The WHO identifies two key factors behind the nutrition paradox in transitioning nations:[28]

- a trend toward decreased physical activity due to the increasingly sedentary nature of many forms of work, changing modes of transportation, and increasing urbanization
- a global shift in diet toward increased intake of energy-dense foods that are high in fat and sugars but low in micronutrients

Transitioning countries are characterized by major migrations from rural to urban areas, less dependence on subsistence farming, more motorized transportation, and better public health measures that increase access to medical care, safe water, and more abundant food. As a transitioning nation's economy improves, employment shifts away from farming,

nutrition paradox   Coexistence of undernutrition and overnutrition in the same region or in the same family.

forestry, and fishing toward service occupations. Work becomes more sedentary, motorized transportation becomes more common, and the daily requirement for physical activity declines. At the same time, the types of foods available change from starchy, low-fat, high-fiber subsistence crops to foods of higher nutrient density, including meats, poultry, dairy products, inexpensive vegetable oils, snack foods, and sweets. Over the past 20 years, foreign investment in companies producing highly processed foods has made energy-dense foods available at lower cost to more people in developing countries. While these changes bring greater dietary variety and alleviate some nutrient deficiencies, they also increase a population's risk of obesity.

The Poverty–Obesity Link

In developing countries, obesity used to be considered healthful and desirable: it demonstrated that the individual was wealthy enough to afford abundant food. In fact, the non-communicable chronic diseases associated with obesity were called "diseases of affluence." But as poor people move from rural farms to take low-paying service jobs in cities, where energy-dense, low-cost foods are widely available, obesity is increasingly being linked to poverty. Energy-dense foods with longer shelf lives, such as vegetable oils, sugar, refined flour, snack foods, soft drinks, and canned goods, are less expensive than perishable foods such as meats, fish, milk, and fresh fruits and vegetables. For example, soft drinks and oils increased in price in the United States less than 40% between 1985 and 2000, whereas the price of fresh fruits and vegetables increased 120%.[29] In addition, cheap, energy-dense foods have a higher satiety value: they cause a person to feel full for a longer period of time at a lower cost. Thus, individuals with limited money to spend are likely to prefer such foods. In short, although the mechanisms by which obesity and poverty are linked are not entirely clear, there is now substantial evidence of the global shift of the burden of overweight and obesity to the poor.

Overnutrition is becoming a problem for impoverished people now that energy-dense foods are becoming widely available.

RecaP

Overnutrition resulting in obesity is now a public health concern not only in developed nations but also in countries transitioning out of poverty. Lack of physical activity and increased availability of low-cost, energy-rich, nutrient-poor foods have shifted the burden of obesity and chronic diseases toward the poor.

How Many Americans Go Hungry?

As we discussed in Chapter 13, overnutrition is becoming a national health crisis. A majority of Americans is now overweight or obese, and the prevalence of type 2 diabetes and other chronic diseases associated with obesity is increasing. But even in the United States, unequal distribution of abundant food leads to undernutrition among the nation's poorest citizens.

As shown in **Figure 19.4**, the U.S. Department of Agriculture (USDA) estimates that just over 11% of U.S. households (about 13 million households) experienced food insecurity in 2007.[30] This means that the people living in these homes were unable to obtain enough food to meet their physical needs every day. Of these 13 million, 4.7 million had *very low food security*, meaning that normal eating patterns of one or more members of the household were disrupted and food intake was reduced at times during the year because they had insufficient money or other resources for food. How do "households" translate into human beings? In 2007, 36.2 million Americans, including 12.4 million children, experienced food insecurity.[30]

The role of poverty in food insecurity is undeniable. In 2007, among households with income below the official U.S. poverty level ($21,027 for a family of four in 2007), 38% experienced food insecurity.

Households with low food security (7%) Households with very low food security (4.1%)

Food-secure households (88.9%)

Figure 19.4 Food security status of U.S. households in 2007. (*Data adapted from:* The Economic Research Service [ERS] using data from the December 2007 Current Population Survey Food Security Supplement. Available at www.ers. usda.gov/Briefing/FoodSecurity/ trends.htm.)

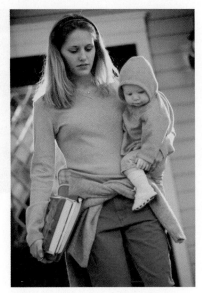

Many single mothers face economic burdens that leave them and their children vulnerable to food insecurity.

At greatest risk for food insecurity are families consisting of single mothers and their children. In 2007, more than 30% of households with children headed by a single woman experienced food insecurity. Also above the national average were African American households (22% food insecure) and Hispanic households (20% food insecure).[30] Other vulnerable groups are the homeless, the unemployed, elderly people living on a fixed income, migrant laborers, and other workers in minimum-wage jobs.

Sometimes physical, psychological, or social factors contribute to food insecurity among Americans. For instance, people with chronic diseases or disabilities may lose paid work hours due to illness, have to accept lower-wage jobs, or have medical expenses that limit money for food. Depression, addiction to alcohol or other substances, and other psychological disorders can similarly limit productivity and reduce income. Divorce frequently leads to financial stressors, especially for women, who may be unable to collect alimony or child support payments and may have jobs that do not provide an income sufficient to provide fully for the family's needs.

Judy
Nutri-Case

"Even with Hannah paying her school tuition and buying her own lunches, I don't seem to be able to make ends meet. I keep thinking that next month will be different, but then I get my paycheck and, by the time I pay the rent and the utilities, not to mention the co-payment for my diabetes medicine, there's almost nothing left! I'm behind on my car payments, I owe the dentist and the eye doctor, and last night, the credit card company called and said that if I didn't send them at least $100, they'd take me to court. I can't tell Hannah we're in trouble, or she might threaten to quit school and work full time. Then she'll end up in a dead-end job like me. So I'll have to take the $100 out of this month's grocery money. I think if I buy cans of soups and beans, powdered milk, some hamburger meat, the store brands of cereal and soda, and bread and crackers from the discount bin, we'll be able to get by."

What, if any, nutrients are missing from Judith's planned food choices for this month? If you had just $50 to spend on a week's groceries for yourself and another adult, what would you buy? (Hint: Review the Nutrition Myth or Fact? box in Chapter 13: Does It Cost More to Eat Right?) What other options could Judy explore to help her get through this month, and to help increase her food security permanently?

What Are Some Solutions to Malnutrition?

The United Nations Millennium Development Goals include the eradication of extreme poverty and hunger.[31] For such a goal to be achieved, both short-term and long-term solutions are needed. Short-term solutions are imperative to prevent famine following natural disasters and in war-torn regions. For example, the U.S. Agency for International Development (USAID) has developed a Famine Early Warning System Network to monitor droughts, floods, and other problems that affect food supplies so that interventions can be provided quickly and efficiently.[32]

Long-term solutions are critical to achieve and maintain global food security. The United Nations identifies the need for the world community to develop a long-term "global partnership for development" involving international, national, community, household, and individual strategies.[33] We discuss some local initiatives and technological strategies to meet these challenges in this section.

Local Initiatives

Local initiatives include programs to encourage breastfeeding, to combat infectious disease, and to promote equitable distribution of available food.

Programs to Encourage Breastfeeding

Among the most important local initiatives for improving the health and nutrition of children worldwide are programs that encourage breastfeeding. As we discussed in Chapter 16, breast milk not only provides optimal nutrition for healthy growth of the newborn but also contains antibodies that protect against infections. Particularly in developing countries, feeding infants with formula is risky: The use of unsanitary water for mixing batches of formula results in diarrheal diseases; and overdilution of formula by families who cannot afford adequate amounts results in inadequate intake. In developing countries, breastfeeding is considered to reduce diarrheal deaths in young children by 50% to 95%.

In 1991, WHO and UNICEF initiated the Baby Friendly Hospital Initiative to increase breastfeeding rates worldwide. Under this initiative, new mothers are educated about the benefits of breast milk, the dangers of bottle-feeding, and the importance of maternal nutrition during lactation. They are encouraged to breastfeed exclusively for the first 6 months of the child's life and to continue breastfeeding as part of the child's daily diet until the child is at least 2 years old.

Programs to Combat Infectious Disease

In 1982, UNICEF began a campaign to eliminate common infections of childhood by four inexpensive local strategies referred to as **GOBI**:

G—growth monitoring to assess childhood well-being
O—oral rehydration therapy to stop death from dehydration during diarrheal diseases using a simple solution containing a balance of fluids and electrolytes
B—breastfeeding
I—immunization against tuberculosis, diphtheria, whooping cough, tetanus, polio, and measles[34]

By 1990, GOBI was estimated to have saved 12 million children. These four successful strategies continue as parts of various local initiatives to reach the United Nations Millennium Development Goals.[33]

In 1998, the Vitamin A Global Initiative was launched by a coalition of international agencies to attempt to increase the intake of vitamin A by fortification of foods and provision of vitamin A–rich fruits and vegetables for home gardens. Because of the critical role of vitamin A in immune defense, these measures also combat infectious disease. In addition, programs for deworming and mosquito control combat not only helminth and malarial infection but their accompanying iron deficiency.

Programs to Promote Equitable Distribution of Food

In the United States, several government programs help low-income citizens acquire food over extended periods of time. Among these programs are the Supplemental Nutrition Assistance Program (previously called the Food Stamp Program), which helps low-income individuals of all ages; the Special Supplemental Nutrition Program for Women, Infants and Children (WIC), which helps pregnant women and children to age 5; the National School Lunch and National School Breakfast Programs, which help low-income schoolchildren; and the Summer Food Service Program, which helps low-income children in the summer.

The United States also has a broad network of local soup kitchens and food pantries that provide meals and food items to needy families. They are supported by volunteers, individual donations, and food contributions from local grocery stores and restaurants. In addition, the U.S. Department of Agriculture distributes surplus foods to charitable agencies for distribution to needy families.

GOBI UNICEF campaign to eliminate common infections of childhood by four inexpensive strategies: growth monitoring, oral rehydration therapy, breastfeeding, and immunization.

Many international organizations help improve the nutrient status of the poor by enabling them to produce their own foods. For example, both USAID and the Peace Corps have agricultural education programs, the World Bank provides loans to fund small business ventures, and many nonprofit and nongovernmental organizations (NGOs) support community and family farms.

Technological Strategies

Technological strategies for increasing the world's food supply include the Green Revolution, the sustainable agriculture movement, and the application of biotechnology, including the use of genetically modified organisms.

The Green Revolution

The **Green Revolution,** one of the major agricultural advances of the past 50 years, has increased the productivity of cultivated land while maintaining environmental quality.[35] As part of the Green Revolution, new **high-yield varieties** of grain were produced by crossbreeding plants and selecting for the most desirable traits. The new semi-dwarf varieties of rice, corn, and wheat are less likely to fall over in wind and heavy rains and can carry more seeds. They have been widely adopted in North and South America and Asia and have doubled or tripled the yield per acre while reducing costs. It is likely that 1 billion people were saved from starvation between 1960 and 2000 by these varieties.[36]

Less success was achieved in creating high-yield varieties of staples traditional to sub-Saharan Africa, such as sorghum, millet, and cassava, which are grown in hot, dry conditions. Thus, Africa has shared least in the alleviation of hunger achieved during the Green Revolution.

Although it has achieved higher yields at lower costs, which greatly benefited farmers and consumers, the Green Revolution has prompted new problems. Because it requires the use of chemical fertilizers, pesticides, irrigation, and mechanical harvesters to reduce labor costs, it has most benefited larger, wealthier landowners and has not helped small, family farms. Environmental damages associated with the Green Revolution have included loss of topsoil due to erosion from heavy tilling, from extensive planting of row crops such as corn and soybeans, and from run-off due to irrigation.

Sustainable Agriculture

In response to these drawbacks of the Green Revolution, a new movement toward **sustainable agriculture** has evolved. The goal of the sustainable agriculture movement is to develop local, site-specific farming methods that improve soil conservation, crop yields, and food security in a sustainable manner, minimizing the adverse environmental impact. For example, soil erosion can be controlled by crop rotation, by terracing sloped land for the cultivation of crops (**Figure 19.5**), by tillage that minimizes disturbance to the topsoil, and by the use of herbicides to remove weeds rather than hoeing. Another practice associated with sustainable agriculture is the use of **transgenic crops,** plant varieties that have had one or more genes altered. Such crops can reduce the need for insecticides or permit the cultivation of marginally fertile land (see Chapter 16).

Meat production is a particularly controversial issue within the sustainable agriculture movement. Promoting vegetarianism, critics emphasize the inefficiency of eating meat from grain-fed cattle instead of eating the grains themselves. They also point out the contribution of livestock production

Green Revolution The tremendous increase in global productivity between 1944 and 2000 due to selective cross-breeding or hybridization to produce high-yield grains and industrial farming techniques.

high-yield varieties Semi-dwarf varieties of plants that are unlikely to fall over in wind and heavy rains and thus can carry larger amounts of seeds, greatly increasing the yield per acre.

sustainable agriculture Term referring to techniques of food production that preserve the environment indefinitely.

transgenic crops Plant varieties that have had one or more genes altered by use of genetic technologies; also called genetically modified organisms, or GMOs.

Figure 19.5 Terracing sloped land to avoid soil erosion is one practice of sustainable agriculture.

to deforestation, release of greenhouse gases, and global warming. Supporters of meat production emphasize the benefits of using livestock to convert otherwise unusable plants to high-quality food, improve the nutritional quality of the diet of people in developing countries, and contribute nonchemical fertilizer to renew the soil.

Biotechnology

Some agricultural scientists see the application of biotechnology, specifically the production of genetically modified foods, as the next step in the Green Revolution. They contend that genetically modified crops can produce higher yields on limited land, allowing peasant farmers to feed their families with disease-resistant crops that can be farmed without chemicals and using traditional methods. In addition, genetically modified crops with improved nutrient density, when grown in areas already being cultivated by the family, can improve nutrient status with no change in farming practices.[37]

As we explored in Chapter 16, however, there is currently considerable controversy surrounding the long-term safety and environmental impact of genetically modified crops. In addition, patents on the technological tools of biotechnology limit their use. Conferring public right to the necessary technological tools would allow more widespread use of advanced technologies for assisting poor farmers to improve food security.[38]

RecaP

Short-term aid prevents death during emergency food shortages. Long-term solutions to global food security include programs to encourage breastfeeding, to combat infectious disease, and to promote equitable distribution of available food, which help maximize local solutions. The Green Revolution, sustainable agriculture practices, and biotechnology are controversial strategies aimed at increasing the world's food supply.

Liz
Nutri-Case

"I wish I could get my dad to stop harassing me about my decision to become a vegetarian. I've tried to explain to him how much grain it takes to produce a pound of beef and how agribusinesses are destroying precious rain forests to provide grazing lands for cows. We're blessed with so much abundance here in the West; if by cutting meat out of my diet I can help preserve the environment and reduce global hunger, then I'm glad to do it! And I wish my dad and mom would do it, too! It's selfish to consume more than our fair share of the world's resources!"

What do you think about Liz's position on vegetarianism? Do her ideas seem radical, sensible, or somewhere in between? Conduct some research to support or refute her claims that eliminating meat from one's diet "can help preserve the environment and reduce global hunger" and that meat-eaters are consuming more than their fair share of the world's resources. In your response, don't neglect to consider the health implications of meat consumption versus vegetarianism. (If necessary, review Chapters 5, 6, and 12.)

What Can You Do to Combat Global Malnutrition?

Two general strategies for combating global malnutrition are to make personal choices that promote food equity and environmental quality and to volunteer with an organization that works to relieve hunger.

Make Personal Choices That Promote Food Equity and Preserve the Environment

The personal choices that each individual makes can contribute to or combat global malnutrition by influencing local and global markets. Choosing to purchase certain foods makes those foods more likely to be produced in the future. If you choose vegetables, fruits, nuts, whole grains, and beans and other legumes, then you will influence greater production of these healthful foods. If you buy organic foods, you encourage reduction in the use of chemical pesticides and herbicides. If you buy produce from a local farmer's market, you encourage greater local availability of fresh foods. This reduces the costs and resources devoted to distribution, transportation, and storage of foods.

To combat overnutrition, the major type of malnutrition in the United States, avoid or limit energy-dense, nutrient-poor choices and encourage your friends to follow your lead. Read labels: Do you really want high-fructose corn syrup in your peanut butter? When large numbers of people stop purchasing foods high in saturated fats or added sugars, the profitability of these foods declines and they are more likely to disappear from the marketplace. And whatever you eat, avoid overconsumption. You'll be leaving more food for others as well as reducing your risk for obesity and its accompanying chronic diseases. Not convinced? Consider the competing philosophies in the Nutrition Myth or Fact? box, next page.

The amount of meat you eat also affects the global food supply. As we noted earlier, the production of plant-based foods requires a lower expenditure of natural resources and releases fewer greenhouse gases than the production of animal-based foods, so making plant foods the main source of your diet preserves land, water, and global energy, and reduces global warming. However, animal-based foods do contribute high-quality nutrients and can be consumed in moderation worldwide without harm to either health or the environment.

Remember that physical activity is important in maintaining health and combating overnutrition, so walk and bike as often as you can in your everyday life. Walking, biking, and taking public transportation also limits your consumption of nonrenewable fossil fuels. When it's time to purchase a car, research your options and choose the one with the best fuel economy.

Bicycling is a healthful option that limits your use of fossil fuels.

Volunteer with an Organization That Fights Hunger

Several times each year, college students from hundreds of campuses all over the United States gather to fight hunger as Members of the National Student Campaign Against Hunger and Homelessness. They hold "Hunger Cleanups," staff relief agencies, solicit donations of food and money, and promote community activism. Their organization is just one of dozens in which you can get involved. You can gather foods for local food banks, volunteer to work in a soup kitchen, help distribute food to homebound elderly, or start a community or school garden. You can also hold fund-raisers and donate cash directly. This financial assistance is urgently needed: for example, in 2005, 24% of U.S. emergency food providers surveyed reported that they had turned away requests for food in the past year due to a lack of resources.[39] And food insecurity in the United States has only increased since then. Check out the Web Links at the end of this chapter for the names of national agencies and get involved!

Because obesity is likely to be as much or more of a problem in your community as hunger, you can also volunteer to fight overnutrition. For instance, you could teach children about healthy eating at after-school programs or on Saturday in the local library. You could help provide opportunities for your neighbors to be physically active. Start a walking group or help with community marathons and "fun runs." You might volunteer to coach after-school sports for children or assist with summer camps that teach children about physical fitness.

You can also get involved with one of the many international agencies that assist developing nations in fighting hunger. Research a few of those listed in the Web Links at the end

Nutrition Myth or Fact?

If You Clean Your Plate, Will It Help the Starving Children in Africa?

It used to be considered polite to finish all the food on your plate and wasteful to throw food away. Children were told, "Clean your plate—it will help the starving children in Africa!" Today, this admonition raises a serious issue that you might want to consider if you are or plan to be a parent or to work with children.

The primary reason for not teaching children that they must clean their plates is that overeating is becoming a worldwide problem, and coaxing children to eat when they are no longer hungry teaches them to ignore their body's hunger/satiation signals. This can set the stage for disordered eating. Instead of overfilling a child's plate, parents and caregivers should serve children a reasonable portion of food (see Chapter 17). If the child eats that and is still hungry, he or she can be given more.

Forcing children to finish meals is not a strategy for fighting global hunger.

In addition, "cleaning your plate" at home does not help children in Africa or anywhere else. If anything, encouraging children at home to eat just the amount of food their bodies need may help children in developing nations by preserving more of the global harvest. Healthful eating behaviors also reduce children's risk of developing obesity and its associated chronic diseases, thereby reducing their use of limited medical resources as they age.

So next time you're tempted to admonish a child to "clean your plate," try something new. Get down on the child's level, and ask the child about it: "I notice you haven't finished your dinner. Check in with your tummy—are you still hungry, or have you had enough?" Your question may not help a starving child in Africa, but it might help the very child you're talking to.

of this chapter. When you find one you like, volunteer time or donate or raise money to help its cause. The following See for Yourself feature identifies more steps you can take to help combat global malnutrition.

If you still wonder whether or not your acts can make a difference, consider the advice of historian and civil rights activist Howard Zinn. He urges us to "just do something, to join with millions of others who will just do something, because all of those somethings, at certain points in history, come together and make the world better."[40]

See for Yourself

What Can You Do to Combat Global Malnutrition?

Have you ever wondered if your actions inadvertently contribute to the problem of global malnutrition? Or whether efforts you make locally can help feed people thousands of miles away? In this exercise, you'll reflect on your behavior in three different roles you play every day: consumer, student, and citizen of the world.

In your role as a consumer, ask yourself:

How can I use my food purchases to promote the production of more healthful, less-processed foods?
Any grocery store manager will tell you that your purchases influence the types of foods that are manufactured and

sold. If people become aware of the benefits of eating whole-grain bread and stop buying soft white bread, stores will stop carrying it and food companies will stop making it. In our global economy, your food choices can even influence the types of foods that are imported.

1. Choose fresh, locally grown, organic foods more often to support local sustainability.
2. Choose whole or less-processed versions of packaged foods. This encourages their increased production and saves energy.
3. Both when you're shopping and when you're eating out, avoid nutrient-poor foods and beverages to discourage their profitability.

How often do I eat vegetarian?

Plant-based sources of protein can be produced with less energy cost than animal-based sources, so reducing your consumption of animal foods saves global energy.

1. Experiment with some recipes in a vegetarian cookbook. Try making at least one new vegetarian meal each week.
2. Introduce friends and family members to your new vegetarian dishes.
3. When eating out, choose restaurants that provide vegetarian menu choices. If the campus cafeteria or a favorite restaurant has no vegetarian choices, request that some be added to the menu.

How much do I eat?

Eating just the calories you need to maintain a healthy weight leaves more of the global harvest for others and will likely reduce your use of medical resources as well.

1. To raise your consciousness about the physical experience of hunger, consider fasting for 1 day. If health or other reasons prevent you from fasting safely, try keeping silent during each meal throughout 1 day so that you can more fully appreciate the food you're eating and reflect on those who are hungry.
2. For 1 week, keep track of how much food you throw away, and why. Do you put more food on your plate than you can eat? Do you allow foods stored in your refrigerator to spoil? Do you often buy new foods to "try" and then throw them away because you don't like them?
3. On a daily basis, check in with your body before and as you eat: are you really hungry, and if so, how much and what type of food does your body really need right now?

In your role as a student, ask yourself:

How can I use what I have learned about nutrition to combat malnutrition in my neighborhood?

1. Visit each of your local fast-food restaurants and ask for information about the nutritional value of their foods. Analyze the information, then summarize it in simple language. Offer to submit a series of articles about your findings to your school or local newspaper.
2. Research what local produce is available in each season. Write an article for your school newspaper identifying the foods in season and include two healthful recipes using those foods.
3. Begin or join a food cooperative, community garden, or shared farming program. Donate a portion of your produce each week to a local food pantry.

What careers could I consider to help combat global malnutrition?

No matter what career you choose, use your unique talents to advocate global food security.

1. You could become a member of the Peace Corps and serve in a developing country.
2. If you're interested in science, you could have a career helping to develop more nutrient-dense or perennial crops, better food-preservation methods, or projects to improve food or water safety.
3. If you plan a career in business, you could enter the food industry and work for the production and marketing of healthful products.
4. If you pursue a career in healthcare, you could join an international medical corps to combat deficiency diseases.

In your role as a world citizen, ask yourself:

How can I improve the lives of people in my own community?

1. You can volunteer at a local soup kitchen, homeless shelter, food bank, or community garden.
2. You can join a food cooperative, that is, a store or farm in which you work a number of hours each week in exchange for discounts on healthful foods.
3. Because obesity is likely to be a significant problem in your community, you can help increase opportunities for physical activity in your community. Start a walking group, or volunteer to coach children in a favorite sport.

How can I improve the lives of people in developing nations?

1. Donate time or raise money for one of the international agencies that work to relieve global hunger. Check out options for charitable contributions and volunteer efforts at www.charitynavigator.org.
2. Join efforts to influence government foreign policies to support global food security.
3. Research the human rights records of international food companies whose products you buy. If you don't like what you find out, switch brands, and write to the company and tell them why you did.

Chapter Review

Test Yourself | Answers

1 (T) Currently, about 11% of the population of the United States are unable to obtain enough energy and nutrients to meet their physical needs every day.

2 (F) The major cause of undernutrition in the world is unequal distribution of adequate food supplies because of poverty.

3 (F) We cannot determine exactly what population size can be supported by the earth because we cannot predict how advances in technology will affect our depletion of the earth's natural resources.

4 (T) Significant evidence supports the theory that physiologic adaptations to poor maternal nutrition made as a fetus is developing help the child during times of food shortages but make the child susceptible to obesity and chronic disease when food is plentiful.

5 (T) Currently, the global burden of obesity is shifting to the poor. For example, the prevalence of obesity in both children and adults in many developing nations is increasing at a faster rate than in developed countries.

Summary

- A nourishing diet contributes to health, wellness, and work capacity, improving the prosperity of everyone worldwide.

- Both undernutrition and overnutrition are significant global problems.

- Undernutrition contributes to wasting, growth stunting, reduced resistance to infection, increased mortality, micronutrient deficiency diseases, and diminished work capacity in adults.

- Fetal malnutrition is associated with increased risk of chronic diseases when undernutrition is relieved during childhood and young adulthood.

- Prevalence of obesity is increasing worldwide.

- Chronic diseases such as diabetes, hypertension, and cardiovascular disease are a significant and growing economic burden worldwide.

- Undernutrition results from famines or chronic food shortages due to overpopulation, poor agricultural practices, lack of infrastructure, disease, and unequal distribution of limited food supplies.

- Because the current global food supply is adequate for the current global population, food insecurity is largely a problem of unequal distribution.

- Overconsumption of energy in developed and transitioning countries is exacerbated by sedentary occupations and motorized transportation.

- Poverty exacerbates overnutrition, perhaps because less-expensive foods are energy-dense with a higher satiety value, widely available, and highly promoted.

- The GOBI initiative of UNICEF combats common infections of childhood by encouraging growth monitoring, oral rehydration therapy, breastfeeding, and immunizations.

- The Green Revolution, sustainable agriculture, and biotechnology are controversial programs with a common goal of increasing the world food supply in a sustainable manner.

- The WHO recognized a need for a global strategy to address prevention and control of obesity and chronic diseases by encouraging healthy patterns of diet and activity worldwide.

- Your efforts to combat global malnutrition are urgently needed.

Review Questions

1. The region of the world where undernutrition is most acute is
   a. Sub-Saharan Africa.
   b. Southern Africa.
   c. Central America.
   d. Central Asia.

2. Which of the following statements about the Green Revolution is true?
   a. It has most greatly benefited small, family farms.
   b. It has dramatically reduced undernutrition throughout South America, Asia, and Africa.
   c. It has dramatically increased worldwide production of rice, corn, and wheat at lower costs.
   d. It has reduced the traditional farmer's reliance on chemical fertilizers and pesticides.

3. Which of the following results of undernutrition is most directly linked to death in childhood?
   a. Decreased work capacity
   b. Reduced resistance to infection
   c. Growth stunting
   d. Impaired cognitive development

4. At greatest risk for food insecurity in the United States are
   a. adults over age 65.
   b. single mothers and their children.
   c. African Americans.
   d. Hispanic Americans.

5. Which of the following health problems has been linked to inadequate intake of vitamin A?
   a. Diarrhea
   b. Malaria
   c. Night blindness
   d. All of the above

6. **True or false?** Worldwide, most malnourished children live in countries with food surpluses.

7. **True or false?** Children with night blindness have an increased risk for premature death.

8. **True or false?** Crop rotation and terracing are farming methods used in sustainable agriculture.

9. **True or false?** The rise in global obesity rates has prompted a rise in rates of communicable diseases.

10. **True or false?** Cotton, coffee, and tobacco are examples of subsistence crops.

11. Why might programs to improve the education of women also improve a nation's food/population ratio?

12. Explain why breastfeeding is an essential element of UNICEF's GOBI campaign to eliminate common infections of childhood.

13. Jeanette is a healthcare provider in a free clinic in an impoverished area of India. She is 5'6" tall. Explain why she is not surprised to hear the patients who come to the clinic refer to her as a giant.

14. Davie is 2 years old and lives in rural Alabama. He is the youngest of three children, all of whom live with their mother in an abandoned van. Their mother relies on a local food pantry for food, and the family drinks water from a nearby pond. Neither Davie nor his siblings have been vaccinated, and they have no regular medical care. Pointing to the interrelationship of several factors, explain why Davie's risk of dying before he reaches age 5 is significant.

15. José grew up in a slum in Mexico City, but his brilliance in school earned him recognition and a patron who funded his education. Now in medical school in the United States, he plans to return to Mexico as a pediatrician and specialize in the treatment of children with type 2 diabetes. Explain why José might be drawn to work with this population.

Web Links

www.actionagainsthunger.org
Action Against Hunger
This site explains the mission of an international organization that helps in emergency situations and also promotes long-term food security and lets you know how to volunteer to help.

www.bread.org
Bread for the World
Visit this site to learn about a faith-based effort to advocate local and global policies that help the poor obtain food.

www.care.org
CARE
This site is the international page that links to CARE organizations in many countries working to improve economic conditions in more than seventy developing nations.

www.feedingminds.org
Feeding Minds Fighting Hunger
Visit this international electronic classroom to explore the problems of hunger, malnutrition, and food insecurity.

www.freefromhunger.org
Freedom from Hunger
Visit this site to learn about an established international development organization, founded in 1946, that works toward sustainable self-help against chronic hunger and poverty.

www.heifer.org
Heifer International
Visit this site to learn how you can give a cow, some rabbits, or a flock of chickens to a community in a developing country so that they are better able to provide food for themselves.

www.hki.org/index.html
Helen Keller International
This site describes sustainable ways of preventing blindness and childhood deaths by fighting poverty and malnutrition.

www.studentsagainsthunger.org
National Student Campaign Against Hunger and Homelessness
Visit this site to learn what students like you are doing to fight hunger, and how you can get involved.

www.oxfamamerica.org
Oxfam America
Oxfam International is a confederation of organizations in more than 100 countries working together for a more equitable world. This Web site explains the American initiatives fighting global poverty, hunger, and social injustice.

www.unicef.org/nutrition/index.html
The United Nations Children's Fund
Visit this site to learn about international concerns affecting the world's children, including nutrient deficiencies and hunger.

www.who.int/nutrition/en
The World Health Organization Nutrition Site
Visit this site to learn about global malnutrition, micronutrient deficiencies, and the nutrition transition.

References

1. Central Intelligence Agency. Sierra Leone. 2009, May 14. *The World Factbook*. Available at www.cia.gov/library/publications/the-world-factbook/geos/sl.html; UNICEF. 2009, June. 68 countdown countries with high mortality: Selected health and nutrition indicators. Data companion to the Annual Report of the Executive Director (p. 5). Available at www.unicef.org/about/execboard/files/UNICEF_Data_Companion_2009_Eng_light.pdf.

2. World Health Organization. 2008, May. Core health indicators: Sierra Leone. *WHO Statistical Information System* (WHOSIS). Available at http://apps.who.int/whosis/database/core/core_select_process.cfm.

3. Aguayo, V. M., D. Garnier, and S. K. Baker. 2007. *Drops of Life: Vitamin A Supplementation for Child Survival, Progress and Lessons Learned in West and Central Africa*. UNICEF Regional Office for West and Central Africa.

4. International Food Policy Research Institute. 2008, October 14. Global hunger index. Available at www.ifpri.org/PUBS/cp/ghi08.asp.

5. FAO. 2008. The spectrum of malnutrition. Available at www.fao.org.

6. World Health Organization/World Food Programme/United Nations System Standing Committee on Nutrition/The United Nations Children's Fund. 2007, May. *Community-Based Management of Severe Acute Malnutrition* Available at www.who.int/nutrition/topics/Statement_community_based_man_sev_acute_mal_eng.pdf; Collins, S. 2007, May. Treating severe acute malnutrition seriously. *Arch. Dis. Child.* 92(5):453–461.

7. WHO. 2002. *The World Health Report, 2002: Reducing risks, promoting healthy life.* Geneva: World Health Organization.

8. Aguayo, V. M., D. Garnier, and S. K. Baker. 2007. *Drops of Life: Vitamin A Supplementation for Child Survival, Progress and Lessons Learned in West and Central Africa*. UNICEF Regional Office for West and Central Africa.

9. Scrimshaw, N. S. 2003. Historical concepts of interactions, synergism and antagonism between nutrition and infection. *J. Nutr.* 133:316S–321S.

10. Ambrus, J. L. Sr., and J. L. Ambrus Jr. 2004. Nutrition and infectious diseases in developing countries and problems of acquired immunodeficiency syndrome. *Exp. Biol. Med.* 229:464–472.

11. Black, R. E., S. S. Morris, and J. Bryce. 2003. Where and why are 10 million children dying every year? *Lancet* 361:2226–2234.

12. Central Intelligence Agency. 2009, May 14. *The World Factbook*. Available at www.cia.gov/library/publications/the-world-factbook/geos/sl.html.

13. Population Reference Bureau. 2008. 2008 World Population Data Sheet. Available at www.prb.org/Publications/Datasheets/2008/2008wpds.aspx.

14. World Health Organization. 2004. Proportion of general population with insufficient iodine intake: Iodine status worldwide. Available at www.who.int/vmnis/iodine/status/summary/iodine_data_status_summary_t2/en/index.html.

15. Aguayo, V. M., D. Garnier, and S. K. Baker. 2007. *Drops of Life: Vitamin A Supplementation for Child Survival, Progress and Lessons Learned in West and Central Africa*. UNICEF Regional Office for West and Central Africa.

16. Demment, M. W., M. M. Young, and R. L. Sensenig. 2003. Providing micronutrients through food-based solutions: A key to human and national development. Supplement: Animal source foods to improve micronutrient nutrition and human function in developing countries. *J. Nutr.* 133:3879S–3885S.

17. Hunt, J. M. 2002. Reversing productivity losses from iron deficiency: The economic case. *J. Nutr.* 132(4 Suppl):794S–801S 2002.

18. Adair, L. S., and A. M. Prentice. 2004. A critical evaluation of the fetal origins hypothesis and its implications for developing countries. *J. Nutr.* 134:191–193.

19. World Health Organization. 2006, September. Obesity and overweight. Available at www.who.int/mediacentre/factsheets/fs311/en/.

20. American Diabetes Association. 2008. Economic costs of diabetes in the U.S. in 2007. Available at www.diabetes.org/advocacy-and-legalresources/cost-of-diabetes.jsp.

21. NASA. Earth observatory: Famine in Niger and Mali. Available at http://earthobservatory.nasa.gov/NaturalHazards/natural_hazards_v2.php3?img_id=13028.

22. Herz, B. 2004. The importance of educating girls. *Science* 305:1910–1911.

23. Population Reference Bureau. 2008. 2008 World Population Data Sheet. Available at www.prb.org/Publications/Datasheets/2008/2008wpds.aspx.

24. UNAIDS. 2008, July 29. Substantial increases in HIV prevention efforts producing results, but not enough to turn back the epidemic. Available at http://data.unaids.org/pub/GlobalReport/2008/080725_GR08_pressrelease_en.pdf.

25. De Waal, A., and A. Whiteside. 2003. New variant famine: AIDS and food crisis in southern Africa. *Lancet* 362:1234–1237.

26. Struble, M. B., and L. L. Aomari. 2003. Position of the American Dietetic Association: Addressing world hunger, malnutrition and food insecurity. *J. Am. Diet. Assoc.* 103:1046–1057.

27. Charlton, K. E., and D. Rose. 2001. Nutrition among older adults in Africa: The situation at the beginning of the millennium. *J. Nutr.* 131:2424S–2428S.

28. World Health Organization. 2006, September. Obesity and overweight. Available at www.who.int/mediacentre/factsheets/fs311/en/.

29. Drewnowski, A., and N. Darmon. 2005. The economics of obesity: Dietary energy and energy cost. *Am. J. Clin. Nutr.* 82:265S–73S.

30. U.S. Department of Agriculture (USDA). 2007. Economic Research Service. Food security in the United States: Key statistics and graphics. Available at www.ers.usda.gov/Briefing/FoodSecurity/trends.htm.

31. United Nations. 2005. The Millennium Development Goals Report. Available at www.un.org/millenniumgoals/.

32. USAID. 2005. Famine early warning system. Available at www.fews.net/.

33. United Nations. 2005. The Millennium Development Goals Report. Available at www.un.org/millenniumgoals/.

34. UNICEF. 1996. Fifty years for children. Available at www.unicef.org/sowc96/1980s.htm.

35. Evenson, R. E., and D. Gollin. 2003. Assessing the impact of the Green Revolution, 1960 to 2000. *Science* 2:758–762.

36. Center for Global Food Issues. 2005. Declaration in support of protecting nature with high-yield farming and forestry, 2002. Available at www.highyieldconservation.org/.

37. Sakamoto, T., and M. Matsuoka. 2004. Generating high-yielding varieties by genetic manipulation of plant architecture. *Curr. Opin. Biotechnol.* 15:144–147; Gibson, R. W., V. Aritua, E. Byamukama, I. Mpembe, and J. Kayongo, 2004. Control strategies for sweet potato virus disease in Africa. *Virus Res.* 100(1):115–22; and Welch, R. M., and R. D. Graham. 2004. Breeding for micronutrients in staple food crops from a human nutrition perspective. *J. Exp. Botany* 55:353–364.

38. Knight, J. 2003. A dying breed. *Nature* 421:568–570.

39. National Student Campaign Against Hunger and Homelessness. 2005, February. Communities in crisis: Survey of hunger and homelessness in America. Available at www.studentsagainsthunger.org/hunger.asp?id2=15761.

40. Zinn, H. 2006. *Original Zinn*, p. 167. New York: Harper Perennial.

41. Anderson, K., and W. Martin, eds. 2006. *Agricultural Trade Reform and the DOHA Development Agenda*. Washington, DC: The World Bank/Palgrave Macmillan.

42. World Trade Organization. Available at www.wto.org/.

43. World Bank Report. 2004. Global agricultural trade and developing countries. Available at www.worldbank.org/prospects/globalag.

44. Fair Trade Overview. TransFair USA. Available at www.transfairusa.org/content/about/overview.php.

Tariffs and Subsidies: Helpful or Harmful?

In response to the global economic downturn, governments throughout the world in 2009 began to consider new measures to protect their farmers, food manufacturers, and consumers from rising prices. Such measures, which traditionally include tariffs, subsidies, and embargoes, can provide economic relief at home, but inevitably increase economic distress among trading partners.

The United States and many countries in Europe protect their farmers' incomes by paying *subsidies,* grants of money legislated and distributed by a region's government, that guarantee a minimum price for a crop even if the market value is lower. This has the effect of increasing the production of subsidized crops, such as wheat and corn and milk, and creating surpluses that lower the prices of these foods for consumers, as well as for companies manufacturing processed foods that use these crops. These subsidized foods also can be exported at lower prices, often to the financial detriment of producers in the countries receiving the exported goods.

At the same time, importing countries worldwide protect their own farmers by charging *import tariffs,*

The European Union requires an import tariff on bananas from Latin America, such as from this Costa Rican farm, but no tariff from some countries in Africa and the Caribbean.

which are taxes on a particular class of goods when they are brought into a country to be sold. These charges increase the price of cheap imported foods so that farmers who grow the same crop locally can charge the price necessary to make a living wage and still be competitive. For example, tariffs in Japan on imported rice from Burma protect Japanese rice farmers but make it difficult for Burmese farmers to market their crop in Japan. Consumers in Japan pay a price higher than they would if they were permitted to buy Burmese rice at *market price,* that is, at the price that results from an interaction of two factors: the supply available and the demand for the goods at a given time. Similarly, the United States maintains the local price of domestic sugar by an import tariff on sugar from other countries. Import tariffs effectively reduce the ability of exporting countries—often developing nations—to compete in markets where the same crop is grown domestically. They also maintain higher prices for consumers, essentially requiring consumers in countries with import tariffs to subsidize domestic production.

Export subsidies, which are grants of money provided by a region's government to exporters of surplus crops, also make it difficult for farmers to compete in international markets. These subsidies are paid, usually by developed countries, to exporters of surplus crops so that they can then sell their crops cheaply abroad. Export subsidies decrease prices for consumers in the country to which the food is shipped but also decrease the income that local farmers in that country can receive at market for the same food.

An *export embargo* is a government-ordered prohibition on exporting a particular product. Export embargos are typically used to protect domestic customers from high prices for a particular crop when farmers could fetch a higher price for it if they were to sell it abroad. One example is the U.S. export embargo on soybeans in the 1970s. This embargo protected American consumers of soybeans but resulted in shortages in other countries.

Subsidies and tariffs are also called *trade barriers.* Their goal is to provide local farmers with a higher and steadier income than might be possible with a free market. For this reason they are sometimes also called *protective trade barriers.* The United States has protective trade barriers for many crops, including the eight major field crops of corn, sorghum, barley, oats, wheat, rice, cotton, and soybeans. The countries in the European Union also support their agricultural producers heavily. On average, about 30% of farm income in developed countries is from a variety of supports.[41]

Part of a nation's protection can extend to the environment. In fact, the growing international concern about global warming and other environmental issues has led to many new proposals for protective trade barriers. Let's say, for instance, that a nation's government has passed legislation prohibiting the use of certain harmful pesticides on a particular domestic crop. This has increased the domestic price of the crop, as farmers have had to use more expensive biopesticides for a reduced yield. Now another country petitions this nation's government to allow it to sell the same crop at a lower price—but its crop was produced with the environmentally harmful pesticide. A variety of protective measures, including an outright prohibition on importation of the crop, are likely to be considered. So-called "green trade barriers" are currently being reviewed not only on food crops, but also on vehicles and other manufactured goods.

As we have seen, certain disadvantages to global welfare result from trade barriers on food. These include a reduced ability of developing agricultural nations to compete in the world market and higher prices for consumers and food companies that use the raw food materials in their products. The mission of the World Trade Organization (WTO) is to reduce protective trade barriers and encourage global free trade by negotiating fair trade agreements and settling trade disputes among its 149 member-countries.[42] The World Bank suggests that removing subsidies for agriculture would reduce poverty in developing countries, particularly those with small urban populations and thus little opportunity for expanding the

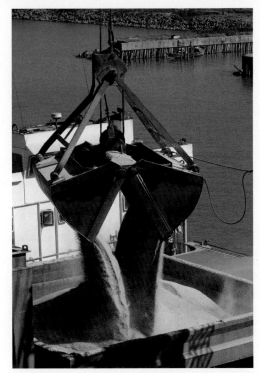

Protective trade barriers may inflate the price of grain sold on the world market.

domestic market.[43] At the same time, removing subsidies for agriculture in rich countries would free public moneys for other uses and encourage development of more competitive products.

However, not everyone agrees that global free trade in agriculture would automatically benefit the world's poor. Those opposed suggest that large multinational corporations and landholders in developing countries stand to gain at the expense of the majority of poor farmers. Fair trade organizations emphasize the need to ensure fair prices for farmers in developing nations and decent living and working conditions for laborers.[44] The latter include access to education, access to working capital, and use of sustainable agricultural practices that protect worker health and the local environment.

The politics of international trade affect the worldwide distribution of healthy food, the stability of farmers' incomes, and access to food by the world's poor. Debate is ongoing about the best ways to provide food security to all.

Critical Thinking Questions

■ Do you think it is ethical for wealthy nations to erect trades barriers that protect domestic farmers and/or consumers but reduce prosperity in developing nations?

■ Why or why not?

■ Do you think that so-called "green" trade barriers are an effective means of protecting the environment?

■ What alternatives to protectionist measures can you envision?

Appendices

Appendices

Appendix A Metabolism Pathways and Biochemical Structures

When learning about the science of nutrition, it is important to understand basic principles of metabolism and to know the molecular structures of important nutrients and molecules. Chapter 8 of this text provides a detailed discussion of the major metabolic processes that occur within the body. This appendix gives additional information and detail on several metabolism pathways and biochemical structures of importance. As in Chapter 8, red arrows indicate catabolic reactions.

Metabolism Pathways

Glycolysis

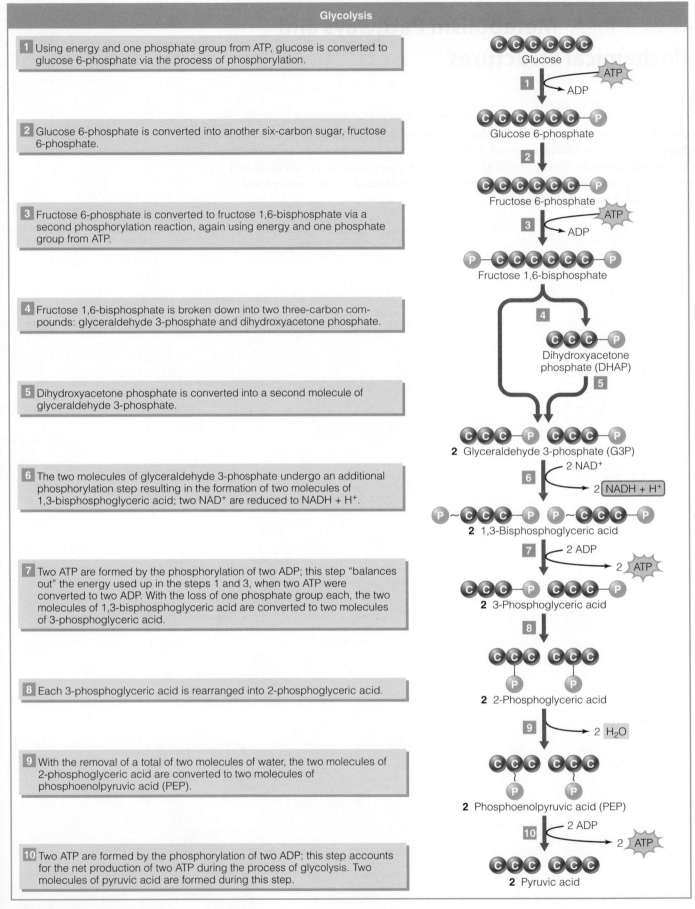

1. Using energy and one phosphate group from ATP, glucose is converted to glucose 6-phosphate via the process of phosphorylation.

2. Glucose 6-phosphate is converted into another six-carbon sugar, fructose 6-phosphate.

3. Fructose 6-phosphate is converted to fructose 1,6-bisphosphate via a second phosphorylation reaction, again using energy and one phosphate group from ATP.

4. Fructose 1,6-bisphosphate is broken down into two three-carbon compounds: glyceraldehyde 3-phosphate and dihydroxyacetone phosphate.

5. Dihydroxyacetone phosphate is converted into a second molecule of glyceraldehyde 3-phosphate.

6. The two molecules of glyceraldehyde 3-phosphate undergo an additional phosphorylation step resulting in the formation of two molecules of 1,3-bisphosphoglyceric acid; two NAD^+ are reduced to $NADH + H^+$.

7. Two ATP are formed by the phosphorylation of two ADP; this step "balances out" the energy used up in the steps 1 and 3, when two ATP were converted to two ADP. With the loss of one phosphate group each, the two molecules of 1,3-bisphosphoglyceric acid are converted to two molecules of 3-phosphoglyceric acid.

8. Each 3-phosphoglyceric acid is rearranged into 2-phosphoglyceric acid.

9. With the removal of a total of two molecules of water, the two molecules of 2-phosphoglyceric acid are converted to two molecules of phosphoenolpyruvic acid (PEP).

10. Two ATP are formed by the phosphorylation of two ADP; this step accounts for the net production of two ATP during the process of glycolysis. Two molecules of pyruvic acid are formed during this step.

Figure A.1 Glycolysis.

Figure A.2 TCA cycle.

Figure A.3 Electron transport chain. ATP is released at various points in the electron transport chain as electrons are passed from one molecule to another. The process, termed *oxidative phosphorylation*, occurs within the electron transport chain.

(a) Sources of energy use and production during glucose oxidation

(b) Energy balance sheet for glucose oxidation

Figure A.4 Net energy production for glucose oxidation.

Fatty Acid Oxidation

Palmitate (16C)

1   CoA

16-carbon fatty acid (palmitate)

Palmityl CoA

CoA

2   FAD → FADH$_2$

14-carbon fatty acid (myristate)

Activated palmityl CoA

CoA

3   H$_2$O

CoA

OH   O

4   NAD$^+$ → NADH + H$^+$

CoA

O   O

5   CoA

Activated myristate (14C)

CoA + CoA   Acetyl CoA (2C)

O

8 Acetyl CoA

1 Before the fatty acid (palmitate, in this example) enters the mitochondria for beta-oxidation, it is converted to a CoA derivative in the cytosol of the cell. The fatty acid–CoA is then transported into the mitochondria for the actual beta-oxidation pathway.

2 In mitochondria, the palmityl CoA is oxidized, resulting in the formation of FADH$_2$.

3 The activated palmityl CoA undergoes hydration (the addition of water).

4 A second oxidation results in the production of NADH and H$^+$.

5 As one molecule of acetyl CoA is cleaved off (leaving a 14-C fatty acid, myristate), a new CoA attaches to the terminal (end) carbon and the cycle begins again, feeding back into step 2.

Figure A.5 Fatty acid oxidation.

Net Energy Production for Fatty Acid Oxidation

Reaction by-product	Number produced	Number of ATP produced per product	Total energy (ATP) produced	Balance of energy from the oxidation of one 16-carbon fatty acid
FADH$_2$	7	2 via electron transport chain	7 x 2 = 14 ATP	
NADH + H$^+$	7	3 via electron transport chain	7 x 3 = 21 ATP	131 ATP
Acetyl- CoA	8	12 via TCA cycle	8 x 12 = 96 ATP	

Energy balance sheet for fatty acid (16-carbon palmitate) oxidation

Figure A.6 Net energy production for fatty acid oxidation (16-carbon palmitate). With each sequential cleavage of the two-carbon acetyl CoA, one FADH$_2$ (which yields 2 ATP when oxidized by the electron transport chain) and one NADH (which yields 3 ATP when oxidized by the electron transport chain) are produced. Each molecule of acetyl CoA yields 12 ATP when metabolized through the TCA cycle. The complete oxidation of palmitate yields 7 FADH$_2$ (14 ATP), 7 NADH (21 ATP), and 8 acetyl CoA (96 ATP), for a grand total of 131 ATP.

Synthesis of Ketone Bodies

1 As acetyl CoA accumulates, it reacts with acetoacetyl CoA to form a short-lived metabolite β-hydroxy-β-methylglutaryl CoA.

2 β-hydroxy-β-methylglutaryl CoA is rapidly cleaved to form acetyl CoA and acetoacetate (a ketone body). During this step, acetyl CoA is released.

3 Acetoacetate can either be reduced to β-hydroxybutyrate (3a) or decarboxylated to form acetone (3b) and carbon dioxide. Both β-hydroxybutyrate and acetone are ketone bodies. All three ketone bodies accumulate during the condition of ketosis.

Figure A.7 The synthesis of ketone bodies.

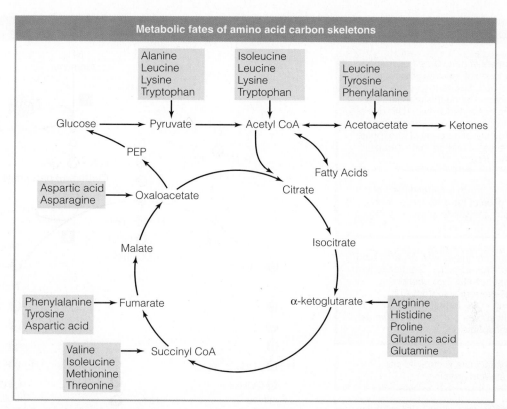

Figure A.8 The metabolic fates of amino acid carbon skeletons. After the deamination of amino acids, their carbon skeletons feed into various metabolic pathways. Glucogenic amino acids can be converted into pyruvate and/or intermediates of the TCA cycle, which can ultimately feed into glucose synthesis. Ketogenic amino acids can be converted into acetyl CoA, which then feeds into the synthesis of fatty acids. Some amino acids have more than one metabolic pathway available.

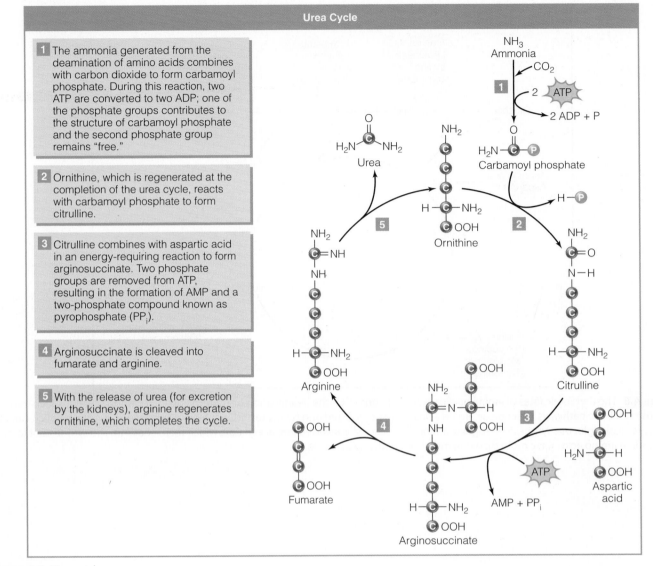

Urea Cycle

1 The ammonia generated from the deamination of amino acids combines with carbon dioxide to form carbamoyl phosphate. During this reaction, two ATP are converted to two ADP; one of the phosphate groups contributes to the structure of carbamoyl phosphate and the second phosphate group remains "free."

2 Ornithine, which is regenerated at the completion of the urea cycle, reacts with carbamoyl phosphate to form citrulline.

3 Citrulline combines with aspartic acid in an energy-requiring reaction to form arginosuccinate. Two phosphate groups are removed from ATP, resulting in the formation of AMP and a two-phosphate compound known as pyrophosphate (PP_i).

4 Arginosuccinate is cleaved into fumarate and arginine.

5 With the release of urea (for excretion by the kidneys), arginine regenerates ornithine, which completes the cycle.

Figure A.9 Urea cycle.

Ethanol Metabolism

Figure A.10 Ethanol metabolism.

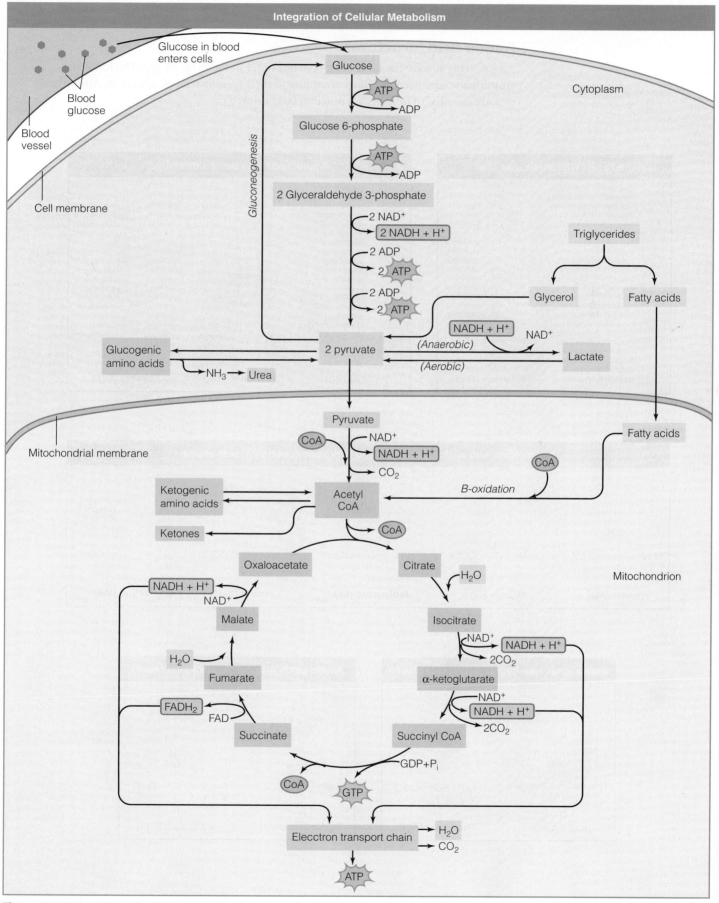

Figure A.11 Integration of cellular metabolism.

Biochemical Structures

Amino Acid Structures

Amino acids all have the same basic core but differ in their side chains. The following amino acids have been classified according to their specific type of side chain. Amino acids that are essential to humans are noted in bold print.

Amino acids with acidic side chains: Aspartate (Asp), Glutamate (Glu)

Amino acids with basic side chains: Arginine (Arg), **Histidine (His)**, **Lysine (Lys)**

Amino acids with aliphatic (carbon- and hydrogen-containing) side chains: Alanine (Ala), Glycine (Gly), **Isoleucine (Ile)**, **Leucine (Leu)**, **Valine (Val)**

Amino acids with hydroxyl (OH) side chains: Serine (Ser), **Threonine (Thr)**

Amino acids with amide (NH₂) side chains: Asparagine (Asp), Glutamine (Gln)

Amino acids with aromatic (ring) side chains

Phenylalanine (Phe)   **Tryptophan (Trp)**   Tyrosine (Tyr)

Amino acids with sulfur-containing side chains

Cysteine (Cys)   **Methionine (Met)**

Imino acid structure (amino group, after losing one hydrogen, forms a ring structure)

Proline (Pro)

Vitamin Structures and Coenzyme Derivatives

Many vitamins have common names (for example, vitamin C, vitamin E) as well as scientific designations (for example, ascorbic acid, α-tocopherol). Most vitamins are found in more than one chemical form. Many of the vitamins illustrated here have an active coenzyme form; review both the vitamin and the coenzyme structures and see if you can locate the "core vitamin" structure within each of the coenzymes. The vitamins found in foods or supplements are not always in the precise chemical form needed for metabolic activity, and therefore the body often has to modify the vitamin in one way or another. For example, many of the B-vitamins are phosphorylated, meaning they have a phosphate group attached.

Water-Soluble Vitamins

Niacin has two forms: nicotinic acid and nicotinamide. Both forms can be converted into the coenzymes nicotinamide adenine dinucleotide (NAD^+) and nicotinamide adenine dinucleotide phosphate ($NADP^+$).

Riboflavin can be converted into the coenzymes flavin adenine dinucleotide (FAD) and flavin mononucleotide (FMN).

Thiamin can be converted into the coenzyme thiamin pyrophosphate (TPP).

Vitamin B$_6$ includes the forms pyridoxine, pyridoxal, and pyridoxamine. The two common coenzymes derived from vitamin B$_6$ are pyridoxal 5′ phosphate (PLP) and pyridoxamine 5′ phosphate (PNP).

Two forms of vitamin B_{12} are cyanocobalamin and methylcobalamin.

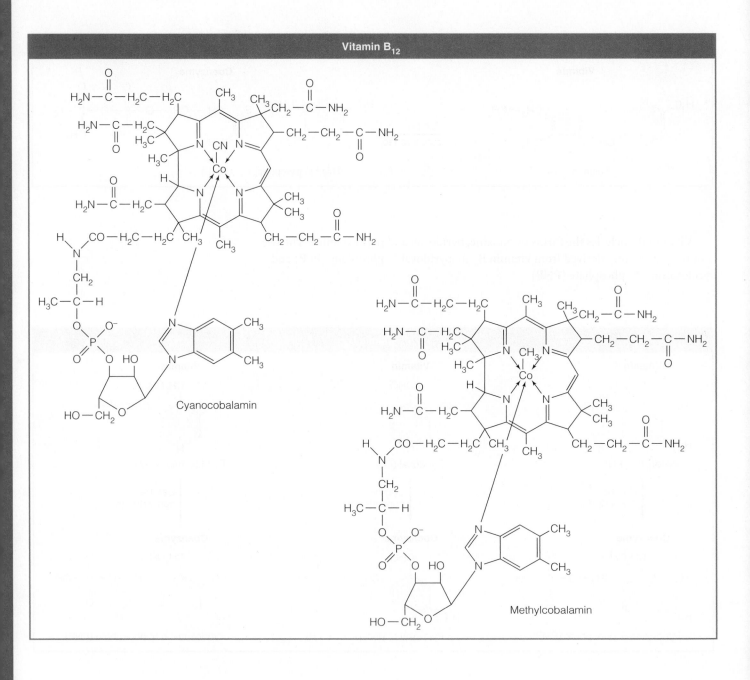

Folic acid is one specific chemical form of folate. This vitamin can be converted into several coenzymes, including tetrahydrafolic acid.

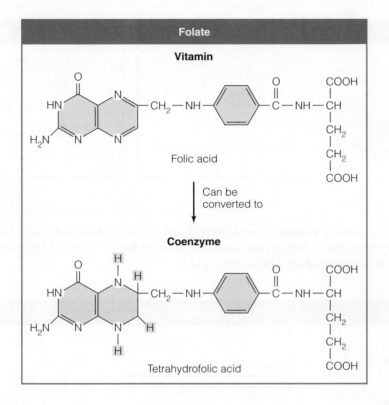

Pantothenic acid is a component of Coenzyme A (CoA).

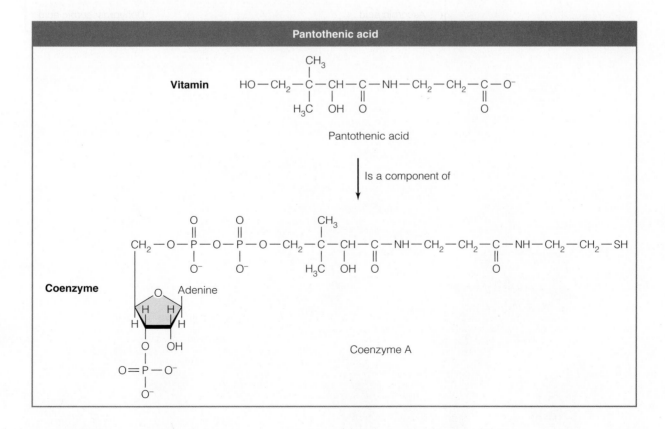

Biotin binds to several different metabolic enzymes. Choline serves as a methyl donor and as a precursor of acetylcholine and phospholipids.

The two forms of vitamin C (ascorbic acid and dehydroascorbic acid) are readily interconverted as two hydrogens are lost through the oxidation of ascorbic acid or gained through the reduction of dehydroascorbic acid.

Fat-Soluble Vitamins

Vitamin A exists as an alcohol (retinol), an aldehyde (retinal), and an acid (retinoic acid). Beta-carotene is a common and highly potent precursor that can be converted into vitamin A by the body.

Vitamin D as cholecalciferol must be activated by two hydroxylation reactions (the addition of one OH group at each step) to form the active form of the vitamin, calcitriol (also called 1,25 (OH)$_2$D).

α-tocopherol is the most active form of vitamin E; the number and location of the methyl (CH₃) groups attached to the ring structure distinguish the four unique forms of the tocopherols.

Vitamin K can be derived from plant sources (phylloquinones) and bacterial synthesis (menaquinones). A synthetic form of vitamin K (menadione) is also available.

Appendix B Chemistry Review

A basic grasp of chemistry is necessary for the introductory nutrition student. You may have taken a chemistry course at your college or in high school; this appendix can help you review concepts about atoms, molecules, pH, chemical reactions, and energy that you have learned previously.

All Matter Consists of Elements

Matter is anything that has mass and occupies space. All matter is composed of elements. An *element* is a fundamental (pure) form of matter that cannot be broken down to a simpler form. Aluminum and iron are elements, and so are oxygen and hydrogen. There are just over 100 known elements, and together they account for all matter on earth. The *periodic table of elements* arranges all the elements into groups according to their similar properties (**Figure B.1**).

Atoms Are the Smallest Functional Units of an Element

Elements are made up of particles called atoms. An atom is the smallest unit of any element that still retains the physical and chemical properties of that element. Although we now know that atoms can be split apart under unusual circumstances (such as a nuclear reaction), atoms are the smallest units of matter that can take part in chemical reactions. So, for all practical purposes, atoms are the smallest functional units of matter.

Figure B.1 The periodic table shows all known elements in order of increasing atomic number.

Even the largest atoms are so small that we can see them only with specialized microscopes. Chemists can also infer what they look like from studying their physical properties (**Figure B.2**).

Electron

Proton

Shell

(a) Hydrogen
1 proton

Neutron

Nucleus

(b) Oxygen
8 protons
8 neutrons
8 electrons
in 2 shells

(c) Sodium
11 protons
11 neutrons
11 electrons
in 3 shells

Figure B.2 The structure of atoms. Atoms consist of a nucleus, comprised of positively charged protons and neutral neutrons, surrounded by spherical shells of negatively charged electrons.

The central core of an atom is called the *nucleus.* The nucleus is made of positively charged particles called *protons* and a nearly equal number of neutral particles called *neutrons,* all tightly bound together. An exception is the smallest atom, hydrogen, whose nucleus consists of only a single proton. Smaller negatively charged particles called *electrons* orbit the nucleus. Because electrons are constantly moving, their precise position at any one time is unknown. You may think of electrons as occupying one or more spherical clouds of negative charge around the nucleus called *shells.* Each shell can accommodate only a certain number of electrons. The first shell, the one closest to the nucleus, can hold two electrons, the second can accommodate eight, and the third shell (if there is one) can contain even more. Each type of atom has a unique number of electrons. Under most circumstances the number of electrons equals the number of protons, and, as a result, the entire atom is electrically neutral.

Protons and neutrons have about the same mass, and both have much more mass than electrons. (Over 99.9% of an atom's mass is due to the protons and neutrons in its nucleus.)

In the periodic table and in chemical equations, atoms are designated by one- or two-letter symbols taken from English or Latin. For example, oxygen is designated by the letter O, nitrogen by N, sodium by Na (from the Latin word for sodium, *natrium*), and potassium by K (from the Latin *kalium*). A subscript numeral following the symbol indicates the numbers of atoms of that element. For example, the chemical formula O_2 represents two atoms of oxygen linked together, the most stable form of elemental oxygen.

In addition to a symbol, atoms have an *atomic number,* which represents the characteristic number of protons in the nucleus, and an *atomic mass* (or mass number), which is generally fairly close to the total number of neutrons and protons.

Isotopes Have a Different Number of Neutrons

Although all the atoms of a particular element have the same number of protons, the number of neutrons can vary slightly. Atoms with either more or fewer neutrons than the usual number for that element are called *isotopes.* Isotopes of an element have the same atomic number as the more common atoms but a different atomic mass. For example, elemental carbon typically consists of atoms with six protons and six neutrons, for an atomic mass of 12. The isotope of carbon known as carbon-14 has an atomic mass of 14 because it has two extra neutrons.

Isotopes are always identified by a superscript mass number preceding the symbol. For instance, the carbon-14 isotope is designated ^{14}C. The superscript mass number of the most common elemental form of carbon is generally omitted because it is understood to be 12.

Many isotopes are unstable. Such isotopes are called *radioisotopes* because they tend to give off energy (in the form of radiation) and particles until they reach a more stable state. The radiation emitted by radioisotopes can be dangerous to living organisms because the energy can damage tissues.

Atoms Combine to Form Molecules

A *molecule* is a stable association between two or more atoms. For example, a molecule of water consists of two atoms of hydrogen plus one atom of oxygen (written as H_2O). A molecule of ordinary table salt (written as NaCl) consists of one atom of sodium (Na) plus one atom of chlorine (Bl). A molecule of hydrogen gas (written as H_2) consists of two atoms of hydrogen. In order to understand *why* atoms join together to form molecules, we need to know more about energy.

Energy Fuels the Body's Activities

Energy is the capacity to do work, or the capacity to cause some change in matter. Joining atoms is one type of work, and breaking up molecules is another—and both require energy. Stored energy that is not actually performing any work at the moment is called *potential energy* because it has the *potential* to make things happen. Energy that is actually *doing work*—that is, energy in motion—is called *kinetic energy.*

Potential energy is stored in the bonds that hold atoms together in all matter, both living and nonliving. The body takes advantage of this general principle of chemistry by using certain molecules to store energy for its own use. When the chemical bonds of these energy-storage molecules are broken, potential energy becomes kinetic energy. The body relies on this energy to power "work" such as breathing, moving, and digesting food.

Matter is most stable when it is at the *lowest possible energy level*, that is, when it contains the least potential energy. This fact has important implications for the formation of molecules, because even single atoms contain energy.

Electrons Have Potential Energy

Recall that electrons carry a negative charge, whereas protons within the nucleus have a positive charge. Electrons are attracted to the positively charged nucleus and repelled by each other. As a result of these opposing attractive and repulsive forces, each electron occupies a specific shell around the nucleus. Each shell corresponds to a specific level of electron potential energy, and each shell farther out represents a potential energy level higher than the preceding one. When an electron moves to a shell closer to the nucleus, it loses energy. In order to move to a shell that is farther from the nucleus, the electron must absorb energy.

Chemical Bonds Link Atoms to Form Molecules

A key concept in chemistry is that *atoms are most stable when their outermost occupied electron shell is completely filled.* An atom whose outermost electron shell is not normally filled tends to interact with one or more other atoms in a way that fills its outermost shell. Such interactions generally cause the atoms to be bound to each other by attractive forces called *chemical bonds.* The three principal types of chemical bonds are called covalent, ionic, and hydrogen bonds.

Covalent Bonds Involve Sharing Electrons

One way that an atom can fill its outermost shell is by sharing a pair of electrons with another atom. An electron-sharing bond between atoms is called a *covalent bond* (**Figure B.3**). Covalent bonds between atoms are among the strongest chemical bonds in nature; they are so strong that they rarely break apart. In structural formulas, a covalent bond is depicted as a line drawn between two atoms.

Hydrogen gas offers an example of how a covalent (electron-sharing) bond fills the outermost shells of two atoms. Each of the two hydrogen atoms has just one electron in the first shell, which can accommodate two electrons. When joined together by a covalent bond (forming H_2, a gas), each atom has, in effect, a "full" first shell of two electrons. As a result, H_2 gas is more stable than the same two hydrogen atoms by themselves. The sharing of one pair of electrons, as in H_2, is called a *single* bond.

Oxygen gas is another example of covalent bonding. An oxygen atom has eight electrons: Two of these fill the first electron shell, and the remaining six occupy the second electron shell (which can accommodate eight). Two oxygen atoms may join to form a molecule of oxygen gas by sharing two pairs of electrons, thus completing the outer shells of both atoms. When two pairs of electrons are shared, the bond is called a *double bond.* In structural formulas, double bonds are indicated by two parallel lines.

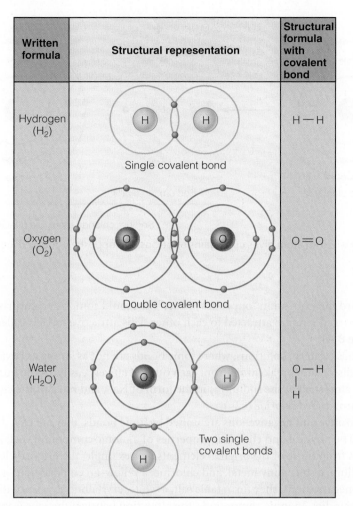

Written formula	Structural representation	Structural formula with covalent bond
Hydrogen (H_2)	Single covalent bond	H — H
Oxygen (O_2)	Double covalent bond	O = O
Water (H_2O)	Two single covalent bonds	O — H $\quad$ O — H with H below

Figure B.3 Covalent bonds. Sharing pairs of electrons is a way for an atom to fill its outermost shell.

A molecule of water forms from one oxygen and two hydrogen atoms because this combination completely fills the outermost shells of both hydrogen and oxygen. The prevalence of water on earth follows from the simple rule described earlier: Matter is most stable when it contains the least potential energy. That is, both hydrogen and oxygen are more stable when together (as H_2O) than when they are independent atoms.

Ionic Bonds Occur Between Oppositely Charged Ions

A second way that atoms can fill their outer shell of electrons is to give up electrons completely (if they have only one or two electrons in their outermost shell) or to take electrons from other atoms (if they need one or two to fill their outermost shell). Such a loss (or gain) of electrons gives the atom a net charge, because now there are fewer (or more) negatively charged electrons than positively charged protons in the nucleus. The net charge is positive (+) for each electron lost and negative (−) for each electron gained.

An electrically charged atom or molecule is called an *ion*. Examples of ions are sodium (Na^+), chloride (Cl^-), calcium (Ca^{2+}), and hydrogen phosphate (HPO_4^-). Note that ions can have a shortage or surplus of more than one electron (for example, Ca^{2+} has lost two electrons). A positively charged ion is called a *cation;* a negatively charged ion is called an *anion.*

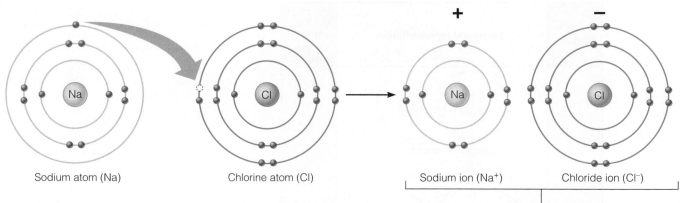

Figure B.4 Ionic bonds. Electrically charged ions form when an atom gives up or gains electrons. The oppositely charged ions are attracted to each other, forming an ionic bond.

Ever heard the expression "opposites attract"? It should come as no surprise that oppositely charged ions are attracted to each other. This attractive force is called an *ionic bond* (**Figure B.4**).

In aqueous (watery) solutions, where ionic bonds are not as strong as covalent bonds, ions tend to dissociate (break away) from each other relatively easily. In the human body, for example, almost all of the sodium is in the form of Na^+, and most of the chlorine is in its ionized form, *called chloride* (Cl^-).

When positive and negative ions are united by ionic bonds, they are called *ionic compounds*. The physical and chemical properties of an ionic compound such as NaCl are very different from those of the original elements. For example, the original elements of NaCl are sodium, a soft, shiny metal, and chlorine, a yellow-green poisonous gas. Yet, as positive and negative ions, they form table salt, a white, crystalline substance that is common in our diet. In ionic compounds, the attraction between the ions is very strong, which makes the melting points of ionic compounds high, often greater than 300°C. For example, the melting point of NaCl is 800°C. At room temperature, ionic compounds are solids.

The structure of an ionic solid depends on the arrangement of the ions. In a crystal of NaCl, which has a cubic shape, the larger Cl^- ions are packed close together in a lattice structure. The smaller Na^+ ions occupy the holes between the Cl^- ions.

Ions in aqueous solutions are sometimes called *electrolytes* because solutions of water containing ions are good conductors of electricity. Cells can control the movement of certain ions, creating electrical forces essential to the functioning of nerves, muscles, and other living tissues.

Weak Hydrogen Bonds Form Between Polar Molecules

A third type of attraction occurs between molecules that do not have a net charge. Glance back at the water molecule in Figure B.3 and note that the two hydrogen atoms are found not at opposite ends of the water molecule but fairly close together. Although the oxygen atom and the two hydrogen atoms share electrons, the sharing is unequal. The shared electrons in a water molecule actually spend slightly more of their time near the oxygen atom than near the hydrogen atoms because the oxygen atom attracts electrons more strongly than do the hydrogen atoms. Although the water molecule is neutral overall, the uneven sharing gives the oxygen end a partial negative charge and the hydrogen end a partial positive charge.

Molecules such as water that are electrically neutral overall but still have partially charged ends, or *poles*, are called *polar* molecules. According to the principle that opposites attract, polar molecules arrange themselves so that the negative pole of one molecule is

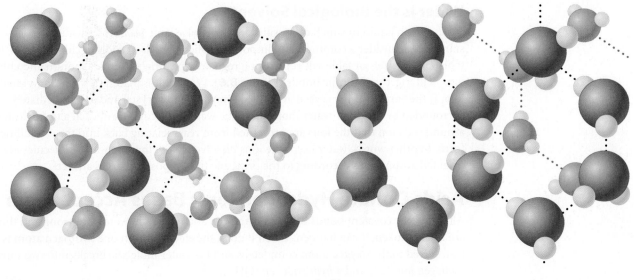

(a)   (b)

Figure B.5   Hydrogen bonds. **(a)** In water, weak hydrogen bonds continually form, break, and re-form between hydrogen and oxygen atoms of adjacent water molecules. **(b)** Ice is a solid because stable hydrogen bonds form between each water molecule and four of its neighbors.

oriented toward (attracted by) the positive pole of another molecule. The weak attractive force between oppositely charged regions of polar molecules that contain covalently bonded hydrogen is called a *hydrogen bond* (**Figure B.5**).

Hydrogen bonds between water molecules in liquid water are so weak that they continually break and re-form, allowing water to flow. When water becomes cold enough to freeze, each water molecule forms four stable, unchanging hydrogen bonds with its neighbors. When water is vaporized (becomes a gas), the hydrogen bonds are broken and stay broken as long as the water is in the gas phase.

Hydrogen bonds are important in biological molecules. They provide the force that gives proteins their three-dimensional shape, and they keep the two strands of the DNA molecule together.

Table B.1 summarizes covalent, ionic, and hydrogen bonds.

The Body Depends on Water

No molecule is more essential to life than water. Indeed, it accounts for between 50% and 70% of body weight. The following properties of water are especially important to the body: water molecules are polar, water is a liquid at body temperature, and water can absorb and hold heat energy.

These properties make water an ideal solvent and an important factor in temperature regulation, as discussed in Chapter 9.

Table B.1 Summary of the Three Types of Chemical Bonds

Type	Strength	Description	Examples
Covalent bond	Strong	A bond in which the sharing of electrons between atoms results in each atom having a maximally filled outermost shell of electrons	The bonds between hydrogen and oxygen in a molecule of water
Ionic bond	Moderate	The bond between two oppositely charged ions (atoms or molecules that were formed by the permanent transfer of one or more electrons)	The bond between Na^+ and Cl^- in salt
Hydrogen bond	Weak	The bond between oppositely charged regions of molecules that contain covalently bonded hydrogen atoms	The bonds between molecules of water

Water Is the Biological Solvent

A *solvent* is a liquid in which other substances dissolve, and a *solute* is any dissolved substance. Consider a common and important solid: crystals of sodium chloride (NaCl), or table salt. Crystals of table salt consist of a regular, repeating pattern of sodium and chloride ions held together by ionic bonds (**Figure B.6**). When salt is placed in water, individual ions at the surface of the crystal are pulled away from the crystal and are immediately surrounded by the polar water molecules. The water molecules form such a tight cluster around each ion that the ions are prevented from reassociating back into the crystalline form. In other words, water keeps the ions dissolved. Note that the water molecules are oriented around ions according to the principle that opposite charges attract.

Acids Donate Hydrogen Ions; Bases Accept Them

Although the covalent bonds between hydrogen and oxygen in water are strong and thus are rarely broken, it can happen. When it does, the electron from one hydrogen atom is transferred to the oxygen atom completely, and the water molecule breaks into two ions—a *hydrogen ion* (H^+) and a *hydroxide ion* (OH^-).

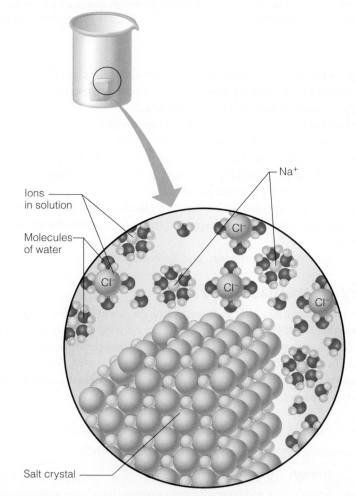

Figure B.6 How water keeps ions in solution. The slightly negative ends of polar water molecules are attracted to positive ions, whereas the slightly positive ends of water molecules are attracted to negative ions. The water molecules pull the ions away from the crystal and prevent them from reassociating with each other.

In pure water, only a very few molecules of water are dissociated (broken apart) into H^+ and OH^- at any one time. However, there are other sources of hydrogen ions in aqueous solutions. An *acid* is any molecule that can donate (give up) an H^+. When added to pure water, acids produce an *acidic* solution, one with a higher H^+ concentration than that of pure water. (By definition, an aqueous solution with the same H^+ concentration as that of pure water is a *neutral* solution). Common acidic solutions are vinegar, carbonated beverages, and orange juice. Conversely, a *base* is any molecule that can accept (combine with) an H^+. When added to pure water, bases produce a basic or *alkaline* solution, one with a lower H^+ concentration than that of pure water. Common alkaline solutions include baking soda in water, detergents, and drain cleaner.

Because acids and bases have opposite effects on the H^+ concentration of solutions, they are said to neutralize each other.

The pH Scale Expresses Hydrogen Ion Concentration

Scientists use the pH scale to indicate the acidity or alkalinity of a solution. The *pH scale* is a measure of the hydrogen ion concentration of a solution. The scale ranges from 0 to 14, with the pH of pure water defined as a pH of 7.0, the neutral point. A pH of 7 corresponds to a hydrogen ion concentration of 10^{-7} moles/liter (a *mole* is a term used by chemists to indicate a certain number of atoms, ions, or molecules). An *acidic* solution has a pH of *less* than 7, whereas a *basic* solution has a pH of *greater* than 7. Each whole-number change in pH represents a tenfold change in the hydrogen ion concentration in the opposite direction. For example, an acidic solution with a pH of 6 has an H^+ concentration of 10^{-6} moles/liter (ten times greater than pure water), whereas an alkaline solution with a pH of 8 has an H^+ concentration of 10^{-8} moles/liter (1/10 that of water). Figure 3.7 on page 83 shows the pH scale and indicates the pH values of some common substances and foods.

The pH of blood is 7.4, just slightly more alkaline than neutral water. The hydrogen ion concentration of blood plasma is low relative to other ions (the hydrogen ion concentration of blood plasma is less than one-*millionth* that of sodium ions, for example). It is important to maintain homeostasis of this low concentration of hydrogen ions in the body because hydrogen ions are small, mobile, positively charged, and highly reactive. Hydrogen ions tend to displace other positive ions in molecules, and this displacement then alters molecular structures and changes the ability of the molecule to function properly.

Changes in the pH of body fluids can affect how molecules are transported across the cell membrane and how rapidly certain chemical reactions occur. pH changes may even alter the shapes of proteins that are structural elements of the cell. In other words, a change in the hydrogen ion concentration can be dangerous because it alters the body's metabolism and threatens homeostasis.

Buffers Minimize Changes in pH

A *buffer* is any substance that tends to minimize the changes in pH that might otherwise occur when an acid or base is added to a solution. Buffers are essential to the body's ability to maintain homeostasis of pH in body fluids.

In biological solutions such as blood or urine, buffers are present as *pairs* of related molecules that have opposite effects. One molecule of the pair is the acid form of the molecule (capable of donating an H^+), and the other is the base form (capable of accepting an H^+). When an acid is added and the number of H^+ ions increases, the base form of the buffer pair will accept some of the H^+, minimizing the fall in pH that might otherwise occur. Conversely, when a base is added that might take up too many H^+ ions, the acid form of the buffer pair will release additional H^+ and thus minimize the rise in pH. Buffer pairs are like absorbent sponges that can pick up excess water and then can be wrung out to release water when necessary.

One of the most important buffer pairs in body fluids such as blood is bicarbonate (HCO_3^-, the base form) and carbonic acid (H_2CO_3, the acid form). When blood becomes too acidic, bicarbonate accepts excess H^+ according to the following reaction:

$$HCO_3^- + H^+ \rightarrow H_2CO_3$$

When blood becomes too alkaline, carbonic acid donates H^+ by the reverse reaction:

$$HCO_3^- + H^+ \leftarrow H_2CO_3$$

In a biological solution such as blood, bicarbonate and carbonic acid take up and release H^+ all the time. Ultimately, a chemical *equilibrium* is reached in which the rates of the two chemical reactions are the same, as represented by the following combined equation:

$$HCO_3^- + H^+ \leftrightarrow H_2CO_3$$

When excess acid is produced, the combined equation shifts to the right as the bicarbonate combines with the H^+. The reverse is true for alkalinity.

There are many other buffers in the body. The more buffers that are present in a body fluid, the more stable the pH will be.

The Organic Molecules

Organic molecules are molecules that contain carbon and other elements held together by covalent bonds. The name "organic" came about at a time when scientists believed that all organic molecules were created only by living organisms and all "inorganic" molecules came from nonliving matter. Today scientists know that organic molecules can be synthesized in the laboratory under the right conditions.

Carbon Is the Common Building Block of Organic Molecules

Carbon is the common building block of all organic molecules because of the many ways that it can form strong covalent bonds with other atoms. Carbon has six electrons, two in the first shell and four in the second. Because carbon is most stable when its second shell is filled with eight electrons, *its natural tendency is to form four covalent bonds with other molecules*. This makes carbon an ideal structural component, one that can branch in a multitude of directions.

Using the chemist's convention that a line between the chemical symbols of atoms represents a pair of shared electrons in a covalent bond, **Figure B.7** shows some of the many structural possibilities for carbon. Carbon can form covalent bonds with hydrogen, nitrogen, oxygen, or another carbon. It can form double covalent bonds with oxygen or another carbon. It can even form five- or six-membered carbon rings, with or without double bonds between carbons.

In addition to their complexity, there is almost no limit to the size of organic molecules derived from carbon. Some, called *macromolecules* (from the Greek *makros*, long), consist of thousands or even millions of smaller molecules. Protein and glycogen are two examples of macromolecules.

Chemical Reactions

In a chemical reaction, original substances (reactants) are changed to new substances (products) with different physical properties and different compositions. All of the atoms of the original reactants are found in the products. However, some of the bonds between the atoms in the reactants have been broken and new bonds have formed between different combinations of atoms to produce the products. For example, when you light a gas burner, the molecules of methane gas (CH_4) react with oxygen (O_2) in the air to produce CO_2, H_2O, and heat.

In another chemical reaction, when an antacid tablet is placed in water, as the sodium bicarbonate ($NaHCO_3$) and citric acid ($C_6H_8O_7$) in the tablet react, bubbles of carbon

Figure B.7 Examples of the structural diversity of carbon. **(a)** In carbon dioxide, a carbon atom forms two covalent bonds with each oxygen atom. **(b)** Lipid molecules contain long chains of carbon atoms covalently bound to hydrogen. **(c)** Carbon is the backbone of the amino acid phenylalanine.

dioxide (CO_2) gas appear. In both these chemical reactions, new properties can be observed. These clues tell you that a chemical reaction has taken place.

Oxidation and Reduction Reactions

In every oxidation–reduction reaction (abbreviated redox), electrons are transferred from one substance to another. If one substance loses electrons, another substance must gain an equal number of electrons. Oxidation is defined as the *loss* of elections; reduction is the *gain* of electrons. Every time a reaction involves an oxidation and a reduction, the number of electrons lost is equal to the number of electrons gained. The following is an example of oxidation and reduction:

$$Zn \rightarrow Zn^{2+} + 2e^{-} \text{ Oxidation of Zn}$$

$$Cu^{2+} + 2e^{-} \rightarrow Cu \text{ Reduction of } Cu^{2+}$$

Enzymes Facilitate Biochemical Reactions

An *enzyme* is a protein that functions as a biological catalyst. A *catalyst* is a substance that speeds up the rate of a chemical reaction without being altered or consumed by the reaction. Enzymes help biochemical reactions to occur, but they do not change the final result of the reaction. That is, they can only speed reactions that would have happened anyway, although much more slowly. A chemical reaction that could take hours by itself might take place in minutes or seconds in the presence of an enzyme.

Without help from thousands of enzymes, most biochemical reactions in our cells would occur too slowly to sustain life. Each enzyme facilitates a particular chemical reaction or group of reactions. Some enzymes break molecules apart; others join molecules together. Enzymes serve as catalysts because, as proteins, they can change shape. The ability to change shape allows them to bind to other molecules and orient them so that they may interact. Figure 6.12 on page 222 depicts how a typical enzyme works.

Free Radicals and Antioxidants

Oxygen free radicals, sometimes simply called free radicals, are an especially unstable class of molecules. Free radicals are oxygen-containing molecules that have an unpaired electron in their outer shell. They are exceptionally unstable because any unpaired electron has a very high potential energy. Consequently, free radicals have a strong tendency to oxidize (remove electrons from) another molecule. They set in motion a destructive cascade of events in which electrons are removed from stable compounds, producing still more unstable compounds. Free radicals damage body tissues, and many scientists believe that they contribute to the aging process.

One of the most destructive free radical molecules is molecular oxygen with an extra electron (O_2^-), called superoxide. Other important free radicals include peroxide (H_2O_2) and hydroxyl (OH). The latter is formed when a hydroxide ion (OH^-) loses an electron. Please refer to Figure 10.2 on page 359 for more detail on free radical formation in the cell membrane.

Some free radicals are accidentally produced in small amounts during the normal process of energy transfer within living cells. Exposure to chemicals, radiation, ultraviolet light, cigarette smoke, alcohol, and air pollution may also create them.

We now know that certain enzymes and nutrients called antioxidants are the body's natural defense against oxygen free radicals. Antioxidants prevent oxidation either by preventing the formation of free radicals in the first place or by inactivating them quickly before they can damage other molecules. Important antioxidants include vitamin E, vitamin C, beta-carotene, and an enzyme called superoxide dismutase.

Condensation and Hydrolysis

Macromolecules are built (synthesized) within the cell itself. In a process called *condensation*, smaller molecules called subunits are joined together by covalent bonds, like pearls on a string. The name of the process accurately describes what is happening, for each time a subunit is added, the equivalent of a water molecule is removed ("dehydration"). The subunits needed to synthesize macromolecules come from the foods you eat and from the biochemical reactions in your body that break other large molecules down to smaller ones.

The synthesis of macromolecules from smaller molecules requires energy. That is one reason why we need energy to survive and grow. It is no accident that children seem to eat enormous amounts of food. Growing children require energy to make the macromolecules necessary to create new cell membranes, muscle fibers, and other body tissues.

Organic macromolecules are broken down by a process called *hydrolysis*. During hydrolysis, the equivalent of a water molecule is added each time a covalent bond between single subunits in the chain is broken. Note that hydrolysis is essentially the reverse of condensation, and thus it should not surprise you that the breakdown of macromolecules releases energy that was stored as potential energy in the covalent bonds between atoms. Hydrolysis of energy-storage molecules is how the body obtains much of its energy. Hydrolysis is also used to break down molecules of food during digestion, to recycle materials so that they can be used again, and to get rid of substances that are no longer needed by the body. Figure 7.4 on page 252 provides an overview of condensation and hydrolysis.

Appendix C Anatomy and Physiology Review

The Cell

Whereas atoms are the smallest units of matter and make up both living and nonliving things, cells are the smallest units of life. That is, cells can grow, reproduce themselves, and perform certain basic functions, such as taking in nutrients, transmitting impulses, producing chemicals, and excreting wastes. The human body is composed of billions of cells that are constantly replacing themselves, destroying worn or damaged cells, and manufacturing new ones. To support this constant demand for new cells, we need a ready supply of nutrient molecules, such as simple sugars, amino acids, and fatty acids, to serve as building blocks. These building blocks are the molecules that come from the breakdown of foods. All cells, whether of the skin, bones, or brain, are made of the same basic molecules of amino acids, sugars, and fatty acids that are also the main components of the foods we eat.

Cells Are Encased in a Functional Membrane

Cells are encased in a membrane called the cell membrane, or *plasma membrane* (**Figure C.1**). This membrane is the outer covering of the cell and defines the cell's boundaries. It encloses the cell's contents and acts as a gatekeeper, either allowing or denying the entry and exit of molecules such as nutrients and wastes.

Cell membranes are composed of two layers, called the *lipid bilayer*, because each layer is made of molecules called *phospholipids*. Phospholipids consist of a long lipid "tail" bound to a round phospholipid "head." The phosphate head interacts with water, whereas the lipid tail repels water. In the cell membrane, the lipid tails of each layer face each other, forming the membrane interior, whereas the phosphate heads face either the extracellular environment or the cell's interior. Located throughout the membrane are molecules of another lipid, cholesterol, which helps keep the membrane flexible. The membrane also contains various proteins, which assist in transport of nutrients and other substances across the cell membrane and in the manufacture of certain chemicals.

Cells Contain Organelles That Support Life

Enclosed within the cell membrane is a liquid called cytoplasm and a variety of organelles (see Figure C.1). These tiny structures accomplish some surprisingly sophisticated functions. A brief review of some of them and their functions related to nutrition is as follows:

- *Nucleus.* The nucleus is where our genetic information is located, in the form of deoxyribonucleic acid (DNA). The cell nucleus is darkly colored because DNA is a huge molecule that is tightly packed within it. A cell's DNA contains the instructions that the cell uses to make certain proteins.
- *Ribosomes.* Ribosomes are structures the cell uses to make needed proteins.
- *Endoplasmic reticulum (ER).* The endoplasmic reticulum is important in the synthesis of proteins and lipids and in the storage of the mineral calcium. The ER looks like a maze of interconnected channels.
- *Mitochondria.* Often called the cell's powerhouse, mitochondria produce the energy molecule ATP (adenosine triphosphate) from basic food components. ATP can be thought of as a stored form of energy, drawn upon as we need it. Cells that have high energy needs contain more mitochondria than cells with lower energy needs.

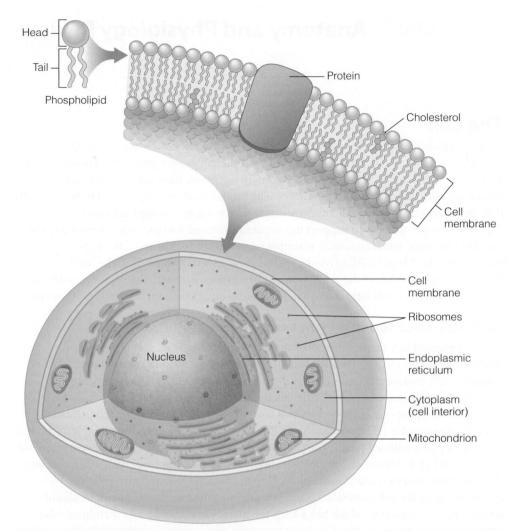

Figure C.1 Representative cell of the small intestine, showing the cell membrane and a variety of organelles.

Molecules Cross the Cell Membrane in Several Ways

Recall that the cell membrane is the gatekeeper that, along with its proteins, determines what goes into and out of the cell. This means that cell membranes are *selectively permeable*, allowing only some compounds to enter and leave the cell.

Passive Transport: Principles of Diffusion and Osmosis

Passive transport is "passive" because it transports a molecule without requiring the cell to expend any energy. Passive transport relies on the mechanism of diffusion.

Molecules in a gas or a liquid move about randomly, colliding with other molecules and changing direction. The movement of molecules from one region to another as the result of this random motion is known as diffusion.

If there are more molecules in one region than in another, then strictly by chance more molecules will tend to diffuse away from the area of high concentration and toward the region of low concentration. In other words, the *net* diffusion of molecules requires that there be a difference in concentration, called a *concentration gradient*, between two points. Once the concentration of molecules is the same throughout the solution, a state of equilibrium exists in which molecules are diffusing randomly but equally in all directions.

Not all substances diffuse readily into and out of living cells. The cell membrane is selectively permeable, meaning that it allows some substances to cross by diffusion but not others. It is highly permeable to water, but not to all ions or molecules. The net diffusion of water across a selectively permeable membrane is called *osmosis*. Osmosis and osmotic pressure are discussed in more detail in Chapter 9.

Most substances cross cell membranes by passive transport. Passive transport always proceeds "downhill" with respect to the concentration gradient, meaning that it relies on diffusion in some way. Three forms of passive transport across the cell membrane are (1) diffusion through the lipid bilayer, (2) diffusion through channels, and (3) facilitated transport.

Diffusion through the lipid bilayer

The lipid bilayer structure of the cell membrane allows the free passage of some molecules while restricting others. For instance, small uncharged nonpolar molecules can diffuse right through the lipid bilayer as if it did not exist. Such molecules simply dissolve in the lipid bilayer, passing through it as one might imagine a ghost walking through a wall. Polar or electrically charged molecules, on the other hand, cannot cross the lipid bilayer because they are not soluble in lipids.

Two important lipid-soluble molecules are oxygen (O_2), which diffuses into cells and is used up in the process of metabolism, and carbon dioxide (CO_2), a waste product of metabolism, which diffuses out of cells and is removed from the body by the lungs. Another substance that crosses the lipid bilayer by diffusion is urea, a neutral waste product removed from the body by the kidneys.

Diffusion through channels

Water and many ions diffuse through channels in the cell membrane. The channels are constructed of proteins that span the entire lipid bilayer. The sizes and shapes of these protein channels, as well as the electrical charges on the various amino acid groups that line the channel, determine which molecules can pass through.

Some channels are open all the time (typical of water channels). The diffusion of any molecule through the membrane is largely determined by the number of channels through which the molecule can fit. Other channels are "gated," meaning that they can open and close under certain conditions. Gated channels are particularly important in regulating the transport of ions (sodium, potassium, and calcium) in cells that are electrically excitable, such as nerves.

Facilitated transport

In facilitated transport, also called *facilitated diffusion*, the molecule does not pass through a channel at all. Instead, it attaches to a membrane protein, triggering a change in the protein's shape or orientation that transfers the molecule to the other side of the membrane and releases it there. Once the molecule is released, the protein returns to its original form. A protein that carries a molecule across the plasma membrane in this manner, rather than opening a channel through it, is called a transport protein (or carrier protein).

Facilitated transport is highly selective for particular substances. The direction of movement is always from a region of high concentration to one of lower concentration, and thus it does not require the cell to expend energy. The normal process of diffusion is simply being "facilitated" by the transport protein. Glucose and other simple sugars enter most cells by this method.

Active Transport Requires Energy

All methods of passive transport allow substances to move only down their concentration gradients, in the direction they would normally diffuse if there were no barrier. However, active transport can move substances through the plasma membrane *against* their concentration gradient. Active transport allows a cell to accumulate essential molecules even when their concentration outside the cell is relatively low and to get rid of molecules that it does not need. Active transport requires the expenditure of energy.

Like facilitated transport, active transport is accomplished by proteins that span the plasma membrane. The difference is that active transport proteins must have some source of energy in order to transport certain molecules. Some active transport proteins use the high-energy molecule ATP for this purpose. They break ATP down to ADP and a phosphate group (P_i) and use the released energy to transport one or more molecules across the plasma membrane against their concentration gradient. Figure 3.14 on page 91 provides an overview of active and passive transport.

From Cells to Organ Systems

Cells of a single type, such as muscle cells, join together to form functional groupings of cells called tissues. In general, several types of tissues join together to form organs, which are sophisticated structures that perform a unique body function. The stomach and small intestine are examples of organs.

Organs are further grouped into systems that perform integrated functions. The stomach, for example, is an organ that is part of the gastrointestinal system. It holds and partially digests a meal, but it cannot perform all system functions—digestion, absorption, and elimination—by itself. These functions require several organs working together in an integrated system. The following sections provide a review of some other body systems.

The Muscular System

Muscle cells are found in every organ and tissue in the body and participate in every activity that requires movement. The most obvious are the *skeletal muscles* that attach to the skeleton and give us strength and mobility. There are two other types of muscle in the body besides skeletal muscle. Rhythmic contractions of the *cardiac muscle* of the heart pump blood throughout the body. Powerful, intermittent contractions of *smooth muscle* in the walls of the uterus contribute to childbirth. Slower waves of smooth muscle contractions push food through the digestive tract and transport urine from the kidney to the bladder. Steady, sustained contractions of smooth muscle in the walls of blood vessels regulate blood flow to every living cell in the body.

A Muscle Is Composed of Many Muscle Cells

A single *muscle* (sometimes referred to as a "whole muscle") is a group of individual muscle cells, all with the same function. In cross section, a muscle appears to be arranged in bundles called *fascicles*, each enclosed in a sheath of a type of fibrous connective tissue called *fascia*. Each fascicle contains from a few dozen to thousands of individual muscle cells, or *muscle fibers*. The outer surface of the whole muscle is covered by several more layers of fascia. At the ends of the muscle all of the fasciae (plural) come together, forming the tendons that attach the muscle to bone (**Figure C.2**).

Individual muscle cells are tube shaped, larger, and usually longer than most other human cells. The entire interior of each muscle cell is packed with long cylindrical structures arranged in parallel, called *myofibrils*. The myofibrils are packed with contractile proteins called *actin* and *myosin*. When myofibrils contract (shorten), the muscle cell also shortens.

The Contractile Unit Is a Sarcomere

Sarcomeres are segments of myofibrils. A single myofibril within one muscle cell in the biceps muscle may contain more than 100,000 sarcomeres arranged end to end. The microscopic shortening of these 100,000 sarcomeres all at once is what produces contraction (shortening) of the muscle cell and of the whole muscle. Understanding muscle shortening, then, is simply a matter of understanding how a single sarcomere works.

A sarcomere consists of two kinds of protein filaments. Thick filaments composed of *myosin* are interspersed at regular intervals within filaments of *actin*. Muscle contractions depend on the interaction between these actin and myosin filaments.

Muscle bundle (fascicle) surrounded by connective tissue

Whole muscle

Single muscle cell (fiber)

Connective tissue sheath

Tendon

Bone

Figure C.2 Muscle structure. A muscle is arranged in bundles called fascicles, each composed of many muscle cells and each surrounded by a sheath of connective tissue called fascia. Surrounding the entire muscle are several more layers of fascia. The fascia join together to become the tendon, which attaches the muscle to bone.

Nerves Activate Skeletal Muscles

Skeletal muscle cells are stimulated to contract by certain nerve cells called motor neurons. The motor neurons secrete a chemical substance called *acetylcholine (ACh)*. Acetylcholine is a neurotransmitter, a chemical released by nerve cells that has either an excitatory or an inhibitory effect on another excitable cell (another nerve cell or a muscle cell). In the case of skeletal muscle, acetylcholine excites (activates) the cells.

When a muscle cell is activated, an electrical impulse races down the inside of the muscle cell. The arrival of that impulse triggers the release of calcium ions from the sarcoplasmic reticulum (a structure similar to other cells' smooth endoplasmic reticulum). The calcium diffuses into the cell cytoplasm and then comes into contact with the myofibrils, where it sets in motion a chain of events that leads to contraction. Muscles contract when sarcomeres shorten, and sarcomeres shorten when the thick and thin filaments slide past each other, a process known as the sliding filament mechanism of contraction (**Figure C.3**).

Muscles Require Energy to Contract and to Relax

Muscle contraction requires a great deal of energy. Like most cells, muscle cells use ATP as their energy source. In the presence of calcium, myosin acts as an enzyme, splitting ATP into ADP and inorganic phosphate and releasing energy to do work.

The energy is used to "energize" the myosin head so that it can form a cross-bridge and undergo bending. Once the bending has occurred, another molecule of ATP binds to the myosin, which causes the myosin head to detach from actin. As long as calcium is present, the cycle of ATP breakdown, attachment, bending, and detachment is repeated over and over again in rapid succession. The result is a shortening of the sarcomere.

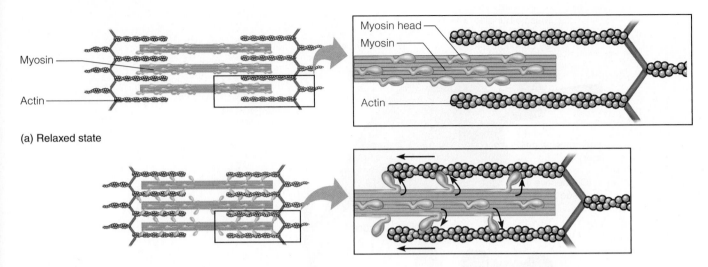

(a) Relaxed state

(b) Contracted state

Figure C.3 Sliding filament mechanism of contraction. (a) In the relaxed state, the myosin heads do not make contact with actin. (b) During contraction, the myosin heads form cross-bridges with actin and bend, pulling the actin filaments toward the center of the sarcomere.

At the end of the contractile period (when nerve impulses end), energy from the breakdown of ATP is used to transport calcium back into the sarcoplasmic reticulum so that relaxation can occur. However, a second requirement for relaxation is that an intact molecule of ATP must bind to myosin before myosin can finally detach from actin.

Muscle cells obtain ATP from several sources

Muscle cells store only enough ATP for about 10 seconds' worth of maximal activity. Once this is used up, the cells must produce more ATP from other energy sources, including creatine phosphate, glycogen, glucose, and fatty acids.

An important pathway for producing ATP involves creatine phosphate (creatine-P), a high-energy molecule with an attached phosphate group. Creatine phosphate can transfer a phosphate group and energy to ADP and therefore create a new ATP quickly. This reaction is reversible: If ATP is not needed to power muscle contractions, the excess ATP can be used to build a fresh supply of creatine phosphate, which is stored until needed.

The combination of previously available ATP plus stored creatine phosphate produces only enough energy for up to 30 to 40 seconds of heavy activity. Beyond that, muscles must rely on stored glycogen. For the first 3 to 5 minutes of sustained activity, a muscle cell draws on its internal supply of stored glycogen. Glucose molecules are converted from the stored glycogen, and their energy is used to synthesize ATP. Part of the process of the breakdown of glucose can be done without oxygen (called anaerobic metabolism) fairly quickly, but it only yields two ATP molecules per glucose molecule.

The most efficient long-term source of energy is the aerobic metabolism of glucose, fatty acids, and other high-energy molecules such as lactic acid. Aerobic metabolism takes place in mitochondria and requires oxygen. The next time you engage in strenuous exercise, note that it may take you a few minutes to start breathing heavily. The increase in respiration indicates that aerobic metabolism is now taking place. Until aerobic metabolism kicks in, however, cells are relying on stored ATP, creatine phosphate, and anaerobic metabolism of glycogen. Weight lifters can rely on stored energy because their muscles perform for relatively short periods. Long-distance runners start out by depending on stored energy, but in less than a minute they are relying almost exclusively on aerobic metabolism. If they could not, they would collapse in exhaustion.

The Cardiovascular System

The heart and blood vessels are known collectively as the cardiovascular system (*cardio* comes from the Greek word for "heart," and vascular derives from the Latin word for "small vessel"). The heart provides the power to move the blood, and the vascular system represents the network of branching conduit vessels through which the blood flows. The cardiovascular system is essential to life because it supplies every region of the body with just the right amount of blood.

Blood Vessels Transport Blood

We classify the body's blood vessels into three major types: *arteries*, *capillaries*, and *veins*. Thick-walled arteries transport blood to body tissues under high pressure. Microscopic capillaries participate in exchanging solutes and water with the cells of the body. Thin-walled veins store blood and return it to the heart.

As blood leaves the heart it is pumped into large, muscular, thick-walled arteries. Arteries transport blood away from the heart. The larger arteries have a thick layer of muscle because they must be able to withstand the high pressures generated by the heart. Arteries branch again and again, so the farther blood moves from the heart, the smaller in diameter the arteries become. Eventually blood reaches the smallest arteries, called arterioles (literally, "little arteries").

Where an arteriole joins a capillary is a band of smooth muscle called the precapillary sphincter. The precapillary sphincters serve as gates that control blood flow into individual capillaries. Extensive networks of capillaries, called *capillary beds*, can be found in all areas of the body, which is why you are likely to bleed no matter where you cut yourself. Capillaries' branching design and thin, porous walls enable blood to exchange oxygen, carbon dioxide, nutrients, and waste products with tissue cells. In fact, capillaries are the *only* blood vessels that can exchange materials with the interstitial fluid.

Figure C.4 illustrates the general pattern of how water and substances move across a capillary. At the beginning of a capillary, fluid is filtered out of the vessel into the interstitial fluid, accompanied by oxygen, nutrients, and raw materials needed by the cell. The filtered fluid is essentially like plasma except that it contains very little protein because most protein molecules are too large to be filtered. Filtration of fluid is caused by the blood pressure generated by the heart. Waste materials such as carbon dioxide and urea diffuse out of the cells and back into the blood.

From the capillaries, blood flows back to the heart through *venules* (small veins) and veins. Like the walls of arteries, the walls of veins consist of three layers of tissue. However,

Figure C.4 The general pattern of movement between capillaries, the interstitial fluid, and cells. For simplicity, only a single tissue cell is shown, but a single capillary may supply many nearby cells.

the outer two layers of the walls of veins are much thinner than those of arteries. Veins also have a larger lumen (that is, are larger in diameter) than arteries.

The Heart Pumps Blood Through the Vessels

The heart is a muscular, cone-shaped organ slightly larger than your fist, located in the thoracic cavity between the lungs and behind the sternum (breastbone). The heart consists mostly of cardiac muscle. Unlike skeletal muscle, cardiac muscle does not connect to bone. Instead, it pumps ceaselessly in a squeezing motion to propel blood through the blood vessels.

The heart consists of four separate chambers. The two chambers on the top are the atria (singular *atrium*), and the two more muscular bottom chambers are the ventricles. A muscular partition called the septum separates the right and left sides of the heart (**Figure C.5**).

The Pulmonary Circuit Provides for Gas Exchange

Review Figure 3.15 on page 92, which shows the general structure of the entire cardiovascular system. Note that the heart is pumping blood through the lungs (the pulmonary circuit) and through the rest of the body to all the cells (the systemic circuit) simultaneously. Each circuit has its own set of blood vessels. Let's follow the pulmonary circuit first:

1. When blood returns to the heart from the veins, it enters the right atrium. The blood that returns to the heart is deoxygenated—it has given up oxygen to tissue cells and taken up carbon dioxide.
2. From the right atrium, blood passes through the right atrioventricular valve into the right ventricle.
3. The right ventricle pumps blood through the pulmonary semilunar valve into the pulmonary trunk (the main pulmonary artery) leading to the lungs. The

Figure C.5 A view of the heart showing major blood vessels, chambers, and valves. The pulmonary vessels are shown in purple to distinguish them from systemic arteries and veins.

pulmonary trunk divides into the right and left pulmonary arteries, which supply the right and left lungs, respectively.

4. At the pulmonary capillaries, blood gives up carbon dioxide and receives a fresh supply of oxygen from the air we inhale. It is now oxygenated.

5. The freshly oxygenated blood flows into the pulmonary veins leading back to the heart. It enters the left atrium and flows through the left atrioventricular valve into the left ventricle.

The Systemic Circuit Serves the Rest of the Body

When blood enters the left ventricle, it begins the *systemic circuit*, which takes it to the rest of the body.

1. The left ventricle pumps blood through the aortic semilunar valve into the aorta, the largest artery.

2. From the aorta, blood travels through the branching arteries and arterioles to the capillaries, where it delivers oxygen and nutrients to all of the body's tissues and organs and removes waste products. Even some tissues of the lungs receive their nutrient blood supply from the systemic circulation.

3. From the capillaries, blood flows to the venules, veins, and then back again to the right atrium.

The Lymphatic System

The lymphatic system is closely associated with the cardiovascular system. The lymphatic system performs three important functions:

1. It helps maintain the volume of blood in the cardiovascular system.
2. It transports lipids and fat-soluble vitamins absorbed from the digestive system.
3. It defends the body against infection and injury.

Lymphatic Vessels Transport Lymph

The lymphatic system begins as a network of small, blind-ended *lymphatic capillaries* in the vicinity of the cells and blood capillaries. The lymphatic system helps maintain blood volume and interstitial fluid volume by absorbing excess fluid that has been filtered out of the capillaries and returning it to the cardiovascular system. Lymphatic capillaries in the small intestine are called lacteals (see Figure 3.13 on page 90 and pick up most lipids and fat-soluble vitamins absorbed in the small intestine and eventually send them to the bloodstream.

Lymph capillaries have wide spaces between overlapping cells. Their structure allows them to take up substances (including bacteria) that are too large to enter a blood capillary.

The fluid in the lymphatic capillaries is *lymph*, a milky body fluid that contains white blood cells, proteins, fats, and the occasional bacterium. Lymphatic capillaries merge to form the *lymphatic vessels*. Located at intervals along the lymphatic vessels are small organs called lymph nodes, described in the following section. Like veins, lymphatic vessels contain one-way valves to prevent backflow of lymph. The lymphatic vessels merge to form larger and larger vessels, eventually creating two major lymphatic ducts: the *right lymphatic duct* and the *thoracic duct*. The two lymph ducts join the subclavian veins near the shoulders, thereby returning the lymph to the cardiovascular system.

Lymph Nodes Cleanse the Lymph

Lymph nodes remove microorganisms, cellular debris, and abnormal cells from the lymph before returning it to the cardiovascular system. There are hundreds of lymph nodes, clustered in the areas of the digestive tract, neck, armpits, and groin. They vary in diameter from about 1 mm to 2.5 cm. Each node is enclosed in a dense capsule of connective tissue pierced by lymphatic vessels. Inside each node are connective tissue and two types of white blood cells, known as macrophages and lymphocytes.

The largest lymphatic organ, the spleen, is a soft, fist-sized mass located in the upper-left abdominal cavity. The spleen has two main functions: It controls the quality of circulating red blood cells by removing the old and damaged ones, and it helps fight infection. Note that the main distinction between spleen and lymph nodes is *which* fluid they cleanse—the spleen cleanses the blood, and the lymph nodes cleanse lymph. Together, they keep the circulating body fluids relatively free of damaged cells and microorganisms.

The thymus gland is located in the lower neck, behind the sternum and just above the heart. Encased in connective tissue, the gland contains lymphocytes and epithelial cells. The thymus gland secretes two hormones, thymosin and thymopoietin, that cause certain lymphocytes called *T lymphocytes* (T cells) to mature and take an active role in specific defenses.

The *tonsils* are masses of lymphatic tissue near the entrance to the throat. Lymphocytes in the tonsils gather and filter out many of the microorganisms that enter the throat in food or air.

The Respiratory System

For the sake of convenience, the respiratory system can be divided into the upper and lower respiratory tracts. The *upper respiratory tract* comprises the nose (including the nasal cavity) and pharynx—structures above the "Adam's apple" in men's necks. The *lower respiratory tract* starts with the larynx and includes the trachea, the two bronchi that branch from the trachea, and the lungs themselves (**Figure C.6**).

The Upper Respiratory Tract Filters, Warms, and Humidifies Air

During inhalation, air enters through the nose or mouth. The internal portion of the nose is called the nasal cavity. The mucus in the nasal cavity traps dust, pathogens, and other particles in the air before they get any farther into the respiratory tract.

Incoming air next enters the pharynx (throat), which connects the mouth and nasal cavity to the larynx (voice box). The upper pharynx extends from the nasal cavity to the roof of the mouth. The lower pharynx is a common passageway for both food and air. Food passes through on its way to the esophagus, and air flows through to the lower respiratory tract.

The Lower Respiratory Tract Exchanges Gases

The lower respiratory tract includes the larynx, the trachea, the bronchi, and the lungs with their bronchioles and alveoli. The larynx extends about 5 cm (2 in.) below the pharynx. The larynx contains two important structures: the epiglottis and the vocal cords. The epiglottis is a flexible flap of cartilage located at the opening to the larynx. When air is flowing into the larynx, the epiglottis remains open. But when we swallow food or liquids, the epiglottis tips to block the opening temporarily. This "switching mechanism" routes food and beverages into the esophagus and digestive system, rather than into the trachea. This is why it is impossible to talk while you are swallowing.

As air continues down the respiratory tract, it passes to the trachea, the "windpipe" that extends from the larynx to the left and right bronchi. If a foreign object lodges in the trachea, respiration is interrupted and choking occurs. If the airway is completely blocked, death can occur within minutes. Choking often happens when a person carries on an animated conversation while eating. The risk of choking provides a good reason beyond good manners not to eat and talk at the same time.

The trachea branches into two airways called the right and left bronchi (singular *bronchus*) as it enters the lung cavity. Like the branches of a tree, the two bronchi divide into a network of smaller and smaller bronchi. The smaller airways that lack cartilage are called bronchioles. The smallest bronchioles are 1 mm or smaller in diameter and consist primarily of a thin layer of smooth muscle surrounded by a small amount of elastic connective tissue.

The bronchi and bronchioles also clean the air, warm it to body temperature, and saturate it with water vapor before it reaches the delicate gas exchange surfaces of the lungs.

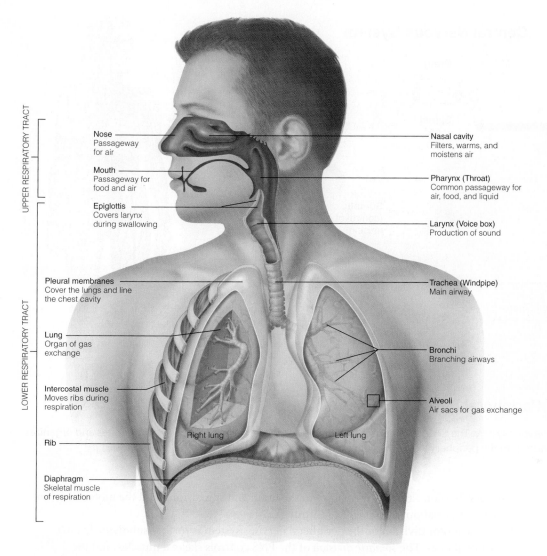

UPPER RESPIRATORY TRACT

LOWER RESPIRATORY TRACT

Nose
Passageway
for air

Mouth
Passageway for
food and air

Epiglottis
Covers larynx
during swallowing

Pleural membranes
Cover the lungs and line
the chest cavity

Lung
Organ of gas
exchange

Intercostal muscle
Moves ribs during
respiration

Rib

Diaphragm
Skeletal muscle
of respiration

Nasal cavity
Filters, warms, and
moistens air

Pharynx (Throat)
Common passageway for
air, food, and liquid

Larynx (Voice box)
Production of sound

Trachea (Windpipe)
Main airway

Bronchi
Branching airways

Alveoli
Air sacs for gas exchange

Right lung

Left lung

Figure C.6 The human respiratory system. The functions of each of the anatomical structures are included.

The Lungs Are Organs of Gas Exchange

The lungs are organs consisting of supportive tissue enclosing the bronchi, bronchioles, blood vessels, and the areas where gas exchange occurs. If you could touch a living lung, you would find that it is very soft and frothy. In fact, most of it is air. The lungs are basically a system of branching airways that end in 300 million tiny air-filled sacs called alveoli (singular *alveolus*). It is here that gas exchange takes place. Alveoli are arranged in clusters at the end of every terminal bronchiole, like grapes clustered on a stem. A single alveolus is a thin bubble of living squamous epithelial cells only one cell layer thick. Their combined surface area is nearly 800 ft², approximately forty times the area of a person's skin. The tremendous surface area and thinness facilitate gas exchange with nearby capillaries.

The Nervous System

The nervous system comprises the central nervous system (CNS) and the peripheral nervous system (PNS). The CNS consists of the brain and the spinal cord. It receives, processes, stores, and transfers information. The PNS represents the components of the nervous system that lie outside the CNS. The PNS has two functional subdivisions: The

Figure C.7 Components of the nervous system. The CNS receives input from the sensory component of the PNS, integrates and organizes the information, and then sends output to the periphery via the motor components of the PNS.

sensory division carries information to the brain and spinal cord, and the motor division carries information from the CNS (**Figure C.7**).

The motor division of the peripheral nervous system is further subdivided along functional lines. The *somatic division* of the PNS controls skeletal muscles, and the autonomic division of the PNS controls smooth muscles, cardiac muscles, and glands. In turn, the *autonomic division* has two subdivisions called the *sympathetic* and *parasympathetic* divisions. In general, the actions of the sympathetic and parasympathetic divisions oppose each other. They work antagonistically to accomplish the automatic, subconscious maintenance of homeostasis within the body.

Neurons

Neurons are cells specialized for communication. They generate and conduct electrical impulses, also called *action potentials*, from one part of the body to another. The longest neurons extend all the way from your toes to your spinal cord.

There are three types of neurons in the nervous system:

1. Sensory neurons of the PNS are specialized to respond to a certain type of stimulus, such as pressure or light. They transmit information about this stimulus to the CNS in the form of electrical impulses. In other words, sensory neurons provide input to the CNS.
2. Interneurons within the CNS transmit impulses between components of the CNS. Interneurons receive input from sensory neurons, integrate this information, and influence the functioning of other neurons.
3. Motor neurons of the PNS transmit impulses away from the CNS. They carry the nervous system's output, still in the form of electrical impulses, to all of the tissues and organs of the body.

All neurons consist of a cell body, one or more dendrites, and an axon. The main body of a neuron is called the cell body. Slender extensions of the cell body, called dendrites, receive information from receptors or incoming impulses from other neurons. Interneurons and motor neurons have numerous dendrites that are fairly short and extend in many directions from the cell body. Sensory neurons are an exception, for their dendrites connect directly to an axon.

An axon is a long, slender tube of cell membrane containing a small amount of cytoplasm. Axons are specialized to conduct electrical impulses. Axons of sensory neurons originate from a dendrite, whereas the axons of interneurons and motor neurons originate from a cone-shaped area of the cell body called the *axon hillock*. At its other end, the axon branches into slender extensions called *axon terminals*. Each axon terminal ends in a small rounded tip called an *axon bulb*.

Action Potentials

An action potential occurs as a sequence of three events: (1) depolarization, (2) repolarization, and (3) reestablishment of the resting potential.

1. *Depolarization: Sodium moves into the axon.* Voltage-sensitive Na^+ channels in the axon's membrane open briefly and Na^+ ions diffuse rapidly into the cytoplasm of the axon. This influx of positive ions causes *depolarization*, meaning that the membrane potential shifts from negative (-70 mV) to positive (about $+30$ mV).

2. *Repolarization: Potassium moves out of the axon.* After a short delay, the Na^+ channels close automatically. But the reversal of the membrane polarity triggers the opening of K^+ channels. This allows more K^+ ions than usual to diffuse rapidly out of the cell. The loss of positive ions from the cell leads to *repolarization*, meaning that the interior of the axon becomes negative again.

3. *Reestablishment of the resting potential.* Because the K^+ channels are slow to close, there is a brief overshoot of membrane voltage during which the interior of the axon is slightly hyperpolarized. Shortly after the K^+ channels close, the resting potential is reestablished. At this point the axon is prepared to receive another action potential. The entire sequence of three steps takes about 3 ms.

Once an action potential is initiated, it sweeps rapidly down the axon until it reaches the axon terminals.

Synaptic Transmission

Once an action potential reaches the axon terminals of a neuron, the information inherent in it must be converted to another form for transmittal to its target. In essence, the action potential causes the release of a chemical that crosses a specialized junction between the two cells called a synapse. This chemical substance is called a neurotransmitter because it transmits a signal from a neuron to its target.

Figure C.8 illustrates the structure of a typical synapse and the events that occur during synaptic transmission. At a synapse, the *presynaptic membrane* is the cell membrane of the neuron that is sending the information. The *postsynaptic membrane* refers to the membrane of the cell that is about to receive the information. The small, fluid-filled gap that separates the presynaptic and postsynaptic membranes is the *synaptic cleft*.

The Endocrine System and Hormones

The endocrine system is a collection of specialized cells, tissues, and glands that produces and secretes circulating chemical messenger molecules called hormones. Most hormones are secreted by endocrine glands—ductless organs that secrete their products into interstitial fluid, lymph, and blood (*endocrine* means "secreted internally"). In contrast, *exocrine* glands secrete products such as mucus, sweat, tears, and digestive fluids into ducts

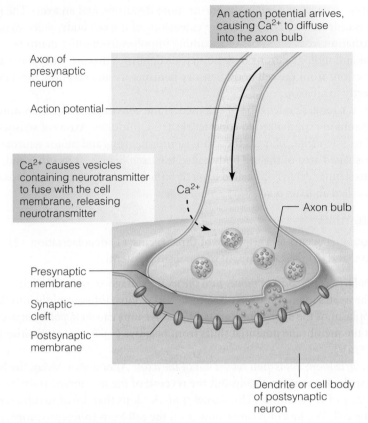

An action potential arrives, causing Ca²⁺ to diffuse into the axon bulb

Axon of presynaptic neuron

Action potential

Ca²⁺ causes vesicles containing neurotransmitter to fuse with the cell membrane, releasing neurotransmitter

Ca²⁺

Axon bulb

Presynaptic membrane

Synaptic cleft

Postsynaptic membrane

Dendrite or cell body of postsynaptic neuron

Figure C.8 Summary of synaptic transmission.

that empty into the appropriate sites. There are approximately fifty known hormones circulating in the human bloodstream, and new ones are still being discovered. Hormones are bloodborne units of information, just as nerve impulses are units of information carried in nerves.

The endocrine system has certain characteristics that set it apart from the nervous system as a communications system:

1. Hormones of the endocrine system reach nearly every living cell.
2. Each hormone acts only on certain cells.
3. Endocrine control tends to be slower than nervous system control.
4. The endocrine and nervous systems can (and often do) interact with each other.

Hormones Are Classified as Steroid or Nonsteroid

Hormones generally are classified into two basic categories based on their structure and mechanism of action. Steroid hormones are structurally related to cholesterol; in fact, all of them are synthesized from cholesterol and all are lipid soluble. Nonsteroid hormones consist of, or at least are partly derived from, the amino acid building blocks of proteins. In general, they are lipid insoluble. The differences in lipid solubility explain most of the important differences in how the two categories of hormones work. Steroid hormones usually enter the cell, bind to an intracellular receptor, and activate genes that produce new proteins. Nonsteroid hormones generally bind to receptors on the cell's surface. Their binding either opens or closes cell membrane ion channels or activates enzymes within the cell.

The Hypothalamus and the Pituitary Gland

The hypothalamus is a small region in the forebrain that plays an important role in homeostatic regulation. It monitors internal environmental conditions such as water and solute balance, temperature, and carbohydrate metabolism.

The hypothalamus also produces hormones and monitors the pituitary gland, a small endocrine gland located beneath the hypothalamus and connected to it by a stalk of tissue (review Figure 3.1 on page 75). The pituitary gland is sometimes called the "master gland" because it secretes eight different hormones and regulates many of the other endocrine glands.

The Urinary System

Excretion refers to processes that remove wastes and excess materials from the body. **Figure C.9** provides a review of the systems involved in managing metabolic wastes and maintaining homeostasis of water and solutes.

Because the excretory capacity of the other organs is limited, the urinary system has primary responsibility for homeostasis of water and most of the solutes in blood and other body fluids. The urinary system consists of the organs (kidneys, ureters, bladder, and urethra) that produce, transport, store, and excrete urine.

Urine is essentially water and solutes. Among the solutes excreted in urine are excess elements and ions, drugs, vitamins, toxic chemicals, and waste products produced by the liver or by cellular metabolism. Some substances, such as water and sodium chloride (salt), are excreted to regulate body fluid balance and salt levels. About the only major solutes *not* excreted by the kidneys under normal circumstances are the three classes of macronutrients. The kidneys keep these nutrients in the body for other organs to regulate.

Water is the most abundant molecule in the body, accounting for at least half of body weight. As discussed in Chapter 9, the urinary system plays a large role in regulating water levels in the blood and body fluids.

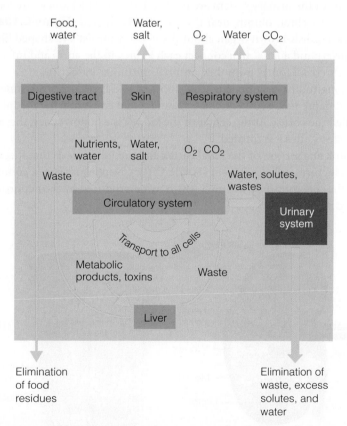

Figure C.9 Organ systems involved in removing wastes and maintaining homeostasis of water and solutes. With the large tan box representing the body, this diagram maps the inflow and outflow of key compounds we consume. The kidneys of the urinary system are the organs primarily responsible for the maintenance of homeostasis of water and solutes and for the excretion of most waste products.

Even though many solutes in the body are essential for life, we continually acquire more of them than we can use. The primary solutes excreted by the urinary system are nitrogenous wastes, excess ions, and trace amounts of other substances.

Nitrogenous wastes are formed during the metabolism of proteins. The major nitrogenous waste product in urine is urea. The metabolism of protein initially liberates ammonia (NH_3). Ammonia is quite toxic to cells; however, it is quickly detoxified by the liver. In the liver, two ammonia molecules are combined with a molecule of carbon dioxide to produce a molecule of urea ($H_2N\text{-}CO\text{-}NH_2$) plus a molecule of water. Although far less toxic than ammonia, urea is also dangerous in high concentrations. A small amount of urea appears in sweat, but most of it is excreted by the urinary system.

Dozens of different ions are ingested with food or liberated from nutrients during metabolism. The most abundant ions in the body are sodium (Na^+) and chloride (Cl^-), which are important in determining the volume of the extracellular fluids, including blood. The volume of blood, in turn, affects blood pressure. Other important ions include potassium (K^+), which maintains electrical charges across membranes; calcium (Ca^{2+}), important in nerve and muscle activity; and hydrogen (H^+), which maintains acid–base balance. The rate of urinary excretion of each of these ions is regulated by the kidneys in order to maintain homeostasis.

Trace amounts of many other substances are excreted in proportion to their daily rate of gain by the body. Among them are *creatinine*, a waste product that is produced during the metabolism of creatine phosphate in muscle, and various waste products that give the urine its characteristic yellow color.

Kidneys: The Principal Urinary Organs

The main organs of the urinary system are the two kidneys. The kidneys are located on either side of the vertebral column, near the posterior body wall (**Figure C.10a**). Each kidney is a dark-reddish-brown organ about the size of your fist and shaped like a kidney bean. A *renal artery* and a *renal vein* connect each kidney to the aorta and inferior vena cava, respectively (*renal* comes from the Latin *ren*, meaning "kidney").

Seen in a longitudinal section (Figure C.10b), each kidney consists of inner pyramid-shaped zones of dense tissue (called renal pyramids) that constitute the medulla and an outer zone called the cortex. At the center of the kidney is a hollow space, the *renal pelvis*, where urine collects after it is formed.

A closer look at a section of the renal cortex and medulla reveals that it contains long, thin, tubular structures called *nephrons* (Figure C.10c). Nephrons share a common final section called the *collecting duct*, through which urine produced by the nephrons is delivered to the renal pelvis.

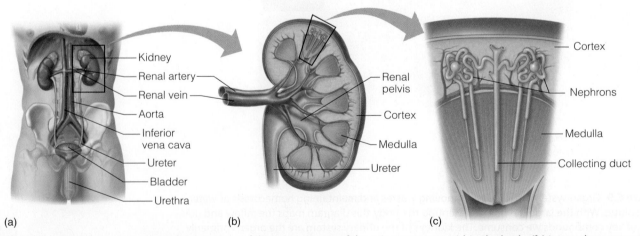

(a)   (b)   (c)

Figure C.10 The human urinary system. **(a)** Locations of the components of the urinary system within the body. **(b)** Internal structure of a kidney. **(c)** The cortex and medulla of the kidney are composed of numerous nephrons.

In addition to being the primary organs of the urinary system, the kidneys regulate the production of red blood cells in the bone marrow, through the secretion of the hormone erythropoietin, activate the inactive form of vitamin D from the liver, and help maintain blood pressure, volume, and pH.

The Integumentary System

The proper name for the skin and its accessory structures such as hair, nails, and glands is the integumentary system (from the Latin *integere*, meaning "to cover").

The skin has several different functions related to its role as the outer covering of the body: protection from dehydration (helps prevent our bodies from drying out), protection from injury (such as abrasion), defense against invasion by bacteria and viruses, regulation of body temperature, synthesis of an inactive form of vitamin D, and sensation (provides information about the external world via receptors for touch, vibration, pain, and temperature).

The outer layer of the skin's tissue is the epidermis and the inner layer of connective tissue is the dermis (**Figure C.11**).

Figure C.11 The skin. The two layers of skin (epidermis and dermis) rest on a supportive layer (hypodermis). Although not part of the skin, the hypodermis provides the important functions of cushioning and insulation.

The skin rests on a supportive layer called the *hypodermis* (*hypo-* means "under"), consisting of loose connective tissue containing fat cells. The hypodermis is flexible enough to allow the skin to move and bend. The fat cells in the hypodermis insulate against excessive heat loss and cushion against injury.

As mentioned in Chapter 11, the skin synthesizes an inactive form of vitamin D. A cholesterol compound in the skin becomes an inactive form of vitamin D when it is exposed to the ultraviolet rays of sunlight. The inactive form must then be modified in the liver and kidneys before it becomes active (see Figure 11.8 on page 421).

Appendix D Calculations and Conversions

Calculation and Conversion Aids

Commonly Used Metric Units

millimeter (mm):	one-thousandth of a meter (0.001)
centimeter (cm):	one-hundredth of a meter (0.01)
kilometer (km):	one-thousand times a meter (1000)
kilogram (kg):	one-thousand times a gram (1000)
milligram (mg):	one-thousandth of a gram (0.001)
microgram (µg):	one-millionth of a gram (0.000001)
milliliter (ml):	one-thousandth of a liter (0.001)

International Units

Some vitamin supplements may report vitamin content as International Units (IU).

To convert IU to:

- Micrograms of vitamin D (cholecalciferol), divide the IU value by 40 or multiply by 0.025.
- Milligrams of vitamin E (alpha-tocopherol), divide the IU value by 1.5 if vitamin E is from natural sources. Divide the IU value by 2.22 if vitamin E is from synthetic sources.
- Vitamin A: 1 IU = 0.3 µg retinol or 3.6 µg beta-carotene.

Retinol Activity Equivalents

Retinol Activity Equivalents (RAE) are a standardized unit of measure for vitamin A. RAE account for the various differences in bioavailability from sources of vitamin A. Many supplements will report vitamin A content in IU, as just shown, or Retinol Equivalents (RE).

1 RAE = 1 µg retinol
12 µg beta-carotene
24 µg other vitamin A carotenoids

To calculate RAE from the RE value of vitamin carotenoids in foods, divide RE by 2.

For vitamin A supplements and foods fortified with vitamin A, 1 RE = 1 RAE.

Folate

Folate is measured as Dietary Folate Equivalents (DFE). DFE account for the different factors affecting bioavailability of folate sources.

1 DFE = 1 µg food folate
0.6 µg folate from fortified foods
0.5 µg folate supplement taken on an empty stomach
0.6 µg folate as a supplement consumed with a meal

To convert micrograms of synthetic folate, such as that found in supplements or fortified foods, to DFE:

$$\text{µg synthetic} \times \text{folate } 1.7 = \text{µg DFE}$$

For naturally occurring food folate, such as spinach, each microgram of folate equals 1 microgram DFE:

$$\text{µg folate} = \text{µg DFE}$$

Conversion Factors

Use the following table to convert U.S. measurements to metric equivalents:

Original Unit	Multiply by	To Get
ounces avdp	28.3495	grams
ounces	0.0625	pounds
pounds	0.4536	kilograms
pounds	16	ounces
grams	0.0353	ounces
grams	0.002205	pounds
kilograms	2.2046	pounds
liters	1.8162	pints (dry)
liters	2.1134	pints (liquid)
liters	0.9081	quarts (dry)
liters	1.0567	quarts (liquid)
liters	0.2642	gallons (U.S.)
pints (dry)	0.5506	liters
pints (liquid)	0.4732	liters
quarts (dry)	1.1012	liters
quarts (liquid)	0.9463	liters
gallons (U.S.)	3.7853	liters
millimeters	0.0394	inches
centimeters	0.3937	inches
centimeters	0.03281	feet
inches	25.4000	millimeters
inches	2.5400	centimeters
inches	0.0254	meters
feet	0.3048	meters
meters	3.2808	feet
meters	1.0936	yards
cubic feet	0.0283	cubic meters
cubic meters	35.3145	cubic feet
cubic meters	1.3079	cubic yards
cubic yards	0.7646	cubic meters

Length: U.S. and Metric Equivalents

¼ inch	=	0.6 centimeters
1 inch	=	2.5 centimeters
1 foot	=	0.3048 meter
		30.48 centimeters
1 yard	=	0.91144 meter
1 millimeter	=	0.03937 inch
1 centimeter	=	0.3937 inch
1 decimeter	=	3.937 inches
1 meter	=	39.37 inches
		1.094 yards
1 micrometer	=	0.00003937 inch

Weights and Measures
Food Measurement Equivalencies from U.S. to Metric
Capacity

⅕ teaspoon = 1 milliliter
¼ teaspoon = 1.25 milliliters
½ teaspoon = 2.5 milliliters
1 teaspoon = 5 milliliters
1 tablespoon = 15 milliliters
1 fluid ounce = 28.4 milliliters
¼ cup = 60 milliliters
⅓ cup = 80 milliliters
½ cup = 120 milliliters
1 cup = 225 milliliters
1 pint (2 cups) = 473 milliliters
1 quart (4 cups) = 0.95 liter
1 liter (1.06 quarts) = 1,000 milliliters
1 gallon (4 quarts) = 3.84 liters

Weight

0.035 ounce = 1 gram
1 ounce = 28 grams
¼ pound (4 ounces) = 114 grams
1 pound (16 ounces) = 454 grams
2.2 pounds (35 ounces) = 1 kilogram

U.S. Food Measurement Equivalents

3 teaspoons = 1 tablespoon
½ tablespoon = 1½ teaspoons
2 tablespoons = ⅛ cup
4 tablespoons = ¼ cup
5 tablespoons + 1 teaspoon = ⅓ cup
8 tablespoons = ½ cup
10 tablespoons + 2 teaspoons = ⅔ cup
12 tablespoons = ¾ cup
16 tablespoons = 1 cup
2 cups = 1 pint
4 cups = 1 quart
2 pints = 1 quart
4 quarts = 1 gallon

Volumes and Capacities

1 cup = 8 fluid ounces
½ liquid pint
1 milliliter = 0.061 cubic inches
1 liter = 1.057 liquid quarts
0.908 dry quart
61.024 cubic inches
1 U.S. gallon = 231 cubic inches
3.785 liters
0.833 British gallon
128 U.S. fluid ounces

1 British Imperial gallon = 277.42 cubic inches
1.201 U.S. gallons
4.546 liters
160 British fluid ounces
1 U.S. ounce, liquid or fluid = 1.805 cubic inches
29.574 milliliters
1.041 British fluid ounces
1 pint, dry = 33.600 cubic inches
0.551 liter
1 pint, liquid = 28.875 cubic inches
0.473 liter
1 U.S. quart, dry = 67.201 cubic inches
1.101 liters
1 U.S. quart, liquid = 57.75 cubic inches
0.946 liter
1 British quart = 69.354 cubic inches
1.032 U.S. quarts, dry
1.201 U.S. quarts, liquid

Energy Units

1 kilocalorie (kcal) = 4.2 kilojoules
1 millijoule (MJ) = 240 kilocalories
1 kilojoule (kJ) = 0.24 kcal
1 gram carbohydrate = 4 kcal
1 gram fat = 9 kcal
1 gram protein = 4 kcal

Temperature Standards

	°Fahrenheit	°Celsius
Body temperature	98.6°	37°
Comfortable room temperature	65–75°	18–24°
Boiling point of water	212°	100°
Freezing point of water	32°	0°

Temperature Scales

To Convert Fahrenheit to Celsius:

$[(°F - 32)\ 5]/9$

1. Subtract 32 from °F.
2. Multiply (°F – 32) by 5, then divide by 9.

To Convert Celsius to Fahrenheit:

$[(°C \times 9)/5] + 32$

1. Multiply °C by 9, then divide by 5.
2. Add 32 to (°C × 9/5).

Appendix E Foods Containing Caffeine

Data from: USDA Nutrient Database for Standard Reference, Release 21.

Beverages

Food Name	Serving	Caffeine/serving (mg)
Beverage mix, chocolate flavor, dry mix, prepared w/milk	1 cup (8 fl. oz)	7.98
Beverage mix, chocolate malt powder, fortified, prepared w/milk	1 cup (8 fl. oz)	5.3
Beverage mix, chocolate malted milk powder, no added nutrients, prepared w/milk	1 cup (8 fl. oz)	7.95
Beverage, chocolate syrup w/o added nutrients, prepared w/milk	1 cup (8 fl. oz)	5.64
Beverage, chocolate syrup, fortified, mixed w/milk	1 cup milk and 1 tbsp syrup	2.63
Cocoa mix w/aspartame and calcium and phosphorus, no sodium or vitamin A, low kcal, dry, prepared	6 fl. oz water and 0.53-oz packet	5
Cocoa mix w/aspartame, dry, low kcal, prepared w/water	1 packet dry mix with 6 fl. oz water	1.92
Cocoa mix, dry mix	1 serving (3 heaping tsp or 1 envelope)	5.04
Cocoa mix, dry, w/o added nutrients, prepared w/water	1-oz packet with 6 fl. oz water	4.12
Cocoa mix, fortified, dry, prepared w/water	6 fl. oz H_2O and 1 packet	6.27
Cocoa, dry powder, high-fat or breakfast, plain	1 piece	6.895
Cocoa, hot, homemade w/whole milk	1 cup	5
Coffee liqueur, 53 proof	1 fl. oz	9.048
Coffee liqueur, 63 proof	1 fl. oz	9.05
Coffee w/cream liqueur, 34 proof	1 fl. oz	2.488
Coffee mix w/sugar (cappuccino), dry, prepared w/water	6 fl. oz H_2O and 2 rounded tsp mix	74.88
Coffee mix w/sugar (French), dry, prepared w/water	6 fl. oz H_2O and 2 rounded tsp mix	51.03
Coffee mix w/sugar (mocha), dry, prepared w/water	6 fl. oz and 2 round tsp mix	33.84
Coffee, brewed	1 cup (8 fl. oz)	94.8
Coffee, brewed, prepared with tap water, decaffeinated	1 cup (8 fl. oz)	2.37
Coffee, instant, prepared	1 cup (8 fl. oz)	61.98
Coffee, instant, regular, powder, half the caffeine	1 cup (8 fl. oz)	30.99
Coffee, instant, decaffeinated	1 cup (8 fl. oz)	1.79
Coffee and cocoa (mocha) powder, with whitener and low-calorie sweetener	1 cup	405.48
Coffee, brewed, espresso, restaurant-prepared	1 cup (8 fl. oz)	502.44
Coffee, brewed, espresso, restaurant-prepared, decaffeinated	1 cup (8 fl. oz)	2.37
Energy drink, with caffeine, niacin, pantothenic acid, vitamin B_6	1 fl. oz	9.517
Milk beverage mix, dairy drink w/aspartame, low kcal, dry, prep	6 fl. oz	4.08
Milk, lowfat, 1% fat, chocolate	1 cup	5
Milk, whole, chocolate	1 cup	5
Soft drink, cola w/caffeine	1 fl. oz	2
Soft drink, cola, w/higher caffeine	1 fl. oz	8.33
Soft drink, cola or pepper type, low kcal w/saccharin and caffeine	1 fl. oz	3.256
Soft drink, cola, low kcal w/saccharin and aspartame, w/caffeine	1 fl. oz	4.144
Soft drink, lemon-lime soda, w/caffeine	1 fl. oz	4.605
Soft drink, low kcal, not cola or pepper, with aspartame and caffeine	1 fl. oz	4.44
Soft drink, pepper type, w/caffeine	1 fl. oz	3.07
Tea mix, instant w/lemon flavor, w/saccharin, dry, prepared	1 cup (8 fl. oz)	16.59
Tea mix, instant w/lemon, unsweetened, dry, prepared	1 cup (8 fl. oz)	26.18
Tea mix, instant w/sugar and lemon, dry, no added vitamin C, prepared	1 cup (8 fl. oz)	28.49
Tea mix, instant, unsweetened, dry, prepared	1 cup (8 fl. oz)	30.81
Tea, brewed	1 cup (8 fl. oz)	47.36
Tea, brewed, prepared with tap water, decaffeinated	1 cup (8 fl. oz)	2.37
Tea, instant, unsweetened, powder, decaffeinated	1 tsp	1.183
Tea, instant, w/o sugar, lemon-flavored, w/added vitamin C, dry prepared	1 cup (8 fl. oz)	26.05
Tea, instant, with sugar, lemon-flavored, decaffeinated, no added vitamin	1 cup	9.1

Cake, Cookies, and Desserts

Food Name	Serving	Caffeine/serving (mg)
Brownie, square, large (2-3/4" x 7/8")	1 piece	1.12
Cake, chocolate pudding, dry mix	1 oz	1.701
Cake, chocolate, dry mix, regular	1 oz	3.118
Cake, German chocolate pudding, dry mix	1 oz	1.985
Cake, marble pudding, dry mix	1 oz	1.985
Candies, chocolate-covered, caramel with nuts	1 cup	35.34
Candies, chocolate-covered, dietetic or low-calorie	1 cup	16.74
Candy, milk chocolate w/almonds	1 bar (1.45 oz)	9.02
Candy, milk chocolate w/rice cereal	1 bar (1.4 oz)	9.2
Candy, raisins, milk-chocolate-coated	1 cup	45
Chocolate chips, semisweet, mini	1 cup chips (6-oz package)	107.12
Chocolate, baking, unsweetened, square	1 piece	22.72
Chocolate, baking, Mexican, square	1 piece	2.8
Chocolate, sweet	1 oz	18.711
Cookie Cake, Snackwell Fat Free Devil's Food, Nabisco	1 serving	1.28
Cookie, Snackwell Caramel Delights, Nabisco	1 serving	1.44
Cookie, chocolate chip, enriched, commercially prepared	1 oz	3.118
Cookie, chocolate chip, homemade w/margarine	1 oz	4.536
Cookie, chocolate chip, lower-fat, commercially prepared	3 pieces	2.1
Cookie, chocolate chip, refrigerated dough	1 portion, dough spooned from roll	2.61
Cookie, chocolate chip, soft, commercially prepared	1 oz	1.985
Cookie, chocolate wafers	1 cup, crumbs	7.84
Cookie, graham crackers, chocolate-coated	1 oz	13.041
Cookie, sandwich, chocolate, cream-filled	3 pieces	3.9
Cookie, sandwich, chocolate, cream-filled, special dietary	1 oz	0.85
Cupcake, chocolate w/frosting, low-fat	1 oz	0.86
Donut, cake, chocolate w/sugar or glaze	1 oz	0.284
Donut, cake, plain w/chocolate icing, large (3-1/2")	1 each	1.14
Fast food, ice cream sundae, hot fudge	1 sundae	1.58
Fast food, milk beverage, chocolate shake	1 cup (8 fl. oz)	1.66
Frosting, chocolate, creamy, ready-to-eat	2 tbsp creamy	0.82
Frozen yogurt, chocolate	1 cup	5.58
Fudge, chocolate w/nuts, homemade	1 oz	1.984
Granola bar, soft, milk-chocolate-coated, peanut butter	1 oz	0.85
Granola bar, with coconut, chocolate-coated	1 cup	5.58
Ice cream, chocolate	1 individual (3.5 fl. oz)	1.74
Ice cream, chocolate, light	1 oz	0.85
Ice cream, chocolate, rich	1 cup	5.92
M&M's Peanut Chocolate	1 cup	18.7
M&M's Plain Chocolate	1 cup	22.88
Milk chocolate	1 cup chips	33.6
Milk-chocolate-coated coffee beans	1 NLEA serving	48
Milk dessert, frozen, fat-free milk, chocolate	1 oz	0.85
Milk shake, thick, chocolate	1 fl. oz	0.568
Pastry, eclair/cream puff, homemade, custard-filled w/chocolate	1 oz	0.567
Pie crust, chocolate-wafer-cookie-type, chilled	1 crust, single 9"	11.15
Pie, chocolate mousse, no bake mix	1 oz	0.284
Pudding, chocolate, instant dry mix prepared w/reduced-fat (2%) milk	1 oz	0.283
Pudding, chocolate, regular dry mix prepared w/reduced-fat (2%) milk	1 oz	0.567
Pudding, chocolate, ready-to-eat, fat-free	4 oz can	2.27
Syrups, chocolate, genuine chocolate flavor, lite, Hershey	2 tbsp	1.05
Topping, chocolate-flavored hazelnut spread	1 oz	1.984
Yogurt, chocolate, nonfat milk	1 oz	0.567
Yogurt, frozen, chocolate, soft serve	0.5 cup (4 fl. oz)	2.16

U.S. Exchange Lists for Meal Planning

Data from: Choose Your Foods: Exchange Lists For Diabetes. © 2008 by the American Diabetes Association and the American Dietetic Association. Reproduced with permission.

Starch List

1 starch choice = 15 g carbohydrate, 0–3 g protein, 0–1 g fat, and 80 cal

Icon Key

☺ = More than 3 g of dietary fiber per serving.

❗ = Extra fat, or prepared with added fat. (Count as 1 starch + 1 fat.)

🧂 = 480 mg or more of sodium per serving.

Food	Serving Size	Food	Serving Size
Bread		Grits, cooked	½ c
Bagel, 4 oz	¼ (1 oz)	Kasha	½ c
❗ Biscuit, 2½" across	1	Millet, cooked	⅓ c
Bread		Muesli	¼ c
☺ reduced-calorie	2 slices (1½ oz)	Pasta, cooked	⅓ c
white, whole-grain, pumpernickel, rye,		Polenta, cooked	⅓ c
unfrosted raisin	1 slice (1 oz)	Quinoa, cooked	⅓ c
Chapatti, small, 6" across	1	Rice, white or brown, cooked	⅓ c
❗ Cornbread, 1¾" cube	1 (1½ oz)	Tabbouleh (tabouli), prepared	½ c
English muffin	½	Wheat germ, dry	3 tbs
Hot dog bun or hamburger bun	½ (1 oz)	Wild rice, cooked	½ c
Naan, 8" by 2"	¼	**Starchy Vegetables**	
Pancake, 4" across, ¼" thick	1	Cassava	⅓ c
Pita, 6" across	½	Corn	½ c
Roll, plain small	1 (1 oz)	on cob, large	½ cob (5 oz)
❗ Stuffing, bread	⅓ cup	☺ Hominy, canned	¾ c
❗ Taco shell, 5" across	2	☺ Mixed vegetables with corn, peas, or pasta	1 c
Tortilla		☺ Parsnips	½ c
Corn, 6" across	1	☺ Peas, green	½ c
Flour, 6" across	1	Plantain, ripe	⅓ c
Flour, 10" across	⅓ tortilla	Potato	
❗ Waffle, 4"-square or 4" across	1	baked with skin	¼ large (3 oz)
Cereals and Grains		boiled, all kinds	½ c or ½ medium (3 oz)
Barley, cooked	⅓ cup	❗ mashed, with milk and fat	½ c
Bran, dry		French fried (oven-baked)	1 cup (2 oz)
☺ oat	¼ c	☺ Pumpkin, canned, no sugar added	1 c
☺ wheat	½ c	Spaghetti/pasta sauce	½ c
☺ Bulgur (cooked)	½ c	☺ Squash, winter (acorn, butternut)	1 c
Cereals	½ c	☺ Succotash	½ c
☺ bran	½ c	Yam, sweet potato, plain	½ c
cooked (oats, oatmeal)	½ c	**Crackers and Snacks**	
puffed	1½ c	Animal crackers	8
shredded wheat, plain	½ c	Crackers	
sugar-coated	½ c	❗ round-butter type	6
unsweetened, ready-to-eat	¾ c	saltine-type	6
Couscous	⅓ c	❗ sandwich-style, cheese or peanut butter filling	3
Granola		❗ whole-wheat regular	2–5 (¾ oz)
low-fat	¼ c	☺ whole-wheat lower fat or crispbreads	2–5 (¾ oz)
❗ regular	¼ c	Graham crackers, 2½" square	3

Food	Serving Size	Food	Serving Size
Matzoh	¾ oz	**Beans, Peas, and Lentils**	
Melba toast, about 2" by 4" piece	4 pieces	*(Count as 1 starch + 1 lean meat)*	
Oyster crackers	20	☺ Baked beans	⅓ c
Crackers and Snacks		☺ Beans, cooked (black, garbanzo, kidney, lima, navy, pinto, white) ½ c	
Popcorn	3 c	☺ Lentils, cooked (brown, green, yellow)	½ c
⚠ ☺ with butter	3 c	☺ Peas, cooked (black-eyed, split)	½ c
☺ no fat added	3 c	🧂☺ Refried beans, canned	½ c
☺ lower fat	3 c		
Pretzels	¾ oz		
Rice cakes, 4" across	2		
Snack chips			
fat-free or baked (tortilla, potato),			
baked pita chips	15–20 (¾ oz)		
⚠ regular (tortilla, potato)	9–13 (¾ oz)		

Fruit List

1 fruit choice = 15 g carbohydrate, 0 g protein, 0 g fat, and 60 cal
Weight includes skin, core, seeds, and rind.

Icon Key

☺ = More than 3 g of dietary fiber per serving.

⚠ = Extra fat, or prepared with added fat.

🧂 = 480 mg or more of sodium per serving.

Food	Serving Size	Food	Serving Size
Apples		Grapes, small	17 (3 oz)
unpeeled, small	1 (4 oz)	Honeydew melon	1 slice or 1 c cubed (10 oz)
dried	4 rings	☺ Kiwi	1 (3½ oz)
Applesauce, unsweetened	½ c	Mandarin oranges, canned	¾ c
Apricots		Mango, small	½ fruit (5½ oz) or ½ c
canned	½ c	Nectarine, small	1 (5 oz)
dried	8 halves	☺ Orange, small	1 (6½ oz)
☺ fresh	4 whole (5½ oz)	Papaya	½ fruit or 1 c cubed (8 oz)
Banana, extra small	1 (4 oz)	Peaches	
☺ Blackberries	¾ c	canned	½ c
Blueberries	¾ c	fresh, medium	1 (6 oz)
Cantaloupe, small	⅓ melon or 1 c cubed (11 oz)	Pears	
Cherries		canned	½ c
sweet, canned	½ c	fresh, large	½ (4 oz)
sweet, fresh	12 (3 oz)	Pineapple	
Dates	3	canned	½ c
Dried fruits (blueberries, cherries, cranberries,		fresh	¾ c
mixed fruit, raisins)	2 tbs	Plums	
Figs		canned	½ c
dried	1½	dried (prunes)	3
☺ fresh	1½ large or 2 medium (3½ oz)	small	2 (5 oz)
Fruit cocktail	½ c	☺ Raspberries	1 c
Grapefruit		☺ Strawberries	1¼ c whole berries
large	½ (11 oz)		
sections, canned	¾ c		

Food	Serving Size	Food	Serving Size
😊 Tangerines, small	2 (8 oz)	Grape juice	⅓ c
Watermelon	1 slice or 1¼ c cubes (13½ oz)	Grapefruit juice	½ c
		Orange juice	½ c
Fruit Juice		Pineapple juice	½ c
Apple juice/cider	½ c	Prune juice	⅓ c
Fruit juice blends, 100% juice	⅓ c		

Milk and Yogurts

1 milk choice = 12 g carbohydrate and 8 g protein

Food	Serving Size	Count as
Fat-free or Low-Fat (1%)		
(0–3 g fat per serving, 100 calories per serving)		
Milk, buttermilk, acidophilus milk, Lactaid	1 c	1 fat-free milk
Evaporated milk	½ c	1 fat-free milk
Yogurt, plain or flavored with an artificial sweetener	⅔ c (6 oz)	1 fat-free milk
Reduced-fat (2%)		
(5 g fat per serving, 120 calories per serving)		
Milk, acidophilus milk, kefir, Lactaid	1 c	1 reduced-fat milk
Yogurt, plain	⅔ c (6 oz)	1 reduced-fat milk
Whole		
(8 g fat per serving, 160 calories per serving)		
Milk, buttermilk, goat's milk	1 c	1 whole milk
Evaporated milk	½ c	1 whole milk
Yogurt, plain	8 oz	1 whole milk
Dairy-Like Foods		
Chocolate milk		
fat-free	1 c	1 fat-free milk + 1 carbohydrate
whole	1 c	1 whole milk + 1 carbohydrate
Eggnog, whole milk	½ c	1 carbohydrate + 2 fats
Rice drink		
flavored, low-fat	1 c	2 carbohydrates
plain, fat-free	1 c	1 carbohydrate
Smoothies, flavored, regular	10 oz	1 fat-free milk + 2½ carbohydrates
Soy milk		
light	1 c	1 carbohydrate + ½ fat
regular, plain	1 c	1 carbohydrate + 1 fat
Yogurt		
and juice blends	1 c	1 fat-free milk + 1 carbohydrate
low carbohydrate (less than 6 g carbohydrate per choice)	⅔ c (6 oz)	½ fat-free milk
with fruit, low-fat	⅔ c (6 oz)	1 fat-free milk + 1 carbohydrate

Sweets, Desserts, and Other Carbohydrates List

1 other carbohydrate choice = 15 g carbohydrate and variable protein, fat, and calories.

Icon Key

🧂 = 480 mg or more of sodium per serving.

Food	Serving Size	Count as
Beverages, Soda, and Energy/Sports Drinks		
Cranberry juice cocktail	½ c	1 carbohydrate
Energy drink	1 can (8.3 oz)	2 carbohydrates
Fruit drink or lemonade	1 c (8 oz)	2 carbohydrates
Hot chocolate		
regular	1 envelope added to 8 oz water	1 carbohydrate + 1 fat
sugar-free or light	1 envelope added to 8 oz water	1 carbohydrate
Soft drink (soda), regular	1 can (12 oz)	2½ carbohydrates
Sports drink	1 cup (8 oz)	1 carbohydrate
Brownies, Cake, Cookies, Gelatin, Pie,		
and Pudding		
Brownie, small, unfrosted	1¼" square, ⅞" high (about 1 oz)	1 carbohydrate + 1 fat
Cake		
angel food, unfrosted	1½ of cake (about 2 oz)	2 carbohydrates
frosted	2" square (about 2 oz)	2 carbohydrates + 1 fat
unfrosted	2" square (about 2 oz)	1 carbohydrate + 1 fat
Cookies		
chocolate chip	2 cookies (2¼" across)	1 carbohydrate + 2 fats
gingersnap	3 cookies	1 carbohydrate
sandwich, with creme filling	2 small (about ⅔ oz)	1 carbohydrate + 1 fat
sugar-free	3 small or 1 large (¾ oz–1oz)	1 carbohydrate + 1–2 fats
vanilla wafer	5 cookies	1 carbohydrate + 1 fat
Cupcake, frosted	1 small (about 1¾ oz)	2 carbohydrates + 1–1½ fats
Fruit cobbler	½ c (3½ oz)	3 carbohydrates + 1 fat
Gelatin, regular	½ c	1 carbohydrate
Pie		
commercially prepared fruit, 2 crusts	⅛ of 8" pie	3 carbohydrates + 2 fats
pumpkin or custard	⅛ of 8" pie	1½ carbohydrates + 1½ fats
Pudding		
regular (made with reduced-fat milk)	½ c	2 carbohydrates
sugar-free, or sugar-free and fat-free (made with fat-free milk)	½ c	1 carbohydrate
Candy, Spreads, Sweets, Sweeteners,		
Syrups, and Toppings		
Candy bar, chocolate/peanut	2 "fun size" bars (1 oz)	1½ carbohydrates + 1½ fats
Candy, hard	3 pieces	1 carbohydrate
Chocolate "kisses"	5 pieces	1 carbohydrate + 1 fat
Coffee creamer		
dry, flavored	4 tsp	½ carbohydrate + ½ fat
liquid, flavored	2 tbsp	1 carbohydrate
Fruit snacks, chewy (pureed fruit concentrate)	1 roll (¾ oz)	1 carbohydrate
Fruit spreads, 100% fruit	1½ tbs	1 carbohydrate
Honey	1 tbsp	1 carbohydrate

Food	Serving Size	Count as
Jam or jelly, regular	1 tbs	1 carbohydrate
Sugar	1 tbs	1 carbohydrate
Syrup		
chocolate	2 tbs	2 carbohydrates
light (pancake type)	2 tbs	1 carbohydrate
regular (pancake type)	1 tbs	1 carbohydrate
Condiments and Sauces		
Barbeque sauce	3 tbs	1 carbohydrate
Cranberry sauce, jellied	¼ c	1½ carbohydrates
Gravy, canned or bottled	½ c	½ carbohydrate + ½ fat
Salad dressing, fat-free, low-fat, cream-based	3 tbs	1 carbohydrate
Sweet and sour sauce	3 tbs	1 carbohydrate
Doughnuts, Muffins, Pastries, and Sweet Breads		
Banana nut bread	1" slice (1 oz)	2 carbohydrates + 1 fat
Doughnut		
cake, plain	1 medium, (1½ oz)	1½ carbohydrates + 2 fats
yeast type, glazed	3¾" across (2 oz)	2 carbohydrates + 2 fats
Muffin (4 oz)	¼ muffin (1 oz)	1 carbohydrate + ½ fat
Sweet roll or Danish	1 (2½ oz)	2½ carbohydrates + 2 fats
Frozen Bars, Frozen Dessert, Frozen Yogurt, and Ice Cream		
Frozen pops	1	½ carbohydrate
Fruit juice bars, frozen, 100% juice	1 bar (3 oz)	1 carbohydrate
Ice cream		
fat-free	½ c	1-½ carbohydrates
light	½ c	1 carbohydrate + 1 fat
no sugar added	½ c	1 carbohydrate + 1 fat
regular	½ c	1 carbohydrate + 2 fats
Sherbet, sorbet	½ c	2 carbohydrates
Yogurt, frozen		
fat-free	⅓ c	1 carbohydrate
regular	½ c	1 carbohydrate + 0–1 fat
Granola Bars, Meal Replacement Bars/Shakes, and Trail Mix		
Granola or snack bar, regular or low-fat	1 bar (1 oz)	1½ carbohydrates
Meal replacement bar	1 bar (1⅓ oz)	1½ carbohydrates + 0–1 fat
Meal replacement bar	1 bar (2 oz)	2 carbohydrates + 1 fat
Meal replacement shake, reduced-calorie	1 can (10–11 oz)	1½ carbohydrates + 0–1 fat
Trail mix		
candy/nut-based	1 oz	1 carbohydrates + 2 fats
dried-fruit-based	1 oz	1 carbohydrate + 1 fat

Nonstarchy Vegetable List

1 vegetable choice = 5 g carbohydrate, 2 g protein, 0 g fat, 25 cal

Icon Key

😃 = More than 3 g of dietary fiber per serving.

🧂 = 480 mg or more of sodium per serving.

Amaranth or Chinese spinach	Kohlrabi
Artichoke	Leeks
Artichoke hearts	Mixed vegetables (without corn, peas, or pasta)
Asparagus	Mung bean sprouts
Baby corn	Mushrooms, all kinds, fresh
Bamboo shoots	Okra
Beans (green, wax, Italian)	Onions
Bean sprouts	Oriental radish or daikon
Beets	Pea pods
🧂 Borscht	😃 Peppers (all varieties)
Broccoli	Radishes
😃 Brussels sprouts	Rutabaga
Cabbage (green, bok choy, Chinese)	🧂 Sauerkraut
😃 Carrots	Soybean sprouts
Cauliflower	Spinach
Celery	Squash (summer, crookneck, zucchini)
😃 Chayote	Sugar pea snaps
Coleslaw, packaged, no dressing	😃 Swiss chard
Cucumber	Tomato
Eggplant	Tomatoes, canned
Gourds (bitter, bottle, luffa, bitter melon)	🧂 Tomato sauce
Green onions or scallions	🧂 Tomato/vegetable juice
Greens (collard, kale, mustard, turnip)	Turnips
Hearts of palm	Water chestnuts
Jicama	Yard-long beans

Meat and Meat Substitutes List

Icon Key

❗ = Extra fat, or prepared with added fat. (Add an additional fat choice to this food.)

🧂 = 480 mg or more of sodium per serving (based on the sodium content of a typical 3-oz serving of meat, unless 1 or 2 is the normal serving size).

Food	Amount	Food	Amount
Lean Meats and Meat Substitutes		*Fish, fresh or frozen, plain:* catfish, cod, flounder,	
(1 lean meat choice = 7 g protein, 0–3 g fat,		haddock, halibut, orange roughy, salmon, tilapia,	
100 calories)		trout, tuna . . . . .1 oz	
Beef: Select or Choice grades trimmed of fat:		🧂 *Fish, smoked:* herring or salmon (lox) . . . . .1 oz	
ground round, roast (chuck, rib, rump), round,		*Game:* buffalo, ostrich, rabbit, venison . . . . .1 oz	
sirloin, steak (cubed, flank, porterhouse, T-bone),		🧂 Hot dog with 3 g of fat or less per oz (8 dogs	
tenderloin . . . . .1 oz		per 14 oz package) (*Note: May be high in*	
🧂 Beef jerky . . . . .1 oz		*carbohydrate.*) 1	
Cheeses with 3 g of fat or less per oz . . . . .1 oz		*Lamb:* chop, leg, or roast . . . . .1 oz	
Cottage cheese . . . . .¼ cup		*Organ meats:* heart, kidney, liver (*Note: May be high*	
Egg substitutes, plain . . . . .¼ cup		*in cholesterol*) . . . . .1 oz	
Egg whites 2			

Food	Amount
Oysters, fresh or frozen	6 medium
Pork, lean	
🧂 Canadian bacon	1 oz
rib or loin chop/roast, ham, tenderloin	1 oz
Poultry without skin: Cornish hen, chicken, domestic duck or goose (well drained of fat), turkey	1 oz
Processed sandwich meats with 3 g of fat or less per oz: chipped beef, deli thin-sliced meats, turkey ham, turkey kielbasa, turkey pastrami	1 oz
Salmon, canned	1 oz
Sardines, canned	2 medium
🧂 Sausage with 3 g or less fat per oz	1 oz
Shellfish: clams, crab, imitation shellfish, lobster, scallops, shrimp	1 oz
Tuna, canned in water or oil, drained	1 oz
Veal: Lean chop, roast	1 oz

Medium-Fat Meat and Meat Substitutes

(1 medium-fat meat choice = 7 g protein, 4–7 g fat, and 130 calories)

Food	Amount
Beef: corned beef, ground beef, meatloaf, Prime grades trimmed of fat (prime rib), short ribs, tongue	1 oz
Cheeses with 4–7 g of fat per oz: feta, mozzarella, pasteurized processed cheese spread, reduced-fat cheeses, string	1 oz
Egg (*Note: High in cholesterol, limit to 3 per week.*)	1
Fish, any fried product	1 oz
Lamb: ground, rib roast	1 oz
Pork: cutlet, shoulder roast	1 oz

Food	Amount
Poultry: chicken with skin; dove, pheasant, wild duck, or goose; fried chicken; ground turkey	1 oz
Ricotta cheese	2 oz or ¼ c
🧂 Sausage with 4–7 g fat per oz	1 oz
Veal: Cutlet (no breading)	1 oz

High-Fat Meat and Substitutes[a]

(1 high-fat meat choice = 7 g protein, 8+ g fat, 150 calories)

Food	Amount
Bacon	
🧂 pork	2 slices (16 slices per lb or 1 oz each, before cooking)
🧂 turkey	3 slices (½ oz each before cooking)
Cheese, regular: American, bleu, brie, cheddar, hard goat, Monterey Jack, queso, Swiss	1 oz
🧂 ❗ *Hot dog:* beef, pork, or combination (10 per lb-sized package)	1
🧂 *Hot dog:* turkey or chicken (10 per lb-sized package)	1
Pork: ground, sausage, spareribs	1 oz
Processed sandwich meats with 8 g of fat or more per oz: bologna, pastrami, hard salami	1 oz
🧂 *Sausage with 8 g of fat or more per oz:* bratwurst, chorizo, Italian, knockwurst, Polish, smoked, summer	1 oz

[a]These foods are high in saturated fat, cholesterol, and calories and may raise blood cholesterol levels if eaten on a regular basis. Try to eat 3 or fewer servings from this group per week.

Plant-Based Proteins

Because carbohydrate content varies among plant-based proteins, you should read the food label.

Icon Key

😊 = More than 3 g of dietary fiber per serving.

🧂 = 480 mg or more of sodium per serving (based on the sodium content of a typical 3-oz serving of meat, unless 1 or 2 oz is the normal serving size).

Food	Amount	Count as
"Bacon" strips, soy-based	3 strips	1 medium-fat meat
😊 Baked beans	⅓ c	1 starch + 1 lean meat
😊 *Beans, cooked:* black, garbanzo, kidney, lima, navy, pinto, white	½ c	1 starch + 1 lean meat
😊 "Beef" or "sausage" crumbles, soy-based	2 oz	½ carbohydrate + 1 lean meat
"Chicken" nuggets, soy-based	2 nuggets (1½ oz)	½ carbohydrate + 1 medium-fat meat
😊 Edamame	½ c	½ carbohydrate + 1 lean meat
Falafel (spiced chickpea and wheat patties)	3 patties (about 2 inches across)	1 carbohydrate + 1 high-fat meat
Hot dog, soy-based	1 (1½ oz)	½ carbohydrate + 1 lean meat
😊 Hummus	⅓ c	1 carbohydrate + 1 high-fat meat

Food	Amount	Count as
😊 Lentils, brown, green, or yellow	½ c	1 carbohydrate + 1 lean meat
😊 Meatless burger, soy-based	3 oz	½ carbohydrate + 2 lean meats
😊 Meatless burger, vegetable- and starch-based	1 patty (about 2½ oz)	1 carbohydrate + 2 lean meats
Nut spreads: almond butter, cashew butter, peanut butter, soy nut butter	1 tbs	1 high-fat meat
😊 *Peas, cooked:* black-eyed and split peas	½ c	1 starch + 1 lean meat
🧂😊 Refried beans, canned	½ c	1 starch + 1 lean meat
"Sausage" patties, soy-based	1 (1½ oz)	1 medium-fat meat
Soy nuts, unsalted	¾ oz	½ carbohydrate + 1 medium-fat meat
Tempeh	¼ cup	1 medium-fat meat
Tofu	4 oz (½ cup)	1 medium-fat meat
Tofu, light	4 oz (½ cup)	1 lean meat

Fat List

Icon Key

1 fat choice = 5 g fat, 45 cal

🧂 = 480 mg or more of sodium per serving.

Food	Serving Size	Food	Serving Size
Unsaturated Fats—		Nuts	
Monounsaturated Fats		Pignolia (pine nuts)	1 tbs
Avocado, medium	2 tbs (1 oz)	walnuts, English	4 halves
Nut butters (trans fat-free): almond butter,		*Oil:* corn, cottonseed, flaxseed, grape seed,	
cashew butter, peanut butter (smooth or crunchy)	1½ tsp	safflower, soybean, sunflower	1 tsp
Nuts		*Oil:* made from soybean and canola oil—Enova	1 tsp
almonds	6 nuts	Plant stanol esters	
Brazil	2 nuts	light	1 tbs
cashews	6 nuts	regular	2 tsp
filberts (hazelnuts)	5 nuts	Salad dressing	
macadamia	3 nuts	🧂 reduced-fat (*Note: May be high*	
mixed (50% peanuts)	6 nuts	*in carbohydrate.*)	2 tbs
peanuts	10 nuts	🧂 regular	1 tbs
pecans	4 halves	Seeds	1 tbs
pistachios	16 nuts	flaxseed, whole	1 tbs
Oil: canola, olive, peanut	1 tsp	pumpkin, sunflower	1 tbs
Olives		sesame seeds	1 tbs
black (ripe)	8 large	Tahini or sesame paste	2 tsp
green, stuffed	10 large	**Saturated Fats**	
Polyunsaturated Fats		Bacon, cooked, regular or turkey	1 slice
Margarine: lower-fat spread (30% to 50% vegetable		Butter	
oil, *trans* fat-free)	1 tbs	reduced-fat	1 tbs
Margarine: stick, tub (*trans* fat-free), or squeeze		stick	1 tsp
(*trans* fat-free)	1 tsp	whipped	2 tsp
Mayonnaise		Butter blends made with oil	
reduced-fat	1 tbs	reduced-fat or light	1 tbs
regular	1 tsp	regular	1½ tsp
Mayonnaise-style salad dressing		Chitterlings, boiled	2 tbs (½ oz)
reduced-fat	1 tbs	Coconut, sweetened, shredded	2 tbs
regular	2 tsp		

Food	Serving Size	Food	Serving Size
Coconut milk		Lard	1 tsp
light	⅓ c	*Oil:* coconut, palm, palm kernel	1 tsp
regular	1½ tbs	Salt pork	¼ oz
Cream		Shortening, solid	1 tsp
half and half	2 tbs	Sour cream	
heavy	1 tbs	reduced-fat or light	3 tbs
light	1½ tbs	regular	2 tbs
whipped	2 tbs		
whipped, pressurized	¼ c		
Cream cheese			
reduced-fat	1½ tbs (¾ oz)		
regular	1 tbs (½ oz)		

Free Foods List

A *free food* is any food or drink that has less than 20 calories and 5 g or less of carbohydrate per serving. Foods with a serving size listed should be limited to three servings per day. Foods listed without a serving size can be eaten as often as you like.

Icon Key

🧂 = 480 mg or more of sodium per serving.

Food	Serving Size	Food	Serving Size
Low Carbohydrate Foods		Salad dressing	
Cabbage, raw	½ c	fat-free or low-fat	1 tbs
Candy, hard (regular or sugar-free)	1 piece	fat-free, Italian	2 tbs
Carrots, cauliflower, or green beans, cooked	¼ c	Sour cream, fat-free, reduced-fat	1 tbs
Cranberries, sweetened with sugar substitute	½ c	Whipped topping	
Cucumber, sliced	½ c	light or fat-free	2 tbs
Gelatin		regular	1 tbs
dessert, sugar-free		**Condiments**	
unflavored		Barbecue sauce	2 tsp
Gum		Catsup (ketchup)	1 tbs
Jam or jelly, light or no sugar added	2 tsp	Honey mustard	1 tbs
Rhubarb, sweetened with sugar substitute	½ c	Horseradish	
Salad greens		Lemon juice	
Sugar substitutes (artificial sweeteners)		Miso	1½ tsp
Syrup, sugar-free	2 tbs	Mustard	
Modified Fat Foods		Parmesan cheese, freshly grated	1 tbs
with Carbohydrate		Pickle relish	1 tbs
Cream cheese, fat-free	1 tbs (½ oz)	Pickles	
Creamers		🧂 dill	1½ medium
nondairy, liquid	1 tbs	sweet, bread and butter	2 slices
nondairy, powdered	2 tsp	sweet, gherkin	¾ oz
Margarine spread		Salsa	¼ c
fat-free	1 tbs	🧂 Soy sauce, regular or light	1 tbs
reduced-fat	1 tsp	Sweet and sour sauce	2 tsp
Mayonnaise		Sweet chili sauce	2 tsp
fat-free	1 tbs	Taco sauce	1 tbs
reduced-fat	1 tsp	Vinegar	
Mayonnaise-style salad dressing		Yogurt, any type	2 tbs
fat-free	1 tbs		
reduced-fat	1 tsp		

Drinks/Mixes

Any food on this list—without serving size listed—can be consumed in any moderate amount.

Icon Key

🧂 = 480 mg or more of sodium per serving.

🧂 Bouillon, broth, consommé	Diet soft drinks, sugar-free
Bouillon or broth, low sodium	Drink mixes, sugar-free
Carbonated or mineral water	Tea, unsweetened or with sugar substitute
Club soda	Tonic water, diet
Cocoa powder, unsweetened (1 tbs)	Water
Coffee, unsweetened or with sugar substitute	Water, flavored, carbohydrate free

Seasonings

Any food on this list can be consumed in any moderate amount.

Flavoring extracts (for example, vanilla, almond, peppermint)	Spices
Garlic	Hot pepper sauce
Herbs, fresh or dried	Wine, used in cooking
Nonstick cooking spray	Worcestershire sauce
Pimento	

Combination Foods List

Icon Key

☺ = More than 3 g of dietary fiber per serving.

🧂 = 600 mg or more of sodium per serving (for combination food main dishes/meals).

Food	Serving Size	Count as
Entrées		
🧂 Casserole type (tuna noodle, lasagna, spaghetti with meatballs, chili with beans, macaroni and cheese)	1 c (8 oz)	2 carbohydrates + 2 medium-fat meats
🧂 Stews (beef/other meats and vegetables)	1 c (8 oz)	1 carbohydrate + 1 medium-fat meat + 0–3 fats
Tuna salad or chicken salad	½ c (3½ oz)	½ carbohydrate + 2 lean meats + 1 fat
Frozen Meals/Entrées		
🧂☺ Burrito (beef and bean)	1 (5 oz)	3 carbohydrates + 1 lean meat + 2 fats
🧂 Dinner-type meal	generally 14–17 oz	3 carbohydrates + 3 medium-fat meats + 3 fats
🧂 Entrée or meal with less than 340 calories	about 8–11 oz	2–3 carbohydrates + 1–2 lean meats
Pizza		
🧂 cheese/vegetarian thin crust	¼ of 12" (4½ to 5 oz)	2 carbohydrates + 2 medium-fat meats
🧂 meat topping, thin crust	¼ of 12" (5 oz)	2 carbohydrates + 2 medium-fat meats, + 1½ fats
🧂 Pocket sandwich	1 (4½ oz)	3 carbohydrates + 1 lean meat + 1–2 fats
🧂 Pot pie	1 (7 oz)	2½ carbohydrates + 1 medium-fat meat + 3 fats
Salads (Deli-Style)		
Coleslaw	½ c	1 carbohydrate + 1½ fats
Macaroni/pasta salad	½ c	2 carbohydrates + 3 fats
🧂 Potato salad	½ c	1½ carbohydrates + 1–2 fats
Soups		
🧂 Bean, lentil, or split pea	1 cup	1 carbohydrate + 1 lean meat

Food	Serving Size	Count as
🧂 Chowder (made with milk)	1 c (8 oz)	1 carbohydrate + 1 lean meat + 1½ fats
🧂 Cream (made with water)	1 c (8 oz)	1 carbohydrate + 1 fat
🧂 Instant	6 oz prepared	1 carbohydrate
🧂 with beans or lentils	8 oz prepared	2½ carbohydrates + 1 lean meat
🧂 Miso soup	1 c	½ carbohydrate + 1 fat
🧂 Oriental noodle	1 c	2 carbohydrates + 2 fats
Rice (congee)	1 c	1 carbohydrate
🧂 Tomato (made with water)	1 c (8 oz)	1 carbohydrate
🧂 Vegetable beef, chicken noodle, or other broth-type	1 c (8 oz)	1 carbohydrate

Fast Foods List[a]

Icon Key

☺ = More than 3 g of dietary fiber per serving.

! = Extra fat, or prepared with added fat.

🧂 = 600 mg or more sodium per serving (for fast food main dishes/meals).

Food	Serving Size	Exchanges per Serving
Breakfast Sandwiches		
🧂 Egg, cheese, meat, English muffin	1 sandwich	2 carbohydrates + 2 medium-fat meats
🧂 Sausage biscuit sandwich	1 sandwich	2 carbohydrates + 2 high-fat meats + 3½ fats
Main Dishes/Entrees		
🧂☺ Burrito (beef and beans)	1 (about 8 oz)	3 carbohydrates + 3 medium-fat meats + 3 fats
🧂 Chicken breast, breaded and fried	1 (about 5 oz)	1 carbohydrate + 4 medium-fat meats
Chicken drumstick, breaded and fried	1 (about 2 oz)	2 medium-fat meats
🧂 Chicken nuggets	6 (about 3½ oz)	1 carbohydrate + 2 medium-fat meats + 1 fat
🧂 Chicken thigh, breaded and fried	1 (about 4 oz)	½ carbohydrate + 3 medium-fat meats + 1½ fats
🧂 Chicken wings, hot	6 (5 oz)	5 medium-fat meats + 1½ fats
Oriental		
🧂 Beef/chicken/shrimp with vegetables in sauce	1 c (about 5 oz)	1 carbohydrate + 1 lean meat + 1 fat
🧂 Egg roll, meat	1 (about 3 oz)	1 carbohydrate + 1 lean meat + 1 fat
Fried rice, meatless	½ c	1½ carbohydrates + 1½ fats
🧂 Meat and sweet sauce (orange chicken)	1 c	3 carbohydrates + 3 medium-fat meats + 2 fats
🧂☺ Noodles and vegetables in sauce (chow mein, lo mein)	1 c	2 carbohydrates + 1 fat
Pizza		
🧂 Cheese, pepperoni, regular crust	⅛ of 14" (about 4 oz)	2½ carbohydrates + 1 medium-fat meat + 1½ fats
🧂 Cheese/vegetarian, thin crust	¼ of 12" (about 6 oz)	2½ carbohydrates + 2 medium-fat meats + 1½ fats
Sandwiches		
🧂 Chicken sandwich, grilled	1	3 carbohydrates + 4 lean meats
🧂 Chicken sandwich, crispy	1	3½ carbohydrates + 3 medium-fat meats + 1 fat
Fish sandwich with tartar sauce	1	2½ carbohydrates + 2 medium-fat meats + 2 fats
Hamburger		
🧂 large with cheese	1	2½ carbohydrates + 4 medium-fat meats + 1 fat
regular	1	2 carbohydrates + 1 medium-fat meat + 1 fat
🧂 Hot dog with bun	1	1 carbohydrate + 1 high-fat meat + 1 fat
Submarine sandwich		
🧂 less than 6 grams fat	6" sub	3 carbohydrates + 2 lean meats
🧂 regular	6" sub	3½ carbohydrates + 2 medium-fat meats + 1 fat

[a]The choices in the Fast Foods list are not specific fast food meals or items, but are estimates based on popular foods. You can get specific nutrition information for almost every fast food or restaurant chain. Ask the restaurant or check its website for nutrition information about your favorite fast foods.

Food	Serving Size	Exchanges per Serving
Taco, hard or soft shell (meat and cheese)	1 small	1 carbohydrate + 1 medium-fat meat + 1½ fats
Salads		
Salad, main dish (grilled chcken type, no dressing or croutons)	salad	1 carbohydrate + 4 lean meats
Salad, side, no dressing or cheese	Small (about 5 oz)	1 vegetable
Sides/Appetizers		
French fries, restaurant style	Small	3 carbohydrates + 3 fats
Medium		4 carbohydrates + 4 fats
Large		5 carbohydrates + 6 fats
Nachos with cheese	Small (about 4½ oz)	2½ carbohydrates + 4 fats
Onion rings	1 serving (about 3 oz)	2½ carbohydrates + 3 fats
Desserts		
Milkshake, any flavor	12 oz	6 carbohydrates + 2 fats
Soft-serve ice cream cone	1 small	2½ carbohydrates + 1 fat

Alcohol List

In general, 1 alcohol choice (½ oz absolute alcohol) has about 100 calories.

Alcoholic Beverage	Serving Size	Count as
Beer		
light (4.2%)	12 fl. oz	1 alcohol equivalent + ½ carbohydrate
regular (4.9%)	12 fl. oz	1 alcohol equivalent + 1 carbohydrate
Distilled spirits: vodka, rum, gin, whiskey, 80 or 86 proof	1½ fl. oz	1 alcohol equivalent
Liqueur, coffee (53 proof)	1 fl. oz	1 alcohol equivalent + 1 carbohydrate
Sake	1 fl. oz	½ alcohol equivalent
Wine		
dessert (sherry)	3½ fl. oz	1 alcohol equivalent + 1 carbohydrate
dry, red or white (10%)	5 fl. oz	1 alcohol equivalent

CDC Growth Charts: United States

Stature-for-age percentiles: Boys, 2 to 20 years

in"

cm

Age (years)

97th
95th
90th
75th
50th
25th
10th
5th
3rd

Published May 30, 2000.
Data from: The National Center for Health Statistics in
collaboration with the National Center for Chronic
Disease Prevention and Health Promotion (2000).

SAFER · HEALTHIER · PEOPLE™

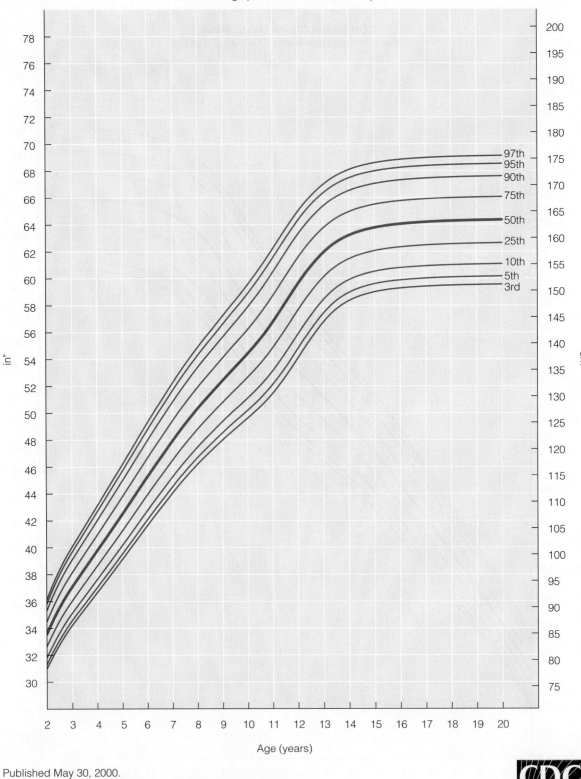

CDC Growth Charts: United States
Stature-for-age percentiles: Girls, 2 to 20 years

Age (years)

Published May 30, 2000.
Data from: The National Center for Health Statistics in
collaboration with the National Center for Chronic
Disease Prevention and Health Promotion (2000).

CDC
SAFER • HEALTHIER • PEOPLE™

Appendix H Organizations and Resources

Academic Journals

International Journal of Sport Nutrition and Exercise Metabolism
Human Kinetics
P.O. Box 5076
Champaign, IL 61825-5076
(800) 747-4457
www.humankinetics.com/IJSNEM

Journal of Nutrition
A. Catharine Ross, Editor
Department of Nutrition
Pennsylvania State University
126-S Henderson Building
University Park, PA 16802-6504
(814) 865-4721
www.nutrition.org

Nutrition Research
Elsevier: Journals Customer Service
6277 Sea Harbor Drive
Orlando, FL 32887
(877) 839-7126
www.journals.elsevierhealth.com/periodicals/NTR

Nutrition
Elsevier: Journals Customer Service
6277 Sea Harbor Drive
Orlando, FL 32887
(877) 839-7126
www.journals.elsevierhealth.com/periodicals/NUT

Nutrition Reviews
International Life Sciences Institute
Subscription Office
P.O. Box 830430
Birmingham, AL 35283
(800) 633-4931
www.ingentaconnect.com/content/ilsi/nure

Obesity Research
North American Association for the Study of Obesity
(NAASO)
8630 Fenton Street, Suite 918
Silver Spring, MD 20910
(301) 563-6526
www.obesityresearch.org

International Journal of Obesity
Journal of the International Association for the Study of Obesity
Nature Publishing Group
The Macmillan Building
4 Crinan Street

London N1 9XW
United Kingdom
www.nature.com/ijo

Journal of the American Medical Association
American Medical Association
P.O. Box 10946
Chicago, IL 60610-0946
(800) 262-2350
http://jama.ama-assn.org

New England Journal of Medicine
10 Shattuck Street
Boston, MA 02115-6094
(617) 734-9800
http://content.nejm.org/

American Journal of Clinical Nutrition
The American Journal of Clinical Nutrition
9650 Rockville Pike
Bethesda, MD 20814-3998
(301) 634-7038
www.ajcn.org

Journal of the American Dietetic Association
Elsevier, Health Sciences Division
Subscription Customer Service
6277 Sea Harbor Drive
Orlando, FL 32887
(800) 654-2452
www.adajournal.org

Aging

Administration on Aging
U.S. Health & Human Services
200 Independence Avenue, SW
Washington, DC 20201
(877) 696-6775
www.aoa.gov

American Association of Retired Persons (AARP)
601 E. Street, NW
Washington, DC 20049
(888) 687-2277
www.aarp.org

Health and Age
Sponsored by the Novartis Foundation for Gerontology &
The Web-Based Health Education Foundation
Robert Griffith, MD
Executive Director
573 Vista de la Ciudad
Santa Fe, NM 87501
www.healthandage.com

National Council on the Aging
300 D Street, SW, Suite 801
Washington, DC 20024
(202) 479-1200
www.ncoa.org

International Osteoporosis Foundation
5 Rue Perdtemps
1260 Nyon
Switzerland
41 22 994 01 00
www.osteofound.org

National Institute on Aging
Building 31, Room 5C27
31 Center Drive, MSC 2292
Bethesda, MD 20892
(301) 496-1752
www.nia.nih.gov

Osteoporosis and Related Bone Diseases National Resource Center
2 AMS Circle
Bethesda, MD 20892-3676
(800) 624-BONE
www.osteo.org

American Geriatrics Society
The Empire State Building
350 Fifth Avenue, Suite 801
New York, NY 10118
(212) 308-1414
www.americangeriatrics.org

National Osteoporosis Foundation
1232 22nd Street, NW
Washington, DC 20037-1292
(202) 223-2226
www.nof.org/

Alcohol and Drug Abuse

National Institute on Drug Abuse
6001 Executive Boulevard, Room 5213
Bethesda, MD 20892-9561
(301) 443-1124
www.nida.nih.gov

National Institute on Alcohol Abuse and Alcoholism
5635 Fishers Lane, MSC 9304
Bethesda, MD 20892-9304
www.niaaa.nih.gov

Alcoholics Anonymous
Grand Central Station
P.O. Box 459
New York, NY 10163
www.alcoholics-anonymous.org

Narcotics Anonymous
P.O. Box 9999
Van Nuys, California 91409
(818) 773-9999
www.na.org

National Council on Alcoholism and Drug Dependence
20 Exchange Place, Suite 2902
New York, NY 10005
(212) 269-7797
www.ncadd.org

National Clearinghouse for Alcohol and Drug Information
11420 Rockville Pike
Rockville, MD 20852
(800) 729-6686
www.health.org

Canadian Government

Health Canada
A.L. 0900C2
Ottawa, ON
K1A 0K9
(613) 957-2991
www.hc-sc.gc.ca/english

National Institute of Nutrition
408 Queen Street, 3rd Floor
Ottawa, ON K1R 5A7
(613) 235-3355
www.nin.ca/public_html/index.html

Agricultural and Agri-Food Canada
Public Information Request Service
Sir John Carling Building
930 Carling Avenue
Ottawa, ON K1A 0C5
(613) 759-1000
www.arg.gc.ca

Bureau of Nutritional Sciences
Sir Frederick G. Banting Research Centre
Tunney's Pasture (2203A)
Ottawa, ON K1A 0L2
(613) 957-0352
www.hc-sc.gc.ca/food-aliment/ns-sc/e_nutrition.html

Canadian Food Inspection Agency
59 Camelot Drive
Ottawa, ON K1A 0Y9
(613) 225-2342
www.inspection.gc.ca/english/toce.shtml

Canadian Institute for Health Information
CIHI Ottawa
377 Dalhousie Street, Suite 200
Ottawa, ON K1N 9N8
(613) 241-7860
www.cihi.ca

Canadian Public Health Association
1565 Carling Avenue, Suite 400
Ottawa, ON K1Z 8R1
(613) 725-3769
www.cpha.ca

Canadian Nutrition and Professional Organizations

Dietitians of Canada
480 University Avenue, Suite 604
Toronto, ON M5G 1V2
(416) 596-0857
www.dietitians.ca

Canadian Diabetes Association
National Life Building
1400-522 University Avenue
Toronto, ON M5G 2R5
(800) 226-8464
www.diabetes.ca

National Eating Disorder Information Centre
CW 1-211, 200 Elizabeth Street
Toronto, ON M5G 2C4
(866) NEDIC-20
www.nedic.ca

Canadian Pediatric Society
100-2204 Walkley Road
Ottawa, ON K1G 4G8
(613) 526-9397
www.cps.ca

Canadian Dietetic Association
480 University Avenue, Suite 604
Toronto, ON M5G 1V2
(416) 596-0857
www.dietitians.ca

Disordered Eating/Eating Disorders

American Psychiatric Association
1000 Wilson Boulevard, Suite 1825
Arlington, VA 22209
(703) 907-7300
www.psych.org

Harvard Eating Disorders Center
WACC 725
15 Parkman Street
Boston, MA 02114
(617) 236-7766
www.hedc.org

National Institute of Mental Health
Office of Communications
6001 Executive Boulevard, Room 8184, MSC 9663
Bethesda, MD 20892
(866) 615-6464
www.nimh.nih.gov

National Association of Anorexia Nervosa and Associated Disorders (ANAD)
Box 7
Highland Park, IL 60035
(847) 831-3438
www.anad.org

National Eating Disorders Association
603 Stewart Street, Suite 803
Seattle, WA 98101
(206) 382-3587
www.nationaleatingdisorders.org

Eating Disorder Referral and Information Center
2923 Sandy Pointe, Suite 6
Del Mar, CA 92014
(858) 792-7463
www.edreferral.com

Anorexia Nervosa and Related Eating Disorders, Inc. (ANRED)
E-mail: jarinor@rio.com
www.anred.com

Overeaters Anonymous
P.O. Box 44020
Rio Rancho, NM 87174
(505) 891-2664
www.oa.org

Exercise, Physical Activity, and Sports

American College of Sports Medicine (ACSM)
P.O. Box 1440
Indianapolis, IN 46206-1440
(317) 637-9200
www.acsm.org

American Physical Therapy Association (ASNA)
1111 North Fairfax Street
Alexandria, VA 22314
(800) 999-APTA
www.apta.org

Gatorade Sports Science Institute (GSSI)
617 West Main Street
Barrington, IL 60010
(800) 616-GSSI
www.gssiweb.com

National Coalition for Promoting Physical Activity (NCPPA)
1010 Massachusetts Avenue, Suite 350
Washington, DC 20001
(202) 454-7518
www.ncppa.org

Sports, Wellness, Eating Disorder and Cardiovascular Nutritionists (SCAN)
P.O. Box 60820
Colorado Springs, CO 80960
(719) 635-6005
www.scandpg.org

President's Council on Physical Fitness and Sports
Department W
200 Independence Avenue, SW
Room 738-H
Washington, DC 20201-0004
(202) 690-9000
www.fitness.gov

American Council on Exercise
4851 Paramount Drive
San Diego, CA 92123
(858) 279-8227
www.acefitness.org

The International Association for Fitness Professionals (IDEA)
10455 Pacific Center Court
San Diego, CA 92121
(800) 999-4332, ext. 7
www.ideafit.com

Food Safety

Food Marketing Institute
655 15th Street, NW
Washington, DC 20005
(202) 452-8444
www.fmi.org

Agency for Toxic Substances and Disease Registry (ATSDR)
ORO Washington Office
Ariel Rios Building
1200 Pennsylvania Avenue, NW
M/C 5204G
Washington, DC 20460
(888) 422-8737
www.atsdr.cdc.gov

Food Allergy and Anaphylaxis Network
11781 Lee Jackson Highway, Suite 160
Fairfax, VA 22033-3309
(800) 929-4040
www.foodallergy.org

Foodsafety.gov
www.foodsafety.gov

The USDA Food Safety and Inspection Service
Food Safety and Inspection Service
United States Department of Agriculture
Washington, DC 20250
www.fsis.usda.gov

Consumer Reports
Web Site Customer Relations Department
101 Truman Avenue
Yonkers, NY 10703
www.consumerreports.org

Center for Science in the Public Interest: Food Safety
1875 Connecticut Avenue, NW
Washington, DC 20009
(202) 332-9110
www.cspinet.org/foodsafety/index.html

Center for Food Safety and Applied Nutrition
5100 Paint Branch Parkway
College Park, MD 20740
(888) SAFEFOOD
www.cfsan.fda.gov

Food Safety Project
Dan Henroid, MS, RD, CFSP
HRIM Extension Specialist and Website Coordinator
Hotel, Restaurant and Institution Management
9e MacKay Hall
Iowa State University
Ames, IA 50011
(515) 294-3527
www.extension.iastate.edu/foodsafety

Organic Consumers Association
6101 Cliff Estate Road
Little Marais, MN 55614
(218) 226-4164
www.organicconsumers.org

Infancy and Childhood

Administration for Children and Families
370 L'Enfant Promenade, SW
Washington, DC 20447
www.acf.dhhs.gov

The American Academy of Pediatrics
141 Northwest Point Boulevard
Elk Grove Village, IL 60007
(847) 434-4000
www.aap.org

Kidnetic.com
E-mail: contactus@kidnetic.com
www.kidnetic.com

Kidshealth: The Nemours Foundation
12735 West Gran Bay Parkway
Jacksonville, FL 32258
(866) 390-3610
www.kidshealth.org

National Center for Education in Maternal and Child Health
Georgetown University
Box 571272
Washington, DC 20057
(202) 784-9770
www.ncemch.org

Birth Defects Research for Children, Inc.
930 Woodcock Road, Suite 225
Orlando, FL 32803
(407) 895-0802
www.birthdefects.org

USDA/ARS Children's Nutrition Research Center at Baylor College of Medicine
1100 Bates Street
Houston, TX 77030
www.kidsnutrition.org

Keep Kids Healthy.com
www.keepkidshealthy.com

International Agencies

UNICEF
3 United Nations Plaza
New York, NY 10017
(212) 326-7000
www.unicef.org

World Health Organization
Avenue Appia 20
1211 Geneva 27
Switzerland
41 22 791 21 11
www.who.int/en

The Stockholm Convention on Persistent Organic Pollutants
11–13 Chemin des Anémones
1219 Châtelaine
Geneva, Switzerland
41 22 917 8191
www.pops.int

Food and Agricultural Organization of the United Nations
Viale delle Terme di Caracalla
00100 Rome, Italy
39 06 57051
www.fao.org

International Food Information Council Foundation
1100 Connecticut Avenue, NW
Suite 430
Washington, DC 20036
(202) 296-6540

Pregnancy and Lactation

San Diego County Breastfeeding Coalition
c/o Children's Hospital and Health Center
3020 Children's Way, MC 5073
San Diego, CA 92123
(800) 371-MILK
www.breastfeeding.org

National Alliance for Breastfeeding Advocacy
Barbara Heiser, Executive Director
9684 Oak Hill Drive
Ellicott City, MD 21042-6321
OR
Marsha Walker, Executive Director
254 Conant Road
Weston, MA 02493-1756
www.naba-breastfeeding.org

American College of Obstetricians and Gynecologists
409 12th Street, SW, P.O. Box 96920
Washington, DC 20090
www.acog.org

La Leche League
1400 N. Meacham Road
Schaumburg, IL 60173
(847) 519-7730
www.lalecheleague.org

National Organization on Fetal Alcohol Syndrome
900 17th Street, NW
Suite 910
Washington, DC 20006
(800) 66 NOFAS
www.nofas.org

March of Dimes Birth Defects Foundation
1275 Mamaroneck Avenue
White Plains, NY 10605
(888) 663-4637
http://modimes.org

Professional Nutrition Organizations

Association of Departments and Programs of Nutrition (ANDP)
Dr. Marilynn Schnepf, ANDP Chair
316 Ruth Leverton Hall
Nutrition and Health Sciences
University of Nebraska-Lincoln
Lincoln, NE 68583-0806
http://andpnet.org

North American Association for the Study of Obesity (NAASO)
8630 Fenton Street, Suite 918
Silver Spring, MD 20910
(301) 563-6526
www.naaso.org

American Dental Association
211 East Chicago Avenue
Chicago, IL 60611-2678
(312) 440-2500
www.ada.org

American Heart Association
National Center
7272 Greenville Avenue
Dallas, TX 75231
(800) 242-8721
www.americanheart.org

American Dietetic Association (ADA)
120 South Riverside Plaza, Suite 2000
Chicago, IL 60606-6995
(800) 877-1600
www.eatright.org

The American Society for Nutrition (ASN)
9650 Rockville Pike, Suite L-4500
Bethesda, MD 20814-3998
(301) 634-7050
www.nutrition.org

The Society for Nutrition Education
7150 Winton Drive, Suite 300
Indianapolis, IN 46268
(800) 235-6690
www.sne.org

American College of Nutrition
300 S. Duncan Avenue, Suite 225
Clearwater, FL 33755
(727) 446-6086
www.amcollnutr.org

American Obesity Association
1250 24th Street, NW, Suite 300
Washington, DC 20037
(800) 98-OBESE

American Council on Health and Science
1995 Broadway
Second Floor
New York, NY 10023
(212) 362-7044
www.acsh.org

American Diabetes Association
ATTN: National Call Center
1701 North Beauregard Street
Alexandria, VA 22311
(800) 342-2383
www.diabetes.org

Institute of Food Technologies
525 W. Van Buren, Suite 1000
Chicago, IL 60607
(312) 782-8424
www.ift.org

ILSI Human Nutrition Institute
One Thomas Circle, Ninth Floor
Washington, DC 20005
(202) 659-0524
http://hni.ilsi.org

Trade Organizations

American Meat Institute
1700 North Moore Street
Suite 1600
Arlington, VA 22209
(703) 841-2400
www.meatami.com

National Dairy Council
10255 W. Higgins Road, Suite 900
Rosemont, IL 60018
(312) 240-2880
www.nationaldairycouncil.org

United Fresh Fruit and Vegetable Association
1901 Pennsylvania Ave. NW, Suite 1100
Washington, DC 20006
(202) 303-3400
www.uffva.org

U.S.A. Rice Federation
Washington, DC
4301 North Fairfax Drive, Suite 425
Arlington, VA 22203
(703) 236-2300
www.usarice.com

U.S. Government

The USDA National Organic Program
Agricultural Marketing Service
USDA-AMS-TMP-NOP
Room 4008-South Building
1400 Independence Avenue, SW
Washington, DC 20250-0020
(202) 720-3252
www.ams.usda.gov

U.S. Department of Health and Human Services
200 Independence Avenue, SW
Washington, DC 20201
(877) 696-6775
www.os.dhhs.gov

Food and Drug Administration (FDA)
5600 Fishers Lane
Rockville, MD 20857
(888) 463-6332
www.fda.gov

Environmental Protection Agency
Ariel Rios Building
1200 Pennsylvania Avenue, NW
Washington, DC 20460
(202) 272-0167
www.epa.gov

Federal Trade Commission
600 Pennsylvania Avenue, NW
Washington, DC 20580
(202) 326-2222
www.ftc.gov

Partnership for Healthy Weight Management
www.consumer.gov/weightloss

Office of Dietary Supplements
National Institutes of Health
6100 Executive Boulevard, Room 3B01, MSC 7517
Bethesda, MD 20892
(301) 435-2920
dietary-supplements.info.nih.gov

Nutrient Data Laboratory Homepage
Beltsville Human Nutrition Center
10300 Baltimore Avenue
Building 307-C, Room 117
BARC-East
Beltsville, MD 20705
(301) 504-8157
www.nal.usda.gov/fnic/foodcomp

National Digestive Disease Clearinghouse
2 Information Way
Bethesda, MD 20892-3570
(800) 891-5389
http://digestive.niddk.nih.gov

The National Cancer Institute
NCI Public Inquiries Office
Suite 3036A
6116 Executive Boulevard, MSC 8322
Bethesda, MD 20892-8322
(800) 4-CANCER
www.cancer.gov

The National Eye Institute
31 Center Drive, MSC 2510
Bethesda, MD 20892-2510
(301) 496-5248
www.nei.nih.gov

The National Heart, Lung, and Blood Institute
Building 31, Room 5A52
31 Center Drive, MSC 2486
Bethesda, MD 20892
(301) 592-8573
www.nhlbi.nih.gov/index.htm

Institute of Diabetes and Digestive and Kidney Diseases
Office of Communications and Public Liaison
NIDDK, NIH, Building 31, Room 9A04
Center Drive, MSC 2560
Bethesda, MD 20892
(301) 496-4000
www.niddk.nih.gov

National Center for Complementary and Alternative Medicine
NCCAM Clearinghouse
P.O. Box 7923
Gaithersburg, MD 20898
(888) 644-6226
http://nccam.nih.gov

U.S. Department of Agriculture (USDA)
14th Street, SW
Washington, DC 20250
(202) 720-2791
www.usda.gov

Centers for Disease Control and Prevention (CDC)
1600 Clifton Rd
Atlanta, GA 30333
(404) 639-3311 / Public Inquiries: (800) 311-3435
www.cdc.gov

National Institutes of Health (NIH)
9000 Rockville Pike
Bethesda, MD 20892
(301) 496-4000
www.nih.gov

Food and Nutrition Information Center
Agricultural Research Service, USDA
National Agricultural Library, Room 105
10301 Baltimore Avenue
Beltsville, MD 20705-2351
(301) 504-5719
www.nal.usda.gov/fnic

National Institute of Allergy and Infectious Diseases
NIAID Office of Communications and Public Liaison
6610 Rockledge Drive, MSC 6612
Bethesda, MD 20892
(301) 496-5717
www.niaid.nih.gov

Weight and Health Management

The Vegetarian Resource Group
P.O. Box 1463, Dept. IN
Baltimore, MD 21203
(410) 366-VEGE
www.vrg.org

American Obesity Association
1250 24th Street, NW
Suite 300
Washington, DC 20037
(202) 776-7711
www.obesity.org

Anemia Lifeline
(888) 722-4407
www.anemia.com

The Arc
(301) 565-3842
E-mail: info@thearc.org
www.thearc.org

Bottled Water Web
P.O. Box 5658
Santa Barbara, CA 93150
(805) 879-1564
www.bottledwaterweb.com

The Food and Nutrition Board
Institute of Medicine
500 Fifth Street, NW
Washington, DC 20001
(202) 334-2352
www.iom.edu/board.asp?id-3788

The Calorie Control Council
www.caloriecontrol.org

TOPS (Take Off Pounds Sensibly)
4575 South Fifth Street
P.O. Box 07360
Milwaukee, WI 53207
(800) 932-8677
www.tops.org

Shape Up America!
15009 Native Dancer Road
N. Potomac, MD 20878
(240) 631-6533
www.shapeup.org

World Hunger

Center on Hunger, Poverty, and Nutrition Policy
Tufts University
Medford, MA 02155
(617) 627-3020
www.tufts.edu/nutrition

Freedom from Hunger
1644 DaVinci Court
Davis, CA 95616
(800) 708-2555
www.freefromhunger.org

Oxfam International
1112 16th Street, NW, Suite 600
Washington, DC 20036
(202) 496-1170
www.oxfam.org

WorldWatch Institute
1776 Massachusetts Avenue, NW
Washington, DC 20036
(202) 452-1999
www.worldwatch.org

Food First
398 60th Street
Oakland, CA 94618
(510) 654-4400
www.foodfirst.org

The Hunger Project
15 East 26th Street
New York, NY 10010
(212) 251-9100
www.thp.org

U.S. Agency for International Development
Information Center
Ronald Reagan Building
Washington, DC 20523
(202) 712-0000
www.usaid.gov

Answers to Review Questions

The answers to Review Questions appear here and also on the Companion Website, at: www.pearsonhighered.com/thompsonmanore.

Chapter 1

1. **d.** micronutrients.
2. **d.** all of the above.
3. **c.** contain 90 kcal of energy.
4. **c.** measurement of height.
5. **c.** "A high-protein diet increases the risk for porous bones" is an example of a valid hypothesis.
6. **False.** Vitamins do not provide any energy, although many vitamins are critical to the metabolic processes that assist us in generating energy from carbohydrates, fats, and proteins.
7. **True.**
8. **True.**
9. **False.** An epidemiological study assesses phenomena of large populations and determines the factors that may influence these phenomena. It is not a clinical trial.
10. **True.**
11. In a well-designed experiment, a control group allows a researcher to compare between treated and untreated individuals, and thereby to determine whether or not a particular treatment has exerted a significant effect.
12. The Estimated Average Requirement, or EAR, represents the average daily nutrient intake level estimated to meet the requirement of half of the healthy individuals in a particular life stage or gender group. The Recommended Dietary Allowance, or RDA, represents the average daily nutrient intake level that meets the nutrient requirements of 97% to 98% of healthy individuals in a particular life stage or gender group. The EAR is used to estimate the RDA.
13. I would explain to Marilyn that the term "nutritionist" does not guarantee that this particular person who suggested the supplements is qualified to give nutritional guidance. I would recommend that she is be better off talking with a qualified healthcare professional about her fatigue. To find reliable nutrition information, I would suggest she talk with a registered dietitian. She can find registered dietitians in her local area by contacting the American Dietetic Association. She can also access free, reliable information from the Web sites of organizations such as the American Dietetic Association, the National Institutes of Health, and the Centers for Disease Control and Prevention.
14. The source of funding can be a good indicator of the level of bias in a research study. For instance, if this particular study was funded by chocolate manufacturers and conducted by their own scientists, the results could be potentially biased in that the chocolate manufacturer could make a substantial profit by discovering positive findings related to chocolate. Having an independent research team conduct the study can reduce this type of bias.
15. There are numerous aspects of this study that limit its relevance to your mother. Some of these are:
   a. Limited number of participants. Only twelve women participated in this study. This very small number of participants significantly limits the ability to generalize the results to a larger population.
   b. Age. The women in the study were all older than your mother.
   c. Blood pressure. Your mother has blood pressure at the upper end of the normal range, and all of the participants in this study had high blood pressure.
   d. Activity level. Your mother is physically active. She walks daily and swims once a week. The participants in this study were sedentary or inactive.
   e. Smoking. Your mother is a nonsmoker, and only half of the participants in this study were nonsmokers, with the other half being relatively heavy smokers.

Chapter 2

1. **d.** The % Daily Values of select nutrients in a serving of the packaged food.
2. **b.** provides enough of the energy, nutrients, and fiber to maintain a person's health.
3. **a.** at least half your grains as whole grains each day.
4. **c.** Being physically active each day.
5. **b.** Foods with a lot of nutrients per calorie, such as fish, are more nutritious choices than foods with fewer nutrients per calorie, such as candy.
6. **False.** There is no standardized definition for a serving size for foods.
7. **False.** Structure-function claims do not need FDA approval.
8. **True.**
9. **True.**
10. **False.** About two-thirds of Americans eat out at least once a week.
11. As humans, we are all different in terms of body size, physical activity level, religious and ethnic beliefs, and disease risk factors. No single diet can meet the needs of every single human being, as our needs are very different. It is necessary to vary a diet based on individual needs.

12. Answers will vary. Be sure labels contain all five of the primary components of information identified in Figure 2.1.

13. Because MyPyramid suggests a range in the number of daily servings of each food group, because our energy needs are dependent upon our physical activity level and body size, and therefore different for everyone. The lower end of the range provided by MyPyramid applies to inactive women and small individuals while the higher end of the range applies to more active people and larger men. In fact, highly active people may need to eat even more servings than those recommended at the higher end of the range. People should not eat fewer than the lowest recommended number of servings because this could lead to nutritional deficiencies.

14. At least 5 grams per serving.

15. It is not accurate. The Mediterranean diet is actually relatively high in fat, not low in fat. However this diet recommends consuming foods that contains more healthful mono- and polyunsaturated fats. Bread and pasta are a daily part of the Mediterranean diet, but this diet does not recommend unlimited consumption of these foods. If Sylvia eats more energy than she expends, even while consuming the Mediterranean diet, she will not be able to lose weight.

Chapter 3

1. **b.** peristalsis.
2. **d.** emulsifies lipids.
3. **c.** hypothalamus.
4. **a.** seepage of gastric acid into the esophagus.
5. **a.** a bean-and-cheese burrito.
6. **True.**
7. **True.**
8. **False.** Vitamins and minerals are not really "digested" in the same way that macronutrients are. These compounds do not have to be broken down because they are small enough to be readily absorbed by the small intestine. For example, fat-soluble vitamins, such as vitamins A, D, E, and K, are soluble in lipids and are absorbed into the intestinal cells along with the fats in our foods. Water-soluble vitamins, such as the B-vitamins and vitamin C, typically undergo some type of active transport process that helps ensure that the vitamin is absorbed by the small intestine. Minerals are elements, which cannot be broken down. They are absorbed all along the small intestine, and in some cases in the large intestine as well, by a wide variety of mechanisms.
9. **False.** A person with celiac disease cannot tolerate products with gluten, a protein found in wheat, rye, and barley.
10. **True.**
11. Our bodies are composed of cells, which are the smallest unit of matter that exhibits the properties of living things. That is, cells can grow, reproduce themselves, and

perform certain basic functions, such as taking in nutrients, transmitting impulses, producing chemicals, and excreting wastes. The human body is composed of billions of cells that are constantly replacing themselves, destroying worn or damaged cells, and manufacturing new ones. To support this constant demand for new cells, we need a ready supply of nutrient molecules, such as simple sugars, amino acids, and fatty acids, to serve as building blocks. These building blocks are the molecules that come from the breakdown of foods. All cells, whether of the skin, bones, or brain, are made of the same basic molecules of amino acids, sugars, and fatty acids that are also the main components of the foods we eat. Thus, we are what we eat in that the building blocks of our cells are comprised of the molecules contained in the foods we eat.

12. **No.** The main function of the small intestine is to absorb nutrients and transport them into the bloodstream or the lymph system. In order to do this effectively, the surface area of the small intestine needs to be as large as possible. The inside of the lining of the small intestine, referred to as the mucosal membrane, is heavily folded. This feature increases the surface area of the small intestine and allows it to absorb more nutrients than if it were smooth. The villi are in constant movement, which helps them to encounter and trap nutrient molecules. Covering the villi are specialized cells covered with hair-like structures called microvilli (also called the brush border). These intricate folds increase the surface area of the small intestine by more than 500 times, which tremendously increases the absorptive capacity of the small intestine.

13. The stomach does not digest itself because it secretes mucus that protects the lining from being digested by the hydrochloric acid it secretes.

14.

Digestive Disorder	Area of Inflammation	Symptoms	Treatment Options
Celiac Disease	Small intestine	• Fatty stools • Diarrhea or constipation • Cramping • Anemia • Pallor • Weight loss • Fatigue • Irritability	Modified diet that excludes foods that contain gluten or gliadin (for example, wheat, rye, and barley)
Crohn Disease	Usually ileum of small intestine but can affect any area of gastrointestinal tract	• Diarrhea • Abdominal pain • Rectal bleeding • Weight loss • Fever • Anemia • Delayed physical and mental development in children	Combination of prescription drugs, nutritional supplements, and surgery

Digestive Disorder	Area of Inflammation	Symptoms	Treatment Options
Ulcerative Colitis	Mucosa of large intestine (or colon)	• Diarrhea (which may be bloody) • Abdominal pain • Weight loss • Anemia • Nausea • Fever • Severe urgency to have bowel movement	• Anti-inflammatory medications • Surgery if medications are not effective

15. It is possible that your roommate could be suffering from heartburn or gastroesophageal reflux disease (GERD). Eating food causes the stomach to secrete hydrochloric acid to start the digestive process. In many people, the amount of HCl secreted is occasionally excessive or the gastroesophageal sphincter opens too soon. In either case, the result is that HCl seeps back up into the esophagus. Although the stomach is protected from HCl by a thick coat of mucus, the esophagus does not have this mucus coating. Thus, the HCl burns it. When this happens, a person experiences a painful sensation in the region of his or her chest above the sternum (breastbone). This condition is commonly called heartburn.

   If your roommate experiences this painful type of heartburn more than twice per week, he may be suffering from GERD. Similar to heartburn, GERD occurs when HCl flows back into the esophagus. Although people who experience occasional heartburn usually have no structural abnormalities, many people with GERD have an overly relaxed or damaged esophageal sphincter or a damaged esophagus itself. Symptoms of GERD include persistent heartburn and acid regurgitation. Some people have GERD without heartburn and instead experience chest pain, trouble swallowing, burning in the mouth, the feeling that food is stuck in the throat, or hoarseness in the morning.

Chapter 4

1. **b.** the potential of foods to raise blood glucose and insulin levels.
2. **d.** carbon, hydrogen, and oxygen.
3. **d.** sweetened soft drinks.
4. **a.** monosaccharides.
5. **a.** phenylketonuria.
6. **False.** Sugar alcohols are considered nutritive sweeteners because they contain 2 to 4 kcal of energy per gram.
7. **True.**
8. **False.** A person with lactose intolerance has a difficult time tolerating milk and other dairy products. This person does not have an allergy to milk, as he or she does not exhibit an immune response indicative of an allergy.

Instead, this person does not digest lactose completely, which causes intestinal distress and symptoms such as gas, bloating, diarrhea, and nausea.
9. **False.** Plants store glucose as starch.
10. **False.** Salivary amylase breaks starches into maltose and shorter polysaccharides.
11. Insulin is a hormone secreted by the beta cells of the pancreas in response to increased blood levels of glucose. When we eat a meal, our blood glucose level rises. But glucose in our blood cannot help the nerves, muscles, and other tissues function unless it can cross into them. Glucose molecules are too large to cross the cell membranes of our tissues independently. To get in, glucose needs assistance from insulin. Insulin is transported in the blood to the cells of tissues throughout the body, where it stimulates special molecules located in the cell membrane to transport glucose into the cell. Insulin can be thought of as a key that opens the gates of the cell membrane, and carries the glucose into the cell interior, where it can be used for energy. Insulin also stimulates the liver and muscles to take up glucose.
12. **a.** Fiber adds bulk to the stools, which aids in efficient excretion of feces.
    b. Fiber keeps stools moist and soft, helping to prevent hemorrhoids and constipation.
    c. Fiber gives the gut muscles something to push on, making it easier to eliminate stools. Diverticulosis can result in part from trying to eliminate small, hard stools.
    d. Fiber may bind with cancer-causing agents and speed their elimination from the colon, which could in turn reduce the risk for colon cancer.
13. Grain-based foods contain carbohydrates, and sometimes these foods are processed, meaning that many of the important nutrients we need for health are taken out of them. Fiber-rich carbohydrates contain not only more fiber, which is important for the health of our digestive tract, but they also contain many vitamins and minerals that we need to be healthy. The foods you listed here are examples of foods in the "grains" group that are processed. Examples of healthier fiber-rich alternative choices include whole-wheat saltine crackers, whole-wheat or pumpernickel bagels, brown rice, and whole-wheat spaghetti.
14. Ben explains to his wife that his doctor told him that diabetes more commonly runs in families, but just because no one in the family has diabetes does not mean that someone cannot get it. Being overweight increases a person's risk for this type of diabetes even if no one else in the family has it. Since Ben is overweight, he is more at risk for type 2 diabetes than he would be if he was not overweight. Overweight and obesity trigger insulin insensitivity, or insulin resistance, which in turn causes the pancreas to produce greater amounts of insulin so that glucose can enter the cells and be used for energy.

Eventually, type 2 diabetes develops because either (1) there is an increasing degree of insulin insensitivity; (2) the pancreas can no longer secrete enough insulin; or (3) the pancreas has entirely stopped producing insulin.

15.

Carbohydrate	Molecular Composition	Food Sources
Glucose	Six carbon atoms, twelve hydrogen atoms, six oxygen atoms	Fruits, vegetables, grains, dairy products; does not generally occur alone in foods, but attaches to other sugars to form disaccharides and complex carbohydrates
Fructose	Six carbon atoms, twelve hydrogen atoms, six oxygen atoms	Fruits and some vegetables
Lactose	One glucose molecule and one galactose molecule	Milk and other dairy products
Sucrose	One glucose molecule and one fructose molecule	Honey, maple syrup, fruits, vegetables, table sugar, brown sugar, powdered sugar

Chapter 5

1. **d.** found in flaxseeds, walnuts, and fish.
2. **b.** exercise regularly.
3. **a.** lipoprotein lipase.
4. **d.** high-density lipoproteins.
5. **a.** monounsaturated.
6. **False.** Lecithin is a phospholipid.
7. **False.** Fat is an important source of energy during rest and during exercise, and adipose tissue is our primary storage site for fat. We rely significantly on the fat stored in our adipose tissue to provide energy during rest and exercise.
8. **False.** A triglyceride is a lipid composed of a glycerol molecule and three fatty acids. Thus, fatty acids are a component of triglycerides.
9. **False.** While most *trans* fatty acids result from the hydrogenation of vegetable oils by food manufacturers, a small amount of *trans* fatty acids is found in cow's milk.
10. **False.** A serving of food labeled *reduced fat* has at least 25% less fat than a standard serving but may not have fewer calories than a full-fat version of the same food.
11. The straight, rigid shape of both *trans* and saturated fatty acids appears to raise blood cholesterol levels and to change cell membrane function and the way cholesterol is removed from the blood. For these reasons, many health professionals feel that diets high in *trans* and saturated fatty acids can increase the risk of cardiovascular disease. Because of the concerns related to *trans* fatty acid consumption and heart disease, manufacturers will soon be required to list the amount of *trans* fatty acids per serving on the food label.

12. Dietary fat enables the transport of the fat-soluble vitamins, specifically vitamins D and K. Vitamin D is important for regulating blood calcium and phosphorus concentrations within the normal range, which indirectly helps maintain bone health. If vitamin D is low, blood calcium levels will drop below normal, and the body will draw calcium from the bones to maintain blood levels. Vitamin K is also important for proteins involved in maintaining bone health.
13. This is not particularly good advice for someone doing a 20-mile walk-a-thon. Fat is a primary source of energy during rest and during less-intense exercise. In addition, we use predominantly more fat as we perform longer-duration exercise. This is because we use more carbohydrate earlier during the exercise bout, and once our limited carbohydrate sources are depleted during prolonged exercise, we rely more on fat as an energy source. Although carbohydrates are an important source of energy during exercise, loading up on carbohydrates is typically only helpful for individuals who are doing longer-duration exercise at intensities higher than those experienced during walking. As the primary goal of this walk-a-thon is to raise money and not to finish in record time, you can walk at a pace that matches your current fitness level. Thus, it would be prudent to consume adequate carbohydrate prior to and during the walk-a-thon, but loading up on carbohydrates is not necessary.
14. Caleb's father probably had a blood test to determine his blood lipid levels, including total cholesterol, LDLs, HDLs, and triglycerides. Unfortunately, switching to cottage cheese and margarine will not improve his blood lipid values. Margarines are high in *trans* fatty acids, and these increase blood lipids and increase our risk for heart disease. In addition, cottage cheese is a relatively high-fat food, and it contains saturated fatty acids, which also increase blood lipid levels. Both *trans* and saturated fatty acids will increase Caleb's father's risk for heart disease. A non-dietary lifestyle choice that might improve his health is regular physical activity. Regular physical activity can help people maintain a more healthful body weight, can increase HDLs, and can also cause other changes that reduce our risk for heart disease.
15.

Type of Fat	Maximum recommended intake (% of total energy intake)	Maximum recommended calorie intake
Saturated fat	7%	140 calories
Linoleic acid	10%	200 calories
Alpha-linolenic acid	1.2%	24 calories
Trans fatty acids	0%	0 calories
Unsaturated fat	None; amount equal to remainder of total fat calories after you account for intake of saturated fat and linoleic and alpha-linolenic acids	336 calories

Calculations used:
- Total energy needs = 2000 calories per day
- Maximum AMDR for fat = 35% of total energy intake = 0.35 × 2000 = 700 calories
- Saturated fat = 7% of total energy intake = 0.07 × 2000 = 140 calories
- Linoleic acid = 10% of total energy intake = 0.10 × 2000 = 200 calories
- Alpha-linolenic acid = 1.2% of total energy intake = 0.012 × 2000 = 24 calories
- *Trans* fatty acids = 0 calories

Chapter 6

1. **d.** mutual supplementation.
2. **a.** rice, pinto beans, acorn squash, soy butter, and almond milk.
3. **c.** protease.
4. **b.** amine group.
5. **c.** carbon, oxygen, hydrogen, and nitrogen.
6. **True.**
7. **False.** Both shape and function are lost when a protein is denatured.
8. **False.** Some hormones are made from lipids.
9. **False.** Buffers help the body maintain acid–base balance.
10. **False.** Depending upon the type of sport, athletes may require the same amount of or up to two times as much protein as nonactive people.
11. Adequate protein is needed to maintain the proper balance of fluids inside and outside of the cells. When a child suffers from kwashiorkor, the protein content of the blood is inadequate to maintain this balance. Fluid seeps from inside of the cells out to the tissue spaces and causes bloating and swelling of the abdomen.
12. In general, only people who are susceptible to kidney disease or who have kidney disease suffer serious consequences when eating a high-protein diet. Consuming a high-protein diet increases protein metabolism and urea production. Individuals with kidney disease or those who are at risk for kidney disease cannot adequately flush urea and other by-products of protein metabolism from the body through the kidneys. This inability can lead to serious health consequences and even death.
13. mRNA, or messenger RNA, transcribes or copies genetic information from DNA in the nucleus and carries this information to the ribosomes in the cytoplasm. Once this genetic information reaches the ribosomes, it is translated into the language of amino acid sequences, or proteins. tRNA, or transfer RNA, binds with select amino acids dissolved in the cyptoplasm and transfers these amino acids to the ribosome so that they can be assembled into proteins. The specific amino acids that are transferred to the ribosome from tRNA are dictated by the amino acid sequence presented by mRNA.
14. There are various classifications of vegetarianism. Many people feel that if a person eats any meat or products

from animals (such as dairy or eggs), then they cannot be a vegetarian. People who eat only plant-based foods are classified as vegans. If you believe this, then you would argue that your Dad is not a true vegetarian. However, there are others who believe a vegetarian is someone who can eat dairy foods, eggs, or both in addition to plant-based foods. There are also people who classify themselves as pescovegetarians, meaning they eat fish along with plant-based foods. Semi-vegetarians may eat lean meats such as poultry on occasion in addition to plant-based foods, eggs, and dairy products. If you believe in these broader definitions of vegetarianism, then you would agree with your Dad's opinion that he is now a vegetarian.
15. Use Figure 6.4 as a guide. Amino acids should be joined at the acid group of one amino acid and the amino group of the next amino acid. Multiple amino acids joined in this way make a protein.

Chapter 7

1. **a.** lactic acid.
2. **b.** power plant.
3. **a.** hydrolysis.
4. **d.** None of the above statements is true.
5. **d.** catabolic hormones.
6. **True.**
7. **False.** The body can only store a small amount of glycogen.
8. **True.**
9. **False.** Catabolism releases energy.
10. **True.**
11. The final stage of glucose oxidation is called oxidative phosphorylation and occurs in the electron transport chain of the mitochondria. In this step, a series of enzyme-driven reactions occur in which electrons are passed down a "chain." As the electrons are passed from one carrier to the next, energy is released. In this process, NADH and $FADH_2$ are oxidized and their electrons are donated to O_2, which is reduced to H_2O (water). The energy released when water is formed generates ATP.
12. Fatty acids released from the adipose tissue or fatty acids that come from the foods we eat are transported on albumin in the blood. They are then transported to the cells that need energy, such as the muscle cells. The fatty acids move across the cell membrane into the cytosol, where they are activated by the addition of CoA and then transported to the mitochondria, where fatty acid oxidation occurs. Once in the mitochondria, the fatty acid is systematically broken down into two-carbon units that lead to the formation of acetyl-CoA, which can enter the TCA cycle for energy production.
13. Without insulin, the body cannot utilize the glucose derived from food. Since glucose cannot enter the cells, the body begins the process of breaking down body fats to fatty acids, which can be used to produced ketones and alternative fuel for the brain when glucose is not

available. These ketones are acidic and can build up in the blood, leading to ketoacidosis. Under these conditions more ketones are produced than can be utilized or eliminated from the body, so they build up in the blood.

14. When children with PKU go off their diet they increase the levels of the amino acid phenylalanine in the body. They cannot metabolize phenylalanine correctly due to a genetic enzyme disorder that can result in the toxic build-up of phenylalanine in the body, which causes organ tissue damage.

15. We can assume that Aunt Winifred has been eating so little food that her need for carbohydrate (to maintain blood glucose) has not been met. Since the brain, red blood cells, and other types of cells, are all dependent on glucose for fuel, her body has no doubt been breaking down muscle protein in order to use some of the amino acids—known as glucogenic amino acids—to synthesize new glucose (gluconeogenesis). So, not only has Aunt Winifred been losing body fat, she has been also losing muscle mass, our main pool of body protein.

Chapter 8

1. **d.** thiamin, pantothenic acid, and biotin.
2. **d.** Choline is necessary for the synthesis of phospholipids and other components of cell membranes.
3. **a.** iodine deficiency.
4. **b.** tuna sandwich on whole-wheat bread, green peas, banana, 1 cup of low-fat milk.
5. **d.** It is water soluble.
6. **True.**
7. **True.**
8. **True.**
9. **True.**
10. **False.** Riboflavin occurs naturally in milk, and niacin deficiency causes pellagra.
11. People from inland regions are more prone to goiter because they consumer fewer seafoods, which are high in iodine.
12. Vitamin B$_6$ is important in the transamination of essential amino acids to nonessential amino acids.
13. Vitamins and minerals added to foods can help improve our nutritional status for these micronutrients. Not everyone will eat enough variety or quantity of the foods they need to get all the micronutrients they need; thus, fortification and enrichment help these individuals maintain their nutritional status.
14. Dialysis can remove water-soluble vitamins from the blood, which need to be replaced with either foods high in these nutrients or supplements.
15. Sally might be suffering from iron-deficiency anemia due to the elimination of all heme iron from her diet. Other micronutrients most likely to be low in Sally's diet are zinc, calcium, and vitamin B$_{12}$. These are all micronutrients that are found in animal products such as dairy and meat. Low vitamin B$_{12}$ may also be contributing to Sally's fatigue.

Chapter 9

1. **b.** It can be found in fresh fruits and vegetables.
2. **d.** a healthy infant of average weight.
3. **a.** extracellular fluid.
4. **b.** It is freely permeable only to water.
5. **b.** normalizing body weight.
6. **False.** In addition to water, the body needs electrolytes, such as sodium and potassium, to prevent fluid imbalances during long-distance events such as a marathon. Because purified water contains no electrolytes, it is not the ideal beverage for preventing fluid imbalances during a marathon.
7. **False.** Our thirst mechanism is triggered by an increase in the concentration of electrolytes in the blood.
8. **False.** Hypernatremia is commonly caused by a rapid intake of high amounts of sodium.
9. **False.** Quenching our thirst does not guarantee adequate hydration. Urine that is clear or light yellow in color is one indicator of adequate hydration.
10. **False.** These conditions are associated with decreased fluid loss or an increase in body fluid. Diarrhea, blood loss, and low humidity are conditions that increase fluid loss.
11. Chronic diarrhea in a young child can lead to severe dehydration very quickly due to his or her small body size. Diarrhea causes excessive fluid loss from the intestinal tract and extracellular fluid compartment. This fluid loss causes a rise in extracellular electrolyte concentration, and intracellular fluid leaves the cells in an attempt to balance the extracellular fluid loss. These alterations in fluid and electrolyte balance change the flow of electrical impulses through the heart and can lead to abnormal heart rhythms and eventual death if left untreated.
12. One possible cause of these symptoms is dehydration. You most likely lost a significant amount of fluid during the cross-country relay race. In addition, you consumed a few beers after the race. Beer is a diuretic, which causes you to lose even more fluid. The "pins and needles" feeling in your extremities is consistent with a fluid loss of about 3% to 5% of body weight. To maintain your health and support optimal performance, it is critical that you make every effort to consume enough fluid (preferably water, a sport beverage, or some other beverage that is not a diuretic) to regain any body water you have lost due to your athletic efforts.
13. Although there are many things to consider when consuming foods prior to exercise, one important factor is consuming an optimal balance of fluid and electrolytes. In this case, lunch (b) would be the better choice. Lunch (a) is very high in sodium. While our bodies need adequate sodium to function properly, lunch (a) is filled with very high-sodium foods, such as chicken soup, ham, and tomato juice. It is likely that consuming lunch (a) will lead to excessive thirst due to a rise in blood sodium levels. This excessive thirst could

cause distraction or even lead to consuming so much fluid that you feel nauseous during practice. Lunch (b) has a more desirable balance of sodium and fluid, should not cause excessive thirst, and should provide ample energy for hockey practice.

14. Most over-the-counter weight-loss pills are diuretics, which means that they cause fluid loss from the body. Your cousin should avoid diuretics as she needs to maintain her fluid levels at a higher-than-normal level due to breastfeeding. If she becomes dehydrated, she cannot produce adequate milk for her infant. In addition, it is possible that the substances in the weight-loss pills could be passed along to her infant in her breast milk, which could cause serious health consequences for the infant.

15. Her muscle cramps may be prompted by an electrolyte imbalance brought on by dehydration.

Chapter 10

1. **d.** It is destroyed by exposure to high heat.
2. **b.** an atom loses an electron.
3. **a.** cardiovascular disease.
4. **d.** nitrates.
5. **a.** vitamin A.
6. **True.**
7. **True.**
8. **False.** Vitamin C helps regenerate vitamin E.
9. **True.**
10. **False.** Pregnant women should not consume beef liver very often, as it can lead to vitamin A toxicity and potentially serious birth defects.
11. Free radicals steal electrons from the stable lipid molecules in our cell membranes. This stealing can destroy the integrity of the membrane and lead to membrane dysfunction and potential cell death.
12. Cancer development has three primary steps: initiation, promotion, and progression. During the initiation step, the DNA of normal cells is mutated, causing permanent changes in the cell. During the promotion step, the genetically altered cells repeatedly divide, locking the mutated DNA into each new cell's genetic instructions. During the progression step, the cancerous cells grow out of control and invade surrounding tissues. These cells then metastasize, or spread, to other sites of the body.
13. Vitamin E may help reduce our risk for heart disease in a number of ways. Vitamin E protects LDLs from oxidation, thus helping to reduce the build-up of plaque in our blood vessel walls. Vitamin E may also help reduce low-grade inflammation. Vitamin E is known to reduce blood coagulation and the formation of blood clots, which will reduce the risk of a blood clot clogging a blood vessel and causing a stroke or heart attack.
14. Trace minerals such as selenium, copper, iron, zinc, and manganese are part of the antioxidant enzyme systems that convert free radicals to less damaging substances that are excreted by our bodies. Selenium is part of the glutathione peroxidase enzyme system. Copper, zinc, and manganese are part of the superoxide dismutase enzyme complex, and iron is a part of the structure of catalase.

15. Yes, you should be concerned. Vitamin E acts as an anticoagulant, and combined with the prescription anticoagulant Coumadin, the effects are magnified, which could cause uncontrollable bleeding. This could lead to both internal bleeding and prevent the cessation of bleeding caused by a cut or other external injury. In some people, long-term use of standard vitamin E supplements may cause hemorrhaging in the brain, leading to a type of stroke called hemorrhagic stroke. It would be prudent to tell your mother about your concerns, and suggest that she stop taking the supplement until she has discussed with her healthcare provider the potential interactions with her medication and this supplement.

Chapter 11

1. **a.** calcium and phosphorus.
2. **c.** has normal bone density as compared with an average, healthy 30-year-old.
3. **d.** It provides the scaffolding for cortical bone.
4. **c.** a dark-skinned retiree living in Illinois.
5. **d.** structure of bone, nerve transmission, and muscle contraction.
6. **True.**
7. **True.**
8. **False.** The fractures that result from osteoporosis cause an increased risk of infection and other related illnesses that can lead to premature death.
9. **True.**
10. **False.** The body makes vitamin D by converting a cholesterol compound in the skin to the active form of vitamin D that we need to function. The body does not absorb vitamin D from sunlight, but when the ultraviolet rays of the sun hit the skin, they react to eventually form calcitriol, which is considered the primary active form of vitamin D in the body.
11. Because vitamins D and K are fat-soluble vitamins, they are absorbed with the fat we consume in our diets. If a person has a disease that does not allow for proper absorption of dietary fat, there will also be a malabsorption of the fat-soluble vitamins, which include vitamins D and K.
12. The two processes behind this phenomenon are bone resorption and bone formation. The combination of these processes is referred to as bone remodeling. To preserve bone density, our bodies attempt to achieve a balance between the breakdown of older bone tissue and the formation of new bone tissue.
    One of the primary reasons that bone is broken down is to release calcium into the bloodstream. We also want to break down bone when we fracture a bone and need to repair it. During resorption, osteoclasts erode the bone surface by secreting enzymes and acids that dig grooves

into the bone matrix. Their ruffled surface also acts much like a scrubbing brush to assist in the erosion process. Once bone is broken down, the products are transported into the bloodstream and utilized for various body functions.

Osteoblasts work to form new bone. These cells help synthesize new bone matrix by laying down the collagen-containing organic component of bone. Within this substance, the hydroxapatites crystallize and pack together to create new bone where it is needed. In young healthy adults, the processes of bone resorption and formation are equal so that just as much bone is broken down as is being built. The result is that bone mass is maintained. At around 40 years of age, bone resorption begins to occur more rapidly than bone formation, and this imbalance results in an overall loss in bone density. This loss of bone density affects all bones, including the vertebrae of the spine, and thus results in a loss of height as we age.

13. This meal does not ensure that your calcium needs for the day are met because our bodies can only absorb about 500 mg of calcium at one time. Although this meal contains more than 100% of the DRI for calcium, you cannot absorb all of the calcium present. To meet your daily calcium needs, it is recommended that you eat multiple servings of calcium-rich foods throughout the day and try to consume no more than 500 mg of calcium at one time.

14. The sunlight is not sufficient in Buffalo, New York, during the winter to provide adequate vitamin D for anyone. Thus, all people living in this climate in winter need to consume vitamin D in foods and/or supplements to meet their needs.

15. **a.** In order to meet expectations of the dance world, Liz is concerned about maintaining a low body weight. If she consistently consumes a very-low-energy diet, this eating pattern can put her at risk for a variety of nutritional deficiencies for both macro- and micronutrients. She complains of always being hungry, which is a good indicator that she is likely not consuming adequate energy to support her higher activity level.
b. Liz is interested in following a very-low-fat diet (less than 10% of total energy from fat). This puts her at risk for inadequate intake of fat-soluble vitamins, including vitamins A, D, E, and K, and also at risk for consuming inadequate amounts of essential fatty acids.
c. Liz is very willing to try any dietary change if it will enhance her physical performance and appearance. In addition to eating a very-low-fat diet, Liz expresses interest in trying a high-protein, low-carbohydrate diet. This could put her at risk for consuming inadequate amounts of many of the B-vitamins, vitamin C, and fiber. In addition, her carbohydrate needs may not be met by a higher-protein diet.

d. Liz consumes a lot of beverages that contain diuretics, such as caffeine. Although her fluid intake appears adequate for her size and activity level, she needs to be careful that she does not become dehydrated by consuming too many diuretics. She also does not consume much milk, which could put her at risk for consuming inadequate calcium.

Chapter 12

1. **b.** vitamin K.
2. **b.** Iron is a component of hemoglobin, myoglobin, and certain enzymes.
3. **c.** a by-product of incomplete methionine metabolism.
4. **a.** plasma cells.
5. **d.** antibodies.
6. **True.**
7. **False.** Iron deficiency causes iron-deficiency anemia; pernicious anemia occurs at the end stage of an autoimmune disorder that causes the loss of various cells in the stomach, which leads to a deficiency of vitamin B_{12}.
8. **False.** Wilson disease is a rare disorder that causes copper toxicity.
9. **True.**
10. **True.**
11. Mr. Katz's doctor probably did not give him the vitamin in pill form because Mr. Katz is 80 years of age, and it is more likely that he suffers from low stomach acid secretion. This is a condition known as atrophic gastritis, and it is estimated that about 10% to 30% of adults older than 50 years have this condition. Stomach acid separates food-bound vitamin B_{12} from dietary proteins. If the acid content of the stomach is inadequate, we cannot free up enough vitamin B_{12} from food sources alone. Because atrophic gastritis can affect almost one-third of the older adult population, it is recommended that people older than 50 years of age consume foods fortified with vitamin B_{12}, take a vitamin B_{12}-containing supplement, or have periodic B_{12} injections. Because Mr. Katz's condition was so severe, it was critical to treat him with a form of vitamin B_{12} that would be guaranteed to enter his system as quickly and effectively as possible; thus, his physician opted to use a vitamin B_{12} injection.
12. Jessica is at a higher risk for iron-deficiency anemia due to her menstrual status and the fact that she consumes only plant-based foods. Plant-based foods contain only the non-heme form of iron, which is more difficult to absorb. Consuming vitamin C enhances the absorption of iron from our foods; thus, it is imperative that Jessica's parents encourage her to eat good plant-based food sources of iron with a vitamin C source to optimize her iron absorption and reduce her risk for iron-deficiency anemia.
13. Based on this diet, Robert does not appear at risk for inadequate micronutrient intake. The foods he

consumes contain all of the necessary micronutrients, and as long as he continues to eat a wide variety of foods from these groups, his risk for inadequate intakes of micronutrients is very low.

14. **a.** Janine is of childbearing age. It is recommended that all women of childbearing age consume adequate folate even if they do not plan to become pregnant. This recommendation is made to reduce the risk for neural tube defects in the developing fetus in case a woman does become pregnant.
b. Janine is avoiding foods that are excellent sources of folate, including many vegetables and enriched grain products. Thus, it is likely that her intake of folate is inadequate. If she continues to avoid these folate-rich foods, a folate supplement may be warranted.

15. Both underweight and obese people have an increased risk of infection, and if they are infected, an increased risk that the infection will be severe. Undernutrition reduces defense against infection because micronutrient deficiencies impair immune function. In obese individuals, most studies show a lower ability of B and T cells to multiply in response to infection. Obese individuals also appear to maintain a low-grade inflammatory state currently thought to increase the likelihood that they will develop asthma, type 2 diabetes, and other disorders that would increase the severity of infection.

Chapter 13

1. **d.** body mass index.
2. **a.** basal metabolic rate, thermic effect of food, and effect of physical activity.
3. **b.** take in more energy than they expend.
4. **c.** all people have a genetic set point for their body weight.
5. **b.** ghrelin.
6. **False.** It is the apple-shaped fat patterning, or excess fat in the trunk region, that is known to increase a person's risk for many chronic diseases.
7. **True.**
8. **False.** Weight-loss medications are typically prescribed for people with a body mass index greater than or equal to 30 kg/m², or for people with a body mass index greater than or equal to 27 kg/m² who also have other significant health risk factors such as heart disease, high blood pressure, or type 2 diabetes.
9. **False.** Healthful weight gain includes eating more energy than you expend and also exercising both to maintain aerobic fitness and to build muscle mass.
10. **True.**
11. A weight that is appropriate for your age and physical development; a weight that you can achieve and sustain without restraining your food intake or constantly dieting; a weight that is acceptable to you; a weight that is based upon your genetic background and family history of body shape and weight; a weight that promotes good eating habits and allows you to participate in regular physical activity.

12. *Dietary recommendations for a sound weight-loss program include:*
a. Set reasonable weight-loss goals. Reasonable weight loss is defined as 0.5 to 2 pounds per week. To achieve this rate of weight loss, energy intake should be reduced approximately 250 to no more than 1,000 kcal/d of present intake. A weight-loss plan should never provide less than a total of 1,200 kcal/d.
b. Eat a diet that is relatively low in fat and high in complex carbohydrates. Total fat intake should be 15% to 25% of total energy intake. Saturated fat intake should be 5% to 10% of total energy intake. Monounsaturated fat intake should be 10% to 15% of total energy intake. Polyunsaturated fat intake should be no more than 10% of total energy intake. Carbohydrate intake should be around 55% of total energy intake with less than 10% of energy intake coming from simple sugars, and fiber intake should be 25 to 35 g/day.
Physical activity recommendation: Set a long-term goal for physical activity that is at least 30 minutes of moderate physical activity most, or preferably all, days of the week. Doing 45 minutes or more of an activity such as walking at least 5 days per week is ideal.
Behavior modification recommendations include:
a. Eliminating inappropriate behaviors by shopping when you are not hungry, only eating at set times in one location, refusing to buy problem foods, and avoiding vending machines, convenience stores, and fast-food restaurants.
b. Suppressing inappropriate behaviors by taking small food portions, eating foods on smaller serving dishes so they appear larger, and avoiding feelings of deprivation by eating regular meals throughout the day.
c. Strengthening appropriate behaviors by sharing food with others, learning appropriate serving sizes, planning healthful snacks, scheduling walks and other physical activities with friends, and keeping clothes and equipment for physical activity in convenient places.
d. Repeating desired behaviors by slowing down eating, always using utensils, leaving food on your plate, moving more throughout the day, and joining groups who are physically active.
e. Rewarding yourself for positive behaviors with non-food rewards.
f. Using the "buddy" system by exercising with a friend or relative, and/or calling this support person when you need an extra boost to stay motivated.
g. Refusing to punish yourself if you deviate from your plan.
13. You can increase your basal metabolic rate by increasing your lean body mass or by using drugs such as

stimulants, caffeine, and tobacco. Stress and certain illnesses can also increase BMR. The most healthful way to increase BMR is to increase your lean body mass by participating in regular strength-training exercises. Attempting to increase your BMR by using drugs or by increasing your stress is not wise and can be dangerous to your health.

14. **a.** Greater access to inexpensive, high-fat, high-calorie foods (for example, fast foods, vending machine foods, and snack/convenience foods)
    b. Significant increases in portion sizes of foods
    c. Increased reliance on cars instead of bicycles, public transportation, or walking
    d. Use of elevators and escalators instead of stairs
    e. Increased use of computers, dishwashers, televisions, and other time-saving devices
    f. Lack of safe, accessible, and affordable places to exercise

15. One primary question for Misty is: what is her idea of her ideal weight? It sounds as if Misty might have significant body image concerns. If this is the case, it is important that she meet with a healthcare provider or nutrition professional who can assist her with improving her body image perceptions.

    Another question is: what weight can she achieve and sustain without trying so hard (in other words, without restricting her food intake or constantly dieting)? The fact that she must try so hard and is still not losing weight is a good indication that she may already be at the weight that is healthful.

    A third question is: how does her current weight and body shape compare to her genetic background and family history? If her body weight and shape are consistent with her genetic makeup and family history, she may have unrealistic expectations of reducing her body weight or significantly altering her shape.

    A final question Misty should consider is whether she is able to maintain her current weight by being regularly active and by eating a healthful, balanced diet. If not, then this is another indication that her body weight goals are unrealistic.

Chapter 14

1. **c.** 64% to 90% of your estimated maximal heart rate.
2. **a.** 1 to 3 seconds.
3. **b.** fat.
4. **c.** can increase strength gained in resistance exercise.
5. **a.** An intensity of 12 to 15, or somewhat hard to hard, is recommended to achieve physical fitness.
6. **True.**
7. **False.** A dietary fat intake of 20% to 35% of total energy intake is generally recommended for athletes.
8. **False.** Carbohydrate loading involves altering duration and intensity of exercise and intake of carbohydrate such that the storage of carbohydrate is maximized.

9. **False.** Sports anemia is not true anemia, but a transient decrease in iron stores that occurs at the start of an exercise program. This is a result of an initial increase in plasma volume (or water in our blood) that is not matched by an increase in hemoglobin.

10. **True.**

11. There are an infinite number of correct answers to this question. The plan outlined here is for a 40-year-old woman who is interested in maintaining a healthful body weight, optimizing her blood lipid profile, reducing her stress, and maintaining aerobic fitness, flexibility, and upper body strength. She works full-time as a research scientist, and most of her occupational activities are sedentary in nature.

    - *Monday and Wednesday:* 60 minutes of fitness walking (including 5-minute warm-up and 5-minute cool-down)
    - *Tuesday and Thursday:* 75 minutes of Power/Ashtanga yoga (including warm-up and cool-down); 45 minutes of morning swimming (substitute with bicycling in the summer months)
    - *Friday:* 60 minutes of fitness walking (including warm-up and cool-down); 30 minutes of gardening
    - *Saturday:* 75 minutes of Hatha yoga (including warm-up and cool-down); 120 minutes of gardening
    - *Sunday:* 30 minutes of Hatha yoga (including warm-up and cool-down); 180 minutes of hiking with a light daypack.

12. To answer this question, you need to know the total energy that is required to maintain body weight and support the previously described activity/exercise routine. This value can be calculated using the simple equation provided in Chapter 13 in the You Do the Math activity on page 497.

    If the woman described in Question 11 weighs 130 pounds:

    Her weight in kg = 130 pounds ÷ 2.2 kg/pound = 59.1 kg

    Her BMR = 59.1 kg × 0.9 kcal/kg body weight/hr = 53.19 kcal/hr × 24 hours/day = 1277 kcal/day

    To estimate the amount of energy she expends to perform daily activities, you can again refer to the You Do the Math activity in Chapter 11. Based on the answer to Question 11, she is assumed to be moderately active, which means her daily physical activity needs are about 50% to 70% of her BMR.

    1277 kcal/day × 0.5 = 638.5 kcal/day
    1277 kcal/day × 0.7 = 893.9 kcal/day

    She expends approximately 639 to 894 kcal/day doing physical activities.

    To estimate her total energy needs for the day, add her BMR value to the estimates for physical activity needs previously calculated:

    1277 kcal/day + 639 kcal/day = 1916 kcal/day
    1277 kcal/day + 894 kcal/day = 2171 kcal/day

She expends approximately 1,916 to 2,171 kcal/day to support her current lifestyle.

This woman is not a competitive athlete and is exercising regularly to maintain health. Thus, it is recommended that she consume about 55% of her total energy as carbohydrate, 20% to 25% of her total energy as fat, and the remainder (20% to 25%) as protein. To simplify our calculations, let's assume that this woman requires 2,044 kcal/day to maintain her present weight and physical activity level (the average of the two values calculated for her total energy needs). To calculate the number of grams that will come from each macronutrient:

For carbohydrate:

2044 kcal/day × 0.55 = 1124 kcal of carbohydrate per day

1124 kcal of carbohydrate/day ÷ 4 kcal/gram of carbohydrate = 281 grams of carbohydrate per day

For fat:

2044 kcal/day × 0.20 = 409 kcal of fat per day
2044 kcal/day × 0.25 = 511 kcal of fat per day
409 kcal of fat/day ÷ 9 kcal/gram of fat = 45 grams of fat per day
511 kcal of fat per day ÷ 9 kcal/gram of fat = 57 grams of fat per day

For protein:

2044 kcal/day × 0.20 = 409 kcal of protein per day
2044 kcal/day × 0.25 = 511 kcal of protein per day
409 kcal of protein/day ÷ 4 kcal/gram of protein = 102 grams of protein
511 kcal of protein/day ÷ 4 kcal/gram of protein = 128 grams of protein

Thus, the correct answer for the woman in question is 281 grams of carbohydrate, 45 to 57 grams of fat, and 102 to 128 grams of protein.

13. The most helpful strategy you might consider is the use of sports beverages. Sports beverages were designed for people who exercise for more than 60 minutes at a time and are specially formulated to replenish the fluid and micronutrients that are lost during intense, long-duration exercise. By consuming sports beverages during training for a marathon, you can ensure that you are maintaining adequate hydration levels and avoid hyponatremia by replenishing sodium.

14. Gustavo is 73 years of age, has high blood pressure, and has a family history of colon cancer. He manages a vineyard. You would need to know a little bit more about his occupation to determine his level of activity at work. However, based on his health status, Gustavo could most likely benefit from participating in a planned exercise program of low to moderate intensity. This type of program will help keep his blood pressure under better control, will reduce his risk for cardiovascular disease,

stroke, and type 2 diabetes, will help Gustavo maintain a healthful body weight, and will assist in maintaining bone density. This type of program may also reduce his risk for colon cancer.

Before Gustavo begins an exercise program, he should get a thorough physical exam by his physician because of his older age and his high-blood-pressure status. His physician can then determine the safest forms of physical activity for Gustavo.

15. Factors that assist Marisa in maintaining a normal, healthful weight include:
    * walking to/from school each day;
    * covering the lunch shift at her college's day care center, which requires that she be on her feet, walk, and perform light lifting two hours each day; and
    * walking on the weekends

    Factors that contribute to Conrad's weight gain include:
    * driving to school each day;
    * working an office job 2 hours each day; and
    * going to the movies on the weekends instead of doing some form of physical activity

Chapter 15

1. **a.** oxygen, heat, and light.
2. **c.** a type of fungus used to ferment foods.
3. **b.** a flavor enhancer used in a variety of foods.
4. **a.** contain only organically produced ingredients, excluding water and salt.
5. **d.** all of the above.
6. **False.** The appropriate temperatures for cooking foods vary according to the food.
7. **True.**
8. **True.**
9. **True.**
10. **True.**
11. No, this food is not 100% organic. This is because it contains whey, which is a protein from cow's milk. This item is not designated as organic. Remember that to be considered 100% organic a food must contain only organically produced ingredients, excluding water and salt. This food also contains food additives; in this case, the additive is salt.
12. The safest choice is to select the pasteurized juice. Unpasteurized beverages (such as juices and milk) may contain a significant number of microbes that can cause food-borne illnesses. Pasteurization does not eliminate all microbes but significantly decreases the numbers of heat-sensitive microorganisms, which tend to be the most harmful. The amount of pesticides found in juice is most likely very low or zero, as the pesticides would have been applied to the trees and oranges with the peel on the fruit. It is highly likely that this juice contains none of the pesticides that may have been used because the peel is not used to make the juice.

13. There are a few different processes of pickling, but this process requires the use of vinegar and also salt. The vinegar used works to destroy microbes that cause food-borne illness (particularly the *Clostridium botulinum* bacteria). The salt used not only adds flavor but also inhibits spoilage and the growth of harmful bacteria.

14. Based on this brief description, it sounds as if the cause of this disease was mercury poisoning. Mercury, a naturally occurring element, is found in soil and rocks, lakes, streams, and oceans. It is also released into the environment by pulp and paper processing and the burning of garbage and fossil fuels. As mercury is released into the environment, it falls from the air, eventually finding its way into streams, lakes, and oceans. Fish absorb mercury as they feed on aquatic organisms. This mercury is passed on to people when they consume the fish. As mercury accumulates in the body, it has a toxic effect on the nervous system. Mercury is especially toxic to the developing nervous systems of fetuses and growing children. Thus, pregnant and breastfeeding women and young children are advised to avoid eating fish that may be contaminated with mercury.

    Based on an Internet search, it appears that Minamata disease was caused by mercury poisoning. A variety of heavy metals were used in a highly successful industrial plant on Minamata Bay. After careful study and elimination of other toxic chemicals used in this industrial plant, it was discovered that the disease experienced by these people was a result of mercury poisoning.

15. **a.** Failure to wash your hands before you removed chicken from the freezer. You touched the chicken when you placed it in the bowl to thaw in the refrigerator.
    b. Failure to wash your hands with hot water and soap prior to putting the chicken breasts on the cutting board.
    c. Failure to wash the chicken breasts thoroughly prior to putting them on the clean cutting board.
    d. Failure to wash your hands with hot water and soap after handling the chicken breasts just prior to touching and rinsing the lettuce, red pepper, and scallions.
    e. Failure to check the temperature of the chicken breasts. Even though they were no longer pink in color, they may not have been cooked to a high enough temperature to kill bacteria.

Chapter 16

1. **b.** neural tube defects.
2. **c.** oxytocin.
3. **c.** iron.
4. **b.** women who begin their pregnancy underweight.
5. **d.** iron-fortified rice cereal.
6. **False.** These issues are most likely to occur in the first trimester of pregnancy.
7. **True.**
8. **True.**
9. **True.**

10. **False.** Newborns of mothers with gestational diabetes are at risk for overly large body size.

11. *Advantages:* Optimal nutritional quality; protects infants from infections and allergies; reduced risk of sudden infant death syndrome; quickens the return of the uterus in the mother to prepregnancy size and reduces postpregnancy bleeding; suppresses ovulation, which lengthens the time between pregnancies and gives the mother's body time to recover before conceiving again; provides for mother–infant bonding and attachment; more convenient than bottle-feeding; less expensive than bottle-feeding.
    Disadvantages: Passage of drugs (caffeine, prescription drugs), alcohol, and irritating components of foods such as onion, garlic, etc.; allergic reactions to foods mother eats such as wheat, peanuts, and cow's milk; transmission of HIV from mother to infant in mothers who are HIV-positive; balancing the challenges of regular breastfeeding with job duties; sleep deprivation of mother due to feeding every 2 to 3 hours; social concerns such as exposing breasts in public and discomfort of others who may observe breastfeeding in public.

12. After reviewing the girl's typical dietary intake, I would discuss the importance of appropriate prenatal weight gain (not too much, not too little), the importance of taking folic acid, iron, and possibly calcium supplements, and the need to avoid alcohol, street drugs, and (unless prescribed by her healthcare provider) medications.

13. It is possible that your cousin is partly right and partly wrong. If she is very careful and consumes a wide variety of nutrient-dense foods she is likely consuming adequate amounts of the macronutrients and many of the micronutrients she needs to support her pregnancy. However, there are some nutrients that are extremely difficult to consume in adequate amounts in the diet during pregnancy, as a woman's needs are very high for these nutrients. One of these nutrients is iron. During pregnancy, the demand for red blood cells increases to accommodate the needs of the growing uterus, placenta, and the fetus itself. Thus, more iron is needed. Fetal demand for iron increases even further during the last trimester, when the fetus stores iron in the liver for use during the first few months of life. This iron storage is protective because breast milk is low in iron.

    Because of these risks, the RDA for iron for pregnant women is 27 mg per day, compared with 18 mg per day for non-pregnant women. Even though your cousin feels her eating habits are sufficient, it is highly likely that she had low iron stores prior to pregnancy, as this is a common problem in many women. Women have a difficult time consuming 18 mg of iron per day in their diets; consuming twice this amount is extremely difficult if not impossible for most women. Thus, women of childbearing age typically have poor iron stores, and the demands of pregnancy are likely to produce deficiency. To ensure adequate iron stores during pregnancy, an iron supplement (as part of, or distinct from, a total prenatal supplement) is routinely prescribed during the last two trimesters. In addition, consuming vitamin C will enhance iron absorption, as do dietary sources of heme iron.

14. Based on this description, it is possible that Katie has a condition referred to as colic. Overstimulation of the nervous system, feeding too rapidly, swallowing of air, and intestinal gas pain are considered possible culprits, but the precise cause is unknown. As with allergies, if a colicky infant is breast-fed, breastfeeding should be continued, but the parents should try to determine whether eating certain foods seems to prompt crying and, if so, eliminate the offending food(s) from her diet. Formula-fed infants may benefit from a change in type of formula. In the worst cases of colic, a physician may prescribe medication. Fortunately, most cases disappear spontaneously, possibly because of maturity of the gastrointestinal tract, around 3 months of age. It is important that Katie's parents discuss her condition with her pediatrician before making any decisions about changing her diet.

15. The primary information to share with this woman is that breastfeeding is recommended for all children up to at least 2 years (or 24 months) of age. Thus, an 11-month-old child is not too old to be breastfed. In addition, it is also possible that this woman is offended by seeing your sister breastfeed in public. If this is the case, it is important to point out that all women have the right to breastfeed in a public place. If this woman is offended, she can leave the area or choose not to observe your sister as she breastfeeds her child.

Chapter 17

1. **d.** greater than that for young children, adults, and pregnant adults.
2. **c.** 45% to 60%.
3. **b.** skipping breakfast.
4. **b.** 2 tablespoons of plain yogurt, 2 tablespoons of applesauce, 2 tablespoons of fortified whole-grain oat cereal, and 1/2 cup of calcium-fortified orange juice.
5. **a.** Cigarette smoking can interfere with the metabolism of nutrients.
6. **True.**
7. **False.** Children are able to understand the basic information about which foods are more nutritious and which foods should be eaten in moderation. Also, parents are important role models for children.
8. **False.** The DRI for calcium remains at 1,300 mg per day up through the age of 18 years.
9. **False.** The Institute of Medicine now recommends that children participate in daily physical activity and exercise for at least an hour each day.

10. **True.** Adolescents typically experience a 9- to 11-in. increase in height during their 2- to 3-year growth spurt. With this increase in height, normal-weight adolescents need to gain a proportional amount of weight. In males, much of that weight is lean body mass, while female adolescents tend to gain a higher proportion of body fat.

11. *Advantages:* Improved access to a wider variety of affordable fresh, healthful foods from around the United States and the world; improved access to nutrition and health information from a variety of sources, including television and Internet sources; improved access to interactive nutrition and healthful lifestyle programs that encourage family participation
    Disadvantages: Reduced energy expenditure due to increased television viewing and computer use leading to obesity; lower fitness levels and higher risk for chronic diseases due to the lack of physical activity; increased exposure to advertisements promoting junk foods and less healthful foods; failure to acquire important physical skills because not much time is spent engaged in physical activities; inhibition of imagination and creativity in young children because they do not have to develop skills necessary for creative play

12. Toddlers are relatively picky eaters, and they are also small individuals and can only consume small amounts of food at any give time. In consuming a vegan diet, the primary sources of quality proteins are restricted to legumes, meat substitutes, and various combinations of vegetables and whole grains. It is highly likely that a vegan diet will be too low in protein for toddlers, as their protein needs are relatively high. Few toddlers can consume enough legumes and whole grains to provide sufficient protein, and many may not prefer the taste of vegetables and meat substitutes. In addition, certain staples of the vegan diet that are high in protein, such as wheat, soy, and nuts, commonly provoke allergic reactions in children. When this happens, finding a plant-based substitute that contains adequate protein and other nutrients can be challenging.

13. There are numerous correct answers to this question. The key to designing a menu for this age group is to keep in mind that these children need adequate fluid, and they do not eat large amounts of food. The foods should also look fun and attractive to encourage regular snacking and should be easy to eat when the children are active. Here are some foods you may want to offer to these children:
    • Ample water in small, colored plastic cups
    • Whole-grain crackers that are small and easy to eat
    • Small chunks of different colors and flavors of cheese to eat with the crackers (or you could make peanut butter/whole-grain cracker "sandwiches")
    • Baby carrot sticks
    • Orange slices

14. Here are three of many lunch choices that you could offer to these students:
    - Menu 1: Bean burrito with salsa; rice; low/no-fat milk; fresh fruit
    - Menu 2: Grilled turkey and muenster cheese sandwich on whole-wheat bread; assorted raw vegetables; pineapple/orange yogurt fruit smoothie
    - Menu 3: Chicken and vegetable teriyaki rice bowl; fruit skewers; low/no-fat milk

15. A registered dietitian would be concerned about (1) Lydia's monotonous and unbalanced diet, (2) her lack of physical activity, and (3) Lydia's potential homesickness and isolation. Her poor dietary habits are probably contributing to a lack of protein as well as most vitamins and minerals. Her poor diet and the fact that she lives in a northern region almost certainly mean that she is vitamin D deficient, and her consumption of soda rather than milk or a calcium-fortified beverage further increases her risk for low bone density. These deficiencies may also account for some of her lethargy and lack of physical activity. By guiding Lydia toward more healthful meals and menus, she would feel more energetic and be more likely to ride a bicycle, take an activity class, or join a gym.

    A regular routine of physical activity would probably stimulate Lydia's appetite, encouraging her to consume greater amounts of food, hopefully healthy food! Lydia's move from Vermont to New York could account for her isolation; she may need additional guidance in finding and developing new friendships. If Lydia had always lived at home, where someone else prepared the meals, she would benefit from specific sessions on planning menus, shopping for healthful foods, and preparing daily meals.

Chapter 18

1. **b.** vitamin D.
2. **a.** dysgeusia.
3. **d.** 122 years.
4. **c.** glycosylation.
5. **c.** palliative care.
6. **True.** Programmed theories of aging imply that the aging process is biologically driven and rarely, if ever, affected by lifestyle traits such as diet.
7. **True.** As humans age, percent body fat typically increases. Even if elderly persons lose weight during their 70s or 80s, body fat increases as a percentage of their total body weight.
8. **True.** Elderly who are overweight or obese have lower rates of mortality compared to those who are underweight.
9. **True.** Vitamin B_{12} found in food sources is often bound to food proteins and is difficult for older adults to digest and absorb due to their lack of adequate stomach acidity. The vitamin B_{12} found in supplements or fortified foods is not protein-bound; therefore, it is easier to absorb.

10. **True.**
11. Lack of adequate stomach acid can lower the absorption of vitamin B_{12}, calcium, iron, and zinc, increasing the risk for deficiencies of these nutrients.
12. **a.** If not fluent in English, an elderly immigrant woman may not be confident enough to go out to shop for food on a regular basis, or may not qualify for a driver's license, which would affect her ability to obtain food. In both cases, she might have to purchase food from the nearest convenience store (not the best source), and/or simply run low on food, leading to possible malnutrition. **b.** If isolated, with no southeast Asian friends or relatives nearby, the woman could easily become depressed, which often results in poor food intake and rapid onset of nutrient deficiencies.
13. Older adults may purposely limit fluid intake to avoid embarrassing "accidents" due to poor bladder control; they may be taking medications that act as diuretics, increasing urinary output; many elderly fail to perceive thirst and may not drink adequate amounts of fluid during the day; and some elderly may not be able to drink enough fluids due to physical limitations related to a stroke, Parkinson's disease, or other neuromuscular disorder.
14. I would first try to determine why my client eats as he does: is he easily tired, does he have a poor appetite, is he inexperienced in planning and producing healthful meals, or is he on a very limited budget? Depending upon his circumstances, I would develop several simple but nutritious meal suggestions that have more protein, fiber, total energy, and a wider range of vitamins and minerals. Finally, I would discuss ways of improving his sleeping habits while limiting alcohol intake. Gentle physical activity during the day, a warm bath before bedtime, and avoiding caffeine during the evening might help him sleep through the night without the need for beer.
15. The death of a spouse often triggers mental and physical declines in older adults. Loss of appetite, depression, loneliness, and fearfulness may contribute to a drastic reduction in food and fluid intake. Malnutrition and dehydration quickly develop, which then contribute to loss of balance, weakness, and fatigue. These factors may have lead to Marta's grandmother's fall and fracture.

Chapter 19

1. **a.** sub-Saharan Africa.
2. **c.** It has dramatically increased worldwide production of rice, corn, and wheat at lower costs.
3. **b.** reduced resistance to infection.
4. **b.** single mothers and their children.
5. **d.** all of the above.
6. **True.**
7. **True.**
8. **True.**

9. **False.** The rise in global obesity rates has prompted a rise in rates of other chronic diseases, such as heart disease and type 2 diabetes.

10. **False.** Cotton, coffee, and tobacco are cash crops. Subsistence crops are those that can be eaten by the farmer, such as cassava or peanuts.

11. Women with access to education are more likely to have increased earning potential, access to information about contraception, and information to use better health practices. These circumstances lead to smaller, healthier, more economically stable families.

12. Breast milk contains antibodies that protect against infections. In addition, there is a danger in developing countries of feeding infants with formula because the use of unsanitary water for mixing batches of formula results in diarrheal diseases. Another problem is that overdilution of formula by families who cannot afford adequate amounts results in inadequate intake for the infant, whereas breast milk is likely to contain adequate amounts of the nutrients needed.

13. When undernutrition is endemic throughout an area, growth stunting becomes the norm. In such a population, a person who is of average height by U.S. standards would be considered unusually tall.

14. The family is dependent on the supplies available at the local food pantry. These supplies may provide for good nutrition, but likely do not provide all nutrients regularly. Therefore Davie's nutrition status is likely to be compromised. Davie is at greatest risk of infection from drinking water from a nearby pond, particularly if his mother does not boil the water prior to consumption. Because they have limited access to medical care, they are likely to wait out infections, prolonging the time that the infection is resolved. This further exacerbates his nutrition status, makes him more susceptible to another infection, and makes it more likely that he will die from a prolonged fight with infection.

15. Mexico is a country experiencing economic growth and the nutrition transition. Obesity is becoming a serious problem for both adults and children. Because of obesity, type 2 diabetes is being diagnosed at younger and younger ages in the Hispanic population. The best solution to diabetes is prevention, and a concerned pediatrician is likely to be able to make a tremendous beneficial difference in the lives of the children he sees.

Glossary

24-hour recall　A data collection that assesses everything a person has consumed over the past 24 hours.

5-A-Day for Better Health Program　A major pubic health initiative developed by the National Cancer Institute to promote nutrition and prevent cancer; recommends that Americans consume at least 5 servings of fruits and vegetables daily.

A

absorption　The physiologic process by which molecules of food are taken from the gastrointestinal tract into the circulation.

Acceptable Daily Intake (ADI)　An estimate made by the Food and Drug Administration of the amount of a non-nutritive sweetener that someone can consume each day over a lifetime without adverse effects.

Acceptable Macronutrient Distribution Ranges (AMDR)　A range of intakes for a particular energy source that is associated with reduced risk of chronic disease while providing adequate intakes of essential nutrients.

acetylcholine　A neurotransmitter that is involved in many functions, including muscle movement and memory storage.

acetyl CoA (or acetyl coenzyme A)　Coenzyme A is derived from the B-vitamin pantothenic acid; it readily reacts with two-carbon acetate to form the metabolic intermediate acetyl CoA.

achlorhydria　Lack of gastric acid secretion.

acidosis　A disorder in which the blood becomes acidic; that is, the level of hydrogen in the blood is excessive. It can be caused by respiratory or metabolic problems.

active immunity　The condition of having memory lymphocytes for protection from a particular disease. Acquired by having the disease once or by being vaccinated for it.

active transport　An absorptive process that requires the use of energy to transport nutrients and other substances in combination with a carrier protein.

acute phase response　A generalized inflammation of the whole body characterized by fever, pain, loss of appetite, sleepiness, and specialized proteins released from the liver into the blood to provide rapid protection against microorganisms.

added sugars　Sugars and syrups that are added to food during processing or preparation.

adenosine diphosphate (ADP)　A metabolic intermediate that results from the removal of one phosphate group from ATP.

adenosine monophosphate (AMP)　A low-energy compound that results from the removal of two phosphate groups from ATP.

adenosine triphosphate (ATP)　A high-energy compound made up of the purine adenine, the simple sugar ribose, and three phosphate units; it is used by cells as a source of metabolic energy. Also, the common currency of energy for virtually all cells of the body.

adequate diet　A diet that provides enough of the energy, nutrients, and fiber to maintain a person's health.

Adequate Intake (AI)　A recommended average daily nutrient intake level based on observed or experimentally determined estimates of nutrient intake by a group of healthy people.

albumin　A serum protein, made in the liver, that transports free fatty acids from one body tissue to another.

alcohol　An organic compound with at least one hydroxyl (OH) group.

alcohol dehydrogenase (ADH)　An enzyme that converts ethanol to acetaldehyde in the first step of alcohol oxidation.

alcoholic encephalopathy　A disorder of brain structure and function caused by alcohol-induced liver failure.

aldehyde dehydrogenase (ALDH)　An enzyme that oxidizes acetaldehyde to acetate.

aldosterone　A hormone released from the adrenal glands that signals the kidneys to retain sodium and chloride, which in turn results in the retention of water.

alkalosis　A disorder in which the blood becomes basic; that is, the level of hydrogen in the blood is deficient. It can be caused by respiratory or metabolic problems.

alpha bond　A type of chemical bond that can be digested by enzymes found in the human intestine.

alpha-linolenic acid　An essential fatty acid found in leafy green vegetables, flax seed oil, soy oil, fish oil, and fish products; an omega-3 fatty acid.

amenorrhea　Lack of menstruation in the absence of pregnancy. Primary amenorrhea is the absence of menstruation by the age of 16 years in a girl who has secondary sex characteristics, whereas secondary amenorrhea is the absence of the menstrual period for 3 or more months after the onset of menstruation.

amino acids　Nitrogen-containing molecules that combine to form proteins.

ammonia　A highly toxic compound released during the deamination of amino acids.

amniotic fluid　The watery fluid contained within the innermost membrane of the sac containing the fetus. It cushions and protects the growing fetus.

anabolic　A substance that builds muscle and increases strength.

anabolism　The process of making new molecules from smaller ones.

anaerobic　Means "without oxygen." Term used to refer to metabolic reactions that occur in the absence of oxygen.

anencephaly　A fatal neural tube defect in which there is partial absence of brain tissue most likely caused by failure of the neural tube to close.

anergy　Severely diminished or absent response to specific antigens.

angiotensin II　A potent vasoconstrictor that constricts the diameter of blood vessels and increases blood pressure; it also signals the release of the hormone aldosterone from the adrenal glands.

anorexia nervosa　A serious, potentially life-threatening eating disorder that is characterized by self-starvation, which eventually leads to a deficiency in energy and essential nutrients that are required by the body to function normally.

antibodies　Circulating proteins produced by plasma cells to a particular antigen in response to a disease or vaccination or acquired passively, also called immunoglobulins.

antidiuretic hormone　A hormone released from the pituitary gland in response to an increase in blood solute concentration. ADH stimulates the kidneys to reabsorb water and to reduce the production of urine.

antigens   Parts of a molecule, usually proteins, from bacteria, viruses, worms, or toxins that are recognized by specific receptors on lymphocytes and induce formation of antibodies or killing of an organism displaying the antigen.

antioxidant   A compound that has the ability to prevent or repair the damage caused by oxidation.

antiresorptive   Characterized by an ability to slow or stop bone resorption without affecting bone formation. Antiresorptive medications are used to reduce the rate of bone loss in people with osteoporosis.

antiserum   Human or animal serum that contains antibodies to a particular antigen because of previous exposure to the disease or to a vaccine containing antigens from that infectious agent.

appetite   A psychological desire to consume specific foods.

ariboflavinosis   A condition caused by riboflavin deficiency.

ascites   Accumulation of excess fluid in the abdominal cavity; often a complication of cirrhosis.

aseptic packaging   Sterile packaging that does not require refrigeration or preservatives while seal is maintained.

at risk for overweight (childhood)   Having a body mass index (BMI) at or above the 85th percentile.

atrophic gastritis   A condition frequently seen in individuals over the age of 50 years, in which stomach acid secretion is low, resulting in decreased production of mucus, HCl, pepsin, and intrinsic factor.

atrophy   A decrease in the size and strength of muscles that occurs when they are not working adequately.

autoimmune   A destructive immune response directed toward the individual's own tissues.

B

B cells   Lymphocytes that can become either antibody-producing plasma cells or memory cells.

β-oxidation (or fatty acid oxidation)   A series of metabolic reactions that oxidize free fatty acids, leading to the end products of water, carbon dioxide, and ATP.

bacteria   Microorganisms that lack a true nucleus and have a chemical called peptidoglycan in their cell walls.

balanced diet   A diet that contains the combination of foods that provides the proper proportions of nutrients.

basal metabolic rate (BMR)   The energy the body expends to maintain its fundamental physiologic functions.

Behavioral Risk Factor Surveillance Systems (BRFSS)   The world's largest telephone survey that tracks lifestyle behaviors that increase our risks for chronic diseases.

beriberi   A disease caused by thiamin deficiency.

beta bond   A type of chemical bond that cannot be easily digested by enzymes found in the human intestine.

BHA (butylated hydroxyanisole)   An antioxidant used primarily to stop rancidity in fats and oils.

BHT (butylated hydroxytoluene)   An antioxidant used primarily to stop rancidity in fats and oils.

bile   Fluid produced by the liver and stored in the gallbladder; it emulsifies lipids in the small intestine.

binge eating   Consumption of a large amount of food in a short period of time, usually accompanied by a feeling of loss of self-control.

binge-eating disorder   A disorder characterized by binge eating an average of twice a week or more.

bioavailability   The degree to which our bodies can absorb and utilize any given nutrient.

biologic age   Physiologic age as determined by health and functional status; often estimated and scored by questionnaires.

biological value   An assessment of how efficiently dietary protein is converted into body tissues; determined by comparing the amount of nitrogen retained in the body with the amount of nitrogen that is consumed in the diet.

biopesticides   Primarily insecticides, these chemicals use natural methods to reduce damage to crops.

biotoxins   Naturally occurring poisonous chemicals.

bleaching agents   Chemicals used to speed the natural process of ground flour changing from pale yellow to white.

bleaching process   A reaction in which the rod cells in the retina lose their color when rhodopsin is split into retinal and opsin.

blood volume   The amount of fluid in blood.

body composition   The ratio of a person's body fat to lean body mass. Also, the amount of bone, fat, and muscle tissue in the body.

body fat mass   The amount of body fat a person has.

body image   A person's perception of his or her body's appearance and functioning.

body mass index (BMI)   A measurement representing the ratio of a person's body weight to his or her height.

bolus   The mass of food that has been chewed and moistened in the mouth.

bone density   The degree of compactness of bone tissue, reflecting the strength of the bones. Peak bone density is the point at which a bone is strongest.

bone strength   A subcomponent of musculoskeletal fitness that is dependent upon the density and mineral content of bone and is related to the risk for bone fractures.

brown adipose tissue   A type of adipose tissue that has more mitochondria than white adipose tissue and can increase energy expenditure by coupling oxidation from ATP production. It is found in significant amounts in animals and newborn humans.

brush border   Term that describes the microvilli of the small intestine's lining. These microvilli tremendously increase the small intestine's absorptive capacity.

buffers   Proteins that help maintain proper acid-base balance by attaching to, or releasing, hydrogen ions as conditions change in the body.

bulimia nervosa   A serious eating disorder characterized by recurrent episodes of binge eating and recurrent inappropriate compensatory behaviors (such as self-induced vomiting, laxative abuse, and so forth) in order to prevent weight gain.

C

calcitonin   A hormone secreted by the thyroid gland when blood calcium levels are too high. Calcitonin inhibits the actions of vitamin D, preventing reabsorption of calcium in the kidneys, limiting calcium reabsorption in the intestines, and inhibiting the osteoclasts from breaking down bone.

calcitriol   The primary active form of vitamin D in the body.

calcium rigor   A failure of muscles to relax, which leads to a hardening or stiffening of the muscles; caused by high levels of blood calcium.

calcium tetany   A condition in which muscles experience twitching and spasms due to inadequate blood calcium levels.

calorie (cal)   A unit of measurement equal to 1/1000 of a kilocalorie.

Calorie   A unit of measurement equal to 1 kilocalorie; sometimes used in food labels and elsewhere with a lowercase "c" to represent the unit of kilocalorie.

calorimeter   A special instrument in which food can be burned and the amount of heat that is released measured; this process demonstrates the energy (caloric) content of the food.

cancer   A group of diseases characterized by cells that reproduce spontaneously and independently and may invade other tissues and organs.

carbohydrate   One of the three macronutrients, a compound made up of carbon, hydrogen, and oxygen that is derived from plants and provides energy.

carbohydrate loading   Also known as glycogen loading. A process that involves altering training and carbohydrate intake so that muscle glycogen storage is maximized.

carbohydrates   The primary fuel source for the body, particularly for the brain and for physical exercise.

carbon skeleton   The unique "side group" that remains after deamination of an amino acid.

carcinogen   Any substance or agent capable of causing the cellular mutations that lead to cancer, such as certain pesticides, industrial chemicals, and pollutants.

cardiorespiratory fitness   Fitness of the heart and lungs; achieved through regular participation in aerobic-type activities.

cardiovascular disease   A general term that refers to abnormal conditions involving dysfunction of the heart and blood vessels; cardiovascular disease can result in heart attack or stroke.

carnitine   A small organic compound that transports free fatty acids from the cytosol into the mitochondria for oxidation.

carotenoids   Fat-soluble plant pigments that the body stores in the liver and adipose tissues. The body is able to convert certain carotenoids to vitamin A.

carrying capacity   The theoretical maximum population that can be supported indefinitely by the earth.

cash crops   Crops grown to be sold rather than eaten, such as cotton, tobacco, jute, and sugar cane.

catabolism   The breakdown or degradation of larger molecules to smaller molecules.

cataract   A damaged portion of the eye's lens, which causes cloudiness that impairs vision.

celiac disease   Genetic disorder characterized by an inability to absorb a component of gluten that causes an immune reaction that damages the lining of the small intestine.

cell   The smallest unit of matter that exhibits the properties of living things, such as growth, reproduction, and metabolism.

cell differentiation   The process by which immature, undifferentiated stem cells develop into highly specialized functional cells of discrete organs and tissues.

Centers for Disease Control and Prevention (CDC)   The leading federal agency in the United States that protects the health and safety of people. Its mission is to promote health and quality of life by preventing and controlling disease, injury, and disability.

cephalic phase   Earliest phase of digestion in which the brain thinks about and prepares the digestive organs for the consumption of food.

ceruloplasmin   A copper-containing protein that transports copper in the body. It also plays a role in oxidizing ferric to ferrous iron (Fe^{2+} to Fe^{3+}).

chemical score   A method used to estimate a food's protein quality; it is a comparison of the amount of the limiting amino acid in a food with the amount of that same amino acid in a reference food.

chief cells   Cells lining the gastric glands that secrete pepsin and gastric lipase.

childhood overweight   Having a body mass index (BMI) at or above the 95th percentile.

cholecalciferol   Vitamin D_3, a form of vitamin D found in animal foods and the form we synthesize from the sun.

chronic dieting   Consistently and successfully restricting energy intake to maintain an average or below-average body weight.

chylomicron   A lipoprotein produced in the mucosal cell of the intestine; transports dietary fat out of the intestinal tract.

chyme   Semifluid mass consisting of partially digested food, water, and gastric juices.

cirrhosis   End-stage liver disease characterized by significant abnormalities in liver structure and function; may lead to complete liver failure.

coal tar   A food additive made from thick or semisolid tar derived from bituminous coal, the by-products of which have been found to cause cancer in animals.

coenzyme   A molecule that combines with an enzyme to activate it and help it do its job.

cofactor   A small, chemically simple organic or inorganic substance that is required for enzyme activity; trace minerals such as iron, zinc, and copper function as cofactors.

colic   Unconsolable infant crying of unknown origin that lasts for hours at a time.

collagen   A protein that forms strong fibers in bone and connective tissue.

colostrum   The first fluid made and secreted by the breasts from late in pregnancy to about a week after birth. It is rich in immune factors and protein.

complement proteins   A family of about twenty different blood proteins made mostly by the liver that can work together to kill bacteria and can also mark invaders for killing by phagocytes.

complementary proteins   Proteins contained in one or more foods that together contain all nine essential amino acids necessary for a complete protein. It is not necessary to eat complementary proteins at the same meal.

complete proteins   Foods that contain all nine essential amino acids.

complex carbohydrate   A nutrient compound consisting of long chains of glucose molecules, such as starch, glycogen, and fiber.

conception (also called *fertilization*)   The uniting of an ovum (egg) and sperm to create a fertilized egg, or zygote.

condensation   An anabolic process by which smaller, chemically simple compounds are joined with the removal of water.

conditionally essential amino acids   Amino acids that are normally considered nonessential but become essential under certain circumstances when the body's need for them exceeds the ability to produce them.

cone cells   Light-sensitive cells found in the retina that contain the pigment iodopsin and react to bright light and interpret color images.

constipation   Condition characterized by the absence of bowel movements for a period of time that is significantly longer than normal for the individual. When a bowel movement does occur, stools are usually small, hard, and difficult to pass.

cool-down   Activities done after an exercise session is completed; should be gradual and allow your body to slowly recover from exercise.

cortical bone (compact bone)   A dense bone tissue that makes up the outer surface of all bones as well as the entirety of most small bones of the body.

cortisol   A hormone produced by the adrenal cortex that increases rates of gluconeogenesis and lipolysis.

covert symptom   A symptom that is hidden from the client and requires laboratory tests or other invasive procedures to detect.

creatine phosphate (CP)   A high-energy compound that can be broken down for energy and used to regenerate ATP.

cretinism   A unique form of mental retardation that occurs in infants when the mother experiences iodine deficiency during pregnancy.

Crohn disease   A bowel disease that causes inflammation in the small intestine leading to diarrhea, abdominal pain, rectal bleeding, weight loss, and fever.

crop rotation   The practice of alternating crops in a particular field to prevent nutrient depletion and erosion of the soil and to help with control of crop specific pests.

cross-contamination   Contamination of one food by another via the unintended transfer of microbes through physical contact.

cystic fibrosis   A genetic disorder that causes an alteration in chloride transport, leading to the production of thick, sticky mucus that causes life-threatening respiratory and digestive problems.

cytoplasm   The liquid within an animal cell.

cytotoxic T cells   Activated T cells that kill infected body cells.

D

Daily Reference Values (DRV)   Standardized food label values for food components that do not have an RDA, such as fiber, cholesterol, and saturated fats.

DASH diet   The diet developed in response to research into hypertension funded by the National Institutes of Health (NIH); stands for "Dietary Approaches to Stop Hypertension."

deamination   The removal of an amine group from an amino acid.

dehydration   Depletion of body fluid that results when fluid excretion exceeds fluid intake.

denature   Term used to describe the action of unfolding proteins. Proteins must be denatured before they can be digested.

denaturation   The process by which proteins uncoil and lose their shape and function when they are exposed to heat, acids, bases, heavy metals, alcohol, and other damaging substances.

de novo **synthesis**   The process of synthesizing a compound "from scratch."

dental caries   Dental erosion and decay caused by acid-secreting bacteria in the mouth and on the teeth. The acid produced is a by-product of bacterial metabolism of carbohydrates deposited on the teeth.

desiccants   Chemicals that prevent foods from absorbing moisture from the air.

diabetes   A chronic disease in which the body can no longer regulate glucose.

diarrhea   Condition characterized by the frequent passage of loose, watery stools.

dietary fiber   The nondigestible carbohydrate part of plants that forms the support structures of leaves, stems, and seeds.

Dietary Guidelines for Americans   A set of principles developed by the U.S. Department of Agriculture and the U.S. Department of Health and Human Services to assist Americans in designing a healthful diet and lifestyle. These guidelines are updated every five years.

Dietary Reference Intakes (DRIs)   A set of nutritional reference values for the United States and Canada that apply to healthy people.

digestion   The process by which foods are broken down into their component molecules, either mechanically or chemically.

dioxins   An industrialized pollutant most commonly attributed to waste incineration.

direct calorimetry   A method used to determine energy expenditure by measuring the amount of heat released by the body.

disaccharide   A carbohydrate compound consisting of two monosaccharide molecules joined together.

discretionary calories   A term used in the MyPyramid food guidance system that represents the extra amount of energy you can consume after you have met all of your essential needs by consuming the most nutrient-dense foods that are low-fat or fat-free and that have no added sugars.

disordered eating   Disordered eating is a general term used to describe a variety of abnormal or atypical eating behaviors that are used to keep or maintain a lower body weight but are not severe enough to make the person seriously ill.

diuretic   A substance that increases fluid loss via the urine. Common diuretics include alcohol as well as prescription medications for high blood pressure and other disorders.

docosahexaenoic acid (DHA)   Another metabolic derivative of alpha-linolenic acid; together with EPA, it appears to reduce the risk of a heart disease.

doubly labeled water   A form of indirect calorimetry that measures total daily energy expenditure through the rate of carbon dioxide production. It requires consumption of water that is labeled with nonradioactive isotopes of hydrogen (deuterium, or ^{2}H) and oxygen (^{18}O).

drink   The amount of an alcoholic beverage that provides approximately 0.5 fl. oz of pure ethanol.

dual energy x-ray absorptiometry (DXA or DEXA)   Currently the most accurate tool for measuring bone density.

dysgeusia   Abnormal taste perception.

dysphagia   Abnormal swallowing.

E

eating disorder   A psychiatric disorder characterized by severe disturbances in body image and eating behaviors. Anorexia nervosa and bulimia nervosa are two examples of eating disorders for which specific diagnostic criteria must be present for diagnosis.

eating disorders–not otherwise specified (ED-NOS)   Atypical eating disorders that meet the definition of eating disorder but not the strict criteria for anorexia nervosa or bulimia nervosa.

eclampsia   Occurrence of seizures in pregnant women with previously diagnosed preeclampsia.

edema   A disorder in which fluids build up in the tissue spaces of the body, causing fluid imbalances and a swollen appearance.

eicosanoids   Physiologically active signaling molecules, including prostaglandins, thromboxanes and leukotrienes, derived from the twenty-carbon fatty acids arachidonic acid and eicosapentaenoic acid.

eicosapentaenoic acid (EPA)   A metabolic derivative of alpha-linolenic acid.

electrolyte   A substance that disassociates in solution into positively and negatively charged ions and is thus capable of carrying an electric current.

electron transport chain   A series of metabolic reactions that transport electrons from NAHD or $FADH_2$ through a series of carriers resulting in ATP production.

elimination   The process by which the undigested portions of food and waste products are removed from the body.

embryo   Human growth and developmental stage lasting from the third week to the end of the eighth week after fertilization.

emulsifiers Chemicals that improve texture and smoothness in foods; stabilize oil-water mixtures.

endocytosis An absorptive process by which a small amount of the intestinal contents is engulfed by the cell membrane (also called pinocytosis).

energy cost of physical activity The energy that is expended on body movement and muscular work above basal levels.

energy expenditure The energy the body expends to maintain its basic functions and to perform all levels of movement and activity.

energy intake The amount of energy a person consumes; in other words, it is the number of kilocalories consumed from food and beverages.

enteric nervous system The nerves of the GI tract.

enterocytes Specialized absorptive cells in the villi of the small intestine.

enterotoxins A type of toxin that targets the gastrointestinal tract cells.

enzymes Small chemicals, usually proteins, that act on other chemicals to speed up body processes but are not changed during those processes.

epinephrine A hormone produced mainly by the adrenal medulla that stimulates the release of glucose from liver glycogen and the release of free fatty acids from stored triglycerides.

epiphyseal plates Plates of cartilage located toward the end of long bones that provide for growth in the length of long bones.

ergocalciferol Vitamin D_2, a form of vitamin D found exclusively in plant foods.

ergogenic aids Substances used to improve exercise and athletic performance.

error theories of aging Aging is a cumulative process determined largely by exposure to environmental insults; the fewer the environmental insults, the slower the aging process.

erythrocyte hemolysis The rupturing or breakdown of red blood cells, or erythrocytes.

erythrocytes Red blood cells; they transport oxygen in the blood.

esophagus Muscular tube of the GI tract connecting the back of the mouth to the stomach.

essential amino acids Amino acids not produced by the body that must be obtained from food.

essential fatty acids (EFA) Fatty acids that must be consumed in the diet because they cannot be made by the body. The two essential fatty acids are linoleic acid and alpha-linolenic acid.

essential nutrients Nutrients for which specific biological functions have been identified and that the body cannot synthesize in sufficient quantities to meet our biological needs. Essential nutrients must be provided through the diet.

Estimated Average Requirements (EAR) The average daily nutrient intake level estimated to meet the requirement of half of the healthy individuals in a particular life stage or gender group.

Estimated Energy Requirement (EER) The average dietary energy intake that is predicted to maintain energy balance in a healthy person.

ethanol A specific alcohol compound (C_2H_5OH) formed from the fermentation of dietary carbohydrates and used in a variety of alcoholic beverages.

evaporative cooling Another term for sweating, which is the primary way in which we dissipate heat.

exchange system Diet planning tool developed by the American Dietetic Association and the American Diabetes Association in which exchanges, or portions, are organized according to the amount of carbohydrate, protein, fat, and calories in each food.

exercise A subcategory of leisure-time physical activity; any activity that is purposeful, planned, and structured.

extracellular fluid The fluid outside of the body's cells, either in the body's tissues (interstitial fluid) or as the liquid portion of the blood or lymph (intravascular fluid).

F

facilitated diffusion The absorptive process that occurs when nutrients are shuttled across the enterocytes with the help of a carrier protein.

FAD (flavin adenine dinucleotide) A coenzyme derived from the B-vitamin riboflavin; FAD readily accepts electrons (hydrogen) from various donors.

failure to thrive (FTT) An unexplained condition where the infant's weight gain and growth are far below usual levels for age and previous pattern of growth.

famines Widespread, acute food shortages that affect a substantial portion of a population, often associated with starvation and death.

fats An important energy source for our bodies at rest and during low-intensity exercise.

fat-soluble vitamins Vitamins that are not soluble in water, but soluble in fat. These include vitamins A, D, E, and K.

fatty acids Long chains of carbon atoms bound to each other as well as to hydrogen atoms.

fatty liver An early and irreversible stage of liver disease often found in people who abuse alcohol and characterized by the abnormal accumulation of fat within liver cells; also called alcoholic steatosis.

female athlete triad Refers to the interrelationship between three conditions seen in female athletes: inadequate energy intake, menstrual dysfunction (for example, amenorrhea), and reduced bone strength (for example stress fractures, osteopenia, osteoporosis).

fermentation The anaerobic process in which an agent causes an organic substance to break down into simpler substances and results in the production of ATP.

ferritin A storage form of iron found primarily in the intestinal mucosa, spleen, bone marrow, and liver.

ferroportin An iron transporter that helps regulate intestinal iron absorption and the release of iron from the enterocyte into the general circulation.

fetal alcohol effects (FAE) A milder set of alcohol-related birth defects characterized by behavioral problems such as hyperactivity, attention deficit disorder, poor judgment, sleep disorders, and delayed learning; also known as fetal alcohol spectrum disorder.

fetal alcohol syndrome (FAS) A set of serious, irreversible alcohol-related birth defects characterized by certain physical and mental abnormalities.

fetus Human growth and developmental stage lasting from the beginning of the ninth week after conception to birth.

FIT principle The principle used to achieve an appropriate overload for physical training. Stands for frequency, intensity, and time of activity.

flavoring agents Obtained from either natural or synthetic sources; allow manufacturers to maintain a consistent flavor from batch to batch.

flexibility The ability to move a joint through its full range of motion.

fluid A substance composed of molecules that move past one another freely. Fluids are characterized by their ability to conform to the shape of whatever container holds them.

fluorohydroxyapatite   A mineral compound in human teeth that contains fluoride, calcium, and phosphorous and is more resistant to destruction by acids and bacteria than hydroxyapatite.

fluorosis   A condition marked by staining and pitting of the teeth; caused by an abnormally high intake of fluoride.

folate deficiency anemia (stage IV)   The stage of folate deficiency in which the number of red blood cells has declined due to lack of folate, and macrocytic anemia develops.

folate deficiency erythropoiesis (stage III)   The stage of folate deficiency in which folate levels are so low that the ability to synthesize new red blood cells is inhibited.

folate depletion (stage II)   The stage of folate deficiency accompanied by low serum and red blood cell folate, with slightly elevated serum homocysteine concentrations.

food   The plants and animals we consume.

food-borne illness   An illness transmitted through food or water; either by an infectious agent, a poisonous substance, or a protein that causes an immune reaction.

food additives   A substance or mixture of substances intentionally put into food to enhance appearance, palatability, and quality.

food allergy   An allergic reaction to food, caused by a reaction of the immune system.

Food Guide Pyramid   Illustration developed by the U.S. Department of Agriculture (USDA) to provide Americans with a conceptual framework for the types and amounts of foods we can eat in combination to achieve a healthful diet.

food insecurity   Condition in which the individual is unable to regularly obtain enough food to provide sufficient energy and nutrients to meet physical needs.

food insecurity with hunger   Condition in which the individual experiences physiological in addition to food insecurity.

food intolerance   Gastrointestinal discomfort characterized by certain foods that is not a result of an immune system reaction.

food/population ratio   The amount of food available for each individual; also food available per capita.

food preservatives   Chemicals that help prevent microbial spoilage and enzymatic deterioration.

food security   Condition in which the individual has access everyday to food with enough energy and sufficiently rich nutrient quality to enjoy a healthy, active life.

food shortage   Condition in which food production and import in an area are not sufficient to meet the needs of the population in that area.

free radical   A highly unstable atom with an unpaired electron in its outermost shell.

frequency   Refers to the number of activity sessions per week you perform.

fructose   The sweetest natural sugar; a monosaccharide that occurs in fruits and vegetables. Also called *levulose*, or *fruit sugar*.

functional fiber   The nondigestible forms of carbohydrate that are extracted from plants or manufactured in the laboratory and have known health benefits.

fungi   Plant-like spore-forming organism that can grow either as single cells or multicellular colonies.

G

galactose   A monosaccharide that joins with glucose to create lactose, one of the three most common disaccharides.

gallbladder   A pear-shaped organ beneath the liver that stores bile and secretes it into the small intestine.

gastric juice   Acidic liquid secreted within the stomach; it contains hydrochloric acid, pepsin, and other compounds.

gastroesophageal reflux disease (GERD)   A painful type of heartburn that occurs more than twice per week.

gastrointestinal (GI) tract   A long, muscular tube consisting of several organs: the mouth, esophagus, stomach, small intestine, and large intestine.

gene expression   The process of using a gene to make a protein.

Generally Recognized as Safe (GRAS) list   A list established by Congress that identifies several hundred substances that have either been tested and found to be safe and approved for use by the FDA in the food industry or that are deemed safe as a result of consensus among experts qualified by scientific training.

genetic modification   Changing an organism by manipulating its genetic material.

genetically modified food   A food product derived from a genetically modified organism.

genetically modified organism (GMO)   An organism in which the genetic material, or DNA, has been altered using recombinant DNA technology.

geriatric failure to thrive   Inappropriate, unexplained loss of body weight and muscle mass; usually results from a combination of environmental and health factors.

gestation   The period of intrauterine development from conception to birth.

gestational diabetes   Insufficient insulin production or insulin resistance that results in consistently high blood glucose levels, specifically during pregnancy; condition typically resolves after birth occurs.

ghrelin   A protein synthesized in the stomach that acts as a hormone and plays an important role in appetite regulation by stimulating appetite.

giardiasis   A diarrheal illness caused by the intestinal parasite *Giardia intestinalis* (or *Giardia lamblia*).

glucagon   A hormone produced by the alpha cells of the pancreas that stimulates the release of glucose into the bloodstream.

glucogenic amino acid   An amino acid that can be converted to glucose via gluconeogenesis.

glucokinase   An enzyme that adds a phosphate group to a molecule of glucose.

gluconeogenesis   The synthesis of glucose from noncarbohydrate precursors such as glucogenic amino acids and glycerol. Also, the generation of glucose from the breakdown of proteins into amino acids.

glucose   The most abundant sugar molecule, a monosaccharide generally found in combination with other sugars. The preferred source of energy for the brain and an important source of energy for all cells.

glutathione   A tripeptide composed of glycine, cysteine, and glutamic acid that assists in regenerating vitamin C into its antioxidant form.

glycemic index   Rating of the potential of foods to raise blood glucose and insulin levels.

glycemic load   The amount of carbohydrate in a food multiplied by the glycemic index of the carbohydrate.

glycerol   An alcohol composed of three carbon atoms; it is the backbone of a triglyceride molecule.

glycogen   A polysaccharide stored in animals; the storage form of glucose in animals.

glycolysis   The breakdown of glucose; yields two ATP molecules and two pyruvate molecules for each molecule of glucose.

glycosylation Addition of glucose to blood and tissue proteins; typically impairs protein structure and function.

GOBI UNICEF campaign to eliminate common infections of childhood by four inexpensive strategies: growth monitoring, oral rehydration therapy, breastfeeding, and immunization.

goiter Enlargement of the thyroid gland; can be caused by iodine deficiency.

goitrogens Substances in certain foods that interfere with the utilization of iodine and, with regular consumption, predispose the consumer to symptoms of iodine deficiency.

grazing Consistently eating small meals throughout the day; done by many athletes to meet their high energy demands.

Green Revolution The tremendous increase in global productivity between 1944 and 2000 due to selective cross-breeding or hybridization to produce high-yield grains and industrial farming techniques.

H

haustration Involuntary, sluggish contraction of the haustra of the proximal colon that moves wastes toward the sigmoid colon.

healthful diet A diet that provides the proper combination of energy and nutrients and is adequate, moderate, balanced, and varied.

Healthy People 2010 An agenda that emphasizes health promotion and disease prevention across the United States by identifying goals and objectives that we hope to reach as a nation by the year 2010.

heartburn The painful sensation that occurs over the sternum when hydrochloric acid backs up into the lower esophagus.

heat cramps Muscle spasms that occur several hours after strenuous exercise; most often occur when sweat losses and fluid intakes are high, urine volume is low, and sodium intake is inadequate.

heat exhaustion A heat illness that is characterized by excessive sweating, weakness, nausea, dizziness, headache, and difficulty concentrating. Unchecked heat exhaustion can lead to heat stroke.

heat stroke A potentially fatal heat illness that is characterized by hot, dry skin, rapid heart rate, vomiting, diarrhea, an increase in body temperature greater than or equal to 104°F, hallucinations, and coma.

heat syncope Dizziness that occurs when people stand for too long in the heat or when they stop suddenly after a race or stand suddenly from a lying position; results from blood pooling in the lower extremities.

helminth Multicellular microscopic worm.

helper T-cells Activated T-cells that secrete chemicals needed to activate other immune cells.

heme The iron-containing molecule found in hemoglobin.

heme iron Iron that is part of hemoglobin and myoglobin; found only in animal-based foods such as meat, fish, and poultry.

hemoglobin The oxygen-carrying protein found in red blood cells; almost two-thirds of all iron in the body is found in hemoglobin.

hemosiderin A storage form of iron found primarily in the intestinal mucosa, spleen, bone marrow, and liver.

hepatitis Inflammation of the liver; can be caused by a virus or toxic agent such as alcohol.

hephaestin A copper-containing protein that oxidizes Fe^{2+} to Fe^{3+} once iron is transported across the basolateral membrane by ferroportin.

high-density lipoprotein (HDL) A lipoprotein made in the liver and released into the blood. HDLs function to transport cholesterol from the tissues back to the liver. Often called the "good cholesterol."

high-yield varieties Semi-dwarf varieties of plants that are unlikely to fall over in wind and heavy rains and thus can carry larger amounts of seeds, greatly increasing the yield per acre.

homocysteine An amino acid that requires adequate levels of folate, vitamin B_6, and vitamin B_{12} for its metabolism. High levels of homocysteine in the blood are associated with an increased risk for vascular diseases such as cardiovascular disease.

hormone Chemical messenger that is secreted into the bloodstream by one of the many glands of the body and acts as regulator of the physiological processes at a site remote from the gland that secreted it.

hormone-sensitive lipase The enzyme that breaks down the triglycerides stored in adipose tissue.

humectants Chemicals that help retain moisture in foods, keeping them soft and pliable.

hunger A physiologic sensation that prompts us to eat.

hydrogenation The process of adding hydrogen to unsaturated fatty acids, making them more saturated and thereby more solid at room temperature.

hydrolysis A catabolic process by which a large, chemically complex compound is broken apart with the addition of water.

hypercalcemia A condition marked by an abnormally high concentration of calcium in the blood.

hyperglycemia A condition in which blood glucose levels are higher than normal.

hyperkalemia A condition in which blood potassium levels are dangerously high.

hyperkeratosis A condition resulting in the excess accumulation of the protein keratin in the follicles of the skin; this condition can also impair the ability of epithelial tissues to produce mucus.

hypermagnesemia A condition marked by an abnormally high concentration of magnesium in the blood.

hypernatremia A condition in which blood sodium levels are dangerously high.

hypertension A chronic condition characterized by above-average blood pressure readings; specifically, systolic blood pressure over 140 mmHg or diastolic blood pressure over 90 mmHg.

hypertrophy An increase in strength and size that results from repeated work to a specific muscle or muscle group.

hyperthyroidism A condition characterized by high blood levels of thyroid hormone.

hypocalcemia A condition characterized by an abnormally low concentration of calcium in the blood.

hypoglycemia A condition marked by blood glucose levels that are below normal fasting levels.

hypokalemia A condition in which blood potassium levels are dangerously low.

hypomagnesemia A condition characterized by an abnormally low concentration of magnesium in the blood.

hyponatremia A condition in which blood sodium levels are dangerously low.

hypothalamus A region of the forebrain below the thalamus where visceral sensations such as hunger and thirst are regulated.

hypothyroidism A condition characterized by low blood levels of thyroid hormone.

I

incomplete proteins Foods that do not contain all of the essential amino acids in sufficient amounts to support growth and health.

indirect calorimetry A method used to estimate energy expenditure by measuring oxygen consumption and carbon dioxide production.

infant mortality   Death of infants between birth and 1 year.

inflammatory response   Localized swelling, pain, heat, and redness at the site of injury.

inorganic   A substance or nutrient that does not contain the element carbon.

insensible water loss   The loss of water not noticeable by a person, such as through evaporation from the skin and exhalation from the lungs during breathing.

insoluble fiber   Fibers that do not dissolve in water.

insulin   A hormone produced by the beta cells of the pancreas that increases cell uptake of glucose and amino acids.

immunocompetence   Adequate ability to produce an effective immune response to an antigen.

immunodeficiency   Decreased ability to respond to an antigen and resolve an infection.

intensity   Refers to the amount of effort expended during the activity, or how difficult the activity is to perform.

interstitial fluid   The fluid that flows between the cells that make up a particular tissue or organ, such as muscle fibers or the liver.

intracellular fluid   The fluid held at any given time within the walls of the body's cells.

intravascular fluid   The fluid in the bloodstream and lymph.

intrinsic factor   A protein secreted by cells of the stomach that binds to vitamin B_{12} and aids its absorption in the small intestine.

invisible fats   Fats that are hidden in foods, such as the fats found in baked goods, regular-fat dairy products, marbling in meat, and fried foods.

iodopsin   A color-sensitive pigment found in the cone cells of the retina.

ion   Any electrically charged particle, either positively or negatively charged.

iron-deficiency anemia (stage III)   A form of anemia that results from severe iron deficiency.

iron-deficiency erythropoiesis (stage II)   The second stage of iron deficiency, which causes a decrease in the transport of iron and leads to a decline in the ability to produce heme and make new red blood cells.

iron depletion   The first stage of iron deficiency caused by a decrease in iron stores.

irradiation   A sterilization process using gamma rays or other forms of radiation that does not impart any radiation to the food being treated.

irritable bowel syndrome (IBS)   A bowel disorder that interferes with normal functions of the colon. Symptoms are abdominal cramps, bloating, and constipation or diarrhea.

K

Keshan disease   A heart disorder caused by selenium deficiency. It was first identified in children in the Keshan province of China.

keto acid   The chemical structure that remains after the deamination of an amino acid.

ketoacidosis   A form of metabolic acidosis caused by elevated serum levels of ketone bodies. Also, a condition that alters basic body functions and damages tissues.

ketogenic amino acid   An amino acid that can be converted to acetyl CoA for the synthesis of free fatty acids.

ketone bodies   Three- and four-carbon compounds (acetoacetate, acetone, and β- or 3-hydroxybutyrate) derived when acetyl CoA levels become elevated.

ketosis   Elevated serum levels of ketone bodies.

ketones   Substances produced during the breakdown of fat when carbohydrate intake is insufficient to meet energy needs. Provide an alternative energy source for the brain when glucose levels are low.

kilocalorie (kcal)   A unit of measurement we use to quantify the amount of energy in food that can be supplied to the body. One kilocalorie is equal to the amount of heat required to raise the temperature of 1 kilogram of water by 1 degree Celsius.

Korsakoff psychosis   An alcohol-induced amnestic condition; often coexists with Wernicke syndrome in chronic alcoholics.

kwashiorkor   A form of protein-energy malnutrition that is typically seen in developing countries in infants and toddlers who are weaned early because of the birth of a subsequent child. Denied breast milk, they are fed a cereal diet that provides adequate energy but inadequate protein.

L

lactase   A digestive enzyme that breaks lactose into glucose and galactose.

lactate (or lactic acid)   A three-carbon compound produced from pyruvate in oxygen-deprived conditions.

lactation   The production of breast milk.

lacteal   A small lymph vessel located inside of the villi of the small intestine.

lactic acid   A compound that results when pyruvate is metabolized in the presence of insufficient oxygen.

lactose   Also called *milk sugar*, a disaccharide consisting of one glucose molecule and one galactose molecule. Found in milk, including human breast milk.

lactose intolerance   A disorder in which the body does not produce sufficient lactase enzyme and therefore cannot digest foods that contain lactose, such as cow's milk.

large intestine   Final organ of the GI tract consisting of cecum, colon, rectum, and anal canal, and in which most water is absorbed and feces are formed.

lean body mass   The amount of fat-free tissue, or bone, muscle, and internal organs, a person has.

leisure-time physical activity   Any activity not related to a person's occupation; includes competitive sports, recreational activities, and planned exercise training.

leptin   A hormone that is produced by body fat that acts to reduce food intake and to decrease body weight and body fat.

leukocytes   White blood cells; they protect the body from infection and illness.

life expectancy   The expected number of years remaining in one's life; typically stated from the time of birth. Children born in the United States in 2003 could expect to live, on average, 77.6 years.

life span   The highest age reached by any member of a species; currently the human life span is 122 years.

limiting amino acid   The essential amino acid that is missing or in the smallest supply in the amino acid pool and is thus responsible for slowing or halting protein synthesis.

linoleic acid   An essential fatty acid found in vegetable and nut oils; also known as omega-6 fatty acid.

lipids   A diverse group of organic substances that are insoluble in water; lipids include triglycerides, phospholipids, and sterols.

lipogenesis   The synthesis of free fatty acids from nonlipid precursors such as ketogenic amino acids or ethanol.

lipolysis   The enzyme-driven catabolism of triglycerides into free fatty acids and glycerol.

lipoprotein   A spherical compound in which fat clusters in the center and phospholipids and proteins form the outside of the sphere.

lipoprotein lipase   An enzyme that breaks down the triglycerides on chylomicrons, very-low-density lipoproteins (VLDLs), and other lipoproteins.

liver The largest auxiliary organ of the GI tract and one of the most important organs of the body. Its functions include production of bile and processing of nutrient-rich blood from the small intestine.

long-chain fatty acids Fatty acids that are fourteen or more carbon atoms in length.

low birth weight A weight of less than 5.5 pounds at birth.

low-density lipoprotein (LDL) A lipoprotein formed in the blood from VLDLs that transport cholesterol to the cells of the body. Often called the "bad cholesterol."

low-intensity activities Activities that cause very mild increases in breathing, sweating, and heart rate.

lymph nodes Small organs of the lymphatic system that filter the tissue fluid called lymph and contain lymphocytes.

lymphocytes Cells of the specific immune system that include cytotoxic T cells that kill infected host cells, helper T cells that produce signaling chemicals, and B cells that produce antibodies.

lymphopenia Fewer-than-normal numbers of lymphocytes in the blood.

M

macrocytic anemia A form of anemia manifested as the production of larger-than-normal red blood cells containing insufficient hemoglobin, which inhibits adequate transport of oxygen; also called megaloblastic anemia. Macrocytic anemia can be caused by severe folate deficiency.

macronutrients Nutrients that the body requires in relatively large amounts to support normal function and health. Carbohydrates, lipids, and proteins are macronutrients.

macrophages Cells of the nonspecific immune system that directly phagocytize invaders and present antigens to lymphocytes.

macular degeneration A vision disorder caused by deterioration of the central portion of the retina and marked by loss or distortion of the central field of vision.

mad cow disease A fatal brain disorder caused by an abnormal form of protein that causes brain damage. Also referred to as bovine spongiform encephalopathy (BSE).

major minerals Minerals we need to consume in amounts of at least 100 mg per day and of which the total amount in our bodies is at least 5 g.

malnutrition A state of poor nutritional health that can be improved by adjustments in nutrient intake.

maltase A digestive enzyme that breaks maltose into glucose.

maltose A disaccharide consisting of two molecules of glucose; does not generally occur independently in foods but results as a by-product of digestion; also called *malt sugar.*

marasmus A form of protein-energy malnutrition that results from grossly inadequate intakes of protein, energy, and other nutrients.

mass movement Involuntary, sustained, forceful contraction of the colon that occurs two or more times a day to push wastes toward the rectum.

matrix Gla protein A vitamin K-dependent protein that is located in the protein matrix of bone and also found in cartilage, blood vessel walls, and other soft tissues.

maximal heart rate The rate at which your heart beats during maximal-intensity exercise.

meat factor A special factor found in meat, fish, and poultry that enhances the absorption of non-heme iron.

medium-chain fatty acids Fatty acids that are six to twelve carbon atoms in length.

megadose A dose of a nutrient that is ten or more times greater than the recommended amount.

memory cells Lymphocytes that differentiate from B-cells and T-cells, recognize a particular antigen for an infectious disease, and remain in the body after the disease is resolved to be ready to respond if the disease is encountered again later. The purpose of vaccination is to create memory lymphocytes.

menaquinone The form of vitamin K produced by bacteria in the large intestine.

menarche The beginning of menstruation, or the menstrual period.

metabolic water The water formed as a by-product of the body's metabolic reactions.

metabolism The sum of all the chemical and physical changes that occur in body tissues when food is converted from large molecules to small molecules.

metallothaionein A zinc-containing protein within the enterocyte; it assists in the regulation of zinc homeostasis.

microcytic anemia A form of anemia manifested as the production of smaller-than-normal red blood cells containing insufficient hemoglobin, which reduces the ability of the red blood cells to transport oxygen; it can result from iron deficiency or vitamin B_6 deficiency.

micronutrients Nutrients needed in relatively small amounts to support normal health and body functions. Vitamins and minerals are micronutrients.

microsomal ethanol oxidizing system (MEOS) A liver enzyme system that oxidizes ethanol to acetaldehyde; its activity predominates at higher levels of alcohol intake.

minerals Inorganic substances that are not broken down during digestion and absorption and are not destroyed by heat or light. Minerals assist in the regulation of many body processes and are classified as major minerals or trace minerals.

moderate-intensity activities Activities that cause moderate increases in breathing, sweating, and heart rate.

moderation Eating the right amounts of foods to maintain a healthy weight and to optimize the body's metabolic processes.

monosaccharide The simplest of carbohydrates. Consists of one sugar molecule, the most common form of which is glucose.

monosaturated fatty acids (MUFA) Fatty acids that have two carbons in the chain bound to each other with one double bond; these types of fatty acids are generally liquid at room temperature.

morbid obesity A condition in which a person's body weight exceeds 100% of normal, putting him or her at very high risk for serious health consequences.

morning sickness Varying degrees of nausea and vomiting associated with pregnancy, most commonly in the first trimester.

mucosal tolerance The ability of gut mucosal cells to ignore proteins in food while preserving the ability to mount an immune response to pathogens in food.

multifactorial disease Any disease that may be attributable to one or more of a variety of causes.

muscle cramps Involuntary, spasmodic, and painful muscle contractions that last for many seconds or even minutes; electrolyte imbalances are often the cause of muscle cramps.

muscular endurance A subcomponent of musculoskeletal fitness defined as the ability of a muscle to maintain submaximal force levels for extended periods of time.

muscular strength A subcomponent of musculoskeletal fitness defined as the maximal force or tension level that can be produced by a muscle group.

musculoskeletal fitness Fitness of the muscles and bones.

mutual supplementation The process of combining two or more incomplete protein sources to make a complete protein.

myoglobin   An iron-containing protein similar to hemoglobin except that it is found in muscle cells.

MyPyramid   A revised pyramid-based food guidance system developed by the USDA and based on the 2005 Dietary Guidelines for Americans and the Dietary Reference Intakes from the National Academy of Sciences.

N

NAD (nicotinamide adenine dinucleotide)   A coenzyme form of the B-vitamin niacin; NAD readily accepts electrons (hydrogen) from various donors.

National Health and Nutrition Examination Survey (NHANES)   A survey conducted by the National Center for Health Statistics and the CDC; this survey tracks the nutrient and food consumption of Americans.

National Institutes of Health (NIH)   The world's leading medical center and the focal point for medical research in the United States.

natural killer cells   Cells that are part of the innate immune system and are effective killers of a wide variety of parasites, bacteria, fungi, viral-infected cells, and cancer cells.

negative folate balance (stage I)   The first stage in folate deficiency, in which serum levels of folate begin to decline.

negative vitamin B$_{12}$ balance (stage I)   The stage of vitamin B$_{12}$ deficiency accompanied by reduced blood levels of cobalamin.

neonatal   Referring to a newborn.

neonatal mortality   Death of newborns between birth and 28 days.

neural tube   Embryonic tissue that forms a tube, which eventually becomes the brain and spinal cord.

neural tube defects   The most common malformations of the central nervous system that occur during fetal development. A folate deficiency can cause neural tube defects.

neurotoxins   A type of toxin that targets the nervous system cells.

neutropenia   Fewer-than-normal numbers of neutrophils in the blood.

neutrophils   Cells of the nonspecific immune system found in blood and in inflamed tissue. A neutrophil is recruited from blood into injured tissue by signaling cytokines.

night blindness   A vitamin A–deficiency disorder that results in the loss of the ability to see in dim light.

nitrates   Chemicals used in meat curing to develop and stabilize the pink color associated with cured meat; also function as antibacterial agents.

nitrites   Chemicals used in meat curing to develop and stabilize the pink color associated with cured meat; also function as antibacterial agents.

nonessential amino acids   Amino acids that can be manufactured by the body in sufficient quantities and therefore do not need to be consumed regularly in our diet.

non-heme iron   The form of iron that is not part of hemoglobin or myoglobin; found in animal-based and plant-based foods.

non-nutritive sweeteners   Also called *alternative sweeteners;* manufactured sweeteners that provide little or no energy.

nonspecific immune function   Generalized body defense mechanisms that protect against the entry of foreign agents such as microorganisms and allergens; also called *innate immunity.*

nucleotide   A molecule composed of a phosphate group, a pentose sugar called deoxyribose, and one of four nitrogenous bases: adenine (A), guanine (G), cytosine (C), or thymine (T).

nucleus   The positively charged, central core of an atom. It is made up of two types of particles—protons and neutrons—bound tightly together. The nucleus of an atom contains essentially all of its atomic mass.

nutrient deficiency   State of malnutrition resulting from inadequate intake of one or more nutrients.

nutrient density   The relative amount of nutrients per amount of energy (or number of calories).

nutrients   Chemicals found in foods that are critical to human growth and function.

nutrition   The scientific study of food and how food nourishes the body and influences health.

Nutrition Facts Panel   The label on a food package that contains the nutrition information required by the FDA.

nutrition paradox   Coexistence of undernutrition and overnutrition in the same region or in the same family.

nutrition transition   The increased availability of food and the change in the types of food available to the population as the economy of a developing country improves; associated with increasing incidence of obesity and chronic diseases.

nutritive sweeteners   Sweeteners such as sucrose, fructose, honey, and brown sugar that contribute calories (or energy).

O

obesity   Having an excess body fat that adversely affects health, resulting in a person having a weight that is substantially greater than some accepted standard for a given height.

oligosaccharide   Complex carbohydrate that contains three to ten monosaccharides.

opsin   A protein that combines with retinal in the retina to form rhodopsin.

organ   A body structure composed of two or more tissues and performing a specific function, for example, the esophagus.

organic   A substance or nutrient that contains the element carbon.

osmosis   The movement of water (or any solvent) through a semipermeable membrane from an area where solutes are less concentrated to areas where they are highly concentrated.

osmotic pressure   The pressure that is needed to keep the particles in a solution from drawing liquid toward them across a semipermeable membrane.

osteoblasts   Cells that prompt the formation of new bone matrix by laying down the collagen-containing component of bone that is then mineralized.

osteocalcin   A vitamin K-dependent protein that is secreted by osteoblasts and is associated with bone turnover.

osteoclasts   Cells that erode the surface of bones by secreting enzymes and acids that dig grooves into the bone matrix.

osteomalacia   Vitamin D-deficiency disease in adults, in which bones become weak and prone to fractures.

osteopenia   A term used to describe a condition of low bone mass that increases the risk for fractures, in which a person's T-score is between −1 and −2.5.

osteoporosis   A disease characterized by low bone mass and deterioration of bone tissue, leading to increased bone fragility and fracture risk.

ounce-equivalent   (or oz-equivalent) A term used to describe a serving size that is 1 ounce, or equivalent to an ounce, for the grains section and the meats and beans section of MyPyramid.

overhydration   Dilution of body fluid. It results when water intake or retention is excessive.

overload principle   Placing an extra physical demand on your body in order to improve your fitness level.

overnutrition   State of malnutrition resulting from regular intake of excess energy and/or micronutrients.

overpopulated   Characteristic used to describe a region that has insufficient resources to support the number of people living there.

overt symptom   A symptom that is obvious to a client, such as pain, fatigue, or a bruise.

overweight   Having a moderate amount of excess body fat, resulting in a person having a weight that is greater than some accepted standard for a given height but is not considered obese.

overweight (childhood)   Having a body mass index (BMI) at or above the 95th percentile.

ovulation   The release of an ovum (egg) from a woman's ovary.

oxidation   A chemical reaction in which molecules of a substance are broken down into their component atoms. During oxidation, the atoms involved lose electrons.

oxidation-reduction reactions   Reactions in which electrons are lost by one compound (it is oxidized) and simultaneously gained by another compound (it is reduced).

P

palliative care   Reducing an individual's pain and discomfort without any attempts at a treatment or cure.

pancreas   Gland located behind the stomach; it secretes digestive enzymes.

pancreatic amylase   An enzyme secreted by the pancreas into the small intestine that digests any remaining starch into maltose.

parathyroid hormone (PTH)   A hormone secreted by the parathyroid gland when blood calcium levels fall. It is also known as parathormone, and it increases blood calcium levels by stimulating the activation of vitamin D, increasing reabsorption of calcium from the kidneys, and stimulating osteoclasts to break down bone, which releases more calcium into the bloodstream.

parietal cells   Cells lining the gastric glands that secrete hydrochloric acid and intrinsic factor.

passive diffusion   The simple absorptive process in which nutrients pass through the enterocytes and into the bloodstream without the use of a carrier protein or the requirement of energy.

passive immunity   The condition of having circulating antibodies to protect you from a disease. These antibodies are used in immune defense but cannot be replaced by the host. Examples are antibodies acquired by an infant in breast milk or injection of an antiserum to snake venom.

pasteurization   A form of sterilization using high temperatures for short periods of time.

pellagra   A disease that results from severe niacin deficiency.

pepsin   An enzyme in the stomach that begins the breakdown of proteins into shorter polypeptide chains and single amino acids.

peptic ulcer   Area of the GI tract that has been eroded away by the acidic gastric juice of the stomach. The two main causes of peptic ulcers are *Helicobacter pylori* infection or use of nonsteroidal anti-inflammatory drugs.

peptide bonds   Unique types of chemical bonds in which the amine group of one amino acid binds to the acid group of another in order to manufacture dipeptides and all larger peptide molecules.

peptide YY (PYY)   A protein produced in the gastrointestinal tract that is released after a meal in amounts proportional to the energy content of the meal; it decreases appetite and inhibits food intake.

percent daily values (%DV)   Information on a Nutrition Facts Panel that identifies how much a serving of food contributes to your overall intake of nutrients listed on the label; based on an energy intake of 2,000 calories per day.

peristalsis   Wave of squeezing and pushing contractions that move food, chyme, and feces in one direction through the length of the GI tract.

pernicious anemia   A special form of anemia that is the primary cause of a vitamin B_{12} deficiency; occurs at the end stage of an autoimmune disorder that causes the loss of various cells in the stomach.

peroxidation   The oxidative deterioration of an organic compound, such as a lipid, resulting in the formation of a peroxide.

persistent organic pollutants (POPs)   Chemicals released into the environment as a result of industry, agriculture, or improper waste disposal; automobile emissions also are considered POPs.

pesticides   Chemicals used either in the field or in storage to destroy plant, fungal, and animal pests.

pH   Stands for percentage of hydrogen. It is a measure of the acidity—or level of hydrogen—of any solution, including human blood.

phagocytes   Cells that engulf and destroy foreign agents.

phospholipids   A type of lipid in which a fatty acid is combined with another compound that contains phosphate; unlike other lipids, phospholipids are soluble in water.

phosphorylation   The addition of one or more phosphate groups to a chemical compound.

photosynthesis   Process by which plants use sunlight to fuel a chemical reaction that combines carbon and water into glucose, which is then stored in their cells.

phylloquinone   The form of vitamin K found in plants.

physical activity   Any movement produced by muscles that increases energy expenditure; includes occupational, household, leisure-time, and transportation activities.

Physical Activity Pyramid   A pyramid similar to the Food Guide Pyramid that makes recommendations for the type and amount of activity that should be done weekly to increase physical activity levels.

physical fitness   The ability to carry out daily tasks with vigor and alertness, without undue fatigue, and with ample energy to enjoy leisure-time pursuits and meet unforeseen emergencies.

phytic acid   The form of phosphorus stored in plants.

phytochemicals   Chemicals found in plants (*phyto-* is from the Greek word for plant), such as pigments and other substances, that may reduce our risk for diseases such as cancer and heart disease.

pica   An abnormal craving to eat something not fit for food, such as clay, paint, etc.

placebo effect   The belief that a product improves performance although it has been proven to have no physiologic benefits.

placenta   A pregnancy-specific organ formed from both maternal and embryonic tissues. It is responsible for oxygen, nutrient, and waste exchange between the mother and fetus.

plasma   The fluid portion of the blood; it is needed to maintain adequate blood volume so that the blood can flow easily throughout the body.

plasma cells   Lymphocytes that have differentiated from activated B-cells and produce millions of antibodies to an antigen during an infection.

platelets   Cell fragments that assist in the formation of blood clots and help stop bleeding.

polychlorinated biphenyls (PCBs)   An industrial pollutant most commonly attributed to discarded transformers.

polypharmacy   Concurrent use of three or more medications.

polysaccharide   A complex carbohydrate consisting of long chains of glucose.

polyunsaturated fatty acids (PUFA)   Fatty acids that have more than one double bond in the chain; these types of fatty acids are generally liquid at room temperature.

portal vein   A vessel that carries blood and various products of digestion from the digestive organs and spleen to the liver.

prebiotics   Fibers that are preferentially fermented by the beneficial lactobacilli and bifidobacteria in gut flora and thus encourage their growth.

preeclampsia   High blood pressure that is pregnancy-specific and accompanied by protein in the urine, edema, and unexpected weight gain.

preterm   Birth of a baby prior to 38 weeks of gestation.

primary deficiency   A deficiency that occurs when not enough of a nutrient is consumed in the diet.

primary malnutrition   Malnutrition caused by inadequate intake of one or more nutrients.

prion   An infectious, self-replicating protein.

probiotics   Live beneficial strains of gut bacteria in food or supplements that help maintain a proactive balance in the gut flora.

processed foods   Foods that are manipulated mechanically or chemically during their production or packaging.

programmed theories of aging   Aging is biologically determined, following a predictable pattern of physiologic changes, although the timing may vary from one person to another.

proof   A measure of the alcohol content of a liquid; 100-proof liquor is 50% alcohol by volume; 80-proof liquor is 40% alcohol by volume, and so forth.

prooxidant   A nutrient that promotes oxidation and oxidative cell and tissue damage.

proteases   Enzymes that continue the breakdown of polypeptides in the small intestine.

protein digestibility corrected amino acid score (PDCAAS)   A measurement of protein quality that considers the balance of amino acids as well as the digestibility of the protein in the food.

protein efficiency ratio   An assessment of protein quality that involves comparing the weight gained by a laboratory animal consuming a standard amount of a test protein with the total amount of protein that is consumed.

protein-energy malnutrition   A disorder caused by inadequate consumption of protein. It is characterized by severe wasting.

proteins   Large, complex molecules made up of amino acids and found as essential components of all living cells.

proteolysis   The breakdown of dietary proteins into single amino acids or small peptides that are absorbed by the body.

provitamin   An inactive form of a vitamin that the body can convert to an active form. An example is beta-carotene.

puberty   The period in life in which secondary sexual characteristics develop and people are biologically capable of reproducing.

purging   An attempt to rid the body of unwanted food by vomiting or other compensatory means, such as excessive exercise, fasting, or laxative abuse.

pyruvate   The primary end product of glycolysis.

pyruvic acid   The primary end product of glycolysis.

R

raffinose   An oligosaccharide composed of galactose, glucose, and fructose. Also called melitose, it is found in beans, cabbage, broccoli, and other vegetables.

rating of perceived exertion (RPE)   A scale that defines the difficulty level of any activity; this scale can be used to estimate intensity during exercise.

reactive oxygen species (ROS)   A specific term used to describe an oxygen molecule that has become a free radical.

recombinant bovine growth hormone (rBGH)   A genetically engineered hormone injected into diary cows to enhance their milk output.

recombinant DNA technology   Type of genetic modification in which scientists combine DNA from different sources to produce a transgenic organism that expresses a desired trait.

Recommended Dietary Allowance (RDA)   The average daily nutrient intake level that meets the nutrient requirements of 97% to 98% of healthy individuals in a particular life stage and gender group.

Reference Daily Intakes (RDI)   Standardized food label values for nutrients with RDAs, including protein and vitamins.

registered dietitian (RD)   A professional designation that requires a minimum of a bachelor's degree in nutrition, completion of supervised clinical experience, a passing grade on a national examination, and maintenance of registration with the American Dietetic Association (in Canada, the Dietitians of Canada). RDs are qualified to work in a variety of settings.

remodeling   The two-step process by which bone tissue is recycled; includes the breakdown of existing bone and the formation of new bone.

renin   An enzyme secreted by the kidneys in response to a decrease in blood pressure. Renin converts the blood protein angio-tensinogen to angiotensin I, which eventually results in an increase in sodium reabsorption.

residues   Chemicals that remain in the foods we eat despite cleaning and processing.

resistance training   Exercises in which our muscles work against resistance.

resorption   The process by which the surface of bone is broken down by cells called osteoclasts.

resveratrol   A potent phenolic antioxidant found in red wines as well as grapes and nuts.

retina   The delicate light-sensitive membrane lining the inner eyeball and connected to the optic nerve. It contains retinal.

retinal   An active, aldehyde form of vitamin A that plays an important role in healthy vision and immune function.

retinoic acid   An active, acid form of vitamin A that plays an important role in cell growth and immune function.

retinol   An active, alcohol form of vitamin A that plays an important role in healthy vision and immune function.

rhodopsin   A light-sensitive pigment found in the rod cells that is formed by retinal and opsin.

ribose   A five-carbon monosaccharide that is located in the genetic material of cells.

rickets   Vitamin D-deficiency disease in children. Symptoms include deformities of the skeleton such as bowed legs and knocked knees.

rod cells   Light-sensitive cells found in the retina that contain rhodopsin and react to dim light and interpret black-and-white images.

S

saliva   A mixture of water, mucus, enzymes, and other chemicals that moistens the mouth and food, binds food particles together, and begins the digestion of carbohydrates.

salivary amylase   An enzyme in saliva that breaks starch into smaller particles and eventually into the disaccharide maltose.

salivary glands   Group of glands found under and behind the tongue and beneath the jaw that release saliva continually as well as in response to the thought of, sight, smell, or presence of food.

salt resistance   A condition in which certain people do not experience changes in blood pressure with changes in salt intake.

salt sensitivity   A condition in which certain people respond to a high salt intake by experiencing an increase in blood pressure; these people also experience a decrease in blood pressure when salt intake is low.

sarcopenia   Age-related progressive loss of muscle mass, muscle strength, and muscle function.

saturated fatty acids (SFA)   Fatty acids that have no carbons joined together with a double bond; these types of fatty acids are generally solid at room temperature.

secondary deficiency   A deficiency that occurs when a person cannot absorb enough of a nutrient, excretes too much of a nutrient from the body, or cannot utilize a nutrient efficiently.

secondary malnutrition   Malnutrition caused by abnormal digestion, absorption, transport, activation, or retention of one or more nutrients.

segmentation   Rhythmic contraction of the circular muscles of the intestines that squeeze chyme, mix it, and enhance digestion and absorption of nutrients from the chyme.

seizures   Uncontrollable muscle spasms caused by increased nervous system excitability that can result from electrolyte imbalances.

selenocysteine   An amino acid derivative that is the active form of selenium in the body.

selenomethionine   An amino acid derivative that is the storage form for selenium in the body.

senescence   The progressive deterioration of bodily functions over time, resulting in increased risk of disability, disease, and death.

sensible water loss   Water loss that is noticed by a person, such as urine output and sweating.

set-point theory   A theory that suggests that the body raises or lowers energy expenditure in response to increased and decreased food intake and physical activity. This action serves to maintain an individual's body weight within a narrow range.

short-chain fatty acids   Fatty acids fewer than six carbon atoms in length.

sickle cell anemia   A genetic disorder that causes red blood cells to be sickle, or crescent, shaped. These cells cannot travel smoothly through the blood vessels, causing cell breakage and anemia.

simple carbohydrate   Commonly called *sugar;* a monosaccharide or disaccharide such as a glucose.

small for gestational age (SGA)   Infants whose birth weight for gestational age falls below the 10th percentile.

small intestine   The longest portion of the GI tract where most digestion and absorption takes place.

soluble fibers   Fibers that dissolve in water.

solvent   A substance that is capable of mixing with and breaking apart a variety of compounds. Water is an excellent solvent.

specific immune function   The strongest defense against pathogens. Requires adaptation of lymphocytes that recognize antigens and that multiply to protect against the pathogens carrying those antigens, also called adaptive immunity or acquired immunity.

sphincter   A tight ring of muscle separating some of the organs of the GI tract and opening in response to nerve signals indicating that food is ready to pass into the next section.

spina bifida   Embryonic neural tube defect that occurs when the spinal vertebrae fail to completely enclose the spinal cord, allowing it to protrude.

spontaneous abortion (also called *miscarriage*)   Natural termination of a pregnancy and expulsion of pregnancy tissues because of a genetic, developmental, or physiological abnormality that is so severe that the pregnancy cannot be maintained.

stabilizers   Help maintain smooth texture and uniform color and flavor in some foods.

stachyose   An oligosaccharide composed of two galactose molecules, a glucose molecule, and a fructose molecule. Found in the Chinese artichoke and various beans and legumes.

starch   A polysaccharide stored in plants; the storage form of glucose in plants.

sterols   A type of lipid found in foods and the body that has a ring structure; cholesterol is the most common sterol that occurs in our diets.

stomach   A J-shaped organ where food is partially digested, churned, and stored until release into the small intestine.

stunted   Shorter stature than expected for chronological age.

subclinical deficiency   A deficiency in its early stages when few or no symptoms are observed.

subsistence crops   Crops grown to be eaten by a family or community, such as rice, millet, and garden vegetables. Surpluses may be sold locally.

sucrase   A digestive enzyme that breaks sucrose into glucose and fructose.

sucrose   A disaccharide composed of one glucose molecule and one fructose molecule; sweeter than lactose or maltose.

sudden infant death syndrome (SIDS)   The sudden death of a previously healthy infant; the most common cause of death in infants more than 1 month of age.

sulfites   Agents that are effective as preservatives, antioxidants, and that prevent browning. Sulfites also have antibacterial properties, are used to bleach flour, and inhibit mold growth in grapes, wine, and other foods.

sustainable agriculture   Term referring to techniques of food production that preserve the environment indefinitely.

system   A group of organs that work together to perform a unique function, for example, the gastrointestinal system.

T

T-cells   Lymphocytes that mature in the thymus gland and are of several varieties, including helper T-cells.

teratogen   Any substance that can cause a birth defect.

texturizers   A chemical used to improve the texture of various foods.

thermic effect of food (TEF)   The energy expended as a result of processing food consumed.

thickening agents   Natural or chemically modified carbohydrates that absorb some of the water present in food, making the food thicker while keeping food components balanced.

thirst mechanism   A cluster of nerve cells in the hypothalamus that stimulates our conscious desire to drink fluids in response to an increase in the concentration of salt in our blood or a decrease in blood pressure and blood volume.

thrifty gene theory   A theory that suggests that some people possess a gene (or genes) that causes them to be energetically thrifty, resulting in them expending less energy at rest and during physical activity.

time of activity   How long each exercise session lasts.

tissue   A sheet or other grouping of similar cells that performs a particular set of functions, for example, muscle tissue.

tocopherol   The family of vitamin E that is the active form in our bodies.

tocotrienol   A family of vitamin E that does not play an important biological role in our bodies.

Tolerable Upper Intake Level (UL)   The highest average daily nutrient intake level likely to pose no risk of adverse health effects to almost all individuals in a particular life stage and gender group.

total fiber   The sum of dietary fiber and functional fiber.

toxin   Any harmful substance; specifically a chemical produced by a microorganism that harms tissues or causes harmful immune responses.

trabecular bone (spongy or cancellous bone)   A porous bone tissue that makes up only 20% of the skeleton and is found within the ends of the long bones, inside the spinal vertebrae, inside the flat bones (breastbone, ribs, and most bones of the skull), and inside the bones of the pelvis.

trace minerals   Minerals we need to consume in amounts less than 100 mg per day and of which the total amount in our bodies is less than 5 g.

transamination   The process of transferring the amine group from one amino acid to another in order to manufacture a new amino acid.

transcription   The process through which messenger RNA copies genetic information from DNA in the nucleus.

transferrin   The transport protein for iron.

transgenic crops   Plant varieties that have had one or more genes altered by the use of genetic technologies.

transitioning countries   Developing countries that are experiencing economic growth.

translation   The process that occurs when the genetic information carried by messenger RNA is translated into a chain of amino acids at the ribosome.

transport proteins   Protein molecules that help to transport substances throughout the body and across cell membranes.

triglyceride   A molecule consisting of three fatty acids attached to a three-carbon glycerol backbone.

trimester   Any one of three stages of pregnancy, each lasting 13 to 14 weeks.

T-score   A comparison of an individual's bone density to the average peak bone density of a 30-year-old healthy adult.

tumor   Any newly formed mass of undifferentiated cells.

type 1 diabetes   Disorder in which the body cannot produce enough insulin.

type 2 diabetes   Progressive disorder in which body cells become less responsive to insulin.

U

ulcerative colitis   A chronic disease of the large intestine, or colon, indicated by inflammation and ulceration of the mucosa, or innermost lining of the colon.

umbilical cord   The cord containing arteries and veins that connect the baby (from the navel) to the mother via the placenta.

undernutrition   Malnutrition resulting from less energy intake than necessary to support optimal growth in children or to maintain a healthy, active body in adults.

underweight   Having too little body fat to maintain health, causing a person to have a weight that is below an acceptably defined standard for a given height.

urinary tract infection   A bacterial infection of the urethra, the tube leading from the bladder to the body exterior.

V

vaccination   Administering a small amount of antigen to elicit an immune response for the purpose of developing memory cells that will protect against the disease at a later time.

variety   Eating a lot of different foods each day.

vegetarianism   The practice of restricting the diet to food substances of plant origin, including vegetables, fruit, grains, and nuts.

very-low-density lipoprotein (VLDL)   A lipoprotein made in the liver and intestine that functions to transport endogenous lipids, especially triglycerides, to the tissues of the body.

vigorous intensity activities   Activities that produce significant increases in breathing, sweating, and heart rate; talking is difficult when exercising at a vigorous intensity.

viruses   A group of infectious agents that are much smaller than bacteria, lack independent metabolism, and are incapable of growth or reproduction apart from living cells.

viscous   Term referring to a gel-like consistency.

visible fats   Fat we can see in our foods or see added to foods, such as butter, margarine, cream, shortening, salad dressings, chicken skin, and untrimmed fat on meat.

vitamin A paradox   The situation in which individuals with low vitamin A status show improved immune function with supplementation, but those with adequate vitamin A status show reduced immune function with supplementation.

vitamin B_{12}-deficiency anemia (stage IV)   This stage of vitamin B_{12} deficiency is characterized by reduced number of red blood cells and the development of macrocytic anemia.

vitamin B_{12}-deficiency erythropoiesis (stage III)   This stage of vitamin B_{12} deficiency is characterized by decreased synthesis of new red blood cells.

vitamin B_{12} depletion (stage II)   This stage of vitamin B_{12} deficiency is characterized by decreased saturation of the transport protein with cobalamin.

vitamins   Organic compounds that assist in regulating physiologic processes.

W

warm-up   Also called preliminary exercise; includes activities that prepare you for an exercise bout, including stretching, calisthenics, and movements specific to the exercise bout.

wasting   A condition of very low body-weight-for-height or extreme thinness.

water-soluble vitamins   Vitamins that are soluble in water. These include vitamin C and the B-vitamins.

weight cycling   The condition of successfully dieting to lose weight, regaining the weight, and repeating the cycle again.

wellness   A multidimensional, lifelong process that includes physical, emotional, and spiritual health.

Wernicke-Korsakoff syndrome   An alcohol-induced syndrome associated with severe thiamin deficiency in chronic alcoholics; it is characterized by ataxia, tremors, abnormal eye movements, memory loss, and psychosis.

X

xerophthalmia   An irreversible blindness due to hardening of the cornea and drying of the mucous membranes of the eye.

xerostomia   Dry mouth due to decreased saliva production.

Z

zygote   A fertilized egg (ovum) consisting of a single cell.

Index

Page numbers followed by an "f" indicate figures. Page numbers followed by a "t" indicate tables.

Credits

Photo Credits

Table of Contents

p. xxiv: Corbis; **p. xxv:** Dorling Kindersley; **p. xxvi:** Randy Sidman-Moore/Masterfile; **p. xxvii:** Dorling Kindersley; **p. xxviii:** David Murray/Dorling Kindersley; **p. xxix:** Ian O'Leary/Dorling Kindersley; **p. xxx:** Clive Streeter and Patrick McLeavy/Dorling Kindersley; **p. xxxi:** Ariel Skelley/Corbis; **p. xxxii:** Eyewire Collection/Getty Images; **p. xxxiii:** David Murray/Dorling Kindersley; **p. xxxv top:** Heinz Tschanz-Hofmann/age fotostock; **bottom:** Jon Feingersh/Image Bank/Getty Images; **p. xxxvii:** Digital Vision/Getty Images; **p. xxxviii:** FoodPix/Jupiter Images/PictureArts Corporation; **p. xxxix:** Ariel Skelley/Corbis; **p. xl:** Ryan McVay/Photodisc; **p. xli:** Kent Gilbert/AP Wide World Photos.

Chapter 1

Chapter Opener: Rosemary Calvert/Getty Images; **p. 3:** Fotocrisis/shutterstock; **p. 4:** Lew Robertson/Picture Arts/Corbis; **p. 5:** Lester V. Bergman/Corbis; **p. 11:** Tom Stewart/Corbis; **p. 12:** Ana Strack/Corbis; **p. 13:** FoodPix/Jupiter Images/PictureArts Corporation; **p. 14:** Andy Crawford/Dorling Kindersley; **p. 17:** Jon Feingersh/Image Bank/Getty Images; **p. 19:** BSIP/Phototake NYC; **p. 20:** Blair Seitz/Photo Researchers; **p. 21:** Stockbyte/Getty; **p. 25:** Stockbyte/Getty Images; **p. 26:** Kristin Piljay; **p. 28:** LA/Tevy Battini/Phototake NYC; **p. 29:** Michael Donne/Photo Researchers; **p. 31:** Rubberball/Getty; **p. 35:** Randy L. Jirtle; **p. 36:** Digital Vision/Getty Images.

Chapter 2

Chapter Opener: Scott Peterson/Foodpix/Jupiter Images; **p. 39:** Frank_U/iStockphoto; **p. 40:** Ariel Skelley/Corbis; **p. 41 top:** Duomo/Corbis; **bottom:** Alex Mares-Manton/Asia Images/Getty Images; **p. 42 top:** Dorling Kindersley; **bottom:** AP Wide World Photos; **p. 43:** Chris Collins/Corbis; **p. 45:** Sky Bonillo/PhotoEdit; **p. 46:** Ned Frisk Photography/Corbis; **p. 49:** David Sacks/Image Bank/Getty Images; **Fig. 2.4:** Creative Digital Visions; **p. 51:** Alexander Walter/Taxi/Getty Images; **p. 52:** Andrew Whittuck/Dorling Kindersley; **p. 54 top:** AGE Fotostock; **bottom:** Andrew Whittuck/Dorling Kindersley; **Fig. 2.7:** Pearson Learning Photo Studio; **Fig. 2.8a left:** Image Source Pink/Alamy; **right:** Envision/Corbis; **2.8b left:** F. Schussler/PhotoLink/PhotoDisc/Getty Images; **right:** Ragnar Schmuck/PhotoDisc/Getty Images; **p. 62:** George Doyle & Claran Griffin/Stockbyte/Getty; **p. 64:** Joe Raedle/Getty Images; **p. 65 top:** Koichi Kamoshida/Getty Images; **bottom:** Sigrid Estrada/Getty Images; **p. 66:** Photodisc/Getty Images; **p. 70:** Pearson Learning Photo Studio; **p. 71 left:** Lars Borges/PhotoDisc/Getty Images; **top right:** Triolo Productions/Getty Images; **lower right:** Cristina Cassinelli/Foodpix/Jupiter Images.

Chapter 3

Chapter Opener: Rosemary Calvert/AGE Fotostock; **p. 73:** Klaudia Steiner/iStockphoto; **p. 74 top:** Jean Luc Morales/Image Bank/Getty Images; **bottom:** Howard Kingsnorth/Image Bank/Getty Images; **Fig. 3.2:** Jon Riley/Stone/Getty Images; **p. 77:** Paul Poplis/Foodpix/Jupiter Images; **p. 78 top:** Matt Bowman/FoodPix/Jupiter Images/PictureArts Corporation; **center:** George Doyle & Claran Griffin/Stockbyte/Getty; **p. 86:** SPL/Photo Researchers; **Fig. 3.13 left:** Steve Gschmeissner/SPL/Photo Researchers; **right:** Dr. David M. Phillips/Getty Images; **p. 92:** Tim Hawley/Foodpix/Jupiter Images; **p. 96 top:** Digital Vision/Getty Images; **Fig. 3.19:** Dr. E. Walker/Science Photo Library/Photo Researchers; **p. 97:** David Murray and Jules Selmes/Dorling Kindersley; **p. 98:** Gerald Zanetti/Foodpix/Jupiter Images; **p. 100:** Rubberball/Getty; **p. 101:** Peter Adams/Getty Images; **p. 102:** Pramod Mistry/Lonely Planet Images; **p. 108:** Scott Indermaur/Jupiter Images; **p. 109:** Cordelia Molloy/Photo Researchers.

Chapter 4

Chapter Opener: Ian O'Leary/Dorling Kindersley; **p. 111:** Anatoliy Samara/shutterstock; **p. 113:** Michael Newman/PhotoEdit; **p. 115 left:** Foodcollection/Getty Images; **right:** Envision/Corbis; **p. 117:** Robert J. Bennett/AGE Fotostock; **p. 118:** Kristin Piljay; **p. 123 left:** Steve Shott/Dorling Kindersley; **right:** Ryan McVay/Getty Images; **p. 124:** Rob Lewine/Corbis; **p. 125:** Jeff Greenburg/PhotoEdit; **p. 126:** Dorling Kindersley; **p. 128:** Justin Sullivan/Getty Images; **p. 129:** Joe Raedle/Getty Images; **p. 131:** Dorling Kindersley; **Fig. 4.15 top to bottom:** Eduard Andras/istockphoto; Darja Vorontsova/Shutterstock; Jurga Rubinovaite/istockphoto; Julie Masson Deshaies/istockphoto; **p. 134 top:** Dorling Kindersley; **bottom:** Photodisc/Getty Images; **Fig. 4.16:** Creative Digital Visions; **Fig. 4.17a:** Rebecca Ellis/istockphoto; **Fig. 4.17b:** Ben Beltman/istockphoto; **p. 138:** Kristin Piljay; **p. 141:** Roche Diagnostics Corporation; **p. 142:** Scott Camazine/Photo Researchers; **p. 143:** Tim Mosenfelder/Getty Images; **p. 144:** George Doyle & Claran Griffin/Stockbyte/Getty; **p. 145:** Dorling Kindersley; **p. 151:** Brian Buckley/Alamy Images; **p. 152:** isifa Image Service s.r.o./Alamy Images; **p. 153:** Andre Jenny/Alamy Images.

In Depth

p. 154: Supapixx/Alamy Images; **p. 155:** Kristin Piljay; **p. 156:** Richard Levine/Alamy; **p. 157:** Stockbyte/Getty; **p. 159:** Jemma Jones/Alamy; **Fig. 4a:** Science Photo Library/Photo Researchers; **Fig. 4b:** Martin M. Rotker; **p. 161:** Enigma/Alamy; **Fig. 6:** George Steinmetz Photography.

Chapter 5

Chapter Opener: Alan Campbell/Stock Food Creative/Getty Images; **p. 167:** martin garnham/shutterstock; **p. 168 top:** Jeff Greenberg/AGE Fotostock; **bottom:** Dorling Kindersley; **p. 171 top:** J. Garcia/Corbis; **bottom:** David Murray/Dorling Kindersley; **p. 172:** AP Wide World Photos; **p. 174:** Dorling Kindersley; **p. 176:** Kip Peticolas/Fundamental Photographs, NYC; **p. 177:** Nino Mascardi/Getty Images; **p. 179:** Quest/Photo Researchers; **p. 181 top:** Andersen Floss/Photodisc/Getty Images; **bottom:** Doug Pensinger/Getty Images; **p. 183 top:** Odd Andersen/Agence France Presse/Getty Images; **bottom:** Corbis; **p. 185:** Rubberball/Getty; **p. 186:** Spencer Platt/Getty Images; **p. 187 bottom:** James Leynse/Corbis; **Fig. 5.14:** Foodfolio/Alamy Images; **p. 192:** Constantine Manos/Magnum Photos; **p. 193:** AP Wide World Photos; **Fig. 5.18a:** Science Photo Library/Photo Researchers; **Fig. 5.18b:** ISM/PhototakeUSA; **p. 198 top:** Sang An/Foodpix/Jupiter Images; **bottom:** Markus Amon/Image Bank/Getty Images; **p. 200:** Ned Frisk Photography/Corbis; **p. 206 top:** Frances Roberts/Alamy Images; **bottom:** Michael Newman/PhotoEdit; **p. 207:** Dorling Kindersley.

Chapter 6

Chapter Opener: D. Amon/photocuisine/Corbis; **p. 209:** Suzannah Skelton/iStockphoto; **p. 210:** Duomo/Corbis; **Fig. 6.9:** Andrew Syed/ Photo Researchers; **p. 218:** Foodfolio/Jupiter Images; **Fig. 6.10:** Creative Digital Visions; **p. 221:** Ian O'Leary/Dorling Kindersley; **Fig. 6.13a:** Geri Engberg; **Fig. 6.13b:** Medical-on-Line / Alamy; **p. 226:** AP Wide World Photos; **Fig. 6.15a:** Jupiterimages; **Fig. 6.15b:** Andrew Holbrooke/Corbis; **Fig. 6.15c:** Alan K. Bailey/Rubberball/Getty Images; **p. 230 top:** Rubberball/Getty; **bottom:** Ranald MacKechnie/Dorling Kindersley; **p. 233:** BananaStock/Alamy Images; **p. 234:** StockFood/ Getty Images; **p. 235:** Jennifer Levy/FoodPix/Jupiter Images; **p. 236:** Dorling Kindersley; **p. 237 top:** Stockbyte/Getty; **Fig. 6.17a:** Paul Almasy/Corbis; **Fig. 6.17b:** AP Wide World Photos; **Fig. 6.18:** Oliver Meckes & Nicole Ottawa/Photo Researchers; **p. 244 top a:** Clive Streeter/Dorling Kindersley; **top b:** Dorling Kindersley; **bottom a:** Glowimages/Getty Images; **bottom b:** Kevin Schafer /DanitaDelimont.

Chapter 7

Chapter Opener: Bagros/PhotoCuisine/Corbis; **p. 247:** Dole/shutterstock; **p. 248:** David Sacks/Getty Images; **p. 254:** Foodfolio/Alamy Images; **p. 259:** Getty Images; **p. 262:** Photodisc/Getty Images; **p. 263:** Ted Tamburo/ WorkbookStock/Getty Images; **p. 266:** Jack Andersen/ Foodpix/Jupiter Images; **p. 267:** Corbis; **p. 268:** Ariel Skelley/Corbis; **p. 270:** Chris Collins/Corbis; **p. 272:** Stockbyte/Getty.

In Depth

p. 280: www.blende11.de/Photonica Amana America/Getty Images; **p. 281:** Steve Terrill/Corbis; **p. 282:** Simon Smith/Dorling Kindersley; **p. 284:** Noe Montes/Foodpix/Jupiter Images; **p. 287 top:** Perry Correll/shutterstock; **bottom:** Lisa Hubbard/Jupiter Images; **p. 288 top left:** James Carrier/Getty Images; **bottom left:** Rubberball/Getty; **bottom right:** Nancy R. Cohen/Getty Images; **p. 289:** Photodisc/Getty Images.

Chapter 8

Chapter Opener: Corbis; **p. 293:** cloki/shutterstock; **p. 294:** PhotoDisc/ Getty Images; **Fig. 8.4 top:** Pearson Learning Photo Studio; **bottom:** Suzannah Skelton/istockphoto; **Fig. 8.5:** Danny Hooks/iStockphoto; **Fig. 8.7 top:** Ross Durant/Foodpix/Jupiter Images; **bottom:** Barry Gregg/Corbis; **p. 300:** Burke/Triolo Productions / Foodpix / Jupiter Images; **p. 301:** Renee Comet/StockFood Creative/Getty Images; **Fig. 8.9 top:** Brand X/Alamy Images; **bottom:** Craig Veltri/istockphoto; **Fig. 8.11 both:** Spauln/Shutterstock; **p. 304:** Brian Hagiwara/Foodpix/Jupiter Images; **p. 305:** David Murray/Dorling Kindersley; **Fig. 8.13 both:** Kelly Cline/iStockphoto; **p. 307 top:** George Doyle & Claran Griffin/Stockbyte/Getty; **bottom:** Corbis; **Fig. 8.16:** Alison Wright/Corbis; **p. 309 top:** Andy Crawford/Dorling Kindersley; **bottom:** Monique le Luhandre/ Dorling Kindersley; **p. 310:** Kristin Piljay; **Fig. 8.17 top:** Rudi Tapper/ istockphoto; **bottom:** Nigel Paul Monckton/Shutterstock; **p. 311:** Dorling Kindersley; **p. 313:** vario images GmbH & Co.KG / Alamy; **p. 314 top:** Allen Polansky/Stock Connection; **bottom:** Stockbyte/Getty; **p. 315:** Robert Fiocca/Picture Arts/Corbis; **p. 320:** Creatas Images/ Jupiter Unlimited; **p. 321:** Kristin Piljay.

Chapter 9

Chapter Opener: Tim Hawley/Foodpix/Jupiter Images; **p. 323:** Valentyn Volkov/iStockphoto; **p. 325:** Arthur Tilley/Taxi/Getty Images; **p. 327:** Theo Allof/Corbis; **p. 329:** Shkind/shutterstock; **p. 330:** Randy Sidman-Gerfile; **Fig. 9.7:** Yong Hian Lim/istockphoto; **p. 332:** ty Images; **p. 333:** Corbis; **Fig. 9.8:** Photodisc/Getty

Images; **p. 334:** George Doyle & Claran Griffin/Stockbyte/Getty; **p. 336:** Network Productions/The Image Works; **p. 337:** Masterfile; **p. 338:** Michael Pohuski/Getty Images; **p. 339:** Al Bello/Getty Images; **Fig. 9.9 top:** Barry Gregg/Corbis; **bottom:** Spauln/istockphoto; **p. 341 top:** Foodcollection/Getty Images; **bottom:** Shaun Egan/Stone/ Getty Images; **Fig. 9.10 top:** Barry Gregg/Corbis; **bottom:** Marco Testa/istockphoto; **p. 343:** Eyewire Collection/Getty Images; **p. 344:** Ned Frisk Photography/Corbis; **p. 345:** Rick Stewart/Getty Images; **p. 346 top:** Creatas Images/Jupiter Images; **bottom:** Stockbyte Platinum/ Alamy; **p. 347:** Clive Streeter/Dorling Kindersley; **p. 349:** Kristin Piljay; **p. 354 bottom:** Tobias Titz/Getty Images.

Chapter 10

Chapter Opener: Garo/Photo Researchers; **p. 357:** Rosemary Buffoni/ iStockphoto; **p. 359:** Deborah Davis/Stone/Getty Images; **p. 361:** Bill Aron/PhotoEdit; **Fig. 10.4 top:** Suzannah Skelton/istockphoto; **bottom:** Craig Veltri/istockphoto; **p. 364:** David Murray/Dorling Kindersley; **p. 365:** Steve Gorton/Dorling Kindersley; **p. 366:** Philip Wilkins/Dorling Kindersley; **Fig. 10.7 both:** Barry Gregg/Corbis; **p. 367:** Photodisc/Getty Images; **p. 370:** United States Department of Agriculture; **Fig. 10.9 top:** Westmacott Photography/istockphoto; **bottom:** Engin Communications/istockphoto; **Fig. 10.12:** Kristin Piljay; **p. 374:** Dorling Kindersley; **Fig. 10.13 top:** Ross Durant/Foodpix/Jupiter Images; **bottom:** Steve Cohen/Foodpix/Jupiter Images; **p. 376:** JLP/Sylvia Torres/Corbis; **p. 377:** Stephen Hayward/Dorling Kindersley; **Fig. 10.15 top:** Stephen Rees/ istockphoto; **bottom:** Brian Hagiwara/Foodpix/Jupiter Images; **Fig. 10.16:** Miranda Mimi Kuo; **p. 381:** Dave King/Dorling Kindersley; **Fig. 10.18a:** St. Bartholomew's Hospital/Photo Researchers; **Fig. 10.18b:** Edward H. Gill/Custom Medical Stock Photo; **Fig. 10.19:** Lauren Shear/Photo Researchers; **Fig. 10.20:** Phototake NYC; **p. 383 top:** Paul Souders/Corbis; **Fig. 10.21:** Dr. P. Marazzi/Photo Researchers; **p. 383 bottom:** Jeff Greenberg/PhotoEdit; **p. 384:** Suzannah Skelton/ istockphoto; **p. 385:** Ned Frisk Photography/Corbis; **p. 386:** Ian Logan/Photographer's Choice/Getty Images; **Fig. 10.22:** National Institute of Health; **p. 393:** Cordelia Molloy/Photo Researchers; **p. 395:** Dorling Kindersley.

In Depth

p. 398 left: Image100/Jupiter Images; **right:** Ian O'Leary/Dorling Kindersley; **Fig. 1 top to bottom:** Southern Illinois University /Photo Researchers; Lew Robertson/Foodpix/Jupiter Images; Image Source Pink/Getty Images; Pixtal/AGE Fotostock America; Carol and Mike Werner /Phototake NYC; **p. 401:** Rob Bartee/Alamy; **p. 402:** Kurt Wilson/Foodpix /Jupiter Images; **p. 403 top:** Amy Etra/PhotoEdit; **bottom:** Mark Thomas/Foodpix/Jupiter Images; **p. 404:** Kristin Piljay; **p. 405 top left:** Eric Risberg /AP Wide World Photos; **top right:** George Doyle & Claran Griffin/Stockbyte/Getty; **bottom:** Dorling Kindersley; **p. 406:** Kristin Piljay.

Chapter 11

Chapter Opener: Andrew Ward/Getty Images; **p. 409:** NASTYApro/ shutterstock; **Fig. 11.4 left:** Science Photo Library/Photo Researchers; **right:** Pascal Alix/Photo Researchers; **p. 414:** Richard Ross/Stone/Getty Images; **p. 417 top:** Dave King/Dorling Kindersley; **middle:** Peter Anderson/Dorling Kindersley; **Fig. 11.6 top:** Bill Varie/Workbook Stock/Jupiter Images; **bottom:** Barry Gregg/Corbis; **Fig. 11.7 left:** Pearson Learning Photo Studio; **right top to bottom:** Brand A Food/Alamy; Pearson Learning Photo Studio; Comstock Images/Jupiter Images; Bill Varie/Workbook Stock/Jupiter Images; Dorling Kindersley; Paul Poplis/ Foodpix/Jupiter Images; **p. 419:** Pearson Learning Photo Studio; **p. 420:**

Kristin Piljay; **p. 422:** Peter Turnley/Corbis; **p. 423:** Dorling Kindersley; **Fig. 11.10 top:** Imagine/Inspirestock/Jupiter Images; **bottom:** Barry Gregg/Corbis; **Fig. 11.11:** Biophoto Associates/Photo Researchers; **p. 425:** Stockbyte/Getty; **Fig. 11.13 top:** Alamy; **bottom:** Darja Vorontsova/Shutterstock; **p. 427 top:** Philip Dowell/Dorling Kindersley; **bottom:** Dorling Kindersley; **p. 428:** Catherine Ledner/Stone/Getty Images; **p. 429:** Spencer Jones/Photodisc/Getty Images; **Fig. 11.14 top:** Greg Nicholas/istockphoto; **bottom:** Suzannah Skelton/istockphoto; **p. 432:** Larry Williams/Corbis; **Fig. 11.15:** National Institute of Dental Research; **Fig 11.16:** Michael Klein/Peter Arnold; **Fig 11.17:** Yoav Levy/Phototake NYC; **p. 434:** Spencer Platt/Getty News; **p. 435:** Duomo/Corbis; **p. 436 top:** Ned Frisk Photography/Corbis; **bottom:** Frances Roberts/Alamy; **p. 437:** Marc Romanelli/Photographer's Choice/Getty Images.

Chapter 12

Chapter Opener: Purestock/Getty Images; **p. 445:** Rohit Seth/shutterstock; **p. 450:** Burke/Triolo Productions/Jupiter Images; **p. 451:** Sara D. Davis/AP Wide World Photos; **Fig. 12.4 top:** Laitr Keiows/Shutterstock; **bottom:** Suzannah Skelton /istockphoto; **p. 457:** Isabelle Rozenbaum & Frederic Cirou/Getty Images; **Fig. 12.7 top:** Dan Peretz/shutterstock; **bottom:** Roger Phillips/Dorling Kindersley; **p. 459:** Ian O'Leary / Dorling Kindersley; **Fig. 12.8 top:** Morgan Lane Photography/Shutterstock; **bottom:** Kelly Cline /istockphoto; **p. 461 top:** Guy Gillette; **bottom:** Dorling Kindersley; **p. 463:** David Young-Wolff/PhotoEdit; **Fig. 12.10 top:** Gretchen Halverson/iStockphoto; **bottom:** Pearson Learning Photo Studio; **Fig. 12.13 top:** Ross Durant/Foodpix/Jupiter Images; **bottom:** Imagine/Inspirestock /Jupiter Images; **p. 467:** Food Features/Alamy Images; **p. 468:** Rubberball/Getty; **p. 471:** Lennart Nilsson/Albert Bonniers Forlag AB; **p. 472 left:** Microworks Color/Phototake NYC; **right:** Dr. Andrejs Liepins/Photo Researchers; **p. 473:** Aaron Haupt/Photo Researchers; **p. 474:** Horizon International Images Limited/Alamy; **p. 475:** Mitch Hrdlicka/Getty Images; **p. 476:** Photodisc/Getty Images; **p. 482 left:** Kristin Piljay; **right:** Burker/Triolo Productions/Brand X/Corbis; **p. 483:** Color Day Productions/Getty Images.

Chapter 13

Chapter Opener: Stockdisc/Getty Images; **p. 485:** Piotr Marcinski/shutterstock; **p. 486:** Eugene Gologursky/WireImage/Getty Images; **p. 489:** R H Production/Robert Harding World Imagery; **Fig. 13.3 top to bottom:** PhotoEdit; Brown/Custom Medical Stock Photo; Phototake NYC; BSIP/Phototake NYC; Life Measurement, Inc.; **Fig. 13.5:** Kristin Piljay; **Fig. 13.6a:** Stockbyte/Getty Images; **Fig. 13.6b:** M. L. Harris/Getty Images; **Fig. 13.6c:** LWA/Sharie/Kennedy/PhotoDisc/Getty Images; **p. 493:** Dorling Kindersley; **Fig. 13.8:** Alix/Photo Researchers; **p. 495:** Xavier Bonghi/Image Bank/Getty Images; **p. 499 top:** Alvis Upitis/Getty Images; **bottom:** istockphoto; **p. 502 top:** Philip Dowell/Dorling Kindersley; **bottom:** Bruce Dale/Getty Images; **p. 503:** Norma Joseph/Alamy; **p. 504:** Mark Douet/Stone/Getty Images; **p. 505:** Photodisc/Getty Images; **p. 507:** Lew Robertson/Corbis; **p. 508:** BananaStock/Jupiter Images; **Fig. 13.11:** Creative Digital Visions; **p. 514 top:** Sheri Giblin/Foodpix/Jupiter Images; **bottom:** Stockbyte/Getty; **p. 515:** Food Alan King/Alamy Images; **p. 517:** Ariel Skelley/Corbis; **p. 519:** Liu Jin/Agence France Presse/Getty Images; **p. 525:** St. Petersburg Times/Newscom; **p. 526:** Chederros/AGE Fotostock.

In Depth

p. 528 left: Oscar Burriel/Photo Researchers; **right:** Eugenio Savio/AP Wide World Photos; **p. 529:** Klaus Lahnstein/Getty Images; **p. 531:** Digital Vision/Getty Images; **Fig. 2:** Laura Murray; **Fig. 3:** Karl Prouse/

Catwalking/Getty Images; **Fig. 4:** Kendall Samantha Alon/SIPA; **p. 534:** Blake Little/Getty Images; **Fig. 6:** Baumgartner Olivia/Corbis; **p. 535:** Roel Loopers/Photolibrary; **p. 536:** D. Hurst/Alamy; **p. 537:** AP Wide World Photos; **p. 538 top:** AP Wide World Photos; **bottom:** Rubberball/Getty.

Chapter 14

Chapter Opener: David Madison/Getty Images; **p. 543:** Olivier Blondeau/iStockphoto **p. 544:** Caleb Kennal/PNI/Aurora Photos; **p. 546:** Photodisc/Getty Images; **p. 547:** AP Wide World Photos; **Fig. 14.3 top to bottom:** BananaStock/Jupiter Images; Alan Jakubek/Corbis; Comstock Images/Jupiter Images; **p. 549:** Will & Deni McIntyre/Photo Researchers; **p. 550:** Marc Romanelli/Image Bank/Getty Images; **p. 551:** George Doyle & Claran Griffin/Stockbyte/Getty; **p. 555:** Corbis Super RF/Alamy; **p. 557:** Stephen Oliver/Dorling Kindersley; **Fig. 14.11:** Laura Murray; **p. 559:** Jens Schlueter/Getty Images; **p. 560:** Photodisc/Getty Images; **p. 562:** Scott T. Smith/Corbis; **p. 564:** Dave King/Dorling Kindersley; **Fig. 14.13 top:** Lily Valde/Pixland/Jupiter Images; **bottom:** Dominic Burke/Alamy; **p. 565:** David Young-Wolff/Getty Images; **p. 568:** Stockbyte/Getty; **p. 569:** KRT/Newscom; **p. 570:** Altrendo/Getty Images; **p. 571:** Derek Hall/Dorling Kindersley; **p. 578 top:** Stockbyte/Getty Images; **bottom:** Sarto/Lund/Getty Images; **p. 579 top:** Image Source/Jupiter Images; **bottom:** Pick and Mix Images/Alamy Images.

Chapter 15

Chapter Opener: Jupiter Images; **p. 581:** Gregory Gerber/shutterstock; **p. 582:** matka_Wariatka/shutterstock; **Fig. 15.1:** Barry Dowsett/Photo Researchers; **Fig. 15.2:** Andrew Syred/Photo Researchers; **Fig. 15.3:** Matt Meadows/Peter Arnold; **p. 587:** Minnesota Historical Society/Corbis; **Fig. 15.4:** Neil Fletcher/Dorling Kindersley; **p. 588:** Jean-Louis Vosgien/shutterstock; **p. 589 top:** Vanessa Davies/Dorling Kindersley; **bottom:** Justin Sullivan/Getty Images; **p. 590:** Digital Vision/Getty Images; **p. 591:** Kristin Piljay; **p. 594:** Alan Richardson/Foodpix/Jupiter Images; **p. 597 top:** Stockbyte/Getty; **bottom:** Owen Franken/Corbis; **p. 598 top:** Liaison/Getty Images; **bottom:** Digital Vision/Getty Images; **p. 599 top:** AKG/Photo Researchers; **bottom:** Lon C. Diehl/PhotoEdit; **p. 603:** Corbis; **Fig. 15.11 left:** Carl Walsh/Aurora Photos; **right:** Brian Hagiwara/Foodpix/Jupiter Images; **p. 605:** Corbis; **p. 606 top:** Red Cover / Alamy; **bottom:** Abbott Laboratories; **p. 607:** Ned Frisk Photography/Corbis; **p. 608:** Paul Gunning/Photo Researchers; **p. 615 top:** Martin Bond/Peter Arnold; **bottom:** Courtesy Syngenta; **p. 616:** Toby Talbot/AP Wide World Photos; **p. 617:** image100/Corbis.

Chapter 16

Chapter Opener: Camille Tokerud/The Image Bank/Getty Images; **p. 619:** Douglas Freer/shutterstock; **p. 620:** David Phillips/The Population Council/Photo Researchers; **Fig. 16.4 top to bottom:** Lennart Nilsson/Albert Bonniers Forlag AB; Lennart Nilsson/Albert Bonniers Forlag AB; Neil Bromhall/Photo Researchers; Tom Galliher/Corbis; **Fig. 16.5:** Ron Sutherland/Photo Researchers; **p. 626:** Ian O'Leary/Getty Images; **Fig. 16.6:** ingret/shutterstock; **Fig. 16.7a:** Biophoto Associates/Science Source/Photo Researchers; **p. 629:** Dave King/Dorling Kindersley; **p. 630:** Carl Tremblay/StockFood/Getty Images; **p. 632:** Dave King/Dorling Kindersley; **p. 633 top:** Brand X Pictures/Getty Images; **bottom:** Dorling Kindersley; **p. 634:** Jim Craigmyle/Corbis; **p. 636:** John Birdsall/AGE Fotostock; **p. 637 top:** Phanie/Photo Researchers; **bottom:** George Doyle & Claran Griffin/Stockbyte/Getty; **Fig. 16.9:** Brigitte Sporrer/Getty Images; **p. 642:** Rick Gomez/AGE Fotostock America; **p. 643:** Darama/Corbis; **p. 644:** Chris Craymer/Stone/Getty Images; **p. 645 top:** Philip Gould/Corbis; **bottom:** Jose Luis Pelaez, Inc./Corbis; **p. 648:** Mel Yates/Taxi/

Getty Images; **p. 649:** Pixland/Getty Images; **p. 651:** Jupiterimages; **p. 652:** Corbis; **p. 653:** Tom Stewart/Corbis; **p. 654:** Anne Flinn Powell/Photolibrary; **Fig. 16.13:** Dr. Pamela R. Erickson; **p. 662:** Goodshoot/Getty Images; **p. 663:** Richard Levine/Alamy.

Chapter 17

Chapter Opener: Jupiter Images; **p. 665:** Carlos Caetano/iStockphoto; **p. 666 top:** Ryan McVay/Getty Images; **bottom:** Michael Newman/PhotoEdit; **p. 671:** Dave King/Dorling Kindersley; **Fig. 17.2:** Laura Dwight; **p. 672 top:** Roger Phillips/Dorling Kindersley; **center:** Foodfolio/Alamy; **p. 673:** debr22pics/shutterstock; **p. 674:** Jaume Gual/AGE Fotostock; **p. 676:** Laura Murray; **p. 677:** Holly Harris/Getty Images; **p. 678:** Bob Daemmerich/The Image Works; **Fig. 17.5 left to right:** Jupiter Images; Rob Melnychuk/Jupiter Images; Getty Images; **p. 680:** Photodisc/Getty Images; **p. 682:** Tom Stewart/Corbis; **p. 684:** Tim Hawley/Foodpix/Jupiter Images; **p. 685:** Adam Gault/Getty Images; **p. 686:** Tome & Dee Ann McCarthy/Corbis; **p. 688:** Banana Stock/AGE Fotostock; **p. 689:** Paul Barton/Corbis; **p. 697:** Johner Images/Getty Images.

Chapter 18

Chapter Opener: David McLain/Aurora Photos; **p. 699:** Compassionate Eye Foundation/Colorblind Images/Getty Images; **p. 700:** Robert W. Ginn/AGE Fotostock; **p. 701 top:** Richard Koek/Stone/Getty Images; **bottom:** Claro Cortes IV/Reuters/Corbis; **p. 703:** Toshio Nakajima/Amana Images/Getty Images; **p. 704:** Raymond Gehman/Corbis; **p. 706 top:** Ariel Skelley/Corbis; **bottom:** Donna Day/Getty Images; **p. 707:** Dr. P. Marazzi/Photo Researchers; **p. 709:** Don Smetzer/Getty Images; **p. 711 top:** Deborah Jaffe/Jupiter Images; **bottom:** Ned Frisk Photography/Corbis; **p. 712:** Jed Share/Getty Images; **p. 715:** Dr. P. Marazzi/Photo Researchers; **p. 716 top:** Dorling Kindersley; **bottom:** Ray Ellis/Photo Researchers; **p. 718:** Mark Richards/PhotoEdit; **p. 720 top:** Karen Preuss/The Image Works; **bottom:** Ansell Horn/Phototake NYC; **p. 726:** Andreas Pollok/Getty Images; **p. 727 top:** IPS/Jupiter Images; **bottom:** ImageState/Alamy.

Chapter 19

Chapter Opener: Mediacolor's/Alamy Images; **p. 729:** Bon Appetit/Alamy; **p. 730:** Peter Turnley/Corbis; **Fig. 19.3:** Geert van Kesteren/Magnum Photos; **p. 733:** Jane Sweeney/Alamy Images; **p. 734 top:** Sheldan Collins/Corbis; **bottom:** Neil Cooper/Alamy; **p. 735:** Reuters/Corbis; **p. 736:** Geert van Kesteren/Magnum Photos; **p. 737 top:** Nik Wheeler/Corbis; **bottom:** Coston Stock/Alamy Images; **p. 739:** David Turnley/Corbis; **p. 740 top:** Purestock/Jupiterimages; **bottom:** George Doyle & Claran Griffin/Stockbyte/Getty; **Fig. 19.5:** Getty Images; **p. 743:** Rubberball/Getty; **p. 744:** Corbis; **p. 745:** Gallo Images/Alamy; **p. 752:** Kent Gilbert/AP Wide World Photos; **p. 753:** jeremy sutton-hibbert/Alamy.

Figure and Text Credits

Fig. 3.2 Adapted from Johnson, M., Human Biology: Concepts and Current Issues, 5/e, Fig. 10.1, Copyright © 2010 Benjamin Cummings. Reprinted by permission of Pearson Education, Inc. **Fig. 3.3** Adapted from Johnson, M., Human Biology: Concepts and Current Issues, 5/e, Fig. 14.1, Copyright © 2010 Benjamin Cummings. Reprinted by permission of Pearson Education, Inc. **Fig. 3.4** Adapted from Johnson, M., Human Biology: Concepts and Current Issues, 5/e, Fig. 3.3, Copyright © 2010 Benjamin Cummings. Reprinted by permission of Pearson Education, Inc. **Fig. 3.5** Adapted from Johnson, M., Human Biology: Con-

cepts and Current Issues, 5/e, Fig. 3.3, Copyright © 2010 Benjamin Cummings. Reprinted by permission of Pearson Education, Inc. **Fig 3.6** Adapted from Johnson, M., Human Biology: Concepts and Current Issues, 5/e, Fig. 3.3, Copyright © 2010 Benjamin Cummings. Reprinted by permission of Pearson Education, Inc. **Fig. 3.8** Adapted from Johnson, M., Human Biology: Concepts and Current Issues, 5/e, Fig. 3.3, Copyright © 2010 Benjamin Cummings. Reprinted by permission of Pearson Education, Inc. **Fig. 3.10** Adapted from Johnson, M., Human Biology: Concepts and Current Issues, 5/e, Fig. 3.3, Copyright © 2010 Benjamin Cummings. Reprinted by permission of Pearson Education, Inc. **Fig. 3.11** Adapted from Johnson, M., Human Biology: Concepts and Current Issues, 5/e, Fig. 3.3, Copyright © 2010 Benjamin Cummings. Reprinted by permission of Pearson Education, Inc. **Fig. 3.7** Adapted from Bauman, R. Microbiology. Fig. 2.14, © 2003 Benjamin Cummings; and Moyes, C. and Shulte, P. Principles of Animal Physiology, Fig. 2.15, © 2006 Benjamin Cummings. Used by permission of Pearson Education. **Fig. 3.18** Adapted from Johnson, M., Human Biology: Concepts and Current Issues, 5/e, Fig. 10.13, Copyright © 2010 Benjamin Cummings. Reprinted by permission of Pearson Education, Inc. **Fig. 4.6** Adapted from Johnson, M., Human Biology: Concepts and Current Issues, 5/e, page 89, Copyright © 2010 Benjamin Cummings. Reprinted by permission of Pearson Education, Inc. **Fig. 4.11** Adapted from Johnson, M., Human Biology: Concepts and Current Issues, 5/e, Fig. 3.3, Fig. 13.5, and page 88. Copyright © 2010 Benjamin Cummings. Reprinted by permission of Pearson Education, Inc. **Fig. 5.7** Adapted from Johnson, M., Human Biology: Concepts and Current Issues, 5/e, Fig. 3.3, Copyright © 2010 Benjamin Cummings. Reprinted by permission of Pearson Education, Inc. **Fig. 6.8a** Adapted from Johnson, M., Human Biology: Concepts and Current Issues, 5/e, page 88, Copyright © 2010 Benjamin Cummings. Reprinted by permission of Pearson Education, Inc. **Fig. 6.8b** From Germann, W. and Stanfield, C. Principles of Human Physiology, Fig. 2.9, Copyright © 2004 Benjamin Cummings. **Fig. 6.8c** From Alberts, B. Molecular Biology of the Cell, 4/e. Garland Publishers. © 2002 by Bruce Alberts, Alexander Johnson, Julian Lewis, Martin Raff, Keith Roberts, and Peter Walter. **Fig. 6.9** Hemoglobin illustration, Irving Geis. Rights owned by Howard Hughes Medical Institute. Not to be reproduced without permission. **Fig. 10.11** From Marieb, E. Human Anatomy and Physiology, 5/e, Fig. 16.7, Copyright © 2003 Benjamin Cummings. Used by permission of Pearson Education, Inc. **Fig. 11.1** From Germann, W. and Stanfield, C. Principles of Human Physiology, Fig. 7.13, Copyright © 2004 Benjamin Cummings. **Fig. 11.5** From Whitney, E. and Rolfes, S. Understanding Nutrition, 10/e, p. 414. © 2005. Reprinted with permission of Brooks/Cole, a division of Thomson Learning. **Fig. 11.8** From Nelson et al. Lehninger Principles of Biochemistry, 3/e, © 2000 W. H. Freeman. Used with permission. **Fig. 12.2** Hemoglobin illustration, Irving Geis. Rights owned by Howard Hughes Medical Institute. Not to be reproduced without permission. **Fig. 13.4** Pearson Science Figure 7, In Depth: Disordered Eating Adapted from Otis et al. 1997. The female athlete triad. Med Sci Sports. 29:i–ix. © Lippincott Williams & Wilkins. Used with permission. **Fig. 16.1** Adapted from Germann, W. and Stanfield, C. Principles of Human Physiology, 2/e, Fig. 22.20a, Copyright © 2004 Benjamin Cummings. Reprinted by permission of Pearson Education, Inc. **Fig. 16.2** Adapted from Germann, W. and Stanfield, C. Principles of Human Physiology, 2/e, Fig. 22.21, Copyright © 2004 Benjamin Cummings. Reprinted by permission of Pearson Education, Inc. **Fig. 16.3** Adapted from Germann, W. and Stanfield, C. Principles of Human Physiology, 2/e, Fig. 22.22, Copyright © 2004 Benjamin Cummings. Reprinted by permission of Pearson Education, Inc. **Fig. 16.6** Adapted from Germann, W. and Stanfield, C. Principles of Human Physiology, 2/e, Fig. 22.25a, Copyright © 2004 Ben-

Dietary Reference Intakes: RDA, AI*, (AMDR)

Life-Stage Group	Carbohydrate—Total Digestible (g/d)	Total Fiber (g/d)	Total Fat (g/d)	n-6 polyunsaturated fatty acids (linoleic acid) (g/d)	n-3 polyunsaturated fatty acids (?-linolenic acid) (g/d)	Protein and Amino Acids (g/d)[a]
Infants						
0–6 mo	60* (ND[b])[c]	ND	31*	4.4* (ND)	0.5* (ND)	9.1* (ND)
7–12 mo	95* (ND)	ND	30*	4.6* (ND)	0.5* (ND)	13.5 (ND)
Children						
1–3 y	130 (45–65)	19*	(30–40)	7* (5–10)	0.7* (0.6–1.2)	13 (5–20)
4–8 y	130 (45–65)	25*	(25–35)	10* (5–10)	0.9* (0.6–1.2)	19 (10–30)
Males						
9–13 y	130 (45–65)	31*	(25–35)	12* (5–10)	1.2* (0.6–1.2)	34 (10–30)
14–18 y	130 (45–65)	38*	(25–35)	16* (5–10)	1.6* (0.6–1.2)	52 (10–30)
19–30 y	130 (45–65)	38*	(20–35)	17* (5–10)	1.6* (0.6–1.2)	56 (10–35)
31–50 y	130 (45–65)	38*	(20–35)	17* (5–10)	1.6* (0.6–1.2)	56 (10–35)
51–70 y	130 (45–65)	30*	(20–35)	14* (5–10)	1.6* (0.6–1.2)	56 (10–35)
>70 y	130 (45–65)	30*	(20–35)	14* (5–10)	1.6* (0.6–1.2)	56 (10–35)
Females						
9–13 y	130 (45–65)	26*	(25–35)	10* (5–10)	1.0* (0.6–1.2)	34 (10–30)
14–18 y	130 (45–65)	26*	(25–35)	11* (5–10)	1.1* (0.6–1.2)	46 (10–30)
19–30 y	130 (45–65)	25*	(20–35)	12* (5–10)	1.1* (0.6–1.2)	46 (10–35)
31–50 y	130 (45–65)	25*	(20–35)	12* (5–10)	1.1* (0.6–1.2)	46 (10–35)
51–70 y	130 (45–65)	21*	(20–35)	11* (5–10)	1.1* (0.6–1.2)	46 (10–35)
>70 y	130 (45–65)	21*	(20–35)	11* (5–10)	1.1* (0.6–1.2)	46 (10–35)
Pregnancy						
≤18 y	175 (45–65)	28*	(20–35)	13* (5–10)	1.4* (0.6–1.2)	71 (10–35)
19–30 y	175 (45–65)	28*	(20–35)	13* (5–10)	1.4* (0.6–1.2)	71 (10–35)
31–50 y	(45–65)	28*	(20–35)	13* (5–10)	1.4* (0.6–1.2)	71 (10–35)
Lactation						
≤18 y	210 (45–65)	29*	(20–35)	13* (5–10)	1.3* (0.6–1.2)	71 (10–35)
19–30 y	210 (45–65)	29*	(20–35)	13* (5–10)	1.3* (0.6–1.2)	71 (10–35)
31–50 y	210 (45–65)	29*	(20–35)	13* (5–10)	1.3* (0.6–1.2)	71 (10–35)

Data from: Reprinted with permission from "Dietary Reference Intakes for Energy, Carbohydrates, Fiber, Fat, Fatty Acids, Cholesterol, Protein, and Amino Acids (Macronutrients)," © 2002 by the National Academy of Sciences, courtesy of the National Academies Press, Washington, DC.

Note: This table is adapted from the DRI reports, see www.nap.edu. It lists Recommended Dietary Allowances (RDAs), with Adequate Intakes (AIs) indicated by an asterisk (*), and Acceptable Macronutrient Distribution Range (AMDR) data provided in parentheses. RDAs and AIs may both be used as goals for individual intake. RDAs are set to meet the needs of almost all (97% to 98%) individuals in a group. For healthy breastfed infants, the AI is the mean intake. The AI for other life stage and gender groups is believed to cover the needs of all individuals in the group, but lack of data prevent being able to specify with confidence the percentage of individuals covered by this intake.

[a] Based on 1.5 g/kg/day for infants, 1.1 g/kg/day for 1–3 y, 0.95 g/kg/day for 4–13 y, 0.85 g/kg/day for 14–18 y, 0.8 g/kg/day for adults, and 1.1 g/kg/day for pregnant (using pre-pregnancy weight) and lactating women.

[b] ND = Not determinable due to lack of data of adverse effects in this age group and concern with regard to lack of ability to handle excess amounts. Source of intake should be from food only to prevent high levels of intake.

[c] Data in parentheses are Acceptable Macronutrient Distribution Range (AMDR). This is the range of intake for a particular energy source that is associated with reduced risk of chronic disease while providing intakes of essential nutrients. If an individual consumes in excess of the AMDR, there is a potential of increasing the risk of chronic diseases and/or insufficient intakes of essential nutrients.

Dietary Reference Intakes: RDA, AI*

	Vitamins													
Life-Stage Group	Vitamin A (µg/d)[a]	Vitamin D (µg/d)[b]	Vitamin E (mg/d)[c]	Vitamin K (µg/d)	Thiamin (mg/d)	Riboflavin (mg/d)	Niacin (mg/d)[d]	Pantothenic Acid (mg/d)	Biotin (µg/d)	Vitamin B_6 (mg/d)	Folate (µg/d)[e]	Vitamin B_{12} (µg/d)	Vitamin C (mg/d)	Choline (mg/d)
Infants														
0–6 mo	400*	5*	4*	2.0*	0.2*	0.3*	2*	1.7*	5*	0.1*	65*	0.4*	40*	125*
7–12 mo	500*	5*	5*	2.5*	0.3*	0.4*	4*	1.8*	6*	0.3*	80*	0.5*	50*	150*
Children														
1–3 y	300	5*	6	30*	0.5	0.5	6	2*	8*	0.5	150	0.9	15	200*
4–8 y	400	5*	7	55*	0.6	0.6	8	3*	12*	0.6	200	1.2	25	250*
Males														
9–13 y	600	5*	11	60*	0.9	0.9	12	4*	20*	1.0	300	1.8	45	375*
14–18 y	900	5*	15	75*	1.2	1.3	16	5*	25*	1.3	400	2.4	75	550*
19–30 y	900	5*	15	120*	1.2	1.3	16	5*	30*	1.3	400	2.4	90	550*
31–50 y	900	5*	15	120*	1.2	1.3	16	5*	30*	1.3	400	2.4	90	550*
51–70 y	900	10*	15	120*	1.2	1.3	16	5*	30*	1.7	400	2.4	90	550*
>70 y	900	15*	15	120*	1.2	1.3	16	5*	30*	1.7	400	2.4	90	550*
Females														
9–13 y	600	5*	11	60*	0.9	0.9	12	4*	20*	1.0	300	1.8	45	375*
14–18 y	700	5*	15	75*	1.0	1.0	14	5*	25*	1.2	400	2.4	65	400*
19–30 y	700	5*	15	90*	1.1	1.1	14	5*	30*	1.3	400	2.4	75	425*
31–50 y	700	5*	15	90*	1.1	1.1	14	5*	30*	1.3	400	2.4	75	425*
51–70 y	700	10*	15	90*	1.1	1.1	14	5*	30*	1.5	400	2.4	75	425*
>70 y	700	15*	15	90*	1.1	1.1	14	5*	30*	1.5	400	2.4	75	425*
Pregnancy														
≤18 y	750	5*	15	75*	1.4	1.4	18	6*	30*	1.9	600	2.6	80	450*
19–30 y	770	5*	15	90*	1.4	1.4	18	6*	30*	1.9	600	2.6	85	450*
31–50 y	770	5*	15	90*	1.4	1.4	18	6*	30*	1.9	600	2.6	85	450*
Lactation														
≤18 y	1200	5*	19	75*	1.4	1.4	17	7*	35*	2.0	500	2.8	115	550*
19–30 y	1300	5*	19	90*	1.4	1.4	17	7*	35*	2.0	500	2.8	120	550*
31–50 y	1300	5*	19	90*	1.4	1.4	17	7*	35*	2.0	500	2.8	120	550*

Data from: Reprinted with permission from the Dietary Reference Intakes series, National Academies Press. Copyright 1997, 1998, 2000, 2001, by the National Academy of Sciences. These reports may be accessed via www.nap.edu. Courtesy of the National Academies Press, Washington, DC.

Note: This table is adapted from the DRI reports; see www.nap.edu. It lists Recommended Dietary Allowances (RDAs), with Adequate Intakes (AIs) indicated by an asterisk (*). RDAs and AIs may both be used as goals for individual intake. RDAs are set to meet the needs of almost all (97 percent to 98 percent) individuals in a group. For healthy breastfed infants, the AI is the mean intake. The AI for other life stage and gender groups is believed to cover the needs of all individuals in the group, but lack of data prevent being able to specify with confidence the percentage of individuals covered by this intake.

[a] Given as retinal activity equivalents (RAE).
[b] Also known as calciferol. The DRI values are based on the absence of adequate exposure to sunlight.
[c] Also known as α-tocopherol.
[d] Given as niacin equivalents (NE), except for infants 0–6 months, which are expressed as preformed niacin.
[e] Given as dietary folate equivalents (DFE).